Contemporary Literary Criticism

Yearbook 1986

Guide to Gale Literary Criticism Series

When you need to review criticism of literary works, these are the Gale series to use:

If the author's death date is:	You should turn to:
After Dec. 31, 1959 (or author is still living)	*CONTEMPORARY LITERARY CRITICISM* for example: Jorge Luis Borges, Anthony Burgess, William Faulkner, Mary Gordon, Ernest Hemingway, Iris Murdoch
1900 through 1959	*TWENTIETH-CENTURY LITERARY CRITICISM* for example: Willa Cather, F. Scott Fitzgerald, Henry James, Mark Twain, Virginia Woolf
1800 through 1899	*NINETEENTH-CENTURY LITERATURE CRITICISM* for example: Fedor Dostoevski, Nathaniel Hawthorne, George Sand, William Wordsworth
1400 through 1799	*LITERATURE CRITICISM FROM 1400 TO 1800 (excluding Shakespeare)* for example: Anne Bradstreet, Daniel Defoe, Alexander Pope, François Rabelais, Jonathan Swift, Phillis Wheatley
	SHAKESPEAREAN CRITICISM Shakespeare's plays and poetry
Antiquity through 1399	*CLASSICAL AND MEDIEVAL LITERATURE CRITICISM* for example: Dante, Homer, Plato, Sophocles, Vergil, the Beowulf poet *(Volume 1 forthcoming)*

Gale also publishes related criticism series:

CHILDREN'S LITERATURE REVIEW

This ongoing series covers authors of all eras. Presents criticism on authors and author/illustrators who write for the preschool through high school audience.

CONTEMPORARY ISSUES CRITICISM

This two-volume set presents criticism on contemporary authors writing on current issues. Topics covered include the social sciences, philosophy, economics, natural science, law, and related areas.

ISSN 0091-3421

Volume 44

Contemporary Literary Criticism

Yearbook 1986

The Year in Fiction, Poetry, Drama, and World Literature and the Year's New Authors, Prizewinners, Obituaries, and Works of Literary Biography

Guest Essay, "Feminist Literary Criticism," by Gayle Greene

Sharon K. Hall
EDITOR

Gale Research Company
Book Tower
Detroit, Michigan 48226

STAFF

Sharon K. Hall, *Editor*

Anne Sharp, *Senior Assistant Editor*

Derek T. Bell, *Assistant Editor, Yearbook*
Joyce A. Davis, *Senior Research Assistant, Yearbook*

Sharon R. Gunton, *Contributing Editor*

Jeanne A. Gough, *Permissions & Production Manager*

Lizbeth A. Purdy, *Production Supervisor*
Kathleen M. Cook, *Assistant Production Coordinator*
Suzanne Powers, Jani Prescott, *Editorial Assistants*
Linda Marcella Pugliese, *Manuscript Coordinator*
Donna Craft, *Assistant Manuscript Coordinator*
Jennifer E. Gale, Maureen A. Puhl, Rosetta Irene Simms, *Manuscript Assistants*

Victoria B. Cariappa, *Research Supervisor*
Maureen R. Richards, *Research Coordinator*
Mary D. Wise, *Senior Research Assistant*
Daniel Kurt Gilbert, Kent Graham, Michele R. O'Connell,
Filomena Sgambati, Laura B. Standley, *Research Assistants*

Janice M. Mach, *Text Permissions Supervisor*
Susan D. Battista, Kathy Grell, *Assistant Permissions Coordinators*
Mabel E. Gurney, Josephine M. Keene, Mary M. Matuz, *Senior Permissions Assistants*
H. Diane Cooper, *Permissions Assistant*
LaWanda R. Austin, Eileen H. Baehr, Martha Mulder, Anita L. Ransom, *Permissions Clerks*

Patricia A. Seefelt, *Picture Permissions Supervisor*
Margaret A. Chamberlain, *Assistant Permissions Coordinator*
Colleen M. Crane, *Permissions Assistant*
Lillian Tyus, *Permissions Clerk*

Special recognition is given to Jean C. Stine for her editorial contributions.

Frederick G. Ruffner, *Chairman*
J. Kevin Reger, *President*
Dedria Bryfonski, *Publisher*
Ellen Crowley, *Associate Editorial Director*
Laurie Lanzen Harris, *Director, Literary Criticism Series*
Dennis Poupard, *Senior Editor, Literary Criticism Series*

Library of Congress Catalog Card Number 76-38938
ISBN 0-8103-4418-1
ISSN 0091-3421

Computerized photocomposition by
Typographics, Incorporated
Kansas City, Missouri

Printed in the United States

Contents

Literary Biography

Preface

Every year, an overwhelming number of new publications and significant literary events confront the reader interested in contemporary literature. Who are the year's notable new authors? What dramas have been introduced on the New York and regional stages? Who won the literary world's most prestigious awards? Which authors have been the subjects of significant new literary biographies, and what approach did the biographer take—factual, interpretive, psychological, critical? Finally, who among our best-known contemporary writers died during the year, and what is the reaction of the literary world?

To answer such questions and assist students, teachers, librarians, researchers, and general readers in keeping abreast of current literary activities and trends, the *Contemporary Literary Criticism Yearbook* is being published as part of the *Contemporary Literary Criticism (CLC)* series.

Standard *CLC* volumes provide readers with a comprehensive view of modern literature by presenting excerpted criticism on the works of novelists, poets, playwrights, short story writers, scriptwriters, and other creative writers who are now living or who died after December 31, 1959. Works covered in regular *CLC* volumes are those that have generated significant critical commentary within recent years, with a strong emphasis on works by established authors who frequently appear on the syllabuses of high school and college literature courses.

To complement this broad coverage, the *Yearbook* focuses in depth on a given year's literary activity and highlights a larger number of currently noteworthy authors and books than is possible in standard *CLC* volumes. The *Yearbook* provides critical overviews of the past year's work in various genres, supplies up-to-date critical commentary on new authors and prizewinning writers whose publications have made recent literary news, and marks the deaths of major contemporary literary figures. In addition, the *Yearbook* expands the scope of regular *CLC* volumes by presenting excerpted criticism on the works of literary biographers, whose growing importance in the literary world warrants increased attention. The *Yearbook* is, in short, a valuable supplement to the regular *CLC* volumes in its comprehensive treatment of the year's literary activity. Since the majority of the authors covered in the *Yearbook* and regular *CLC* volumes are living writers who continue to publish, an author frequently appears more than once in the series. There is, of course, no duplication of reprinted criticism.

Scope of the Work

CLC Yearbook 1986 includes excerpted criticism on over 70 authors and provides comprehensive coverage of the year's significant literary events. As with the regular volumes of *CLC,* the authors covered include those who are now living or who died after December 31, 1959. In addition, the *Yearbook* also includes essays commissioned exclusively for this publication. The *Yearbook* is introduced by a Guest Essay and divided into five sections: The Year in Review, New Authors, Prizewinners, Obituaries, and Literary Biography.

Guest Essay—The Guest Essay is an article devoted to a special topic in contemporary literature or literary criticism. This year the Guest Essay focuses on feminist literary criticism, with Gayle Greene providing a broad overview of the field. Greene is a professor of English at Scripps College, Claremont, California, and an active contributor in the field of literary criticism. She has coedited, with Carolyn Ruth Swift Lenz and Carol Thomas Neely, a collection of feminist readings of Shakespeare, *The Woman's Part: Feminist Criticism of Shakespeare* (1980), and coedited, with Coppélia Kahn, *Making a Difference* (1985), a collection of essays aimed at defining and developing feminist literary criticism. In her essay Greene describes the beginnings of feminist criticism, details its development in the 70s and 80s when critics both reinterpreted the literary canon from a feminist perspective and discovered the work of many neglected women writers; she then examines the split between French and Anglo-American feminist critics, and closes with speculations about the future.

The Year in Review—This section includes specially commissioned essays by prominent literary figures who survey the year's new works in their respective fields. In *CLC Yearbook 1986* we have the advantage of viewing "The Year in Fiction" from the perspective of Dianne Donovan, *Books* editor, and John Blades, *Books* critic, for the *Chicago Tribune.* Donovan and Blades are both members of the National Book Critics Circle, and Blades serves on NBCC's

Board of Directors. "The Year in Poetry" is presented by Sidney Burris, who is a poet, critic, and assistant professor of English at the University of Arkansas. Burris's poetry has appeared in the *Atlantic Monthly, Poetry, Prairie Schooner, Missouri Review,* and *New Virginia Review,* and both a collection of his poems and a critical study of Irish poet Seamus Heaney are in press. "The Year in Drama" is reviewed by Robert Cohen, author of numerous books on the theater, including *Giraudoux: Three Faces of Destiny* (1969), *Creative Play Direction* (1974), and *Theatre* (1982). Cohen is also chair of the drama department at the University of California, Irvine. Finally, "The Year in World Literature" is discussed by William Riggan, who as associate editor of the quarterly *World Literature Today* is in a unique position to comment on important international literature; Riggan specializes in Third World, Slavic, and Anglo-American literatures. These annual survey essays on fiction, poetry, drama, and world literature are a special feature of the *Yearbook* and provide a focus that is outside the scope of our regular *CLC* volumes.

New Authors—*CLC Yearbook 1986* introduces eighteen writers whose first book, or first book in English-language translation, was published during 1986. Authors were selected for inclusion if their work was reviewed in several sources and garnered significant criticism. Although the regular *CLC* volumes often cover new writers, the *Yearbook* provides more timely and more extensive coverage of authors just coming into prominence. This expanded coverage includes writers of poetry, short stories, plays, and novels. *CLC Yearbook 1986,* for example, presents the playwright Reinaldo Povod, short story writers Peter Cameron, Linda Collins, Norman Rush, and horror writer Thomas Ligotti. The *Yearbook* also features newly-translated novelists, namely German-born Patrick Süskind and Russian-born Yuz Aleshkovsky, as well as new American novelists such as Sue Miller, who offers a timely narrative of a child-custody battle, and Lisa Grunwald, who tells a heartfelt story of a family's struggle with a mother's death by cancer.

Prizewinners—This section of the *Yearbook* begins with a list of Literary Prizes and Honors Announced in 1986, citing the award, its recipient, and the title of the prizewinning work. *CLC Yearbook 1986* then highlights twenty major prizewinners who will be featured in this volume. A Prize Commentary follows, discussing each award featured in the *Yearbook;* the Prize Commentary indicates the year the award was established, the reason it was established, the awarding body, how the winner is chosen, and the nature of the prize (money, trophy, etc.). After the Prize Commentary, entries on individual award winners are presented. Recipients of established literary honors, such as the Pulitzer Prize, are included as well as authors who have won less established but increasingly important prizes, such as the PEN/Faulkner Award for Fiction, the only award given by writers to writers. In addition to the winners of major American awards, recipients of several outstanding international prizes are also covered. Thus we include England's distinguished Booker-McConnell Prize, awarded to Kingsley Amis, and Canada's Governor General's Literary Awards, presented to Margaret Atwood for Fiction, George F. Walker for Drama, and Fred Wah for Poetry. We have, of course, also featured the literary world's most prestigious award, the Nobel Prize in literature, bestowed on Nigerian dramatist, novelist, and poet Wole Soyinka.

Obituaries—This section begins with a Necrology of *CLC* authors. Following the Necrology, individual author entries are included for the more prominent writers whose influence on contemporary literature is reflected in the obituaries, reminiscences, tributes, or retrospective essays included in their entries. *CLC Yearbook 1986,* for example, presents entries on Simone de Beauvoir, Jorge Luis Borges, Frank Herbert, John D. MacDonald, and Bernard Malamud, among others.

Literary Biography—Since literary biographies are outside the scope of works covered in regular *CLC* volumes, the *Yearbook* provides an opportunity to offer comprehensive commentary on these prominent and popular works. This part of the *Yearbook,* then, is devoted to criticism on literary biographies of authors who are within the *CLC* time period. We do not, therefore, include biographies of authors of the early twentieth century or of previous centuries. Besides giving a biographical perspective on the authors who are the subjects of the literary biographies, this section also introduces readers to today's biographers, their methods, styles, and approaches to biography. This *Yearbook* discusses twelve literary biographies, including Richard P. Graves's biography of the early years of his uncle, *Robert Graves: The Assault Heroic;* Andrew Field's controversial biography of Vladimir Nabokov, *VN: The Life and Art;* and Barbara Branden's *The Passion of Ayn Rand,* considered by critics surprisingly fair and well-balanced given that Branden's husband was Rand's lover for many years.

Format of the Book

With the exception of the Guest Essay and the essays in The Year in Review section, which are written for this publication, the *Yearbook* is comprised of excerpted criticism. There are approximately 515 individual excerpts in

CLC Yearbook 1986 drawn from hundreds of literary reviews, general magazines, distinguished newspapers, and scholarly journals. The excerpts included reflect the critical attention the authors and their works have received by critics writing in English and by foreign criticism in translation; critical books and articles not translated into English have been excluded.

Since the *Yearbook* is designed to complement other *CLC* volumes, *Yearbook* entries generally follow the same format with some variations and additional features. *Yearbook* entries variously contain the following elements:

- The **author heading,** which is included in entries in the New Authors, Prizewinners, and Obituaries sections, cites the author's full name. The portion of the name outside the parentheses denotes the form under which the author has most commonly published. If an author has written consistently under a pseudonym, the pseudonym will be listed in the author heading and the real name given on the first line of the author entry. Also located at the beginning of the author entry are any important name variations under which an author has written. For New Authors and Obituaries, the author's name is followed by the birth date, and, in the case of an obituary, the death date. Uncertainty as to a birth or death date is indicated by question marks. For Prizewinners, the author's name is followed by the title of the prizewinning work and the award received.

- The **book heading,** which is included in entries in the Literary Biography section, cites the complete title of the book followed by the biographer's name.

- A brief **biographical and critical introduction** to the author and his or her work precedes the excerpted criticism in entries in the New Authors and Prizewinners sections.

- **Cross-references** have been included in entries in all sections, except The Year in Review, to direct the reader to other useful sources published by the Gale Research Company: *Contemporary Authors*, which includes detailed biographical and bibliographical sketches on more than 86,000 authors; *Children's Literature Review*, which presents excerpted criticism on the works of authors of children's books; *Something about the Author*, which contains heavily illustrated biographical sketches on writers and illustrators who create books for children and young adults; *Contemporary Issues Criticism*, which presents excerpted commentary on the nonfiction works of authors who influence contemporary thought; *Dictionary of Literary Biography*, which provides original evaluations of authors important to literary history; and the new *Contemporary Authors Autobiography Series*, which offers autobiographical essays by prominent writers. Previous volumes of *CLC* in which the author has been featured are also listed. Cross-references are provided for both the authors and subjects of literary biographies. In *CLC Yearbook 1986,* for example, the entry on Dorothy Herrmann's *S. J. Perelman: A Life* cites additional sources of information on both Herrmann and Perelman.

- A list of **principal works,** including the author's first and last published work and other important works, is provided in entries in the Obituaries section in order to reflect the author's entire literary career. The list is chronological by date of first book publication and identifies the genre of each work. In the case of foreign authors where there are both foreign language publications and English translations, the title and date of the first English-language edition are given in brackets. Unless otherwise indicated, dramas are dated by first performance, not first publication.

- A **portrait** of the author is included, when available, in entries in the New Authors, Prizewinners, and Obituaries sections; in the Literary Biography section, **illustrations** of the subject, representing different stages in his or her life, are included whenever possible.

- Illustrations of **dust jackets** are included, when available, to complement the critical discussion in entries in The Year in Review, Prizewinners, and Literary Biography sections.

- An **excerpt** from the author's work is included, when available, in entries in the New Authors, Prizewinners, and Literary Biography sections, in order to provide the reader with a sampling of the author's theme and style.

- The **excerpted criticism,** included in all entries except those in The Year in Review section, represents essays selected by the editors to reflect the spectrum of opinion about a specific work or about an author's writing in general. The excerpts are presented chronologically, adding a useful perspective to the entry. All titles featured in the entry are printed in boldface type, which enables the reader to easily identify the works being discussed.

- Selected critical excerpts are prefaced by **explanatory notes** that give important information regarding critics and their work and also provide a summary of the criticism.

- A complete **bibliographical citation** designed to help the user find the original essay or book follows each excerpt.

Other Features

- A list of **Authors Forthcoming in CLC** previews the authors to be researched for future volumes.

- An **Appendix** lists the sources from which material in the volume has been reprinted. Many other sources have also been consulted during the preparation of the volume.

- A **Cumulative Index to Authors** lists all the authors who have appeared in *Contemporary Literary Criticism* (including authors who are the subjects of works of literary biography covered in the *Yearbook*); *Twentieth-Century Literary Criticism, Nineteenth-Century Literature Criticism,* and *Literature Criticism from 1400 to 1800,* along with cross-references to other Gale series: *Children's Literature Review, Authors in the News, Contemporary Authors, Contemporary Authors Autobiography Series, Contemporary Authors Bibliograpical Series, Dictionary of Literary Biography, Something about the Author, Something about the Author Autobiography Series,* and *Yesterday's Authors of Books for Children.* Users will welcome this cumulated author index as a useful tool for locating an author within the various series. The index, which lists birth and death dates when available, will be particularly valuable for those authors who are identified with a certain period but whose death date causes them to be placed in another, or for those authors whose careers span two periods. For example, F. Scott Fitzgerald is found in *Twentieth-Century Literary Criticism,* yet a writer often associated with him, Ernest Hemingway, is found in *Contemporary Literary Criticism.*

- A **Cumulative Nationality Index** listing the authors featured in *CLC* alphabetically under each nationality, followed by the volume numbers in which they appear, is included in alternate volumes of *CLC.*

- A **Cumulative Title Index** listing titles reviewed in *CLC* from Volume 1 through the current volume is included in alternate volumes of *CLC.* A separate offprint of the Author, Nationality, and Title Index is also available.

Acknowledgments

The editors wish to thank the copyright holders of the excerpted articles included in this volume for permission to use the material and the photographers and other individuals who provided photographs for us. We are grateful to the staffs of the following libraries for making their resources available to us: Detroit Public Library, the Library of Congress, and the libraries of Wayne State University, the University of Michigan, and the University of Detroit.

Suggestions Are Welcome

The editors welcome the comments and suggestions of readers to expand the coverage and enhance the usefulness of the series.

Authors Forthcoming in *CLC*

Contemporary Literary Criticism, Volumes 45 and 46 will contain criticism on a number of authors not previously covered in the series and will also feature criticism on newer works by authors included in earlier volumes.

To Be Included in Volume 45

Kathy Acker (American novelist and scriptwriter)—Acker has attracted critical attention for her experimental novels *Great Expectations* and *Don Quixote,* in which she uses pornography, plagiarism, autobiography, and dream fragments to subvert literary conventions and to attack traditional social values.

Eric Bogosian (American performance artist)—In *Drinking in America,* a series of satirical monologues, Bogosian examines the psyches of several obsessed male characters. This work shared the 1986 Obie Award for best off-Broadway play.

Guillermo Cabrera Infante (Cuban-born novelist, short story writer, journalist, and critic)—In his recent novel, *Infante's Inferno,* Cabrera Infante continues the use of humorous wordplay and narrative experimentation that won him international recognition with his earlier novel, *Three Trapped Tigers.*

J. P. Donleavy (American-born Irish novelist, dramatist, short story writer, and nonfiction writer)—Donleavy is best known for his first novel, *The Ginger Man,* in which his protagonist searches for love and stability amid a hostile society and a chaotic personal life. Among the recent novels to be covered in his entry are *Schultz, Leila,* and *De Alfonce Tennis.*

William Humphrey (American novelist, short story writer, and essayist)—Humphrey's fiction is usually set in the American Southwest and depicts families and individuals struggling to survive in an often hostile environment. His recent publications include *The Collected Stories of William Humphrey* and *Open Season: Sporting Adventures,* a volume of essays.

Joseph Kesselring (American dramatist and scriptwriter)—An author of popular Broadway comedies during the 1940s and 1950s, Kesselring is best remembered for his domestic farce *Arsenic and Old Lace.*

Ursula K. Le Guin (American novelist, short story writer, poet, and essayist)—A respected award-winning author of fantasy and science fiction, Le Guin is best known for her *Earthsea Trilogy.* Her recent works include *Always Coming Home* and *The Eye of the Heron.*

Thomas McGuane (American novelist, short story writer, scriptwriter, and essayist)—A leading contemporary American satirist, McGuane writes irreverent fiction that focuses on what he terms America's "declining snivelization." Works to be covered in his entry include the novels *Nobody's Angel* and *Something to Be Desired* and the short story collection *To Skin a Cat.*

Alice Munro (Canadian short story writer and novelist)—Munro writes humorous, well-crafted stories about the disturbing undercurrents that affect the ordinary lives of her characters, who inhabit a rural area in southwestern Ontario. Her recent collection, *The Progress of Love,* has attracted significant critical attention.

Lewis Nkosi (South African novelist, critic, and dramatist)—Nkosi, who has lived in exile in England, the United States, and Zambia for over twenty-five years, is well known for his essays on contemporary African literature. His first novel, *Mating Birds,* centers on a young Zulu man who is sentenced to die by the South African government for allegedly raping a white woman.

Charles Tomlinson (English poet, translator, and critic)—Considered one of England's most distinguished post-World War II poets, Tomlinson writes verse that displays his precise attention to detail and his concern with metaphysical themes. Tomlinson's recent collections include *The Flood* and *Notes from New York and Other Poems.*

Rex Warner (English novelist, nonfiction writer, poet, and translator)—Warner was a scholar of classical literature and history whose novels evidence his early interest in Kafkaesque techniques, his concern with contemporary political and social issues during the World War II era, and his later use of historical narratives to focus on universal themes.

To Be Included in Volume 46

Alice Adams (American novelist and short story writer)—In her fiction, Adams often explores the emotional lives of upper-middle-class professional women. Her recent works include a novel, *Superior Women,* and a short story collection, *Return Trips.*

Louise Bogan (American poet, critic, editor, translator, and autobiographer)—A distinguished figure in twentieth-century American literature, Bogan wrote classically structured poetry that passionately explores the extremes of experience. Her collections of verse have been complemented by the publication of *Journey around My Room: The Autobiography of Louise Bogan.*

Len Deighton (English novelist, short story writer, nonfiction writer, and scriptwriter)—Deighton is a highly popular author of spy thrillers who delighted critics and readers with the parodic elements in his first novel, *The Ipcress File.* Recent works to be covered in his entry include *Mexico Set* and *London Match.*

Jean Genet (French dramatist, novelist, and poet)—Described by Jean Cocteau as France's "Black Prince of letters," Genet was a controversial author who sought to replace Western values with his own system of antimorality. Among his most respected writings are the plays *The Maids* and *The Balcony* and the prose works *The Thief's Journal* and *Our Lady of the Flowers.*

Ken Kesey (American novelist, essayist, and short story writer)—Best known for his experimental novel *One Flew Over the Cuckoo's Nest,* Kesey has ended a long publishing hiatus with *Demon Box,* a collection of essays and short stories.

John Montague (American-born Irish poet, short story writer, and editor)—Montague's recent volumes of verse, *Selected Poems* and *The Dead Kingdom,* have secured his reputation as one of contemporary Ireland's leading poets.

Alberto Moravia (Italian novelist, short story writer, essayist, critic, dramatist, and scriptwriter)—Regarded as one of the foremost twentieth-century Italian literary figures, Moravia often presents a world of decadence and corruption in which his characters are guided primarily by their senses and by sexual obsession. Recent works to be covered in his entry include *Erotic Tales* and *The Voyeur.*

Vladimir Nabokov (Russian-born American novelist, poet, short story writer, essayist, dramatist, and critic)—Considered one of the greatest stylists of twentieth-century literature and renowned for his experimentation with language, Nabokov has gained renewed attention with the posthumous publication of his novel *The Enchanter.*

John Cowper Powys (English novelist, poet, autobiographer, essayist, and critic)—A prolific author in several genres, Powys is admired for the depth of imagination, ornate prose style, and philosophical beliefs displayed in such novels as *Wolf Solent, A Glastonbury Romance,* and *Weymouth Sands.*

Bernard Slade (Canadian-born dramatist and scriptwriter)—A popular Broadway dramatist best known for *Same Time Next Year, Tribute,* and *Romantic Comedy,* Slade combines humor with emotionally affecting situations in plays about marital and familial love.

Tristan Tzara (Rumanian-born French poet, dramatist, and essayist)—Tzara was the founder of Dadaism, an intellectual movement of the World War I era that espoused intentional irrationality and repudiated traditional values of art, history, and religion. Tzara's nihilistic precepts continue to influence contemporary artists of all genres.

Anzia Yezierska (Russian-born novelist and short story writer)—Yezierska is best known for her fiction detailing the experiences of female Jewish immigrants in the United States at the beginning of the twentieth century. Since her death in 1970, several of Yezierska's works have been reissued, prompting renewed critical interest in her writings.

Guest Essay

Guest Essay

Feminist Literary Criticism
by Gayle Greene

Beginnings

Feminist literary criticism originated in the women's movement of the sixties and is part of the larger efforts of feminism to liberate women from the structures that have marginalized them. Inspired by early feminist analyses of the social construction of gender (by Simone de Beauvoir, Juliet Mitchell, Shulamith Firestone, and others), women in the early seventies began taking a new look at the "great books" that we had read in graduate school.

Re-reading the canon from a feminist perspective, we saw that women and men played different roles in literature. Throughout all periods of western culture and in all literary genres, women were the objects, but rarely the initiators of quests, and were praised for qualities (such as chastity, obedience, meekness, humility) that encouraged them to accept their subordination. In the Golden Age of Renaissance literature, women were defined in a particularly narrow and sexual way—reviled as whores or adulated as love objects. In the nineteenth century, the great age of the novel, even the most unconventional of writers—Tolstoy and George Eliot—subjected their heroines to the conventional endings of marriage or death; and the more extraordinary a female protagonist was, the more likely she was to end up dead. Whereas we had been taught that literature expressed "universal truths," we came to see that it expressed the ideas of male writers in specific historical situations and that it passed for "true" because it affirmed prevailing ideology—an ideology that consistently, throughout all ages in our culture, subordinated women. We realized that the canon, far from being "natural" or divinely ordained, was as much a construct of culture as gender itself, and that the standards of literary excellence on which it was based were determined by historical and political circumstances. We came to the startling realization that we had been studying an alien tradition—that the literary and critical tradition was androcentric (male-centered) and defined in a way that excluded women's accomplishments. Such realizations were confirmed by our experience of higher education, since many of us had gone through entire Ph.D. programs without ever taking a course from a woman professor.

We began to ask questions: what accounted for the stereotyping of women in "the great books"? On what basis had these books been "canonized"? And why did the canon include so few women writers? Where were the women writers who might offer an opposing voice, who might suggest an ideal of female character and conduct that provided an alternative to the narrow stereotyping we found in the canon? Such questions constituted a challenge to the androcentric assumptions of literary studies, and it soon became clear that they would re-shape the discipline; for the assumptions of a discipline determine what it deems significant, what constitutes evidence and methodology, and asking new questions brings into existence new evidence and calls for new methodology. Since its inception in the early seventies, feminist criticism has developed in breadth and in theoretical sophistication, and, together with other radical approaches, has made a significant impact on the study of literature. But feminists today are by no means agreed about goals—whether, for example, we wish to add women writers to the existing canon, establish a "counter-canon" of women writers, or eliminate literary canons altogether; and (a related question) whether we wish to "mainstream" women's studies into the traditional curriculum or to establish separate women's studies programs.

Having defined gender as socially constructed—"one is not born, but rather becomes, a woman," in Simone de Beauvoir's famous phrase (p. 273)—feminists were in a position to reconstruct it. That a category which had seemed as "natural," as "essential" and divinely ordained, as gender, could be perceived as a cultural construct was itself a view which was made possible by the more general dethroning of authority that had been begun by Freud, Marx, and Saussure. Saussurean linguistics, which analyzed language as a system of signs; structuralism and semiotics, which analyzed culture as a set of signifying systems; and Derridian deconstruction, which revealed language as a system of differences—all helped to undermine the idea of a transcendental signified to which language refers, and with it, a center or source. Though feminists in the early seventies might not have seen it this way, feminism was part of these larger twentieth-century intellectual movements.

If categories, systems, and cultural paradigms are constructed, then they can be deconstructed and reconstructed. Feminist scholars in literature, as in history and the social sciences, embarked on this two-fold task: deconstructing male paradigms of knowledge and reconstructing new paradigms which include a female perspective. In literature, this took the form of rereading the canon and rediscovering neglected or lost women writers. Elaine Showalter terms these two projects "the feminist critique" and "gynocritics" (1979, p. 25). Sydney Janet Kaplan describes the two foci as originating in different impulses in the reader: the former, originating in the "urge to reveal the diverse ways women have been oppressed, misinterpreted and trivialized by the dominant patriarchal tradition" and the latter, originating in "love for women writers" (1985, p. 37). Her reminder that criticism begins with the individual reader is important, especially since feminist criticism seeks to restore the "I" to reading, urging recognition that literary standards which have passed for "universal," objective, and gender-free, are in fact subjective and gendered.

Rereading the Literary Canon

Those critics who focused on re-reading the canon addressed "images of women" and explored ways in which "structures of primarily male power" "have been—and continue to be—reified in our literature and by our literary criticism" (Kolodny, 1980-a, p. 20). Thus Katharine M. Rogers, *The Troublesome Helpmate* (1966), discussed misogyny in the Bible and classics, and throughout major works of the nineteenth and twentieth centuries. Carolyn Heilbrun's *Toward a Recognition of Androgyny* (1973) traced sexual polarization and an ideal of androgyny throughout the western literary tradition. Kate Millett's *Sexual Politics* (1970) discussed sexism in works of twentieth-century writers Henry Miller, D.H. Lawrence, Norman Mailer, and Jean Genet. Annette Kolodny's *The Lay of the Land* (1975) and Judith Fetterley's *The Resisting Reader* (1977) examined stereotyping of women in American fiction. Mary Ellmann's *Thinking About Women,* (1968), Elizabeth Janeway's *Man's World, Woman's Place,* (1971), and Germaine Greer's *The Female Eunuch,* (1971) participated in similar efforts to liberate women from cultural stereotypes. Feminist critics of Shakespeare—in *The Women's Part: Feminist Criticism of Shakespeare,* eds. Carolyn Ruth Swift Lenz, Gayle Greene, Carol Thomas Neely (1980)—looked at the different roles women and men play in Shakespeare's works and discussed the relation of Shakespeare's plays to Renaissance ideology of woman. The collaborative nature of this anthology was characteristic of much of the new feminist criticism; anthologies, often compiled by two or more editors and including the work of a dozen or more scholars, played a vital role in defining and developing feminist criticism. (Others included Arlyn Diamond and Lee R. Edwards, *The Authority of Experience,* 1977; Cheryl L. Brown and Karen Olsen, *Feminist Criticism,* 1978; Hester Eisenstein and Alice Jardine, *The Future of Difference,* 1980; Elizabeth Abel, Marianne Hirsch, and Elizabeth Langland, *The Voyage In: Fictions of Female Development,* 1983; Gayle Green and Coppélia Kahn, *Making a Difference,* 1985.)

Rediscovering Women Writers

Of those critics who were concerned with women writers, Elaine Showalter has been the leading proponent in American feminist criticism of a "women's literature" and "women's literary tradition." Her pioneering *A Literature of Their Own: British Women Novelists from Bronte to Lessing* (1977) set the example for the study of women writers which she later termed "gynocriticism": "the history of styles, themes, genres, and structures of writing by women" (1981, pp. 181-85), the development of "new models based on the study of female experience" and "female culture" (1979, p. 28). Feminist studies of this sort include Patricia Meyer Spacks's *The Female Imagination* (1975), Sydney Janet Kaplan's *Feminine Consciousness in the Modern British Novel* (1975), Ellen Moers's *Literary Women* (1977), Sandra Gilbert and Susan Gubar's *The Madwoman in the Attic* (1979), Annis Pratt's *Archetypal Patterns in Women's Fiction* (1981).

The rediscovery of women writers could not have been accomplished without the reprinting of women's writings. The Feminist Press in America and Virago Books in England reissued works such as Rebecca Harding Davis's *Life in the Iron Mills* and Charlotte Perkins Gilman's *The Yellow Wallpaper,* as well as novels by Dorothy Richardson, May Sinclair, Sarah Grand, Antonia White, Agnes Smedley, Zora Neale Hurston, Paule Marshall. Commercial presses have also been reissuing women's works, and novels by such writers as Penelope Mortimer, Ann Petry, Jean Rhys, and Joanna Russ are now available in inexpensive paperbacks. The Women's Press in England publishes an extensive selection of contemporary fiction by women. Anthologies play a role in this part of the enterprise also: Mary R. Mahl and Helene Koon's *The Female Spectator* (1977) compiled previously unpublished women's writings before 1800; poetry anthologies were edited by Louise Bernikow (1974), Florence Howe and Ellen Bass (1973) and Cora Kaplan (1975); Mary Helen Washington's *Midnight Birds: Stories by Contemporary Black Women Writers* (1980) and Dexter Fisher's *The Third Woman: Minority Women Writers of the United States* (1980), also deserve mention, along with Sandra M. Gilbert and Susan's Gubar's *Norton Anthology of Literature by Women* (see Sydney Janet Kaplan for discussion of this aspect of feminist criticism [1985]).

Revisioning Literature

Whether we were rereading the canon or rediscovering women writers, feminist critics embarked on what Annette Kolodny terms "a revisionist rereading of our entire literary inheritance" (1980-b, pp. 464-65). Adrienne Rich defines "re-vision"—"the act of looking back, of seeing with fresh eyes, of entering an old text from a new critical direction"—as the main task of feminist criticism; and she adds that for women this is "more than a chapter in cultural history: it is an act of survival" (p. 35). Whether reading works by women or by men, feminist critics found themselves challenging the criteria on which the canon was based. We came to see that women writers had been excluded from the canon because we had learned how to read and formed our criteria of "excellence" from a canon which excluded them—which meant that we had never learned how to read them.

Revising our ways of reading, we found ourselves opposed to the basic assumptions of so-called "new criticism," the critical approach which originated in the fifties and prevailed throughout the sixties and which had been the staple of our graduate educations. New criticism engaged in close readings of texts with a view to discovering their "unity" and the "universal truths" they expressed, which meant that it asked questions that isolated literature from its social and historical context and tended to de-politicize literary studies. Feminists insisted that the social and historical conditions that produced texts mattered, and that to deny the political implications of literary studies was in itself a political statement. While not abandoning the techniques of close reading learned from new criticism, we enlisted them to different ends; and we differed from other approaches not by being more "political" in our ends and assumptions, but by more openly acknowledging the political implications of our own and of all other critical approaches.

The two foci of feminist criticism—rereading the canon and reading women writers—lead to different questions and concerns. The "patriarchal critique" attended to the representation of women and inscription of ideology in works written by men; "gynocriticism" asked questions about a women's style, "women's tradition," and a counter-canon of women's writings. But the two enterprises also intersected in various ways, as questions raised by the reading of women writers inevitably challenged the accepted categories of the androcentric discipline—categories such as periods and genres. In the same way that including women in history modified traditional notions of periodizaton—showing, for example, that there had never been a "Renaissance" for women—so did the reading of women writers begin to reshape definitions of literary periods, altering, for example, our understanding of modernism, its causes and characteristics (see Kaplan, 1985, p. 48). Traditional definitions of the *Bildungsroman* turn out to be based, not surprisingly, on male experience and a male norm of development. Since women's search for adulthood conflicts with gender norms that dictate that "girls grow down rather than up" (Pratt, p. 168), female development takes a different course—it is often a "voyage in"; and definitions of the genre are altered when fictions of female development are taken into account. Feminist critics seek wider generic definitions that can accommodate women's stories (see Abel, Hirsch, and Langland, 1983).

In the decade and a half since its inception, the emphasis in feminist criticism has shifted from a critique of the canon to a study of women writers, and this shift reflects a larger shift in feminism. Early feminist efforts, influenced by such works as Simone de Beauvoir's *The Second Sex* (1952), aimed at equality for women—an ideal which assumes a basic similarity between the sexes or the desirability of similarity. Heilbrun's argument for androgyny implied that women should become less like women and more like men; and she went further, to argue that women should emulate "male" qualities such as autonomy, independence, and selfishness, that we "revinvent womenhood" on the male model (1979). But a second stage of feminist thought emphasizes "differences," differences which have been reconceptualized to women's advantage, and this change was corroborated by revisionist analyses in the social sciences. Jane Flax, Nancy Chodorow, Dorothy Dinnerstein, Jean Baker Miller, Carol Gilligan, were redefining female identity in positive terms: that women conceive of themselves in terms of relationship and have more fluid ego boundaries than men do is viewed as a strength rather than weakness. These qualities constitute not a failed adulthood, which they were when judged by "male" standards of maturity—autonomy and separation—but a different (and some claimed, a better) kind of maturity. Hester Eisenstein accounts for this change in terms of the situation of the women's movement historically: whereas initially we needed to prove women's worth in men's terms—that "differences between women and men had been exaggerated, and that they could be *reduced*" (1980, p. xvi)—this need became less urgent at a later stage.

Differences in French and Anglo-American Feminism

This shift characterized feminism in France as well, where "a new generation of French feminists. . .reject de Beauvoir's desire for equality as a covert attempt to force women to become like men" (Moi, p. 98). But otherwise French feminist theory developed according to principles which were different from those which informed Anglo-American feminist criticism, proceeding according to assumptions concerning language, text, and the relation of text to experience unlike our own. Implicit in gynocriticism is the assumption that women's writing "reflects" women's experiences. But in French feminist theory, which derives from post-Saussurean linguistics, structuralism, and Derridian deconstruction, language is not assumed to be a "reflection" of experience, a transparent medium on a pre-existent reality, but is, rather, viewed as a set of signifying practices which is constitutive of reality; as such, it is not neutral, but ideologically complicit. Feminist critics who accept these assumptions—Toril Moi, Alice Jardine, Mary Jacobus—argue that the view of texts as unproblematically transmitting "truth" is precisely the view on which the canon has been predicated, that it conceals assumptions about language and literature which have been the basis of the traditional paradigm of knowledge, and that it thereby reaffirms the system we should be challenging. Whereas Anglo-American feminist criticism aims at liberating women from cultural sterotypes, Franco-feminism aims at dismantling the system that has produced these stereotypes, enlisting Derridian deconstruction to "deconstruct" the binary oppositions which are the basis of western thought and of the hierarchies that dictate women's subordination. (For the logic of opposites—male/female, light/dark, order/chaos, presence/absence—inevitably leads to the valuation of one term at the expense of the other, which has always meant the valuation of male over female.)

The most fundamental difference between French and Anglo-American feminism concerns the question of language. If language is a construct inscribing patriarchal ideology, woman cannot express or represent herself in it, let alone use it to challenge the system which has oppressed her; and whether she can write or even speak using the tools of the oppressor becomes a central question. Thus French feminists Hélène Cixous and Luce Irigaray advocate an alternative discourse which is based on female physiology and sexuality—*"l'écriture féminine,"* writing the body. The complex physicality of female experience, the rhythms and sensations of the female body, represent a challenge to conventional structures and provide the basis of a "new insurgent writing" (in Cixous's terms in "The Laugh of the Medusa," the manifesto of *"l'écriture féminine"*). Julia Kristeva maintains that women's experience of *joissance* (pleasures repressed by patriarchal culture) can be the source of subversive energy and of an alternative discourse.

Since 1980, when Domna Stanton articulated this "Franco-American disconnection" (pp. 78-9), the differences between French and American feminist critical practice and theory have emerged as a focus of feminist discussions (Homans, Moi, Greene and Kahn, Jardine, Marks). Some efforts have been made at bridging this disconnection, but the approaches differ in basic ways. Franco-feminism is in certain respects more radical; it goes to the "root" of women's oppression in challenging the system which is the source of the problem; though it is also true that the ideal of *"l'écriture féminine"* reaffirms notions of "essential" femaleness which feminism has supposedly repudiated. Anglo-American feminism is less theoretical, but it has been more effective in practical terms; it has brought about changes within academic institutions, established women's studies programs, and been instrumental in curricular reforms. Moreover, whereas French feminist theory has produced little practical criticism, especially of women writers, Anglo-American feminism has not only succeeded in recovering many lost or neglected women writers, but has addressed the critical issues they raise.

In England feminists have always had a clear sense of the relation of women's subordination to the economic and social system. British feminism sees women's oppression as an instance of the exploitation of all people by capitalism and views the feminist revolution not as a matter of women seizing men's privileges, but of a radical transformation in the structures of society. The leading British feminists—Michele Barrett, Juliet Mitchell, Cora Kaplan, Rosalind Coward—enlist Marxist analyses of economic and class structures and the ideology and institutions of literary production.

One of the challenges facing American feminist criticism today is to incorporate the findings of British and French feminism—Marxist and deconstructionist analyses—into its own positions, in order to develop a theory and practice true to the most radical implications of its critiques. We cannot ignore French theory because it is in France that thought has most fully responded to the disruptive movements of the twentieth century and the most radical analytical tools have developed. And without a socialist understanding of class and economics, feminist criticism narrowly privileges gender in isolation from other forms of social determination. Feminist criticism must also attend to issues of race. Though it developed as a white, middle-class, academic movement, it must not remain parochial; it must not practice the same exclusion of others that has been practiced against women. The existence of works by women of color and lesbian writers raises questions analogous to those posed by women's writings in relation to a male-dominated tradition: is there a lesbian and black women's tradition? How will women's literature be altered when the work of lesbian and black black women writers is not merely added to but incorporated into it? (Robinson, 1983; Smith, 1982).

Feminist criticism must also decide whether it wishes to propose a counter-canon of women writers. My own feeling is that if we substitute one canon for another we will perpetuate the terms which we are trying to challenge, reduplicate the basic assumption—of woman as "other," separate and apart—that we are trying to change, and that this will relegate the study of women's writing to a women's studies ghetto. This question reflects a further argument, whether we should be building separate women's studies programs or "mainstreaming" the study of women into traditional parts of the curriculum. But I would agrue that the terms of this argument are themselves misleading, another version of the binary oppositions Franco-feminism has rightly challenged: surely we ought to insist on *both* women's studies programs *and* the incorporation of women into the curriculum.

The Future of Feminist Criticism

From rereading the canon to recovering women writers, feminist criticism is now moving into what Showalter terms a "third phase": "what we are demanding is a new universal literary history and criticism that combines the literary experiences of both women and men, a complete revolution in the understanding of our literary heritage," "a radical rethinking of the conceptual grounds of literary study, a revision of the accepted theoretical assumptions about reading and writing" (1985, pp. 10, 8). This "new universal literary history and criticism" should be inclusive of literature by women and men. By considering works by women and men in relation to one another, feminist criticism will not join the "mainstream," but will rather, redirect it, widening the field of literary studies as it alters the paradigm on which it is based; and it should ask not whether a text has been written by a woman and reflects her experience of life or how it compares to other works by women, but how texts work as signifying processes which inscribe ideology. Though it may be more logically consistent to dispense with the literary canon altogether, since any privileging of one work over another reasserts the hierarchy we are opposing, nevertheless, in practical terms, some sort of canon is probably necessary. But we should remember—and this is one of the main lessons of feminist criticism—that the canon is culturally produced rather than "universal"; that it is a process rather than a product; and that it is always being written, always in formation. Feminist literary criticism also needs to be responsive to revisionist scholarship in other areas; since "the production of 'woman' in discourse. . . traverses many different discourses—medical, legal, biological, psychoanalytic. . . The proper study of 'woman' is consequently a trans-disciplinary venture" (Ruthven, 1984, pp. 74-5).

Thus feminist literary criticism faces the challenge of incorporating feminist scholarship from other disciplines and approaches in order to develop a theory and practice that are truly revolutionary. In this enterprise its eclecticism is a strength. From the beginning, it had the capacity to enlist whatever tool or method worked, whether new critical, psychoanalytic, socio-historical, or Marxist. In 1980, Annette Kolodny noted this "playful pluralism" and praised feminist criticism for being "responsive to the possibilities of multiple critical schools and methods, but captive of none" (1980-a, p. 19); and though other critics have attacked it for having no methodology (as though other critical approaches have "a methodology"), I think she was right to see this pluralism as enabling. I am not suggesting that feminist criticism strive to be free of theory (as though this were possible): but that, rather than trying to slot ourselves into a single critical "methodology," we recognize that feminist criticism encompasses a range of subjects and diversity of approaches, and that its method varies according to subject and approach. Feminist criticism of Shakespeare works differently from feminist criticism of women writers; and Marxist-feminist critics of Shakespeare enlist methods different from those enlisted by feminist psychoanalytic critics of the plays. And if Marxist feminists draw on Marx, and psychoanalytic feminists on Freud or Lacan, and structuralists on Derrida, this does not mean that we are recuperating authorities we ought to be repudiating or slavishly following the law of the fathers; it means, rather, that we are enlisting the most radical analyses of culture to our purposes.

Some recent feminist criticism exemplifies the sort of theoretically-rigorous and radical eclecticism that I am advocating as a feminist critical practice. In *Writing Beyond the Ending: Narrative Strategies of Twentieth-Century Women Writers* (1985), Rachel Blau DuPlessis describes the project of twentieth-century women writers as "cultural critique," and her own work is itself exemplary of the sort of cultural critique she addresses. DePlessis begins from a discussion of narrative as an "expression of ideology" (p. x) which combines Marxist analyses of ideology with revisionist psychoanalytic analyses of the gendering process. She demonstrates that the romance plot, which centers on love and culminates in woman's marriage or death, ratifies traditional assumptions about "femininity" and is "a trope for the sex gender system" (p. 5). Both marriage and death reinforce the same rules: heterosexuality, the hierarchy of the sexes, woman's confinement to the domestic space. But twentieth-century women novelists and poets write beyond the ending—beyond the telos of romance—in a variety of ways, using narrative to "dissent from social norms as well as narrative forms" (p. 20). DuPlessis argues that the aesthetic that emerges from women's *Künstlerromane*—a "poetics of domestic values," an art "immersed in human relations" and "charged with the conditions of its own creation" (p. 97)—is different from the aesthetic that emerges from *Künstlerromane* written by men. Again, as with the *Bildungsroman,* we see that a consideration of women's writings results in a revision of traditional generic definitions. DuPlessis's book makes clear the larger implications of feminist criticism, its revisionary efforts to change our society by changing our stories.

Works Cited

Abel, Elizabeth, ed. *Writing and Sexual Difference.* University of Chicago Press, 1983.

——. With Marianne Hirsch and Elizabeth Langland, eds. *The Voyage In: Fictions of Female Development.* Hanover, NH: University Press of New England, 1983.

Barrett, Michele. *Women's Oppression Today: Problems in Marxist Feminist Analysis.* London: Villiers Publications, 1980.

Bernikow, Louise, *Among Women.* New York: Harmony-Crown, 1980.

Brown, Cherly L., and Olsen, Karen, eds. *Feminist Criticism: Essays on Theory, Poetry, and Prose.* Metuchen, NJ: Scarecrow Press, 1978.

Chodorow, Nancy. *The Reproduction of Mothering: Psychoanalysis and the Sociology of Gender.* Berkeley: University of California Press, 1978.

Cixous, Hélène. "The Laugh of the Medusa." *Signs* 1 (1976): 875-93; rpt. in Marks and Courtivron, *New French Feminisms,* 245-64.

Coward, Rosalind. *Language and Materialism: Developments in Semiology and the Theory of the Subject.* London: Routledge and Kegan Paul, 1977.

de Beauvoir, Simone. *The Second Sex.* New York: Vintage, 1952.

Diamond, Arlyn, and Edwards, Lee R., eds. *The Authority of Experience: Essays in Feminist Criticism.* Amherst: University of Massachusetts Press, 1977.

Dinnerstein, Dorothy. *The Mermaid and the Minotaur.* New York: Harper and Row, 1976.

Donovan, Josephine, ed. *Feminist Literary Criticism: Explorations in Theory.* Lexington: University of Kentucky Press, 1975.

DuPlessis, Rachel Blau. *Writing Beyond the Ending.* Bloomington: Indiana University Press, 1985.

Edwards, Lee R. *Psyche as Hero: Female Heroism and Fictional Form.* Middletown, CN: Wesleyan University Press, 1984.

Eisenstein, Hester, and Jardine, Alice, eds. *The Future of Difference: The Scholar and the Feminist.* Boston: G.K. Hall, 1980.

Ellmann, Mary. *Thinking About Women.* New York: Harcourt, Brace and World, 1968.

Fergusson, Mary Anne. "The Female Novel of Development and the Myth of Psyche," in Abel, Hirsch, and Langland, *The Voyage In,* 228-43.

Fetterley, Judith. *The Resisting Reader: A Feminist Approach to American Fiction.* Bloomington: Indiana University Press, 1978.

Firestone, Shulamith. *The Dialectic of Sex: The Case for Feminist Revolution.* New York: Bantam, 1970.

Fisher, Dexter, ed. *The Third Woman: Minority Women Writers of the United States.* Boston: Houghton Mifflin, 1980.

Flax, Jane. "The Conflict Between Nurturance and Autonomy in Mother-Daughter Relationships and within Feminism." *Feminist Studies* 4 (1978): 171-89.

Gilbert, Sandra M., and Gubar, Susan. *The Madwoman in the Attic: The Woman Writer and the Nineteenth-Century Literary Imagination.* New Haven: Yale University Press, 1979.

____. Eds. *The Norton Anthology of Literature by Women.* New York: W.W. Norton, 1985.

Gilligan, Carol. *In a Different Voice: Psychological Theory and Women's Development.* Cambridge: Harvard University Press, 1982.

Greene, Gayle, and Kahn, Coppélia. *Making a Difference: Feminist Literary Criticism.* London, New York: Methuen, 1985.

Greer, Germaine. *The Female Eunuch.* New York: McGraw Hill, 1971.

Heilbrun, Carolyn G. *Toward a Recognition of Androgyny.* New York: Knopf, 1978.

____. *Reinventing Womanhood.* New York: Norton, 1979.

Homans, Margaret, "'Her Very Own Howl': The Ambiguities of Representation in Recent Women's Fiction." *Signs* 9 (1983): 186-205.

Hull, Gloria T.; Scott, Patricia Bell; and Smith, Barbara, eds. *All the Women Are White, All the Blacks Are Men, But Some of Us Are Brave.* New York: Old Westbury, Feminist Press, 1982.

Howe, Florence, and Bass, Ellen, eds. *No More Masks! An Anthology of Poems by Women.* Garden City, NY: Doubleday, 1973.

Irigaray, Luce. *This Sex Which Is Not One.* Translated by Catherine Porter with Carolyn Burke. Ithaca, NY: Cornell University Press, 1985.

Jacobus, Mary, "The Difference of View," in *Women Writing and Writing About Women,* ed., Jacobus. New York: Barnes and Noble, 1979.

____. "The Question of Language: Men of Maxims and *The Mill on the Floss.*" *Critical Inquiry 8* (Winter 1981); rpt. in Abel, *Writing and Sexual Difference.*

____. "Is There a Woman in This Text?" *New Literary History* 14 (Autumn 1982).

Janeway, Elizabeth. *Man's World, Woman's Place.* New York: Penguin, 1971.

Jardine, Alice. *Gynesis: Configurations of Women and Modernity.* Ithaca and London: Cornell University Press, 1985.

Kaplan, Cora, ed. *Salt and Bitter and Good: Three Centuries of English and American Women Poets.* New York: Paddington Press, 1975.

____. "Pandora's Box: Subjectivity, Class, and Sexuality in Socialist Feminist Criticism," in Greene and Kahn, *Making a Difference,* 146-76.

Kaplan, Sydney Janet. *Feminine Consciousness in the Modern British Novel.* Urbana: University of Illinois Press, 1975.

____. "Varieties of Feminist Criticism," in Greene and Kahn, *Making a Difference,* 37-58.

Kolodny, Annette. *The Lay of the Land: Metaphor as Experience in American Life and Letters.* Chapel Hill, N.C.: University of North Carolina Press, 1975.

____. "Dancing through the Minefield: Some Observations on the Theory, Practice, and Politics of a Feminist Literary Criticism." *Feminist Studies* 6 (Spring, 1980-a): 1-25.

____. "A Map for Rereading; or, Gender and the Interpretation of Literary Texts." *New Literary History* 11 (Spring, 1980-b): 451-67.

Kristeva, Julia. *Revolution in Poetic Language.* Translated by Margaret Waller. New York: Columbia University Press, 1984.

Lenz, Carolyn Ruth Swift; Greene, Gayle; and Neely, Carol Thomas, eds. *The Women's Part: Feminist Criticism of Shakespeare.* Champaign: University of Illinois Press, 1980.

Mahl, Mary R., and Koon, Helene, eds. *The Female Spectator: English Women Writers Before 1800.* Bloomington: Indiana University Press, 1977.

Marks, Elaine. "Women and Literature in France." *Signs* 3, no. 4 (1978).

____. With de Courtivron, Isabelle, eds. *New French Feminisms: An Anthology.* Amherst: University of Massachusetts Press, 1980.

Mitchell, Juliet. *Woman's Estate.* New York: Vintage, 1971.

Miller, Jean Baker. *Toward a New Psychology of Women.* Boston: Beacon Press, 1976.

Miller, Nancy K. *The Heroine's Text: Readings in the French and English Novel, 1722-1782.* New York: Columbia University Press, 1980.

____. "Emphasis Added: Plots and Plausibilities in Women's Fiction." *PMLA* 96, no. 1 (1981).

Millett, Kate. *Sexual Politics.* Garden City, NY: Doubleday, 1970.

Moers, Ellen. *Literary Women: The Great Writers.* Garden City, NY: Anchor Press, Doubleday, 1977.

Moi, Toril. *Sexual/Textual Politics.* New York: Methuen, 1985.

Pratt, Annis. *Archetypal Patterns in Women's Fiction.* Bloomington: Indiana University Press, 1981.

Rich, Adrienne. "When We Dead Awaken: Writing as Re-Vision," in *On Lies, Secrets, and Silence: Selected Prose, 1966-1978,* 33-49. New York: W.W. Norton, 1979.

Robinson, Lillian S. "Treason Our Text: Feminist Challenges to the Literary Canon." *Tulsa Studies in Women's Literature* 2, no. 1 (Spring): 83-98.

Rogers, Katharine M. *The Troublesome Helpmate: A History of Misogyny in Literature.* Seattle: University of Washington Press, 1966.

Ruthven, K.K. *Feminist Literary Studies: An Introduction.* Cambridge: Cambridge University Press, 1984.

Showalter, Elaine. *A Literature of Their Own.* Princeton: Princeton University Press, 1977.

____. "Literary Criticism." *Signs* 1, no. 2 (1975).

____. "Towards a Feminist Poetics." *Jacobus* (1979): 22-41.

____. "Feminist Criticism in the Wilderness." *Critical Inquiry* 8, no. 2 (1981): 179-205.

____. "Women's Time, Women's Space: Writing the History of Feminist Criticism." *Tulsa Studies in Women's Literature* 3, (Spring/Fall 1984).

____. Ed. *The New Feminist Criticism.* New York: Pantheon, 1985.

Smith, Barbara. "Towards a Black Feminist Criticism," in Hull, Scott, and Smith, *All the Women Are White, All the Blacks Are Men, But Some of Us Are Brave.*

Spacks, Patricia Meyer. *The Female Imagination.* New York: Knopf, 1985.

Stanton, Domna C. "Language and Revolution: The Franco-American Dis-Connection," in Eisenstein and Jardine, *The Future of Difference: The Scholar and the Feminist,* 73-87.

Wasington, Mary Helen, ed. *Midnight Birds: Stories by Contemporary Black Women Writers.* New York: Doubleday, 1980.

The Year in Review

The Year in Fiction

by Dianne Donovan and John Blades

The year was made memorable less by the appearance of stunning new books than by the remarkable stamina of several old ones, whose anniversaries were marked with reissues, facsimile copies, and at least one unlikely celebration. A. A. Milne's ***Winnie the Pooh*** celebrated its sixtieth year in print, and Munro Leaf's ***Ferdinand the Bull*** turned fifty along with Margaret Mitchell's ***Gone With the Wind. Catch-22,*** Joseph Heller's hilarious and jaundiced look at a military at war with itself, was still in print after twenty-five years—and the Air Force threw a party to celebrate.

Celebration, though perhaps of a less literary sort, also was in order for publishers of the blockbuster best sellers of 1986, led off by Stephen King's *It* and James Clavell's *Whirlwind,* two of the year's biggest books in both size and sales. King, the self-described "McDonald's of literature," once again tapped into the dark night of childhood guilts and fears for his opus (1,138 pages) on the tracking down of a "presence" living in the sewers beneath an outwardly peaceful Maine town. Clavell veered from his traditional Japanese locale with ***Whirlwind,*** a thriller set in Iran in the days just before the fall of the Shah.

But as in years past, a place on the best-seller list did not guarantee a place on the perennial bookshelf occupied by Winnie and Ferdinand; indeed, the bedroom, not the library, seemed the most appropriate spot for novels by top-selling veteran titillators Jackie Collins (***Hollywood Husbands***), Danielle Steel (***Wanderlust***), and Judith Krantz (***I'll Take Manhattan***).

In the same vein, journalist Sally Quinn's embarrassing ***Regrets Only,*** a story of sex, power, and ennui in Washington made best-seller lists across the country even as critics marveled at its wooden writing and plot deficiencies. Faring somewhat better was Karleen Koen's historical epic ***Through a Glass Darkly,*** which came in for more attention than might ordinarily be paid a first novel because of the $350,000 Random House paid housewife Koen for writing it.

Another relative newcomer, Tom Clancy, had a top seller in 1986 with the naval thriller ***Red Storm Rising.*** Clancy, a former insurance salesman, had seen his first novel, *The Hunt for Red October,* gain national attention in 1985 when President Reagan called it "a perfect yarn."

And near-perfect is what a number of lower-profile critics called Pat Conroy's ***The Prince of Tides,*** the story of a man haunted by memories of a cruel and violent past dominated by a tyrannical father. The book, set in Conroy's familiar South Carolina territory, managed to be both a commercial and critical success.

Also enjoying both literary and commercial success—though more the former than the latter—was John Updike's ***Roger's Version,*** a novel that was in many ways a departure for Updike in that it dealt more explicitly with science and theology than with sex. The book, which matched a young computer wizard against a divinity professor in an attempt to prove the existence of God, was technically impressive, but chilly and schematic. It seemed less like a novel than a very calculated virtuoso performance, a showcase for Updike's intellectual and reportorial skills, his authoritative grasp of computer technology, and, above all else, his fulsome prose.

Like Updike, Robert Stone is a writer obsessed with moral issues, though his refusal to make explicit moral judgments has caused him to be accused, wrongly, of amorality. ***Children of Light*** was the most alienating of his four novels, the story of a spiritually depleted, drugged-out actor-writer who pursues his former lover, an unbalanced Hollywood actress, to a Mexican film location, where they act out all their most degraded, and ultimately fatal, fantasies. Stone's compassion for his characters was admirable, but so cold-blooded that it was impossible to warm up to them or the book.

On the other hand, it was impossible not to respond sympathetically to the youthful lovers in Thomas Williams's ***The Moon Pinnace.*** A writer who's never quite connected with a wide readership despite much critical praise and numerous prizes (including a National Book Award for *The Hair of Harold Roux*), Williams was at his best in this, his ninth novel. Set during the summer of 1948, ***The Moon Pinnace*** (a whimsical reference to the shape of a lima bean) was a charming, circuitous love story that had the allusory quality of an adult fairy tale.

Both Williams and Updike were among the nominees for National Book Critics Circle Awards, an honor that went to Reynolds Price for his graceful and remarkably perceptive ***Kate Vaiden.*** The story of Kate, a bright but emotionally confused woman who abandons her baby, is told in her voice and spans her life from girlhood to age fifty-seven. The creation of this tough, touching, and very real narrator was a triumph for Price.

Also an NBCC nominee, Louise Erdrich—who won the award in 1984 for *Love Medicine*—proved with the 1986 publication of ***The Beet Queen*** that she had not lost her touch for creating memorable characters living everyday lives that reflect universal themes. A critical and popular success, this story of abandonment and love, of victims and survivors in small-town North Dakota was in many ways a reprise of the earlier novel, with large doses of laugh-out-loud humor.

Another NBCC also-ran, Peter Taylor, nominated for his novel, ***A Summons to Memphis,*** went on to win the Pulitzer and the Ritz Paris Hemingway Award, neither of which can be considered consolation prizes. Taylor's story was narrated by Philip Carver, a transplanted Southerner living in Manhattan, whose sisters summon him home to Memphis when their aging and recently widowed father threatens to marry a younger woman. Though it pleased most critics, a few felt Taylor was out of his element, that his novel didn't have the precision of his best short stories.

If Taylor had temporarily abandoned the short story, it wasn't suffering from neglect by other old and young hands. So many collections appeared in 1986, as well as in previous years, that there was talk of a short story renaissance—talk discouraged by Ted Solotaroff, who as an editor at Harper & Row, formerly of the *New American Review,* is considered one of the chief preservationists of the story. "For some reason the market seems to be interested in short story collections," said Solotaroff, "and since they need to put a fancy term on it for media consumption, it's called a renaissance. What's happening, though, is that there's a *trend* for the short story."

Whatever it's called, trend or renaissance, there's no question that this was an uncommonly productive year for the short story, with books by Ann Beattie, Thomas McGuane, Joyce Carol Oates, Shirley Ann Grau and Ellen Gilchrist, among many others. For Beattie, her new collection, ***Where You'll Find Me,*** was a return to the form, after having published a novel the year before. Beattie was not at the top of her form, however; the fifteen stories in the book were often so elliptical and fragmentary that they read like parodies of her earlier, influential work.

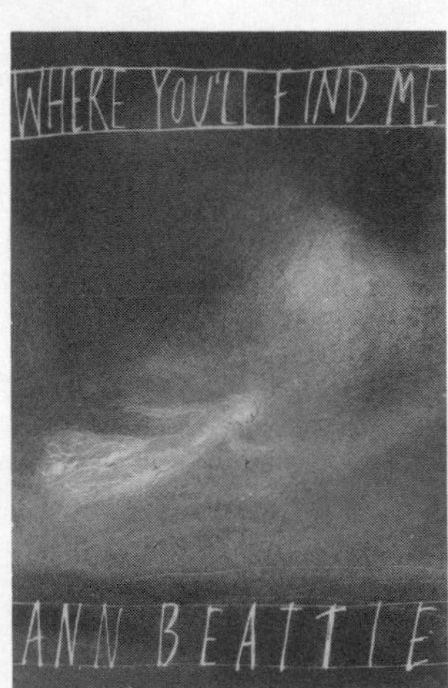

Dust jacket of Moon Pinnace, *by Thomas Williams. Doubleday, 1986. Jacket painting by Bill Creevy. Jacket typography by Hideo Ietaka. Courtesy of Doubleday & Company, Inc. Dust jacket of* The Beet Queen, *by Louise Erdrich. Henry Holt, 1986. Jacket design and illustration copyright © 1986 by Wendell Minor. Courtesy of Henry Holt and Company, Inc. Dust jacket of* Where You'll Find Me, *by Ann Beattie. Linden Press, 1986. Jacket design by Carin Goldberg. Jacket illustration by Vivienne Flesher. Courtesy of Simon & Schuster, Inc.*

The Beattie influence, especially her use of the present tense and her "minimalist" technique, was evident in Peter Cameron's ***One Way or Another,*** brittle, entertaining, but transparently derivative stories about the post-Beattie generation. Cameron's stories were unintentionally minimalist, perhaps—missing the emotional resonance of Beattie's best work, which was largely missing in her new collection as well.

For pure trendiness, though, it was hard to top Tama Janowitz's ***Slaves of New York,*** stories set in and around the SoHo art scene. That the book became a best seller was due as much to Janowitz's beguiling appearances on television as for its literary merits, though they weren't negligible. More substantial and impressive, in some ways, than either of these first collections was Robert Boswell's ***Dancing in the Movies,*** grim, violent stories, centering on a lost generation of druggies and drifters, that won the author the Iowa School of Letters Award for Short Fiction.

Joyce Carol Oates was unfailingly cheerless in ***Raven's Wing,*** a group of stories notable, as her stories and novels inevitably are, for their undercurrents of psychological and spiritual violence, for their Gothic permutations. By contrast, Pulitzer Prize-winning novelist Shirley Ann Grau seemed almost high-spirited in ***Nine Women,*** even though her stories somberly examined the ways in which her various heroines "come to uneasy terms," as one critic put it, "with a world that lacks sense." Where Grau's fiction concentrated exclusively on feminine traumas, the emphasis in Russell Banks's ***Success Stories*** was on male disorders, which he made amusing as well as painful.

The stories in Ellen Gilchrist's ***Drunk with Love*** had their abrasive edges, too, with glimpses into adolescent love, premature marriage, and family misfortune, but these were softened by the author's buoyance and humor, qualities that helped her win an American Book Award for an earlier collection, *Victory over Japan.*

Tom McGuane's ***To Skin a Cat*** included a fifty-page novella about a spoiled young man who aspires to be a pimp, but most of the dozen shorter, finely crafted works were about outdoorsmen and -women, whose emotionally chaotic lives were out of harmony with their bucolic environment. McGuane's fellow Montanan, Rick DeMarinis, won a Drue Heinz Literature Prize for *Under the Wheat,* adult fairy tales with contemporary and black comedic twists.

Perhaps the year's most unconventional and off-center collection was Ian Frazier's ***Dating Your Mom,*** irreverent but in no way incestuous stories. These weren't so much short stories as satirical vignettes, revealing what one critic called a "strange and wondrous mind at play."

That description could just as easily fit Donald Barthelme, whose playfully abstract stories, like Frazier's, regularly show up in *The New Yorker*. This year brought not another book of short fiction from Barthelme but his third novel, ***Paradise.*** This was the story of a fiftyish architect, an empty nester, who abandons wife and practice, then moves to a New York apartment, another empty nest that he turns into "hog heaven" with two women he picks up in a bar. Though this mock immorality tale was marked by Barthelme's stylish idiosyncracies and his verbal ingenuity, it was also considered his most accessible fiction yet.

If Barthelme's novel portrayed a fantasy Paradise, then Denis Johnson's third novel, ***The Stars at Noon,*** took place in a real inferno, contemporary Nicaragua, as seen through the eyes of a whore posing as a freelance journalist. While it superficially resembled a Third World thriller, Johnson's novel was actually a labyrinthine passion play, with overtones of spiritual torment and betrayal; intensely mystical and poetic, the novel had all the texture and illogic of a nightmare, which seemed only fitting for a country that threatens to detonate into a Central American Vietnam.

Peru provided the title but not the setting for Gordon Lish's second novel. In fact, the book's only allusion to the South American country came in a reference to a TV newsclip showing an act of terrorism there; Lish, who is perhaps better known as an editor than a writer, used this reference to trigger the memories of a man who years earlier had killed a six-year-old playmate in a sandbox. ***Peru*** is a highly fragmented story that was impossible to appreciate, as one reviewer observed, unless you feel comfortable reading the monologues of inarticulate, psychotic characters.

Also generally disappointing was Scott Spencer's ***Waking the Dead.*** With the thoroughly unlikable Fielding Pierce at its center, this tale of ambition and hopeless love predictably was compared to his previous novel, the critically acclaimed *Endless Love,* and found inferior.

Ernest Hemingway's ***The Garden of Eden*** became his second posthumous book (after *The Dangerous Summer*) to appear on best-seller lists in two years. Unfinished at his death, the novel had to be drastically edited before it was published by Scribners; but the prose was vintage Hemingway, even if the allegedly autobiographical plot—which featured androgyny and bisexuality among American expatriates in France—was not. Though reviews were generally approving, ***The Garden of Eden,*** as edited, was the target of blistering criticism by Barbara Probst Solomon, who, after comparing the cut version with the 1,500-page manuscript, pronounced it a "travesty" of Hemingway's intentions.

A posthumous short novel (or perhaps long short story) written by Vladimir Nabokov in 1939 also saw first publication in 1986. ***The Enchanter*** was more a curiosity than a finished work, interesting primarily because this story of an unnamed middle-age jeweler and a twelve-year-old roller-skating vixen contains the embryonic characters that would become Lolita and Humbert Humbert.

Spiritual exhaustion was the crucial element in Richard Yates's ***Cold Spring Harbor,*** a novel that, like the author's other fiction, depicted life (or perhaps living death) in suburban America with relentless dispassion and deadpan prose. Beginning just before Pearl Harbor, the book followed its male protagonist, who has more affection for cars than people, through marriage, infidelity, divorce, years of hard drinking—all the morbidly fascinating ingredients that have been so fundamental a part of Yates's novels and stories, from *Revolutionary Road* to *Young Hearts Crying*.

Geoffrey Wolff's fourth novel, ***Providence,*** was a tightly written almost-thriller that moved from tragedy to tragedy with a grace undeserved by a contrived and ultimately sordid plot, which revolved around five characters who worked out their destinies over the course of one long summer in Providence, R.I.

Almost equally downbeat was Richard Ford's ***The Sportswriter,*** with the title character a divorced, burned-out novelist, whose creative bankruptcy has forced him to employ his talents on a slick sports magazine. It was a measure of Ford's talent, his empathy and insight, that he made the reader respond to the emotional plight of his alienated hero. A paperback original from Vintage, ***The Sportswriter*** was also notable for the sensitive but unsentimentalized way the author handled the death of the hero's young son.

Death was treated far more casually in Cathie Pelletier's ***The Funeral Makers,*** a mordant joyride through rural Maine ("the land of pulp and guns"), and T. E. Pearson's ***Off for the Sweet Hereafter,*** a funereal comedy set in the Gothic South. For those not turned off by gross irreverence and unsophisticated gallows humor, Pelletier's first novel was as funny as any book this year, as it satirized, ridiculed, and maligned not just our solemn

Dust jacket of Waking the Dead, *by Scott Spencer. Knopf, 1986. Jacket design by Paul Bacon. Courtesy of Alfred A. Knopf, Inc. Dust jacket of* Providence, *by Geoffrey Wolff. Viking, 1986. Jacket design by Neil Stuart. Jacket design copyright © 1986 by Viking Penguin Inc. Reproduced by permission of Viking Penguin Inc. Dust jacket of* Golden Days, *by Carolyn See. McGraw-Hill, 1986. Jacket illustration by Fred Marcellino. Reproduced by permission of Fred Marcellino.*

death rituals but everything that's sacred about American life, including family solidity, rustic comforts, and small-town piety.

When he was on target, Pearson could be just as outrageously funny and sacrilegious—his ghoulishly humorous scenes of gravediggers boxing, bagging, and transplanting corpses, for example. But, structurally, ***Off for the Sweet Hereafter*** was a series of poky comic digressions, with its mock Bonnie-and-Clyde plot and many of the laughs buried in mock-Faulknerian prose. Though he's an inspired folk humorist, Pearson seemed so intent on imitating (or parodying) his master's voice that it was impossible to take him seriously, except as a master mimic.

A corpse also figured prominently in Robert Coover's "post-modernist" farce, ***Gerald's Party.*** The discovery of the body at the party set off this wildly absurd and erotic excursion into Cooverland, which, as one reviewer put it, is the "terrain between fact and fiction, peopled with a cast of thousands engaged in grand-scale orgies, madcap chases, and continual metamorphoses into Beauty and the Beast." But, as in his previous fiction, Coover's humor was often so broad and acidic that (some) readers were more antagonized than amused.

In his own, vastly different way, Jimmy Breslin is as funny, distinctive, and unconventional a novelist as Coover. Winner of a Pulitzer Prize for his New York newspaper columns, Breslin located his fifth novel, ***Table Money,*** in the territory he knows best, the Irish-American homes, bars, and streets of his native Queens. This story of sandhogs, cops, mobsters, their wives and children was club-fisted and preachy in places, and written with Breslin's calculated inelegance, but it was also a forceful composite of working-class lives, lives of noisy desperation, which is exactly what his readers expect of Breslin.

Carolyn See put a humorous twist on the Big Bang books with ***Golden Days,*** a light-hearted look at nuclear holocaust. Although it turned out not to be the hoped-for "breakthrough" novel for See, attracting less attention, perhaps, than it deserved, ***Golden Days*** stood out as the only novel of the Doomsday genre with wit, charm, and a happy ending. Set in Los Angeles, it was the quintessential California novel, featuring the friendship between Edith, who is twice divorced and gives investment seminars to rich housewives, and Lorna, four times divorced and a devout follower of a pop psychologist. The book was called by one critic a "richly intelligent, culturally discerning novel."

Literary humor of a more traditional sort was provided by the indefatigable Peter DeVries with ***Peckham's Marbles,*** a goofy if not wholly satisfying romp about an acerbic ex-English professor and a looney bin called Dappled Shade. Michael Malone's ***Handling Sin*** was compared favorably to *A Confederacy of Dunces* and described as "a hilarious success" by one reviewer. And satirist Christopher Buckley turned Capital Hill upside down with ***The White House Mess,*** the wacky mock memoir of fictional presidential advisor Herbert Wadlough.

In a grimmer vein, veteran travel writer and novelist Paul Theroux escorted readers fifty years into the future with ***O-Zone,*** an unlikely story about life after a nuclear accident, when the world is divided into pockets of safety for the very wealthy (Manhattan is one of them) and the rest of the planet is inhabited by "aliens."

Also global in scope, but in an ultimately more satisfying way, was Mary Lee Settle's ***Celebration,*** a novel of love and death that, while it does not span centuries as her Beulah Quintet did, globetrots from the British museum to Africa to Hong Kong with ease.

Paternalism was the common denominator in fiction by a trio of skilled novelists, who also have in common a dedication to their craft that is not as widely recognized or appreciated as it ought to be, even if they do have devoted readerships. Frederick Busch's tenth novel, ***Sometimes I Live in the Country,*** was a potentially maudlin subject—a 13-year-old boy who, after the breakup of his parents's marriage, moves to Upstate New York with his father—that the author made painfully honest and touching.

Then there was Craig Nova's ***The Congressman's Daughter,*** an emotionally engaging, if somewhat contrived, novel in which an upright New England congressman's refusal to accept his daughter's pregnancy (by a married man) leads to an all-American tragedy. Finally, Richard Stern's ***A Father's Words,*** his seventh novel, was a witty, affectionately autobiographical account of a divorced man's relationships with his four children, especially a favored son, who is the source of as much apprehension as pride or joy.

Autobiographical elements were also unmistakable in a new work by Ken Kesey, onetime *wunderkind* of the literary world, who turned fifty in 1986 and published ***Demon Box,*** which he called a novel and most critics called a "collection." Some twenty-four years after the publication of *Sometimes a Great Notion,* his last major work, ***Demon Box*** showed flashes of brilliant styling and evocative prose—but those flashes made even more plaintive the crying need for a cohesive plot to tie together the splintered narrative.

Joyce Carol Oates, who doesn't let years, much less decades, roll by between novels, checked in with ***Marya: A Life*** in 1986. This story of a woman's rise from humble origins to success as a writer was, somewhat like ***Demon Box,*** a piecemeal account, many of the eleven episodes having been previously published as separate stories. However, in Oates's case, the pieces ultimately fit to make what one critic called an "absorbing" whole.

Suspicions of autobiography were also unavoidable with ***Expensive Habits,*** Maureen Howard's moving account of a writer's reconstruction of her life told in a letter to her son (a character every reader must fall in love with and mourn for) when she fears she is going to die.

Africa was the scene for two superior works of fiction by American writers, one of which, Norman Rush's ***Whites,*** was a nominee for an American Book Award. In his collection of six stories, Rush, a former codirector of the Peace Corps in Botswana, brought home the painful collapse of our idealism and technology in that "emerging" nation. A South African-born novelist (who now lives in San Francisco), Lynn Freed suggested in ***Home Ground*** that her native land is an alien place even for those who make it their home.

Africa was used for more nefarious purposes (as were countries in almost every other corner of the planet, with the possible exception of Fredonia and Ruritania) in the dozens of espionage novels. Among the better and/or more popular thrillers were Bill Granger's ***Hemingway's Notebook*** and Robert Ludlum's ***The Bourne Supremacy,*** both of which, with their contorted plots and quintuple crosses, attempted to follow in the footsteps of John Le Carre (whose *A Perfect Spy* was a nearly perfect

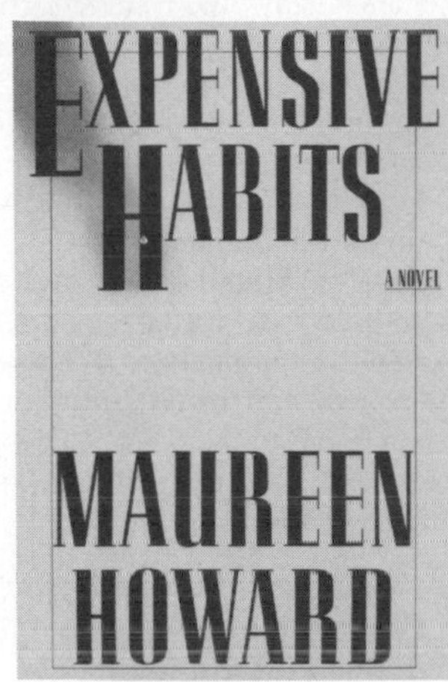

Dust jacket of Whites, *by Norman Rush. Knopf, 1986. Jacket illustration and design by Renee Klein. Courtesy of Alfred A. Knopf, Inc. Dust jacket of* Conspiracy of Knaves, *by Dee Brown. Henry Holt, 1986. Jacket design copyright © 1986 by Paul Bacon Studio. Courtesy of Henry Holt and Company, Inc. Dust Jacket of* Expensive Habits, *by Maureen Howard. Summit Books, 1986. Jacket design © 1986 by Lawrence Ratzkin. Courtesy of Simon & Schuster, Inc.*

spy story). But the only writer who came close to filling them was Robert Littell. In ***The Sisters,*** Littell cunningly told how the title characters, a pair of diabolical (male) villains named Francis and Carroll, try to pull off a perfect international caper, one that involved those ubiquitous and equally amoral agencies of terror and death, the CIA and the KGB. "What Elmore Leonard is to mysteries . . . ," wrote Susan Isaacs, "Robert Littell is to the novel of intrigue."

As for Leonard, the industrious author considered by many connoisseurs of fictional crime and violence to be America's supreme pulpmeister was represented at his familiar, if erratic, best in ***Bandits*** (which showed up in bookstores late in '86, though it wasn't officially published until January of '87). This was a muscular, pungent but occasionally windy shoot-'em-down in which an ex-con formed an unholy partnership with an ex-nun, and assorted unsavory characters, to steal $2 million intended for Nicaraguan contras.

The robbery of a Union payroll by Confederate agents figured in the plot of ***Conspiracy of Knaves,*** a vigorous Civil War spy story by Dee Brown, who is considered our foremost chronicler of Indian history after *Bury My Heart at Wounded Knee*. Brown's novel was one of several major Westerns published in 1987, which, after the success the previous year of Larry McMurtry's *Lonesome Dove* and James Michener's *Texas*, seemed to prove that there's still plenty of life left in that timeworn genre.

Although Louis L'Amour, with his sure-fire formula for success, was the only writer of Western lore to make it onto the year's best-seller list (with ***Last of the Breed***), a number of more literary authors in that genre were worthy of attention as well, including Robert Douglas Meade for ***Heartland*** and Greg Matthews for ***Heart of the Country.***

Other notable '86 Westerns were Edward Hoagland's ***Seven Rivers West,*** which deftly combined adventure and naturalism in a tall tale about a pair of fortune hunters; ***Fool's Crow,*** by James Welch, a novelist of Indian blood who told of the disintegration of a Montana Blackfoot tribe; and ***Deadwood,*** a bawdy folk yarn about Wild Bill Hickok, by Pete Dexter, a former Philadelphia newspaper columnist.

Before closing the book on 1987 fiction, mention should be made of some other honorable works: Larry Heinemann's ***Paco's Story,*** a powerful Vietnam postmortem; Steven Millhauser's hallucinatory ***From the Realm of Morpheus,*** which traced a young man's descent into the underworld; Paul West's ***Rat Man of Paris,*** an imaginative biography of a legendary Parisian derelict; Martin Booth's ***Hiroshima Joe,*** a harrowing World War II survival tale; and Ishmael Reed's ***Reckless Eyeballing,*** which a critic described as a discursive bludgeoning of "Clint Eastwood's Dirty Harry, feminists, neoliberals, and the new right."

Dianne Donovan, *Books* Editor
John Blades, *Books* Critic
The Chicago Tribune

The Year in Poetry

by Sidney Burris

Critics who praise a great many contemporary poets are, necessarily, bad critics—that, at least, was Randall Jarrell's opinion in the summer of 1955 when he reviewed a batch of books for *The Yale Review.* Statistically his logic is precise and punishing. Each century of English and American literary history offers us a handful of major poets, a dozen or so minor poets, and scores upon scores of poetasters. In 1986, the waning years of the century, critics of contemporary poetry might issue an even harsher imperative than Jarrell's. We have already identified our century's major poets—they might proclaim—and we leave the rest to fight for their places among the lower ranks. The corollary seems gloomy; if we do not confine our twentieth-century reading list to the work of some twenty poets, then we are reading poems that will never be read again. As our standard literary anthologies indicate, posterity is parsimonious when handing out its laurels.

Contemporary writing is difficult to judge because the contours of its forest are continually being altered by its insistent saplings. And we must remember that each century has its embarrassments, its mistakes in judgment. Edward Young's long poem, *Night Thoughts (1742-1745),* catapulted the poet to Olympian heights during his own time. Even the European community embraced the work with passion and devotion; Robespierre, for example, slept with a copy of the poem under his pillow, and Diderot greatly admired it. Today the poem is virtually unknown to the general reader. Nor must we forget that we read with pleasure many poets whose reputations have consigned them to the dungeons of minority; I enjoy, for example, John Clare's verse far more than William Blake's verse, but I will readily admit that Blake is the major poet, Clare the minor (although his stock is currently rising); and in the twentieth century, I am far happier with Edwin Arlington Robinson's best lyrics than I am with Pound's, and Pound nowadays seems the major, Robinson the minor poet. So, if we are not so immodest that we claim prophetic powers in assessing a contemporary poet's final resting place on the ladder of literary value, then we can, in fact, enjoy, even praise, a great many contemporary poets. We will not value every poem by every poet, and many will either escape or numb our discerning sensibilities; but even in those poets whose work we suspect will not survive, we are occasionally surprised by the odd line, the arresting image that startles us with its sudden illumination, and this is one of the joys of reading the poet unheralded by historical reputation. Contemporary poetry, in its bewildering diversity, often requires of its readers gymnastic sympathies, but healthy literary cultures demand well exercised readers, and there is no better way to strengthen ourselves than by intelligently enjoying the verse of our own time.

Younger American Poets

Contemporary American poetry comprises styles, prosodies, images, dictions, and perspectives of such a broad range that only the glibbest generalities corral the array of voices. Accentual variations of the American language, of which there are many in the United States, influence the various musics of our poets; and geographical variations, which are stark and pronounced, nourish the diversity of imaginative topographies we encounter in even the most casual survey. Terese Svoboda's ***All Aberration*** (University of Georgia Press) begins in the plains of the Midwest. Her poems are authentic and unencumbered by affectation, and she has the talent for selecting the one detail that precisely locates the experience in the Midwest. In "Dust Storm," for example, she ends the poem with an observation that is certainly commonplace to plains dwellers but one that will introduce everyone else to a fundamental feature of that landscape: "I found the car yards from a curb / imprisoned by tumbleweeds / with its headlights glaring / for miles." For miles? Not in Virginia or Arkansas or California; this is Midwestern poetry, and Svoboda's eye is sensitive to its distinguishing features. But she is equally at home on snowy hillsides, and she has a good ear for the solid phrase; riding with several friends on a sled in "Downhill Romance," she is "jammed cock to buttock," a succinct assessment that uncovers the erotic energies hidden in the casual occasion. This is Svoboda's first book, and its foreboding strengths would seem to promise the development—already well under way—of a vigorous voice.

Wild Gratitude (Knopf), Edward Hirsch's second book, follows *For the Sleepwalkers,* a book that received widespread praise and admiration. There is a breathless, rhapsodic quality to these poems that Hirsch contains by the judicious use of syntactic parallelism. In "Excuses," for example, a poem of thirty-one lines and seven sentences, we find the conditional clause "If only I . . ." repeated five times, knitting the poem together in a classically rhetorical manner, and it is a technique that he uses in other poems. The imaginative progression of those poems is often dazzling; he is one of the few writers whose poems are utterly unpredictable, but whose poems seem, upon finishing them, utterly logical. And, most characteristically, he is a deeply celebratory poet who insists in "Wild Gratitude" that Christopher Smart's cat "Jeoffrey—and every creature like him— / . . . can teach us how to praise—purring / In their own language, / Wreathing themselves in living fire."

Over the past few years, both poets and critics have been noticing with astonishment, glee, or sorrow the return to American letters of traditional form. What is meant by the phrase "traditional form" is difficult to know, but those who pride themselves on having attained it speak warmly of rhyme, meter, and regular stanzaic forms, while those who avoid it inveigh against it with the spirit of liberalism cultivated by their free forms. Brad Leithauser has written both prose and poetry that defend and exemplify his own version of traditional form. His second book ***Cats of the Temple*** (Knopf) is brimming with the strengths and pitfalls that are gradually becoming characteristic of several young poets. Most prominently, marvelous invention—a seahorse is a "like-winged, light-winged /

Pegasus''—parades side by side with innocuousness foolishness—''oh, / those lovable / black bunny eyes!'' And Vikram Seth's new book, ***The Golden Gate*** (Random House), is not, as its cover proclaims, a novel, but a long sonnet sequence. Witty, satirical, and by implication, reverential, the book finds its kindred spirit in Byron's *Don Juan,* and although it pales with that comparison, it is nowadays a unique accomplishment to have walked, even at arm's length, with that behemoth of Romanticism. In ***The Whole Truth*** (North Point Press), James Cummins has constructed a series of twenty-four sestinas that chronicle the further exploits of Perry Mason, Della Street, Paul Drake, and Hamilton Burger. Cummins, I suspect, has talents more formidable than those in abundant evidence here; his task, however difficult, was a narrow one, and I titillate myself by envisioning the book that would have paired this accomplished piece with a collection of lyrics.

Individual talents receive and interpret the poetic tradition in different ways. Our literary forebears deserve our respect, and the poet's emerging voice demands a jealous faithfulness; the compromise, retaining something essential, introducing something new, will often seem to part from the more obviously traditional work we associate with rhyme and meter. Dana Gioia's new book, ***Daily Horoscope*** (Graywolf Press), however, offers us a poetry, as he puts it in ''In Cheever Country,'' of ''the modest places which contain our lives;'' and these modest places are so modestly asserted, with such grace and effervescence, that we resort ultimately to the poetry's *technique* to assess the poetry's splendid accomplishments. Whether insinuated or announced, such concern for craft is an integral part of the English and American literary tradition, and Gioia's poetry brings a much needed freshness to our often hidebound notions of traditional form. R. S. Gwynn, in ***The Drive-In*** (University of Missouri Press), makes a virtue of terseness; as he says in ''Ars Poetica,'' ''Sweet music makes the same old story new. / That is a lie, but it will have to do.'' His poems, controlled, largely rhymed, have the inevitability of one of Aesop's fables: we are not asked to believe them because they arrive in such an unalterable way—I had wanted to say ''in such an unalterable form,'' but that is too limiting. We deal with these poems as we deal with the fables: quizzically, thankfully, and respectfully.

The Language Student (Louisiana State University Press) by Bin Ramke is a book of serious philosophical aspirations, and Ramke is an intelligent man. Although he is attracted by words such as ''lubricious,'' ''insinuant,'' and ''diaphanous,'' he is, of the younger poets, one of those most capable of providing the proper dramatic contexts for abstract diction. The Yale Series of Younger Poets was awarded to George Bradley whose ***Terms to be Met*** (Yale University Press) belies the awkwardness of the passive infinitive in his title; his poems are fluent, analytical, detached, and occasionally incomprehensible in a fashionable way. Uncomfortable with abstractions, Chase Twichell's ***The Odds*** (University of Pittsburgh Press) exhibits nonetheless a gift for finding the phrase that unites idea and image; ''Jack's Flashlight'' begins: ''Three years old, my nephew / strafes the dark pines / from the porch with his flashlight.'' And Deborah Digges's ***Vesper Sparrows*** (Atheneum) introduces us to a poet whose wisdom lies in secular benedictions, one aspect of our Romantic inheritance: ''I can bless a death this human, this leaf / the size of my hand. . . .'' Her verse moves skillfully between the hard edges of the world and the renovating cadences of prayer.

Other poets are doing other things in other ways. Rita Dove's second book ***Thomas and Beulah*** (Carnegie-Mellon University Press) is a two-part sequence, each telling one side of her story; but along with the discursive tapestry of the writing, she has interwoven elements of song and dialect. Often, her ear for the mellifluous phrase is so keen (*''Done right, the sheen jags / and the grit shines through''* in ''Nothing Down''; or ''Towards winter his skin paled, / buckeye to ginger root'' in ''Taking in Wash'') that her phrases distract our attention from the narrative, but that is her gift, and we are richer for her indulgences. The roomy poems of ***The Bus Home*** by Shirley Bowers Anders (University of Missouri Press) make you feel as if you were talking with the poet—always a good sign—and learning something from the conversation; these are poems whose high ambitions are often hidden by the hospitality of the language.

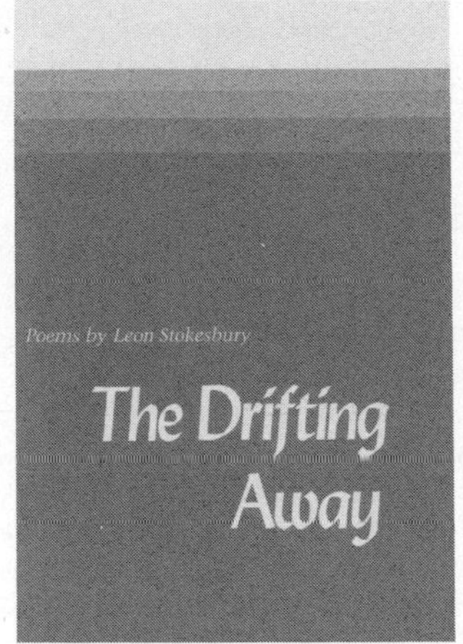

Dust jacket of The Drifting Away, *by Leon Stokesbury. The University of Arkansas Press, 1986. Courtesy of the publisher. Dust jacket of* The Golden Gate, *by Vikram Seth. Random House, 1986. Jacket design by Bob Aulicino. Jacket illustration by Yuri Kritchever. Courtesy of Random House, Inc. Dust jacket of* The Whole Truth, *by James Cummins. North Point Press, 1986. Jacket illustration by George Grosz. Jacket design by David Bullen. Courtesy of North Point Press.*

Dominion (Knopf), Brooks Haxton's second book, will be aligned indiscriminately under the aegis of Southern literature, but that is because Southern literature will want very much to claim him. The notion of regional literature is far too constricting to describe this book. The long poem which begins the collection,

"Breakfast ex Animo," follows the organic form of the ode and rambles through its natural surroundings with a Lucretian complexity. David Baker's ***Haunts*** (Cleveland State University Press) is a much gentler, quieter book, but in its rich evocation, for example, of "the summer Sally Millsap fell from the graceful / perch we shared . . . ," Baker shows great dexterity in handling the sobering comedies of our adolescence; these subjects often seem shop-worn, but they are given a new luster by Baker's hand. Leon Stokesbury's ***The Drifting Away*** (University of Arkansas Press) makes fine reading just when you thought humor, a sophisticated, incisive humor, had vanished from contemporary writing. His assimilative imagination is devouring; how else could he begin a poem entitled "Chance of Showers" with such a simile: "Like the greatest steak house / salad bar you ever saw, there is some- / thing varied but, I am afraid, all / too familiar in this big autumnal air."

RECOMMENDED: J. D. McClatchy, ***Stars Principal*** (Collier Books); Margaret Gibson, ***Memories of the Future: The Daybooks of Tina Modotti*** (Louisiana State University Press); Don Bogen, ***After the Splendid Display*** (Wesleyan University Press); Christianne Balk, ***Bindweed*** (Collier Books); Roy Bentley, ***Boy in a Boat*** (University of Alabama Press).

Contemporaries

Both Stanley Kunitz and David Ignatow have been giving us a steady stream of poetry for a very long time. Kunitz, the octogenarian, and Ignatow, the septuagenarian, provide us with fit examples of the vigorously aging imagination. Ignatow's ***New and Collected Poems, 1970-1985*** (Wesleyan University Press) brings together well over 250 poems; Kunitz's ***Next to Last Things: New Poems and Essays*** (Atlantic Monthly Press) is a much slimmer volume—his monumental collection of fifty years of poetry came out several years ago—and includes thirteen new poems along with nine essays. Reading these two volumes convinced me that it is inappropriate—perhaps rude—to pass judgment on such unabashed, ceaseless energy. Kunitz is the quieter, more discriminating poet, Ignatow, the more public, Whitmanesque poet. Both have worked long and hard, both have shown exceptional devotion to their craft. I do not have to ask myself if I *like* these poets (although I do); I simply revel in the old fashioned feeling that I am a better person because I have *read* these poems.

What to say about Adrienne Rich's new book ***Your Native Land, Your Life*** (W. W. Norton)? Or rather, what to say about Adrienne Rich? That she elicits fear, or anger, or hesitation, or—what is worse—ignorance from her male reviewers would be easily demonstrable; that she too is having a long and productive career is equally obvious; and that she is delighted by both of these aspects of her work would be my suspicion. From the first book, *A Change of World* (1951), which Auden chose for the Yale series and complimented for "display[ing] a modesty . . . which disclaims any extraordinary vision," then more forcefully in the two volumes of essays in the late 'seventies in which she revealed for us the genealogy of her feminist theory, to the collections of lyrics which have been regularly appearing every three years or so—Adrienne Rich's work has clearly voiced the concerns and beliefs of many within the feminist movement. It is difficult to think of another American poet as socially influential as she has been. Although I cannot point to a volume of lyrics stronger than *The Dream of a Common Language* (1978), the present collection continues her incessant experimentation with form, exercises her prodigious and often overlooked talent for understatement (in "Baltimore: A fragment from the Thirties," she speaks of a "segregated morgue"), and, most important of all, fortifies her position as a poet of perspicacity and endurance.

Miller Williams's latest book of poems—there are eight others—is entitled ***Imperfect Love*** (Louisiana State University Press), the adjective of which aptly misrepresents the perfection of the poems contained therein. Williams's poems have always been restoratives, reminders that there is no substitution for the well made verse, and what amazes most is that his insistent disciplines continually yield poems that are surprising, unpredictable, magical—all of the terms used whenever we suspect that Ariel has unpacked his bags. Williams is a gifted and prolific translator too, and perhaps that accounts for the exotic fertility of his imagination; but he is—and always has been—a formalist very much in the American grain who makes the popular migration toward "traditional form" seem stuffy and ill-informed, yet he has—and always has had—an imagination of such diversity, that his work makes less formal, ostensibly unfettered poems seem pale and anemic.

Seamus Heaney chose Jack Myers's ***As Long As You're Happy*** (Graywolf Press) as one of the winners of the National Poetry Series, and, unfairly, I came to the volume with high expectations because, after all, is not Seamus Heaney one of the most widely and highly regarded living poets? I am sure that Mr. Myers—"Please! I am not my captor," I hear him say—would rather be judged on his own terms. Those terms are two: 1) That the poetic mind, the mind that creates, is only part of his existence, and that the other parts often irritatingly, often humorously vie for his attention (see "Do You Know What I Mean"); 2) That his poems, because of the creative pluralism indicated in (1), will seek their wisdom anywhere ("In this business of watching everything," he remarks in "Air Mail Shoes," "everything happens once and for all"). And everything that happens is fair game for a poem, a good poem, by Jack Myers. Dave Smith chose ***Local Time*** (Quill / William Morrow) by Stephen Dunn as another of the winners in The National Poetry Series. With its staggered tercets, Dunn's verse looks, at first glance, much like the famous tercets of William Carlos Williams's "Asphodel, That Greeny Flower"; and the delicate, difficult-to-categorize modulations of each line recall Williams's lifelong attempt to perfect what he termed the "variable foot" in American prosody. But whereas Williams was the iconographer of wheelbarrows and plums, the everyday objects of our lives, Dunn is the connoisseur of a "favorite cheese" ("The Night the Children Were Away"), the adjective emphasizing the ordinary individuals that share our lives and enjoy our cheese. His formidable accomplishment lies in the fact that he neither proclaims nor denigrates the trappings of middle-class America; the "unaffordable house" ("Local Time") that all Americans of this sprawling class inhabit, the "locker room," a forum for the sexual exploits of men ("Among Men"), and the "turnpike" traveled on the way to the movies ("Accident in the Snow on the Way to 'Amadeus'")—these form the distant, but carefully etched background to the personal relationships that are the subject of his poems. He has given these mundane icons a subdued and permanent place in his work.

Mary Oliver's *American Primitive* won the Pulitzer Prize for poetry in 1983; her latest offering is ***Dream Work*** (Atlantic Monthly Press), which, the dust jacket claims, follows "chronologically and logically" the award-winning volume. Of course, and perhaps. Oliver is a poet of inspired observation whenever she turns to fish, weathers, flowers, geese, clams, egrets, hawks, turtles, and Stanley Kunitz. In fact, these poems fit most easily

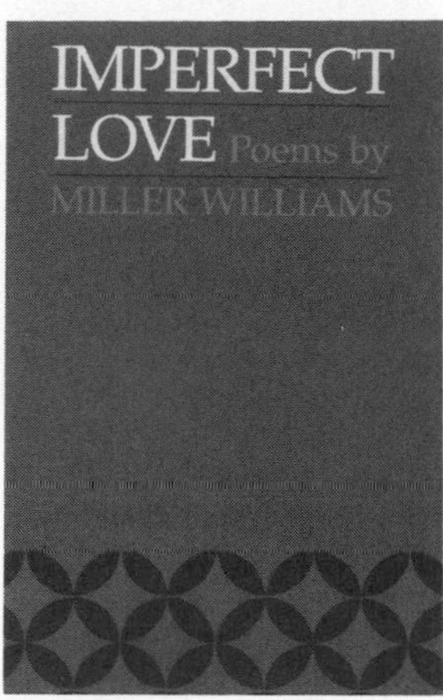

Dust jacket of Next-To-Last Things, *by Stanley Kunitz. Atlantic Monthly Press, 1986. Copyright © 1985 by Stanley Kunitz. Jacket photo by Renate Ponsold. Jacket design by Steve Snider. Reprinted by permission of the Atlantic Monthly Press. Dust jacket of* Imperfect Love, *by Miller Williams. Louisiana State University Press, 1986. Courtesy of the publisher. Dust jacket of* Collected Poems, *by Geoffrey Hill. Andre Deutsch, 1986. Jacket illustration is a detail from "The Vision after the Sermon," by Paul Gauguin, National Gallery of Scotland. Reproduced by permission of Andre Deutsch Ltd.*

into the Thoreauvian tradition, and I can imagine him writing these poems were he alive today; but if he were alive today, writing these poems, he would nonetheless stake his literary reputation on his prose. Ai's new book ***Sin*** (Houghton Mifflin) engages, most prominently, most successfully, the dramatic monologue; we hear from a journalist who saw a Buddhist nun incinerate herself in Viet Nam and from J. Robert Oppenheimer, the nuclear physicist whose science is grimly portrayed by his confession that "what we as a brotherhood lack in imagination / we make up for with curiosity." Although Ai's verses occasionally lack the subtlety of accurate phrasing and resonant implication, her poems are self-assured, clear, decisive, and—without damaging the intricate tensions of her poems—full of purpose. Audre Lord's "Every Traveler Has One Vermont Poem" is the best poem of her new volume, ***Our Dead Behind Us*** (W. W. Norton). Poets who write Vermont poems, of course, face the titular old man who gave that state its poetic prominence; I hear a pun in the first line of the second stanza: "Two nights of frost / and already the hills are turning / curved green against the astonished morning. . . ." How quickly and skillfully, though, Lorde evokes the Frostean harvest, and how devastating she subverts it:

Tanned boys I do not know
on their first proud harvest
wave from their father's tractor
one smiles as we drive past
the other hollers
nigger
into cropped and fragrant air.

I certainly would not burden any poet with the label "political"; but as soon as that label becomes honorific, properly shorn of its shrillness, Audre Lorde should be the first in line to receive it.

Both Fred Chappell and Norman Dubie have new books, and I mention these two very different poets in the same breath because my first judgment about both of these writers has always been—and I am confident, will always be—identical: "I have never read anything like that," I say when I finish their books. As with many poets of radical originality, a little verse tells a lot. Here is the second and final stanza of the title poem of Chappell's ***Source*** (Louisiana State University Press):

The gray-eyed peasant
leans on his scythe, the barge enters his reverie
and noses toward the source of light,
the source of ravens. A bell has spoken once only,
then that long tower of sound wavers and dissolves.

Finally, I feel unequal to this stanza. It seems, oddly, to be a very old stanza—four centuries, at least—yet it does not seem antiquarian. I hear "bard" for "barge," and I imagine the one nosing toward inspiration, the other toward sunrise. I know that bells do not "speak" unless we are meant to notice the silence of everything else, including the silence of a bard nosing toward inspiration; and my attention when the tower of sound "wavers and dissolves" returns to the river, which appeared in the first stanza. On one level—the level that matters most—I am convinced that this is a poem about poetic inspiration, but I cannot offer a rational, watertight argument to convince you. And that is, perhaps, the point. Chappell is a poet of the first order.

In ***The Springhouse Poems*** (W. W. Norton), Dubie continues to construct his versions—no other word will do—of the natural world, and it is the perspective of the poems that so startles the reader. "Wintry Night, Its Reticule" is Dubie's celebration of the coming of spring:

There are suffering mice

Down low between the thatch, down
Where the wind lifts red berries
That float and roll with snow
Across a frozen marsh, young deer
Watch while a few berries
Drop into the green muck of their tracks—

The lady's-slipper with its fleshy sac,
The bones of a lost hunter strewn
Through sumac—

Spring, at last.

From the "suffering" mice to "the bones of a lost hunter," the poem rolls along on the backs of "red berries" that will flower in the "green muck" of the deer's tracks. Presumably, the hunter missed his deer; at any rate, Nature gets along fine without us, which is what Shelley said at the foot of Mont Blanc. And in many ways, Dubie is the poet of a late and vital Romanticism. James Applewhite's fourth volume, ***Ode to the Chinaberry Tree and Other Poems*** (Louisiana State University Press) begins in the spring of the year also. The title of the poem is "Jonquils," and the language is visually inventive: there are "armatures of honeysuckle,"and "Baskets of weed-wire," and the poison oak is "thicker than adders." He is a very brave poet because he is a Southerner who will still write poems about what it means to be a Southern poet. "Southern Voices" will not interest the unobsessed, but the theory he propounds in the poem is essentially correct and should ease the tiringly proud xenophobia of much regionalist writing: "This clay of vowels, this diffidence / Of consonantal endings, murmurs *defeat*. . . ." Perhaps there is a bit too much of the enraptured linguist here, but Applewhite reminds us, as do the hordes of Faulkner scholars in Japan, that Southerners are the only Americans who have suffered defeat—in the old fashioned sense—in a major war. It is a fact elegant in its simplicity and pervasive in its influence; Applewhite's poems, while registering its influence, embody its eloquence.

RECOMMENDED: Turner Cassity, ***Hurricane Lamp*** (The University of Chicago Press); Philip Dacey, ***The Man with the Red Suspenders*** (Milkweed Editions); Jonathan Holden, ***The Names of the Rapids*** (The University of Massachusetts Press); William Logan, ***Difficulty*** (David R. Godine); William Pitt Root, ***Faultdancing*** (University of Pittsburgh Press); John Stone, ***Renaming the Streets*** (Louisiana State University Press); C. K. Wright, ***Further Adventures With You*** (Carnegie-Mellon University Press).

English, Irish, and European

Geoffrey Hill published his ***Collected Poems*** (Oxford) this year, and that alone makes for a bumper crop. Reading poem after poem—the volume spans twenty-seven years of writing—I found myself struggling to characterize the verse. Austere? Theological, or rather Pentecostal, one of Hill's favorite festivals? Mythopoeic? Historical? As my watchwords changed, I felt a constant sense of importance that lingered after I read the poems, as if they said, "You may not be able to categorize me, but you cannot deny my importance." And indeed I cannot. The early poems insist on a severe, but inspired accuracy; "In Memory of Jane Fraser" ends, "She died before the world could stir. / In March the ice unloosed the brook / And water ruffled the sun's hair. / Dead cones upon the alder shook." What precision this is; but what poetry too. And whether it is the *Mercian Hymns,* those grand prose-poems that fall midway through the collection, or the long narrative devoted to Charles Peguy which ends the collection, Hill's poetry fastidiously cultivates the virtue of accuracy. American readers will find him both difficult—as the English do—and eccentric—as the English do not—but all readers will return to his poems, wondering if they are as important as they seemed at the last reading. They were, and are.

Stephen Spender—yes, the one who was pals with Auden and Isherwood—has also given us a ***Collected Poems, 1928-1985*** (Random House), and I had forgotten what a fine poet he is when addressing the political issues of the 30s and 40s. Auden's "Spain, 1937" seems flat and contrived beside the thirty lines of Spender's "In 1929." Auden's sensibilities gravitated toward the morality of war and politics—and hence toward abstraction—while Spender's confront the individual, harried by the events he is trying to understand. Spender lacks Auden's range and technical virtuosity, but his best poems, like his elegy for Auden, are permanent additions to the language. Charles Tomlinson too has collected over thirty years of writing in his ***Collected Poems*** (Oxford), and the American reader unfamiliar with his verse will take to it immediately. Among other things, he writes well about nature, the untouched, untouchable nature of the frontier; and Americans, both our poets and our readers, cherish that vision. He is comfortable with the short, wide poem as well as the long, skinny one, so his prosody will not seem snobby, an American desideratum. And, in fact, for American readers wishing to test the waters of contemporary English poetry, here is a fine place to begin.

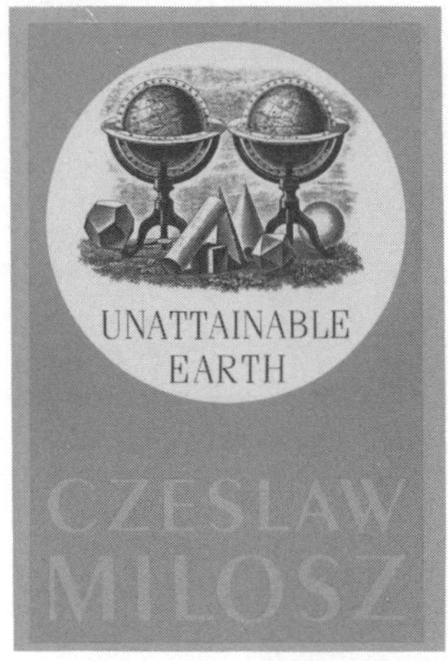

Dust jacket of Stephen Spender: Collected Poems, 1928-1985, *by Stephen Spender. Random House, 1986. Jacket design by Catherine Hopkins. Courtesy of Random House, Inc. Dust jacket of* Charles Tomlinson: Collected Poems, *by Charles Tomlinson. Oxford, 1986. Jacket illustration by Charles Tomlinson. Reproduced by permission of Oxford University Press. Dust jacket of* Unattainable Earth, *by Czesław Miłosz. Ecco, 1986. Jacket © Cynthia Krupat. Reproduced by permission of The Ecco Press. Dust jacket of* Paul Celan: Last Poems, *by Paul Celan. Translated by Katharine Washburn and Margaret Guillemin. North Point Press, 1986. Jacket design by David Bullen. Courtesy of North Point Press.*

Thomas Lynch, an Irish poet currently living in America, published his first book this year, and it is called ***Skating with Heather Grace*** (Knopf). Because I received the uncorrected galleys, I am unable to quote from the poems, but were I able to do so, you would exclaim, "How much he knows about the United States, Roethke, Tennessee Williams, daughters, serious comedy, marriage, and divorce." These are poems of youthful energy well aware that the world is often a hard place in which to live; the balance is a difficult one to achieve, and for the reader the spectacle is invigorating. Mr. Lynch has made an admirable debut.

Turning to the European writers, I begin with concessions. Most of us, I believe, who read contemporary American poetry on a regular basis and who reside in one of the fifty states feel drastically ill-equipped to speak for any length of time on the poetry currently being published in Europe. There are two reasons for this, one practical and defensible, the other practical and sad. First, the poems are inaccessible—unless we live near a major research library, we simply cannot get at them; and second, if we do live near such a library, we often cannot read them—we are not known for our linguistic diversity. Rilke, bless his soul, is regularly hoisted up in epigraphs to poems, in translations, and in those things we call "versions" as evidence that we are trying very hard to save our monoglot souls. But there is something desperate about this, and, as I said, sad.

So we are very thankful that the Nobel prize winner from Poland, Czeslaw Milosz currently lives in the United States and writes a good deal of his material in English, and that what he writes in Polish is translated for us by Robert Hass. ***Unattainable Earth*** (Ecco), Milosz's latest book, is a collection of poems, journal entries, prose poems, fragments from personal letters, and favorite poems he has read over the past several years—an attempt, he claims, to "approach the inexpressible sense of being." Whitman's "Sparkles from the Wheels" is included, and that is a poem everyone should know—it is one of his best and least known short lyrics. North Point Press has done a series of distinguished translations, and Katharine Washburn and Margaret Guillemin's bilingual edition of Paul Celan's ***Last Poems*** will further solidify that reputation. The introduction by Washburn is informative, level-headed, and devoted to its subject in just the right way—having finished it, I was anxious to read the poems, although I had previously read and translated many of them. Celan has often been labeled a Surrealist *Wunderkind,* but he is much more than that; his devotion to language is Shelleyan in intensity; and in German, a language capable of such expansive compounds, this devotion becomes labyrinthine in its verbal modulations. William Arrowsmith has translated Eugenio Montale's ***The Storm and Other Things*** (Norton), and it represents another of his impeccable translations. The poem was first published in Italy in 1956, and is widely recognized as a masterful work. American readers who have not read this poem, but have been properly indoctrinated by Pound's *Cantos* and Eliot's *The Four Quartets* will begin to believe that there must be something in the Mediterranean air whispering *epic, epic, epic*. It is the work of a dense and burnished imagination, and our notions of the modern long poem, its possibilities and limitations, must confront the brooding achievement of this poem.

RECOMMENDED (English and Irish): Basil Bunting, ***Collected Poems*** (Moyer Bell Limited); Hugo Williams, ***Writing Home*** (Oxford); Oliver Reynolds, ***Skevington's Daughter*** (Faber).

RECOMMENDED (European and other): Yannis Ritsos, ***Exile and Return: Selected Poems, 1967-1974*** (The Ecco Press); George Faludy, ***Selected Poems of George Faludy*** (University of Georgia Press).

The University of Arkansas

The Year in Drama

by Robert Cohen

This essay has always centered on the theater in New York, but to do so in the late eighties would require retitling the piece "Last Year In Drama" or "Two Years Ago in Drama," for rarely do New Yorkers see a play, anymore, that has not already surfaced, enraptured audiences, and won quite a few prizes elsewhere. This year's report, therefore, includes not only the major openings on and off Broadway, but works that should be appearing in New York in 1987 or 1988.

New York Theater

It wasn't a great year in New York anyway. *Vogue* claimed 1986 "the dullest Broadway season ever," and there wasn't much still playing by year's end that could be considered serious drama. There were, however, at least three important openings in the city: including major works by the present polar opposites of the commercial theater, Neil Simon and Sam Shepard, and an extraordinary play for one woman by Jane Wagner. I'll talk about the Wagner piece, entitled ***The Search for Signs of Intelligent Life in the Universe,*** first, partly because it was my favorite, and also because it is a fruitful starting point for considering the good and bad of the current American stage.

Wagner's play was written to be performed by Wagner's long-time friend and partner, Lily Tomlin; Tomlin plays all the roles, and has been doing so during the play's two year developmental phase—through workshop productions in San Diego, Los Angeles, Seattle, Portland, Houston, Lexington, Atlanta, Aspen, and Boston according to the production program. While Tomlin is often brilliant in her multi-character portrayals (she won the Tony as Best Actress for doing them), it is not at all clear to me that Tomlin's performance is required for the play to succeed, nor indeed that the play is best served by a solo acting performance. That Wagner's play was popularly known around New York as "the Lily Tomlin show" masks the fact that Wagner's play is an independent masterpiece which should be fully recognized apart from Tomlin's immediate (and quite splendid) contribution.

Lily Tomlin in Jane Wagner's The Search for Signs of Intelligent Life in the Universe. *Courtesy of PMK Public Relations.*

Intelligent Life centers on the public reflections of Trudy, a delightful Manhattan (see "Chaillot") madwoman, who has assumed the duties of an earthly tour guide for visiting outer space aliens (see "Sezuan"). Using her umbrella hat as a satellite dish, Trudy brings in signals from a stream of representative earthlings who then appear on the stage: a punk performance artist, a bored and aging socialite, two Broadway whores, three women friends from the women's movement, and an odd assortment of wives, husbands, grandparents, kids, gays, straights, drunks, and even a prescient dog. Somehow we keep them all straight, and by the end there's at least a semblance of a story, and a tying up of three or four of the play's several dozen loose ends. Not all of them of course, for, as Trudy concludes, "At the moment you are most in awe of all there is about life that you don't understand, you are closer to understanding it all than at any other time."

Wagner's story isn't the critical element here, it's the unflagging wittiness of her observations, the wry, unsentimentalized look at our past decade and a half of self-delusions ("ending world hunger through tofu consciousness"), and the reflexive running commentary on her own writing ("I have been on heavy metaphor maintenance all day," says Agnus Angst, the punk performance artist) that have us in her grasp.

Indeed, Wagner's play flirts dangerously with the metatheatrical as well as the metaphysical; at play's end Trudy tells her alien comrades to go to a Broadway play so they can experience human goose bumps; they do—and, in fact, they go to ***The Search for Signs of Intelligent Life***—and, in fact, they get goose bumps. This would be a disaster, of course, if we didn't get goose bumps too, but we do, bushels of them, and the play and the audience collide at the end in an absolutely remarkable burst of shared feeling, which the author, through Trudy, talks about just as we experience it: "a group of strangers sitting together in the dark, laughing and crying about the same things." She's describing us! All this leads to a rather monumental curtain call for the play's solo performer. This alone may justify the solo performance, but I suspect the play will also work (and in some ways work better) with a division of roles amongst a full cast. In any event, make no mistake about it; this is NOT the Lily Tomlin show, and the chief artist of the evening is not Lily Tomlin, it's Jane Wagner.

This was a year, by the way, of one-person shows in and around Broadway. There were at least four, and one, Eric Bogosian's ***Drinking in America*** at the slightly-off-Broadway American Place Theater, garnered some wonderful reviews. I report this, but not happily; I thought the material was purely Home Box Office, with Mr. Bogosian giving clever and witty, but hardly novel, impressions of various of our lowlife archetypes, including a coke-snorting Hollywood agent and a jovial ("Yuk, yuk") killer-rapist. It was good high-voltage stuff, with some real grimy laughs, but I was baffled at the extravagant reviews—Bogosian has none of the cathartic drive of writer-actor Jeff Weiss, who's been doing a similar but much better show (*And That's How the Rent Gets Paid*) further downtown for, off and on, more than ten years. Unlike Weiss, Bogosian lets you feel very safe, which is comfortable but hardly inspiring. Nor does his work draw you upwards from that safety, as Wagner's does, into new appreciations. On the other hand, I never saw the end of ***Drinking in America,*** nor did anyone else in the audience that night; two-thirds of the way through, Bogosian's voice gave out, and he spent the balance of the evening offering ticket exchanges. I felt safe; he probably didn't.

The other big hit on Broadway, and deservedly so, was Neil Simon's ***Broadway Bound,*** which opened in December; *Time* magazine called it the "play of the decade," and it clearly shows Simon working not only at the top of his form, but working in a new form altogether. ***Broadway Bound*** caps the autobiographical "BB" trilogy Simon has been working on for several years (*Brighton Beach Memoirs* and *Biloxi Blues* are the earlier works); this play carries Simon's self-portrait of the artist as a young man up to his emergence as a radio comedy writer, seen here collaborating with his brother on a CBS series satirizing a Jewish family in Brooklyn. Thus, like the Wagner play, ***Broadway Bound*** is self-reflexive: it's an autobiographical comedy about a young man who is writing autobiographical comedy. But Simon's play has meat, and it has depth; it is his *Death of a Salesman,* and, indeed, the parallels between these plays are astonishing: two brothers upstairs in the bedroom, planning to go into business with each other (as comedy writers in Simon's play, as sporting goods merchants in Miller's); dad coming home exhausted from work, relieved but guilt-ridden by his sexual infidelities; loyal Mom and tormented Dad fighting it out, mostly silently, in the downstairs kitchen-dining room, and the sons coming to Mom's support when the other woman gets mentioned; all of this set in Brooklyn in the late 1940's. Simon's play is openly Jewish, Miller's implicitly so; in Simon's play dad finally leaves home, in Miller's play he leaves life, but the men's motives and desperation are closely similar. Simon also borrows the younger-brother-as-author theme from *Long Day's Journey Into Night* (his young hero is named "Eugene," which may be a testimonial,) and there are young-writer echoes also from Miller's *A Memory of Two Mondays* and Williams' *The Glass Menagerie*. So make no mistake about it, this is written within the tradition of the great American autobiographical play, and it pretty much succeeds at that level; I think we'll be admiring ***Broadway Bound*** for a long time to come.

Simon's gift in the play is to create characters that are genuinely funny, and funny without realizing that they're funny; one of the recurring themes is that Eugene's sense of comedy comes not out of a mere predilection for joketelling, but out of his clear-sighted observation of the life around him. I wouldn't have to write comedy, he suggests, if I could just bring the audience into my house. Which of course is what Simon has done in this play. The play's subjects, meaning Simon's family, taken by themselves, are grim enough. The grandfather is incontinent. The father is unfaithful. His mistress is dying. The mother is all but irrevocably closed down to living. Nobody listens to each other much; nobody outwardly seems to love each other; even the weather is impossible. Somehow Simon has parlayed these irreconcilable differences, and this level of familial inattention, to a rare and entirely fulfilling harmony. One feels, at the end of ***Broadway Bound,*** that Simon's success as a writer came from the fact that nobody paid any attention to him as a child, and that his extraordinary prolificacy (22 Broadway plays and 18 feature films, in 25 years) comes from trying to be heard. One also feels a level of love that emerges almost like a force of nature in these deeply frustrated and antagonistic family relationships. It is heartwarming in a pleasantly unsentimental way, and Simon evokes a deeper sense of affection in this play than I have ever seen in an American Drama.

The depth of Simon's play, of course, comes from its autobiographical density; these characters are deeply felt and drawn with great specificity. There are certain actions in the play which are there presumably only because they really happened in Simon's life; this gives the play, at a few moments, a documentary nature I found arbitrary and unwelcome; still I wouldn't dream of trading them for the more synthetic comedies of Simon's past. And as the play discusses comedy, and the generation of comedy from life's seriotragic realities, it is also a document of the creative process, which it dramatizes beautifully; this is one of ***Broadway Bound***'s greatest assets.

I do wonder if we would be so interested in this play were we ignorant of Simon's subsequent and celebrated success—it is also interesting to speculate if we would find *Long Day's Journey Into Night* of such interest did we not know of its author's own journeys and dilemmas—for some of the impact of these memorial plays comes from our preknowledge that the young writer in the story (Eugene in Neil's work, Edmund in Eugene's) went on to achieve his sought-for literary success, and, in fact, has written the play we are now seeing. We are always aware of this in ***Broadway Bound;*** much in the play works through our sharing the author's hindsight and recognize the many ironies. As with Sophocles' *Oedipus,* we know how this one turns out, and we know when to look between the lines.

Sam Shepard was also represented in New York this year, and his ***A Lie of the Mind*** won the Critics' Circle Play of the Year award (it actually opened in late 1985, but since it was not discussed in this space last year, I will mention it here.) I would not have predicted that I should prefer the Simon play to the Shepard, but such was the case; I found Shepard's work quite compelling on an image to image and scene to scene basis, but quite a failure in its totality; by the end I felt I was looking at my watch as much as at the stage. ***A Lie of the Mind***

Jonathan Silverman and Jason Alexander in Neil Simon's Broadway Bound. *Photograph by Martha Swope & Associates.*

concerns two stage families, joined by an ill-conceived marriage between Jake at stage right and Beth at stage left; at the play's opening, Jake calls his brother to tell him he has just beaten and murdered his wife. He hasn't, as it turns out; Beth survived, but barely; she has to relearn talking, walking, just about everything, and she is helped by, among others, Jake's brother Frankie who crosses the stage gulf to find her. This play has brilliant images, and, as directed by the author, some of them are simply unforgettable; Jake smashing his receiver on the highway payphone while calling his brother; Beth's father, in hunter's orange covered with a camouflage vest, bringing in Frankie after shooting him with a rifle; Beth's brother coming in with, over his shoulder, the severed hindquarters of a deer he's just killed; Jake putting on his dead father's World War II flying jacket while, in memory, he sees Beth before the assault, oiling her half-naked body in her room across the stage; Jake, failing to attack her this time, blowing his late father's ashes into the moonlight. All this, of course, is pure Shepard, and it works beautifully, for the moment. Pure Shepard won't carry me through an evening any more, however, and while I have some appreciation for the appropriateness of his concerns and the density of his symbols—the emasculated American male and the urbanization of Western American life among them—I am beginning to resist the author's easy and sudden sensationalism. It all doesn't add up to very much. When Anne Wedgeworth, playing Meg, asked author/director Shepard about the meaning of her (and the play's) last line, ("Looks like a fire in the snow. Who can that be?"), Shepard replied "I just have the feeling that that's the way the play should end." Well, I suppose, but then please don't ask us to think much about it either.

And that was it in New York, for the most part. The only 1986 shows lasting into 1987 were the musical ***Drood*** (music, book, and lyrics by Rupert Holmes), and the comedy ***Social Security*** by Andrew Bergman, neither of which were a contribution to the art of drama. ***Drood,*** which won the Tony Award for best musical, is simply the worst thing I've seen on Broadway in forty years of constant theatergoing. It's an "interactive" musical, by which I mean that the cast, using the conceit that this is a play within a (music hall) play, continually exhorts the audience to applaud, laugh, cheer, and boo; also shilling us on are some clacquers in civilian dress behind us. We are also asked to vote on how the play should conclude, and presumably there are a number of rehearsed endings, although it doesn't seem that more than three or four are used; all this hectoring of the audience made me feel as if I were in the studio of a television game show. The music and lyrics seemed to me banal, and the only reason for the Tony award seemed to be that ***Drood*** was the only musical that survived the season (one of the ways of making it survive was cutting down the name in mid-run, from ***The Mystery of Edwin Drood,*** presumably to make for flashier advertising impact); this is all a very bad show for the Big Way. ***Social Security*** is a diverting debut play by a distinguished novelist and screenwriter; it concerns a trendy middle-aged Eastside couple—they are both art dealers—and the wife's aging mother: in the first act Mom arrives mean, sick, and nasty, clomping her walker up the stairs; and in the last she leaves, cheerily free-striding and elegantly attired, off for a vacation in France with her new lover, a celebrated 98 year old painter. The moral is that old people should reject the trendiness of the Eastsiders (don't call it mousseline of pike if it's really gefilte fish) as well as the 1950's morality of the wife's sister: rather they should marry rich celebrities and make love in fancy apartments. ***Social Security,*** then, is a fantasy posing as a realistic comedy, and it works acceptably on a TV sitcom level (a sitcom with dirty jokes, anyway). There are some good lines and a few pratfalls, and the story moves fairly easily through the two acts and three scenes. With but one set and six characters, it will clearly have a long future in the dinner theater/community theater market (and ***Drood*** will undoubtedly survive for a generation or so in the high school play business), but one hopes for its author the kind of development that followed Neil Simon's early comedies, which ***Social Security*** resembles.

It was, as I've said, a bad year in New York: the Broadway season attendance in 1985-86 was only about six and one-half million, representing a 40% drop over the last five years. The number of productions at season's end was a record low, and the wait for half-price theater tickets at the TKTS booth in Times Square, on a February weekday in early 1987, was virtually zero; I have spent over an hour in that line in previous seasons.

Regional Theater

Elsewhere in the country the theater was quite lively, however. The year was big in classical revisions (and I mean revisions, not revivals.) I'm afraid I missed Peter Sellar's version of Sophocles' ***Ajax,*** which played at the American National Theater in Washington's Kennedy Center; although it was followed by Sellar's (forced? requested?) indefinite leave as the ANT artistic director, the production had its followers, and toured successfully to La Jolla. But I did see, and enjoy, Robert Wilson's version of Euripides' ***Alcestis*** at the American Repertory Theater in Cambridge, with a wholly adapted text (by Wilson, with contributions from Heiner Muller and others) and Wilson's characteristically original—and often miraculously inventive—staging and lighting. Euripides' play is considered such a minor work that I can recollect no professional staging of it in my lifetime, and Wilson's version cannot possibly have an afterlife except in Wilson's own inventive hands, but his visual effects—a mountain which collapses, stone by stone, in slow motion; a river through which the actors laboriously wade up to their knees; a nineteen-foot, seemingly self-illuminated Cycladic statue floating above the audience; trees which become Corinthian columns, which become industrial smokestacks belching fire—these leave indelible impressions. I had reservations, however. ***Alcestis*** in the original is scarcely quaint, and Wilson's succession of images tamed rather than revivified Euripides' vision, lending the staged events a rather pleasant but pointless surreality; added to this, a rather jocular and what-the-hell acting style predominated (''It made very little sense to me, but I'm willing to ride,'' said Paul Rudd, who played Admetus, in a subsequent interview), so that one finally had little sense of a play, even a postmodern non-diachronic play;

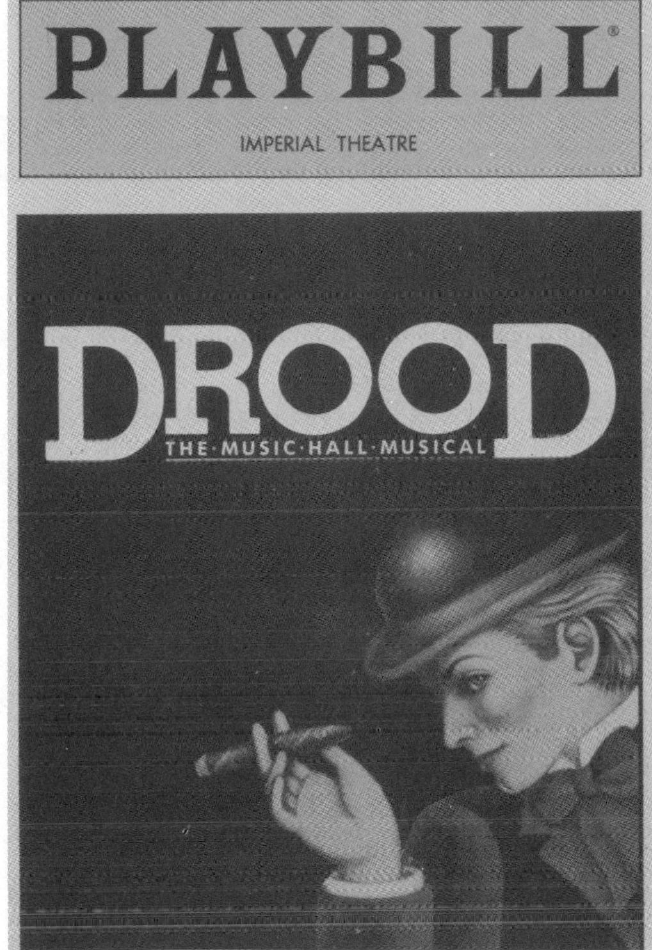

Playbill for Rupert Holmes's Drood. Playbill® *is a registered trademark of Playbill Incorporated, N.Y.C. Used by permission.*

still it was the sort of aesthetic experience I found deeply satisfying, as did the Cambridge audiences and subsequent crowds in Paris where the ART toured it in the summer.

The ART won the special Tony Award this year, by the way, for its continuously provocative repertory over the past few years. No argument from here on that one.

A more conventional revision of a heretofore ignored play by an acknowledged master was ***Wild Honey,*** which English author Michael Frayn adapted rather freely from Anton Chekhov's early manuscript, generally known to Chekhov enthusiasts as *Platanov,* after its leading character. Coproduced in America by Great Britain's National Theater, with the English actor Ian McKellen (as Platanov) supplemented by an otherwise all-American cast, ***Wild Honey*** proved a bright and sometimes poignant comedy success in both Los Angeles and New York.

This was apparently Chekhov's first play; in it we can see sketches of portraits more fully developed in *The Cherry Orchard* and *The Three Sisters,* and a romantic wistfulness, leading to tragicomical consequences, which is familiar in all of the author's work. Platanov, a provincial schoolteacher and failed intellectual, is the town rake, the town wit, and the town drunk; into his life comes Anna Petrovna, landowner, in hot pursuit; and Sofya, former student, full of recrimination at

Platanov's wasted life and wastrel ways. Anna after Platanov, and Platanov after Sofya, and all others (Platanov's wife, Sofya's fiance, Anna's suitor) hurrying to keep up. It is the ever-turning wheel of farce—at which Frayn excelled in ***Noises Off***—but with wry Chekhovian observation hung from every spoke. Why should we live up to our potential, anyway? And is it really living "up?" These ruminations are not new, but Chekhov's play, in Frayn's fine adaptation, is fresh, and the questions do not go begging. If the farce is, in the end, too exasperatingly relentless to let us take the play seriously, and if Ian McKellen is too much the ham to let us take Platanov seriously, (even seriocomically), well then that's the price we pay for digging into the vault and extracting this hundred-plus year old unfinished play by an unknown twenty-one year old author—and putting it in the hands of one of England's most exquisite virtuosos of the actor's art. Christopher Morohan directed, quite effectively, (although those seeing both New York and London productions preferred the English cast), and John Gunter designed the wonderfully wooded set, which included a terrific surprise in the final moments: most Chekhov plays end with a whimper, this one reaches closure with the bang of a steam locomotive.

The classic adaptation market had yet another entry with Charles Marowitz' ***Shrew,*** which intersperses parts of the Katharine—Petruchio scenes from Shakespeare's play with some original and contemporary scenes concerning a young (American?) couple. First produced in England several years ago, ***Shrew*** made its American debut under Marowitz' direction at the Ensemble Studio Theater in Hollywood, with Jenny Agutter as Katharine. Marowitz has quite intelligently excerpted everything in Shakespeare's play that is brutal, dehumanizing, and psychotic, and has directed them down to a word by word, breath by breath depiction of wife abuse; it is almost as savage as ***Blue Velvet*** which premiered on California screens at about the same time. In Marowitz' version, which is completely faithful to the restricted selections of Shakespeare's text, Petruchio is a grinning punk fascist (Mark Lindsay Chapman played the role), and Grumio and Hortensio are his gang member associates; Baptista, equally terrorized, is concerned only with saving face as his daughter is brutalized. Katharine is starved, humiliated, beaten, and sodomized, emerging by play's end as only tenuously sane; a virtual automaton, spouting (and abjectly accepting) her husband's doctrines. It is more moving than any holocaust drama I have ever seen (see below), and neither removed from reality nor from the fundamental notions in Shakespeare's play. Still, the modern scenes, while interesting in themselves, are not highly original in any way, and do not lead to anything of very much importance; nor do they contribute anything to the Katharine—Petruchio dialogues. They appear, essentially, as fillers (the rest of the play wouldn't last an hour), and need to be rethought if Marowitz' play is to have a substantial future. The actors, under Marowitz' guidance, were superb.

The theater world always awaits a Stephen Sondheim musical with excitement, and consequently the Old Globe Theater in San Diego was awash in ticket orders from Los Angeles and New York for the premiere of Sondheim and James Lapine's ***Into the Woods,*** which opened there in December, "en route" to Broadway. The route will be tortuous, I suspect. ***Into the Woods,*** like all of Sondheim's musicals, rewrites the form: here we have a show which opens with three Grimm Brothers' fairy tales, and which compounds them with the integrated admixture of five or six more; all the tales, by play's end, are interwoven in a tapestry which seems, finally, to proclaim its unendingness. In Sondheim's mind, apparently, fairy tales do not end happily ever after simply because they cannot end at all. As Prince Charming abandons Cinderella to chase after Sleeping Beauty ("I was trained to be charming, not sincere," he explains), and as Jack the Giant Killer has to perform the follow-up of killing Jack the Giant's revenging wife, the Sondheimian life becomes a cyclical adventure into and out of the woods, a ***Midsummer Night's Dream*** woods, which is filled with song, with witches, ogres, and good fairies, but which is ultimately uninhabitable. Sondheim's music is, as ever, replete with wondrous complexities, and echoes the eternal intertwining of Lapine's stories with musical lines wrapped around each other as tightly as the collective chromosomes of Western culture—the final resting place, I'm sure, of fairy tales. But the production is exquisitely cold, even for a Sondheim show, as it is impossible to develop much feeling for any of this compilation of fairy tale figures: they cannot die (when they do, they pop right back to life), and they cannot love or suffer finitely, being creatures of absolute time. Without duration, I might say, they become unendurable, which is exactly how I found them two hours into the evening—which had yet an hour to go. Sleepers outnumbered wakers in my row during the second act, and the mechanisms to keep them awake were basically limited to some very cheap parodic gags (a twerpish Little Red Riding Hood insisting on looking on her Grandmother's corpse, because, with a stamp of her pretty little foot, "I've never seen a dead person before!") Parodying your own subject matter is the easiest way to get a laugh, but the gag compromises the rest of the evening, and I cannot feel confident that this is going to be a play for grownups—yet. But that's what workshops are for, and I'm sure we will hear more of ***Into the Woods*** in the coming year.

Although nearly destroyed by a lumpish production at the Mark Taper Production in Los Angeles, Joshua Sobol's ***Ghetto,*** an enormous success in Europe in 1985, should have some running room in the American theater. Only trouble is, Americans have some difficulties trying to stage these post-Brechtian multidimensional works. ***Ghetto*** is set in the Vilna Ghetto during the Nazi Occupation of what is now Lithuania; the play depicts the real and imaginary activities of a Jewish theater troupe whose existence was encouraged, and, for a time, protected by the German authorities under SS officer Hans Kittel. Kittel, Sobol suggests, seems to have patronized the company's activities to forestall a ghetto rebellion, because he possessed somewhat schizophrenic appreciation of Jewish culture; certainly the troupe's ensuing performances provide him and his SS cohorts with wry amusement and psychosexual pleasures. Most of the Vilna Jews, including local police chief Jacob Gens, support the Jewish theater (as well as a local Jewish garment factory) as a means to save at least some Jewish lives, and to preserve a measure of Jewish heritage; contrarily some Jews, represented in the play by librarian Herman Kruk, bitterly opposed the theater as nothing other than collaboration with the Nazis and a destruction of Jewish honor.

Taper Director Gordon Davidson clearly articulates ***Ghetto***'s major question—"What is the value of solidarity, and the cost of survival?"—and says it's "unanswerable;" unfortunately, however, the question also may prove unfocusable, as it did in Los Angeles where the play never brought the matter to a climax. Sobel even abandons his dialectic towards the end of the play, as Kruk suddenly and inexplicably reverses his ideological stance; however correct this may have been historically, it sabotages ***Ghetto***'s dramaturgy, and Sobel is reduced to melodrama and sentimentality to achieve closure. One might also wonder about the possibility, any more, of holocaust drama; after all, drama traditionally tries to sensitize us to the phenomena we ordinarily take for granted ("Hath not a Jew eyes?" "A man is not a piece of fruit,") but we need little sensitizing, at this point, about the holocaust, particularly by the theater. If there's something new for us to learn, let's have it, but ***Ghetto*** doesn't deal with very much we haven't already thought through to the point of quite diminished returns.

Nonetheless, the play's potential is high: it's a big theater piece that combines entertainment and savagery; Jewish music and humor with world-wise catastrophe. The Los Angeles ***Ghetto*** featured a fine sculptural set (by Douglas Stein) with slatted (boxcar) walls and a mountain of discarded clothing in the middle; the dialectic of the play was destroyed, however, by its syrupy stage lighting (by Paulie Jenkins) which treated the play as a picaresque romance, and by a clarinetist who had escaped from *Fiddler on the Roof* to tell us how we were supposed to feel about all this. Blind sentimentality has always been the nemesis of the Mark Taper Forum, if not Los Angeles theater in general, and it certainly held back ***Ghetto*** in its American debut there.

Keith Reddin's ***Rum & Coke*** was a strong success at the New York Public Theater in January, following its world premiere at the South Coast Repertory Theatre in California and a subsequent spot in Yale's Theaterfest in New Haven. Reddin's play is about the Bay of Pigs, and takes place in various spots in Washington, Miami, Guatemala, and Cuba: there is even a flashback where the young hero, Jake, helps Richard Nixon out of his famous Fourth Crisis in Caracas, Venezuela. The strongest point of ***Rum & Coke*** is the satirical CIA caricatures Reddin creates, and the pathetically earnest logistics involved in, among other things, sprinkling Thallium salts on Castro's shoes to make his beard fall out, and shipping American whores to service Cuban "freedom fighters" in Guatemala. Presidentially-autographed bibles and key-shaped Israeli cakes, anybody? Reddin's play often borders on the tried and trite (CIA types mockingly call Jake "Joe College:" is this early Miller or early O'Neill?), and the gullibility of the U. S.-loyal Cubans is a bit inappropriately unflattering (as is the resounding naivete of the Americans). But the fact remains that the Bay of Pigs was a monstrous stupidity, and not only in hindsight: my own memory is that every American I talked with during that period was quite certain the invasion would fail, as it did. How in the world could John Kennedy not know that? How could he be stupider than the undergraduates at Berkeley I was hanging out with at the time? Reddin knows of the stupidity, but doesn't quite get at the reasons why; the CIA operatives and Kennedy were probably cleverer than he gives them credit for, but clever in a way so devious and wrongheaded that none of us really understand it, even yet. Still, anyone curious about the current goings on in Managua, Tripoli, Beirut, or Tehran will find something to think about here, and the play moves along rapidly, wittily, and persuasively. Richard Nixon and Fidel Castro put in brief appearances, and John and Jackie Kennedy hover around the multi-episodic and slightly rambling plot.

Aunt Dan and Lemon, by Wallace Shawn, won the 1986 Obie Award for best play; it has premiered at the Public Theater in 1985, but since it wasn't in last year's review, I'll report on it here. Some critics consider this the most important play of the year, and while I don't, I found much of it very stimulating in the 1986 Magic Theater production in San Francisco. Aunt Dan (for Danielle) is a brilliant neo-fascist, post-Bloomsbury Oxfordian; she fascinates and dominates a sickly young girl, Lemon, with exceptional tirades in praise of Henry Kissinger and the American bombing of North Vietnam; Lemon survives her, but barely, and the play is a series of flashbacks where Lemon lives alone with her fruit drinks, and her preoccupation with Nazi atrocities. "There's something I find refreshing about the Nazis," she concludes, "because they sort of had the nerve to say, 'Well, what *is* this compassion? . . .' And they all had to admit that they really didn't know what the hell it was." Shawn throws some of our very basic prejudices into a cruelly bright light, and finds enough conflicts there to make us work on them long after the curtain has fallen, and Maud Winchester, at the Magic, made Lemon a most giddily likable Hitlerphile. But I don't think Shawn has tied his play's very particular characters to their ideas very well (what made *Dinner with Andre* so successful was that the characters simply were the actors who played them, and the ideas were already theirs), and the events of the play are neither terribly illustrative, amusing, nor affecting. I suspect that ***Aunt Dan*** will claim more partial successes around the country in the next few years (it played an extended run at the Magic, and has already been published in a trade paperback by Grove), but I cannot imagine it emerging in the next few years as much more than a provocative conversation starter.

Two new and important plays centered on comically awkward middle-class American dinner parties. In Craig Lucas' ***Blue Window,*** one of the characters wishes aloud for people to have windows in their bodies, so that one can see what they're really thinking; in the other, Stephen Berkoff's ***Kvetch,*** they have such windows: Berkoff has them speak their thoughts, taking up a hoary device invented by Eugene O'Neill in *Strange Interlude*.

Berkoff's play is the more intermittently brilliant, but Lucas' is the more satisfying, and the more polished at this point; ***Blue Window*** will probably have a future beyond its early successes at the New York Production Company, the New Haven Long Wharf, and the South Coast (California) Repertory Theater. In the play's long and sole act, three couples and a stray male prepare for a party; then they have it; then three couples and the stray reflect at home on the party experience—but the stray and one of the semi-attached males have switched places, and each of the relationships has more or less been affected by the goings on. I say "more or less" because Lucas doesn't get any more definite than that, and neither do the characters involved; nor are the characters individually memorable, except perhaps for Libby, who physically survived a seven story fall and has a nice speech about it: apparently her mind is still falling off the balcony. Otherwise, much of the talk is simultaneous (even when it takes place in separate apartments), and much more of it is innocuous, but when the talk is all over you feel you know quite a bit more about the individuals than they know about themselves; you also feel that they're more worth knowing than they realize. These are not easy characters to write, and Lucas has done a beautiful job with them. The play ends in hugging, not talking, and then no windows are needed, even for the characters.

Berkoff's ***Kvetch,*** as directed by the author at the Odyssey Theatre in Los Angeles, opens with two wickedly funny scenes; the first in a bar, when Frank invites Hal over for dinner; the second at Frank's home, after Hal has the bad taste to accept. The dinner party is a complete disaster, for which everyone—Frank, Hal, Frank's wife, and Frank's mother-in-law—blames himself or herself, in vitriolic thought-monologues, delivered while the others freeze. The actors were well into the run when

Marcia Mohr, Mitch Kriendel, Kurt Fuller, Laura Esterman, and Ken Tigar in Steven Berkoff's Kvetch. *Courtesy of Odyssey Theatre Ensemble.*

I saw this, and their timing was absolutely sensational; the audience (of 99, since the play was produced under Equity waiver restrictions) was in acute hysterics through the intermission, when things unfortunately bogged down. "***Kvetch*** is a study of the effects of anxiety," Berkoff writes in his program note, and nobody since Moliere has, to my knowledge, tapped an audience's insecurity as well as Berkoff has in this play's first hour. Berkoff's conclusion is, as I've said, a let down, although not a disaster; Hal and Frank become homosexual lovers, Frank's wife runs off with Frank's boss, and new levels of anxiety are broached; the structure of the play does not effectively lead to these new developments (nor to the new character), and the anxiety seems all of a sudden too particularized. ***Kvetch*** is not a fully operational play at this point, but if Berkoff can shape its conclusion, he may have his first New York success. Laura Esterman, Kurt Fuller, and Mitch Kreindel were stunning in the principal roles at the Odyssey premiere.

America's heartland did not come up with its annual surprise hit this year, at least not at Louisville, where for years the celebrated Humana Festival of New American Plays has spewed forth such important premieres as *A Gin Game, Crimes of the Heart, Agnes of God, Extremities, Getting Out,* and *Execution of Justice*. This year's offerings had no such winners ("Festival Portends a Dreary Season" headlined the Washington *Times*), but I very much enjoyed Mary Gallagher's ***How to Say Goodbye,*** the well wrought story of a young couple, their friends, and their hydrocephaloid child, engaging and disengaging through the 1970's. It is a touching story and beautifully written; Gallagher has as much dramaturgical authority as anyone now writing plays, and her dialogue absolutely pulses with human vitality and enthusiasm. The subject is a bit limited, however, and the voice is generalized: one senses, if not the direct influence, then the indirect heritage, of *Loose Ends, Joe Egg,* and a dozen or so movies of the week. I also would like to urge a ten year moratorium on the poignant cheering up of children with unbearably tragic nursery songs: ***How to Say Goodbye*** is, among other things, variations on the theme of "In a cabin in a wood, / A little man by the window stood," wrung for every drop of sentiment affordable (at least it wasn't "Hush little baby, don't say a word," the current record-holder for dramatist-abused nursery songs.) ***How to Say Goodbye*** opened and closed in New York late in the season, and was barely noticed; clearly this is not a masterpiece of drama, but I feel Ms. Gallagher bears our very close attention from here on.

The other plays I saw at Louisville were not worth reporting on; however, one I didn't see, ***Some Things You Need to Know Before the World Ends: A Final Evening with the Illuminati,*** by Larry Larson and Levi Lee of Atlanta's Southern Theater Conspiracy, garnered some respectable reviews. Such was not the case for another Georgia export, and the Atlanta Alliance Theater came a cropper when it brought Sandra Deer's ***So Long on Lonely Street*** to Broadway; after a rapturous and extended run in Atlanta, ***Lonely Street*** collapsed utterly in New York, to the complete consternation of its backers and producers. But there is almost nothing of value in this old fashioned 19th century Southern melodrama, complete with its will reading scene, its birth certificate-ex-machina denouement, its Poe-spouting incestuous intellectuals, its maid named Annabel Lee, and its ancestral home, founded by "Big Jack" and "Miss Beulah," which is about to be turned into a shopping center named "Beulahland." Ms. Deer, sad to report, intends this all quite seriously. The author's introduction to the printed version says, "These are realistic characters, not Southern types," but the fact is that they *are* Southern types, no matter what the author thinks, and the plot is a ludicrous Southern-Gothic melange. How the late Cheryl Crawford (and others), who produced it, could have thought this had a chance in New York is one of the year's biggest mysteries.

There's little question but that the regional stages are our most vigorous theater groups today. In addition to the new plays coming out of these companies, there are also a host of distinguished revivals, including, among those I caught this year, Garland Wright's stunning ***Good Woman of Sezuan*** at the Washington (D.C.) Arena Stage, and the same director's lovely ***The Seagull*** at the Denver Theater Center. Leslie Reidel did an exquisite job, too, with ***Two Gentlemen of Verona*** at the Colorado Shakespeare Festival, and there were a number of productions about which I heard glowing reports from around the country. *American Theater* does a fine job of providing schedules for most of this activity, but, sadly, that journal's actual coverage consists mainly of puff pieces by and about its constituent members (the magazine is put out by the Theater Communications Group), and aside from the irregular "Resident Legit Review" in *Variety* (the best source), or the occasional national newsmagazine coverage of one city's theatrical season, (Chicago and La Jolla have been so honored this year), there is little timely critical guidance as to what important works are playing in the country; nothing in the nation's periodical press that provides, say, what *Theater Heute* provides for the West German theater, or *Theater der Zeit* for the East German. Anyone seriously interested in studying the contemporary U.S. drama scene, therefore, had best have lots of friends in diverse places, and make lots of phone calls, before hopping on a plane. Still, the effort will prove rewarding. The high levels of theater artistry in the country, and the pertinent intelligence and imagination of the best of our playwrights, make for a national theater (uncapitalized) which is infectious in its energy, and increasingly assured in its accomplishment.

The University of California, Irvine

The Year in World Literature

by William Riggan

The literary year 1986 got off to an inauspicious start with January's fractious International PEN Congress in New York, as invective and political posturing dominated both the proceedings and the daily headlines. The spectacle and the results were less than edifying, to say the least. Happily, the events in no way presaged the rich, bountiful array of first-rate works that were to emerge from European and Third World writers alike or the introduction of important writers from less-accessible languages to large, worldwide reading audiences via new translations. The posthumous revelation of previously unpublished materials by deceased twentieth-century classics provided an additional boon to readers everywhere.

European Literature

The German-speaking countries enjoyed a particularly strong year both in the breadth and the depth of the newest works by their leading authors. Günter Grass, one of the most outspoken and provocative participants at the January PEN meeting, produced ***Die Rättin* (The She-Rat),** a grim though undeniably imaginative vision of an imminent apocalypse that will leave rats as the dominant surviving species. Earlier Grass characters such as Oskar Matzerath and Anna Koljaicek (from *The Tin Drum*) put in cameo appearances, as in a swan song or a summa, and the book is indeed rumored to be Grass's final novelistic effort, as he turns exclusively to his art work and to global politics. The Austrian author Peter Handke's newest novel ***Die Wiederholung***—whose title means both "Repetition" and "Retrieval"—also points toward the aftermath of a possible future cataclysm, but reaches that end via more mythic-poetic means, tracing a young writer's twenty-five-year quest for his vanished brother in the Slovene countryside; the work is Handke's most substantial and important in several years and has reignited the critical attention and acclaim that marked the young novelist's early career. His startlingly prolific countryman Thomas Bernhard produced *his* most comprehensive work as well in 1986, the six-hundred-page novel ***Auslöschung* (Extinction)**, whose writer-protagonist seeks to obliterate all ties between himself and his now-abhorred parochial hometown of Wolfsegg through literary exaggeration and excess, to "extinguish all that I associate with Wolfsegg and all that Wolfsegg is." A bigger popular success among Austrian readers was Gerhard Roth's intellectual thriller ***Am Abgrund* (At the Edge of the Abyss)**, which turns such Kafkaesque themes as guilt, justice, and power inside out via a complex triple narrative perspective. In East German letters only ***Bronzezeit* (Bronze Age)**, five interrelated tales by Hermann Kant featuring his recurrent protagonist, the accountant Farssman, proved noteworthy for its "stylistically unique mixture of nineteenth-century idiom and contemporary cheekiness," as one critic noted; the depiction of a lighter side to life in the Democratic Republic, moreover, points significantly toward a "new ease" and a so-called "end of administration" that are beginning to appear there. In West Germany new novels by Max von der Grün and Hermann Lenz as well as intriguing short-story collections by Luise Rinser and Hermann Burger attracted respectful interest but were overshadowed by Grass's new book, by the 1944-46 installment of Thomas Mann's voluminous and continuing diaries, and by what must surely be of the most-discussed and least-bought or -read German novels in decades, Marianne Fritz's ***Dessen Sprache du nicht verstehst* (Whose Language You Do Not Understand)**, a three-volume, thirty-four-hundred-page "epic of collective memory" about the experience of World War I that has been compared in richness and complexity by some to Robert Musil's *Man without Qualities* and Karl Kraus's *Last Days of Mankind*. Parenthetically one might note, in connection with the Germanic literatures, the publication of an expanded and now complete Dutch edition of ***The Diaries of Anne Frank,*** including manuscript facsimiles and the author's early verses, all overseen in painstaking and authoritative detail by the Royal Dutch Institute of Documentary Research; translations into the major Western languages are certain to follow soon.

French literature enjoyed a strong year as well, led by such longtime mainstays as Claude Mauriac and Julien Green. With the ninth and penultimate installment of his "Temps immobile" (Immovable Time) series, ***Mauriac et fils* (Mauriac & Son)**, Mauriac weaves a vibrant, lyric chronicle that transcends autobiography to reflect the author's entire epoch, dwelling particularly on the mysteries of transmission—of heritage, of culture, of sensibility—while offering a continuous counterpoint of personal drama and public events in what one critic describes as a kind of "Goncourt journal as revisited by the New Novel." The octogenarian Green weighed in with ***Chaque homme dans sa nuit* (Each Man in His Night)**, a novel of love, murder, and forgiveness but also a kind of "sentimental education" leading to a fuller knowledge of love and the heart. Robert Sabatier completed his best-selling tetralogy with ***David et Olivier,*** a moving yet infectiously joyous chronicling of an adolescent's explorations in 1930s Montmartre. The Academician Jean Cayrol focused on the denser, darker, less-congenial world of an orphaned youth's country estate in ***Les châtaignes* (The Chestnuts)**, a stripped-down récit devoid of psychological probing and fixated on the overt gesture, the spoken word, the palpable odor *à la nouveau roman* of three decades ago. Michel Butor, once a leading practitioner of the New Novel, continued along his own imaginatively unique literary road with the fifth and final volume of ***Matière de rêves* (The Stuff of Dreams)**, a fanciful and free-flowing weave of fact and fiction that follows the associative logic of dreams, here blending the work of e.g. Baudelaire and Huysmans with his own inventions and fantasy. The popular young author J. M. G. Le Clézio followed his previous year's success *Le chercheur d'or* (The Seeker of Gold) with ***Voyage à Rodrigues,*** inspired by the adventures of the author's grandfather and by the latter's visit to the island of Rodrigues while exploring his ancestor's life and legend.

Of equal note in French letters in 1986 were two voices from an earlier day: ***Le passé défini*** **(Past Definite)**, the second volume of Jean Cocteau's diaries, covers the year 1953, by which time the 1920s charmer had soured considerably toward friends and fame but was nevertheless still the compulsively gregarious public *artiste* striving to convince the world that he was a serious, dedicated talent; and the letters of Max Jacob to a young friend, ***Lettres à Michel Manoll,*** on a wide range of artistic and literary topics provide a valuable historical addendum to the great writer-artist's career.

New releases by two of Italy's most accomplished prose writers, Primo Levi and the late Italo Calvino, highlighted that country's relatively modest literary production in 1986. Levi continued his series of inspired, insightful, deceptively simple accounts of his death-camp experiences during the war with ***I sommersi e i salvati*** **(The Submerged and the Saved)**. Calvino's posthumously published book ***Sotto il sole giaguaro*** **(Under the Jaguar Sun)** gathered a series of narrative "exercises," his own formal structural invention combining indirect narration, a "geometric" framework, fantasy, myth, and the tangible evidence of the senses. Spain's authors meanwhile continued in 1986 to mine the fertile field of their country's civil war, as in Francisco Umbral's ***Pío XII, la escolta mora y un general sin un ojo*** **(Pius XII, the Moorish Escort, and a One-Eyed General)**, although writers such as Gonzalo Torrente Ballester did turn to other historical subjects, as in ***El golpe de estado de Guadalupe Limón,*** about revolutionary upheaval in a New World colony resembling Mexico; Torrente Ballester's novel, like many works appearing in Spain during the last ten years, is actually a very early work only now being at last published in the author's native country.

Eastern European Literature

Several important publications by East European writers marked the literary year in that region. The 1984 Nobel laureate, the late Czech poet Jaroslav Seifert, was at last made more widely accessible to non-Czech readers through the publication of the 194-page ***Selected Poems*** in fine English translations by Ewald Osers and George Gibian; included as a bonus in the volume are excerpts from the poet's charming memoir of his later years, *All the Beauties of the World.* The eminent Czech playwright Václav Havel set the scholar-hero of the drama ***Largo desolato*** not only against the infernal machinations of state authorities displeased with his latest book, but also against the pressures of friends and colleagues to act this way or that in his dilemma. The year's biggest sensation in Czech literature, however, was created by first-time novelist Jan Pelc with ***. . . a bude hur*** (a slang phrase meaning roughly "It will be worse"), a radically innovative and exaggeratedly scatological work centered on the lowest stratum of contemporary Czech society in all its squalor and nihilism—thereby presumably illuminating the deficiencies of the current political system, in the view of most critics; several editors at home and abroad have refused to comment on the book at all, citing its pornographic nature and its "insults to Czech national dignity."

Dust jacket of Mauriac et fils, *by Claude Mauriac. Grasset, 1986. © Jeanne François Mauriac. Courtesy of Éditions Bernard Grasset. Dust jacket of* Unattainable Earth, *by Czesław Miłosz. Ecco, 1986. Jacket © Cynthia Krupat. Reproduced by permission of The Ecco Press.*

On a loftier plane, the 1978 Nobel recipient, Polish-born Czeslaw Milosz, issued a new volume of his verse in translation, ***Unattainable Earth,*** wherein he moves away from the largely historical themes of his earlier work and into the realm of metaphysics and ontology as he approaches the stately age of seventy-five; Milosz's addition of his translations of other poets enhances both the serene sense of community evoked in the original material and the richness of the poet's own verse.

Latin American Literature

In the New World itself, Peru's outstanding writer Mario Vargas Llosa led the way with two new books: ***Quién mató a Palomino Molero?*** **(Who Killed Palomino Molero?)**, a marvelously cerebral, phantasmagoric, yet politically astute account of the convoluted events surrounding the murder of a young military pilot—a plot recalling that of the author's first successful novel, *La ciudad y los perros* (Eng. *The City and the Dogs*) nearly twenty years ago; and the play ***La chunga*** **(The Vixen)**, a study in sordid local realism wihin a primitive *machisto* urban setting in northern Peru. Alfredo Bryce Echenique proved again that Peru has more than one writer of world-class talent with his new novel ***El hombre que hablaba de Octavia de Cádiz,*** an urbanely comic turn on the theme of the charming but ne'er-do-well young bohemian. ***Quintuples*** **(Quintuplets)**, a play by Puerto Rico's Luis Rafael Sánchez, and ***Anteparadise,*** presenting the excellent poetry of Chile's Raúl Zurita in a bilingual format, were also noteworthy for their respective efforts to bring to the stage the verbal inventiveness that characterized Sánchez's earlier novel *Macho Camacho's Beat* and to evoke the collective trauma of post-Allende Chile in apocalyptic verse of passion, urgency, and uniquely evocative talent.

Brazil was, if anything, even better represented in the year's production than was Spanish America. ***A Polaquinha*** **(*The Polish Girl*)**, Dalton Trevisan's first full-length novel, stretches the author's limits somewhat but excellently captures the sound and rhythm of modern Brazilian Portuguese and presents in the title figure one of Brazilian literature's most memorable characters in recent years. The young Luiz Berto Filho penned one of the year's most popular and best-selling works, ***O romance da Besta Fubana,*** about the founding of the Revolutionary Republic of Palmares in 1953. Rubem Fonseca, whom Vargas Llosa calls "one of those contemporary writers who have absconded from the library to create high-quality literature with materials and techniques stolen from mass culture," came to the attention of American readers in an English-language edition of ***High Art,*** a carnivalistic parody of detective fiction's excesses and unrealities, all carried out with good humor and engaging intellect.

Dust jacket of Quintuples, *by Luis Rafael Sánchez. Ediciones Norte, 1986. Dust jacket of* O Romance da Besta Fubana, *by Luiz Berto. Courtesy of Luiz Berto. Dust jacket of* The Anti-Soviet Soviet Union, *by Vladimir Voinovich. Harcourt Brace Jovanovich, 1986. Jacket design © Bob Silverman, Inc. Jacket illustration by Rick Geary. Used with permission.*

Russian Literature

Russian-language literature was most ably represented in 1986 both at home and in the diaspora. Konstantin Simonov, one of the mainstays of Soviet Russian prose in the postwar years, published ***Sofia Leonidovna,*** a novelette written twenty-six years earlier which tells in compassionate and surprisingly enlightened fashion the stories of three women active in the resistance movement against the Nazi occupation forces in 1941. Two other leading Soviet Russian prose writers, the gracefully Jamesian Andrei Bitov and the psychologically astute Yuri Nagibin, were introduced to Western audiences via the translated story collections ***Life in Windy Weather*** and ***The Peak of Success*** respectively. Bitov is something of a loner and a gadfly whose demanding, consistently high-quality works challenge the view that Soviet literature is essentially socialist-realist and esthetically conservative; in addition to James, the writers he most brings to mind in theme and style are Proust, Nabokov, and Chekhov. Nagibin, considered by many critics as the best active Soviet short-story writer and known in some circles for his screenplay of the award-winning film *Dersu Uzala,* has been most often compared with Bunin and Chekhov as a "psychologically sensitive and disciplined author with clear, uncomplicated moral values tempered by a sense of irony and compassion," in the words of one Western commentator. The outstanding Russian émigré poet Joseph Brodsky turned to prose in 1986 with ***Less than One,*** a volume of essays in English covering such disparate topics as postwar Leningrad, older fellow writers such as Akhmatova and Mandelstam, Russian classics such as Pushkin and Dostoevsky, and a good many foreign authors, including Cavafy and Montale. Vladimir Voinovich, whose hilariously satiric novels about the good soldier Chonkin and other matters have placed him squarely in the tradition of Gogol and Saltykov-Shchedrin in Russian-language letters, turned to nonfiction prose in ***Antisovetskii Sovetskii Soiuz*** (Eng. ***The Anti-Soviet Soviet Union***), a collection of wryly moving anecdotes and elaborated reports on everyday facets of life both in the USSR and in emigration.

African/West Indian Literature

In the African-Caribbean literary realm, the outstanding poet-playwright Derek Walcott of Trinidad again led the way, following the previous year's highly acclaimed *Collected Poems* with the volume ***Three Plays;*** the best of the three, ***Beef, No Chicken,*** is a farcical diagnosis of progress in the West Indies and the corruption, "commodification," and total lack of nostalgia for the old ways that characterize the march of modernization there. Ronald Dathorne of Guyana explores the nature of emerging political leadership in the Caribbean in his novel ***Dele's Child,*** finding mostly bald ambition and venality instead of the political-administrative skills and intelligence needed for the region's future. The tragic and largely forgotten genocide visited upon Haiti's Indian and Carib peoples by Spanish explorers and colonizers around 1500 is movingly evoked by native son Jean Métellus in ***Anacaona,*** particularly in the novel's central, emblematic episode: the crucifixion of Queen Anacaona by Christopher Columbus's sailors. The work's much-praised elegance of construction and luxuriance of language convey as well an enormous measure of indignation and revulsion at the events depicted. The consensus of critical opinion thus far is that Métellus has with this work written the first great epic of the Haitian people.

From Africa proper came several works of note, including ***The Scaffold*** by the South African writer Edward Lurie, who uses the cynical conversion of a welfare complex for "coloreds" into a monstrous "hypermarket" as a concrete emblem of apartheid's all-pervasive, destructive nature. The exiled black South African writer Lewis Nkosi produced in ***Mating Birds*** a more personal, muted, and agonizing narrative on the same subject, using the now-familiar metaphor of forbidden yet irresistible sexual attraction between a black man and a white woman to expose the anguish generated by the sociopolitical circumstances. The poet Daniel Kunene, like Nkosi a black émigré from South Africa but one who has recently begun to publish at home as well as abroad, brought out his first collection of stories, ***From the Pit of Hell to the Spring of Life.*** "Through careful observation of character and a subtle understanding of the relationship between the individual and his community," one perceptive critic has written, "Kunene portrays people facing significant choices and explores the complexity of the choice, its implications, its potential to enslave or liberate." Nearly a continent away, the Sudan's Francis Mading Deng offered a thinly disguised and self-proclaimed political novel in ***Seed in Redemption.*** Following the saga of three generations of a Sudanese family from slavery to trusted government service in the office of the country's charismatic but unstable president, the work presents, in one commentator's words, "a sweeping panorama of history and politics, of violence, intrigue, tenderness, and love, painting a terrifying future for the Sudan, but one that can be salvaged." Kenya's Ngugi wa Thiong'o bade "farewell to English as a vehicle for [his] writings" in ***Decolonising the Mind,*** a collection of essays and lectures "on some of the issues in which I have been passionately involved for the last twenty years in fiction, theater, criticism, and in teaching of literature." Ngugi plans to publish all his future works in his native Kikuyu, possibly following up with English versions by himself or others.

Prominent African Francophone publications in 1986 included ***Naissance à l'aube*** (***Birth at Dawn***) by Algeria's Driss Chraïbi, ***L'enfant de sable*** (***The Child of Sand***) by Tahar Ben Jelloun of Morocco, and the first English translation from the work of Ivory Coast novelist Bernard Dadié, ***The City Where No One Dies.*** Of particular merit was ***The Seven-Headed Serpent,*** a translation of the newest novel by Chraïbi's countryman Ali Ghanem, which records the picaresque odyssey of a young Berber orphan from his primitive mountain village, through the liberation war, to university study in France, to success and recognition in the film industry for this "good Muslim youth" struggling to find his niche in the world.

Dust jacket of Dele's Child *by Ronald Dathorne. Three Continents Press, 1986. Jacket illustration and design by Max K. Winkler. Courtesy of Three Continents Press, Inc. Cover of* Anacaona, *by Jean Métellus. Libraire Hatier, 1986. Dust jacket of* Decolonising the Mind, *by Ngugi Wa Thiong'o. James Curry Publishers, 1986 (also published in 1986 by Heinemann, Inc. and Heinemann, Nairobi, Kenya). Reproduced by permission of James Curry Publishers Ltd., London. Dust jacket of* Mating Birds, *by Lewis Nkosi. St. Martin's Press, 1986. Jacket art by Melanie Marder Parks. Jacket design by Paolo Pepe. Reproduced by permission of St. Martin's Press, Inc.*

Near Eastern Literature

Egyptian writers dominated the year's production from the Near East, led by the most-translated and most highly skilled Arabic prose writer of today, Naguib Mahfouz. Not one but *two* Mahfouz novels were added to the growing list of his books available in English: ***Autumn Quail,*** the 1962 tragedy of a government official in King Farouk's regime who is purged following the revolution; and ***Wedding Song,*** a story of sordid intrigue and hatred within the Egyptian theater world. Nawal el-Saadawi attracted international attention several years ago with her sociocultural study *The Hidden Face of Eve* but has now produced two much-discussed novels as well, including 1986's ***Two Women in One,*** whose teen-age heroine is pushed gradually from small symbolic rebellions to violent open revolt against what she perceives as stifling social conventions and a repressive political order. ***The Net*** by Sherif Hetata recounts the victimization of a political activist who proves powerless against the combined forces of corruption, sycophancy, and secretive machinations born of sheer expediency; the result is a "searing commentary on the moral changes wrought by the Sadat era on Egyptian society." Yaakov Shabtai's ***Past Continuous,*** issued almost simultaneously in Hebrew and English, highlighted the year in Israeli literature, with its complexly structured, demanding evocation of the dynamism that characterizes modern-day urban life in Israel and the concomitant clash of generations and values. ***Sevgilim Istanbul*** (***Istanbul My Love***) by Nedim Gürsel, which appeared a year earlier in French, was the most important of Turkey's many fine new publications in 1986, a collection of eighteen interrelated stories that—despite the title—are set in a number of world capitals and explore the theme of alienation and solitude. Gürsel's newest novel, ***La première femme*** (***The First Woman;*** again appearing in French prior to publication in Turkish), tracks the coming of age of a young provincial newly arrived in Istanbul, deftly interweaving four archetypal feminine figures—mother, whore, legendary Turkish heroine, and Istanbul itself—who play important roles in his maturation. Across the strait, the 1979 Nobel laureate Odysseus Elytis's Greek poetry of the last seven years was adequately rendered into English by Olga Broumas in ***What I Love,*** half of which is occupied by the book-length 1983 poem "Maria Nephele."

Asian/Pacific Literature

Significantly, the year 1986 brought the first publication and/or translation of a number of fine recent works by writers from Asia and the Pacific region. ***The Uncollected Stories of Christina Stead*** rounded off the late Australian author's successful career in unfortunately uneven fashion but with a sufficient quantity of unexpected treasures to warrant the collection several times over. In ***The Matriarch*** the Maori novelist Witi Ihimaera delves deeply into New Zealand history, interweaving fact and fiction while recounting the story of his narrator's legendary grandmother, the beautiful and cunningly ruthless priestess-ruler who led the fight to reclaim native lands against Pakeha (white European) encroachment. ***The Birth and Death of the Miracle Man,*** a collection of stories by Samoan writer Albert Wendt, focuses on several intriguing and complex island figures whose tales offer a highly original, variegated tapestry of their Pacific community as an only slightly exotic microcosm of the modern world.

From the Asian mainland came the latest work by India's grand old man of letters, R. K. Narayan; set in the now-famous fictional town of Malgudi, ***Talkative Man*** gently satirizes a perceived continuing subservience and gullibility among the author's countrymen via the story of an ambitious but garrulous and sometimes naïve journalist's efforts to assist—and report on—a mysterious fair-haired stranger who insinuates himself secretively into the life of both the reporter and the entire community.

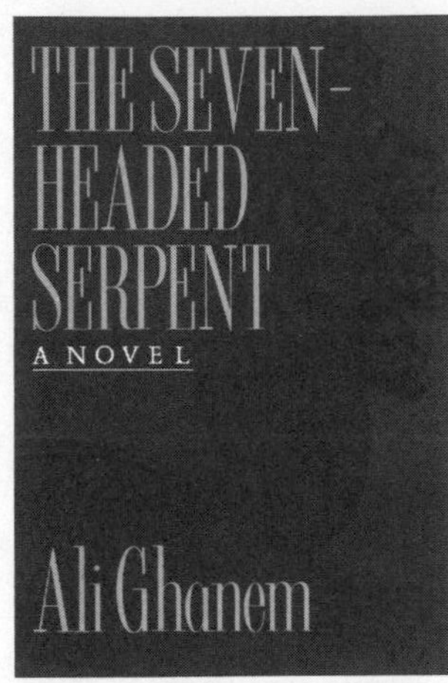

Dust jacket of L'enfant de sable, *by Tahar Ben Jelloun. Roman Seuil, 1986. Courtesy of Georges Borchardt, Inc. Dust jacket of* The Seven-Headed Serpent, *by Ali Ghanem. Harcourt Brace Jovanovich, 1986. Jacket design by Laurie Dolphin. Reproduced by permission of Laurie Dolphin. Dust jacket of* Past Continuous, *by Yaakov Shabtai. The Jewish Publication Society, 1986. Jacket design by Adrianne Onderdonk Dudden. Used through the courtesy of The Jewish Publication Society. Dust jacket of* The Matriarch, *by Witi Ihimaera. Heinemann, 1986. Jacket artwork by Sally Hollis-McLeod/Moscow. Courtesy of William Heinemann Ltd.*

The first translation of major works from the late 1930s and from a leading contemporary author plus one completely new novel stood out in the Chinese literary year. Xiao Hong's accomplished and compelling 1936 novel ***Market Street*** recounts the poverty, hardship, and Confucian misogyny the author encountered at the start of her abbreviated career, all in prose that is both unadorned and lyrical. Cao Yu's skillful 1940 play ***Peking Man,*** on the other hand, offers hope for better times in its portrait of the decline of the traditional family and the awakening humanitarian ideals of the younger generation. ***Love Must Not Be Forgotten*** is the first comprehensive selection of stories by Zhang Jie, perhaps the most widely hailed of today's Chinese women writers. In the words of no less an authority than Harrison Salisbury, "Zhang Jie is one of the most exciting and gifted of the new writers who are beginning to come out of China; she has a powerful interest in human problems, particularly those of women and their relationships to their environment, and writes with a comprehension and sympathy which is certain to appeal across any boundaries of nation or viewpoint." The young Taiwanese novelist Li Ang, finally, reports in ***The Butcher's Wife*** the harrowing, factually based story of a young peasant woman who, brutalized by her pig-butcher husband and by a male-dominated superstitious society, is driven to madness and ultimately to murder; despite the stark prose and macabre subject matter, the work is being praised as the finest example of Chinese fiction in recent years.

The work of Japan's Kenzaburo Oe continued to find a wide audience in the West in 1986 with the publication of an English edition of his 1985 book ***A Story of M/T and the Mysteries of the Forest,*** a Utopian novel that evokes both the mythological power of the Matriarch and Trickster figures and the mystical life forces that, for Oe, lie hidden in nature and in humankind, even in present-day Japanese society. Wholly different in tone and manner is Saiichi Maruya's prizewinning novel ***Singular Rebellion,*** a wonderfully clever and lightfooted comic work that is as insightful about Japanese ways as it is humorous in satirizing them. ***Waves*** presents for Western readers two novellas by the octogenarian prose master Masuji Ibuse, whose speciality is the realistic-satiric historical novel: the title story takes us back to the Japanese "War of the Roses," the twelfth-century confrontation between the Heike and Genji clans, and conveys much of the turbulence, cruelty, and beauty of a world on the brink of cataclysmic change; "Isle-on-the-Billows," on the other hand, is an ironically humorous portrait of eighteenth-century Japanese class conflict, hypocrisy, and bureaucratic snarls that prove not so distant from present-day Japanese society as first assumed. Finally, ***The Showa Anthology*** offers twenty-one stories dating from 1926 to the present (i.e., the Showa Era) by writers both famous in the West (Oe, Kawabata, Endo, Abe) and hitherto unfamiliar to most Western readers (Jun Ishikawa, Toshio Shimao, Junzo Shono); the selections themselves range from autobiographical sketches to surrealistic pieces, lyrical interludes, intellectual discourses, pastorals, and studies of war, constituting in sum a reasonable cross section of contemporary Japanese writing styles and literary themes.

World Literature Today

New Authors

Yuz Aleshkovsky

1929-

Russian novelist.

Although he published four novels in the Soviet Union from 1963 through 1973, Aleshkovsky was more widely recognized for his children's books and popular songs. *Kangaroo* (1986), his first novel published in English, was written in 1975, prior to his emigration. "The moment I sensed the image of *Kangaroo,* the moment I got the hang of the whole, I became awfully agitated. For suddenly I realized the possibility of finding myself inside the medley of history—yet not in the capacity of a victim or a scholar—no: I found myself inside it as a writer. . . ."

© Jerry Bauer

Kangaroo is the story of Fan Fanych, a small-time criminal whose forced confession to the rape and murder of an elderly kangaroo results in a surreal journey through the Soviet penal system. In this satire of the Stalinist show trials and the ideology from which they developed, Aleshkovsky writes in the Russian mode of skaz, a slangy, first person narrative, which allows Fanych to tell the story in his own profane, criminal vernacular. Some critics fear that Americans may know too little of Soviet culture for Aleshkovsky's satire to be completely effective, but they praise its energy and originality.

Aleshkovsky currently resides in the United States and is working on two novels, one of which concerns a Russian exile in America.

PUBLISHERS WEEKLY

[In Aleshkovsky's ***Kangaroo***], the first of his novels to appear in English, his narrator, smalltime criminal Fan Fanych, (aka Citizen Etcetera), is peremptorily requested by the KGB to appear at the Lubyanka in the year 1949. He is accused of the "vicious rape and murder of an aged kangaroo in the Moscow zoo on a night between July 14, 1789 and January 9, 1905." In an acid-soaked monolog Fan addresses the KGB agent and beyond him the nation and the world, ranging up and down the dark corridors of Soviet history, allowing no one and nothing—no prominent figure, no infamous event, no ideological peculiarity—to escape his scalding notice. Not a novel in any conventional sense, this is a sustained cry of rage and despair delivered at the top of the lungs—unremittingly foulmouthed, deadly, on-target, seditious and mirthlessly funny.

A review of "Kangaroo," in Publishers Weekly, *Vol. 229, No. 10, March 7, 1986, p. 82.*

JOHN UPDIKE

The dire results of [the Russian] revolution are, with the bewildering mixture of slapstick and rage that used to be called "black humor," tumbled before us by the expatriate Yuz Aleshkovsky in his novel ***Kangaroo***. . . .

[***Kangaroo***] makes no compromise with the American reader, who is expected to know and care, without benefit of footnote or appendix, who or what Ordzhonikidze, the Chelyuskin, Mikhail Zoshchenko, Chekists, Ilya Ehrenburg, Ivan Pyriev, Radishchev, Zoya Fyodorova, Tukhachevsky, Kirov, Karatsupa, Kulaks, Zhdanov, Voznesensky, Yuri Levitan, Bukharin, Rykov, Zinoviev, Kamenev, Zelinsky-Nesmeyanov gas, Joseph Vissarionovich, and zeks are or were. Our daunted American reader is further expected to pick the serious satirical strands from a grotesque, scatological, backward-looping farrago involving the conviction of a Russian pickpocket and criminal by name of Fan Fanych, alias Etcetera, alias Cariton Ustinych Newton Tarkington, for "the vicious rape and murder of an aged kangaroo in the Moscow Zoo on a night between July 14, 1789, and January 9, 1905." . . . Fan Fanych remembers while under durance or en route his earlier curious involvements with Hitler in 1929 and the Yalta Conference in 1945; he returns to a de-Stalinized Moscow in 1955, finds his apartment full of sparrow nests, and falls in love with a now grown-up girl he glimpsed just before packing to go to the Lubyanka. Finally, he locates his old friend Kolya, to whom he is somehow telling all this, much as Portnoy is delivering his complaint to a psychiatrist. The analogy with Philip Roth's exuberant demolition of bourgeois inhibitions may illuminate why ***Kangaroo*** struck me as so grindingly unfunny, albeit prankish: to relish unrepressed prose, we must have had some experience of the repression, and we must be able to hear the voice. ***Kangaroo*** is told in that heavily slangy Russian which drives translators to revive such stale English expressions as "mug," "screwball," "shoot the breeze," and "off his (her, its) rocker." While a patriotic citizen of the free West must be politically flattered by so detailed and vehement a blasphemy against the Soviet system, it makes deadly reading if you've never been a believer and don't know the iconography.

Only when ***Kangaroo*** floats free of its political burden does it stir a smile. In inflation-plagued Germany, our down-and-out hero has his overcoat and suit "turned"—torn apart and resewn inside out, to show the unworn side of the cloth. His clothes take revenge, with an animation that recalls the bedevilled and bedevilling objects of the old Chaplin films: "For some reason my whole body's twitching inside the suit, as if there's a flea biting me, or a sharp little splinter scratching me. . . . I can tell my rotten jacket's doing it on purpose, just to make me look like an idiot, and my pants are giving it moral support. They're riding up my knees in creases, and keep rustling. And my pockets are moaning like seashells, 'Oo-oo-oo.'" Here the referent—wearing clothes—is generally human, and the absurd can be measured against the actual and its degree of exaggeration appreciated. But in this Soviet system conceived as sheer demonism—"sucking people's blood just for laughs, destroying innocent souls, wearing out their strength and keeping the human spirit humiliated for half a century"—we do not quite know where we are, and hardly dare laugh in the dark. ***Kangaroo*** translates a work whose intended readers can all read Russian. (pp. 120-22)

John Updike, in a review of "Kangaroo," in The New Yorker, *Vol. LXII, No. 10, April 28, 1986, pp. 120-22.*

An Excerpt from *Kangaroo*

"I'll be brief," I said. "Your era's intellect and honor and conscience can all go to hell as far as I'm concerned. I've never wanted to change the world. I've never taken alms from nature by force, I've just expropriated what the big guys don't need. I've ripped off a lot of governments, but I've never touched ordinary people. And I could have—I know six and a half languages. I refuse to help build such a dubious future on principle. I left behind me outside a whole museum of all the wallets, briefcases, and monocles I've swiped from big political activists from Poland, Rumania, England, Japan, Morocco, Germany, Costa Rica, et cetera. I've had the clap twice. I raped and viciously murdered a kangaroo called Gemma in the Moscow Zoo on a night between January 9, 1789, and July 14, 1905. That's why the People's Court in Krasnaya Presnya put me away for twenty-five years. And now," I wind up, "benefactors of mankind, friends of the people, night-night, it's sleepy-time."

They muttered to each other, went into a huddle, and finally passed a resolution which said that jailing a recidivist criminal alongside the most senior members of the party, the men who stormed the Winter Palace and fought at Lenin's side, was horrible cynicism and violated the Geneva Convention's ruling on treatment of political prisoners. They resolved not to shake hands with me and not to call me comrade, but rejected Chernyshevsky's amendment proposing a Red Terror against me. They said it went against Leninist norms of polemical discussion with an ideological enemy. I told them a whole lot more about the country's internal situation, starvation, imprisonment, the greatest commander of all times and all peoples, who should have been hauled up before the law for killing and dismembering millions of soliders, about making you do time for being late for work that an animal shouldn't have to do, about how the peasants were starving to death while the big guys told them fairy tales about serfdom and the glorious kolkhoz life. I told them how an ordinary guy who has to go from one end of Moscow to the other to get to work squeezes himself into streetcars and not enough trolleybuses, scuffles with other poor bastards just like him, worried to death by government loans and meetings, puts in the extra hours when they have elections to the people's courts, all the time getting madder than a hungry wolf. And it's only because he's afraid they'll shove him inside that he tucks his tail between his legs and just bares his teeth after a little glass of vodka.

"Maybe, but we've got the cheapest housing in the world!" said Chernyshevsky to me, his dull eyes suddenly shining.

JOHN GLAD

Yuz Aleshkovsky, popular as an underground songwriter in his native Russia but still virtually unknown as a novelist, has revived the tradition of Gogol. ***Kangaroo,*** his first novel published in English, is a great satire based on fantasy. It will stand as a landmark for literary historians and Russian writers of the future.

Aleshkovsky sees himself as a maker of myth, which he uses to create an absurd, phantasmagorical novel about a crook, a kangaroo and a kangaroo court. The main character in ***Kangaroo,*** Fan Fanych, is selected for a special public-relations event intended to celebrate the anniversary of the KGB's "very first case." The event will be a mock trial, with charges dreamed up by a computer, since Party henchmen are falling behind schedule and not producing convictions fast enough. . . .

In exchange for his cooperation in the show trial, he is promised unlimited Western movies, his choice of cell mates, Western newspapers, etc. during his imprisonment, because, of course, conviction is a certainty. . . .

Russian writers in exile are now renewing the rich artistic currents which characterized Russian literature in the early years of this century. At the same time, they are returning to the Western roots from which Russian literature grew. In the case of ***Kangaroo,*** the affinities are with Kafka's *Trial,* but even more so they are with a Russian work—Nabokov's *Invitation to a Beheading.*

To truly appreciate ***Kangaroo,*** it is important to understand the context from which it arises. Censorship for Soviet writers has taken on a role analogous to that of rhyme and meter in traditional poetry. The writer's message, just like the poet's sonnet, must fit into very specific conventions. Many Russian writers come to place such importance on slipping at least something past the censor that it becomes a goal in and of itself. And without that goal, many emigre writers become disoriented, lack a sense of direction. Not so Aleshkovsky. He continues in his role as mythmaker, fantasist.

Myth in the context of the official Soviet literary code of Socialist Realism is just as impossible as political satire. And what of Socialist Fantasy? This sort of literature just does not exist in Soviet Russia today, except for the work of a few authors like Arkady and Boris Strugatsky, whose science fiction novels are likewise frowned upon by the official critics.

Kangaroo is replete with specifically Soviet references. Western readers will have to do their homework to appreciate everything that is going on. The translator's heroic efforts notwithstanding, an entire dimension of obscenities and criminal slang is inevitably lost, and even if the flavor of such elements in the original could be rendered in English, the impact of such language in the jaded West is necessarily of a lesser magnitude than in the relatively puritanical atmosphere of Russian letters.

But this is a problem which arises with virtually all Russian novels translated into Western languages. The question of how well literature "travels" from one country to another is a particularly sore point for Russian writers. Literature in the Soviet Union has been developing along separate lines for so long that no Soviet novel has become popular in the West without there first being a political hullabaloo. Certainly, the straits in which the satirist finds himself are the cruelest of all, since his Western audience is unfamiliar with the context he is satirizing.

But despite all these drawbacks, this is both a funny novel and a novel with a serious message about the evils of totalitarianism. And as you follow Fan Fanych's efforts to work himself into the role of a sex fiend lusting after elderly kangaroos, you will remember Gogol's "laughter through the tears."

John Glad, "Russian Satire Lives: Marsupial Madness at the Moscow Zoo," in Book World—The Washington Post, *May 4, 1986, p. 5.*

RONALD FLORENCE

The repressive world of *samizdat,* of dog-eared, hectographed manuscripts, circulated in repressed secrecy, takes its toll on writers. Yuz Aleshkovsky is a veteran of that world, and in ***Kangaroo,*** he takes his revenge with a torrent of scatological satire that leaves few targets in Soviet history or society untouched. The slangy Russian and sexual descriptions that read like 1950s hard porn leave no doubt that the intent of the author is vehemence. The targets of the satire, unfortunately, are not easily deciphered.

The plot is a complex recursive loop from the conviction of the hero, a Russian pickpocket named Fan Fanych, for the rape and murder of an aging kangaroo in the Moscow Zoo, to scenes in a spaceship, to the Yalta Conference, to a Siberian prison camp where Fanych engages in debates with fervent old Bolsheviks. Keeping track of the narrative and the whirls of fantasy, sorting out the scenes in which the hero is a kangaroo, a rat-catcher with a third eye at the back of his head, or debating Hitler, puts considerable demands on a reader. Making sense of the myriad obscure references will challenge the most avid historians and students of Soviet pop culture. The reader also must contend with Ordzhonikidze, Mikhail Zoshchenko, Ivan Pyriev and dozens of other proper names, few of which can be parsed from context, and none of which is explained.

The real problem with ***Kangaroo,*** for an American reader, is that the book does not convey a reality against which to measure the satire. What is it in Soviet life that inspires recurrent themes like characters constantly soiling their pants or the crude sexual fantasies of the hero? Hit by a broadside barrage, we are left wondering how to rank the pains and suffering: Which is worse, the excesses of repression, the dulling debates of arcane ideology, the warehouse camps of Siberia, the lack of privacy in crowded communal apartments, or the failure of technology that leads to mistaken indictments and convictions? ***Kangaroo*** hints at the questions, but the characters are so remote and the reality so obscure that we cannot feel or begin to comprehend the human impact of that culture.

Ronald Florence, in a review of "Kangaroo," in Los Angeles Times Book Review, *July 6, 1986, p. 6.*

DAVID HOLAHAN

Underpinning the continuous fantasies that embody ***Kangaroo*** is a powerful satiric allegory worthy of George Orwell's *Animal Farm.* The more the novel's protagonist, Fan Fanych, feels a growing empathy with animals, particularly those caged in zoos, the more he is oppressed by his Soviet keepers. Fanych frequently proposes that he and his friend Kolya (to whom the book is narrated) toast members of the animal kingdom: "Let's drink to anteaters and armadillos, who yearn for their native jungles forever. God give their children freedom someday, or at least their grandchildren."

Like the author, Yuz Aleshkovsky, a Russian emigree who spent time in the Gulag, Fanych is an independent-minded Jew, an *a priori* criminal stoically awaiting an official charge. When he is finally called in by the KGB in 1949, he has a choice of 10 crimes to be accused of. . . .

His trial, as might be expected, is a phantasmagoric journey into the unreal jungle of the Soviet legal system. Having first made up the crime, the authorities must now concoct the evidence: Fanych offers to write a screen play for the movie which will convict him. Instead of allegedly duplicating life, Socialist Realist art has become reality. The defendant finds himself caught up in his own propaganda. As the film rolls on, he begins rooting for the state and against himself.

After the show, parasite Fanych is sentenced to a labor camp containing purged comrades of Lenin, sad old Bolsheviks who, despite their cruel fate, still cling to their faith in the inevitable worldwide triumph of Soviet communism. They have risen above their individual tragedies, seeing themselves as martyrs to the cause of Historical Necessity. Isolated from the world—even from state disinformation—they cheer wildly when Fanych tells them that Winston Churchill is being tried in the Moscow City Court. In a nation built on unreality, their little sphere is simply more unreal than others.

During his incarceration, Fanych reminisces about the time he happened upon the meeting of Stalin, Roosevelt and Churchill at Yalta in 1945. Hidden in the basement, he looks out through a grate and can see only the feet of the world's great leaders. At one point, he is observing Stalin sitting alone when the dictator's own right foot starts a rebellion: "Hey, Stalin. You're a s—." The self-abuse continues and the leader of world revolution ponders his choices. A foot's not a conscience, so he can't shut it up. Amputation is a possibility but then, "Can you rely on the left foot?" The answer is no, of course, when enemies and traitors are everywhere.

Fanych is eventually freed, after Stalin's death, and returns to Moscow to look up his KGB prosecutor. He is nowhere to be found and there is no record of his ever having existed. There is also no record of Fanych's bestial crime. He goes to the zoo and determines that a kangaroo named Gemma actually had been murdered. He wishes that the animals in the zoo and the people of the Soviet Union might one day be free of their unnatural worlds. Like a zoo, Fanych concludes, the Soviet state is a crime against nature; and "The world doesn't forgive men who try to turn it inside out."

Some readers may not forgive Aleshkovsky for his flights of fancy. At times, his magic-carpet rides are too long or simply without redeeming significance. Also, the novel was written in 1975 in the Soviet Union for a Russian audience, and therefore many of the indigenous references will be lost on Westerners. Still, ***Kangaroo*** will reward those who persist through the flawed and disorienting stretches. Delivered with a searing and insightful wit, Aleshkovsky's message is universal and compelling: humankind should be free, or at least struggling to be so.

David Holahan, "Worthwhile 'Kangaroo' a Real Zoo," in Chicago Tribune, *July 13, 1986, p. 47.*

COMMENTS OF YUZ ALESHKOVSKY TO *CLC YEARBOOK*

In writing, Aleshkovsky says, "My main motivation is my gift, given to me by God, that is a passionate desire to create with the help of the Word, some World unknown and unseen before."

"I was inspired to write [*Kangaroo*] by my life in a totalitarian state. But it demanded not just a political protest, but an artistic expression because the art of prose was always my calling and my love."

"I did not do any research. The historical background of the novel was absolutely fresh in my memory, and its plot was evolving by itself, fed by the time."

Even when he could not get his later novels published in his own country, Aleshkovsky did find an audience through foreign publications. "I had no problems publishing [*Kangaroo*] in the West. I'm very thankful to the late Carl Proffer who was the head of the Ardis Publishing House . . . , and who smuggled my book from the U.S.S.R. and later published it."

"The unforgettable and wonderful experience of writing *Kangaroo* changed my life. I understood that I would not be able to write a single word under censorship. This, in some mysterious way, led me to the happy encounter with my beloved wife, Irene, and to the decision to emigrate to the West: to run away from a humiliating existence to a more difficult but free one."

"I would like the whole world to be my audience," writes Aleshkovsky, "but I'm absolutely ready and able to write only for myself, my wife, and a few close friends, getting full satisfaction and enjoyment from the creative process."

About his works in progress Aleshkovsky comments, "At this moment I cannot begin either of my two new novels. I've been thinking every morning for the past two months how true the Russian proverb is: If you chase after two hares, you won't catch either of them."

Peter Cameron

1959-

American short story writer.

With his short story collection *One Way or Another* (1986), Cameron made his debut as one of the year's acclaimed new exponents of the minimalist style in fiction. Like such other young American writers as Jay McInerney and Amy Hempel, Cameron employs a terse, objective prose reminiscent of the restrained narrative technique pioneered by Ann Beattie, Raymond Carver, and other writers of the previous generation. Also in the minimalist tradition, Cameron's protagonists in such stories as "Fear of Math" and "Fast Forward" are disaffected young people unable to achieve satisfying relationships with others.

Reviewers observe that Cameron severely limits the expression of his characters' emotions and inner conflicts in order to achieve the cool effect of objective realism. The result, allege critics John Blades and Rosellen Brown, is a set of beautifully crafted stories lacking human interest. The strength of Cameron's collection, several commentators agree, lies in Cameron's witty approach to his subjects and his ability to reflect the dilemmas of many in his generation.

MARCIA TAGER

The stories in Cameron's first collection [***One Way or Another***] are succinct and sometimes memorable. Many deal with need, particularly the ripple effect of one person's need on another. Thus, in **"Fast Forward"** a young woman asks a casual male friend to accompany her on a visit to her dying mother. She lets the dying woman believe him to be her fiancé, fulfilling her own need to fulfill her mother's need. In **"Fear of Math"** Julie's need to pass calculus masks her need to separate from her separating parents. In **"Odd Jobs"** a young woman's need for rituals hides her need for connection to her lover. Cameron gives us a sharp, almost photographic picture of each character's external features and inner reality simultaneously, and though not all the stories are equally successful, they contain irony, tenderness, and sharp wit. This work deserves a place in all contemporary short story collections.

Marcia Tager, in a review of "One Way or Another," in Library Journal, *Vol. III, No. 12, July, 1986, p. 105.*

CAMPBELL GEESLIN

As more and more volumes of short stories, especially by young writers, are published, it becomes clear that the novel today isn't nearly as lively or fresh as it once seemed. The short story is where more of the finest creative juices are flowing, and Cameron is one of the form's best practitioners. His subtle, witty prose [in ***One Way or Another***] is admirably clean. His characters are mostly young, bright, sweetly puzzled by life. They can't find or even define a love that might prove lasting. **"Memorial Day"** is about an angry teenage boy who is trying to deal with his parents' divorce and his mother's new—and much younger—husband, a 29-year-old who is "too uptight to go barefoot. He would step on a piece of glass immediately." In **"Fear of Math,"** a young woman takes a summer course in calculus so that she can enter an MBA program. Her parents argue, and when her mother talks to her about it, the daughter thinks, "Don't tell me this, don't say any of this. I don't want to know you're unhappy." Particularly moving is **"Fast Forward,"** in which a young woman asks a friend to pretend that he is her fiancé because her mother is dying and wants desperately to believe the daughter's future has some substance.

Campbell Geeslin, in a review of "One Way or Another," in People Weekly, *Vol. 26, No. 3, July 21, 1986, p. 13.*

ROSELLEN BROWN

[Most] postsixties fiction writers have embraced a style that is unabashedly impersonal and that attempts to defy the inevitability of point-of-view. They have flaunted a shrinkage of range, of fascination with the world at large; a concomitant reduction in emotional volume; and perhaps a super-refinement of taste that is embarrassed by the sloppiness of passion and exuberance. It is as if Jack Webb stood over their word processors urging, "Just the facts, Ma'am." Ann Beattie, Raymond Carver, Bobbie Ann Mason—such "minimalist" writers do not presume to tell us what to think, or to evaluate their protagonists or their protagonists' lives. Their efforts are all for self-effacement, a kind of trompe l'oeil of narrational nonpresence, as if it is enough that these characters live, speak, see; honesty and integrity demand that no one (not even the parental author) yank them around, tell us what to think or what any of it means. . . .

The newest advocates of minimalist fiction, yoked together by hype-sters more because of their youth than their craft (most are in their early and mid-twenties), are writers much favored by the *New Yorker* like Peter Cameron and Tama Janowitz. Cameron's characters rarely commit themselves to an acknowledged emotion. . . . These writers, like their progenitors, give the impression that to comment on the lives of their protagonists or invite judgment on them, or to prod a story into any shape more complex than the simplest chronology (Cameron's are all in the present tense, as if no event had a history), is to spoil the purity of their observation. (p. 7)

[In ***One Way or Another***] the very young Peter Cameron substantiates the precise place his characters occupy on the demographic scale, somewhere between old-style feckless hippies (people have jobs cutting hair or stencilling wicker furniture) and new-style well-turned-out yuppies. He tells us, for example, that a mother and son discuss her separation from his father while they drink "brewed decaffeinated coffee." Every now and then a writer gives away his game by a single gesture. Cameron, who is very good at what he does (if you like to feel you've been somewhere very real but you don't much care what it's *like* there) tells us in that three-word phrase that he has been scrupulously bent on getting it right, showing as precisely as a poll-taker what these people would (of course) have to be drinking. Whether it matters—why it should matter—is a different question. . . .

Peter Cameron's stories end, one after another, in emotional disengagement that does not quite acknowledge its poignance. (p. 8)

Rosellen Brown, "The Emperor's New Fiction," in Boston Review, *Vol. XI, No. 4, August, 1986, pp. 7-8.*

An Excerpt from *One Way or Another*

Stephen and I had, in our one short week together, established a ritual. We went out together after class for a beer. The middle of the afternoon, I discovered, was a nice time to frequent bars. I'd never much liked them at night in Ann Arbor when they were noisy and crowded and dark and sticky. But in the afternoon no one played the jukebox, the sun shone in the open door, and the people in the soap operas swam through their complicated lives on the TV above the bar like fish in an aquarium.

Stephen was drawing a diagram on a soggy cocktail napkin, trying, as always, to explain something I didn't understand. I was half watching him and half watching a large white cat thread himself through the legs of the bar-stools, savoring the touch of each leg against his fur.

"See," Stephen said, pushing the napkin across the table. I looked at it but couldn't make any sense of it, so I turned it around.

"No," Stephen said. "This way." He turned it back around.

Something about the blurry diagram on the cocktail napkin depressed me. I couldn't believe it had come to be an important part of my life. It had no message for me. I leaned back against the vinyl booth.

"Can we forget about it for a while?" I said.

"Sure." Stephen crumpled the napkin and punted it to the floor with his fingers. "What's the matter?" he asked.

"I've been thinking," I said. "Maybe this is a bad idea."

"What?"

"This," I said. "Us."

"Oh," said Stephen. "Why?"

"I just feel like I should get through this myself. I mean I think I should pass calculus by myself and then we can decide if we want to see each other."

"But you can't pass calculus by yourself. You need a tutor."

"I'll get another tutor," I said.

"It's too late to get another tutor. We just have one more week. Julie, you know, no one expects you to pass calculus yourself. It's not some big deal. This isn't the Girl Scout merit-badge contest."

"I know," I said. "I can't explain. I just think this is wrong."

Stephen drained his beer glass. "Why won't you let me help you?" he asked.

"I told you," I said. "I think it's wrong."

"But it's not wrong. There's nothing wrong about it. You just want to get rid of me."

I didn't say anything. I watched the cat. We sat there for a moment. I felt like I was making a terrible mistake, only I wasn't sure what it was: if it had to do with love or calculus. I felt I was probably losing on both counts.

ALICE H. G. PHILLIPS

"What is it about your life you don't like? What is it you want to change?", one of Peter Cameron's characters [in ***One Way or Another***] asks his cat, which has been cowering in its litterbox for days.

All the human protagonists of these fourteen short stories in Cameron's first collection think they might want to change, or at least get started with, their lives (the youngest is fifteen, the oldest in his early thirties). Distanced from their (often tacky) surroundings, "inarticulate" with their lovers, not very interested in a career or even in rock videos, they seem to have floated through the America of the 1980s.

The narrator of **"The Last Possible Moment"** is typical. He visited a friend in Maine and stayed there because it seemed "safe". In the summer, he worked on boat trips to Seal Rock, where no live seals ever appeared; now he is on welfare. He reads self-improvement books and abandons them. He realizes he isn't in love with his girlfriend, but hangs around because he's lonely.

Similarly, the boy in **"Jump or Dive"** feels himself pulled towards homosexuality and is unable to say yes or no, to enjoy the plunge or jacknife out of it. Other Cameron characters make choices—a healthy trend in this fiction. The teenage narrator of **"Memorial Day"**, who has not spoken to his mother and young step-father for months because he has nothing to say to them, relents when his mother tells him quietly that he is breaking her heart. Julie, in **"Fear of Math"**, releases her boyfriend the math tutor and passes calculus on her own.

The preoccupations are those of young adults, wrapped up in their own problems, surprised that other people can feel pain. But Cameron handles deftly his characters' serious unhappiness and vague hopes, going easy on the *Angst,* not giving anything more weight than it deserves. The situations are nicely everyday—a family weekend at which the father doesn't show up, a man getting his ear pierced—but have a muted urgency. Cameron's style is smooth, perhaps too much so (his different voices could be more distinct, too); its coolness is enlivened with flashes of humour. Cameron is best when he bounces his craft off the wall, as in **"Freddie's Haircut"**, or when he allows himself to be swept away by his characters' uncertainties, making them his own.

Alice H. G. Phillips, "A Pained Surprise," in The Times Literary Supplement, *No. 4353, September 5, 1986, p. 978.*

JOHN BLADES

You really do have your ear to the ground . . . ," a character in an Ann Beattie story remarks. "You . . . could be the town crier." Among contemporary writers, Beattie has indeed become the town crier. With her short stories and novels, she has urgently spread the word about her spiritually disaffiliated generation—children who came of age in the '60s. In this task, Beattie has rarely raised her voice, but it is one that has been clearly heard and widely imitated throughout the land. . . .

Consider this passage: "Guess what my monogram is,' asks Mark. He is sitting at the porch table eating a bowl of Froot Loops: first the pink, then the yellow, and finally the orange circles. The bowl keeps changing colors." So begins an archetypal Ann Beattie story, except it is a not a Beattie story at all but one that appears in a new collection by Peter Cameron, ***One Way or Another***. . . .

The opening lines of any of these 14 stories . . . might illustrate the point just as well. Yet Cameron is not simply an Ann Beattie impersonator. He is younger, for one thing, and he writes about people of a later generation, who are indelicately balanced between adolescence and adulthood. But in addition to Beattie's techniques, Cameron shares so many of her mannerisms and obsessions—with lovers (straight and gay), animals, snow, brand names—that it is impossible to ignore the connections.

What's missing in Cameron's stories is the emotional resonance of Beattie's best work. . . . Many of his stories are brisk and entertaining. Unless I'm misled by Cameron's deadpan style and fail to get the message, however, they don't exactly reverberate with meaning. Like Beattie, Cameron could well become the town crier for the spiritually crippled children of his generation. But if the stories in this book are an accurate indication of all that's troubling them, I'm not convinced that there's a whole lot worth shouting about.

John Blades, "Ann Beattie's Influence No Present for Readers," in Chicago Tribune, *October 5, 1986, p. 3.*

LAUREL SPEER

In ***One Way or Another*** . . . , Peter Cameron will knock you down by resonance and understatement. He'll present a situation or series of events, never overplaying his hand as a writer, and give you plenty of clues as to the greater meanings of a kid who refuses to speak because of family upset, another who grapples with the smashing of his dog by staying out've school, or another who tries to understand and beat out the cruelty of an adult by playing her superior brain against his determination to bludgeon her feelings. He writes beautifully; he has a superior sensibility and he'll move you to the deepest feeling without ever sentimentalizing the hardest situations we face in life. (pp. 9-10)

Laurel Speer, in a review of "One Way or Another," in The Small Press Review, *Vol. 19, No. 3, March, 1987, pp. 9-10.*

Linda Collins

1931-

American short story writer.

From the couple who find that their cottage has been badly damaged in "When the Pipes Froze," to the father quietly attempting to bridge the gulf that separates him from his son in "Going to See the Leaves," the eight stories in Linda Collins's first collection, *Going to See the Leaves* (1986), explore the hidden tensions within human relations. Critics praise Collins for the subtle manner in which she evokes the fragile and complex emotions of ordinary relationships, particularly those within families. Reviewers note that Collins excels both in observing the small, telling details that make up everyday life and in probing domestic scenes to disturbing effect.

© Evan Eames, 1985

KIRKUS REVIEWS

[***Going to See the Leaves*** is a] first collection of eight distinctive stories, each recording with great sympathy and precision the ways in which small emotional changes resonate through the domestic lives of ordinary, thoughtful men, women and children.

The most moving of these stories are the most purely domestic: **"A Summer's Day"** in which an affluent young husband and wife, their 10-year-old daughter and the wife's father are spending the summer together in the country and find their small misreadings of one another deepening into alienation; **"When the Pipes Froze,"** an evocation of the stages of marriage, seen through the eyes of a middle-aged woman whose husband's and her hopes for a cozy country weekend are dashed by the discovery of frozen pipes in their house (and in themselves); and perhaps best of all, **"Meditation on Play, Thoughts on Death,"** in which a mother, regretting the end of her son's wild and imaginative babyhood, stands at the edge of a winter pond and watches a dead swan begin to move with the roiling of the water, reflecting that "Everything had seemed immobile utterly still, and when I noticed the slight swerve of the floating world I felt my chilled body sway in response. I saw, as time slowed, that what had seemed frozen and fixed was in motion . . . all moving in the same direction . . . I made a strange sound in my throat. I felt it leave my mouth and wing away."

Collins' stories are not dark, but they are rich and somber, full of subtlety and force. All in all, an impressive debut. (pp. 2-3)

A review of "Going to See the Leaves," in Kirkus Reviews, *Vol. LIV, No. 1, January 1, 1986, pp. 2-3.*

PUBLISHERS WEEKLY

[***Going to See the Leaves*** is a collection of] impressively forceful stories—eight strong pieces that leave one eager for more fiction from Collins. With uncommon skill, she manages to hurl the reader smack into the center of diverse situations. Collins has a knack for portraying the simultaneous fulfillment and disappointment of love relationships: husband-wife, parent-child. Her story lines range from the ordinary (a husband and wife arrive at their Vermont weekend home to find that the pipes have frozen: so have the emotional bonds of their marriage. Another couple has a near-accident on the highway en route home from a family funeral) to the extraordinary (a New York attorney discovers he is pregnant and gives birth to a son). Some of the tales are quietly devastating, demonstrating how those who are closest to one can seem like the coldest strangers. This is a wonderful collection.

A review of "Going to See the Leaves," in Publishers Weekly, *Vol. 229, No. 4, January 24, 1986, p. 63.*

JOANNE WILKINSON

[In ***Going to See the Leaves***] Collins takes the small domestic events of everyday life and overlays them with a certain menace so that the routine becomes ominous. An evening meal, a tennis game, a scenic drive—all are parlayed into searing analyses of the fragility of family life. . . . Collins is a consistently interesting writer; she shoots such tension through these tenuous, trivial events that reading about them is chilling yet compelling.

Joanne Wilkinson, in a review of "Going to See the Leaves," in Booklist, *Vol. 82, No. 3, March 1, 1986, p. 944.*

SHERRIE TUCK

Most of the eight short stories in [***Going to See the Leaves***] deal with the gray areas of human relationships—the unacknowledged tensions between husband and wife, parent and child, friend and friend. The characters are outwardly successful, but they derive little satisfaction from their achievements. . . . Collins's method depends in part on the accumulation of details. Although an effective style results, at times her observations on modern life threaten to become lost in the specifics.

Sherrie Tuck, in a review of "Going to See the Leaves," in Library Journal, *Vol. 111, No. 4, March 1, 1986, p. 106.*

JOE DAVID BELLAMY

As the American baby boomers begin to enter their 40s, perhaps the experience of middle age will become a more serious subject for our literature, and the midlife crisis will be recognized as more than a sociological chestnut dismissible by yet another Hollywood cackle. If so, the baby boom generation may have found a sympathetic interpreter in Linda Collins, whose work has appeared previously in many magazines, though this is her first collection of stories. ***Going to See the Leaves*** describes the trials and poignancy of transit into the middle years with sobering precision and shows evidence of a mature talent.

In [**"Going to See the Leaves"**], a middle-aged couple invites their grown son and his wife to a weekend outing in New England for the ostensible purpose of enjoying the fall foliage. The son accepts; the two couples make the trip together; outwardly everything is pleasant and sociable. They picnic in a meadow, attend a concert. Yet the trip is subtly full of anguish. It is an occasion during which all four characters are exposed to the author's penetrating vision. Surrounded and stunned by the strangeness and loveliness of the natural world, they are privately and desperately struggling with the disparity between youthful expectations and the responsibilities of adulthood, with implacable barriers between themselves and those they love the most. Mrs. Collins's strength lies in her ability to evoke these elusive feelings with delicacy and credibility.

Similarly, in the story **"Intimacy,"** Mrs. Collins's characters seem locked into lonely isolation, unable even to understand their own motives or impulses yet yearning to please one another. We glimpse the tensions, the helplessness, the subterranean precipices her characters somehow manage to scale as they strain through domestic rituals together. This story and several others are, in fact, meditations on the difficulties and fragility of intimacy, written in a prose style that is alternately dispassionate and lyrical.

In **"When the Pipes Froze,"** a middle-aged philosophy professor and his wife arrive at their newly remodeled Vermont vacation home in January to find that the heat has gone off, the pipes have frozen and their dreams have turned to rubble. Full of remorse, the wife recalls meeting the previous owner of the house, a dotty, likable old fellow whose second wife and her daughter were intent on selling the place out from under the old man in order to slip him quietly into a nursing home. She considers, ironically, how their own best intentions have led to a further erosion of what the old man had worked a lifetime to build.

Except for one story, **"Meditation on Play, Thoughts on Death,"** that may strike some readers as sentimentalizing childhood, Mrs. Collins's evocation of children in ***Going to See the Leaves*** most often is one of her more notable talents. Her treatment of the ways the child stubbornly persists in the adult personality is psychologically acute and especially appropriate to a fictional world so steeped in parable and allegory and so determined to measure the distance between what we were and what we eventually become.

In several stories Mrs. Collins follows a pattern of leapfrogging from one point of view to another, creating an intense, brief sense of closeness to a character, then a quick, omnipotent detachment reminiscent of James Joyce. At times Mrs. Collins seems to be calmly paring her nails from a celestial purchase somewhere above the jetstream.

The effect of this technique and of Mrs. Collins's thematic focus throughout is to infuse the prose with spiritual implications in every vista, every encounter, no matter how ordinary. The real action of these stories, then, takes place on a subjective plane while external events seem mostly undramatic and unexceptional.

This is true even in the one explicitly surreal or fabulous story in the collection, the novella-length **"Doctor's House,"** in which the overcontrolled, hyper-real world of a Manhattan attorney approaching midlife suddenly gives way (after the sudden deaths of two close colleagues) to myth, parable or madness.

In what may seem a bizarre collaboration between the Kafka of *The Metamorphosis* and the Tolstoy of *The Death of Ivan Ilyich,* the lawyer hero goes to a doctor complaining of stomach cramps and dizziness and learns that he is, in fact, four months pregnant. His pregnancy is not to be understood as either a misdiagnosis or a medical impossibility, and to Mrs. Collins, it is certainly not a joke. It is every bit as real as Kafka's hero's insect body and as much an affliction, in a way, as Ivan's illness. He must give birth.

Dealing with his miraculous transformation leads the protagonist on a nightmarish spiritual passage accompanied by an elderly Jewish doctor at an overgrown cottage somewhere in the wilds of Long Island. The outcome tugs at the heart with unexpected force.

Joe David Bellamy, "The Hero Was Pregnant," in The New York Times Book Review, *March 9, 1986, p. 27.*

An Excerpt from *Going to See the Leaves*

We sat in silence. My husband drove. Above the snowy hillsides white hills rose; beyond them, a white sky. Perhaps we were not going to escape the new snowstorm. We were driving a little too fast, considering the snowbanks crowding the road and the slippery patches and the cars in our lane and in the other, driving too fast themselves and subtly urging us to keep up.

We sped along, curving with the curves of the highway. I turned on the radio and tried up and down the dial to find something for us to listen to, but after a while I switched it off and sat back. At once, the silence between us swelled. It would not be muffled by the sound of the tires on the pavement, of the engine accelerating and slowing, by the clicking of the turn signal or the flashlight rolling in the glove compartment. In it, my thoughts followed with the tail of one stuck in the jaws of the one behind. My thoughts were so thick that to isolate one you would have had to unravel the whole. They made a terrific din in my head. But they refused to be translated into speech.

Perhaps in my husband's head a parallel loom clattered. No doubt it did. I have on occasion, on other drives, for instance, asked him, "What are you thinking about?" And he would answer, "I was calculating the mileage," or "I hear a little knock when you accelerate. There, do you hear it?" Now I leaned away from him against the armrest and closed my eyes. What might span our two silences? What would I say if he asked me what I was thinking about?

"Oh, look!" I said. "Look at the little stairway going all the way to the top of the slag heap. It's so delicate. Like twigs in the snow."

And responding no doubt to the foolishness of my remark, my husband said nothing.

We drove on.

AMY HEMPEL

Linda Collins is a writer who can win a reader's trust in a very few pages. In her first book of stories, ***Going to See the Leaves,*** she illumines the fragility and complexity of "ordinary" life with confidence and skill; it is quickly evident that if a situation merits her attention, it must also be worth our own. . . .

In **"When the Pipes Froze,"** a household disaster is amplified to the point of allegory. A couple arrives for a weekend at their country house to find the power off, the new copper pipes frozen and cracked. They are struck not only by the extent of the cost and inconvenience, but also by "something more deeply distressing, something that evoked shame, . . ." These are people who "believed that love and work were shields against failure." The ruin of their carefully restored house is, then, a *personal* failure. . . .

In **"Fears,"** a young boy watches the assassination of Egyptian President Anwar Sadat on TV. "He could have thought he was looking at a movie," his mother hopes. But that night it is the boy's *father* who wakes from nightmares.

"Comfort is close by," Collins writes in **"Intimacy,"** but not before she has said plenty about the violation of "domestic covenants," and the queasy feeling of betrayal when we find out our lives are not charmed. Catching the right gesture, avoiding too-tidy endings, Collins writes with grace and strength about the tenuous quality of life.

Amy Hempel, "Linda Collins Finds Complexity in the Ordinary," in Chicago Tribune, *July 13, 1986, p. 41.*

LESLIE CARPER

Newcomer Linda Collins displays skill and originality in her first collection of seven stories and one novella. Although the precise prose and unexpected twists of plot invite comparison with better known writers, such a comparison would indeed belie the distinction that is ***Going to See the Leaves.***

Collins focuses on details of overlooked moments as ordinary men and women go about everyday life. Sympathetically, she explores the emotional resonances in the passions and fears, large and small, in our lives. In **"Driving Back From the Funeral,"** the subtle dangers encountered by a couple heading home through the snow bring their feelings of malaise into perspective. The shifting points of view in **"A Summer's Day"** explore the lonely preoccupations of family members as they arrive at separate understandings of a single event. Collins has the sure touch of a master. The slow, almost imperceptible, layering of tiny, banal exchanges builds to powerful conclusions rendered with a delicate touch.

Leslie Carper, in a review of "Going to See the Leaves," in Belles Lettres, *Vol. 2, No. 2, November-December, 1986, p. 12.*

Ellen Currie

19??-

American novelist and short story writer.

Currie's well received first novel, *Available Light* (1986), is the result of the author's recovery from a debilitating writer's block of more than twenty years. Currie had enjoyed success with her short fiction in the 1950s, publishing stories in *The New Yorker* and *New World Writing* and garnering two O. Henry awards before the paralyzing block developed. "All I wanted to do was write, but I just couldn't. I read plenty of books about writer's block, but none was of any use. I know it's supposed to be self-indulgence and foolishness. I tried and tried. I just could not do it." Currie credits her eventual breakthrough to her ten years of attendance at poetry workshops, where she could write without pressure by working in a genre she did not consider her own. Finally, Currie entered a fiction class taught by novelist Maureen Howard and created the first chapter of *Available Light* for a course assignment. Encouraged by this success, Currie spent her free time in the next three years shaping the rest of the novel. "Writing that book felt like it must feel when you've been limping all your life and you wake up one morning not limping. I was delighted—also exhausted."

The story of Kitty and her errant lover, Jack Rambeau, *Available Light* centers on the unexpected sense of loss Kitty feels when her relationship with Rambeau ends. Kitty's crisis occurs amidst the lives of, among others, her sister, Eileen, whose inability to conceive a child is leading to an emotional breakdown; Eileen's pompous husband, Gordon; Gordon's recently impregnated teenage girlfriend, Dorinda; and Kitty's mother, Mick, an elderly Irish refugee full of spiky wit.

Available Light is warmly praised for its well-drawn and engaging characters, and for its remarkably energetic prose. "I know it's an odd, extravagant book," Currie observes, "but I thought being such an elderly beginner, I might as well swing for the fences." Reviewers note that Currie's artistic vision focuses on the complexities of family and male-female relationships, offering a comic and compassionate view of human frailty and human dignity. The novel's title symbolizes her theme: "In photography," she explains, "the phrase 'available light' means using only what light you have, without augmenting it. And I guess that's what we're all obliged to do in our own lives."

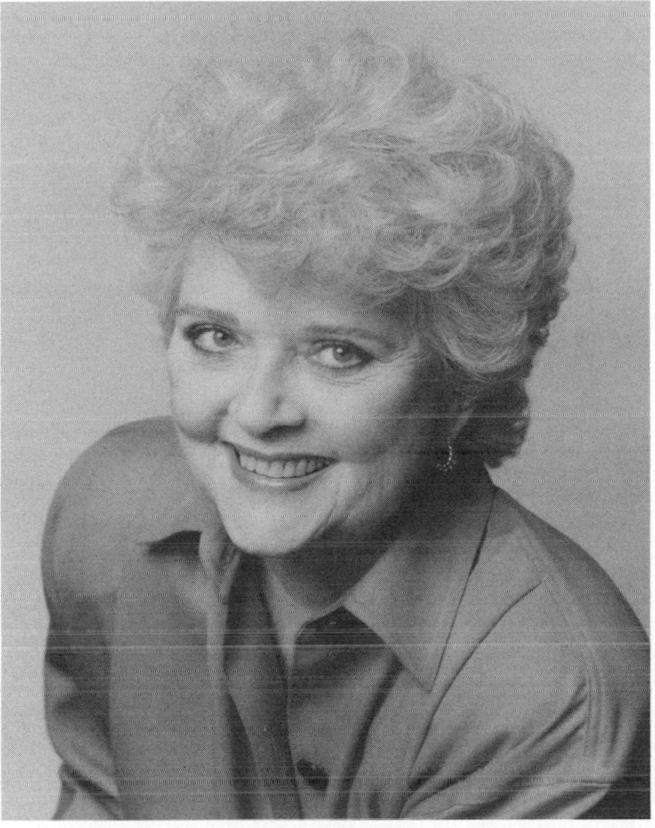

PUBLISHERS WEEKLY

There is pathos underlying the rollicking comedy in Currie's inspired debut [***Available Light***], but readers gleefully rocketing at top speed from page to page will not be consciously aware of it until they are brought up short in the novel's final chapters. Written with deadpan, irreverent comic verve, with dialogue so saucy that one keeps wanting to say, "Listen to this!", the book has as memorable a cast of characters as we'll see this season. There's vulnerable, engaging Kitty, in her mid-30s and waiting for her life to begin, only to realize, when her lover Rambeau leaves her, that he *is* her life; there's softhearted Rambeau, saxophone player and gambler on a permanent losing streak, who takes up with Drindy and vows to take care of her baby; there's huge, amoral Drindy, whose baby's father is smarmy Gordon, married to Kitty's sister Eileen, who desperately wants to be pregnant; there's Mick, mother to Kitty and Eileen, possessed of blue eyes like a sword's flash and a tongue to match; there's diminutive Mr. Gordon, poet manqué and baby snatcher; and there's Rambeau's dog, a duplicitous creature who bites Kitty and dotes on everyone else.

The antics of this eccentric crowd, as they weave in and out of hilarious scenes rife with wild but cannily managed coincidences, sometimes remind one of Fay Weldon's novels. But Currie has a unique and original voice, and she reveals the dark secrets in her characters' hearts with a wit and bravado that ennobles what she calls "the whole human escapade."

A review of "Available Light," in Publishers Weekly, *Vol. 228, No. 25, December 20, 1985, p. 57.*

RICHARD EDER

Rambeau could be a contemporary suburban Don Juan as redesigned by the editors of Ms. magazine at some inebriated late-evening session. He is a footloose but home-loving male in Ellen Currie's remarkably voiced first novel; an outsized, untidy man, a lover and lovable; and seen through the consciousness of a heroine who is even more outsized and even less tidy.

That is two "outsizes" in one paragraph, so I'll try to be exact. The characters in ***Available Light,*** despite one or two wild cards and wild touches, are middle class and lead reasonably ordered lives. They seem eccentric, yet, again with a glaring exception or two, their eccentricity roots firmly in their normality.

Currie has made their voices and reflections rampage wildly through their own confines, so that when these confines buckle or budge, we have the sense that our own peace is being shattered. Her characters grow varicolored jungles in their small backyards. All backyards—and this is what the novel was invented to tell us—have jungle spores, though not all sprout as funny and particular as those in ***Available Light.***

The novel is about the separation and reunion of Kitty and Rambeau, two frazzled lovers approaching middle age. More essentially, it is about the battering that life has given to them and to the other characters, mostly Kitty's family, that they move among. More essentially still, because Currie's people are far more than their circumstances, it is about their retorts to the battering.

Umberto Eco, asked what his novel, *The Name of the Rose,* was really about, replied that it was about adverbs. ***Available Light*** is about the words, spoken or meditated, of Kitty, Rambeau, Kitty's mother, her sister, brother-in-law and one or two others. Their words marvelously delineate them, much more than the occasionally contrived actions and personalities that Currie has arranged for them.

Kitty is a stylist for fashion photography; Rambeau plays saxophone in an Atlantic City cafe. Neither of these things defines them nearly as much as their capacity to console each other, and to miss each other when they separate. The separation has no particular reason for it, other than the sense that life is too much. The novel recounts this too-muchness, how Kitty and Rambeau eventually get through it and how others don't. . . .

Their mutual yearning, and the comic expedients they use to resist it or express it, provide much of the book's drive. Rambeau's letters sum up a wandering biography. He was close to his mother and sisters—hence his domestic talents—but they abandoned him when he was a child. His father was an alcoholic wreck, but he gave Rambeau an image of wildness before he bled to death in a drunken accident.

Available Light is, among other things, a utopia of contemporary male-female relations. Rambeau has a voice of his own, but he tends to fit too squarely into post-feminist fantasy. His mother, nurturing and then ditching him, allows a feminine streak without effeminacy; his father, dying, provides a male example without overwhelming him. He is a wild rover who cooks; he loves many women, but Kitty most of all; and finally he comes back to her. It is a bit too tidy.

Still, there are plenty of crosscurrents to mess things up. Kitty's sister, married to a total modern disaster named Gordon—he emerges as caricature, yet paradoxically fuzzy—gradually goes mad in her effort to conceive a child. Doreen, a comical but coarsely realized character, takes sealed bids on the baby she may have conceived by Rambeau, Gordon or a number of other men. Conrad, a Hungarian pornographer, floats in and out, alternately cheering Kitty up and depressing her.

Finally, there is Kitty's mother, an Irish woman who is a blend of firm convention and an endless wandering imagination. "Our Lady of the Perpetual Cardigan," Kitty names her, and her stalwart and idiosyncratic decline in a chaotic world is one of the best and most moving things in the book.

Kitty is the very best thing, though she has a touch or two of the utopian convenience that mars Rambeau. She is no stereotypic free spirit. Comic and grave, she moves through her passions and reverses with a spirit that is utterly her own. . . .

Currie gives us no still center, but the entrancing ricochets of a character who darts, determined and half-blinded, into life.

Richard Eder, in a review of "Available Light," in Los Angeles Times Book Review, *February 23, 1986, p. 3.*

ROBERT WILSON

Every spring, it seems, a handful of first novels, among the dozens and dozens published, manages to get most of the attention. Let's be optimistic and say that this handful generally deserves it. Even if that is so, there are puzzling exceptions.

Ellen Currie's first novel, ***Available Light,*** strikes me as one. It's already getting ink that most seasoned novelists would kill for, and the blurbsters on the back jacket are more impressive than the usual suspects. Why? Why? Why?

Probably the novel's unusual and, at first, exciting energy is to blame. Currie's prose is supercharged, something like Grace Paley (one of the blurbsters) on hallucinogens. As it careers along, the prose trails behind it a plot as manic as itself, featuring, among other things, patricide, generous portions of "motel love" (an Updikism), a little incest and, perversely, considering all the unnecessary coupling going on, an immaculate conception.

If this sounds like fun, you're probably the sort who enjoys hearing your friends recount their dreams in stupefying detail. Because that's what the chaos into which this novel descends most resembles: a long, determinedly amusing and suffocatingly dull dream.

The artistic intention behind all this, if I'm not mistaken, is to explore the massively unsettling effects of love gone awry. . . .

Some of this is funny. Currie's characters—especially Mick, with her strange and convincing brogue—do have fresh and individual voices. But—I'm sorry—none of it means anything.

Robert Wilson, "Left in the Dark over 'Available Light'," in USA Today, *February 28, 1986, p. 4D.*

T. GERTLER

"This is not trouble we're having, this is just life we're having," Eileen tells her sister, Kitty, who answers, "I sincerely hope you are mistaken." They're both right. Life, as it happens in this first novel, isn't trouble-free or just. It's funny, menacing and more than a little skewed—as if Fra Angelico's "Annunciation" had been retouched by Salvador Dali and used as a backdrop for a rock video. This is a tall tale told with high good humor and respect for unshared but universal secrets.

At first ***Available Light*** seems straightforward enough. . . . As the couple's paths separate, though, the story widens too, stretching familiar patterns of love into amazing events.

Ellen Currie nudges reality and uncovers a vein of the fabulous. Hints of magic, of destiny arranged by coincidence, wind through the book. The bizarre happens matter-of-factly: In the parking lot of a New Jersey mall, a fetus flees a young woman and enters Eileen's womb. "Her womb made a mouth and gobbled it. It seats itself with a suck and a pop, socked into her tissues as a pitched ball socks into a waiting glove." On a visit to Mexico, a man has a vision of a horseman dressed in gray and feels that he has "swallowed a hard knob of grace." A dog is a reincarnation of Kitty and Eileen's mean-tempered father; their mother, Kitty observes, "worships Chaos, the oldest of the gods."

Tart-tongued, witty, raucous people do terrible and ordinary things to one another and to themselves. . . .

[The] twists and shifts and curlicues of the book spin along in vibrant prose. Miss Currie's language is so rich and compelling that, even in places where the story falters, her voice invites the reader to continue. With the exceptions of Mr. Conrad and some minor characters, the people sound true. They may be eccentric, but they're also recognizable in all of us. Their pain and self-discovery are startlingly familiar.

Miss Currie does her characters a disservice, though, with three chapters called "Dreams and Secrets," in which she describes their dreams. Since their longings and loathings are vivid from their speech and actions, accounts of their dream lives add nothing to the story. As Eileen's psychiatrist tells her, "This isn't new material."

Another problem lies in the author's discomfort with the uncanny undercurrents she evokes so well: how children murder fathers, how mothers own children, how love exhausts lovers. From deep sources of wonder she strays to trivia, as if, having created a splendid example of life's messiness, she wishes fervently to clean it all up. Finding herself out of work, Kitty suddenly becomes an actress, playing the Apple Witch, in an advertising campaign and learns that one variety of apple is called the Summer Rambo. Very neat and symbolic and tiresome stuff. With her talent and imagination, Miss Currie doesn't need neatness; she needs only confidence in her own quirky vision.

Still, ***Available Light*** should be greeted with celebration. It takes risks and its sound is original.

T. Gertler, "Rambeau—Not Rimbaud or Rambo," in The New York Times Book Review, *March 2, 1986, p. 15.*

An Excerpt from *Available Light*

"Would you like to take down this number? Because I'm in a phone booth and I haven't any change and any minute now they'll cut us off."

"They'll no such a thing," her mother says firmly. "Why are you out at this hour of the morning and no money in your pocket and you in a dirty telephone booth that some dirty man passed his water in? And you with a perfectly good telephone at your own home with nothing at the end of it but a nasty, rude answering machine?"

"No dirty man passed anything in this phone booth, it's far too breezy."

"Why do you contradict each word I say?"

"I don't."

"You see there you did it again. Give me that number, do, though God knows I can't see a thing without my specs. And I haven't a pencil, I'll write it with my nail."

"Oh dear," Kitty says, squinting and straining, "I can't quite see it either. I forgot to tell you I did something to my eye."

"Your *eye,*" Kitty's mother says, as Kitty knew she would. "How could you be so careless?"

"Maybe I should just call you later."

"Do then," her mother says. "For I haven't had sight or light of you for this long time and I'm worried. And I have a little tidbit I think will interest you."

"Okay, then," Kitty says; she feels no faintest interest, only deep fatigue. "Call you later."

"Jock Rambeau was here," says Mick.

The receiver slips from Kitty's hand and swings at the end of its cord, banging and thudding. Kitty rescues it. All her joints have gone liquid, great shudders travel up the backs of her legs and down the backs of her arms. She presses her head against the coin slots and closes one eye. She shouts the number at her mother, who shouts it back, incorrectly. They do this another time while Gordon's twenty-dollar bill, crushed in Kitty's palm, grows wetter. When Mick at last has the number right, they wait. Nothing happens.

Then Kitty says, "Thank God."

"I gave him a meal and a place to put his head," Mick says. "And I gave him no news and he gave me no news. I hope I did the right thing, Kitty."

"Where is he? He was with you last night? He slept there last night?"

"He slept in your bed in your room. He showed up on my doorstep with a stewing hen and he asked me to make him a chicken fricasee and I did and the two of us sat down and ate it. And he mended the float in the toilet tank that's been broken this long while. Then this morning he pulled down the curtains for me and he took his leave just as the telephone was ringing. And I said, 'That will be Kitty, I know her by the telephone's ring. It's like the banshee's lonely wail,' I said. 'It is,' he said. 'I'll be off, then,' he said. And off he went."

"Where did he go? What's his address? Where can I get hold of him?"

"He never said and I never asked."

WALTER CLEMONS

Kitty, the heroine of Ellen Currie's astounding first novel [***Available Light***], has been deserted by her man, the gambling, saxophone-playing Jack Rambeau. Desolate, Kitty insists that it was just an interim attachment: "I can't get involved, not really involved, with a man like that—I've got a life coming up. I'm just stretching my hamstrings before I take the run. Of course I've been doing that a while now, but I'm a staller, that's my nature."

A horrendous dresser herself, Kitty is a photographic fashion stylist who rounds up clothes and props for advertising shoots. . . .

The photographic term in the novel's title applies to the unaided knowledge the characters have of each other and of themselves. . . .

Currie is exceptionally daring. For a while, her plotty book looks like a collage of voices that we contentedly listen to without expecting that much will happen. The splintered points of view deepen into a humane vision of concealed lives. Mick, a comic scourge to her daughters, tells only Rambeau the story of her tragic early life in Ireland, of which Kitty knows puzzling fragments. Mick, Kitty and Eileen each consider themselves murderously responsible for the accidental death of the girls' brutal father. Even the "priggish and lascivious" Gordon has a dimension the other characters don't know about.

The resolution of this pungent, ferociously funny tale is unusually moving. "This is very scary," Kitty says. "What is this I'm feeling? This is alarming; I don't know what to call it." "This is called requited love," says Rambeau. "Nobody has much experience in it.

Walter Clemons, "Swinging for the Fences," in Newsweek, *Vol. CVII, No. 9, March 3, 1986, p. 66.*

JACQUELINE AUSTIN

This first novel [***Available Light***] reads like anything but. The pacing is sure and consistent. The voice is so warm it glows at the edges. The plot—except for a few overdone "metaphysical" coincidences—is exuberant. And if the characters are autobiographical, they hide their origins beneath peacock plumes of wit.

Boy denies girl, re-finds girl: what matters is how it's done. The boy, Jack Rambeau, is a jack of many trades and master of all, particularly those which involve lip, such as talking, kissing, and playing horn. The heroine, Kitty O'Carolan, fortyish, sardonic and sexy, is made for him as he is made for her. Blessed with a heavenly gift of gab, kooky but genuine Kitty narrates and exposits and confesses with the best of 'em. She starts strong and continues that way. . . .

Kitty has prematurely white hair and Rambeau's family members tell him she's an old bag. But readers, who are privy to her cute, svelte, conditioned body and her spicy thoughts, know better. They see that Kitty takes in strays. She's good to animals. She has an animal side of her own. She's a true person and even a true New Yorker. The secondary characters who surround her are as unpredictable as she, and as successful in filling their narrative function, which is to postpone the reconciliation of Jack and Kitty until Ellen Currie has played out her hand.

Kitty's mother, conservative sister, pompous brother-in-law, Gordon, and business associates all operate as she does, teetering gracefully between the sentimental and the grotesque, without falling into either trap. And Rambeau's descriptions of his mother and grandmother and daughter Cherokee skip lightly from memory to document to real-time incident. His letters to Kitty are deeply idiosyncratic and sexual, sometimes taking poetic, almost surreal shortcuts, but they never break the reader's tension of belief. "The first communication I had from my mother, after she left (my father for) Zeke, was a box of chocolates and two snapshots of her in a playsuit, ass to the camera in a Betty Grable pinup pose smiling down over her shoulder. My grandmother took the snapshots away from me. She snipped out the little heads. She returned the little heads to me on a saucer."

Reorganizing the dangers of life by playing with their properties is Currie's method of transcending them: she defangs Scylla and Charybdis by renaming them Scyllis and Charybda. Sometimes this game works and sometimes it doesn't. Currie is at her best when she favors naturalism. Her most metaphysical character, Dorinda, is a punk fertility goddess who sleeps with Rambeau, Gordon, and the rest of Kitty's clansmen, too patly complicating the plot, too neatly tying up thematic loose ends.

Dorinda is pregnant with Gordon's child. The only person in the book who doesn't want the baby, Dorinda is at once earth mother and perpetual adolescent. She's so much larger than life that she squashes it. And her fetus, Everybabe, is supposed to be all things to all parents. Kitty's mother (who in her own child-bearing years lost an infant son) prepares a little nest, helped by Rambeau. Kitty's romantic, pathetic, somewhat vampirish platonic lover, Mr. Conrad, steals the child. Kitty's sister Eileen, in her umpteenth year of trying to become pregnant, does—possibly with the same fetus, miraculously transferred to her own womb when she spots Dorinda in a parking lot. Here the Currie's overcooked.

But this flaw is hardly as significant as the book's many strengths. It's a problem of too much enthusiasm, and how terrible is that? This same trait is positive when it charges descriptions, transforms characters into people, and gives language vitality. Kitty's and Rambeau's worlds mesh because they both, under all their problems, have an identical *joie de vivre*. That all their friends and family interact, vertically through the generations as well as horizontally, in bed, across the usually sanguine strictures of consanguinity, is a bonus. When a character such as Eileen is presented first in one context, then another, as sister, wife, mother, and daughter, she gains resonance.

Currie knows her people. She can see the ways in which they transfer energy and essence to each other, making love, having children, thinking, talking, performing multiple functions. ***Available Light*** is funny, literate, fabulously verbal, and completely accessible. It deserves to be read on a sunny spring day. Though the title might sound a little vague, as though pointing to some cloud in idea heaven, the book is both comedy and communion. I hope Currie gives us more and yet more of the same.

Jacqueline Austin, "Hello Kitty," in The Village Voice, *Vol. XXXI, No. 20, May 20, 1986, p. 56.*

CRAIG STOLZ

From the moment I learned the male lead in [***Available Light***] is named Rambo, I wanted to toss the thing aside. After the very first page explained that Rambo spells his name Rambeau, wears long red hair spilling down his shoulders and delights in ironing ruffled women's clothing, I was ready to write off Ellen Currie as a lazy jokester on men.

But it turns out that Currie is anything but lazy, anything but derivative and—although she can be painfully funny—anything but a jokester. Currie is a powerful writer who has managed, in her first novel, not only to create people who are vital and original, but also to shake them by the ears and let us hear the brainstems rattle. This is a relentless book, one that takes the ancient stuff of family love—mothers and sons, fathers and daughters—and rubs its edges raw. . . .

Although the events of the book have the random feeling of life itself, they are connected by a vision that seems reconciled with its difficulty. Currie's people do not work through conflicts to resolutions; they thrash along, directed by forces they don't understand, battering the ones they love along the way. They live in a difficult world where opposites are not opposite, but adjacent. Hate rages right along with love, and usually in direct proportion; sterility nuzzles fertility; death circles near birth, demonic dogs sniff around angelic babies. Love between parent and offspring multiplies and twists, leading either to sex or to death; sex between lovers diminishes, and will not bring along new life.

Throughout ***Available Light,*** Currie combines the urgency of somebody telling a story for the first time with the certain mind of one who has been telling stories all her life. And better still, by the time the book ends, Currie has earned complete forgiveness: "Rambo" turns out to be a variety of green apple—old-fashioned, strange to look at, but good to eat.

Craig Stolz, in a review of "Available Light," in Saturday Review, *Vol. 12, No. 2, May-June, 1986, p. 70.*

LESLIE CARPER

Family love, with its terrible and wonderful connections, is the bedrock of Ellen Currie's novel, ***Available Light.*** Caught in circumstances that would be tragic if they were not so hilarious, are Kitty; her gambling saxophonist lover, Rambeau, who has left her; Eileen, so desperate to get pregnant that she has absorbed another woman's implanted womb in a New Jersey parking lot; fat, disagreeable Dorinda, pregnant by Eileen's husband, Gordon, but living with Rambeau; and the sisters' mother, Mick. . . .

How these enchanting characters resolve their different desires requires plotting worthy of Shakespeare. Currie never fails to garner our rapt attention and affection for the characters and for their credence, dignity, and tart wit. Chapters juxtapose Kitty's first-person narrative with Rambeau's confessional letters and everybody's "Dreams and Secrets." The hilarity is periodically halted by passages outlining pasts of almost unrelieved misery: Rambeau's abandonment by his mother, Mick's abandonment by her Irish husband, Kitty's terrible conviction that she caused her own father's death. . . .

Currie's perspicacious prose hurtles through intriguing new uses of verbs and completely bypasses peripheral scenes of little consequence. The story's unexpected twists and turns are perfectly aligned with a voice and style that are sure, deft, and wizardly. Currie's mastery of the one-liner begs reading aloud: "If you don't straighten out your life, Kitty, I am going to tell your mother." "You must know more about sex than I do, you're single." . . .

The things that support and sustain these characters are not their jobs or professions, not the material possessions they seek comfort from, not even their hopes and dreams. They find dignity and direction, despite their meandering shenanigans, in the connections they have with each other. A surfeit of love and goodwill informs all of their actions. Currie is telling us that we learn, as well as we are able, from what we do, and we do the best we can.

Leslie Carper, "First in Fiction," in Belles Lettres, *Vol. 1, No. 6, July-August, 1986, pp. 7-8.*

Amitav Ghosh

1956-

Indian novelist.

Born in Calcutta, Ghosh was raised in East Pakistan, Sri Lanka, Iran, and India. An Oxford educated teacher and social anthropologist, he admits, "The only thing I ever wanted to do was write a novel." *The Circle of Reason* (1986), Ghosh's first novel, was inspired by his reading of *Moby Dick*. "Reading Melville's chapter on whales, I remember thinking, 'This is something I want to be able to do.'"

Just as the protagonist, Alu, weaves individual strands into complex tapestries, so Ghosh weaves a multitude of characters and events into *The Circle of Reason*. A picaresque novel, it details the diverse adventures of the guileless Alu in three main settings, which comprise the three sections of the novel: a traditional village in East Bengal that recalls Alu's youth—his adoption and apprenticeship; Alu's escape after the murder of his family to the hastily modernized city of al-Ghazira; and his subsequent travels in Algeria.

Most critics agree that the narrative is overly ambitious, lacking sufficient unity and suffering from too many characters and distracting digressions. Nevertheless, Ghosh has received unanimous praise for his arresting language and his dazzling style, which animate many of the peripheral episodes with rich and exotic descriptions. Several reviewers have likened Ghosh to the acclaimed Indian novelist Salman Rushdie, seeing in both writers the flavor of the magic realism so popular with Latin American writers, most notably Gabriel García Márquez. While the blend of fantasy and reality characteristic of magic realism is apparent in Ghosh's fiction, some reviewers trace his style back to Indian folk tales and legends, and one commentator observes that Rushdie and Ghosh are both "heirs to a technique of story-telling in which, as in *The Thousand and One Nights,* the skill lies in ensuring that the story never finishes." Despite the belief of many critics, then, that *The Circle of Reason* would have benefited from greater authorial restraint, it is, nevertheless, considered a work of original talent and wildly inventive imagination.

LIZ HERON

Yarn-spinning is an intended analogue as well as a conscious metaphor in ***The Circle of Reason,*** whose central character acquires a phenomenal mastery of weaving.

But this is a first novel whose length and mega-ambitions overwhelm the skills and experience of its author and remind us that the epic fabulist's art isn't easily achieved. A mix of historical events, reference to the politics of the Indian subcontinent, family mythologies and magic realism points at first to Salman Rushdie territory. The comparison calls for more narrative ingenuity than is evidenced; intermittent lively stretches suggest that Amitav Ghosh has genuine talent, but the book is over-hurried in its plotting and overburdened with characters, none of whom comes adequately into focus; as it staggers to a close, after the long trek from Bengal to Algiers, it's still impossible to discern any shape or meaning in the whole.

Liz Heron, "Lost in the Labyrinth," in New Statesman, *Vol. 111, No. 2866, February 28, 1986, p. 27.*

JOHN MELLORS

Amitav Ghosh has chosen to make his literary début with a long, rambling, picaresque novel, with umpteen characters, and diversions that are sometimes so long and winding that we feel we shall never get back to the main narrative. In the early chapters of ***The Circle of Reason*** the reader feels confident enough. We appear to be in the hands of a capable, accomplished writer who is creating characters we can believe in, however eccentric their behaviour, and whose descriptions of place combine exotic colouring with a draughtsman's precision. A boy of eight comes to the village of Lalpukur, about a hundred miles north of Calcutta. He looks extraordinary. His head is several times too large and 'curiously uneven, bulging all over with knots and bumps'. Someone says it is like an *alu,* a potato, so the boy is nicknamed Alu. He has come to live with his uncle, Balaram, and aunt, Toru-debi, after his parents have been killed in a car crash. Balaram and Toru-debi are childless, although Toru-debi has her Singer, a sewing machine 'seen for the first time on the morning after the traumas of her wedding night' and, therefore, to her, a sort of child.

The reader's initial confidence in the author's skill and sense of direction is likely to last for as long as we are in Lalpukur. There are plenty of bizarre happenings but they embellish rather than obscure the main stream of the narrative. For example, when Alu is sixteen he has one of the oddest sexual initiations. He has been apprenticed to a weaver and is working away at a loom when the weaver's daughter straddles him. She tells him to keep the loom going so that her father will not hear anything suspicious, and 'bouncing with the rhythm of his legs as they pushed the pedals' she presses her knees to his ribs until the sky bursts. That is not a poetic way of indicating orgasm. An aeroplane has come down on to the nearby school.

However, ***The Circle of Reason*** is over four hundred pages long, and about a third of the way through the book the author gets overcome by his own inventiveness. When Alu sails over the Indian Ocean to al Ghazira the story begins to disintegrate. Alu is trapped, unhurt, under a building that collapses because of faulty workmanship. The reader begins to feel trapped, too, as the book falls down on him, and for him there is no near-miraculous rescue, as there is for Alu. However, although the plot meanders and at times seems to go round in circles that are beyond reason, there are still some fascinatingly vivid oases where the wearying reader can find refreshment: for example, a description of a man dancing 'the joys of bridegrooms', his movements 'both absolutely erotic and absolutely abstract, both love-making and geometry'; and, towards the end, a very funny argument between two Indian doctors in Algeria about the cleaning of a Hindu corpse. One looks forward to seeing what Amitav Ghosh can do with his creative exuberance when he can bring himself to give his fancy freedom but not unbridled license. (pp. 100-01)

John Mellors, "Fancy Free," in London Magazine, *n.s. Vol. 25, No. 12, March, 1986, pp. 98-101.*

PRABHU S. GUPTARA

Ghosh is a disillusioned Marxist, and he has made compelling fiction out of his distress at the world's refusal to conform to his ideas, hopes and desires. More significantly, ***The Circle of Reason*** is about the constrictions of mere reason, whose delusive quality is both explored and revealed by this funny, tragic and quite original novel.

Balaram takes to his orphaned nephew, Alu, because the boy has a knobbly head—an incomparable subject for his single passion, phrenology. Balaram's early enthusiasm for Rationalism had given place to this science because it appeared to him to establish a connection between the outside appearance of people and their inner character. His phrenological predictions turn out to be wildly inaccurate, but Balaram carries on believing, so coming to stand for all those who put their trust in reason. Balaram's friend, Gopal, trusts in common sense, but does not seem to do any better.

There is a whole gallery of characters, eccentric, wild, harmless, with peculiar interests and passions, whom a grown-up Alu meets when he sets off to travel through the Middle East and into the Sahara desert. Town, village and desert, in India and other countries, are brilliantly evoked in the picaresque course of Alu's adventures, before he arrives at a highly individual salvation. The beginning, middle and end of the story are stitched on to the threefold Indian notion of *sattwa* (reason), *rajas* (passion), and *tamas* (death), which form the three sections of the novel. Though this book recalls surrealist as well as continental novels, its antecedents are in fact in Indian folktale and legend, as should be clear by comparing Ghosh's work with that of other Indian writers of the same vein: G. V. Desani, Sudhindranath Ghose, Zulfikar Ghose, Salman Rushdie.

Prabhu S. Guptara, in a review of, "The Circle of Reason," in British Book News, *April, 1986, p. 240.*

NEVILLE SHACK

Alu [the protagonist of Amitav Ghosh's ***The Circle of Reason***] is a boy with a potato-shaped head and a persona fitting him for picaresque fiction; things happen to him, but he retains a certain innocence in a world marked by guile. Balaram, his cranky uncle, adopts him as a young orphan. Their village in Bengal then becomes the starting-point for a series of capers, chases and mysteries which take Alu westwards to the Arab world. His companions are never less than the rummest types, doing their extravagant best to bedevil the plot with a tangent here, a conspiracy there, and a scattering of energies everywhere else. Alu enters this madcap Indian diaspora, eventually joining up again with the beloved book of his life, a biography of Louis Pasteur. Just when you suspect that randomness is all, an old thread reappears, to weave a motif out of a contingency.

Appropriately enough, this Indian tale sets great store by the act of weaving on a loom, although Alu's aunt is no slouch with a Singer sewing machine. Balaram, a schoolmaster, amazes people when he apprentices Alu to the weaving trade. Mechanical man is a fine example indeed, using his mind to create a unified world; reason should inform everything. Balaram's ridiculous delusions, strange ideas and experiments with the free use of carbolic acid certainly make for incident. He lashes out at a friend for allowing his mind to become a dumping-ground for the West. Balaram might as well be indicting himself. The Pasteurized cosmos, and character assessments of the human skull in the pseudo-science of phrenology, are particular obsessions of his; the Indian mind chafes at its European chains while it tightens the links. The Rationalist motto "Reason rescues Man from Barbarity" becomes a pretext for Balaram's absurd brand of village terrorism. He establishes a Pasteur School of Reason, dedicated to the French conqueror of evil microbes, but the project is predictably doomed.

After the close of that truly wacky chapter, the action moves across the Arabian Sea, with more angles thrown in along the way. A displaced teacher-cum-charlatan, a salesman of laxatives, and Zindi, madam-extraordinary, meet up with Alu on the boat journey. Zindi turns out to be a vital catalyst in the town of al-Ghazira, a jerry-built jumble of a place. One of the many expatriate Indian merchants there, Jeevanbhai Patel, owner of the Durban Tailoring House, involves himself with Zindi and even more shady business. Another curious character, Nuri, sells eggs and trades stories, a living reject from the *Arabian Nights*. Every egg is an epic for him, a thousand-page song of love, death and betrayal. So (over the course of 420 pages here) one story leads inexorably to another, in a dyslexic game of consequences, always colourful, but giving a slipshod feel to the narrative as a whole.

Alu meanwhile fades out, apparently crushed to death by a collapsing building. But he survives, as if by a miracle, to preach against the horrors of the cash-nexus. This formerly silent, inscrutable figure must be taking on his uncle's mantle. Pasteur got it right, obviously. The old microbiologist wanted purity but had failed finally to track down the definitive germ, money, and eradicate it. Now, perhaps, it is all a question of metaphors, a picaresque farrago alive with phantoms of morality. If events become too flighty and crazed for a level-headed kind of reader, Zindi will offer some counter-poise. What would happen, she asks, if we all spent our time chasing every new madness that sweeps over us? Never underestimate the task of staying alive and keeping the house together, even if it is a thoroughly disreputable establishment. This particular fictional world, though, crawls with shysters; it does not know such a thing as domestic stability.

Onwards, to Algeria, with some reflections on that country provided by the most serious deracinated Indian so far, Dr Mishra. The tone in this final phase of the novel becomes poignant and thoughtful. Knowledge, whether of microbiology or anything mechanical, has a human value: no small relief after such a roistering trail, on which pedagogy served to confuse the issue, whatever that was. This free-wheeling juggernaut of a story, the making of Alu, inevitably generates more heat than light. A very lively style has it going in all directions, on escapades and wheezes, letting rip until some kind of rationale is added at the end to convey sobriety.

Neville Shack, "Rational Capers," in The Times Literary Supplement, *No. 4332, April 11, 1986, p. 382.*

An Excerpt from *The Circle of Reason*

It's so simple, Alu said with a conqueror's elation. It took no more than a day to learn, just a matter of co-ordination: tug on the shuttle-cord once and the shuttle flies across with the weft, press the right pedal and the warp closes on the weft, push the reed once towards you and the cloth grows by another minute fraction of an inch, then tug the shuttle-cord again. . . . like a dance, one way, then another, hands and feet together.

Yes, said Shombhu Debnath. Plain white cloth, like you're weaving, is simple. You'll find out how simple it is if you ever get past that.

Alu paid him no attention. He had his reward at last: a five-yard length of cloth. Maya cut it from the cloth beam for him. You'll never learn, she said, folding it. Go back to your books. But she smiled.

Alu walked sedately out of the courtyard, the cloth folded under his arm. When he reached the bamboos he began to run. He bounded into Balaram's study and shouted: Look, the first bit of cloth I've woven. But Balaram was away, dousing the village in antiseptic.

It didn't matter, for Alu was already in a dream. It took him barely a week to master the weaving of ordinary white cloth. At the end of the week the loom, rattling faster than it ever had before, had thrown out a waterfall of cloth.

But Shombhu Debnath curled his lip. He looked at the bale Alu had woven, and snorted: How old are you?

Fifteen, Alu said, sixteen soon.

Shame, said Shombhu. We used to do better than that when we were ten.

But, again, Maya smiled.

ANTHONY BURGESS

The magic realism of Amitav Ghosh's first novel, ***The Circle of Reason,*** is a genre much developed in Latin America, a continent where the condition of the people is not conducive to novels of rational cause and effect. India, with its pullulating poor and its superstitions, has recently given us, though the book was written in London, Salman Rushdie's *Shame,* which belongs to the tradition of Gabriel García Márquez and Mario Vargas Llosa. Mr. Ghosh, who teaches in the sociology department of the Delhi School of Economics, follows the same line of extravagance in the service of truth.

His title would seem to disclaim any magical content, though the contradiction in it cancels the rational in favor of the cyclical. His characters think they are walking a straight line, but they are going round, powered by hope, in that nonproductive circle that life too often imposes on the poor.

Mr. Ghosh writes at least as well as Mr. Rushdie. When we read some of the fictional output of America and Britain these days, we despair of the future of the English language. The subcontinent, on the evidence of this and some other Indian novelists, is a preserve of unassailable syntax and elegant force.

The hero of ***The Circle of Reason*** is named Nachiketa Bose, but he is called Alu, which means "potato." This is because of the shape of his head, knobby, bumpy and far too big. A deformed protagonist is to be expected in some brands of magic realism. . . .

Alu is brought up in a village called Lalpukur in East Bengal. . . . Balaram is the schoolmaster. . . . He believes in science, having read a life of Pasteur, and one of his achievements is to drench the village in carbolic acid. If he stands, in his demented way, for progress, the talent that the growing Alu evinces is traditional: he learns how to weave, and well.

Mr. Ghosh has a Tolstoyan concern with realities, which leads him to teach the reader himself how to weave, at the same time pouring on him an entire history of the craft. From *Anna Karenina* you can learn how to make strawberry jam; here you can learn how to join the warp to the weft. Ancient craft and carbolic acid cohere in a beneficient synthesis, but the modern world pushes itself in without help from Balaram. (p. 6)

The picaresque narrative, crammed with characters who would do well in Cervantes, comes to an end without having taught us anything. Mr. Ghosh reserves the didactic for his courses in sociology at Delhi.

We are, of course, wrong when we expect a work of the imagination to illustrate some moral profundity. That is not what fiction is about. Mr. Ghosh succeeds in his main aim, which is to show the bewildering diversity of a world very remote from *Dallas* or *Dynasty,* though we can't doubt that those two parodies of the life of the rich are being watched in al-Ghazira. But American fiction itself is only occasionally convincing in showing real human struggle, which has relatively little to do with the rights of blacks, homosexuals or women. In the teeming subcontinent and its outposts, life is pared to essentials but, paradoxically, breeds an obsession with particularities, which are the stuff of fiction.

We in the West are too generalized, too abstract: it is with us that the true paring down is at work. And we are, of course, deodorized. ***The Circle of Reason*** smells of cow-dung fires, and it tastes of chilies. It is a remarkable achievement, though not without faults. We expect more from Alu than we get. There are divagations, episodic disquisitions on, for instance, the history of al-Ghazira, that hold up the narrative. Not that the narrative was really intended to take us anywhere.

If much British fiction is effete and American fiction overcommercialized, Indian fiction, on the showing of Mr. Rushdie and now Mr. Ghosh, is alive. It has been alive for a long time, though not with sharp eyes and ears for the riches of postmodernism. This novel is not merely a highly contemporary construct: it looks ahead. Technically, a lot of us can learn from Mr. Ghosh. Finally, it is the intelligence, manifested in a brilliant handling of language, that most impresses us. Many Western novels these days exhibit little more than the resources of a perverse sensorium. Here is a brain. (p. 7)

Anthony Burgess, "A Little Dementia in the Name of Progress," in The New York Times Book Review, *July 6, 1986, pp. 6-7.*

THE ECONOMIST

Mr Amitav Ghosh's hero, in his novel ***The Circle of Reason*** is a weaver. So is Mr Ghosh. The pleasure of his book lies in the stories which spin off and then are looped back into the loose plot. In that, he is rightly compared to Salman Rushdie: both of them heirs to a technique of story-telling in which, as in *The Thousand and One Nights,* the skill lies in ensuring that the story never finishes.

The Circle of Reason is Mr Ghosh's first novel. In India, it has received less than its due acclaim. Indians, particularly Mr Ghosh's fellow-Bengalis, are ambivalent about people who write in English. (p. 14)

This puts Mr Ghosh in a tricky position. He is writing for a largely non-Indian audience about Indian matters. He says, for instance, that it is difficult for anybody who has not been through the sort of debates that Indian socialism indulged in during the 1960s and 1970s to understand one of his main themes: that you cannot apply rational solutions to problems while ignoring the history of the people you are practising on. Indian socialism, he says, has always been more international, less rooted in its own soil, than European socialism—which perhaps partly accounts for its evident failure to turn India into a socialist country.

Mr Ghosh's book is scattered with failed reformers: in its first part, one character becomes obsessed with the idea of disinfecting a village with carbolic acid, and is eventually killed by an alliance between the local bigwig, whose preeminence he threatens, and the police, who believe him (quite rightly) to be an "extremist".

The book is in three parts: it moves from Bengal to a mythical place of eccentric sheikhs, oil and migrant labour called Al Ghazira, to El Oued in Algeria, a small town in the north-east of the Sahara desert. . . . In each place, reason—symbolised by a copy of *The Life of Pasteur* which appears in Bengal and re-emerges through a series of coincidences in El Oued—struggles and fails to impose itself on a disorganised world.

The Middle Eastern locations are chosen partly because Mr Ghosh liked them. But the migrations of plot reflect another of Mr Ghosh's preoccupations—that exile, or restlessness, is the normal condition of people in Asia and the Middle East. It is only the Europeans, he maintains, for whom "home" is an attribute of a particular place. For Arabs and Asians, home is something you construct wherever you happen to be. (pp. 14, 16)

Al Ghazira takes migration to extremes—as the real Gulf states do. Money has sucked in an international work-force: the combination of the two is destroying the traditional society of the Gulf. Whence emerges Mr Ghosh's third theme: the nobility and pathos of people from an old world trying to cope with a new one. (p. 16)

"An Enthralling Yarn," in The Economist, *Vol. 300, No. 7457, August 2, 1986, pp. 14, 16.*

HANIF KUREISHI

The Circle of Reason is a huge, ambitious novel with a crowd of characters and themes, set in a number of countries: India, Yemen, Egypt, and Algeria. It is like an immense pot into which scores of more or less random ingredients have been thrown. Some of those ingredients are those that make good books. There is the conflict between reason and superstition, mind and feeling, criminality and the law, the collective and the individual. But although Ghosh's pot swills with life and parts of the stew are delicious, it is not cooked all the way through. Parts of it are indigestible, in fact; and they take so long in the chewing that the jaws of your brain will ache with the effort.

In its form the book recalls *The Tin Drum* or, more closely and slightly suspiciously, *Midnight's Children.* The style is multidimensional, ironic, a mixture of the bizarre and the ordinary. It seethes with stories, odd characters, terrible journeys, strange occurrences. Ghosh takes it for granted, as Salman Rushdie said in a recent interview, "that reality is not realistic," and that "magical realism" through its torrent of entertaining lies comes closer to telling us how the world is than something that attempts to reproduce the surface of everyday life. (p. 40)

In addition to [the] central, rather convoluted story, there are numerous others, often askew in relation to the rest of the book. And there are numerous other characters, including Nury the egg salesman, who knows everything about everyone in al-Ghazira. His eyes are at such odd angles "it was said of him that when other people only saw Cairo he could see Bombay as well." He has his head bitten off by a camel.

Ghosh's writing is certainly more lively than a good deal of contemporary fiction, at least in Britain. India seems full of stories of a kind that England, for instance, isn't. . . .

But Rushdie lives in Britain, and one of his virtues—in this he is an example to British novelists—is his brilliant, creative thieving, his eclecticism. He has taken from India, from England, from both German and South American literature, using these influences to forge a new style, a unique voice. And what he is able to do, in a way that Amitav Ghosh cannot, is to unite the personal and the political. Rushdie's characters, however bizarre or idiosyncratic, always live in a real world of political pressures. We are able to see, in his work, the many complicated ways in which public politics determines private behavior.

Ghosh's novel, in contrast, is set in a kind of timeless no-man's-land of the imagination. His characters have a set of eccentric traits that he has pinned onto them. They have no depth; it is almost impossible to care about them. Some of the prose is terrific, vivid, and original; some of the descriptions are marvelous. But the book is overextended and broken-backed, lacking in all narrative drive and tension. Ghosh's numerous and overwhelming details don't add up, and ideas once introduced are inexplicably and irritatingly dropped. The book is fascinating, but it is a first draft rather than a complete and successful object. (p. 41)

Hanif Kureishi, "A Feast of Words," in The New Republic, *Vol. 195, No. 5, August 4, 1986, pp. 40-1.*

LOIS BRAGG

[***The Circle of Reason***] establishes Amitav Ghosh . . . as one of our contemporary greats. Ghosh's transcendent vision is as imaginative as that of Garcia Marquez, his fictional universe is as expansive as Joyce's, his affirmation of the human spirit in the face of political terror as joyous as I. B. Singer's, his power to shape a narrative from multiple voices as astonishing as Faulkner's, and his metaphoric style as evocative as that of Gunter Grass. In addition, Ghosh presents the kind of integrated double vision that one finds in the best third-world novelists with first-world readerships, such as V. S. Naipul or the South African J. M. Coetzee, although Ghosh's novelistic vision is diametrically opposed to Naipaul's and Coetzee's dark world views, and is most reminiscent of Garcia Marquez.

Ghosh's story is complex and his cast of characters large. The one character who remains in the book from first page to last is the character we learn least about, an impenetrable core to whom the many profoundly developed characters adhere.

Ghosh's plot, characterization, and symbolism would each alone make this novel worth reading, but it is his power of language that makes it great. Ghosh sums up his own ability in speaking of Zindi, whose story-telling changes "mere incidents to a palpable thing . . . she could bring together empty air and give it a body just by talking of it."

Lois Bragg, in a review of, "The Circle of Reason," in Best Sellers, *Vol. 46, No. 6, September, 1986, p. 203.*

Lisa Grunwald

1959-

American novelist.

When Grunwald began the novel *Summer* (1986) in the summer of 1980, the idea for her fiction was not prompted by her mother, *Women's Wear Daily* columnist Betty Grunwald, who had at that time recovered from recent cancer surgery. She was remembering instead her comment to her parents a few years earlier when they were leaving for a trip, "I'd rather have the two of you crash in the same plane than have either of you die alone." The motivation to write the novel took a different turn, however, when six months later Grunwald's mother died of cancer. For the next three years, Grunwald, who is an associate editor for *Esquire* magazine, and whose father, Henry Grunwald, is editor-in-chief of Time, Inc. magazines, fashioned her story of a close-knit family during the mother's last bout with cancer. Grunwald observes that the novel was not emotionally difficult to write, adding, "It was helpful to write this. I had to write it."

Summer is told from the point of view of Jennifer Burke, the youngest daughter of renowned sculptor Milo Burke and his wife Lulu. In the summer following her freshman year in college, Jennifer learns that Lulu is dying of cancer, and to prevent her parents' separation, she plans to sabotage Milo's plane so that both will die. But her father's absorption in his work, her own first experience with love, and her mother's stern refusal to behave like a dying woman, lead Jennifer to abandon her plan; she achieves instead a greater understanding of love and of the complexities of its expression.

While several reviewers find the plot device of the airplane accident unconvincing, and some observe that the first-romance theme falters, most commend Grunwald for her solid portrait of the last stages of the mother's life and death by cancer and her family's anguished response. Lending power to this story, critics note, is Grunwald's ability to render a sensitive subject without sentimentality, using realistic dialogue and a spare prose style.

(See also *Contemporary Authors,* Vol. 120.)

KIRKUS REVIEWS

[***Summer*** is a] darting, very sad little book about a young woman's coming-to-terms with her family's mortality—more specifically, the mortality *of* family, how its seemingly eternal unit in fact changes and passes away. Jennifer Burke is one of the two daughters of Milo and Lulu. They're the closest of couples, these two; he's a well-off sculptor; she runs a Boston art gallery but serves more importantly as an artist's dream-wife: intuitive, smart, graceful, patient. If Milo and Lulu have to some degree shut their children out of their love affair with each other, they've also provided (at least to Jennifer) an almost Edenic romance of continued marital absorption.

But this summer in question, spent as all others are on an island off Cape Cod, Lulu is in the last stages of bone cancer and she won't live out the summer. Milo, in grieving self-defense, spends more and more time in the studio; Jennifer's sister Hilary, an actress, makes intermittent appearances to help attend to Lulu's dying; and Jennifer, opportunely and not, a little embarrassedly, finds herself really in love for the first time, with a local boy who gives flying lessons at the small airport on the island where Milo keeps his plane.

The plane—and the flying lessons—figure prominently at first: Jennifer has decided to sabotage the airplane, so that Milo and Lulu might die together at the end of the summer, thus to be unseparated. It's a plan that she finally abandons—seeing that both Milo and Lulu have found a way to say goodbye to each other already . . . and a good thing for the book, too: it's the most melodramatic element in a book otherwise fairly free of it. Grunwald lets her (sometimes too-good-to-be-true) characters drift too far out of focus at times, and the clippedness of many scenes is too bejeweled; yet sentimentality is kept to a minimum, and the hard narrative job of allowing complication its own rhythms through time—which is the book's chief idea—is deftly handled.

A good debut. (pp. 1152-53)

A review of "Summer," in Kirkus Reviews, *Vol. LIII, No. 21, November 1, 1985, pp. 1152-53.*

DONNA KITTA

The Burkes are an unusual family. Milo is a world-famous sculptor; Lulu is his wife, model, muse, and protectress. Their two daughters are beautiful, precocious, and talented. The elder, Hillary, is an actress, and Jennifer, [***Summer*** 's] narrator, is an 18-year-old who's just had a book of photographs published. The family spends their summers on an island off Cape Cod, but this will be Lulu's last—she's dying of cancer. Grunwald examines the process of grief as it evolves from shock, denial, and fear to grim acceptance. What finally emerges and triumphs is the irresistible tug of life—the intricacies of love, the uplifting power of art, the challenge of growing and learning. The narrator's photographic sensibility creates careful, framed, static descriptions animated by staccato conversation. A story of death becomes a story of life in this strong first novel.

Donna Kitta, in a review of "Summer," in Booklist, *Vol. 82, No. 7, December 1, 1985, p. 531.*

ELISE CHASE

Eighteen-year-old photographer Jennifer Burke returns from college for summer vacation [in the novel ***Summer***] to find her close-knit family in crisis: mother Lulu, all-wise, all-nurturant, is dying of cancer. In a desperate attempt to stave off chaos and pain, Jennifer schemes to rig a plane accident so her devoted parents will die together. If this perverse plan never quite rings true—it seems, somehow, more artistic contrivance than either dark comedy or a valid expression of character—the rest of the novel is very real indeed. Lulu's disintegration and the family's anguish are marvelously rendered, as is Jennifer's first love affair, which ultimately helps her transcend her desire symbolically to "photograph" her parents' "perfect" marriage in a joint death. Stylistically, Grunwald has a good ear for dialogue, and her narrative is crisp, witty, and moving. All in all, a fine first novel.

Elise Chase, in a review of "Summer," in Library Journal, *Vol. 111, No. 1, January, 1986, p. 102.*

CATHERINE BANCROFT

Lisa Grunwald's first novel [***Summer***] begins as the Burke family is going up to an island off Cape Cod for the summer; the father flies them in his own plane, and they have familiar jokes and rituals to attend the opening of the summer house. Everyone is too perfect—the heroine already has had her photographs accepted for a book. The conflict in the story appears when Jennifer plans to make her parents die together so their love will not be lost. But not until we start to see Jennifer's anger at her mother, late in the book, do we perceive a struggle with the power to engage us. ***Summer*** draws an opposition between two kinds of art: art that celebrates life's power to change, and art that is man's attempt to control what he cannot. When her father responds to his wife's imminent death with a fresh view of his own sculpture, his uninhibited reaction spurs Jennifer to abandon her attempt to make her mother's death as neat as a photograph. Revolving around the improbable plot device, this theme never has a chance to achieve subtlety; we are less convinced by Jennifer's rite of passage than by the haunting images of her dying mother, curled in bed, leaving behind those whose stratagems to preserve her are finally futile.

Catherine Bancroft, in a review of "Summer," in The New York Times Book Review, *January 26, 1986, p. 20.*

An Excerpt from *Summer*

It was three o'clock. Daddy had worked in the morning and come back up to the house for a swim with Lulu. No problem with that, Dr. Irving had said. Good for her to get exercise.

Daddy's cries for help mingled with the cries of the gulls, and Hillary and I, lazing in the sun, did not understand, at first, what was happening.

By the time we reached the beach, running as fast as we could down the long staircase, Daddy had already pulled Lulu from the water. They were lying side by side on the shore, panting and sandy.

"What happened?" Hillary and I shouted together, running toward them. They were too winded to answer, and at some point in the frozen moment waiting to hear their voices, Hillary and I reached for each other. We figured that out hours later, when we both found small red welts where our nails had dug into each other's hands.

"A cramp in her back," Daddy finally managed to say.

"Lulu?" Hillary said to her, kneeling beside her, efficient, ready to help.

"She couldn't swim," Daddy continued. His eyes filled with tears. "She started to sink."

I realized that I couldn't move. I was standing perhaps five yards from Lulu and I was scared of her, scared that she would get sick, or pass out, or scream in pain. It wasn't until she sat up and forced a smile that she was Lulu again and I could draw closer. It was the same as the night she had fallen. She had ceased to be Lulu, and in some strange way that I did not understand then and am only beginning to understand now, I ceased to be me as well. This was the reality I had been waiting for, and I found myself completely unequipped to deal with it.

She could not quite straighten up and so we supported her from three sides, nearly carrying her up the stairs back to the house. We put her in bed, wet bathing suit and all, because she did not want us to have to change her clothes for her. I was relieved, and ashamed of my relief.

She smiled at Daddy and reached for his hand.

"Scared me," he said.

"Nothing to be scared of."

After she had fallen asleep, I walked back down to the beach. The sun was throwing an electric current of light across the waves, so bright it had no color. I stared at the spot where she might have died, and at the beach, where I had been unable to help her.

I imagined myself as a helpless infant with soiled clothes. I imagined all the messy intimate moments: Lulu teaching me to blow my nose, scrape my teeth, clean my ears, get sick. She had done the same for Hillary. Our bodies and smells and illnesses had not repelled her. We had been, somehow, an extension of her. And I could not, at least not yet, summon the same courage for her. I wanted to be far away so she wouldn't see my fear, and I knew she'd already seen it.

I went back to the house after the sun set. Lulu was still asleep. Hillary drove to town with Daddy, and for the first time in my life I was afraid to be alone with my mother. I sat at the living room table, avoiding my reflection in the glass and praying that she would not wake up needing something I couldn't give.

SHARON DIRLAM

If you can accept the premise that a reasonably normal 18-year-old girl would seriously consider killing her father in order to spare him the grief of living without her mother, who is dying of cancer, then [***Summer***] may speak volumes to you. It houses some marvelous dialogue, introduces a group of attractive characters, and contains a love story that is both fragile and robust. This is a study of a tightly bound family, sufficient unto each other, and what happens when the mother begins to die and the world comes unraveled and still life goes on. The author has a tendency to lead the reader by the hand; her first-person narrator says that the idea of causing her parents' plane to crash "was simply never a crime," and that her behavior in the initial throes of infatuation was "still embarrassing for me to recall."

The thoughts presented and the actions taken have not the slightest need for signposts pointing the way to appropriate response. And yet, the telling of this story is generally so compelling and the youthful zest shines through with such charm that one forgives the rough edges as one forgives the younger self for thinking that the world should make sense. Lisa Grunwald's fictional milieu is peopled with characters who are intriguing and situations that keep one interested right to the final sentence.

Sharon Dirlam, in a review of "Summer," in Los Angeles Times Book Review, *February 9, 1986, p. 4.*

CATHLEEN McGUIGAN

Like everyone in Lisa Grunwald's first novel, ***Summer*** . . . , the narrator, Jennifer Burke, is terribly accomplished. Even the townie she falls for on Sanders Island (read Martha's Vineyard) turns out to have gone to Yale. At 18, Jennifer is about to have a book of photographs published and she yearns for those around her to be frozen in time, like the pictures she takes. "I stored up my memories like ammunition," Jennifer tells us. When she learns her mother is dying of cancer, she can't bear the idea that her parents' symmetry will be destroyed. Admirably well crafted, this novel can seem, at times, emotionally muffled. But ***Summer*** takes on real power when the narrator finally cracks into fury and grief, in taut scenes in which she, the daughter, must become the parent to her withering mother.

Cathleen McGuigan, in a review of "Summer," in Newsweek, *Vol. CVII, No. 7, February 17, 1986, p. 71B.*

STEFAN KANFER

The appeal of an island is older than prose. It is a universal symbol, as valid for the isolated state as for the besieged heart. In this lean, piercing novel [***Summer***], Lisa Grunwald renews the metaphor by making Sanders Island, off Cape Cod, Mass., a garden and a desert. The narrator, Jennifer Burke, is the younger daughter of what seems an ideal couple: Milo and Lulu Burke are so devoted that they have always refused to fly in separate planes because "they wouldn't have *wanted* to go on without each other."

But from this summer onward, Milo, a vastly successful sculptor, will have to take off alone: Lulu is dying of inoperable cancer. Yet of the four members of the immediate family, she seems the least affected. Under the relentlessly cheerful sun, Jennifer and her sister Hillary bicker with each other, flirt with young men and fend off the questions of concerned friends. Milo disappears into his work. Only Lulu perseveres as if nothing untoward were happening, presiding at parties and amiably chatting with celebrities. "She would not act like a dying woman," Jennifer resentfully observes, "would not grant us the haven of feeling sympathy and outrage and pity and sorrow."

Like many new novelists, Grunwald tends to oversymbolize a first affair (this one concerns a romantic flying instructor), and the consolations of art and life are a bit too neatly programmed. But on the journey to maturity, she displays a knowing eye for the arrangements of society and color in a place where "the summer residents were tan, the weekenders were sunburned, and the islanders were pale," and she is wholly immune to the first novelist's affliction of elaboration and repetition.

Whether the author, who is 26, can sustain her intensity and self-discipline remains to be read. For now, she has found an intonation and an idiom entirely her own, and if her novel brims with pain, it also fulfills Francis Bacon's famous and difficult demand that ideally the "heart is no island cut off from other lands, but a continent that joins to them." (pp. 77-8)

Stefan Kanfer, "New Pleasures and Promises," in Time, *Vol. 127, No. 7, February 17, 1986, pp. 77-8.*

DIANE COLE

In ***Summer,*** Lisa Grunwald . . . attempts to recapture a part of the past—in this case, a dying mother's final summer with her husband and two daughters. But in remembering the progress of that season, 18-year-old Jennifer discovers that life does not lose its power to surprise or disturb, and that it is simply a myth "that families freeze, that they never smile or argue while it's going on." Rather, her mother's presence resembles "the ocean's sounds in our house, sometimes clear and specific, more often not."

Nonetheless, that background noise grows progressively louder as the summer continues, and its persistent roar affects each family member differently. (p. 84-5)

With care and precision, Grunwald dramatizes the various strategies each of these characters adopts to avoid, confront, and at last accept the reality that they yearn to deny. Grunwald's tone is calm and cool, as if to follow the advice Milo, the sculptor, gives Jennifer, the budding photographer: "You just *can't* make people *feel* things if you've got 'Feel Things' written over everything you do." Instead, Grunwald has crafted a wise and subtle work that tells us of the end of many things—of a mother's life and, with it, the end of her children's childhood. (p. 85)

Diane Cole, "Three First Novels Confront the Ultimate Loss," in Ms., *Vol. XIV, No. 10, April, 1986, pp. 83-5.*

Thomas Ligotti

1953-

American short story writer.

In *Songs of a Dead Dreamer* (1986) Ligotti demonstrates what horror novelist Ramsey Campbell calls "one of the few consistently original voices in contemporary horror fiction." Most of the stories in this collection originally appeared in British and American small press magazines devoted to horror fiction, including *Nyctalops, Fantasy Tales*, and *Grimoire*. *The Penguin Encyclopedia of Horror and the Supernatural* cites Ligotti's work found in small presses as "outstanding fiction" deserving "wider appreciation." Reviewers praise Ligotti's arresting, highly distinctive style; at the same time, they note, he follows the literary, neo-Gothic tradition of such distinguished fantasy writers as H. P. Lovecraft, Arthur Machen, and Campbell.

Reviewers commend Ligotti most highly for his imagination and versatility. The stylistic approach of the tales in *Songs of a Dead Dreamer* varies, from the realism of "The Frolic" to the surrealistic dream imagery in "Dr. Voke and Mr. Veech" to the deconstructionist fantasy "Notes on the Writing of Horror: A Story." Like Lovecraft and Campbell, critics note, Ligotti for the most part avoids explicitly gruesome subject matter and deemphasizes plot. Instead, he relies on subtle atmospheric effects to evoke a sense of awe and existential terror. As critic Rosemary Pardoe describes it, "Ligotti's supernatural fiction invariably features characters who struggle on (and usually topple over) the edge of a strange and sometimes hideously beautiful madness." Reviewers also applaud Ligotti's wit, the atemporal quality of his narrative, and his exceptional skill in introducing mainstream avant-garde literary techniques to the conventions of the horror genre. Above all, they emphasize, it is the compellingly nightmarish quality of the tales that makes *Songs of a Dead Dreamer* an important contribution to supernatural literature.

RAMSEY CAMPBELL

[*Campbell is an English novelist, short story writer, and critic specializing in supernatural literature. Writing in a style influenced by the neo-Gothic tradition of H. P. Lovecraft and M. R. James, Campbell has won acclaim for his short stories, included in such collections as* Demons by Daylight *(1976), and for his novels,* The Doll Who Ate His Mother *(1976) and* The Hungry Moon *(1986), among others. In the following excerpt from his introduction to* Songs of a Dead Dreamer *Campbell praises Ligotti's subtlety, wit, and originality.*]

I don't know when I have enjoyed a collection of an author's horror stories more than the book you now hold in your hands [***Songs of a Dead Dreamer***], if hands they are. I'll go further: it has to be one of the most important horror books of the decade. . . . Ligotti is one of the few consistently original voices in contemporary horror fiction, one of the few whose work is instantly recognizable.

He belongs to the most honourable tradition in the field, that of subtlety and awesomeness rather than the relentlessly graphic. At times he suggests terrors as vast as Lovecraft's, though the terrors are quite other than Lovecraft's. He's capable of writing tales as dismayingly horrifying as any of his contemporaries— **"The Frolic"**, for example—yet even there one finds a hint of more than horror, an extra dimension of awe. Others of his tales—**"The Troubles of Dr. Thoss"**, **"The Greater Festival of Masks"**, **"Dr. Voke and Mr. Veech"**—read like dreams prompted by memories of M. R. James, dreams stranger than anything the good doctor ever wrote: perhaps the dreams of the consciousness glimpsed behind one of Ligotti's most elaborate stories, **"Dream of a Mannikin"**. Despite faint echoes of writers he admires, however, Ligotti's vision is wholly personal. Few other writers could conceive a horror story in the form of notes on the writing of the genre, and I can't think of any other writer who could have brought it off.

In **"The Consolations of Horror"** (a companion piece, published in *Dark Horizons* 27, to **"Professor Nobody's Little**

Lectures"), Ligotti defines the consolations of the genre thus: "simply that someone shares some of your own feelings and has made of these a work of art which you have the insight, sensitivity and—like it or not—peculiar set of experiences to appreciate." In his case the consolations also include an elegant and witty style, an inimitable imagination, a willingness to expand the genre, and a timelessness which ought to mean that his fiction will be read with as much pleasure a hundred years from now. May this book bring him the acclaim which he certainly deserves. (pp. 5-6)

Ramsey Campbell, in an introduction to Songs of a Dead Dreamer *by Thomas Ligotti, Silver Scarab Press, 1986, pp. 5-6.*

MICHAEL A. MORRISON

"There is more than one way to write a horror story," notes the narrator of Thomas Ligotti's **"Notes on the Writing of Horror: A Story."** In his first collection [***Songs of a Dead Dreamer***], Ligotti sets out to prove this point, ringing extravagant changes on the style and substance of the tale of terror. His purview embraces metafictional commentary (**"Professor Nobody's Little Lectures on Supernatural Horror"**), wry retellings of archetypal horror stories (**"The Excruciating Final Days of Dr. Jekyll, Englishman"** (". . . Hyde died days ago in an unfortunate accident of science. The man would drink anything he could get his hands on, and he was totally ignorant of chemistry!"), enigmatic dark fables, (**"The Greater Festival of Masks"**) and the (slightly) more traditional stories that comprise the rest of this book.

Like the elderly authoress who is subjected to a tenuous but terrifying haunting in **"Alice's Last Adventure,"** Ligotti is "a conjurer of stylish nightmares." Working in the tradition of Arthur Machen, Robert Aickman, and Ramsey Campbell, he eschews graphic scenes of mutilation and death for a subtler approach, writing in an experimental rather than jugular vein. Using modernist stylistic devices and an array of narrative forms, Ligotti strives to induce a sense of cosmic terror and awe rather than to horrify or revolt. Many of his stories are Lovecraftian in effect and structure, but his style is quite unlike Lovecraft's and his voice wholly original. In some tales, such as **"Les Fleurs,"** he fumbles, leading us not into a whirlpool of terrified awe but into a miasma of muddled quasi-mysticism. But more often than not he succeeds; stories such as **"Dream of a Mannikin, or the Third Person"** or **"Drink to Me Only with Labyrinthine Eyes"** tickle our subconscious with intimations of "demonic powers lurking just beyond the threshold of sensory perception."

The wellspring of horror in Ligotti's most effective stories is the uncertainty of identity in the modern world. His tales are filled with images of frozen, shifting, or lost identity: the dolls, puppets, mannikins and ventriloquists' dummies of **"Dream of a Mannikin"** and **"Dr. Voke and Mr. Veech"**; the "missing faces" and masks of **"The Greater Festival of Masks."** This is an acutely relevant theme for the horror story of the eighties, and Ligotti's modernist style is perfectly suited to it. . . . Ligotti is an ambitious, original, provocative writer, and his promising debut collection is well worth your attention. (pp. 23-4)

Michael A. Morrison, "Delights of the Cosmic Macabre," in Fantasy Review, *Vol. 9, No. 6, June, 1986, pp. 23-4.*

NEAL WILGUS

[Wilgus is an American critic who has written extensively on science fiction, fantasy, and horror literature. In the following excerpt Wilgus observes that the strongest stories in Songs of a Dead Dreamer *rely on stylish writing rather than plot for their effect.]*

Thomas Ligotti has a unique and arresting style that more than makes up for the rather weak plots in this collection of eleven stories and seven prose poems [***Songs of a Dead Dreamer***]. I particularly liked **"Drink to Me Only with Labyrinthine Eyes,"** in which a hypnotist takes his audience for a rather revolting ride, and **"The Troubles of Dr. Thoss,"** in which a mindless young artist is "taken" in a gruesome manner—but all of the stories are well done and many are excellent. Two stories-as-lectures-on-horror-fiction are the weakest and least successful, though even they have their moments—as do the "poems" retelling the lives of famous horror figures. (p. 44)

Neal Wilgus, in a review of "Songs of a Dead Dreamer," in Science Fiction Review, *Vol. 15, No. 3, August, 1986, pp. 44-5.*

An Excerpt from *Songs of a Dead Dreamer*

"Voke," Cheev calls out. "Doctor, are you here?"

Within the darkness ahead a tall cubicle suddenly appears, like a ticket-seller's booth at carnivals. The lower part is composed of wood and the upper part of glass; its interior is lit up by an oily red glare. Slumped forward on its seat inside the booth, as if asleep, is a well-dressed dummy: nicely-fitting black jacket and vest with bright silver buttons, a white high-collar shirt with silver cufflinks, and a billowing cravat which displays the same moons-and-stars pattern as the wooden half of his cell. Because his head is forwardly inclined, the dummy's only feature of note is the black sheen of its painted hair.

Cheev approaches the booth a little cautiously. He fails to notice, or considers irrelevant, the inanimate character of the booth's inhabitant. Through a semi-circle cut out of the glass, Cheev slides his hand into the booth, apparently with the intention of giving the dummy's arm a shake. But before his own arm creeps very far toward its goal, several things occur in succession: the dummy casually lifts its head and opens its eyes . . . it reaches out and places its wooden hand on Cheev's hand of flesh . . . and its lower jaw drops open to dispense a forced laugh—yah-ha-ha-ha-ha, yah-ha-ha-ha-ha.

Wresting his hand away from the lurid dummy, Cheev staggers backward a few chaotic steps. The dummy continues to give forth its mocking laughter, which flaps its way into every niche of the evil loft and flies back as deranged and horribly peculiar echoes. The dummy's face is vacant and handsome; its eyes roll like mad marbles. Then, from out of the shadows behind the dummy's booth, steps a figure that is every bit as thin as Cheev, but much taller. His outfit is not unlike the dummy's, but the clothes hang on him, and what there is left of his sparse hair falls like old rags across his bone-white scalp.

"Did you ever wonder, Mr. Veech," Voke begins, parading slowly toward his guest while holding one side of his coat like the train of a gown, "did you ever wonder what it is that makes the animation of a wooden dummy so horrible to see, not to mention to hear. Listen to it, I mean really listen. Ya-ha-ha-ha-ha; a stupid series of sounds which become unspeakably eloquent when uttered by the Ticket Man. They are a species of poetry that sings what should not be sung, they are a sub-class of music that speaks what should not be spoken. But what in the world is it laughing about. Nothing, it would seem. No clear motives or impulses make the dummy laugh, and yet it does! Ya-ha-ha-ha-ha, just as pure and as evil as can be.

"'What is this laughter for?' you might be wondering, Mr. Veech. It seems to be for your ears alone, doesn't it? It seems to be directed at every nameless secret and also every triviality of your being. It seems . . . knowing. Indeed, it is knowing, but in another way from what you suppose, in another direction entirely. It is not you the dummy knows, it is only itself. The question is not: 'What is this laughter for,' not at all. The question is: 'Where does it come from?' This is the essence of the horror, in fact. The dummy terrorizes you, while he is really the one in terror.

"Think of it: *wood waking up*. I can't put it any clearer than that. And let's not forget the paint for the hair and lips, the glass for the eyes. These too are aroused from a sleep that should never have been broken; these too are now part of a tingling network of dummy-nerves, alive and aware in a way we cannot begin to imagine. This is something too painful for screams and so the dummy laughs in your face, trying to give vent to an evil that was no part of his old home of wood and paint and glass. But this evil is now the very essence of its new home—our world, Mr. Veech. This is what is so horrible about the laughing Ticket Man. Go to sleep now, dummy. There, he has his nice silence back. Be glad I didn't make one that screams, Mr. Veech. And be glad the dummy is, after all, just a device."

ROSEMARY PARDOE

[*Pardoe is an English short story writer, critic, and editor of* Ghosts and Scholars, *a journal devoted to supernatural fiction in the tradition of M. R. James. In the following excerpt Pardoe praises the unique, eerie effect of Ligotti's tales.*]

[***Songs of a Dead Dreamer*** is a] very stylish publication featuring a selection of Thomas Ligotti's powerful and eerie prose. . . . Ligotti's supernatural fiction invariably features characters who struggle on (and usually topple over) the edge of a strange and sometimes hideously beautiful madness. There is no other writer producing anything quite like this, and while I doubt whether his work will ever be *entirely* to my taste, I would be the first to admit that stories like **"Dream of a Mannikin"**, **"Notes on the Writing of Horror: A Story"** and **"The Troubles of Dr Thoss"** are very fine indeed (the latter is even a little Jamesian).

Rosemary Pardoe, in a review of "Songs of a Dead Dreamer," in Haunted Library Newsletter, *November, 1986.*

ROBERT M. PRICE

[*Price is an American educator and critic whose writings are principally devoted to his two main fields of expertise: Christian theology and the works of H. P. Lovecraft. He is the editor of* Crypt of Cthulhu: A Pulp Thriller and Theological Journal. *In the following excerpt Price commends* Songs of a Dead Dreamer *as an original and effectively nightmarish work in the tradition of H. P. Lovecraft and Ramsey Campbell.*]

It was the lateness of the hour, not the content of the book, that made me drop off to sleep after finishing several of the stories in ***Songs of a Dead Dreamer.*** I recall dimly wondering if I would have nightmares influenced by the stories. What I dreamed actually seemed to be kind of *like* one of the stories: it seemed that the very dream itself was a thought, an experience telepathically stolen from someone else and written down, and my dream-awareness was actually the subjective self-awareness *of* the written account! "I" struggled with the realization that I was but the echo and not after all the identity I felt myself to be. What kind of book prompts dreams of this kind?

It is the kind of book that moved Ramsey Campbell to call it, in his Introduction, "one of the most important horror books of the decade" [see excerpt above]. Again, "I don't know when I have enjoyed a collection of an author's horror stories more." Such praise coming from Campbell is rather striking, and I have to admit it's what got me to set other things aside and take a look. (p. 57)

Ligotti's stories are not all cut from the same predictable cloth as some authors' are. His premises and characters have the same appearance of unselected variegatedness as reality itself, as if Ligotti's imagination were a radar dish set to pick up signals from any and every corner of the universe of nightmare. Uniting all the stories is a narrative style that is confident, fluid, and sensitive to arresting metaphor. There is an eerie suggestiveness reminiscent of HPL and Clark Ashton Smith, but the stories are perhaps more like the work of Ramsey Campbell than anyone else I am familiar with. However, such comparisons are easily misleading. Let me rather say that if you like Campbell, you will very likely enjoy Thomas Ligotti. (p. 58)

Robert M. Price, in a review of "Songs of a Dead Dreamer," in Crypt of Cthulhu, *Vol. 5, No. 6, June 15, 1986, pp. 57-8.*

JESSICA AMANDA SALMONSON

[*American novelist, short story writer, and editor Salmonson won a World Fantasy Award for her short story anthology* Amazons! *(1979). Her novels include* Tomoe Gozen *(1981) and* Ou Lu Khen and the Beautiful Madwoman *(1985). In the following excerpt Salmonson observes that Ligotti follows the traditions of Symbolist and Expressionist literature rather than the pulp magazine fiction emulated by many American horror writers.*]

I first encountered the work of Thomas Ligotti in the macabre-surrealist journal *Grimoire*. . . . Ligotti has been creating a fierce stir among the fanatic devotees of horror literature. But his voice is perhaps *too* original for instant recognition among the typical editor or anthologist of horror fiction, a field where conservatism invariably translates *artistic* as being *pretentious* and where even a microscopic moment of the experimental creates paroxysms of disdain. You see, Thomas Ligotti is not a fellow whose chief inspiration can be seen to be the dreary horror of the pulp era. He tempers this inspiration with an easy comprehension of the gloomier aspects of the German expressionism and French symbolism long before "the pulps" degraded fiction to the level of comic book scripting. (pp. 187-88)

Jessica Amanda Salmonson, in an introduction to "Masquerade of a Dead Sword," in Heroic Visions II, *edited by Jessica Amanda Salmonson, ACE Fantasy Books, 1986, pp. 187-88.*

WILLIAM J. GRABOWSKI

Watch for the fireworks.

If you haven't already spotted them, don't worry: you will. To that wrinkled and stained list—your Catalogue of the Craven—onto which are scrawled the names of your favorite authors, please add one Thomas Ligotti. I have; and while I hate to tell you what to do you'll quickly realize that ***Songs of a Dead Dreamer*** is fresh and quality stuff.

The strongest story in this collection has to be **"Dr. Voke and Mr. Veech,"** in which a fellow called Cheev (who, enigmatically, becomes "Veech" only upon entering the nightmarish loft of Voke) visits the reclusive doctor searching for some way to eliminate a man who is courting the woman who tickles Cheev's fancy. Particularly memorable is the scene where Cheev, in the wake of being cackled at by an unmanned ventriloquist's dummy, encounters Voke whose attire is ". . . not unlike the dummy's, but the clothes hang on him . . . " Then Voke inquires: "Did you ever wonder . . . what it is that makes the animation of a piece of wood like that dummy so horrible to see, not to mention to hear. Listen to it, I mean really listen. Ya-ha-ha-ha-ha . . . " Ligotti has the ability to make one ponder certain things one would rather not. (What *is* it about ventriloquists' dummies?) The logic in his fiction is that of the dream, of paranoia. I think you'll gulp as forcefully as did I when you ascertain just *how* the good doctor dispatched Cheev's problem. It is a skilled writer indeed who can suggest a horror so shocking that one is grateful it was kept offstage. Ligotti makes one feel precisely that dizzy dread which blooms within the stomach an instant before one lays eyes onto a gruesome auto accident.

His opening story, **"The Frolic,"** shares that same aura of timelessness possessed by such classic screamers as "The Monkey's Paw" and "A Rose For Emily," yet derives its potency from the visionary end of the spectrum—closer to Machen than, say, Lovecraft. You'll honestly be astonished, after reading these stories, when you consider that before now Ligotti has never seen professional publication. Some of his work has appeared in *Nyctalops* and *Eldritch Tales,* but I don't see his future as one in which his truly disturbing yarns are going to be strictly a part of low-circulation magazines—and that of course is up to Ligotti, and you.

I've got Ramsey Campbell backing me up on this.

"(***Songs of a Dead Dreamer***) has to be one of the most important horror books of the decade," he proclaims in his introduction [see excerpt above]. And as all of us know by now, Ramsey Campbell is one chap who takes his horror seriously. Thomas Ligotti is another. (p. 32)

William J. Grabowski, in a review of "Songs of a Dead Dreamer," in The Horror Show, *Vol. 5, No. 2, Spring, 1987, pp. 32-3.*

COMMENTS OF THOMAS LIGOTTI TO *CLC YEARBOOK*

In various ways, the stories in *Songs of a Dead Dreamer* reflect—however imperfectly—my attachment to a type of horror tale that is no longer practiced to any significant extent. Some of its most obvious traits are: an idiosyncratic prose style, characters who are abnormal in striking ways, an intensely dreamlike atmosphere created primarily by means of visual images, and an ultimately dark view of human existence. Some of its best known practitioners were: Edgar Allan Poe, Sheridan LeFanu, Arthur Machen, and H. P. Lovecraft. In my opinion, it is among the works of these authors that the horror tale may be found *in its essential form,* assuming one is concerned with such things. Always a rare phenomenon, even throughout the flourishing of literary supernaturalism in the nineteenth and early twentieth centuries, this species of horror is today, perhaps necessarily, all but extinct."

Carole Maso

19??-

American novelist.

Ghost Dance (1986) is the story of Vanessa Turin's struggle to endure the disintegration of her family. Wandering through worlds of reality and imagination, Vanessa remembers her lonely grandmother, spiritual grandfather, silent father, and politically radical brother, and their individual withdrawals from her life. But, above all, there is her mother, Christine—the genius poet whom Vanessa fiercely loves—and the memory of her recurring psychosis and tragic death.

Reviewers note that Maso's episodic narrative disregards plot and chronology, following instead a musical structure. Within this form, critics point to the novel's main themes of love and separation, its images that weave like leitmotifs throughout the narrative, and its lyrical prose, blending the real and surreal with only minor lapses. Citing the novel's flaws, a few reviewers fault the repetition of sentences and paragraphs, and some complain that certain events are overwrought, including the novel's closing scenes. Overall *Ghost Dance* is praised for its ambitious canvas of personal and public affairs and its highly imaginative rendering of a poignant family story.

KIRKUS REVIEWS

[***Ghost Dance*** is an] ambitious and wide-canvassed history-of-a-family novel (the author's first) that has many graceful moments, but that degenerates into a shrill diatribe against the crassness of corporate America.

Central here is Christine Wing, distinguished American poet, mother of two children, great beauty—and quite mad. As they grow up, the children struggle with their genius-touched mother's bouts of psychosis—including the time she forced the family to huddle on one bed (she wrapped twine around the four bedposts to keep them "in") against the imagined threat of sure destruction, or the time she made a drunken public display of great vulgarity before giving a poetry reading at the Guggenheim Museum (by this time she'd had her picture on the cover of *Time*). In an emotion-charged and montage-like narrative that roams freely from deep in the past right up to the present, daughter Vanessa Turin tells the whole story of her beauty-seeking family: a maternal grandfather who, widowed, goes back home to Armenia; a grandfather on the paternal side who becomes mystically enamored of the American Indians; a father who speaks seldom of his past, but who, in his quiet, intelligent way, seeks the purity of perfected beauty (as he did, too, in marrying his exquisite poet-wife); and a brother, Fletcher, whose sensitive conscience leads him to a life of paralyzed outrage at America's long history of exploitation and greed. Unfortunately for the novel, it is this latter impulse that emerges as dominant in the closing sections. Christine Wing is killed when the family's Ford Pinto is hit from the rear at a toll booth and then burns, an event that lets loose a clumsy flood of anti-corporate polemic ("You stupid bastards! . . . you can poison us, you can hack us into little bits, you can burn us in your furnaces . . ."). Before book's end, daughter Vanessa will make love with her dead mother's longtime lesbian lover, Sabina; brother Fletcher will report in anguish on popular causes and injustices ranging from asbestos poisoning to untested drugs to ending the Vietnam war; and Marta, Vanessa's troubled friend and lover at Vassar, will *not* die from slit wrists and "at least thirty" barbituates.

Trying for a song-of-America breadth, the novel declines slowly from a more focused and dramatic poise to a harrying clutter of the soap-operatic and trendy. Better for openers than as a whole. (pp. 572-73)

A review of "Ghost Dance," in Kirkus Reviews, *Vol. LIV, No. 8, April 15, 1986, pp. 572-73.*

PUBLISHERS WEEKLY

Comparable more to musical than to literary forms, [***Ghost Dance***] resembles a tone poem: its whispering minor-key passages rush suddenly into sexual ecstasy and return to, vary and enlarge upon the agonizing theme of death. Vanessa is the daughter of beautiful, crazed poet, Christine Wing, who is killed in an automobile accident. Although this tragedy takes place in the last pages, it is presaged by all that goes before, adding urgency to Maso's depiction of Christina, whose 25-year lesbian love affair in no way altered or diminished the often passionate, always gratifying course of her marriage. Maso also makes it clear that Vanessa, too, is as erotically moved by women as by men. This is a restless book, inveighing against corporate power that gets away with murder, sketching brilliant pictures of farm life and lost customs, summoning the frustration that culminates in a strapped arm and heroin in the vein. Yet all these vignettes of anger and fear and searching are in the end the author's lyric expression of love.

A review of "Ghost Dance," in Publishers Weekly, *Vol. 229, No. 17, April 25, 1986, p. 66.*

RON BURNETT

How do you relate an event so shattering that merely telling what happened fails to state the truth? Carole Maso, in her first novel, ***Ghost Dance,*** implies an answer: ignore normal narrative sequence and let the manner of telling be as important, even more important, than the ostensible subject.

Ghost Dance recounts how Vanessa Turin, who has known a tragic life (a friend's attempted suicide, violent death, insanity, drugs, difficult family life), sorts out events and values in order to come to some understanding of what life means. But because she hasn't discovered the logic of her "story" at the moment the novel starts, her "telling" cannot be in neat rhetorical packages.

Thus, what the reader witnesses is not so much a "story" as a mode of recall by a narrator who really isn't telling a story at all but trying to build a rationale for her own existence. Because she cannot face certain horrible moments in her past, she tells us about things she is more comfortable with, and, at first, they seem to come forth in random fashion. We read the early episodes without knowing if they are cause or effect.

In the final analysis, the reader will decide if the book is worth the effort. Some will be tempted, as I was, to put it aside. I finally opted—and others may also—to make a list of events, characters, and relationships in order to put together the puzzle of Vanessa Turin's story.

There is satisfaction in that. Satisfaction, too, in seeing the picture in the puzzle begin to emerge. It is a touching, if horrific story that unfolds. And the final scene seems, I repeat, *seems,* to suggest that Vanessa makes peace with the past. But I wonder if, for a first novel, author Maso hasn't been too self-indulgent, too fascinated with the lyric of her prose, and less concerned than she ought to be with the fiction she assumedly wants us to read about.

If puzzles aren't your game, this isn't your book.

Ron Burnett, "Sorting Out the Puzzle of a Tragic LIfe," in The Christian Science Monitor, *July 18, 1986, p. 22.*

MEREDITH SUE WILLIS

In Carole Maso's exquisitely written and ambitious first novel [***Ghost Dance***], a college student descends into a snow-white hell in search of her family. The novel tells of Vanessa Turin's coming to terms with the disintegration of her family through death, disappearance and insanity. Imagery ties together the book's short sections. Snow, for example, is at once cocaine, the asbestos in a worker's lungs and the setting for the massacre of Native Americans at Wounded Knee. Fire is Christmas candles, a rich variety of sexual experimentation and exploding Ford Pintos. This breadth of imagery is typical of the ambition of a novel that attempts to combine themes of family estrangement with references to historical offenses committed by the United States military and by American business. Often this combination works, but sometimes the book tries too hard for profundity. The most powerful passages are about the narrator's obsessive love for her mother, a brilliant, seductive, mad poet. "The snow is blindingly white. She is smiling. She is bathed in apricot. The poem is complete." Other family members are also captured with vivid poignancy. In one of the longer sections (a fine short story in its own right) the family attends the opening day of the 1964 World's Fair. The father and daughter visit Michelangelo's "Pieta", meanwhile, the grandfather and little brother are arrested in a civil rights demonstration. Here family and public affairs blend wonderfully. Some other sections, however, fall into melodrama. Unfortunately, several of these come at the end, during the final unraveling of mysteries. The strongest impression left, however, is of the power and beauty of many bravura passages.

Meredith Sue Willis, in a review of "Ghost Dance," in The New York Times Book Review, *July 20, 1986, p. 18.*

An Excerpt from *Ghost Dance*

My mother never listened to the weather report and consequently was almost always dressed unsuitably for the ever-changing whims of the Connecticut climate. I can see her shivering in a thin navy-blue cloth jacket in November or sweating in April in her lined raincoat, her whole face flushed.

"Why didn't you tell me?" she'd ask, shedding layers of sweaters, or, hunched over in another season, her arms clutching a manuscript against her chest in an attempt to ward off wind and cold, "Why?"

"But, Christine, I did," my father would say, nearly inaudibly. It seemed to me that he suffered from my mother's discomfort more than she did. To my father, I think, my mother's problem of dressing was a symbol of all her suffering, and because of this he could hardly bear to witness these lapses in judgment.

"Why must she suffer so much?" he wondered day after endless day, night after sleepless night, as she typed. It moved him terribly to see my mother in the middle of January in a thin cotton blouse and cardigan sweater. He seemed wounded by it.

But I thought it was a good sign, a reassuring sign when my mother knew she was dressed improperly. What I feared more than anything in the world was when she felt no weather at all—no cold, no heat, no rain—when she would walk through a rainstorm, come back drenched, and sit down to work at her typewriter, without changing her clothes, or even wiping her brow; when she came in from a walk in the snow in her sandals, her feet bright red and numb, and she, completely unaware of them. When she felt no weather, when weather did not matter, I knew it would not be long before the doctors would come and she would not be allowed out of bed. And so these days of complaining, of discomfort, of my mother questioning my father and Fletcher and me eased me in a strange way.

"Why didn't you tell me about this terrible heat?" she would ask again and again, taking off a sweater, cocking her head and squinting slightly as if to say, "If you told me, then why can't I remember?"

Her mind could not be trusted completely. It stopped, it skipped, it added, it forgot. It changed things.

"I did tell you, sweetheart," my father whispered into her ear. He held her in his strong arms. She would not go mad, he said to himself. She would not.

A simple thing like dressing for the weather might have made my mother feel more at home here, day to day, had she only somehow known how to listen to such things. She knew, though, that she had only so much energy and, considering the demanding nature of her mind, she could not afford to pay attention to everything, every conversation, every news broadcast. She knew how easily she tired. If she allowed herself to see and hear everything, she would not have survived, for everything to her was a challenge, imperfect, asking to be transformed, rearranged, made over. But she would not allow it; above all my mother was a survivor.

CYRA McFADDEN

Intensely demanding and rewarding, ***Ghost Dance*** is a novel about family, especially the bond between Christine Wing, a poet, and her daughter Vanessa.

The mother, a celebrated beauty, is greatly gifted, "an elaborate inventor, who looked squarely into the invisible. . . ." Her husband, Turin, is a quiet man whose vocation is to love Christine, and insofar as possible, to protect her; the poet fades in and out of madness.

Fletcher, their son, is an activist, a believer that human beings can and must reclaim a purer world. . . .

Daughter Vanessa shares her mother's gift for relentless and tormenting introspection. . . .

Like Christine, Vanessa is a human seismograph, acutely attuned to sensory impressions, the rest of her family's dreams and disappointments, the world swirling around her and creating a vortex.

Her first-person narrative shifts between imagination and memory; the present and the past; the real and the surreal. It's Vanessa who finally has a vision of "the Topaz Bird," symbol of her poet-mother's madness but also her creativity.

At the beginning of ***Ghost Dance*** with Christine drifting off into her private world, she follows her mother's gaze and imagines that she, too, sees the Bird, "its terrible claws, its beak curved and sharp, its feathers brutal, sharpening into points." In the novel's final pages, it reveals itself to her as it revealed itself to Christine. "I see it perfectly, I do not turn from it and it does not fly away." This time, she and Fletcher "are nearly blinded by its brilliant, jewel-like light."

Christine is dead. Turin has disappeared, off on a solitary pilgrimage whose nature only he knows. Fletcher has reappeared after his own long absence, his sense of possibility shattered, as is the family. When he and Vanessa enact an American Indian ritual, one of letting go of the dead, they're seeking to undo what Vanessa sees as the Wings' curse: "We love too much."

Written in dense, lyrical language, Carole Maso's first novel takes enormous risks, juggling level upon level of metaphor—the Topaz Bird, the mathematical theory of "the Golden Ratio," Indian mythology, Grace Kelly and Jacqueline Onassis as women and icons, facets of Christine. The book's repetition of sentences and entire paragraphs, while incantatory, eventually grates. Its eroticism has an unreal quality, sex seen through a grainy lens, and leads Maso into rare lapses of control, when her prose shades into purple. Vanessa's lover, Jack, is "a man so large he might blot out the sun with his body." (p. 3)

No more convincing are Vanessa's addiction, first to cocaine and then heroin, on an impulse so slight, "impulse" seems too strong a word. Christine's accident confirms Fletcher's view of a planet ruled by corporate criminals. Vanessa has an affair with her mother's female lover of 25 years, a "love call . . . to the other side of death, where we were sure my mother was, whole, smiling, waiting for us."

The book's strengths are greater than its flaws, however, and the flaws are honorable, born of ambition and abundant talent. I can't remember a more striking depiction of madness, or the labyrinth of family ties.

Cyra McFadden, in a review of "Ghost Dance," in Los Angeles Times Book Review, *July 27, 1986, pp. 3, 7.*

ALICIA DULAC

[***Ghost Dance***] is Carole Maso's first book. Despite the label on the dust jacket, I do hesitate saying it is a "novel." Carole writes beautifully, with a depth of imagination and fine descriptive power—but plot, continuity, and climax generally conceded to a novel are most difficult to pull from the thick cloudy context of ephemeral memories.

There is a story of sorts. Vanessa Turin has lost all her family, her safeguards of sanity and security. Only her brother still lives, somewhere far away. So, one roams within Vanessa's mind in her memories, her dreams, and her recollections as she seeks this missing and elusive contact with reality—her departed family. On the way, she remembers her mother, Christine Wing, a poet. Christine's loving attention comes alive in Vanessa's dreams. Vanessa sees her hazily at college graduation ceremonies as the key speaker and as a bejewelled figure in Grand Central Station.

Vanessa spreads her finely-tuned words in small separate paragraphs among her parents, her brother Fletcher, her friend Natalie, her grandparents, and others who have somehow entered her life in the past.

No doubt all of us, particularly those of us designated as "Seniors," have many flashing memories of this or that day, or of this or that person. Vanessa has captured this—drifting in ghostly space with no regard to time or continuity.

Toward the end of these ghostly flights of fancy, an ocean liner is suddenly introduced into the story. It steams into New York harbor with Vanessa and brother Fletcher aboard. Then come the few most beautiful and sane words in the entire book: "And over there, I say, pointing to the shining waters, have you ever seen anything like it before? So pure and perfect in its form—it is the Brooklyn Bridge!" Then it would seem Vanessa and Fletcher join hands and float over the tall Manhattan buildings, calling to the departed souls. "Goodbye. We can't come yet. We must live."

Those who dream and drift instead of living and working may be able to empathize with Vanessa and her kin. The book is beautiful, but it's my bet that it will prove too incomprehensible and irrelevant for the majority of readers. And I'll vote with that majority, Brooklyn Bridge notwithstanding.

Alicia Dulac, in a review of "Ghost Dance," in Best Sellers, *Vol. 46, No. 6, September, 1986, p. 204.*

E. M. BRONER

We writing women are connected to one another, in permission given, trials encountered, styles developed. Part of the linkage of Carole Maso's brilliant first novel [***Ghost Dance***] is her debt to Maxine Hong Kingston's *The Woman Warrior*. Kingston used family as archeology, taking the stones of a family telling and arranging them on the beach of extended memory. . . . Kingston taught us to make the personal an epic and the family tale a mythos.

Which is what Maso has done. The characters in her book are the typical American family of four, mother, father, sister, brother, living in the typical American town, Mystic, Connecticut. The difference is that this family, the Turins, has inherited or created the legends they live by.

As summer entertainment, the children research the lives of the previous inhabitants of their house. They train themselves to become the keepers of the past, the genealogists of their family, of memory, even inventing memory. To save themselves, ultimately, this sister and brother have to allow history to settle in its dust and the dead to die.

The mother of the family is a poet of world renown, Christine Wing. Christine's mother Alice was an invalid who saw the shadow of a bird over her newborn child and knew it was a bird of promise and genius, a bird spotted twice before in the German family's history. This bird will flutter, soar within the daughter's life. But she also knows it hovers over her, and sometimes sinks its talons into her brain.

Christine's presence in the life of her family is more mythic than actual. . . .

The mother and daughter meet, for the last time, in Grand Central Station. The daughter is returning to school, the mother stands in the middle of the station, over-dressed, confused. The daughter tries to wipe off the excess makeup, to remove some of the bracelets. As the daughter leaves the mother calls out, "I have loved you all my life." The small departures prepare us for greater ones. . . .

The father of the family is a romantic, present but distant. His reality is the silver screen, Grace Kelly's marriage to Prince Rainier. His sounds are not of life, of the children in the house, but of his sound-proofed room where the phonograph plays.

There are dances in the book—lyrics of songs, characters declaring themselves while dancing. The parents meet at a dance, whirl and marry. The grandmother has been forbidden to carry her Old World ways with her by her husband who is anxious for them to become Americans. The last day of her life, she rises, dresses herself in traditional Italian costume and dances the tarantella.

The children observe marriages of opposites, parents and grandparents. Their father is silent, their mother's life and living are words. Their Italian grandmother is practical; her husband is a visionary, a moralist who, in old age, travels out West to learn the secrets of the Indians. The children are the heirs of these symbiotic traits. Vanessa, the eldest, inherits her mother's physical form, and, like the mother, writes. Fletcher, the brother, a year younger, speaks out for the silent things that have no speech themselves, flora, fauna, the environment. While the daughter is the chronicler, her brother is the activist. . . . It is Fletcher, the most sensitive, who is the most injured. It is he, the speaker, who falls silent. Vanessa opens her door to Jack the Lover, who forces her, hurts and loves her back into life. . . .

In these days when many of our most distinguished writers are writing a minimalist fiction, momentary, sketchy, the mirror clouded by the breath of the narrator, the lives bounded by the immediate, one has to applaud that other strain of what Linsey Abrams in the *Mississippi Review* (Winter, 1985) calls "maximalism." Here there is texture, embrace of the larger theme, the past and future equally necessary, the family not the entity but the political part of the text. One thinks of a print-maker's "ghost print," where the second image of a monoprint floats beneath the surface as minimalism. Tapestry and the extended self are the art form of Carole Maso.

Maso's book is interrupted chronology, sometimes antichronology, the history pushed forward, backward, the narrator hearing lyrics of popular songs, names of composers chanted by the father, sayings of American Indian leaders. All that has affected the writer/narrator must be included in this book. It is like a calliope, a turn and a fragment, the brilliance of children, a segment of parents, a focus on grandparents, the tail-feathers of a bird that flits through the story.

The novel seldom falters. (The section on Vanessa's college years is weaker because no characters can be as vivid, can compete with the family.) Its great scenes are orchestral. There is a rare family outing: the grandparents, parents, children go to the 1963 New York World's Fair. As the father and daughter look at the *Pieta,* sent from Italy, the 67-year-old grandfather, with his perky bow tie, and his 5-year-old grandson Fletcher wander into a demonstration. It is a sit-in of Blacks, objecting to business as usual, calling "Freedom Now." The surrounding crowd, inconvenienced by them, begins to shout such terrible racial epithets that the grandfather enters the circle of protesters, still holding Fletcher's hand; the two of them, in the pouring rain, lie down and are arrested. From then on, Fletcher knows he must take government to task, put himself at risk. Towards the end, when he has lost connection, he can only send postcards to his sister from the various cities of his wandering, detailing which industry has polluted the surrounding land.

As in other recent beautiful novels that have crossed my desk, death is the hunter, the stalker. The losses are so great, the characters have to ask themselves why they continue to live. In Maso's book, where the sins of the nation are so grave that the idealistic young people are silenced, a way has to be found to hope. The way, between sister and brother, is familial love and ritualistic healing, as well as connection with the ancient lore of the land, the Indian lore.

E. M. Broner, "Dance of Life," in The Women's Review of Books, *Vol. III, No. 12, September, 1986, p. 13.*

LESLIE LAWRENCE

Ghost Dance is a stunning first novel, extraordinarily ambitious and just as successful.

The book does not proceed chronologically, nor is it organized into chapters. Structured more like a musical composition than a conventional novel, it is divided into five unnamed parts, each one further divided into sections, some as short as one sentence, others several pages long. Epic in proportion (though less than 300 pages), the novel contains dozens of characters, subplots, and motifs that are threaded through the whole—elaborated here, compressed there, turned upside down and inside out. . . .

All of this is told to us by the daughter, Vanessa Turin, who at times is recalling the past and at other times is relating what is happening to her in the present. (Despite her wondrous lover, we gather she is in a bad way, nearly catatonic, rarely leaving her shabby Greenwich Village apartment.) What makes this all a little more complicated and a lot more unusual is that, although the novel is essentially first person, many of the sections are rendered in the third person, as if Vanessa had intimate and perfect knowledge of other character's unspoken thoughts, of places she's never seen, of lives lived before she was born. Scenes that we first take as fact we come to realize are works of Vanessa's imagination. And it becomes increasingly clear that the imagination is the real heroine of this novel. . . .

The memories/fabrications in the early part of the novel are rosy and suspect. . . .

By the middle of the novel, however, Vanessa begins to let in some of the less pretty truths until, little by little, she can let in the ugliest truth of all: something terrible has happened to her mother, something so terrible Vanessa can't imagine it. Yet she realizes she must—must say and envision this tragedy in her mind's eye—or she will never get to the center of her pain, never get started with the mourning she must do in order to save her own life.

Ghost Dance's unconventional structure is not a pretentious, arty overlay. The structure is born of necessity; the story could be told no other way. This is not a novel about character development or about how one event leads to another. It is a novel that succeeds in conveying the enormity and fertility of one woman's mind. It reminds us that at every moment we are all that we have ever known, witnessed, believed, experienced, dreamed, imagined. . . . Time, in Maso's world, is not linear but eternal; the present is infused by both the past and future. Given this, it would be nice if we could take in ***Ghost Dance*** all at once, as we do a painting. Since we cannot, this is a novel that begs to be read at least twice.

Which is not to say that ***Ghost Dance*** is rough going the first time around. We may not, at every point, know what Maso is up to, but we quickly learn that we can trust her: she is a marvelous travel guide, giving us just enough information so that we have the pleasure of making our own discoveries in the lush, exotic world she creates. Nevertheless, in our second reading (as in our second hearing of a symphony) we can experience the beginning differently, now knowing what we do about what comes next, and we can appreciate the whole even more, knowing how all the parts relate. In short, ***Ghost Dance*** gives us the best of both worlds—the aesthetic pleasures of a beautifully wrought work of art, and the dramatic and emotional pleasures of a good read.

Ghost Dance is distinctive in other ways, too. Vanessa may be most at home in her imagination, but other characters and events in the novel demand that she acknowledge the power of political and cultural forces, and, as readers, we come to see how her private grief is inextricably linked to the grief of a nation that has lost its way. Grief, in fact, is the cord that binds the book's seemingly disparate motifs.(p. 38)

Sorrow, yes, loss, longing, outrage—these permeate ***Ghost Dance.*** And yet the book is in no way dreary. It appeals to the senses as much as to the mind and heart. Maso's prose is passionate and lyrical, sumptuous and erotic, fresh and charming at every turn. . . . Even if ***Ghost Dance*** were not so magnificently conceived and controlled, it would dazzle on the strengh of its language.

Yes, ***Ghost Dance*** has some flaws. A few of the very brief sections seemed gratuitous, the topaz bird symbol wore thin, and at times the apotheosis of the imagination seemed forced. I was irritated by the fact that none of the women in the several lesbian relationships suffered any discomfort over how the world might regard them. There were too many climaxes in the last section, and the final scene struck me as operatic; I couldn't but it.

But these are quibbles. The characters are splendid and the novel is rich, moving, and wise. (pp. 38-9)

Leslie Lawrence, "'Ghost Dance': A Stunning Success," in Sojourner, *Vol. 12, No. 4, December, 1986, pp. 38-9.*

THE VIRGINIA QUARTERLY REVIEW

Carol Maso's first novel [***Ghost Dance***] is a family chronicle, a hazy, unfocused story, written in sometimes poetic, more often hallucinatory prose, stretching over lumps of quotations, and interspersed with bits of wisdom that have the ring of "insights" from an old college notebook. All the family members are, to some degree, unstable. . . . Maso tries, without success, to employ the musical technique of repeating motifs, and too frequently skates over the edge into fantasy. . . . This is a disturbing book by a gifted writer hypnotized by her own prose; her occasional clichés, and the misuse of 'like' for 'as' are puzzling, coming from a writer so dedicated to style.

A review of "Ghost Dance," in The Virginia Quarterly Review, *Vol. 63, No. 1 (Winter, 1987), p. 21.*

Daphne Merkin

1954-

American novelist, critic, short story writer, and editor.

Enchantment (1986), Merkin's first full-length work of fiction, impressed critics with its compelling depiction of a young woman obsessed by memories of her painful childhood. Merkin is a senior editor at Harcourt, Brace, Jovanovich and a contributing editor of *Partisan Review*. Her literary and film criticism, as well as her short stories, have appeared in many distinguished journals including the *New Leader, Commentary,* and *The New York Times Book Review;* part of her novel originally appeared in *The New Yorker*.

Enchantment consists of a long confessional narrative by Hannah, a twenty-six-year-old from a wealthy Orthodox Jewish family on New York's East Side, painstakingly recounting her childhood traumas in an attempt to understand the emotional problems she suffers in adulthood. At the heart of the novel is Hannah's disturbing, unresolved relationship with her mother—a cool, detached woman with rigid views of child rearing—from whom Hannah hopelessly longs for warm, maternal affection. Hannah's ruminations irritated many critics with their self-absorption, bordering at times on self-pity, but reviewers also emphasize that Merkin compensates for this weakness by her subtle humor and her rare powers of insight and observation. Above all, reviewers state, it is Merkin's evocative vignettes of family life and the candid portrayal of Hannah herself that give *Enchantment* its haunting fascination.

KIRKUS REVIEWS

In outline, [***Enchantment***] is rather familiar, unpromising material: poor neurotic little rich girl, from an Upper East Side orthodox Jewish family, kvetches about her parents in relentlessly confessional prose. But that's where convention ends, and one of the most unusual voices in contemporary fiction begins. Not even a novel by most standards, Merkin's debut organizes itself through the controlling consciousness of its narrator, Hannah Lehmann, a 26-year-old self-described shlump who is haunted by an obsession with her past.

At the center of her "black thoughts, doubt, and malice," is her family, "a kind of closed system," difficult to "penetrate from the outside." So instead she circles and circles around it, providing snapshots, vignettes, seemingly random insights and images, as well as an "emotional geography." A truly Proustian effort to conquer time, her painful, humiliating, and self-pitying narrative nevertheless burnishes some indelible portraits in the reader's memory. The siblings: two sisters and three brothers in constant, frenzied rivalry for the affection and attention that comes mainly from a staff of servants. Their number include the kind but inaccessible Negroes—the cook, the laundress, the chauffeur—and the cruel European nurse whose vicious spankings in the past provide Hannah the eroticized model for her present S&M encounters. There's her father, busy all the time at the work Hannah doesn't bother to learn about. But it's the tyrannical influence of her German-born mother that Hannah is trying most to escape. A woman toughened by "war and death and loss," she is the ultimate object of Hannah's divided self, driven by love and hate. The book progresses by such contraries—victim/victimizer, pleasure/pain—but also with a "wit deflecting anxiety."

It's hard not to think that, having gotten this always elegant and intellectual, but at times infuriatingly self-involved, book out of her system, Merkin just may well write a truly great one next time out. (pp. 964-65)

A review of "Enchantment," in Kirkus Reviews, *Vol. LIV, No. 13, July 1, 1986, pp. 964-65.*

PUBLISHERS WEEKLY

This piercing evocation of family life [***Enchantment***] chronicles a child's obsessive enchantment with her mother—a "hopelessly entangling skein of anger and need and pain." If this memory of self-described, anal-retentive Hannah Lehmann, who grows up in material wealth but emotional deprivation, incorporates too much therapy-talk (right down to accounts of steaming feces) as well as a self-absorbed whine, it is also gifted with rare insight and a deft and witty style. Merkin . . . weaves fragments of Hannah's past and present from the protagonist's claustrophobic and relentless vantage, vividly rehashing every last familial grudge and longing as she masterfully unfolds the tragedy of Hannah's paralyzing inability to exorcise an oppressive parental omnipresence, which is mostly of her own making. Her mother wishes that she wouldn't make "mountains out of molehills"; Hannah does so with such candor and lack of sentimentality that the reader is forced to bear witness with frustration to her self-pity; with fear to her capacity for self-destruction; with empathy to her painful transition from needy child to responsible adult. Elegant depictions of the ordinary, such as a favorite pair of washed-out cotton pajamas or the contents of an almost-bare refrigerator, and the accurate portrayal of Orthodox Jewish life are especially skillful.

A review of "Enchantment," in Publishers Weekly, *Vol. 230, No. 3, July 18, 1986, p. 79.*

RALPH NOVAK

The focus of this sorrowful, disturbing first novel [***Enchantment***] is a young woman whose hopeless love-hate relationship with her mother dominates her life. The "enchantment" of the title is what most people would call a curse: "the spell that bound me, a desolate adjunct, to (my mother's) side." Hannah Lehmann comes from a wealthy New York family and has never been mistreated in any overt way, yet she has grown up wanting to belong to other parents. "I am 26," she says, "but I am really 6, looking to be special." This is really a long rumination by Hannah, with little in the way of action, yet Merkin sustains it, largely through the emotional energy the daughter exerts in trying to undo the irrevocable. On the one hand, she wants to be rid of her mother; on the other, she wonders, "Without my mother, who will cut up the world into bite-size pieces for me?" Hannah's relentless self-pity can get annoying; her mother's abuse of her seems subtle and chilling, yet the daughter courts that abuse, and perhaps imagines some of it. (Hannah's insistence on feeling abused has become a major part of her problem.) That self-pity is neutralized, however, by Hannah's sense of humor and the rueful kind of wisdom she displays. When her father takes a break from nagging a taxi driver to tell her how tired he is, for example, she muses that "he is tired because it is very tiring to trust no one—neither daughters nor cabdrivers." The ending avoids the melodramatic, though Hannah's masochistic relationship with her lover seems ominous enough. The book could have been better edited. Hannah cites the same quote from the Alfred Hitchcock film *Vertigo* twice to no purpose, and at another point she says she smiled exaggeratedly for a picture, "like a cheetah," when Merkin apparently meant "chimpanzee." Nonetheless, Merkin . . . has created a vivid character who commands sympathy even when she is not being very likable. Her turmoil carries the impact and burden of reality.

Ralph Novak, in a review of "Enchantment," in People Weekly, *Vol. 26, No. 9, September 1, 1986, p. 16.*

An Excerpt from *Enchantment*

Doesn't everyone begin happy? More or less inclined to embrace the world (I'm taking those innate differences of temperament child psychiatrists are always arguing about into account) but basically content to be born? Or are there those who sense the sorrow the world has in store for them already in the cradle, furrowing their infant brows in an adult manifestation of distress?

My mother didn't believe in cuddling babies too much, in giving them ideas. The experts like Dr. Spock may have advised against letting a child cry longer than fifteen minutes, but there I am in a baby photograph screaming myself wild. I am holding on to the bars of a playpen set in the garden, wearing nothing but diapers; I can't be more than a year old, yet my hair looks as if it has turned white and my face wrinkled from crying. Even now, in those conversations about styles of mothering that take place all around her, my mother insists on the dangers of picking up babies too quickly when they cry. "Americans," she says, "with their one or two babies apiece! Americans let their babies rule the house!"

Perhaps this Teutonic training in early self-control should have hardened me, thickened my infant skin into something reptilian, capable of surviving the jungle. But what if it has effected the opposite result, created a permanent weakening of my ability to distract myself with small pleasures? If such a process did in fact occur—and I've come to believe it has—it must have begun way back then, with the mobile of plastic ducks in cheerful primary colors that hung over my crib and failed to inspire a gurgle of joy. Without that image of consolation flashed and reflashed on my early brain like a winning ace in a deck of cards—The Mother who ran to pick me up when I cried—how was I to develop faith in the coming end of sorrow?

JOHN GROSS

When Hannah Lehmann was 10 years old, she went to summer camp. Desperately homesick, she sent her mother a succession of tear-blotched letters: "I love you so much. I miss you terribly. Please let me come home." Her mother tore up the first of the letters and sent it back to her with an accompanying note: "This is what I will do with each and every one of these letters." Hannah persisted, even so, and in the end the family driver came to collect her in an enormous car—the talk of the camp. When she got back, her mother wasn't home.

By the time we learn about this particular episode, near the end of ***Enchantment***, it comes as no great surprise. In the course of the novel, Hannah has already plied us with examples of the emotionally constricted atmosphere in which she was brought up, and the "coolly punitive approach" to which she and her brothers and sisters were subjected. Her mother, it has been made clear from the outset, is "citric rather than lactic," incapable of showing her children unconditional love or allowing for the free play of their personalities. Naturally enough, one of her favorite complaints is that none of them has inherited her joie de vivre.

And father? He makes money, down on Wall Street, he attends endless fund-raising dinners, he is fond of words like "clout"; when he flies into a rage, "he is a red crayon scrawled every which way across a paper until it is all covered." Hannah doesn't find him very seductive—but then, while she was still a little girl, she recognized that he wasn't "seducible," either, "that he took me in without being in any way stirred by the proposition that I existed."

Her thwarted love for her mother affects her far more deeply. It is an addiction, an obsession, the "enchantment" of which the novel's title speaks. She feels it smothering her, like a witch's cloak, or worse—the Lehmann parents originally came from Germany, as refugees, and, in the darkest moments of her adolescence, Hannah used to fantasize that before her mother married her father she had been an officer in a concentration camp.

Now she can look back, with the unflinching gaze of a patient who hasn't been cured but who knows almost everything there is to be known about her condition. ***Enchantment*** is an unsentimental family album; in her mid 20's Hannah takes stock, mixing past and present, summoning up scenes that still reverberate and incidents that still smolder. Many of the things she recalls she would rather forget, but her memories refuse to go away. *"You are stuck with us,* they say. *Try getting friendly."*

Much of the power of ***Enchantment*** comes from its directness—almost, at times, its brazenness—and from its determination to hold nothing back. But for a writer to be unembarrassed by the material she puts into a book is no guarantee that the result is not going to be embarrassing. In the wrong hands, the inside story of the Lehmann family, dirty linen and all, could easily have made uncomfortable reading. As it is, thanks to Daphne Merkin's subtlety and sureness of touch, it is a story that draws the reader on unresisting.

For a start, everything in the book is firmly realized—the inner workings of the family, the distinctive style of each of the children, the penumbra of cousins and neighbors, the Jewish background (a religious one), the Germanic echoes. Then, witch's spell or not, it is a book about growing up, and one that convincingly conveys the flavor of adolescence in, roughly speaking, the Beatles era. It is also very much a book about New York, the Upper East Side in particular, and the New York locales with which it deals are lovingly and freshly delineated. ("Lovingly" in the artistic sense, which certainly doesn't exclude "satirically"—it is often very funny.)

Still, in the end ***Enchantment*** stands or falls by Hannah, and Hannah seems to me doubly successful, both as character and narrator. As a narrator, she inspires confidence; at any rate, you feel that most of her perceptions are accurate, and that you can sense when they are exaggerated or distorted. As a character, she is wholly credible and, in her way, formidable. She recognizes her compulsions—the urge not to throw anything away, for instance, since the things she keeps are evidence that she exists, that she isn't just "an important figment in my own snarling imagination." She understands, all too clearly, the forces that have made her what she is. And yet not everything can be explained by external circumstances. She is left with an indefinable sense of wrongness, denied the full luxury of self-pity by "the dull clang of my self-dislike."

One result is a pattern of relationships first spelled out in her infatuation (hauntingly described) with another girl at school, who boycotts her and torments her until she begs forgiveness—not for anything she has done but simply for being who she is. If the dismal affair she is having with a kinky, cold-blooded lawyer at the end of the book is any guide, this is the masochistic shape of things to come.

What we hear very little about, on the other hand, are her time at college, her job, any of the ways in which her intelligence and force of character might have helped her to carve out a life, or part of a life, beyond childhood's emotional thrall. And though she comes to see that her mother must once have suffered crippling blows, too ("at some predetermined moment I was designated as the carrier of my mother's unspoken fears"), the insight isn't enough in itself to break the fatal spell. Right to the end, ***Enchantment*** continues to describe a closed world—but with a liberating energy and wit that make one very curious to know what Miss Merkin is going to write next.

John Gross, in a review of "Enchantment," in The New York Times, *September 8, 1986, p. C18.*

JANET HADDA

"Desires that aren't met don't go away, they just get twisted," muses Hannah Lehmann, the opulently temperamental protagonist of Daphne Merkin's ***Enchantment.*** Hannah . . . is consumed by unrequited love, but you will find scant ordinary romance in this memorable, eccentric first novel.

Hannah's passion centers on her mother, in whom perfumed softness and rigid, punishing authoritarianism are seamlessly combined. Margot Lehmann subjects her daughter to unpredictable, apparently random treatment; kindness alternates with indifference and sheer cruelty, the last no less tormenting for being verbal and frequently subtle. Hannah is hooked, driven by an obsessive suspense that, to her, means being alive. Again and again she must navigate the shifting boundary between approval and rejection, never knowing on which side she will come to rest.

Despite its gloomy preoccupation, ***Enchantment*** is a lively, evocative, often amusing work. Through Hannah's voice, Merkin deftly captures the concentration on self-definition—as well as the doubt and frustration—of dawning womanhood. In this respect, the novel is deeply female. The adolescent's uneasy blend of childishness and maturity emerges brilliantly in scenes such as one that features Hannah shopping with her mother. Forced to comply with parental choice, she finds herself possessed of a dull but utilitarian winter coat. "I'll look like a doorman," she wails, helpless and close to tears. Yet moments later, transformed, she sits in Lord & Taylor's coffee shop, chatting demurely with her recent enemy.

Hannah struggles doggedly to maintain her dignity, but success is capricious and fleeting. At 14, sufficiently mature and skillful to advise her mother on up-to-the-minute cosmetic tricks, she must nonetheless remain at home with her fantasies and a host of siblings, while Margot, luminous in fur and diamonds, sweeps off to join her husband at the Waldorf-Astoria.

Hannah's is an unusual Jewish family—at least as represented in current American fiction: wealthy, ritually observant, German. At first glance, this is possibly the most intriguing aspect of ***Enchantment***, and it is therefore disappointing that the depiction is so lackluster. Nothing about Hannah's parents stands out as distinctly German Jewish except, perhaps, their discomfort with emotional excess and Margot's penchant for Spartan discipline.

In contrast, Hannah's grandparents, cameo figures in the novel, exemplify the strange mix of European and Jewish sensibilities that epitomizes German Jewish culture: The grandfather, his bearded face reminiscent of Freud's, is secretly more at home reading Thomas Mann than dissecting religious texts; the grandmother, product of an aristocratic British secretarial/finishing school, devotee of "shoes, *marrons glaces,* linens," smells cleanly of 4711 cologne and is wispily out of place in the bustling heat of Jerusalem. They earn the name *yekke,* a sobriquet for German Jews that implies admiration as well as disdain—depending on the user.

The prototypical *yekke* was urbane, earnest, discreet, and, above all, proud to be German. Reflexes of this personality, attenuated to be sure, still survive today. In Merkin's rendition, the German Jewish psyche becomes a vague and faded realm, comprising a handful of German expressions and, mainly, Margot Lehmann's harshness. This poorly serves a refined, if perplexing, heritage.

At the same time, however, the pallid version of Hannah's immediate environment is crucially important, because it dramatizes the stifling nest in which she is trapped. Late in the novel, she comments: "Somewhere in this story is a tragedy, but it is nearly impossible to see." Hannah's is a quiet sorrow, stemming from years of inconspicuous brutality: She writes a frantic, pleading letter from summer camp, only to have it returned in pieces, together with a note: "This is what I will do with each and every one of these letters"; Margot, in retaliation for an insult, ignores her despairing child for 10 excruciating days. Such inflictions, often accepted with the wretched conviction that they are deserved, form the basis of miserable, even tortured lives.

Enchantment is a pioneering novel, although probably not to everyone's taste, for it is strong medicine. The author insists that the bedrock of psychological development lies in primary bonding experiences. Sexuality, independence, creativity—even obsession and so-called masochism—are influenced by the child's first relationships.

At issue is not instinct but love, love of the most basic sort: neither perfect nor all-encompassing, since that is hardly possible, but steady, affirming, robust. Where there is no fundamental belief in one's own acceptability, the result is a terrified and vulnerable self. Merkin refuses to relent: Hannah, a victim of inconsistent nurturing, may forever be doomed to cling, waiting for the improbable day when her beloved finally sees the light. (pp. 2, 12)

Janet Hadda, in a review of "Enchantment," in Los Angeles Times Book Review, *September 14, 1986, pp. 2, 12.*

PATRICIA HAMPL

The enchantment Hannah Lehmann endures in Daphne Merkin's first novel [***Enchantment***] is really a thralldom. "Who will ever see my mother as I do," she asks, "the consuming irritant of my life, my unrequited love?"

Hannah insists that she has a mother problem, but her plight is considerably richer. This is a family story, a first-person narration told in photo album style. (p. 7)

Mrs. Lehmann, a refugee from Hitler's Germany, immigrated first to Palestine and later to America. But as a girl, Hannah entertains the fantasy that her mother is really Ilse Koch, chief female SS officer at Auschwitz. She recognizes that the notion is "ludicrous" but sees it "as a measure of the lengths I went to try and make sense of her arbitrary cruelties."

The trouble is, there aren't enough arbitrary cruelties here to make a villain. Perhaps Mrs. Lehmann is a woman who simply copes too well: "If mothers were merely arrangers," Hannah says, "she would have made a marvelous one." Mrs. Lehmann remains a curiously indistinct personality who is analyzed far more completely than she is embodied.

On those rare occasions when she is allowed to appear in an extended vignette, she seems not unfeeling, but possessed of a peasant faith, an airy confidence in life's habit of righting itself. "Hannah, it'll be fine," she says in her signature phrase, repeated several times in ***Enchantment.*** "You'll see. Nothing's so terrible."

"Stop griping," Hannah's sister Lily admonishes her; she seems to be speaking for everyone Hannah knows, and thereby bedevils her still further. Even Dr. Klein, one of her several psychiatrists, reminds Hannah that "by your age . . . the problems reside within you. Your mother has no real power over you anymore, other than what you give her."

Hannah can't seem to fasten onto the generative power of taking that responsibility, however; she remains impotent though enraged—"burdened with all this insight." One of the unfortunate effects of what Hannah calls her "ferociously interior" temperament is that what is meant to be her pain often reads as torpor.

"Why do I remain loyal to the pain of childhood?" she asks in one of the many questions that punctuate the novel. "If your heart is broken early enough, do you begin to mistake pain for love?" "What happens if the people you want to save . . . don't want the scenario you're offering?" The questions are meant to stitch together the narrative, to locate past and present episodes in the hive of Hannah's reflections.

They are the genuine conundrums of the novel, of Hannah's heart—and perhaps contain the mystery of family bondage. Hannah never answers them, but that alone does not explain the disappointment of this novel. Such questions do not require answers so much as enactment.

Here these questions promote the static insight Hannah bemoans but clings to. More significantly, they rob the narrative of dramatic potential. There is little dynamism in the way people hurt each other in this novel. The force keeping pain alive is Hannah's intelligence, her "insight." Hannah would not need to be an appealing character to make her unhappiness come alive. But her obsession with her family's past needs to be seen against the backdrop of her daily life, about which we hardly know anything, not even if she has a job. Hannah's memoiristic voice rarely displays detachment; and though her insight is indeed acute, she uses it largely to make judgments.

This is a pity, because in individual scenes—a walk with her grandmother in Jerusalem, a limousine ride to a benefit dinner with her father—Ms. Merkin . . . allows Hannah a fine regard for the eloquence of gestures and banal conversation. There is elegance, even dignity, in much of the writing at the level of the sentence, but it all plays back into the pool of Hannah's insight, which in the end becomes her vanity.

Insight is valuable insofar as it propels a character to the threshold of action. But Hannah maintains the value of insight as a thing in itself, her lonely bastion of sensibility. She is so aware of having been inadequately loved that she allows herself the supreme hatred—not of her mother, but of her own future. It feels like a strange, disembodied suicide. (pp. 7, 9)

Patricia Hampl, "Hannah, with Her Implacable Needs," in The New York Times Book Review, *October 5, 1986, pp. 7, 9.*

PATRICK PARRINDER

Daphne Merkin's first novel, ***Enchantment,*** has the obsessively circular and cyclical quality of a bad dream. The story is little more than an accumulation of episodes in which Hannah Lehmann, a contemporary New Yorker in her mid-twenties, picks away at the scars left by her unhappy childhood in a large, wealthy and strictly Orthodox Jewish family. If families, according to Hannah, are like locked trunks, this particular trunk and its contents are relentlessly scrutinised from the inside. ***Enchantment*** is a memorable portrait of narcissistic self-hatred, in which the author's wit and powers of invention succeed in maintaining the interest and pace of a narrowly confessional and therapeutic narrative. (pp. 16-17)

Daphne Merkin is rightly unapologetic about the financial comfort and social privilege that underpin Hannah's situation. Nevertheless, it is hard to imagine such a self-absorbed narrative emerging from many novelists of an earlier generation. A subtle feature of ***Enchantment*** is its use of a sustained though highly indirect and discreet mode of allusion to recent Jewish history. Hannah reflects, in the mode of *qui s'excuse s'accuse,* that she and her contemporaries have 'no Hitler to wake us out of our dreams of self'. She is bored by Jewish history lessons, unresponsive during her visits to grandparents in Israel, and capable of indulging in casual terrorist fantasies. More serious are the stereotypes she would like to impose on her mother and father. The unloving father becomes a Shylock figure, her tough-minded mother a Jewish Nazi. For all her lucidity, Hannah does not begin to achieve the objectivity and compassion needed to view her parents as the victims, not the agents, of historical oppression. Their lives, as we piece them together from the scattered hints that she lets fall, must have been very much harsher than anything within the range of Hannah's experiences. She is all too ready to pass judgement on her parents but, imprisoned by her own self-projection as the Sleeping Beauty, she cannot learn to forgive their inadequacies. Here Daphne Merkin, an elegant writer with an acid cutting-edge, has created an all-too-believable heroine. (p. 17)

Patrick Parrinder, "Charmed Lives," in London Review of Books, *Vol. 9, No. 8, April 23, 1987, pp. 16-17.*

Sue Miller

19??-

American novelist and short story writer.

The Good Mother (1986), Miller's widely acclaimed novel, is the result of a lengthy apprenticeship, both in writing and in life. Miller credits her highly praised portrayal of the mother-child relationship, the heart of the book, to her own role as a single parent and to her eight years of work in a day-care center. "It was the best thing I ever did. I saw millions of families, millions of people, and I intersected with their lives at a very vulnerable point. It gave me more insight into human experience than anything else I could have done."

Miller had published several short stories in literary journals and had written two earlier novels, which she considered unworthy of publication. It wasn't until *The Good Mother* that Miller felt she had sufficiently found her voice. It is informed, she observes, by her moral perspective. Miller is influenced by her ecclesiastical family—her father is an ordained minister and both her grandfathers were Protestant clergymen. Several reviewers note the novel's moral viewpoint. "It *is* a didactic book and finally that's the kind of person I am and that's the kind of writer I am," Miller explains. "The fiction I care about has that sort of attitude. That's part of the deep pleasure of reading, and that's what I aspire to. It sounds terribly grandiose but that's it, that sense of making a turning that lifts the narrative beyond being 'just a story.'"

The story of *The Good Mother* is told from the point-of-view of Anna Dunlap, a woman struggling after her divorce to build a life for herself and her four-year-old daughter, Molly. She becomes involved with Leo Cutter, a local artist, and though their relationship brings Anna greater happiness and sexual fulfillment than she had thought possible, an accusation of sexual irregularities between Leo and Molly creates an irrevocable change. While several reviewers note that Anna shares a dilemma similar to her literary forbears, Anna Karenina and Emma Bovary—the choice between erotic love and mother love—it is apparent, too, that Anna Dunlap is no tragic heroine. Neither is she a character impelled by feminist energies or self-help formulas; she is, some critics observe, passive to her fate. This stance is purposeful, notes Miller, and is part of the novel's moral message. "For me, the book is about the sense—the false sense—that we are essentially in charge of our destiny. It's about what suffering and sorrow mean in our lives. . . . I was also interested in the meaning of the heroic in domestic life—I mean, a life that's constrained by ties to other people. It seems to me that when life is constrained that way our ability to be heroic takes on a whole different meaning. To me Anna is heroic, although she doesn't stand up in court and say, 'The hell with this—I'm going to do it my way.' When you have other people's lives at stake and other people's emotions involved, I think you need to look at different definitions of heroism—domestic definitions."

Though few events in the novel are autobiographical, critics observe that *The Good Mother* seems remarkably realistic, effecting an absorbing story on a timely topic with vivid and believable characters. In addition to the integrity and sincerity with which Miller explores the difficult issues of divorce, child custody, child sexual abuse, and passion and responsibility, reviewers praise her ability to sustain an intense narrative pace, rich in psychological detail. While some commentators quarrel with the qualities of the protagonist or the message conveyed, most agree that the novel delivers a provocative and honestly written fiction.

© Jerry Bauer

ROBERT WILSON

The Good Mother, Sue Miller's pretty good first novel, explores in a serious way the struggles between passion and order, the individual and society, the bohemian and the bourgeois, the feminine and the masculine. And yet it manages to tell the particular, affecting story of a mother's custody battle for her daughter.

Miller's prose is poised, if not inspired, and tends toward reflection, so that every so often it throws off observations and perceptions that stick in the mind. Her main characters, even including Molly, the disputed child, are plausible and complex, and her minor characters emerge cleanly.

But among all these virtues lingered a vice that very nearly spoiled the book for me. In one of its aspects ***The Good Mother*** tells of its first-person narrator's awakening as a woman. The familiarity of this as a subject is not the problem. What bothered me was Miller's penchant for some of the conventions of such novels—what you might call the menstruation syndrome.

It's not only menstruation, of course, it's also masturbation, flatulence, flaccidity and its opposite, all the little details of sexual and bodily function, both female and male. I hope I'm not just being squeamish. For me, fiction does not follow function. We all function in much the same way, and besides we read about it ad nauseam in novels of a decade or so ago. This sort of detail tells nothing about character and little about life. It makes ***The Good Mother*** sometimes seem a throwback to a kind of novel we've simply outgrown.

Even so, a certain amount of sexual detail *is* important to Miller's story. Her narrator, Anna Dunlap, has split up with her uptight lawyer husband, Brian, who immediately marries Brenda, another uptight lawyer, and moves from Cambridge, Mass., to Washington, D.C. Molly, who is 4, stays with Anna, who is determined to support them as best she can, teaching piano lessons and working a part-time job running rats through mazes for a professor.

Into her life comes Leo Cutter, a painter who introduces her to passion. There follows a long romantic swoon, during which everything about Anna's world becomes sexually charged. She and Leo get careless about Molly in a sexual way that seems almost natural in the context of their relationship. (It's to Miller's credit that she can make it seem so.)

When Brian finds out about it, though, he takes Anna to court to fight for custody of Molly. In the cold light of the law, Anna and Leo's relationship seems quite different. Miller makes the court case both dramatic and convincing, and effectively interweaves the impersonal legal machinations with the almost devastatingly intense emotions Anna feels for Molly and Leo.

The Good Mother is an intricate and mature novel. It's so much better than most of those other books suffering from the menstruation syndrome that I wish it didn't so often bring them to mind.

Robert Wilson, "The 'Good Mother' Who Loved Too Well," in USA Today, *April 4, 1986, p. 4D.*

MICHIKO KAKUTANI

A quick summary of the plot of ***The Good Mother*** tends to sound like a standard soap-opera scenario. . . . As it turns out, however, ***The Good Mother*** does not resemble a soap opera at all. Thanks to Sue Miller's gift for precise psychological detail, her sure sense of narrative and her simple compassion for ordinary lives, this powerful novel proves as subtle as it is dramatic, as durable—in its emotional afterlife—as it is instantly readable. In Anna, the "good mother" of her story, Mrs. Miller has created a hip, passionate narrator, a modern heroine, who suffers not from alienation and malaise—those staple afflictions of so many fictional characters today—but from a surfeit of feeling for two people in her life, her daughter and the man she loves.

As we learn in several flashbacks, Anna is someone who has always defined herself in terms of family: her mother's family, a somewhat snobbish clan of overachievers, who are fond of nicknames and holiday celebrations; her father's family, a more taciturn group, who value neither ceremony nor chatty endearments, and, until recently, her own family—her husband, Brian, a minister's son, and their 4-year-old-daughter, Molly.

Anna, it quickly becomes apparent, is both an articulate and persuasive narrator—though her voice is not particularly distinctive, its very directness proves highly compelling—and we come to experience her life through her own eyes. Her sense of hurt over her failed marriage; her fierce caring for her daughter; her shifting feelings of selfishness, pride, tenderness and passion—all are made palpable to us by Mrs. Miller.

A woman who came of age during the 50's and 60's, Anna often feels caught on the margins of changing morality—torn between the old rules that differentiated between "good" girls and "wild" girls, that held up marriage, respectability and decorum as the large ideals; and the hectic, new imperatives of sexual freedom and self-fulfillment. In fact, in her attempts to reconcile the conflicting demands of freedom and responsibility, Anna reminds the reader less of any recent heroine than of those troubled men in John Updike's fiction, who are always trying to mediate between their need for independence and their yearning for safety and a home.

For a brief space of time, Anna believes that she's actually managed to put everything in her life into perfect balance. Having just come out of a seemingly amicable divorce, she's met a wonderful new man, an artist named Leo, who's "everything my family, Brian, I, were not"—poor, self-sufficient and somewhat reckless, someone who's good at pickup conversations in bars and subways, someone who's emotionally committed to his work and a vision of the world, and perhaps most importantly, someone who's unabashedly sensual and passionate.

Not only do Anna and Leo rapidly assemble a brave, new life together, but her daughter, Molly, also seems to share their happiness—she likes Leo, maybe even loves him; and the three of them give the impression of being a perfect family. "I felt I'd never been so happy," Anna recalls, "and perhaps I never was. Our lives seemed magically interpenetrated, commingled, even as we each separated into all the day's complicated activities. I had never expected it to seem so graceful and easy, but Molly's seemingly complete comfort with Leo was like a benediction on all aspects of the relationship, even the sexual."

Suddenly, however, this happy little world comes flying apart: one day Anna's ex-husband calls to tell her that he's keeping Molly for good, that she's been sexually molested by Leo, that she—Anna—has been grossly negligent as mother. Is it possible, Anna wonders, that Leo is capable of such a thing, that she's never really known him at all? Is it possible that her sweet daughter has maligned him—for the sake of winning attention in the wake of the divorce? Is it possible that she has brought all this about by some private failure?

By the time the custody hearing's begun, it's fairly clear that several misunderstandings lie at the center of the accusation—in the novel's one real lapse of narrative, the explanation offered seems muddled and glossed over—but already the damage has been done. Anna's feelings—toward Leo, toward her ex-husband and even toward Molly—have been irrevocably altered, and in her loss of innocence, she is forced both to reassess her own role in the unfortunate spiral of events and to accept a sad, new configuration of emotions.

In relating Anna's story, Mrs. Miller raises a lot of questions about the nature of sin and guilt and redemption; and, by indirection, she also addresses various questions about modern sexual morality and familial duty. Yet if she evinces a somewhat irritating tendency to turn her male characters into stereotypes—the ploddingly devoted, unsexy husband, the wild and crazy boyfriend—her novel bears little resemblance to those preachy feminist tracts so popular a few years ago. Mrs. Miller is not interested in making any sort of argument for—or, for that matter, against—liberation. She is interested in examining the ambiguous consequences it has had on the lives of individual women, men and children; and in doing so, she's written a remarkably assured first novel.

Michiko Kakutani, in a review of "The Good Mother," in The New York Times, *April 23, 1986, p. C20.*

CATHERINE PETROSKI

Readers may expect first novels to follow certain conventions: first-person narratives of personal education, introspective, given to excesses of lyrical language and short on plot. ***The Good Mother*** may be Anna Dunlap's own story of the aftershocks of her marriage's dissolution, but Sue Miller is absolutely no ordinary first novelist. ***The Good Mother*** would be an extraordinarily skillful piece of fiction from a veteran, so as a first book it is a very remarkable accomplishment.

Certainly this is one book that's not short on plot. Anna Dunlap's story mesmerizes the reader till the last page is turned. . . .

Sue Miller has an eye for the perfect detail to crystallize the emotional impact of her character's situation. We see the author's canniness in her choice of starting the novel after the breakup; Anna's taken Molly on a "vacation" and though Molly is rather a pain, we are charmed by her language—full of unconscious ironies and the distractableness of a child's voice.

Later in the book, we smell the paints in Leo's studio, pick through the creative clutter with Anna. During the custody battle, we and Anna are surrounded by double-standards and biases of lawyers, case workers, even judges. Beyond the wonderful detail, the novel's pacing is authoritative, the transitions bold, the story engrossing.

Yet some may not be completely comfortable with ***The Good Mother*** and, as much as I am in awe of the book's accomplishment, I confess I am such a reader. Fiction's business needn't be to comfort, but some readers want—after having read a novel—to feel that its characters and their relationships are either finally back in some sort of order or that they tried desperately to achieve some kind of order, not that people and relationships are so hopeless they're not worth worrying about. ***The Good Mother*** asks us to consider what, in this day and age, is a "good mother?" As much as one wants to like Anna, she's not a basically admirable character because she perpetually operates in the default mode. Because she never does take charge in any significant way, we're left with the nagging suspicion that Anna's brought her problems on herself. She inevitably responds to other's actions rather than initiating her own. Anna never transcends her confusion of self-fulfillment and selfishness, so her spirit never really wins me.

Catherine Petroski, "'Good Mother': A 1st Novel in a Class by Itself," in Chicago Tribune, *April 27, 1986, p. 45.*

LINDA WOLFE

Every once in a while, a first novelist rockets into the literary atmosphere with a novel so accomplished that it shatters the common assumption that for a writer to have mastery, he or she must serve a long, auspicious apprenticeship. The novel arrives, all its parts gleaming, ticking, and we are filled with awe. However did the novice learn to build this thing? We marvel. But the question is beside the point, which is that the thing exists, has form, energy and power. This is the case with Sue Miller's ***Good Mother,*** the work of a writer who has thus far published only a handful of short stories.

The book is about the passionate attachments of Anna Dunlap, the devoted mother of a lively toddler. Like that other famous Anna before her, this one loves two people—the child she has had with her husband, a humorless, conventional lawyer, and a man who is not that husband. But Anna Dunlap is divorced, and therefore, presumably, free to love where she will. That she cannot, that "life without limits" is not, in the end, possible for Anna Dunlap any more than it was for Anna Karenina—although for subtly different reasons—is one of the many fascinations of this novel about the risks and responsibilities of love. (p. 1)

In a way, what Miss Miller is telling us here is an old story. Tales of women who, married, feel no sexual passion, only to discover such passion outside marriage and pay dearly for the pleasure, have haunted literature since its inception. Indeed, the first account with which I'm familiar was written in Egypt sometime during the 18th dynasty by an unknown scribe recording an even more antique legend. It told of a woman known simply as "Ubau-anir's wife," a fool for love who lost her high station, and eventually her life, because she felt passion not for her husband, but for another, less eminent but more enticing man.

The risk-laden predicament of women who love men other than those to whom they are married seems always to have preoccupied writers, and certainly it inspired the creation of some of the most memorable heroines of Western poetry and prose: Phaedra, Isolde, Francesca da Rimini and, coming to more recent times, Hester Prynne, Madame Bovary, Edna Pontellier in Kate Chopin's novel *The Awakening,* and, of course, Anna Karenina. All these heroines paid dearly for their passion, usually with their lives. Still, one would have thought that in the age of divorce, the old story would have lost its bite. Not so, Miss Miller tells us. Ecstasy out of wedlock can be costly even to divorced wives.

The price exacted from Anna Dunlap is different from that demanded of most of her literary forebears, but it is probably no accident that Miss Miller has given her heroine the same name as Tolstoy's. Among the great 19th-century novelists who wrote about women in love with men not their husbands, it was only Tolstoy whose heroine is attached as keenly to a child as she is to a lover or lovers. Emma Bovary, in pursuit of her sexuality, is neglectful of her daughter. Edna Pontellier, in pursuit of hers, scorns what she calls "mother-women" and considers her children antagonists. But Anna Karenina, living with her lover Alexey, is in despair over being separated from her son, Seryozha. "Do you see," she confesses to a friend shortly before she kills herself, "I love—equally, I think, but both more than myself—two creatures, Seryozha and Alexey, (and since) I can't have them together . . . I don't care about the rest.'' She is speaking about life.

This duality of affection is Anna Dunlap's burden. And so it is interesting that when this Anna is confronted by Anna Karenina's dilemma, or at least by what she perceives as the same dilemma, the need to choose between child and lover, she sacrifices the lover. When Leo urges her to show some self-respect and fight for her right to have both him and her child, she tells him, ''I just want Molly. I don't care about *dignity,* or *pride,* or any of that stuff.'' Even more interesting is the fact that this Anna eventually voluntarily incriminates herself for the acts of adult sexuality that Molly may have witnessed, and shoulders all the blame. She doesn't, as a 1960's or 70's heroine might have done, excoriate society or the men in her life for her predicament; rather, she accepts, even invites, her punishment, believing that the truly good mother, which is what she ultimately most longs to be, would never have succumbed to a ''euphoric forgetfulness of all the rules.''

Miss Miller, it becomes clear, is ringing a clever change on the old literary preoccupation. It is a change that could only have been composed now, when women, having thoroughly explored the possibilities inherent in sexual gratification so long out of bounds to them, appear to have discovered that a passionate attachment toward a child may not be just equal to, but more powerful than, the ties that arise through erotic love.

The novel is constructed on several levels. It is a suspense story for Anna as well as the reader: What has Molly seen? What, if anything, has Leo done to the child? Will Anna succeed in regaining custody? It is also a novel about a problem—is it damaging for a child to be exposed to episodes of adult sexuality? Has Anna in fact injured her precious offspring? Wasn't she herself, as she supposes, injured as a child by her own parents' secretiveness about sex, which gave her the feeling that ''even *having* flesh was a form of mortification''?

And, on a third level, the book is a traditional first novelist's effort, an autobiographical exploration of the familial forces that have gone into creating a central character's consciousness. Thus, Miss Miller focuses not only on Anna's present relationships with Molly, Brian and Leo, but on her past involvements with her parents, cousins and grandparents. She is the only child of an ineffectual father and an ambitious mother, and the granddaughter of a wealthy New England inventor and investor who, although now retired, will let no one in the family forget his power and authority. Anna's mother, perhaps to curry favor with the grandfather, wants Anna to make something of herself, and pushes her toward a musical career.

Anna rejects the career. She knows she hasn't got real talent and, besides, she scorns the family's emphasis on achievement, competition and financial success, stern goals that overlook more human, emotional possibilities. She has seen several of her female relatives destroyed by this family predilection, among them her devil-may-care aunt Babe and her kindly, nurturing grandmother. Specifically, they have both lost children, an anguish about which they rarely speak because, according to patriarchal values, as exemplified by the grandfather, the subject is not quite fit for dwelling upon.

Nevertheless, as Anna comes to realize, her relatives' unspoken, unspeakable losses eroded and corroded their spirits. (The subject of maternal attachment, long brushed aside as limp or trivial by male and female writers alike, is hardly an unfit one, in life or literature, Miss Miller seems to be saying. And certainly the scenes devoted to the subject are remarkably vigorous—particularly one in which the long-subdued grandmother comes to Anna's economic rescue.)

In part, it is the complexity of this novel, its three levels, that saves it from being soap opera. But even more, what makes the book truly remarkable is its authenticity. Miss Miller speaks, in the book, of ''the healing beauty of everything that is commonplace,'' and I found the phrase significant, for one of the greatest pleasures of ***The Good Mother*** comes not from its lively story or its timely topic, but from the author's skillful rendition of the ordinary, particularly the commonplaces of motherhood. I think virtually no one has done it better.

Here is Anna eating out with her daughter: ''I never tired of looking at her. Sometimes she'd find it annoying, as though I were taking something from her by loving her so greedily with my eyes, ''Don't *look* at me, Mommy,' she'd say, and cover her eyes with her hands as though then I couldn't see her anymore.''. . . .

Anna herself is so finely drawn, so particularized, that she is almost as rich as John Updike's Rabbit Angstrom. And because her creator has endowed her with acute psychological sensitivity, her observations about herself and others are often quite profound. Of the failure of her marriage, she speculates, ''Brian . . . was as stern, as judgmental with himself as I was with myself. I thought that I would slowly, with his solicitousness, his loyalty as a support, become a more and more passionate person. . . . But then I saw that he couldn't change me, that we were too alike, really, to lift the other out of himself.'' . . .

Nor is it Anna alone who is fully developed. This is no narcissistic one-character novel. Miss Miller introduces us to a large cast of idiosyncratic and vivid individuals, not just Aunt Babe and the grandparents, but Anna's histrionic friend Ursula, her baby-faced lawyer Muth, her argumentative uncles and gossipy aunts.

Having said all this I must add that I have not revealed the full complexities of the plot or the book's moving conclusion. Do I have any quibbles? Well, perhaps the custody trial reads a bit too much like a court transcript. Perhaps little Molly is at times a shade too clever, the kind of wiseguy waif in whom films specialize. But in view of how rarely something this good comes along, it would be foolish to be faultfinding about ***The Good Mother.*** (p. 40)

Linda Wolfe, ''Men, Women and Children First,'' in The New York Times Book Review, *April 27, 1986, pp. 1, 40.*

RON BURNETT

The ingredients author Sue Miller brings together in ***The Good Mother*** are not unusual in modern fiction. (p. 21)

What is unusual about this first novel is the skillful treatment and evocative presentation of several complex moral dilemmas.

Miller's first-person narrative embraces two time frames: In the present are Anna's day-to-day struggles as a single mother; in the past, a recollective account of her childhood. In the narrative of present time there is a sharp, almost startling, clarity of focus.

But the episodes drawn from childhood are slightly misted; the novelist allows her lens to blur the background landscape, thus highlighting the figures in the foreground: Anna, her parents, grandparents, relatives, friends.

Memories of the past are redefined by Anna's measurement of them against the needs of the present. She finally understands that what appeared to be inattention on the part of her paternal grandparents was, instead, a kind of freedom she had never known until she spent a summer vacation at their home.

And her Aunt Babe, seen through Anna's childhood eyes as a kind of wondrous free spirit (though a black sheep to the rest of the family), is ultimately understood as a rebel testing—and defeated by—the confines of her father's (Anna's grandfather's) rigorously contained world.

Childhood, Anna discovers, is not always what it seemed to be.

What are the moral dilemmas Anna faces?

To remain in a loveless marriage with her husband for the sake of Molly, or seek self definition on her own. To live a celibate life as a single mother or enter into sexual liaisons with some of the men she meets. Whether to place her daughter for a portion of the day in a day care center, while she works part-time in a university laboratory. Whether to allow her daughter and her lover, Leo, to develop a quasi father-daughter relationship without the protection afforded by marriage.

The fulcrum on which the novel's plot pivots is the allegation by Anna's ex-husband that Anna's lover has molested Molly, and the ensuing custody trial.

Miller's treatment of this high point of tension in the novel is dramatic, discreet, compassionate.

Each development in the legal process increases the tension. The drama heightens, the suspense builds, character is further developed, and the latitude for choice logically narrowed.

Like a final judgment, the custody decision breaks over reader and character alike.

Everything required for an assessment of the rightness or wrongness of the events we have been witness to is in place. But the option is solely the reader's.

I found myself pondering the ambiguities, identifying and measuring my own guidelines, and then applying them to the fictive questions to see if they would fit.

Some measure of the novel's ability to get under the reader's skin is, perhaps, indicated by the fact that regardless of the direction my own adjudications took, I was left unsettled and unsatisfied by their ultimate implications.

While many readers may be put off by Miller's graphic treatment of her protagonist's relationship with her lover, I feel they will be drawn inexorably into the bind and bite of the novel's cause-and-effect world. (pp. 21-2)

Ron Burnett, "Custody Battle Is the Focus in a Sensitive First Novel," in The Christian Science Monitor, *April 30, 1986, pp. 21-2.*

An Excerpt from *The Good Mother*

Still we were trying to keep it from Molly. We didn't discuss it much, and by now Leo was spending three or four nights a week in my bed, but he got up faithfully each morning he slept over and was out of the house before she emerged from her room. Once or twice it was the noise of her beginning to putter in her room which woke us, but then Leo would kiss me, rise swiftly from the bed and pull on his clothes, and be gone barefoot down the long hall nearly as quickly as the half-formed memory of my dreams faded from me.

I'm not sure why we didn't tell her. She seemed irrevocably to like Leo, so it wasn't the fear that it would threaten their friendship. Perhaps part of it was simply that I didn't understand what significance it might have to her to know that he and I were sleeping together, and so wasn't sure how to explain it. As for Leo, he was again following my lead. It was a fatal part of his sweetness to follow me, even in my confusion, to assume always that I knew what I was doing with her, around her. I fostered it. I never articulated to him my anxiety, the sudden rush of feeling I sometimes had with her that I was doing everything wrong. He saw my mothering her, her relationship with me, as implacably monolithic, a given, what was meant to be, and took all his cues from that. Even the grace of his uncomplaining rising in the morning—the quick tilt back of his hips to zip his fly, the wings of his half-buttoned shirt flying out as he turned to enter the hallway—seemed emblematic to me of his assumption of rightness in whatever I was doing with Molly.

JONATHAN YARDLEY

[***The Good Mother*** is] a first novel, with all the predictable characteristics and shortcomings of apprentice work: a self-absorbed first-person narrator, labored expository passages, prose that reaches for an excess of lyricism, and a plethora of extraneous detail. Yet though its artlessness can be distracting and irritating—especially in the first 150 pages, before Sue Miller gets command of her story—***The Good Mother*** is redeemed by its author's not inconsiderable strengths: a willingness to cope with serious, complex issues, and a sincerity that is genuinely appealing. . . .

There are elements of courtroom and domestic melodrama in [***The Good Mother***] just as there were in the considerably more artful *Kramer vs. Kramer,* but they are of less consequence than the serious issues Miller raises. The central one is that there is no such thing as "life without limits" and that one of an adult's most important obligations is to discover what those limits are: to learn, that is, the rules by which one's life must be lived. . . .

The most effective scene in the novel occurs when Anna, confronted with her lawyer's $2,500 retainer for the custody case, goes to her grandfather for money; not merely does the encounter place her in direct conflict with the world of her past, it also shows the unexpected divisions and rivalries within that world itself. From her grandparents as from the court, she learns that you can't have it all.

That's one of several sound, refreshingly adult conclusions that Miller reaches in ***The Good Mother,*** so it's all the more a pity that the novel is considerably less successful as a work of fiction. If ever an author has had a show-and-tell problem it is Miller, who belabors her thematic material to a fare-thee-well; though she has woven this material quite successfully into her story, she insists on examining it didactically as well, apparently not trusting the reader to discover it on his own. She also takes far too long to get her tale into place; not until she has given us prolonged, repetitious background material on Anna does she at last move into the heart of the book, the custody case, and only then does ***The Good Mother*** come alive. She gets high marks for seriousness and sincerity, but—even though ***The Good Mother*** can be recommended as intelligent and provocative—low ones as a novelist.

Jonathan Yardley, "A Family Divided: Living, Loving, and Losing," in Book World—The Washington Post, *May 4, 1986, p. 3.*

JOSEPHINE HUMPHREYS

Anna Karenina was not a good mother. Sex distracted her from maternal interests. In horror she finally realized that obsessive love for Vronsky had crowded out her love for Seryozha, her son. Emma Bovary wasn't a good mother, either. Poor Berthe whimpered at home while Emma and Léon rolled through the streets of Rouen in that ominous carriage of love, windows closed against the world.

Fiction since Emma and Anna has tended to follow the rule implied by Flaubert and Tolstoy: the sexual misbehavior of mothers will be punished, if not by loss of life then by harm to children, an even more gruesome penalty. (I'm thinking particularly of two recent novels, Louise Shivers's *Here to Get My Baby Out of Jail* and John Irving's *The World According to Garp*.)

Sue Miller's stunning first novel, ***The Good Mother,*** examines the issue of mothers in love with a thorough attention to contemporary mores. Her Anna (surely the name is not an accidental choice) is married to a man not unlike Alexei Karenin or Charles Bovary. The crime of these husbands is that they are boring. Brian Dunlap is not a bad man, not a bad father. In a moment brilliant with the pain of divorce, Anna hears her 4-year-old daughter, Molly, say to him, "I really hate my mom, don't you? We *hate* her, right?" And Brian's answer is at least as wise as the advice books. "No," he says, "I can still love Mom even though she and I don't want to live together anymore. And you can still love her, even though you're being with me for a few days. You can always love us both."

But Anna doesn't love Brian; he has become "peripheral" to her life. The divorce is amicable and clean; one wonders what might have become of Emma and Anna K. if they could have got divorces and custody and flextime jobs, as Anna D. does. She gets a chance to start over again, to live happily in Cambridge with her daughter—poorer, to be sure, because she is a piano teacher and will never earn as much money as Brian, a lawyer, but she doesn't mind. She is a strong, independent woman, without much interest in money.

And she's a good mother. Not a Supermom, but a mother who loves and respects her child while leaving room for her own growth. The dialogue between Molly and Anna is beautifully written; it reveals an unusually comfortable friendship between mother and child.

Everything goes smoothly. Anna succeeds in establishing her independence not only from Brian but also from a set of controlling parents and grandparents, and she finds a job to supplement her income from the piano lessons. She even meets a man, the dark and shaggy Leo, artist and enthusiastic lover. (p. 648)

Things go so well, in fact, that one begins to glance around nervously for the story here. The pace of the narrative has been an easy lope; halfway through the novel there is still no major conflict, certainly no hint of the clash between "two powerful sets of feelings, the erotic and the maternal" promised on the dust jacket. (pp. 648-49)

It is a mark of Sue Miller's masterful narrative technique that when the plot suddenly rounds a bend upon an enormous surprise, it seems at once an unexpected and inevitable turn. The story is off and running, building a momentum that never flags. The surprise, as enormous to Anna as to us, is this: Brian sues to regain custody of Molly, alleging that Leo is guilty of "sexual irregularities" with the child.

Anna's world changes. In an instant, outsiders—lawyers, social worker, psychiatrist, judge—converge on the threesome that had seemed to Anna so magically happy. The court must decide whether Leo is guilty of the charges, and to what extent Anna can be held responsible for the atmosphere of permissiveness that allowed such an incident to occur. Anna is sure of Leo's innocence, or at least of the innocence of his intent: the charges are based on an accidental meeting of Molly and Leo in the bathroom, when Molly, seeing Leo naked, asked if she could touch him, and he, in confusion and in the spirit of openness that Anna had established in the household, said yes.

After the rich, introspective first half of the novel, the second half is streamlined and cinematic, made up of courtroom dialogue and interviews instead of Anna's thoughts. It's as if her thoughts had drained away under the scrutiny of the public eye. Since there are no criminal charges, there are no limits to the inquiry, and custody will be awarded by the subjective decision of a judge. Anna's whole existence is relevant. No question is left unasked. A caseworker discovers in the course of an interview that Anna and Leo once made love while Molly was asleep in their bed with them. A lawyer wins from Leo an admission that he involuntarily "responded sexually" the time Molly touched him. Anna begins to understand the sort of nightmare she is in, one in which private truth begins to look grotesque.

Sue Miller manages the emotional drama of these scenes so expertly that one is not likely to notice that the original issue has turned murky. What was the question? Whether erotic and maternal love can coexist? But they did, easily; the trouble came from elsewhere. Whether sexually miscreant mothers are punished by society? But this mother got her divorce fair and square, and surely nobody is suggesting that she and Leo ought to have got married before sleeping together. Not even Brian's lawyers say that. The issue now has become whether a woman can lose her child if the man she loves makes a mistake, and how hard she will fight to defend him.

But Anna doesn't fight at all. She betrays Leo instead of defending him. How are we to read this ending? She loses custody of Molly anyway, as it was obvious she would. Lawyers prevail. Her surrender is an act of fear rather than courage. Anna knows Leo is not to blame—but she blames him, losing her child and her integrity at once, and for no great cause.

It is true that custody cases are regularly lost in this ignoble way. The novel is realistic, timely, important. But Anna looked at first as if she might prove to be heroic. Instead she does herself in, as surely as if she had gone under the wheels of a train or stuffed her mouth with arsenic. In her acceptance she resembles another antecedent, Hester Prynne. "You never even *tried,* Anna," a friend says after the case is lost and Anna has begun her new existence, diminished and passionless, her hope as intense as an orphan's.

How brave that a first novel should attempt these extraordinarily difficult questions, questions so emotionally tough that they complicate the usual business of the novel, the expectations of character and plot. And how brave of Sue Miller to avoid easy answers, to leave the puzzle finally unsolved. Because her Anna is, in the end, human rather than heroic, the novel is all the more disturbing and powerful. (pp. 649-50)

Josephine Humphreys, "Private Matters," in The Nation, *New York, Vol. 242, No. 18, May 10, 1986, pp. 648-50.*

MARY PINARD

Sue Miller's elegant and penetrating first novel, ***The Good Mother,*** is Anna Dunlap's story. Newly divorced, Anna tries to adjust to life as a single parent: Molly, her four-year-old daughter is precocious, energetic, demanding. This character is so real, so true to the integrity and independence of a four-year-old, I don't remember when I've met such an accurately drawn child in fiction. . . .

Anna's "new" single life forces her to look closely at herself. This kind of attention and consideration has never been encouraged in her life. In general, women don't have the time (or the support) to ponder their own lives, their intimate selves. After all, that would mean taking oneself seriously. But in the course of the novel, Anna manages to see herself in situations she never thought possible. What she observes is at once comforting and disturbing. . . .

The Good Mother is a finely crafted novel. I felt an odd grief when it ended; I did not want the connection I felt with the characters to end. The narrative intensity and lush prose style make it an absolute pleasure to read. But it is also the first novel I've read that deals in such an adroit way with the often paradoxical make-up of the mother who strives to be "good" despite her own needs. Sue Miller gives us a gift in the character of Anna Dunlap whom we can love and learn from. A woman who in her perceptive, intimate reflections does justice to the complexity of women's responsibilities in our culture and shows how there is always more courage, more self-knowledge, more strength than we can imagine.

Mary Pinard, "Caught between Motherlove and Passion," in New Directions for Women, *Vol. 15, No. 4, July-August, 1986, p. 10.*

JOANNE KAUFMAN

In style and content, ***The Good Mother,*** a first novel by Sue Miller . . . , is certainly more ambitious and more sophisticated than most of its current neighbors on the best-seller lists. But despite its incendiary subject—a divorcee's fight for custody of her four-year-old daughter because of her lover's sexual brush with the child—***The Good Mother*** is an arid business.

The characters—Anna Dunlap, the eponymous good mother; her artist lover, Leo; her ex-husband, Brian; and her daughter, Molly—seem distant, as though being viewed through the wrong end of a telescope, or vaguely distasteful.

It's not that Anna's situation doesn't demand empathy. She either will lose her daughter (under the circumstances, one can only wish that Ms. Miller had made Molly more appealing; unfortunately, she's a wispy-haired whiner) or she will lose the first man with whom sex has meant pleasure, then incalculable joy (under the circumstances, one can only wish that Ms. Miller had made Leo more appealing; unfortunately, he's a bit too irresponsible, a bit too cranky to be anyone's Prince Charming). That Anna herself is so ineffectual makes it difficult to summon up interest in her plight, let alone sympathy.

"Now there was nowhere in my life I felt at home," writes Ms. Miller describing Anna as a high school student. "I feel completely false to myself, that there wasn't any center to me." It seems an apt description of the adult Anna as well.

Though the book does occasionally come alive, notably when Anna goes to borrow money from her autocratic grandfather to finance her custody fight, as well as during the custody fight itself, such scenes are not enough to give ***The Good Mother*** lasting resonance.

Joanne Kaufman, "Heft and Heavy Breathing," in The Wall Street Journal, *September 10, 1986, p. 28.*

CHRISTOPHER LEHMANN-HAUPT

There is a gun in Sue Miller's best-selling first novel, ***The Good Mother,*** about a divorced woman named Anna Dunlap and her legal fight to keep custody of her 4-year-old daughter, Molly. And that gun eventually gets fired, just as Chekhov would have insisted it must. But the circumstances under which its trigger finally gets pulled aroused such strong and ambivalent feelings in this reader that its report has continued to echo in my head with a volume that surpasses the dramatic power of Ms. Miller's story.

The gun is planted, somewhat gratuitously, about a third of the way into the novel, when Anna Dunlap is describing her new lover, Leo Cutter—the man who has awakened her sexually for the first time in her life—and how life "seemed to reach in and touch" him "in a way it never did me." "Once he even bought a gun, not because he wanted or needed it, but because he'd never owned a gun before." He buys it from a black man in a bar and puts it in his bureau drawer.

Then, at the climax of the novel, when Anna's world has collapsed around her. . . . Anna, in despair, goes to Leo's apartment, digs out the gun from the bureau drawer, and heads out to commit some as yet undefined act of violence.

At this point, my mind neatly divided itself into two opposing emotions. The brute part of me shared Anna's rage and much wanted to see her commit some extreme act of violence, whether against her former husband, her lover, her daughter, or even herself, it didn't much matter. But at the same time the more civilized part of me realized that there was no appropriate object for this rage. To kidnap Molly at gunpoint, as Anna consciously plans to do, would destroy whatever few rights as a mother she still had left to her. To kill anybody, including herself, would be pointless. Anna has her rage, but it is trapped by reason.

As it turns out, Anna ends up firing the pistol harmlessly at a sand dune. She throttles her rage, faces the reality of her loss, and decides to accept the humiliation of seeing her daughter on her former husband's terms. For all her discontents, civilization has finally prevailed.

My rage continued to boil for Anna, nonetheless. Why could she not have exacted some form of revenge? If she were a gunfighter in a western, someone would be made to pay for her suffering. Why, if she were any man, she would find some way of striking back. It's because she's a woman that violence isn't done. It's the schoolmarm against the cowboy again. Whenever there's a woman around, violence must be repressed and civilization prevail.

But then I got to thinking of the many violent women in serious and popular literature. . . . Plenty of women have acted out violent forms of retaliation in literature. . . .

Plenty of women have pulled triggers, too: Frankie, who shot Johnnie in the popular song, because "he done her wrong"; Ibsen's Hedda Gabler, who "dies beautifully" by putting a bullet through her head because, unlike Anna Dunlap of ***The Good Mother,*** she can't bear to be manipulated by someone with power over her; and of course the wife in Ernest Hemingway's short story "The Short Happy Life of Francis Macomber," who shoots her husband when he at last begins to assert his masculinity.

But the most apt parallel to Anna Dunlap has to be Medea of Greek mythology, who murders her two children by Jason when he repudiates her to marry the daughter of Creon, and whose story has been repeated sympathetically in several plays and operas. Why, it occurred to me on finishing Sue Miller's novel, could she not have written a *Medea* in modern dress, and make Anna fire that pistol with more tragic effect?

The answer to my question was supplied by a couple of shrewd women I know. They pointed out what I'd failed to recognize, that ***The Good Mother*** is really an attempt to dramatize the common female fantasy that if a woman lets herself go sexually she loses control of her world, including her ability to mother. Anna's loss of Molly is her punishment for allowing herself to be sexually awakened by Leo. She accepts her penalty with shoulders bowed and fires her pistol into the sand.

Christopher Lehmann-Haupt, "How a Good Mother Expresses Rage," in The New York Times, *September 15, 1986, p. C12.*

DARCIE CONNER JOHNSTON

The word *passion* pervades the current flurry of reviews and articles about ***The Good Mother***. . . . Responses to Sue Miller's first novel have been no less than passionate, but I wonder if the spotlight on Anna Dunlap's sexuality . . . is blinding readers to both the book's finest points and its flaws.

This is a book about Anna more than passion, and certainly more than sexual passion. In many ways, yes, passion is central, if self-control can be considered its other side. Anna's sexuality is only one arena where passion and restraint hang in a balance; it is a template duplicated in her approach to her child, her work as a musician, her relationships, and even herself. And contrary to what most of the writing about ***The Good Mother*** indicates, Anna's scales are heavily weighted in favor of control.

Often this control is an admirable strength, but at other times it is a handicap. For example, when her ex-husband Brian calls to announce, passionately, that he is keeping their daughter Molly, Anna stifles panic and disbelief and tries to deal calmly with someone who is clearly irrational. It does not work. Tragically, the impression she gives is one of falsity. Indeed, her internal state is far from calm during the conversation, but Brian interprets her composure as lies about her ignorance, as complicity in the "crimes" against Molly. If passion had been met with passion at this critical point, the story might have ended far differently.

When Anna's passion does flare, she describes those moments with detached wonder. The feeling she conveys in the sexual scenes with her lover Leo is more one of awe than abandon: "Is that me?" she seems to muse. Similarly, in a crescendo of emotion toward the end of the book, when passion and control vie at their highest pitch, her detachment gives way to fragmentation:

> I was driving carefully, slowly, because the rational part of me understood that I mustn't be stopped, I mustn't get caught with the gun in my purse. Courteously, while I wept and talked to myself about what a sensible thing I was doing, I yielded the right of way coming on to Route 93, I let other cars slip ahead of me as we merged from eight lanes down to two at the Callahan Tunnel.

"After this experience," she says, "I forever understood the expression *beside yourself.*"

The scene culminates when Anna fires the gun over and over until its bullets are spent. Even this frenzied act, though, is tempered by its having taken place on an isolated beach, with Anna firing the bullets downward into the sand. Ultimately she buries the gun, afraid someone might have heard her, and runs away. It is perfect: Anna's passion, Anna herself, hidden beneath a smooth surface and deserted.

This is where the beauty of ***The Good Mother*** lies—in the consistency and depth of its central character. Anna Dunlap is real. Other praiseworthy aspects of the book include the subtle, even ingenuous, power play enacted between Brian and Anna; the many other believable characters, most notably Anna's antithesis, Leo; and the feast of rich, true scenes and dialogue, such as Anna and Leo's first fight, the sessions with the psychiatrist, and the courtroom meetings.

So much of ***The Good Mother*** is so sharp that the flat characters (few) and scenes (several) are startling. The contrast makes one wonder how much of the book is autobiographical, a speculation to which first novels and their authors are vulnerable, and this debut work in particular has the tone of a journal. Perhaps the less successful scenes are those that Miller had to invent to fill out the plot. Or perhaps she diminishes actual events and people in order to protect someone: For example, the characters of Anna's parents are almost entirely absent, and the daughter Molly becomes strangely vague as the story progresses. Or, some of the scenes that do not work may be real events that Miller simply burned to commit to paper.

Most notably, the reflections on Anna's youth, though they are engaging, do not seem integral to the plot. One way they could have contributed would have been by providing insight into why the adult Anna thinks and acts as she does. What were her parents like? What was her place, what was expected of her, and what were her relationships like within her extended family, whose members, but not the interpersonal dynamics, are described in detail? Years later, Anna is restrained to the point of passivity, and in fact, she could be considered a victim. Focusing on the relationships might have deepened the reader's understanding and unified the novel.

In spite of its weaknesses, ***The Good Mother*** deserves attention. Unfortunately, much of what has been written is superficial, and some even distorts the book. For example, the jacket claims a "stubborn emergence of courage, acceptance, hope" for Anna, and reviews for the most part do not contest this summary. Yet the prevailing atmosphere in the final pages—masterfully evoked by Miller—is more one of resignation, frustration, and despair.

Perhaps the publicity emphasizing the book's passion is designed to increase its popular appeal. . . . But in the end, this one-dimensional treatment could do the book, its author, and its audience a disservice. The subjects of divorce, custody, and self-exploration—in all forms—are also timely and compelling enough to draw a wide audience. To nurture Miller's gifts and provide honest feedback, as a good mother would, is to ensure her growth as a good writer.

Darcie Conner Johnston, "Blinded by the Light," in Belles Lettres, *Vol. 2, No. 2, November-December, 1986, p. 13.*

DEBORAH NAVAS

> "Babe lifted her head and shivered. For a moment she sat staring across the dark lake at the spot the music seemed to come from. Then she bent her head and gently kissed first one, then the other of her bare knees. She shuddered again and pulled her sweatshirt over them. Never, even later in her most overt wildness, did she seem more aberrant to me, more separated from what I understood my family to be, than in that moment of tenderness to her own body. . . . I came to think of Babe as a cautionary tale."

This is Anna Dunlap speaking, [the central character of ***The Good Mother***]. She is describing her favorite aunt, Babe, who so perversely loves her body and is the family renegade. She becomes pregnant out of wedlock and is hustled off by an older sister to Switzerland, where she delivers and gives up her baby. A few years later, drunk, Babe dives out of a rowboat into the lake that borders the family's Maine summer home, and drowns. It is a cautionary tale indeed, and emblematic of Anna's larger story.

Babe's story is a familiar cautionary tale to more than Anna Dunlap. Its message—that female sexuality is equated to sin, and the wages of sin is death—has been preserved and passed down through the descendants of New England Puritans such as Anna Dunlap's propriety-serving family, and passed along by religious traditionalists everywhere. It would be nice to believe that the sexual revolution did away with such an unenlightened view of morality, but ***The Good Mother*** makes it clear that such an assumption, for Anna Dunlap anyway, is simply wishful thinking.

Chapter One opens with Anna in an interlude before her divorce, spending a few weeks with her three-year-old daughter, Molly, in a rented New Hampshire cottage. . . .

Anna's idyll with Molly is jarred to a conclusion when she has to find a notary to witness her signature on a divorce-related document. . . .

Anna's divorce goes through—a civilized divorce where she and her lawyer ex-husband, who has fallen in love and plans to marry another woman, compete in niceness—and she gains custody of Molly. Sue Miller is a fine and observant writer, and so the familiar fictional territory of Anna's reentry as a single person—her voluntary adjustment to less affluence, difficulties with her family, new friendships, a new job—seem fresh and poignant. Inevitably, Anna finds a new love too. The erotic scenes are a pleasure to read on both an artistic and sensual level. If the sexual revolution hasn't affected attitudes much, at least it has affected writing about sex; few writers, before, treated the subject with this combination of honesty and discriminating sensibility.

Euphoric with her sexual awakening, Anna includes Molly in this new bodily joy, wanting to impart an openness about sex to her daughter that she was denied as a child. Molly accompanies Leo into the bathroom when he showers; once she crawls into bed when Anna and Leo are making love, thereby laying the grounds for a custody suit from Anna's enraged ex-husband. The novel turns on the resolution of the suit. In order to get her daughter back, Anna comes to believe that she must give up her love and her sexual fulfillment in order to be a good mother to Molly. The denouement is beautifully and meticulously wrought, absolutely true to the purposeful and accidental pain people inflict on their children and each other in the name of love.

The Good Mother is a powerful book, powerfully felt. Having Anna tell her own story in first person narrative rather than the more cosmic omniscient third person point of view was a deft choice. An omniscient narrator would have given this story a different dimension and breadth—more like *Anna Karenina,* which is as much a political story as it is a personal tragedy. Reviewers have made much about the allusion to *Anna Karenina* in Sue Miller's choice of her protagonist's name, but ***The Good Mother***'s intention is different; the allusion simply adds resonance. First person makes it an unavoidably personal story; Anna's character is revealed through her voice as much as by what she does. . . .

The Good Mother never intended the grand political scale of *Anna Karenina,* declaring that a mother who pursues sexual passion is doomed to become train fodder. Its intention, as I see it, is to show how Anna Dunlap, like her aunt Babe, is ultimately bowed by the sheer weight of a repressive value system—her family's values and the values of society in the form of an antiquated court system. Encouraged to believe that her sexuality was a poor second alternative to a career as a concert pianist, she came to believe that her options boiled down to jettisoning her sexual self in order to keep her daughter. That misperception of events was Anna's tragedy—she didn't have to abandon Leo, she only saw it that way because of the persuasive weight of her upbringing, her passive nature, and her masochism—what her grandfather referred to as her "perspective . . . on suffering."

It surely can be argued that women are manipulated by society at large and family at close hand to be doomed to such a regrettable choice, and the story illustrates how well those forces do their work. But ***The Good Mother***'s strength is that it's not a simple cautionary tale, and Anna is not simply a victim. Anna did have a choice: she could have fought back, as her friend Ursula pointed out to her.

Sue Miller's first novel is a tour de force—fully developed and satisfying, artfully written, packed with meticulous and original small observations, and informed with fine intelligence and hard honesty. My only criticism is a niggling one. ***The Good Mother*** raises an interesting question: How shall we live a moral life as mothers and sexual creatures in this post-revolutionary age? ***The Good Mother*** doesn't say, but the fictional acknowledgment that women have a moral as well as sexual and maternal life is a new idea on the literary front. I hope Sue Miller will tackle it again with her next novel.

Deborah Navas, "Home Deliveries: Cautionary Sex & Violence," in New Letters, *Vol. 1, No. 1, Spring, 1987, pp. 9-10.*

Susan Minot

1956-

American novelist and short story writer.

Monkeys (1986), the title of Minot's first novel, is also Rosie Vincent's affectionate term for her children. As seen through the eyes of Sophie, Rosie's second child, *Monkeys* is a portrait of the Vincent family, extended over thirteen years in which the monkeys grow up, their father fades into an alcoholic silence, and Rosie dies.

Like her characters, Minot was raised in a northern suburb of Boston. She began writing the stories that would later become *Monkeys* in 1981, publishing several in *Grand Street* and *The New Yorker*. Reviewers note the warm tone evident throughout the novel and praise Minot's precise prose style and skillful use of detail in evoking the complex and enduring nature of family relationships.

KIRKUS REVIEWS

[In ***Monkeys*** you] can hear the voices of the masters—the descriptive economy of Hemingway, the imaged delicacy of Virginia Woolf, and, above all, the informing echo of J. D. Salinger (darkness and breakdown lurking just under a middle-class things-as-usual surface)—in these spare, carefully wrought, and often moving stories. A rather well-off family in Massachusetts with seven children (the "monkeys" of the title) has a father who drinks too much, a mother who dies in a car accident, and a future that somehow must be lived.

In "Hiding," earliest of these chronological pieces, mother and children "hide" from Dad (in an upstairs closet) only to find, rather shakenly, that he doesn't come look for them, but turns on the TV. "Thanksgiving Day" shows grandparents entering senility and despair after lives that were once, it seems, exotic and rich. "Allowance" takes the family to a Bermuda vacation, where Dad is worried about "things at the bank," drinks too much, empties a glass of water over his head at the restaurant table. "Wildflowers," tugging heartstrings to the danger point, shows the death of an infant, the birth of another. "Party Blues," the one real failure in the volume, tackles adolescent love, inflates it beyond what it can bear, and falls flat. Dad's drinking is handled with a similar overdramatization in "The Navigator," as is, but more forgivably, a son's acting out of grief in "Accident." "Wedlock" (beautifully) sketches the first Christmas after the mother's death; "Thorofare" is the scattering of her ashes at sea.

The risk of a mere fashionableness is here, in the peculiarly "literary" quality of aesthetic contentedness while studying, purportedly, the manifestations and effects of half-nameless but pervasive anxiety and fear. Much, though, in the stories is tone-perfect, and much, escaping convention, will bring moments of recognition to readers, and feeling.

A review of "Monkeys," in Kirkus Reviews, *Vol. LIV, No. 5, March 1, 1986, p. 332.*

SHERIE POSESORSKI

In his poem "Chansons Innocentes," e.e. cummings encapsulated in his "mud-luscious . . . puddle-wonderful" childhood world those exhilarating, evanescent moments of sheer joy experienced by children tumbling and leaping through their lives. That mud-luscious paradise is where we first meet the seven rambunctious Vincent children (affectionately called monkeys by their mother), in Susan Minot's striking and original first novel [***Monkeys***]. In a series of interconnected stories spanning 13 years, Minot chronicles the mundane and miraculous moments that characterize family life.

Few novels have captured, as Minot beautifully does, the octopuslike collectivity of family life. In her novel, she is not as much concerned with characterizing the individual members of the Vincent family as she is with portraying the experiential and spiritual growth of a family's collective identity. In prose that is exactingly realistic yet delicately lyrical, she so vividly depicts the lively and frenzied lives of the Vincents that the book twitches with nervous energy. She reinforces her creation of the family's communal presence with her masterful use of a narrative voice and point of view that functions almost as a collective chorus.

In the stories of early childhood, Minot depicts the experiences of the children through their leapfrogging jumble of sights, sounds and emotions. As they reach adulthood, they perceive their lives with a discriminating intricacy.

As undeniably powerful as these stories are, the discursive quality of the narrative has a tendency to become a jumble of visual images. In addition, the ballet corps movement of the family's life results in a portrait that is over-sentimentalized and too generic—leaving the reader with his face pressed up against the windowpane of the Vincent home, straining to make out who's who, and what's what.

The joys and frustrations inherent in family life ultimately lie in the struggle of idiosyncratic and warring individuals to be themselves while sustaining the identity and bonds of their family. ***Monkeys*** does not develop these individual aspects; nevertheless few novels have so powerfully displayed the collective unity—and joy—of family life.

Sherie Posesorski, ''Joys of Family Life on Display in 'Monkeys','' in Chicago Tribune, *April 27, 1986, p. 45.*

A. R. GURNEY, JR.

[***Monkeys***] is a book about an upper-middle-class family with seven children—a rare phenomenon in America these days. It is also a rare book—a subtle, funny and often extremely moving first novel. Set in those times of cultural upheaval between 1966 and 1979, it chronicles various moments in the life of the Vincent family, particularly its children, called ''monkeys'' by their mother, as they grow up in a suburb north of Boston and at a summer resort in Maine. Not since J. D. Salinger has an American writer so feelingly evoked the special affections and loyalties that may develop among children in a large family, and there are passages in Susan Minot's ***Monkeys*** that may also remind one of Faulkner's *Sound and the Fury,* when the Compson children attempt to decode the strange perplexities of the adult world.

A short work, ***Monkeys*** is composed of nine chapters or sections, seven of which have been previously published as short stories in either *The New Yorker* or *Grand Street*. These chapters are now presented chronologically, beginning when the children are all quite young, and ending 13 years later as all but the youngest move into tentative adulthood. Each chapter is devoted to a crystalizing incident that either threatens the coherence of the family or reasserts it. Most, but not all, of these events are perceived primarily through the eyes of Sophie, the second daughter and second child. Furthermore, while each of these chapters is complete in itself, there are flashbacks and foreshadowings, echoes and adumbrations, that give the work a compelling unity as a whole.

The sociological background of the book is more complicated than it might at first seem. The Vincent family lives in the fictitious Marshport, on the north shore of Boston, and summers at North Eden, in Maine. They ski in Vermont and New Hampshire and take occasional trips to Bermuda. Yet even though they seem to touch all the right bases, this is a ''mixed marriage.'' Augustus Paine (Gus) Vincent, who went to a country day school and played hockey for Harvard, has married Rose Marie O'Dare, who skated on the Boston Common and once dated a football player from Boston College. The names of their seven offspring reflect either their Yankee or Irish roots (Caitlin Marie Vincent, Chase Endicott Vincent), and much of the tension in the novel comes from the subtle clash between these two strong traditions.

Rose, always called Rosie by Gus (''after the schoolteacher in *The African Queen* who dumps out all of Humphrey Bogart's gin''), holds on to little from her past but her Catholicism. We never meet her parents, though we see a good deal of Gus's. We never learn where she went to school or college. She seems to have absorbed unquestioningly the manners and morals of the Brahmin world into which she has married, even down to her hectic colloquialisms and the bright colors of her clothes. . . . Yet occasionally we see a chink in her bright armor: her fears about money, her sense of futility about her husband's drinking, a moment when she is seen in her bedroom, alone and crying. And of course the very fact that she bears seven children testifies that she is finally and fundamentally an Irish Catholic mother. . . .

On the other hand, Gus Vincent, the father, has become an empty man. Fastidiously polite in his behavior, archaically stuffy in his language, he manages to disengage himself from any real emotional involvement with his family until the end of the book.

Within this troubled nest, the seven Vincent children struggle toward maturity, forging complicated bonds and connections among themselves that enable them to cope with the evasions of their father, the dissolution of the genteel values their mother holds so dear, and ultimately their mother's death and burial. Like Mr. Salinger's Glass children, they pay a psychological price for their commitment to each other. The girls find it difficult to connect with outside boys, while their brothers smoke dope, drink too much and crack up cars. Yet unlike Mr. Salinger's broodingly mystical clan, these ''monkeys'' remain anchored in the world. They may give up going to mass, but they maintain a wonderfully ceremonial sense of life. All of them become strikingly appealing characters, achingly real in their attempts to grow beyond the family even as they remain passionately loyal to it.

Susan Minot tells this tale with a fine economy. She conveys the special texture of life in a large family through such details as mitten baskets hanging by the back door, wobbly children's tables at Thanksgiving and the thrilling mysteries of grandmother's attic. She evokes the horrors of a blighted family vacation in Bermuda simply through the sound of rain as it ''drummed down on a metal table out on the terrace.'' She knows how parkas ''crinkle in the cold car,'' after ice skating, and how records can become ''hopelessly warped'' when left in summer houses over the winter. She also has a first-rate ear for what people say or don't say. ''You're giving me a mental heart attack,'' says a sister to a brother. ''Yoo-hoo,'' calls Rose to her drunken husband at the end of the table, trying to engage him in the family conversation. That's all she says, and that says it all.

In her finely observed accounts of human gesture and behavior, Miss Minot is even more effective. Rose religiously refolding the laundry after the kids have messed up the linen closet, Gus ineptly asserting his paternal dignity as his children organize dinner after their mother's death, the family delicately trying to persuade their father to give up drinking—all these are memorable moments, rich in the tensions and releases of family life.

Most memorable of all, however, is the final chapter, as the seven children and their father come together to improvise a burial ceremony for Rose's ashes. The book begins with a mass, and ends with this, as each member of the family takes a handful of her dust and tosses it into the sea. Here the Vincents become their own congregation, and the ritual they devise not only celebrates their splendid mother but also enables them to assert their own individuality, as one by one they make their throws. It's a heartbreaking scene, transformed by the virtuosity of the writing and the author's pervasive love for her characters into something exhilarating as well. (pp. 1, 27)

A. R. Gurney, Jr. "Men, Women and Children First," in The New York Times Book Review, *April 27, 1986, pp. 1, 27.*

RALPH NOVAK

Worlds of emotional ache and love—both repressed in the most painful ways—are compacted in [***Monkeys,*** an] affecting fiction about a Massachusetts family with seven children. . . . Minot, 29, is an exacting, economical writer; the deceptive gentleness of her language masks its virulent bite. At one point, while the family is gathered around the breakfast table, the father stops to pantomime a golfer hitting a putt: "There was a gentle craning of necks as the invisible ball rolled over the straw carpet. When Dad unfroze, it meant the ball had stopped so they could stop paying attention. He frowned, unhappy with the stroke. But Dad never looked satisfied with anything he did." Minot also creates, in the most understated way, a backdrop of surpassing warmth among the siblings that endures everything from a querulous Thanksgiving dinner to a tragic accident. She invokes characters whose lives and problems seem familiar—all too familiar, in some cases—addressing the deeper philosophical issues only obliquely, the way most of us do. This first novel is a startling penetrating experience.

Ralph Novak, in a review of "Monkeys," in People Weekly, *Vol. 25, No. 22, June 2, 1986, p. 14.*

An Excerpt from *Monkeys*

I try to teach Delilah how to skate backwards but she's flopping all over the ice, making me laugh, with her hat lopsided and her mittens dangling on strings out of her sleeves. When Gus falls, he just stays there, polishing the ice with his mitten. Dad sees him and says, "I don't care if my son is a violin player," kidding.

Dad played hockey in college and was so good his name is on a plaque that's right as you walk into the Harvard rink. He can go really fast. He takes off—*whoosh*—whizzing, circling at the edge of the pond, taking long strides, then gliding, chopping his skates, crossing over in little jumps. He goes zipping by and we watch him: his hands behind him in a tight clasp, his face as calm as if he were just walking along, only slightly forward. When he sweeps a corner, he tips in, then rolls into a hunch, and starts the long side-pushing again. After he stops, his face is red and the tears leak from the sides of his eyes and there's a white smudge around his mouth like frostbite. Sherman, copying, goes chopping forward on collapsed ankles and it sounds like someone sharpening knives.

Mum practices her 3s from when she used to figure skate. She pushes forward on one skate, turning in the middle like a petal flipped suddenly in the wind. We always make her do a spin. First she does backward crossovers, holding her wrists like a tulip in her fluorescent pink parka, then stops straight up on her toes, sucking in her breath and dips, twisted, following her own tight circle, faster and faster, drawing her feet together. Whirring around, she lowers into a crouch, ventures out one balanced leg, a twirling whirlpool, hot pink, rises again, spinning, into a blurred pillar or a tornado, her arms going above her head and her hands like the eye of a needle. Then suddenly: stop. Hiss of ice shavings, stopped. We clap our mittens. Her hood has slipped off and her hair is spread across her shoulders like when she's reading in bed, and she takes white breaths with her teeth showing and her pink mouth smiling. She squints over our heads. Dad is way off at the car, unlacing his skates on the tailgate but he doesn't turn. Mum's face means that it's time to go.

R. Z. SHEPPARD

Susan Minot's first novel [***Monkeys***] is a way to understand the familial instinct at a time when young women have other demands made on their minds and bodies. The point of view is largely that of Sophie, the second daughter, who coolly focuses on incidents that span some dozen years. . . .

Father's melancholy and Mother's sunny disposition determine the weather that pervades the book. It breaks over the breakfast table at Thanksgiving dinner and during vacations at the family's summer house in Maine. Time takes big jumps, and each episode finds the Vincents older. The girls begin dating, smoking and drinking, and the boys start sneaking off for marijuana nightcaps. Dad grows increasingly predictable ("nothing more normal than for him to be standing in the shade at a family picnic holding a can of beer"), and then Mother is dead.

The bad news is conveyed casually. In one chapter we are gunkholing with all the Vincents in their motorboat, and in the next an indeterminate amount of time has passed, and we learn that Rosie was killed when a train hit her car. It is an effective narrative trick that Minot might have learned from John Irving, who could have got it from Evelyn Waugh. Like them, Minot also knows how to blend the touching and the macabre. ***Monkeys*** ends with the Vincents each taking a handful of Rosie's ashes ("rounded and porous, like little ruins") and scattering them in the channel that flows past their summer house. The event requires a double take because it appears at first glance that the family is posing for the Lands' End catalog. Saying goodbye to Rosie is a scene not quickly forgotten, executed by a gifted writer whose debut cannot easily be ignored. (pp. 70-1)

R. Z. Sheppard, "Really Rosie," in Time, *Vol. 127, No. 23, June 9, 1986, pp. 70-1.*

MARGARET WALTERS

Susan Minot's first book—nine stories covering the lives of the seven Vincent ***Monkeys,*** as their mother Rosie lovingly labels them—evokes the rituals and warmth of belonging in a big family. It also catches the unblinking directness with which children register adult unhappiness: their mother's forced attempts at gaiety, their father's irritated detachment and heavy drinking. The stories both celebrate family and record its breakdown. By the end, after Rosie's death in a car accident, and their father's rapid remarriage, the family hardly exists. Yet the children still cling to childhood memories of coherence; in spite of jobs and boyfriends and travel, it remains their only source of identity. A fascinating theme that's tantalisingly undeveloped. Susan Minot's exquisite short story craft, her skill at small-scale effects and significant moments, restricts the fuller exploration the characters demand.

Margaret Walters, "Variations on a Theme," in The Observer, *August 24, 1986, p. 20.*

THOMAS HINDE

Susan Minot's ***Monkeys*** is . . . [a] group of short stories described as a novel. There is, however, . . . justification for the description: the same characters occur in each, and they are arranged in chronological order.

These characters form a Massachusetts family at first consisting of father, mother and six children, later of father, new wife and seven children. Mostly they do the sort of things you'd expect a middle class Massachusetts family to do: hide in an airing cupboard to play a trick on father when he comes home; visit grandparents for Thanksgiving; get drunk and smoke pot at teenage parties. . . . [All] is in the telling, and Susan Minot's is a delight.

Her large cast of children give her a problem, and the reader needs time to sort them out, but the re-introducing of the family at the start of each chapter (required when they were short stories) is a help and she manages it with admirable economy.

Admirable, too, is her sense of what should be told when it occurs and what should occur, as it were, off stage. Three of the most dramatic events—the mother's fatal accident, the father's drunken return on hands and knees from a party he didn't want to go to, a son's car crash—emerge only in other characters' memories of them. But they are none the less vivid (film makers note), indeed, Susan Minot excels at catching a whole scene in a singe perfectly chosen detail.

In all of this Susan Minot's trainer might be John Updike and her stable *The New Yorker*. A young American writer could have worse luck, and if her skills may develop into mannerisms, that is all the more reason for enjoying them while they are fresh.

Thomas Hinde, "Bursts of Lucidity," in Books and Bookmen, *No. 371, September, 1986, p. 37.*

KATHERINE BUCKNELL

Susan Minot's first novel ***Monkeys*** began as a group of short stories. She has not attempted to disguise this. It is mildly annoying to be told more than once, in so slim a volume written in so spare a style, that there are seven children in the Vincent family, that Sophie is the second eldest between Caitlin and Delilah, that Sherman is the middle brother, or that the Vincent girls "have parties at the house—huge ones". But otherwise the short story form gives ***Monkeys*** sharp focus. Thirteen years of privileged family life north of Boston, with holidays in Maine and Bermuda, are skilfully suggested in nine lightly sketched episodes. Minot shapes these episodes neatly, making them irresistibly true to life, but only rarely allowing them to display a ragged edge.

Virginia Woolf once suggested that *To the Lighthouse* was not a novel but an "elegy". ***Monkeys*** is an elegy for Mrs Vincent; it is the charm of Mrs Vincent and the response which that charm arouses in her children that animate the book. . . .

Only the children feel the full force of Mrs Vincent's charm, and understand instinctively its sensual character. Mrs Vincent thrives on love. She is "thrilled" by the attention of the wealthy and handsome Mr Kittredge; she is even more "thrilled" when she nurses her late-born eighth child. . . .

Mr Vincent's apparent indifference provides a chilling contrast. In a pained interview, he assures his children "I won't drink", but the contentment of a family picnic is soon shattered by the sound of a beer can being opened. For Mrs Vincent there is "nothing so thrilling" as nursing a baby at her breast; for Mr Vincent there is "nothing more normal" than nursing himself on drink. . . .

After their father breaks his promise not to drink, the Vincents begin to fall. When their mother is killed in an accident, the shock is "absolute", and the Vincents find themselves in hell: "the Devil had swooped down and had landed and was lingering with them all, hulking in the middle of the kitchen table, settling down to stay". Mr Vincent's example impels his sons towards self-destruction. His eldest daughters turn coolly away from his misery, happy when he soon finds a new wife. But the Vincents still believe what Caitlin insists on—"We're a family"—and struggle to reanimate the love which once held them in a charmed circle.

Within the tale of the Vincent family there is another, more personal story about Sophie's struggle to discover, on her own, who she is. In the picture of Sophie preparing to cast her share of her mother's ashes into the sea near the Vincent summer house in Maine is perhaps a picture of the author who, before she can let go, must examine her mother and childhood and see them clearly. There is relief in Sophie's recognition that "This is just like anything else you throw overboard", but also an awareness that "this" is not at all like anything else. It is Minot's special talent to depict for us why not.

Katherine Bucknell, "The Children of Charm," in The Times Literary Supplement, *No. 4353, September 5, 1986, p. 978.*

DEBORAH NAVAS

The dust jacket proclaims [***Monkeys***] a novel, but that feels like an arbitrary classification. This small work is composed of nine short stories. . . . The stories are related in subject: a bumptious upper-middle-class family of seven children, an alcoholic father, and extraordinary mother who has managed to maintain and share with her children her *joie de vivre* despite the circumstances.

The stories' points of view jump from child to child, and occasionally to an omniscient narrator who seems to be in league with the children, observing events from their concrete perspective. Beginning with the first story, "Hiding," told by

Sophie, who seems to be the focal intelligence in this collection, we sense that for all of the lollypops, Sunday night treats and BLTs, this is not as happy a family for the adults as it is for the children. (p. 9)

[In] these cleanly written, minutely detailed stories, which grow progressively sadder as the children grow up and perceive more of their father's drinking problem. The heroine of this collection is Mum, who singlehandedly provides the momentum and magic for the entire family. . . . (pp. 9-10)

But sadly, for us, we only see Mum obliquely, in vivid glimpses. . . , as the children see her. . . .

The stories are highly controlled and finely written with a wealth of the pleasing details of childhood—mittens dangling from sleeves, and sniffing seaweed by smushing it to your face. But as separate stories, complete in themselves, they lack the substance and character development of a true novel. These stories are like a mirrored ball that reflects brilliant flashes and pleasing images, but we can't see much beyond that shimmering surface. There are hints of a bigger story here—what about the mysterious death of baby Frances? And was Mum having an affair with Wilbur Kittredge, and if so was she driven to it by Dad's indifference, or did the affair provoke his drinking and loutish behavior? Such hints add resonance to a short story, but beg the issue—sidestep the depth of characterization and larger dimension that a novel demands.

Monkeys is a fine and precisely written collection of short stories, but it just doesn't deliver as a novel. Like Louise Erdrich's *Love Medicine,* it's a hybrid form, a writer's cautious half-step from short story to novel. But, no risk, no gain; it is no greater than the sum of its parts. (p. 10)

Deborah Navas, "Home Deliveries: Cautionary Sex & Violence," in New Letters Review of Books, *Vol. 1, No. 1, Spring, 1987, pp. 9-10.*

Taghi Modarressi

1931-

Iranian-born novelist.

Modarressi, who previously published two works in Persian, pictures the Iran of his youth in his first English publication, *The Book of Absent People* (1986). The novel, set in the 1960s during the last years of the Shah's regime, revolves around the search by the narrator, the artistic Rokni, for his long absent half-brother, the revolutionary Zia. Rokni discovers an intricate web of relations in his aristocratic family, who have maintained an internal split between the clan members who are artisans and those who are socially aware. Reviewers note that Modarressi's engrossing tale of this complex family mirrors the conflict of the country, where an ancient and revered but repressive Persian culture falls to the domination of a modern, terrorizing, and theocratic regime. Critics praise Modarressi's achievement in creating such a rich and haunting story.

Modarressi left Iran as a young man, completing his medical education in America, where he specialized in psychiatry. *The Book of Absent People* is his first fiction in twenty-five years. Modarressi notes that it was inspired by "a new contact with Iranians and Iranian culture after the revolution since many Iranians immigrated to this country." Modarressi, who is married to novelist Anne Tyler, is the director of the Center for Infant Study at the University of Maryland. He is currently working on his next novel, the story of a history professor "who is trying to make sense of contemporary events."

Courtesy of Taghi Modarressi

PUBLISHERS WEEKLY

Modarressi's first English novel [***The Book of Absent People***] . . . is surreal and labyrinthine, capturing the plight of a cultivated family between two eras. While spectral gunfire and tear-gas drift from alleys strewn with Pepsi bottles, Rokni's kinsfolk cite ancient proverbs as guides for living, and the physician pores over classical tomes of herbal medicine. Clan snapshots and photos of war atrocities depict the new order; the past is beautifully summoned by Rokni's trancelike visions of Homayundokht, his dead stepmother, gazing at the stars or in a jewelled mirror like a Persian miniature. Although the novel sometimes reads like an awkward translation, it affords a first-hand glimpse of contemporary Tehran that will fascinate most readers. (pp. 57-8)

A review of "The Book of Absent People," in Publishers Weekly, *Vol. 228, No. 25, December 20, 1985, pp. 57-8.*

JANETTE TURNER HOSPITAL

During the tense days of the Iranian hostage crisis, there were no doubt many of us who pondered the paradox of stern mullahs sitting beneath the sensuous ceilings of Isfahan, and who asked ourselves in bewilderment: *How? Why?* What was the route from Persia the Magnificent to modern Iran? Rokni, 23-year-old son of the dying patriarch of the Heshmat Nezami family, and narrator of ***The Book of Absent People,*** embarks on a quest to solve those very riddles.

This wonderful novel by Taghi Modarressi . . . is set in the last years of the Shah's regime, though for Rokni the angry crowds are less real than his father's beautiful first wife, Homayundokht, long dead but given to drifting in and out of Rokni's vision in a white lace gown. She looks over her shoulder and lures him into the labyrinth of family history. Rokni plunges in, for—at his dying father's request—he is searching for his half-brother Zia, Homayundokht's son, who must not be spoken of and whose room has been sealed. Zia has been missing for 11 years, and Rokni, innocent as a child, knows nothing. Or so it seems.

Gradually we realize that he has long known far more than he wants to. Like Scheherazade, when he feels the horror coming too close he staves it off with another tale, always about the family. We ramble in circles through the maze of the family. But the family, it transpires, is Iran in microcosm, and if Rokni can unravel all the tribal mysteries and unlock all the sealed rooms in the ancestral mansion, he may also solve the riddle of his country. . . .

But Rokni's tunnel vision—and ultimately the novel's—disappoints. "I wasn't used to being away from my family," he says. "We didn't belong to any place or any person except our own relatives. Wherever we went, whatever we touched, we behaved as if we had no connection with anyone." Quite so, to the very end. And we want to demand: but what about those people shaking the gates, those people without family mansions or even ordinary houses or food?

When a passerby in a riot-torn street asks the way to Khaniabad, we wait for Rokni the painter to *draw* that passerby, to throw just a smidgen of light on someone beyond the pale of the aristocratic families. But Rokni, obsessed with personal confusion, answers, "It's not possible to get to Khaniabad from here."

At times, too, the business of Rokni's repression of awareness is problematic—either too heavily hinted at in psycho-mystical terms, or simply tedious, as he indulges in yet another childish whim or denial tantrum. But this is mere caviling, for Rokni's tale is exquisitely told, and the book . . . is a veritable enchantment. Like Scheherazade's sultan, we are beguiled. As for the unanswered wider questions, well, perhaps you really can't get to Khaniabad from here.

Janette Turner Hospital, "Obsessed in Iran," in The New York Times Book Review, *February 9, 1986, p. 21.*

TOM LeCLAIR

Before the remedial geography lessons of the late '70s—"Here is Iran between Russia and the Persian Gulf"—and before our televised cultural education—"Many of these people chanting 'Death to America' are Shiite Moslems"—Iranians were to most Americans an absent people, governed by a shah, sometimes seen skiing in Switzerland, who, it was rumored, made some subjects disappear into his political prisons. Now that propaganda has replaced ignorance, Iranians are no less absent to us.

Taghi Modarressi's novel [***The Book of Absent People***] helps fill the void. He creates a large clan of people with their own fingerprints and desires, with individual histories and a shared present, the Tehran of 1963, a time of popular uprisings against the shah. . . . If, for readers, his characters are far away and alien, Modarressi too is absent, an exile who can only remember and imagine, not rejoin, his people and native place.

The Book of Absent People is told by Rokni Nezami, a 23-year-old art student who, at the end of his account, leaves Iran. The novel's action takes place within a few weeks and has as its framing events Rokni's father's retirement from medicine and his death. This domestic upheaval forces Rokni back into a family past previously absent to him, a past he finds connected to a hundred years of Iranian history and to the then current violence in Tehran streets.

Rokni discovers that the generations-old clan split—between the realistic, hard-working and respectable Nezamis and the artistic, passionate and convention-defying Azhdaris—is not due to the genetic difference he assumed but is the result of a political argument between brothers over foreign influence in 19th-century Iran. Closer to home, Rokni also learns that his respected "Khan Papa Doctor" once participated in a peasant slaughter and that the doctor's first wife, the Russian-born Homayundokht Azhdari, killed herself because she, as a "foreigner," was ostracized by Nezami women.

The dying doctor asks Rokni to find his first-born son, Rokni's half-brother Zia, absent for 11 years after being arrested by the Shah's secret police. To find Zia, Rokni has to investigate present-day politics and needs help from the suspect Azhdaris—from Masoud, a childhood friend now a SAVAK agent; from cousin Massibi, who sells opium and gives away, perhaps, secrets. Even more important, to unwind the novel's several plots and discover his own identity, Rokni must learn from women, the longest absent people: a half-sister sunken into mental illness, his provincial mother hiding behind her veil, and his long-neglected aunt Badi Zaman, family interpreter of the Koran.

The book's authority—the presence and import of its people—comes from the combination of Rokni's innocence, his naive questioning and recording in a voice accented with the youthful simplicity of non-native English, and Modarressi's sophistication, his suspenseful plotting and careful twisting of Rokni's family recognitions into clan complexities and national knots.

Early in his story, Rokni confesses to talking as if he "were reading from an ancient tale." Paradoxically, it is this "bookishness" that expresses the elaborate formalities of a culture with strong remnants of oral traditions and clan relations. Rokni alludes to unfamiliar texts, historical events, and customs without explaining them, another way for the author to create insider authority. Modarressi also has Rokni use Persian forms of address, verbal tags, and folk sayings, though occasionally American colloquialisms (such as "stick it to him") slip in and disrupt the effect. Because Rokni believes in religious visions and cultural mysteries, a Persian magic suffuses his whole account. In Modarressi's narrator the Azhdaris' art and the Nezamis' social awareness fuse to produce a complex version of the Iranian—an Iranian's—mind.

It seems fair to ask who has been left out of ***The Book of Absent People.*** Modarressi records an aristocracy "decaying" into an elite professional and civil servant class, the Iranians seemingly best served by the shah's policies. Had Modarressi included other people—the Tudeh Communists, peasants, or Islamic fundamentalists—the internal conflicts of the Nezami-Azhdari clan, its split loyalties to various visions of what Iran could be, would have been more comprehensible. Another exile with a family background similar to Rokni's, Vladimir Nabokov, chose to enshrine his memories of Russia with inward-turning art. Modarressi's effect is centrifugal: sending the reader outward from Rokni to his family and, finally, to the library. An intervening stage between his invented clan and historical facts—other absent people—would have made this fine novel a better book.

Tom LeClair, "Figures in a Persian Carpet," in Book World—The Washington Post, *February 16, 1986, p. 9.*

An Excerpt from *The Book of Absent People*

All my family used to say that I was an imagining person, that I believed whatever came to my mind. It was true. Eleven years ago, in fact, I imagined that I saw Homayundokht, God forgive her soul. It was when I was standing in front of the old fig tree. I looked through the dirty, cobwebbed windowpanes into the room of Homayundokht, God forgive her soul. I tried to make out the details of the alarm clock that her Dear Daddy, the late Mirza Yousef, had brought her from Petersburg. In the darkness, I couldn't see very well. I could just discern the vague, borderless outlines of the dolls that she herself had knitted with her own hands and arranged on the mantel with such artistry and good taste. A big copy of *The Queen of Birds* hung on the opposite wall. The Queen of Birds held her palms together and turned her passionate, innocent gaze upon the sky. And what pearl and emerald necklaces she wore on her white crystal neck, and what diamond and topaz rings on her slender hands! A paragon of beauty, popularity, and virtue.

Now, my family says this is just more of my showing off, something to make me seem dramatic—a self-indulgence, like my habit of talking as if I were reading from an ancient tale—but the truth of the matter is, that night eleven years ago I was inspired to take the hurricane lamp from the niche, climb the stairs, and go to the rooftop. In the middle of the stairs, I was overcome by the sensation of a presence. I felt goose bumps and a cold breeze on my skin. A few steps higher stood Homayundokht, God forgive her soul, with a green umbrella in her hand. I couldn't believe it. It knocked the wind out of me. For a twelve-year-old boy to be granted such a privilege? She wore a white lace gown and she raised the umbrella over her head and looked at me intensely. I gathered my voice and asked, "Homayundokht, is that you? Are we asleep? Are we awake? Where are we?"

She didn't answer. Just like a new bride who has painted her face with seven brushes, she went up the stairs and I followed. On the rooftop, we saw the sky decorated with half a million stars, dazzling our eyes. She beckoned to me. When I stepped forward, the smell of her lavender perfume made me giddy. She put her hand inside her glass bead purse, took out the dark mirror of the Master Assar, and held it up so she could watch the world with the eyes of a painter. What a strange mirror! All around it was enamelwork and jewel-studded patterns. And how elegantly Homayundokht, God forgive her soul, held its silver handle with those fingers which, in their satin gloves, looked white as snow! I told myself, Oh, my God, who am I to be in this royal court? She conveyed to me that I must seize the moment, that the nightingale had no more than an instant to sing. I didn't understand. I thought she wanted me to sing a song. I started singing, "'Portrait maker and painter of china, go and see the face of my beloved . . .'" She listened and didn't shift her gaze from the sky. When I stopped, she smiled regretfully. I sensed that we had lost our chance and would have to endure until our next turn. She spun her green umbrella over her head and disappeared in the dark.

BETH CLEWIS

The setting and background of a novel can sometimes offer the greatest challenge to the reader. In pulp epics the setting is often an exotic locale, like India or China, which is carefully introduced to the reader in manageable portions, never overwhelming with a feeling of alienation. But other books require that the reader understand and relate to greatly different sets of values, background history, and lifestyles. And what country now seems more alien to Americans than Iran? The reader who can comfortably submerge himself in the world of modern Iran will find the most satisfaction from ***The Book of Absent People.***

The plot concerns the reunion of a scattered family upon the death of its patriarch, Khan Papa Doctor, who recruits his dreamer son Rokni to find his other son Zia, a revolutionary missing for 10 years. Rokni, the narrator, eventually effects Zia's return, but spends most of the book in a search for his family's secret history, fascinated as he is by his father's first wife, who died under mysterious circumstances. While Rokni is able finally to answer some of his questions about the family, the answers do not change the family for the better. Instead, Rokni himself joins "the world of absent people."

Modarressi's style is elegant and insightful, but while I came to know a great deal about this family, I never felt that I understood them or connected with them. I was intrigued by the glimpses of the life of women in Iran (though it should be noted that the events take place before the fall of the Shah). The story remained an intellectual curiosity; it never touched my heart.

Beth Clewis, in a review of "The Book of Absent People," in Best Sellers, *Vol. 46, No. 2, May, 1986, p. 48.*

KATE MILLET

Few societies go so fast from the frying pan into the fire as Iran has. A great and lovely culture ravaged now; 25 years of state terrorism under the Shah followed by seven baleful years of a fanatic theocracy which probably has already far exceeded the Shah's reign in executions and in the widespread use of torture, informers and surveillance. . . .

Taghi Modarressi [in ***The Book of Absent People***] can tell you what it was like under the former regime in the walled house of a "good family": uncles and cousins and grandfathers in and out of favor with the shahs of many generations, a family whose men were generals and bureaucrats—there is even a cousin in Savak, the Shah's secret police. . . .

Modarressi's sensitive, subtle, impressionistic and atmospheric novel is something of an allegory. Everything goes back to one riddle—the death of Homayundokht, mother of Iran, who stood on a roof one day and burned herself alive. Brilliant and instinctive being that she was, educated and permitted real freedom in her youth, she discovered one day, in what had been almost a good marriage, that she was in fact her husband's serf—and she would not tolerate a life without freedom. At that point Iran fell silent. Zia galvanized himself to become the new terror whose extent we do not yet foresee, and Rokni vanishes into exile on an airplane, the magic bird of those who are lucky.

Kate Millet, in a review of "The Book of Absent People," in Chicago Tribune, *June 8, 1986, p. 36.*

DONNE RAFFAT

The Book of Absent People is [Modarressi's] first novel in English and reads somewhat like a literal translation. The prose aside, however, Modarressi brings to English all his acumen as a virtuoso Persian storyteller.

The tale unfolds with a growing sense of intricate symmetry—slowly and obscurely, then with increasing speed and clarity. What is gained thereby is a deepening insight into a generational family conflict. A dying father bids his young son to find his older brother, missing for 11 years after a mysterious outburst. The search takes the youth through the streets of prerevolutionary Tehran, only to bring him back with more questions. Not until his father's death and burial, however, do all the pieces fit together and do the absent members of the family reunite, only to separate again.

The final disclosures are poignant and rewarding. All the reader needs is patience getting there. Meanwhile, one wonders how much more appealing this haunting, probing tale would have been in the author's native language.

Donne Raffat, in a review of "The Book of Absent People," in Los Angeles Times Book Review, *June 29, 1986, p. 4.*

COMMENTS OF TAGHI MODARRESSI TO *CLC YEARBOOK*

Modarressi observed that when writing *The Book of Absent People,* he had in mind "the American public, with the hope of influencing their perception of Iranian culture, and Iranians themselves, who had not heard from me in a long time."

The book did not develop rapidly, Modarressi noted. It "had to be revised three times because it took wrong directions. I had to overcome my tendency to stick to realistic details and allow my own imagination to take over."

"I sent the manuscript to Timothy Seldes, and he sent the manuscript to eight publishing houses before being accepted by Doubleday."

After a twenty-five year writing hiatus, Modarressi reveals a new purpose in his fiction writing: "to get in touch with my background, to have a sense of being an Iranian living in this country, and to give a sample of Iranian culture and Iranian style of living in contrast to what people usually read in the press."

Reinaldo Povod

1959-

American dramatist.

The son of a Puerto Rican mother and a Cuban father of Russian descent, Povod grew up in New York's East Village and later studied at New York's American Academy of Dramatic Arts. His first full-length play, *Cuba and His Teddy Bear* (1986), took only two weeks to write; Povod notes, however, that he had been brooding over the play for a longer period, as it is reminiscent of his own childhood. *Cuba and His Teddy Bear* is a seamy, naturalistic slice-of-life story concerning the complex relationship between Cuba, a drug dealer on Manhattan's Lower East Side, and Teddy, his sensitive teenage son who aspires to be a writer. Though Povod was raised by his paternal grandmother, he experienced a relationship with his father similar to Teddy's, both loving and fearing his father. Povod recalls, "I was his valet, so to speak. But I liked it. My father was a hero to everybody on the block. He was a rough man on the streets, and he was respected and feared."

Most critics find *Cuba and His Teddy Bear* too long to sustain audience interest—particularly since it lacks a developing plot and offers no resolution of its themes or actions—and attribute its appeal to the performance of Robert DeNiro, for whom Povod wrote the role of Cuba. Reviewers nevertheless see *Cuba and His Teddy Bear* as a strong first effort and praise the authenticity of Povod's urban-Hispanic milieu with its unromanticized characters and raw, realistic dialogue.

Povod adapted *Cuba* for the screen and has completed his second play, *La Puta Vida Trilogy,* which will be produced by the New York Shakespeare Festival in the 1987-88 season.

© 1986 by Marianne Barcellona

DOUGLAS WATT

Cuba and His Teddy Bear . . . is a sort of lowlife *Father Knows Best*. . . .

This first play by 26-year-old Reinaldo Povod is a comedy, despite the fact that the father figure, a native Cuban, is a drug peddler who has done time. In fact, though it's tiresomely long, it's very close to farce.

Cuba . . . has hoped to raise his teenage son Teddy . . . honestly by doing his apartment drug dealing, accompanied by occasional snorts of coke, right out in the open.

When Cuba isn't punching the wall or pacing up and down or cursing out his supplier pal Jackie . . . , he's pushing Teddy around and yelling at him for just sitting there thinking.

What Teddy is thinking about is being a writer; he is inspired by a drug-addicted Hispanic playwright named Che . . . who won a Tony sometime back. But Cuba doesn't approve of this friendship, insisting that if Teddy wants to shoot up, he should do it with dad.

Actually, Teddy, who does try shooting up, doesn't want to do drugs, alcohol or any crime, and has little use for anything Spanish, including the music and language.

But this badly written and poorly motivated play dawdles on, with repetitive gab about a promised coke deal for Cuba and the possible unloading of two pounds of pot by Jackie.

None of these things come to pass—the melodramatic flourishes in the second half include Cuba's attempt to shoot himself and his partial desecration of the saint's statue occupying a prominent place in the seedy flat.

In the end, everybody's played out, including the audience.

Douglas Watt, "Father Knows Worst," in Daily News, *New York, May 19, 1986. Reprinted in* New York Theatre Critics' Reviews, *Vol. XLVII, No. 9, Week of July 7, 1986, p. 265.*

CLIVE BARNES

Life is tough—particularly if you are a drug addict. For that matter, life's pretty tough even if you are a dealer. But it *is* a life. And junkies and pushers *are* people.

And that is virtually the burden of the drug-infested Lower East Side story that 26-year-old Reinaldo Povod has to tell in his striking first full-length play, ***Cuba and His Teddy Bear***. . . .

Ever since Maxim Gorky's *The Lower Depths*, right at the beginning of the century, our theater has played various variations on themes of seamy naturalism, and Mr. Povod is here adding some Hispanic cooking to a slice of life on the wrong side of the needle tracks.

Not that the scene, and even the characters, are not at least partially familiar. But Mr. Povod seems to write straight from the ear, and his play vibrates and tingles with an authority that goes beyond the cleverly applied local color of mere verismo atmosphere, into truth.

There is no real plot; things happen, but in chaos rather than order, and at the end nothing is resolved, nothing fundamental has changed. No tidy ends have been wrapped around a dramatic bundle.

Cuba . . . is a smalltime Cuban dope dealer—chiefly in cocaine, but with a little marijuana on the side. His main supplier and best friend, Jackie . . . is a fat Jewish slob who, like Cuba, is struggling to make a dishonest living.

Cuba, with his finicky regard for the way he looks, his macho manner, and amoral aggressiveness, could be any dope hustler, except for one thing—he has a 16-year-old son Teddy,. . . whom he adores, and, in his odd, topsy-turvy way, tries to protect. . . .

The play meanders through this oddly domesticated and seemingly normal sub-world of drugs with a miasmic sense of reality. . . .

Cuba, with his fierce love for his son and dead mother, his unapologetic lifestyle, his superstitious version of religion, his doomed sense of God's retribution, is matched by the other characters, all just as aptly rounded. . . .

Like drugs, I guess the play promises more than it eventually delivers. The denizens of Mr. Povod's world are just a little too predictable, and in the event, its own events interest rather than illuminate.

But this is an important debut, and a play that grips you with its tendrils of actuality. The sound has not been turned up, the colors have not been heightened; this, you feel, is the way it was, or could have been. (pp. 263-64)

Clive Barnes, "De Niro and Co. Shoot the Works," in New York Post, *May 19, 1986. Reprinted in* New York Theatre Critics' Reviews, *Vol. XLVII, No. 9, Week of July 7, 1986, pp. 263-64.*

MEL GUSSOW

[***Cuba and His Teddy Bear***] has atmospheric authenticity. . . . But at its core, this is an overly schematic story about an illiterate immigrant father and his misunderstood son. Both the plot and the morality of the tale are imprecise, while the play itself is too long for its limited dimension.

The father believes that drug dealing is on a higher level than drug addiction. From his point of view, he is performing a professional service and making money in order to improve his son's status. He has never hidden his occupation; therefore, his son should respect him. If the youth should ever want to try drugs, he says, he should not do it on the streets but with his father, just as the two once went to ball games together. . . . For a long time, the father is as oblivious of the son's drug problem as he is of his artistic leanings; he even forgets the youth's exact age. More important to him are such concerns as keeping his house in order and praying before a religious statuette on a corner cabinet. Late in the second act, there is a showdown between father and son, a scene that momentarily ignites the play, but it remains only a scene, not a catharsis or a climax. . . .

Despite the potential explosiveness of the situation, however, the play has a tendency toward lassitude. ***Cuba and His Teddy Bear*** lacks the vibrancy of, for example, Miguel Pinero's *Short Eyes*, which also dealt with the Hispanic underclass.

Mel Gussow, in a review of "Cuba and His Teddy Bear," in The New York Times, *May 19, 1986, p. C11.*

ALLAN WALLACH

A towel wrapped around his middle, Cuba stands on the scarred linoleum of his Lower East Side apartment looking down at his son. With his full black beard, ponytail and hooded eyes, he could be some fierce 20th-Century pirate. But he reassures the boy, "You don't have to be afraid of me. I will never hurt you."

The terrible irony of Reinaldo Povod's ***Cuba and His Teddy Bear*** is that the loving father hurts Teddy as surely as if he'd stuck a heroin filled needle in his arm. . . .

Raw and unpolished, ***Cuba and His Teddy Bear*** rips at us like a club fighter . . . At times it becomes almost unbearable to watch, but harsh and crude as it is, the play rivets us. Povod, a 26-year-old Hispanic playwright born and raised on the Lower East Side, makes even his beginner's mistakes contribute to the scorching impact of his first full-length play. (p. 266)

What happens to the boy and two men has to do with Teddy's feelings about his father and a junkie named Che . . . , a Tony-winning playwright who has inspired his own inchoate writing. It also has to with the boy's ambiguous feelings about being white, having no taste for Spanish music, food or even people. . . .

Hoping to become part of his father's world, the boy volunteers to sell two pounds of pot to Che. But his impulse leads to a harrowing encounter with Che and a menacing dealer . . . , followed by an explosive confrontation with Cuba.

Povod underscores the irony and spells out his cautionary message too heavily, even using the fun-loving Redlights to deliver some final words of wisdom. But he makes these and other flaws seem unimportant. Like Jack Gelber's *The Connection*, his play convinces us that this is the way it is for people who live, one way or another, with drugs. At the end, all fury spent, Cuba and the others are as desolate as the family Eugene O'Neill observed in *Long Day's Journey Into Night*, defeated by Mary Tyrone's morphine addiction. (p. 267)

Allan Wallach, "Inside a Drug Dealer's World in 'Cuba'," in Newsday, *May 19, 1986. Reprinted in* New York Theatre Critics' Reviews, *Vol. XXXXVII, No. 9, Week of July 7, 1986, pp. 266-67.*

JOHN BEAUFORT

"What do you want?" asks a baffled Cuba . . . of his teen-age son Teddy . . . at one point in ***Cuba and His Teddy Bear.***

"I want to be valued highly," replies the hapless youth. The odds against Teddy are all but insurmountable. Twenty-six-year old dramatist Reinaldo Povod explores them relentlessly in his first full-length play. . . . (p. 23)

Cuba, a drug-dealing ex-convict, conducts his illicit business openly from his lower East Side Manhattan apartment. He theorizes that what Teddy sees going on will fortify him against involvement with drugs. As in most other respects, Cuba has woefully miscalculated. Teddy is already on the road to heroin addiction. . . . (pp. 23-24)

Cuba and His Teddy Bear proves to be a grimly sardonic ordeal. While its dialogue is authentically sharp (and insistently foul-mouthed), the slice-of-life drama tends to lose the spectator in its profusion of unresolved themes. (p. 24)

John Beaufort, "A Grim Drama," in The Christian Science Monitor, *May 21, 1986, pp. 23-4.*

An Excerpt from *Cuba and His Teddy Bear*

JACKIE (Reading): I love my father. I wanna be a man's man, like him. "What?" Cookie says to me. I hold Cookie closer and I think of what could happen to my father in jail . . . with long hair . . . the guards pulling at it—shouting, drug dealer! He yells in pain—I love my father. His hair gets longer—down to his ankles. They tie his arms behind his back with his long hair—I love my father—his feet. I love my father. He yells, NO! No, I love my father—I love him. The guards kick him and call him drug dealer—I love my father. They shove his hair down his throat—choke on it, drug dealer. I love him. I love you I say, when they cut his throat. I love you, Pop. I love you, I love you. . . . (Stops reading) It jus' goes on like that, Cuba, you know, I love you, I love you—
CUBA: Yer nuts. You want people to read that?
TEDDY: It's jus' a story—
CUBA: Why you write that? For what?
JACKIE: Don't worry him, Cuba, you know whachu do?
CUBA: Whaddayou want me to say after hearin' somethin' like that?
JACKIE (With the pad in his hand): Don't say nothing. I'll tell ya whachu do. (Show CUBA the pad) You see here, it says: "And Pop yanks my underwears"? You take it and you go all the way down to the end here—where it says "worst than to be—accused of"—you know, with the brother— (Quickly) and you cross it all out—all of it. You keep this here: "I love my father. I wanna be a man's man like him." Beautiful. That's friggin' writing. That you keep. And that other stuff about you gettin' hurt in jail—that can go too.
TEDDY: It's just a story—it's not real.
CUBA: I dunno . . . I dunno. . . . Why didn't you write a story like, you know, where I jumped in the water somewhere and saved yer life—or something like, I ran into a building that was on fire and I pulled you out? Ha? Or when I use to take you to the Yankee games. The Knicks. I use to take you to the Garden to see the Knicks play. The circus. Anythin' you wanted I tried to get for you. You wanted a horse—I couldn't get you a horse—but what did I get you?
JACKIE: A goldfish?
TEDDY: You put me in a horseback riding academy.
CUBA: How much that cost me?
TEDDY: Twenty-five dollars an hour.
JACKIE: You coulda saddled me for twenty. Lookit that?
CUBA: How much shit did I have to sell to pay them twenty-five bucks an hour? You think things you shouldn't think about.
TEDDY: I know, Pop, I think I'm wrong.
CUBA: Yer hurtin' yerself—yer hurtin' me. Yer imagining things that don't do you any good—don't do me any good. I know you gotta problem—I might be the problem—but how the fuck I'm gonna know if you don't tell me? I gotta find out—finding a needle in my sink where I shave and brush my teeth. Hearing whachu wrote it makes you sound like a freak! What's yer problem, tell me?
TEDDY: I'm the problem. Me!
CUBA: Whachu mean, me?
TEDDY: Me. Me, Pop. Look at me.
CUBA: You don't like yerself? You don't like the way you look. You look like yer mother.
TEDDY: I look white.
CUBA: You look American—yer in America—what do you wanna look like? Yer better off.
JACKIE: I wish my problem was lookin' white. I gotta little dick. That's whachu said, Cuba, ya hard-on.
CUBA: I treated you better than anybody. I didn't teach ya Spanish on purpose. I did that, this way you be something better. You know, better than me. Get a better chance.
TEDDY: I'm . . . better?
CUBA: *Yeah!*
TEDDY: I gotta better chance? I'm the only kid on the Lower East Side that don't speak Spanish.
CUBA: You think I hurt you by doin' that?
TEDDY: I don't like Spanish food.
CUBA: What's wrong with a cheeseburger?
JACKIE: Gimme a pretzel anytime.
TEDDY: Spanish music.
CUBA: You gonna be a dancer?
TEDDY: Spanish people.
CUBA: What?
TEDDY: Spanish people.
CUBA: You don't like Spanish people?
TEDDY: I do—but it's . . . just. . . . Most of the Spanish people I know that . . . you know, come here, are—you know—
CUBA: What—say it.
TEDDY: Like you.
CUBA: Like me. (To JACKIE) Like me. You hear that? Low-life, he means. (To TEDDY) I never stuck a needle in my arm. *That's* low-life.

MICHAEL FEINGOLD

Joseph Cuba, Teddy's widowed father [in ***Cuba and His Teddy Bear***] . . . is a small-time coke dealer whose supplier has stuck him with two pounds of that unfashionable penny-ante drug, pot. Seventeen-year-old Teddy, who is having a hard time trying to tell his loved-and-hated father that he wants to be a poet like Che, comes up with a somewhat Freudian project: By getting Che's dealer friend to unload the unwanted grass, he will simultaneously win Cuba's respect and reconcile his two opposing father-figures. Teddy ends, of course, both ripped off and disillusioned; the last scene isn't a glib burst of violence, but a sad, unresolved fadeout.

Povod's material is familiar on two fronts, and much of its interest comes from the extra resonances you get when two genres of play are combined; the social story, the drugs-and-violence cycle of the slums, with the personal one, the artist and his uncomprehending parent. When a writer hears well, as Povod does, the merger makes rich, ripe ambiguities: Cuba's love for his son is complicated for us by the fact that he deals drugs, which makes the audience distrust him by definition. Povod has no pretentions about Teddy's art, either; it's shown half-comically as the heart-rending struggle of a young writer's instinctive taste against the mawkish pomposity of adolescence. The close-to-the-bone street life keeps Povod from romanticizing his characters. The junkie-poet is caught in all his flamboyant charm and fraudulence; the crass supplier, the desperate dealer, the petty-thief best friend are all nailed linguistically; and I don't know any other play in which a father, learning of his son's literary aspirations, immediately asks, "Are you gonna kill me in your stories?"

I don't mean to suggest that Povod has hopped into the theater a full-fledged master. ***Cuba and His Teddy Bear*** needs at least 10 minutes of repetitions trimmed out, including its heavy-handed prefigurations of the violence to come. The important motif of Teddy's adventures with junk is badly integrated in the story; the one female character is superfluous. . . .

Still, Povod's promise is real.

Michael Feingold, "Cuba Si, Teddy No," in The Village Voice, *Vol. XXXI, No. 21, May 27, 1986, p. 99.*

JOHN SIMON

The death of realism (and of its twin, naturalism) has been often announced, but always prematurely. Realism remains with us, even as portrait painting remains. Certain faces will always be worth preserving in paint, even as certain raw facts (invented perhaps, but still facts) will want, indeed demand, to be presented undoctored, unsophisticated, uncooked. Naturalism is the steak tartare of literature: good, even if not recommended as a steady diet.

Cuba and His Teddy Bear is the first full-length play by Reinaldo Povod, a "26-year-old Hispanic playwright born and raised in New York's Lower East Side." . . . The name Povod, however, suggests some Slavic, perhaps Jewish, ancestry and has, at any rate, a racy melting-pot smell to it. Lower East Side suggests lower depths, and, sure enough, the play is a *Lower Depths* mixed with *Short Eyes, The Connection,* and even a bit of Kaufman and Hart. A zesty enough stew for a young playwright to cut his teeth on, and if you think stew is not hard enough for tooth cutting, you haven't tried this one.

Cuba is a Lower East Side Hispanic drug pusher who collaborates with Jackie, a Brooklyn Jew and godfather to his son, Teddy, who is pushing seventeen. Cuba, whose wife left him to return to Puerto Rico, is a good father, according to his lights—"You were the only kid walking around the Lower East Side in 250-dollar suits," he lectures Teddy. But he is almost illiterate, has been shot at and jailed, snorts some of the coke he sells right before Teddy, and is, for all his pious (though mumbo jumbo-infested) Catholicism, not the ideal parent for a sensitive boy with literary talent and aspirations who simultaneously loves and execrates him.

The theme—as the play, which tends to wear its meanings on its sleeve, keeps reminding us—is retribution, but differently interpreted by Cuba and Teddy. For even as the sins of the fathers are visited on the sons, the ingenious offspring come up with related sins to visit on their progenitors. Teddy, loving and obedient as he is, dishes out as good as he takes. And Jackie stands by commenting—approvingly, wryly, or hysterically, to suit the occasion. Others, too, get into the act: Che, the addict turned playwright ("I am a junkie who steals, but I'm a junkie who steals with a Tony award"), whom Teddy deludedly reveres, and the sinister black dealer, whom Che brings along to deal with Cuba and Jackie. Also Redlights, a Hispanic client of Cuba's, and his girl, Lourdes, used mostly for comic, or comic-sexy, relief.

A motley crew they are, their doings as dark as they are ludicrous. But for all the violence and decadence (Che has evolved far enough to encompass both), there is not very much going on in ***Cuba and His Teddy Bear***—which could also be described as a lower-Hispanic *Long Day's Journey Into Night;* indeed, when the characters shout all at once, as they repeatedly do, a Jonathan Millerized *Long Day's Journey*. Without, needless to say, the genius of its prototype, but not entirely without its compassion. A junkie's blood, the play informs us, is thin; and so, for all its churning and occasional spurting, is the blood of this play. "Are you happy?," Cuba keeps asking his son, who waffles and, when pressed, "How happy?," responds with "A little happy." We, likewise, feel a little happy about this overlong play: sometimes amused, occasionally slightly moved, and quite frequently bored.

John Simon, "Lower East Side Depths," in New York *Magazine, Vol. 19, No. 22, June 2, 1986, p. 64.*

EDITH OLIVER

Cuba and His Teddy Bear [is] a strong first full-length play by Reinaldo Povod about a drug dealer called Cuba and his fifteen-year-old son. They live on the lower East Side of this city, and Cuba is bringing up the boy alone. The mother, who has deserted husband and son, is a Puerto Rican, and the boy, Teddy, is considered "white." Mysterious. He has no taste for anything Hispanic, doesn't even speak Spanish, hates the music. He wants to be a writer, natch, but fortunately literature is skimped in the action almost to the end. As the play opens, Cuba is sitting at a table with his supplier, Jackie, who is preparing—cutting? pulverizing? (my terminology is shaky in these matters)—cocaine for him. Jackie has brought along a couple of pounds of marijuana as well, which he is eager to dispose of. Teddy, also present, suggests that a friend of his, an addict and writer called Che, handle it. Cuba, a rigorous parent, is very angry, and leery of Che, as well he might be; he refuses to go out and meet Che but agrees to allow him to come to the house. There is much paternal counselling—rough and stylish stuff, absolutely believable. But when Che arrives with an extremely sinister dealer, Cuba sizes them up and, gun in hand, throws them out. He and Jackie leave, and Teddy gets out his secret cache of heroin and tries successfully to shoot up. Che, a flamboyant, pretentious homosexual, returns with the silent dealer, who has got wind of the marijuana and wants it. Considerable activity ensues, much of it frightening (and a lot of it stagy and melodramatic), before Cuba and Jackie return. . . .

If there are better tidings for the theatre than a real play by a new playwright, I cannot imagine what they would be. The first act runs a long time, but not a minute too long for me; I was captivated throughout. The second of the two acts is flawed: Che, once we get to know him, is rather a letdown (unlike the terrifying dealer), and the excerpts from a manuscript of Teddy's, which his father discovers and reads aloud, become very trying. The point, though, is that these flaws don't matter a damn; what does matter is the characters and their speech and the life they lead and the story that is being told. Mr. Povod knows the people he is writing about; he is not slumming or daydreaming. What is fascinating—and is always true when an unfamiliar world is brought to light—is what is taken for granted. Cuba and his supplier, for example, talk shop constantly in front of Teddy, who frequently joins in, yet no boy was ever more carefully watched or disciplined. The sense of a drug-drenched Hispanic community is maintained throughout; a pair of Cuba's friends, a man and a woman high on cocaine and dedicated to a good time, are like messengers from the streets. (p. 74)

Edith Oliver, in a review of "Cuba and His Teddy Bear," in The New Yorker, *Vol. LXII, No. 15, June 2, 1986, pp. 74, 76.*

JACK KROLL

[***Cuba and His Teddy Bear***] is the first full-length play by 26-year-old New Yorker Reinaldo Povod, who clearly knows his subject intimately. What's interesting is that this is a family play: so pervasive has the drug culture become that Joe Cuba is a drug dealer just like Ralph Kramden was a bus driver. In fact, ***Cuba and His Teddy Bear*** has a strong element of comedy; Povod's problems come when he must fuse the comedy and the terror into an inevitable dramatic resolution. Povod doesn't bring it off, but along the way he's turned out a play about drug people that has an almost startling warmth, friendliness and humanity. Povod is a writer of real promise.

Jack Kroll, "De Niro Takes Center Stage: A Family Drug Drama," in Newsweek, *Vol. CVII, No. 22, June 2, 1986, p. 78.*

WILLIAM A. HENRY III

[***Cuba and His Teddy Bear***] has much incident but not a lot of plot. [Povod] relies on arbitrary action more than character development and takes too long reaching an ending. Moments might be cathartic except that these people, with the exception of the son, are not the sort to learn from their mistakes. But Povod knows his terrain, his dialogue is sharp and colorful yet fits the characters, he never bogs down in exposition, and he sentimentalizes nothing.

William A. Henry III, "De Niro, Drugs and a Bold Debut," in Time, *Vol. 127, No. 22, June 2, 1986, p. 77.*

Norman Rush

1933-

American short story writer.

Originally attracted by the adventure of a tenure in Africa, Rush and his wife volunteered for the Peace Corps in 1978. They spent the next five years overseeing the organization's concerns in the country of Botswana. Using his time there to travel and observe, Rush began to write of that southern African nation upon his return to America. "I wasn't able to do any actual composition of stories while I was in Africa. What I did was to accumulate an immense quantity of notes and ideas. I was overwhelmed by the cultural and emotional ironies of the situation, and returned with cartons of undigested material." Six of these stories, four of which appeared in the *New Yorker*, comprise Rush's first collection, *Whites* (1986).

Rush's stories deal with the inability of whites to come to terms with the African culture in which they temporarily reside. From Bruns, the young Dutchman who drowns himself in an attempt to attain revenge against a powerful Boer, to Ione, the attractive wife of an American dentist, whose interests in sexual conquest and black magic lead her to some startling revelations, each character finds their fantasies shattered by the reality of a country they do not understand.

Critics note Rush's ability to evoke place, through brief, telling detail. And while a few critics note problems in the structures of his stories, most find his work effective in combining the social realities of Africa with the more personal concerns of his characters.

© Jerry Bauer

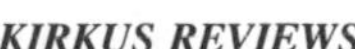

KIRKUS REVIEWS

Six stories about Africa and about the whites—Dutch, Boers, British, but mainly Americans—who live there or who are posted there as workers in government-aid programs.

The publisher tells us that Rush [the author of ***Whites***] was co-director of the Peace Corps in Botswana from 1978 to 1983, and his eye is clearly that of the insider; these stories, though, crisp, observant, and informative as some of them are, don't add a great deal that's new to the well-worked themes of Americans and Europeans abroad. In **"Instruments of Seduction,"** the wife of an American dentist (he advises African governments on dental-care systems) devotes herself to the seduction of men (she's on her 313th) and finds unexpected titillation in a brush with Black revolutionary politics. In **"Official Americans,"** this same woman, priding herself on being fashionably knowledgeable about local ways, arranges for a nervously exhausted and insomnia-plagued American agency bureaucrat to see a medicine man; but the medicine man is a fraud, and the American comes close to death. The stories are fresh in spots, less so in others. In **"Bruns,"** a quietly messianic young Dutchman drowns himself to get back at a bullying and incorrigibly egocentric Boer (wonderfully described) by pinning the death on him. **"Near Pala,"** though, however sharp in its details, is a Hemingway-esque rerun of smug European callousness in the face of local suffering.

On balance, these are stories often better in their details than in their conceptions. Hovering somewhere between the slick and the really perceptive, they will be rewarding in any case to those curious about the lives of career civil servants and agency workers in the harsh sordidness of the poverty- and drought-stricken veldt. (pp. 15-16)

A review of "Whites," in Kirkus Reviews, *Vol. LIV, No. 1, January 1, 1986, pp. 15-16.*

PUBLISHERS WEEKLY

The most extraordinary aspect of these stories [***Whites***] set in Botswana is the absolute authenticity of each of the narrative voices. All are stripped, even severe, but readers will easily distinguish among them. The narrator in **"Bruns,"** a fanatic determined to impose his own moral code on the Boers, who hate him, is distinctively different from the character Frank, **"Alone in Africa"** while his wife is on vacation, leaving him to a bottle of good Riesling and the quirky sexual ministrations of a nubile Botswanan. The heartbreak of everyday tragedy, as evoked in **"Near Pala"** by three women in the drought-parched land beseeching the passengers in a car for water, is heightened by a joltingly ironic ending. Most moving of all, speaking as it seems from the heart of Africa, is the voice of Mokgalagadi, the righteous boy born of a tribe destined for misfortune and thrown out of his mission school. At once innocent and disingenuous, he protests against thieving, yet is saved by thieves, begs on behalf of God, yet is reduced to begging from the houses of God. It is wonderful to hear the click of African syllables in counterpoint to the genteel English of petty officials. In their variety, their pointblank aim, their refusal to editorialize, these six stories raise the curtain on the dark, restless drama of present-day Africa.

A review of "Whites," in Publishers Weekly, *Vol. 229, No. 1, January 3, 1986, p. 43.*

HAZEL ROCHMAN

As in the African stories of Doris Lessing and Nadine Gordimer, Rush [in ***Whites***] integrates complex personal and sexual relationships with a strong sense of the social and political scene. . . . The characters are mainly American expatriates and foreign service officials and their wives, happy to be in Africa "to help" but just passing through. . . . Several stories combine the absurd with violence and suffering. "It was baroque," says an American anthropology doctoral student in her account of a Dutch religious pacifist who challenges the Boer and tribal corruption. Although not all the stories are of equally high quality, Rush vividly evokes the wide, drought-stricken landscape and the overwhelming poverty; he also has a subtle ear for the local nuances of bureaucracy, prejudice, and cultural conflict.

Hazel Rochman, in a review of "Whites," in Booklist, *Vol. 82, No. 12, February 15, 1986, p. 850.*

CHRISTOPHER LEHMANN-HAUPT

Whites. The title of Norman Rush's first collection of stories has an abruptness bordering on a curse. The setting—the south African republic of Botswana (formerly Bechuanaland)—and Mr. Rush's credentials as a co-director of the Peace Corps there from 1978 to 1983 further suggest that we are in for at least a taste of ideology in what follows, one that is not likely to place white people in an especially favorable light.

What a surprise then that the white protagonist of the opening story, **"Bruns,"** turns out to be a hero. He is admittedly a quixotic, even Billy Budd-ish sort of hero, a Dutch pacifist who, by committing suicide, destroys the Boer-dominated power structure of a town near the border of South Africa. "The ruin is absolute. It is a real Götterdämmerung," concludes the narrator, almost chortling. What a surprise that **"Bruns"** is essentially a comedy, since Bruns with his religious zealotry invites little sympathy. What a surprise that the narrator, an American anthropologist ("We are thick on the ground"), is a woman, sexually drawn to the physically "very beautiful" Bruns.

We are caught off guard by **"Bruns,"** just as we are kept off balance by the five other pieces in Mr. Rush's powerful and original collection. In **"Near Pala,"** an English mining engineer reacts to the suffering of three bushwomen by attempting to humiliate his wife. In **"Thieving,"** Paul Ojang, a native boy, recounts in singsong English how "God chose me for a thief" even though "I was very much in churches," "was foremost in singing of hymns, praising God most highly" and "only sought to prosper with good English-speaking." The voices in the stories keep changing, always convincingly authentic sounding. The ironies keep cutting in new directions.

The incidents dramatized in ***Whites*** often strike the reader as having actually happened. . . .

Oddly, this illusion of actuality is heightened by Mr. Rush's occasional failure to transform with perfect seamlessness his raw material into art. Here and there, his endings are a trifle abrupt or heavy-handed. There are passages where the characters' behavior is psychologically fuzzy. It is almost as if the stories were too strong to be tamed by artifice, and it seems quite possible that the author has lapsed intentionally to heighten this effect.

For example, I found it a little hard to believe that Carl Schmoll, in **"Official Americans,"** could be driven so far around the bend by the barking of his neighbor's dogs at night that he would hire a "sangoma" to exercise a form of witchcraft that involves mutilating Carl himself. There is something unreal about this story, something hallucinatory, at least as far as Carl is concerned. Yet that is precisely the point. For Carl, Botswana is an exotic setting exactly suitable for fantasies to be acted out. The story isn't about where he's driven by his fears but rather where he wishes to transport himself.

For most of the foreigners in ***Whites,*** Botswana is a setting for fantasies. And as is often the case with exotic lands, the fantasies inspired are mainly sexual. The narrator of **"Bruns"** is thrilled by its hero's masochistic death. There is an implied sexuality between Paul, the native boy of **Thieving,"** and the wealthy banker's wife who corrupts him with kindness. . . .

One might expect Mr. Rush to condemn the projection of white fantasies onto black Africa. But **"Alone in Africa,"** the highly comic concluding story, effectively resolves that particular issue. A perfect little sexual psychodrama, the story traps Frank the dentist between Moitse, the black temptress who has come to see him when his wife is away, and Benedict Christie, who might as well be Frank's superego. Is Moitse merely a passive sex object, a projection of Frank's fantasy? Not at all. After urging her out of the house and proving to the prying Christie that no hanky-panky is going on, Frank breathes a figurative sigh of relief. "He lays down on the bed. He felt his pulse slowing. Tears came to his eyes for a while. He was near sleep."

And then come the concluding lines of the story and the book: "There was a scraping sound at the window above him, the sound of nails on the flyscreen. He recognized it. He sat up straight. She was back.

"She was back."

Christopher Lehmann-Haupt, in a review of "Whites," in The New York Times, *February 27, 1986, p. C21.*

An Excerpt from *Whites*

"Would you like to see my *tokoloshi*?" she asked, crossing her legs.

He stopped chewing. She warned herself not to be reckless.

"Dream animals!" she said. "Little effigies. I collect them. The Bushmen carve them out of softwood. They use them as symbols of evil in some ceremony they do. They're turning up along with all the other Bushman artifacts, the puberty aprons and so on, in the craft shops. Let me show you."

She got two *tokoloshi* from a cabinet.

"They call these the evil creatures who come to you at night in dreams. There are some interesting features. What you see when you look casually is this manlike figure with what looks like the head of a fox or rabbit or zebra at first glance. But look at the clothing. Doesn't this look like a clerical jacket? The collar shape? They're all like that. And look closely at the animal. It's actually a spotted jackal, the most despised animal there is because of its taste for carrion. Now look in front at this funny little tablet that looks like a huge belt buckle with these X shapes burned into it. My theory is that it's a Bushman version of the Union Jack. If you notice on this one, the being is wearing a funny belt. It looks like a cartridge belt to me. Some of the *tokoloshi* are smoking these removable pipes. White tourists buy these things and think they're cute. I think each one is a carved insult to the West. And we buy loads of them. I do. The black areas like the jacket are done by charring the wood with hot nails and things."

He handled the carvings dutifully and then gave them back to her. He murmured that they were interesting.

He took more tea. She stood the *tokoloshi* on an end table halfway across the room, facing them. He began contemplating them, sipping his tea minutely. Time was passing. She had various mottoes she used on herself. One was, Inside every suit and tie is a naked man trying to get out. She knew they were stupid, but they helped. He was still in the grip of whatever was bothering him.

LESLIE MARMON SILKO

A childhood spent on the Laguna Pueblo Reservation in New Mexico brought me to the conclusion that the third world is not just poor, developing nations. The third world is any place dogs roam freely, howl and bark all night, and defecate and breed on the streets. Last autumn in southern China I discovered that the Chinese understand what dogs are good for—good for lunch, good for dinner, and tasty with noodles and greens. The way the Chinese explained it, European colonialists used to feed their pet dogs while Chinese starved. Plains Indian tribes had good dog recipes too, until Christian missionaries arrived with their sentimentality for their pets.

Dogs and attitudes toward them reveal a great deal about the values of a culture. In ***Whites,*** an admirable collection of short stories set in Botswana, a nation that shares a border with South Africa, Norman Rush shows that he understands this. . . . In **"Official Americans,"** Carl, a middle-aged State Department official stationed in Botswana, has his personal and professional life virtually destroyed by barking dogs that belong to his neighbor, the powerful Minister of Labor. He is beset by a maze of conflicting values and his own weakness and lack of conviction. When a local police commander recommends an arsenic compound for the dog problem, Carl is sure that this is commonly done but is uncomfortable with the directness of the Botswana approach. But nights of lost sleep take their toll and he consults Ione, a colleague's wife who passes the time dabbling in the occult.

Ione is a spiritual shopper, moving from one belief or cult to another. Contemporary American culture seems to offer her no more than this. Ione knows that something peculiarly American rejects commitment to any belief. Absence of real commitment is what's attractive about overseas assignments. . . . She persuades Carl to try a local shaman who claims to have a cure for dogs that bark all night. When he undergoes a ritual in which he is given a series of cuts on his back, Carl first experiences "the sensation of conviction. The ritual felt real to him for the first time." But Carl lacks the courage to keep this conviction. He panics, assumes the ritual wounds are infected, and attempts to hide them from his wife and the doctors. Carl does all the wrong things, treats himself with antibiotics and nearly dies. But his confusions over the legitimacy of the shaman's ritual and his moment of conviction are resolved. . . .

The "new" Africa Mr. Rush reveals in his stories is full of contradictions. It is a cross-cultural hybrid that grew out of African independence and ancient tribalism, but also out of hundreds of years of white colonialism and apartheid both official and unofficial. But many of the cultural elements Europeans shoved down African throats have lost their charm for whites. In **"Bruns,"** an anthropologist from Stanford University goes into the bush to study indigenous nutrition, but learns "the sad fact is you go into the middle of nowhere and people are eating Simba chips and cornflakes and drinking Castle lager."

Where different tribal cultures once coexisted with only sporadic raiding or battles, the danger of genocide now looms. After all, black Africans have had intensive instruction from European colonialists, the best teachers of racism and genocide. In **"Thieving,"** the narrator suffers because of de facto apartheid still operational even in the "new" African nations like Botswana, which gained independence in 1966.

Whites is about disillusionment and loss of conviction. Whether it was the Peace Corps in Botswana or Vista volunteers on the Laguna Pueblo Reservation in the 1960's, a sizable portion of a generation set out with great enthusiasm to share what they believed was valuable: white America's wealth of information and technical resources. The failure of American idealism and technical resources that Mr. Rush describes in these stories, and the subsequent disillusionment—both national and personal—are second only to the Vietnam War in their continuing impact on the direction of American foreign and domestic policy today. Mr. Rush's whites can no longer tote the "white man's burden" because they can't even lift themselves—their loss of conviction is so profound.

Mr. Rush attempts to articulate what Americans or whites in general may be able to salvage where the legacies of apartheid and colonialism make it almost impossible to live and remain decent human beings. His characters struggle to maintain a connection with the world, always hoping for even a small measure of grace. Most whites in Mr. Rush's Botswana are too weak to grasp the considerable opportunities Africa offers them. Occasionally his characters manage to secure a little personal integrity, but only at great cost. Carl is deaf. Mokgalagadi, the narrator in **"Thieving,"** is crazed. In **"Bruns,"** the anthropologist narrates with such icy detachment that she might as well be reporting from Uranus.

A middle-aged American woman in **"Instruments of Seduction"** becomes a seductress, a choice that's hers, a role in which she is not just going through the motions or fooling anybody. Only this woman, and a dentist, Frank, in **"Alone in Africa,"** manage to grasp the possibilities for personal salvation Africa offers them despite all its contradictions and ugly colonial legacies. By choosing the profession of sexual seduction, the woman makes wonderful use of Botswana's "certain atmosphere of allusion to death." She not only fashions a sense of self and identity that keeps her humanity intact, she also manages to realize how the terrifying atmosphere of Botswana can actually be used to deliver her from isolation and loneliness.

Frank, the dentist, actually has Botswana's bounty of generosity, intelligence and vitality rain down on him in the person of Moitse, a woman who comes and proposes to be his maid while his wife is out of town. The voluptuous warmth of all that is good in Botswana is offered to this man as a simple gesture of kindness, an offer of comfort that is both humane and wise. Yet Frank must make the choice. All the arguments, the inhibitions he could succumb to, must be swept aside. In the end, there's probably still enough grace available in Botswana alone to save us all. All that's required is the vision to see it and the courage to open the door.

The cynicism and self-loathing, or worse yet, the self-righteousness that often appear in fiction about whites in the third world are a dead end, whether the writer be black, "colored" or white. It isn't just whites who must face up to moral and political failures in the third world today, Mr. Rush seems to be saying. ***Whites*** is an admirable beginning; because the longer stories work best, I hope he will deliver us a novel soon. The world could use a few more books from human beings like Mr. Rush.

Leslie Marmon Silko, "Grace Abounding in Botswana," in The New York Times Book Review, *March 23, 1986, p. 7.*

JONATHAN YARDLEY

The complex relationships among black natives and white settlers in Africa have long fascinated British novelists, and have produced numerous first-rate works of fiction, but the subject has never really caught on among American writers: perhaps because Africa has never been the object of much imperialist interest in this country, perhaps because black-white relations here at home are quite complex enough in themselves and have produced a rich body of work by black and white writers alike. Whatever the case, apart from a number of novels and stories by Ernest Hemingway and Paul Theroux, little significant American fiction has been set in Africa, and even for these two qualifications must be noted; Hemingway's African fiction deals almost entirely with whites, and Theroux's is mostly apprentice work that, rightly or wrongly, does not have much to do with the high esteem in which he is now held.

So Norman Rush, who is American and who does write about how blacks and whites get along in Africa, has the field pretty much to himself. ***Whites,*** his first book, is a collection of six low-keyed yet forceful stories set in Botswana, where Rush lived from 1978 to 1983. Occasionally there is evidence in them of those who have gone before—Evelyn Waugh, Graham Greene, William Boyd—but there is an important difference. While the British writers focus on colonialism, the Africa about which Rush writes is post-colonial and the whites who come to it are more likely to do so as governmental emissaries or would-be angels of mercy than as rank exploiters; their lives tend to be more immediately intertwined with those of the black natives and their relationships with them are, if anything, even more complex and ambiguous.

That having been said, oddly enough the most successful story of the six is not about American settlers, but about two British couples. It is called **"Near Pala"**; as in most of the stories a central image is the terrible drought afflicting southern and central Africa. The couples are taking a long drive in a Land-Rover through desolate country. Nan, talking in the back seat with Tess, grows increasingly voluble about the shortcomings of white behavior towards blacks—"Truly," she asks, "are we so superior as we think?"—while in the front seat Gareth, her husband, becomes more and more impatient with her: "Might I ask where you have the least proof of that? You don't know a bloody thing about it. We can't set a foot right if we're white, can we? Regular litany with you, Nan. You're becoming tiresome!"

As the conversation grows steadily sharper, the vehicle enters an especially difficult part of the journey. There, while Gareth struggles to keep them on course, Nan pleads with him to stop and help three women and a child, all pleading for water. Gareth refuses; after a heated argument Nan at last flings the precious water bottle out of the car, whereupon Gareth grinds the car to a halt and demands that she fetch the bottle. There the story ends, but what finally happens is beside the point. Without oversimplification, Rush has presented in Nan and Gareth opposing white attitudes toward Africa, and by placing them inside a single marriage has shown how intimately connected they are. Nan is decent but a little foolish, Gareth is cruel but practical; in the white presence in Africa, there are elements of all of these.

In **"Near Pala"** as in several other stories, a woman is the most sympathetic figure. Of the other women, by far the most interesting is Ione, an American nearing 50 who appears in three stories; she has come to Africa with her husband, Frank, who has "a contract to advise African governments on dental care systems." He is on the road much of the time; being a sensuous and independent woman, she takes advantage of his absences to play the game of seduction. Botswana is exactly the locale for that game:

"This place had been designed with her in mind. The furniture the government provided even looked like it came from a bordello. And Botswana was unnerving in some overall way there was only one word for: conducive." . . .

For Ione as for the other whites, Africa is a place where the ordinary rules do not apply. They are in a country that is not their own, in a civilization they do not understand, cannot really connect to, and feel no obligation toward. They may be deeply pained by the drought, the widespread suffering among Africans, the pervasive conviction that matters will get not better but only worse, yet they are at a distance from this because they are white and because, of course, they can always go home. In these strange lives, everything matters and nothing matters; they are under strong constraints, especially those who work for their government, yet in a sense they are utterly free.

In this odd situation they do what people ordinarily do: they reach out, however clumsily and ineffectively, to each other or to the Africans. In a bleak landscape, surrounded by privation and death, they seek the comforts of the flesh and the consolation that affection brings. They often come up short of either, but that probably would be just as true if they were back home. What matters, as Rush emphasizes over and again, is that they try.

Jonathan Yardley, "Our Man in Botswana," in Book World—The Washington Post, *March 23, 1986, p. 3.*

GEORGE PACKER

The flap copy of Norman Rush's new collection of stories, ***Whites,*** suggests that they depart from the apolitical conventions of contemporary American fiction. Set in independent Botswana, where Rush was a Peace Corps country director for five years, they occur, we are told, "at the intersections where whites and emerging Africa meet, . . . where ancient and modern and changing worlds come together with dizzying effect." From this, and from the book's blurbs and early reviews, I imagined something resembling the short fiction of Nadine Gordimer aand V. S. Naipaul, stories about individual lives caught in, and inseparable from, the brutal history of our age.

The jacket misleads; ***Whites*** is not about "the complex relationship . . . between blacks and whites in Africa today." It is not really about blacks or Africa at all, though the setting may be enough to fool some readers. The author's title is accurate: most of the stories examine whites—Americans, English, Dutch and Canadians—whose lives amid hors d'oeuvres and adultery and hair spray are as close to life back home as they can possibly make them. It's true that Botswana is here on every page. Rush has a brilliant eye for landscape and a talent for singling out what is not just exotic but also banal and therefore real about Africa—"late-afternoon light the color of glue." And yet the setting is basically irrelevant, a landscape without figures. The only African characters to appear in these six stories are the young Batswana narrator of **"Thieving"** and the adolescent seductress in **"Alone in Africa."** The other Africans who pass through are no more than figments of the whites' fantasies or obsessions or irritations. If these stories were moved to Katmandu, or Cleveland, a thousand details would have to change, the atmosphere and ironies would shift a litle, but at least half of the stories would remain the same.

This is because Rush's subject is not blacks and whites in Africa, or even (Naipaul's theme) Westerners caught in the throes of the contemporary Third World. It is the moral and spiritual quandaries of middle-class foreigners who happen to be stuck out in Botswana. And this theme Rush handles with great wit and sympathy. (p. 738)

"Official Americans" is typical of the intricate structures and ironic themes of the other stories. Rush is a master at plot—something that has almost disappeared from the razor-thin slices of life we nibble at in contemporary short fiction—and these stories all have a touch of O. Henry. . . .

His stories often end with an ironic inversion on a nearly farcical chain of events that exposes the self-deception his characters use to detach themselves from any meaningful connection to other lives. They are naïvely cynical in a peculiarly American way, and their lack of conviction haunts them without initiating deep change. Frank, the protagonist of **"Alone in Africa,"** is alarmed at how easily he succumbs to a Batswana girl while his wife, Ione, is away in Italy. The girl exposes Frank to the pious suspicions of his British neighbor Christie—a snooping Jeremiah—and then rescues him. But the scare humiliates Frank, and at the end of the evening's farce he is faced with the small hollow core at the center of his life. . . .

Rush's eye is unsparing, but beneath the irony and near-slapstick plots there is also a kind of sad compassion.

Although the stories concern moral moments in his characters' lives, Rush, the esthetician, savors puns and surprises, and he enjoys a trick that intrudes on every story: the habit of stepping back like a solicitous stand-up comic to wink at the reader. "This is a wonderful story. . . . This is extraordinary!" the woman in **"Instruments of Seduction"** exclaims as the doctor she is seducing describes a menacing encounter with a South African refugee. "The story was a brilliant thing, a gem." Frank and Ione appear in several stories, and their re-entry is so subtle that Rush seems to be testing his readers' cleverness—if you don't get it, then part of the story is lost on you. The writing is too good to need these prompting nudges and self-satisfied winks. They indicate that Rush has his eye on something other than "the complex relationship . . . between blacks and whites in Africa today." (p. 739)

The situation of whites in independent Africa is charged with politics, and in spite of their evasions a message can be culled from the accumulated details of these stories: Simply put, any effort at change does more harm than good, though vanity and naïveté will delude us into trying. . . . The vision—bathetic, not tragic—is of political futility. The stories generally have the point of view of the anthropologist, a self-described relativist who watches the demise of Bruns and the provincial town with a wan, detached smile.

In this sense ***Whites*** is saying something about "whites and blacks in modern Africa," but its point, except in **"Bruns"** and **"Thieving,"** emerges on the periphery, in details that aren't essential to the heart of the story. After Carl explains the irresponsibility of whites in Africa, he goes on to say that he has discovered the meaning of his life. And not surprisingly, it has nothing to do with the explanation he's just given: "It's about women. Women are the meaning of my life." That is the basic gesture of ***Whites:*** a glance at the larger issue the situation raises, and then a return to the really important thing, the private matter that makes these lives no different from ones lived in San Francisco or on the Upper West Side.

The gesture has its risks. One story, **"Near Pala,"** shows what happens when a writer introduces politics as a device and then loses his grip. Two English couples in a Land-Rover are driving across the bush. Nan and Gareth, unhappily married, argue about the Batswana—whether they are inherently good (Nan's position), or incompetent (Gareth's). These positions resolve into the extremes of sentimentality and cynicism. . . . The arguments are obvious and static; the story's real concern, of course, is the marital tension, with a subtle focus on Nan's unwanted pregnancy. . . . The story might have been one of Rush's strongest. It fails because its politics turn into caricature. Gareth, who can't spare a drop of water for the drought-stricken women, becomes a monster, while all decency flows to Nan.

"Near Pala" is the only failure in the collection. Elsewhere Rush is superb at the kind of story an American in Africa probably has to write. There is something honest in his refusal to cross the frontier and take on Africa and Africans. One theme of ***Whites*** seems to be, You know what you are. A more "political" collection might have appeared ambitious and sounded only hollow. (pp. 739-40)

George Packer, "Alone in Africa," in The Nation, *New York, Vol. 242, No. 20, May 24, 1986, pp. 738-40.*

STEVE KATZ

Whites is a terrific book, important for our understanding of white people in the world, particularly of the roles of whites in Botswana. Everyone should read it. . . . Norman Rush is an extraordinary writer. To every sentence he has given the intelligence of his absolute attention, the passion of his political intensity, and his humanity. . . . [He] pays scrupulous attention to the operation of the language, and to his subject, the lives of white people in Botswana. . . .

For instance, "It was the next day." is the opening paragraph of a story about the conflict of an insomniac man with his neighbor's barking watchdogs. It is a simple statement, in essence, but rich in strategy. It sets us up for insomnia, makes us feel uneasy about something we should know from the night before. It's a great relief to the character that the next day has come, and a canny strategy for the author to unsettle the reader, make him think he should know what happened on the days before, tweaking the expectation that tomorrow comes next, whereas in accepting the convention of this opening paragraph you agree that yesterday has to come next. This creates a certain narrative tension, suspense, a mild headache, not unlike what the character himself is feeling. . . .

Whites in Botswana live in the luxurious buildings. Blacks and coloreds live as best they can according to their position and privilege, of which there is very little for blacks. The whites enjoy every available privilege, and almost every white in the book goes there for that reason, vague idealisms and intellectual pursuits notwithstanding. (p. 12)

[The] privileged whites, this woman anthropologist, for instance, makes observations like, "They [the Boers] still pay their farm labor in sugar and salt and permission to crawl underneath their cows and suck fresh milk. It is baroque." Since she is an anthropologist, "baroque" is not a judgment. Privilege is again slyly exposed by irony when she says, "You know a drought is bad when cattle come into town and bite the brass taps off the cisterns." You know she will never feel this drought parch her throat, and that she can leave Botswana if everything gets too thirsty.

An **"Official American"** from the story by that title has these thoughts about his wife, "She was his second wife, and she was perfect. Her skin was perfect for Africa—the way she tanned beautifully. She loved Botswana's dry climate, and in fact that reminded him to remind her to be sensitive about the drought when she was enthusing about the climate in front of people." The levels of personal irony in this are worthy of Chekhov, and carry beyond the personal to a broader political irony unique to ***Whites***. (p. 13)

Whites is the most effective political fiction. Without moralizing, the stories reveal characters blinded by their cultural biases. Norman Rush never preaches about them, but lets them condemn themselves with their own words and actions. The judgment is more frightening because everyone is so familiar, and it's easy to find these attitudes among one's own friends, like that young couple you know going off to work in the Peace Corps. The whites are even sympathetic, like you and me, with good intentions. . . . If we are honest with ourselves we have no trouble isolating the contradictions and ironies in the attitudes of Carl, Ione, Frank, etc., in our own hearts. We can be grateful to Norman Rush for identifying them with so much wit and compassion, so that the healing might begin.

In the most difficult, most rewarding tour de force of the stories, **"Thieving,"** a young Botswana black man tells the story of his conversion from his own predisposition to Christian virtues and honesty, to a life of survival by stealing from church collection boxes. At one point he reflects on his conversion, "Because at times I was idling there, I fell more to reasoning as to God's ways. When I set myself against thieving, always God punished me, I said. And if I go near thieving, . . . always I am saved. I said if only one time God can see me a thief full-made, and then see me in straits, lamenting, He shall know His error." The young man's logic is inevitable in the story, and peels back the hypocrisy of the colonialists professing through their missionaries, and provides us also a paradigm for the bizarre reflection of imperialist brutality we've seen during the last decades in independent Africa.

Norman Rush is an effective political writer because he has the experience and talent to give us the political forces operating in the lives of ordinary, imperfect people. Their political blind spots are more a result of self-involvement and distraction than of malice and greed, and that makes the indictment hit home. (pp. 13, 16)

The pace of these stories makes one look for more. The characters could easily inhabit a longer work and I suspect the stories could be episodes from a novel abandoned. It would be rich to relax with a long narrative, a big novel by Norman Rush. . . .

One of the richest books of the last ten years. Twenty years? However you like your superlatives. It should be required study for anyone entering the foreign service or Peace Corps. I wish there were more books in print by Norman Rush. I would read them now. (p. 16)

Steve Katz, "Armed to the Teeth, Having Fun," in The American Book Review, *Vol. 9, No. 2, March-April, 1987, pp. 12-13, 16.*

Mona (Elizabeth) Simpson

1957-

American novelist and short story writer.

Anywhere but Here (1986), Simpson's first novel, is the result of four years of dedicated novel writing. Previously, Simpson had dabbled in poetry—"the usual, on life, death, love, and regret"—before immersing herself in fiction. Her short fiction has been published in *Ploughshares, Iowa Review, North American Review,* and *Paris Review,* where Simpson works as a senior editor. Some of Simpson's pieces have been distinguished by their selection for the anthologies *Best American Short Stories 1986, The Pushcart Prize XI,* and *Twenty under Thirty*.

"I think with a first novel, all the years of your life up to the one you are writing in give inspirations, ideas, nagging threads of . . . what, something? and you try, in some way, to get them all in," Simpson commented. "With this book, I actually began with an image of a woman on a clean highway, putting her kid outside by the road, driving off and then coming back, the kid standing in the ditch, waiting, touching his arms." This vignette of abandonment and reconciliation became the novel's opening scene, dramatizing the ambivalent relationship between Adele, a charming but emotionally disturbed woman, and her young daughter Ann. With dreams of making Ann a child actress, Adele abandons her husband and home in Bay City, Wisconsin (modeled after Simpson's native Green Bay), and takes Ann to California. The squalid life they encounter there contrasts with Adele's manic fantasies of glamor and success. Ann relates the main story, while in separate chapters Adele's sister and mother, and finally Adele herself, provide additional commentary. Explained Simpson: "The book is about the people who stayed in their hometowns and put down their roots and the people who went west and tried to get more from life, because that seems to me the story of life in America." She confessed that, although she originally disliked Adele, her affection for the character grew as the novel progressed. "Adele is unstable, but troubled by American troubles: by the striving for gentility, the striving for a higher station. I wanted her dreams to be what got her into trouble."

Most critics discount the Wisconsin chapters, finding them unnecessary additions to Ann's narrative, though admitting that they add historical perspective to the emotional struggles between Ann and her mother. Adele emerges as an overwhelming presence in both Ann's life and the novel, and reviewers note that while her behavior is often exasperating or unsettling, Simpson portrays her with objectivity and sympathy as well as humor. The author further enriches her story, critics observe, by her precise and provocative descriptions of settings and characters. According to several commentators, Simpson has achieved in *Anywhere but Here* a successful blend of family and social themes, for she not only offers a poignant exploration of the mother-daughter relationship, but with her portrait of the restless, irresponsible Adele exposes the darker aspect of American values and aspirations.

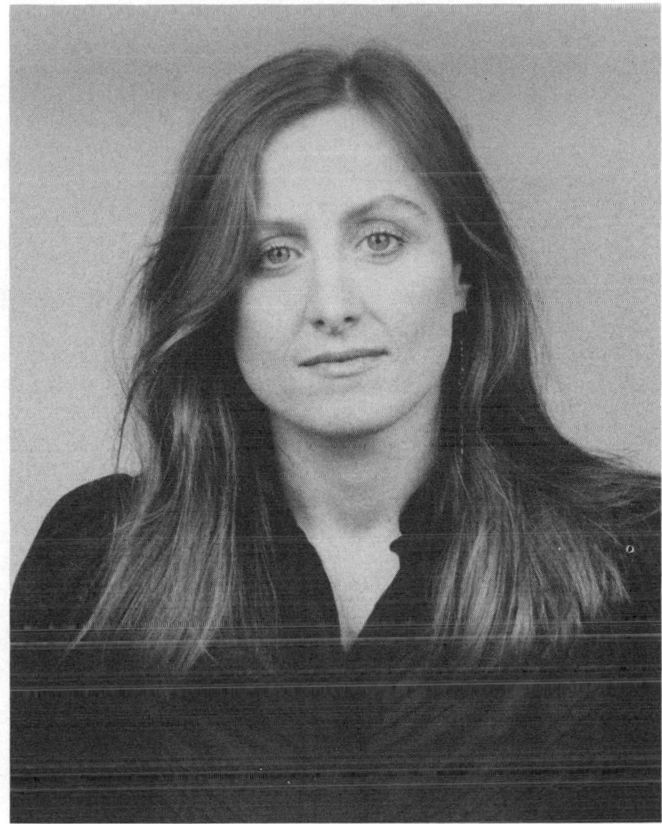

About her future plans, Simpson reports, "I'm writing another novel—this one about a fictitious town in the west and a history of its families. Particularly, the book focuses on the moment in characters's lives when they struggle most with their idealism—the ways in which they try to express it (some become revolutionaries, some do-gooders) or learn to abandon it."

KIRKUS REVIEWS

Simpson's fictional debut [***Anywhere but Here***] no doubt intended as an oddly touching tale of a romantically neurotic woman, catalogues in sordid detail that same woman's truly disturbing behavior—her pathological relations with her mother, sister, and daughter, all of whom speak here at length in the similar, flat cadences of their native Midwest.

When Adele August finally gets in a word edgewise, in the last few pages of this rambling and anecdotal novel, she's well beyond redemption. Her final bit of West Coast psychobabble is self-serving, to say the least, a pathetic apology for a lifetime of lies and deceptions. Her daughter, Ann, the main narrator here, chronicles her mother's manias, compulsions, and vanities with a deadpan weariness that seems to mask a genuine horror. It's left to her long-suffering and plain-speaking grandmother, Lillian, to sum up Adele—"she wasn't quite all there." And that partly explains why Adele drags nine-year-old daughter Ann with her cross-country in an unpaid-for Lincoln, California-dreaming all the way. Unhappy with her job as a teacher, her second husband, and pretty much everything else about Bay City, Wisconsin, Adele hopes "to catch us a man" out West and see Ann become a star, the latter a pipe dream fed only by Adele's hyperactive imagination. After more years of living beyond their means, frazzled mother and embarrassed daughter find themselves down and out in Beverly Hills, broke, hungry, and lonely. More a cut-and-paste assemblage of memories than a well-plotted novel, the disjointed and open-ended narrative wanders through time and place, filling in the ugly particulars of Adele's malfeasance, with Ann providing numerous pseudo-insights ("Our conversations were always like that, like lighting single matches." "You remember the places you've lost to").

By the time you finish this overly long, warts-and-all family portrait, you just might wish, as the title inadvertently suggests, that you'd been somewhere else all along.

A review of "Anywhere but Here," in Kirkus Reviews, *Vol. LIV, No. 21, November 1, 1986, p. 1611.*

PUBLISHERS WEEKLY

Through the engaging vision of Ann, her protagonist, Simpson brings a fresh perspective [in ***Anywhere but Here***] to the much plumbed mother-daughter relationship. In less skilled hands, Adele, an overbearing single mother who shares a bed and shoplifts with her daughter, could have become a caricature. But Simpson astutely balances the tense desires of this primal symbiotic attachment. Adele's discontented wanderlust, capriciousness, paradoxically generous/selfish nature and inveterate lying and pipe-dreaming alienate as well as enchant and endear. . . . Simpson keenly describes the vulnerability of childhood through a daughter's gradual, painful realization that her mother is "not responsible enough to take care of herself, not to mention another person." She also displays a knack for provocative phrasing that commands the reader's attention. Unfortunately, Simpson silences Ann's clear voice with short, intrusive sections written from the points of view of her unfulfilled women relatives. This artifice may fill in informational gaps, but it strains an otherwise masterful debut that sings with authenticity. For its grasp of human relationships and sheer readability, Simpson's novel may well be this season's *The Good Mother*.

A review of "Anywhere but Here," in Publishers Weekly, *Vol. 230, No. 19, November 7, 1986, p. 54.*

MICHIKO KAKUTANI

Mona Simpson's stunning first novel [***Anywhere But Here***] opens simply with a glimpse of a mother and a daughter driving westward in a Lincoln Continental. They are driving from their hometown of Bay City, Wis., to California so that the girl—Ann—can become a child star. In lieu of eating at restaurants, they steal vegetables from convenient farm trucks, and they use a borrowed credit card to charge gasoline and one-night stays at cheap motels. Behind them, to the east, is their old life, a life of modest expectations, modest comforts and modest rewards; ahead lies California, and all the glittering promises of that golden land.

In relating the story of Ann and her mother, Adele, Ms. Simpson not only creates a compelling tale of family love and duplicity, but she also takes on—and reinvents—many of America's essential myths, from our faith in the ever-receding frontier to our uneasy mediation between small-town pieties and big-time dreams. As in so much contemporary fiction, the fragmentation of the family stands as one of this novel's central themes, as is the dichotomy between rootlessness and freedom, domesticity and suffocation. But if ***Anywhere But Here*** carries echoes of the "on the road" novel, the "small town" novel and the Western-pioneer novel, Ms. Simpson also succeeds in creating a wholly original work—a work stamped with the insignia of a distinctive voice and animated by two idiosyncratic and memorable heroines.

At once optimistic and frightened, self-sacrificing and selfish, Adele thinks little of using or hurting other people. Having been abandoned by Ann's father—a vacuum-cleaner salesman who trades his dreams of becoming a songwriter to marry a wealthy woman—she cavalierly leaves her second husband, Ted, and sets out to begin a new life, tabula rasa. In the process, she lies about her education, her job and her past, and she deludes herself, as well, as to her prospects: convinced that one unlikely man after another will marry her, she ends up disappointed but unbroken—one set of dreams replaced by yet another.

As a mother, she shamelessly tries to manipulate her daughter—she threatens suicide when Ann goes out on a date, and whines about sacrificing to give her daughter opportunities she actually craves for herself. Awful as Adele seems, she is also a fiercely protective mother, and as seen through Ann's ambivalent eyes, her pretensions (serving chateaubriand in a barely furnished apartment, coining "tasteful" remarks, calculated to be overheard in public places) are both touching and pathetic. Like the mother and daughter in *Terms of Endearment,* she and Ann are bonded together by love and hate and history, and as ***Anywhere But Here*** progresses, we observe both the differences that separate them, and the similarities that bind them together. Ann learns how to lie and steal from her mother, and while she yearns for a "normal" life free of carelessness and self-delusion, she also inherits Adele's resentments and her capacity to survive.

In the course of the novel—through flashbacks and looping reminiscences delivered from disparate points of view—we see Ann grow from childhood into adolescence and beyond, and thanks to Ms. Simpson's artistry, we are made to feel both the pull of family history and the redeeming role of individual will. In addition, we are given a wonderful montage of scenes that fix her life in our minds with the clarity of snapshots from a photo album: Ann, as a child, watching her father drive away from home for the last time in his brown Valiant with his vacuum cleaners and a new suitcase; Ann, slightly older, clutching a package of brightly colored headbands, given to her as a gift from her absent father; Ann, at age 12, driving across the country with her mother, learning how to apply makeup in gas-station restrooms, and Ann, as a teen-ager, sharing an ice-cream sundae with her mother, in an effort to forget the humiliation of being down and out in Beverly Hills.

Having carefully mapped out the dreams that Adele and Ann have borrowed from slick magazines, Ms. Simpson goes on to delineate the reality of their furtive, attenuated existence in California, orchestrating tiny social details and larger emotional ones to give the reader a sense of the texture of their daily life: Adele's increasingly desperate attempts to catch herself a husband; Ann's desultory attempts to become a television star, and their growing antagonism toward one another. In the interests of opening out her story to embrace a larger slice of contemporary history, she occasionally cuts away from Ann and Adele to sketch in the very different lives chosen by their relatives, who stayed behind in Wisconsin. Although some of these digressions seem unnecessary, even distracting—we don't really need to hear about childhood friends shipped off to Vietnam or the infidelities of assorted friends—these other stories do lend ballast to the tale of Ann and Adele; and they give ***Anywhere But Here*** the specific gravity of a shared history.

Indeed, it is one of Ms. Simpson's many achievements in this sad, fierce novel that she makes us understand about families—how we are trapped by them and how we can escape; how we are irrevocably shaped by the defections and betrayals of others, and how we may transcend those losses through love and will. She makes us understand the idea of home and what it means to lose that idea of safety and place; and in doing so, she makes us apprehend the darkness that lies just beneath the brightly painted surfaces of daily life.

Michiko Kakutani, in a review of "Anywhere but Here," in The New York Times, *December 24, 1986, p. C16.*

RICHARD EDER

Mistrust a character who is larger than life. Billboards are larger than life too, and much emptier.

There are times in Mona Simpson's remarkably gifted first novel [***Anywhere but Here***] when the continual surging of her protagonist, Adele, arouses some such feeling. To voice it is to charge the wave. And after voicing it, this reviewer finds himself up-ended and lifted far up the beach. . . .

Adele is the flimflam woman of the year, lighting up and blighting whatever she touches. Years before, she ruined her older sister Carol's wedding by spending the whole time in the one bathroom, thus forcing the 150 guests to squeeze home early. On the road and in California, she is a mixture of Auntie Mame, Blanche Dubois and Willy Loman. She is avid and fretful, fiery and frail, credulous and tricky, unstoppable and never arriving. Under Adele's dazzlement, and the disconcerting precision with which Simpson handles a wealth of detail about Midwestern small towns, the slummy edges of Beverly Hills glamour, and a varied range of American lives and pseudo-lives, she does two big things.

One is to anchor her story securely to a real theme. Like Sam Shepard's *Curse of the Starving Class,* though with vastly different means, ***Anywhere but Here*** tells of the famished underside of our culture of glamour and success.

Drifting from one small job to another, Adele insists on living in ramshackle quarters to be inside the Beverly Hills High School district, where Ann can make useful friends and connections. They are obsessed with food and often go without. When they have a little money, she and Ann eat cold steak right out of the ice box; when they don't, they subsist on ice cream, the symbol of instant well-being and nutritional disaster.

The second big accomplishment is artistic. Adele is the most conspicuous thing in the book but not the most important. Colorful, funny and alarming, she is a feint, a diversion. Under the fireworks, something else is happening. Ann, the narrator, is watching, learning, growing up, growing tough and breaking away.

Her "I," seemingly overshadowed, is the book's real force. She is not omniscient and not aloof. She is dazzled by her mother and fights her. She knows that Adele's fantasies about a series of affluent lovers are so many ships that unfailingly sink as they come in. They are holed at the waterline. Yet when one of the putative lovers, a psychiatrist, confirms that Adele's affair with him is imaginary, Ann feels something collapse inside her.

As wild in her own way as her mother, Ann fights a child's underground battle to survive; and wins it. Adele's dream of getting her into show business comes true. At an audition, Ann puts on a display of hysterical energy, very much like Adele's, in fact. It impresses a producer and she becomes a minor TV star. The audition was secured—just as her mother had counted on—by a Beverly Hills connection. The terrible thing, in fact, about Adele's cloudy visions and relentless struggling is that they sometimes work.

Simpson makes the scatty cloud-battling of Adele's and Ann's lives grotesque, funny and bitingly real. But she is not engaged in easy judgment. Into their story, she inserts episodes from the lives of Adele's family back in Wisconsin.

Taken by themselves, Adele's and Ann's choices seem tinselly and foolish. Taken in contrast to what they have left behind, the matter is not so simple. Simpson's vision is very dark. Love, hope and a decent and humane life are as elusive in the old America as in the new one.

Anywhere but Here has its flaws. The interweaving of the Wisconsin and the California episodes is sometimes awkward. It is important for us to get fed up with Adele's hysterical beguilements, so we can see Ann better; but even so, it might have helped to curtail her a little.

But the book's rich texture and its ingenious tracking of our far-fetched normalities mark Simpson as a brightly talented new writer. Something deeper and more exciting than bright talent is suggested by the stony pain of Carol's narration, and by subtle variations of Ann's outbursts and silences, with their light and a few terrible shadows.

Richard Eder, in a review of "Anywhere but Here," in Los Angeles Times Book Review, *January 4, 1987, p. 3.*

SVEN BIRKERTS

In the opening scene of Mona Simpson's ***Anywhere But Here,*** 12-year-old Ann August stands at the edge of a flat Western highway, watching with growing panic as her mother's white Continental turns into a dot on the horizon. Car and mother will reappear, but only after the girl is convinced that *this time* they are gone forever. For Adele, the mother, is an engineer of histrionic effects: she is willing to put Ann through the terrors of abandonment again and again in order to offer her the miracle of rescue. . . .

A psychologist would probably describe the relations between mother and daughter as "symbiotic." In Adele's case, she would note a problem with boundaries; she does not know where she leaves off and her daughter begins. . . .

Simpson's novel achieves its force not so much through plotting as through the steady accumulation of sharply drawn scenes. In less skilled hands, such narration could easily become shapeless and repetitious. But Simpson has a sure instinct for the flash points of love and rage in her characters and she softpedals nothing. Though ***Anywhere But Here*** is Simpson's first novel, she has already earned a place beside domestic pioneers like Anne Tyler and Alice Munro. She has not only shaken the family tree, she has plucked it from its soil to expose its tangled system of roots.

Sven Birkerts, "Boundless Love," in Chicago Tribune, *January 11, 1987, p. 6.*

An Excerpt from *Anywhere but Here*

It did something for my mother, every time she let me off on the highway and then came back and I was there. She was proving something to herself. When she drove back, she'd be nodding, grateful-looking, as if we had another chance, as if something had been washed out of her.

Years ago, when I was small, she chased me to the kitchen table and swiveled between her long arms on each side of it.

"Now where are you going to go?" she'd said.

This was when we were all living in my grandmother's house back at home.

I ducked under the table and saw everyone's legs. Jimmy's blue uniform slacks, Ben's bare knees with scrapes and white scars, my grandmother's stiff, bagging, opaque, seamed orange stockings in black tie-up shoes, my mother's tall freckled legs in nylons. The muscles in her calves moved like nervous small animals. I knew I couldn't get away. So I lunged out and grabbed my uncle's blue legs, holding on hard, sobbing in yelps, not letting go. I thought Jimmy was the strongest one there. Carol stood with her back to us, wiping the counter with a sponge.

Jimmy ran his hand over my head and down my spine. He hugged me hard, but then he pried my fingers off and pulled me away from him. His face was blank and large. "I have to let your mother have you."

My mother was screaming, "Jimmy, you give her to me. She's my child. Mine."

Jimmy pushed me forward with his knuckles on my back, and then she had me. When she shook me against the refrigerator, Ben ran out the door. None of them looked while we fought. They turned their backs. Jimmy left then, too, the screen door slamming. Carol followed, shaking her head, and they were gone—a family.

I fought back, I kicked and bit and pulled hair. I fought as if I were fighting to live. She always said I turned animal, wild. And there was something in that. I could feel something, the way my lips went curled on my teeth, the backs of my knees.

Later, I'd be in bed, swollen and touchy, not moving, and the house would seem absolutely still. The sheet felt light, incredibly light on my skin. My grandmother made up her own bed for me, with new sheets dried out on the line. They helped me after, but then I didn't care anymore.

When I was better again, up and running around, my mother still hadn't forgiven me. She drew it out. Those days she ignored me, came in the house like a stranger, as if she had no relation. She left me to my grandmother's care. She'd roll up her pants from the ankles and push up her shirt sleeves to show her cuts and bruises.

"Look what she did to me," she told the mailman on the porch. "She's wild. A little vicious animal."

Maybe it was the same as later, for her it was all one circle, coming back to the same place, when we made up. In the middle of the night, she woke me and wanted to talk. She looked hard into my eyes, sincere and promising, touched me where I didn't want her to touch, told me again and again that she'd never leave me, when I wasn't worried that she would.

"Okay," I always said.

LE ANNE SCHREIBER

"We fought" are the opening words of Mona Simpson's challenging first novel, ***Anywhere but Here.*** The "we" is Ann and Adele August—the most exasperating, insupportable and credible mother-daughter duo to make their presence felt in recent fiction. "Fought" is an understated reference to the war of words, wills and fists that rages between them from the first to last page of this very trying and unique novel. . . .

"The fights came when I thought she broke a promise. She said there'd be an Indian reservation. She said that we'd see buffalo in Texas. My mother said a lot of things. . . . Places she said would be there, weren't." Ann can't stand broken promises and Adele lives on them, or, more precisely, on desperate hopes that turn into broken promises. When the anger between mother and daughter becomes too great, they repeat a ritual of abandonment and reconciliation that allows them to go on. Adele stops the car, tells Ann to get out and leaves her with the sound of wheels spinning in her ears; when enough time has passed to make Ann feel her mother may really not come back, Adele drives up, opens the door and suggests they go look for ice cream.

Ann grows up on a steady diet of broken promises and ice cream. For this, she hates Adele. But things are never that simple between mother and daughter. "Strangers almost always love my mother," Ann observes. "And even if you hate her, can't stand her, even if she's ruining your life, there's something about her, some romance, some power. She's absolutely herself. No matter how hard you try, you'll never get to her. And when she dies, the world will be flat, too simple, reasonable, too fair."

The novel, narrated mostly but not entirely by Ann, makes us privy to the shifting combinations of love, hate, fear, need, loyalty, incestuous longing and sheer confusion that bind Ann to her mother. Ann is a survivor, a clearheaded, stronghearted girl; she knows her beautiful mother is untrustworthy, a check bouncer, a misser of meals, a dreamer: "Forty-four years old and every night of her life she made a wish on a star.'' Still, Ann depends on her mother for food, shelter, love. She has to trust her sometimes, and besides, it's not always easy for a child to spot delusions. Maybe the psychiatrist treating her mother really is in love with her, about to marry her and pay the bills she is racking up in anticipation of their impending wealth.

As a portrait of a daughter in thrall to a nearly lethal mother, ***Anywhere but Here*** is brilliant, funny, at times astonishing. But, finally, the novel is as exasperating as Adele, whose allure and destructiveness we come to know intimately and yet understand not at all. It's as if the author wants the reader, like Ann, to keep circling obsessively around Adele without ever getting to her. . . .

The last chapter of the novel is narrated by Adele herself, and we expect some revelation. But when we enter Adele's head, all we find is delusion. After 406 pages we are still stranded outside the character, like a baffled child denied the information that might explain the mysteries of adult behavior. Adele has a secret, but the author prefers not to share it with the reader.

There is an evasion, an absence, at the heart of this novel. What's missing—from Ann's life, from the recollection of Adele's girlhood, from the women's reckoning of their relations to one another—is fathers. Fathers are mentioned, yearned for, their now distant deaths and departures mourned, but mostly they are a silence, a secret the women keep from one another.

To fill the silence, perhaps to distract us from what's hidden, Ms. Simpson gives us the world. ***Anywhere but Here*** overflows with detail. Every sight, sound, taste, touch her narrators experience is described with uncanny precision—the way ankles feel when they're taken out of ice skates, the sound of a just-caught fish thumping in a metallic pail, the way the air changes when a train is coming through, the texture of a gooey cake made with liqueur in the batter, the feel of an Easy-boy recliner tilted just right.

For the most part, these are not telling, New Yorkerish details that fix a character in his demographic niche. More often, they are details for their own sake, generous irrelevancies—the author taking time out from her characters and their battling to enjoy the world that contains them and us. The density of the material world created in ***Anywhere but Here*** adds immensely to the credibility of the characters, but also diverts our attention from them. By sheer profusion, the details become a digression, a distraction, a compensation for secrets withheld. They almost steal the show.

In one scene, Ann, alone at night and scared of the dark, walks home through country fields. ''I picked up the cold flashlight from the ground by my feet, touched the metal, fumbled it on and the night changed. . . . With the flashlight, you could see one thing at a time, the fitted seeds of one weed, a rough milkpod stem.''

Seeing ''one thing at a time'' is a poet's skill. Seeing the tangle of things, particularly the tangle of families, is a novelist's skill. To judge from ***Anywhere but Here,*** Ms. Simpson is both a novelist and a poet, and her talents are prodigious. At times, however, she lets them work against one another. The novelist creates Adele, places her in a matrix of complicated family relations and begins to explore the intricate ways this family shapes its members. Then, when the novelist seems about to penetrate certain mysteries of character, the poet intervenes, pulls back, asks us to see ''one thing at a time,'' asks us to accept an awed child's view of her mother: ''She's absolutely herself.''

Anywhere but Here tries one's patience as much as it rewards it, which, I guess, makes this novel very much like most families.

Le Anne Schreiber, ''In Thrall to a Lethal Mother,'' in The New York Times Book Review, *January 11, 1987, p. 7.*

LAURIE STONE

We know this mother and daughter, aged 32 and 10. We've watched them, or been one of them, or dreamed of them. They're wearing the same outfit, which makes the woman look frantically girlish, the kid appear prematurely yanked into puberty. The mother senses they're off kilter, and when strangers are around, she makes sitcom noises, mentioning mythical home-baked cookies and planned slumber parties, goading her daughter to say cute kid things, so they can pass for normal. Mostly, the two are alone, though, because the mother has trouble with men. In the company of her daughter, she's herself: uncertain and ambitious, dumb and canny, fragile and overbearing—and lonely. She doesn't have enough self to fill a life; her daughter's got to share it. One life, two people. That's workable.

The daughter sleeps with one eye open. Not really, but it's almost true, the way she stays on guard, figuring out things about sex and sadness and danger she'd rather not know. Her awareness feels like a defect, bad breath or worse, a missing faculty for love, or trust, or whatever it is other people always say they feel. She counts the days until she can grow up, leave. Meanwhile, she helps her mother, jollies her, frustrates her, adores her, takes on her ways—the only ways she knows. She has no choice.

In Mona Simpson's brilliant, true first novel, ***Anywhere But Here,*** this girl is called Ann, her mother Adele. They start out in Bay City, Wisconsin, where both were born, then hatch a plan to go to California, because Adele thinks Ann is cuter than Buffy on *Family Affair* and can make it on TV. When Ann is 12, they cut out on Adele's second husband, Ted—a skater who used to be in *Holiday on Ice*—taking his gas credit card, which only gets them rooms in crummy motels. They drive the white Continental Adele deems survival gear for Beverly Hills. And they get to California and live there, in a series of apartments that never have furniture. Life isn't that different from being in Bay City, where they also lived without furniture. Adele keeps latching on to unlikely men, and Ann makes desultory stabs at TV stardom.

That is more or less the plot for 400 pages, but these familiar females and unmomentous events are made vital, necessary, and new through the force of Simpson's prose: through the original idiom of Ann, who narrates, and through dialogue that emblazons character, drawing the reader on like a siren song. The novel thinks about other novels—road books such as *Huckleberry Finn* and Kerouac's travel meditations. Simpson knows how the world's doubts about women feed Adele's wormy self-image. And she recognizes the American nature of Adele's wishes for clean starts and amnesia about the past. But literary and social themes are embedded in the book's muscle: intimate daily exchange. ***Anywhere But Here*** is a tonic for minimalist toxins, for fiction sure about surfaces but uncertain why it's being written. Simpson's concern is the feeling life. Meaning and emotional power gather around the effort of her mind, hard at work, free of restraint.

Adele is a woman without boundaries where her daughter is concerned. "I'm really bleeding. . . . It's just all over. And thick," she says. After Ann's father leaves home, Adele sleeps with her child, feeling free to pat her naked ass whenever she wants. She even cajoles her 10-year-old daughter to skip out nude in front of her friends. "I'd just like them to see what a cute little shape you have. Come on, won't you please, Ann? Just run out. Just for a second." Partly in response to this treatment, Ann acts out sadistic scenarios with several neighborhood kids. She strips them, takes their pictures, and insists they lie still while she runs her hands along their flesh and probes their mouths with her fingers. "People are so easy to boss," she observes of one victim. "I could have reached down and killed her, she was just lying there, trusting me." By not shielding us from the gory details of this mother/daughter relationship, Simpson takes the same liberties with the reader that Adele takes with Ann, and the effect on the reader, as on the girl, is to excite and alarm. But after a while, under the spell of Simpson's candor, we become like one of Ann's subjects. This writer can do anything with us. We'll listen.

She takes risks all the time that read like inevitabilities, reminding us what a mysterious ragtag a novel is. Suddenly, amid a family scene, Ann stops describing to reflect: "The trouble with serenity is that it can turn. The trees seem to lose their souls and look again like painted scenery. You hug your knees and kiss them as if chilled. You pinch yourself. Then you turn to other people, talk, you trust only human beings again, as if nature has abandoned you. Christianity must have been born in twilight." Elsewhere, a detail is worked to an insight. "In every person's face, there is one place that seemed to express them most accurately. With my grandmother, you always looked at her mouth. Her teeth seemed to balance at the very tips of each other, just touching, her lips held and nervous while she listened to a question."

Sometimes, description contains all needed information: "Once a week, she broiled a châteaubriand, which Ted sliced for her. She arranged the pink rectangular pieces on a plate and kept them in the refrigerator under a sheet of Saran Wrap. We ate them cold, with salt. She made us steak tartare for breakfast. She bought ground tenderloin and mixed it with pepper and capers and two egg yolks. We ate breakfast at the counter, standing up. We spread the meat on buttered whole wheat toast." Other times, the analysis is straightforward, unvarnished. "It was stubbornness. My mother didn't want this to be our life. She'd do it a day at a time, she'd put up with it, but she wasn't going to *plan* for it. We didn't pay bills, we didn't buy groceries, we bounced checks. Accepting our duties might have meant we were stuck forever. We made it so we couldn't keep going the way we were; something had to happen. But the thing was, it never did."

Some aspects of the novel worked less well for me than the book as a whole. At several points, Ann's aunt and grandmother narrate. These sections are beautifully crafted, and the women's voices thicken the atmosphere of family origins, but by diverting the focus from Ann and Adele, they seem diffusive. When treating volatile material, such as the sadistic sequences, Ann uses the phrase "It was something I did then." Given her sophisticated understanding of psychological motive, it strikes a coy note. But these are minor hitches. ***Anywhere But Here*** begins with a scene of breathless anxiety—Adele dumping a petulant, 12-year-old Ann out of the car, then driving off. It's so awful, it's intoxicating, the mother's bravado show of power, the child's instant refuge in storing details, down to weeds in the road. This is hard stuff to top, and it's on page one, but Simpson keeps the thrills coming.

A trip to Disneyland with Ann's elusive father leaves a bloody trail of unarticulated longing on the pages. Through one California Christmas, Adele insists they scrub and polish their shabby flat, managing to spend the day in her grimy T-shirt and deprive Ann of a party, their one possibility for celebration. The chapter is a masterpiece of frustration. After each little murder, it seems impossible that quotidian pain—and the tolerance for it—can deepen, but Simpson shows they can.

For Ann, both revenge and freedom lie in remembering everything. Sometimes she loves Adele, sometimes she hates her. Always she's fascinated by her, and that absorbed attention lifts them both. Every detail Ann supplies makes the child-woman-monster Adele realer, more human, less prey to reductive summary. Ann's dry-eyed clarity—the awareness that once felt burdensome—saves her from her mother's addiction to self-dramatization, the endless casting of herself as the one acted upon and never in control of her fate. Ann's honesty, which lays her mother out, is also, ironically, a gift to her mother, proof that she was, after all, something of a success as a mom. Adele madly competes with Ann, but she gives what she never had: a vision of self-worth. To Adele, her kid-the-child-star is talented, resilient, lovely, and smart. Her phrase "You can make it, honey"—which is partly a mantra for herself—grows in Ann, gathering the shape of a good parent, the necessary ingredient for escaping childhood in one piece. Ann does—we see her briefly at college, on her own. ***Anywhere But Here*** is a book about two women, but Simpson makes them seem like the world.

Laurie Stone, "Motherhood Is Powerful," in The Village Voice, *Vol. XXXII, No. 5, February 3, 1987, p. 47.*

COMMENTS OF MONA SIMPSON TO *CLC YEARBOOK*

Simpson recalls the experience of writing and publishing *Anywhere but Here:* "I wrote the first draft very fast, over one summer at Yaddo, and it was very long and loose. It was like a sketch, all structure, needing everything—color, detail, nuance, shading, life. Then I worked slowly, over a long time (almost four years)—the best I could do every day. I was working part-time jobs, some happy, some not, but I came back to the book every day, giving it what affection, what love and attention I could. I wrote over scenes many, many times, more than ten, until it seemed there was nothing more I could do to it." For inspiration, she reports, "I took a few trips, I looked at certain pictures tacked up near where I worked. One was of an old brick orphanage with yellow, waxy light coming out of small windows. The other was of a group of children with braces, cerebral palsy children, sitting in a group in plastic chairs. . . .

"I kept the book to myself a long time. At one point, I finally thought I was finished. Then I showed the book to three friends. They had distressingly good criticism. Their suggestions seemed right, true. But I couldn't stand to work on the book anymore. I'd lost all perspective. So I put it away for four miserable months. Then I took it out again, spent six more months working on it with absolute certainty as to the changes I was making, then sent it to my agent. She sold the book two weeks later."

When asked what motivates her to write, Simpson replied: ''It seems to be my way, the way I live, writing. It's been at the center of my life for so long, the practice of writing, that it is hard to say what motivates me. What do I hope to accomplish; I hope to write beautiful enduring work that makes people feel, understand, learn about how to live. And to come to understand some questions and their possible answers myself, through the simple long days of writing. . . . I hope to reach the readers who read the way I read, passionately and with much yearning and abandon, readers ardently questioning how they should live, both personally and in a larger context of community and world-wide community, and [who] find the context for their questioning to be books and the process of reading.''

Irini Spanidou

1946-

Greek-born American novelist and short story writer.

Anna, the narrator of *God's Snake* (1986), relates a series of vivid, stark recollections of her childhood in Greece during the aftermath of the Second World War. Like Spanidou herself, Anna is the daughter of an army major; the relationship between Anna and her cruel, authoritarian father forms the central theme of the novel. Several critics assume that Anna's tales are thinly disguised autobiography of Spanidou, who emigrated from her native Thessaly to New York when she was eighteen. Spanidou, however, denies that Anna represents herself. "The actual events as I knew them were more real," she stated. "Writing the novel, the characters took over and began to have their own say." She added: "I wanted to write a book about innocence, our start in the world, what's mysterious. We're born with expectations of love and not with knowledge of evil. The first time anyone hurts us, it's a surprise. My aim was to show how a child comes to terms with hurt. The world of children, the anger and feelings, is a microcosm of the world of adults."

Spanidou struggled, as a beginning writer, with the language of her adopted land. "When I realized I was never going to be an 'American writer', I took a leap of faith. I decided, 'I am going to write out of myself,'" she recalled. "Once I made the decision, all inhibition was gone. It was like accepting my accent." In fact, reviewers praise Spanidou for the elegance and power of her prose, which Christopher Lehmann-Haupt describes as "an idiomatic English that sounds translated and yet achieves eloquence."

God's Snake takes the form of short story-like chapters in which Anna's memory moves back and forth in time, discounting chronological order as she presents her childhood experiences. Spanidou impressed critics with her skill in evoking the atmosphere of Anna's childhood, with its strange and compelling incidents, capturing the essence of postwar Greece as well as the grandeur of the country's historic and mythic past. Writer Doris Lessing found an echo of mythology in the novel. "This story," she observed, "has something of the hard simplicity of a Greek myth, for this is what I was seeing as I read: these figures, each sharply outlined, as if by the clear light of Greece, in an ancient landscape—a very old story, as much as it is a new one." *God's Snake* is deeply rooted in its author's native land; the events in the novel, Spanidou emphasized, could never have taken place in America. "The characters are very Greek: their pride, sense of fate, the way they go to extremes, their articulateness."

Reviewers express admiration for Spanidou's powerful use of imagery. A particularly striking example, they note, is the symbolic use of a series of animals that Anna's father abuses in order to teach his stern value system to his daughter. In these sequences, commentators agree, Spanidou succeeds in making statements of universal significance, particularly in demonstrating the consequences of tyranny.

Spanidou plans to continue her chronicle of Anna in her next novel, *Fear*.

KIRKUS REVIEWS

[***God's Snake*** is a] lyric first novel, in storylike episodes, of a sensitive young girl living in post-WW II Greece.

Because her father is an officer in the Greek army, Anna Karystinou and her family are not only moved frequently from place to place, but Anna is confronted from her earliest years by her father's rigid military bearing and by his stoic, sometimes cruel sense of what constitutes a proper dignity and honor. In "Bitch," her father trains a pet dog with such severity that it dies, and the grieving Anna declares that "Never again would I love." Love is lost again in "Little Wolf," when a pet wolf proves untameable (given to her by her father, it keeps biting Anna), an event paralleled by Anna's close friend moving away after the death of the friend's mother from TB. Filled with expanding symbol and recurrent image, these pieces range from family present to family past (there are mother, uncles, aunts, cousins, and, especially, there are grandparents) in an effort to capture the whole of Anna's poetically (and sexually) searching and troubled world, but often the result is commonplace, within however exotic a setting. Anna, at age 11, watches a carnival's lights "sad with longing," and determines that "It's not the fair that's full of life . . . It's life." There's an episode in the woods with a child molester ("The Man"), young love for a schoolmate ("Longing"), and a final test of deep-water "courage" forced upon Anna by her destructive yet life-giving father ("My Father's Daughter").

Ambitious, painted on a color-filled and half-hallucinatory canvas reminiscent of the South American novelists, the growing up of Anna is richly poignant at moments, but will seem unnecessarily exhaustive and slow-paced to many for the very slight new light it sheds. Half-wonderful.

A review of "God's Snake," in Kirkus Reviews, *Vol. LIV, No. 13, July 1, 1986, p. 971.*

CHRISTOPHER LEHMANN-HAUPT

"The first snake I saw was dead," reads the opening of Irini Spanidou's fervent, visionary first novel, ***God's Snake***, "and so were those of a long time after, but that first snake my father brought home and threw at my feet saying, 'A dead snake.' His orderly Manolis picked it up with some tongs and carried it out of the house, and I went back to my homework. It was an unusual occurrence, but that would be that, I thought. No so."

Not so, indeed. For Manolis the orderly, complying with his master's insistence that the narrator "learn all I could learn about the ways of nature," will bring more snakes to 10-year-old Anna Karystinou. Snakes will twine through her imagination until she becomes convinced that God has sent His snake to watch her: "There the snake was, coiled on top of the armoire opposite my bed, its head thrust out like a person's resting his chin on an open palm, looking at me as though to decide if I was indeed good."

And this is only the first in a series of waking nightmares lived through by a fiercely brave and imaginative young girl growing up in postwar Greece, the daughter of a rigidly disciplined army officer and his bitterly disillusioned wife. These ordeals involve a series of unhappy encounters with animals, gradually ascending the evolutionary scale: a crow, a deer, a wolf, a German shepherd and finally, in a passage that brilliantly illuminates the developing themes of phallus and thanatos, a man who, impersonating a soldier-friend of Anna's come back from the dead, takes her into the woods and exposes himself.

How does Anna survive these trials, not to speak of the oppression of her parents, who are so at odds with each other that her father, provoked by his wife while out on a drive, endangers the family by racing the car into "a street of short steep steps that went five blocks downhill"?

Part of the answer is the physical and intellectual Greece that Ms. Spanidou captures in ***God's Snake,*** a land of warm sunlight and lucid philosophy. Part of it is Anna's extended family, which the author . . . makes memorable in a series of droll, Chekhovian scenes of a neurasthenic, ectomorphic uncle inspired in early childhood to emulate the stolid habits of an ox, or a grandmother so encompassing in her love for Anna that she attempts to absorb her into her body and her dreams, or a grandfather so prim in his manners that even in retirement he dons a three-piece suit to read the evening newspaper.

Still another reason that Anna survives is her passionate heart. No matter how hard she is put down, she keeps bouncing back up, thanks to her capacity for love and hate. But her strongest defense is her imagination, which possesses the power to transform the bizarre into the comic, the unreal into the real, and the dead into the living. Imagination is ultimately what this novel is about, as Ms. Spanidou—in an idiomatic English that sounds translated and yet achieves eloquence—portrays the developing artist who will some day write ***God's Snake.***

Christopher Lehmann-Haupt, in a review of "God's Snake," in The New York Times, *September 4, 1986, p. C20.*

RICHARD EDER

The earliest moment of this haunting childhood memoir [***God's Snake***] is recorded in an old newspaper clipping. It shows the grave black eyes and the tentative smile of a 2-year-old girl, framed in a life preserver. "Man Carrying Child Crosses the Narrows of Euripus," the caption reads.

The sea-borne child is Anna; the man is her father, a Greek army officer and an implacable challenger of life. Not content with swimming the treacherous straits himself, he clamped a rope between his teeth and towed behind him the daughter he doubtless wished were a son; and from whom he demanded a sternly masculine prowess.

Later, when Anna, age 9, swam in these same waters, and the tide turned, her father forbade a friend who started out to help her. "The mother of the brave shall mourn," the father said.

God's Snake is fictional in form; but it is impossible not to assume that Anna is at least a partial projection of the author, Irini Spanidou. It is too harsh, too direct, too much a set of concrete memories that glow with a wider and terrible sense of life, to be a pure invention. Call it "Portrait of the Artist as a Young Maenad."

The baby in the life preserver is its emblem. Anna's growing-up is a journey; and we are made to think of her compatriot, Odysseus, wandering in strange places and encountering emblematic forms of love, fear, malice, delusion and knowledge. The people in Anna's young life appeared to her not as domesticated complexities, but as craggy archipelagoes, jutting out of the sea and inhabited by baffling and disquieting spirits.

Anna was a barracks child, moved from outpost to outpost as her father was transferred around Greece; often in areas that had supported the Left in the Civil War, recently ended; and where the army had something of the quality of an occupying force.

There were no roots except Greece as a whole; the language, the history, the mythology. The gods literally help to form Anna's imagination; and one of the achievements of Spanidou's writing is to make us, so far from these gods, sense the impoverishment of their absence.

For instance, a main theme is Anna's effort to discover herself as a female despite the vigorous presence of the masterful father she adored; and the vacancy of a depressed and fastidious mother whom she almost could not see. "What kind of man are you?" the father demands when she fails at something; and mythology gives her an image with a terrible question: "It was as though I'd sprung out of my father's head like Athena from the head of Zeus,'' she thinks.

There is no peace in the image. From loving her father, she comes to reject, even to loathe, him; and to identify with her distant mother's warm and gentle mother. But Anna's violence and extremism *are* her father's. She recalled his startling pleasure when, on one occasion, she defies him. She cannot escape him; she is divided against herself.

This divided field of force gives rise to the strange and electric sensibility of ***God's Snake.*** Anna lives in a landscape where meanings are disguised and reveal themselves in unexpected forms: as animals, trees, rocks or in the mysterious shifts of the adult world.

Manolis, her father's orderly and her nanny and playmate, is commanded to educate her in snakes. He kills them and brings them to her, their heads crushed and unrecognizable. How can she be interested, she thinks—her reason asserting itself against her child's tendency to believe—in distinguishing species whose faces she cannot see.

What she does pick up, and this was her father's purpose, is that the world is full of dangerous enemies. Later, when an aunt tries to persuade her that God made all things to be beautiful, she thinks of snakes; and particularly, of slugs, which the peasants called God's Snake. ''I had seen it. Amidst flowers, amidst his love, I had seen it creeping, black and vile.''

Snakes, though, lead her to make friends with her father's commander, who shows her a South American snakeskin he keeps on his wall. The general is a gentle intellectual, held in contempt by his officers for lacking their absolute certainties. Anna is won by his gentleness, yet offended by his distinctions. When he tells her that Greek snakes are nothing compared to foreign ones, she protests: ''You mustn't judge by looks. Our snakes are shrewder. They are the sliest.''

The general punctures her father's Spartan code. Fear, he tells Anna, must be acknowledged. ''It is as shameful to deny fear as to run away from danger.''

And he also tells her: ''Now, beauty makes you love and ugliness makes you think. When you grow up, ugliness will make you love and beauty, think.'' It is a prelude to a more than fatherly caress, one that shatters her love and revolts her. Beauty and ugliness.

A soldier lures Anna into the woods and, because she trusts all her father's men, she follows; only to see him expose himself. Later, she says, she came to sleep with many men, but only once with each, and always without pleasure. This seems grandiloquent and forced, perhaps; but it is the way she wrestles with this twinned beauty and ugliness. They are always together, but they never merge in a compromise that, farther to the West, we call civilized maturity. They are always tragic.

Her father gives her a fawn; then he takes it from her and gives it to her little sister. The younger child neglects it, and the fawn gets sick and dies. Anna, in her offended pride, refuses to help. After the death, she reflects: ''Now, I felt love and it was no good.''

The friendships with other children are a mixture of passion and pain. The world offers itself and betrays. Her only wholehearted love is for her maternal grandmother, a stout, innocent woman with an abundant cleavage ''like a smile.'' Anna, who lived with her three years, follows her about continually. Later, back with her parents, she kisses a photograph of her grandmother so often that it becomes ''a gray, scary blur.''

What Anna—her father's child—loves, she can't be; and what she is, she can't love. She moves through her magical and blighted childhood without real comfort, except for those sheltered three years; and with a mixture of exaltation and pain whose only reward is to see clearly with the blackest of eyes.

Anna's world is solitary and full of signs. It is exotic to us and very distant; it can seem melodramatic and wrought up. Yet over and over, her voice, abrupt and charged, brings to us the universal truths of a remote, provincial and mythological childhood. They are truths we recognize because we share some and, equally, because we are starved of others.

Richard Eder, in a review of ''God's Snake,'' in Los Angeles Times Book Review, *September 7, 1986, p. 3.*

An Excerpt from *God's Snake*

With anguish I thought of how I had not given Kyroula my love, how I watched her suffer at my father's hands without protesting.

She was my father's dog. I had believed it was wrong to love her. You can only love what is yours, I had thought. Only what is yours you love. A toy, a doll, a friend, you love them because they are yours. When you crave another child's toy you don't love it. It has to be yours before you love it. That's why you want to have it—so it can be yours, so you can love it.

I could not have Kyroula. It was hopeless to want her. Covetous to love her.

I was wrong, I thought now. Wrong! When you love something, it *is* yours—it *is* yours, even if someone else has it. If you don't love something, it isn't yours. You have no right to it. No right!

My love for Kyroula, a love I had held in, uneasy longing lingering in shame, now bursting free—outraged, despairing—tearing apart, trampling the piety and loyalty that bound me, acquiescent, to my father, let me see his cruelty bare-faced.

He had no right to torture her, I thought. No right! It doesn't matter if you torture someone you love. It's like you're torturing yourself then—you suffer. But he did not love Kyroula. He tortured her without love. That is evil. Evil! My father is evil.

If Kyroula dies, he'll be a murderer, I thought.

I felt horror.

''Don't make my father a murderer, God dear,'' I prayed. ''Don't let Kyroula die.''

But the horror chilled and hardened my heart. My heart did not unbend to pray. I said, ''Please, God. Please . . .'' but my heart was dismayed.

God looks down from the sky and sees, I thought. He knows all this. He knows! It is He who made my father—who made the evil in him. It's His doing all this! And I should pray to Him?

"You're mean," I said to God. "I'm saying to You: You are mean!"

I wasn't frightened to say it. I thought it, and I said it, and I wasn't frightened.

"I hate you," I said to God.

Full of Yourself, powerful, all-too-powerful You are, wallowing in Your might, mean. Be mean! I thought. My love, ungiven, makes of Your power short shrift. *Be* mean!

This is why some people say He does not exist, I thought. They have seen through Him—they know He can't make them love Him.

"You don't exist," I said to God. "Hear me? You don't exist! You think You can do what You want—You think You can be mean. Be mean! *Be* mean! I say, You don't exist!"

Suddenly I felt no more fear. I felt nothing—a strange nothing, as though I had no feelings at all, as though I never had had feelings. There's nothing inside me, I thought. There's nothing inside me and I'm no one. I thought I was my father's daughter but I'm not his daughter. I'm not like him. I thought I was like him but I'm not like him. I don't love him. I loved him when I thought he was like me, but I don't love him and he's not like me. I'm no one. No one will ever love me because I'm no one. I'll be alone, I thought. All my life I'll be like this—no one. There is Anna, people will think. See her? She's no one.

NICHOLAS BROMELL

Childhood seems to be the almost inevitable subject of contemporary first novels. What the child saw and felt and suffered, how the future author gradually discovered artistic sensibility and vision—these have been the commonplace materials of first novels at least since Joyce wrote *A Portrait of the Artist as a Young Man*.

Irini Spanidou's contribution to the genre is nevertheless remarkably fresh and vigorous. ***God's Snake*** traces about nine years in the life of Anna, a young girl whose father is an officer in the Greek military and whose family follows him from post to post across Greece in the 1950's. Through a series of sharply drawn and occasionally piercing incidents, we see Anna stumble her way to some understanding of herself, her sexuality and her future vocation.

Her path is not easy. Major Karystinou is a man of inflexible principles. He regulates his entire life and that of his family according to two verbs: to obey and to command. He dominates his beautiful but pathetic wife and imposes a harsh discipline on his two daughters. Perhaps because he has no sons, he treats Anna, his eldest, as though she were a raw recruit in boot camp—ordering her to walk and speak and think and feel "like a man." It was as though I'd sprung out of my father's head like Athena from the head of Zeus," Anna muses, "as though I was entirely my father's child. . . . His love was a proud, selfish love, the love he had for himself, as though I was his flesh, his image, his self remade."

Anna's growth turns on three kinds of incidents: her relations with men, principally her father; her relations with women, principally her grandmother; and her relations with animals, whose fragile but exotic status outside human life seems to mirror Anna's own sense of alienation. She worships and fears, adores and despises these creatures, just as she alternately accepts and denies her own eccentric character. In one of the novel's most poignant episodes, Anna, manipulated by her father, sinks to his level of cruelty. When the Major capriciously takes back a pet deer he has given her and bestows it on her little sister, Maritsa, Anna deals with her pain by utterly extinguishing her love for the animal. Maritsa soon grows tired of the deer and stops feeding and caring for it, but Anna refuses to rekindle the affection she once felt. "When I came down, it tried to run to me—always it tried to run to me. I pushed it aside. I did not look at it. It suffered—I knew it suffered and hated it, despised it sometimes. It suffers like a weakling, I thought. It has no strength, no pride." Eventually the deer weakens, wastes away and dies.

Anna does receive some human love—from her aunts, from her father's orderly Manolis (an endearing Buster Keaton-like man) and above all from her maternal grandmother. But her most important relationship is her struggle with her father. It is against his conception of her that she must fight. It is against his masculine ethos of unfeeling self-discipline that she must preserve her own fragile sensibility. And yet, as Ms. Spanidou suggests, it is his inhuman commitment to principles that gives Anna the model she will need to become an artist. He is heroic, larger than life. His example teaches her that human feelings must be wrought into an enduring artifact—whether a military code or a work of art. He points to deep waters beyond the shores of common experience and virtually forces Anna to swim in them. "I was swimming," she says in the book's last sentence, "out where the waters, reaching back beyond memory, drenched in history, were immortal."

Ms. Spanidou's novel has two flaws, both minor. By arranging events in nonchronological order, she mirrors the fragmentation of Anna's life but runs the risk of confusing readers. The author . . . has also written in an idiom that occasionally makes Anna sound more like a Valley Girl than a child growing up in Greece 30 years ago. "It's weird of the general to like snakes, I thought. And it's weird of me to like a weird general." But ***God's Snake*** is an impressive achievement. It freshly evokes the beauties and terrors of childhood, illuminating how a girl emerges from the coils of family to become an artist.

Nicholas Bromell, "A Raw Recruit Named Anna," in The New York Times Book Review, *September 14, 1986, p. 13.*

JOAN K. PETERS

[***God's Snake***] is an arresting first novel about a girl, Anna Karystinou, coming to terms with her brutal but compelling father, the "tall, dark, muscular, handsome, fierce" major in the Greek army. While the book reads more like a memoir than a novel, it makes up for a lack of narrative force with powerful characterization, spare, startling scenes, and fine imagery. To weave in the depiction of Anna herself with that of post-civil war Greece where she grows up, Spanidou intermingles present and past with considerable skill. In certain critical scenes, she even moves gracefully into the remote past, which Anna, the narrator, cannot have known.

Anna's mother, we are told, held her newborn child "as though they had handed her an unjust sentence." She is cold and withdrawn, brooding on what Anna finally learns is hatred for her husband, who "raped and brutalized" her soul. "I was a good soul . . . believe me, Anna," her mother pleads. Anna does, understanding for the first time the danger she herself is in.

The mother's disclosure appears in a chapter called "Bitch," which describes the last in a series of animals Anna's father brings home. Each previous one—a dead snake, a frozen crow, a fawn, and a newborn wolf—has revealed to Anna more of her own compassion and her father's perplexing cruelty. The "bitch," a German shepherd pup, marks the end of Anna's innocence. Her father beats the dog mercilessly for her "gentleness, her affectionate nature," until "she crouched toward (him), peeing along the way—incontinent, docile, limply wagging her tail." In the end, when the dog dies, Anna confronts the truth: "He tortured her without love. That is evil. Evil! My father is evil."

Anna's own case is more complex. Her father tortures her, but not without love. He wants her to be "manly" and beats her when she behaves in ways he finds girlish. He teaches her that trusting is for fools, poetry for idiots, and tears for the weak. He loves her the way he loves his soldiers, and in return she adores him. But Anna cannot be like her father; her female self rebels. Fortified by a kind general who tells her to "trust what's good in (herself)," a gentle orderly assigned to look after her, countless aunts and uncles, and a doting grandmother, Anna reconciles her father's destructive strength with her own loving vision.

The two-decade bounty of women's fiction has produced all too few father-daughter portraits. I am grateful for Spanidou's excellent, albeit upsetting, one. Like *Final Payments, Machine Dreams,* and *In Another Country, God's Snake* demonstrates how much can be explained about women's lives through knowing our fathers, and how rich a subject we've just begun to explore.

Joan K. Peters, in a review of "God's Snake," in Ms., *Vol. XV, No. 4, October, 1986, p. 80.*

ANN SNITOW

It's a wise child who knows her own father. Anna, the narrator of Irini Spanidou's first novel [***God's Snake***] is such a child, and wants such knowledge. When she was born, her father "made the sign that signifies 'cunt,' . . . announcing (she) was female with a leer." He taught her that "being a woman was a character defect—like being a swindler or a quack," and his precocious firstborn soon decided, "I'm not going to be a woman when I grow up." Spanidou tells her story as the subtly resifted memories of this little girl.

The scene is an exhausted, diminished Greece after World War II. Anna's father is an officer in the Security Force still fighting internal skirmishes with Communists. He is a man whose job is a perfect fit: "he believed in the cause of the army, its function in society, its service in turning youths into men going out in the world as though reborn, passed through a new womb to adult life."

In a world where proper birth is rational and comes only after excruciating male rites of passage, Anna's mother reels off center, her dignity and occupation gone. Beautiful but humiliated by her impotence, she lives with her family in a succession of barrack towns like a dethroned queen incognito in a sty. Occasionally she flares out with the plain truth, spoken like a morose Cassandra, without any hope of changing anything or even of being heard:

> "You're poisoned with your own venom and want to see everyone else poisoned and destroyed, crawling at your feet," my mother said (to my father). "Power! All you want is power. You don't have it, Stephane. You can kill, you can destroy. You killed me. But you don't have power."
>
> "Who has power?"
>
> "Love has power."
>
> "Such as yours?"
>
> "I have no love. I have no self-respect anymore."
>
> "Did you ever?"
>
> "Before you trampled my soul."
>
> "Words."

"Words" this harsh that have no effect are doubly frightening: small children hear them and witness, too, the vacuum into which a mother's most powerful knowledge is always fated to fall. "She opposed my father in everything," writes Anna, but her mother's utter failure to move her husband one inch off any of his intentions has the quality of nightmare.

God's Snake is among other things a naked story of inequality: a handful of men are the leaders; they rule. Other men, women, children, servants, and animals are helpless in opposition to them. Their only hope is, somehow, to join the strong—as the clever Anna sometimes contrives to do—or to enjoy the rare moments of their capricious mercy. Granted sexual power but patronized on every other front, Anna's mother goes on lifelong strike, while her father expands and expands, appropriating first birth, then nurture, then education. He loves his daughter; she is his pride; and so she must never be hugged, petted, or indulged lest she become a whining weakling, a woman.

In this atmosphere of gender warfare, Anna's lessons can be confusing:

> "There *is* no God," said my father.
>
> "Who made the world then?"
>
> "It made itself."
>
> "How?"
>
> "How did *God* make it?" he said.
>
> "Some people believe God made the world," my mother said. "Some people believe it made itself. There's no proof either way. You'll have to make up your own mind."
>
> "Now?"
>
> She laughed. "You have a long time—till you grow up . . ."
>
> "What if I make up my mind now?"
>
> "You can't now. You're too young. You must believe in God—children must believe in God."
>
> "Children believe what they're told," said my father.

"Do you believe in God, Ma?"

"Yes, Anna," she said. "I believe in God."

For the most part, however, Anna's mother, "like a wild animal caged when young," maintains a "peeved sadness" and leaves meaning like a fallow field to be cultivated by Anna's father. ("Men do not like things to grow unless they plant them.")

Anna's education proceeds like a fairy tale. The family's kind servant, Manolis, is instructed to bring her snakes so she can learn the animals, face down the devil fear, and the trembling, fallible Eve. She has the luck and sense to see that fear is never a winning card and stolidly accepts the snakes. As she grows, more animals arrive at the decree of her father or as his representative: loving fawns or biting wolves. Each one comes like the animals in fables, moral attached, but what Anna learns is not always quite what her father intends. He labors to define the rules of experience; his loyal daughter—at times an honorary son because of her pluck, at times a mere disgraced girl—believes in his rules, observes all he shows her, but assiduous and smart, keeps coming upon rival postulates.

Her father seems to think you can learn what a snake is from its corpse. (But live snakes turn out to be very different, more alluring and quite mysterious.) He seems to think you can compel a baby wolf to be tame. (But you can't. Wolves stay wild, says the wise Manolis, and when this one has mauled Anna often enough the father decides to shoot it rather than set it free, because "he had his chance.") If a crow freezes, it is dead, so says the master of the household as he holds out a bundle of black feathers to his daughter. (But Anna's dead crow defrosts. So powerful is her father's word that at first she thinks the bird is a ghost. When it shits all over her room though, she *knows:* her father was wrong; the crow still lives; life can slip through the net of the father's word.) . . .

Are these the usual lessons of childhood, or do these particular fables have an added spin? Just how sharp a knife does Spanidou mean to hold at the throat of patriarchy? Some of her tales of the father are certainly terrifying and cut deep. The central episode of the novel, "Bitch," is a tour de force, a philosophical essay about gender, developed with the most gruesome of illustrations. Anna's father brings home and tries to train a female dog, Kyroula. . . . (p. 14)

In the end, the father locks Kyroula in a shed and makes the family live with her piteous cries until she dies from her long hysteria in the dark. He is cruel in part because he hasn't the slightest comprehension that Kyroula *doesn't understand*. The fool thinks the dog is rational—or *could* be if she only would. He sees her inability to become a trained, ferocious watch dog in six weeks as he might see insubordination among his soldiers. Kyroula's puppy love and charm make the women of the family love her unconditionally. She has only to bound around and be alive to delight them. But the father, imprisoned in his miserable will, can only approve Kyroula if she is at heel, and worthy. The hideous ignorance behind his call to mastery is finally more threatening than his bad temper, though in the powerful, bad temper alone can be a sentence of death.

In contrast to the horror of "Bitch," other sections of ***God's Snake*** seem equivocal in their judgment of what once was. Spanidou moves in and out, changing tone, yet beautifully integrating Anna's different ages. This is how memory works, an assemblage of moments linked by meaning more than real time. Anna at three, at eleven, at six: There's no announcement of the shift, just a growing feeling that one anecdote is about a small child, while another is obviously about a teenager. Sometimes we learn a particular age, but the edges of that time soon bleed into other times and places. The abiding effect is of a fascinating childhood in which oppression alternated with love and wonder.

Many of the memories are of traumas most children know: early hints of sex and loss, sibling hatred, family quarrels, a near-molestation, a dark bedroom crawling with snakelike shadows. The law of the father is terrible, but it is not everywhere absolute or the same. The book is full of secret loopholes. From age six to nine, Anna escapes the wandering army life altogether and lives with her grandparents, experiencing a love like Eden, a world without snakes. And even in her father's house, there is Manolis, a man entirely unlike her father, tender and empathic, one of the novel's substitute mothers. While the dog dies, he hustles the children out to see the moon. And when her father insists that ugly women are worthless, there is even a lesbian aunt to remind him in Anna's hearing that this is not a law but only an opinion. The novel probes the father's rigidity like a persistent sore until it finds the source of the raw wound in his own childhood. Once motherless, now he rejects the sticky love of mothers. The law is mortal; it had a childhood, too.

So the story breathes, in-out, terrible-wonderful. Anna is damaged, but so is everyone. The book moves toward the nauseating brutality of the central animal episodes of "Deer" and "Bitch," then subsides again, leaving a mixed residue, the law of the father and the energy of the nimble daughter who makes her half-escape. After all, does anyone do more than half escape childhood?

One looks hard at the end of a book that seesaws like this. If the author wants things both ways—trauma and survival, cruelty and kindness—she must find a successfully equivocal resting place for her final words. If she means us to feel that the father is death without resurrection, the end will land us somehow back in the fatal atmosphere of "Bitch," in which women and children stand by unable to save a dog from the arrogance of male discipline, the irrationality of male order. But if this childhood is a memory treasured for itself, whatever the pain, remembered in a tranquility which no longer brings tears of injury or outrage, then the book must mellow, lead us toward a moment of reconciliation. After all, Anna has survived, she is writing these words, as definite and powerful in their way as any her father ever spoke. Anna is grown up, and the law of the father—however powerful—can never be quite the same again as it was during the special slavery of childhood.

Down which path does Irini Spanidou lead us? She has us firmly by the hand because she writes like a dream—vitally, with the elegant and powerful simplicity of her native Greek, though this is not translation but a supple, direct English. At the end, she takes us to the sea for one more primal scene between father and daughter, played out half under the waves, in the unconscious. Anna is nine, recently returned from the good, loving years in her grandmother's happy house. Her father has been snubbing her for days because he found her crying while reading that "sentimental trash," *Lassie, Come Home*. Today he has relented (who can ever fathom why *today?*) and asks her to come along with him and her godfather, his oldest friend, to the Narrows of Euripus, the treacherous sea where first he taught her to swim and where, in the lost heroic age, the Greek hero drowned. The men sit on the beach as Anna swims far out.

> Suddenly, the keen absolving joy I had felt when I first dove in the water drained from me. I felt empty inside, a heavy emptiness, weighing me down.

She calls for help, panicking in the tug of the current. Is she right to fear or is she only a sissy girl? How can one ever know where to draw the line between daring and foolishness, between caution and cowardice? The father draws *his* line without hesitation, wrestling with Anna's godfather on the beach to keep him from coming after her. She sees they will not help and swims furiously back to kill her fear—and to live. (pp. 14-15)

And so the novel ends. Loving her father has made Anna resemble him, but she will always be haunted, too, by the shame and emptiness he cannot help bequeathing to any girl. The word *nothing* thrums through ***God's Snake,*** each time with a different meaning: "Nothing" is what they tell children about sex; it is God and eternity; it is the loss of the father, which is loss of meaning, order, a fixed universe. And "nothing" is female, a vacuum between the legs. Finally, "nothing" is larger than father and mother. Even the powerful are empty—Anna's father's well-kept secret. Though he can give her his love, it cannot fill her up. She must rely on herself—and on her rage—to get her to shore.

But when she gets there, her reward is always and only the accolade of the father. Because he has ventured her, taken the risk she might drown, he dubs her brave, worthy, an honorary man. What snake offers a more sweet or treacherous seduction than this, to win at the father's game, to wish to please him and—perilous moment—*to succeed?* The book ends in the atmosphere of this dangerous, double-edged elation: Anna defeats her emptiness, beats down her fear, and joins her proud father and the other Greek heroes.

After all that Spanidou says about family warfare and the drama of gender, is ***God's Snake*** also a book about how pride can be inculcated and kept alive in the heart of a discouraged people, once glorious, now rendered female by defeat? Does Spanidou join the father in the end, for a brief moment preferring him to the softness of helpless victims, preferring rigidity which beats the waves to plasticity which risks sinking beneath them? The book keeps spiraling around these alternatives; it comes to rest with an only partly ironic image of national pride.

All the same, the momentum of the question posed by the mother and the father, the two unequal pillars of the ancient childhood universe, keeps us moving, leaves us wondering and admiring. Men may heap laurel leaves on Anna, but the formless, flowing stuff—water, mother, memory—keeps lapping at the shore. It will never go away no matter how many times Anna and her father beat their narrow, triumphant path to dry and rational land.

Unresolved though I am about where to place these memories between the savage and the serene accounts of childhood that I know, ***God's Snake*** is a wonderful first novel, one that feels distilled from a hard struggle to face what loving the father gives and what it takes away. The fathers are dreadful, dreadful, and the Annas love them anyway. Such love has its cost, but Spanidou never believes love is a mistake. (p. 15)

Ann Snitow, "Sins of the Father," in VLS, *No. 49, October, 1986, pp.14-15.*

Patrick Süskind

1949-

German novelist, dramatist, and scriptwriter.

Süskind, a Munich-based scriptwriter and dramatist, never anticipated the success of his first novel, *Das Parfum* (1985; *Perfume: The Story of a Murderer*.) He claims that he wrote it in secret and that his friends and family did not even know of its existence until it was published. "I thought it was such an absurd story that if I ever finished it it might have a certain level of readers, people interested in history and literature," Süskind recalled. When critics and readers throughout Western Europe hailed the novel as an astonishing tour de force—it has been translated into more than twelve languages—Süskind responded warily. He granted few interviews and refused to accept a five thousand dollar literary prize from the Frankfurt newspaper that had originally presented the novel in serial form, vowing he would never accept an award for his writing.

Perfume is a bizarre, ironic, yet disturbing tale focusing on an alienated anti-hero. Jean-Baptiste Grenouille is a despised outcast orphan who roams through eighteenth-century France murdering beautiful young women in order to distill their bodily scents into a perfume that will make him the most desirable and powerful man on earth. Critics variously describe the novel as a fairy tale, a philosophical novel, and an allegory of political megalomania. In this last instance, some critics draw parallels between Grenouille and Adolf Hitler. Süskind confirmed the observation. The Third Reich, Süskind explained, "was for my generation always in the back of our minds. It doesn't matter whether you write poems, plays, or novels. Even then it is the theme." Süskind notes with interest that French and Anglo-Saxon critics grasp the political allegory of his tale, whereas German critics often fail to do so.

Reviewers compliment Süskind on his splendid evocation of Paris and the French countryside in the 1700s. They also praise the fascinating, detailed discourses on perfume-making woven throughout the novel. One of the most outstanding aspects of *Perfume,* most critics agree, is its use of odors, both sensuous and repellent, as a recurrent motif. Critic John Updike calls this "reconstruction of the world in terms of scent" a "charming tour de force." Süskind recounted his method of research as a submersion into the world of odors for the two years he spent writing the novel. He would travel through the perfume-producing country of southern France on a motor-scooter: "With goggles I could hardly see and with the helmet on I couldn't hear anything," he recalls. "Smelling was practically the only sense I had functioning on the Vespa."

Some critics protest that several crucial aspects of the story seem contrived, in particular its denouement. Also cited is the incongruity that one of Grenouille's monstrous traits is a complete lack of body odor, yet by coincidence he also possesses an uncannily keen sense of smell. Perhaps more disarming to reviewers, however, is the lack of characters in the novel, and Süskind's failure to create a sympathetic character in his protagonist. Nevertheless, reviewers point to Grenouille's ability to fascinate and engage the reader's curiosity. Most critics conclude that Süskind's absorbing and imaginative narrative permits them to suspend disbelief. Like Umberto Eco's *The Name of the Rose, Perfume* is a historical fable that relies on invention, not realism, to intrigue and delight its readers.

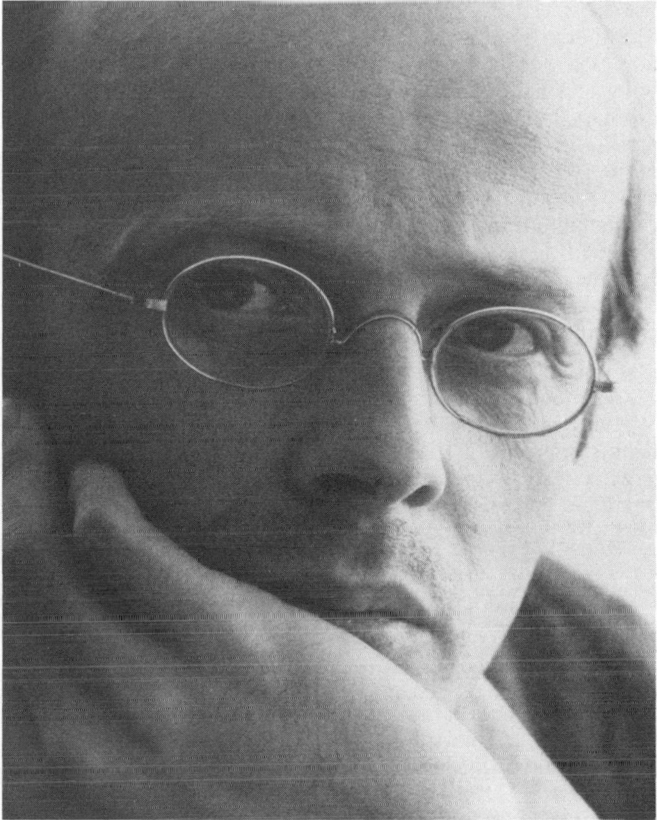

NICHOLAS MURRAY

Perfume, a striking first novel by Patrick Suskind . . . , is set in 18th century France. It is the story of the 'gifted abomination', Jean-Baptiste Grenouille, who murders 25 young women not for their bodies but in order to extract their peculiar odour—from which he will create the ultimate perfume which will allow him to be loved by the humanity he despises. Thus Grenouille becomes apprenticed to a Parisian perfumer, Baldini, from whom he learns the craft of perfumery even though he can astonish the old man (and revive his flagging fortune) by creating, with sublime disregard for the proper procedures of the craft, marvellous scents merely by exercising his instinctual and preternatural sense of smell.

After a seven year mock-Zarathustran interlude on a bare mountain Grenouille returns to the stench of the city to complete his abominable mission. He descends on the perfume centre at Grasse where he carries out the murders and then creates the extraordinary perfume which at first saves his life when he is apprehended for the murders and later is the cause of his destruction when a motley crowd encountered on his return to Paris tear him apart with murderous desire. He is destroyed by the synthetic illusion of love.

The theme of illusion and reality—Grenouille himself, as his horrified wet-nurses were to discover, has no odour on his own body and has to create scents which give him the illusion of ordinary humanity—of artifice and naturalness, coupled with the Enlightenment milieu give this novel something of the feel of the 18th century *conte philosophique*. The author, who maintains a discreet, ironic presence in what is otherwise a very conventional and straightforward narrative, satirises the aristocratic scientific quack, the marquis de la Taillade-Espinasse, epitome of the Enlightenment philosophical amateur, whose comic obsessions parallel the more abominable obsessions of Grenouille.

Perfume-making for Grenouille is 'a cunning apparatus to snatch the scented soul from matter. That scented soul, that ethereal oil, was in fact the best thing about matter, the only reason for his interest in it.' The pursuit of the scented soul of matter is what destroys him and causes him to destroy others, making this lucid and absorbing narrative a parable of the destructiveness of single-minded obsession. (pp. 31-2)

Nicholas Murray, "Obsessions," in Books and Bookmen, *No. 371, September, 1986, pp. 31-2.*

CHRISTOPHER LEHMANN-HAUPT

How can you help being intrigued by the title of this first novel, ***Perfume;*** or by the subtitle, *The Story of a Murderer;* or by the painting of the nude woman on the dust jacket, a detail from Watteau's "Nymphe et Satyre"; or by the jovial yet ironic voice of the narrator? "In eighteenth-century France," he begins, "there lived a man who was one of the most gifted and abominable personages in an era that knew no lack of gifted and abominable personages." He continues, "His story will be told here. His name was Jean-Baptiste Grenouille, and if his name . . . has been forgotten today, it is . . . because his gifts and his sole ambition were restricted to a domain that leaves no traces in history: to the fleeting realm of scent."

Combined, these various elements offset each other in such a teasingly incongruous way that one of the first attractions of Patrick Süskind's remarkable fable is simply to watch the pieces of the puzzle fit together.

Which they quickly do. The abominable personage is a bastard child born in a Paris fishmonger's stall on July 17, 1738. Nobody wants the infant because something is wrong with him: his body has no smell. And yet no scent is not discerned by him. At the age of 6, "he had completely grasped his surroundings olfactorily." "Perhaps the closest analogy to his talent is the musical wunderkind, who has heard his way inside melodies and harmonies to the alphabet of individual tones and now composes completely new melodies and harmonies all on his own. With the one difference, however, that the alphabet of odors is incomparably larger and more nuanced than that of tones; and with the additional difference that the creative activity of Grenouille the wunderkind took place only inside him and could be perceived by no one other than himself."

And the nude on the dust jacket represents what Jean-Baptiste will eventually seek in his quest for the ideal scent—the "essence absolue" of life itself, a perfume made from beautiful women. And of course, as we soon come to realize, for these women to yield their fragrance, they will have to be murdered.

And once Mr. Süskind gets us involved in his puzzle, he can do whatever he wants with us. He can make us root for his monstrous genius and delight in such extravagant scenes as the one in which Grenouille—who is repeatedly likened to a disgusting spider or a tick waiting for a host to drop onto—confounds one of Paris's master perfumers by composing, as if he were "a child busy cooking up some ghastly brew of water, grass, and mud," a perfume that, compared to the most popular brand of the day, is "as a symphony is to the scratching of a lonely violin."

He can make us sympathize with Grenouille. He can make us rise with him to ecstatic heights when, alone and God-like, he populates his solipsistic world with the memories of countless smells and debauches himself on them like an alcoholic in a distillery. Or he can make us sink with him into existential panic when he discovers his own lack of odor, for him the equivalent of lacking an identity.

And he can make us scheme with him as first he concocts a series of aromas that make him smell human, and then he discovers "a scent so terrifyingly celestial that once it had unfolded its total glory, it would unleash a perfume such as the world had never smelled before." And this smell, when captured by Grenouille the spider and tick, will make him beloved by all the world, a veritable god among men.

What does it mean, this latter-day Grimms' fairy tale . . .? . . . ***Perfume*** means many things. It is a fable of criminal genius. It is a commentary on connoisseurship, surpassing even what John Fowles attempted to do in *The Collector*. It debates the relative importance of art and people and comes out, just barely, on the side of the humanity.

Perfume is a guide to the banality of evil. It is a parable of the rise and fall of Hitler and a thinly disguised anatomy of Germany's collective guilt. It mocks by implication every sort of charismatic figure from the religious guru to the rock star.

And yet Mr. Süskind's tour de force never groans beneath the weight of its meaning. Its logic is so surprising yet inevitable that it toys with our expectations at every twist and turn of its plot. Its point of view is so balanced and controlled that we are perfectly divided in our sympathy between the murderer and his victims. Even when Mr. Süskind runs out of tricks and is forced to wind up his parable of evil, he remains resourceful. We are almost sorry to see Jean-Baptiste Grenouille leave the pages of ***Perfume,*** for we have come begrudgingly to admire the perversity of his genius.

Christopher Lehmann-Haupt, in a review of "Perfume: The Story of a Murderer," in The New York Times, *September 16, 1986, p C21.*

PETER ACKROYD

Patrick Suskind's novel [***Perfume: The Story of a Murderer***] is a book of smells—the odors of history, in fact—and on the first page 18th-century Paris is anatomized into its component stinks. In its most fetid spot, beside a mephitic cemetery and beneath a fish stall, the hero of ***Perfume,*** Jean-Baptiste Grenouille, is born. But the point, the miraculous point, is that he has no smell at all. He is an orphan whose absence of body odor turns him, also, into an outcast—both damned and blessed, pariah and magician. . . .

The novel begins as a historical document and ends as a metaphysical mystery.

That this is in every sense an olfactory novel gives a striking sensory immediacy to the fiction itself. ***Perfume*** is a historical novel but one in which the sheer physicality of its theme lends it an honorary present tense. And if Grenouille is the hero of the novel, his obsessions are also its informing presence. Just as he has difficulty with words "designating non-smelling objects, with abstract ideas and the like," so the novel itself creates an elemental world in which such abstract matters are only of token significance. The nose is defined here by a priest as "the primitive organ of smell, the basest of the senses," with its powers springing from "the darkest days of paganism"; but it flourishes in Grenouille, even in an age of "enlightenment," and the unspoken message of ***Perfume*** is that it flourishes still. The point about genuine historical fiction is that it is primarily concerned with the contemporary world. This is not a historical romance, full of "Prithees!" and strange objects known as poniards, but a meditation on the nature of death, desire and decay.

The idea behind the book is actually a simple one, Grenouille being a conflation of Dracula, Charles Maturin's Melmoth the Wanderer—that damned soul of early 19th-century fiction—and the assorted inhabitants of Gothic literature. Mr. Süskind's fastidious but sonorous prose (and John E. Woods's translation from the German is a marvelous piece of work) bears a striking resemblance to that of Oscar Wilde in his more sentimental moments, and ***Perfume,*** with its languorous catalogue of scents and its interest in the esthetics of horror, is strangely reminiscent of *The Picture of Dorian Gray*.

Of course, certain writers are drawn to the past precisely in order to explore such interests; history becomes, as it were, an echo chamber of their own desires and obsessions. But this cannot be conveyed by some easy trick of style: the generally debased standard of historical fiction springs from the fact that most novelists think it sufficient to create approximately the right "atmosphere." But the important things are the details. Without details nothing can live, and one of the pleasures of reading ***Perfume*** is the unmistakable sense that Mr. Süskind has deftly employed the fruits of what must have been long and arduous research into the more arcane aspects of 18th-century French life.

This is Patrick Süskind's first novel . . . and the fact that he has turned at once to historical fiction suggests the current revival of that genre. The point is that it represents a way of abandoning the constrictions of conventional naturalism without falling into the familiar trap of a self-conscious "experimentalism" or "modernism." It accommodates a realism that has nothing whatever to do with ordinary social or psychological observation, but that retains the strength of a fable. As a novel of character or incident, ***Perfume*** is at best tentative, therefore; but as a disquisition on sensibility and as an instrument of historical analysis, it is both well conceived and carefully sustained. Just as Grenouille can manufacture a perfume that infallibly conjures up the same response in anyone who senses it, so Mr. Süskind creates words that provide a satisfying illusion of another time. Grenouille the perfumer becomes a kind of novelist, creating phantom objects in the air, but Mr. Süskind himself is a perfumer of language. This is a remarkable debut.

Peter Ackroyd, "A Killer, Haunted by Smells," in The New York Times Book Review, *September 21, 1986, p. 9.*

JONATHAN KEATES

A term much in vogue among American readers and reviewers is the adjective 'important.' Important writers, generally not writing in English, are those whom you wish to be seen reading and who have something to say, in the form of parable or allegory, on what is vaguely called the Human Condition. Patrick Süskind having been deemed important, his novel [***Perfume: The Story of a Murderer*** has] accordingly sold 400,000 copies in its original German edition and been hailed as a worthy successor to that earlier monster of literary importance, *The Name of the Rose*.

The book is also, let it be said, expertly constructed, grounded with unremitting firmness in its historical context, witty, stylish and ferociously absorbing. Unlike many other quality bestsellers of recent years, what is more, it plays no arch little games with the reader, nor does it seek to delude him with notions of his own intelligence. What the author has to say is expressed trenchantly: sophistication is used here as a technical weapon rather than as a device to distract attention.

Süskind's *ancien régime* Paris is an immense olfactory paradox, rank with stenches and drenched in ambrosial odours, fish guts and dead cats against neroli and patchouli. Out of the scented maelstrom, like a genie from an uncorked bottle, springs apprentice perfumier Grenouille, a dwarfish grotesque who uses his sinisterly precise nasal memory to fulfil the lusts kindled by a girl he has smelt cleaning plums in the Marais. The fact that he himself gives off no identifiable savour lends a ghastly effectiveness to his murderous quest for the scent which will confer on him the ultimate allure.

The tensions within the story are subtly induced by blending eighteenth-century narrative styles, whether in the matter-of-fact haphazardness with which a perfumier's shop tumbles entire into the Seine, in the prodigy of Grenouille's survival as a hermit in an Auvernat cave, or the preposterous self-destruction of an enlightened aristocratic experimenter. If we believe in the hideous efficacy of a single tyrannical nose, it is because of the peculiar distillation of credulity and curiosity in which the novel invites us to share.

What it also requires us to accept is the concept of monomaniacal destructiveness, yoked to anarchic imagination, represented by Grenouille himself: 'To be a giant alembic, flooding the whole world with a distillate of his own making, that was the daydream to which Grenouille gave himself up.' The parallel with more modern world-disturbers and uncreators is no less gripping for its obviousness, yet the ambiguity of Süskind's attitude to his protagonist, mingling fascination with horror, is deepened with a sense of the menace intended by such figures to our increasingly desperate rage for order and discipline—a menace conveyed with all the power of the writer's elegant unease.

Jonathan Keates, "Led by the Nose," in The Observer, *September 21, 1986, p. 31.*

RHODA KOENIG

[***Perfume: The Story of a Murderer***] is one of those European literary successes that seem to come not just from another continent but another planet. . . . In essence (so to speak), ***Perfume*** is a traditional Book-of-the-Month-Club historical, full of quaint customs and long lists of exotic ingredients, overlaid with a sick Germanic creepiness and some elements of the fantastic. The novel is almost punitively obsessive in its narrow focus—there are no important characters besides Jean-Baptiste, and he himself is a silent, brutal creature, a kind of idiot savant of smell. ***Perfume*** is not a badly written book, but it is more peculiar than interesting.

Rhoda Koenig, in a review of "Perfume: The Story of a Murderer," in New York *Magazine, Vol. 19, No. 37, September 22, 1986, p. 163.*

ANDREW HARVEY

One of the hardest kinds of novel to write is the allegorical, which can seem an empty and predictable virtuosic exercise. Patrick Süskind's allegory, ***Perfume*** . . . , avoids with remarkable finesse this pitfall by virtue of its clear and pungent writing and its scalding vision of history as tragic farce. ***Perfume*** has been a best-seller in Europe, and it is easy to see why. It is full of a thoughtfulness that is never pompous or mechanical; it brims with challenging ideas; it is as inventive as Eco's *The Name of the Rose* without being as determinedly "smart" (or as long). And like all true allegories. ***Perfume*** works on a number of different levels.

On one level, it is the biography, set in the mid-eighteenth century, of Jean-Baptiste Grenouille, a man who goes from being possessed by a passion for perfumes and scents of all kinds to becoming a murderer of beautiful young girls. On another, it is a meticulous study of obsession: what drives Grenouille to murder is his search for a scent—one he distills from the hair and bodies of murdered girls—that will at last make him lovable and human. On yet another level, ***Perfume*** is a sustained, intricate meditation on the relationship between estheticism and cruelty, inner emptiness and the rage to power, romanticism and the rise of the amoral, destructive modern spirit. Süskind's achievement is to make the reader aware of all these levels without ever being pedantic or haranguing.

Andrew Harvey, "Genres and Giants," in Vogue, *Vol. 176, No. 10, October, 1986, p. 268.*

PETER S. PRESCOTT

Readers who make best sellers of books are a cautious breed, which is why one best seller is very like another. Here's an exception: a highly literate first novel [***Perfume: The Story of a Murderer***] from West Germany that has had a great commercial success in Europe even though the best sellers it resembles—*Candide* and *Rasselas*—are a couple of hundred years old. Like many a philosophical tale, ***Perfume*** attempts to define the essence of the human condition. Because ***Perfume*** is a story of impeccable cynicism, that essence is—well, an essence; our humanity resides in our human odor. Patrick Süskind goes further: his inhuman protagonist can distill not only those scents that give us our individual odors, but the base of all human odor—a mix of excrement, fat and oil.

This most antirational of stories is appropriately set in France at the time of the Enlightenment. In the most odoriferous corner of Europe's most stinking city—Paris, of course—Jean-Baptiste Grenouille is born amid the offal of a fish market. Two qualities distinguish the baby at once: he has no interest in love or affection and he has no odor at all. . . .

After a sequence of picaresque adventures (Süskind takes his 18th-century models seriously), Grenouille invents several scents for his odorless self and then sets out to invent a scent that will make him smell like an angel, thus causing the world to love him. His quest prompts him to murder 25 radiantly lovely maidens. It also violates one of Süskind's lessons: you cannot have both love and life; to demand both is to come to a grisly end. Süskind's plot grows sillier as his story progresses, but it doesn't matter because by then he's caught us with his metaphor and teased us by the variations he works on it. For a moment he persuades us that the sense that most of us least value defines our lives.

Peter S. Prescott, "By His Scent Shall Ye Know Him," in Newsweek, *Vol. CVIII, No. 14, October 6, 1986, p. 75.*

An Excerpt from *Perfume: The Story of a Murderer*

All at once great contentment came over him. Not a drunken one, as in the days when he had celebrated his lonely orgies in the bowels of the mountain, but a very cold and sober contentment, as befits awareness of one's own power. He now knew what he was capable of. Thanks to his own genius, with a minimum of contrivance he had imitated the odor of human beings and at one stroke had matched it so well that even a child had been deceived. He now knew that he could do much more. He knew that he could improve on this scent. He would be able to create a scent that was not merely human, but superhuman, an angel's scent, so indescribably good and vital that whoever smelled it would be enchanted and with his whole heart would have to love him, Grenouille, the bearer of that scent.

Yes, that was what he wanted—they would love him as they stood under the spell of his scent, not just accept him as one of them, but love him to the point of insanity, of self-abandonment, they would quiver with delight, scream, weep for bliss, they would sink to their knees just as if under God's cold incense, merely to be able to smell *him*, Grenouille! He would be the omnipotent god of scent, just as he had been in his fantasies, but this time in the real world and over real people. And he knew that all this was within his power. For people could close their eyes to greatness, to horrors, to beauty, and their ears to melodies or deceiving words. But they could not escape scent. For scent was a brother of breath. Together with breath it entered human beings, who could not defend themselves against it, not if they wanted to live. And scent entered into their very core, went directly to their hearts, and decided for good and all between affection and contempt, disgust and lust, love and hate. He who ruled scent ruled the hearts of men.

Grenouille sat at his ease on his bench in the cathedral of Saint-Pierre and smiled. His mood was not euphoric as he formed his plans to rule humankind. There were no mad flashings of the eye, no lunatic grimace passed over his face. He was not out of his mind, which was so clear and buoyant that he asked himself why he wanted to do it at all. And he said to himself that he wanted to do it because he was evil, thoroughly evil. And he smiled as he said it and was content. He looked quite innocent, like any happy person.

ROBERT M. ADAMS

From start to finish, ***Perfume*** is a ridiculously improbable piece of verbose claptrap which the author himself evidently found impossible to take seriously for very long at a time.

The central personage, named Grenouille (it means "frog," but the batrachian implications aren't emphasized), is a medical anomaly, but otherwise devoid of character. Born a bastard and quickly orphaned, he starts life in the absolute pits of Parisian slum society. Though endowed with a preternaturally acute sense of smell, he otherwise possesses little sensitivity of any sort, whether verbal, intellectual, or auditory; he feels no human sympathies whatever, neither lust nor hate nor kindliness, and is generally regarded by those who come into passing contact with him as a rather loathsome little creature. Throughout the book he hardly speaks at all, and does little thinking, in the usual sense of the word: he smells. His physical body is naturally devoid of any odor at all; sometimes the author remembers this fact and makes use of it for a particular occasion, mostly not.

Growing up in the brutal Parisian underworld, Grenouille is hired and exploited by an established perfumer. For reasons never very clearly explained, he leaves this position and the city of Paris to live for seven years (on raw salamanders and dry lichen) in a cave atop a mountain in the Auvergne. He does this to be rid of the smell of other human beings, an odor that distresses him unspeakably on this occasion, but doesn't bother him particularly elsewhere in the book. Descending from his mountain peak, he makes his way to Grasse, takes employment again as a perfumer's apprentice, and embarks on a secret career of murdering young women in order to extract their essential aromas for the manufacture of a superperfume. He does away with no fewer than twenty-five of them—but at about this point the story gets so preposterous that your reviewer is ashamed to summarize the rest of it. Süskind implies it is an allegory of the Third Reich. But this does not quite account for the way Grenouille, after anesthetizing people in Grasse, is literally eaten up by people in Paris. As allegory, it is more portentous than clear.

Since very little happens within Grenouille's mind, and he achieves with other characters no relations capable of development, the book requires a good deal of stuffing to achieve the dimensions of a small novel. The best of this material is several different listings of the materials and procedures involved in perfume making. Süskind has done his homework on the topic, and regales us with many words like "opopanax," "pelargonium," "bergamot," "tuberose," etc. Less successful are the author's ventures into minor characters. Giuseppe Baldini, Grenouille's first employer in Paris, delivers a nine-page soliloquy on the state of the world that fills space, to be sure, but serves no other point. Then there is an episode with the marquis de La Taillade-Espinasse, which takes up twenty pages without accomplishing anything. When he is finished with both of these peripheral characters, Süskind, displaying an admirable sense of economy, kills them off as with a cleaver. The writing of the book is verbose and theatrical. A typical passage tries to explain why Grenouille, having got up on his mountain, decides to come down. The answer is, "a catastrophe." . . .

In brief, the catastrophe is a physiological peculiarity, however improbable in itself, about which the reader has known since page 10. I think it was Dr. Johnson who said, "A man might write such stuff forever, if he would *abandon* his mind to it." (p. 26)

Robert M. Adams, "The Nose Knows," in The New York Review of Books, *Vol. XXXIII, No. 18, November 20, 1986, pp. 24-6.*

PETER WHITTAKER

Patrick Süskind's ***Perfume*** . . . yearns to be this year's *Name of the Rose*. But this slight tale of Grenouille, an unloved orphan, compensated for his own lack of bodily odour by a superhumanly developed sense of smell, is too frail a craft to carry the freight of allegory with which Süskind loads it.

After a promisingly olfactorial start—the clash of stenches, smells, and perfumes in the streets of 18th century Paris lovingly evoked—the novel founders on the rock of its central premiss; the murderous and eventually self-destructive quest of Grenouille for the perfect perfume which will bring him the unquestioning love he so desires. It would have been easier to accept the rather obvious artifice of the novel and enter into Grenouille's world—as, for instance, we do readily with Grass or Rushdie—if we were allowed for an instant to have a sympathetic understanding of *any* of the characters. A world composed of pure evil and banal stupidity defeats belief.

Peter Whittaker, "The Smell of the Rose?" in Tribune, *Vol. 50, No. 47, November 21, 1986, p. 8.*

JOHN UPDIKE

There are no monsters like European monsters; they need Gothic nooks and crannies and the icy swirls and trompe-l'oeil of the Baroque to give them their nurture and setting. Patrick Süskind's ***Perfume: The Story of a Murderer*** . . . takes place in a beautifully researched yet fancifully ominous eighteenth-century France; its monstrous hero, Jean-Baptiste Grenouille, is born in July of 1738 into the redolence of the Cimetière des Innocents in Paris—"the most putrid spot in the whole kingdom." . . . A kind of olfactory Superman, he rises from this humblest of beginnings amid the fish offal to become the greatest perfumer in the world and from there to distill out of the aromas of slain adolescent beauties a perfume so captivating that its wearer could rule the world.

Could, but of course does not, for history, until this brilliant fable . . . , bears no trace of Grenouille, whom the author ranks, for moral deformity, with de Sade and Saint-Just and Napoleon. Like the creator of any superman, Mr. Sskind has some trouble generating significant obstacles to his hero's progress: with his fabulous nose, Grenouille can detect a thread of scent a half mile away, can sniff his way through the dark, can mix masterly perfumes with the ease of Mozart scribbling divine melodies, and in the end can subject an enormous crowd to his will. He also, we are asked to believe, can entertain himself for seven years of utterly eremitic life in a cave on an extinct volcano, drugging himself with symphonies of remembered scent. True, he is a superman fearfully handicapped at the outset; since his refusal to die at birth exposes his mother's previous successful attempts at infanticide, she is soon beheaded, and the orphan is cast on the mercy of a world that finds his bent body, inarticulate speech, and lack of human scent repulsive. Though his name means "frog" in French, the tick—"the lonely tick, which, wrapped up in itself, huddles in its tree, blind, deaf, and dumb, and simply sniffs, sniffs all year long, for miles around, for the blood of some passing animal that it could never reach on its own power"—is the creaturely image most frequently associated with Grenouille as he and his monstrous talent mature under a succession of harsh caretakers and taskmasters. The casual squalor and brutality of ordinary eighteenth-century life form one of the tale's subtexts, and its opening portrait of the crowded, smelly, disease-ridden ferment of Paris ("Paris produced over ten thousand new foundlings, bastards, and orphans a year") plausibly blends with its unfolding savageries.

The authenticity, never labored, of the historical background, and the fascinating elucidation of the procedures of perfume-making, as revealed first in a Paris shop and laboratory and then in the essence-extracting cottage industry of Grasse, carry us quite pleasurably along. The writing has the light-handed authority of Mr. Süskind's fellow-Münchner Thomas Mann, and John E. Woods has produced a translation of exceptional energy and grace. The reconstruction of the world in terms of scent is a charming tour de force. Babies, we learn from a wet nurse, have a variety of smells: "Their feet, for instance, they smell like a smooth, warm stone—or no, more like curds . . . or like butter, like fresh butter . . . And their bodies smell like . . . like a griddle cake that's been soaked in milk. And their heads, up on top, at the back of the head, where the hair makes a cowlick . . . is where they smell best of all. It smells like caramel." For Grenouille, smells are subtle and numerous beyond reckoning: there is "the odor of glass, the clayey, cool odor of smooth glass," and the "cool, musty, brawny smell" of a brass doorknob, and the "moist, fresh, tallowy, and a bit pungent" aroma of a dog. (p. 124)

Another subtext of ***Perfume,*** and perhaps the major one, is Sartre's aphorism that hell is other people. People stink, nauseatingly; when Grenouille, to help give himself a human personality and presence, mixes up the odor normal people have, "the scent of humanness," his ingredients are half a teaspoon of cat excrement, "still rather fresh," plus vinegar, salt, and some decomposing cheese. . . . Wearing dabs of this complex concoction, overlaid with perfume, he ventures into the street, timidly, "because he could not imagine that other people would not also perceive his odor as a stench." They do not. For the first time in his existence, he is favorably noticed; he exerts an effect on people; he casts a proper, customary olfactory shadow. Seldom since Gulliver described the Brobdingnagian women from up close ("They would often strip me naked from top to toe, and lay me at full length in their bosoms; wherewith I was much disgusted; because, to say the truth, a very offensive smell came from their skins") has our bodily being been the object of such merciless comedy. Along with the existential nausea is the proposition, borne out by modern scientific studies, that we are more sensitive and responsive to odors than we realize—that the great buried language of smell is still being spoken, subconsciously, by our brains. Whether that language is loud enough to carry instantly to the back of a great crowd and disarm ten thousand people of their reason seems unlikely but, in a land and city mesmerized within living man's memory by the unprepossessing Hitler, perhaps worth imagining.

Having invented his monster and run him through society like a hot knife through butter, Mr. Süskind doesn't quite know how to finish him off, short of calling in armies; the ending is the weakest part, an abrupt and bitter whiff capping a delicious book. ***Perfume*** slightly disconcerts us in being, like Grenouille's fabrication of human odor, so bluntly a concoction: it seems a fiction in which all personal and involuntary elements have been sublimated, a book that animates, with readily summoned erudition and flair, only its ideas. It is characteristically cavalier of Mr. Süskind, in framing his fable, to assign his hero two physiologically quite unrelated extreme attributes—a superkeen sense of smell, which pertains to the olfactory membrane high in the nose, and an utter lack of body odor, which the skin and the glands generate. We close the book with the presumably postmodern sensation of having been twitted. Calvino's fantasies, though more genial, leave something of this same impression, as does Umberto Eco's *The Name of the Rose*—that of an adroit and dazzling playing at novel-writing, which has become, in our age of deconstruction, a smaller art than it used to be, a trick almost contemptibly well within an intelligent man's reach. (pp. 124-25)

John Updike, "Old World Wickedness," in The New Yorker, *Vol. LXII, No. 43, December 15, 1986, pp. 124-25.*

SIMON SCHAMA

Süskind's novel [***Perfume: The Story of a Murderer***] is a fable about the Enlightenment in the guise of a gothic fantasy. . . . Süskind, who studied history in Munich, has provided one of the very best accounts of the topography, the social flavor, and the material life of 18th-century Paris to be found anywhere, inside or outside historical scholarship. He has quite obviously assimilated not only the great contemporary accounts—by Sébastien Mercier, Réstif de la Bretonne, and the like—but also a great deal of recent scholarship on a great variety of topics from wet nursing to the postal system of the ancien régime. He gets straight A's for his social history. More important, he does so without the footnotes swarming over the narrative like a plague of flies.

Süskind the novelist, moreover, is happily free of the obligations of Foucault-decreed cultural chronology. But he is no historical innocent. (p. 30)

Süskind's book is much more ambitious than its gripping gothic plot suggests. Grenouille is invented in the double image of the cultural world into which he is summarily deposited. He is the perfect acolyte of the Enlightenment's belief in the world as a machine, of humanity as a bundle of sensory and chemical matter (*l'homme machine*) that could be made to react in predictable ways through the administration of organized knowledge. The deists have demoted God to the status of the Great Clockmaker, and Grenouille becomes a little god, a Supreme Mechanic of the Nose. Through the Ultimate Olfactory Filing System he comes to believe that he too can create a disembodied essence of Humanity. Unlike the materialist and mechanist philosophes, however, Grenouille is a misogynist rather than a benefactor—an extreme case of scientific dispassion.

And yet there also stirs within him the budding counter-Enlightenment urge to become some sort of human "I." Without the Romantic suspension of disbelief, and without the innate gifts of Nature, he is obliged to manufacture a synthetic nature from the materials of his accumulated expertise. In the end, he is a victim of his own success at supplying an olfactory version of the sublime. In the admittedly rather overstretched climax, Grenouille surrenders himself contemptuously to the crowd, which has been deceived by his perfume into imagining a humanity that might be fragrant.

The eccentrically beautiful prose of ***Perfume*** is itself an alchemical shop of images of the Enlightenment—its fixation with process (set out, for example, in the engravings of the *Encyclopédie*) and the codification of acquired knowledge, and its relentless search for an improved version of Homo sapiens. Among the novel's most memorable creations is the Master Perfumer (working, as Süskind accurately represents, with *both* floral and animal essences), depressed by his inability to keep pace with the speed of changing fashion. In a very important passage, Grenouille as *sauvage* becomes the protégé of a crackpot marquis philosophe. His conviction that air breathed from close to the rotting earth was the source of modern ills is much less bizarre than a great deal of what actually passed for scientific speculation at the end of the 18th century. . . .

Perfume, then, is argument by narrative insinuation and historical parable. Leading us by the nose through a highly specified time and place, it manages to engage with matters of universal significance: essense and existence, sense and spirit. That it should do so in the form of a stunningly imagined chronicle is of great importance, since it adds to a growing list of profound works of fiction and brilliantly executed works of imagination that use history in ways wholly compatible with what ''professionals'' suppose to be the recovery of an authentic past.

The great historical novels of our time are not to be found in the ponderous costume epics that fall off the airport book racks. (These merely mirror the pathetic fallacies of the 20th century.) They are to be found, rather, in works like Carlos Fuentes's *Terra Nostra,* Graham Swift's *Waterland,* Umberto Eco's *The Name of the Rose,* Salman Rushdie's *Midnight's Children,* and now Patrick Süskind's ***Perfume.*** These books go beyond historical decor to grapple with the elusive poignancies of time, memory, and persistence. Historians sometimes imagine fondly that the indeterminate boundaries between fantasy, historical narrative, and authorial argument in all these works sets them sharply aside from their own ''scientific'' endeavors to recover the past *wie ist eigentlich gewesen.* But if the rise of a new kind of historical novel does nothing else than dispose of these childish relics of a collapsed positivism, they will have been worth the writing. Meanwhile they stand as an urgent reminder that in a present where the past has a dauntingly short shelf life, history is becoming too important to leave to the historians. (p. 31)

Simon Schama, ''Scratch 'n' Sniff,'' in The New Republic, *Vol. 196, No. 8, February 23, 1987, pp. 27-31.*

Richard Wiley

1944-

American novelist.

Soldiers in Hiding (1986) is Wiley's third novel, though it is his first to be published. While living in Japan, Wiley befriended an elderly gentleman who later became the basis for Teddy Maki, the protagonist of *Soldiers in Hiding*. "He was a Japanese-American," Wiley recalls, "a musician, who ended up drafted into the Japanese army. He had gone over there from Los Angeles before Pearl Harbor and couldn't get out. . . . Afterward, he lost his American citizenship. . . . What happened to him, the divided life he was forced to endure, remained fixed in my mind." The key event that informs *Soldiers in Hiding* occurs when Maki, despite his attempts to remain neutral, is commanded to shoot a fellow American or face death for refusing to do so. The incident haunts him for more than thirty years, fueling the ambivalence and alienation Maki feels towards both Japan and the United States.

Besides his deft coverage of post-World War II Japanese culture, Wiley is highly praised for his controlled style. In a story that could be weakened by melodrama, critics observe that Wiley sustains a subtle and sombre tone while creating a believable drama of honor, guilt, and revenge. Wiley's interest in language—he's taught English in Korea, Japan, and Nigeria and served as bilingual coordinator for Tacoma, Washington, Public Schools—also surfaces in *Soldiers in Hiding*. "I wanted the rhythm of the language to represent Japanese patterns as well as English ones," Wiley observes. Critic Christopher Lehmann-Haupt comments on reaching the climax of the story, "By this time we've entirely forgotten that it is an American who wrote *Soldiers in Hiding*."

Wiley, now living in Nairobi, Kenya, and serving as executive secretary for the Association of International Schools in Africa, is also working on his next novel. *Small Crimes of the Nineteen-Sixties* is "set in America and Nigeria during the later part of the decade."

Photograph by Gigi Wiley. Courtesy of Richard Wiley.

PUBLISHERS WEEKLY

[In ***Soldiers in Hiding***] Japanese-American jazz musician Teddy Maki, now a star on Japanese TV, has been carrying a heavy burden of guilt since World War II. He and a fellow musician, Jimmy Yakamoto, had been trapped in Japan after the bombing of Pearl Harbor and forced to join the Japanese army, although they were still loyal to America. Jimmy had been killed by ruthless Major Nakamura for refusing to shoot an American prisoner, and Teddy had then carried out the very command his friend had died defying. He has never been able to confide these details to his wife or son—because she was Jimmy's widow and their son is actually Jimmy's child. A chance sighting of the major offers Teddy the prospect of revenge and redemption, but it seems the major has likewise been waiting all these years for a similar encounter. Wiley's first novel is a work of exceptional power and imagination, especially in his portrayal of his protagonist's "listless remorse" and cross-cultural alienation. Although the weight given Teddy's living hell is disproportionate to that given his eventual resurrection from it, Wiley's debut is an auspicious one nonetheless.

A review of "Soldiers in Hiding," in Publishers Weekly, *Vol. 228, No. 25, December 20, 1985, p. 58.*

CHRISTOPHER LEHMANN-HAUPT

"It gives me pleasure to hinder American tourists occasionally. It is a small pleasure, to be sure, but a real one, and it is so very un-Japanese." So goes the opening of Richard Wiley's ***Soldiers in Hiding,*** and its mischievousness seems reason enough to go on reading this unusual first novel. . . .

[Wiley] has achieved a tour de force of compression and impersonation, wresting from his dramatic material a tragicomedy of cultural conflict.

By the time Teddy tells his story he has become Japan's most popular and vulgar television entertainer, the host of "Teddy Maki's Original Amateur Hour" ("Does that ring a bell?" he asks.) He has taken his own rendition of "Mood Indigo" as his theme song, the very tune with which General MacArthur used to introduce his speeches when he was running Japan and "wanted us unhappy in shades of the rainbow the Japanese could not even recognize." And he is dedicated to reducing Japanese culture to the lowest denominator it shares with America, as if to parody Japan's response to the West and to mock the ambiguity of his own situation.

Mr. Wiley's touch is not infallible. The scenes in which Teddy's wife gives birth to their son during a bombing attack are a little too fraught with symbolism, as is Teddy's fixation on the scars of a bar-girl who carries "the shadow of bomb burns" from her childhood in Hiroshima. The statement, "I became the central raiser of my child" seems needlessly clumsy, especially coming from a source that elsewhere describes himself as being "like a man on a rotisserie turning evenly but thoughtlessly through time," or who describes with relative grace the co-conception of that child by himself and Jimmy Yamamoto: "And as my seed set sail on its miraculous voyage I saw, in the cat's cold eye, that I was bathing the growing baby with the ingredients of myself and that he would be a mutation, a hybrid: Jimmy's boy but Teddy Maki's too." . . .

Yet such lapses seem minor in the light of all the dazzling effects Mr. Wiley pulls off, from a scene in which a Buddhist monastery burns down to the parody of a Christmas visit with which the novel ends. That ending is a showdown between Teddy Maki and Major Nakamura intended to expose the major's war crimes. But nothing turns out as planned, and the threads of the novel's complex themes are twisted into a surprising new pattern. By this time we've entirely forgotten that it is an American who wrote ***Soldiers in Hiding.*** At least to a Western ear, it is the voices of Japanese culture and history that are so dramatically declaiming.

Christopher Lehmann-Haupt, in a review of "Soldiers in Hiding," in The New York Times, *February 3, 1986, p. C26.*

An Excerpt from *Soldiers in Hiding*

We stood before American officers while a staff artist drew a depiction of our poor postures, our unrepentant attitudes.

"Teddy Maki of Los Angeles," the court clerk called, so I stepped forward.

A colonel spoke softly, asking me, "Did you, Mr. Maki, fight for the Japanese during the recent war?"

"No, sir."

"You did not?"

"I didn't fight, sir."

"Did you wear the Japanese army uniform? Did you eat with the Japanese soldiers? Did you speak Japanese with them and share their jokes?"

"I had no choice."

"Then the answer is yes."

"Yes."

"Are you aware that taking up arms against the forces of the United States is grounds for imprisonment? Grounds for loss of citizenship?"

"I have recently been told so."

"You are a popular singer, are you not, Mr. Maki? Do you think it is right that you should go free after having turned against your country so?"

"I haven't done anything wrong," I said. "I've turned against no one. Circumstances caused me to do what I did. Any other course would have cost me my life."

I had said, already, more than I wanted to, more than I'd told myself I would when I arrived. Most of my acquaintances were dead. Who would care what happened to me?

The colonel looked back and forth, his face all haughty from my listlessness, my lack of remorse.

"What would your family think, Mr. Maki, if they knew what you'd done?"

From what I could gather my father had lost his land and my uncle his grocery store a few months before they'd enlisted. My mother and brothers and younger cousins waited for them in a makeshift prison, somewhere in the desert, east of where the farm had been.

"They are all scattered," I said. "Victims of the war."

The colonel seemed to tire of me but cleared his throat and asked, "Are you a communist, Mr. Maki? Have you ever been?"

"I am not a communist. I don't care," I said.

The colonel stood and stretched his legs but let me stay standing before him. Finally he asked, "Do you swear that everything you have said is true?"

"Do you mean today?" I asked him.

He was irritated by my insolence but there were many others waiting so he let me go, keeping with him my American citizenship, invisible though it was. When I turned toward the small and silent audience the first face I saw was Milo's, and he was smiling.

"You did well, Daddy," he said, as we were leaving by the back door. He held by its broken strings a toy guitar I'd given him and trailed it slowly along the lockers that lined the hall.

BRAD LEITHAUSER

Teddy Maki, the narrator and aging hero of Richard Wiley's first novel, ***Soldiers in Hiding,*** is the host of a popular Japanese television program called the "Original Amateur Hour." The show always begins and ends with Maki's rendition of Duke Ellington's "Mood Indigo" on the guitar. He addresses his audience in both English and Japanese, although he reads the latter poorly and must have his cue cards written out in roman letters rather than ideographic characters. Maki delights in occasionally misdirecting lost American tourists. He has a son named Milo and a mistress named Sachiko, whose scarred torso recalls the blast that razed her hometown of Hiroshima when she was a little girl.

Maki has constructed, then, a curious, incongruous, trans-Pacific mix of a life for himself, although one that takes on its own forceful coherence as his story falls into place. He recounts his tale in a voice of measured deliberation, beginning with his boyhood in Los Angeles as the eldest son of Japanese emigrants. The disaster—or string of disasters—that is to befall him in early manhood scarcely darkens these early reminiscences. Yet when Maki and his friend Jimmy Yamamoto set out for Tokyo in the summer of 1941 to make their fortunes as jazz musicians in the land of their forebears, the reader knows that nothing good can come of their journey. Pearl Harbor is only months away.

With the outbreak of war, Maki and Yamamoto are suddenly transformed into foreigners behind enemy lines. Fearing imprisonment, and seeing no other means of escape, the two friends pass themselves off as natives and enlist in the Japanese Army. Their plan—which they never formulate very clearly—is to play a bystander's role in the armed forces, perhaps as members of a military band, while waiting out the war's close. But violence stalks them, inexorably. In the end, Yamamoto lies dead and Maki finds himself with a rifle in his hands and a helpless American prisoner of war before him. And he is ordered to execute the prisoner.

As even this sketchy summary should make clear, Mr. Wiley has devised a promising and ingenious plot for his novel, one rich enough that he need not strain after profundity or effect. Indeed, the most welcome characteristic of ***Soldiers in Hiding*** may be the author's self-restraint. He has created in Teddy Maki a remarkably apt symbol for the dislocations of World War II: Maki is an American fighting against American forces, a Japanese who daily fears detection that he is not a "true Japanese." The reader may initially be tempted to call Maki a victim, and will certainly sympathize with someone buffeted so helplessly, and over such great distances, by a war he neither desired nor foresaw. Yet the story's development requires the reader eventually to come to terms with the notion of Maki's complicity.

Soldiers in Hiding wobbles just a bit at the outset. Although I have no clear notions as to the sort of tone that might reasonably emerge from a sixtyish Japanese-American television host and jazz musician, it did appear to me that the book's language wasn't always of a piece. Maki at times can turn out quite a burnished phrase. "Yet it seems to me," he says of his mistress, "that she is connected as I am, fused by the very blanching of her skin, to the life and technology of North America." At other times his locutions may remind the reader of that twisted, grunted hokum that Hollywood was forever placing in the mouths of Indian chiefs in the heyday of the western. "Her husband stood with her wearing slacks of many colors," Maki says of an American tourist on the first page of the novel, "the kind that stretch a little and hug the knees." And at one point, quite confusingly, Maki's former major offers a pun that, while clever enough in English, would not be available in the Japanese he is presumably speaking.

A more serious problem (although one I raise tentatively, unsure whether many readers will be as troubled as I was by it) arises from the book's attempts to incorporate both realism and fabulism; ***Soldiers in Hiding*** at times seems to hover between a naturalistic novel and a fable. Mr. Wiley has obviously taken considerable care to lend his strange story a firm plausibility, and one must commend the book for wearing its research so lightly. And yet there are times when—the plot's believability being momentarily lost—Maki's explanations as to how or why something happened can look clumsily contrived. Still, given the novel's quiet but sizable ambitions, and its high level of achievement, the reader may want to overlook any such shortcomings.

The blast of a rifle echoes through ***Soldiers in Hiding.*** Although that shot was fired in the Philippines, decades before Teddy Maki sat down to tell his story, it lingers in his mind. The success or failure of this novel depends, in large measure, on Maki's evocation of that triggering moment: the reader needs to believe that was indeed a moment that could haunt a man 20, 30, maybe 40 years later. And the scene succeeds brilliantly. The firing of that rifle will roar for some time in the reader's mind as well.

Brad Leithauser, "Whose Side Are You On, Teddy Maki?" in The New York Times Book Review, *February 9, 1986, p. 13.*

D. J. ENRIGHT

Teddy Maki [the narrator of ***Soldiers in Hiding***] has his own television programme, the "Original Amateur Hour". When it began in the early 1950s it featured serious acts, but now it resembles something dug up by Clive James to make British viewers feel superior: contestants win by drinking water through their noses or farting a tune. Maki, who speaks perfect English, takes a mean, similarly cynical pleasure in misdirecting American tourists in Tokyo.

He and his friend Jimmy Yamamoto were Americans, Los Angeles Japanese, who happened to be in Japan, playing in a band, when war broke out. Both of them fell in love with Kazuko, sister of their local agent, Ike, and Jimmy married her. *Faute de mieux,* they joined the Japanese army, and found themselves in the Philippines, guarding American prisoners. Jimmy refused to shoot an officer who had outraged Major Nakamura by his incorrect attitude—he showed himself insufficiently defeated—and was thereupon shot by the major. When Maki was ordered in turn to shoot the American, he complied. Discharged, he found his way to Tokyo and married Kazuko—an admirable, unromanticized figure—who bore a son, ostensibly his, actually Jimmy's. Except for his devotion to the child, named Milo, Maki is a ghost, estranged, belonging nowhere, "like a man on a rotisserie turning evenly but thoughtlessly through time". He cannot forget that he was able to kill where Jimmy preferred to die.

Thirty years after his supposed death in the jungle, Ike returns, having posed as a Filipino, settled in Manila, even married there. Such things did happen. With Milo, now a pop star, and Ike, Maki plans an act of revenge: to have ex-Major Nakamura on his show, "the amateur of that particular hour". On Christmas Day—an American irony, this—they and a camera crew, all dressed in miscellaneous army uniforms from the studio wardrobe, interview Nakamura in a warehouse which the major, now a pharmacist, has turned into a theatre. In a weird climax which avoids staginess by the haphazardness of its events, they don Noh masks and recite lines from an old play. The shooting in the Philippines is very nearly reenacted. For Nakamura is just a mad old man. "All soldiers die" is the conclusion; "None of them are guilty." This—after all those years—

is no sentimental cop-out. Surely no one should suffer at the same time both the pangs of conscience and the pangs of age. For what life is left to him, Maki is released from his guilt, more or less mended. Now he will help lost foreigners to find their way.

Précis makes the story sound melodramatic; in its telling the novel is controlled and sombre, unportentously thoughtful, persuasively low-key. Traces of awkwardness in the writing, as if it were a painstaking translation, add to the impression of honesty; and incidents are the more effective in that "local colour" is applied with a light brush. During a fire raid the neighbours take water from a public bathhouse: never mind the tatami, the matting, the owner tells them, "and quickly the tatami was soaked and torn, the heels of street shoes turning its straight straw lines into twisted sores, like the blooms of an awful flower". A nearby temple is on fire, and the large image of the Buddha changes its expression into one of faint surprise as it begins to melt; the faces of the dead monks have no expression, show no surprise.

After Hiroshima, Maki knows there won't be much trouble, the Japanese will surprise the Americans by being model prisoners: "That had been Major Nakamura's point." And when the Emperor, on the radio, announces the surrender to his subjects, what is extraordinary is not what the Emperor says but the fact that he is speaking. "Our losses were incalculable", Maki reflects, whole cities wiped out, but what is interesting is that now they are crying for the greatest loss of all, "the virginity of the Emperor's voice".

This first novel has a dignity, a decency and a humanity so rare in contemporary fiction as to make one wish for more resounding terms of commendation. It takes the nominally exotic and, without deracinating it, without straining after programmatic effects, reveals it as universally authentic.

D. J. Enright, "Model Prisoners," in The Times Literary Supplement, *No. 4350, August 15, 1986, p. 894.*

COMMENTS OF RICHARD WILEY TO *CLC YEARBOOK*

Wiley cites several reasons behind *Soldiers in Hiding:* it was inspired by "life in Tokyo in the early 1970s. The idea of war, between Japan and America—the idea that it was a cultural and linguistic misunderstanding, and therefore a tragedy."

Though *Soldiers in Hiding* required little research—"I looked up the Japanese Emperor's surrender speech and checked on the dates of certain bombings and battles, but nothing more"—it demanded much work. Wiley confides the novel was the product of "constant rewrites over six years. The book made itself known to me slowly, the fullness of the story not revealing itself until nearly the end of my six years of work. It was a process of constant tightening and of reworking the ending until it became magical."

Like his two earlier novels, *Soldiers in Hiding* met with a number of rejections. "When the book was finally taken I was dumbfounded, realizing only after the fact that I had given up hope." Although publication has not changed his life, "it has," he says, "given me renewed confidence and the will to go on."

Wiley's hoped-for audience for the novel *Soldiers in Hiding* is "anyone at all. Those who read it purposefully or by accident." He adds, "I would love to have the book translated into Japanese for the same people."

Asked what motivates him to write, Wiley asserted, "writing is my only connection to the gods, my only tap into the heart of things—writing is not, for me, something through which one accomplishes something else. The writing is the thing, an end in itself."

Prizewinners

Literary Prizes and Honors

Announced in 1986

ACADEMY OF AMERICAN POETS AWARDS

FELLOWSHIP OF THE ACADEMY OF AMERICAN POETS
Irving Feldman
THE LAMONT POETRY SELECTION
Jane Shore, *The Minute Hand*
IVAN YOUNGER POETS AWARD
Rita Dove, Rodney Jones, Timothy Steele
WALT WHITMAN AWARD
Chris Llewellyn, *Fragments from the Fire*

AMERICAN ACADEMY AND INSTITUTE OF ARTS AND LETTERS AWARDS

GOLD MEDAL FOR DRAMA
Sidney Kingsley
AWARD OF MERIT MEDAL FOR POETRY
Kenneth Koch
AWARDS IN LITERATURE
Russell Banks, Frederick Busch, Robert A. Caro, Robert Kelly, Barry Lopez, David Mamet, Marsha Norman, and Lore Segal
E.M. FORSTER AWARD
Julian Barnes
HAROLD D. VURSELL MEMORIAL AWARD
Gretel Ehrlich, *The Solace of Open Spaces*
JEAN STEIN AWARD FOR POETRY
Gregory Corso
MORTON DAUWEN ZABEL AWARD
Philip Whalen
RICHARD AND HINDA ROSENTHAL FOUNDATION AWARD FOR FICTION
Richard Powers, *Three Farmers on Their Way to a Dance*
ROME FELLOWSHIP IN LITERATURE
Richard Kenney
SUE KAUFMAN PRIZE FOR FIRST FICTION
Cecile Pineda, *Face*
WITTER BYNNER PRIZE FOR POETRY
C.D. Wright

THE AMERICAN BOOKS AWARDS

FICTION
E.L. Doctorow, *World's Fair*
NONFICTION
Barry Lopez, *Arctic Dreams*

BOLLINGEN PRIZE IN POETRY

Stanley Kunitz

BOOKER McCONNELL PRIZE FOR FICTION

Kingsley Amis, *The Old Devils*

COMMONWEALTH POETRY PRIZE

Lauris Edmond, *Selected Poems*

DELMORE SCHWARTZ MEMORIAL POETRY AWARD

Brenda Hillman

DRUE HEINZ LITERATURE PRIZE

Rick DeMarines, *Under the Wheat*

EDGAR ALLAN POE AWARDS

BEST NOVEL
L.R. Wright, *The Suspect*
FIRST NOVEL
Jonathan Kellerman, *When the Bough Breaks*
SHORT STORY
John Lutz, "Ride the Lightning," in *Alfred Hitchcock's Mystery Magazine*
CRITICAL/BIOGRAPHICAL
Peter Lewis, *John Le Carré*
GRAND MASTER AWARD
Ed McBain (Evan Hunter)

PRIX GONCOURT

Michel Host, *Valet de Nuit*

GOVERNOR GENERAL'S LITERARY AWARDS

FICTION
Margaret Atwood, *The Handmaid's Tale*
DRAMA
George F. Walker, *Criminals in Love*
POETRY
Fred Wah, *Waiting for Saskatchewan*

HUGO AWARDS

NOVEL
Orson Scott Card, *Ender's Game*
NONFICTION
Tom Weller, *Science Made Stupid*
NOVELLA
Roger Zelazny, *Twenty-Four Views of Mount Fuji,* in *Isaac Asimov's Science Fiction Magazine*
NOVELLETTE
Harlan Ellison, "Palladin of the Lost Hour," in *Twilight Zone Magazine*
SHORT STORY
Frederik Pohl, "Fermi and Frost" in *Isaac Asimov's Science Fiction Magazine*

JAMES TAIT BLACK MEMORIAL PRIZES

FICTION
Robert Edric, *Winter Garden*
BIOGRAPHY
David Stokes, *Jonathan Swift: A Hypocrite*

JERUSALEM PRIZE

J.M. Coetzee

LENORE MARSHALL/NATION POETRY PRIZE

Howard Moss, *New Selected Poems*

LOS ANGELES TIMES BOOK AWARDS

FICTION
Margaret Atwood, *The Handmaid's Tale*
POETRY
Derek Walcott, *Selected Poems, 1948-1984*
BIOGRAPHY
Maynard Mack, *Alexander Pope: A Life*
HISTORY
Geoffrey Hosking, *The First Socialist Society: A History of the Soviet Union from Within*

THE NATIONAL BOOK CRITICS CIRCLE AWARDS

FICTION
Anne Tyler, *The Accidental Tourist*
POETRY
Louise Glück, *The Triumph of Achilles*
CRITICISM
William Gass, *Habitations of the Word*
BIOGRAPHY
Leon Edel, *Henry James: A Life*
NONFICTION
J. Anthony Lukas, *Common Ground: A Turbulent Decade in the Lives of Three American Families*

NEBULA AWARDS

NOVEL
Orson Scott Card, *Ender's Game*
NOVELLA
Robert Silverberg, *Sailing to Byzantium*
NOVELLETTE
George R.R. Martin, "Portraits of His Children," in *Isaac Asimov's Science Fiction Magazine*
SHORT STORY
Nancy Kress, "Out of All Them Bright Stars," in *Magazine of Fantasy and Science Fiction*
GRAND MASTER AWARD
Arthur C. Clarke

NEUSTADT INTERNATIONAL PRIZE FOR LITERATURE

Max Frisch

NEW YORK DRAMA CRITICS CIRCLE AWARD

Sam Shepard, *A Lie of the Mind*

NOBEL PRIZE IN LITERATURE

Wole Soyinka

OBIE AWARD

Eric Bogosian, *Drinking in America*
Martha Clarke, *Vienna: Lusthaus*
John Jesurun, *Deep Sleep*
Lee Nagrin, *Bird/Bear*
Wallace Shawn, *Aunt Dan and Lemon*

O. HENRY AWARDS

Alice Walker, "Kindred Spirits"

PEN AWARDS

PEN/FAULKNER AWARD FOR FICTION
Peter Taylor, *The Old Forest and Other Stories*
EARNEST HEMINGWAY FOUNDATION AWARD FOR FIRST FICTION
Alan V. Hewat, *Lady's Time*
PEN MEDAL FOR TRANSLATION OF PROSE
Barbara Bray, for *The Lover,* by Marguerite Duras
PEN MEDAL TRANSLATION FOR POETRY
Denis Tedlock, for *Popol Vuh: The Mayan Book of the Dawn of Life*

PULITZER PRIZES

FICTION
Larry McMurtry, *Lonesome Dove*
POETRY
Henry Taylor, *The Flying Change*
BIOGRAPHY
Elizabeth Frank, *Louise Bogan: A Portrait*
HISTORY
Walter A. McDougall, *The Heavens and the Earth: A Political History of the Space Age*

NONFICTION

Joseph Lelyveld, *Move Your Shadow: South Africa, Black and White;* and J. Anthony Lukas, *Common Ground: A Turbulent Decade in the Lives of Three American Families*

TONY AWARDS

BEST PLAY

Herb Gardner, *I'm Not Rappaport*

WORLD FANTASY AWARDS

NOVEL

Dan Simmons, *Song of Kali*

NOVELLA

T.E.D. Klein, *Nadelman's God*

SHORT STORY

James Blaylock, "Paper Dragons"

LIFETIME ACHIEVEMENT

Avram Davidson

YALE SERIES OF YOUNGER POETS AWARD

Julie Agoos, *Above the Land*

Prizewinners

Featured in 1986 Yearbook

Kingsley Amis
The Old Devils
Booker-McConnell Prize for Fiction

Margaret Atwood
The Handmaid's Tale
Governor General's Literary Award: Fiction

Orson Scott Card
Ender's Game
Hugo Award
Nebula Award

E. L. Doctorow
World's Fair
The American Book Awards: Fiction

Max Frisch
Neustadt International Prize for Literature

Herb Gardner
I'm Not Rappaport
Tony Award

Louise Glück
The Triumph of Achilles
The National Book Critics Circle Award: Poetry

Jonathan Kellerman
When the Bough Breaks
Edgar Allan Poe Award: Best First Novel

Sidney Kingsley
American Academy and Institute of Arts and Letters: Gold Medal for Drama

Kenneth Koch
American Academy and Institute of Arts and Letters: Award of Merit for Poetry

Larry McMurtry
Lonesome Dove
Pulitzer Prize: Fiction

Sam Shepard
A Lie of the Mind
New York Drama Critics Circle Award: Best Play

Dan Simmons
Song of Kali
World Fantasy Award: Best Novel

Wole Soyinka
Nobel Prize in Literature

Henry Taylor
The Flying Change
Pulitzer Prize: Poetry

Peter Taylor
The Old Forest and Other Stories
PEN/Faulkner Award for Fiction

Anne Tyler
The Accidental Tourist
The National Book Critics Circle Award: Fiction

Fred Wah
Waiting for Saskatchewan
Governor General's Literary Award: Poetry

George F. Walker
Criminals in Love
Governor General's Literary Award: Drama

L. R. Wright
The Suspect
Edgar Allan Poe Award: Best Novel

Prize Commentary

American Academy and Institute of Arts and Letters: Gold Medal

The Gold Medal, established in 1909, is the most prestigious award given by the American Academy and Institute of Arts and Letters. Each year the prize is given in two separate categories of the arts and these categories are repeated every six years; in all, twelve categories of the arts are recognized, including architecture and history, poetry and music, drama and graphic arts, criticism and painting, biography and music, and fiction and sculpture. The award honors the recipient's entire body of work and can be given to a member of the Institute as well as to other individuals.

American Academy and Institute of Arts and Letters: Award of Merit

The Award of Merit, established in 1942, is one of the most prestigious prizes bestowed by the American Academy and Institute of Arts and Letters. Rotating annually, the prize consists of a medal and 1,000 dollars and recognizes outstanding achievement in painting, sculpture, fiction, poetry, or drama. The award is given to individuals who are not members of the award-giving body and recognizes their entire work.

The American Book Awards

Administered by the Association of American Publishers, The American Book Awards, which were revised in 1984, are given annually "to honor and promote books of distinction and literary merit." Books written by American citizens and published in the United States are submitted by publishers and reviewed by the nominating committees; three titles are nominated in each of the three categories: fiction, nonfiction, and first work of fiction. The winner in each category is judged by the Academy of The American Book Awards. Nominees receive 1,000 dollars, and winners receive 10,000 dollars. The American Book Awards were established in 1980 and are the successors of the National Book Awards, which were established in 1950 by the National Book Committee.

Booker-McConnell Prize for Fiction

Britain's most important prize for fiction, the Booker-McConnell Prize is awarded to the writer of the year's most distinguished full-length novel written in English by a citizen of the British Commonwealth and published in the United Kingdom. Publishers submit the books for consideration and a five-member committee selects the winner of the 10,000 pound award. The prize was established in 1968 by the international food company Booker-McConnell Limited and is administered by the National Book League.

Edgar Allan Poe Awards

Informally known as the "Edgars," the Edgar Allan Poe Awards were established in 1945 by the Mystery Writers of America and are given annually for the year's outstanding works in the mystery genre. The winners are selected by the General Awards Committee from works submitted by publishers. Scrolls are awarded to all nominees, and the winner in each category receives a ceramic bust of Edgar Allan Poe.

Governor General's Literary Awards

Established in 1936 by the Canadian Authors Association, the Governor General's Literary Awards are now administered through the Canada Council. The prize is given for superior works of fiction, poetry, drama, and nonfiction published during the year by Canadian authors. Awards are given both for works in English and works in French, bringing the total annual number of awards to eight. The winners, who are chosen by an eighteen-member committee, receive a specially bound copy of the award-winning work in addition to a cash prize of 5,000 dollars.

Hugo Awards

The Hugo Awards, established in 1953, are sponsored by the World Science Fiction Society and are chosen through the vote of the people who attend the Annual Science Fiction Convention. The Hugo is awarded for notable science fiction works in several categories. Each winner receives a trophy of a chrome-plated Rocket Ship. Informally named after Hugo Gernsback, an early publisher of science fiction, the award's official title is the Science Fiction Achievement Award.

The National Book Critics Circle Awards

Awarded for books published in the previous year, The National Book Critics Circle Awards honor superior works by American authors. The purpose of The National Book Critics Circle, which was founded in 1974, is "to raise the standards of the profession of book criticism and to enhance public appreciation of literature"; awards are bestowed for the best fiction, poetry, biography, criticism, and nonfiction. The winners are judged by the twenty-four members of the National Book Critics Circle Board of Directors; each winner receives an honorary scroll.

Neustadt International Prize for Literature

Dubbed "the American Nobel" by several international newspapers, the Neustadt International Prize for Literature is endowed by the Neustadt family and administered by the University of Oklahoma's publication *World Literature Today*. First bestowed in 1970, the award is presented every other year to a living author and recognizes significant and continuing contributions in poetry, fiction, or drama, thus honoring the author's entire career rather than one particular work. An international committee of twelve judges both nominates and selects the winner; this jury changes for each award. Nominees must have a representative amount of their work available in French or English. The chosen laureate receives 25,000 dollars, a certificate, and a Silver Eagle Feather that represents, in the words of Doris Neustadt, the writer's "need for freedom and the desire to rise to greater heights." In addition, a special issue of *World Literature Today* is devoted to the winner's works. The award was formerly known as the *Books Abroad* International Prize for Literature.

Nebula Awards

Established in 1965 and bestowed by the Science Fiction Writers of America, the Nebula Awards merit significant works (in several categories of the science fiction genre) that are published in the United States during the previous year. Winners are nominated and chosen by the organization's membership. The trophy awarded is a lucite sculpture embedded with a Nebula formation.

New York Drama Critics Circle Awards

The purpose of the New York Drama Critics Circle Awards is to encourage continued excellence in playwriting by recognizing the year's best play (American or foreign), best foreign play (when the "best play" is American), and the best musical. Eligible dramatists are those who have had a new play produced during the year on or off Broadway in New York City; winners are chosen by the vote of members of the Circle. The award has been given by the New York Drama Critics Circle since 1935 and includes a scroll and 1,000 dollars for the best play and a scroll for the other playwrights.

Nobel Prize in Literature

One of six Nobel Prizes given annually since 1901, the Nobel Prize in Literature is generally considered to be the highest recognition a writer can receive. Established under the terms of the will of the Swedish-born Alfred Bernhard Nobel, the Nobel Prizes are given to those "who, during the preceding year, shall have conferred the greatest benefit on mankind." Nobel willed the literary portion of the award to go to "the person who shall have produced in the field of literature the most outstanding work of an idealistic tendency." The award recognizes the author's entire body of work and is open to writers of any nationality. The Nobel Committee of the Swedish Academy nominates candidates and selects the winner. The Nobel laureate receives a gold medal, a certificate, and a honorarium that varies each year but always exceeds 100,000 dollars. The awards are presented in Stockholm, Sweden.

PEN/Faulkner Award for Fiction

The PEN/Faulkner Award for Fiction, sponsored by the PEN South and the PEN American Center in New York—organizations comprised of writers—is judged and mainly supported by writers. First presented in 1981, the award recognizes the year's superior work of fiction by an American writer and continues the tradition of William Faulkner who donated funds to the Nobel Prize to help honor other writers. Each nominee receives 1,000 dollars, while the winner is awarded 5,000 dollars. To emphasize the national nature of the prize, the award committee moved its offices to the Folger Shakespeare Library in Washington, D.C.

Pulitzer Prizes

The Pulitzer Prizes were established in 1904 by Joseph Pulitzer, founder of the *St. Louis Post Dispatch,* and have continued through his willed endowment since 1917. Administered by the Graduate School of Journalism at Columbia University, the prizes recognize outstanding American works that address some aspect of American life; they are awarded in various categories within journalism, music, and literature. The fifteen-member Pulitzer board receives nominations from the separate juries of each category. The winner in each category is awarded 1,000 dollars.

Tony Awards

Formally titled the Antoinette Perry Awards, the Tony Awards were founded in 1947 by the American Theatre Wing "to award the achievement of excellence in the theater" and are administered by the League of New York Theatres and Producers. The awards recognize the year's best play produced at one of the eligible Broadway theaters and also honor many other categories related to dramatic production. From a list of nominees, winners are selected by some 560 people involved in various aspects of the theater. The award itself bears images of the masks of comedy and tragedy on one side and the profile of actress Antoinette Perry on the other.

World Fantasy Award

The World Fantasy Awards, established in 1975, honor outstanding writers and publishers in the fantasy genre. Works of original fiction are eligible for awards in three categories: novel, novella, and short story. The award statuette is the sculptured metal caricature of horror writer Howard Phillips Lovecraft; informally, the prizes are known as Howards. Like the older Science Fiction Achievement Awards, or Hugos, the Howards are connected with a prestigious annual convention. Each year registered members of previous World Fantasy Conventions nominate their award candidates by mail-in ballot. A panel of five distinguished judges is chosen each year to select the winners, who are announced at the next convention.

Kingsley (William) Amis

The Old Devils

Booker-McConnell Prize for Fiction

(Also writes under pseudonyms of Robert Markham and William Tanner) English novelist, poet, critic, essayist, nonfiction and short story writer, and journalist.

Judges for the Booker-McConnell Prize praised *The Old Devils* (1986), their selection for the 1986 fiction award, for its "brilliant comic insight." Many critics regard Amis as one of England's foremost contemporary comic novelists, comparable to Evelyn Waugh in his witty social commentary and command of satirical idioms. Since the publication of his first novel, *Lucky Jim* (1954), Amis has produced a substantial body of work in other genres, including poetry, short stories, science fiction, and espionage tales. He attracts his most devoted following, however, with his humorous novels.

During the 1950s, critics identified Amis, because of his iconoclastic attitude, with the "Angry Young Men" movement of working-class British writers that emerged after World War II. Jim Dixon, the disgruntled hero of *Lucky Jim,* became for many readers a symbol of rebellion against the conservative establishment. As his career progressed, however, Amis began to shock liberal admirers with his increasingly right-wing social and political observations. Though the object of his satirical comedy remained social manners and mores, in particular cultural snobbishness, in this later period Amis turned his comic and pessimistic scrutiny toward many modern trends. His intense antifeminist rhetoric in *Stanley and the Women* (1984) offended many English critics and made American publishers reluctant to distribute the novel. "You can't make nasty remarks, or humorous or critical remarks, about a group without seeming to be attacking it," Amis complained in a 1986 interview. "Look at the things I'm supposed to have attacked: universities, Americans, women, young people, old people. . . . I mean, you wouldn't bother to be critical about something which you didn't like to start with."

The Old Devils takes place in Wales, where Amis worked as a university lecturer during the 1950s and 1960s; satirical references throughout the novel convey his disapproval of modern, gentrified Wales. The novel deals with the aging process, a phenomenon Amis treated previously in his novel *Ending Up* (1974). Whereas the elderly protagonists of *Ending Up* are mostly unpleasant, the group of friends in *The Old Devils* elicit reader sympathy as they attempt to cope with failing health and old romantic entanglements. These characters, mainly upper-class retirees in late middle age, appealed to reviewers despite their Tory prejudices, obsession with bodily functions, and heavy alcohol consumption. Amis stated that he used their drunkenness as a device to lower their defenses and reveal their true emotional states. Besides, he reasoned, "the people in my book are affluent enough to afford to be drunk the whole time, so why not? There's nothing to stay sober for."

Reviewers agree that *The Old Devils* is Amis's least vitriolic and most humane novel to date. Amis mutes his customary sarcasm, they observe, showing tolerance for both his male and female characters and depicting the physical and emotional rigors of aging with compassion as well as humor. Some reviewers also comment that *The Old Devils* features Amis's most accomplished work from a technical standpoint, involving the reader in the story with his impressive prose, engaging dialogue, and startling paradoxes. Anthony Burgess declares in his review: "There is one old devil who is writing better than he ever did."

(See also *CLC,* Vols. 1, 2, 3, 5, 8, 13, 40; *Contemporary Authors,* Vols. 9-12, rev. ed.; *Contemporary Authors New Revision Series,* Vol. 8; and *Dictionary of Literary Biography,* Vols. 15, 27.)

ANITA BROOKNER

[Brookner, an English novelist, nonfiction writer, and critic, published several scholarly works on art history, including The Genius of the Future: Studies in French Art Criticism *(1971), before*

writing her first novel, A Start in Life *(1981). Her other novels include* Hotel du Lac *(1984), which won the Booker-McConnell Prize, and* Family and Friends *(1985). In the following excerpt Brookner praises* The Old Devils *as one of Amis's most mature works.*]

The old devils of the title [***The Old Devils***] are a party of not too viable friends, on the wrong side of 60, who spend the days of their semi-retirement together, apparently dedicated to the proposition of drinking Wales dry. It is impossible to overestimate the amount of drinking done in this novel. While the men are pouring down cascades of whisky and water or torrents of gin and slimline tonic, the latter out of deference to their ruined outlines, their wives are tearing into cases of Soave, Frascati, and Yugoslav Riesling. The two sexes rarely drink together. The husbands peel off in the early morning for a session at the Bible and Crown, breaking off for a more or less liquid lunch at the Glendower, before finishing the afternoon or evening in one or other of their houses attacking more whisky and listening to old jazz records. Their wives are rarely in attendance since they are visiting one another for 'coffee', and tend to spend the day among overflowing ashtrays and empty bottles saying things in an oblique fashion which matches well with the style of the hospitality. Occasions like holidays, a weekend excursion, a wedding, or the unveiling of a plaque to the local hero, Brydan, poet and boozer, are seen as occasions for further refuelling, yet it cannot be said that anybody is any the better for any of this drinking. Serious curtailments of physical well-being are on offer, constipation here, overweight there, anxiety attacks of considerable proportions, and finally a fatality, none of which are seen as more than minor inconveniences, to be brushed aside or erased from the consciousness by the further intake of alcohol.

All this takes place under lowering Welsh skies, and the subject most usually under discussion is what degree of Welshness is permitted to the *honnête homme* and at what point does authentic Welshness deteriorate into token Welshness, a condition liable to interfere with the moral fibre of the principality.

This preoccupation is brought to the fore when the old devils—Malcolm, Charlie, and Peter—await, with varied reflections, the return of their erstwhile comrade Alun (born Alan) Weaver and his wife Rhiannon. Alun Weaver has been all things Welsh on English television for some years and is consequently a figure of some local importance, a professional white-haired charmer given to long rolling sentences when on the job and shorter ones when off it. He is intent on visiting parts of Wales for a television series provisionally entitled, 'In Search of Wales'. Many will recognise it although it was never made. It was never made because Alun, using his shorter sentences, optimises his non-drinking time by bringing a little cheer into the lives of all those girls he left behind him, although they now happen to be married to Malcolm, Charlie, and Peter. Age and girth prove no obstacle to Alun until one unexpected evening, the details of which become a little hazy, as Kingsley Amis cleverly lets us ride along on an exhausting tide of alcohol before turning serious and providing a timely reminder of his habitual craftsmanship.

The serious note on which the book ends is introduced halfway through when it becomes clear that Rhiannon, unlike her husband, has inspired lasting and real love in at least two of the characters, Malcolm and Peter. Just why she has done this is less certain for she is barely differentiated from the other wives, all of whom seem distressingly inter-changeable. But Rhiannon is a heroine because the author loves her: that is how female characters in novels get to be heroines, for they are rarely distinguished by their qualities or actions. What might have been a touching story of love among the elderly is in fact something more grotesque and occasionally painful, something too which hints at the shortness of endeavour that characterises the amorous lives of men who have drowned their joys as well as their sorrows. The book gives off a savage whiff of powerful dislike before allowing itself a backward glance of real or at least remembered affection.

In undistinguished weather the talk ranges back and forth over two topics: Alun's Welshness and Brydan's Welshness. Both are seen to be hedged about with prohibitions since it is felt to be underhand to be too lyrical when sober and not much more defensible when drunk. Yet as the vista of slag heaps, caravan parks, pubs decorated with old team photographs, and more recently introduced Burger Bars unfolds, it is clear to the reader, particularly to the reader who is not Welsh, that this subject is one of the utmost importance, and can be, and indeed is, discussed at great length throughout the entire book. Indeed it is one of two subjects that Kingsley Amis is apparently prepared to take entirely seriously, the other being the steady pursuit of more drink.

There are times in the novel when both subjects become monotonous, when the author's famous irascibility begins to have too weak an edge to it. The equally famous misogyny is less horrendously uninhibited than usual. It is possible to feel rather sorry for these old girls in their trouser suits, despite the handicaps that the author visits on them: loquaciousness, lack of sympathy, infidelity, a daily habit of overindulgence. In a way he is no ruder about the women than about the men. This I take to be a sign of the mature Amis. The mood of the novel might be described as serious dislike buried in affection, or antipathy masked by nostalgia. Were it not for that brief moment of true feeling at the end and the consciousness that the author has not brought us all this way for nothing, the note struck would be unremittingly sour.

For the non-drinker the novel is puzzling. Drinking here is not undertaken to outwit the oppressions of the state or to celebrate natural good fortune; it is undertaken for the sole purpose of getting drunk. It is unaccompanied by wit, satire, courage, or joy. It takes place in unheated bars while veils of rain drift outside the windows. Far more seriously, it does not advance the action of the novel until death unfairly claims a victim: the news of this fatality is on the whole received calmly, drink and Welshness by that stage having done their worst or possibly their best, preserving the survivors in their single-minded pursuit of the ideal state, which would seem to be a greater proportion of drink to that of Welshness.

The author's testiness is in fact as sad as the weather, as sad as the alterations brought about by age. Laughter is absent from the final pages, which quicken the action of the entire book. It is these final pages that reveal the writer Amis at his best, and it is with a genuine sense of the passing of time and of the way in which that same passing leads one to the lip of truth that the author at last reveals something of himself, something not always on show, and in doing so awakens in the reader a wry smile of empathy. (pp. 31-2)

Anita Brookner, "Another Little Drink Wouldn't Do Us Any Good," in The Spectator, *Vol. 257, No. 8253, September 13, 1986, pp. 31-2.*

ANTHONY BURGESS

[*An English novelist and critic, Burgess is well known for his satires of contemporary society in which he uses black humor the most famous of these is his novel* A Clockwork Orange *(1962). Burgess's experimentation with language is widely acclaimed, and his interest in linguistics is reflected in his critical studies of James Joyce, notably, the popular* Here Comes Everybody: An Introduction to James Joyce for the Ordinary Reader *(1965); published in America as* Re Joyce, *(1965). His recent works include* Flame into Being: The Life and Work of D. H. Lawrence *(1985) and* The Pianoplayers *(1986). In the following excerpt Burgess commends Amis for his amusing yet touching portrayal of the aging characters in* The Old Devils.]

Malcolm Cellan-Davies [in ***The Old Devils***] has a mouth suitable for chewing crustless toast only in one selected area; he is also shaken by pain in one testicle which could be cancer, though he is cheered by news of the low mortality rate from this allotrope of the disease. He also passes a little blood from the anus. Charlie Norris, approaching the terminal phase of alcoholism, has nightmares about men whose faces are composed of carpeting and is desperately scared of the dark. Peter Thomas is grossly fat and can only very rarely cut his toenails. When he does, he conducts the operation in the garden, where hallucal chunks of rock fly like bullets at the sparrows.

All these men are old, as are Garth Pumphrey, Owen Thomas (no relation to Peter), Tudor Whittingham, others. Hence they are *ipso facto* comic. Whether they are tragic is not—if we take the strict Aristotelian view—a question to be asked. Old age happens, but it strikes neither pity nor terror in the hearts of those who have not yet reached it. It is probably wholly comic, but we have to expand our conception of what the comic is. Kingsley Amis has been helping us to do this for a long time.

These men, as some of their names indicate, are Welsh, and the locale in which they await 'the old latter end' (***Take a Girl Like You***) is a town in Monmouthshire, which a bureau in London has decided must now be called Gwent. The appeal to ancient history is as factitious and embarrassing as the TAXI/TACSI sign outside Newport station (the Cymric transliteration is for Welshmen unfamiliar with the letter X). The Owen Glendower restaurant (no Owain Glyndŵr crap, thank you very much) has uneatable archaeology like chicken in honey on the menu, also *pys* and *tatws*. Cymric patriotism is a dead scene.

The men drink, chiefly in a backroom of The Bible and Crown, because there is nothing else to do. Their wives drink also, mainly Soave from the two-litre flask at what they call coffee parties. They have not succumbed to the grossness of senility and are smart if raddled in trouser suits. They have no respect for their husbands. Peter's wife is from Yorkshire, and she tells him how unattractive he is before pissing off and leaving him with no roof over the head. It is all a pretty miserable set-up, though the region is ennobled by the memory of a great dead poet, Brydan (1913-60) who died a bit too late to be Dylan Thomas, despite his devotion to *Astounding Science Fiction* and Jack Daniels bourbon.

The alcoholic torpor is lightened by the return of Alun Weaver CBE, together with his wife Rhiannon, to his native land. A phony epigone of Brydan, artificially snowy-haired and full of Taff bullshit on TV, he has been selling Wales to England and even America, as a Mr Llywelyn Caswallon Pugh, an official of the Cymric Companionship of the USA, makes clear to the hungover Charlie at the unveiling of a sculptural andromorph in memory of the dead bard. Rhiannon, a great beauty in her day, and still attractive with her Polygripped dentures, once had an abortion subsidised by a thinner Peter, and Malcolm loved her too, though hopelessly. The past arrives to make the present more painful.

Having assembled his characters, what can Mr Amis do with them? Alun, whose CBE disparages unjustly his creator's own, has to go in search of Wales, which may result in 'In Search of Wales.' This entails massive pub-crawling with his pals in areas defaced by Arab-owned Indian restaurants where the Indian cook comes on duty at six, and by the drinking unemployed young. If there is to be any violence it must be mainly verbal and directed by pub landlords against the bibulous old. If there is to be death it is going to come without any outside help, and suspense is sustained by our wondering whom precisely death is going to hit.

It hits the man whom we least expect to be singled out, which is as it should be. The women survive. Very movingly love is declared toward the end, and not by the fire in the blood that prodigally lends the tongue vows. When decrepit obesity declares it we had better believe it.

Mr Amis has written of Wales before and his preliminary note shows that he has been back to Swansea to renew his knowledge of that sad principality. He has also, in ***Ending Up,*** written of age and death. Age and death in South Wales are doubly senile and lethal. The preacher's *hywl* is no longer available to enlighten human decay with visions of hell, and a local chapel has been turned into a two-screen pornographic cinema. The mines are exhausted and the docks are dead save for a Yugoslav freighter. There is only drink, and the Welsh are, except for weak bitter beer, not natural drinkers. They do not even have a spirituous liquor of their own. They are Celts given to rugby football and lechery, but all our ageing Celts are past both, though Alun tries to live up to his sub-bardic reputation by inviting former girlfriends to an afternoon's dalliance.

The women, being women, are dismayed neither by the betrayals of history nor the decrepitude of their men. Their self-sufficiency, assisted by flagons of white Burgundy, and their own capacity for betrayal, don't awaken the kind of misogyny that made ***Jake's Thing*** and ***Stanley and the Women*** so explosive. We are into a twilight zone which could be called stoical.

This is a brilliant novel of great honesty. It moves without contrivance and it confers, in language of large cunning but no pretension, a curious dignity on that physical decay which Mr Amis, at 64, and his present reviewer, at 69, have to face as no mere novelistic datum but as an all too palpable reality which most literary artists shy from. It is sadly comic and comically sad but, in the wonderful paradox of art, both consoling and stimulating. There is one old devil who is writing better than he ever did.

Anthony Burgess, "Ending Up in Wales," in The Observer, *September 14, 1986, p. 27.*

JOHN BAYLEY

[Bayley, an English critic, poet, novelist, and editor, is best known for such critical works as Tolstoy and the Novel *(1966) and* Shakespeare and Tragedy *(1981). In the following excerpt Bayley discusses the techniques Amis uses to make* The Old Devils *such an engaging novel.]*

We often have the feeling with an Amis novel that we are just not going to be able to keep up: that the flow of sophistication, perception, wittiness, up-to-the-momentness, will reduce our powers of novel-reading repartee, as it were, to helpless silence. But we are wrong, fortunately. Amis is the kindest of novel-talkers in that he does always, and very considerately, wait for us to catch up and make—at least notionally—our own little point.

This is just as well, because the verbal texture of ***The Old Devils*** is richer, more unremitting, than ever before; less, and less prepared, with every clause, to let us slump back into the comfortable old worn fauteuil that every novelist hollows out for us sooner or later. No reposing on the past, or our own sense of Amis's. Indeed that is the theme of the novel: that the past is never safely in place but keeps coming round again in the obsessive chatter of the continuum. Older people need each other because of it. It keeps them young by reminding them that youth is a state we carry helplessly around in our peer-group: those who are just beginning life can be seen to be much more grown-up. All the infirmities of age—white wine swilling, importunate bladders, evenings beginning after breakfast—thrust us firmly back into the needs and the atmosphere of being young together.

And so Alun (at school it was plain Alan) Weaver and his wife Rhiannon come back to South Wales together, to re-encounter their student peer-group, who are disintegrating talkatively together in the snug suburbs of an unspecified South Welsh town. Alun has become a famous professional Welshman and poet, renowned and financially successful not only for his own Welshness but for having been a friend of the fabulous Brydan, doyen of all local poets and topers. He at once reopens relations with Sophie, at one time 'the surest thing between Bridgend and Carmarthen town', wife of Charles Norris, one of the male group who meet at the Bible, who is a co-owner in the restaurant business with his brother Victor: 'Absolutely not my cup of tea. He's . . . you know.' 'What, you mean. . . .' 'Well, we're not supposed to mind them these days but I can't help it. I came to them late, sort of.'

This exchange is between Rhiannon and Gwen, wife of Malcolm, who was once in love with Rhiannon though Peter was much more so, so much so that she had to have an abortion in consequence. The two are talking in Gwen's kitchen, where 'with a small start Rhiannon noticed that the bottle of white wine on the table in front of her was not the same as the one they had started on quite a short time earlier. This had a green instead of a blue and white label and was also about half-empty already.' A little later:

> Gwen got up quickly and toddled to the litter-bin behind Rhiannon. There, having let the empty bottle rustle and thump down inside, she was to be heard knocking out the ashtray on the edge of the bin. Silence followed while she presumably regrouped. When she spoke it was clear from the acoustics that her back was turned. Rhiannon shifted uneasily on her chair.
>
> 'You know, Malcolm was absolutely knocked sideways when your letter came. We'd heard talk but nothing definite. Knocked him completely sideways.'
>
> 'Not with horror, I hope.'
>
> 'Of course not with horror. With delight. With joy.' A loud smacking pop indicated what Gwen had been up to while out of sight. 'But something else as well, Rhi, you know that.'
>
> Gwen came into view again with the new bottle and the empty but still dirty ashtray and rather flung herself down in her seat at the table.
>
> 'You were his first love,' she said matter-of-factly.

All Amis's verbal skills are present here, in a concentration much stronger than the white wine. The military 'regrouped', the brilliantly suggestive economy of 'rather' ('rather flung herself down in her seat'), even the unobtrusively alcoholic absence of question-marks—all show that the old master is firmly in the saddle and has a better seat than ever. But it is significant, too, that these special ways of taking us with him combine with clichés from a multitude of other novels ('first love . . . matter-of-factly . . . something else as well'). Deconstructionists would say it could hardly be otherwise, but Amis has a special way of profiting from the situation, so that we join with him all the more intimately by reason of his way with more public conventions. This donnée about the past, and the way it haunts us, he contrives to make his own, and original, despite the difficulty of its obviously novelish usefulness. Elizabeth Bowen did the same, believing with a certain inner passion, or so her novels indicate, that we remain secretly arrested by early and terminative emotional experiences, smoking away for the rest of our lives and perhaps relit at intervals. ***The Old Devils*** has something in common here with *The Little Girls,* or *The Death of the Heart,* as well as with William Trevor's *The Old Boys*. Naturally enough, all three distinguished novelists contrive to keep the subject clear of the standard treatment given it by afternoon plays on the BBC ('Stephanie has come back in middle age to the town where fate once dealt the card' etc, etc), yet we may still have a sneaking feeling that the truest word on the subject for most people was Anthony Powell's in *A Dance to the Music of Time,* where the narrator re-encounters an old flame and finds it barely credible that he could have ever had a physical or any other kind of relationship with her.

Stanley and the Women continued what had become the usual Amis plot of compelling our loyalty to the hero-narrator no matter what appearances might indicate. Stanley, like Jim and Jake and the Fat Englishman and all the others, might appear unsatisfactory in many ways, but he saw and *understood* things—a great Amis denominator—in ways inaccessible to both the nicer and nastier persons in the novel. Complacency between writer and reader lies at the heart of the novel form, and through his heroes Amis exploited it with great cunning. But ***The Old Devils*** has no single hero or narrator, and the change is technically and morally interesting: all the persons in it start with the same powers, and are allotted the same number of 'understanding' counters. All exercise the same wry charity that is exercised on them.

Yet there are drawbacks. As a novel, it is far from wishing to woo us, or not to bore us. Like Henry James, almost, it seems too intent and majestically preoccupied with its conversational nuances to imagine that this could happen. That is impressive, just as it is in Henry James. There may be a slight overkill on the principle of imitative form: the old devils are so preoccupied with themselves and their drinks and recollections that they seem to have no time to remember they are in a novel which someone is reading. But here again Amis's skill reveals itself more and more surely as the novel progresses. Slowly but surely we are ingested and become one of the elderly party, who know that nothing much will happen (apart from one of us—I won't reveal who—dropping dead) and that nothing of interest will be said. The effect is the exact opposite of the comic principle as met with in the novels of Patrick Hamilton, say, or of Anthony Powell (who is rather engagingly referred to, by one of the Welshmen, as an author presumably Welsh, and who remarked that more marriages come to grief from envy than from jealousy).

This is quite an important matter. Jane Austen, whom Amis has never much cared about, made a fictional principle out of boredom, but it was not implemented by boringness. In showing us just how tedious and restricted her characters' lives were, she liberated us from the tedium they endured and embodied. Mr Woodhouse and Miss Bates are as tiresome as Amis's Old Devils, but this is transcended, so far as the reader is concerned, by Jane Austen's ability to make them entertaining. . . .

And the importance of the matter does not end there. If you are prepared to bore your reader in the name of fictional integrity, you will also be prepared to disgust, terrify and upset him, embarrass him and make him feel small. He becomes a legitimate target for the new terrorism of mimesis. Long ago a purveyor of Gothic novels, Mrs. Barbauld, wrote an essay on 'The Pleasure to be Extracted from Objects of Terror', and this was of course just the same as the pleasure to be extracted in Jane Austen's art from all the boring people. The novel has always accepted the point involved, and yet has always seemed to rebel against it. In many 'experimental' novels the rebellion becomes systematic, accepted policy. It would be surprising to find such an arch-conservative as Amis writing an experimental novel, but that, in a sense, is what has happened, whether or not he intended to do so.

Perhaps this is a rather large claim to make for a novel so sturdily based on all Amis's prejudices, tricks, jokes, domestic details; one, too, that ends, more or less, with a death and a wedding. Amis himself might well retort that all good novels are experimental in the sense that they try to do something not done before. He has approached the study of a group of elderly people, living mostly in pubs and on drinks, in an open-minded spirit, and he is entitled to ask for a little co-operation from the reader. It is noticeable today that novels do seem to get older, and more about the old. A. N. Wilson, the young fogey, has just produced an eloquent fiction about senile dementia and though he sticks to Jane Austen's method on the whole, one would rather skip the pages where his old dear really has her head. One of Amis's triumphs in ***The Old Devils*** is to portray the young as attending caringly and courteously upon their elders, while seeming at the same time completely opaque and mysterious, necessarily left out of the fictional enclave. That is no country for young men any more.

Of course there's a lot of kidding on the level. Dorothy is the drunkest and most boring of the lot. Everyone flees from her when she starts in on how to learn Russian or the customs of New Guinea, and the reader flees too. When it is time to go, Percy, her husband, 'put his hands under her arms and hauled sharply upward, using great but seemingly not excessive force. Dorothy shot to her feet as smartly as a nail responding to a claw-hammer.' (Force in unexpected directions is one of the novel's motifs, as if the elderly still had force to exercise but only in unexpected directions. Going to bed, Alun stood on one leg 'and shook the other with tremendous force to rid it of that part of his trousers'.) But when one of the old devils has a bit of a breakdown Dorothy's 'words of comfort far outdid the others' in range and inventiveness', and she 'was obviously having a whale of a time distinguishing herself in fields like responsibility, compassion etc'. There is something very just about all this, though it may seem like having things both ways. Amis is quite aware that the warmest impulses ('caring . . . compassionate') must be made fun of if they are not to seem intolerably self-righteous: and yet he gives those things their real due with unemphatic force. One of the best things the book does and gives is the sense in which old devils feel warm for each other and try to look after each other, with a little help from the young: so that this seems not a moral but a fact.

And even if our attention wanders, Amis's sentences keep plucking it back. Someone's cereal is of 'a resolutely inauthentic type'; Muriel soothes her husband as well as needling him by observing that those who don't have days on forget that others have days off. Out of the pub, amid 'door-slamming and the whinnying of starters', it might be felt that 'now was a time for the years to roll back. But no, they stayed where they were.' The women decide that 'women have an awful way of feeling things there's no point in them feeling.' Jokey low-key benevolence extends even to the Brydan industry, and its horrible manifestations of the poet's seats, pubs, and shoppes along the coast. Amis might have been expected to go to town on this large fat target, but no, he refrains, implying, rather in the spirit of Malcolm Brinnin's book on Dylan Thomas, that the whole business was repetitively sad rather than wonderfully awful. Press on, and never say die, is the general impression, both of the author and of his characters. 'As number one, Alun had naturally secured the front passenger seat, and he was soon twisted most of the way round in it to push on with conversation.'

John Bayley, "Pushing On," in London Review of Books, *Vol. 8, No. 16, September 18, 1986, p. 12.*

An Excerpt from *The Old Devils*

'I'd just like an explanation,' said Malcolm. 'Just the merest hint of an explanation. That's all.'

'You're the feeblest creature God ever put breath into,' said Alun. 'Why any woman should have spent thirty-three minutes married to you, let alone thirty-three years, defies comprehension. You've no idea in the world of what pleases a woman: in other words'—he seemed to be choosing these with care—'you're not only hopeless as an organiser of life in general, you're a crashingly boring companion into the bargain and needless to say, er, perennially deficient in the bedroom. Correct?'

'That about sums me up. Oh, I'm also cut off.'

'Cut off?'

'Cut off from real people in my own little pathetic fantasy world of dilettante Welshness, medievalism and poetry.' Malcolm drained his glass.

'*Poetry?* You ought to be ashamed of yourself, a great big hulking fellow like you. What are your other shortcomings?'

'That's all I can remember for the moment. And as I say I'd love to know the explanation. There'd been no row before, no upset, nothing. It's most odd. Anachronistic in fact. She hasn't spoken to me in that strain for God knows how long.'

'M'm.' Alun pursed his lips and blinked at the wall, as if reflecting upon one or two mere theoretical conceivabilities, preparing to eliminate them for form's sake. He said, 'She didn't happen to, er, mention anybody else, I suppose, *refer* to anybody who in any way might have . . . ?'

'Not a soul. I'd have remembered if she had.'

'Yes.' Now an expression of considerable relief appeared for an instant on Alun's face before he added quickly, 'That's a, that must be a considerable relief to you. Well, quite a relief.'

Malcolm nodded and sighed. His neck was aching and he wriggled his shoulders around to ease it. 'But of course what's bothering me, what I'm trying to work out is the connection between this and the way she flew off the handle at you. Which I may say I'm very sorry ever happened.'

'The . . . ?'

'Last night in the Golf Club,' said Malcolm, himself starting to blink slightly.

'Oh. Oh yes. Yes. Yes, I wondered when we'd get round to that. Yes, quite a little hatful of words, wasn't it? What did she say to you about it?'

'Well, I had to drag it out of her. But I wasn't going to let it pass.'

'Quite right, it doesn't do. Never. Anyway . . . '

'Well, she was tired, she'd had a few, she was a bit under the weather, and the rest of it was, quite frankly, Alun, I mean I'm being quite frank now, she was furious with you, no not furious, annoyed. Irritated. Some linguistic point which I must confess I didn't really—'

'Oh, I know. She grew up in Capel Mererid speaking Welsh and I didn't. I know. To be frank with you in return, Malcolm *bach,* she thinks I'm a fraud, and worse than being a fraud I peddle Wales to the Saxons, so of course I irritate her. No no, don't . . . We won't argue about it, it's not the topic under discussion. Talking of which . . .' Alun leant forward and said emphatically, but in a lowered voice, 'Don't take what she said at its face value, not any of it. There's something more basic at work there, and yes, you're right, it's connected with what she said to you this evening. Now, the whisky's in the front room.' He spoke to the purpose, in that he and Malcolm had retired to the kitchen for this part of their talk. 'Can I freshen that? Come on, it'll do you good.'

'Do you really think it will? All right, just a small one. Thank you.'

After getting up, Alun laid his hand gently on Malcolm's arm. 'It's all right, boy. I'll explain it to you now. It's not easy but it's all right.'

'I'll give it to you in one word. Jealousy. Plain old-fashioned jealousy. Also envy, which isn't by any means the same thing, but no better. I was reading where someone made that point recently—envy's worse for a marriage than jealousy. Welsh writer too. Can't think who for now. Anyway. Something nice, something a little bit romantic has come your way, to wit, Rhiannon. Nothing like that has come her way, poor old Gwen's,' he said, staring quite hard at Malcolm. 'You have a nostalgic day out, you come back in triumph, she punishes you. Simple as that. Don't think hardly of her. Happens all the time wherever there are women. Like a reflex.'

'But I wasn't in triumph, I thought of that, I'm not a complete fool, I guarded against that. I said it was quite fun, food nothing much, bit chilly and so on and so on.'

Foreseeably, Alun had started shaking his head before the last was half over. 'Listen, you come back after that sort of jaunt anything short of minus your head and you come back in triumph, got it? That's how they all . . . oh Christ.'

'But you're saying she was just trying to hurt me.'

'Check.'

'But I wasn't trying to hurt her.'

A fervent groan suggested the hopelessness of any kind of answer to that one.

JEREMY LEWIS

Nothing, one imagines, can be more frustrating for a writer than to be best-remembered for his first novel, written some thirty years ago, and to have every subsequent book referred back to it, more often than not in terms of a falling-off. The blurb for Kingsley Amis's [***The Old Devils***] makes familiar, well-worn claims ('The most outrageously funny yet poignant Amis novel since ***Lucky Jim***'), and follows this up with equally predictable intimations of hilarity. ***The Old Devils*** is a marvellous novel, melancholy rather than—as some might expect—misanthropic, and shot through with indignation and a sense of the absurd, but readers in search of a laugh a minute, or the Tom-Sharpe type of crudities that are all too often in the offing when blurb-writers reach for the 'hilarious', may find themselves temporarily baffled and ill-at-ease.

The Old Devils in question consist of a clutch of pensioners living on suburban estates somewhere in South Wales. They have known one another since their early twenties, meet regularly in a pub called The Bible and Crown, and are uncomfortably aware of being on the wrong side of sixty-five. (p. 96)

The Devils are stirred from their grumbling torpor when an old friend, Alun Weaver, decides to return to his home town from the literary life in Highgate. Weaver is a professional Welshman who has made his fame and fortune writing books about a Dylan Thomas-like poet called Brydan, 'whom he had run into on several occasions and once spent most of an evening with'. Hardly has he stepped off the train from Paddington and delivered his all-purpose patter about the joys of returning home ('Heart is where the home is, and the heart of a Welshman . . .') before he is dreaming up a television series 'In Search of Wales'. Although—not surprisingly—he finds it hard to be told the truth, even by one of his oldest friends, Weaver is a ham and a fraud: but, as one of the Devil's wives points out, 'We need a few fakes to put a dent in all that bloody authenticity.'

There sounds the essential Amis note, echoed later in the novel when one of the Devils complains—apropos a newly-erected piece of modern sculpture—'When Labour councillors in South Wales start blathering about bringing art to the people everyone's in deep trouble': yet the matter of 'authenticity' not only provokes some pleasing ironies and crusty paradoxes, but provides the novel with much of the poignancy quite correctly referred to in the blurb. Weaver is a light-weight, and seems as such beside the resident Devils (with the possible exception of the medically-minded Garth Pumphrey, who once 'as good as chaired an impromptu Brains Trust on false teeth' in The Bible): far more disturbing is the effect his elegant, grey-eyed wife Rhiannon has on two of their number, Peter Thomas and Malcolm Cellan-Davies. Peter . . . is cynical, bad-tempered and enormously over-weight, so much so that he drives his car with the seat pushed full back to accommodate his stomach, and his arms and legs stretched stiffly out before him (as the car lunges forward an empty tonic bottle rolls out from under his seat); he tucks into cream cakes and profiteroles with defiant zeal, eats a breakfast cereal which 'by his preference was of a resolutely inauthentic type', and ridicules bilingual road signs and anything that smacks of arty or folksy Welshness.

Malcolm, by contrast, is proud of having kept his figure and his hair, is keen on roughage and 'the body's equilibrium', has spent much of his life translating mediaeval Welsh poetry (contributing a slim volume of his own as well) and is more likely to discuss the weather or church architecture than to join his fellow-Devils in complaints about the unemployed or the black economy; as Rhiannon ruefully points out, 'Of all the men she knew, he was right out in front the likeliest to be ignored at the bar, given a table the kitchen door banged into, brought his first course while late arrivals were drinking up their coffee, or overcharged.'

Both men, it seems, were involved with Rhiannon when young—Peter on intimate terms, Malcolm from an adoring distance—and thirty-five years later the pattern repeats itself. Malcolm's attempt to take Rhiannon on a trip down 'Memory Lane' provides the novel with a scene of cringe-inducing pathos, in the course of which it turns out that she remembers absolutely nothing of the incidents so fondly referred to, try as she may: Amis's head may be with the carnivores, relishing the Devils' mischievous delight in seeing 'who could say the most outrageous things' about 'trade unions, the education system, the penal system, the health service, the BBC, black people and youth' or singing the praises of 'President Reagan, Enoch Powell, the South African Government, the Israeli hawks and whatever his name was that ran Singapore', but on the evidence of this subtle and oddly likeable novel part of his heart at least goes out to the herbivores. (pp. 96-8)

Jeremy Lewis, "Bible Punchers," in London Magazine, *n.s. Vol. 26, No. 7, October, 1986, pp. 96-8.*

BRIAN MORTON

The Old Devils continues the (senior) Amis renaissance, and it is certainly his most humane and clear-sighted novel yet. Alun and Rhiannon Weaver cause a mild sensation (mild in prospect, even milder in actuality) by announcing their return from England to the Welsh surroundings of their youth. Their old friends are these days grouped in drinking cliques along strict gender lines and have different cause to remember the Weavers. Rhiannon is still the light of more than one liverish, middle-aged life; Alun, best of both worlds, still a game bed-hopper and reliable drinking companion. His English fame, as a kind of professional Welshman, has been minor enough not to cause uneasiness, substantial enough to inspire proprietary pride among his old pals.

Veteran of television shows and popular books about Wales, Alun's own poetic career has been overshadowed by his association with the valleys' true Famous Son, the great Brydan. Lest anyone miss who this roaring boy might be, there's a hefty allusion to *Adventures in the Skin Trade*. When you get to these characters' time of life, though, personality does not peel away in delicate, translucent layers. The surface is thickened and desensitised and only comes free in painful, jarring lumps.

Amis's grip on the narrative is superb and his chapter transitions—a trademark—have never been more effective. A conversation begins at the end of one and *appears* to continue at the beginning of the next. There is a death and then a preparation for church, but for a later wedding, not for the funeral. What the Weavers bring about isn't whole cloth but a series of psychological knots and lumps. They act as catalysts—less important for what they are than for what they set in motion.

Brian Morton, "Suspects," in The Listener, *Vol. 116, No. 2982, October 16, 1986, p. 22.*

ROBERT FLINT

It's always a pleasure for American admirers of Kingsley Amis to find that someone in his native land is giving him his rightful homage. John Bayley's review of ***The Old Devils*** [see excerpt above] is gratifyingly imaginative, comprehensive, and to the point. But I'm more than a little puzzled that Mr Bayley considers this novel to be Mr Amis's first foray into the higher comic gerontology. Way back in 1974 Mr Amis published ***Ending Up,*** a mordantly funny, wonderfully well-organised book about a group of septuagenarians living together out in the country in a house called Tuppenny-Hapenny Cottage. Like ***The Old Devils*** as Mr Bayley describes it, ***Ending Up*** has no central 'hero-narrator', satisfactory or unsatisfactory, but is a straight comic extravaganza equally indebted, I would think, to the more economical Waugh and to the more efficiently plotted stage comedies that Mr Amis may have seen and read.

I find it most peculiar that no one should have prompted Mr Bayley to have a look at this prior adventure in the genre. But the jacket blurb may provide a clue. Its ill-concealed prurient disapproval, just barely sweetened by phrases like 'wickedly enjoyable', suggests that 1974 was not a banner year for Mr Amis, that he may indeed have fallen under a small cloud during the Seventies. It is greatly to be hoped that he is now re-established in his true catbird seat as Waugh's only serious heir and successor. One welcomes the day when the Powellites are finally put to rout.

Robert Flint, "Pushing On," in London Review of Books, *Vol. 8, No. 21, December 4, 1986, p. 5.*

MICHIKO KAKUTANI

Kingsley Amis's most recent novel, ***Stanley and the Women*** (1985), was a rude, ill-considered complaint against life. Diatribes and nasty jokes about women and Jews, psychiatrists, intellectuals and children dominated the narrative, and the reader came away with the impression that the book's hero (and perhaps his creator, too) was not only a misogynist but an unreconstructed misanthrope as well. Mr. Amis's talent for social satire, it seemed, had hardened into something darker and more unpleasant.

Happily, ***The Old Devils*** . . . is a book with an altogether different outlook. While the author has by no means lost his comic edge, he has discovered a compassion for his characters, and as a result ***The Old Devils*** possesses a depth and emotional chiaroscuro new to Mr. Amis's work. It is, at once, a satire of the problems and pretensions of a group of provincials in their declining years and an elegiac portrait of the disappointments—and consolations—of old age.

Structured like a traditional comedy—the novel even closes with a marriage and the promise of another happy, if unlikely, romance—***The Old Devils*** begins with the disruptive announcement that a couple named the Weavers are returning to their hometown. To their old friends, schoolmates and lovers in Wales, this is highly disturbing news: it has been nearly 30 years since Alun Weaver—and his beauteous wife, Rhiannon—left for the literary big time in London, and his return now as a prodigal son stirs up festering resentments, jealousies and hopes. . . .

Some of Mr. Amis's acerbic descriptions of a newly yuppified Wales are very funny—as is his depiction of Alun's attempts to rip off the memory of a celebrated Welsh poet named Brydan. In the end, however, the reader is less engaged by the slapstick elements of this book than by its thoughtful, even melancholy, portrayal of its characters' attempts to come to terms with the past: Malcolm's realization that Rhiannon's affection for him in the present almost makes up for her inability to remember the details of their former romance; Alun's realization that he should have pursued his own course in poetry instead of apprenticing himself to a dead master, and Peter's realization that he should not have let cowardice keep him from going back to Rhiannon, the girl he really loved.

Instead of making fun of his characters' dilemmas, Mr. Amis has chosen this time to write each of them—men *and* women—from the inside, and this decision invests the novel with a greater emotional density and burnishes the entire narrative with the luster of redemption. Indeed, we finish ***The Old Devils*** feeling that the characters have somehow succeeded in their attempts to accept the past and that their creator, too, has managed to accept them as flawed but sympathetic human beings.

Michiko Kakutani, in a review of ''The Old Devils,'' in The New York Times, *February 25, 1987, p. 20.*

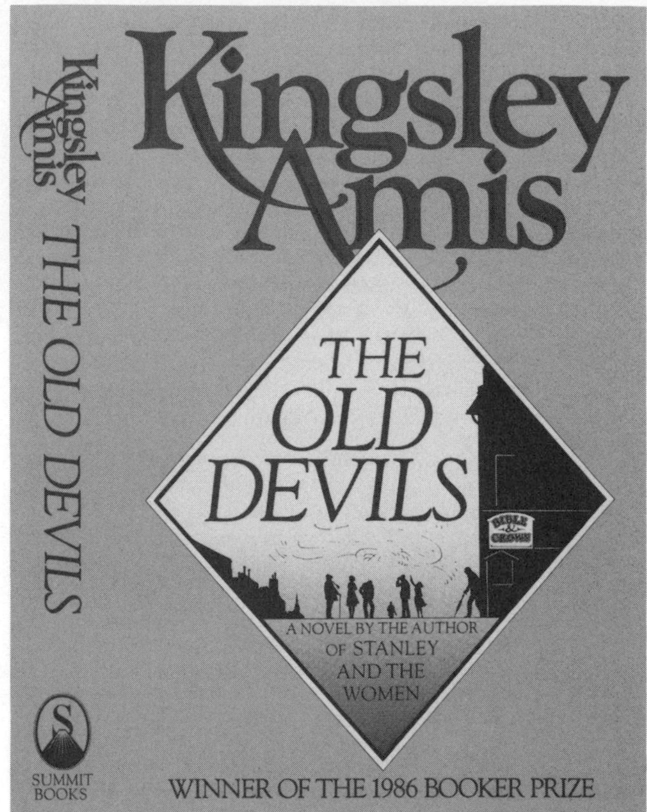

Dust jacket of The Old Devils, *by Kingsley Amis. Summit Books, 1986. Jacket design by Paul Bacon. Courtesy of Simon & Schuster, Inc.*

DAVID LODGE

[Lodge is an American novelist, dramatist, critic, and editor. His novels and plays, including Out of the Shelter *(1978) and* Small World *(1985), are known for their comic accounts of academic life and of changing attitudes in the Catholic community. Lodge is also highly regarded for his work as a literary critic and as the editor of several works on nineteenth- and twentieth-century British authors. His interests in both writing and theory are evident in his books of criticism, which include* The Novelist at the Crossroads and Other Essays on Fiction and Criticism *(1971),* Modes of Modern Writing: Metaphor, Metonymy and the Typology of Modern Literature *(1977), and* Write On *(1986). In the following excerpt Lodge comments on Amis's treatment of the themes of old age and Welshness in* The Old Devils.*]*

Kingsley Amis's first novel, ***Lucky Jim*** (1954), did more than inaugurate a British version of the campus novel already established by Mary McCarthy and other American writers. It made its author, willy-nilly, the standard-bearer for a whole new school of British novelists, who refused the mythopoeic streams of consciousness of the great modernists, and the somewhat specialized social and spiritual preoccupations of their successors, like Greene and Waugh, in favor of an observant and irreverent rendering of the texture of ordinary life, especially provincial life, in Britain, as the nation sluggishly tried to free itself from the constraints of the prewar class system.

This fiction was the prose equivalent of the poetic ''Movement'' of the Fifties, to which Amis also contributed, and ***Lucky Jim*** was dedicated to the most gifted and original of the Movement poets, Philip Larkin. Amis, indeed, had more in common with Larkin than with novelists like Alan Sillitoe and John Braine with whom he was journalistically linked under the heading of the ''Angry Young Men.'' It was not really anger that fueled Amis's writing, but rather an acute sensitivity to affectation and hypocrisy in social and personal behavior. This he was able to convert into farcical comedy and a very distinctive prose style, superficially inelegant, but in fact full of artful and amusing rhetorical device. Kingsley Amis belongs to a very British tradition of novel writing that goes back to Dickens, Smollett, and Fielding, which uses irony and humor to explore serious subjects, such as madness and death. Even in the lighthearted and high-spirited ***Lucky Jim*** there is the troubling theme of Margaret's hysteria, and as Amis went on publishing novels (which he has done with remarkable regularity) they have become progressively darker in tone, their comedy steadily blacker.

Comedy and humor, however, do not always travel well, and one has the impression that readers in other countries, including the United States, are somewhat baffled by Amis's work and the esteem in which it is held in Britain. In this respect he is again representative. ''If the postwar English novel figures on the international stage as winsomely trivial,'' John Updike uncharitably declared in a review of ***Jake's Thing*** (1978),

"Kingsley Amis must bear part of the blame . . . his ambition and reputation alike remain in thrall to the weary concept of the 'comic novel' . . . there is no need to write 'funny novels' when life's convolutions, set down attentively, are comedy enough." More recently, Kingsley Amis met even stronger resistance in America: his ***Stanley and the Women*** (1984), widely acclaimed in England, could not for some time find an American publisher, allegedly because a feminist cabal among New York publishers, outraged by the novel's misogynism, conspired against it; but one can't help feeling there must have been some pretty strong literary reservations among male editors as well.

Amis's latest novel, ***The Old Devils,*** may get a more sympathetic reception, for it is much more evenhanded in its treatment of the war between the sexes than anything else he has written, and it has very little of the rather artificial comic plotting that wearied John Updike. I would hazard a guess, however, that many American readers will be puzzled why it was a popular and for once uncontroversial choice for the 1986 Booker Prize. ***The Old Devils*** is Amis at his most mellow, most disarming, but it is still an intensely, defiantly, almost inscrutably British novel.

I say "British" rather than "English" because, although Kingsley Amis himself is very much an Englishman (indeed presents himself as almost a caricature of one these days), ***The Old Devils*** is set in Wales and is partly concerned with the concept of "Welshness"—in itself a source of potential puzzlement to the foreign reader. Politically and socially, Wales is more closely linked to England than either Scotland or Northern Ireland, but it has a long and distinctive cultural tradition of its own. Its sense of self-identity is, however, split between cultural nationalists (mainly from the North) who struggle to preserve and extend the Welsh language as a weapon against English "imperialism," and those, mainly living in the industrialized south, who regard themselves as no less Welsh because their mother tongue is English and tend to resent the fanaticism of the nationalists.

Most of the characters in ***The Old Devils*** are Welsh of the second type. All of them, with some minor exceptions, are old. Old age, and the problems of coping with its indignities, frustrations, and regrets, is the real subject of the novel; but the theme acquires a special piquancy, and poignancy, from its Welsh setting. . . .

The circle includes Malcolm, a sentimentalist with feeble poetic aspirations and fond memories of Rhiannon, and his wife Gwen, one of Alun's old flames; Sophie, another old flame, and her husband Charlie, a rather childlike boozer; Peter, an overweight ex-academic once deeply entangled with Rhiannon, now married to the shrewish (and English) Muriel; and two other couples, Garth and Angharad, and Percy and Dorothy. Garth keeps boasting about his health and quizzing the others about theirs, and Dorothy gets uncontrollably and volubly drunk at every opportunity. Since all the other characters have more or less alarming physical symptoms to worry about and drink is their chief pleasure in life, this makes Garth and Dorothy particularly tiresome company. But one of the themes of the novel is the necessity of putting up with boring and exasperating friends because you have known them for years and it is too late to escape from them. (p. 15)

The main source of suspense in this novel would appear to be the question of who will die first, and whether it will be from heart failure or cirrhosis of the liver (it would be unfair to reveal the answer here).

The unhealthiness of these lives is partly connected with a lack in their marriages. Peter and Muriel have not touched each other for ten years. Charlie sleeps in a separate cot so as not to disturb Sophie when he comes in drunk to bed or wakes in the night with the horrors. Malcolm is treated by Gwen with affectionate contempt, sometimes just contempt. Angharad's once potent sexuality has been destroyed by a drastic hysterectomy and Dorothy was never known to have had any. Only Alun and Rhiannon seem still to have an appetite for life and love as well as drink, and in Alun's case it is vitiated by a streak of selfishness that leads him to disgrace himself in the eyes of all the others.

Although the surface texture of the novel is amused and amusing, one feels that it is a very fragile integument covering an appalling abyss of pain, despair, and anxiety. There is a dark irony in the spectacle of people for whom "the evening started starting after breakfast" (all Amis's rhetorical cunning is in that apparently redundant "starting") who are both oppressed by the mounting evidence of their own mortality yet incapable of occupying the time left to them with anything more creative than boozing, reminiscing about the past, and grumbling about the present. Alun, admittedly, plans to write a novel in retirement, but the vanity of this ambition is exposed in one of the best sequences of the book. (p. 16)

The human condition as depicted in ***The Old Devils*** is not so far removed from the bleak vision of Samuel Beckett as it might seem, or as Mr. Amis might like to think. Devils are dead metaphors, and the Bible a meaningless metonym for a pub. It would seem one is not, in Yeats's phrase, a soul fastened to a dying animal, but just a dying animal. When one of the characters dies, the reaction of the others is either devastating banality or impotent irony. . . .

Two things soften, or are intended to soften, the darker implications of the story. One is the marriage of Rosemary, the Weavers' daughter, to William, the son of Peter and Muriel. Their wedding concludes the novel and is intended as a conventional symbol of continuity and renewal—too conventional, I must say, for this reader. The characters of the young couple are not sufficiently realized to make the hope invested in them by their parents seem more than sentimental. More persuasive—indeed, genuinely moving—are the relationships of Rhiannon with her two old admirers, Malcolm and Peter, on whom she has the effect of Eliot's April, mixing memory and desire, stirring dull roots with spring rain. This is slightly embarrassing for Rhiannon, especially with respect to Malcolm, but Rhiannon gamely submits to being taken by Malcolm for a sentimental outing to some site of their courting days which she has quite forgotten; while to Peter she extends a hand of forgiveness and friendship.

The Old Devils is unusual among Amis's novels in being narrated partly from the point of view of women—principally, Rhiannon, but also Gwen and Muriel for a time. The perspective shifts frequently between these three and the four principal male characters, Malcolm, Charlie, Peter and Alun. It is not always easy to remember who is who, and married to whom, and there is presumably a point to this. As we grow older, we grow more like each other, our anxieties and desires become restricted to a narrower and narrower range (the fear of death and of loneliness, the desire for animal comfort and peace of mind). In this phase of life, ordinary, unaffected human kindness counts for a lot. It is because Alun and Garth lack this generosity of spirit that the novel ultimately comes down hard on them. Amis has always been a very traditional moralist.

And what has all this to do with Wales? In a sense, nothing. The theme of old age could be explored in any regional context, as well as in the imaginary landscape of the later Beckett. But there is an elegiac quality about the topography of South Wales, romantic scenery interspersed with the relics of decayed industry, that makes it an appropriate setting. And in this novel the subject of Wales and Welshness is locked into an ironic double bind that is characteristic of Kinglsey Amis's work. It is very hard to find in the novel an attitude to Wales that is both positive and authentic. All enthusiasm for things Welsh, all celebrations of the Welsh language or the Welsh character, are made to seem bogus—but only the Welsh are allowed to say so. From anyone else such criticism would be arrogant and unwarranted. The consequence is that, as Rhiannon says to Peter, "Wales is a subject that can't be talked about. Unless you're making a collection of dishonesty and self-deception and sentimental bullshit." The same, it seems, goes for death—the skull beneath the genially smiling surface of this novel, Mr. Amis's best for many years. (pp. 16-17)

David Lodge, "Closing Times," in The New York Review of Books, *Vol. XXXIV, No. 5, March 26, 1987, pp. 15-17.*

JAMES WOLCOTT

Kingsley Amis's ***The Old Devils*** is so dense with booze that the book seems sunken, subaquatic, its retired Welsh sots trying to remain standing in an aquarium stocked with gin and drifting hunks of scenery. They don't always succeed. "Siân Smith fell down on her way out but soon got up again and made it into the hall." Even sitting can be a trial. "There came a noise that began rather like a fart of heroic proportions but soon proved to be made by the exhaustive ripping of the canvas seat of Peter's chair under his buttocks." These pratfalls are set within a movieish swirl of clinking bottles, lingering smoke, and confidential asides ("I never realized how much he drank till the night he came home sober. A revelation, it was"). By morning, Amis's wasted wrecks feel as if heavy furniture has been pushed around in their heads. Everyone recalls the hangover in ***Lucky Jim*** ("His mouth had been used as a latrine by some small creature of the night, and then as its mausoleum"), and a casualty here wakes up taking similar inventory ("He felt as if about two-thirds of his head had recently been sliced off and his heart seemed to be beating somewhere in his stomach, but otherwise he was fine . . ."). Another dreams amorously of Mrs. Thatcher, who tells him that "without him her life would be a mere shell, an empty husk." Teenagers who crave kicks might envy the lifestyle of these aimless ruins, with their pensions and pills. This crew can get oiled until their eyeballs float and there's nobody around to tell them, "Mind your elders." They *are* the elders. Nearly everyone they had to mind is kaput.

Not that they're merry sods, waving mugs in time to songs at ye olde ale-house. . . . Booze as they might, Amis's ornery types are sandbagged in being. But what being! ***Ending Up,*** an earlier Amis tale of age and collapse, was an elaborate mousetrap of black humor snapping the spindly necks of its set-up cast. ***Stanley and the Women,*** trying so hard to provoke, was little more than a cranky fit—phlegm passing itself off as bile. But ***The Old Devils*** has a tough honest crust and scuttling sideways humor. Nowhere in it does Amis attempt shapely sentences or lyrical, dying falls. His is an aesthetic of the anti-beautiful. The book's astringency feels just right. It's the best novel on the delinquencies of the old since Muriel Spark's *Memento Mori.*

The sheer cussed readability of ***The Old Devils*** is a constant reward. Bam, right from the start Amis tunes in to the morning chat of one of his couples as if it were a long-running radio show. Malcolm, the male half of this team, smokes a single cigarette in the morning to get his insides going. He doesn't hold with the laxatives that his wife, Gwen, recommends. "He thought it a bit thick for a man not to be able to win an argument about his own insides, even one with his wife." Along with Malcolm and Gwen, the couples treading time in ***The Old Devils*** are Alun and Rhiannon, Charlie and Sophie, Garth and Argharad, Percy and Dorothy, Peter and Muriel. There's also a young pair consisting of William (son of Peter and Muriel) and Rosemary (daughter of Alun and Rhiannon), whose wedding takes up the novel's least riveting chapter. I've provided a line-up because a number of reviewers in England, where the novel won the Booker Prize, have complained about not being able to tell the players without a scorecard. . . . At a time when so many novels are vehicles for a single vote (*Edisto, The Counterlife, Tough Guys Don't Dance,* whatever), Amis provides a distinct party mix. He moves a small troupe of actors across the page, and their voices never fritz through crosswiring, as in George V. Higgins's lowlife broadcasts. They have their own individual swing. (pp. 33-4)

Mimicry has always been one of Amis's specialties, vocal and facial. The poet Philip Larkin recounted that at Oxford Amis had a rich repertoire of riffs. "Kingsley's masterpiece, which was so demanding I heard him do it only twice, involved three subalterns, a Glaswegian driver and jeep breaking down and refusing to restart somewhere in Germany. Both times I became incapable with laughter." It was Larkin who encouraged Amis to put more faces into ***Lucky Jim.*** (Larkin himself seems to be making faces in ***The Old Devils.*** Echoes abound, from a rephrasing of one of his most famous lines—"Life is first boredom, then fear" becomes "Life is first boredom, then more boredom"—to a replay of their shared love for old jazz: "Through a roaring fuzz of needle-damage the sounds of 'Cakewalkin' Babies' emerged.")

The mimicry that Larkin admired was and is more than imitation. Amis has a brilliant handle on how theatrical bits of business infiltrate daily life until they become casual shtick. . . . Amis has always been marvelous on the subtle gradations of the slightly off.

For Amis, slightly off isn't a bad state to be in, considering the surrounding mess. Happiness he locates at the margins, away from the madding crowd and media megahype. Like Larkin (with whom he shares a distrust of the transcendent sublime—e.g., his poem "Against Romanticism"), he sees the century choking on its own unrest and coughing up weeds. No Shelleys await to lift the planet high. Useful purpose is petering out, not only in the old devils but in Wales, the world. (pp. 34-5)

Kingsley Amis being something of an old devil himself (asked what he was going to spend his prize money on, he replied, "Booze of course"), it's hardly surprising that the book has an air of complicity. What is surprising is that the air is so cool and clear. Despite the age of its cast, ***The Old Devils*** doesn't tiptoe near the sunset waters of *On Golden Pond* to engage in gallant reverie. Its rambling yet pointed dialogue, snapshots of decay, and noisy misdemeanors are very much in the present tense. Amis's old devils don't look backward, to youth, or forward, to death, but just far enough ahead to get through the livelong day. Each morning becomes a matter of getting the machinery going. Few novels contain this much crowded sensation. Fewer still show such fidgety control of their funny-sad effects. Like Alun, Amis has a stay-awake mind that sees through muck and stupor. Sobriety sits in his forehead like a Cyclopean eye, always open for business. Business here is brisk. (p. 35)

James Wolcott, "Do Not Go Sober," in The New Republic, *Vol. 196, No. 3767, March 30, 1987, pp. 33-5.*

BARBARA EVERETT

[English critic and editor Everett is the editor of Poets in their Time: Essays on Poetry from Donne to Larkin *(1986). In the following excerpt from an essay in which she examines the deliberately philistine approach to literature adopted by Amis and his friend, the poet Philip Larkin, Everett discerns a romantic quality in Amis's novels, including* The Old Devils.*]*

The success of ***The Old Devils*** was just: it's a considerable novel, and if anything improves with rereading. But there's a certain disjunction between the book and what might be called its notional character. Critics seem agreed that the book is not only set in Wales but is actually about Wales and Welshness. Certainly Amis writes here with his usual brilliancies of comic realism, and gives a whole 'social geography' of location and behaviour. But as to the people in his book, some reservations have been expressed. One or two reviewers complained that Amis's characters have begun, in this late novel, to blur together, to talk and think too much like each other. The problem struck me in a slightly different way. If this is a story of Wales, then it has to be said that the people in it aren't Welsh—that under all the carefully-assembled Welsh locutions the psyches of the characters remain obstinately English, or at least obstinately Amisian. Celts just don't come like this.

One of the book's major themes is the very loss of national and racial identity: Wales and Welshness, it is said, hardly 'exist' now except as a form of charlatanism, or a bane. Yet, just as this lament has its own moral counterpoise—what the individual does not find outside himself, he must find inside—so it offers a clue to certain of Amis's aesthetic methods. . . . In ***The Old Devils,*** uncertainty about Wales and Welshness, and indeed about the whole characterisation of individuals, can act more as a positive than a negative, and lead the attention to where the book has its real strength and character. Amis is concerned here, as he has mostly been (and as the whole novel genre has usually been, insofar as it is a social medium), with love and friendship: the love, in this case, of men for women, and the friendship of men for men—and theoretically, too, the love of women for men, and the friendship of women for women. Wherever the story nominally takes place, the book is constructed in a series of emotional confrontations, the chapters being given (as in Henry James's 'dramatic' novel, *The Awkward Age*) the names of the leading actors in each, and the 'awkward age' being in this case nearer 67 than 17. The plot concerns retirement and homecoming, ending and reconciliation, and the Welsh setting as Amis evokes it—a faded provincial distance—is therefore relevant. But this is a story of 'coming home' in a more inward sense. In the course of the book the all-male and all-female drinking-bouts that pass for 'social life' evolve to something closer to simple human loving-kindness, where human beings actually talk to each other. The relationship of parents to grown children becomes important, and there is even, in the form of a nice Labrador puppy, a kind of surrogate grandchild: it too, in the wedding that acts as grand finale, has become a grown-up dog.

This action falls naturally into dramatic encounters, sometimes chorus-like, more critically between person and person. Characteristic, though gentler than most, is the outing shared by Malcolm and Rhiannon in Chapter Five ('Rhiannon'): their jaunt a climax obscurely awaited by the reader from the novel's opening pages, with Malcolm's narratorial thoughts of the returning Alun and Rhiannon. The occasion, seized by Malcolm to make his declaration of lifelong passion for the still pretty, 'ordinary', kind and sensible Rhiannon, is hopeless, for he is not only married—and he not only knows that Rhiannon loves him as little as does his wife, as well as being herself married and in love with someone else again who only ambiguously loves her—but is himself 'hopeless', a virtuously clumsy sexless loser. Yet something does come out of the touching communion of these two most innocent of the characters, and begins to affect the rest of the action.

The landscaping of Malcolm's and Rhiannon's outing, apparently west along the coast from Swansea, leaves even the most sympathetic reader not very clear about what it was all like: the writer is obviously so much more interested in the pathetic persons of the drama, trying to talk to each other. And the intensity of this encounter can best be explained in terms of its echoic nature. Their comic but weeping conversation seems to be a richer replay of the terrible evening-out of Jenny and Graham in ***Take a girl like you,*** the best novel of Amis's earlier years. That previous heroine was, in theory, North Country English, and the hero's sad grotesque friend a Thames Valley Scot. But the Welsh Rhiannon and her Malcolm (whom the end of the novel leaves not altogether unhappily putting his love into his translation of Welsh Medieval verse) are to all intents and purposes Jenny and Graham met again almost thirty years later. The whole point of their second encounter seems to lie, not in anything that has to do with shifts of localisation, but in that peculiar permanence of the characters, and in the burden and release of the phrase 'thirty years later'. It matters that the devils of this book are *old* devils.

Chief Devil is Rhiannon's husband Alun—famous, faithless, shallow, engaging—the story's catalyst, as he is the source of the book's dark vitality. He is in many ways sharply characterised, with a formidable resource of observed contemporaneity—Media Man in motion. Yet, for all his TV hair-do's, he, too, has an ancestry like that of Rhiannon and Malcolm; he is surely descended from the incorrigible Patrick of the earlier book who lamentably rapes the gentle Jenny instead of marrying her the first time round: an attractive and intelligent if callow cricket-playing Classics master, as 'English' an archetype as one could find in the modern novel. Alun and Patrick have something important in common: what might be called a formally demonic quality in the judgment of the writer of their novels. Both are forgivable—or at least Alun is finally forgiven by some of his friends in the light of their own moral frailties, and Patrick, being to a large extent the empathetic, if not sympathetic central consciousness of his story, its ego if not its hero, can as little be absolutely rejected in the end by the reader of the novel as by Jenny herself. But the actions of both men are obviously repulsive to the moral sense. And the greedily erotic, vain and venomous Alun—brought by the dramatic method of the book as inwardly close to us as anyone else in it—would quite plainly have continued his escalating violences had not the developing logic of the story stopped him (by death: one of the few things to be said in favour of death, so the book reminds us, is that it kills off the destroyers). His homecoming is an ending in a sense he didn't expect. But it also offers the novel a conclusion in a rather different sense: it serves to suggest intellectually that love and friendship can't exist *just* to be defined in practice as hatred and enmity. The novel's real achievement is to make its action follow this simple, strong, moral logic, adding to it the bringing-about from unpromising beginnings of several acceptable if quiet happy endings: a whole group of genuinely touching reconciliations, all dependent on first the arrival and then the stopping of the vital but deathly Alun, regarded by the little gang of ageing cronies, the Old Devils of the title, as their star and centre.

From this point of view, the novel conveys through its jovial title a faint luminosity of meaning more than merely colloquial. Its action really is a casting-out of Old Devils: the set of epically drink-sodden old boys gets not once but twice thrown out of pubs, the second time—epoch-markingly if not for ever—from their own headquarters, their den, the cramped cosy cubby-hole in Tarquin Jones's public-house, the Bible and Crown, known throughout the narrative as 'the Bible'. In this haunt of the Old Devils there is something strikingly reminiscent of one of Larkin's most potent small poems, the Dutch 17th-century genre-painting of a tavern, at once radiant and very gross, which he called 'The Card-Players'. The Larkin poem possesses a rich calm moral abstraction that works against and yet through its earthy image of what happens when, in the company of 'Jan van Hogspeuw' and 'Dirk Dogstoerd', someone behind 'Old Prijck' eternally sings his love-songs. It is possibly harder for a reader absorbed in Amis's more densely naturalistic novel to recall that Tarquin (not the most commonplace of Welsh names) was a Roman who, like the hero of ***Take a girl like you,*** raped an innocent woman.

There are always good reasons for *not* reading allegory into work that succeeds at the vividly realistic level. Yet it perhaps does not harm to extend the number of ways in which a good novel can be good. And the English novel has often found a place for the *psycho-machia,* the 'battle for the soul'. Even the best novel critics don't always leave room for the distinctness of the English novel tradition, but identify it with the kind of 19th-century realism in which Tolstoy and Balzac are supreme. Such criteria may not help in judging the more romantic English genre that contains Richardson and Jane Austen and Dickens, all as different from each other as they could be, yet not precisely a realist. Smaller in scale, Amis is—like Evelyn Waugh, in some respects an influence on him—a comedian, a comic artist: yet neither fails to be a novelist.

The Old Devils in particular shows what very various elements can go together to make up the idiosyncratic English novel. If it lacks the economy of the more savage ***Ending up*** (another dark comedy of age), and even something of the hard-hitting sociology of ***Stanley and the Women,*** and of the (lesser) ***Jake's Thing, The Old Devils*** has a real largeness of its own that is more than a matter of its sprawling form. And this extra breadth and depth is owed to its quality of 'Romance' in several interlinked senses. Mainly this is a question of reliance on looser yet more abstract literary disciplines: forms rights for the definition of love as reflected through life's randomness, through social dispersion and simple human ageing—a treatment which we meet, for instance, in the Late Romances of Shakespeare (one of which, *Cymbeline,* even takes its action into wild Wales, where it finds things not altogether unlike England). (pp. 3, 5)

Barbara Everett, ''Philistines,'' in London Review of Books, *Vol. 9, No. 7, April 2, 1987, pp. 3, 5-8.*

Margaret (Eleanor) Atwood

The Handmaid's Tale

Governor General's Literary Award: Fiction

Canadian novelist, poet, critic, and short story writer.

The Handmaid's Tale (1985) earned Atwood her second Governor General's Literary Award. Twenty years previously, she had received the prize for her poetry collection *The Circle Game* (1966). *The Handmaid's Tale* is Atwood's sixth novel, as well as her twenty-third published book. It is also her first experiment in the genre of speculative fiction. "The main difficulty with writing this book," Atwood commented, "was that when I started it I thought it was wacko. I thought it was loony. But this is true about a lot of the things I do. I mean I had the same reaction to *Surfacing* [1972], that this was a really crazy book to be writing." Like her earlier novel *Surfacing,* now regarded as a modern feminist classic, *The Handmaid's Tale* met with international critical success. Reviewers hailed it as a powerful dystopian allegory in the tradition of *Brave New World* and *1984*.

Like George Orwell and Aldous Huxley before her, Atwood extrapolates sociopolitical trends from the present day into a chilling vision of society's future. The novel is set in Cambridge, Massachusetts, during the early twenty-first century, after Christian fundamentalists have transformed the United States into the fascistic theocracy of Gilead. Atwood's dystopian conception differs from those of Orwell and Huxley in that her narrator-protagonist is female, and the appalling nature of the society she describes is revealed through its cruel, repressive treatment of women. The narrator, a young woman known only as "Offred," has been kidnapped by her government, separated from her husband and child, and forced into slavery as a Handmaid, or surrogate mother, for a powerful but childless couple. Aware that Offred's story might be dismissed as a mere feminist nightmare, Atwood pointed out in several interviews that virtually every indignity suffered by female Gileadeans has an authentic historical precedent. For instance, the restrictive clothing and rules of conduct imposed on Offred are similar to those known by Puritan women in colonial New England. *The Handmaid's Tale,* incidentally, is dedicated to an American Puritan ancestor of Atwood's who was sentenced to hang for witchcraft but managed to foil her persecutors. "They went to cut her down in the morning," Atwood explained, "and she wasn't dead, and under the law of double jeopardy you could not execute a person twice for the same crime, so she remained alive. Tough neck." Similarly, a postscript to *The Handmaid's Tale* offers hope that Offred will escape from the Gileadean regime.

Many critics compare *The Handmaid's Tale* favorably with *1984, Brave New World,* and other distinguished dystopian novels for its disturbingly convincing evocation of its imaginary world. Some commentators call it Atwood's best novel to date, evidencing both her customary theme of a woman struggling to survive in a male-dominated world and her distinctive sardonic wit. Other reviewers contend that *The Handmaid's Tale* is not as fully realized in its imaginative details as *1984* or

Brave New World, or perhaps even Atwood's earlier novels. However, most deem it a success, both as a powerful suspense thriller and a cautionary allegory against political extremism, which, the novel implies, inevitably leads to totalitarian oppression. The question of whether the extremism Atwood cautions against is of the right-wing fundamentalist or left-wing feminist variety provides a subject of lively critical debate. Atwood herself observed: "Speculative fiction is a logical extension of where we are now. I think this particular genre is a walking along of a potential road, and the reader as well as the writer can then decide if that is the road they wish to go on. Whether we go that way or not is going to be up to us."

(See also *CLC,* Vols. 2, 3, 4, 8, 13, 15, 25; *Contemporary Authors,* Vols. 49-52; *Contemporary Authors New Revision Series,* Vol. 3; and *Dictionary of Literary Biography,* Vol. 53.)

BRAD HOOPER

Atwood's trying novel [***The Handmaid's Tale***] takes the form of a transcript of a taped narrative by a woman called Offred who is living in the Republic of Gilead (a futuristic society that was once the U.S.). Offred is a handmaid, someone who is used for reproduction purposes by members of the male elite whose wives can't bear children. Atwood has taken both the socioecological excesses and the burgeoning conservatism that exist within the contemporary U.S. and has extrapolated them to their most extreme point, furnishing us with a lesson on how terribly monitored our future lives might be. This cri de coeur is certainly impassioned, and Atwood's adept style renders the grim atmosphere of the future quite palpably. But the didacticism of the novel wears thin; the book is simply too obvious to support its fictional context.

Brad Hooper, in a review of "The Handmaid's Tale," in Booklist, *Vol. 82, No. 7, December 1, 1985, p. 514.*

VICTORIA GLENDINNING

[*Glendinning, an English biographer, critic, and bibliographer, is the author of* Edith Sitwell: A Unicorn among Lions *(1981) and* Vita: The Life of Vita Sackville-West *(1983). In the following excerpt Glendinning, while praising* The Handmaid's Tale *as a cogent feminist allegory, expresses regret that it is not informed by the same humorous wildness as Atwood's earlier novels.*]

When Canada curls up with a good book this winter, that book is likely to be Margaret Atwood's startling new novel, ***The Handmaid's Tale.*** It's extraordinary, and it's very good, but it's not her best. It must be infuriating for a writer to hear that her earliest work is thought better than what has come after; but Atwood has never, in prose, surpassed her first published novel, ***The Edible Woman.*** It is an amazingly original and funny book, while containing in embryo all the themes elaborated in her later fictions.

I'm playing the devil's advocate with Canada's best-known woman writer. This is possible for me because I am English, living thousands of miles away, in London. Margaret Atwood is known and respected here by the loose community of literary people and by those others, mostly women, who regularly read the new novels praised in the newspapers. Her novels have been reissued in the U.K. by Virago Press in their Modern Classics series: this is recognition. But her signal does not bleep so strongly here as in Canada; she is not a household name as a novelist, still less as a poet.

This is understandable. The British are notoriously parochial when it comes to literature. It is only recently that they have been compelled to recognize the energy coming out of the rest of the English-speaking world. The American novel has always been part of our mental furniture. But I am thinking now of what was once considered the periphery, writers dependent on the British cultural heritage, from India, Africa, Australia, New Zealand, and Canada. The critic George Steiner has identified this new wave as "the flight from the centre," and there is no doubt that column inches and literary prizes have, in the past few years, recognized these foreign-familiar writers. Salman Rushdie is only the most celebrated case in point. They seem to be revitalizing both the language and the form of fiction, much as the outer parts of a herbaceous plant, given their own space, will produce better blooms than the exhausted centre.

Yet the blooms of the centre—the homegrown British novelists—are still thick on the ground. There are, for example, half a dozen established women novelists living within a mile's radius of where I sit, in a not notably cultured quarter of north London. We have a great deal to absorb, from both within and without, and the nearer signals still tend to be picked up most clearly.

The liveliest British women novelists—writers such as Muriel Spark, Beryl Bainbridge, Alice Thomas Ellis, and Caroline Blackwood—tend to counter black realities with an even blacker wit. North American women are still sufficiently optimistic to tackle problems straight up and head on. Margaret Atwood, prominent in the vanguard of an expanding national literature, is a builder and not an iconoclast. Nevertheless, I mourn the fact that she has lost, or dropped, much of her zany humour. Writers become serious when they are taken seriously. As the British novelist William Boyd said recently, you lose your guilelessness, you watch yourself with "the dreadful third eye of you the writer." This may be specially true of someone such as Atwood. Steeped in the history and tradition of the novel, she is a teacher and critic of literature who now finds herself solemnly written about as part of that tradition.

Losing her innocence, Atwood became self-conscious and responsible. Her writing is not anarchic, even when it treats of madness and alienation. ***Surfacing,*** her second published novel, expressed an intense female pantheism which was seized upon by feminist writers such as Francine du Plessix Gray, and which provoked serious critical debate about the nature of women's spiritual quest and Atwood's own religious symbolism. No place here for jokes, nor for anarchy. She became fodder, to use an Atwoodian image, for the literary theorists; and like the edible woman herself, she connived in the process to the extent that her later novels often seemed neatly tailored for the purpose of analysis and deconstruction in the seminar room.

Atwood and her heroines are fascinated by language; the Handmaid of ***The Handmaid's Tale*** uses litanies of words and derivations "to keep sane." Yet the young woman in ***Surfacing*** longed to get beyond words: "Language divides us into fragments, I wanted to be whole." It's as if Atwood the conscientious scholar and critic were at odds with Atwood the artist. The hyperliterary quality of her work, though it attracts flattering critical attention, may paradoxically be an impediment to her gifts.

What seems to ignite her talent is fear—fear of being consumed by others' expectations, as in ***The Edible Woman,*** fear of world catastrophe, as in her great short story **"When It Happens,"** which describes in a few terrifying pages the transformation of a comfortable farmer's wife into a lonely bundle of animal instincts bent on survival. ***The Handmaid's Tale*** too is a postcatastrophe story, an ingenious futuristic fantasy which is disturbingly believable.

The reader, mystified at first, picks up what has happened in the world through cracks in the narrative. The story is set in the Republic of Gilead (formerly the U.S.). We learn that sometime in the mid-1980s the president of the U.S. was assassinated and the constitution suspended. During the chaos of the last two decades of the twentieth century there has developed an authoritarian regime based on "a return to traditional values" and fundamentalist Christianity. Not that the population is allowed to read the Bible. ("Who knows what we'd make of it . . .?") Rebellious Quakers and Baptists are hunted down and killed by the military, known now as the Angels of

Light. The police are called Guardians of the Faith, and the secret police the Eyes; this theological Orwellian newspeak filters down into the way individuals talk among themselves.

In this new American society women are needed as breeders. "The air got too full, once, of chemicals, rays, radiation, the water swarmed with toxic molecules." Atomic power plants exploded, a new strain of syphilis raged. (One of the effective horrors of Atwood's scenario, which amounts to a curse laid on the U.S., is that disaster is inevitable whether or not the bombs are dropped.) The birth rate has plummeted, and potentially fertile young women are a protected species: they are the Handmaids, allotted to high-status childless couples as surrogate wombs. Our heroine lies in the marital bed between the Commander's Wife's spread thighs, being serviced by the Commander—after which she creeps back to her room. The Handmaid is anxious to conceive, since failures, declared Unwomen, are sent to die in lethally radioactive districts.

It may be a vision of the future, but it's also a mutant vision of the past, a nasty version of *Upstairs, Downstairs,* and a story that could not have been conceived by someone who had not read *Grimm's Fairy Tales* or the lives and works of the Brontës. That's precisely why it's so oddly believable; it's a vision reflecting not only the atavism of the moral majority but the myths and memories of all Western culture. The Handmaid's world is like a nineteenth-century school, ruled by taboos. The Handmaids all wear red, and must walk in twos; the Wives wear blue and the Marthas (the domestic servants) wear green. All wear habits down to the ground, and long sleeves; the Handmaids, "modest and impenetrable," are also blinkered by nunlike coifs, lest they catch the eye of a man other than the stud to whom they belong. Death, a ritual dismembering by one's peers, is the penalty for transgression.

The Commander's house is Victorian, and the Handmaid, pausing on the curving stairs in her nightgown, her hair down her back, could be Jane Eyre. This literary nostalgia underlines a ticklish ambiguity, as if the author acknowledges the perverse, familiar masochism of what she is proposing. The women enforce the norms on one another with little need for male coercion, since "people will do anything rather than admit that their lives have no meaning."

But whatever the accepted norms there will always be dissidents, and our Handmaid is one of these. What has been overlooked by the regime is the subversive force of love. On this the plot turns, as in all romantic narratives since the world began.

At first glance ***The Handmaid's Tale*** seems to be a new departure for Margaret Atwood, yet the themes of her previous novels are all here, turned on their head and brought out into the open. Instead of pre-history, post-history. The way clothes and bodies determine the roles one plays is here pushed up front, instead of forming a subtext. Atwood has, subtly, always been writing costume gothics, like her heroine in ***Lady Oracle; The Handmaid's Tale*** is pure costume gothic, pitched in a future that is a disturbed reflection of an internalized past.

The heroine in ***Surfacing*** painted fairy-tale princesses. Often, Atwood's fat, plain heroines have had desirable alternative selves. The Handmaid in her Pre-Raphaelite robes is the captive princess of all these fantasies, undergoing ordeals, rites of passage, and fateful flights. No doubt Atwood is aware of these parallels; what is impossible to know, either from her writing or her own remarks about her work, is whether there is any self-irony in what she does.

Atwood's novels have been concerned with power and powerlessness. She is justly claimed by the feminists, in that power struggles for a woman tend to be with men. But in Atwood's work the struggles are also between Canada and the U.S., wife and mistress, man and nature, parent and child. ***The Handmaid's Tale*** is clearly an "oppression" story; but equally it is about the way women connive passively with that oppression for the sake of survival and even for their own satisfaction.

The question of what freedom for women really is has always concerned Atwood's heroines. The protagonist of ***The Edible Woman*** said seventeen years ago that if you were never specifically forbidden to do anything you feel "actually forbidden to do everything." (This is a very shrewd perception, and explains why children of liberal parents can end up riddled with guilt.) The Handmaids, trained by Aunts armed with electric cattle prods, are told that "there is more than one kind of freedom. . . . Freedom to and freedom from." In the old days—i.e., nowadays—women had "freedom to," sex was "too easy," and the Handmaids are reminded of the rape, pornography, and devaluation of women that were the result. The Commander claims that women can under his regime "fulfil their biological destinies in peace" with support from men; all the regime has done is to "return things to Nature's norm". Our Handmaid's mother had been a feminist, and she says to her mother in her heart: "You wanted a woman's culture. Well, now there is one. It isn't what you meant, but it exists."

We are living in a period in which a great many women novelists worldwide are contributing to a body of fiction that is unique in literary history, and it's in this dense and feisty international context that Margaret Atwood really belongs. The tensions and ambivalences—between action and reaction, conformity and revolt, tradition and change, order and chaos—fuel her writing and, one must suspect, form part of her own personality. Atwood seems compelled to classify and systematize, to make patterns, in one part of her mind, while an alternative self glimpses a more fluid reality, a creative surreality.

This latter self is the one that makes comic-sinister magic out of everyday things—as in the scene in ***The Edible Woman*** in which a distraught and weeping woman in a lavatory cubicle eyes "the roll of toilet paper crouched in there with me, helpless and white and furry, waiting passively for the end." This is the Atwood that carries a major charge, inventive and eccentric. Between her respect for the literary tradition and the earnest scholarly respect that her own writing now commands, there is only a small space left in which that charge can explode. (pp. 39-41)

Victoria Glendinning, "Lady Oracle," in Saturday Night, *Vol. 101, No. 1, January, 1986, pp. 39-41.*

CHRISTOPHER LEHMANN-HAUPT

It's a bleak world that Margaret Atwood opens up for us in . . . ***The Handmaid's Tale***—how bleak and even terrifying we will not fully realize until the story's final pages. But the sensibility through which we view this world is infinitely rich and abundant. And that's why Miss Atwood has succeeded with her anti-Utopian novel where most practitioners of this Orwellian genre have tended to fail.

To begin with, there's the matter of technique, which Miss Atwood, a Canadian with an international reputation, has honed in five previous novels (***Surfacing, The Edible Woman*** and ***Life***

Before Man are the best known of them), two works of short fiction and 10 volumes of poetry. Confined as we are in ***The Handmaid's Tale*** to the viewpoint of an anonymous woman living in some oppressive society of the near future, we realize only gradually and with the utmost dramatic effect that she is a slave whose sole function is to bear children for the under-populated theocracy called the Republic of Gilead that was once the United States.

She doesn't even have a name. She is a cipher called Offred, presumably because the Commander of the household in which she is the only fertile member has the given name of Frederick.

Fortunately, however, she is an incompletely successful product of the Rachel and Leah Re-education Center, literally named for the passage in Genesis where Rachel tells Jacob, "Behold my maid Bilhah, go in unto her; and she shall bear upon my knees, that I may also have children by her." While she partly enjoys her oppression, which lends the novel an arresting ambiguity, she also knows better, understands the psychology of tyranny and feels guilty for submitting.

She is sensitive to the landscape around her, which is not a mere decorative background but plays a role in the novel's thematic development. She never stops scheming to escape, occasionally considering the route of suicide that her predecessor turns out to have taken. Most important of all, she never loses her acute sense of language; she never gives up her freedom to play with words.

"I wait," she muses, "for the household to assemble. *Household:* that is what we are. The Commander is the head of the household. The house is what he holds. To have and to hold, till death do us part. The hold of a ship. Hollow." Later, as the book approaches its chilling climax, she comments: "Today there are different flowers, drier, more defined, the flowers of high summer: daisies, black-eyed Susans, starting us on the long downward slope to fall."

This sensitivity to language is vital, and not only because it keeps the book alive. Women are absolutely forbidden literacy in the Republic of Gilead; "Our big mistake was teaching them to read," says the member of the Sons of Jacob who is thought to have orchestrated the massacre of the President and Congress (as we learn from an epilogue called "Historical Notes"). "We won't do that again." Or, as one of the Center's mottos puts it, "Pen is Envy."

It's of special meaning that the only clue to her predecessor's existence that Offred finds in her bedroom, besides the decoration on the ceiling where the light fixture from which she hanged herself was once attached, is the old joke-Latin sentence, "Nolite te bastardes carborundorum" ("Don't let the bastards grind you down"). And one of the novel's wittiest touches is that when Offred's Commander has her brought to him illegally, at great risk to her, late at night, it is because, as he explains when she arrives, "I would like—I'd like you to play a game of Scrabble with me."

What usually works against this genre of fiction—one thinks of Marge Piercy's *Woman on the Edge of Time,* Ira Levin's *This Perfect Day,* one or two of Doris Lessing's later novels and, to a lesser extent, Thomas Berger's *Regiment of Women*—is that what makes the imagined society narrow and oppressive also serves to limit the work in which it is described. This can also be said of ***The Handmaid's Tale;*** among other things, it is a political tract deploring nuclear energy, environmental waste, and antifeminist attitudes.

But it [is] so much more than that—a taut thriller, a psychological study, a play on words. It has a sense of humor about itself, as well as an ambivalence toward even its worst villains, who aren't revealed as such until the very end. Best of all, it holds out the possibility of redemption. After all, the Handmaid is also a writer. She has written this book. She may have survived.

Finally, if it is an ideological jeremiad, it happens also to be a sadomasochistic fantasy, what one might even call a cerebrated version of Pauline Reage's *Story of O.* The tension between these two ways of reading it makes even more interesting what is already a rich and complex book. ***The Handmaid's Tale*** is easily Margaret Atwood's best novel to date, and the long-awaited fulfillment of the earlier promise of ***Surfacing.***

Christopher Lehmann—Haupt, in a review of "The Handmaid's Tale," in The New York Times, *January 27, 1986, p. C24.*

JOYCE JOHNSON

We must think of ourselves as tourists, travelers in time. These streets are familiar, yet it would appear we have entered the Dark Ages. We are in a well-tended suburb in New England. Pleasant old houses, manicured lawns. A college town, perhaps Cambridge, although it is evident that the university has been closed permanently. Hooded bodies hang from hooks against an old brick wall, black vans with eyes ominously painted on them patrol the streets, uniformed men are stationed at checkpoints. On these streets there is an absence of children and old people. Everyone is also white.

Women are dressed oddly in floor-length costumes that appear to delineate caste. . . .

It is some time around the year 2000. Those who were in college in 1986 (children of parents from the Sixties generation) are now in their mid-thirties. They grew up in the culture that is so familiar to us today—they remember punk hairstyles, Humphrey Bogart festivals, painted toenails, adultery, women's liberation, paper currency, the TV shows that from time to time featured leaders of the Moral Majority. We would share their frame of reference, yet we would have immense difficulty adjusting to the demands of this new, austere, regimented society. Life as we know it in the U.S.A. no longer exists. We have entered the Republic of Gilead.

Recently the Canadian poet and novelist Margaret Atwood was asked to describe her religious views for her listing in *Contemporary Authors.* "God is everywhere, but losing," was her answer. In ***The Handmaid's Tale,*** her fifth and most powerful novel, she looks into the clouded glass of the future and, fully attuned to some of the negative signals in the present, envisions startling but by no means illogical consequences. In opening her imagination to what we might find some years down the road, Atwood joins the company of Doris Lessing, J. G. Ballard and Anthony Burgess, literary writers of future shock fiction—a genre whose pioneers include H. G. Wells, Aldous Huxley, and George Orwell.

In a period when the novel of bourgeois life increasingly suffers from a poverty of subject—when we read over and over again about the attenuated sufferings of those in comfortable circumstances who should be a little happier than they are—the novel of the disastrous future offers the writer of fiction rejuvenated possibilities. Characters are placed in extremis, calling upon all their resources of courage and ingenuity in order to survive. Rebels defy the rules of society, risking everything to retain their humanity. If the world Atwood depicts is chilling, if "God is losing," the only hope for optimism is a vision that includes the inevitability of human struggle against the prevailing order. (pp. 1-2)

Just as the world of Orwell's *1984* gripped our imaginations, so will the world of Atwood's handmaid. She has succeeded in finding a voice for her heroine that is direct, artless, utterly convincing. It is the voice of a woman we might know, of someone very close to us. In fact, it is Offred's poignant sense of time that gives this novel its peculiar power. The immense changes in her life have come so fast that she is still in a state of shock and disbelief as she relates to us what she sees around her. Her present reality is constantly invaded by painful memories of what she has lost—everyday life as we ourselves know it. Vestiges of the recent past take her by surprise.

In Atwood's Gilead, even the male leaders are not immune to longings for the illicit pleasure of the past, to "an appreciation of the old things," although Offred's elderly commander points out to her that men used to suffer because sex used to be too easily come by. "Anybody could just buy it. There was nothing to work for, nothing to fight for." The double standard still prevails, however. Offred's commander takes it upon himself to break the rules, summoning her to visit him alone in his private study. She goes to the assignation expecting, as the reader does, whips and chains, sexual perversion. Instead there is a marvelously comic turn. What he wants is to play a game of Scrabble with her, and he wants to be kissed as if she means it. In return, she asks for a bottle of hand lotion to use on her face and—because women have been deprived of knowledge—she makes a classic demand for something even more valuable and forbidden: "I want to know," she says. "Whatever there is to know. What's going on."

The Handmaid's Tale is a novel that brilliantly illuminates some of the darker interconnections of politics and sex, and it will no doubt be labeled a "feminist *1984*." Yet it is Atwood's achievement to have produced a political novel that avoids the pitfall of doctrinaire writing. Offred lives and breathes. She is defiant in her own way, but no Superwoman. She resembles neither her mother, a militant feminist leader of drives against pornography, nor her friend Moira, a gay activist who refuses to become a handmaid and briefly manages to join the underground. She is simply a warm, intelligent, ordinary woman who had taken for granted the freedoms she was to lose—the freedom to love, the freedom to work, the freedom to have access to knowledge. Gilead threatens those who break its rules with extinction. Yet for Offred, the price of obedience is even higher—the death of the senses, the death of the spirit. She catches herself in the absurd contradiction of smearing butter on her face to preserve her complexion and simultaneously contemplating hanging herself from a hook in her closet. Overwhelming loneliness and boredom afflict her even more than oppression, "Nobody dies from lack of sex," she discovers. "It's a lack of love we die from. There's nobody here I can love, all the people I could love are dead or elsewhere. Who knows where they are or what their names are now? They might as well as be nowhere, as I am for them. I too am a missing person."

Offred's plight is always human as well as ideological, and so is her inevitable assertion of her needs. Her tale, in Atwood's masterful hands, is extraordinarily satisfying, disturbing and compelling. (p. 2)

Joyce Johnson, "Margaret Atwood's Brave New World," in Book World—The Washington Post, *February 2, 1986, pp. 1-2.*

ELAINE KENDALL

America in Atwood's bleak, unnerving novel is the theocracy of Gilead, established by religious fanatics who have dismantled the republic, liquidated the opposition and replaced our present political system with a quasi-military infrastructure. The northeastern United States has been transformed into Gilead with terrifying swiftness and remarkably little resistance, the transition eased by a lingering Puritan tradition fortified by neo-fundamentalism. The overriding concern of this regime is human reproduction; the time is the foreseeable future, when a devastating combination of chemical pollution, radiation and epidemic venereal disease has caused the national birthrate to fall below replacement level. For an assortment of good, bad and indifferent reasons, too few children have been born in the preceding decades to keep America from extinction. Arthur Campbell, a demographer quoted in the Jan. 13 issue of *Newsweek,* believes that more than a fifth of the women born in the 1950s may never have a child. By the time ***The Handmaid's Tale*** begins, he has been proved right and reforms long advocated by radical elements of the Moral Majority have become law.

Unlike science fiction, which is sharply fanciful, this sort of speculative literature merely extrapolates from past and present experience to a future firmly based upon actuality, beginning with events that have already taken place and extending them a bit beyond the inevitable conclusions. ***The Handmaid's Tale*** does not depend upon hypothetical scenarios, omens, or straws in the wind, but upon documented occurences and public pronouncements; all matters of record. For contemporary American women, ***The Handmaid's Tale*** could be the ultimate Doomsday Book; a man's reaction may well be ambivalent. In Gilead, such distinctions between the sexes have been revived and emphasized with a vengeance.

As the proclaimed moral guardians of the nation, the High Commanders of Gilead have declared all second marriages and unsanctified unions between men and women invalid. Fertile female partners in these liaisons have been seized and forced into the role of childbearers to the ruling elite; the offending males have been killed, exiled or imprisoned. After a period of indoctrination in their duties to their master and the state, the handmaids are incarcerated in the Commanders' houses, guarded by attendants called Marthas, women who for racial or other reasons are unfit for childbearing. Though the legal wives of the Commanders occupy an exalted position in this society, by the time their husbands have reached Commander status, the wives are too old to have children. A vicarious arrangement has been devised for their benefits; a "ceremony" in which the real wife is present while her husband attempts to impregnate his handmaid. The handmaid's only outside activity is shopping for food, but after each of these carefully monitored excursions, she must return to her cell-like room. Handmaids are not allowed to read, hold jobs or own property; an abrogation of rights justified by the Scripture-quoting theocrats in power. Radio, television and films have apparently been abolished; coffee, tea, tobacco and cosmetics are forbidden to the breeders. Categories of women are identified by their costume, as in feudal societies before the industrial revolution enabled the lower orders to imitate the privileged. (pp. 1, 12)

The narrator of the tale is Offred; the literary mode a diary of her circumscribed existence. Offred's young daughter has been kidnaped, her husband apparently shot while trying to cross the border into Canada; her mother and a close friend, both outspoken feminists, have vanished without a trace. Offred herself is living on borrowed time. Each handmaid has three years in which to produce a healthy child for a Commander. Should she fail to become pregnant in that time, she too will disappear, either to "The Colonies," where infertile women are used to clean up toxic waste, or if she is more fortunate, to forced labor on a farm. The third option is a secret bordello set up to stimulate the Commanders' lagging interest in sex, which tends to wane under the circumstances. Because the birthrate has not yet been raised by these Draconian measures, even more heroic tactics may soon be required. As it stands, life in Gilead exceeds the grim primitive reality described by Hobbes in *Leviathan,* "no arts, no letters, no society, and which is worst of all, continual fear and danger of violent death." The university system has been demolished, public executions are frequent, the economy is faltering, secret police are everywhere, and virtually all civil rights gained by women and minorities during the last century have been rescinded.

Given conducive circumstances, every one of the atavistic changes in this novel could be implemented virtually overnight, smoothly and efficiently. The legislative machinery is already in place, the communications networks established; vast sums of money available to the advocates of such a system. As a Harvard educated Canadian with a particular interest in Puritan history, Atwood can observe these changes from a privileged vantage point; close enough for involvement, sufficiently removed for perspective. In a recent CBC interview she said, "Canada's role in this novel is the role Canada has always taken in bad times in the United States . . . so Canada's position would be to do what she always does: to try to remain neutral without antagonizing the superpower to the South."

Atwood has created a spirited and engaging narrator and surrounded her with an array of active and passive supporting characters, each of whom represents a type familiar in America today. She has rounded off her icy cautionary tale with a desperately needed and hilarious spoof of an academic convention in the year 2195, at which time Gilead is a defunct society, regarded by all as a trivial aberration in cultural history, but despite this full complement of literary virtues, the power of the book comes not from Atwood's inspired flights of fancy or felicities of style but from her deliberate subjugation of imagination to demonstrable fact. Only the form of ***The Handmaid's Tale*** is fiction, as the form of *Mein Kampf* was autobiography. (p. 12)

Elaine Kendall, in a review of "The Handmaid's Tale," in Los Angeles Times Book Review, *February 9, 1986, pp. 1, 12.*

MARY McCARTHY

[McCarthy is an American novelist, critic, and essayist. She is highly regarded for her unflinchingly honest portrayal of modern society in her novels, including The Company She Keeps *(1942),* The Group *(1963), and* Cannibals and Missionaries *(1979), as well as her mordant commentary on drama, literature, and politics. She has published a number of nonfiction volumes, including the essay collections* On the Contrary *(1961) and* Occasional Prose *(1985). In the following excerpt McCarthy concludes that* The Handmaid's Tale, *as a cautionary dystopian allegory, lacks the biting satirical wit and imaginative conviction that Aldous Huxley and George Orwell brought to* Brave New World *and* 1984.]

Surely the essential element of a cautionary tale is recognition. Surprised recognition, even, enough to administer a shock. We are warned, by seeing our present selves in a distorting mirror, of what we may be turning into if current trends are allowed to continue. That was the effect of *Nineteen Eighty-Four,* with its scary dating, not 40 years ahead, maybe also of *Brave New World* and, to some extent, of *A Clockwork Orange.*

It is an effect, for me, almost strikingly missing from Margaret Atwood's very readable book ***The Handmaid's Tale,*** offered by the publisher as a "forecast" of what we may have in store for us in the quite near future. A standoff will have been achieved vis-à-vis the Russians, and our own country will be ruled by right-wingers and religious fundamentalists, with males restored to the traditional role of warriors and us females to our "place"—which, however, will have undergone subdivision into separate sectors, of wives, breeders, servants and so forth, each clothed in the appropriate uniform. A fresh postfeminist approach to future shock, you might say. Yet the book just does not tell me what there is in our present mores that I ought to watch out for unless I want the United States of America to become a slave state something like the Republic of Gilead whose outlines are here sketched out.

Another reader, less peculiar than myself, might confess to a touch of apathy regarding credit cards (instruments of social control), but I have always been firmly against them and will go to almost any length to avoid using one. Yet I can admit to a general failure to extrapolate sufficiently from the 1986 scene. Still, even when I try, in the light of these palely lurid pages, to take the Moral Majority seriously, no shiver of recognition ensues. I just can't see the intolerance of the far right, presently directed not only at abortion clinics and homosexuals but also at high school libraries and small-town schoolteachers, as leading to a super-biblical puritanism by which procreation will be insisted on and reading of any kind banned. Nor, on the other hand, do I fear our "excesses" of tolerance as pointing in the same direction. Liberality toward pornography in the courts, the media, on the newsstands may make an anxious parent feel disgusted with liberalism, but can it really move a nation to install a theocracy strictly based on the Book of Genesis? Where are the signs of it? A backlash is only a backlash, that is, a reaction. Fear of a backlash, in politics, ought not to deter anybody from adhering to principle; that would be only another form of cowardice. The same for "excessive" feminism, which here seems to bear some responsibility for Gilead, to be one of its causes. The kind of doctrinaire feminism likely to produce a backlash is exemplified in the narrator's absurd mother, whom we first hear of at a book-burning in the old, pre-Gilead time—the "right" kind of book-burning, naturally, merely a pyre of pornographic magazines: "Mother," thinks the narrator in what has become the present, "you wanted a women's culture. Well, now there is one." The wrong kind, of course.

The new world of ***The Handmaid's Tale*** is a woman's world, even though governed, seemingly, and policed by men. Its ethos is entirely domestic, its female population is divided into classes based on household functions, each class clad in a separate color that instantly identifies the wearer—dull green for the Marthas (houseworkers); blue for the Wives; red, blue and green stripes for the Econowives (working class); red for the Handmaids (whose function is to bear children to the head of the household, like Bilhah, Rachel's handmaid in Genesis, but who also, in their long red gowns and white wimple-like headgear, have something of the aura of a temple harlot); brown for the Aunts (a thought-control force, part-governess, part-reform-school matron). The head of the household—whose first name the handmaid takes, adding the word "of" to show possession—"Offred," "Ofwarren"—is known as the Commander. It is his duty to inseminate his assigned partner, who lies on the spread thighs of his wife.

The Commanders, presumably, are the high bureaucracy of the regime, yet they are oddly powerless in the household, having no part in the administration of discipline and ceremonially subject to their aging wives. We are not told how and in what sense they govern. The oversight perhaps accounts for the thin credibility of the parable. That they lack freedom, are locked into their own rigid system, is only to be expected. It is no surprise that our narrator's commander, Fred, like a typical bourgeois husband of former times, does a bit of cheating, getting Offred to play Scrabble with him secretly at night (where books are forbidden, word games become wicked), look at his hoard of old fashion magazines (forbidden), kiss him, even go dressed in glitter and feathers to an underground bunny-type nightclub staffed by fallen women, mostly lesbian. Nor is it a surprise that his wife catches him/them. *Plus ça change, plus c'est la même chose*. But that cannot be the motto for a cautionary tale, whose job is to warn of change.

Infertility is the big problem of the new world and the reason for many of its institutions. A dramatically lowered birth rate, which brought on the fall of the old order, had a plurality of causes, we are told. "The air got too full, once, of chemicals, rays, radiation, the water swarmed with toxic molecules." During an earthquake, atomic power plants exploded ("nobody's fault"). A mutant strain of syphilis appeared, and of course AIDS. Then there were women who refused to breed, as an antinuclear protest, and had their tubes tied up. Anyway, infertility, despite the radical measures of the new regime, has not yet been overcome. Not only are there barren women (mostly shipped to the colonies) but a worrying sterility in men, especially among the powerful who ought to be reproducing themselves. The amusing suggestion is made, late in the book at a symposium (June 25, 2195) of Gileadean historical studies, that sterility among the Commanders may have been the result of an earlier gene-splicing experiment with mumps that produced a virus intended for insertion into the supply of caviar used by top officials in Moscow.

The Handmaid's Tale contains several such touches of deft sardonic humor—for example, the television news program showing clouds of smoke over what was formerly the city of Detroit: we hear the anchorman explain that resettlement of the children of Ham in National Homeland One (the wilds of North Dakota) is continuing on schedule—3,000 have arrived that week. And yet what is lacking, I think—what constitutes a fundamental disappointment after a promising start—is the destructive force of satire. *Nineteen Eighty-Four* had it, *A Clockwork Orange* had it, even *Brave New World* had it, though Huxley was rather short on savagery. If ***The Handmaid's Tale*** doesn't scare one, doesn't wake one up, it must be because it has no satiric bite.

The author has carefully drawn her projections from current trends. As she has said elsewhere, there is nothing here that has not been anticipated in the United States of America that we already know. Perhaps that is the trouble: the projections are too neatly penciled in. The details, including a Wall (as in Berlin, but also, as in the Middle Ages, a place where executed malefactors are displayed), all raise their hands announcing themselves present. At the same time, the Republic of Gilead itself, whatever in it that is not a projection, is insufficiently imagined. The Aunts are a good invention, though I cannot picture them as belonging to any future; unlike Big Brother, they are more part of the past—our schoolteachers.

But the most conspicuous lack, in comparison with the classics of the fearsome-future genre, is the inability to imagine a language to match the changed face of common life. No newspeak. And nothing like the linguistic tour de force of *A Clockwork Orange*—the brutal melting-down of current English and Slavic words that in itself tells the story of the dread new breed. The writing of ***The Handmaid's Tale*** is undistinguished in a double sense, ordinary if not glaringly so, but also indistinguishable from what one supposes would be Margaret Atwood's normal way of expressing herself in the circumstances. This is a serious defect, unpardonable maybe for the genre: a future that has no language invented for it lacks a personality. That must be why, collectively, it is powerless to scare.

One could argue that the very tameness of the narrator-heroine's style is intended as characterization. It is true that a leading trait of Offred (we are never told her own, real name in so many words, but my textual detective work says it is June) has always been an unwillingness to stick her neck out, and perhaps we are meant to conclude that such unwillingness, multiplied, may be fatal to a free society. After the takeover, she tells us, there were some protests and demonstrations. "I didn't go on any of the marches. Luke (her husband) said it would be futile, and I had to think about them, my family, him and her (their little girl)." Famous last words. But, though this may characterize an attitude—fairly widespread—it does not constitute a particular kind of speech. And there are many poetical passages, for example (chosen at random): "All things white and circular. I wait for the day to unroll, for the earth to turn, according to the round face of the implacable clock." Which is surely oldspeak, wouldn't you say?

Characterization in general is weak in ***The Handmaid's Tale***, which maybe makes it a poet's novel. I cannot tell Luke, the husband, from Nick, the chauffeur-lover who may be an Eye (government spy) and/ or belong to the "Mayday" underground. Nor is the Commander strongly drawn. Again, the Aunts are best. How sad for postfeminists that one does not feel for Offred-June half as much as one did for Winston Smith, no hero either but at any rate imaginable. It seems harsh to say again of a poet's novel—so hard to put down, in part so striking—that it lacks imagination, but that, I fear, is the problem. (pp. 1, 35)

Mary McCarthy, "Breeders, Wives and Unwomen," in The New York Times Book Review, *February 9, 1986, pp. 1, 35.*

PETER S. PRESCOTT

Margaret Atwood's [***The Handmaid's Tale***] . . . belongs to that breed of visionary fiction in which a metaphor is extended to elaborate a warning: *Caution: The author has concluded that present social trends are dangerous to individual welfare*. Wells, Huxley and Orwell popularized the tradition with books like *The Time Machine, Brave New World* and *1984*—yet Atwood is a better *novelist* than they. Unlike those English gentlemen, she can create a nuanced character. The dystopia she has imagined may be more limited than theirs, but it's fully as horrifying—and achieved without recourse to special effects. Human brutality being what it is, gene splitting and electronic surveillance aren't necessary to a totalitarian state: the most advanced technological device in Atwood's story is an electric cattle prod.

The time is only a few years in the future; the place, Cambridge, Mass. The religious right in America has staged a coup and proclaimed the Republic of Gilead. Lawyers and universities have been abolished. Jews have been offered a choice—conversion or emigration—and blacks are being resettled in North Dakota. Atwood isn't really interested in these details. Her concern is with the role of women in a theocracy whose social values have reverted to those of *Genesis*. . . .

All such visionary novels have the same plot. At first the bewildered protagonist accepts his lot, then rebels. He hears a rumor of a resistance movement, then unexpected sex assuages his pain for a while, before he's eased to his doom or escape. Atwood sees no need to vary the formula. Her novel works as well as it does for several reasons. First, it is not, as the unwary might suppose, a departure from her usual theme. Atwood's novels have always been about women's survival in a hostile, male-dominated world: woman's refusal, as she wrote in ***Surfacing,*** to be a victim. Next is her cruel amplification of an area of immediate political concern. The novelist's imagination, his skill at extending a metaphor, enables him to suggest not what he believes *will* happen, but what *could* happen because the machinery is in place and the guards who are supposed to supervise that machinery are dozing at their desks. Huxley and Orwell didn't mean to tell us that totalitarianism is inevitable, nor does Atwood. In this kind of fiction, exaggeration makes clear the dark side of current attitudes we too easily accept.

Then there's Atwood's irony, which begins with her title, reminiscent of Chaucer's great poem which incorporated precisely what has disappeared from Gilead: the juice and joy of living. "We are for breeding purposes," Offred says. "There is supposed to be nothing entertaining about us." More ironic is the feminine nature of this slave society. Gilead is designed by men, to be sure, but it's the women who make it work, who keep each other in line. It is, as Offred observes, a woman's culture, if hardly what the feminists had in mind.

Finally, there's Offred's tone of voice, beautifully modulated and as different from Atwood's other narrators as they are from each other. Offred at first accepts assurance that the new order is for her protection: "Modesty is invisibility," the Aunts have taught her. "To be seen is to be penetrated." But she remembers her past, her weak husband (all the men in Atwood's novels are weak) and the child that was taken from her: "I am like a room where things once happened and now nothing does, except the pollen of the weeds that grow up outside the window, blowing in as dust across the floor."

Peter S. Prescott, "No Balm in This Gilead," in Newsweek, *Vol. CVII, No. 7, February 17, 1986, p. 70.*

An Excerpt from *The Handmaid's Tale*

There was no one cause, says Aunt Lydia. She stands at the front of the room, in her khaki dress, a pointer in her hand. Pulled down in front of the blackboard, where once there would have been a map, is a graph, showing the birthrate per thousand, for years and years: a slippery slope, down past the zero line of replacement, and down and down.

Of course, some women believed there would be no future, they thought the world would explode. That was the excuse they used, says Aunt Lydia. They said there was no sense in breeding. Aunt Lydia's nostrils narrow: such wickedness. They were lazy women, she says. They were sluts.

On the top of my desk there are initials, carved into the wood, and dates. The initials are sometimes in two sets, joined by the word *loves. J. H. loves B. P. 1954. O. R. loves L. T.* These seem to me like the inscriptions I used to read about, carved on the stone walls of caves, or drawn with a mixture of soot and animal fat. They seem to me incredibly ancient. The desk top is of blond wood; it slants down, and there is an armrest on the right side, to lean on when you were writing, on paper, with a pen. Inside the desk you could keep things: books, notebooks. These habits of former times appear to me now lavish, decadent almost; immoral, like the orgies of barbarian regimes. *M. loves G. 1972.* This carving, done with a pencil dug many times into the worn varnish of the desk, has the pathos of all vanished civilizations. It's like a handprint on stone. Whoever made that was once alive.

There are no dates after the mid-eighties. This must have been one of the schools that was closed down then, for lack of children.

They made mistakes, says Aunt Lydia. We don't intend to repeat them. Her voice is pious, condescending, the voice of those whose duty it is to tell us unpleasant things for our own good. I would like to strangle her. I shove this thought away almost as soon as I think it.

A thing is valued, she says, only if it is rare and hard to get. We want you to be valued, girls. She is rich in pauses, which she savors in her mouth. Think of yourselves as pearls. We, sitting in our rows, eyes down, we make her salivate morally. We are hers to define, we must suffer her adjectives.

I think about pearls. Pearls are congealed oyster spit. This is what I will tell Moira, later; if I can.

All of us here will lick you into shape, says Aunt Lydia, with satisfied good cheer.

JANE GARDAM

[Gardam, an English novelist, short story writer, and critic, is the author of such novels as A Long Way from Verona *(1971) and* Crusoe's Daughter *(1985), as well as short story collections, including* A Few Fair Days *(1971). In the following excerpt Gardam praises* The Handmaid's Tale *for its clear, sensuous prose that evokes both the beauty and horror of Atwood's fictional dystopia Gilead.]*

Twenty years ago Margaret Atwood, now 'the star of Canadian letters', then still at college, wrote an enormously entertaining novel called ***The Edible Woman*** about a young woman's reluctance to be devoured by husband and children. At the time all she knew of feminism was what she 'had read of Betty Friedan and Simone de Beauvoir behind closed doors'. 'I am not clairvoyant,' she says and did not know that she was blazing the trail for the long and usually much more lumbering caravan of feminist literature to come.

In 1972 in an extraordinary and maybe wider book, ***Surfacing,*** she has a heroine looking for a different freedom, the freedom of the spiritual life. She puts the girl—as Emily Brontë had done before—out into the physical world and causes her to live wild in the forest, for a time to become the forest and even what causes the forest to grow. Her attempt to achieve the negation of self is the same battle waged by the mystic and the nun.

Now in . . . ***The Handmaid's Tale,*** she has by no means finished with nuns, or with the nature of female freedom but this is a far from willing nun in a nightmare nunnery deprived of the marriage and child she was running from in ***The Edible Woman*** and cut off from physical freedom too. She has not a chance in hell—and she is in hell—of finding oneness with nature or with anything or anyone. The monastic ideals are horrors imposed, and the neglect of them punishable by death, death without hope of after-life let alone heaven.

It happens in a place called Gilead, once part of the United States, and to a girl called Offred. There has been a government coup. Women have been deprived of money (credit cards invalid and bank accounts frozen) and thrown back on their men's charity. Offred with her man and child has tried to escape 'over the border'—there are still a few flight lines—but they are all caught. Man and child disappear and are now almost certainly dead. Offred as a healthy, proven child-bearer is taken off to the terrible Rachel and Leah Centre where she is conditioned to serve the state as a breeding machine. (p. 29)

This terrible world, like Orwell's England (Airstrip One) is not meant to be totally in the future. *1984* we know was only the year in which the book was written with the last two digits reversed, and Gilead we are told in the 'Historical Note' at the end, written in 2195, described many events of the late 20th century. Romania for instance 'had anticipated Gilead in banning birth-control, imposing compulsory pregnancy tests and linking promotion and wage increases to fertility,' and there was already in the world artificial insemination and the use of surrogate mothers. The nightmare nunnery is also heavy with religious symbolism of what is still expected of women today in, for instance, Iran.

Gilead has not perhaps the dreadful grey eternal nature of Airstrip One however and, though things can happen fast—as in Hungary—can one really believe that the power of the American woman could be removed by a swoop upon her credit cards overnight? Considering the American women one meets it seems very unlikely, even though Margaret Atwood believes that real feminism has made little progress in 20 years.

What gives her picture of Gilead its force is that in all its vileness it is strangely beautiful. Margaret Atwood is now an internationally acclaimed poet as well as novelist and there are echoes in ***The Handmaid's Tale*** of the sensuous delights of 19th century poetry. The recurring image of red-veined tulips for example is reminiscent of Browning's

Big red bubbles of blood
For the children to pick and sell

and the picture of the floppy old wife of the Commander, tending her garden under a blue-veiled hat, is Tennysonian. The landscape of the country is dream-like, glitteringly clear like a mirror-image of the medieval heavenly landscape of the poem, "Pearl", that wonderful lament for a dead child. There is even a horrible beauty in the heroine's plight—her quiet reverie of better days, her dignity and sorrow, her courageous rationing of recollection of times past so that she will be able to bear them. And there are nice vignettes: her 1960s feminist mother, banner-carrying, hard-drinking, jolly, believing in the pursuit of pleasure; and Offred's man, Luke, teasing the women about being incapable of abstract thought and they teasing him back, as he cuts up the carrots ('I enjoy cooking.' Mother: 'You don't know how many women's bodies the tanks had to roll over just to get that far. Once they'd have called you queer.') And there are poignant memories of the small daughter who returns to Offred at angles of the stairs and with the smell of baby-soap in the bath. Flashes of old, unregarded happiness. Even the horrors are beautifully described in a clear pure prose that looks easy until you try to list the layers of its imagery, symbols and concepts.

The Handmaid's Tale is also exciting. It is not all reverie. A great deal happens and there's a fine dénouement which reads almost like Graham Greene—or John Buchan! And time does march on even in Gilead. Anthropologists will be reassured by the post-script as the common reader will be reassured that there are nightmares from which one does eventually wake up. (pp. 29-30)

Jane Gardam, "Nuns and Soldiers," in Books and Bookmen, *No. 365, March, 1986, pp. 29-30.*

JOYCE MAYNARD

[Maynard, an American novelist, nonfiction writer, critic, and editor, is book editor of Mademoiselle. *She is the author of* Looking Back: A Chronicle of Growing Up Old in the Sixties *(1973),* Baby Love *(1981), and* Camp-Out *(1985). In the following excerpt Maynard praises* The Handmaid's Tale *as an absorbing, moving, and provocative meditation on the future of American society.]*

I had intended to talk about a whole bunch of novels this month. I'd read some good ones. Then almost as an afterthought I picked up Margaret Atwood's ***The Handmaid's Tale***. . . . I had read on the jacket that it was set in the near future, and since I don't like science fiction much (I like books that speak to my life, situations I can recognize), I didn't imagine this one would hold a lot of interest.

That's what I told myself at around 10 P.M., but half an hour later I was transfixed, and as things turned out, I finished the novel in one sitting. As for those other books—all of them good—I can't think about them right now, I'm so consumed by this one. I read it late into the night and into the morning, because I knew that even if I turned out the light I wouldn't get to sleep, and that even if I could, I'd have troubled dreams. ***The Handmaid's Tale*** will change anyone who reads it, which is to say, anyone who picks it up.

It's a vision of hell, nothing less, that Atwood's giving us here, but she calls the place the Republic of Gilead. It was once known as the United States. It's sometime in the future, but not all that far into the future, we know, because our narrator remembers the things that are part of our lives right now: Feminist marches. Fashion magazines. Rock music. Ice cream. All of that has vanished—and been replaced by an ultra-conservative puritanical regime in which men rule over women, and some of the women rule over the rest of the women. The handmaid telling this tale is somewhere near the bottom of the social hierarchy. She is in her early thirties, which probably means she was born around 1986. We know her only as Offred and never learn her real name. (p. 114)

The situation may sound unreal and remote, but it doesn't as Offred the handmaid describes it. Margaret Atwood has constructed a whole world here, detailing not only the basic rules and structures by which Gilead operates, but a thousand small, odd, harrowing particulars too: the design of the floating, nunlike garment worn by the handmaids to obscure their faces. The stores where Offred shops—all of them with names from the Bible: Loaves and Fishes; Lilies of the Field; All Flesh. (That one's the butcher's shop. Here, as so often, Atwood manages to be grim and funny at the same time.) We get the feeling she's navigated every street of Gilead (even the ones she doesn't show us), and worked out in her mind the way inhabitants of this new world cope—not only with the enormous, overwhelming alterations in their way of life, but all the small losses too. For instance, Offred hides her daily allotment of butter in the toe of her shoe, to rub over her skin, later, as moisturizer. Not because she's worried about wrinkles, we can see, but because she needs to believe that there will be some better future to stay unwrinkled for.

The Handmaid's Tale reads like some wonderfully rich childhood game of invention—the kind of game that spreads itself over an entire bedroom floor, and out into the hall, and calls into service Barbies and blocks, G.I. Joes and Matchbox trucks, old toilet-paper rolls and construction paper and tape. And like most made-up worlds, too, this one is full of recognizable elements: shuffled up, recast, but still familiar. That's the chilling part. Just as we're beginning to allow ourselves the comfort and ease of a little distance (saying this is only a story, this is only a story), a character comes along talking about AIDS or Agent Orange, or some of the other elements that led, ultimately, to the creation of this new world. Because of that, what we have here is not a bizarre horror story to read with interest and detachment. It's more like one of those images a fun-house mirror reflects back—twisted and misshapen, but also, unmistakably our own.

Part of the brilliance of ***The Handmaid's Tale*** is the way the world it creates comes not only to seem real, but like all real places, to evolve. It's not a static, National Geographic account of Gilead that Atwood gives us here; it's a picture of the way corruption begins to erode even the most rigid and restrictive societies (those most of all, maybe). By the time we're three quarters of the way into ***The Handmaid's Tale,*** we have Fred the Commander (who is supposed to have disavowed all romantic attachment to his handmaid) setting up a secret nighttime rendezvous with Offred, providing her with forbidden black-market copies of old fashion magazines and cheap, foulsmelling skin lotion. We have the handmaid herself falling into something like love with the Commander's chauffeur, Nick. There is even a place called Jezebel's, officially sanctioned by the very government that has forbidden all forms of wanton, lustful behavior, where prostitutes are made available for Commanders and visiting dignitaries. Fred takes Offred there one night—dresses her up in old, sequined lingerie for the occasion, has her put on makeup, and makes love to her. Has sex with her, anyway.

It's a society—formed in reaction to one form of corruption—that begins corrupting its own rules, and we can almost feel the tremors as this new, hastily constructed edifice of sanctity—Gilead—begins to topple. Things are getting out of control: There are the handmaids's feelings for Nick, her chauffeur lover; the Commander's for the handmaid. The handmaid may be pregnant. Her best friend may be dead. Danger is everywhere: Offred has a confidante named Ofglen who teaches her a secret password and gives her hope of an escape. But maybe Ofglen is really a spy, planted to test Offred's loyalty. Or maybe she's a genuine resister who will be caught, only to have Offred's name tortured out of her. Maybe Nick will turn her in to the Commander. Who to trust? What to believe? The handmaid's situation is worse than death—so much worse that even suicide has become a pleasant fantasy.

But along with the grim, terrible situation Atwood creates, there is, amazingly, devastating humor here: black, sardonic wit in the voice of the narrator and a kind of devilish glee on the part of Margaret Atwood herself. She names the Aunts after women whose names were once (in the old days) attached to commercial products: Elizabeth Arden and Sara Lee. She has the Commander keeping Scrabble scores on a Happy Face notepad, and a pitiful, sanctimonious handmaid named Ofwarren coming out with lines like "Have a nice day." There is a kind of comedy even in Atwood's description of what is called "the Ceremony," meaning the (presumably monthly) event in which Offred, the Commander and his wife arrange themselves together on the Commander's bed so that Offred might be inseminated. ("Maybe I'm crazy and this is some new kind of therapy," Offred thinks to herself.)

Our handmaid is a worthy guide in this strange new world: wry, dispassionate, realistic and detached, but sometimes, too, sunk in despair. She's haunted by the disappearance of her husband and child (during their attempted escape at the time of the revolution), and their conjured images both comfort and torment her. Sometimes she'll construct a scenario in which her husband escapes. Sometimes on her daily walks she'll look at the dead, tortured bodies of "traitors," hanging upside down at a place called The Wall, and expect to see him there. It may be the novel's one clear failing that we hear so much less of Offred's feeling over the loss of her daughter. I can believe—seeing how deeply Atwood has allowed herself to enter into the handmaid's experience—that fully exploring the loss of the child might simply have been more than she could bear. Still, we can imagine Offred's pain, as the Commander's wife allows her a quick, furtive glance at a Polaroid of her missing daughter now with a new mother, heading rapidly toward the day when she, too, will become a child-bearing vessel.

I won't tell—must not tell—where the book leaves Offred the handmaid, and where it leaves the world of Gilead. I can say, though, that in the end, ***The Handmaid's Tale*** forces us to think not so much about the repression and intolerance of Atwood's mythical republic, but the climate and events in our own time which (Atwood suggests) could make it possible for a Gilead to come into being.

It would be easy to get preachy here, or to suggest (mistakenly) that Atwood is getting preachy herself. She never says, "Look what could become of us if we don't watch it with the toxic wastes," or, "Keep your eye on Jerry Falwell; he could be mobilizing to take over the White House." Atwood has written an intensely political novel here, but it's too rich and subtle to be distilled into a single, humorless, cautionary message about where we're headed. Inevitably, though, she focuses the reader on the small, easily ignored rotten spots surrounding us, and forces us to consider where that decay could leave us. And it must be said, she's evenhanded in the warnings. If she makes rigid fundamentalists her most sinister villains, she sounds something of a warning (*alert* might be the better word) about elements from the other side as well. Abortion isn't the crime here, and neither is feminism. But still, Atwood seems to suggest that there is something in the shrillness of extremism, coming from any direction, that leads a society to danger.

The warning is there, all right. But the reason we hear it so piercingly in ***The Handmaid's Tale*** is because Margaret Atwood has written such an unforgettable and moving story. You might not want a message this month. You might not be losing any sleep over the national birthrate or nuclear wastes. You might just want to read a novel that will make you cry, or keep you up all night. In which case you should read this book. ***The Handmaid's Tale*** will do those things to you all right. And then some. (pp. 118, 120)

Joyce Maynard, "Briefing for a Descent into Hell," in Mademoiselle, *Vol. 92, March, 1986, pp. 114, 118, 120.*

BARBARA EHRENREICH

[Ehrenreich, an American nonfiction writer and critic, writes about health care reform, feminism, and other issues from a socialist viewpoint. She coauthored several books about health care, including The American Health Empire *(1970) and* For Her Own Good: One Hundred Fifty Years of the Experts's Advice to Women *(1978). Her other works include* The Hearts of Men: American Dreams and the Flight from Commitment *(1983) and* Re-Making Love: The Feminization of Sex *(1986). She is also a contributing editor of* Ms. *In the following excerpt Ehrenreich observes that while* The Handmaid's Tale *is not as compelling a portrait of dystopia as George Orwell's* 1984, *it offers a fascinating exploration of feminist issues.]*

The feminist imagination has been far more productive of utopias (from Charlotte Perkins Gilman's *Herland* to Marge Piercy's *Woman on the Edge of Time*) than of dystopias, and for good reason. Almost every thinkable insult to women has been tested and institutionalized at one time or another: foot-binding, witch-burning, slavery, organized rape, ritual mutilation, enforced childbearing, enforced chastity, and the mere denial of ordinary rights to own property, speak out in public, or walk down a street without fear. For misogynist nastiness, it is hard to improve on history.

Yet there has been no shortage of paranoid folklore about what the future may hold for women. Since the early 1970s, one important strand of feminist thought (usually called "cultural" or "radical" feminist) has tended to see all of history as a male assault on women and, by proxy, on nature itself. Hence rape, hence acid rain, hence six-inch high heels, hence the arms race, hence (obviously) the scourge of pornography. Extrapolating from this miserable record, cultural feminists have forseen women being driven back to servitude as breeders and scullery maids, or else, when reproductive technology is refined enough to make wombs unnecessary, being eliminated altogether. The alternative, they believe, is to create a "women's culture," envisioned as intrinsically loving, nurturing, and in harmony with nature—before we are all destroyed by the toxic effects of testosterone.

Margaret Atwood's [***The Handmaid's Tale***] is being greeted as the long-awaited feminist dystopia, and I am afraid that for some time it will be viewed as a test of the imaginative power of feminist paranoia. Is Atwood's brave new world really so bad? Is it as ingeniously awful as *1984?* And, by implication, are the fears—or for that matter, the concerns—of feminism worth taking all that seriously? Atwood's book has, for better or worse, taken the most obvious route from here to hell: the Moral Majority, or some group of similar persuasion, has taken over the United States, extirpated the printed word, hunted down the heretics, and established a medieval-style theocracy that is almost as boring, in a day-to-day sense, as it is grisly.

It is not only women who are in trouble in the new Christian nation. The "Children of Ham" are being relocated from the cities to their new "homeland" in North Dakota. Jews have been packed aboard ships supposedly headed for Israel. It's open season on Catholics, Quakers, former abortionists, and "gender traitors" (male homosexuals), all of whom are likely to end up hung from hooks on the wall that runs along the city of Gilead. But women are in a particularly tight spot. (pp. 33-4)

What we see through the eyes of the handmaid narrator, Offred (of-Fred, her current Commander), is mostly the narrow household in which she must mate, once a month, and wait passively for signs of pregnancy. The real power in the household lies with the regally blue-robed Wife, who was in the old days, we are pleased to learn, a celebrated right-wing evangelical TV personality, and is now festering with resentment at a world in which women are barred from any visible public role. There are also two servants, generically called "Hannahs" and consigned to dull green outfits, and a cocky chauffeur called Nick, who may or may not be an "Eye," a spy for the central authorities, whoever they are. And, as in *1984,* there is a resistance movement, which Offred learns of through a handmaid in a neighboring household; but, also as in *1984,* the only truly subversive force appears to be love. Fred, the bumbling, wistful Commander, falls in love with Offred, who in turn falls for the inscrutable Nick.

It is not the plot, however, or even the novel social setting, which accounts for the peculiar grip of ***The Handmaid's Tale.*** Atwood has woven a fantasy of regression that is almost as seductive, in a perverse way, as it is repellent. Offred had been a happy yuppie in "the time before," with a husband, a daughter, a job, money to spend, decisions to make, and of course, a name of her own. Now her only responsibility is to conceive; otherwise it is to sit quietly and stare out through a window of shatter-proof glass. There is not much to think about except the time of the month and the next meal, which will invariably feature soft bland offerings like canned pears and milk. Offred cries a lot and lives in fear of finding her erstwhile husband hanging from a hook on the wall, but when she is finally contacted by the resistance, she is curiously uninterested. She has sunk too far into the incestuous little household she serves—just as the reader, not without intermittent spasms of resistance, sinks into the deepening masochism of her tale.

My own resistance came from wanting to know more about this nightmare world, much more than Offred cares to find out. As a dystopia, this is a thinly textured one; and it is hard to know whether to blame the author or the narrator, who is forced, after all, into a kind of tunnel vision by the wimple she must wear along with her red handmaid's uniform. Offred spends a lot of time on aimless mental word games: "I sit in the chair and think about the word *chair*. It can also mean the leader of a meeting. It can also mean a mode of execution. It is the first syllable in *charity,*" and so forth.

Maybe this is how people think when they are depressed and have nothing to read. Still, one yearns for a narrator with a little anthropological imagination. Who's in charge here? Is there still a central government? The consumer culture has been almost obliterated, but has capitalism itself been routed by the fundamentalists? And if printed matter is illegal, what do they do without operating manuals for the cars and computers that are still very much in use? Yet when Offred finally rouses herself to put a question to the Commander, all she can come up with is a weak request to know "whatever there is to know.... What's going on."

But if Offred is a sappy stand-in for Winston Smith, and Gilead seems at times to be only a coloring book version of Oceania, it may be because Atwood means to do more than scare us about the obvious consequences of a Falwellian coup d'état. There is a subtler argument at work in ***The Handmaid's Tale,*** and it is as intellectually interesting as the fictional world she has housed it in. We are being warned, in this tale, not only about the theocratic ambitions of the religious right, but about a repressive tendency in feminism itself. Only on the surface is Gilead a fortress of patriarchy, Old Testament style. It is also, in a thoroughly sinister and distorted way, the utopia of cultural feminism.

There is, for example, no pornography in the new world (even the Bible is kept under lock and key); there are no cosmetics or other artifices to insult the natural female form, and the punishment for rape is to be torn to bits by a mob of women. Men, including physicians, have been barred from the scene of childbirth, which is now assisted by a ritual circle of chanting handmaids. In the Red Center where handmaids are trained for service, the presiding "Aunts" indoctrinate their charges in a twisted proto-feminist ideology: women were once subject to hideous abuse by men, but now they are "free" from all that, while men have been reduced, for all practical purposes, to stud service. Aunt Lydia even offers oblique praise for the more separatist feminists of our own time, and dreams of a future in which "Women will live in harmony with each other... Women united for a common end!" The irony is not lost on Offred, whose own mother had been something of a feminist termagant, fond of pornographic book burnings. "You wanted a women's culture," Offred thinks, addressing her mother. "Well, now there is one. It isn't what you meant, but it exists."

Revolutionaries seldom do get exactly what they want, but at least with ***The Handmaid's Tale*** we stand warned. There *has* been an ominous convergence between some of the ideas of the anti-feminist right and those of the cultural feminist militants. The antifeminists would like to get us all back to the kitchen, but they are also responsible for some of the most strident female supremacist literature to come out of the last two decades' gender wars. (See, for example, Phyllis Schlafly's *The Power of the Positive Woman.*) The cultural feminists, for their part, would like women to be free agents in the public sphere, but other feminists argue that their views on sex may be ultimately repressive to women. On the issue of pornography, the two sides appear to agree wholeheartedly, although just what it is, and whether it might even be defined to include a thoroughly feminist nightmare like ***The Handmaid's Tale,*** no one can say.

This tale is an absorbing novel, as well as an intra-feminist polemic. Still, it does remind us that, century after century, women have been complicit in their own undoing. Like the sadistic Aunts in ***The Handmaid's Tale,*** it was women who bound their granddaughters' feet, women who turned over their little girls for clitoridectomies, and often even women who denounced their neighbors as witches. In the long sorry story of human cruelty and pillage, women are actors as well as victims, even when, like Offred, we choose to turn our backs and burrow into the narrow world of daily life. We can do better—we *have* to do better, because that hard rain or toxic waste will fall not only on those who conspired to torture nature, but on those who merely swooned and simpered. (pp. 34-5)

Barbara Ehrenreich, "Feminism's Phantoms," in The New Republic, *Vol. 194, No. 11, March 17, 1986, pp. 33-5.*

ANN SNITOW

There's a chill on all that Margaret Atwood writes. Among the least cozy of novelists, she prefers the unimpassioned judgment to empathy, and finds—everywhere she looks—anesthetized hearts. As the years roll by and Atwood (who is also a fine poet) gives us a sixth novel—cerebral, dry, intricately written—her coldness feels bracing, a tonic against familiar sentiment; her difficulties whet the appetite for the difficult. Too, she seems to be finding substitutes for passion that burn like passion. She's simply getting better and better.

Atwood's latest, ***The Handmaid's Tale,*** is a philosophical disquisition on the idea of history (also of freedom and of hope), disguised as an intense good read, almost a game or a puzzle, but with changeable rules. One day in the early 21st century, a woman, who seems familiar enough, goes out for a pack of cigarettes and is told her money card is invalid; at work the same day, men with machine guns tell her and the other women to go home; at home she learns from her husband, who is a shade less regretful than she might wish, that all women's bank accounts are now in their husband's name; all women's jobs

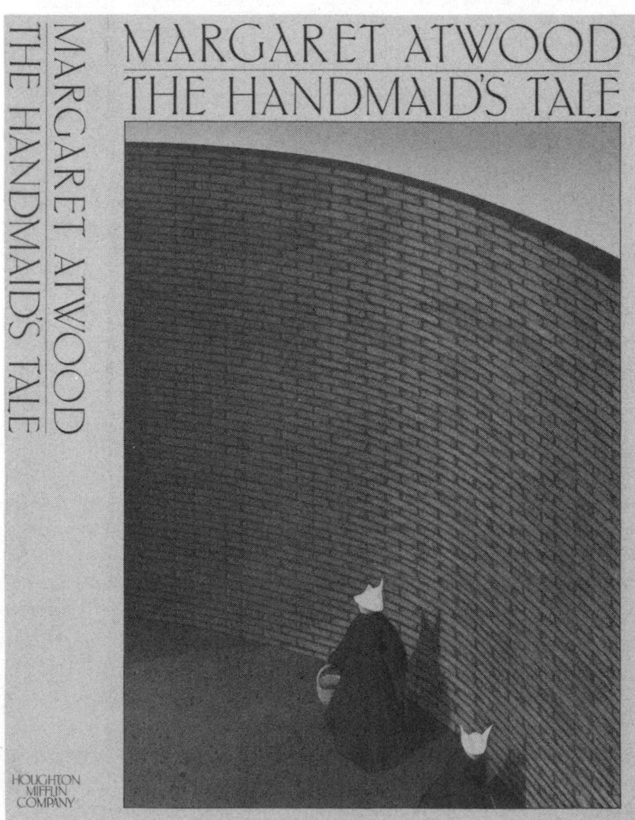

Dust jacket of The Handmaid's Tale, *by Margaret Atwood. Houghton Mifflin Company, 1985. Jacket illustration/design Fred Marcellino © 1985. Courtesy of Houghton Mifflin Company and Fred Marcellino.*

will now be done by men organized into a new, post-constitutional government. Overnight, fascism has come to America, hand in hand with religious fundamentalism. From now on, the U.S.A. is Gilead, a center of orthodoxy fighting endless skirmishes with heretics on its fluctuating margins.

The mass presence of women in public space—on the streets, at work—turns out to have been a momentary aberration of the late 20th century (or is Gilead the aberration? This is just the kind of question the writer of history finds hard to answer), and now women are again what they have been so often—disenfranchised, stripped of property, reduced to their relationships to men. . . . (p. 59)

In "the time before," Offred was one of those passive inheritors of the right to abortion and other women's freedoms fiercely won for her by her mother's generation. Now, she has to start from scratch to reinvent the concept "choice" in a world where young virgins wear white, marry by arrangement, and have never heard of feminism. The State knows Offred is "transitional," a tiny point of consciousness connecting Then with Now. The Commanders keep her and her kind prisoners of sex and hope to wait their memory out, but ironically, life as a "two-legged womb" leaves one an awful lot of freedom to think. Thinking is the loophole available at this particular place and time and Offred slips through it, making retrospection her daily occupation. She wanders among the generations, hungry for clues, a mental time traveler, gradually, a historian. She craves to know what the relationship might be between the prodigality of choices she once had in a late capitalist, consumer society and the bitter restriction in which she now lives.

Once upon a time she complained about the lack of ceremony in her busy mother's life; now her days are nothing if not ceremonious. The boredom of routine is broken only by the intensity of controlled ritual when women gather in crowds to attend births or to tear rapists apart. At a Birth Ceremony, Offred sits among the panting, excited women and thinks a little speech to her mother, now old and probably banished to the Colonies (a euphemism for areas that are, among other things, permeated with lethally toxic waste): "You wanted a women's culture. Well, now there is one. It isn't what you meant, but it exists. Be thankful for small mercies." These are the wry, threatening ironies of ***The Handmaid's Tale***. Things we think of as crisp opposites wilt and sag toward each other over historical time. "A women's culture," once such an achievement, is a mockery of itself in Gilead.

Yet when Offred thinks of "the time before," neither feminism nor freedom beckons unambiguously. She tries to remember: "They'd been in a march that day; it was during the time of the porn riots, or was it the abortion riots, they were close together. There were a lot of bombings then: clinics, video stores; it was hard to keep track." Memory has distorted and conflated what were once rival rages, but distance has also yielded its own species of truth: whether an abortion clinic or a porn store, a bombing is a bombing.

Continuity/Discontinuity: The Commander is a very familiar man. In "the time before" he was in marketing research, a manager. He smuggles Offred into his private room at night to tell her the oldest, most banal of secrets: his Wife doesn't understand him. Choking back laughter at the absurd, Offred agrees to play Scrabble with him during their illicit meetings. He is breaking all the rules especially for her (women are no longer allowed to read and write), and Offred dives into this forbidden pleasure, calling up the freedom of profligate knowledge in words like *prolix, quandry, quartz*.

One day he goes further and shows her a treasured antique, a copy of *Vogue*. In an exquisitely complex reaction. Offred calls back her faint memory of these women with their painted mouths and sassy poses, so flagrant and fearless. Red lips and slave shoes form a cultural oxymoron with audacity and freedom of choice. To Offred, the women in *Vogue* look free, though she vaguely recalls a feminist critique of these lacquered monsters of vanity.

Offred longs for the lost days of love and female mobility pictured in *Vogue,* but like the other sequestered women of the new order, she is also encouraged to remember the horrible, naked side of that former life, a time when "women were not protected." She remembers makeup, embarrassingly short skirts, rape in alleys, the anomic side of free love, and the hidden deaths buried in romance. Now, all that is changed. As the Commander reminds her, in the old days, women were always complaining—about loneliness, low pay, no child support or day care. In Gilead, he smugly notes, no one complains. (In Gilead, complainers end up dead on hooks.)

Of course, Atwood never prefers the brutal stringencies of Gilead to the free and easy rapacity of a former consumerism, but she is mesmerized by the difficulty of such relative judgments. Among the absolutes of Gilead, dualities are tempting; "either/or" feels true. Offred is tempted to ask: Which is more obscene, pornography everywhere or sexuality as a dirty secret? Which is more sexy, free love, or love so repressed it boils over? Which is better, being controlled by men or raped by them? Finally, though, she climbs off this seesaw, becoming a philosopher who rejects the simplification of opposites. Fascist Gilead is terrible, which doesn't make 1986 wonderful. Now is far better than Gilead, but Now carries the seeds of that blasted future in its womb. In either case—and even at the worst of times—change keeps working.

In fact, under the repressive surface, things are teeming in Gilead. Touch is forbidden but so intensely longed for that the brush of a hand is enough to tumble all restraint. Passwords are mumbled between seemingly docile slaves of the State. Gilead, which aspires to an iron stasis, is actually mad with angst, ripe for overthrow. The end teeters between possibilities. Does Offred escape—or not?

But this "either/or" doesn't end the story. To her Tale of Then and Now Atwood suddenly adds a third temporal dimension, tossing her readers out of Gilead and into a time 200 years later. A symposium of historians is discussing an antique text—***The Handmaid's Tale.***

It's nice to know Gilead is not the Future Atwood imagines but only a fragment of it in a larger frame. But how advanced are the historians of the 22nd century? Both women and men take part in the symposium, so here's a world where women can speak in public once more. But there's still the old pomposity of the lectern, the rumble of false objectivity, and a familiar sexist jest about the charming "chair" who introduces the meeting. Perhaps Gilead was such a terrible detour that it has taken 200 years to return to a social terrain similar to our own?

We readers can know Offred better and fear her life more; we're closer to her. In the late 20th century, we drive off in our own direction in cars, sometimes in illicit pairs; we stay in hotels with room service, thick towels, absolute privacy; we buy this and we do that. But our fragile, expensive privileges can perhaps be dissolved within days and our independence, once so taken for granted, may be contracted, like the Handmaid's, into the space of our own minds. (pp. 59-60)

Ann Snitow, "Back to the Future," in Mother Jones, *Vol. XI, No. III, April-May, 1986, pp. 59-60.*

MARY PINARD

In her new novel, the ***The Handmaid's Tale,*** Margaret Atwood creates a disturbing vision of what our near future must logically be like if we continue in the direction we're going now. You will recognize yourself in the voice of the narrator, Offred. You will feel as though you have been to the Republic of Gilead, the setting of the novel. And in a way, you have.

Based on elements of the United States of the 1980s (and before) Gilead is ruled by a male elite (the High Commanders). Here, the Bible is taken literally as a kind of Constitution. Here, it is against the law to speculate, plan, doubt. Those who do are killed and hung from large hooks on the Wall, centrally located for public viewing. Here, women are not allowed to read, own property, hold jobs, think. Here, women are sorted and uniformed according to age, economic status, the viability of ovaries. . . .

The plot is not linear; Offred's narrative is like a journal, shifting from the present to the past, from her most intimate reflections to her wry, dispassionate assessment of daily life in Gilead. Events leading up to the Gileadean era are revealed in passing by Offred, and it is eerie to realize that her past is our present. This gradual accumulation of detail makes reading the novel like reading a compelling mystery.

Atwood's brilliance as a novelist (this is her sixth) is due in part to her poetic abilities. Her prose, like her poetry, is taut, relentlessly specific, ironic. She knows both the strength of language and its vulnerability, the ease with which it can be compromised and manipulated. Such is the case in Gilead and Offred's narrative—recorded in secret, lost, and recovered in the course of the novel—it stands as proof that true language means survival.

The final section of the book puts the entire story into historical perspective. It is both delightful and disconcerting because you see that we are implicated, that we are part of the plot after all. To call this novel speculative, futurist or even cautionary allows us to distance ourselves from it and its message. In many ways, however, Offred and the Gilead she must tolerate are closer than we think.

Mary Pinard, "A Cautionary Tale," in New Directions for Women, *Vol. 15, No. 3, May-June, 1986, p. 15.*

BRUCE ALLEN

This visionary satire [***The Handmaid's Tale***], in part a feminist reworking of Orwell's *1984,* is set in the near future in an America now known as the Republic of Gilead and ruled by a savage Puritanism which has sprung up in reaction to uncontrolled violence, pornography and related forms of social license. . . . Atwood has imagined this dystopian horror in detail that's at first exhilarating, then gradually grows tiresome; there isn't enough here to power the story forward, and it eventually lapses into self-conscious linguistic trickery and predictable ironies. The protagonist Offred ("of Fred") endures a succession of representative abuses, is further victimized by her own emotions and ends up a marked woman fleeing from a death sentence. There is real substance, and suspense, in Offred's memories of her earlier life and her family, and especially in the concluding "Historical Notes" that look backward (from the year 2195) at the story we've been reading, and place it in a context of chilling irony. The book has the shape and pace of a thriller, but not the content. Only sporadically does Atwood's imagination rise to the challenge she has set herself. It's a very disappointing novel.

Bruce Allen, in a review of "The Handmaid's Tale," in Saturday Review, *Vol. 12, No. 2, May-June, 1986, p. 74.*

GAYLE GREENE

[Greene, an American professor, editor, and critic, is coeditor of The Woman's Part: Feminist Criticism of Shakespeare *(1980) and* Making a Difference: Feminist Literary Criticism *(1985). In the following excerpt Greene contrasts* The Handmaid's Tale, *with its implied critique of radical feminism, with the more doctrinaire feminist fantasies of Marge Piercy, Doris Lessing, and others.]*

Considering how many feminist writers have been turning to science fiction lately, it is not surprising to find Margaret Atwood's [sixth novel] . . . set in the future. But whereas Doris Lessing, Marge Piercy, Joanna Russ and Ursula K. Le Guin use science fiction to explore utopian societies, ***The Handmaid's Tale*** is a cautionary tale, the Republic of Gilead a dystopia in the tradition of *1984* and *Brave New World.*

The Handmaid's Tale offers a horrific vision of things to come based on an extrapolation from things as they are. In this "future history," Cambridge, Massachusetts is the center of the Republic of Gilead, a Christian fundamentalist theocracy. Threatened by a drastically declining birth rate, Gilead has institutionalized control of the female population "for breeding purposes." Atwood's narrator Offred is a handmaid: "We aren't concubines, geisha girls, courtesans. On the contrary . . . There is supposed to be nothing entertaining about us . . . We are two-legged wombs, that's all: sexual vessels, ambulatory chalices." Handmaids are given three opportunities to produce a healthy baby, three two-year duties with a "Commander of the Faithful" whose name they take (Offred's Commander is Fred). Sterility can only be her fault, since "there is no such thing as a sterile man . . . there are only women who are fruitful and women who are barren, that's the law." Failure will get her sent to the dreaded "Colonies," where she will be put to work cleaning up toxic wastes. Offred is down to her last chance.

Gilead justifies its polygamy on the basis of Old Testament precedent and "nature" (which "demands variety, for men . . . [as] part of the procreational strategy"), for, like all social orders, this one claims its practices as "natural"; "All we've done is to return things to Nature's norm.". . .

The power of Atwood's tale is in its gradual unfolding, and this second-hand account of it gives no sense of the novel's complex structure or of its delicate interplay of wit and horror. Because of Offred's lowly position in her society's hierarchy, she does not see the total picture, and we share her bewilderment and disorientation. We experience what she calls her "reduced circumstances," a circumscribed environment in which "a chair, a table, a lamp" are the world. We feel the weight of the scarlet nun's habit which is her official garb, the way it restricts movement and vision. We participate in her changed sense of her body which, no longer "an implement for the accomplishment of [her] will," becomes something which "determines" her, something "congealed around a central object, the shape of a pear." We experience her changed sense of time, "blank time," "unfilled time," time measured by the arrival of "the daily egg" on the breakfast tray and "the inevitable egg" of the monthly cycle—time as a medium to be "endured . . . heavy as fried food or thick fog." Much of this world is familiar—the house, the garden, the block, the shops, the university wall that borders Offred's neighborhood. Yet the ordinary is repeatedly defamiliarized: hooded bodies hang on the wall of what once was the Harvard Yard. "Context is all," Offred says more than once.

As Offred learns more, so do we; together we gradually piece together a picture of this society. We discover its social practices: the Birth ceremony, a communal event in which all classes of women participate in orgiastic celebration of female physicality; "Prayvaganzas" (Women's Prayvaganzas are for group weddings . . . men's are for military victories . . . the things we are supposed to rejoice in the most"); "Salvagings" (public executions); "Particicution" (in which the women are given the opportunity to tear a male limb from limb). Once a month, in "the Ceremony," the Commander tries to inseminate the Handmaid as she lies between the legs of his wife. These public, communal scenes alternate with private scenes, where the narrator, alone with herself in chapters called "Night," wonders what it all means.

Offred is no hero. She is more like a "good German" than a freedom fighter, unlike her friend Moira, a rebel and lesbian separatist whose courage she does not share but does need to believe in: "I don't want her to be like me. Give in, go along, save her skin. . . . I want gallantry from her, swashbuckling, heroism, single-handed combat. Something I lack." Offred identifies herself with the many people who, in "the time before," tried to survive by "lying low," who "lived by ignoring.":

> Ignoring isn't the same as ignorance, you have to work at it . . . there were stories in the newspapers . . . but they were about other women . . . How awful, we would say, and they were, but they were awful without being believable . . . We were the people who were not in the papers. We lived in the blank white spaces at the edges of print. It gave us more freedom. We lived in the gaps between the stories.

But Gilead, like Nazi Germany, has been brought into existence by just such "ignoring."

Offred is contrasted not only with Moira, but also with her mother, a feminist who was active in "Take Back the Night" protests, in rallies against pornography and for abortion, and who used to harangue her daughter for being "a backlash": "you young people don't appreciate things . . . You don't know what we had to go through, just to get where you are . . . how many women's lives, how many women's *bodies,* the tanks had to roll over." Offred, in short, grew up as a postfeminist. But the thoughtful reader takes the mother's feminism more seriously than the condescending daughter: "history will absolve me," says the older woman, and in ***The Handmaid's Tale*** it does.

But the feminism of the novel is not simple, for feminism too is a target of Atwood's satire. Gilead pretends to foster a "women's culture" in which women live and work together, sharing traditional female activities. After participating in the birth ceremony, the narrator thinks, "Mother . . . Wherever you may be . . . You wanted a women's culture. Well, now there is one. It isn't what you meant, but it exists." Of course Gilead is not really a women's culture, for "there's no doubt who holds the real power." But there is a spooky resemblance between the pornography burning that Offred's mother took part in and the book-burnings carried out by the right; there is a suggestion that feminist sentimentalization of women's bodies and "women's work" produces new forms of old stereotypes. The narrator criticizes Moira's separatism: "if Moira thought she could create Utopia by shutting herself in a women-only enclave she was sadly mistaken. Men were not just going to go away . . . You couldn't just ignore them," and in fact Moira's kind of ignoring has effects as disastrous as the narrator's. Atwood offers a cruel refutation of separatism when she has Moira find her separatist utopia with a vengeance at "Jezebel's," an officially-sanctioned nightclub-brothel where unassimilable females, professional women and lesbians end up—"butch paradise," as Moira calls it. The parody carries the warning that feminists must not lose sight of the larger issues. Gilead has happened partly because of the *failure* of feminism to effect social change.

As in *1984* and *Brave New World,* the authoritarian society of the future makes us long for the world of the present; and this is the aspect of ***The Handmaid's Tale*** that will spark argument and disagreement among feminists. The restrictions of Gilead make today's "rules" seem like freedom: "I remember the rules . . . Don't open your door to a stranger . . . Don't go to a laundromat, by yourself, at night," and in one of her many nostalgic "attacks of the past," the narrator goes on to "think about laundromats. What I wore to them . . . what I put in them. I think about having such control." As bad as our society is, when compared to the repressions of a totalitarian regime it is "free," for "freedom, like everything else, is relative." Laundromats represent freedom, as do short dresses, high heels, make-up—"When I think: I used to dress like that. That was freedom."

But to reject Gilead seems to leave us no alternative but to endorse the old system—our system. The Commander compares it unfavorably with his brave new world: "We've given (women) more than we've taken away. Don't you remember the singles' bars, the indignity of high school blind dates? The meat market. Don't you remember the terrible gap between the ones who could get a man easily and the ones who couldn't? . . . Think of the human misery . . . What did we overlook?" "Love," Offred answers, "falling in love"; and it is tempting to hear Atwood's voice in this reply, for a world that forbids any personal relationships, friendships or alliances makes even our own look good.

Yet Atwood's voice echoes in the Commander's rejoinder too—"oh yes, he said, I've read the magazines, that's what they were pushing, wasn't it?" Offred herself thinks about "falling in love" in a way that appears to corroborate the Commander's scepticism: "It was the central thing; it was the way you understood yourself . . . *God is love,* they once said, but we reversed that, and love, like heaven, was always just around the corner. The more difficult it was to love the particular man beside us, the more we believed in love. . . . It's strange to remember how we used to think, as if everything were available to us, as if there were no contingencies, no boundaries, as if we were free to shape and reshape the ever-expanding perimeters of our lives." *As if we were free:* if we are free, why do our ideas of ourselves, the way we define and redefine ourselves, return so insistently to the well-worn ruts of "falling in love"? Why hasn't freedom allowed us to imagine more various shapes for our lives?

Was (is) our freedom real or is it a sham? The narrator recalls women in films: "women on their own, making up their minds . . . They seemed to be able to choose. We seemed to be able to choose, then." Looking at images of women in an old copy of *Vogue,* Offred sees in their "candid eyes" "no quailing, no clinging . . . Pirates, these women." She thinks about those magazines: "What was in them was promise. They dealt in transformations; they suggested an endless series of possibilities . . . They suggested rejuvenation, pain overcome and transcended, endless love. The real promise was immortality." But isn't this promise a media hype that makes women the more miserable for continually failing at what they are told they have the "freedom" to do? Offred says "I want everything back, the way it was," but does Atwood?

I think, finally, that she does. Despite her reservations, Atwood implies that our society is preferable not only to Gilead, but to any planned society that can be imagined. Even feminist utopias have their horrors, and, as the Commander says, "Better never means better for everyone. It always means worse, for some." "Consider the alternatives," says another defender of the new order; "You see what things used to be like"; and Atwood seems to concur that these are "the alternatives"—a "free society," with all its perils, risks and abuses, or a planned society, which may entail worse. But, in the words which conclude her earlier novel, ***Surfacing,*** "there ought to be other choices." Indeed, there have to be other choices, for the alternatives allowed us by a complex industrial world are not likely to be a "free" or a "planned" society, but a choice of how society will be planned and who will do the planning.

Atwood anticipates the criticism she knew this tale would incur when she has the Handmaid say, "I wish this story were different . . . I wish it showed me in a better light." I too wish for a "different story," not in the sense that I require a more heroic protagonist, for I think ***The Handmaid's Tale*** offers something more important than a story of swashbuckling heroism by demonstrating that there is no safety in "ignoring" and that the greatest danger is in the illusion that there is. But what I do miss is some suggestion of an ideal, some sense of a better way of organizing society that will enable us to become other than we are. As one of the characters points out, "There is more than one kind of freedom . . . Freedom to and freedom from." Though Atwood questions how much freedom our society allows us, she still implies that our "freedom to" is preferable to the new order's "freedom from." But isn't there yet another kind of "freedom to" that she is not seeing—a freedom to do or be in ways that are qualitatively different from anything we who have been conditioned by this society, with its impoverished notion of possibility, can yet imagine?

Perhaps I am unfairly asking Atwood to be the utopian she is not; and I must admit to finding this novel more interesting than the more "politically correct," straightforward feminist utopias precisely because it does not offer easy solutions. Finally, perhaps, this is the tale's greatest value—its power to disturb.

Gayle Greene, "Choice of Evils," in The Women's Review of Books, *Vol. III, No. 10, July, 1986, p. 14.*

ROBERT LINKOUS

Although Margaret Atwood's [***The Handmaid's Tale***] is set in the future, it is not science fiction, but rather "speculative fiction," as she insists, because its milieu is an "extrapolation" not an invention.

The novel is the first-person narrative of a woman called Offred and is ostensibly transcribed from some thirty cassette tapes discovered not very long before the year 2195: "Elvis Presley's Golden Year" and "Boy George Takes it Off" were among the collection. Like other women in second marriages or adulterous relationships, Offred had her real name and freedom taken from her in the wake of something analogous to a coup by the Moral Majority. In the new regime, Commanders and their Wives constitute the ruling class, and Handmaids like Offred are their chattel. . . .

"There is nothing in ***The Handmaid's Tale,*** with the exception maybe of one scene, that has not happened at some point in history," Atwood told *MS* Magazine recently. "I was quite careful about that. I didn't invent a lot. I transposed to a different time and place, but the motifs are all historical motifs." But a conglomeration of "National Homelands," book burning, practices of the early Puritans, and other souvenirs of world oppression, past and present, does not necessarily add up to a convincing dystopia; nor is the prevalence of the most banal elements of the abolished culture (e.g., hamburgers, bad TV, hand lotion, Scrabble, and *Reader's Digest* treated as hard-to-acquire furtive delights) enough to render it suitably grim. What is requisite is a grinding regimen, torturous denial, and some pervasive, monstrous power of which Offred's rather hapless Commander and Wife are hardly adequate avatars, and an unremitting flood of lurid and grotesque imagery such as the largely inarticulate and undiscerning Offred manages to summon up only rarely.

But Offred had to be dim, Atwood rationalized, because hers "is only the view of one woman who lives in that society. It would be cheating to show the reader more than the character has access to. Her information is limited. In fact, her lack of information is part of the nightmare."

Cheating? Writing fiction is *lying;* and if there was such a thing as a code of ethics regarding the novel, it would dictate that the author chose the point of view that best illuminates the milieu, except when diminished perception augments mystery or can be made poignant. (Besides, if Offred's "lack of information" is part of her nightmare, it is the least part; she agonizes over the whereabouts of her daughter and the girl's father, but she could be privy to the widest array of the regime's secrets and still not know that.) Moreover, the presumptive code of ethics also would decree that a literary work must be eloquent on every page, but Offred's monotonous manner of expression just drones and drones.

Nor is this Handmaid, despite her victimization, altogether sympathetic. Her will to revolt is mainly puerile: she contemplates spitting on the Commander, tells herself "small meanminded bitter jokes" about the Wife. Occasionally, she experiences flashes of hot lust for violence, but her resentment never accumulates into obsession or rage, or motivates her to formulate a daring plan and act upon it.

The Handmaid's Tale has been compared, by the author and some critics, to *Brave New World* and *Nineteen Eighty-Four,* but the comparisons are either gratuitous or unflattering to Atwood's novel. The latter novels are legitimately compelling, even terrifying. Atwood, however, seems to regard chronological plotting as another way of cheating, and she habitually defuses suspense long before it can develop by revealing what is going to happen before it does.

"I began this novel several years ago but backed off, because I thought it was too crazy," Atwood has admitted. She should have trusted her instincts.

Robert Linkous, "Margaret Atwood's 'The Handmaid's Tale'," in San Francisco Review of Books, *Fall, 1986, p. 6.*

AMIN MALAK

[*In the following excerpt Malak examines how Atwood in* The Handmaid's Tale *infuses the conventions of the dystopian genre with her own distinctive artistry.*]

One of [***The Handmaid's Tale***'s] successful aspects concerns the skillful portrayal of a state that in theory claims to be founded on Christian principles, yet in practice miserably lacks spirituality and benevolence. The state in Gilead prescribes a pattern of life based on frugality, conformity, censorship, corruption, fear, and terror—in short, the usual terms of existence enforced by totalitarian states, instance of which can be found in such dystopian works as Zamyatin's *We,* Huxley's *Brave New World,* and Orwell's *1984*. (pp. 9-10)

What distinguishes Atwood's novel from those dystopian classics is its obvious feminist focus. Gilead is openly misogynistic, in both its theocracy and practice. The state reduces the handmaids to the slavery status of being mere "breeders." . . . The handmaid's situation lucidly illustrates Simone de Beauvoir's assertion in *The Second Sex* about man defining woman not as an autonomous being but as simply what he decrees to be relative to him: "For him she is sex—absolute sex, no less. She is defined and differentiated with reference to man and not with reference to her; she is the incidental, as opposed to the essential. He is the Subject, he is the Absolute—she is the Other." This view of man's marginalization of woman corroborates Foucault's earlier observation about the power-sex correlative; since man holds the sanctified reigns of power in society, he rules, assigns roles, and decrees after social, religious, and cosmic concepts convenient to his interests and desires.

However, not all the female characters in Atwood's novel are sympathetic, nor all the male ones demonic. The Aunts, a vicious élite of collaborators who conduct torture lectures, are among the church-state's staunchest supporters; these renegades turn into zealous converts, appropriating male values at the expense of their feminine instincts. One of them, Aunt Lydia, functions, ironically, as the spokesperson of antifeminism; she urges the handmaids to renounce themselves and become non-persons: "Modesty is invisibility, said Aunt Lydia. Never forget it. To be seen—to be *seen*—is to be—her voice trembled—penetrated. What you must be, girls, is impenetrable. She called us girls." On the other hand, Nick, the Commander's chauffeur, is involved with the underground network, of men and women, that aims at rescuing women and conducting sabotage. Besides, Atwood's heroine constantly yearns for her former marriage life with Luke, presently presumed dead. Accordingly, while Atwood poignantly condemns the misogynous mentality that can cause a heavy toll of human suffering, she refrains from convicting a gender in its entirety as the perpetrator of the nightmare that is Gilead. Indeed, we witness very few of the male characters acting with stark cruelty; the narrative reports most of the violent acts after the fact, sparing the reader gory scenes. Even the Commander appears more pathetic than sinister, baffled than manipulative, almost, at times, a Fool.

Some may interpret Atwood's position here as a non-feminist stance, approving of women's status-quo. In a review for the *Times Literary Supplement,* Lorna Sage describes ***The Handmaid's Tale*** as Atwood's "revisionist look at her more visionary self," and as "a novel in praise of the present, for which, perhaps, you have to have the perspective of dystopia." It is really difficult to conceive Atwood's praising the present, because, like Orwell who in *1984* extrapolated specific ominous events and tendencies in twentieth-century politics, she tries to caution against right-wing fundamentalism, rigid dogmas, and misogynous theosophies that may be currently gaining a deceptive popularity. The novel's mimetic impulse than aims at wresting an imperfect present from a horror-ridden future: it appeals for vigilance, and an appreciation of the mature values of tolerance, compassion, and, above all, for women's unique identity.

The novel's thematics operate by positing polarized extremes: a decadent present, which Aunt Lydia cynically describes as "a society dying . . . of too much choice," and a totalitarian future that prohibits choice. Naturally, while rejecting the indulgent decadence and chaos of an anarchic society, the reader condemns the Gilead regime for its intolerant, prescriptive set of values that projects a tunnel vision on reality and eliminates human volition: "There is more than one kind of freedom, said Aunt Lydia. Freedom to and freedom from. In the days of anarchy, it was freedom to. Now you are being given freedom from. Don't underrate it." As illustrated by the fears and agonies that Offred endures, when human beings are not free to aspire toward whatever they wish, when choices become so severely constrained that, to quote from Dostoyevsky's *The Possessed,* "only the necessary is necessary," life turns into a painfully prolonged prison term. Interestingly, the victimization process does not involve Offred and the handmaids alone, but extends to the oppressors as well. Everyone ruled by the Gilead regime suffers the deprivation of having no choice, except what the church-state decrees; even the Commander is compelled to perform his sexual assignment with Offred as a matter of obligation: "This is no recreation, even for the Commander. This is serious business. The Commander, too, is doing his duty."

Since the inhabitants of Gilead lead the precarious existence befitting victims, most try in varied ways to cope, endure, and survive. This situation of being a victim and trying to survive dramatizes Atwood's major thesis in her critical work ***Survival: A Thematic Guide to Canadian Literature,*** in which she suggests that Canada, metaphorically still a colony or an oppressed minority, is "a collective victim," and that "the central symbol for Canada . . . is undoubtedly Survival, *la Survivance*." Atwood, furthermore, enumerates what she labels "basic victim positions," whereby a victim may choose any of four possible options, one of which is to acknowledge being a victim but refuse "to accept the assumption that the role is inevitable." This position fully explains Offred's role as the protagonist-narrator of ***The Handmaid's Tale.*** Offred's progress as a maturing consciousness is indexed by an evolving awareness of herself as a victimized woman, and then a gradual development toward initiating risky but assertive schemes that break the slavery syndrome. Her double-crossing the Commander and his Wife, her choice to hazard a sexual affair with Nick, and her association with the underground network, all point to the shift from being a helpless victim to being a sly, subversive survivor. This impulse to survive, together with the occasional flashes of warmth and concern among the handmaids, transmits reassuring signs of hope and humanity in an otherwise chilling and depressing tale.

What makes Atwood's book such a moving tale is its clever technique in presenting the heroine initially as a voice, almost like a sleepwaker conceiving disjointed perceptions of its surroundings, as well as flashing reminiscences about a bygone life. As the scenes gather more details, the heroine's voice is steadily and imperceptively, yet convincingly, transfigured into a full-roundedness, that parallels her maturing comprehension of what is happening around her. Thus the victim, manipulated and coerced, is metamorphosed into a determined conniver who daringly violates the perverted canons of Gilead. Moreover, Atwood skilfully manipulates the time sequence between the heroine's past (pre-Gilead life) and the present: those shifting reminiscences offer glimpses of a life, though not ideal, still filled with energy, creativity, humaneness, and a sense of selfhood, a life that sharply contrasts with the alienation, slavery, and suffering under totalitarianism. By the end of the novel, the reader is effectively and conclusively shown how the misogynous regime functions on the basis of power, not choice; coercion, not volition; fear, not desire. In other words, Atwood administers in doses the assaulting shocks to our sensibilities of a grim dystopian nightmare: initially, the narrative voice, distant and almost diffidently void of any emotions, emphasizes those aspects of frugality and solemnity imposed by the state, then progressively tyranny and corruption begin to unfold piecemeal. As the novel concludes, as the horror reaches a climax, the narrative voice assumes a fully engaged emotional tone that cleverly keeps us in suspense about the heroine's fate. This method of measured, well-punctuated revelations about Gilead connects symbolically with the novel's central meaning: misogynous dogmas, no matter how seemingly innocuous and trustworthy they may appear at their initial conception, are bound, when allowed access to power, to reveal their ruthlessly tyrannical nature.

Regardless of the novel's dystopian essence, it nevertheless avoids being solemn; on the contrary, it sustains an ironic texture throughout. We do not find too many frightening images that may compare with Oceana's torture chambers: the few graphic horror scenes are crisply and snappily presented, sparing us a blood-curdling impact. (Some may criticize this restraint as undermining the novel's integrity and emotional validity.) As in all dystopias, Atwood's aim is to encourage the reader to adopt a rational stance that avoids *total* "suspension of disbelief." This rational stance dislocates full emotional involvement in order to create a Brechtian type of alienation that, in turn, generates an ironic charge. This rational stance too should not be total, because Atwood does want us to care sympathetically about her heroine's fate; hence the emotional distance between reader and character must allow for closeness, but up to a point. Furthermore, Atwood is equally keen on preserving the ironic flair intact. No wonder then that she concludes ***The Handmaid's Tale*** with a climactic moment of irony: she exposes, in a hilarious epilogue, the absurdity and futility of certain academic writings that engage in dull, clinically sceptic analysis of irrelevancies and inanities, yet miss the vital issues. . . . The entire "Historical Notes" at the end of the novel represents a satire on critics who spin out theories about literary or historical texts without genuinely recognizing or experiencing the pathos expressed in them: they circumvent issues, classify data, construct clever hypotheses garbed in ritualistic, fashionable jargon, but no spirited illumination ever comes out of their endeavours. Atwood soberly demonstrates that when a critic or scholar (and by extension a reader) avoids, under the guise of scholarly objectivity, taking a moral or political stand about an issue of crucial magnitude such as totalitarianism, he or she will necessarily become an apologist for evil; more significantly, the applause the speaker receives gives us a further compelling glimpse into a distant future that still harbours strong misogynous tendencies.

While the major dystopian features can clearly be located in ***The Handmaid's Tale,*** the novel offers two distinct additional features: feminism and irony. Dramatizing the interrelationship between power and sex, the book's feminism, despite condemning male misogynous mentality, upholds and cherishes a man-woman axis; here, feminism functions inclusively rather than exclusively, poignantly rather than stridently, humanely rather than cynically. The novel's ironic tone, on the other hand, betokens a confident narrative strategy that aims at treating a depressing material gently and gradually, yet firmly, openly, and conclusively, thus skilfully succeeding in securing the reader's sympathy and interest. The novel shows Atwood's strengths both as an engaging story-teller and a creator of a sympathetic heroine, and as an articulate craftswoman of a theme that is both current and controversial. As the novel signifies a landmark in the maturing process of Atwood's creative career, her self-assured depiction of the grim dystopian world gives an energetic and meaningful impetus to the genre. (pp. 11-15)

Amin Malak, "Margaret Atwood's 'The Handmaid's Tale' and the Dystopian Tradition," in Canadian Literature, *No. 112, Spring, 1987, pp. 9-16.*

Orson Scott Card

Ender's Game

Hugo Award
Nebula Award

American novelist, short story writer, critic, and editor.

Ender's Game (1985) is a novel-length expansion of Card's short story of the same name published by *Analog* in 1977. A prolific author who earned two previous Nebula and Hugo nominations for his short fiction in 1979 and 1980, Card claimed that as his novel-writing skills developed in the early 1980s, his stories kept unexpectedly burgeoning into book-length works. "By the time I was through with *Hart's Hope* [1983], *The Worthing Chronicle* [1983], and *Woman of Destiny* [1984], long treatments felt natural," he explained. "I got used to having room to flesh things out. To linger a little. To build through lots of scenes." Both Card's science fiction and mainstream writings are informed by his life-long commitment to the Mormon church. As a religious man, he commented that he often feels like an outsider in secular circles, even among other science fiction writers: "Those of us who grew up in Mormon society and remain intensely involved are only nominally members of the American community. We can fake it, but we're always speaking a foreign language."

Although in *Ender's Game* Card employs the familiar science fiction premise of a super-being who must save Earth from alien invaders, critics note that Card nonetheless creates a gripping story. Card's hero is Andrew "Ender" Wiggin, a child genius whom reviewers find likable but unbelievable, trained in space battle games in preparation for actual warfare against insect-type extraterrestrials. Reviewers commend Card for maintaining reader sympathy for Ender, despite the brutal fights he engages in, by portraying his essential innocence and empathy for the beings he must kill in order to protect humanity. Some critics judged the novel's subplot, in which Ender's sadistic brother plots to take over the world, to be a distraction, serving only to pad out the original *Analog* tale to novel length. Most agree, however, that Card's narrative gifts make Ender's story both compelling and satisfying. Card has written a sequel, *Speaker for the Dead* (1986), which continues the adventures of Ender.

(See also *Contemporary Authors,* Vol. 102.)

Photograph by Jay Kay Klein

KIRKUS REVIEWS

[***Ender's Game*** is a] rather one-dimensional but mostly satisfying child-soldier yarn which substantially extends and embellishes one of Card's better short stories ([from] ***Unaccompanied Sonata and Other Stories,*** 1980). Following a barely-defeated invasion attempt by the insect-like alien "buggers," a desperate Earth command resorts to genetic experimentation in order to produce a tactical genius capable of defeating the buggers in round two. (A counterinvasion has already been launched, but will take years to reach the buggers' home planet.) So likable but determined "Ender" Wiggin, age six, becomes Earth's last hope—when his equally talented elder siblings Peter (too vicious and vindictive) and Valentine (too gentle and sympathetic) prove unsuitable. And, in a dramatic, brutally convincing series of war games and computer-fantasies, Ender is forced to realize his military genius, to rely on nothing and no-one but himself . . . and to disregard all rules in order to win. There are some minor, distracting side issues here: wrangles among Ender's adult trainers; an irrelevant subplot involving Peter's attempt to take over Earth. And there'll be no suspense for those familiar with the short story. Still, the long passages focusing on Ender are nearly always enthralling—the details are handled with flair and assurance—and this is altogether a much more solid, mature, and persuasive effort than Card's previous full-length appearances.

A review of "Ender's Game," in Kirkus Reviews, *Vol. LII, No. 21, November 1, 1984, p. 1021.*

ROLAND GREEN

Expanded from a novella of the same title, Card's latest novel [***Ender's Game***] is one of his best. . . . Card has taken the venerable sf concepts of a superman and an interstellar war against aliens, and, with superb characterization, pacing, and language, combined them into a seamless story of compelling power. This is Card at the height of his very considerable powers—a major sf novel by any reasonable standard.

Roland Green, in a review of, "Ender's Game," in Booklist, *Vol. 81, No. 7, December 1, 1984, p. 458.*

MICHAEL LASSELL

Some people swear by science fiction, others swear at it. Fortunately, or unfortunately—depending on one's cosmic consciousness—some of the greatest writers of the century have turned their talents to it, some to create fictions that later became realities.

Orson Scott Card is not a great writer, nor does [***Ender's Game***] break any new ground. Card manages clean, fluid prose and has storytelling talent, but he has not mastered structure. His tale is too expansive and detailed throughout—too fascinated by its own hardware—but foreshortened in its conclusion. The climax of ***Ender's Game*** is a trick (on the reader as well as on Ender) for which there is no adequate preparation. This may be legitimate in an O. Henry short story . . . , but it is cheating in a novel.

The diminutive protagonist of Card's fancy is Andrew Wiggin, nicknamed Ender, the third child of an ordinary American couple. In this future America, however, third children are illegal, and Ender is stigmatized from birth. Six years old when the book begins, Ender, like his brother Peter and sister Valentine, is of superior intelligence. He is under study by the Interplanetary Forces, the supreme military organization, which is in great and hurried need of a fleet commander. (The third invasion of the dreaded "buggers," it seems, is imminent, and nowhere in the galaxy is there a genius sufficient to the task of commander.)

Ender, unknown to him, is the last hope of humankind; he's taken off to a space station Battle School. The action of the book tracks Ender's military education from age 6 to 10, as he is manipulated by omniscient adults who isolate him from family and potential friends. Card's uninspired notions of Ender's training involve increasingly complex, increasingly surreal video games and mock battles in zero gravity. Much of this material is time-worn, though the imagery is often vivid and the child hero genuinely likable. He is, however, utterly unbelievable as a child his age, genius or no.

Whether one allows oneself to become engaged in this world, I suspect, is related to one's commitment to science fiction as a genre. There are few girls in Card's future, and every non-Caucasian or non-American is designated by origin or racial characteristics. The Warsaw Pact nations are still Earth villains in the rather jingoistic subplot, and the sad lesson taught is that self-preservation is the highest human virtue.

It also is difficult to cheer Ender's string of successes, even though he is sympathetically rendered. Ender's adversaries are unworthy of him, straw boys rather than true nemeses. Whether Card intends this story for adults or children is entirely unclear, and having Ender sleep through the war on Earth after saving mankind from buggerdom is most unsportsmanlike writing.

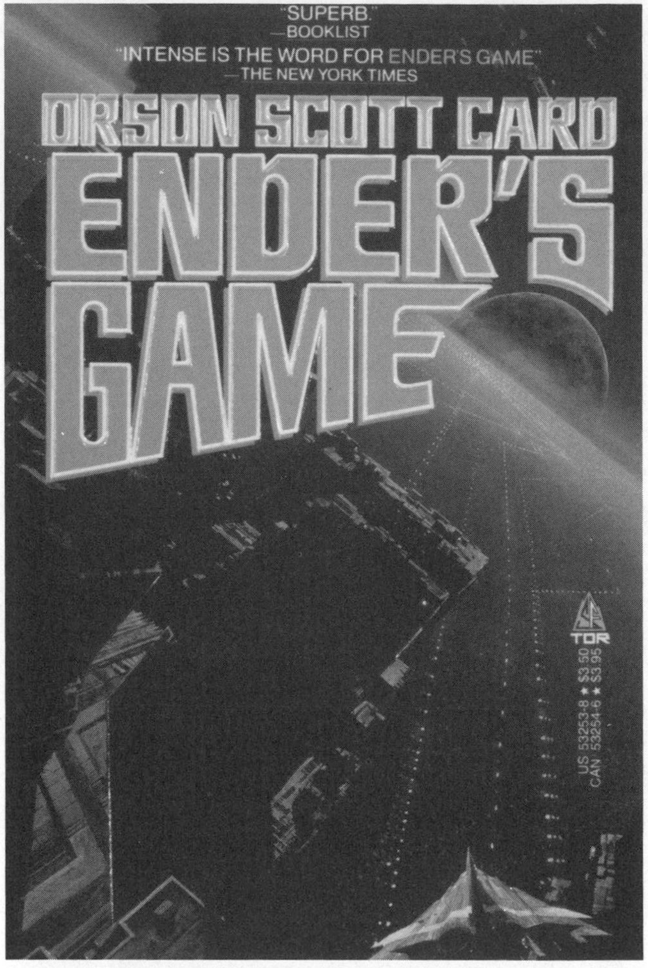

Cover of Ender's Game, *by Orson Scott Card. Tor Books, 1985. Cover art by John Harris. Reproduced by permission of Tor Books/Tom Doherty Associates.*

And, although the entire novel is marred by a dangerous value system, Card tries to redeem the militarism of his book by turning Ender into a kind of life-affirming seer for the remainder of his days. Generally speaking, Card promises more than he delivers; although it shows signs of literary life, his book will most likely be enjoyed by precocious youngsters and dedicated science-fiction fans only.

Michael Lassell, "A Youngster Saves the Planet," in Los Angeles Times Book Review, *February 3, 1985, p. 11.*

An Excerpt from *Ender's Game*

Ender turned seven. They weren't much for dates and calendars at the Battle School, but Ender had found out how to bring up the date on his desk, and he noticed his birthday. The school noticed it, too; they took his measurements and issued him a new Salamander uniform and a new flash suit for the battleroom. He went back to the barracks with the new clothing on. It felt strange and loose, like his skin no longer fit properly.

He wanted to stop at Petra's bunk and tell her about his home, about what his birthdays were usually like, just tell her it was his birthday so she'd say something about it being a happy one. But nobody told birthdays. It was childish. It was what landsiders did. Cakes and silly customs. Valentine baked him his cake on his sixth birthday. It fell and it was terrible. Nobody knew how to cook anymore, it was the kind of crazy thing Valentine would do. Everybody teased Valentine about it, but Ender saved a little bit of it in his cupboard. Then they took out his monitor and he left and for all he knew, it was still there, a little piece of greasy yellow dust. Nobody talked about home, not among the soldiers; there had been no life before Battle School. Nobody got letters, and nobody wrote any. Everybody pretended that they didn't care.

But I do care, thought Ender. The only reason I'm here is so that a bugger won't shoot out Valentine's eye, won't blast her head open like the soldiers in the videos of the first battles with the buggers. Won't split her head with a beam so hot that her brains burst the skull and spill out like rising bread dough, the way it happens in my worst nightmares, in my worst nights, when I wake up trembling but silent, must keep silent or they'll hear that I miss my family, I want to go home.

JACKIE CASSADA

Chosen as a six-year-old for his potential military genius, Ender Wiggin spends his childhood in outer space at the Battle School of the Belt. Severed from his family, isolated from his peers, and rigorously tested and trained, Ender pours all his talent into the war games that will one day repel the coming alien invasion. Card's [***Ender's Game***] is both a gripping tale of adventure in space and a scathing indictment of the militaristic mind.

Jackie Cassada, in a review of "Ender's Game," in Library Journal, *Vol. 110, No. 3, February 15, 1985, p. 182.*

GERALD JONAS

Intense is the word for Orson Scott Card's ***Ender's Game***. . . . Aliens have attacked Earth twice and almost destroyed the human species. To make sure humans win the next encounter, the world government has taken to breeding military geniuses—and then training them in the arts of war from the time they are 6 years old. The early training, not surprisingly, takes the form of "games," both physical and computer-assisted. Ender Wiggin is a genius among geniuses; he wins all the games. At the age of 10 he is assigned to Command School. He is smart enough to know that time is running out. But is he smart enough to save the planet?

I am aware that this sounds like the synopsis of a grade Z, made-for-television, science-fiction-rip-off movie. But Mr. Card has shaped this unpromising material into an affecting novel full of surprises that seem inevitable once they are explained. The key, of course, is Ender Wiggin himself. Mr. Card never makes the mistake of patronizing or sentimentalizing his hero. Alternately likable and insufferable, he is a convincing little Napoleon in short pants.

Gerald Jonas, in a review of "Ender's Game," in The New York Times Book Review, *June 16, 1985, p. 18.*

TOM EASTON

In ***Ender's Game,*** Card shows us a future threatened by the buggers, insectoid aliens who lack all speech, communicating telepathically; who feel nothing in common with nontelepaths; and who seem intent in two attacks on the solar system on exterminating the human species. To beat them, Earth needs a military leader of unsurpassed genius: quick to respond, creative, uncompromisingly violent yet empathic enough to sense an enemy's intent. To get this paragon, the generals select a couple whose genes show promise and draft their infants. But the first proves *too* violent and the second not violent enough. The third—a despised Third in a world that allows each couple only two children—is Ender Wiggin. At age six, he is removed to the orbiting Battle School to learn tactics, strategy, and leadership under extreme pressure. He plays games like any child, but the games are not always games, and the final victory becomes tragic in more ways than one.

Meanwhile, back on Earth, Ender's hateful brother and loving sister, geniuses both, are using the world's computer net. Wearing adult guises to hide their preteen ages, they are writing, debating, and influencing the masses. Their intent? To pull power for themselves from the wars to be fought on Earth after victory over the buggers. The brother especially wants to rule the world.

Game is a tale of manipulation, verbal and nonverbal, of children and mobs, of emotions and fleets. It succeeds because of its stress on the value of empathy. Its greatest villain lacks this quality most. The governmental agents who rule young Ender are as guilty of despicable acts, but they are saved by their ability to bleed for the souls they mangle.

We need not agree that empathy is a brute's saving grace to appreciate the problem Card confronts. Clearly, the evil ones of history—or, better, literature—care nothing for their victims. They relish pain and savor death, and thus in truth do we define evil. Yet heroes can cause as much damage, and if we are thoughtful we must ask just what is the difference between hero and villain.

The historian and the cynic alike say the hero is on our side. He does evil for the sake of good. Of course, the historians of the villain's side say the same, and the labels are cast in bronze medals by the winners of wars. Think of the Holy Inquisition, Vietnam, Israel, etc., ad infinitum.

The relativity of reality defies our wish for absolutes. One task of the fictioneer is thus to reconcile truth and dream, perhaps to find absolutes where there are none. Card, like many others before him, suggests that the absolute *is* empathy, and he does so very well. (pp. 180-81)

Despite his stress on empathy, he goes to great pains to shield Ender's childish innocence from truth, to keep us from calling him one more brute of history.

Read and enjoy, my friends. And reserve your skepticism of Ender's talents, remarkable enough in an adult, much less a little kid. Remember—the kid's a genius. (p. 181)

Tom Easton, in a review of "Ender's Game," in Analog Science Fiction / Science Fact, *Vol. CV, No. 7, July, 1985, pp. 180-81.*

E(dgar) L(aurence) Doctorow

World's Fair

The American Book Awards: Fiction

American novelist, short story and novella writer, editor, essayist, and dramatist.

With *World's Fair* (1985), his sixth novel, Doctorow continues the experimental blending of historical fact and invention that characterizes his work. Like his novel *Ragtime* (1976), which earned both the National Book Critics Circle and American Academy of Arts and Letters awards, *World's Fair* won laurels for its imaginative recreation of a period in American history.

A former book editor and publisher, Doctorow is one of the rare contemporary bestselling authors who attracts serious attention from critics while entertaining a general audience. Reviewers called *Ragtime* an ingenious panorama of life in New York during the early twentieth century, with its juxtaposition of actual events and historical figures with fictional ones. They also praised the skill with which Doctorow, in *The Book of Daniel* (1971), uses the case of Julius and Ethel Rosenberg, the American couple executed in 1953 for espionage, as the basis for fictional speculation. In *World's Fair,* Doctorow draws upon his personal experiences as a child growing up in New York during the Great Depression. His narrator, a middle-aged man named Edgar, relates anecdotes about his childhood crowned by his visits to New York's famous World's Fair in 1939. Reviewers note that numerous details of Edgar's life, including his parents' first names and his boyhood street address, correspond to biographical information about Doctorow himself. From this several critics conclude that *World's Fair* is not a genuine novel but thinly disguised autobiography. Doctorow called the book an ''illusion of a memoir.'' He also explained: ''I make books for people to live in, as architects make houses. I lived in it by writing it. Now it's the reader's turn. When an architect does a house, do you say to him, 'Is this house autobiographical?' ''

Reviewers praised *World's Fair* as a well-researched, accurate impression of the 1930s. Edgar's anecdotal recreation of his boyhood failed to interest some critics, but the majority observed that, in describing the mundane settings and occurrences in Edgar's life, Doctorow infuses them with their own engaging narrative tension. Edgar's reminiscences, a few critics averred, invoke nostalgia for a Jewish childhood in Depression-era New York even in those who never lived in Edgar's particular time and place. Many reviewers also found merit in Doctorow's portrayal of the young Edgar's development from infancy to age nine, comparing his confrontations with mortality and sexuality and his growing writer's conciousness to those of Stephen Daedalus in James Joyce's *A Portrait of the Artist as a Young Man.* States critic T. O. Treadwell, ''Doctorow's portrait of the artist when young may not be in the Joycean class, . . . but it is a considerable achievement.''

(See also *CLC,* Vols. 6, 11, 15, 18, 37; *Contemporary Authors,* Vols. 45-48; *Contemporary Authors New Revision Series,* Vol. 2; *Dictionary of Literary Biography,* Vols. 2, 28; and *Dictionary of Literary Biography Yearbook: 1980.*)

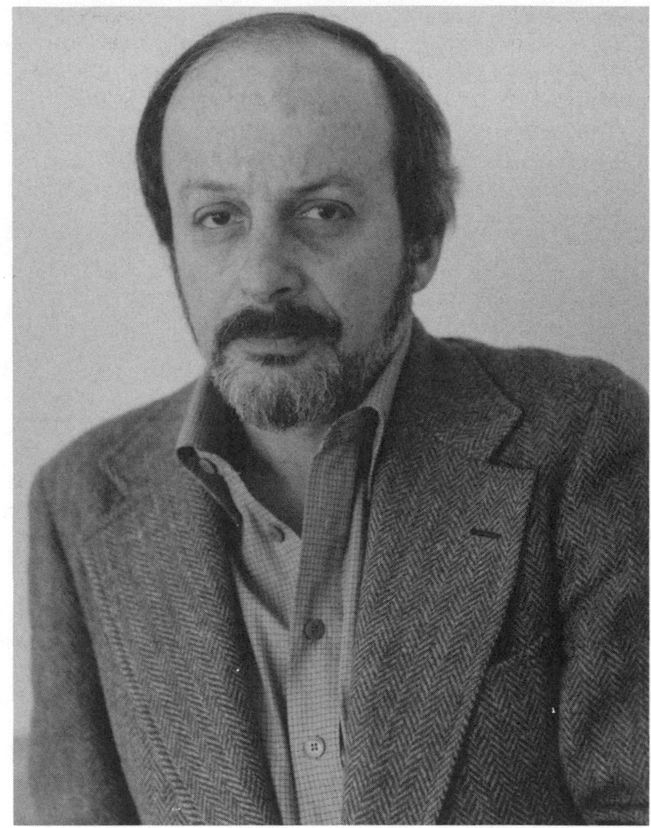

PUBLISHERS WEEKLY

In his most powerful book to date [***World's Fair***], Doctorow (***Ragtime, Lives of the Poets,*** etc.) fashions a moving story from obviously autobiographical material. Edgar Altshuler, like Doctorow, and bearing his first name, grows up in the Bronx in the 1930s. The tensions between his parents, Rose and Dave (again, the names of Doctorow's mother and father) are dimly perceived by the child and become more clear as he gets older. Similarly, events in the outside world—the Depression, the war in Europe—impinge on his consciousness with increasing clarity. When Rose and the family's older son, Donald, take over the narration, they add their own, somewhat differing impressions of a period when the family's fortunes are sinking and the future seems precarious. The final scene of the book, a visit to the 1939 World's Fair, is an ironic reminder of the fair's hopeful theme, ''The World of Tomorrow,'' and a crucial event in Edgar's rite of passage.

Doctorow's impressive accomplishment here is to calibrate the novel's tone with marvelous precision. The narrator's memories are always appropriate to his chronological age, significant and believable. They are the kinds of things a boy would remember: the arrival of the coal delivery truck, Sunday visits to grandparents, catching sight of the German zeppelin *Hindenburg,* listening to *The Shadow* on the radio—idyllic events underscored by a primeval fear, "enormous looming fearful attacks of unnamed chaos of the heart." An emergency operation for appendicitis has the elements of myth in seeming to leave the boy vulnerable to mysterious evil. In addition to capturing the universals of childhood, however, Doctorow evokes the specific condition of being a Jewish child in that time and place. He does it so well that the book should immediately become a classic.

Lyrical in its telling, resonantly expressive of the universal aspects of human life, this wise and tender novel will haunt readers with its resurrected memories.

A review of "World's Fair," in Publishers Weekly, *Vol. 228, No. 11, September 13, 1985, p. 124.*

CHRISTOPHER LEHMANN-HAUPT

When you finish reading E. L. Doctorow's marvelous new novel, ***World's Fair,*** you shake your head in disbelief and ask yourself how he has managed to do it. After all, the book is about nothing more than a lower-middle-class boy growing up in the Bronx between the years 1936 and 1940. And beyond the experience of most boys between the ages of 5 and 9, not all that much happens to Edgar Altschuler—a burst appendix, the discovery of his grandmother's corpse on the morning she dies, an attack at knifepoint by a couple of anti-Semitic bullies. Yet you get lost in ***World's Fair*** as if it were an exotic adventure. You devour it with the avidity usually provoked by a suspense thriller.

The most obvious if superficial explanation is the book's nostalgic appeal, at least for anyone who happens to have experienced a New York City childhood in the 1930's. Though chocolate egg creams never appear in these pages, everything else does from Fleers Double Bubble Gum to the Green Hornet, from the lyrics of "Deep Purple" to the words of the Little Blue Book, *Ventriloquism Self-Taught.*

Yet these aren't simply evoked as totems of childhood. They are savored in retrospect by a mature intelligence whose memory of childhood is uncannily vivid yet who keeps his unsentimental distance with the mock solemn prose that has become Mr. Doctorow's inimitable music. He has never played that music more charmingly than in these pages. "I did not like Humpty Dumpty, who lacked all manly definition and was so irrevocably fragile. Georgie Porgie, Jack Horner, Jack and Jill, all seemed to me unnatural abstractions of child existence; there was some menacing propaganda latent in their circumstances but I couldn't quite work out what it was. It was a strange planet they lived on, some place of enormous fearful loneliness and punishment. Or it was as if they were dead but continued to be alive."

The frequent mention of death in the novel also draws the reader on. Not that one expects some unforeseen catastrophe. Indeed, we know the worst—and the best—of the family's fate in advance through intermittent statements in the text made by Edgar's mother, Rose, and various other relatives; these statements serve both to speed up and brake the narrative's momentum. But death is associated with some nameless dread that bothers Edgar intermittently. Death, a fear of suffocating, and grief "for the dark mysterious things that my parents did in the privacy of their relationship"—these anxieties are linked to Edgar's idea of growing up. They impel him to seize the future for better or for worse. They impel us to learn how he will survive the confrontation.

And then of course there is the symbol of that future, the 1939 World's Fair, which was mounted in the Queens Flushing meadowlands. The fair isn't even mentioned until page 185 of the novel, but its presence in the title and its representation in the phallic Trylon and Perisphere that decorate each chapter heading, serve to arouse our curiosity in the role it will play. And in the novel's final hundred pages, it looms large over the story's landscape. How will Edgar ever get there? Will his unreliable father fulfill a promise to take him? Will he win an essay contest that holds out the chance of free admission? Or will he go with a playmate whose mother works there in some questionable capacity? The answers to these questions come to matter considerably.

And what symbolic use will Mr. Doctorow make of the fair? To many who remember it and to some who don't, the 1939 New York World's Fair has become a heavy irony, a symbol of the streamlined future displayed at a moment in history when the very idea of the future had begun to look a little grim. And in the subsequent half century, the future that the fair envisioned has been mocked by traffic jams and industrial pollution.

Yet if irony is what Mr. Doctorow has in mind with his use of the fair, he leaves it to the reader to supply it. The only character who makes ideological hay of the fair is Edgar's politically leftist father, but his voice doesn't count for much in the novel. In any case, it is always dangerous to equate the radical voices embodied in Mr. Doctorow's fiction with the voice of the novelist himself. Only if one is confused about the point of view of ***The Book of Daniel, Ragtime,*** and ***Lives of the Poets*** is one likely to read politics into ***World's Fair.***

What the novel is really about is the idea of the future in the mind of a developing child, how hope wins out over the threat of death and annihilation. As Edgar grows, he becomes aware of his father's failing business, of his parents' failing marriage, of the world's failing chances for peace. But his vision of the World's Fair, rendered erotic by the novel's subtle interplay of plot and fantasy, serves to arm him and give him strength.

The middle-aged narrator looks back on his childhood with amused amazement at the disasters he survived. The Hindenburg crashed, after looming over him like "an enormous animal leaping from the sky in monumental slow motion." But the Trylon and Perisphere thrust its spire into the sky. The drama of these balancing events is so vivid that one might mistake it for autobiography. It is far more than that. It is E. L. Doctorow's most accomplished artistic performance to date.

Christopher Lehmann-Haupt, in a review of "World's Fair," in The New York Times, *October 31, 1985, p. C23.*

WALTER CLEMONS

E. L. Doctorow has long been attracted to the idea of a novel as "false document"—Kenneth Rexroth's phrase for one of the first modern fictions, Defoe's *A Journal of the Plague Year.* He has repeatedly tried to dissolve the boundary between the factually verifiable and the invented and make us believe his fiction is "true." ***Ragtime*** (1975) was boldly different from the traditional historical novel in which public figures made stately appearances. If Napoleon in *War and Peace* had made love to Natasha, there might have been a precedent for the mix-up of Father, Mother and Younger Brother with Emma Goldman, Evelyn Nesbit and Harry Houdini in Doctorow's extravaganza. Readers excitedly asked whether Henry Ford and J. P. Morgan ever "actually" met. "They have now," Doctorow calmly said. ***Ragtime***'s extremely graceful, mock-documentary prose was a triumph of stylistic aplomb that Doctorow's next books, ***Loon Lake*** and ***Lives of the Poets,*** failed to match.

"You always try to make people believe what you're writing so they'll say, 'Gee, did that really happen? Was it true?'" Doctorow told an interviewer [in 1984] when his quasi-autobiographical sequence of linked stories, ***Lives of the Poets,*** was published. Some years earlier he told a questioner that his excellent first novel, ***Welcome to Hard Times,*** taught him "my strength, which was *not* autobiographical writing. Somehow I was the kind of writer who had to put myself through prisms to find the right light—I had to filter myself from my imagination in order to write." He said that ***The Book of Daniel*** "has to be done in *his* voice, not my own."

It would be incautious, then, to take Doctorow's new book, ***World's Fair,*** for what it seems. It's the apparent reminiscence, from bed-wetting babyhood to the age of nine, of a boy named Edgar—born on the same day as Edgar Laurence Doctorow—whose parents bear the same first names as Doctorow's own. Mother plays the piano, Father runs a music store on Sixth Avenue in New York's old Hippodrome building, as Doctorow's parents did. Almost the only visible fictional invention, late in the book, is that the family's name is Altschuler.

Young Edgar responds to the sights, smells and sounds of Eastburn Avenue in the Bronx, where Doctorow grew up. The boy enters elementary school, idolizes his older brother, overhears his parents' quarrels with a child's imperfect understanding and eventually wins honorable mention in an essay contest on the theme of The Typical American Boy, which of course Edgar isn't. His essay wins him and his family passes to the 1939 World's Fair, and the climax of the novel is the family's visit to that great, futuristic exhibition on the eve of World War II.

In producing an entirely convincing facsimile of a loving, discursive, rather tedious memoir by a long-winded middle-aged author, Doctorow has successfully suppressed any detectable evidence of novelistic invention, plot complication or fictional surprise. Was this worth doing?

One picks one's way through exquisitely rendered details of a lost way of life in New York 50 years ago. . . .

Doctorow successfully avoids the pitfall of false naiveté likely to afflict a boyhood narrative of this kind. His tone is measured and exactly gauged, his prose is rapt and steady. I would like to like his book better. When the Altschuler family finally arrives at the World's Fair, they have a terrific time. . . . Some cheap thrills would be welcome—a faint trace of plot, maybe, to pep up the glacierlike progression of Edgar's days. Doctorow's exact contemporary Philip Roth, in *Zuckerman Bound,* recently completed a stinging, comic quasi-autobiography that Doctorow's ruminations don't even approach in shrewdness, seriousness and sheer fun. Of course, ***World's Fair*** is only a childhood memoir. The later years of Edgar Altschuler may prove more exciting. ***World's Fair*** is a work of austere majesty, slow, pretty and dull.

Walter Clemons, "In the Shadow of the War," in Newsweek, *Vol. CVI, No. 19, November 4, 1985, p. 69.*

PETER CONN

E. L. Doctorow's ***World's Fair*** is a story of growing-up, consisting almost entirely of Edgar Altschuler's recollections of his childhood in the Depression and told in a stripped down language that avoids bravura. The key to the novel's point of view lies in lines from Wordsworth that Doctorow quotes as his epigraph: "A raree-show is here, / With children gathered round . . ." Through Edgar's eyes, the 1930s become a raree-show, a world more of spectacle than politics.

The main events in the novel are those that happen inside the family. The global history of the '30s intrudes, but only as it becomes part of the boy's own experience. Thus, the Depression means primarily a sequence of ever-smaller houses into which Edgar and his family move.

Lists are not literature, and Doctorow relies rather too often on catalogues of brand names as a sentimental short-cut to the past. (p. 1)

However, Doctorow's main purpose in creating a narrator of such extreme simplicity is not to evade history but to confront it more directly. Edgar is intended as a kind of emotional and moral perspective device, whose own innocence and transparency permit the facts he reports to speak powerfully for themselves. The history of the Depression and the slide into war becomes the education of a young boy, and the calamitous events of the 1930s are thereby rescued from familiarity and regain something of their outsize scale.

Doctorow has always been stronger as a maker of separate scenes than as a storyteller, and the autobiographical technique of ***World's Fair*** enables him to offer a series of episodes that reveal his thematic purposes. He invents some of the episodes, while he borrows others—as in ***Ragtime*** and ***The Book of Daniel***—from history. When Edgar is 3, for example, his older brother builds an igloo in the backyard. At first, this is a mysterious, inviting habitat. After a week or two, it becomes dirty, misshapen, boring, and then it simply melts. Here is an emblem for the decay of childhood wonder, the transience of human achievement, and the futility of utopian dreams.

Several years later, in 1936, one of Edgar's most exalted moments occurs when he sees overhead the airship *Hindenburg,* silver and huge and mighty, tilted toward him "as if she was an enormous animal leaping from the sky in monumental slow motion." That same evening, while listening to *The Answer Man* and *I Love a Mystery,* Edgar hears the news bulletin that the *Hindenburg* has crashed at Lakehurst, New Jersey. The symbolic point is obvious: the effort to soar above the jumble of the world leads to catastrophe.

It is above all the 1939-1940 World's Fair itself that provides Doctorow with his most extended and resonant cluster of images. What had been a swamp in Flushing, Long Island—"the valley of ashes" in Scott Fitzgerald's *The Great Gatsby*—suddenly became the World of Tomorrow.

The Fair's inspirational symbolism was calculated and timely. The country was mired in the 10th year of the worst depression in its history. Despite the palliatives of the New Deal, recovery was not yet clearly in sight. The Fair inspired hope: like its sleek, modern buildings, America would rise out of stagnation and create a prosperous, carefree future. For a few hours at least, visitors could leave behind the dreariness of unemployment and class struggle and enter an ideal world of rational planning in which social problems found elegant solutions.

History, as usual, had other plans. Within a few months of the Fair's opening, Hitler invaded Poland and the dream of tomorrow became the nightmare of war and holocaust. In the fall of 1940, as America inched closer to entering the war, the World's Fair quietly closed, and demolition of its buildings commenced more or less immediately.

In short, simply to juxtapose the Fair and the war is to create a kind of morality play, in which history becomes cautionary myth. The irony in all this is intense, almost theatrical, and Doctorow finds it irresistible. As he manipulates Edgar's wide-eyed responses, Doctorow dramatizes both the power and the limits of illusions. The Fair is dazzling, but it is ersatz, and its World of Tomorrow is on a tiny scale. It has the charm and irrelevance of a toy.

When Edgar makes his second visit to the Fair, just before it closes down, he walks up to the Trylon and Perisphere, those famous linked symbols of the future. Edgar notices for the first time the gypsum board of which the two structures are made. In the sunlight, the whiteness of the Perisphere turns silver and "I could imagine it as the flank of a great airship. Then I could see where the paint was peeling." Here Doctorow knits several of his major motifs together: The Perisphere resembles both a great airship, such as the doomed *Hindenburg,* and the igloo Edgar had entered seven years earlier.

Near the end of the novel, Edgar watches a newsreel of the burial of the Time Capsule, that extraordinary attempt to communicate with the future by sealing up an assortment of the commonplace objects that filled the material world of 1939. Then, in the novel's final scenes, Edgar buries his own time capsule, stuffed with some of his own possessions: a Tom Mix Decoder badge, a handwritten four-page biography of Franklin D. Roosevelt, a harmonica. The real time capsule, of course, is this novel, filled with the memorabilia of Doctorow's own childhood. It is his effort to decode, reconstruct and chronicle a personal version of the 1930s, that receding but tumultuous and decisive decade. (p. 4)

Peter Conn, "E. L. Doctorow's Time Capsule," in Book World—The Washington Post, *November 17, 1985, pp. 1, 4.*

RICHARD EDER

World's Fair is E. L. Doctorow's portrait of the artist as a young child. The author's alter-ego, Edgar Altschuler, grows into an awareness that the world stretches far beyond the protective confines of a Bronx Jewish household.

It was a quieter passage than Stephen Daedalus' vehement breakout from a constricted Dublin youth, and conducted with far greater cautiousness. Yet in some ways, Edgar's constriction, because more cherishing, was greater; the great world more ominous, and his passage more painful.

Less grand too, and less universal. E. L. Doctorow, like everyone else, perhaps including the author of *Finnegans Wake,* is no James Joyce. What he is, though, is a writer of implacable intelligence. The subject of growing up is not so much a literary theme as a literary subspecies. Yet ***World's Fair,*** like a superior marathon runner, starts in a crowd of thousands and bit by bit—there's Philip Roth, right beside you; and watch out for Saul Bellow's left elbow—is running, not necessarily in front, but unmistakably by itself. . . .

The Altschulers live in a comfortable Bronx apartment, then in a slightly less comfortable one. A second move takes them to even smaller quarters in a less desirable neighborhood, but still in the secure brick Jewish section and away from the Irish and Italian slums. The family is trying to stay in the middle class but is never entirely free from threat.

David, an expansive, vaguely unsound businessman, loses his downtown music store and takes a salesman's job. Rose, on a dollar a day for housekeeping, is dutiful, intelligent and angry. Donald, Edgar's brother and eight years older, is both distant and kind. If the Depression and a crooked business partner constitute outside threats, there are tensions on the inside that run beneath the love and nurturing.

There is nothing remarkable about this nor about any of the events and memories of Edgar's childhood. What gives ***World's Fair*** its character is its quality of recollection and narration; the mingling of experience as a child sees it and as an adult remembers it; and above all, the sense of a consciousness breaking through its shell.

There is a curious evolution. The youngest memories are rendered with a marvelous clarity and perfect detail. There are games, family visits and expeditions. There are the neighborhood shops: for example, the Great Atlantic and Pacific Tea Co.—before its metamorphosis into the A&P supermarket—with sawdust on the floor, a pervasive smell of coffee, and the clerk toting up the purchases with a pencil on the edge of a shopping bag.

Everything is evoked with singular perfection, yet it lies inert. There is none of the feeling of transcendence, mystery, or possibility that marks other childhood accounts. Edgar was a young prince, but a prince resembling Zigismund in *Life Is a Dream:* imprisoned. He was dominated by his need to feel special and by his dependence upon grown-ups to provide him with that feeling.

He couldn't stand Mother Goose, for example, nor tales of the gods or saints, nor anything that suggested the random commonality and capriciousness of life. Only as he grows older, more independent, more powerful, do his recollections change from perfect pictures to something that stirs. Life was not what happened to you but what you could do.

It is a double stirring, away from his family's ability to define him and into his own possibilities. "One had as resources only one's self, one's brother, one's parents and then, perhaps, President Roosevelt," a narrator writes of his early sense of circumscription. Later, at the circus, he watches the clown who begins by clumsily imitating the aerialists and suddenly emerges as the star of the high wire. "It was not merely that I, the sniffler with the red nose, would someday in my good time reveal myself to be a superman among men. . . . What was first true was then false, a man was born from himself."

Doctorow evokes Edgar's gradual maturing with something close to magic. His account of a near-fatal peritonitis manages to convey a child's sense of death from the inside; it may be the most remarkable passage in the book.

School, where Edgar does well both socially and in his work, is a kind of flowering. Portents drift in. A runaway car smashes a pedestrian through the school fence, killing her. One afternoon, the German zeppelin Hindenburg passes overhead, a ship of dreams and, as the pride of Nazi Germany, of menace. An hour or two later, it will explode and burn in Lakeville, N.J.

Each of these things engages Edgar's sensibility, luring it gradually out of fortified childhood. He makes friends with Meg, whose mother, a burlesque dancer, is everything that Edgar's family detests. She and Meg, whom Edgar is half in love with, make something approaching a second home for him.

And they take him to the World's Fair where Meg's mother has a job as a striptease swimmer. This exuberant vision of the half-possible, half-impossible future, set in Queens, most prosaic of New York boroughs and home of thousands of families like the Altschulers, becomes for Edgar and for us an utterly convincing emblem of his transplanting. The following year, having won his essay prize, he will affirm the emblem by treating his family to a Fair visit: the provider instead of the provided-for.

Doctorow, leading Edgar into the world on his own shaky legs, has renewed an old theme in his quite individual way. His Daedalus lacks wings, but manages perfectly well on the subway.

Richard Eder, in a review of "World's Fair," in Los Angeles Times Book Review, *November 24, 1985, p. 3.*

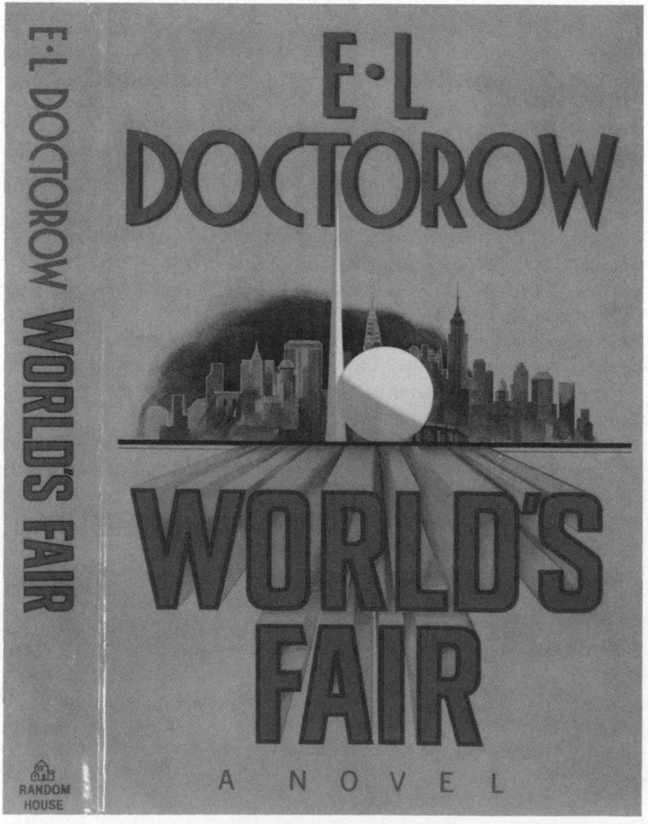

Dust jacket of World's Fair, *by E. L Doctorow. Random House, 1985. Jacket illustration and design by Paul Bacon. Courtesy of Random House, Inc.*

J. HOBERMAN

Is E. L. Doctorow that "reborn novelist" whose coming Leslie Fiedler prophesied 15 years ago in *Playboy* magazine? Or is he that dream's instant recuperation? From ***Welcome to Hard Times*** to ***The Book of Daniel*** to ***Ragtime***—that is, from revisionist western (Fiedler's privileged form) to countercultural critique to outlandish commercial success—Doctorow has operated in the gap between elite and mass culture. Although Fiedler has never to my knowledge deigned to acknowledge it, Doctorow's themes—not to mention his trajectory—suggest, more than those of any other contemporary writer, Fiedler's "popular, not quite reputable, a little dangerous" practitioner of "mythological Americanism."

Perhaps because three of his novels have been turned into movies, Doctorow seems to be part of mass culture. He is often bracketed with Robert Altman, the ace genre deconstructor, who was originally supposed to direct the film version of ***Ragtime.*** But, in another sense, Doctorow is just as close to that arch genre reconstructor Steven Spielberg. ***Loon Lake,*** in particular, is as complex, calculated, and nostalgic a pastiche as *Raiders of the Lost Ark*—except, instead of *Casablanca* and *King Solomon's Mines,* Doctorow is mining Theodore Dreiser and F. Scott Fitzgerald, John Dos Passos and James M. Cain, *Nightmare Alley* and *The New Masses*.

Doctorow, in short, is full of contradictions. Here is a best-selling author who is also a serious artist (the measure of commitment his brave plunge from the giddy heights of ***Ragtime*** into the icy depths of ***Loon Lake***), a left-wing novelist who gets his picture on the cover of *The New York Times Magazine,* a writer of historical fictions whose best known book is a little fugue of outrageous factoids. ***World's Fair*** is another reversal: the man who has always eschewed autobiography (as recently as 1980 he declared, "I don't take characters directly from my own life or experience") has written what appears to be, on the surface at least, a sentimental memoir of his Bronx boyhood.

A constant in Doctorow is his particular fascination with the American past, a recognition of the logic by which period styles and/or the history of artistic fashions come to stand for history itself. Along with Spielberg, if to different ends, Doctorow perceives America as theme park. This is explicit in the title of ***World's Fair,*** but not for nothing does ***The Book of Daniel,*** still Doctorow's most passionate and disturbing novel, use Disneyland—"a technique of abbreviated shorthand culture for the masses, a mindless thrill, like an electric shock, that insists at the same time on the recipient's rich psychic relation to his country's history and language and literature"—as the backdrop for one of its major revelations. (Indeed, with its immediately graspable formal relation to television or *People,* ***Ragtime*** is sort of a mindful thrill, a left-wing Disneyland.) . . .

Doctorow has suggested that ***The Book of Daniel*** is "not about the Rosenbergs but about the idea of the Rosenbergs" and that ***Loon Lake*** is "about our idea of the Thirties." In much the same sense, I imagine, he recently called ***World's Fair*** "the illusion of a memoir"—although this undoubtedly seems a perverse description of a mainly first-person, highly episodic narration in which the hero shares Doctorow's first name (Edgar), age, family configuration (older brother named Donald, mother named Rose), and childhood address.

World's Fair takes Edgar from his earliest memory (wetting the bed at age two, "startled awake by the ammoniated mists . . .") through a half-dozen years' worth of accidents, seders, and radio shows, to a triumphant pair of trips to the 1939-40 World's Fair—half honky-tonk, half utopia and altogether more august than the SoCal cartoonland where Daniel and Selig Mindish meet face to face. The novel's epigram comes from *The Prelude* but, *pace* Wordsworth, ***World's Fair*** might well be subtitled "Intimations of Mortality." Death is the underlying theme—first Edgar's dog, then his grandmother. A fatal car accident outside his school foreshadows the Hindenburg disaster (in one of the novel's set pieces he sees the great airship sailing overhead "like a scoop of sky come down to earth"). Oblivion looms even closer when Edgar's appendix ruptures and then again when a pair of Christian bullies put their knives to his gut after he wanders from the confines of his own Bronx neighborhood.

Almost brutally prosaic, Doctorow resolutely glosses over those scenes redolent of magic realism (a hospital ward full of dying children, the revelation that Edgar's Yiddish-speaking grandma smokes pot for her asthma). What counts is the mimesis of total recall—minute sensations and critical judgments. For every inspired account of suffering through the fall sale at Klein's or discovering, under the boardwalk at Rockaway, "an item so loathsome, so evil, that the very word itself was too terrible to pronounce," there are two additions to the ongoing litany of brand names and radio serials.

Like America itself, ***World's Fair*** is overloaded with fastidiously drawn pop culture artifacts. "The Shadow had no imagination," Edgar decides. "He neither looked at naked women nor thought of ridding the world of dictators like Hitler or Mussolini. If his program hadn't been on a Sunday afternoon, I would probably not have listened to it." (As a kid's observation this is convincingly banal. On the other hand, making Edgar's favorite film star Frances Farmer is so blatantly oversophisticated there can be no excuse except that this was actually true of young Doctorow.)

Despite its naturalism, the Doctorow novel that ***World's Fair*** most resembles is clearly ***Ragtime***. It's just as wrapped in the web of the media; its language is as controlled in its way as the coolly unadorned declarative sentences that contributed to ***Ragtime***'s tour de force. The razzmatazz quotient, however, is far lower. The voice here is solemn and overprecise: Edgar emerges as a self-important, slightly pedantic child. (Is Doctorow satirizing Wordsworth's sense of himself as a chosen being even as he substitutes the universe of comic books, movies, and radio shows for the English Romantic's natural world?) Although he sometimes falters, Doctorow manages to effect a double style, at once mature and childish—occasionally drawing on "oral history"-type observations from mother or brother to help out. (The child may be father to the man, but the father in ***World's Fair*** never really jells.) "In my own consciousness I was not a chilld," Edgar recalls. "When I was alone, not subject to the demands of the world, I had the opportunity to be the aware sentient being I knew myself to be." What's striking about ***World's Fair*** is how conscientiously Doctorow maps the expanding perimeters of Edgar's awareness—his growing consciousness of his mother's unhappiness, his father's failure, the fragility of peace and order. What's equally striking is just how calculated a construction Edgar's worldview is.

Edgar is the seven-year-old as intellectual: "I did not like Humpty Dumpty, who lacked all manly definition and was so irrevocably fragile. Georgie Porgie, Jack Horner, Jack and Jill, all seemed to me unnatural abstractions of child existence, there was some menacing propaganda latent in their circumstances . . ." It's one of the book's jokes that after nearly 300 pages of Edgar's narration, Doctorow inserts the prize-winning essay—the ***Ragtime,*** in a sense—that will provide the boy with a triumphant trip to the World's Fair: "The typical American Boy is not fearful of Dangers. . . . He roots for his home team in football and baseball but also plays sports himself. He reads all the time. It's all right for him to like comic books so long as he knows they are junk . . ."

As an attempt to recreate a child's consciousness, ***World's Fair*** has little in common with Andrei Bely's *Kotik Letaev,* certain stories by Bruno Schulz, Freud's *The Sexual Enlightenment of Children,* or Henry Roth's *Call It Sleep*. The Roth Doctorow suggests is Philip. ***World's Fair*** belongs to the tradition of the Bronx-Brownsville-Newark bildungsroman. Were it not so thin, it could almost be a deadpan satire of *Making It, New York Jew,* or *A Margin of Hope*. The landscape, the moral seriousness, and even the issues are the same. Like Howe or Kazin, Edgar is grappling with art, politics, sex, money, family, ambition, and Jewishness—except from the perspective of a middle-aged kid. And just as surely, his writing leads him to the Promised Land.

That shining city, incidentally, is surprisingly benign. . . . A bonanza of experimental progaganda techniques and futuristic consumerism, the 1939-40 World's Fair (also known as the "World of Tomorrow") seems almost too juicy a metaphor, but Doctorow is curiously restrained. His account of Edgar's two trips to Flushing Meadow (one in the company of a little girl whose mother works there under somewhat sleazy conditions, the other with his own more proper family) are the most compelling aspects of the novel. Yet the landscape resists the visionary—the illusion of sentimentality is far too real.

World's Fair ends with Edgar burying his own time capsule in imitation of the Westinghouse exhibit at the fairgrounds. He includes a Tom Mix Decoder badge, a school assignment biography of FDR (for which he received a 100), a harmonica, two Tootsy Toy rocket ships, a book on ventriloquism self-taught, and one of his mother's silk stockings. History may be made of these, but as the recipe for a novel it's not enough.

J. Hoberman, "Back to the Future," in The Village Voice, *Vol. XXX, No. 48, November 26, 1985, p. 57.*

WHITNEY BALLIETT

You never know what kind of hat E. L. Doctorow will be wearing when he writes a new book. During the past twenty-five years, he has written a Western, a science-fiction novel, a tract novel, a historical docu-novel, a play, a Horatio Alger romance, and a collection of allegorical-surrealist short stories capped by a quasi-autobiographical novella. Now we have the puzzling ***World's Fair***. . . . The book appears to be a novel in the form of a memoir set down by a middle-aged man about his growing up in the Bronx during the thirties. But Doctorow likes to play games with his readers. He grew up in the Bronx, and the narrator and his family have the same general makeup and the same given names that he and his family have. In an interview with Bruce Weber in the Sunday *Times Magazine,* Doctorow said that the book is "the illusion of a memoir." Then he said in the daily *Times* that it is "really a story about memory," that "in a sense, my whole book is a time capsule." This last is accurate, if incomplete. What the book is is fragments of a novel embedded in a kind of catalogue of the everyday detritus of the thirties. The catalogue is taken from a rich archive. . . .

World's Fair begins when Edgar Altschuler (Doctorow was named after Edgar Allan Poe) is four and ends when he is ten and goes to the 1939 World's Fair. . . .

All the while, Doctorow attempts to graft heavy-duty sensibilities onto Edgar which would have astonished the child had he been able to understand them. (p. 157)

Doctorow surrounds Edgar with his accurately researched lists of the artifacts of the thirties. But two-thirds of the way through the book the novel hidden within it begins to be visible. It concerns the intense and abrasive relationship between Rose and Dave [Edgar's parents]. They are opposites, inextricably entwined by tradition and propriety, and they give off intense heat. We learn much of this from brief interludes that occasionally break the narrator's drone and are offered almost as oral reports by Rose and [Edgar's older brother] Donald and Frances—a beautiful sister of Dave's who is married to a successful lawyer and lives in Pelham Manor. We also learn from Edgar, who overhears this perfect patch of dialogue one night:

> "The phone bill," my mother was saying. "Consolidated Edison. Today I didn't even have the money to get your shirts out of the Chinese laundry."
>
> "I have some money for you."
>
> "You've been saying that for three days."
>
> "I drew something against my commissions this morning. I don't like to do that, since it puts me in the hole."
>
> "I'll tell you what puts you in the hole. Your card playing puts you in the hole."
>
> "Does this go with dinner? What course is this?"
>
> "Tell me of any other wife who waits to twelve o'clock to serve dinner? Where have you been? What have you been up to?"
>
> "If you don't let me eat in peace, I'm going to walk right out of here."
>
> "Walk. You don't frighten me. Do I ever have your company? Would I know the difference?"

By the time we read this, it is too late. The book has only forty pages left, and we have already been told that Edgar's father dies before his time. (The first short story in Doctorow's ***Lives of the Poets,*** which preceded ***World's Fair,*** can be read as an epilogue to it. It's as if the idea for ***World's Fair*** had grown backward out of the story.)

Doctorow tends to be showy. Either his sentences are short and clipped or they limp on, making commas do the work of periods or dashes. . . . He stops where Saul Bellow begins. Doctorow's descriptions of Edgar's trips to the World's Fair are the climax of his book. They remind us that if that jubilant, visionary exhibition failed to improve urban design in this country it changed our gastronomy. (pp. 157, 160)

Whitney Balliett, "Mel-O-Rols, Knickers, and Gee Bee Racers," in The New Yorker, *Vol. LXI, No. 42, December 9, 1985, pp. 153, 157, 160.*

ISA KAPP

E. L. Doctorow has always had a considerable and mystifying talent for persuading critics that his works are inventions. About ***Ragtime,*** a silvery cavalcade of picturesque public figures like Houdini, Emma Goldman and J. P. Morgan, he confided that he "wanted to create something not as intimate as fiction nor as remote as history," a dubious ambition. In ***Loon Lake,*** which reads like a loony Marxist pamphlet on class conflict, camouflaged by layers of instant dreamwhip lyricism, the narrator (according to his creator) "throws his voice, and the reader has to figure out who and what he is," an unprofitable enterprise. Doctorow is under the impression that "the convention of the consistent, identifiable narrative . . . now has been torpedoed."

Since both books are, despite broad hints of ominous social undercurrents, essentially frivolous, the author's arbitrary tactics and sententious glosses are of relatively small consequence. But ***The Book of Daniel,*** dealing with an actual event as disturbing and complicated as the 1951 spy trial of Julius and Ethel Rosenberg, who were convicted of giving atomic secrets to the Soviets, should have impelled him to become more systematic and, above all, honest; to deepen, not slant according to his needs, our understanding of the accused couple and the issues they were involved in.

Instead, the story of the fictional Isaacsons is narrated by their son, making the account as far from objective as it could possibly be. Profligate with such details as the physical effect of electrocution, it bypasses entirely the question of moral delinquency on the part of the defendants or an examination of the fellow-traveling mentality that could not admit Soviet atrocity for fear of losing complacency in its own familiar political judgments. The burden of proof is further lightened by omitting almost any mention of the trial proceedings or the evidence as to guilt or innocence.

It is curious that the only Doctorow story the reader can participate in emotionally is the real one of the Rosenbergs. Yet here again, in keeping with his usual method, facts masquerade as fiction and fiction masquerades as fact. Until very recently, this writer has felt that rather than pursue either to its logical conclusion, he could use one to provide what he lacked in the other. Somewhat in the manner of comedian Victor Borge at the piano, he tinkered about, cutting out a snippet for use here, borrowing a tune there, blending old prejudices into new shapes, and smugly serving up the outlandish pastiche to his audience.

In his new book [***World's Fair***], however, a less pretentious Doctorow than we are accustomed to has finally undertaken a subject he is equipped to handle: his autobiography from ages four to 10. The publishers, apparently loath to make him face the truth at this late date, have let him pretend that he has written another novel. And prosaic and literal though ***World's Fair*** is . . . , the author's dogged faithfulness to his 1930s childhood in the West Bronx turns it into his best effort so far.

His grandmother's highlaced black shoes, the baked potato he ate for lunch, the price of admission to the Surrey Theater on Mt. Eden Avenue (10 cents), the see-through blouse worn by his mother's friend, Mae—a kaleidoscope of images has affixed itself to Doctorow's prodigious memory. "My grandfather had a wonderful way of paring an apple, with his own pocketknife, so that the peel came off in one continuous strip . . . he was partial to a tan cardigan . . . he liked me to press my palm against his to measure our hands. . ." In such plain, matter-of-fact, Yiddish-inflected prose, Doctorow records everyday occurrences; by sheer incremental persistence, he conjures up that lost chunk of Jewish family life from decades ago.

Building characters has never been his strong suit, so members of the cast often slide by on a single mannerism or trait: an attractive woman will wink at Edgar good-naturedly; his paternal grandmother will make a spiteful remark about her daughter-in-law's extravagance. But the touch of the immediate family is strong and unmistakable, and for once, true to the Jewish middle-class experience, family is not synonymous with perversion, cruelty or violence. Doctorow keeps returning to the jaunty image of his father, restless, full of surprises, reciting puns and limericks, happy in his Manhattan radio and record store till late at night. "To journey up the broad Grand Concourse with my father was to be somehow in the proper rhythm of the day, like everyone else. He cheered up, too, outside the house. He loved to be going somewhere."

Also authentic is the figure of brother Donald, seven years Edgar's senior, efficient, protective, a model of normality. This memoir of the passive, dreamy Edgar is punctuated by the stages of Donald's life—he forms a swing band and the kid brother learns "Deep Purple" by heart; he gets his first job and the hero, left to his own devices, turns with a vengeance to radio serials like *The Green Hornet* and *The Lone Ranger*.

But the star Edgar is endlessly gazing at, that looms up in ***World's Fair*** like an artist's model, captured in every pose and light, is his mother, who "ran our home and our lives with a kind of tactless administration that often left a child with bruised feelings, though an indelible sense of right and wrong. . . . Her stories dazzled me. Their purpose was instruction. Their theme was vigilance." Whether plumping up pillows or striding through the chaos of Klein's department store in search of bargains, she seems magnificent to him. He admires her metaphors. "Patience wearing thin was very fine. A little later she would say, 'If you don't walk like a human being, I'm going to knock the spots out of you.' That was good too, although I never quite understood the etymology of it."

For the first time in his career, Doctorow is being attentive to psychological fluctuation and creating a substantial person. He has managed to convey a small boy's uneasy sense of the conflict between parents he adores, who are affectionate to him and each other, yet unalterably opposed in temperament, separate in their satisfactions. Genuinely novelistic as well is the recollection of his stoical but intimate friendship with his schoolmate Meg, from ages seven to 10, and her mother Norma, more easygoing and natural than the women he was used to, and therefore viewed disapprovingly by his own mother.

Certainly, Doctorow is writing "like a human being" in ***World's Fair***. Nevertheless, tangibles still very much preoccupy him—foods he liked, exhibits he went to at the World's Fair, streets he traversed in the West Bronx, the local transit routes he delineates with the zeal of a cartographer. He roams the valley of Webster Avenue, the stores on 174th Street, the Tremont library—before he was 10, the protagonist was already a veteran walker in the city.

Doctorow can go on forever about the igloo built in his backyard or the technicalities of a coal truck delivery. To a reader like myself, who lived a block away on the Grand Concourse and had two "best friends" on Eastburn Avenue where the hero of ***World's Fair*** lived, this passion for the concrete can be exasperating. Of the people in one of New York's loveliest and liveliest neighborhoods, whose Claremont Park was humming with political discussion, brilliant teenagers and energetic, gossipy women—a fascinating brew of high-pitched middle-class Jewry—Doctorow seems to remember only Mr. Rosoff, the drugstore owner. Choosing to write about the very early years was calculated to limit his scope, stopping him circumspectly before the age of intellectual risk. In part, the small-scale solipsism is an advantage. A change in family fortunes or a move to a cheaper apartment, for example, is so clearly a jolt to his vulnerable young self that there is no need for sentimental embellishment.

Even when he reverts to his former obligation to sketch in historical vibrations, Doctorow settles for a child's view. Edgar hears whispers of frightening events in Germany; and after his grandmother (who spoke Yiddish and lit candles for her dead husband) dies, he comments oddly, "I had the distinct impression that death was Jewish." Then, illogically, recalling how his grandmother treated her asthma with marijuana, he speaks with the hindsight of a 54-year-old writer: "But to this day the smoke of grass produces in me memories of the choking harsh bitter rage of an exile from the shtetl, a backfired life full of fume and sparks like a fourth of July held in an open grave and projecting on the night a skull's leer and a clap of crossed bones." One indulgence of the adult world Doctorow cannot forgo is rhetorical blowup.

The identical grandmother who pleases Edgar when she gives him a few pennies and frightens him when she intermittently believes her food is being poisoned appeared in ***The Book of Daniel***. So did the scene of the boy seeing a car crash into a mother in the schoolyard of PS 70 and knock her to death two stories below. Why are these admittedly potent episodes almost literally repeated? Partly, I suppose, because imagination, along with character, plot and idea, the necessary components of serious fiction, are in short supply for Doctorow. Perhaps more distressingly, because of a particular attribute of this writer: capricious selection. I never quite know why certain occurrences or images recommend themselves to him, why he dwells on some events, like the zeppelin Hindenburg looming over Bronx housetops before it expired in New Jersey. I'm sure many will be quoting his lengthy descriptions of the General Motors Futurama at the 1939 World's Fair. It is one of those impersonal crowd experiences that the author is especially at home with, and does well, but leaves me absolutely indifferent. On the other hand, I did enjoy the prize essay Edgar sent to the World's Fair contest on the subject of "The Typical American Boy," though I don't believe for a minute that he could have written it. . . . (pp. 5-6)

On second thought, why not? E. L. was probably a smooth operator by the time he was 10. (p. 6)

Isa Kapp, "Tales of the Bronx," in The New Leader, *Vol. LXVIII, No. 16, December 16-30, 1985, pp. 5-6.*

An Excerpt from *World's Fair*

I had a keen eye for contests. Many were false and ridiculous, and only the innocent would enter them. They usually required you to say what you liked about a product in twenty-five words or less and send in your remarks with a boxtop or label. The contest was really designed to get you to buy the product. My friend Arnold had made up a contest for Castoria, the laxative. "I like Castoria because it's foul-tasting and gives you terrible diarrhea, and we all know what fun that can be."

But this was different. This was run not by a company but by the World's Fair. I read the rules carefully. They wanted original thought. Whoever won would have a statue made of him by a famous artist, and the name of the statue would be "The Typical American Boy." There were other prizes too, including free trips to the Fair, all expenses paid. My mind began to race.

In the old days Donald and I had collected coupons from newspaper promotions of various sorts. Enough coupons and you collected your premium—in one memorable instance the *New York Evening Post* offered a set of ten volumes called *The World's One Hundred Best Short Stories*. That had taken a year of coupons. We had been very methodical and efficient, cutting the coupons out on the dotted line, keeping them in order in packs, slipping rubber bands over them and storing them in a cigar box. But there were contests too of an intellectual sort, puzzles, rebuses, tests of vocabulary and grammar. With success you could earn subscriptions to magazines or even money. All these were means of entry in my mind to a just and well-regulated world of carefully designed challenges to boys. By accepting these challenges you advanced yourself. So I recognized this World's Fair essay contest. I recognized it. In my early days I had joined secret organizations run by Tom Mix and Dick Tracy, among others. I had in the depths of my desk drawers numerous artifacts of entry, a Jack Armstrong whistle ring, little lead Buck Rogers rocket ships with wheels, water pistols, magnifying lenses, badges, secret code cards, and so on. For each of them I had once eagerly awaited the mail. The mail was very much a part of all this. There were rules of postmark to consider and specifications as to format. Wherever you were, at whatever far edge of the world's consciousness, one three-cent postage stamp could vault you into the heart of things.

Under the printing of the contest rules were the palest, most meaningful shadows of the Trylon and Perisphere. Only gradually did I perceive them. They emerged in my mind as a message just for me, a secret summons, wordless, indelible.

I fully understood why our family hadn't gotten to the World's Fair. Nobody had said anything, but I knew. Boldly I asked the librarian if I could borrow a pencil. I asked also for a piece of paper. I didn't care if she smiled. I copied down the information on the poster. My heart was beating wildly. I worried that the old people trying to read their periodicals would hear it and the derelict men nodding in their hard chairs would wake up, and all of them would give me dirty looks.

R. Z. SHEPPARD

Like generations of authors before him. Edgar Laurence Doctorow blends fact and fancy and calls the results novels. His tragedy of political passion, ***The Book of Daniel,*** was based conspicuously on the Rosenberg atom-spy case. Although he changed names and broadened perspectives, it was impossible to turn a page without thinking about Julius and Ethel Rosenberg on their way to the electric chair. The real had again overpowered the imagined.

Ragtime solved this problem in high style. Its storybook setting in America before World War I gave Doctorow enough distance to rewrite history. Nobody complained when Sigmund Freud visited Coney Island, Henry Ford conspired with J. P. Morgan, or Evelyn Nesbit (the Girl in the Red Velvet Swing) was converted by Anarchist Emma Goldman. Wrapped in nostalgia, Doctorow's dramatizations of rapacious capitalism, racism and revolution was defused of controversy. Unlike ***Daniel,*** a dredger of bad memories and mixed feelings, ***Ragtime*** was a safe book.

By comparison, ***World's Fair*** is downright guarded. Doctorow calls it a novel. But the book reads like a memoir. . . .

Little Edgar is a witness to the nation's possibilities. He has been to the 1939-40 World's Fair, with its models of superhighways, bullet-shaped automobiles, electrical appliances and television, or "picture radio." He has, in fact, been there twice. The first time he accompanied a friend whose mother worked with Oscar the Amorous Octopus, a titillating sideshow at the amusement park. He returned on a family pass that he had won for his fawning entry in a typical-American-boy contest. The essay is heavy with irony. It also introduces a writer who knows what it takes to get on the bestseller list. . . .

World's Fair is not a happy book. The dreariness of the '30s and the strains of family life appear to have had a bad effect on Edgar's style. He is either too terse or verbosely academic, as if the boy grew up to be a literary critic rather than a novelist. Evocations of his time and place are frequently bloated with pretentious prose. . . .

Doctorow's artifacts have a familiar, wistful charm. Yet there is a curious defensiveness to his enterprise. Tone seems to have been substituted for emotion; artiness replaces vitality. Doctorow aims for a myth that would link a nation on the edge of war and a boy approaching adolescence, but he is too cautious with his material. He calls the book a novel, yet it has few of the elements usually associated with the form. A melancholy Edgar ticks off his experiences and observations; his mother, brother and aunt make brief personal appearances, while the father remains silent and remote. Even the Bronx is incompletely perceived. Granted that it is not New York City's most glamorous borough, it is home to the Yankees and one of the world's great zoos. Neither attraction appears in the book, understandable if Doctorow had written a memoir, but a lost opportunity in a novel about growing up with "King Kong" Keller and other great apes in the neighborhood.

R. Z. Sheppard, "The Artist as a Very Young Critic," in Time, *Vol. 126, No. 20, December 18, 1985, p. 100.*

ROBERT TOWERS

In a world of ideal literary forms, autobiography, however fictionalized in certain of its aspects, would exist as a genre distinct from the novel, however much the latter might be derived from the author's personal experience. Often the distinction is clear enough: for a variety of reasons involving style, rhetoric, narrative organization, and the presentation of the protagonist, we are not likely to regard *Stop-Time* as a novel or *Look Homeward, Angel* as an autobiography. When a blurring of the two genres occurs, the result can be dismaying if issues of public significance are concerned (Lillian Hellman's memoirs come to mind—just where does the purportedly factual account of an episode slide into self-aggrandizing fantasy?) or harmless enough, as in the case of Doctorow's ***World's Fair,*** a work of substantially autobiographical prose that is called a novel.

Just what in ***World's Fair*** is indeed fictional? Presumably Doctorow wishes to provoke the question, for he has experimented with such blurring of genre before. In the recent novella called ***Lives of the Poets,*** certain publicly known facts of Doctorow's own life are used as a scaffolding on which to hang invented encounters and relationships. More closely aligned to ***World's Fair*** is the short story called **"The Writer in the Family"**—clearly the same family that figures in the new "novel." In ***World's Fair*** even the disguising of the names is largely dropped. . . .

World's Fair progresses in an unhurried way through a series of episodes, major and minor, that contribute in different ways to the boy's growing awareness of himself in the world. In the narration of these episodes (ranging in significance from Edgar's fourth birthday party to a ruptured appendix that nearly kills him) Doctorow makes use of a double perspective—that of the re-created child who experiences an event and that of the reflective adult who remembers it. (p. 23)

There is nothing remarkable about many of the events in ***World's Fair:*** the grandmother's death, a Sunday visit to the paternal grandparents, a Seder celebrated at rich Aunt Frances's house, a near mugging at the hands of anti-Semitic toughs from the East Bronx, a Tom Sawyer-like romance with a child named Meg. The material is familiar from a dozen novels, from books on the Depression era, and from memoirs of growing up Jewish in New York. But to it Doctorow brings so much observed period detail that a reader who has lived through the Thirties will experience repeated tremors, if not shocks, of recognition. The trivia of those years is lavishly spread on nearly every page: the radio programs (the *Chase and Sanborn Hour, Major Bowes' Original Amateur Hour, Information Please*) and the radio personalities (Gabriel Heatter, H. V. Kaltenborn, Walter Winchell), the popular songs ("Deep Purple," "I Must See Annie Tonight"), the movies, the newsreels. It is pleasurable to be reminded of such things, to submit to the tug of a nostalgia in which I suppose even much younger readers can vicariously participate. As a period autobiography, ***World's Fair*** is authoritatively documented and evocative.

Its claims to being a novel reside chiefly in the re-created dialogue with which the scenes are embellished and in the elaborate mounting of set pieces, such as Edgar's first enraptured visit to the World's Fair with Meg and her "disreputable" mother, who performs in an erotic underwater sideshow in the fair's Amusement Zone. But the characters, while convincingly reproduced and analyzed, are not really memorable, and the book as a whole lacks the movement and suspense of good fiction. The ongoing conflict between Rose and Dave, which might have been crucial in the development of a real novel, generates surprisingly little tension; it is expertly recalled but never fully dramatized. Much of the same is true of young Edgar's fear of death and his growing awareness (and apprehension) of sex. The mislabeling of ***World's Fair*** by no means spoils one's enjoyment of many passages in the book, but it does result in a degree of aesthetic smudging and the raising of expectations that remain unfulfilled. (pp. 23-4)

Robert Towers, "Three-Part Inventions," in The New York Review of Books, *Vol. XXXII, No. 20, December 19, 1985, pp. 23-5.*

PETER LEWIS

Edgar Doctorow is one of those fortunate novelists to have achieved bestsellerdom and academic respectability, although his critical reputation, based mainly on ***The Book of Daniel*** and ***Ragtime,*** wobbled precariously after the publication of ***Loon Lake.*** Even some of his admirers have expressed uneasiness about the apparent ideological and philosophical confusion at the heart of his work, arising from his ambitious and idiosyncratic attempt to fuse the social, political and historical concerns of the realistic tradition with the absurdism and reflexivity of metafiction. Doctorow has displayed an interest in the postmodernist deconstructive enterprises of his avant-garde contemporaries without sharing their belief in the non-referential autonomy of language and literary forms, and his commitment to the truth-telling function of fiction is manifest in his essentially realistic ***World's Fair***. . . . The thirty-one numbered chapters of ***World's Fair*** are a first-person account of a Jewish boyhood in New York, covering the period from Doctorow's own birthyear of 1931 until the American involvement in World War II. This narrative reads like an autobiographical memoir, and although Doctorow reveals fairly late in the novel that the 'I' is Edgar Altschuler, not Edgar Doctorow, the deliberate withholding of the narrator's name for so long helps to blur the distinction between fictional and real selves, between imagination and reality. To confirm the status of ***World's Fair*** as fiction rather than autobiography, there are seven short unnumbered sections dispersed throughout the main narrative, each presenting a viewpoint other than Edgar's, mainly his mother's. Unfortunately Doctorow's use of these 'inserts' is insufficiently developed to add much to the novel except in the early stages; here, the mother's inserts provide valuable information about the family background not available to Edgar himself, and the time-shifts involved create an interesting counterpoint between past and present. Having established this technique early in the novel, Doctorow was faced with either abandoning it, which would appear incompetent, or extending it fruitfully throughout, which he fails to do. The inconsequential inserts in the middle and later stages serve to underline this failure.

Where Doctorow does succeed is in his portrait of the artist as a very young man, even though his tendency to overwrite, to indulge in that characteristically American vice of uneconomic and uncontrollable volubility, mars parts of the book. In his *Portrait,* Joyce uses an appropriate idiom for each stage of Stephen's development, whereas Doctorow's Edgar seems to emerge from the womb in a state of euphuistic hyperarticulacy: 'Startled awake by the ammoniated mists, I am roused in one instant from glutinous sleep to grieving awareness.' Doctorow's linguistic impasto can be off-putting, but it is worth persevering with ***World's Fair*** because it steadily improves as it advances in time and acquires a symbolic dimension. The significance of the title, referring to New York's famous prewar Fair with its optimistic vision of the future, emerges only gradually. Rather like Araby in Joyce's story of that name, the World's Fair possesses an imaginative significance for Edgar that cannot live up to the reality, especially at a time when the shadows of Hitler and a second world war are falling on Western civilization. In his relative 'innocence', Edgar is only marginally aware of the adult reality of 'experience' surrounding and threatening him, but the later stages of the novel owe their power to Doctorow's implicit contrast between Edgar's developing apprehension of the world and the reader's knowledge of the nightmare already engulfing Europe, especially the Jews. Doctorow's subtle way of involving the reader's historical consciousness allows him to expand the scope of what is a type of *Bildungsroman* to accommodate his preoccupation with the relationship between the private and the public, the personal and the historical. (pp. 100-02)

Peter Lewis, "Half-Baked Alaska," in London Magazine, *n.s. Vol. 25, No. 11, February, 1986, pp. 100-03.*

HILTON KRAMER

Rather late in the day, long after he has become an established, best-selling author, E. L. Doctorow has written a "first novel" called ***World's Fair***. . . . By actual count, of course, ***World's Fair*** is Mr. Doctorow's seventh novel, having been preceded by such celebrated fictions as ***Ragtime*** and ***The Book of Daniel.***

Yet, both in its subject matter—the author's boyhood in the Bronx—and in its unabashed sentimentality, ***World's Fair*** certainly reads like a prototypical first novel. The only thing it lacks in this regard is the aura of "promise" that such novels are usually presumed to have for their readers. In Mr. Doctorow's case, alas, we already know what this promise holds in store.

Like many first novels, ***World's Fair*** is written on the assumption that every jejune scrap of experience recalled from the author's childhood, no matter how shopworn it may be as fictional material, will still resonate for the reader with the undiminished charm and significance it has for the author himself. In a young, inexperienced writer, such an assumption, however callow, is understandable. Given the requisite talent, it may even be endearing. But what are we to make of the spectacle of a mature writer attempting in middle age to impersonate this posture of literary innocence? What does he hope to accomplish by it?

The story of ***World's Fair,*** if one can call something so devoid of narrative interest a story, has the kind of school-primer simplicity that is the special hallmark of Mr. Doctorow's fiction. Its principal narrator, Edgar, who is also, of course, the author, purports to tell us what it was like to grow up between the ages of four and 10 in a troubled but fondly remembered Jewish family in the West Bronx in the 1930s. Everything from memories of bed-wetting to his parents' quarrels to the popular songs of the Depression era is recalled in picturesque detail and enveloped in a roseate glow of family piety and period nostalgia. Even the death of the boy's grandmother is described in a way that makes it seem more like a remnant from the folklore of a sweet but distant period than a vivid personal experience.

We can scarcely be surprised, then, when at last we reach the elaborate set piece toward which this sentimental journey into childhood memories has been heading all along: the description of the narrator's encounter with the 1939 World's Fair. The World of Tomorrow (as the famous General Motors exhibit was called) is a subject ideally suited to Mr. Doctorow's gift for tinsel documentary. One can almost hear the author sigh with relief as he abandons all pretense of dealing with the complexities of human experience and gives himself over entirely to the evocation of technological fantasy and utopian spectacle. Once freed from the need to pay even cursory attention to human relationships, the narrator of ***World's Fair,*** which is to say, Mr. Doctorow himself, experiences a kind of liberation of the spirit. It is on this note of escape into fantasy that this curious "first novel" abruptly concludes.

Perhaps for minds that, like Mr. Doctorow's, feed on fantasy and technological artifice, this denouement will prove entirely satisfactory. For the reader who looks to fiction for a convincing account of life, however, ***World's Fair*** is little more than a contrived trifle, a period romance filled with stock characters and stage-set decor. Its every emotion conforms to a convention that has been familiar to the literate reader for half a century, ever since Clifford Odets and numerous other writers of the 1930s first established it.

Yet the fact that everything in this novel is conventionalized to the point of abject cliche is, oddly enough, what makes this material so appealing to a writer of Mr. Doctorow's sensibilities. He is essentially a writer of historical romances. That is the genre to which ***Ragtime*** and ***Welcome to Hard Times*** belong, and it is really the genre to which ***World's Fair*** belongs as well. Now that the Depression era has acquired the kind of patina that makes it painless and picturesque for readers who know little or nothing about it, and any number of novelists, memoirists, stand-up comics and television scriptwriters have made a Boyhood-in-the-Bronx into an archetype of American popular culture, Mr. Doctorow can approach the story of his own life as if it were an impersonal fable. All the emotion is gone. What remains is the literary equivalent of a retouched photograph, complete with staged poses and faked expressions.

It tells us something—perhaps everything we need to know—about the author's talent, that he could not finally deal with his own childhood in fiction until it, too, could be rendered as a historical romance, with its principal characters—the Jewish mother, the older brother, the failed father, et al.—drawn straight from central casting.

This, I think, explains why Mr. Doctorow had to wait so long to produce a "first novel."

Hilton Kramer, "Yesterday's World of Tomorrow," in The Wall Street Journal, *February 7, 1986, p. 19.*

T. O. TREADWELL

Both ***World's Fair*** and [James Joyce's *Portrait of the Artist as a Young Man*] have as their subject the gradual extension of an individual consciousness from pure self-absorption, outward through an awareness of the reality of other people and relationships, to a sense of the complexity of the world and the place of the self in it; both novels begin with infantile bed-wetting and end with their narrators' determination to embrace the multiform experiences of life and, by implication at least, to turn them into art. Doctorow's prose at moments becomes so Joycean that it flirts with parody. . . .

But while Stephen Dedalus has to undergo the trials of adolescence and young manhood before grasping his destiny, Edgar's quest for a sense of himself and his place in the world reaches its climax at the age of ten. Doctorow's symbol for this goal is the New York World's Fair of 1939, with its centrepiece, the Futurama, a giant mechanical model of the city of the future which offers a thrilling and optimistic vision of adult possibility. But the World's Fair also incorporates a grim exhibition of freaks and monsters, and a tawdry burlesque show where Edgar faces the fierce and upsetting power of sexuality. Multiple meanings, it turns out, reside in Doctorow's title. ***World's Fair*** moves Edgar towards the great exhibition of 1939 as a symbol of adult acceptance, but it is also much concerned with questions about the fairness of the world in terms both of beauty and equity.

Doctorow conveys childish fearfulness and uncertainty with great skill: Edgar's bafflement in the face of the forces that motivate the adult world around him is reflected in his sense of the horror and cruelty lurking in nursery rhymes and religious iconography. As he grows older, the boy becomes aware of tension in the relationship between his parents and between his mother and his father's family. Death occurs both in the family and, with shocking randomness, in a street accident, while reports of the persecution of German Jewry by the Nazis become less abstract when Edgar is mugged by antisemitic louts in the East Bronx. But though his world can be a frightening place, this novel also succeeds in rendering the richness of the child's experience, his sense of loving and being loved and the familiar artefacts and comforting rituals of his everyday life. In the end, Edgar achieves the "World's Fair" twice, once as a consequence of his affection for a serenely beautiful little girl, the second time as a reward for his performance in an essay competition on the theme of the typical American boy; as lover and artist, he enters the glittering world of the future.

For the adult Doctorow, ***World's Fair*** also functions as a way into the past. In the final pages of the novel Edgar and a friend, inspired by an exhibition at the World's Fair, construct a time capsule from a mailing tube and bury it in Claremont Park in the Bronx. In this they place. . . . trivial objects from a middle-class boyhood in the New York of forty-five years ago. Their recovery in this novel suggests that ***World's Fair*** is itself a time-capsule, an evocation of the spirit of a lost era through a rendering of the texture of its daily life, but that life as seen in childhood, when the ordinary surfaces of things are at their most threatening and wonderful. Doctorow's chronicle of a child's experience is often comic, and never patronizing or coy. By narrowing its focus to the life of one family, ***World's Fair*** offers a profounder sense of the past than the elaborate historical fantasizing of Doctorow's ***Ragtime*** (1975), and it communicates its themes the more effectively by dropping the stylistic extravagances of ***Loon Lake*** (1980). Doctorow's portrait of the artist when young may not be in the Joycean class—not to be Joyce is, after all, no disgrace—but it is a considerable achievement.

T. O. Treadwell, "Time-Encapsulating," in The Times Literary Supplement, *No. 4324, February 14, 1986, p. 163.*

CLANCY SIGAL

Toward the end of E. L. Doctorow's comfortable, comforting, amazingly evocative but curiously standoffish account of his Bronx childhood in the Thirties [***World's Fair***], he and a friend bury a time capsule in a local park. It has an old harmonica, toy rocket ships, Edgar's handwritten history of F.D.R., a Tom Mix decoder badge—all sorts of wonderful boys' gimcracks and doohickeys, just like what the book itself is remarkably full of.

I had a childhood not unlike Doctorow's and can testify to his genius for accumulating detail, whether of the smell of asphalt in the summer or the peculiar dusty look of a primary school classroom with the afternoon sun burning through the half-lowered shade, in a way that immediately assaults the sympathetic reader's senses. His talent is for sensation in the best sense.

As one saw from ***Ragtime*** and even ***Loon Lake,*** Doctorow has a tendency to sweeten up the past. Growing up in the Bronx in the Depression—despite Hitlerite rumblings in the east, despite pennypinching and parental anxieties—was a curiously stable experience. Doctorow is marvellous at conjuring up the separate and disconnected parts of such a boyhood, although he is not above a bit of too much "foine" writing ("I had the opportunity to be the aware sentient being I knew myself to be," or when his grandmother dies he perceives her "declared inanimateness".) But was it only my boyhood that was darker, bloodier, more plagued with irrational tides, ghosts and nightmares?

His well-barbered, leftish and genial cardplaying father Dave lived on hope and puns that delighted his two kids, young rather sickly Edgar and the older brother Donald. As in many Jewish families mother Rose "was forever calling him to account," blasting his hopes as fantasies, incessantly wondering if he had a doxie somewhere.

Doctorow's parents are curiously not-quite there in contrast to his toys and illnesses; perhaps that's how kids protect themselves from the bitter threatening quarrels of their mothers and fathers. But Doctorow is so determined, rosily nostalgic that my pleasure in his book was occasionally disrupted by a slight question about what had happened to all the emotion-induced stomach-aches, unvoiced terrors and dark formless clouds that must have also been an authentic part of his growing up.

Perhaps, as they say in the movies, it's all in the visuals. There is a truly impressive scene when the German Zeppelin Hindenburg practically stops life in the Bronx by flying overhead. . . .

A few hours later the giant airship crashed in flames, a perhaps too-easy metaphor for what was about to happen to Doctorow's family and his world in general.

Clancy Sigal, "A Better Yesterday," in Manchester Guardian Weekly, *February 23, 1986, p. 21.*

CAROL IANNONE

World's Fair features Doctorow at what he does best, capturing with painstaking, sometimes exquisite accuracy a certain kind of intensive family life that we are being told on many sides has passed into history. (The short story, **"A Writer in the Family,"** is another example.)

The Altschuler fortunes are delicately chronicled by the younger son Edgar, now a middle-aged man. Along with the little joys and satisfactions of Edgar's family, he records an increasing sense of loss and disappointment as the marriage grows cooler, the father's business fails, and the older brother flunks out of college and soon leaves home. Edgar's growing perception of life's bewitching and often mournful seriousness is especially well evoked through the rich details of his 30's Bronx boyhood.

Despite being a boyhood memoir, ***World's Fair*** has the tone of an elegy. The sense of fated inevitability and the gradually shrinking possibilities that Edgar chronicles in his family turn gently ironic when juxtaposed against the brash, infinite possibilities presumably represented by the 1939 World's Fair, which the family visits at the end of the book. That fair, we know, has become something of a negative *locus classicus* for the Left, a monument to the worst excesses of capitalist technology and mindless futurism. Doctorow, however, underplays all this, never departing from Edgar's tone of impeccable editorial reserve, leaving the implications to the reader.

It might thus seem in ***World's Fair*** that this resolutely anti-bourgeois author has succumbed to the lures of "the little world of personal experience." But not quite. For Doctorow has here forgone still another classic staple of fiction, the engagement of characters in action that tests and defines them. His characters are never allowed to become individuals whose consciousness can shape their circumstances; rather, they passively preside over an existence conditioned by various factors beyond their ken and beyond their control. (p. 56)

Carol Iannone, "E. L. Doctorow's 'Jewish' Radicalism," in Commentary, *Vol. 81, No. 3, March, 1986, pp. 53-6.*

GENE BLUESTEIN

Novelist E(dgar) L(aurence) Doctorow likes to mention that he was named after Edgar Allan Poe. He doesn't usually discuss his middle name, but it may have been the source of his penchant for using initials, perhaps after D(avid) H(erbert) or T(homas) E(dward) Lawrence. Doctorow may come from the German-Yiddish word *dichter,* which means author or poet.

The names are of some interest since the main characters in ***World's Fair*** are a young boy named Edgar, his older brother, and his parents, named Dave and Rose. Since the last two are the real names of Doctorow's parents, many reviewers object to the subtitle, *A Novel,* and insist that the book is a memoir or autobiography and not fiction at all. But that is to underestimate Doctorow's skill and miss the carefully wrought strategies that support this brilliant reconstruction of the life and mind of a young boy's first ten years in the Bronx.

As in his other novels, Doctorow centers on an American family, this one called Altschuler—the name means Old Scholar, or perhaps a student of old times. And indeed Doctorow has engaged in a prodigious effort to research the details of life in the 1930s, concluding in 1939-1940 with the World's Fair in Flushing, Long Island. Under the influence of the Fair's time capsule, which is intended to acquaint finders five thousand years hence with the outlines of our civilization, Edgar buries his own version in Claremont Park. . . . As Doctorow has also noted, the book itself is a time capsule. Things change so quickly in America, he feels, that they will be lost forever if the writer does not salvage them.

Doctorow's strategy to accomplish this is a carefully managed and controlled narrative point of view. He begins with a brief section from Edgar's mother that explains something of the family's European background. Then most of the narrative comes from Edgar himself, with occasional asides from his brother and an aunt but, significantly, none from his father. Not that Edgar rejects his father. On the contrary, although his father was clearly unreliable, he was fun: "He was a child's ideal companion, full of surprises and animal energy . . . a free soul tethered, by a generous improvidence not terribly or shrewdly mindful of itself, to the imperial soul of an attractive woman."

Young Edgar displays a magical marshalling of objects and activities which clearly foreshadow the work materials of a writer. If you grew up elsewhere they may leave you cold or, on the other hand, you may be fascinated by Doctorow's almost compulsive memorization. Having grown up in Brooklyn around the same time, I was amazed at how many details could be dredged up. His commentary includes games like stoop ball, punch ball and stickball, slug, and hit the stick. He remembers his first punchboard, his first scumbag on the beach, Melorols, a coal truck dumping its load on the sidewalk, trips to the "country," excursions all the way to the beach in Far Rockaway, and a first experience with anti-Semitism. (I bristled at his comment that Brooklyn was a foreign country—this was exactly what we used to say about the Bronx.)

Underlying the plot is the constant bickering of Edgar's mother and father: "The conflict between my parents was probably the major chronic circumstance of my life. They were never at peace. They were a marriage of two irreducibly opposed natures. Their differences created a kind of magnetic field for me in which I swung this way or that according to the direction of the current."

Like all important works of art, Doctorow's ***World's Fair*** moves from personal to universal insights, constantly recreating events and ideas he couldn't possibly have literally recalled from his childhood. It is perhaps not a book for everyone. If you're not interested in the culture of cities, you may not be moved. If you need the stimulation of rape, outrageous violence, uncontrollable passion, it is not here. There are several superb moments of incipient sexuality in the play of Edgar and his first real friend, Meg; he essentially shows the human solidarity of two children before the world imposes its skewed values.

The final trip to the World's Fair is brilliantly researched. Who can remember that the narration in the Perisphere was by H. V. Kaltenborn or that the music for that exhibit was by the black composer William Grant Still? I doubt that the underwater nudie show in which Meg's mother took part actually existed. Here as elsewhere, there are lots of fictions in this lovely and quietly passionate work. (pp. 42-3)

Gene Bluestein, "Time Capsule," in The Progressive, *Vol. 50, No. 3, March, 1986, pp. 42-3.*

D. KEITH MANO

'On the kitchen ceiling was a wooden rack with a clothesline strung up on it; you let it down like a shade by means of a rope attached to the wall, and you dried your clothes that way." I read this sentence and, time warp, was back in our 1947 apartment on Thayer Street. To feel again the mossy groping of wet hems hung from that weird trellis. And our kitchen water pipe, whose spent, blistered silver paint I broke open under my five-year-old thumbnail. While Mother let me play postman with old World War II ration-stamp books. Or let me turn the meat-grinder handle, cuisine-sweat, C-clamped to our cabinet shelf edge. Or . . .

Well, ***World's Fair*** is sure a sweet mnemonic device. I was enfolded by it: first time I've felt nostalgia for someone else's life. Doctorow can punch a special inner clock. Narrative line, in fact, was often disrupted by my wild, elaborate associations. Yet the protagonist, Edgar, and I aren't an exact fit: I'm younger, Christian not Jewish, born several New York City miles south. Would this novel patch into the vibrating diaphragm of, oh, some twenty-year-old from San Francisco? Am I an inappropriate reporter here: is my enthusiasm particular? Maybe. Then again, a twenty-year-old from San Francisco would probably prefer Gestalt-O-Rama to fiction. Doctorow has had success, in part, because he writes for our last live reading generation. The rest is MTV and topless radio.

I've never gotten my *déjà vu* second hand before. And Doctorow is a past master not merely because he took good three-by-five-card notes or "recreated the period." Because, unlike Proust, he can isolate just that piece of *madeleine* we *both* have eaten. His imagery is commonplace, yet central: some trite object, some event forgotten now and not well perceived even then. The *tshotchkes* of life that, suddenly brought up, flag widening recollection. Think now, you who were born before 1945—how many of these resonate in your past *perdu*. Dumbwaiter rope. Punchboard. The block pedals on a bike. Sulfanilamide. Your pencil box. A wool bathing suit. Kazoos with tissue membrane. The Green Hornet. A postage-stamp union label on rye bread. Stan Lomax's voice. Emmett Kelly. The thin rubber tube in a fountain pen. I have this fading portrait of me: apparently the same photographer went far south down from Doctorow's neighborhood to snap my picture on his old, unscenic, blindered pony.

In 2500 A.D., you realize, Jewish-American experience will dominate and shade our historical record. The documentation can only overwhelm archivists. What comparable evidence is there for black or Hispanic or even WASP culture in America? We will all be Hittites, just about: known to have existed from occasional mention in the Semitic chronicle. This is probably so because Jews possess a terrific historical sense—maybe because they also possess a developed sense of exposure and impending annihilation. Anne Frank *wrote*. Life should be registered: with written memorabilia you can preserve a fragile race (and a fragile personality). All people, to be sure, have some historical instinct, but the Jewish is most democratic. Not just U.S. Grant's cigar, but one your father smoked as well. Hero and battle and political act—and that washboard leaning diagonally in a sink. Jews are persuaded that self, even least self, will gather significance around: intellect or art can extrapolate from it. This is, indeed, the modern novelist's central, leveling sensibility.

Yet, in that familiar genre—urban Jewish *Bildungsroman*—Doctorow doesn't quite play first chair. He misses, for instance, the reach and special votive light of *Old World, New World* by Mark Dintenfass, which treated wholly similar material. Doctorow has an ingratiating, frank style, but his trivial finesse itself is distortive. Major incidents—appendix removal, *Hindenburg*, 1939 fair—seem unspecific and cursory in contrast with those elegant minutiae. After all I never saw the *Hindenburg* and I've still got an appendix: that overhead kitchen rack is more momentous. Good as they are, by comparison they feel contrived, *fictional:* and, unfortunately, they also bear Doctorow's plot thrust—a progress from myopic childhood vision to that larger household furniture, Trylon and Perisphere, to what they symbolize both for America and for Edgar on his way up, out. A lens change is needed, that or more text: otherwise you can't easily rack-fade from close-up to master shot without some consequential blurring.

In 1939 the time capsule was buried. They "put articles of common use . . . like a wind-up alarm clock, a can opener, and a toothbrush." In imitation Edgar will inter his Tom Mix Decoder Badge and two Tootsy Toy lead rockets. And now Doctorow has made yet another deposit here. A time capsule can have its own instructive and delicious purpose, beyond the quibble of literary criticism. (pp. 54-5)

D. Keith Mano, "That Trivial Finesse," in National Review, *New York, Vol. XXXVIII, No. 4, March 14, 1986, pp. 54-5.*

DEAN FLOWER

[There] is little to prevent the reader from taking [***World's Fair***] as personal history, a subjective document all right but not one refracted through fiction's usual lenses. Doctorow seems to be reconstructing his first decade not so much to understand himself or ascertain his identity, the way Joyce Carol Oates does, as to evoke the period, passing around a whole lot of old snapshots, setting it down for posterity and the sociologists. (p. 310)

The narrative is free from the excessive manipulations that made ***Ragtime*** and ***Loon Lake*** such bogus exercises in historicism; it has instead something of the clarity and specific gravity of ***The Book of Daniel,*** still Doctorow's best novel. The style of ***World's Fair*** ranges from the declarative simplicity of a young boy's consciousness to the elegant, carefully-shaped evocation of the remembering adult: "And in my sleep figures would loom in threatening gesture and just as suddenly recede into colored swirling points, as if I myself had been spread-eagled on a wheel spinning so fast that the colors melted together and became a target." But it remains a somewhat disappointing book. For all its elegance and clarity, it's a document of the period instead of the person. When the story ends Edgar is still too young to have taken distinctive shape. The single most revealing detail about him emerges only at the end, when he and another boy bury a "time capsule" of symbolic artifacts . . . for the enlightenment of posterity. At the last minute Edgar decides not to bury his copy of *Ventriloquism Self Taught*, a portent of the writer whose voice he will learn to "throw" into his characters. Trouble is, ventriloquism has become a stunt Doctorow is only too good at; he will impersonate almost anyone but himself. Indeed, he has in a sense no real voice of his own, only the ones he hears in the history books and the family narratives, in the novels and newspapers of his American past. Doctorow's art is to parody those voices in the service of a tireless nostalgia. (p. 311)

Dean Flower, "Fables of Identity," in The Hudson Review, *Vol. XXXIX, No. 2, Summer, 1986, pp. 309-21.*

Max (Rudolf) Frisch

Neustadt International Prize for Literature

Swiss novelist, dramatist, diarist, and journalist.

The 1986 Neustadt Prize for Literature is one of many honors, including the 1958 Georg Büchner Prize, earned by Frisch as one of Switzerland's most distinguished and versatile men of letters. In addition to being one of the finest contemporary novelists writing in German, Frisch, along with fellow dramatist Friedrich Dürrenmatt, brought international recognition to the postwar Swiss theater through innovative plays written for Zurich's Schauspielhaus. Also Frisch published diaries valued by critics for their revelations of the writer's mind at work and as documents of such significant literary events as Frisch's meetings with Bertolt Brecht, recorded in his *Tagebuch 1946-1949* (1950; *Sketchbook, 1946-1949*) and *Tagebuch 1966-1971* (1972; *Sketchbook, 1966-1971*).

As a youth, Frisch learned about drama by studying on his own the plays of Henrik Ibsen; at age sixteen he sent his first play, *Stahl,* to producer-director Max Reinhart in Berlin. Frisch went on to major in literature at the University of Zurich, until his father's death interrupted his studies, whereupon he went to work as a journalist, writing sports and travel articles for several newspapers. Critics regard the early fiction written during this period as relatively conventional, interesting mainly as precursors of more important works to come. In 1936 Frisch decided he had been unsuccessful, and he made a ceremonial bonfire of all his early writings, including his diaries. He then returned to school to train as an architect, the profession his father had practiced. During World War II Frisch served in the Swiss army, which was mobilized against a possible invasion. He recorded his army experiences in what became his first literary diary, *Blätter aus dem Brotsack* (1940). His indignation at Switzerland's neutrality towards Hitler became a central theme of his postwar works.

After the war, Frisch began a successful career as an architect in Zurich. Although his early novels contain no hint of politics, professional involvement with urban planning led him to adopt the socialist views that characterize his mature work. Also at this time, Kurt Hirschfeld, director of the Zurich Schauspielhaus, encouraged Frisch to write a play for his theater, which reawakened Frisch's literary interests. *Nun singen sie wieder* (1945), a bitter antiwar statement, was Frisch's first drama to appear onstage. Other productions at the Schauspielhaus followed, and Frisch was hailed as a topical allegorist in the tradition of Brecht. Frisch scholars later agreed that although Frisch became an enthusiastic admirer of Brecht in the 1940s, the Swiss writer had experimented in his novels with Brechtian devices, such as the alienation technique, years before he became familiar with the writings of his German colleague. The two authors eventually met in 1947 and became friends. Frisch, however, always remained skeptical of Brecht's Marxist beliefs, as well as his custom of delivering moral lectures through his plays. Many of Frisch's most highly-regarded dramas, including *Andorra* (1961) and *Biedermann und die Brandstifter* (1958; *The Firebugs*), are Brechtian parables, in form if not in content. However, Frisch ultimately rejected the parable form as too limited for his purposes. In his later plays, *Biographie: Ein Spiel* (1968; *Biography: A Game*) and *Triptychon* (1978; *Triptych*), he approaches his theatrical ideal. He attempts to demonstrate, without conventions of naturalism, didacticism, or logical temporal constraints, not only what a given set of characters think and do, but what they might experience if they acted on all possibilities open to them. This striving towards a "theater of permutations" is also reflected in his novels, notably *Stiller* (1954; *I'm Not Stiller*), *Mein Name sei Gantenbein* (1964; *A Wilderness of Mirrors*), and *Blaubart* (1982; *Bluebeard: A Tale*). In these narratives, Frisch presents his heroes's fantasies about their lives as no less important or true than what actually happens to them.

Courtesy of German Information Center

In 1950 Frisch retired from architecture to devote himself to writing. "I write my plays and novels alternately," he reported. "When I write a play I embark on a kind of dialogue with a problem. If I go on to another play it also is shaped by that dialogue. But if I turn to writing a novel I forget the dialogue and am forced to create something new."

Some critics theorize that while Frisch's plays deal with social and political problems, such as prejudice in *Andorra* and nuclear war in *Die Chinesische Mauer: Eine Farce* (1947; *The Chinese Wall*), his novels confront problems of a personal nature. But the main thrust of Frisch's work, whether personal or public, is, according to many critics, the exploration of human identity. Frisch repeatedly pits his protagonists against social forces that threaten to distort or extinguish their personalities. To force an individual into a social role against one's own true nature, Frisch believes, is a deadly sin, a violation of the Biblical commandment: "Thou shalt not make unto thee any graven image." Frisch is praised by reviewers as a superb ironist; often, his fictional works present a profoundly serious theme couched in terms of playful humor.

Frisch's diaries have provided a rich field of study for critics. They serve as study aids to the plays and novels, as well as literary works in their own right. Frisch always writes his *Sketchbooks* with publication in mind, not as personal records. They are not strictly autobiographical, as they contain elements of fiction and other narrative forms that do not fit the diary genre. Some reviewers comment that this methodical blurring of truth and invention in Frisch's writings reached its fullest expression in *Montauk* (1975), his novelized account of an actual weekend he spent on Long Island with an amorous young admirer. Again, however, according to critic Barbara Saunders, Frisch's true subject is the nature of identity. "Frisch is a very fascinating writer," stated Ivar Ivask, long-time editor of *World Literature Today* and founder of the Neustadt International Prize. "He maintains a personal engagement in the questions he asks and the problems he depicts. This very fine awareness, this moral sensitivity, characterizes everything Frisch has written."

(See also *CLC*, Vols. 3, 9, 14, 18, 32 and *Contemporary Authors*, Vols. 85-88.)

ALAN PRYCE-JONES

[*English critic and dramatist Pryce-Jones was editor of the* Times Literary Supplement *from 1948 to 1959. He has also served as drama critic for* The Observer *and* Theatre Arts *and contributed to many other periodicals. His works include* The Spring Journey *(1931),* The Rise and Fall of the Man of Letters *(1969), and* The Bonus of Laughter *(1986). In the following excerpt Pryce-Jones comments on Frisch's weaknesses as a dramatist.*]

[Max Frisch] was born in Zurich before the first World War: that is, he has had a prolonged experience of neutrality at the central point of Europe. He has watched—and "watched" is the operative word—the rise and fall of tyrannies, of insane experiments in government, of unexampled horrors in peace and war; and he has done so against an orderly background of luxury shops on the Bahnhofstrasse, splendid plumbing, rapid and regular electric trains, Ovaltine, and a curiously striated form of life in which there is little difference—to judge from the headlines in Swiss newspapers—between the small drama of a bicycling accident lovingly reported and the extreme brutality practiced by local murderers.

Like his near contemporary, Friedrich Dürrenmatt, he has been appalled by this double experience. All around him lies the most prosperous, and certainly the most comfortable, island of civilization in the world. It is very small, and it exists only because the prowlers over the hill all find it convenient that a neutral zone for the safekeeping of money and the promotion of high-minded conversation be kept intact. In the village of the world Switzerland, and especially the Swiss banking system, is in the position of the medieval church. It offers sanctuary.

This state of things is not, however, maintained without strain. Like the Swedes, the neutral Swiss have developed a high degree of neurosis. They feel themselves imperfectly loved by less fortunate neighbors; they suspect that neither Voltaire nor Madame de Staël would have lived long among them if they could conveniently have returned to Paris; they are well aware that there is more, in their healthy atmosphere, of cheese than champagne.

The reaction to this of Frisch was two-fold. On the one hand he adopted one of the most orderly of professions, that of architect; on the other, he broke early out of Swiss seemliness in order to explore the turbulent Balkans. The influence of Brecht upon him has been considerable; likewise that of Paul Claudel. Jointly with Dürrenmatt, and considerably assisted by the goodwill of the Zurich Schauspielhaus, which has allowed him to use its stage as a testing ground, he has set himself up as the conscience of Switzerland—a function which he has extended from the stage to the novel. His plays are carefully worked over. Like Brecht, he writes and rewrites, so that ***Count Oederland,*** for one, has been presented in several forms over ten years, and the germ of ***Andorra*** only matured after fifteen. His first play, ***The Chinese Wall,*** . . . was written in 1946 and revised in 1955.

The prophetic stance which he has adopted is a highly personal one. In his play about Don Juan, for instance, Juan turns out to be, at heart, no lover but a mathematician: a kind of deutero-Frisch, in fact. And in each of the three plays upon which his reputation abroad is chiefly founded—***Count Oederland, The Firebugs*** and ***Andorra***—the same voice rings through, at once generous and querulous, insistent, and often exasperatingly grumpy. It can already be heard in ***The Chinese Wall.***

Much the best of these plays is ***The Firebugs***. . . . It is a warning against the "long littleness of life" and the inevitable punishment which falls upon those who accept their subordinate role too easily. Its protagonist is Herr Biedermann—a name which in German not only connotes Everyman but carries with it overtones of contempt. Biedermann, then, is the *Spiessbürger*, the Little Man who will never dare be himself and who consequently deserves exactly what he gets. In this particular case, he takes into his house two fire-raisers, knowing full well what they are. Not only does he welcome them, he allows them to store tin drums of petrol in his attic. He offers them a banquet. He is all ingratiation. (pp. 22-3)

It is the logical end of the argument that it is Biedermann himself who finally produces the matches which allow the firebugs to light their conflagration.

A weakness of Frisch's plays, however, is that he does not know when to stop. The main structure of ***The Firebugs*** is spoiled by a long afterpiece in the next world, carrying fantasy dangerously close to the Higher Whimsy. Frisch has adopted a Claudel-like technique, with a group of firemen to act as ironic chorus. For six scenes his writing is beautifully economical, pointed, and rapid. Then, unable to resist dotting the "i's" of his theme, he slackens control. Similarly, in ***Count Oederland,*** which begins with great verve, fantasy finally turns to incoherence. The play itself is oddly reminiscent of Dürrenmatt's *Die Ehe des Herrn Mississippi (The Marriage of Mister Mississippi)*. Both deal with a public prosecutor who finds himself unable to bear the tidiness of his daily life, the predictability, the rectitude. In Frisch's drama the public prosecutor gets to work with an axe: he hacks his way to control of the state, via a revolutionary episode in the sewers of the city. The trouble with this evolution, however, is that it is far too forced. It seems likely that Frisch is remote from the fantasist he conceives himself to be. An ironist, yes: he has a fine deflationary sense; he can very well turn an epigrammatic stretch of dialogue at the expense of convention. But when he tries to sublimate his criticism of society in the realm of the fabulous he loses his way: the stratosphere is no home for the Swiss German, and his fable evaporates in mere intellectual oddity.

Similarly, ***Andorra*** fails as a statement about anti-Semitism—the kernel of its lesson—because it deals largely in clichés. There is something peculiarly exasperating about its title, to begin with. "The Andorra," says a note, "of this play has nothing to do with the real small state of this name, nor does it stand for another real small state; Andorra is the name of a model." Why, then, Andorra? Why not Erewhon, or Laputa, or a modern equivalent? Why go back to a forgotten style, by naming the characters, with the exception of two principals, "The Innkeeper," "The Priest," and so on? The situation into which they are plunged is so particular that they never acquire the universality which alone might justify this procedure. For the plot turns on the dilemma of a young man who has been adopted in a moment of impulse by "The Schoolteacher," who not only is his real father, but adds one deception to another by pretending, in the name of tolerance, that his son is a Jew. This exposes the son to danger at the hands of extremists from a hostile neighboring state; it also sets him up as an object of ridicule to his own countrymen. (pp. 23, 70)

This might be a moving tragedy, but it is spoiled by a melodramatic insistence which reduces it to the scale of an early nineteenth-century shocker like *The Lady of Lyons:* at any moment, one feels, the characters might break into blank verse. They are cutouts, not people, and their dilemma is the less striking for being wholly artificial. What is designed as a kind of morality play becomes a charade, redeemed from triviality only by being so patently and heavily "on the right side" in a genuine clash of minds.

To sum up, then: let us salute in Max Frisch a dramatist who is sincerely concerned by the complacent society in which he lives and into which he was born. He contemns its values, its littleness revolts him. He has a keen sense of theatre, and an acrid wit at command. But I suspect that his skill would have been more apparent at the beginning of this century when plays were written with a cabinetmaker's precision. The note of fantasy which he strikes does not ring quite true. It becomes forced, it swamps the argument it was meant to express. If it were still permissible to write problem plays in the manner of Arthur Pinero, Frisch would be better at home than in the fashionable world of Brecht, Genet and Beckett. (p. 70)

Alan Pryce-Jones, "Max Frisch: The Sage of Bahnhofstrasse," in Theatre Arts, *Vol. XLVII, Nos. 8-9, August-September, 1963, pp. 22-3, 70.*

ALEX NATAN

[*Natan edited the critical essay collections* German Men of Letters: Twelve Literary Essays *(1964) and* Swiss Men of Letters *(1970). In the following excerpt from his introductory essay in* German Men of Letters *Natan discusses the recurrent theme in Frisch's fiction of the individual's search for identity in an alienating society.*]

While his Swiss compatriot Dürrenmatt exerts himself to express the gnawing uneasiness of our conscience through daring and often fantastic situations and visions, Max Frisch is concerned with the complexity of the human character which must be ultimately held responsible for this uneasiness. A mathematician and architect by training, he pays much attention to balance and form when describing his experiences in our times. His central theme is the questionable or even lost identity of the individual and his self. Frisch enjoys the full support of readers who acutely feel uneasy when considering the dubiety of life in the atomic age, who are inclined to resignation and have grown tired of moral protests. On the other hand, Frisch has met with the opposition of those who still believe they are firmly protected by strong convictions. "The man who has a conviction", says the writer, "is able to cope with everything. Convictions proffer the best safeguard against being drowned in truth and reality". What caused the complete failure of his hitherto most successful play ***Andorra*** in New York, apart from bad translation and production, was the optimistic belief of an enlightened world in the powers of plain common sense. What Europeans have experienced in human suffering and degradation has never touched the core of the white Americans. The mass seduction of a whole community, and of a whole nation, was considered impossible in the country of maximal consumer seduction.

Stiller and Faber, the leading characters in his two best novels, are in search of their own real selves. This quest is a simple attack on the prevailing lethargy and on a resigned attitude to everything which might have nihilistic implications. Frisch, the bringer of new enlightenment, will yet preserve an element of romanticism, Frisch, the dispenser of irony, will always point a clear moral, and Frisch, the rationalist without illusions, will yet retain some strands of vivid imagination. In other words, Frisch undertakes to prove that the true self of a man is not necessarily identical with the image, which history or his fellow-men have given him. In his witty parody ***Don Juan oder die Liebe zur Geometrie*** Don Giovanni tilts against his reputation of being the eternal lady-killer, because he wants to follow his real passion, the pursuit of mathematics. Because of his real love, he devalues all existing values, and is even prepared to end his life as a "bon bourgeois" with wife and child.

This theme of the true identity behind an artificial mask, the destruction of false conventions, and the freeing of the self from deeply ingrained prejudices, is developed in ***Biedermann und die Brandstifter*** and in ***Andorra.*** The former play is a "Morality without a Moral" which shows the influence of Bert Brecht. Who are the wanton fire-raisers: the incendiaries or the bourgeois Everyman who would love to appease the world? The villains serve obviously as foils to the real question of whether a peace-loving good man "in his moral corruption and uncertainty of conviction, can defend himself at all, and indeed whether, being no better than the avowed criminals, he even deserves to be saved". In the end Biedermann confesses what he does not mean and does what he would avoid doing because he is afraid of the truth. The truth, however, is the inability of our world to come to its senses. In ***Andorra*** Frisch is concerned with pointing the moral that nobody in our present world is really free to use "his" qualities but that certain anonymous impulses exist whose dynamic forces compel him to act at a given moment, irrespective of whether this was his intention or not. In ***Andorra*** the ostensible innocence of a community is treated with biting irony in the beginning when a house is whitewashed. It becomes the writer's intention to leach the veneer and to reveal the ground-colours. Such an undertaking demands victims. The innocent falls a prey to the delusion, whether of himself or of the society he lives in, for it is always evil delusion which prevents the identification of man with his self and destroys his fundamental goodness and love instinct. Evil is not satisfied with inactivity. It must attack, it must get hold of man, it must feed on human flesh. Even awareness of prevailing evil will no longer stop or change the course of history. Frisch's technique as a writer is the analytical method. His novels and plays usually have a long history to look back upon, which can be traced in his diaries and occasional writings. But Frisch, like Dürrenmatt, is also an inveterate rewriter who is never satisfied with the final result. Once a theme has got hold of him, it proves expandable in many ways. He published reflections on his ***Don Juan*** play and a postscript to ***Biedermann.*** It is this variability of approach which is fascinating to the reader and allows the author so many interpretations of his central theme.

Attention has been drawn to the resemblance of Frisch's main characters to the traditional type of the romantic hero in German literature who has lost his identity, e.g. Kleist's *Amphitryon* and Chamisso's *Peter Schlemihl*. [Soergel-Hohoff, *Dichter und Dichtung der Zeit, Vol. II,* 1963] has even cited Dr. Faust, the archetype of a man who has lost his identity. This analogy appears rather far-fetched, for Frisch's novels and plays are set in a world which has largely become schizophrenic and has thus forced its inhabitants to adapt themselves to such an unusual situation. Amphitryon, Peter Schlemihl and Faust, moreover, consciously part with their selves for material lucre, while Stiller and Graf Oederland, Biedermann and Andri are desperately engaged in distilling their true selves out of the welter of present-day chaos. On their brows is written: Thou shalt not make to thyself any graven image. (pp. 26-8)

Alex Natan, in an introduction to German Men of Letters: Twelve Literary Essays, Vol. III, *edited by Alex Natan, 1964. Reprint by Oswald Wolff, 1968, pp. 1-33.*

MICHAEL BUTLER

[*Butler, an English critic, poet, and editor, is the author of a poetry collection,* Nails and Other Poems *(1964). He has written two critical surveys of Frisch's works,* The Novels of Max Frisch *(1976) and* The Plays of Max Frisch *(1985). In the following excerpt from* The Novels of Max Frisch *Butler examines five major novels by Frisch. He identifies several central themes in Frisch's fiction, particularly that of the "eccentric" individual at odds with society.*]

An important preoccupation of twentieth-century German literature has been the sense that man has lost his vital centre. Writer after writer has struggled with the problems produced by the collapse not just of traditional values but also of the self, the human personality, which this loss of centricity has induced. Hofmannsthal, Rilke, Kafka, Hesse, Musil, Böll, Grass and Frisch are some of the many writers who have sought in their different ways to throw light on an apparently increasing disintegration of human individuality and who have wrestled with the difficulties of portraying man in fiction that this involves. A poem written at the mid-point of the century by Gottfried Benn, whose roots stretch back to pre-First World War Expressionism, seemed to articulate a widely shared and persistent experience: . . .

> This is contemporary man,
> his centre a vacuum,
> continuity of personality
> is preserved by clothes
> which, if of good quality, last ten years.

The imagery of this poem with its characteristic title, "Fragmente," remarkably foreshadows Max Frisch's ***Mein Name sei Gantenbein*** which appeared fourteen years later—a novel in which a fictive narrator tries on 'stories' like clothes in an attempt to capture a sense of identity and restore continuity and substance to a fractured personality. But the sense of lost centricity to which Benn alludes affects, in one way or another, all the characters who people Frisch's narrative world. For they are eccentric individuals in that they are shown as living at odds with an environment which, far from exerting any central stabilising power, has itself a void at its core. The frightening nature of this void is disguised from the apparently centric majority only by habit and the repetitive shape of everyday routine. Frisch's characters, indeed, are embedded—the exception is perhaps the hero of his first novel, ***Jürg Reinhart*** (1934)—in the well-defined context of a modern bourgeois society which is depicted as deeply flawed. For by the conformity which it demands of its members, the rôles which it expects them to perform, and the pressures to which it subjects them, this society is shown to be indifferent, if not inimical, to the maintenance and development of personal integrity. The linchpin of this social system is marriage, and Frisch uses the institution as a microcosm of the larger community beyond. It is not therefore surprising that marriage—and in particular the problematical nature of its supposed centripetence—is the fundamental experience to which all Frisch's protagonists are exposed.

In this way the picture Frisch draws of mid-century European society—and certain pages of ***Stiller*** (1954) and ***Homo Faber*** (1957) suggest that in his view the American way of life is not dissimilar—is given an essentially negative character. Society does not reveal within itself, nor offer to the individual, any viable centric principle. Paradoxically, therefore, those who commit themselves to the system, whilst on the surface appearing satisfied and integrated, are in fact disastrously lacking in wholeness and genuine centricity. The reader of Frisch's narrative fiction is thus presented with not one but two poles of eccentricity—a positive and a negative one. Around the latter are clustered such characters as the Oberst, Ammann and Hauswirt (***Die Schwierigen,*** 1943, revised and reissued in 1957), Julika, Bohnenblust and Sturzenegger (***Stiller***) and Frantisek Svoboda (***Mein Name sei Gantenbein***). Such men and women live on the surface of life, clinging to facts or ideologies as guarantees of stability. Around the other pole (the one which most clearly attracts Frisch himself) are gathered Jürg Reinhart, Anatol Stiller, Walter Faber and, in the last novel, Felix Enderlin—that is, 'die Schwierigen' who are suddenly brought face to face with the hollowness of everyday life, for whom the 'facts' lose their coherence without warning and who consequently suffer a severe degree of dislocation. In the grey area between the two are to be found those characters like Yvonne and Hortense (***Die Schwierigen***), Rolf and Sibylle (***Stiller***) and Hanna Landsberg (***Homo Faber***) who have experienced a comparable sense of alienation from themselves and society but who have settled for an uninspiring, melancholy compromise.

With the exception of the first novel it cannot be said that Frisch depicts the outcome of his heroes' endeavours to locate a centric principle with any optimism. At best the issue is left open. After the straightforward account of the mature Jürg Reinhart's search for a more integrated existence and his failure to discover it in ***Die Schwierigen,*** Frisch turned to the examination of one individual's attempt to return to society as a 'new man'. Anatol Stiller is brought to realise that his 'angel' experience, which he felt and hoped would function as a dynamic centre around which he could build a new life, is not strong enough to withstand the pressures of a society which can offer nothing but rôle-playing as an alternative. Not only does society in this way offer Stiller a false centricity, it also refuses to brook autonomous eccentricity within its own gravitational field. The effects of such societal intransigence on personality are illuminated by the case of Walter Faber. The danger of total conformity to current social 'normality' is that there exists no guarantee that society's opiates will remain permanently effective. The protagonist of ***Homo Faber*** is one individual for whom the narcotic effects of a false centricity wear off. The awareness of his life-long 'negative' mode of eccentricity, however, comes too late to give him much more than a tantalising glimpse of what true centricity might be—indeed, the novel is the record of Faber's struggle against precisely this awareness. Finally, with the fictions of his anonymous narrator in ***Mein Name sei Gantenbein*** Frisch has presented his most radical exposition to date of this fundamental theme. Marriage and the problem of human transcience move to the forefront of an intensely private exploration of personal dislocation and inadequacy.

In this narrative world only the 'Schwierigen' come close to perceiving a centre to which they might relate their lives, but they fall victim to the pressures inherent in the very eccentricity which ensures that they are truly alive at all. For it is not possible, Frisch seems to be saying, to live an integrated life on the periphery. Neither love between man and woman nor any form of transcendental faith (posited only in ***Stiller***) is shown as ultimately viable. The one is too difficult to sustain in the face of human rigidity and the hostile nature of time, the other depends, as the Christian theologian would put it, on Grace: that is, it cannot be commanded by the autonomous individual. The paradox is deep and bitter: only the 'positive' eccentric has any chance of achieving 'das wirkliche Leben', but the very condition of his eccentricity militates directly against such wholeness.

That Max Frisch should be attracted to the theme of eccentricity is readily understandable when one particular but important aspect of his Swiss intellectual background is considered. This aspect was both investigated and given a name by the Swiss scholar Karl Schmid in his book *Unbehagen im Kleinstaat* (1963). Schmid's study of five Swiss men of letters (C. F. Meyer, Henri-Frédéric Amiel, Jakob Schaffner, Jacob Burckhardt and Max Frisch) makes clear the existence and nature of a persistent malaise which runs contrary to what is generally—and in Switzerland almost exclusively—held to be the central Swiss literary tradition, exemplified by such writers as Albrecht von Haller, Jeremias Gotthelf, Gottfried Keller and Jean-Henri Pestalozzi. This malaise is shown to have three principal sources: the feeling of living on the periphery of historical developments; an unease at occupying an ill-defined position between the great nations and cultures of Germany, France and Italy; and thirdly, as a consequence, the lack of any opportunity to face and take influential decisions in the world. Thus the 'Kleinstaat' with its historical principle of neutrality is felt by these writers to have no central rôle to play, to be condemned to what Schmid calls 'Schicksalslosigkeit'. The surrender of Jakob Schaffner to the temptations of the Third Reich can be seen as an example of the disorientation brought about by such a loss of social, political and human relevance. On the other hand, Frisch's work, despite or because of its pessimistic features, is testimony to the creative possibilities inherent in an eccentricity which is recognised, defined and explored in a positive way.

Another writer whom Schmid could equally have chosen for his argument, and one who deeply influenced the younger Frisch, is Albin Zollinger. Zollinger, indeed, has been called the 'key figure in contemporary Swiss German literature', and it is he who expresses in his novels more than most this feeling of 'Unbehagen im Kleinstaat', particularly acute during the fateful years that saw the Depression, the Spanish Civil War and the rise and initial success of National Socialism. Zollinger's novels, which all appeared during this period, depict protagonists who are 'difficult' in Frisch's sense of the term, 'Sonderlinge' who stand out from their parochial and not infrequently hostile environment by virtue of their troubled scepticism and unwillingness or inability to accept their society's myths, conventions and norms. . . . It is not difficult to see in Zollinger's eccentrics prototypes for Frisch's own characters, but it must be said that nowhere does Zollinger achieve the subtlety, depth and unity of Frisch's narrative fiction. As Frisch himself put it in his belated obituary of the older writer: 'Albin Zollinger was in the situation of an emigrant who never emigrated . . . Zollinger had no other hinterland but the country in which he lived, and it proved too small to be a productive environment in itself, a country which has lacked a history for too long to yield a true model of the world.'

In a speech accepting the Büchner Prize in 1958 Frisch declared his own solidarity with all those literary figures, from Georg Büchner himself to twentieth-century contemporaries, who are linked by 'das Emigrantische'. But this solidarity has its roots in a very different world from the one Zollinger left so abruptly in 1941: 'The notion of emigration which unites us is not expressed in the fact that we neither can nor wish to speak for our mother countries, but that we feel our homes—whether we change them or not—to be merely temporary ones in the world of today.' The physical and moral devastation of Hitler's War, the use of the atomic bomb and the permanent threat of an ultimate, all-embracing holocaust have underlined to a degree hardly imaginable by Zollinger and earlier writers, not only the savage consequences of human disintegration and lost centricity, but also the fact that the eccentric dilemma, the sense of personal and intellectual homelessness, is not simply a Swiss problem but a universal malaise. It is this which has enabled Frisch in his novels and dramas to attain the international relevance which was denied Albin Zollinger.

Ironically, the very marginality, 'Schicksalslosigkeit', which obsessed C. F. Meyer, Amiel and others, can be said to have contributed to Switzerland's defence against the encircling Axis powers during the Second World War. At the same time, although isolated and cut off from the great events in the outside world, a writer like Frisch found himself face to face with an extraordinary paradox: whilst the comprehensive nature of the mid-century upheaval left Switzerland the only corner of Europe unscathed, it made him simultaneously aware of the depths of his roots in the wider culture of Germany. The year 1945, it is true, did not represent for him 'das Jahr Null' in quite the same way as it did for many writers living in or returning to a shattered Germany. Neither was there the same need for Frisch to share in the linguistic 'Kahlschlag' which such writers as Weyrauch, Eich, Andersch and Hans Werner Richter felt was necessary to oppose the aesthetic pretensions of older writers and in particular to eradicate the poisonous undergrowth nurtured by Goebbels' Propaganda Ministry which had threatened to suffocate the German language itself. Nevertheless, Frisch did feel a deep sense of personal involvement in the German catastrophe, an involvement which found immediate expression in his second play, ***Nun singen sie wieder*** (1945), and many pages of his ***Tagebuch 1946-1949*** (1950)—despite the fact that he was not burdened directly with the guilt of a recent and appalling past. Furthermore, Frisch certainly *is* heir to a specific German language scepticism which arose at the beginning of the century—most urgently and interestingly in the peripheral capitals of Prague and Vienna—and which gained powerful impetus from the impact of National Socialist ideology upon the use of language. With Frisch it is not so much the feeling that certain words and phrases, distorted and manipulated by the Nazis, have become unusable, as that language in its literary form has in itself always possessed an element of intractable strangeness. For Max Frisch, as indeed for all Swiss Germans, there exists a basic tension between *Schriftdeutsch* and everyday speech. In a sense, therefore, some aspects at least of that linguistic alienation felt by many of the immediate post-war generation of writers in Germany have long been familiar to Swiss German writers who have chosen not to write in their native dialect. And this fact may help to explain Frisch's own early fascination with the problematic nature of language.

It was, of course, a moment of intense irony for a Swiss German writer to look across the border from his self-conscious position as a 'Verschonter' on the periphery of a rich and dominant literary tradition and to observe that tradition's apparent collapse. It is thus not surprising that Frisch's novels are among the first in the post-war period to raise such significant issues as the problem of identity and to explore the negative and positive tensions which exist in the search for centricity in a shifting, pluralistic world. Despite obvious differences, it is not difficult to see the close relationship of Frisch's eccentrics to such figures as Keetenheuve in Koeppen's *Das Treibhaus* (1953), Oskar Matzerath, Joachim Mahlke and Eddi Amsel in Grass's 'Danzig Trilogy' (1959-63), Hans Schnier in Böll's *Ansichten eines Clowns* (1963) or Leni, the heroine of *Gruppenbild mit Dame* (1971). These novels show, like those of Frisch, the disintegrating effects on human personality and relationships of a social reality which is essentially lacking in health and wholeness. Furthermore, in Frisch's mature fiction narrative continuity itself is disrupted in order to render this reality confusingly opaque and to prevent the reader from assembling simple social and biographical data into comfortable patterns in which to imprison his protagonists. It is this quality of opacity that offers points of contact with such novels as Uwe Johnson's *Mutmaßungen über Jakob* (1959) and *Das dritte Buch über Achim* (1961), Hildesheimer's *Tynset* (1965) or Peter Bichsel's *Die Jahreszeiten* (1967). These authors all reject or modify traditional narrative assumptions, share a common interest in abstaining from reassuring statements about external reality and leave their characters' personalities fluid and hypothetical. The novels of Max Frisch, written over a time-span of thirty years, form an impressive body of fiction in their own right; they can also be seen as central to the contemporary German language novel as it has developed since the end of the Second World War. (pp. 9-16)

Despite Frisch's own oblique admission of the novel's immaturity, ***Jürg Reinhart*** is still of some interest in that it reveals many of the thematic preoccupations of the later novels. It is however true that little in the book anticipates the complexity of ***Die Schwierigen,*** the unique power of ***Stiller*** or the sensitive handling of character in ***Homo Faber.*** Nor is there more than the faintest hint of that quality of irony which transfigures all three later novels, but most subtly, perhaps, ***Mein Name sei Gantenbein.*** The novel, in fact, is a straightforward account—in the tradition of the *Bildungsroman*—of the central character's progress from a hesitant and self-conscious adolescence to the threshold of manhood via confrontation with love, suffering and death. The name Frisch gives to his eponymous hero immediately indicates the author's debt to Gottfried Keller whose *Der Grüne Heinrich* Frisch once called 'the best father anyone could have' (***Tagebuch 1946-1949*** . . .). Like Heinrich Lee before him, Jürg has left the narrow confines of his native Zürich to seek wider experience abroad. Although he too has a gift for painting, he is now a tyro writer earning his living as a composer of newspaper articles and short stories. To borrow a phrase Keller applied to his Grüne Heinrich, Jürg is 'a private and solitary individual'. Frisch calls him significantly 'dieser Sonderling' (*'this eccentric'*). It is precisely this quality of apartness, seen also in varying degrees in the other characters of the novel, that links the book most securely with the later narratives. It is a quality that affects not only the character's appraisal of himself, but also vitiates his relationships with others. An investigation of the thematic elements of the novel must therefore proceed from this dual perspective.

The setting provides a pertinent backcloth for the analysis of these relationships: a 'Fremdenhaus' aptly named *Hotel Solitudo* which is run by Frau von Woerlach and her daughter, Inge, impoverished remnants of the Prussian nobility and close cousins to Fontane's similarly placed Poggenpuhls family. It is a place where people come to unburden themselves, to seek momentary relief from their everyday worries. Its attraction is precisely its anonymity, a sense of freedom comes from the knowledge that they can leave before their true selves are discovered. 'For they liked the idea of being heard sympathetically without having to commit themselves, as if they were aware that they themselves were not capable of love'. . . . Indeed, the capacity for love, the need to extend it and the problem of how to preserve it, can be seen as the basis of all Frisch's writing. Here the wilful obscurity of people's attitudes towards each other is contrasted with the purity and delicacy of the Adriatic spanned by an immensely clear blue sky, the description of which is placed as a *leitmotiv* at key moments in the novel.

Dr Svilos, of all the characters, is the only one native to this environment—and even he is a black sheep with a prison record for surgical negligence. The rest are strangers, displaced aristocrats or lost souls like the Baron and his younger wife who spend their lives in bored and aimless travel. The lack of a valid contact with their environment points to a similar failing in their personal relationships. A possible exception may be found in the friendship between Frau von Woerlach and Frau von Reisner, the guest whose selflessness and personal commitment contrast sharply with her son's unpleasantness. However, this friendship hardly rises in its treatment above the conventional and serves mainly to highlight the younger people's predicament, in particular Inge's loneliness and vain love for Jürg. And it is this latter relationship—the one that leads to the hero's apparent ultimate self-realisation—which forms the core of the novel. In its frustrations and convolutions it epitomises the dominant theme of the existential aloneness of human beings, their lack of a viable centric principle around which they can build their lives, which has occupied Frisch for over thirty years. It is true to say, however, that this state of affairs is only diagnosed with clarity in the later work; for ***Jürg Reinhart*** is made to end on a note of optimism which is not unequivocally deducible from the novel's internal logic. (pp. 17-19)

Occasionally the quality of the writing adds to the reader's unease: far too often it is strained and prone to purple passages which come close to bathos. Nor are some of the ideas free from banality, and the central preoccupation of Part One, Jürg's obsessive sexual modesty and his tendency to emotionalism, strike today's reader as faintly comic. There is an element of shock in the euthanasia theme—no doubt even stronger in the 1930s—but its final link with Jürg's maturation must be declared tenuous. The novel is at its strongest in the straightforward depiction of relationships, but a weakness for melodrama and the 'important statement' betrays the youthfulness of the author.

Despite such criticisms, however, it is fascinating to see the tentative exploration of themes which, in a more intricate form, are to become the unmistakable hallmark of Frisch's mature fiction: the eccentricity of his characters' stance, their sense of personal dislocation, the fundamentally centric nature of the man/woman nexus and the early beginnings of the 'graven image' theme, seen in Jürg's struggle with his sense of what he is and what he thinks others see him as. They undergo a further intensification in Frisch's second novel, ***Die Schwierigen,*** in which we meet an older Jürg Reinhart in a wider and more complex context. (p. 25)

Frisch was clearly disappointed at the lukewarm reception accorded to his first novel, and this may have accounted for the delay of almost a decade before the appearance of his second, ***J'adore ce qui me brûle oder Die Schwierigen*** in 1943. The first edition had as its opening section a chapter entitled 'Reinhart/ oder die Jugend' which in fact was a version of the earlier novel, condensed to a third of the original text. Frisch is on record as stating that this opening section was provided—against his own inclination—at the behest of his publisher and after the novel had been completed. It is not surprising, therefore, that when he decided to reissue the novel in 1957 with the reversed title, ***Die Schwierigen oder j'adore ce qui me brûle,*** Frisch should obey his earlier instinct and suppress the first section which he had always regarded with some reserve. (p. 26)

The reversal of the title, though an obvious and simple device to distinguish the two editions, can be seen to have a further signficance: by taking the emphasis away from the idiosyncratic gallicism and placing it more squarely on 'Die Schwierigen', Frisch indicates where the real tensions of the novel lie. His main characters have difficulty in fitting into society, in finding suitable rôles with which they can identify. And as society is made up of a complex system of personal relationships, checks and balances, it is the problem of such relationships that is in the forefront. In this novel—in contrast to ***Jürg Reinhart***—these are seen more clearly, and therefore more convincingly, in their *social* context.

The greater complexity of this work enables us to isolate and contrast a number of essential themes, the discussion of which can best illustrate the problematic nature of Frisch's characters and the critique of society which it implies. These themes can be subsumed under three main headings: (a) the problem of marriage, (b) the problem of the Artist in Society, and (c) the search for 'das wirkliche Leben'. However, these problems are not mutually exclusive but all three closely interwoven. For marriage, perhaps more than any other institution, is the one which most tightly links men and women to the social system, and if the artist is aware of his relationship to society as a problematic one—and it is argued here that *all* Frisch's protagonists can be seen as eccentric figures in their society—then the question of marriage is likely to be a central preoccupation. It naturally follows that the concept of 'das wirkliche Leben' in this novel can only be explored in relation to these two central areas. (pp. 26-7)

With the publication in 1954 of ***Stiller*** Max Frisch established a claim to major status in the history of the novel in post-war Germany and Switzerland. Hitherto respected, like his fellow countryman Dürrenmatt, as a leading dramatist in the German-speaking world, Frisch suddenly produced a narrative work of unsuspected depth and fascination. Although his powers as a novelist had been refined and intensified since the earlier novels by the composition of his ***Tagebuch 1946-1949,*** this was the first occasion they had been put to the test in a sustained narrative. . . . The novel has been discussed variously and cogently as an examination of the 'problematic and tragic nature of marriage', as an 'artist-novel in an age of reproduction' and as an exposition of Kierkegaard's existentialism. Faced with such widely divergent interpretations (and each has its specific strengths as well as weaknesses), the reader must look for a common denominator that will allow each emphasis its due weight. For to grant any one view exclusivity would be to impoverish a very rich structure. This common denominator—the creative principle which joins the disparate parts and themes of the book together—is *irony*.

It is only in the ironic mode that ***Stiller*** achieves its unity as a novel, for practically every page reveals an essential ambivalence that Anatol Stiller himself characterises: . . . 'Every word is false and true, that is the nature of words'. . . . Viewed thus, the 'Postscript by the Public Prosecutor', for example, ceases to be a *Formbruch* and becomes a kind of 'Eighth Notebook' giving a final but none the less subjective perspective to the story of Anatol Stiller. Other ironic features of the novel are similarly striking. The most obvious and the most complex, of course, is the device of 'Mr White' writing about Stiller as a third person; it enables Frisch to achieve a high degree of ambiguity which means that no account can be taken at its face value but each is relativised by the others. Furthermore an essential paradox is contained in the idea of Stiller as the centre of the other characters' world, a 'prisoner' to whom the 'free' come to tell the important stories of their lives. Ironic, too, is the contrast between the freedom Stiller appears to secure in prison and the constraints to which he falls victim once he is released. The many parodistic literary associations and the fact that Stiller's defence counsel proves hostile and the prosecuting counsel sympathetic are examples of the mode in minor key.

An interpretation of the novel, therefore, will actively involve the reader's experience to a high degree. He must play a *creative* rôle in piecing the evidence together and coming to his own conclusion. His own experience and view of life will lead him to give more credence, now to this character, now to that. Frisch himself has declared in his ***Tagebuch 1946-1949*** that the principle enjoyment in reading is that 'the reader above all discovers the richness of his own thoughts'. . . . The truth itself is inexpressible in words—a sceptical attitude towards language Frisch shares with many twentieth-century German writers—

but it can perhaps be located in the tension between what is said and what is meant: 'One makes statements which never express our true experience which remains inexpressible; such statements can only circumscribe the truth as closely and accurately as possible; reality, the inexpressible, emerges at best as the tension between our statements'. . . . It is this scepticism which has led Frisch to prefer the fragment form, the 'sketch', as an expression of mistrust of premature 'wholeness', of formal perfection which cannot correspond to his experience of an essentially fragmented world. Stiller's concern is the same: he relates his fragmentary stories in an attempt to escape the finished image ('Bildnis') other people are intent on fixing upon him. (pp. 54-5)

Stiller's response to his defence counsel's demand that he write down 'the plain, unvarnished truth' . . . is entirely in tune with the Diary entry quoted above. Stiller begins to tell stories as a method of approaching, obliquely and tentatively, the expression of his unique experience. At the same time he is aware—in the third sentence of the novel—of the danger he is in, although his attitude at this early stage is one of defensive humour: 'For experience has taught me that without whisky I'm not myself, I'm open to all sorts of good influences and liable to play the part they want me to play, although it's not me at all'. . . . Indeed, the novel's opening exclamation—'I'm not Stiller!'—coupled with the breathless hypotaxis of this sentence (it covers fourteen lines of text), underlines the fragile nature and the tensions of the position Stiller is trying to hold. The stories he tells constitute an effort to preserve intact the vision of a new self and to forestall society's desire to recapture its fixed image of its 'lost' citizen.

The stories vary a good deal both in their length and in their importance. Although they are ultimately meant for his defence counsel, Dr Bohnenblust, the actual audience varies from Bohnenblust himself to Knobel (who receives the bulk of the tales), and from Julika to Rolf, the holder of the State's brief. Two appear to be written primarily for himself (i.e. the first version of 'Isidor' and the final version of the Florence story). They occur predominantly in the first Notebook, in which Stiller's attempt to escape his identity still seems possible, and finally in the third Notebook after which they cease. And they cease for the good reason that their essential function—the gradual revelation of Stiller's personality culminating in the 'experience with his angel'—is taken over by the stories the *others* tell *him* and the increasingly painful self-analysis this forces upon White/Stiller until the two identities are, legally at least, synthesised.

That the stories consist of a gradual revelation of true experience can be seen if their nature is examined. They progress from the relatively lighthearted story of the murder of the 'hair-oil gangster' Schmitz, via the apeces of the Isidor, Rip van Winkle and Jim White episodes, to the bitter honesty of the real story of Florence the mulatto girl. In other words, the actual relation of the stories slowly turns against the narrator's intention of establishing beyond doubt his identity as Mr White. (pp. 55-6)

It is Max Frisch's particular *tour de force* in ***Stiller*** that his chosen form prevents the reader from jumping to conclusions about events and characters. An integral part of the method is the sacrifice of the traditional omniscient narrator. Thus even at the end of the book one cannot be absolutely sure about anything. One cannot, for example, say with the grotesque confidence of Stiller's former friends: 'I know you!' For Frisch 'everything which is complete ceases to accommodate the human spirit'. It is in this sense of posing questions and then leaving them open, of refusing to seize the neat and comfortable answer, however 'real' it might seem to be, that Frisch demonstrates most clearly his gifts as a subtle and humane ironist. (p. 87)

Having drawn in ***Stiller*** the portrait of a man intensely aware of a personal eccentricity in a world that has itself lost its centre, in ***Homo Faber*** Frisch turns the problem through a hundred and eighty degrees. Whereas Anatol Stiller's story begins with the recognition of such a severe dislocation, Walter Faber's ends with it. For fifty years Faber has lived, as it were, at the dead centre of an ostensibly stable world, his rôle circumscribed by precise problems and precise solutions. In fact, Faber's life has been what Stiller feared most: repetition, routine, banality.

If ***Stiller*** explored the artistic temperament, it was in a sense a logical step for Frisch the architect to proceed to an examination of a technologist who might represent that other sphere of human activity with which the novelist himself has been most closely involved. However, technology as such plays surprisingly little part in the novel. Frisch makes no attempt, for example, to describe its rôle and impact in the modern world. . . . What the reader is shown instead is a certain attitude of mind rooted in rigid mental categories which Frisch has observed before in other fields of human endeavour—for example, the Law (Bohnenblust), the Army (Ammann), Architecture (Sturzenegger) and Commerce (Hauswirt). Such an attitude enables men to take refuge in practical affairs and neglect the more difficult problems of the spirit. Precisely the process of showing an individual confronted with the disastrous one-sidedness of this type of thinking gives ***Homo Faber*** its particular shape and interest.

Faber's 'report' is composed at two unexpected moments of inertia (confinement to his hotel room in Caracas and to his sickroom in an Athens hospital) amidst a flux of normally undifferentiated sense impressions. Clearly, the writing of a report can hardly be seen in itself as an unusual activity for a UNESCO engineer, but what is abnormal is the fact that Faber should be turning his scientific training—i.e. in the observation, enumeration and assessment of data—on to *himself*. The tragic loss of his daughter forces him to go over the past and search in it for a pattern—or rather, to deny the existence of a pattern only to create one by the choice of those memories which he deems significant. What the undertaking undoubtedly demonstrates is that his mental attitude and the style and language which reflect it, however suitable for the evaluation of technical problems and achievements, are simply not capable of dealing with the larger imponderables of human behaviour.

During the course of his story Faber becomes—whatever he may himself think—more than a 'typical' engineer or technologist, just as Stiller similarly became more than a 'typical' sculptor and artist. Indeed, it is arguable that if they did not achieve such individuality their stories would not hold the reader as they do. Both are, of course, representative of problems general to life in mid-twentieth-century society, but both wrestle with intensely private concerns. In Faber's case it is his fear of human involvement—'Menschen sind anstrengend' ('People are a strain')—a fear he hides behind the system of neat conventions which is technology. For technology provides Faber with an escape route to the periphery of life where he can avoid being sucked into the dangerous vortex—Stiller's 'black hole'—of real experience. This personal, 'technocratic' rigidity strongly recalls that of Bohnenblust—but with one crucial difference: unlike Bohnenblust Faber is struggling against a suspicion, faint but nagging, which he would dearly be rid of, namely that society and his rôle in it are no longer in meaningful conjunction. Bohnenblust never questions surface reality, the apparent stability of the world, but what we read in the opening pages of ***Homo Faber*** are the words of a man who, however self-confident his motivation, has begun to move in a fateful direction: that of an attempt to assert that life, his life, is congruent, understandable and therefore controllable. With typical Frisch irony he achieves the precise opposite of this. But, paradoxically enough, the very destruction of his preconceptions gives Faber—too late, perhaps—that vision of genuine centricity which can only be gained by the recognition of centrifugal extremes and the consequent necessity to steer a path between them. (pp. 88-9)

A remarkable feature of ***Homo Faber*** is the fact that well over half its pages concern travel of one sort or another. Like a modern Ahasuerus Walter Faber covers thousands of miles in an apparently endless criss-crossing of continents. On closer inspection, however, all this toing and froing reveals one common characteristic: circularity. (p. 90)

If distortion and incongruity are seen as the common feature in Faber's relationship to the environment and to people, it is not surprising to find the same characteristics reflected in his choice and use of language. Faber sets out to compose a factual report on his recent and not-so-recent past in the obvious hope that it will prove his innocence and uphold his view of life as a system of unemotional orderliness in which all phenomena are satisfactorily accounted for. To succeed in this task, his instrument-language ought to possess the very virtues of sobriety and order which he desires to affirm. It is precisely these virtues, however, that disintegrate under the pressure of Faber's memories as he relives crucial moments of past experience. The fundamental irony of his report lies in that Faber's language *catches him out,* i.e. the discrepancy between what he says and what he thinks he says becomes increasingly evident, until the point is reached when he himself can no longer overlook it. It is in this sense that the novel constitutes the gradual process of unmasking Walter Faber. Language, indeed, is the mask behind which Faber hides his real self (even from himself); and the composition of the report is the unexpected means by which he is made to recognise this fact. (p. 106)

Walter Faber can be seen, therefore, as a 'negative' eccentric, his natural reflexes thoroughly blunted by the rôle he has chosen to play in society. From the very first pages we see him as drained, both physically (stomach cancer) and emotionally (Ivy)—a fitting member of Bohnenblust's docile, anonymous society. Faber is the sort of person Bohnenblust wanted Stiller to be, and thus the novel carries forward that particular strand of social criticism. The paradox here is that as Faber becomes aware of his eccentricity, he catches at the same time a glimpse of a possible cure. In doing so he rises above the level of comfortable anonymity and becomes an individual. The centric principle . . . is posited but not achieved. The novel ends, as do ***Stiller*** and ***Die Schwierigen,*** pessimistically. Nevertheless, Frisch shares that indomitable humanism of Albert Camus: 'Etre privé d'espoir, ce n'est pas désespérer.' And in ***Mein Name sei Gantenbein*** he returns yet again to the problem of eccentricity with imagination and irony undiminished. (p. 120)

The lack of a vital centre which precipitated Stiller's crisis of identity and led to Faber's total dislocation is also the dominant theme of ***Mein Name sei Gantenbein.*** However, whereas in ***Stiller*** and ***Homo Faber*** we witness one man run out of energy and another out of time, as they struggle from opposite points to harmonise their experience of themselves and of the world, here the problem is posed in a radically different manner. The reader is no longer invited to observe the behaviour of a man under stress in a prison cell or of a man caught in a web of habit which fails to sustain his weight at the critical moment. On this occasion he is placed squarely inside the skull of an anonymous narrator who, by an effort of imaginative reflection, endeavours to define and come to terms with his experience. In Frisch's view, the removal of traditional plot structure gives his narrator a better opportunity to explore at will the latent potentialities of his situation. By inventing a number of separate identities the latter achieves an ironic detachment from his fictions which enables him (and the reader) to observe more accurately their relationship to those experiences which triggered off the need to explore in the first place.

In one sense, of course, this technique had been adumbrated in ***Stiller,*** whose protagonist invents stories to express an existential experience. It is also true that the fundamental experience playfully encircled and probed in ***Mein Name sei Gantenbein*** is quite as eccentric as any illustrated in the earlier novels. However, in this book the fictive narrator is presented as completely isolated, and the fact that most of what he narrates is put forward unambiguously as fiction leads to a much more radical expression of Frisch's old belief that experience cannot be directly or absolutely captured in language, that truth will always remain fluid and elusive as quicksilver. 'Confessions are more masklike than silence, one can say everything and the secret merely slips back behind our words'. . . . Nevertheless, to try and enmesh the secret of human experience Frisch stakes out a subtle net of verbal fictions. Exploiting humour and irony to the full, he prevents the reader from seizing on any particular fiction and thereby fracturing what is in fact a rich, if unfathomable, totality. Thus he has his narrator construct personae, each of which relativises the other, as the narrator identifies with, and retreats from, each in turn. In this way 'a very ordinary story' . . . is revealed as paradoxically full of extraordinary potentialities, potentialities that were alive enough for, and therefore part of, the individual whose story it is. For it is an essential Frisch insight that 'experience' is not just something that has 'happened' but is also coloured by what has been neglected, by the fact that certain paths, certain decisions have *not* been taken. Frisch here attempts to penetrate the surface level of biography, which is normally all that is accessible to others, in order to reach the underlying pattern of experience ('Erlebnismuster') whose contours are much more fascinatingly varied than the superficial topography would lead one to suspect. . . . In a key essay entitled **"Unsere Geir nach Geschdichten,"** published four years before ***Mein Name sei Gantenbein,*** Frisch declared:

> Experience is an insight, not a result of external events. A single external event can serve a thousand experiences. Perhaps there is no other way to express experience than by narrating events, i.e. stories, as if our experience sprang from stories. I believe it is the other way round. Stories spring from experience. Experience wants to make itself intelligible and so it invents a reason for itself, preferably a past. Once upon a time . . . Stories are sketches ('Entwürf') projected into the past, games of the imagination which we pass off as reality.

These 'games of the imagination' are a means of defining the quality of experience more accurately, more openly. If truth cannot be expressed directly (as Stiller knew) because of the subjective nature of perception, then stories must be invented in the hope that they will act as a relatively objective mirror to the reality experienced by the individual. This, for Frisch, is a general and necessary principle: 'There is no other way of coming face to face with our pattern of experience.' Experience is only comprehended and controlled, he goes on significantly, when the story invented to express it has the aura of credibility.

The implications for the narrative technique of ***Mein Name sei Gantenbein*** are obvious. An experience (or pattern of experience) is searching for stories in which to express itself, much as Pirandello's six characters search for an author who might articulate their particular experience in dramatic form. In this sense fictions as a product of experience have a reality all of their own: 'I believe decisive changes in a person's life can stem from events which have never really happened, from ideas produced by an experience which is there before a story appears to act as a cause. The story merely expresses the experience.' It follows that an examination of the stories an individual invents, whether instinctively or deliberately, should lead to the basic pattern of experience that determines their shape and the individual's identity. The more complex the pattern of experience (i.e. the more complex the individual personality and particularly his degree of self-awareness), the greater will be the variety of the stories needed to reflect it. This is the nexus of problems behind ***Mein Name sei Gantenbein.*** (pp. 121-23)

In one of the answers to a series of imaginary questions on the nature and themes of his new novel, published under the title **"Ich schreibe für Leser,"** Frisch revealed his intentions vis-à-vis his fictive narrator: 'I wanted to show the reality of a man by having him appear as a white patch ('als weißer Fleck') outlined by the sum of fictional identities congruent with his personality. Such an outline, I thought, would be more precise than any biography which is based, as we know, on speculation. A negative procedure, if you like. There is no investigation of where and when something happened . . . The story is not told as if an individual could be identified by his factual behaviour; he betrays himself in his fictions.' And indeed Frisch's narrator does remain 'ein weißer Fleck' at the centre of the book, an ironic non-character searching for a reflected identity in the characters he invents.

Frisch's fictive narrator is thus clearly motivated by that same dissatisfaction with 'biographical' reality which we have already noted in Stiller and which similarly inspires the ironically named Kürmann in ***Biografie.*** The experience of such men (or perhaps their heightened awareness of it) is plainly too rich to find adequate expression in the mere objective facts of their lives. Nevertheless, although Frisch has his narrator declare: 'I try on stories like clothes!' . . . , he makes him at the same time aware of the ironic nature of his enterprise: although these 'clothes' will hide his nakedness and thus protect him against a world which is only too swift to seize on his vulnerability, they will not give him a *new* life—'the same creases always develop in the same places, I know that'. . . . Instead the 'clothes' are seen as a possible route to the discovery of his true identity. For they allow playful variations on his static, but fundamentally fragmentary biography. (pp. 123-24)

[Faced] with the problem of defining and recreating his experience of reality on the basis of his imagination, the narrator has a simple choice: either he could cut himself off altogether from empirical reality and enter a world of fantasy or he could keep alive his roots in that reality with the hope that his inventions would then produce that sense of personal integrity which he lacks in his everyday life. Although the variations, the stories he tries on like a man tries on clothes, are openly presented as fictions, it is obvious the narrator has chosen the second course. For the stories gain in credibility the more they approximate to his fundamental experience—that is, acts of pure imagination become a method of defining a pattern of experience which is rooted in a clear fictive reality.

Although Krolevsky's remark to Kürmann in ***Biografie,*** 'ab posse ad esse valet, ab esse ad posse non valet', is obviously correct, such a law is inadequate to grasp an experience whose rich ramifications require imaginative interpretation if it is to be fully understood. By giving form to such experience, exploration and delineation of the fictive narrator's identity becomes a viable proposition. The process of writing thus becomes a method of revealing the true self in all its contradictions, and ***Mein Name sei Gantenbein*** can be seen accordingly to link up closely with the earlier narratives ***Stiller*** and ***Homo Faber.*** The novel demonstrates Frisch's belief that 'the individual is a sum of various possibilities, not an unlimited sum, but one which goes beyond his biography. Only the variations reveal the common centre.' (pp. 148-49)

A close analysis of Max Frisch's novels has demonstrated that the concept of eccentricity is the key to the understanding of his narrative world. In all five works the theme of lost centricity can be seen to be of prime importance. Such thematic consistency over thirty years is remarkable in itself, but Frisch's achievement is best gauged by the fact that he has been able to treat the theme of eccentricity in such a complex and continually fascinating way. It has proved indeed to be a starting point for an intense exploration of problems that have shown themselves to be endemic in contemporary German literature. His heroes, whilst retaining their essential individuality, can be seen as symptomatic of a whole society. Their acute sense of dislocation, their feeling of crisis in terms of personal identity—whether caused by the collapse of marriage as a centric principle or by scepticism towards the claims of language to express experience adequately or by the inevitability of old age and death—are magnificently caught in narratives of extraordinary diversity.

It is true that Jürg Reinhart, Anatol Stiller, Walter Faber and the fictive narrator of ***Mein Name sei Gantenbein*** never attain 'das wirkliche Leben' which they all, sooner or later, acknowledge to be the only goal worth striving for. They are all brought face to face with the same central dilemma: surface reality is simply not adequate to reflect human experience and values. Realisation of this fundamental truth separates them from their fellows, turns them—irrespective of their wishes—into 'Sonderlinge' and reveals dimensions to life that are wholly unsuspected by an apparently centric majority. Their uneasy narratives bear witness to the fact that they cannot escape from the pain of being alive. They have each had a glimpse of the meaning of integrated personality, and there can be no going back to the unreflective life represented at its most positive by the Oberst in ***Die Schwierigen*** and at its most negative by Dr Bohnenblust in ***Stiller.***

All five models are informed by this concern for personal centricity and affirm essential human values in a world which appears itself to have lost its centre. Frisch himself is well aware of the difficulties of writing such novels in a situation where personality is constantly under attack from increasingly fearsome abstractions. In ***Mein Name sei Gantenbein,*** for example, he has his narrator remark—significantly in parenthesis: 'I, too, often have the feeling that any book which isn't concerned with the prevention of war, with the creation of a better society and so on, is senseless, futile, irresponsible, tedious, not worth reading, inadmissible. This is no time for ego stories.' Yet he goes on ruefully: 'And yet human life is fulfilled or goes wrong in the individual ego, nowhere else'. . . . As a novelist, therefore, Frisch sees his work as asserting itself in that ironic tension which is generated between two polar opposites: the absurdity of 'ego stories' and the necessity for their existence. Thus he is led to re-affirm the importance of the individual personality and proclaim what he once called his 'individuelles Engagement an die Wahrhaftigkeit'. This 'personal commitment to truthfulness' has enabled him in an age of widespread depersonalisation to put forward a consistent body of fiction which has thrown a sharp, critical light on those pressures within the individual and within society that threaten integrity and prevent the attainment of genuine centricity.

The five novels which have formed the basis of this study all underline [the] essential perception: human reality is too complex and the individual's transient experience of it too fluid to be captured either in a neat set of statistics or in a simple 'story'. Each human being has to come to terms with the consequences of this predicament in his own way. For Frisch offers no global solutions to the problems he delineates so clearly in his books. The vital, integrating centre is not finally located but remains tantalisingly beyond his protagonists' grasp.

What the reader witnesses and recognises, however, when confronted with Max Frisch's narrative world, is a unique and creative paradox: in an eccentric environment only those eccentric individuals, the 'Schwierigen', who are alive to their condition and who strive to find the lost centre, come close to personal integrity. Like Camus' Sisyphus, Jürg Reinhart, Anatol Stiller, Walter Faber and the protagonist of ***Mein Name sei Gantenbein*** realise their essential identity only to the degree with which they commit themselves to the struggle to make sense of their lives and their environment. Though they fail, the nature of their failure is both impressive and illustrative of their common humanity. Max Frisch's versatile and imaginative handling of the theme of eccentricity, with its characteristic irony, humour and subtlety, has established for the Swiss novelist a strong claim to a position of central significance in the history of post-1945 German fiction. (p. 155)

Michael Butler, in his The Novels of Max Frisch, *Oswald Wolff, 1976, 176 p.*

BARBARA SAUNDERS

[*In the following excerpt Saunders discusses the ambiguous boundaries between fiction and autobiography in Frisch's work, exemplified in* Montauk.]

The importance of a creative and critical application of memory to the problems of personal identity is both catalyst and theme of Max Frisch's prose work ***Montauk*** (1975). Firstly, this book represents a new stage in the author's treatment of the relationship between "fiction" and "reality" in the life of the individual. Secondly, it embodies Max Frisch's most radical attempt to examine the personal consequences of his literary thought for his own private life. Through its confrontation of fantasy and fact ***Montauk*** breaches the sensitive boundaries of autobiography and poses questions which extend far beyond the thematic emphasis of the work itself. It also foreshadows a decisive departure from the distinctive kind of autobiographical narrative with which Frisch has long been associated.

Many literary critics have been quick to integrate ***Montauk*** with Frisch's earlier creative work by isolating those themes and stylistic techniques which are already familiar to readers from novels such as ***Stiller*** (1954), ***Homo Faber*** (1957) and ***Mein Name sei Gantenbein*** (1964). In this way, however, they deprive ***Montauk*** of much of its individual force. True, questions of narratorial, social and personal identity are fundamental to all Frisch's prose, but it is dangerous to assume on the basis of earlier work that each dramatization of the "identity crisis" is ultimately an evasive one on Frisch's part. In ***Montauk*** Frisch pursues his exploration of the potential boundlessness of personal relationships, but broadens the perspective of this investigation by introducing his own presence as author and subject of the text. The entrenched self-criticism which underlies this work limits the degree to which Max Frisch as narrator can employ irony as a means of distancing his personality from the questions raised by his reflective prose. In ***Montauk*** he plays far less than in his previous novels with imaginative modes of behaviour and their potential consequences for human personality. He does not invent his characters (e.g. Ingeborg Bachmann, Peter Huchel and Christa Wolf are some of those mentioned) and the situations are fixed in a specific location and at a precise time. In the novels Frisch makes no attempt to discuss an autobiographical intention, and the impulse towards integrating views of the self is less obvious and not the prime objective of the narrator. In ***Montauk*** Frisch concentrates explicitly upon the deterministic effect of certain recurrent patterns in his life which continue to influence his emotional responses as a 64-year-old man. Thus, the problems presented are treated in direct relation to the resolution or portrayal of a personal dilemma. Clearly, in literature with as strong a psychological emphasis as the work of Frisch, it is tempting to become preoccupied with thematic comparisons and to neglect formal insights. It is unsatisfactory, however, to ignore the transition from the ambiguity and ambivalence of his early first person narratives to the more self-confident stance of narrator and persona in ***Montauk.*** Frisch emphasizes that authorial identity is in part created by narrative technique, and therefore that these two components are inseparable in autobiography. It is precisely through their interaction that it becomes clear that the author views identity as open to interpretation and change, whilst at the same time seeing in his own life at this stage disturbing signs of repetition.

Earlier in his career Frisch wrote two short autobiographical narratives. One forms a short section entitled "Autobiographie" in his first ***Tagebuch of 1946-9,*** the other is an account of his military service in 1939 called ***Blätter aus dem Brotsack*** (1940). Both of these are direct artistic expressions of Frisch's attitude to autobiography, although neither monitor more than isolated stages of his career. In the former the author resorts to writing about himself when, during a stay in Paris, he is reluctant to add to the many descriptions of life in the capital, whilst in the latter he consolidates his early war-time observations in literary form. In ***Montauk,*** however, Frisch changes the emphasis and content of these early narratives and transforms them into a distinctive personal variation of self-analysis. Here, he focuses on a personal crisis whose immediacy highlights particular personal experiences of the past in relation to their emotional impact in the present. Frisch chooses a brief relationship with a woman 30 years younger than himself through which to reflect upon his personal and literary life. Their weekend trip to Montauk (on Long Island) offers him a variety of constantly interacting perspectives on his self-image. Particular memories, hopes, failures and dreams are mirrored in an emotional investment in his short relationship with Lynn. In comparison with ***Montauk,*** "Autobiographie" appears like a traditional "Lebenslauf" which describes Frisch's family life from birth in social terms, whilst ***Blätter aus dem Brotsack*** combines diaristic anecdote and philosophical reflection in its depiction of the suddenness of war. Neither of the two achieve the same intensity of self-scrutiny and self-criticism evident in ***Montauk.*** Frisch sets the scene for this more extensive personal autobiography in his ***Dienstbüchlein*** of 1974 where he re-examines critically the whole of his military service during the war and relates ritualised attitudes to authority to wider political issues in modern Switzerland.

Frisch has said that he is not fully aware of the personal significance of his work as he is writing—or even when the work is complete—since he does not view it as an objective outsider whose job it is to trace plot and character development. Similarly, he did not realise the extent of self-revelation contained in ***Montauk*** until he had completely exhausted the exploration of personal identity in autobiographical form, "When I published it, the freedom was complete, and I am finished with that form. I don't know what I will write in the future, but if it is fiction it will be pure invention and will contain nothing autobiographical." Admittedly, this work could also be approached as pure fiction. It is designated an "Erzählung", although this does not negate the validity of autobiographical terms of reference within the text. And yet, it does to a certain extent condition the reader to expect a "fictional" narrative before he starts to read. The stylistic devices within the work itself, however, emphasize a sense of commitment to an autobiographical purpose on Frisch's part, rather than a surrender to the "fictional". The use of "Erzählung" as designation in relation to the whole text broadens our view of form and content rather than restricting it. It allows the material to be interpreted in many ways and gives Frisch room for autobiographical experiment. We are invited to question genre boundaries and definitions and to consider how arbitrary genre designation can be in relation to the relative "authenticity" of the text itself. Above all, ***Montauk*** stresses that the force of material presented depends not upon concepts of fiction or individuality external to the text, but upon interacting stylistic devices with strictly autobiographical connotations and preoccupations. Those who read ***Montauk*** closely will find it difficult to avoid identifying with the human needs, aspirations and doubts recorded here by explaining them away into "pure invention".

Readers must also be careful not to confuse Frisch's conception of autobiography with Montaigne's. Although Frisch frequently refers to Montaigne both in the motto of the preface and in quotations integrated into the text, we do not know whether Frisch conceives of Montaigne as a model autobiographer or suspects him of insincerity. There is a danger of using his Montaigne quotations to support any critical argument we choose. In Frisch's text clear guidelines as to how to read Montaigne's essays or Frisch's references to them are absent. Once again, this ambiguity emphasizes that the evaluation of "irony" and "insincerity" in this work depends upon the individual reader's response to the standards and values set up by the author in the text *as a whole,* and not simply upon isolated references to other autobiographers or to the role of fantasy.

Perhaps with Frisch more than many modern writers we are conscious of a view of behaviour as a role which the individual adopts in order to make his experience appear credible to himself and to the outside world. Frisch has demonstrated that men take on fictional identities at will and need a plausible myth to sustain meaning in their lives. His protagonists are led into conflicts in personal relationships where it is dangerous to define other people in terms of how one would like to see them, although the key to development and self-discovery lies in close relationships of this kind. Frisch's view of experience as "Erlebnismuster" or "Einfall" rather than as an "Ergebnis aus Vorfällen" has led him to portray characters whose past is "eine Fiktion, die nicht zugibt, eine Fiktion zu sein"—"fiction" because experience consists of fluid patterns and not conclusive events. The use of "fiction" in this sense is not inimical to "subjective truth", indeed, it is this very confrontation of individual "Erlebnismuster" which constitutes Frisch's "individuelles Engagement an die Wahrhaftigkeit". It is not difficult, then, to understand why Frisch has singled out one of his own personal relationships in ***Montauk*** in order to re-evaluate his past. Both the experience itself and his narrative technique are fragmentary, avoiding the constrictions of linear chronology and superfluous detail. Economy of expression gives sharp contours to the recurrent emotions and interacting perspectives. Frisch is not concerned with the presentation of an integrated, rounded personality which is widely thought to be an anachronism in the twentieth century and an inappropriate measure of modern consciousness. The associations of his relationship with Lynn are part of more complex conditioning in his life and at the same time representative of his organization of experience. Whilst it is important to be aware of traditional autobiographical criteria when reading this work in order to understand its individual force, the modern mistrust of total personality is a dilemma Frisch inherits but for which he is not responsible. In ***Montauk*** his chosen style and theme must be seen as a personal *and* a contemporary attempt to come to terms with the autobiographical tradition, not as an inevitable rejection of its achievements.

In the essay **"Öffentlichkeit als Partner"** (1958), Frisch claims that readers and literary critics alike often severely misinterpret works which radically challenge their own moral views, "(. . . auch die zünftige Kritik neigt dazu . . . Arbeit künstlerisch besser zu finden, wenn sie ihre eigenen Meinungen moralischer Art bestätigt findet oder wenigstens nicht in Frage gestellt sieht)". A work such as ***Montauk*** poses moral and literary questions about the changing genre of autobiography. For many, it also transgresses the boundaries of personal and public discretion. It is not surprising, therefore, that its reviewers have exposed their own glaring inadequacies in the face of its broad artistic questions, thus prejudicing their appraisal of the work itself. Clearly Frisch has never underestimated public resentment, but his freedom of exploration as a writer demands a certain indifference to a specific audience. He has to endeavour to write without thinking of his prospective readers in order to attain a redefined authorial standpoint. . . . The social pressures accompanying literary success and personal change are shown in ***Montauk*** to have precipitated in Frisch a need to review his responsibility as a writer whilst at the same time stressing his dependence on others for effective self-criticism.

Frisch is also well aware of the curious fact that readers are apt to see fiction in autobiography and autobiography in fiction and that they prefer to measure personal confession according to criteria of social acceptability, while allowing poetic imagination to enjoy superior artistic standing. (pp. 212-16)

Frisch's emotional investment in his task and his responsibility towards the people he mentions highlight the errors of those critics who accuse him of inventing pretexts for recollection in order to mask insincerity and indecision. Far from evading the charge of conceit and vanity, Frisch takes pains to confront any hint of emotion resembling jealousy and pride in his conditioned responses as well as his attitudes to "success" and "wealth". His approach to these less socially acceptable sentiments derives not from a misplaced sense of glory or self-deception. On the contrary, it is precisely the potential destructiveness of acquired behaviour which Frisch is anxious to examine for its intellectual and emotional insight. Many critics are unable or unwilling to accept the risk involved in applying Frisch's strategy to their own personal lives and thus reject an opportunity to support his commitment to individual growth.

The skilful use of language is the crucial agent of a sense of authenticity in ***Montauk.*** Frisch writes modestly yet boldly about intimate experience without appearing either to disguise or to embellish deliberately. His selectivity and discretion contribute to a sense of precision and poignancy which play a vital role in creating visual and emotional tension. ***Montauk*** represents an extension and an adaptation of the diaristic style with which we are familiar from both Frisch's earlier prose works and his ***Tagebücher I*** and ***II.*** In every case this technique serves to build up subjective impressions of experience without suggesting conclusive definition. In the novels this emphasizes individual uncertainty and the fluidity of role; in the diaries the swift changes in subject matter pose questions of a more directly personal nature whilst relating them to more general literary and social issues. In ***Montauk,*** this form of writing makes it possible for the autobiographer to describe irrevocable conditioning in his past without appearing to close his identity through a story. Throughout, Frisch is aware of the possibility of self-delusion and the danger of fitting experience into a reality he wants to see, yet he knows that even those who accept themselves and are open to the future are not safe from "story telling". He suppresses the chronology of events and juxtaposes impressions of himself in relation to various others so that the reader is less tempted to decipher cause and effect and the order in which relationships came than encouraged to question the role of memory in self-appraisal. The connections between each relationship cannot be established without Frisch's intervening subjective interpretation of the impressions presented, so that attention is focused upon his critical perception. Place names of the past and present, questions addressed to Lynn, himself and to the reader, quotations from his own and others' literary work which have particular significance for his personal life, excerpts from interviews, responses of the public and abrupt, one-word sentences interact to sustain the tension of self-scrutiny and to invite the reader's emotional investment in the text. We are repeatedly challenged to use Frisch's recognition . . . as a springboard for our own evaluation. . . . "Wahn" is our capacity for inventing for each human relationship a different emphasis in order to avoid repetition, although we thereby often perpetuate our original dilemma.

Frisch's concentration on the lasting consequences of particular experiences for his behaviour in the present sustains the sense of impatience and urgency he wishes to convey throughout the period of composition. A deliberate tension is maintained in the present between intimacy and indiscretion, personal development and social taboo, memory of the past and awareness of the moment. (pp. 217-18)

Naturally, this kind of autobiography has not failed to raise doubts as to its artistic standing, with the result that several critics reject Frisch's portrayal of intimacy in this work. For them it has a place in fiction but autobiography should be distanced if it is to avoid pure self-indulgence. Ironically, it seems to be precisely because ***Montauk*** confronts the theme of self-scrutiny in an original way that reviewers fail to reconcile the artistry of the work with their own rigid generic criteria for autobiography. They see the problem of honesty as a trap, feeling ill-treated and confused by an author whose text is loyal to artistic criteria *and* factual accuracy, thus raising an illusory conflict between "life" and "art". Often this results in the work being rejected both as art and as autobiography, whereby formal originality is overlooked or dismissed. (p. 220)

Montauk is not a simple book to read, although this does not mean that it is deliberately confusing or abstruse. For Frisch, whose work has always confronted the themes of "authenticity" and "role", the variations of autobiographical narration are complex. As the "absolute" criteria for autobiography are rendered inappropriate due to a breakdown of faith in self-fulfilment, traditional models and historical progress, the nature of a private work such as ***Montauk*** is of great importance and prime significance. The enigma of identity and the paradox of role are clearly boundless in the modern world. Memory is not always productive and forgetting does not always protect. The originality of ***Montauk*** lies in its determination to explore the human consequences of these problems in one life. Since this occurs through the medium of literature, artistic criteria are also on trial. The great autobiographies of world literature appear serene and unequivocal in comparison with Frisch's slim volume, yet although ***Montauk*** dispenses with their serenity and supreme self-confidence in life's meaning, it lacks none of their traditional conviction. It combines a search for self with an exploration of original and significant modes of expression. As such it attempts to isolate "(die tönende) Grenze", the point at which language captures the causal nexus of experiences in aesthetic terms, in this case, the roots of Frisch's individual emotional conditioning which continue to influence the present. Upon critical reflection, Frisch rediscovers the patterns of his growth through personal relationships. The portrayal of "das geschichtliche Ich in seinen realisierten Möglichkeiten und nicht mehr in seinen variablen Entwürfen" characterizes the change in emphasis in this prose work. It also emphasizes the potentially destructive effects of language upon an individual's responses to emotion, since the recurrence of certain semantic images in this work occur in conjunction with particular unresolved experiences in Frisch's past, fragments of which can be found in his earlier prose work. The crux of each emotional experience lies, as Michael Butler realizes, in the difficulty of forming personal relationships in which the partner has sufficient independence to allow individual and mutual growth. Butler also sees that throughout ***Montauk*** Frisch refuses to pose "poetry" and "truth", "fact" and "fiction", "honesty" and "deception" as "antinomies" of "alternatives" and that experience can only be expressed as a mixture of each, as a "permanent confrontation between fact and fiction".

Uwe Johnson predicted that Frisch would find himself in an aesthetic corner after exhausting the diary form and "memoir" through ***Montauk.*** So far Frisch has not broached the autobiographical narrative again. His latest works—***Triptychon: Drei szenische Bilder*** (1978) and ***Der Mensch erscheint im Holozän*** (1979)—mark a turning point in his writing. The former dispenses with self-conscious form, although its concern with social and individual attitudes to life in the face of death and "eternity" retains Frisch's focus on problems of identity. The latter depicts the effect of a prolonged storm on the existence of an old man living alone in the Swiss Alps. Both substantiate

Frisch's own assertion that he is "finished" with the autobiographical form. ***Montauk*** indicates the climax of a progression towards positive self-appraisal and has enabled Frisch to develop beyond the preoccupations of ambivalent personal identity. (pp. 222-23)

Barbara Saunders, "Confronting 'Fictions,' Past and Present: Max Frisch's 'Montauk' as Autobiography," in Forum for Modern Language Studies, *Vol. XVIII, No. 3, July, 1982, pp. 212-23.*

MANFRED JURGENSEN

[*Jurgensen, a critic and professor of German, is the author of the critical study* Max Frisch *(1968); his other works include* Frauenliteratur *(1982) and* Keith Leopold: Selected Writings *(1985). In the following excerpt Jurgensen discusses the evolution of several major themes in Frisch's drama.*]

As early as 1931 Frisch, then twenty years of age, had begun his literary career with an analysis of role playing, both in the theater and outside it. His essay **"Mimische Partitur?"** (Mimic score?), which appeared on May 27, 1931, in the *Neue Zürcher Zeitung* came to the conclusion that all fiction was derived from some kind of dialogue. It was easy to see that with such a concept of fiction this writer would sooner or later turn to drama as an appropriate form of artistic self-expression. Frisch had discovered quite early that in entering into a dialogue with himself, he would inevitably turn his own preoccupations into dramatic manifestations of a fictional I. Any individual identity could therefore only be involved in role playing; it is forever in search of an alter ego willing to be part of his self-dialogue. Frisch's fictionalization of the I clearly serves the function of self-knowledge. While his literary works may be highly entertaining, they are primarily intellectual, concerned with bearing witness to the reality of man, to the existential problems of individual authenticity.

This fictional form of self-dialogue expressed itself in Frisch's many diaries. From ***Blätter aus dem Brotsack*** to ***Tagebuch 1966-1971,*** the author questions himself; as a representative I he calls himself into doubt. In the novels ***Jürg Reinhart*** and ***Die Schwierigen,*** Frisch gives an epic account of the same existential dialogue with himself. The literary genre may have changed; his central preoccupation, however, has remained the same: Frisch's subject continues to be the art of self-reflection. In his arabesque ***Bin oder Die Reise nach Peking,*** the dialogue between ego and alter ego may be followed most clearly. Significantly, Frisch is not interested in any psychoanalytical interpretations of subjective individuality. The other I identifies itself as an expression of existential self-consciousness. Although this alter ego develops more and more into a brotherly You, revealing "the other" as a manifestation of the social I, Frisch's diaries (and their form-fictional applications to novels and, in ***Biografie: Ein Spiel*** [**Biography: A Play**], the drama) remain essentially lyrical. Frisch then has made use of all genres in his attempt to realize a fiction of self-dialogue.

The interaction of various genres in the works of Frisch is therefore an expression of different kinds or different states of self-examination. His "Romance" ***Santa Cruz*** embraces all three genres: Pelegrin and Pedro are narrative personae who at the same time enact (or re-enact) their epic accounts dramatically while they remain throughout the play personifications of lyrical longing. The central theme of the play is that of all Frisch's early works: *Sehnsucht* (longing). What better way to express the longing for another life than in the form of a dialogue with another, a different I? The I itself becomes a dramatis persona: in splitting itself, it realizes the dreams and hopes of a socially identified and personally restricted individual.

But there is another way in which Max Frisch expresses the longing of a limited I: throughout his work, but particularly in its early phase—a period characterized by dramatic lyricisms—he presents the theme of self-realization, the very search for a self, in terms of a pilgrimage, an excursion, a journey. The destinations of such journeys remain beyond the reach of the socially restricted I; they are places of fantasy, dreams, and longing: Peking, Santorin, or Santa Cruz. Frisch introduces a new concept linked to the longing for self-realization: repetition. It too finds its appropriate expression in dialogue; the exchangeability not only of experience itself but also of the very idea, the longing for an experience is a natural consequence of the interchangeability of the personality, of the dramatic splitting of the I. Consequently, the *Sehnsucht*-journey of the I can only be undertaken in the company of the other I: in ***Bin oder Die Reise nach Peking*** the I is accompanied by its *"Bin,"* i.e., its existential projection of self-realization; in ***Santa Cruz*** the wandering performer (Vagrant) becomes the dramatic symbol of Elvira's and the captain's self-alienation and self-discovery. The two themes of the play which relate to its central issue of self-discovery are repetition and the journey of the self. In his program notes on the occasion of the first performance of ***Santa Cruz*** in Zurich, Frisch summed up the interaction of these themes: "Santa Cruz, that is the name of a foreign, apparently Spanish, harbor, but one shouldn't look it up on the map—if at all, one will most readily find it in his own experience, in that area of recognition that everyone has already had, of that dream-like, surprising experience of standing before a certain situation in life and knowing: I have already experienced that, I don't know when or where, but basically it's exactly the same, and wherever I go, I will experience it again and again.—That's Santa Cruz." In many ways this drama could be described in the same terms that Frisch applied to ***Bin oder Die Reise nach Peking***: both are "Träumereien" (dream pieces). There is overwhelming evidence that ***Santa Cruz*** was meant to be a dream play. The wandering performer himself (the Vagrant) is a dream figure; both Elvira and the captain relate to him only in their dreams. Significantly, they are introduced into the play by the wandering performer; only with his help can they enact their dreams. There can be little doubt then that ***Bin oder Die Reise nach Peking*** and ***Santa Cruz*** belong, not only historically, to the same period of Frisch's development. It is well known that Frisch habitually expresses certain themes and preoccupations in various, and to him experimental, literary genres (cf. ***Gantenbein*** and ***Biografie*** or ***Stiller*** and ***Andorra*** or, generally, the "pretexts" in the diaries).

It is all the more remarkable then that this "dream play" ***Santa Cruz*** incorporates into its enactment of dreams a very acute social conscience. There is no withdrawal from harsh social realities in the dream analysis. (pp. 4-6)

Only in dreams can social freedom be realized. Frisch's critics have, on the whole, reacted negatively to this play because it seemed to them to avoid the burning issues of contemporary society. It is the well-known objection to Frisch's alleged subjectivity. No one who has read (or seen) this play, the first of ten, with an open mind can fail to recognize the social dimension of our dreams, of our longings. Frisch shows marriage as the most intimate social relationship, not as a purely private affair. In the same way, our most intimate dreams and ambitions are revealed to be social in character and consequence. The fact that we can share a dream makes our longings too part of an overall, i.e., social, pattern of repetition. (p. 7)

Already at this early stage Frisch moves in the direction of the "model theater." One of the most important aspects of his drama ***Santa Cruz*** lies in its parabolic nature. In that, too, it is a rewriting of ***Bin oder Die Reise nach Peking.*** On the stage too now the I is on its way in search of its "Bin," its alter ego, its social I—in search of its audience.

Frisch's second play (although the first to be performed on stage), ***Nun singen sie wieder*** (**They're Singing Again Now**), bears the subtitle *Versuch eins Requiems* (Attempt at a Requiem). In his own introduction to the printed edition (1946), Frisch spoke of "a far-off sadness" and "the involuntary force of dreams" which prompted and informed this drama. He was very much aware of his own unique position regarding the war; as a Swiss, apparently unaffected by the conflict surrounding his own country, Frisch could only attempt to present the lessons of the war from a bipartisan point of view. This he does in ***Nun singen sie wieder*** not only by representing both sides of the warfaring factions, but also by enacting the lamentation of his requiem in staging a realm of death where friends and foes are equals.

In dealing with the German dilemma, Frisch analyzes dramatically the dichotomy of *Geist* (spirit) and *Macht* (power). The theme is summarized neatly in an entry in his ***Tagebuch 1946-1949*** where, under the heading of "Café Delfino" (written during October 1946), we read:

> I'm thinking of Heydrich, who played Mozart, as an example of a definite experience. Art in this sense, art as a moral schizophrenia, if one can say so, would in any case be the opposite of our task; and all in all it is questionable whether the artistic and human task can be separated. A sign of the spirit that we need is not primarily a talent representing some plus, but rather responsibility. Especially the German people, who were never lacking in talents, or minds that felt themselves beyond the demands of the common day, the Germans were the ones who supplied the most, or at least the first, barbarians of our century. Shouldn't we learn something from that? . . .

The character of Herbert personifies this moral schizophrenia in an exemplary fashion. Art as a cultural alibi is exposed for what it is: aestheticism, formal rhetoric without humane values. The lengthy discussions between Herbert and Karl in the first part of the play tend to have the effect of set pieces in a Platonic dialogue. It is fair to say that up to ***Graf Öderland*** (**Count Öderland**) the argumentative nature of Frisch's plays meant that very little real dramatic interaction took place on the stage. Set speeches, quotations, and montages take the place of dramatic plot and interaction in the traditional drama. Indeed, some of Herbert's reflections read like diary entries; one of his speeches seems to reflect the despair Frisch expressed in his diary on the occasion of the atomic bombing of Bikini—exemplifying the interrelationship between some of the themes in ***Nun singen sie wieder*** and the ***Tagebuch 1946-1949.*** In the play Herbert explains: "We reached for power, for the ultimate force in order to encounter the spirit, the real one; but the cynic was right, there is no real spirit, and we have the world in our pocket, whether we need it or not; I don't see any limit to our power—that's the despair." A year later, Frisch reacts in rather similar fashion to the possibility of a total nuclear destruction of the world: "The progress that led to Bikini will yet take the last step also: the deluge will be feasible. That's what's grandiose. We can do what we want; at the end of our progress we're standing where Adam and Eve stood; for us there still remains only the moral question." . . . This is an updated version of the same dilemma which lies at the center of the play ***Nun singen sie wieder***: the conflict between spirit and power.

Stylistically, the drama relies heavily on narrative passages with intensely lyrical overtones. In addition, Frisch makes extensive use of quotations which in turn are used as leitmotivs. In juxtaposing identical passages spoken by opposing forces, he literally plays out one viewpoint against the other without seeming to take sides himself. (pp. 7-8)

Frisch uses them not merely for characterization; he interrelates them, combines and redesigns them, until they amount to a kaleidoscope of prejudice, anguish, and despair. These leitmotivs accumulate to a reflective statement per se; the exchange of dialogue is more like the self-reflection of a diary. Max Frisch stages his own thoughts on the war, uses the theater as a pretext for a visualization of the self-reflective dialogues in his diaries. No wonder that in his comments on the play he wrote: "The place where these scenes take place always emerges from the spoken word. Scenery should be present only to the extent that the actor needs it and in no case would it attempt to simulate reality. For the impression of a play must remain preserved throughout." . . . The place of action clearly is Frisch's own consciousness and his conscience. One theme which seems to have been overlooked by most critics is the theme of all Frisch's early works: *Sehnsucht* (longing); the longing for a better world, a meaningful life as well as the longing of fiction, of illusion, of all art. In that sense, Frisch's theater itself is an expression of the author's *Sehnsucht,* more than a full realization of all the potentials of the stage. Eduard's speech in the third scene of the play clearly sums up Frisch's concept of the piece, a concept he retained right up to one of his last dramas, ***Biografie: Ein Spiel.***

> EDUARD: I believe in illusion. Even that which never occurs in the world, even that which one cannot grasp with his hands and cannot destroy with his hands, even that which occurs as a desire, as a longing, as a goal going beyond everything existing at hand. . . .

All theater, all fiction is in this context a rehearsal, an attempt to play out possibilities that cannot be realized outside the realm of art. The theatrical rehearsal held a deep fascination for Frisch. It is significant that his *Probe*-concept (testing in rehearsal) is, by its very nature, related to the montage of quotations. Play, *Spiel,* then, is the interaction of quotations used as self-characterizations, quotations of a self which can never be defined but only rehearsed.

One theme that proved to be of major significance for many of his later works, Frisch introduces as a dream: the Rip van Winkle folktale, a legend by Washington Irving. (p. 9)

Frisch also wrote a radio play entitled ***Rip van Winkle*** and, more importantly, revived the myth in his best-known novel ***Stiller.*** In addition, the short tale **"Schinz"** in his ***Tagebuch 1946-1949*** offers yet another variation of the Rip van Winkle theme. To my knowledge, its early appearance in the play ***Nun***

singen sie wieder has been virtually overlooked by all Frisch critics and scholars.

In Frisch's drama, dreams and nightmares, hopes and longings, projections and flashbacks all form part of a moral, intellectual, and existential totality. From the earliest diary ***Blätter aus dem Brotsack,*** the subsequent novel(s) of Greece, and the "dreamings in Prose" ***Bin oder Die Reise nach Peking,*** there is a natural progression to the "Romance" ***Santa Cruz*** and the "Requiem" ***Nun singen sie wieder.***

The characterization of his plays indicates Frisch's own development not only as a dramatist but also as a writer of growing political awareness. His next play ***Die Chinesische Mauer*** (**The Chinese Wall**) bears the subtitle "A Farce." Again, broad use is made of quotations as a structural device. Frisch separates his dramatis personae into "figures" and "masks." Of the former it may be said that they relate specifically to the play concept; they are in fact introduced in the first speech of "Der Heutige" (The Present-day Man) as figures of the play. Frisch again plays them out against each other; in the place of a traditional dramatic conflict there is a figurative exchange of beliefs, attitudes, and views. We are dealing here with purely figurative speech quoted by the theater; or, better, with figurative language quoting the stage. None of these figures are dramatic characters controlled by a personal psychology. The masks, on the other hand, are rather more obvious and direct quotations, either from history or from literature. They are, as the present-day man states in the first scene of the play, "figures that populate our brain, and to the extent of being figures of our thinking, . . . still alive throughout." Ultimately, then, both "figures" and "masks" fall under the heading of Frisch's play concept.

The play begins with a visual quotation of the Great Wall of China. In describing it, the present-day man quotes from the encyclopedia. If this drama in its most literal sense is a play and the dynamics of this play are provided by a structural interaction of quotations, its immediate and ultimate theme is history. Frisch's more recent play ***Biografie: Ein Spiel*** applies the same logic to the history of an individual. In ***Die Chinesische Mauer*** Frisch follows the principle of the encyclopedia: he quotes from history and stages a conversation piece which, even under the designation of a farce, remains a playful exercise, lacking the dimensions of a dramatic realization. It must be obvious that the very choice of theme dictated the limitations of this play. If it is the playwright's intention not to write about one particular period in history but to embrace the entire course of European civilization, his presentation can only take the form of selective quotations.

But Frisch does not simply quote from literary or political history. Frequently he quotes himself. The most striking example is the repeated warning of the present-day man: "The deluge is feasible. . . . That is: we stand before the choice whether there should be a humanity or not." Readers of the ***Tagebuch 1946-1949*** are familiar with the corresponding entry (written in 1946, the same year as ***Die Chinesische Mauer***): "The deluge is becoming feasible. . . . It depends on us whether there is humanity or not." The Nanking of his play is clearly a quotation and variation of the Peking in ***Bin oder Die Reise nach Peking.*** Furthermore, the dilemma of Hwang Ti, summed up in the Exclaimer's statement "The world is ours," the entire power-versus-spirit theme which forms the highlight of ***Die Chinesische Mauer,*** is unmistakeably a representation of the central conflict in Frisch's earlier play ***Nun singen sie wieder.*** Here too he relates the power/spirit trial of strength to a purely aesthetic concept of culture. Hwang Ti's master of ceremonies, Da Hing Yen, declares the conscience of the present-day man as poetic and awards him the "golden chain around his neck"—a national prize for cultural achievement: "What would it be—the most powerful empire in this world, victorious over all barbarians—what would it be without the streaming glory and decoration of its spiritual forces? That's why it's an old custom for us to reward and honor the spiritual forces that we have listened to with joy." Significantly, this award and its announcement are themselves a quotation. Not only Brecht was to experience this kind of honor; the capitalist West has found its own form of reconciling spirit and power: the countless industry prizes to writers and artists speak for themselves. (pp. 10-11)

It is clear . . . that Frisch's use of (self-) quotations is not restricted to themes, ideas, and characterization; it applies as much to the formal structure of the play. Only in the overall composition of figurative and masklike alienated quotations does it find its ultimate identity.

One form of quotation lies at the very center of this play: it is the theater quoting itself. This occurs in the obvious sense that major characters address themselves directly to the audience to reveal their theatricality. . . . The concept of theater is clearly extended beyond the limits of the stage, as is expressed in the corresponding definition of the play as a farce. . . . Clearly, Frisch's concept of the theater here is a sociopolitical analogy, an extension of pretense, role playing, and make-believe. Theater and "reality" (i.e., history) interact in their respective quotations. If we are arguing that in Frisch's ***Chinesische Mauer*** the theater is quoting itself, it is necessary to add that this kind of self-quotation can only take place in a confrontation with history. What Goethe expressed in reference to himself, "I have become historical to myself," now applies to the consciousness of our whole century, to the totality of modern literature. Frisch's protagonist, the present-day man, can only be understood in these terms. He is then above all a representative of modern, contemporary theater—and as such a forerunner of the later Frisch-protagonists (Stiller, Faber, Gantenbein) who are all authors, producers, and directors of their particular brand of a "theater of the self." Nothing could be more misleading therefore than the attempts of various Frisch critics to psychoanalyze this concept of a theatrical self-rehearsal. In Frisch's works it is always a social and political, not merely a private, individual; an individual in search of his place in contemporary society and history. The identity crisis of Frisch's protagonists is not an expression of a subjective neurosis but a manifestation of an existential crisis. The *Ich* itself has been reduced to a sociopolitical quotation. In a society consisting of a totality of such self-quotations (and in literature of similar quality), Frisch's present-day man despairs at the end of this theatrical piece of history. . . . (pp. 12-13)

In Frisch's concept of the theater we are presented with an existential confrontation: that of man's fiction and his authenticity. In the formal use of quotations he expresses the epitome of this dilemma. It is, of course, a polarity which in one form or another has been the determining factor of human existence from the beginning of time. Authenticity can be a deadly exercise, both individually and collectively. Gantenbein explains: "I thirst for betrayal. I would like to know that I am. Whatever doesn't betray me falls under the suspicion of living only in my imagination, and I'd like to get outside of my imagination, I'd like to be in the world. I'd like to be betrayed in the innermost depths." (p. 13)

Frisch defined his fourth play, ***Als der Krieg zu Ende war*** (**When the war was over**), as belonging to the genre of historical plays (afterword to the edition of 1949). Yet he is anxious to turn historical events into paradigmatic fiction, the "factual event" acquires the moral and aesthetic qualities of a parable. History in this case too came to Frisch in the form of a quotation; revisiting Germany immediately after the war he listens to countless "stories from the so-called Russian period." Thus Frisch experiences this history of the immediate past through "stories," i.e., as fiction. ***Als der Krieg zu Ende war*** is an "epic drama," both in its nature and in its origin. The first lines of Agnes Anders are not even disguised as a monologue; they are in fact quotations (indicated in the text by quotation marks) of an epic narrative. A great deal depends on how successfully the actress playing Agnes Anders manages to convey in her speech the quality of a quotation. We are witnessing here in the stylistic device of such narrative quotation the genesis of the play. Agnes's role playing includes a constant act of self-alienation; in her epic self-stylization she uses the third person. (p. 14)

All moral conflicts are raised and discussed on this narrative level of the play, hardly ever in the dramatic re-enactment of a historical event. No doubt the influence of Bertolt Brecht was greatest on Frisch during the late 1940s, as the ***Tagebuch 1946-1949*** verifies. In ***Als der Krieg zu Ende war*** the alienation effect of Brechtian epic drama has been used for its own ends and, one might add, with considerable effect.

Frisch's second war play is the earliest example of a theatrical treatment of his diary theme "Thou shalt not make unto thee any graven image" (1946). It reintroduces the enemy image of the earlier farce ***Die Chinesische Mauer***. . . . Frisch's play ends rather pessimistically. Like the earlier war play ***Nun singen sie wieder,*** the love of Agnes and Stepan does not suffice to overcome the graven image. Love is affirmed as a source and expression of human recognition, but ultimately it too cannot put an end to man's inhumanity to man. (pp. 14-15)

Frisch's extensive use of quotations as a means of epic drama ultimately leads to his very own brand of theater, the "model piece." In ***Biedermann und die Brandstifter*** ([Philistine and] the firebugs, 1957-1958), ***Andorra*** (1958-1961), and ***Biografie: Ein Spiel*** (**Biography: A Play,** 1967), Frisch's drama reaches its high point. Although his truly great plays were not written until the 1950s and 1960s, their genesis lies in the development of his early dramatic experiments. A transition to the model and play concept of his later plays is marked by the "ballad in twelve scenes" ***Graf Öderland*** (**Count Öderland**). . . . Clearly, ***Graf Öderland*** no longer belongs to the group of Frisch's early plays of the forties, plays which were not only conceived during the immediate postwar period but completed and performed in those years. The influence of Brecht on the young Frisch is most evident in ***Die Chinesische Mauer*** and ***Als der Krieg zu Ende war.*** In the years 1947 and 1948 Frisch's contact with Brecht was at its most intense. An entry in his ***Tagebuch*** from the year 1948 underlines the impact Brecht had on the young Swiss playwright: "Our association goes most smoothly when the conversation, which Brecht always leaves up to the notions and requirements of his partner, revolves around questions of the theater, of directing, acting, questions concerning also the writer's trade, which, handled soberly, inevitably lead to something of substance." . . . Predictably, Brecht showed great interest in ***Als der Krieg zu Ende war,*** Frisch's renewed attempt to write an epic drama dealing paradigmatically with the events of recent history. It is, as Frisch himself noted, a historical play, dramatically dated perhaps; its epic structure, however, bears the portents of Frisch's political, parabolic model theater. Thus the history of the playwright's own development illustrates the genesis of all fiction. The play as a model is not a stylistic device of "timeless" aesthetics; Frisch's play concept emerges as the highest stage of historical fiction.

"We were both dreaming." This sudden realization by the public prosecutor in the final act of ***Graf Öderland*** draws an obvious parallel with Max Frisch's first play ***Santa Cruz.*** Both dramas are "dream plays" which lead to a return of the original dilemma; their conclusions reiterate a status quo which cannot be overcome. They are plays of repetition, suggesting the eternal recurrence of paradigmatic conflicts. In ***Santa Cruz,*** Frisch explores the dream of reconciling marital faithfulness with a longing for individual freedom. As such the play draws an analogy between the relationship of marriage partners and the individual's limited freedom in society. Frisch portrays marriage as the most intimate social relationship. In ***Graf Öderland*** the dream has turned into a nightmare: the dichotomy is now between social power and individual freedom. Again the marriage, in this case that of the public prosecutor and Elsa, is in a symptomatic state of crisis; again it is the "order" of this social institution which has become indicative of a deadly order characterizing the whole of society, a society or state that Frisch calls Öderland. It could be said that ***Graf Öderland*** is a politicized ***Santa Cruz.*** Frisch's public prosecutor rebels against the very order he himself represents. In his attempt to break out of this social order he merely exemplifies the nightmare of personified power: "Whoever overthrows the present powers in order to be free takes over the opposite of freedom, the power," says the president at the conclusion of the play, "and I completely understand your personal fright." The public prosecutor's only response to this analysis of revolution is his desperate and helpless appeal "I was just being dreamed . . . Wake up—now, quickly—now: Wake up—wake up—wake up!" The nightmare of an inescapable social order consists of repetitions of interchangeable patterns of power, of an eternal recurrence of the same status quo.

Of all plays, Frisch's ***Graf Öderland*** seems the most relevant in our present sociopolitical situation. It is indeed surprising to see that over the last decade of increasing political terrorism in the Federal Republic, only a handful of German theaters have included this play in their repertoire. Yet it clearly deals, in the form of an almost Brechtian ballad or "Moritat," with two of the most challenging issues of contemporary Western society: revolution and anarchy. In a series of didactic scenes (Frisch calls them "Bilder") the play demonstrates the cyclic sequence of revolution and restoration, of anarchy and order. It takes up one of the themes of the earlier war play ***Nun singen sie wieder,*** when it analyzes the totality of power. "I don't want any power!" exclaims the public prosecutor as revolutionary leader. "I want life!" This then is the central theme of ***Graf Öderland***: how to live with power. The longing for freedom—in ***Santa Cruz*** primarily, though not exclusively, a matter of private self-assertion—inevitably leads to the use of violence. . . . Freedom to Frisch seems an almost Kierkegaardian grace, a spiritual concept in conflict with political realities. . . . This play of Frisch's concerns itself with the totalitarianism inherent in power. As soon as any challenge to social power succeeds in the name of freedom, it turns against itself and restores the original pattern of restrictions, laws, regulations, prohibitions, and control over the individual. It is this type of violent order which cannot be overcome by violence, it can only return to itself. Frisch shows the inevitable logic of such a process. He demonstrates that freedom is relative and in fact a concept which is, more often than not, an aspect of power and violence itself. This play then has a political urgency and relevance far surpassing Frisch's earlier dramas, and it is its further development toward a model theater which enables it to exemplify its lesson paradigmatically. (pp. 15-18)

[***Don Juan oder Die Liebe zur Geometrie***] re-presents in the form of a comedy several of Frisch's earlier preoccupations. The most obvious theme of the play is the search for an individual identity. ***Don Juan,*** however, is above all a drama about marriage—in the incongruity of the Don Juan theme and the subject of marriage lies the basis for its treatment as a comedy. In one sense, ***Don Juan oder Die Liebe zur Geometrie*** continues Frisch's dramatic analysis of marriage and as such stands in line with his earlier plays ***Santa Cruz*** and ***Graf Öderland.*** It is hardly a coincidence that ***Don Juan*** opens with a scene "before the castle" and ends with a mock idyllic scene in the "castle in Ronda." As in ***Santa Cruz,*** the castle is a symbol of marriage. . . . (p. 18)

As in ***Santa Cruz*** and ***Graf Öderland,*** Frisch's first comedy is preoccupied with the uniqueness of love and personal identity. Both are related but cannot be regulated or institutionalized, as in marriage. . . . Frisch introduces a theme that was to become central in his later novel ***Mein Name sei Gantenbein*** (**Wilderness of Mirrors**). It is only through betrayal that the uniqueness of the individual can be identified. (pp. 18-19)

The authentic I can be experienced wherever it is betrayed or itself betrays. . . . Love, to Frisch, is the unknown, including the unknown qualities and characteristics in the beloved. Lovers then are by definition individuals in search of each other, unknown to themselves. Sexual love is experienced by Don Juan as an eternal repetition of the same, exchangeable emotions. . . . Repetition of reality, on the other hand, is a theatrical device, it is a re-enactment of something unique. That is why during the "wild night" of pre-Christian times everyone who participated in the sexual promiscuity also wore a mask. . . . Don Juan's life too is turned into a theatrical spectacle, the social consequence of his individual theater of the self. . . . He expresses Frisch's own concept of the theater when he declares: "Truth cannot be shown, only invented." Repetition too is such an invention. Ultimately, therefore, authenticity and truth can only be imagined; which in turn must mean that our imagination cannot be merely repetition or reduplication. (pp. 19-20)

Frisch calls his ***Biedermann und die Brandstifter*** (**The Firebugs,** 1957-1958), rather flirtatiously a didactic play without a moral (Lehrstück ohne Lehre). In the context of the play, the subtitle is borne out by the closing lines of the Chorus:

> Much is senseless, and nothing
> More senseless than this story:
> Which, namely, once enkindled,
> Killed many, ah, but not all
> And changed nothing at all.

It is fair to say that ***Biedermann*** is the most Brechtian of all Frisch's plays. Like the later ***Andorra*** (1958-1961), it offers a dramatic analysis of social behavior. In ***Biedermann,*** however, Frisch relies rather more heavily on the spoken word than on the kind of theatrical demonstration which makes ***Andorra*** an altogether more dramatic performance. It is easy to trace ***Biedermann*** back to its origin as a radio play. In Frisch's *Lehrstück,* unlike Brecht's epic drama, the rhetoric of the argument is not balanced by its sensuous staging. The grotesque humor of ***Biedermann*** derives almost entirely from linguistic misunderstandings or a particular kind of hypocrisy which expresses itself in language. In the most literal sense, the pattern of this play is predictable. (p. 20)

[***Biedermann*** is] an analysis of social hypocrisy, complacency, and inaction. Frisch draws a bourgeois Biedermann who will not identify himself, even where his attitudes are ludicrously obvious. By contrast, his opponents make no attempt to hide their identities, without being recognized by Biedermann. As so often in the drama of Max Frisch we are witnessing a spectacle of confusion. It is no longer simply individual role playing which leads to deception and frustration; now the theater of the self is replaced by a theater of society. Both the anarchic fire raisers and the bourgeois Everyman are violent; the only difference is that Schmitz and Eisenring do not disguise their intentions. Biedermann on the other hand characteristically reconciles his violence with certain bourgeois values: "I'm too good-natured," he agrees with his wife, "you're right: I'm going to twist this Knechtling's throat around." (p. 21)

Biedermann und die Brandstifter logically progresses from Frisch's earlier farce ***Die Chinesische Mauer.*** Here, too, the protagonists address themselves directly to the audience (Biedermann, Babette, Dr. phil., Chor). However, in this *Lehrstück* these speeches serve less as a dramaturgical device of alienation than a directly didactic purpose. . . . By comparison with ***Die Chinesische Mauer*** this is a far more provocative play, designed to involve the audience to a much greater extent. No doubt, despite its subtitle, Frisch's ***Biedermann*** hopes to incite in his audience a willingness to political action. Of his earlier plays, one similarity with ***Graf Öderland*** cannot be overlooked. Both are "revolutionary plays," both are nonspecific about the political identity of the forces determined to overthrow the social status quo. And as in ***Graf Öderland,*** the maid announces at the end of the play: "The sky is burning!" Both dramas amount to an appeal for greater political consciousness, for a more articulate identification of social values.

The spectator must be reminded that he is watching a model, as indeed is the nature of theater, Frisch wrote with reference to his best known play ***Andorra.*** He simply calls it "A drama in twelve scenes." If it stands in the tradition of ***Die Chinesische Mauer, Graf Öderland,*** and ***Biedermann und die Brandstifter,*** developing as it does the concept of model theater, it also has at least one other thing in common with ***Graf Öderland***: both plays are structurally divided into twelve scenes or "Bilder." The "Bild" holds a special significance for Frisch; it is not simply a dramatic scene but also the graven image toward which his theater directs itself. In the context of the drama of Max Frisch, the "Bild" has a very special dramaturgical significance: it is neither an attempt to represent realistically a place of action nor an anti-illusionary device to shock his audience into a state of sociopolitical self-alienation. Frisch speaks of a basic image/scene (Grundbild) for the whole play, which is in fact the market square of this fictitious Andorra. This basic "Bild" is meant to be ever present throughout the play; all other scenes appear as reflections of this "Grundbild" of Andorra. In other words: Frisch's theatrical "Bild"-concept presents the image of an image. As he directs in his annotations to the play: "All scenes that do not take place on the plaza of Andorra are presented in front of it." The entire drama unfolds as a reflection and projection of the real creator of images: the society based on fear and prejudice called Andorra. It is in this sense that Frisch remarks: "Andorra is the name for a model."

The line of the bishop in the earlier play ***Don Juan oder Die Liebe zur Geometrie,*** "Truth cannot be shown, only invented," refers specifically to the interaction of prejudice and images staged by society's own brand of theater. It is therefore not only the basis of Frisch's own drama but raises a general question extending far beyond the function of the stage. How can social play acting be revealed for what it is, political role playing in relation to power? With reference to ***Andorra***: how can the truth of individual and social role playing be exposed? Clearly, not by imitating it but, according to Frisch, by analyzing the dynamics of this social process. His theater therefore uses "Bilder" which are neither fictional nor antifictional but which offer a critical anatomy of society's own staging of prejudice and persecution of the individual in the name of an image of man based on power and the right of might. ***Andorra*** is, above all, a play about truth; the staging of it and its "unstaging." It is obvious that Frisch owes a great deal to Bertolt Brecht, yet his own model theater is characterized by its own kind of didactic intent.

Another line from ***Don Juan*** could be seen as the basis of Frisch's special brand of "epic drama." It is Celestina's lament "Why does truth have it so difficult in Spain?" Again and again Frisch analyzes social distortions, manipulations, and exploitations of truth. It is a truth which, for him, identifies itself most clearly in the uniqueness of the individual. Only the integrity of an individual can bear witness to the truth. Society's treatment of individual beings therefore is indicative of its attitude to truth. A social outsider is almost always an articulate critic of social hypocrisy and violence. Truth in that sense has a difficult time in all societies, not only in Spain, not only in Andorra. What the teacher says to the carpenter lies at the basis of Frisch's model theater: "I see what's there and I say what I see, and all of you see it too." ***Andorra*** is a play about the difficulty of speaking the truth in a society determined to pretend it does not exist. "They will be amazed when I tell them the truth," claims the teacher. Yet truth is manipulated to such an extent that none of the witnesses who take the stand after their fateful betrayal of Andri (the "other" Andorran) admits to any guilt or part in his downfall. Andri appeals in despair: "How is it that you all are stronger than the truth?" The answer lies in his gradual realization that they can defeat truth by being stronger; their very power can manipulate and destroy truth. . . . Society cannot be forced to accept the truth of individual rights and the freedom of personal existence. Frisch makes it clear that society must want to face truth, and that only individuals can appeal to it. (pp. 22-4)

Andri is the only one who reaches an understanding of truth which is both personal and social. As he says to the priest, "Already now I don't need any more enemies, the truth is sufficient." It is the need for imaginary opponents, antisocial forces, and "enemies" which has taken our societies further and further away from truth. . . . Social power is forever in need of a scapegoat; any individual who challenges its principles of order must be made an example of. That is the fate of Andri. He is gradually becoming aware of the pattern of individual persecution in the name of a social truth. Frisch reintroduces a theme so prevalent in his earlier plays: that of repetition and recurrence. "What's coming has all already happened before," says Andri to Barblin, expressing his newly gained understanding of the model kind of behavior which surrounds him. The complementary remark from the Andorran establishment is made by the doctor at the opening of the final "Bild"; for him there is no doubt that despite the "invasion" of the blacks, "Everything's remaining as before. . . . Andorra is going to remain Andorran." That too is an expression of a social pattern, a model of social existence, a paradigm of social survival. It is easy to see then why for Frisch the theme of repetition is linked with his concept of a model theater. Almost all his plays end with a return to the social status quo. They are, to a greater or lesser extent, "Lehrstücke ohne Lehren." In that, however, lies the challenge, even provocation of the drama of Max Frisch.

Biografie: Ein Spiel (**Biography: A Play,** 1967) is the culmination of all Frisch's earlier dramas. Most of the major themes reappear in this, the most comprehensive play he has written. Here the spheres of private and public life intermingle; the individual identity finds itself defined both by personal and by social forces. The play of biography is no longer merely a theater of the self, nor is it the exclusive domain of society at large. ***Biografie*** balances the private self-definition of ***Santa Cruz*** with the public role playing of ***Andorra.*** Dramaturgically, this means that in Frisch's more recent drama the theater is enacting itself. Instead of subjective self-projections and/or the creation of prejudicial images by society, instead of a private *Ich-Theater* or a socially oriented *Gesellschafts-Theater,* the newer play ***Biografie*** emerges as total theater. And it is specifically the absence of any dogmatically held view by Frisch or the play itself which makes the theatrical rehearsal the intellectual, moral, and artistic basis of this drama. One important aspect of a rehearsal is of course repetition, a central theme in all Frisch's dramas. Here repetition is neither accepted nor rejected as in so many of his earlier plays; it is simply reconciled with the logic of an all-embracing self-expression. It is in harmony with the very medium of representational self-expression. The stage has become, more than ever before, a realm of self-reflection. As such, it is the center of the play, it is the center of conflict, the essence of our consciousness. In ***Biografie*** the theme itself is presented as a variation. Max Frisch explores the identity of choice, the private and public existence based on freedom. As such, the play analyzes the mechanics of historical existence, the process of gradual identification. Only this development is inevitable, its influences, both private and public, may alter and are largely a matter of choice. The reconstruction of an individual identity does not demonstrate the fatefulness of its biography, it merely illustrates the inevitability of acquiring any identity. Identity is inescapable; biography, a game played according to its rules. Kürmann's freedom of choice lies in the playful range of his selfdom, his performance in the game is limited by the need to be identified. This play of Frisch's is a sublime comedy about man's imprisonment in his self-styled freedom. If he wants to find himself, he is in need of identification, both privately and publicly; once he is discovered though, he has lost the freedom of continuous individual choice.

The theme of repetition—*Wiederholung*—well known from Frisch's earlier plays, is introduced by a quotation from Anton Chekov's drama *Three Sisters*. Vershinin's contemplation of a second chance to live his life reaches its peak in his conviction "Each one of us would then endeavor, so I think, above all to not repeat himself.—" (pp. 24-6)

The clash of social and private life lies at the center of Frisch's comedy. ***Biografie,*** like so many of Frisch's plays, is a drama about marriage. It is in marriage that the private and social identities merge, it is again the most intimate social relationship. (p. 27)

How to realize oneself socially has remained the overriding theme of the drama of Max Frisch. It was appropriate then that marriage should play such a central part in his theater. In the discovery of the marriage partner as a complementary alter ego lies the root of a social self-acceptance. The "holy cross" of marriage and the egotistical playfulness of a Don Juan can once again be reconciled and harmonized to a "play" of identity which is both exploratory and enjoyable. . . . ***Triptychon*** (1978) appears to be a counterversion of ***Biografie.*** It analyzes the finality of life from a theatrical realm of death. Not time but death determines the inevitability of an individual biography. This is not a new insight, not even in the works of Frisch; already ***Homo faber*** (1957) saw death as the executor of a personal history. Nor is it new that Frisch stages a sphere of death: both ***Nun singen sie wieder*** (1946) and the epilogue to ***Biedermann und die Brandstifter*** (1958) cast the dead as reflections of their self-projection in life. ***Triptychon*** is by no means the play of an old man afraid of death. The subject of death has always been a central aspect in Frisch's dramatic analysis of man's identity.

Triptychon is made up of three, loosely interrelated, "scenes," each with its own dramatis personae (even if a few overlap). It does not claim to add up to a "play"; instead, it offers repeated attempts to relate death back to life: to our social values, to our concepts of science, philosophy, and religion, to our relationships in love, hate, and indifference. Frisch's "death" is a theatrical device, the pretext for a dramatic analysis of human reality, of man's identity, of his self-concept. Despite the religious model from which the work takes its title, Frisch at no stage glorifies or mystifies death. His scenic triptychon is clearly an expression of faith on the altar of the theater. Only the stage can realize death and use it as a means of social analysis. Again, Frisch has made extreme use of the theater, because he knows that it allows him to rehearse, to demonstrate, and to recognize behavior in a concrete, sensuous, and exemplary fashion.

The discovery that unites all three scenes is a secularized eternity of being: death perpetuates our lives. What may have appeared to be a mere coincidence is turned into an inevitable fate. Death makes our life count, it makes it valid. In a rather Nietzschean manner it rules over an eternal recurrence of the same. Theatrical repetition, varied re-enactment through rehearsals, emerges as a lively exercise; life itself appears, by comparison, to be deadly and final. The ultimate triumph of the stage is that it can treat death as a variation, as a technical device, as a rehearsal. Frisch's theatrical realm of death serves the art of self-knowledge; it allows for change, its model demonstration aims at a new understanding, a different kind of being. It does not want to perpetuate our life, such as it is, but strives to alter it. Frisch's theater is an agent of change. (pp. 27-8)

As always with Frisch, the theater serves the function of enlightening man, not in the form of abstractions or with philosophical pretensions, but as a model, in sensuous analysis. In this way, man becomes more and more identified with the theater—indeed, he is the theater. His life consists of role playing. He is quoting not only classical literature but increasingly his own identity as well. Death is seen as the eternal repetition of the self-quotations we have lived. . . . Death is demythologized by the theater; it becomes another tool of analyzing and assessing social behavior. Frisch offers a dialectical definition of death: it is both repetition and redefinition. The social dimensions of a death which continues to define our age are unmistakeably articulated in the form of political criticism. . . . Frisch shows in his ***Triptychon*** how all acts, thoughts, and misunderstandings are repeated in death; death becomes the stage for re-enacting our lives. The finality does not lie in death but in our unthinking life, in our inability to do anything other than repeat ourselves. Life itself is seen as a form of deadly self-quotation. As such, it is unsocial, sterile, uncommunicative. It seems that in both life and death only repetition or silence are possible. . . . (pp. 28-9)

Not a play dealing with the fear of death then but scenes reflecting on man's seemingly incurable social laziness, his inability to change, intellectually, emotionally, morally. Death in this case can only confirm the triviality of such being. Katrin puts it most explicitly when she says at the end of the second scene: "eternity is banal." . . . What Frisch means as well is that human banality too seems eternal. ***Triptychon*** has more in common with ***Biedermann*** than may at first appear. It shares above all the lament over man's incorrigible selfishness and his inability or unwillingness to learn, to change, to think dynamically. As such, these scenes must be seen as an appeal to live creatively, socially, and intelligently. The moralist Frisch has written another "Lehrstück ohne Lehre," both in content and form. His scenes do not therefore add up to the total unity of a traditional play concept. . . . ***Triptychon*** was written by a social moralist who . . . realizes that death is gradual but who sees signs of this death all around him, who does not restrict death to the individual, any more than life. ***Triptychon***'s real subject is a social death, in fact: the death of society. (pp. 29-30)

Manfred Jurgensen, "The Drama of Frisch," in Perspectives on Max Frisch, *edited by Gerhard F. Probst and Jay F. Bodine, The University Press of Kentucky, 1982, pp. 4-30.*

HORST STEINMETZ

[*In the following excerpt Steinmetz examines Frisch's literary diaries in relation to his fiction.*]

One of the trivialities in Frisch scholarship has been to point out the close connection between Frisch's ***Tagebuch*** (Diary) ***1946-1949*** and the rest of his work. To discover the inseparable interweaving of his diary and literary work does not require any great acumen. The interconnection, moreover, has been increased with the appearance of the second ***Tagebuch*** in 1972. A whole series of dramas is present in the ***Tagebuch 1946-1949*** in the form of either a conceptual outline or at least a motif inventory; namely, ***Graf Öderland, Andorra, Als der Krieg zu Ende war, Biedermann und die Brandstifter,*** **"Schinz".** In addition, a great number of individual motifs are found there that are encountered again in almost all the literary works; for example, the motifs of repetition and self-acceptance. Also smaller details that appear later in the works already exist in the diary, such as the angel that Stiller will meet, or observations about jealousy and unfaithfulness that return in ***Mein Name sei Gantenbein.*** By no means, however, can the ***Tagebuch I*** be treated as merely a type of motif or content source for Frisch's dramas or novels, nor as, in addition, something like a poetic of Frisch's.

Naturally it has also been noticed how often Frisch uses the diary as both form and motif in other works. . . . This regular resort to diary forms or similar structures unmistakenly points toward the fact that the relationship between Frisch's diaries and literary work is closer and more intensive than is the case with other authors who during their other poetical writing might have kept a diary and published it later—even during their lifetimes. In Frisch there is manifested a relationship that goes much beyond connections of motif and content. Thus Jürgen Schröder correctly determined: "A boundary line between his diaries and other work can hardly be drawn." Actually it is necessary to go a step further, since a boundary cannot be drawn at all. The reciprocal crossover of the boundary not only applies to individual aspects of subject matter, content, and form but also characterizes the structure and essence of Frisch's entire oeuvre. The congruency between diary and work is so great that finally all his literary works have to be defined as components of a comprehensive diary. After all it is inconsequential whether one designates the literary work as sections of the diaries or the diaries as literary products.

An unprejudiced view of the diaries has been obstructed repeatedly by among other things the fact that so many of Frisch's works have been anticipated in motif or sketch in ***Tagebuch I.*** That has been misleading above all in the sense of understanding it to be a type of idea storehouse. In actuality, however, these sections, partly carried out and partly mere literary projections, have their own function in the ***Tagebuch,*** serving the elucidation of the problems discussed and portrayed in the diary. For as in ***Bin oder Die Reise nach Peking, Stiller, Santa Cruz,*** or ***Biografie,*** there stands in the center of the diaries a man or person, an ego that wants to find information about himself. And the so-called literary inserts are not primarily the first conceptions or formulations that are later completed and merely jotted down or noted at the time of the diary's composition; rather they are attempts to objectify one's own self, they are the expression of the wrestling carried out to delimit the nonself. Used already in ***Tagebuch I*** as well as later in other works was the "invented example," employed for the elucidation of experiences, for the attempt at objectification in parable form of the elements incapable of direct expression.

Only from the perspective of the later publications, not from the perspective of ***Tagebuch I,*** do the sketches of ***Graf Öderland, Andorra,*** or ***Biedermann*** constitute first drafts or projections. Read in the context of ***Tagebuch I,*** they constitute alienating self-analyses of the diary-self and descriptions of his relationship to the world. In them are documented the play character and consciousness, and the artistic element, for whose creation Brecht's techniques were already used even before they were reflected upon in ***Tagebuch I.***

Therein is revealed the especially close interconnection of the diary form and the techniques of an alienating portrayal. In Frisch they are inseparable. They develop and complement each other, and in a type of reciprocal amalgamation they lead to art forms, to forms of fiction and illusion that are characteristic of Frisch's oeuvre and alone capable of suitably rendering his special themes and problems, of portraying them at all. (pp. 56-7)

One encounters in almost all observations and investigations of ***Tagebuch I*** the concept of a "literary diary," which is considered to be a special genre of diary, to which Max Frisch's work also belongs.

All the problems that the diary as literary genre can proffer seem to be combined in Frisch's ***Tagebuch I.*** It conveys the impression that it was begun and at least in some sections kept as a private diary; at the same time it was from the beginning manifestly written for readers. It is a "writer's workshop," at least it can evoke that impression; on the other hand there is no doubt that it is "artistically constructed," composed as a complete whole. That can be readily recognized in the recurring place names, which have replaced to a large extent the dates characteristic of a diary, and announce with their recurrence as "chapter headings" certain thematic complexes (Café de la Terrasse, Café Odeon). The diary appears full of contradictions—but only as long as it is read as a personal diary of Max Frisch, that is, as long as it is viewed simply as private notations brought into the public eye, notations—as expected in the case of a writer—that have been interspersed with literary inserts, with sketches of literature, similar to poetical études.

The dedication to the reader, however, attempts at the very beginning to hinder such a reading of the book. It warns against understanding the book merely as a traditional diary: "The reader would be doing this book a great favor if he, rather than leafing back and forth according to whim and chance, observed the compositional sequence; the single stones of a mosaic, and such a mosaic is at least the intention of this book, can hardly justify themselves individually." . . . Thus individual passages as isolated sections do not convey the intention of the author; only the book as a whole is capable of achieving the effect. The diary does not thereby reveal the intimate sphere of the author.

Yet an additional fact relativizes the ***Tagebuch*** as a diary in the usual sense. The author hardly ever expresses a concern about eventually rereading his own notations. This diary was evidently made for his own use in a different sense. When the writer speaks of reading his diary, he almost never does it in regard to himself. More interest is shown for the writing itself, for the act of writing. "Writing constitutes reading one's self" . . . states the central sentence in the section "Of the sense of a diary." And even in the various entries on the theme of writing, writing is emphasized not only in its meaning concerning the activity of an author but directly concerning its existential value for the person writing.

The challenge to the reader to read the book as a whole and not as a traditional diary, as well as the recurring reflections and statements about the sense of writing are keys for the structure and understanding of ***Tagebuch I.*** They underline the inner structure of the work, whose unity is not to be found in the author's biography or in the chronology of his notated experiences. These statements are at the same time a first indication of the fictionality of the whole.

Frisch himself explicitly stated that his ***Tagebuch I*** was not to be confused with the "private diary that one once kept as a young man"; here he has used the diary as a "literary form." His ***Tagebuch I*** went beyond the "log book of chronological events," it was a diary that sought reality not only in the facts but equally in fiction. It is not inconsequential that Frisch avoids the term "literary diary" and speaks of a "diary in literary form." Thus he emphatically indicates the fictional character of ***Tagebuch I,*** which does not claim to be a literary diary in the traditional sense but rather belongs to literary forms and structures.

How then can the fictionality of a diary be developed when it doubtlessly contains a great number of autobiographical facts? How can the "I" of this diary, which also undeniably exists outside of the work, lose his demonstrable reality and become a fictional figure? The answer can be found in one of the numerous statements of the diary-self about himself: "Every experience remains basically unrelatable as long as we hope to be able to express it with the actual example that befell us. Only that example which is as distant from me as it is from the listener is capable of expressing me: namely, the fictional example. Only what has been poetisized, transposed, transfigured, only what has been formed is, in essence, capable of conveying." . . . With these words the constitutive relationship is sketched out in which the expressive values of fact and fiction stand in relation to the self of the diarist. Facts have only a limited value because the self involved in them cannot appropriately express itself. That is better achieved, if not solely, with the "fictional example." This amounts to nothing other than the fact that the self becomes observable in its true nature only when it uses fiction for self-recognition and self-representation. And that again means that the reader, if he wants to gain insight into the personality of the diarist, cannot refer to or invoke those statements of the writer that appear to agree with a reality beyond the framework of the book. Precisely those passages that apparently contain Frisch's actual experiences are the ones that do not concern the true self and whose reliability is therefore suspect.

To be touched upon only marginally is the problem that arises when the reader cannot with ease distinguish between fact and fiction. The criterion for his decision is gained through comparison with the reality outside of ***Tagebuch I.*** However, this procedure naturally does not guarantee any correct results. Even where we seem to be dealing with facts from the life of the writer Max Frisch—and in most cases the reader is only able to surmise as much—we could in principle still be dealing with fiction. (pp. 59-60)

One can easily make a test, as an example, of the diarist's words according to which not the "real" but only the "fictional" sample can express his nature. In the midst of the notes is found an autobiography of the author. This autobiography is mostly limited in its length of seven and a half pages to external dates and locations, such that there emerges a type of brief life story. It is not much more than a sketchy outline of the writer's life's story. Sober, objective, limiting itself almost completely to verifiable facts, the author courteously places the external data of his life at the disposal of those who call for such a biography and expect none other. Absent is the rendering of all personal information. Thus it has not been without secret irony that Frisch scholarship has made thorough use of this "autobiography" to impart specific information about Frisch. It is with yet greater irony that apparently no one has remarked until now in what great contrast the autobiography stands to many other sections of ***Tagebuch I.*** It portrays an image that corresponds to the requirements of many Frisch readers. Precisely therein lies, however, the distancing of the diarist from this image. The fact is degraded to an image so that in this "autobiography," it is precisely the self of the diary that cannot be found. (p. 61)

The autobiography and its "antinomian" relationship to the other parts of ***Tagebuch I*** shed light precisely upon those sections that seem to be linked with the nonfictional reality. These parts convey a reality that is real in a superficial sense but do not include the "actual" reality nor even at best approach it. Corresponding to the image of the self shown in the autobiography is the image of the world. This image comprises the person's superficial aspects, representing a relative value. It practically forces the diary writer to go beyond it, to replace it with other images more appropriate to reality, if not at least to enlarge upon it. What the diarist is seeking in his depiction of the world and of the confrontation of his inner self with it is "realms of life yet unknown, unexperienced realms, a world that has not yet been described" . . . , that lies concealed in or behind the actual reality. Hence the numerous travel impressions—"Under way" (Unterwegs) reads the programmatic heading of a series of entries—hence also the strong hope felt throughout (but thwarted at the end of the book) that the catastrophe of the Second World War might have changed the rigid image of the world along with the conduct of men relative to such a world view. Out of this hope speaks the conception that the present image of the world and the individual is merely provisional; one can and must overcome that world. In this context the hesitant and objective descriptions of life in the ruined German cities, of Theresienstadt, of the sojourns in Poland and Russia are to be movingly felt. Consequently the author refrains from almost any interpretation. He is reluctant to draw conclusions from the image he sees. The image is not permitted to be transposed into the "actual." From the standpoint of the observer, however, there does not become visible any "new world that should be brought to light through epic discovery but rather only the distorted face of the old one that we know and that is worthy of mention only in its aberrance; that is to say, the ruin presupposes that we know, or at least have a sense of, its earlier wholeness, the ruin is almost nothing without the background of its yesterday, it is worthy of mention only by comparison, with reflection." . . . Coming to terms with the world, to which process his autobiography belongs, as well as with all the experiences of the self which affect its existence in the world basically occurs in light of a double perspective. The diary keeper recognizes the parallel between his existence and the image of the world. He writes a diary in order to escape the one-sideness of these images. Finally, coming to terms with the world takes place for the sake of his own self. The decisive goal is the battle for self-recognition on the part of the essentiality lying behind the, as it were, official autobiography. The diary has its center point in the "thought, whether it would be possible that our life could have proceeded differently." (pp. 62-3)

From this vantage point reality is seen as only one of the possibilities standing open to the self for realization. Therefore, as a fact, the irrefutability of this self-materialization is called into question. In principle it is replaceable with a different reality. In this manner the solidity of reality is diminished. And with it the verifiable reality of the author Max Frisch is relativized to such an extent that it borders on the reality form of fiction according to its essence and constitution as only one realization of different possibilities. It has no more argumentative force than the fiction.

The insight and recognition of this state of affairs establish the point of departure for composing the diary, and simultaneously this insight and recognition are to be substantiated with the aid of the diary. By writing, forming first of all the images into words, the author is able to see through the provisory value of reality. "Writing amounts to reading one's self." The act of writing has in this context both a negative and a positive aspect. With the rendering of the existing reality, one is first of all in a position to read what one is not. One can only describe the image, depict it as that which is. If, on the other hand, one attempts by means of the writing process to express (directly) the "actual," then the undertaking's dubiousness is revealed in all its severity, and that has to be overcome if writing is to have meaning. Language turns out to be closely affiliated with the image, to be part of the reality that comprehends merely the surface:

> Our concern, the actual, can at best be paraphrased, and that means most literally: One writes around and around it. One encloses it. One makes statements that never contain our actual experience, which remains inexpressible; these statements can only encircle it, as close and exact as possible; and the actual, the unutterable appears at best as the tension between them.

> Our endeavor is presumably to express everything that is utterable. Language is like a chisel that hews everything away that is not secret; and all saying means removing. In that respect it should not disconcert us that everything that comes to words lapses into a certain emptiness. One says what life is not. One says it for the sake of life. (pp. 63-4)

In view of this situation, self-understanding presents itself to the writer only in a roundabout way. His only other alternative is to represent the nonreal, in which language also contains, at least in part, other truth. This is the alternative of art, genuine invention, the "fictional example." This alternative offers him the possibility of exemplifying himself in other images. Here also they remain images since here also language forms the basis upon which rest the varying projections of the self. However, the noncommittalness now amounts to freedom; the replaceability becomes an advantage. The examples are, in the true sense of the word, samples. They achieve something of the character of theatrical roles. They resemble theatrical situations, testing, playing, creating the illusion of an artificially projected reality that, though not real, is yet true. Thus it is not coincidental that the diary writer repeatedly speaks of his fascination with the theater. He recognizes in the situation created by the theatrical "framework" what he is otherwise incapable of seeing: people. (p. 64)

The fictions in ***Tagebuch I*** in this manner become proofs for the existence of the true self veiled for the greatest part by images. The numerous so-called literary inserts are thus not to be conceived as the first jottings down of the works of the author Max Frisch but rather as self-projections that express the true self. In any case they are supposed to contribute to suspending (Aufheben) one-sidedness and the falsifying limitation of factual (yet already relativized) life, or at least to make it perspicuous. The unity and totality of ***Tagebuch I,*** which Frisch in the dedication postulates as something to be accepted by the reader, is brought about by this correspondence between foreground reality and exemplary fiction structured in the manner just discussed. The ***Tagebuch I*** does not divide into two parts, as it were, with the one comprising a private diary and the other containing literary sketches. Rather they complement each other; together they result in a work of literature.

The close interweaving and homogeneity of the "fictional examples" and of the other entries of ***Tagebuch I*** are not recognizable solely on the basis of the writer's comments but are demonstrated by the text itself. As a rule the fictional episodes follow sections in which their general theme is reflected upon; and then the simple sequence is usually transformed into a near dialectical relationship. The insight of the reflections is transposed, as Frisch likes to say elsewhere, into a "story" (Geschichte) or, better, into a type of play action. To a great extent this process corresponds in its model form to the conditions and forms of the Brechtian theater. Seen from the factual form of its life, the self alienates itself within the fictions of certain play situations, where its unrealized existential possibilities and variants gain contour. In this manner, as in Brecht, the factualness of supposedly irrevocable occurrences is suspended in favor of an alteration intended to further the truth. For the portrayal of his specific "self" subject matter (Ich-Problematik), Frisch in ***Tagebuch I*** employs a technique similar to the Brechtian alienation. And he apparently has not fully recognized the significance of the technique developed and applied in this work when he speaks of how enticing it would be to apply Brecht's theory of alienation to the novel as well. . . . He has already done what appears to him to be merely an enticing idea. (pp. 64-5)

Thus, on almost every page the unity of the basic theme and the associated expansion and fictionalization of the author-self can be observed. In this manner ***Tagebuch I*** is divested of the one-sided, pragmatic character of being the depiction of the thoughts and experiences of an empirical person, and it is transferred into the realm of fiction and literature. Hans Werner Richter is one of the few who have recognized this basic structure, although he also was not able finally to let go of the idea, both that a literary diary is supposed to remain in its very essence a statement of an empirical person and that a disintegration of its basic form is inadmissable:

> Objective? Yes, am I moreover honestly objective? In attempting it, I am already departing from the truth. I am no longer taking notes, I am telling tales. I am telling tales for the diary reader, my diary reader of tomorrow. Is that the sense of a diary?
>
> In many literary diaries I discover this propensity not to note down but rather to tell tales. That is what makes it worth reading to the consumer.
>
> Max Frisch is an example of that. He writes a novel and presents it as a diary. It is almost always not the novel of his life but rather of how he imagines his life, his thoughts, and his experiences. These imagined conceptions correspond to the conceptions of Max Frisch's reader.

Richter is right to the extent that he determines that the book is directed in its intention toward the readers. That also cannot be any different since we are, to be sure, not dealing with a private diary. On the contrary, we are dealing with literature that is just as much fiction and illusion as Frisch's dramas and novels and that addresses itself to readers just as all literature does. Frisch himself stated these facts unequivocably. In his conversations with Horst Bienek he pointed out that the diary form was "specifically characteristic (eigentümlich) for the author with my name." In such a formulation, strange only at first glance, we can perceive the adequate mirroring of the basic structure of the diary-self. The formulation emphasizes the fact that Frisch is conscious of the special form that he had been able to give to the diary as literary genre. Characteristically Frisch does not speak of a literary diary, but rather of a "diary as literary form." However we might interpret the sentence that the diary form is specifically characteristic for the author with his name, the unusual statement makes one thing evident: the diary writer is not the citizen Max Frisch but rather an author bearing his name. Thus in ***Tagebuch I*** the same relationship prevails between the author Max Frisch and the diary-self as between the author of a first-person novel and the first-person narrator appearing in it. With Frisch they both merely bear the same name. From this fact came the misunderstanding that ***Tagebuch I*** was a book of personal notes rather than the fictional work that it actually is, standing in its essential nature closer to the novel than to the genuinely private journal. (pp. 68-9)

Horst Steinmetz, "Frisch as a Diarist," translated by Jay F. Bodine, in Perspectives on Max Frisch, *edited by Gerhard F. Probst and Jay F. Bodine, The University Press of Kentucky, 1982, pp. 56-70.*

ROLF KIESER

[Kieser is a Swiss-born American critic and professor of German history and literature. His critical study Max Frisch: Das literarische Tagebuch *(1975) lauds Frisch as "an innovator of the concept of prose fiction by creating an artistic narrative genre (the diary) which reflects the linguistic and philosophical principles of a literature increasingly irreverent of distinctions between literary genres." In the following excerpt Kieser analyzes Frisch's intentions in presenting his Don Juan as a lover of geometry who settles for a middle-class marriage.]*

Whenever Max Frisch's ***Don Juan*** play is discussed by the critics, their attention unfailingly focuses on the story of that archetypal protagonist of *Macho* who, as Frisch insists, prefers geometry by far to the fairer sex.

The author, on the other hand, strongly emphasizes that his ***Don Juan*** has little in common with Tirso de Molina's Glorious *Burlador de Sevilla* since he intends to show "Don Juan as a developing character, which is only possible at the price that he is no real Don Juan anymore but a man who (for one reason or the other) acquired the role of Don Juan."

"The love of geometry" is a symbol for what Frisch considers "a male intellect which is an affront because it is aiming for completely different goals than a woman does and which considers woman from the beginning a sheer episode—with the well-known result, to be sure, that the episode eventually swallows up the whole life."

Frisch wanted his Don Juan to be a "spiritual figure," which means that we find in him the opposite of the traditional genius of sensuality, "the incarnation of the flesh or the animation of the flesh through the flesh's proper spirit," as Kierkegaard put it. "His fame as a seducer (which accompanies him as fame although he does not identify with it) is a misunderstanding from part of the ladies," says Frisch. "Don Juan is an intellectual although well-built and without glasses. It is indeed his spirituality which makes him irresistible for the ladies of Seville."

Far from being a "libidinous libertine" . . . in the fashion of Casanova, Frisch's Don Juan in fact challenges the laws of nature which divide humanity into two sexes. "His opponent is creation proper." By denying his need for a permanent love relationship with a woman he also forecloses fatherhood: "Don Juan," says Frisch, "is childless, even if there were 1003 children."

By characterizing Don Juan as a "parasite of creation," Frisch depicts him not as a rebel against Christian morality but as a lonely researcher for "the virginal," for paradise lost.

It is, as we know, not the first time that Frisch uses biblical metaphors in his own capricious way. In the ***Sketchbook 1946-1949*** we find the passage which has become the leitmotiv for Frisch's whole work: *Thou shalt not make unto thee any graven image* where we find the following remarks about love: "That is the exciting, the unpredictable, the truly gripping thing about love: that we never come to the end of the person we love: because we love them; and as long as we love them . . . Once we feel we know the other, love is at an end every time, but the cause of that, and the consequence of it, are perhaps not quite as we have always imagined. It is not because we know the other that we cease to love, but vice versa: because our love has come to an end, because its power is expended, that person is finished for us." (pp. 119-20)

Don Juan's rebellion against heaven is stimulated by his interest for geometry: something in the creation is out of tune. Don Juan wants to find out, "was stimmt," ("what harmonizes," one of Frisch's favorite expressions.) His attempt to prove that permanent love does not exist makes him particularly attractive in the eyes of each one of the ladies who wants to prove the opposite, namely that she alone is the answer to his heart's desire. Don Juan gives up when transitoriness, "Vergängnis," catches up with him. An aging seducer who considers himself a spiritual figure is an embarrassment. Don Juan plans his escape from the ladies by staging the farce of the Stone Guest. Ironically he ends up where he started: in marriage.

It is perhaps the strange combination of farce (Frisch himself calls his comedy "ein Kostümstück") and venerable literary tradition that has prevented the critics from seeing the play in its own context: Frisch's intention to write a parody of the Don Juan myth is only secondary. Among the notes in his ***Gesammelte Werke in zeitlicher Folge*** we find the interesting remark that the author during his first journey to the United States worked on a novel with the tentative title *Was macht ihr mit der Liebe*. At the end of the same year he began to work on his ***Don Juan*** while dropping temporarily his novel-project. Later he caught up with it. It developed into ***Stiller.*** If we consider the simultaneity of the creation of novel and drama we are able to realize some meaningful parallels.

Already in ***The Chinese Wall,*** Don Juan appears as one of the figures "who inhabit our brain." "I have just come out of the Hell of literature," he explains and complains that nobody, not even Brecht and his Ensemble, understand him. In ***Stiller*** we find a parallel reference to literature shaping our consciousness: "How am I to prove to my counsel that I don't know my murderous impulses through C. G. Jung, jealousy through Marcel Proust, Spain through Hemingway, Paris through Ernst Jünger, Switzerland through Mark Twain, Mexico through Graham Greene, my fear of death through Bernanos, inability ever to reach my destination through Kafka, and all sorts of things through Thomas Mann?" Don Juan is faced with a similar problem. How can he prove to the world that he is not identical with the myth which bears his name, and that his interest is geometry rather than women? "I am not Don Juan!" he insists, yet his fame is so overwhelming that not even the frank disclosure of the theatrical mechanisms of his planned descent to hell will shatter his reputation. His only way to gain anonymous privacy is to accept Miranda's offer. As father and henpecked husband he blends with a life of mediocrity, just as Stiller does at the end.

Frisch's treatment of the Don Juan myth makes his hero a close relative not only of Stiller but also of other male protagonists such as Walter Faber, Gantenbein, Enderlin-Svoboda, Kürmann, and all the other expressions of a self in search of identity. Their forefather is Don Juan. With him they share their narcissism, their intellectual male chauvinism and their inability to accept woman as more than an episode in their lives. This is the reason why, with rare exceptions, Frisch's female figures do not live an existence of their own. They are focal points of male attention or stumbling blocks such as Antoinette Stein in ***Biografie,*** the proverbial "Stein des Anstosses" (stumbling block).

"Le Donjuanism" as Camus defined it in his *Mythe de Sisyphe* is a salient principle in Frisch's interpretation of the relationship between man and woman. When the lover of the clear logic of geometry and admirer of the law that parallels meet in eternity sets out in a Faustian effort to find out what holds the world together in its innermost being, he realizes in the end that his existence is absurd. There are only two choices left for him: death or capitulation. Frisch's Don Juan chooses the middle-class solution. His fall from the sublime to the ridiculous is tremendous yet inevitable. It is not the descent to hell of the classical Don Juan, and the formula that in Frisch's interpretation marriage equals hell is no more than a pun. For Frisch's Don Juan is not "ein glänzendes Scheusal" (a brilliant monster) as Brecht called Molière's seducer, but an existential searcher whose greatest fear is the fear of repetition. Thus marriage is a metaphor for repetition, and one of Frisch's metaphors for a man threatened by it is Don Juan. (pp. 120-22)

Frisch's transformation of a literary myth into a middle-class marriage story does not thoroughly succeed. The author plays with the knowledge of the average theater-goer in reference to Don Juan. Ironically, the intensity of the old fable wins an easy victory over Frisch's intellectual Anti-Hero by putting him under its charm. His position of geometry remains unauthenticated even if the author points out the contingency of that cipher: "It is still too early, it would still be shocking, but sometime one should write a comedy with a noble ending: 'Don Juan Or the Love For the Duino Elegies'—the story of the last Don Juan in our time who dismissed all women because they bothered him in his ten years of waiting (to write) the Elegies." (p. 122)

Rolf Kieser, "Wedding Bells for Don Juan: Frisch's Domestication of a Myth," in Perspectives on Max Frisch, *edited by Gerhard F. Probst and Jay F. Bodine, The University Press of Kentucky, 1982, pp. 119-123.*

FRANZ P. HABERL

[Haberl, a German-born Canadian critic and professor of German language and literature, is the author of Im Stil Unserer Zeit *(1967), as well as a contributor to scholarly journals. In the following excerpt Haberl discusses themes of death and aging in* Triptych *and* Man in the Holocene.*]*

Anyone familiar with Max Frisch's works knows that the topics of death and dying occur frequently, both in his fiction and in his dramas. In his very first novel, ***Jürg Reinhart*** (1934), the protagonist carries out an act of euthanasia. In one of his earliest dramas, ***Nun singen sie wieder*** (1945; Eng. ***Now They Sing Again***), the twenty-one dead hostages are integrated in the dramatic action. In Frisch's ***Tagebuch 1966-1971*** (1972; Eng. ***Sketchbook 1966-1971***) the problems of aging, dying, and death figure very prominently. . . . However, no matter how prominently the subject of death may be featured in Frisch's early as well as mature writings, it is fair to say that his main concern in these works is life, the ongoing, ever-changing process of living.

In the course of his artistic creation Frisch developed a theory of "permutation" which applies equally well to his dramas and to his fiction. In essence, this theory consists of repeatedly asking the question, "What would happen or how would a given character behave if certain circumstances or premises were changed?" and of then having the character act out the new scenario. (p. 580)

In his 1965 speech upon accepting the Schiller Prize, Frisch justified the application of his theory of permutation to his dramas in the following words: "Wherever life takes place we see something much more exciting (than dramatic peripeteia): it is the sum of actions which are often accidental, and each time it (life) might have been different; there is no action and no omission that does not permit variants for the future. The only occurrence that does not permit a variant any more is . . . death." Pondering this statement and considering the happy events in Frisch's life during 1965 and over the next three or four years (the move to his house in Berzona and his relationship with and marriage to Marianne Oellers, all so movingly recounted in ***Montauk***), one might be tempted to believe that the positive, life-affirming aspects of his theory would continue to dominate his works.

In fact, however, the period from 1966 to 1971 is the time when he wrote the abovementioned ***Sketchbook 1966-1971,*** with its marked preoccupation with death. (pp. 580-81)

On a personal level, Frisch's concern with aging and death certainly culminates in ***Montauk*** (1975). This *Erzählung* or "tale" is really a *journal intime,* an utterly frank account of certain aspects of his life, his thoughts and feelings, his relationships with women, his joys, fears, feelings of guilt, et cetera. Within this emotional-intellectual kaleidoscope, Frisch's concern with aging and death is *one* constituent part, not the predominant preoccupation it had been in the ***Sketchbook 1966-1971.*** (p. 581)

[It] is fitting to remember the intellectual and conceptual groundwork which Frisch laid in his ***Sketchbook 1966-1971*** and in ***Montauk*** when one considers his ***Triptychon*** (1978; Eng. ***Triptych***) and ***Der Mensch erscheint im Holozän*** (1979; Eng. ***Man in the Holocene***). Contrary to Frisch's previous practice, wherein the death of a character (or even of several characters) was an incidental part of the dramatic or epic plot, in these two works death (actual or impending) is the central concern; it constitutes the very agon of the plots.

Triptych was written during 1976 and 1977 and published in 1978. It is therefore Frisch's first drama since the original version of ***Biography*** (1967)—i.e., there was a hiatus of some ten years in his dramatic production. As Jürgen H. Petersen has pointed out, this hiatus seems to be due to the problems Frisch faced when he tried to realize his "drama of permutation." The main difficulty which Frisch perceived in presenting the "variants" of human actions on the stage lay in the medium of theatre itself, in the reactions of the audience to the "games" on the stage: "As soon as something is played onstage, no matter how short the variant of a scene may be, the audience thinks that the action has really occurred." The difficulty of direct dramatic representation notwithstanding, Frisch continued to be preoccupied with the principle of permutation. However, in ***Triptych*** this principle is not acted out on the stage; the dramatic action is transferred to the brain and the imagination of the spectator or reader. Indeed, these three "scenic panels" (as the subtitle labels them) demand at least as much attention from the spectator as do great paintings containing many details.

There are only a few tenuous links between the central panel (which was written first and was originally intended to stand alone) and the first and third. The "action" of the first consists of a social gathering after the funeral of Matthis Proll, who has died at the age of seventy. Proll and several of the guests reappear in the central tableau. Two of the guests from the first panel (Roger and Francine) do not take part in the central tableau; they are the protagonists in the third.

In the first tableau Roger and Francine meditate on the nature of life and death. Roger establishes the axiom that "human consciousness must have a biological basis"—i.e., that there can be no consciousness after the brain stops functioning. In this sense, death is something trivial, a mere confirmation of the laws to which all of nature is subjected. What is "mystical" about the death of a human being is that it bestows finality upon human life: "It is *what* we have lived that counts. The various events of our lives, each one in its own place and time—there they stand, unalterable. . . . " This principle is aptly illustrated during the long harangue which "the widow" addresses to her deceased husband, who suddenly appears, sitting on a rocking chair, unperceived by the guests. She berates him for real and imaginary wrong-doings, halfheartedly apologizes for having a clergyman at his funeral (which he had forbidden), and, after twenty-six years of marriage, during which time she must have had ample opportunity to realize that he did not believe in Christianity, she expresses her belief that she will see him again in the afterlife. At the end of the tableau, the deceased gets up from the rocking chair and walks away. The fact that the deceased never speaks a word during the widow's harangue, together with his final silent disappearance, suggests that the lack of communication between Proll and his wife is meant to extend beyond their lifetimes into eternity. Moreover, the fact that all the characters in the first panel (except Roger and Francine) are designated by generic terms ("the deceased husband," "the widow," "a young clergyman," "her [the widow's] daughter"), as well as the formalized, conventional utterances by the guests (condolences, statements to the effect that "seventy is a good age, after all," et cetera), suggests that the lack of genuine interpersonal communication, of thoughtfulness, and of empathy is meant to be general, to extend to human society as a whole.

Most of the characters in the first panel are cast as types. Their utterances do not provide much occasion for the minds of the audience to speculate on how things might have been different, if. . . . In other words, the static quality of the tableau does not facilitate the operation of a "theatre of permutation" even in the imagination of the audience. This is not the case in the second, or central, panel, which takes place in Hades, presented very much like the real world from which the characters have departed. There is a cement-covered ditch (meant to represent the River Styx) where "the old man" (Matthis Proll) fishes without ever catching a thing, just as he did during his lifetime. There is the rocking chair from the first panel, and birds chirping intermittently. On the "wide and empty and white" stage there appear a variety of people, who talk about their past lives and ask questions of each other without ever receiving any meaningful answers. As the eighteen characters interact in various ways, one all-pervading concept is expressed again and again: namely, the finality of death. There are no further developments, there is no growth, there are no permutations in Hades. (pp. 581-82)

Most of the episodes are related realistically and vividly; some of them even recall elements from Frisch's autobiographical accounts. For instance, the fact that Matthis Proll's mother was not adequately provided for when her husband died evokes a statement in ***Montauk*** to the effect that Frisch's father had debts when he died. The entire fabric of the numerous bits of memories recounted by the various characters is held together, as it were, by several leitmotivs such as Proll's fishing, his service in the Spanish Civil War, the story of Katrin's life, or the man with the flute who continually plays the wrong tune. Eventually all the characters have expressed themselves; their memories are "dried up," to use the tramp's words . . . , and the action ends with Katrin's remark, "Eternity is banal." . . . In presenting a cross section of society in the central panel, Frisch seems to suggest that for most people, existence in Hades is as unsatisfactory as life on earth. Katrin's final words are an obvious counterstatement to the clergyman's affirmation that "a light will come, a light such as we have never seen before, and a birth without flesh," . . . The vacuity of the statement is underscored by the speaker's purposeless meandering throughout the middle tableau: he simply does not have a useful role to play.

In the third panel Roger and Francine, the probing intellectuals whom the audience had met in the opening tableau, reappear. They are sitting on a park bench in Paris and spend a night talking about their lives and their nature as human beings. Roger is fifty years old and still alive. Francine is dead; she was thirty-three at the time of her death. Francine's contributions to the conversation are almost exclusively words she had spoken during the time when she was living with Roger, and particularly during their night of leavetaking in the same park. Most of the scene is a reenactment of that night several years ago, a fact emphasized by the repetitive phrase, "That's what you said," spoken by Roger after most statements made by Francine. (pp. 582-83)

As Roger recapitulates their life together, he raises the fundamental question about their child, about procreation: "Why didn't you want to have our child?" . . . A little later he admits his own acquiescence, if not complicity, in the abortion which Francine had undergone: "I didn't insist on it (having the child), no, I certainly didn't." . . . These sentences echo similar ones in ***Montauk*** . . . and thus express very personal concerns of the author, yet their real significance for the present discussion is that for Francine and Roger there is no afterlife through any offspring, that their deaths are not transcended through procreation.

When Francine eventually breaks out of the mold of her set phraseology, when she addresses Roger directly, she describes the great love they shared and offers her definition of life, of being alive: "At that time I really did believe I could rethink things, you could rethink things. We weren't dead, Roger, never dead—as we are now." . . . Seen in this light, death is inflexibility, one's inability to alter one's thought processes. This idea is further illustrated by Francine's reference to Lenin's head, which she had seen in his mausoleum in Moscow and which had nauseated her: "His wise head empty of thought for the past fifty years. . . . The dead don't rethink." . . .

As the night progresses, Roger attempts to *umdenken*, to "rethink things," to reshape their story, to eliminate the discord that had led to their separation; but of course it is too late. When Francine eventually responds to his agonized outcry, "Say something!" . . . , she tells him the truth about his own essence, at least as she sees it: "You have never loved anybody, Roger, you are not capable of that, and you will never love anybody." . . . Since Roger is still alive, he does not have to accept this dictum, does not have to go on existing with this blemish on his character; he can still *umdenken*, can still develop. In this sense, Roger's suicide at the very end of the scene may be seen as a contradiction of Francine's verdict, as an effort to rejoin her, as a *Liebestod*. Frisch's final stage instructions (". . . daylight: the bench is empty, the traffic sounds, now loud") seem to make a statement to the effect that life goes on, that individual fates are contained and submerged in the flow of human traffic.

In ***Triptych*** the topics of death and transcendence are presented in a direct and obvious manner; the protagonists are, for the most part, dead and now reflect upon their previous lives. In ***Man in the Holocene*** Frisch deals with the subject of approaching death; the protagonist is still alive, but his life-forces are slowly and inexorably petering out. Though ***Holocene*** was published one year after ***Triptych,*** the genesis of both works seems to have been more or less simultaneous; indeed, Frisch may well have begun working on ***Holocene*** before he started writing ***Triptych.*** (p. 583)

The plot, in its barest outline, is as follows: seventy-four-year old Herr Geiser lives alone in a house in a remote village in the Onsernone Valley in Ticino. It has been raining for several days; there are some landslides, one of which blocks the only road to the outside world. The telephone is out of order, and intermittent power failures deprive Geiser of television and of some of his food, since it thaws in the freezer. Still, he copes. There is always something to do, such as building a pagoda from pieces of crisp bread. However, as the days pass and the rain continues, Geiser starts asking questions: about previous landslides and rock slides in the valleys of Ticino, and about the Flood in Noah's time. He examines with a telescope the big rock which overshadows the village to see whether a fissure has developed. This leads him to inquire into the various periods of geology and into the evolution of life. He finds the answers to these questions in various encyclopedias but soon realizes that he cannot retain the information. In an effort to fight his progressive loss of memory, he cuts the appropriate articles out of the encyclopedias and pins them to the living-room walls. Eventually Geiser sets out on a perilous expedition to leave his valley. He climbs up a steep mountain pass and down to another valley. When he can already hear the church bells in the other valley, when he has to descend only another 313 meters, when he knows he can escape, he decides not to and undertakes the even more dangerous climb up to the pass and back down to his valley. After his return, Geiser locks himself in his house and carries on an increasingly difficult struggle for physical and spiritual survival. Finally he suffers a stroke; a few days later his daughter arrives from Basel to take care of him.

The entire narrative is interspersed with references to Geiser's lapses of memory, of which he is conscious and which he tries to counteract by means of the notes he writes for himself and the articles from the encyclopedias which he pins to the walls. There are also numerous references to his dead wife; in fact, Geiser carries on a sort of dialogue with her. He wonders how she would react to certain situations; he knows she would shake her head about the walls that are covered with pieces of paper, et cetera. Ultimately his forgetfulness, some of his odd actions, and just sheer bad luck result in a general aura of deterioration in the house, which in turn infringes on his dogged, steadfast will to survive. (pp. 583-84)

After his stroke, Geiser suffers a partial loss of memory; he cannot remember several facts pertaining to the present, but he vividly recalls episodes from the distant past such as the climb of the Matterhorn that he undertook with his brother fifty years ago. This narrative is another breathtaking tour de force, a detailed account of mortal danger shared and survived by the two brothers. As Geiser muses about such past events, the present intrudes into his reflections; past and present become fused in his mind. The last five clippings which he cuts from his lexicons are the definitions of *eschatology* and *coherent* and descriptive entries on chestnut canker, the Roman colony in Locarno, and apoplexy (stroke). The complete definition of *eschatology* reads, "theology of 'the last things,' i.e., the final fate of the individual human beings and of the world." . . . By having Geiser clip these articles and arrange them in this order, the author suggests that there is a "coherence," an organic connection between dying trees, the downfall of empires, and the death of individual human beings. The abovementioned clippings are followed by a description of Geiser's village after the rains have stopped. The village is "unharmed" and full of plant, animal, and human life. The serenity and peace and the continuing life of the village seem to encompass Geiser. By remaining in his community, surrounded by "his" mountains, Geiser transcends his individual death, because he is part of a larger process of birth, life, and death, a process that extends beyond the span of an individual human life. In "Fragment" Frisch had said, "A human life is nothing at all. . . ." In the final version of ***Holocene*** he seems to say that a human being is (and will remain, even beyond his physical death) a part of a larger order of things, a part of his geological age (the Holocene), and hence a part of the universe.

There is an abundance of autobiographical references in ***Holocene.*** First of all, the village in the Onsernone Valley is obviously meant to be Berzona, where Frisch has lived off and on since 1965. . . . Another autobiographical reference is the set of symptoms exhibited by Geiser after he has suffered his stroke: the left eyelid is paralyzed and insensitive. These are precisely the symptoms which Frisch mentions in describing his own physiognomy in ***Montauk***. . . . Given these autobiographical references, it seems justified to consider the philosophic statements contained in ***Holocene*** as a most significant expression of Max Frisch's personal eschatology. (pp. 584-85)

Franz P. Haberl, "Death and Transcendence in Max Frisch's 'Triptych' and 'Man in the Holocene'," in World Literature Today, *Vol. 60, No. 4, Autumn, 1986, pp. 580-85.*

MARGA I. WEIGEL

[*Weigel is a German critic and professor of German language and literature. In the following excerpt Weigel compares the protagonist of* Bluebeard *to similar characters in Frisch's earlier works.*]

Following acquittal on charges of murdering a prostitute, Felix Theodor Schaad, M.D., begins to search [***Blaubart*** (1982; ***Bluebeard: A Tale***)] for the reasons why his life has been a failure. The public cross-examination in the courtroom is followed by Schaad's private cross-examination, an attempt to determine his guilt which ultimately drives him to confess the murder and shortly thereafter to attempt suicide. In the last analysis he is indeed convinced that he is guilty, although he has consistently maintained, both to the court and afterward to himself, that he did not commit the murder. . . .

As far as the title ***Bluebeard: A Tale*** is concerned, the best judgment is Walter Faber's: "None of it is true"; it is neither a tale in the usual sense, nor is it about a fairy-tale Bluebeard who kills his seven wives.

To be sure, the link with the tale of Charles Perrault is made in the text . . . ; however, the motif of the tyrannical man is inverted. Unlike Bluebeard, Schaad is not characterized by authoritarian power, but rather by powerlessness caused by a weak sense of self. (p. 589)

[The] ''laconic'' narrator Schaad contrasts sharply with Frisch's earlier protagonists. Those men, who delighted in their ability to tell tales and maintained sovereign command of their narrative, paraphrased their situation in imaginative attempts at stories for the purpose of making available to the reader their reality, that which moved them. Schaad, however, for want of language, imagination, and vitality, is unable to flee into stories. He makes good on what Stiller merely promised: ''We possess language in order to become mute.''

Tortured by guilt feelings, Schaad attempts to discover what really happened, but he is unable to do so because he does not know himself and because he represses a great deal. (pp. 589-90)

A year after the murder, Schaad is sitting wordlessly in a tavern. Pursued by hallucinations as though by the Erinyes, he tries to call his dead wife . . . , possibly to warn her of her murderer. In ever-increasing isolation—patients and friends, as well as his seventh wife, have long since deserted him—he works himself more and more into the role of the murderer. He is now convinced that he is the person others consider him to be—an attitude identical to the reaction of Andri in ***Andorra,*** who is forced into an identity by others and is thereby destroyed. With its headlines ''Bluebeard in Court'' . . . , the press not only has contributed to the destruction of his reputation, but has also been instrumental in convincing him of his own guilt. . . .

Schaad seems familiar to us, for we have already gotten to know his predecessor Anatol Stiller, who also maintained that he had killed his wife and who in fact did so in his dreams. . . . The latent aggressiveness of both protagonists is suppressed in the waking state and thus leads to feelings of guilt and to silence. Each makes the ''terrifying discovery'' that he has no language for his reality. . . . Stiller explains that his reality lies not in the role he plays, but rather in the *kind* of role which he unconsciously assigns to himself. . . . (p. 591)

Frisch, in selecting Schaad for his new story, chose a figure astonishingly similar to Stiller. New, however, is the narrative technique, which in its linguistic parsimony mirrors the inner condition of the protagonist. Schaad lacks the language which, by allowing him to articulate his problems, could have provided clarity for him in his search for guilt and identity. With the medium of language it would have been possible for him to put aside misunderstandings and defend himself against a hostile press, which with its Bluebeard caricature made life impossible for him both as a doctor and as a private person. Frisch explained the function of language early on, in a 1946 entry in his first ***Sketchbook.***

> Like the sculptor plying his chisel, language works by bringing the area of blankness in the things that can be said as close as possible to the central mystery, the living element. There is always the danger that in doing so one might destroy the mystery, just as there is the danger that one might leave off too soon, might leave it as an unshaped block, might not locate the mystery, grasp it, and free it from all the things that could still be said; in other words, that one might not get through to its final surface.

For his part, Schaad decides not to use language any longer as a means of communication, a way of attaining renewed vitality in his state of inertia. During the entire first-person narrative (which begins only after his acquittal), he does not conduct a single conversation, except at the police station. Language is employed only to cross-examine himself or imagined witnesses, including dead ones, in the attempt to ascertain his own guilt. ***Bluebeard*** may well be a ''work comprised of dialogues'' (*Dialogwerk*), as was ***Triptych*** (1978) before it; however, there are no longer any conversations in either work, or in ***Man in the Holocene*** (1979), which appeared shortly after ***Triptych.*** Thus language is used neither as an anchor, in order to begin anew after defeat and draw closer to the ''mystery,'' nor, as Frisch had hoped, as a means with which ''to rebel, to change one's way of thinking, to revise, and not to stagnate prematurely.'' Like the protagonists of the late works after ***Montauk*** (1975) in particular, Schaad chooses to fall silent or, as Frisch expresses it, chooses ''that which is lethal'' (*das Tödliche*). Instead of joining battle, instead of using the weapon of language to defend his position and his reality, Schaad flees into amnesia and, once this is cured, into the labyrinth of his hallucinations, so that we must finally wonder whether he will ever find his way back into a life in which he can feel at home. (pp. 591-92)

Marga I. Weigel, '''I Have No Language for My Reality': The Ineffable as Tension in the 'Tale' of Bluebeard,'' in World Literature Today, *Vol. 60, No. 4, Autumn, 1986, pp. 589-92.*

Herb Gardner

I'm Not Rappaport

Tony Award

American dramatist and scriptwriter.

Gardner traces the origins of his Tony Award-winning comedy, *I'm Not Rappaport* (1985), to an amusing vignette he observed in progress on a bench in New York's Central Park, an alter-office where he spends much time. "There was an old white guy and an old black guy," he reported. "They'd be silent for long periods, and then they'd be yelling. And yet they would come back every day; they wouldn't sit with anybody but each other. They were obviously friends, and getting a big kick out of hollering at each other. . . . I started imagining what these two old guys were yelling, and why they were friends, and it just kind of took over." The resulting play involves two octogenarians, Nat and Midge, who meet on a Central Park bench and help each other cope with the vicissitudes of old age and urban life.

Like other comedies Gardner has written for the stage and cinema, *I'm Not Rappaport* shows the triumph of individual eccentricity over an inhumane society. Similar to the heroes of Gardner's plays, *A Thousand Clowns* (1962) and *The Goodbye People* (1968), Nat is a lovable nonconformist, in this case a former left-wing activist now raging against society's unfairness to senior citizens. Midge serves as the foil for his outrageous antics. Many of these dramatic characters, Gardner comments, are formed from his childhood images of older men. "I grew up with these people who lived at the top of their voices," he explains. "Some of them were in my family, some were just around. There were these cafeterias, and these guys in berets and goatees would sit and yell about Trotsky, and about wars long since fought that were vivid to them. I remember those guys hollering—and caring that much, still. Against all evidence to the contrary, they had not given up an image of a better world. If they didn't argue about Lenin, they argued about the egg salad."

Reviewers praise Gardner's play for its skillful blending of warmth and wry humor, exemplified in the engaging, joke-filled dialogue shared by Nat and Midge. The play's title, incidentally, is taken from a classic vaudeville routine referred to by the characters. A number of critics, however, complain of the play's weak, formulaic plot, finding Gardner's attempts to add interest to the static situation of the park bench dialogue through subplots of street violence and drug dealing forced and melodramatic.

In addition, though Gardner attests that in all his plays he intends to write comedy, the result is a mix of seriousness and humor, sometimes perplexing to critics and audiences. "The only thing I'm aware of is that most funny stuff is born of a certain kind of pain," Gardner muses. "But when you ask me why things keep coming out like that in my plays, the most honest answer is, I don't know. And yet I think of every one of these things as enormously hopeful. To me the fact that these people are hopeful is what makes them not hopeless. I guess I think of these people as survivors." Not surprisingly, reviewers find Gardner's typical blend of wit, sentiment, and philosophizing in *I'm Not Rappaport* as unsatisfying. Some critics observe, for example, that although Gardner intends to deliver a serious message about the problems of senior citizens, he undercuts his aim with an excess of frivolous humor and theatrical technique. While many reviewers conclude, then, that *I'm Not Rappaport* fails to move the audience to the plight of the elderly, most agree that it succeeds in being abundantly and warmly entertaining. "My ambition," confides Gardner, "consists entirely of being able to do it well enough that they let me do it again—and to avoid public disgrace."

Courtesy of Jeffrey Richards & Associates

VARIETY

In this (so called) comedy [***I'm Not Rappaport***], Herb Gardner has created two memorable characters, Nat . . . , a former Communist, backer of lost causes, and a spinner of wild tales, and Midge . . . , superintendent of a Central Park West apartment house. The two old men, each 81, have a meeting place at benches near a path in Central Park. Their long running tête-à-tête has Midge a sometimes grudging listener to Nat's stories of his past(s), with the recurring query: "Who are you, anyway?"

Nat's daughter wants to move him from his familiar hotel to a retirement home in Great Neck, and Midge is about to lose his job after many years of faithful service. Nat has many ideas about how Midge can be recompensed for his years of work. Although the material is not obviously comic, the two oldsters grow in stature and interest as the play enfolds, with some funny lines in the longish running time.

In between fretting over pragmatic problems, the two emerge as witty, strongminded, and (at times) funny. Premise seems to be how badly elders are treated in our society, but the two geezers are so much more alive and juicy than the other characters that the point is weakened.

Interspersed with the conversations between the quick and chameleon-like Nat and the slower, more reserved Midge, there's some action from an inept mugger, a woman art student, pursued by an evil drug pusher, The Cowboy, and Nat's daughter Clara. These minor characters are mostly background noises, except for the daughter, who has a solid scene in which she seems to convince the father he'd be better off in a retirement home. . . .

Final scene has the two friends meeting for a farewell. Nat is going to the retirement home; Midge has lost his job, with little severance pay, and holds this against Nat. But the parting isn't quick. Nat lures Midge back to the bench to hear his latest scheme: a move to California to be a "mogul." So the oldsters end the play, as they began it, deep in shared, warm conversation.

A review of "I'm Not Rappaport," in Variety, *January 23, 1985, p. 113.*

CLIVE BARNES

There is something stealthily attractive and winning about Herb Gardner's rambunctiously funny play ***I'm Not Rappaport***. . . .

In somber terms it is about the importance of illusions in the ugly face of fact, but this is, by no means or intent, a somber play.

Gardner has cooked up a delightful fantasy comedy with real characters poised delicately in an egg-shell world of reality.

It is also a play about ageing—and people's fear of age, seeing in it their own future.

Mind you, Gardner's principal characters, two octogenarians, one white, one black, coming to grips with life from the vantage point of a bench in Central Park, are only old in calendar terms.

Their responses remain frisky—in the case of Nat, a crusty curmudgeon, by profession and by fate a Jewish battler from the workers' barricades of the '30s, probably too frisky for his own good.

Certainly too frisky for the good of his reluctant friend, Midge, who favors a somewhat lower profile as a recipe for geriatric survival. He at least still has a job—or at least had one until Nat tried to help him.

Nat chooses to live in a strangely hard-edged fantasy world. When we first meet him he is explaining to his new acquaintance, and explaining with a wealth of circumstantial flim-flam, that he is an undercover agent posing as a Cuban terrorist.

There is not a word of literal truth in the story, but it possesses the special truth of internal conviction. . . .

Having gotten his two old men, Sam Beckett-style, on his bench—one still waiting for Lefty, the other waiting for God knows what—Gardner is compelled to do something with them.

Convention demands—although it never demanded it of Beckett, but that was, and is, a higher matter—something usually referred to as a plot. And here, to be honest, Gardner is not on quite such secure ground as with his characters and their attitudes.

It doesn't matter. In fact you might well hardly notice its absence. Events, not events nearly as likely as the people inhabiting them, do vaguely event. (p. 224)

What actually happens is as unimportant to the play's inner life as is its title, which is based on a Second Avenue vaudeville routine.

The play triumphantly exists in its concept—and in this aspect it recalls Gardner's earlier hit, ***A Thousand Clowns***—and performance. . . .

I'm Not Rappaport is precisely the kind of play, full of middle-brow brilliance and crafty craft, that Broadway needs to survive. One trusts that the play will move there with dispatch. Its presence, and that of its two master-clowns, would add luster to the newly born season. (p. 225)

Clive Barnes, "Comic 'Rappaport' Takes Illusion Lightly," in New York Post, *June 7, 1985. Reprinted in* New York Theatre Critics' Reviews, *Vol. XLVI, No. 11, Week of September 16, 1985, pp. 224-25.*

FRANK RICH

No one can accuse Herb Gardner of betraying his convictions to keep up with changing times. Almost 25 years after his first Broadway success, ***A Thousand Clowns,*** he is still writing roughly the same play—the comedy about the cranky but endearing New York eccentric who refuses to capitulate peacefully to the crass workaday world. Mr. Gardner's new variation on the theme . . . is titled ***I'm Not Rappaport,*** and there's a valor to it. During much of this playwright's career, nonconformity has been fashionable, but these days, it's not. Mr. Gardner, like his on-stage heroes, stubbornly continues to say what he thinks.

One only wishes that he did so with more dramatic verve and less preaching. In spite of its occasionally funny, flavorsome lines and pervasive sweetness, ***I'm Not Rappaport*** often seems didactic and repetitive. Mr. Gardner's characters tend to be either lovable lunatics or uptight pills, and the outcomes of their unambiguous confrontations are always predictable. While the author wants the audience to wake up and question the humdrum patterns of bourgeois life, his stacked theatrical technique achieves the reverse effect: We're lulled into tranquillity, rather than stimulated into self-examination, by the easy moral victories that the hero achieves over his antagonists. . . .

For much of the play . . . , two old geezers perform a series of mild, cross-cultural "Sunshine Boys" routines. Some of the bits are canned—"I was smoking dope when you were eating matzoh balls," says Midge—but a few are amusing: Nat reenacts the comic Willie Howard's most famous vaudeville sketch (the source of Mr. Gardner's title), and Midge pays vocal tribute to his own idol, Joe Turner. While the pals' other conversations are often treacly reveries about long-lost loves or urban decline, Mr. Gardner's writing rises to an affecting pitch when Midge describes the sad deterioration of his eyesight or when Nat mourns Stalin's betrayal of his lifelong ideals. . . .

The plotting is clumsy—and, in Act II, preposterously melodramatic—but it does allow [Nat] to perform some set comic turns. To disarm intruders, Nat spins the tallest of imaginary tales and variously impersonates an undercover agent, a hot-headed litigator and even a Mafia Godfather. . . .

While the iconoclastic Nat tirelessly insists on "shaking things up," his free spirit is domesticated by Mr. Gardner's refusal to shake up the formula that tames his independent-minded play.

Frank Rich, "Gardner's 'I'm Not Rappaport'," in The New York Times, *June 7, 1985, p. C3.*

EDITH OLIVER

[In ***I'm Not Rappaport***] Nat is a fiery, defiant Jewish radical—a former Marxist and a liar and impersonator. . . . Midge is the quiet, canny black superintendent of an apartment house nearby, who gets the news that he is about to be retired. Nat springs into action, posing as Midge's lawyer and his union representative, and threatening a public hearing and picketing and the rest of the activist paraphernalia, over Midge's weary protests. Nat drives Midge crazy with his non-stop talking, but the bond between the two men is strong, and when Nat brings out marijuana the results are engaging. These characters, it must be said, are synthetic, as are all the other characters. . . . The play has no plot, but it does not lack for incidents, somewhat casually assembled. . . . Although Mr. Gardner's thoughts on aging alone in this city, which are meant to provide a sombre undertone to the play, don't come to much, his jokey dialogue and jokey ideas are frequently amusing. His is indeed a practiced hand, and if his purpose is to entertain he has accomplished it. . . . (pp. 118-19)

Edith Oliver, in a review of "I'm Not Rappaport," in The New Yorker, *Vol. LXI, No. 17, June 17, 1985, pp. 118-19.*

JOHN SIMON

In ***A Thousand Clowns,*** [Herb Gardner] had hit upon a serviceable comic formula: the figure of the oddball nonconformist (in this case, a pair: a precocious child and a childlike adult), who, spouting a string of one-liners from a seemingly endless bundle, outwits or, at any rate, outtalks the establishment stiffs trying to impose their conventionality. Though a success on stage . . . ***A Thousand Clowns*** proved barely one clownsworth on screen. Gardner's movie ***Who Is Harry Kellerman and Why Is He Saying Those Dreadful Things About Me?*** had a run shorter than its title. Next, Gardner wrote one of the phoniest plays within human memory, ***The Goodbye People***. . . . Still, it was made into a movie, or bibelot, and has been sitting on the shelf awaiting a Gardner stage hit to carry it.

Then came the play ***Thieves*** and its movie version, both flops. . . . A further Gardner effort, the musical ***One Night Stand,*** belied its very title and closed in previews. Does this make Gardner sound like a master confectioner and heir to Simon? Not quite, but that he could fool enough people into backing him suggests he is at least a sit-*con* artist. Now Gardner is back, with ***I'm Not Rappaport,*** where his steady formula is as unalive and sticky as ever but has, this time round, a number of reviewers vying to pronounce it viable.

We have here two old-timers grudgingly sharing a bench in Central Park. There is the octogenarian Jew, Nat, whose identity, career, even true name are a mystery and who keeps spinning rabble-rousing yarns about his Marxist past and present, but failing to impress his black benchmate, Midge, an aged janitor without portfolio in a West Side building, where they haven't the heart to sack him for decrepitude. But as Danforth, the new head of the tenants' committee, tries to fire Midge with minor severance pay, Nat assumes one of his many fictitious "official" identities and scares Danforth into more pay and less severance. Midge and Nat become friends, the black man forgiving the Jew his nonstop, but seemingly life-enhancing, lies.

There follow diverse more or less (but usually more) preposterous adventures of the oldsters. One involves a park punk, who charges a sizable fee for safely escorting old gents out of the park after nightfall. They could, of course, leave calmly before nightfall and go home to watch TV, but then there would be no play. Another involves a sweet, lovely young woman who, having unconvincingly gotten hooked on cocaine, is brutally mauled and blackmailed by a pusher. Nat's schemes to overcome these two hoods land first himself, later Midge, in the hospital. The graveyard would be more likely, but then there would be no play. Nat also has a decent, hardworking but conformist daughter who wants to take him into her family home ("Scarsdale Siberia" he calls it) or provide an excellent nursing-home accommodation (equally rejected). Nat could easily be declared legally incompetent (would that certain playwrights could!), but then there would be no play.

I'm Not Rappaport consists of endless borscht-belt one-liners from fast-talking Nat, with an obbligato of black (ethnic, not literary) comedy much more cautiously and colorlessly (aesthetically, not ethnically) written, because here Gardner knows himself on shakier ground. Though neither the characters nor the story can stand up, there are some fairly funny lines from Gardner the stand-up comedian. And he has one more trick: Instead of a speciously sentimental happy ending, he provides a speciously sentimental not-so-happy ending. A highly sentimentalized form of evil is shown victorious; but good, equally doused in sentimentality, goes to gentle defeat unreconstructed and head unbowed. And a largely unconvincing rapport (if not Rappaport) between a Jew and a black has been contrived for soft-hearted liberals to feel that everyone is winning in the race between the races.

As beautiful as genuine humanitarianism is, so distasteful is Gardner's formulaic and fake pandering. (p. 72)

John Simon, "Faking It," in New York *Magazine, Vol. 18, No. 25, June 24, 1985, pp. 72-3.*

JULIUS NOVICK

Herb Gardner, the author of ***A Thousand Clowns*** and ***The Goodbye People,*** has written a sentimental comedy [***I'm Not Rappaport***] about a feisty old Jewish man and a grumpy old black man who sit on a bench together in Central Park. The Jewish man likes to tell elaborate, imaginative stories about himself: "Not lies—alterations. I make certain alterations. Sometimes the truth doesn't fit, I take in here and let out there." The black man says he doesn't want to listen, but he never goes away, because then what would happen to the play?

The Jewish man is an old radical who refuses to give up the fight; no going gentle into that good night for him. He is constantly meddling in other people's affairs, in the interests of social justice and generating a plot. With grumbly, comical reluctance, the black man assists him. The play includes a what-are-we-going-to-do-with-you scene between the Jewish man and his loving, exasperated daughter, the 2763rd such scene I have witnessed in my 30 years of theater-going. There are also some uncomfortable patches of melodrama, so that nobody can say nothing happens in Mr. Gardner's play. . . .

I'm Not Rappaport is not what I need or particularly want in my life, but it does no harm: its advocacy of hare-brained quixoticism in the old is not likely to be acted upon by many. I hope it finds its audience.

Julius Novick, "Herb without Spice," in The Village Voice, *Vol. XXX, No. 26, June 25, 1985, p. 110.*

An Excerpt from *I'm Not Rappaport*

MIDGE: (Truly outraged)
Hold it now! Hold that mouth right there! You tellin' *me* how to live? *You* tellin' *me*? You talkin' to an *employed* person here, Mister!
(Retrieving his newspaper from NAT's bench, returning with great dignity to his own)
Midge Carter; you talkin' to Midge Carter here, boy— Super-in-tendent in charge of Three Twenty-One Central Park West; *run* the place, *been* runnin' it forty-two years, July. They got a furnace been there long as *I* have—an ol' Erie City Special, fourteen *tonner*, known to *kill* a man don't show he's boss. Buildin' don't move without that bull and that bull don't move without *me*. Don't have to make up nobody to be when I *am* somebody!
(Setting himself proudly on small bench)
Shake things up, huh? Don't shake *nothin'* up. How you figure I keep my job? Near fifteen years past retirement, how you figure I'm still Super there? I ain't mentioned a raise in fifteen years, and they ain't neither. Moved to the night-shift three years ago, outa the public eye. Daytime a buncha A-rab Supers has come and gone, not Midge. Dozen Spic Doormen dressed up like five-star generals, come and gone, not Midge. Mister, you lookin' at the wise old invisible man.

NAT: No, I'm looking at a dead man!
(Points cane at him)
Fifteen years, no raise; it's a dead person, a ghost! You let them rob you!

MIDGE: They don't rob me; *nobody* robs me, got a system. You see that boy come every day, five o'clock? That's Gilley; give him three bucks, nobody robs me. Ten blocks from here to my place, walks me there, protects me.

NAT: From who?

MIDGE: Him, for one. Fifteen a week, he don't rob me—but nobody *else* neither, see; now *that's* social security—

NAT: (Laughing)
Oh, God—

MIDGE: Keep chucklin', sugar; ain't nobody dyin' of old age in *this* neighborhood.

NAT: Job! I see what your *job* is. Groveling! You're a licensed groveler!

MIDGE: (Rises from bench, shouting)
Super at Three Twenty-One, still got a *callin'*—only thing people got to call *you* is "hey, old man!"

NAT: What do *you* know? What does a *ghost* know?
(Rising proudly)
People *see* me; they *see* me! I *make* them see me!
(His cane in the air)
The night they rushed me to Lenox Hill for the by-pass, as they carried me out on the *stretcher,* six tenants called the Landlord to see if my apartment was available. Now, every *day,* ever day at dawn I ring their bells, all six of them—the door opens, I holler "Good morning, Vulture; Four B is still unavailable!" I hum the first two bars of "The Internationale" and walk away.

MIDGE: (Moving towards him)
Old *fool,* crazy old fool; they can't see *you.* They can hear ya, but they sure can't *see* ya. Don't want to *look* at your old face; mine neither—I just help 'em out. Don't you get it, baby?—*both* of us ghosts only *you* ain't noticed. We old and not rich and done the sin of leavin' slow. No use to fight it, you go with it or you break, boy; 'specially bones like *we* got.

NAT: (Shouting)
Traitor! Traitor in the ranks! It's people like you give old a bad name—

DAVID SHANNON

Like the films *Cocoon* and *On Golden Pond,* [***I'm Not Rappaport***] treats old men as frail, fractious and thoroughly endearing. It shows them to be victims of a society which worships old furniture and cars, but rarely gives a stuff about old people.

"The only way you can tell the live ones from the dead ones," says Midge, of some of his contemporaries, "is by how old their newspapers are."

Midge . . . is so blind he can't tell a tree from a lamp-post. Nat is also going blind and fighting attempts by his daughter to put him "in a home for the ridiculous". "Last time I made love," he admits, "was July 10th, 1971."

"Was your wife still alive?"

"I certainly hope so." . . .

The play is a little sentimental, the two men a little too cute to be true. The wit of the script . . . , though, more than [makes] up for its shortcomings. . . .

The jabbering of two geriatrics may not sound like electrifying drama. In this case it is.

David Shannon, in a review of "I'm Not Rappaport," in Today, *July 7, 1986. Reprinted in* London Theatre Record, *Vol. VI, No. 14, July 2-July 15, 1986, p. 717.*

BENEDICT NIGHTINGALE

The problem with ***I'm Not Rappaport*** is the problem with a good deal of American drama these days. Its author has some not-insignificant points to make and the skill to embody them in situation and dialogue. But there's a level at which he just doesn't trust the seriousness of his audience. So he tries too often, too hard, to beguile and charm it.

Dialogue increasingly comes to consist of wry quips, waggish retorts. The characters insidiously become that awful thing, lovable and, at times, they even become cute. It's an affliction one might call Neilsimonitis, after its best-known current sufferer, and it's not one to take lightly. It can be terminal, deadly to truth and art alike.

Rappaport, it's true, resists the worst ravages of this killer-virus. For instance, it does not finally pretend, as at first seems likely, that a murderous drug baron can be outwitted by an aged prankster who puts dark glasses over his eyes, a carnation in his buttonhole, white gloves on his hands and announces himself as the celebrated mafioso Tony the Cane. The accomplishments with which Herb Gardner credits the old pretender he calls Nat are slighter and smaller than that. Nevertheless, he clearly finds his impishness captivating, his games-playing enchanting and, by the end, has custom-built a front-running candidate for apotheosis as one of the *Reader's Digest*'s Most Memorable Characters I Ever Met. (pp. 26-27)

The real trouble with the evening, though, isn't the gullibility of some of Nat's dupes. It's that his author sees him as a blend of oracle and champion of the oppressed—or, at any rate, asks him to carry more moral weight than he can manage. He's an ex-officio grey panther, sombrely warning the young that he and his peers are what they'll become. He's also a bit of a radical, sufficiently committed to have been a union activist in his youth and now to mount exemplary sorties against butchers' shops in protest against the price of meat. Indeed, his daughter ruefully remembers that she was the only student at the great Columbia sit-in 'whose father turned up to coach'.

But his author doesn't see the character's revolutionary instincts as much more than eccentricities, his socialism as one of those wayward traits that make the old fellow such a marvellous old card. The effect is not, to be sure, as sentimental as might have been. . . . Consequently, the old trickster's attempt to convert a passing mugger to working-class solidarity is a bit more than a joke and his grim diatribe against youthful insensitivity verges on the impressive. And yet, as one leaves him defeated but indefatigable, still spinning his tales, an old rogue who'll be doing a vaudeville routine inside his coffin, one can't help feeling the character has been patronised as winsome, his predicament trivialised as droll. (p. 27)

Benedict Nightingale, "Lovable Types," in New Statesman, *Vol. 112, No. 2885, July 11, 1986, pp. 26-7.*

FRANCIS WHEEN

Two old codgers are sitting on a bench in Central Park, New York, at the start of Herb Gardner's play ***I'm Not Rappaport.*** A couple of hours later they are still there.

You might think this doesn't sound like a lively evening's entertainment, but you'd be wrong. Gardner's script is gentle yet funny. . . . Only someone with a heart made of reinforced concrete could fail to be affected. . . .

Midge is an 81-year-old black man who has worked for more than 40 years as a janitor in a nearby apartment block. . . . Nat, also 81, [is] a wily old socialist in a black beret who lives his life like a variation of *Call My Bluff*. At various points in the play he pretends to be an FBI agent ("I think they got me in what they call deep cover"), a mafia boss, a hotshot lawyer and many other unlikely creatures. . . .

Nat's alterations to the truth are often done for the best of motives, but they invariably end in tears. One of the comic highlights of the play occurs when Nat dons a pair of sunglasses and impersonates a mafia godfather in an effort to save a young woman from being mangled by an irate drug dealer. "I pick up a phone, you disappear," Nat growls at the dealer—who, utterly unimpressed, proceeds to beat him up.

Nat has rather more success, though only temporarily, when he presents himself as Midge's fierce lawyer. The yuppie tenants in Midge's block have decided to turn it into a co-op and dispense with his services. When the tenants' leader Danforth . . . jogs along to Midge's park bench to break the news, he is given an ear-scorching by Nat. People like Danforth, Nat says, collect old furniture, old pictures, old cars; why can't they show a similar respect for old people? The answer, he continues, is that old people "look like the future, and you don't want to know".

This is the main serious point that Herb Gardner is trying to make in the play, and it seems uncontroversial enough: let's treat old people like human beings. Yet I wonder if his picture of the American attitude is quite right. A nation which elects a septuagenarian president can hardly be wholly hostile to oldsters. My feeling is that Americans often err in the other direction, being over-sentimental about characters like Reagan purely because of their age. And if Gardner's play has a fault, it is that he is not immune to this temptation. Nat and Midge are ceaselessly loveable, but aren't they a little too good to be true?

Still, I don't want to sound churlish about what is, by West End standards, a decent, intelligent and hugely enjoyable play.

Francis Wheen, in a review of "I'm Not Rappaport," in Sunday Today, *July 13, 1986. Reprinted in* London Theatre Record, *Vol. VI, No. 14, July 2-July 15, 1986, p. 718.*

JUDITH CHERNAIK

Herb Gardner's ***I'm Not Rappaport*** is certainly the most amiable play about old age, father-daughter relations, and the terrors of life in New York to have surfaced recently. It is not surprising that it won Broadway's Tony Award for Best Play, since New Yorkers like to think their city and its huddled masses retain at least a shred of humanity, grace and humour—qualities stressed in this cheerful production, to the exclusion, perhaps, of harsher realities. Autumn leaves are falling in Central Park, menace lurks in the bushes; but the human spirit survives. The audience loved it.

Two old men, one black, one white, share a park bench, trading jokes and insults, stories and memories. . . .

This is hardly Beckett's grim view of old age, despite a few common elements; though Gardner's old men are half-blind and lame, they are not crawling towards death. Nor does Gardner share Arthur Miller's vision of the ruthless nature of American capitalism, and the true dimensions of American narcissism and bigotry (no apartment house on Central Park West would have hired a black superintendent forty or even ten years ago). Again there are common elements, softened and neutralized in Gardner's benevolent version of old men on the dust heap. He is aware of the pathology of the city, and allows his play to approach or hint at it: the first act ends with Midge crying out to the invisible passers-by (and the audience) "Help!" over the prostrate body of his friend. But five minutes into the second act, we know the menace is not real, not tonight, anyway.

Judith Chernaik, "With the Blunt End," in The Times Literary Supplement, *No. 4348, August 1, 1986, p. 842.*

Louise (Elisabeth) Glück

The Triumph of Achilles

The National Book Critics Circle Award: Poetry

American poet and essayist.

The Triumph of Achilles (1985) marks a development of the spare, eloquent style Glück displayed in earlier verse collections such as *Firstborn* (1968) and *Descending Figure* (1981). "The word 'stark' comes up often in discussions of her style," comments critic Robert B. Shaw. "It may be more illuminating to say that it is classically severe. . . ." Glück uses this restrained, intellectual method of expression to temper the passionate emotional content of her work. Though in *The Triumph of Achilles* the poet treats her customary themes of pain, loss, and betrayal, some critics contend that the poems reveal a broader vision and sharper diction than Glück's earlier work. Above all, critics praise the technical precision and sensitivity Glück demonstrates in this collection.

(See also *CLC,* Vols. 7, 22; *Contemporary Authors,* Vols. 33-36, rev. ed.; and *Dictionary of Literary Biography,* Vol. 5.)

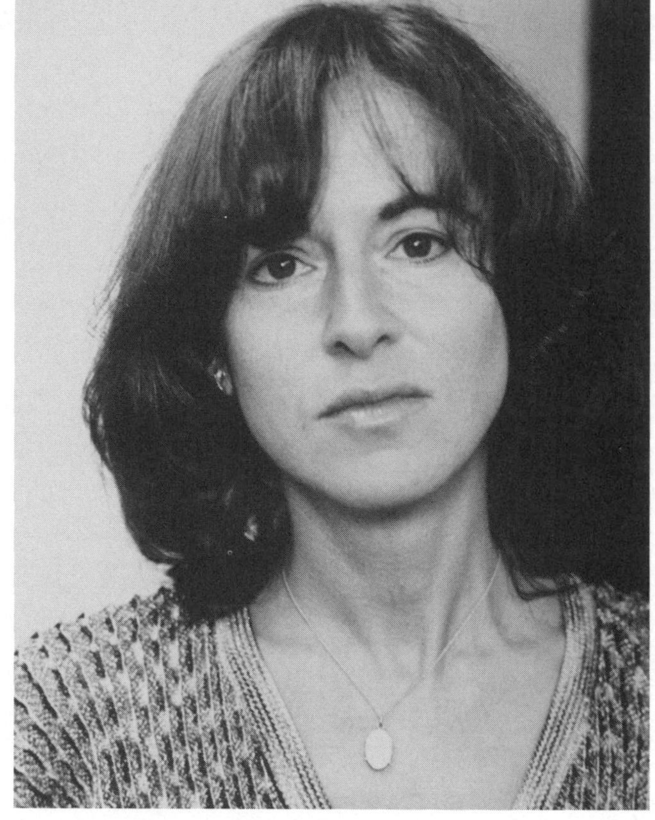

PETER STITT

On one hand, [the speaker in ***The Triumph of Achilles***] finds herself drawn to the physical world, its forever dying beauty and love, while on the other she longs for the unchanging, the eternal, an imperishable bliss. Readers of Glück's earlier volumes are familiar with her attraction to the ideal; her controversial poem **"The Drowned Children"** (from ***Descending Figure***), for instance, has been criticized for the way it denies reality to the children, treating them instead merely as an idea on which one would not waste much feeling.

"The Embrace," a love poem that opens the second section of ***The Triumph of Achilles,*** expresses the tension that lies at the heart of the volume; the speaker distrusts and resists physical love because it draws mankind away from the angelic and towards the bestial:

> She taught him the gods. Was it teaching? He went on
> hating them, but in the long evenings of obsessive talk,
> as he listened, they became real. Not that they changed.
> They never came to seem innately human.
> In the firelight, he watched her face.
> But she would not be touched; she had rejected
> the original need. Then in the darkness he would lead
> her back—
> above the trees, the city rose in a kind of splendor
> as all that is wild comes to the surface.

The female speaker is so attracted to the gods that she resists the amorous advances of the man to whom she speaks, who (crudely stated) represents the physical. At the end of the poem, however, she gives in to an experience that is not just accepted but enjoyed and found to be transforming.

The book is replete with references to gods and demigods, metamorphoses from flesh to spirit or spirit to plant. In [**"The Triumph of Achilles"**] Glück obliquely expresses the attitude that comes to rule this volume. One would expect the triumph of Achilles to be found in his battle with Hector, but such is not the case. Instead, Glück locates it in his loss of Patroclus, an event that makes Achilles human:

> In his tent, Achilles
> grieved with his whole being
> and the gods saw
> he was a man already dead, a victim
> of the part that loved,
> the part that was mortal.

On the face of it, this may not sound like a positive conversion. However, the book is saturated with references to the truth enunciated by Wallace Stevens, that "Death is the mother of beauty": only by embracing his mortality could Achilles learn the meaning of love. It was his human side that fell in love with Patroclus, his human side that triumphed over a sterile, immortal godliness that could never know the truth of Stevens' observation.

Glück's poem **"Winter Morning,"** in fact, is a flattened, free-verse rewriting of Stevens' "Sunday Morning." It ends:

Winters are long here.
The road a dark gray, the maples gray, silvered with
  lichen,
and the sun low on the horizon,
white on blue; at sunset, vivid orange-red.

When I shut my eyes, it vanishes.
When I open my eyes, it reappears.
Outside, spring rain, a pulse, a film on the window.

And suddenly it is summer, all puzzling fruit and light.

Though the texture of the writing is enormously different, these lines have the same feeling and theme that one finds at the end of Stevens' poem—a bittersweet appreciation for change and decay, for the seductive but heartbreaking beauty of the physical world. Or, as the poet asks and answers more prosaically elsewhere, "Why love what you will lose? / There is nothing else to love."

The thematic seriousness of this book is established primarily in its first two sections. More relaxed, the third section benefits—in poems that embody, without worrying, the theme—from the rigor that has gone before. **"Day Without Night,"** for example, rewrites the legend of Moses' early days by making him an entirely human baby, without hints of demigodliness. The poem is even funny, as when Glück speaks of the Pharaoh's daughter:

You did not press this woman.
She said she came upon
a child in the rushes;
each time she told the story,
her handmaidens recreated
their interminable chorus of sighs.
It had to be . . .

Glück coyly suggests that Moses, rather than being a divinely inspired waif chosen for special protection by a designing God, was instead the illegitimate offspring of the princess's unwed lust.

Despite their thematic preoccupation with an essentially emotional topic, the necessity of love in a mortal world, the poems in Louise Glück's ***The Triumph of Achilles*** present a surface determined by logic and the intellect. Theme is primary in her work: idea is dominant over feeling, statement dominant over image. The opening of **"Metamorphosis"** is entirely typical:

My father has forgotten me
in the excitement of dying.
Like a child who will not eat,
he takes no notice of anything.

The simile is used to add logic to the statement, not sensuousness. Still, feeling and image are both more prevalent here than in Glück's earlier books—one notes a definite change, for example, since ***The House on Marshland,*** of which Helen Vendler correctly observed: "Glück's poems bear almost no relation to the 'real' world, realistically perceived." Her writing is spare, pared down to essentials, deeply suspicious of flourishes of form and grand linguistic gestures. Glück is the epitome of the exclusive poet, as that mode has been defined here; and as such, she is among the important poets of our age. (pp. 855-56)

Peter Stitt, "Contemporary American Poems: Exclusive and Inclusive," in The Georgia Review, *Vol. XXXIX, No. 4, Winter, 1985, pp. 849-63.*

RHODA YERBURGH

From the opening line [of ***The Triumph of Achilles***] ("It is not the moon, I tell you") Glück claims absolute control of subject, craft, and perception. We see what we are instructed to see; we understand what Glück insists we understand. Glück's sensitivity to emotional nuance is extreme: "I ask you, how much beauty / can a person bear? It is / heavier than ugliness, even the burden / of emptiness is nothing beside it." Her genius lies in her passionate restraint, a mingling of plain and elevated diction, a reliance on indirection and understatement. Resolution and revelation arise from the stately balance of poems which demand order from anarchy: "Why love what you will lose? / There is nothing else to love." Glück is foremost among her generation of poets. . . .

Rhoda Yerburgh, in a review of "The Triumph of Achilles," in Library Journal, *Vol. 110, No. 15, September 15, 1985, p. 84.*

LIZ ROSENBERG

[*Rosenberg, an American poet, is the author of* The Angel Poems *(1984) and* Fire Music *(1986). In the following excerpt Rosenberg praises* The Triumph of Achilles, *calling it Glück's most mature collection to date.*]

I had always thought of Louise Glück as our foremost poet speaking for adolescent angst—her work struck me as having that kind of intensity, chaos and self-centeredness—and I admired it only at a distance. I never wanted to re-enter those terrible years. So I was especially delighted to see a poet of so much sensitivity and talent moving forward in her newest book, ***The Triumph of Achilles.*** It is in all ways a more mature book—the fine poetry of a woman rather than an unhappy girl. Many of these poems are charged with the mythic overlay implied by the book's title, and these are good, better than most such poems, smart and elegant. . . . Better still are poems that partake of a mythic largeness indirectly, the unexpected Jewish humor of poet-as-philosopher:

Today, when I woke up, I asked myself
why did Christ die? Who knows
the meaning of such questions?

Or one about the dying father who becomes more and less than human in his **"Metamorphosis":**

Once, for the smallest
fraction of an instant, I thought
he was alive in the present again;
then he looked at me
as a blind man stares
straight into the sun, since
whatever it could do to him
is done already.

Then his flushed face
turned away from the contract.

Miss Glück's language is clearer, purer and sharper than ever before, and sometimes ravishing and sexy:

> The sighing gardens, all the young girls
> eating chocolates in the courtyard, slowly
> scattering the colored foil.

Several of the poems have a superluminous dream quality that reminds me, oddly enough, of Robert Bly: "He leaned against the railing: in the dark bay, he saw the city waver; / cells of light floated on the water, they rocked gently, held by white threads."

There are some problems in the book. The poetic voice has a stiff formality, like a woman trying to dance in heavy brocade. The longest love poem sequence, **"Marathon,"** is at best uneven, and not nearly as touching or deep-reaching as the lovely, shorter **"Summer,"** which shows Miss Glück at her newfound best:

> Then the circles closed. Slowly the nights grew cool;
> the pendant leaves of the willow
> yellowed and fell. And in each of us began
> a deep isolation, though we never spoke of this,
> of the absence of regret.
> We were artists again, my husband.
> We could resume the journey.

(pp. 22-23)

Liz Rosenberg, "Geckos, Porch Lights and Sighing Gardens," in The New York Times Book Review, *December 22, 1985, pp. 22-3.*

DON BOGEN

The first poem in a book is inevitably an introduction, with all the potential for pleasure or disaster this entails. Most poems approach this task cautiously, or at least politely: they want to be liked. [***The Triumph of Achilles***], in contrast, demands our attention from the start by its severity, its negation of all that is commonly expected:

> It is not the moon, I tell you.
> It is these flowers
> lighting the yard.
>
> I hate them.
> I hate them as I hate sex,
> the man's mouth
> sealing my mouth, the man's
> paralyzing body—
>
> and the cry that always escapes,
> the low, humiliating
> premise of union—

(**"Mock Orange"**)

The opening of ***The Triumph of Achilles*** is hardly an attempt to cozy up to the reader by striking a familiar pose. We are compelled, rather, by the urgency of the voice and the harsh originality of its claims. **"Mock Orange"** is an outrageous poem; it takes huge risks in subject and tone. Its stance is extreme, blunt, unaccommodating, and Glück has the poetic control to present it without melodrama or portentousness. Her word choices, particularly the verbs "sealing" and "escapes," are startling in their precision. The way she caps the scene with a characteristic abstraction—that "premise of union"—gives a distance that heightens rather than dulls the immediacy. Fierce yet coolly intelligent, Glück's poem disturbs not because it is idiosyncratic but because it defines something we feel yet rarely acknowledge; it strips off a veil.

Glück has never been content to stop at the surfaces of things. Among the well-mannered forms, nostalgia and blurred resolutions of today's verse, the relentless clarity of her work stands out. Her subject is human loss; her vision is tragic. From ***Firstborn*** (1968) through ***The House on Marshland*** (1975) to ***Descending Figure*** (1980), Glück has narrowed and deepened the focus of her work, paring away extraneous concerns, excess verbiage, ornamentations of form and style. In lines that grow more stringent with each book, she examines and rejects all the traditional consolations for loss: fond memories, a benign god, love. Even the lonely achievement of art, that last hope for transcendence from flawed life, is revealed as a perverse obsession, a "need to perfect, / of which death is the mere byproduct" (**"Dedication to Hunger"**). Her poetry is grounded in fundamental skepticism. Its allegiance is not so much to beauty as to truth. If some poets resemble painters in their fluid creation of whole worlds across blank pages, Glück reminds us more of the sculptor chipping at resistant stone until its essence is clear.

Glück's new collection is in some ways a departure from this mode. Her basic subjects and tone haven't changed, but the range of the work has expanded. Larger and more varied than her earlier books, ***The Triumph of Achilles*** shows her experimenting with new types of poems, from Orientalist attempts to capture the moment to songs, narratives and long mixed sequences. Language is looser, embracing the casual as well as the concise, and Glück's sense of the line has broadened too. While some of the poems in this book, like **"Mock Orange,"** have the pared-down elegance of her earlier work, others are by turns airier, denser or more intricate. Her free verse is more generally free to linger over a detail, to lope along or, as in these lines from **"Morning,"** to soar:

> it is pleasant to wake like this,
> with the sun rising, to see the wedding dress
> draped over the back of a chair,
> and on the heavy bureau, a man's shirt, neatly folded;
> to be restored by these
> to a thousand images, to the church itself, the autumn
> sunlight
> streaming through the colored windows, through
> the figure of the Blessed Virgin, and underneath,
> Amelia holding the fiery bridal flowers—

Not all of this new work is equally successful. Some of the shorter poems and sequence sections—**"Hawk's Shadow,"** parts of **"From the Japanese"**—seem a bit too entranced with the ephemeral, and Glück's occasional reliance on parable, as in **"The Mountain,"** can make for thin reading. But the book as a whole keeps the power of the early work while extending its reach.

Glück's new poetic resourcefulness serves her well in **"Marathon,"** a group of nine poems tracing the phases of erotic life. Arousal appears in the sequence as a turgid, long-lined song, gradually reaching lucidity as obstacles are swept aside. In **"First Goodbye,"** jealousy takes the form of a taunt to the lover, cutting in its sibilants, bleak abstractions and sudden shifts in the line break:

> Go back to them,
> to increment and limitation: near the centered rose,
> you watch her peel an orange

so the dyed rind falls in petals on her plate. This
is mastery, whose active
mode is dissection: the enforced light
shines on the blade.

"The enforced light," "the centered rose"—these severe, almost awkward phrases give a jagged edge to the lines that fits the mood perfectly. It's in such choices—vocabulary, word placement, images—that the poet's skill is most apparent. **"Marathon"** is also impressive for its analysis. While Glück has not given up her distrust of easy transcendence, the sequence looks closely at the genuine ecstasies sex can provide. **"Night Song"** goes beyond standard romantic visions to show how desire ultimately isolates as much as it unifies. In the title poem that concludes the sequence, Glück evokes that realm

where only the dream matters
and the bond with any one soul
is meaningless; you throw it away.

Her picture of this strange place is haunting yet familiar. No poet since D. H. Lawrence has explored the terrain with such insight.

Though Glück's poems are intimate, they are not personal in the way we expect. A reader looking for the comforting minutiae of everyday existence (or a way to link the poems with the biographical notes) would be disappointed. Glück is too strict to indulge in easy generalizations from her own life. Even in a love poem to her husband or a study of her father's death, the perspective is distanced, careful, analytical. It respects both her subject and her own role. There is deep self-awareness behind this work, but that's the starting point for the poem, not its goal. Instead of relying on the illusion of personal authenticity—"this really happened, I was there"—Glück trusts the craft and thought in the work itself to prove its claims.

She also trusts the imagination. One of the real pleasures in ***The Triumph of Achilles*** is the wealth of characters, viewpoints and settings created here. Glück has always done well with family scenes and the landscape of Judeo-Christian mythology. In the new book she expands her domain. A Victorian husband rebukes his barren wife in the blunt closing poem, **"Horse." "Baskets,"** in contrast, is brimming with abundance as an old woman wanders a village market among "crates of eggs, papaya, sacks of yellow lemons." **"Hyacinth,"** one of several fine poems on classical themes, conjures a passionate world in which courtiers run weeping through a "glittering grove" and gods sink "to human shape with longing." The idea of something beyond human capability has long been central to Glück, and the Greek gods seem particularly suited to her purposes. Aloof yet still afflicted with desire, they are both apart from us and part of us. She uses them to clarify what being human means.

Louise Glück's basic concerns—betrayal, mortality, love and the sense of loss that accompanies it—are serious. She is at heart the poet of a fallen world. If this world offers us triumph, it will come like that of Achilles in [**"The Triumph of Achilles"**]: not in his crowing victory over Hector but in his grief for his lost friend Patroclus, his accession to "the part that loved, / the part that was mortal." Glück's work to define that mortal part shows dignity and sober compassion. (pp. 53-4)

Don Bogen, "The Funda
Nation, *New York, Vol. 2*
1986, pp. 53-4.

WENDY LESSER

[Lesser, an American editor, has been described as "a leader in providing direction to publishing and literary activities in San Francisco and the Bay Area in general." She is editor of the Berkley literary journal The Threepenny Review. *In the following excerpt Lesser examines the characteristics of Glück's distinctive poetic style.]*

Louise Gluck has one of the most distinctive voices in current American poetry, as she demonstrates once again in ***The Triumph of Achilles.*** The strength of that voice derives in large part from its self-centeredness—literally, for the words in Gluck's poems seem to come directly from the center of herself. "Direct" is the operative word here: Gluck's language is staunchly straightforward, remarkably close to the diction of ordinary speech. Yet her careful selection for rhythm and repetition, and the specificity of even her idiomatically vague phrases, give her poems a weight that is far from colloquial. This becomes most apparent in her powerful last lines.

You're like me tonight, one of the lucky ones.
You'll get what you want. You'll get your oblivion.

is the way she closes **"Night Song,"** while **"Adult Grief"** ends:

But you will not grow,
You will not let yourself
obliterate anything.

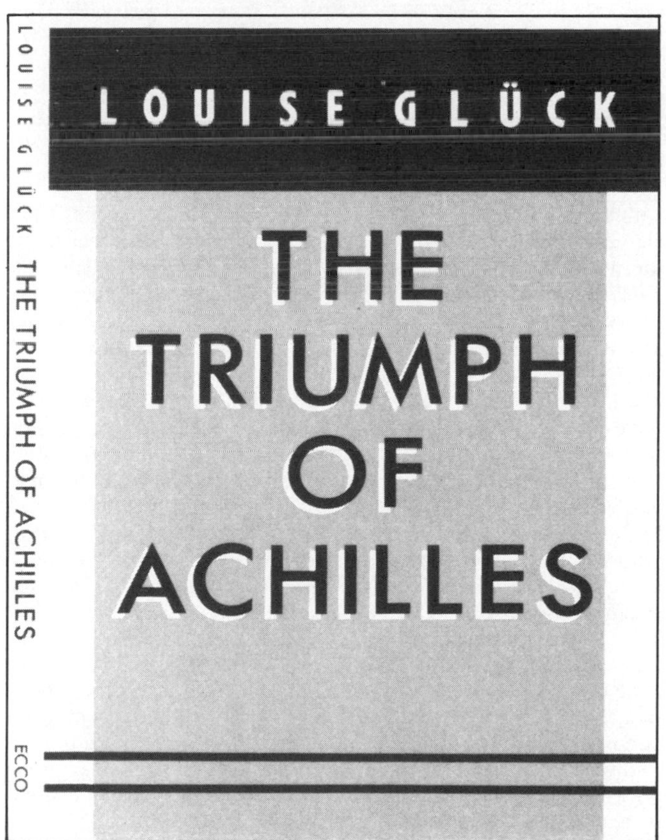

Dust jacket of The Triumph of Achilles, *by Louise Glück. Ecco, 1985. Jacket © JoAnne Metsch. Reproduced by permission of The Ecco Press.*

In both these instances, 'you'll'' or ''you will'' becomes the internal rhyme around which the colloquial language shapes itself into a poem.

Gluck speaks to a ''you'' by virtue of being an ''I.'' Her poems, especially in this book, are usually a claustrophobic conversation between two people, one of whom is absent. Whether she's speaking to a lost lover or a dead father, it is the loss itself which provides the occasion for the poem. She acknowledges as much when she says in the collection's excellent title poem:

Always in these friendships
one serves the other, one is less than the other:
the hierarchy
is always apparent, though the legends
cannot be trusted—
their source is the survivor,
the one who has been abandoned.

Gluck's intense poems are the impassioned cries of ''the one who has been abandoned.'' Her griefs are self-dramatizing and excessive, but even this quality of center-stage breast-beating is accounted for by the poetry. ''But nakedness in women is always a pose,'' she says in one poem, admitting that her self-exposure is in fact a consciously modeled piece of art. Yet if she can see herself from the outside (''I can imagine how my face looks, / burning like that, afflicted with desire—''), she does so from the enclosed vantage point of her own imagination.

Wendy Lesser, ''Poetic Sense and Sensibility,'' in Book World—The Washington Post, *February 2, 1986, p. 11.*

ROBERT B. SHAW

Louise Glück is a very considerable poet; but heavens, isn't she grim! Charm is not her stock in trade; she is not out to be ingratiating. The female speaker in the first poem [in ***The Triumph of Achilles***], **''Mock Orange,''** hates the eponymous flowers, she says, ''as I hate sex.'' The male speaker in the last poem, **''Horse,''** thinks his wife loves the animal better than she does him: ''What does the horse give you / that I cannot give you?'' he asks. People don't, in Glück's view, have a very good time of it. It might be easier to dismiss her message if she were a glib cynic; but she's disquietingly more than that: someone who has seen all the way to the bottom, and consequently has no illusions. It is not only what she says, but the way she says it, that is forbidding. The word ''stark'' comes up often in discussions of her style. It may be more illuminating to say that it is classically severe; some of her poems, like those of H. D., are reminiscent of Greek fragments, both in their elegance and their jaggedness. People who like their poems well-furnished will find Glück's austere. There is little description, and a good deal of uncomfortable pronouncement. Sometimes (as also happens with H. D.) Glück's manner becomes so stylized that we are likely to resist it. Addresses to Greek gods were not carried off by H. D. altogether without embarrassment, and Glück may have arrived too late in history to begin **''The Reproach''** like this:

You have betrayed me, Eros.
You have sent me
my true love.
On a high hill you made
his clear gaze;
my heart was not
so hard as your arrow.

This is trying too hard to return to the roots of Western poetry, and it rings false.

Having said this, it must also be said that Glück's successes, in which her style is beautifully gauged to match her deeper insights, well outnumber her failures. I was particularly struck by her treatments of dominance, of power, which she sees as emotionally barren and morally bankrupt. [**''The Triumph of Achilles''**] exposes the emptiness of Achilles's triumph over the Trojans after the death of Patroclus. Though semidivine, the hero's life has lost all meaning with the loss of his friends. . . . (pp. 42-3)

In **''Liberation''** a hunter and a rabbit stare hypnotized at one another, and the hunter realizes that in this confrontation his own eyes ''have to be blank / because it is impossible / to kill and question at the same time.'' Identifying with his victim, he blinks (''the shutter snapped'') and

the rabbit went free. He flew
through the empty forest

that part of me
that was the victim.
Only victims have a destiny.

And the hunter, who believed
whatever struggles
begs to be torn apart:

that part is paralyzed.

This paradox of power as impotent recalls Simone Weil's great essay, ''The *Iliad:* A Poem of Force,'' or, for that matter, much of our great tragic drama from *The Trojan Women* on. This, so unlike versified editorializing, is the kind of anti-war poetry which touches and endures. Some other fine, remorselessly honest poems are **''Summer,''** **''Hawk's Shadow,''** **''Elms,''** **''Legend,''** and **''Morning.''** However one may hanker after charm, wisdom is a rarer commodity, and Glück has it to offer in an uncompromising fashion few of her contemporaries can match. If her manner is at times attenuated, it is never shoddy, and that, in these days, is a distinction. (p. 44)

Robert B. Shaw, in a review of ''The Triumph of Achilles,'' in Poetry, *Vol. CXLVIII, No. 1, April, 1986, pp. 42-4.*

An Excerpt from *The Triumph of Achilles*

Mythic Fragment

When the stern god
approached me with his gift
my fear enchanted him
so that he ran more quickly
through the wet grass, as he insisted,
to praise me. I saw captivity
in praise; against the lyre,
I begged my father in the sea
to save me. When
the god arrived, I was nowhere,
I was in a tree forever. Reader,

pity Apollo: at the water's edge,
I turned from him, I summoned
my invisible father—as
I stiffened in the god's arms,
of his encompassing love
my father made
no other sign from the water.

HELEN VENDLER

[*Vendler is an American academic critic specializing in modern poets. Her own works include* On Extended Wings: Wallace Stevens's Longer Poems *(1969), studies of John Keats and William Butler Yeats, and* Part of Nature, Part of Us: Modern American Poets *(1981). In the following excerpt Vendler examines Glück's style of lyric poetry, particularly her use of myth, in* The Triumph of Achilles.]

Louise Glück [author of ***The Triumph of Achilles***] has tried in her poetry to give experience the permanent form of myth. Hers is the sort of lyric poetry that turns away from specific details and observations (names, places, dates, quotidian details—what Lowell, for instance, made the stuff of poetry) to an abstract plane, sometimes narrative, as in the Greek myths, sometimes archetypal, as in the encounter of Man with Woman. The tendency for lyric to turn mythical is often irritating to readers who yearn for biography (Who was the Fair Youth? Who was the Dark Lady? Who, for that matter, was Shakespeare?) as if facts would resolve meaning. We all began as sophomores in this respect; but we learn as we read more poetry that it is possible for novelistic detail to obscure, rather than reveal, fictive experience—that the lean shape of myth is the nakedness guaranteeing all stories.

A better argument for mythical lyric is that the beauty possible in mythical or archetypal poetry—with its own lexicon and thesaurus of images—is different from the beauty of the historical quotidian (which too has a lexicon of its own, a specific museum of images). In the treatment of Christian anecdote, for instance, there have always been what one could call artists of essence (those, e. g., who painted hieratic crucifixions showing a monumental and untormented Christ in glory on the cross) and, on the other side, artists of the actual (those who painted crucifixions exhibiting a tortured corpse in a realistic social setting).

The chief obstacle in writing mythical or archetypal poetry is that the story is already known, its conclusion familiar. Interest consequently has to center almost entirely on interpretation and manner. (It is no accident that Milton, who decided to retell archetypal stories that every literate person already knew by heart, became the poet with the most highly developed manner in our history.) Glück retells, in **"Mythic Fragment,"** Ovid's story of the myth of Daphne, saved from Apollo's advances by her father the river god Peneus, who turned her into a laurel tree. The lyric poet, facing a narrative, must choose the point at which the lyric aria will occur: Glück gives us Daphne's postmetamorphic voice. The tree, once a girl, retells the myth with the brevity proper to lyric. . . .

This may be the first time that the myth of Daphne has been retold as a Freudian story, the tale of a girl too much in love with her father to accept a lover. "Reader, pity Apollo," she says; we are to reflect on the many young men who lose the young women they pursue to that unacknowledged rival, the father. And pity Glück's Daphne: begging her father to save her, she imagines that the result will be Apollo repelled, herself unchanged. Instead, she stiffens into the wood of the sexually unresponsive. Her last words are, "Of his encompassing love / my father made / no other sign from the water." The blankness of that vista—as the stiffened bark looks to the silent father—is characteristic of Glück's poems of desolation and impossibility. In this Oedipal retelling of the myth there are no compensatory moments—no laurels bound about Apollo's brow, no ecstatic, Straussian joy in leafiness. The manner of the poem has changed the manner of the myth, turning Ovid's story into a demystifying modern story of virginity, revealing its roots in incestuous desire.

Glück's poems bend erotic stereotypes into her own forms of mannerist anguish:

I have been looking
steadily at these elms
and seen the process that creates
the writhing, stationary tree
is torment, and have understood
it will make no forms but twisted forms.

That splendid Yeatsian close states the poetic of Glück's book: writhing, to be stationary; stationary, to be writhing. This is the poetic of myth—animating what is eternal, freezing what is temporary and vanishing. As Glück's two adjectives imply, motion does not cease, but any notion of "progress" or "advance" or "improvement" ceases. Yeats at one point called himself a marble triton growing old among the streams; that moment when a poet becomes marble is the moment of myth. Myth and archetype offer themselves as the only formally tenable vehicles for a sense of the unchangingness of writhing human experience. The older we get, the more we "progress," the more we find our situations anticipated in Ovid, in Homer, in Genesis.

It is no accident that aphorism suits archetype. Glück shows an aphoristic talent that harks back to the Greek Anthology:

You have betrayed me, Eros.
You have sent me
my true love.

"Only victims," she says elsewhere, "have a destiny." And she offers these Yeatsian lines:

Why love what you will lose?
There is nothing else to love.

This couplet may resemble, in content, Yeats's lines in "Nineteen Hundred and Nineteen," "Man is in love and loves what vanishes, / What more is there to say?" But the chill of Glück's preordained universe is different from the historical turbulence of Yeats's interpenetrating gyres; his manner is tragic rather than fatalistic. Glück's manner suits her matter; the manner is as stationary, as foreseen in its pastness, as her myths.

Glück's nonmythic poems here, chiefly about love, are as ahistorical and nonquotidian as her myths. A long love affair which has come to an end is reviewed in a sequence called **"Marathon."** Some of it seems to me to topple over the line that separates self-scrutiny from self-dramatization: "We have acted a great drama." On the other hand, Glück's harsh and self-incriminating valedictory to the lover who has made her conscious of her greed in passion sticks powerfully in the mind:

Sooner or later
you'll begin to dream of me. I don't envy you
those dreams. I can imagine how my face looks,
burning like that, afflicted with desire—lowered

face of your invention—how the mouth betrays
the isolated greed of the lover
as it magnifies and then destroys:
I don't envy you that visitation.

I don't recall this precise human moment elsewhere in poetry. One aim of lyric poetry is to trace a contour not recorded before; saying the unsaid is a mark of the poet's courage, and Glück is not lacking in it. (p. 47)

Helen Vendler, "In the Zoo of the New," in The New York Review of Books, *Vol. XXXIII, No. 16, October 23, 1986, pp. 47-52.*

EDWARD HIRSCH

[Hirsch, an American poet, critic, short story writer, and nonfiction writer, is the author of two poetry collections, For the Sleepwalkers *(1981) and* Wild Gratitude *(1986), winner of the National Book Critics Circle Award. In the following excerpt Hirsch praises* The Triumph of Achilles *and analyzes the themes of conflict used by Glück in the collection.]*

Thinking about Louise Glück's . . . ***The Triumph of Achilles,*** I keep remembering two early watercolors by Picasso, both done in late 1904 when he was only twenty-three years old, that have always moved me. The paintings are curtain-raisers, as Leo Steinberg terms them, to a theme that Picasso returned to with haunted constancy for the rest of his life: the theme of the sleeper and the watcher. Both of Picasso's watercolors, "Sleeping Nude" and "Meditation," portray a young woman (Fernande Olivier) asleep on a corner bed. Pooled in warm light, with one arm cradled behind her head, she rests calmly, naturally, happily. Her face—to borrow one of Glück's phrases—is filled with "mild expectancy," her body is all lightness and youth. In one painting she is nude, in the other she wears a flimsy nightshirt, but in both she is a figure of ease and grace. By contrast, both paintings show a male observer, a figure of the artist, watching her with dark, selfconscious gloom. In "Sleeping Nude" a ghostly-looking man stands staring down at her with his hands plunged into his pockets. Sullen and thoughtful, with his head tilted, his long hair uncombed, and his eyes blackened, he is a portrait of exhaustion in modern dress, a premonition of the harlequin figure who would begin to appear in Picasso's work the next year. In "Meditation" (or "Contemplation") the tired, thoughtful observer is Picasso himself. He sits at a table with his chin in his palm staring at his mistress with a puzzled, even bewildered gloominess, an exile from the body. The contrast is striking: the dreamer and the watcher, the body and mind dichotomous, the supple female figure in light, her sharp and angular lover in darkness. The paintings are so intimate, Leo Steinberg concludes that the traditional theme of sleeper and watcher entered Picasso's work almost like a personal confession.

The theme of the sleeper and the watcher is crucial to Louise Glück's [***The Triumph of Achilles***] also—it, too, enters her work with the openness and intimacy of a confession. How she articulates and handles that theme, how she limns it with her own particular and even eccentric meanings, can be seen in a poem like **"Night Song,"** the fifth part in the sequence **"Marathon"** and one of the book's crucial lyrics. Here a vigilant speaker dramatically addresses her sleeping lover. The speaker's tone is urgent, her voice low, reckless, intent. "Look up into the light of the lantern," she tells him. "Don't you see? The calm of darkness / is the horror of Heaven."

We've been apart too long, too painfully separated.
How can you bear to dream,
to give up watching? I think you must be dreaming,
your face is full of mild expectancy.

I need to wake you, to remind you that there isn't a
future.
That's why we're free. And now some weakness in me
has been cured forever, so I'm not compelled
to close my eyes, to go back, to rectify—

The lovers are exhausted, spent, cold. The specifics of their situation are sketchy, but we infer from the previous poems in the sequence that they have come together after a long and possibly final absence, remembered their severed past, acted their parts in a "great drama," made love as if branding or stamping each other's bodies. Now while one sleeps and dreams—expectant, oblivious—the other keeps herself awake by talking to him with a passionate, perhaps even terrified intensity, telling him what she has come to understand, bringing him her urgent message:

I have to tell you what I've learned, that I know now
what happens to the dreamers.
They don't feel it when they change. One day
they wake, they dress, they are old.

Tonight I'm not afraid
to feel the revolutions. How can you want sleep
when passion gives you that peace?
You're like me tonight, one of the lucky ones.
You'll get what you want. You'll get your oblivion.

I take this to represent one of the book's central oppositions: the difference between waking and sleeping is also an opposition between clarity and dreaming, consciousness and forgetfulness, living in the present moment against expecting a future. The speaker's vigilant intensity, her doomed foreknowledge, is contrasted to her lover's mildness, his escape from conscience, consciousness, self, his faith in a future which she believes doesn't exist. We have to watch ourselves in the moment, she seems to be telling him; we have to live inside it. Sleep is an escape. Consciousness is the only weapon against an oblivion that separately will be claiming each of us.

In an illuminating essay about **"Night Song"** (in *Singular Voices* . . ., 1985), **"The Dreamer and the Watcher,"** Glück suggests that for her the sleeping lover is a figure of Eros, ravishing god of love, whereas the watcher is a version of Psyche, the mortal woman who, at whatever cost, insists on knowledge. Unlike Picasso's watcher, Glück's observer doesn't long for the lightness of the body; rather the poet valorizes the presence of the watcher, the heroic artistic consciousness. Most important, for Glück the theme of sleeper and watcher is part of a larger argument about the integrity of the human self. Throughout ***The Triumph of Achilles*** she poses the circumstantial and the ideal, the mortal and the god, the existential necessity for solitude against the lover's longing for dissolution.

The situation of sleeper and watcher—even when it is not literally realized—indicates the characteristic voice and tone of the book. The speaker in these poems often seems to be addressing a lover who is close by but somehow just out of reach, speaking intimately and directly in what is for Glück an unusually open and informal language. . . . These poems speak with recognizable Glückian intensities, but they seem less carved out of marble than her previous work, more casual and colloquial, a little closer to common speech than before.

By contrast, it is as if the language in her two previous and mature books, ***The House on Marshland*** (1975) and ***Descending Figure*** (1980), was always being held at a slight distance. Reading that work I have sometimes felt as if I were encountering brilliantly rendered translations, say, from the German. The voice in those books is often oracular and hermetic: passionate but also chilly, flawless, almost pietà-like, impersonal even in its most personal pronouncements. In Glück's work there has always been a great dissatisfaction with the world as it is, an almost religious longing for perfection, a strong aspiration towards a pure poetry. In this she resembles no poet so much as T. S. Eliot. Critics like Calvin Bedient and Helen Vendler have praised her work for its difficult intensity, its gnostic longing for Origin and infinity, its exclusive, unswerving imaginative severity and harsh impatience with the daily and the circumstantial, its abiding, authoritative love for the unearthly and absolute. And yet having concurred in those judgements, I now find myself compelled by Glück's more open and intimate style and manner. Her most humane book thus far, ***The Triumph of Achilles*** is empowered by a complex struggle to live in the world as it is, to accept what the poet has learned to believe is the only world there is, to come to terms with the hard Stevensian proposition that "Death is the mother of beauty."

One basic difference from her previous work is that the reader implied by ***The Triumph of Achilles*** is seldom listening to an oracular voice, a voice that seems autonomously generated by the language itself; instead he or she is more often put in the position of someone listening in on and overhearing a deeply personal, albeit one-sided conversation. To borrow critical terms that Glück has herself employed, these poems speak with a voice of invitation rather than of exclusion. That voice is low, close, direct, absorbing—we grasp its tone before we understand its assertions. It is a voice located in a genuine moment, a real present tense, an irreplaceable *now,* and it seems much more reckless and vulnerable, more tethered to earth, the voice of a lover. Love is the ground situation in a large number of these poems, their dramatic occasion. Yet poems like **"Mock Orange," "Summer," "Marathon,"** and **"Horse"** are something slightly different than traditional love poems. Within the format of a dramatic personal lyric, Glück's new poems are mostly arguments and meditations about the self and the other, the circumstantial and the permanent.

The argument which Glück carefully constructs—the sexual reunion is usually the dramatic occasion—is about two opposite human longings: on one side, the desire to construct a self, to establish personal boundaries; on the other side, the equally powerful longing to give that self up to another, to lose distinction. . . . Glück treats the sexual desire to lose the self to another as an erotic version of the longing for oblivion and death, a joyous but nonetheless terrible illusion. She poses that longing against the artistic consciousness, the desire to leave "exact records." Throughout ***The Triumph of Achilles*** sexual union is equated with muteness, with a frightening silence, a loss of self. She treats erotic need and desire as a mockery of the struggle to create a distinguishing and integral self, and at times exhibits a radical, almost gnostic hatred of sex. In **"Mock Orange"** she writes:

I hate them.
I hate them as I hate sex,
the man's mouth
sealing my mouth, the man's
paralyzing body—
and the cry that always escapes,
the low, humiliating
premise of union—

This helps to explain the watcher's characteristic and severe discontent after lovemaking, her angry sleeplessness. Later in **"Mock Orange"** the longing to merge, "the low, humiliating premise of union," is treated as a mockery since, inevitably, the lovers are split back into two entities, the "tired antagonisms" of self and other. With the fervor of a former mystic crying out against god, the speaker asks rhetorically, "Do you see?" and then announces

We were made fools of.
And the scent of mock orange
drifts through the window.

How can I rest?
How can I be content
when there is still
that odor in the world?

It is this sense of mockery and discontent, of being both needful of and humiliated by the premise of completion, the human need to fully experience another, that deeply fuels Glück's love poems.

One of Glück's recurrent oppositions is between sex and art—the desire for linkage and completion against the need for solitude and labor. The opposition is clearly rendered in **"Summer"** where the lovers lie for days in their first intense passion, a human embodiment of the fullness and ripeness of summer. In one way the lovers seemed happy, but in another they were "lost," drifting far from their "true" natures, moving towards a place where they'd discover "nothing." In the argument of the poem, they had given up their uniqueness, could see only what "anyone could see."

Then the circles closed. Slowly the nights grew cool;
the pendant leaves of the willow
yellowed and fell. And in each of us began
a deep isolation, though we never spoke of this,
of the absence of regret.
We were artists again, my husband.
We could resume the journey.

Here the lovers' fullness and sexuality is associated with the fertility and plenitude of summer—a cooling of passion is associated with the deaths of autumn. And yet by relinquishing the consuming physicality of their passion, the lovers can return to being artists. To be an artist again is to be solitary, flawed, incomplete, but it is also to love distinctions and to leave behind precise records of experience; it is to know a deep, necessary isolation—the self attending to its higher nature. That's why **"The Reproach"** can begin

You have betrayed me, Eros.
You have sent me
my true love.

and why the poem can equate sex with muteness:

I lie awake; I feel
actual flesh upon me,
meaning to silence me—

Against that silence, the poet raises the "twisted forms" of art. Thus the argument about sex becomes attached to the artist's struggle against the inarticulate, the mute, the void.

The other side of this erotic argument—the desire and longing for another, the genuine need for a love that will keep us attached to the world—is articulated in the book's final poem, **"Horse."** Here a husband watches his barren wife riding a horse across an empty field and rebukes her for her "scorn," her "hatred of marriage," her "haste to die" before he dies. "Look at me," he tells her at the conclusion of the poem:

> You think I don't understand?
> What is the animal
> if not passage out of this life?

To the nameless husband of this poem, his wife's riding is a way of rushing headlong towards oblivion; her furious isolation is also her way of escaping the world, of leaving it behind. Whereas he would bring her back into the world, the horse carries her away from it. And where is she going? Her longing for transcendence is equated with a powerful longing for death itself.

In Glück's work, there is but a short jump from the argument about sexual love to the argument about art. **"The Mountain"** and **"Elms,"** two key poems in the book's third and final section, are little parables about the making of art. Didactic and even moralizing, they present in capsule form one of the book's essential oppositions, different sides of the argument about transcendence. In **"The Mountain"** the poet-teacher begins by telling her students the story of Sisyphus as a parable of the life of the artist as "a life of endless labor," in its own way joyous, self-sacrificing, difficult, doomed. But as she tells the story she begins to feel the falseness and even the patness of her explanation—the students, too, are undeceived—until finally she retracts the myth.

> I tell them it occurs
> in hell, and that the artist lies
> because he is obsessed with attainment,
> that he perceives the summit
> as that place where he will live forever,
> a place about to be
> transformed by his burden: with every breath,
> I am standing at the top of the mountain.
> Both my hands are free. And the rock has added
> height to the mountain.

Here the speaker reveals an essential romanticism—her sense of the heights, her obsession with attainment and completion, her feeling of glory and belief in art as a weapon against time, a place of personal and permanent transformation. Like David in a poem about David and Goliath (**"A Parable"**), the successful artist is a hero who has "attained / all he is capable of dreaming."

But **"Elms,"** a later poem in the book, presents the other side of the argument, the artist's inability to distinguish "need from desire." . . . This poem suggests that artists, too, must live in a fallen, imperfect world, far from a Platonic absolute. The forms of art—the planed wood, the words themselves—can only be made from the "twisted forms" available in the temporal world. At the same time, the poem recognizes that flawed forms are the only forms that can exist in a flawed world. Some of the poems in [***The Triumph of Achilles***] show a fresh affection for the ephemeral and the changing (**"From the Japanese," "Baskets"**), but others like **"Elms"** evidence an equally powerful sadness and dissatisfaction with the imperfect world, a nostalgic longing for the unchanging and eternal.

Throughout ***The Triumph of Achilles*** Glück's argument about the circumstantial and the ideal is also framed in terms of classical stories, legends, and myths; indeed, one of the striking features of her fourth book is its fascination with classical themes, its somewhat Stevensian and certainly post-Freudian preoccupation with gods and heroes, and what they offer us as embodiments of our imaginative needs, desires, and projections. Consequently, one finds poems about the gods as entities (**"Hyacinth," "The Embrace"**), about the death of Christ (**"Winter Morning"**), about Daphne and Apollo (**"Mythic Fragment"**), and about Jewish heroes like David (**"A Parable"**) and Moses (**"Day Without Night"**). In these poems Glück is preoccupied with the moment when "the gods sank to human shape with longing" (**"Hyacinth"**) and obsessed by the modernist fact that there is no "true god"; indeed that "there is no god / who will save one man" (**"The End of the World"**). In Stevens's formulation: "The death of one god is the death of all." Partially because these traditional subjects of poetry were so exhaustively mined by American poetry in the fifties, I find myself less emotionally convinced by these poems, though they are no doubt essential to the book's central tension and argument about the imperfect temporal world.

The title poem, **"The Triumph of Achilles,"** enacts one of the dilemmas of mortality. The poem takes place at that moment in *The Iliad* (Books 18-20) when Achilles (who, in Glück's characterization, "was nearly a god") begins his fierce, inconsolable grieving over the death of his close friend, Patroclus. Achilles—the survivor, the abandoned one—experiences a singular, personal grief. The loss of Patroclus is more real to him than the fate of the Greek ships on fire. . . . Achilles' grief, his desolate sense of a permanent and irreplaceable loss, is also a sign of his "triumph," an affirmation that, in his victimization, he has become truly human. Dead to the gods, he is nonetheless fully alive in the fallen, mortal world of human beings, a world held together by love between individuals. As Glück has written elsewhere: "Love connects one irreplaceable being to another; the payment is terror of death, since if each person is unique, each death is singular, an eternal isolation." Achilles is thus similar to the friend in the poem **"Adult Grief"** who refused to prepare herself for the death of her parents and now, after those deaths, refuses to "obliterate anything." Desire and memory: the inseparability of love and loss: the struggle for a contact that makes us vulnerable and leaves us hostages both to fortune and to each other—these are what Glück defines as an essential part of the human contract. "Why love what you will lose?" she asks in an unusually bald and aphoristic moment in **"From the Japanese."** The answer is final: Because "there is nothing else to love."

Despite its deep skepticism and tremendous longing for a perfect and unchanging world, ***The Triumph of Achilles*** ultimately affirms the impermanent, mortal, tainted world of human beings. To my mind, it is just this complex and earned affirmation which makes it her most moving collection of poems to date. (pp. 33-6)

Edward Hirsch, "The Watcher," in The American Poetry Review, *Vol. 15, No. 6, November-December, 1986, pp. 33-6.*

RUBY RIEMER

Louise Glück writes poems that probe hidden meanings. Glück's latest volume [***The Triumph of Achilles***] sustains an ability she has shown in her three previous works (especially ***Descending***

Figure) to touch her own feelings and still search in them for some collective archaic experience. Yet, until the third section of ***The Triumph of Achilles*** she fails to make either her feelings or that experience very compelling. The leaps she is capable of are missing here. Many of the poems lack a familiar subtlety expressed through intimate family figures who have the power to summon up archetypes in the poet's imagination.

In her poem **"The Embrace"** Glück does manage, however, to retrieve some of the loveliness that borders on the erotic in her work. Without offering the reader a feminist direction of her own, she moves quickly to assert the need for transcendence. Male gods are everywhere in these poems. In **"Marathon"** that need to transcend appears in conflict with her physical self, revealing to us how central in her poetry is the theme of the denial of the body: "But nakedness in women is always a pose, / I was not transfigured. I would never be free." Lacking a feminist vision, therefore, Glück also lacks the power to overcome the female imperative of self-denial. In **"Marathon"** she longs for a loss of boundaries, suggesting a characteristically feminine belief regarding the self and the world. "Last night I dreamed we were in Venice; / today, we are in Venice. Now, lying here, / I think there are no boundaries to my dreams, / nothing we won't share." This feminine vision in conflict with the need for transcendence pervades her thinking, even if in her ambivalence she has to admit: "All my life / I have worshipped the wrong gods."

Still, flashes of brilliance break through in these poems. One occurs in the last section of **"Day Without Night:"**

> The context
> of truth is darkness: it sweeps
> the deserts of Israel.
>
> Are you taken in
> by lights, by illusions?
>
> Here is your path to god,
> who has no name, whose hand
> is invisible: a trick
> of moonlight on the dark water.

[Alicia] Ostriker reminds us in *Stealing the Language* "of the conviction that 'love' and 'song' are opposed choices for a woman. . . . That she is forbidden to be both lover / beloved and artist . . . retains considerable force within our culture and within women's minds. [It] is one way of saying that 'woman poet' is a contradiction in terms." Glück, nevertheless, in her own nonfeminist way defies that contradiction as do both Rich and Ostriker, who are proclaimed feminists. The definition of woman poet is one that extends, therefore, beyond class and ideology. (p. 6)

Ruby Riemer, "Women as Poets/Poets as Women," in Belles Lettres, *Vol. 2, No. 2, November-December, 1986, pp. 6, 14.*

RUSH RANKIN

[*In the following excerpt Rankin praises the "terribly intense evocations" of Glück's poems.*]

I believe Louise Glück [author of ***The Triumph of Achilles***] is the great poet of our time, in fact, of this century, surpassing even Eliot; in fact, she's the greatest American poet, period. That's merely an opinion, of course. But if true, it would be hard to believe because here she is alive and well, suffering through dinner parties and flying about the country to read her work. She reads *against* her poems, her voice compressed and flat, in order to avoid inflating their content with any vocal lyrical intensity. She has the slightly rasping voice of a surgeon who has spent all day opening bodies. Her poems, the most painful ever written, embody this strain, with an originality and complexity lacking in Plath and Sexton, for example. The speaker in one poem announces to her husband:

> you want me to touch you; you cry out
> as brides cry, but when I look at you I see
> there are no children in your body.

This is an overwhelming truth. How can we bear to know ourselves this fiercely? As T. S. Eliot writes, "After such knowledge, what forgiveness?"

There is a bleakness in Glück's vision connected to the poetic heritage of New England, to Emily Dickinson and Robert Frost (along with Eliot and William Carlos Williams, the only American poets to compare her to). One way to discover a poet's real power is to submit her poems to intense public analysis. A poem read privately may speak to our personal needs in a way that obscures the poem's limitations. Reading late at night, we often conspire with the poem to protect our sentimentality. The intimate bedside lamp then softens, flatters, enhances the impersonality of print. But teaching American poetry recently, I followed T. S. Eliot with Louise Glück, expecting to find, in that comparison, the weaknesses in Glück's work. Instead, I saw that her words, even when examined under such artificially concentrated light, continue to deepen, to take us even farther into our most elusive compulsions. Of course, if we read Glück, or any other romantic poet, in a skeptical mood, say after signing or missing an alimony check, then her drama sounds like melodrama. But not even Republicans, don't you think, would willingly reduce life to the mundane?

I sense, from perhaps too eccentric a point of view, that part of the harshness of her perspective comes from her feminine suspicion of one version of feminine nature, of what she calls in one poem in an earlier book, "blossom and subterfuge." Sumptuous beauty and deceit are qualities traditionally attributed by men to Eve, the archetype, the elemental. In her fierceness, in fact, and oratorical density, Gluck does not have a Biblical sense of the awesome, of the weight of life, and a Greek sense (echoed in her seemingly archaic use of myth) of fatalism. But for Glück, beauty itself is the deceit, the lie men tell to gratify desire and deny death. Louise Glück's a romantic who subscribes only to the second phrase of Keats' mystical aesthetic formula. Rather than beauty being truth, for Glück, only truth is beautiful.

But what really animates her work, its ferocity, originates, I believe, in her nearly mystical identification of truth with power, a connection that has an erotic edge to it, as though the act of telling the truth, its force, sexually opens and compels. Such a mythic compulsion implies, of course, that social and political distinctions, though possibly valid, are inherently superficial. If anyone really could see into life, into the heart of the molecule, would not the sight, that sudden revelation of life's eruption, wouldn't that sight be obliterating? Consider the "fearful symmetry" of Blake's tyger as radical energy, formally realized, the forged explosion of life into consciousness; Melville's Pip losing his mind at the moment of his intuition of God's dimensions; the "terrible beauty" of revolutionary death that Yeats lamented and celebrated at the same time; and Emily Dickinson's impossible reverie on death as the concentration of consciousness to a single blue buzzing. Jon Anderson has written that "the secret of poetry is cruelty."

I seldom know as I first read them what Louise Glück's poems mean, but I experience them intuitively as terribly intense evocations. Her poems teach us to read poems not with our mind, but rather with our life, with the mysterious focus of personality. Her poems manifest a reality as tangible and elusive as our bodies. Though obviously I revere her power, often I long for some consoling warmth, some endearing lie. The only affirmation she permits, her eloquence, her originality of perception, must sustain us, as it does even in her most frightening and greatest poem, **"Marathon,"** which appears in her most recent book, ***The Triumph Of Achilles,*** a collection not as consistently powerful as her earlier ***Descending Figure*** and ***House On Marshland,*** but still a wonderful book.

In **"Marathon,"** a long poem of nine sections, the last part concludes with a brutal, inescapable dictum that the earlier parts, in effect, have meditated on:

> and the bond with any one soul
> is meaningless; you throw it away.

The first four sections of the poem present a sequence of emotional facts about a love affair in extraordinary concentrated and mythic language: There's the fact of grief and the impossibility of freedom from self (or in self); the fact of innocence and a hint at the end of innocence as the narrator contemplates the beginning of the affair; the fact of craving; and the fact of erotic obliteration seen as a cultural and seismic power. In contrast, the next four sections document dreams, life itself as a trance: the dream of satisfaction, yet of dreams ending; the dream of longing compared to decency as the betrayal of self; the dream of loss and need; and the dream of joy.

The poem's final section presents a heart-rending exposure of the erotic drama as proof of the sadness, the tragedy, of all those dreams and facts. The woman narrator, asleep, hears two men enter her room. Passive, yet sensually, almost unnaturally alert, she registers their presence just by feeling a torch being moved. One of the men explains to the other how to make love to her and describes her body:

> how it responded, what
> it would not do. My back was turned.
> I studied the voices, soon distinguishing
> the first, which was deeper, closer,
> from that of the replacement.
> For all I know, this happens
> every night: somebody waking me, then
> the first teaching the second.
> What happens afterward
> occurs far from the world, at a depth
> where only the dream matters
> and the bond with any one soul
> is meaningless; you throw it away.

The poem's nearly unbearable sadness comes from its flat announcement of erotic compulsion, its passive recognition of the mathematics of desire, its obliquely offhanded acceptance of the emptiness, the death, at the center of our deepest moment of personal connection to another person. Even warmhearted women, maybe especially warmhearted women, read Glück with a sense of relief and pleasure I personally find terrifying. Since Louise Glück sleeps with her eyes open, she compels her readers to witness what happens in the dark. (pp. 3-4)

Rush Rankin, "Knowing Ourselves So Fiercely," in New Letters, *Vol. 1, No. 1, Spring, 1987, pp. 3-4.*

Jonathan (S.) Kellerman

When the Bough Breaks

Edgar Allan Poe Award: Best First Novel

Photograph by Michael Dunn

American novelist, nonfiction writer, essayist, and short story writer.

Like Alex Delaware, the protagonist of *When the Bough Breaks* (1985), Kellerman is a Los Angeles-based clinical psychologist specializing in childhood stress disorders. His professional publications include a medical textbook and *Helping the Fearful Child* (1980), a guide for parents written in a popular psychology format. Kellerman is also an essayist and short story writer whose work has appeared in *Newsweek,* the *Los Angeles Times,* and other periodicals, including *Alfred Hitchcock's Mystery Magazine.*

A devotee of mystery fiction, Kellerman said in a 1982 interview, "While I have written a bit of fiction (satire, mystery story, etc.) my goal is to write a first class detective novel in the tradition of Chandler, MacDonald, etc.—a work in which I can put my psychological training to use in creating something suspenseful, entertaining, and insightful." With *When the Bough Breaks* Kellerman has, according to reviewers, accomplished his objective. Critics observe that Kellerman's professional knowledge of child psychology adds authority and credibility to his first published novel, which is set in Los Angeles and focuses on child molestation. The novel's narrator, psychologist Delaware, uncovers a sinister network of pedophilic criminals while aiding police in a homicide investigation. Some reviewers comment on the timeliness of this theme of child sexual abuse; the novel's publication coincided with a national uproar over allegations of criminal sexual abuse at the McMartin nursery school in southern California. Although a few critics question the plausibility of some details in Kellerman's intricate plot, most commend his suspenseful presentation of a gruesome yet compelling story. *When the Bough Breaks* was adapted for television in 1986.

(See also *Contemporary Authors,* Vol. 106.)

PUBLISHERS WEEKLY

At the age of 33, Dr. Alex Delaware, a rising psychologist with a specialty in pediatrics, burned out and retired to an easy California life. But when it seems that the gruesome murder of a psychiatrist may have been witnessed by a little girl who isn't talking, a friend on the police force persuades Delaware to see if the child has any information, and the psychologist takes his first step into an intricate and brutally believable case of widespread organized child molestation. Motivated by concern for the child and growing suspicion that present events might be linked to the case that precipitated his own emotional breakdown half a year earlier, Delaware follows leads that take him deep into L.A.'s Latino enclave and up the northern coast to an elite island community of inbred wealth and far-reaching power. Writing with authority and humor, sensitivity and more than considerable skill, the author [of ***When the Bough Breaks***] . . . has produced a timely, complex and carefully plotted first novel that encompasses—as all good stories do—the best and the worst in human nature.

A review of "When the Bough Breaks," in Publishers Weekly, *Vol. 227, No. 4, January 25, 1985, p. 88.*

BARBARA CONATY

There is plenty of gore, violence, and suspense in this first novel from Kellerman, [***When the Bough Breaks***]. . . . His insights into the realities of children under stress give haunting credibility to his otherwise slick and polished cop drama. Discerning readers will be grateful for sparkling characterizations and realistic details of scenery that evoke the best of the L.A. hi-lo vistas.

Barbara Conaty, in a review of "When the Bough Breaks," in Library Journal, *Vol. 110, No. 4, March 1, 1985, p. 103.*

JOHN GROSS

Jonathan Kellerman is a clinical psychologist, specializing in the care of children, who lives in southern California. Alex Delaware, the hero of his first thriller, is a clinical psychologist, specializing in the care of children, who lives in southern California. Dr. Kellerman, it would appear, knows whereof he writes, and ***When the Bough Breaks*** marks an assured and more than promising debut. Some of the ingredients may have a familiar look—memories of 100 television programs hover somewhere in the background—but they have been whipped together with skill and conviction, and the result is an exceptionally exciting story. . . .

Dr. Kellerman is particularly good in the scenes where Delaware succeeds in prizing open the life of secluded enclaves with something to hide—a home for problem children that is a little too bland to be true; an inbred island community where a group of rich families have shut themselves away for generations; a Mickey Mouse college where their children are hedged in with privilege and prejudice. (Some neat satire here, and an amusing sketch of an ancient beady-eyed professor who has managed to retain a measure of independence.)

One aspect of the book left me uneasy. While nobody loves a child molester, some of the violence meted out to the offenders in the story (admittedly the more vicious of them) does seem disturbingly vindictive—particularly coming from a psychologist. But this is the only real blemish (unless you count the romantic interest, which is eminently skippable) on an otherwise compelling performance.

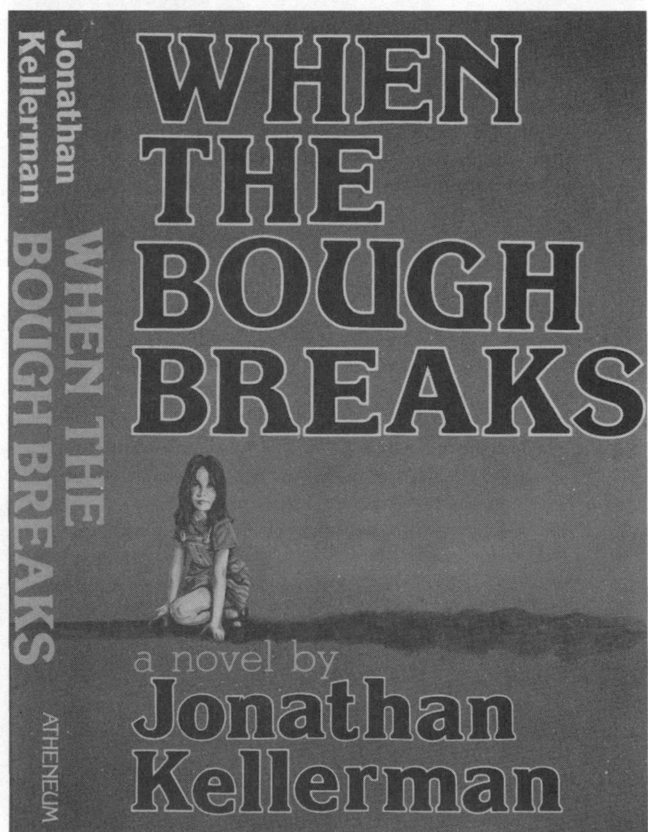

Dust jacket of When the Bough Breaks, *by Jonathan Kellerman. Atheneum, 1985. Jacket design copyright © 1985 by Bill Tinker. Courtesy of Bill Tinker.*

John Gross, in a review of "When the Bough Breaks," in The New York Times, *March 12, 1985, p. C17.*

JOHN BROSNAHAN

A psychologist [in ***When the Bough Breaks***] turns detective when he is called upon to interview a young girl who is the only living witness to a brutal dual murder. Whatever the girl may have seen, the actual crime veils an even more horrible contemporary phenomenon: a ring of child molesters at a school in Southern California. The psychologist is soon out of his professional depth in pursuing clues and leads, but he plods onward to solve the case, nearly at the expense of the girl's and his own life. Kellerman's story is long on sensational descriptions and short on believable disclosures—too many of the good turns of fortune seem coincidentally opportune—but as a suspenseful drama, the novel does rack up its points.

John Brosnahan, in a review of "When the Bough Breaks," Booklist, *Vol. 81, No. 14, March 15, 1985, p. 1030.*

An Excerpt from *When the Bough Breaks*

He stood and looked out the window, gazing out over the tops of pines and eucalyptus. From where I sat I could see smoke rising in indolent swirls from a distant fireplace.

"It's really nice up here, Alex. Does it ever bore you, being in paradise with nothing to do?"

"Not a hint of ennui."

"Yeah. I guess not. You don't want to hear any more about Handler and the girl."

"Stop playing passive-aggressive, Milo, and spit it out."

He turned and looked down at me. The big, ugly face showed new signs of fatigue.

"I'm depressed, Alex." He held out his empty cup like some overgrown, slack-jawed Oliver Twist. "Which is why I'll tolerate more of this disgusting swill."

I took the cup and got him a refill. He gulped it audibly.

"We've got a possible witness. A kid who lives in the same building. She's pretty confused, not sure what she saw. I took one look at her and thought of you. You could talk to her, maybe try a little hypnosis to enhance her memory."

"Don't you have Behavioral Sciences for that?"

He reached into his coat pocket and took out a handful of Polaroids. "Look at these beauties."

I gave the pictures a second's glance. What I saw turned my stomach. I returned them quickly.

"For God's sake, don't show me stuff like that!"

"Some mess, huh? Blood and crud." He drained his cup, lifting it high to catch every last drop. "Behavioral Science is cut down to one guy who's kept busy weeding weirdos out of the department. Next priority is counseling the weirdos who slip through. If I put in an application for this kind of thing I'll get a request to fill out another application form. They don't want to do it. On top of that, they don't know anything about kids. You do.''

''I don't know anything about homicide.''

''Forget homicide. That's my problem. Talk to a seven-year-old.''

I hesitated. He held out his hands. The palms were white, well-scrubbed.

''Hey, I'm not expecting a total freebie. I'll buy you lunch. There's a fair-to-middling Italian place with surprisingly good gnocchi not far from the . . .''

''Not far from the abattoir?'' I grimaced. ''No thanks. Anyway, I can't be bought for noodles.''

''So what can I offer you by way of a bribe—you've got everything—the house in the hills, the fancy car, the Ralph Lauren gear with jogging shoes to match. Christ, you've got retirement at thirty-three and a goddamn perpetual tan. Just talking about it is getting me pissed.''

''Yes, but am I happy?''

''I suspect so.''

''You're right.'' I thought of the grisly photos. ''And I'm certainly not in need of a free pass to the Grand Guignol.''

''You know,'' he said, ''I'll bet underneath all of that mellow is a bored young man.''

''Crap.''

''Crap nothing. How long has it been, six months?''

''Five and a half.''

''Five and a half, then. When I met you—correct that, soon *after* I met you, you were a vibrant guy, high energy, lots of opinions. Your *mind* was working. Now all I hear about is hot tubs, how fast you run your goddamned mile, the different kinds of sunset you can see from your deck—to use your jargon, it's *regression*. Cutesy-poo short pants, roller-skating, water play. Like half the people in this city, you're functioning on a six-year-old level.''

I laughed.

''And you're making me this offer—to get involved in blood and crud—as a form of occupational therapy.''

''Alex, you can break your ass trying to achieve Nirvana Through Inertia, but it won't work. It's like that Woody Allen line—you mellow too much, you ripen and rot.''

HERB. KEIMIG

Jonathan Kellerman is a practicing Clinical Psychologist. . . . It is from this background that Dr. Kellerman has produced a first rate mystery novel that exposes the ramifications of abuses in child care agencies with its attendant cases of child abuse and the sexual exploitation of children.

The scene is Southern California and the area around Los Angeles that has figured recently in newspaper and television accounts of the sexual molestation, exploitation, and in some cases the actual murder of children and adults involved in these scandals. . . .

[***When the Bough Breaks***] is much more than a good mystery, it is a novel with a moral and an indictment of the times in which we live as indicated in one discourse by the narrator Dr. Alex Delaware: ''There's a large segment of the population that views the sight of anyone too young or too old as offensive. It's as if nobody wants to be reminded from whence they come or where they certainly will go. That kind of denial, coupled with face lifts and hair transplants and makeup, creates a comfortable little delusion of immortality. For a short while.''

This book is for thinking and mature adults who realize that the death of value systems opens the door to a veritable chamber of horrors. Read it—it's that good a book.

Herb. Keimig, in a review of ''When the Bough Breaks,'' in Best Sellers, *Vol. 45, No. 1, April, 1985, p. 18.*

MARY DRYDEN

If you are like me, the year begins in the autumn. January 1st is a nice holiday, but the calendar year starts in September. Whether this is a remnant of my academic life or simply the brisk sense of new purpose that fall always brings, I know not. But if you share this view, pick up ***When the Bough Breaks.***

Jonathan Kellerman's first novel is a straightforward murder mystery. What might give one pause before reading it, however, is its subject matter—child molesting. Not only does this appear to be in dubious taste, but there is also the niggling suspicion that someone had cashed in on the most unspeakable crime of the year. These doubts are quickly dispelled. The reader rapidly will gather that neither the child molesters nor the children themselves are exploited. Further, the author . . . had written and submitted this novel for publication many months before the McMartin case surfaced. Kellerman's treatment of children in the novel is, in fact, sensitive and restrained.

What is not restrained is the rip-roaring, pell-mell pace of the story. The author has constructed an intricate web of events and characters which alternately fascinate and repel the reader. The swiftness with which things happen climaxes in a classic high-speed chase involving a car and a motorcycle that can only be described as the literary equivalent to the famous car chases of *Bullitt* and *The French Connection*. Kellerman has a lingering touch when it comes to character development. Tertiary figures such as Kim Hickle, the Korean wife of a convicted child molester, take on a perspective unusual in any modern novel, let alone a first attempt. The only exception is the protagonist's romantic interest, the artisan Robin, who remains thoroughly and stubbornly uninteresting. . . .

To describe any more of the whodunit is to spoil it for others, so suffice it to say that nothing is quite what it seems—the status quo for the genre. What I can tell you is that Kellerman has a gift for using synesthesia to describe a situation or to evoke a time or place. His frequent references to music and weather serve as touchstones for a reader starved for rich prose.

When the Bough Breaks is set primarily in Los Angeles, and the author's observations of the various parts of the city are a special treat to those of us who live here. His description of the mountainous part of Malibu is an exercise in the sinister.

Make no mistake, this is not Great Literature, nor does it attest to be. What it is, is highly readable fiction of a superior level. ***When the Bough Breaks*** should be an enormous success for its novice author. I await with interest his next endeavor.

Mary Dryden, in a review of "When the Bough Breaks," in Los Angeles Times Book Review, *September 8, 1985, p. 5.*

Sidney Kingsley

American Academy and Institute of Arts and Letters: Gold Medal for Drama

(Born Sidney Kieschner) American dramatist and scriptwriter.

The 1986 Gold Medal is the second tribute the American Academy and Institute of Arts and Letters has paid to Kingsley during his career as a dramatist. He received the Academy's Award of Merit Medal in 1951. Kingsley made his first, and many critics feel his most important, contributions to American theater in the mid-1930s with his plays *Men in White* (1933) and *Dead End* (1935). These introduced what became known as the standard Kingsley style, an absorbing blend of melodramatic plot and realistic detail. "I know no contemporary American," wrote critic Joseph Wood Krutch in 1949, "who can take a topic—slum children in *Dead End* or doctors and nurses in *Men in White*—and turn out a more stage-worthy piece, full of shrewd if not too profound observation crisply and humorously embodied in recognizable types."

Men in White, Kingsley's first produced play, is a series of vignettes which center on a young medical intern in a teaching hospital. Critics ascribe a great deal of the impact of the original Broadway production of *Men in White* to the innovative staging given it by the Group Theatre under the direction of Lee Strasberg. It proved to be the Group Theatre's first commercial success, and in 1934 Kingsley received a Pulitzer Prize for the drama. His next play, *Dead End,* astonished audiences with its lifelike depiction of a dead end street near the East River, complete with the river (in the orchestra pit), the wharf, a tenement juxtaposed with a luxury apartment building, and authentically foul-mouthed street urchins. Representatives from a children's welfare society held up the opening night performance of *Dead End* for half an hour, insisting that Kingsley censor the shocking language he had written for his child actors. Kingsley acquiesced, but joked later that he had heard the boys use even worse profanities offstage. Several of these young actors also appeared in the film version of *Dead End* and became popular stars, recreating their roles in a number of motion pictures as "the Dead End Kids." More significantly, Kingsley's vivid dramatization of poverty and juvenile delinquency helped expose deplorable slum conditions in New York City, inspiring an increase in charitable contributions as well as government measures to improve life for tenement dwellers.

Throughout his career, Kingsley continued to be identified with the "social realist" style of his early successes. Starting with *Dead End,* he usually directed his own plays on Broadway, and his productions received much admiration for the authenticity of their settings, carefully researched and ingeniously staged. Kingsley took care to recreate a convincing steam laundry in *The World We Make* (1939), a New York City police headquarters in *Detective Story* (1949), and, although in a more expressionistic vein, a Manhattan after-hours club in *Night Life* (1962). Some reviewers complain, however, that Kingsley's dramas rely on contrived, melodramatic plot lines and stereotyped characters. These devices do work in a surface theatrical sense, they admit, but make his plays artistically unsatisfying.

Neal Boenzi/NYT Pictures

Patriots (1943) won New York Drama Critics Circle Award, according to the prize committee, for its "dignity of material, its thoughtful projection of a great American theme, its vigorous approach to the characters portrayed, and, in spite of certain limitations, its driving final effect on the stage." Written with the assistance of his wife, actress Madge Evans, the drama chronicles the conflict between the democracy-loving Thomas Jefferson and the plutocrat Alexander Hamilton. This patriotic theme appealed strongly to wartime audiences. Kingsley received New York Drama Critics Circle Award again in 1951 for his adaptation of Arthur Koestler's novel *Darkness at Noon* (1951). His anti-Soviet subject matter was wisely chosen to suit the temper of the times, just as *Dead End* had captured the mood of progressive social reform in the early Depression years.

Thereafter, however, Kingsley seemed to lose his skill for capturing the trend of the moment. His attempt at a popular farce, *Lunatics and Lovers* (1954), displeased many reviewers who pronounced it an unworthy attempt at vulgar commercialism. Eight years later, he tried to update his standard realist style with experimental narrative techniques in *Night Life,* but failed to impress critics familiar with more sophisticated avant-garde theater. Kingsley's dramas seemed irredeemably outdated by the 1960s, and have not come back into fashion despite revivals in recent years. "He was never Ibsen," declared critic Richard Gilman in his review of *Night Life*. "He was only Elmer Rice." Nevertheless, his simple, suspenseful semi-documentary style influenced numerous dramatists, from Paddy Chayefsky to the writers of television hospital dramas.

(See also *Contemporary Authors,* Vols. 85-88 and *Dictionary of Literary Biography,* Vol. 7.)

BROOKS ATKINSON

[*As drama critic for* The New York Times *from 1925 to 1960, Atkinson was one of the most influential reviewers in America. In the following excerpt Atkinson praises* Men in White *for its powerful dramatic impact as well as its credible portrayal of doctors at work.*]

Although Mr. Kingsley is not a medical man, [in ***Men in White***] he has written about the ideals and conflicts of loyality of the medical profession with fervent convictions, disclosing uncommon familiarity with his subject. It is a good, brave play, despite a certain austerity in the writing and a slavish fondness for medical terms. . . .

It is Mr. Kingsley's thesis that medicine is a ruthless master. Those who take the Hippocratic oath are embracing a religion. Young Dr. Ferguson, interne at St. George's Hospital, may become a brilliant surgeon if he works hard and selflessly at his profession for the next five or ten years. But the rich young lady to whom he is engaged looks forward to a marriage in which there may be pleasure as well as professional labor. With her wealth she can buy Ferguson's advancement. She might have done that. But while she is in the midst of preparations for the wedding Ferguson is ordered to assist in a critical operation to save the life of a nurse who has just been through an abortion. Ferguson is responsible for her calamity. This situation in all its torturing ramifications settles the question of loyalties more resolutely than any of the discussions could. Ferguson plunges back into medicine as a refuge. The young lady to whom he is engaged is now willing to take him on those ruthless professional terms.

Although this is Mr. Kingsley's first play to reach professional production, he has the gift of dramatic concreteness. ***Men in White*** abounds in scenes that have impact in the theatre. It dramatizes the hospital. It progresses from the interne's library to a patient's room, the director's room and the operating room. In most of the nine scenes some matter of human destiny is at stake. You may question the logic of the story. You may criticize the continuity and the writing. But ***Men in White*** has force in the theatre. It is warm with life and high in aspiration, and it has a contagious respect for the theme it discusses.

Brooks Atkinson, "Men of Medicine in a Group Theatre Drama—'Kultur' of Modern Germany," in The New York Times, *September 27, 1933, p. 24.*

JOSEPH WOOD KRUTCH

]*Krutch is regarded as one of America's most respected literary and drama critics. Noteworthy among his works are* The American Drama since 1918 *(1939), in which he analyzes the most important dramas of the 1920s and 1930s, and* "Modernism" in Modern Drama *(1953), in which he stresses the need for twentieth-century playwrights to infuse their works with traditional humanistic values. In the following excerpt Krutch hails* Men in White *as an important and successful drama.*]

To say that [***Men in White***] is by far the best thing which has appeared this season would be praise far too faint; even to say that it may very probably remain the year's most satisfying demonstration of what the theater can do would still be not enough. The thing must, on the contrary, be praised in terms absolute rather than relative. It furnishes an experience which is thrilling and absorbing, genuine and complete.

No one, I think, is likely to accuse me of being usually prejudiced in favor of either the play with a purpose or the good intentions of "experimental" groups with nothing except experimentalism in their favor. Indeed, when I heard in advance that the present play was to deal with a hospital and, more particularly, with the conflict between love and duty in the breast of a young interne, my feelings were largely composed of that resignation to which any dramatic critic must school himself. But ***Men in White*** stands firmly on its own merits as a dramatic production and needs no apology based upon extraneous considerations. It is not merely "an interesting experiment." Neither is it one of those plays of which we feel that we ourselves could afford to miss it but that the other fellow ought to see it because it "would make him think." It is, on the contrary, so immediately interesting, so completely absorbing, that one forgets to ask whether or not it is "significant" or "important." And that, I submit, is one of the signs by which a genuine work of art may be recognized.

Most of my confreres on the daily press have agreed with this judgment in advance. . . . On the one hand, it can hardly be said that there is anything completely new in the theme or that we have not heard before of the conflict between love and duty as revealed in the life of a young physician. Neither, on the other hand, can it be claimed that the somewhat cinematographic technique is in itself a novelty. Indeed, there is a vague resemblance between this play and such efforts as *Merry-Go-Round* and *Precedent*. . . . But the resemblance is, after all, as unimportant as the resemblance must always be between something which succeeds and something which fails. Where other plays of the sort were shrill or hysterical, ***Men in White*** is eloquent with the eloquence of calm understatement. Where the machinery of the others whirred and creaked and groaned, this play moves with a seemingly effortless inevitability. The final result is that one is left, not in a state of vague exasperation, but merely with the sense of having passed through a vivid self-justifying experience. Doubtless this effect is made possible by the fact that Sidney Kingsley . . . has realized the necessity of resolving the emotional discords and has made the audience feel that the tragic triumph of his hero is worth his struggles and his partial defeat. (pp. 419-20)

Joseph Wood Krutch, "An Event," in The Nation, *Vol. CXXXVII, No. 3562, October 11, 1933, pp. 419-20.*

JOSEPH WOOD KRUTCH

When Sidney Kingsley's ***Men in White*** drew the Pulitzer Prize, . . . it was generally admitted that his success was primarily a theatrical one: the play was effective, not because it was either very original or very profound, but because the author gave an able acting company a script which was eminently actable even at moments when it was not anything else. In his new play ***Dead End*** he now demonstrates the fact that this first success was no mere accident. With the sure instinct of the first-rate theatrical craftsman he again selects a theme which is genuinely significant but which has been treated often enough to be easily manageable in terms of various concrete situations whose effectiveness has already been demonstrated. Thus he himself is relieved of the necessity of working out either characters or predicaments which will serve as satisfactory symbols, and the audience is, at the same time, relieved of the necessity of discovering what their significance is. The author can devote himself to the expert manipulation of easily comprehensible material, and the spectator can surrender himself to a series of swift, colorful, clearly outlined incidents.

On the former occasion Mr. Kingsley devoted himself to the problem of the young doctor who discovers that his profession demands a surrender of the right to much of what the ordinary man regards as an indispensable part of normal human life. In the new play he is concerned with a problem at least as real—with the corrupting influence of poverty, particularly as it affects those children of the slums whose education in the streets really prepares them adequately for no career except the career of the gangster. It is hard to see how this problem could be made to serve as the basis for a more rapidly moving or more exciting melodrama than the one which Mr. Kingsley has written, with its striking setting along what may well be the Sutton Place waterfront, where the apartments of the rich shoulder the tenements of the poor, and with its effective conjunction of the story of a youthful gang with the story of a graduate now become Public Enemy No. 1. For perfectly understandable and not too reprehensible reasons it will probably outlast any other dramatic production made so far this season, despite the fact that no judicious person would be likely to claim that it is in any sense a great play. Doubtless the most grimly earnest of its spectators will argue that the moderately happy ending which promises at least a temporary, if somewhat fortuitous, rescue for the youthful gang leader offers a solution which is not a general one and therefore weakens the social effectiveness of the play. But that is not the real reason why ***Dead End*** remains essentially theatrical. The real reason is that, without being false, it lacks either that originality of incident or that freshness of feeling at least one or the other of which is necessary to make a play great. Its quality varies from the sleazy cheapness of its conventional love story to what seems to me the one touch of near-greatness in the scene between the mature gangster and his mother. But during four-fifths of the time it is running on the level of first-rate melodrama, which grips without actually ceasing at any time to be obviously a play and without turning up any situation or any thought not essentially familiar. ***Dead End*** is, to put it brutally, very high-grade hokum. (pp. 575-76)

Joseph Wood Krutch, "Sure Fire," in The Nation, *Vol. CXLI, No. 3671, November 13, 1935, pp. 575-76.*

EDITH J. R. ISAACS

[*Isaacs, an American editor and critic, was editor of* Theatre Arts Magazine *(later* Theatre Arts Monthly*) from 1918 to 1946. She also wrote nonfiction works including* Theatre *(1927) and* The Negro in the American Theatre *(1947). In the following excerpt Isaacs observes that the finest and most relevant aspect of* Dead End *is its vivid portrayal of New York tenement life.*]

It is strange how recurrently, year after year, time sets its mark on certain plays and avoids all others. It is stranger still that the plays so marked are not the most journalistic and immediate, but those that most clearly show the theatre catching up to the artist, often the best plays in each season. All around and about them there are sure to be productions that might just as well have come last year, ten years ago, a generation ago, except for a shift of argot, an alteration in a 'news-slant', or a bit of intellectual fashion that has drifted across the roads of art. They are the routine matter of a routine theatre, and are as unimportant when they are written 'in a good cause' as when they are written simply to make money—which is a good enough cause in a good theatre. Then, suddenly, there appears a play like *Winterset,* like ***Dead End,*** which seems to be stamped at once with the seal of its day. When ***Dead End*** opened . . . , people said, 'This is like *Winterset.*' And so it is, in the major fact that it is 1935 theatre.

Dead End is like *Winterset,* too, in that its theme is social injustice, its form is melodrama, its place of action is New York City, . . . it has boldness and freedom of attack, it is full of excitement and strong currents, of resentment and of pity. But there the resemblance ends, and the whole character of the authors' work divides as clearly as the material of the two settings. Instead of the giant tower of a Manhattan bridge, . . . [***Dead End*** is set in] the vacant space at the dead end of a riverfront street within whose narrow confines you can almost see the whole pattern of New York life spread out. (p. 888)

The material of Sidney Kingsley's play is as commonplace as city life, as well charted as the distance between riches and poverty. The story has been told on the stage a hundred times and a hundred times more, from *The Streets of New York* to *Street Scene*. Even of idea and of social argument there is nothing new in ***Dead End.*** If you pit a crowd of effervescent, keen-witted youngsters, hungry for life, against the immovable forces of social slavery, ill health, bad food, damp rooms, something is bound to happen, and it happens more quickly than usual when you keep steadily before their eyes the contrast with vast wealth. A pretty obvious story. No New Yorker who wanders from Fifth Avenue east to the river, or west to the river, needs a theatre to show him these facts, or needs Sidney Kingsley to add up the facts and give him the answer, namely, that these strong children of the underworld will, as sure as Fate, hew out their own quick road to wealth in the best way they know, which, in our generation, is through the gang and by means of the gangster's tools—the lie, the bludgeon, the knife and the gun. Our newspapers keep us informed of that.

But what we are forever in need of is a stage on which theatre artists can transmute these facts, so that we shall see the river and the children and the dead end of their street before us while we walk along Fifth Avenue, so that, not through argument but through the influence of the beautiful thing—a fine play finely presented—we may remember the ugly thing which is the black border of our city life, and remember it so insistently that finally we must do something about it to escape from it ourselves. This thrust is what ***Dead End,*** at its best moments, achieves.

If we had a repertory theatre where we could see ***Men in White*** tonight and ***Dead End*** tomorrow, we could measure the distance that Kingsley has traveled since he wrote the play that won him the Pulitzer Prize. He has learned the playwright's way of telling a story, how to choose words and details of action, how to set movement and speech and emotion pulling together or one against another to build his climax (working with the

Group Theatre on ***Men in White*** may well have taught him that). What Kingsley does not yet know clearly is how to define individual character instead of type. . . . (pp. 891-92)

As long as he knows his people and cares enough about having them alive in his play, Kingsley is on safe ground. T B, Tommy, Dippy, Angel and Spit use the language of the streets exactly—you know it is right by the sound and the stress of it—and you soon know, too, that word upon word and speech upon speech it has been put together like the links of a chain, until it is both speech of the street and speech of the theatre. . . . But Mr. Kingsley's rich folks are never real, not lighted from within, not even real types, only a playwright's puppets. Although he has avoided the error of making all of them stupid and vulgar and cruel, it is perfectly clear that they do not interest the playwright, that they are used only as foils. (pp. 892-93)

Edith J. R. Isaacs, "See America First," in Theatre Arts Monthly, *Vol. XIX, No. 12, December, 1935, pp. 888-902.*

BROOKS ATKINSON

After ***Men in White*** and ***Dead End*** comes Sidney Kingsley's third play, ***Ten Million Ghosts***. . . . In it he drives headlong into his boldest subject—the manufacturers of munitions. He has documented his program with excerpts from books and newspapers about Zaharoff, the Krupps, the de Wendels and William B. Shearer, who represented steel and shipbuilding at the 1927 Geneva conference. . . . Mr. Kingsley has discharged a broadside of accusation and indignation at the world's merchants of death. His anger, his muscular strength and the grim importance of his subject are the most concrete virtues his kaleidoscopic drama has. ***Ten Million Ghosts*** is not the sort of play a man can politely ignore, nor rise up from in a composed frame of mind. Nor can he honestly ignore the fact that the characters are placard stencils and that the drama is a cumbersome snarl of story. On his biggest subject Mr. Kingsley has written his least spontaneous play.

In saying so one feels like a traitor to the cause of peace and of man's integrity to man. For ***Ten Million Ghosts*** groans under the weight of many ominous things that have become public property in the last few years when students of war have turned realistic. Mr. Kingsley's most imposing villain is one Zacharey, the most enterprising man in Universe Forges, Inc., dealers in machines of death. From a provincial business Zacharey has made it international by agreements and large-scale salesmanship. When the World War is on the point of breaking out he and his associates have sufficient political influence to save the Briey and Dombasle mines from destruction by the French and the Germans, respectively. According to John Gunther's *Inside Europe,* which Mr. Kingsley quotes in the program, "the war would have ended two years sooner" if both these mines had been destroyed by normal warfare.

This is the basic fact in Mr. Kingsley's passionate indictment of the munitions manufacturers and it is also the turning point in his drama. For the daughter of Zacharey's partner is in love with a French aviator who is stationed on the Briey sector and wonders why the army command forbids an attack upon German munitions plants that are highly vulnerable. He finds out why in a stormy interview with Zacharey and his fiancée's father but in defiance of orders he bombs the plants alone, hoping by his quixoticism to open the eyes of the world. All he achieves is death for himself, misery for his sweetheart and silence from the world. In the last scene, laid in Geneva in 1927, Mr. Kingsley suggests that the munitions manufacturers are still in control of the peace and war of the world.

If this story could be told with the naturalistic conviction of ***Dead End*** it would be sensational in the theatre as well as in thought. But it is too big a subject for the reportorial style of playwrighting; and instead of scaling it down to dimensions that are practicable Mr. Kingsley has tried to make it all-embracing. In the heat of his indignation he has also made the munitions manufacturers solely responsible for all the evils of this tense and trembling world. The war spirit can be artfully stimulated, but it is not so simple as ***Ten Million Ghosts*** implies. . . .

If this column reports that neither the parts nor the acting is very persuasive, it hopes that no one will be reading this far down in the column. For Mr. Kingsley's honest anger in a common cause is exhilarating to encounter along Broadway, no matter how stubbornly his drama resists it.

Brooks Atkinson, "Sidney Kingsley Attacking the Munitions Manufacturers in 'Ten Million Ghosts'," in The New York Times, *October 24, 1936, p. 23.*

BROOKS ATKINSON

Although Millen Brand's novel, *The Outward Room,* may not seem like ideal stage material, Sidney Kingsley has made a deeply moving play out of it. ***The World We Make*** he calls it. . . . Mr. Brand's novel told the haunting story of a mentally unbalanced girl who escaped from an institution and healed herself by living a normal life with normal people. For the childish purpose of dazzling the audience . . . , Mr. Kingsley has plunged one scene into the steamy clatter of a laundry, and he takes pains to squeeze all the current significance he can out of a story that is rooted in individual anguish.

But the theme can stand it, since it is soundly motivated, and Mr. Kingsley has not lost the compassion of a fine study of character fulfillment. . . . Although Mr. Kingsley's ***Dead End*** made a broader show, ***The World We Make*** is an infinitely more sensitive glance into the shadowy mind of a human being. It is brave, original and fervent in conviction, and an ornament to our theatre.

In the prologue Virginia is confined to a sanitarium for mental cases. Strangely obsessed by the violent death of her brother, she is ridden with nameless terrors and cannot face the jangle of the world. But she escapes, ventures into a steam laundry in search of a job, takes refuge with a decent young man who works there, goes helplessly to live in his tenement room and falls in love with him. After the realistic sensationalism of the steam laundry scene, ***The World We Make*** settles down into a gusty chronicle of Virginia's warm and affectionate life with the tenement dwellers in a frowsy building, the pungent normality of the real world gradually triumphing over her terror until she perceives that one corner of the world needs her as much as she needs it. The victory is so simple that it is profoundly stirring—the miracle of nature no longer resisted. . . .

Mr. Kingsley's realistic writing for the character bits in the tenement, his portrait of life swirling helter-skelter through this battered room and the dank hall outside it and his reticent description of the affection Virginia has for the man she has discovered and taken into her heart make ***The World We Make*** a cheerful, merry and also poignant drama of a part of life that is usually sacrificed to political causes in modern writing. Although Mr. Kingsley talks a little too much in his last scene, most of his writing admirably understates the meaning and some of it he has the courage to leave to pantomime. . . .

Like a showman, Mr. Kingsley is lavish with local color. But like a dramatist he can appreciate the fragility and valor of a human being. The theatre should be proud of the world he . . . made out of awareness and integrity.

Brooks Atkinson, "Sidney Kingsley's 'The World We Make' Is Stage Version of 'The Outward Room'," in The New York Times, *November 21, 1939, p. 19.*

CHARLES ANGOFF

[*Angoff, a Russian-born American editor, novelist, essayist, nonfiction writer, and poet, is best known for his autobiographical novels, including* Winter Twilight *(1970). He also worked on the editorial staffs of several prestigious magazines, including* The American Mercury, Nation, American Spectator, *and* North American Review. *In the following excerpt Angoff faults Kingsley for his unconvincing portrayal of working-class urban life in* The World We Make.]

Sidney Kingsley's ***The World We Make,*** based upon Millen Brand's novel, *The Outward Room,* attempts to probe a few miles deeper into the human soul than *Life With Father,* but unfortunately it succeeds only moderately. The tale has to do with a young girl, become mentally unbalanced since the death of her brother, and who finally achieves liberation from her pathology by finding love in the arms of a man who sinks into despair when his own brother dies, and whom she pulls back into the normal world with her tender understanding and limitless affection.

A story of this nature may be placed in a cellar or in a palace, for its problem depends only very little upon environment. Mr. Kingsley places it in a cellar, so to speak, with the apparent belief that he can tell it better in such a locale, but before the play has gone into the third scene one feels that the locale has got the better of the human problem, which almost gets lost in the settings and the gabble they naturally call forth. Scene I, Act I shows probably the most elaborate laundry ever put on the stage, steaming and noisy—and engulfing the girl and the ailment plaguing her. The next seven scenes take place in a shabby tenement, which, alas, always gets in the way of the central theme and the central character.

Even the proletarian background, which swallows the play, has grave deficiencies of delineation. Mr. Kingsley may have had first-hand contact with the proletariat, but he still writes about it from above, as a life subscriber to *Spur* magazine would describe a group of East Side urchins playing in the park. His ***Dead End*** showed the same condescension and lack of insight. The story there had considerable slickness, but that did not hide its pulp character.

Similarly with the story of Virginia and John in ***The World We Make.*** The "earthy" talk and happenings in their flat seem designed to bring forth tears and sighs, but they have little relation to actual proletarian life. Downtown, as uptown, girls do not run to neighbors to boast of their pregnancy, men do not suddenly become mush in public when offered a job after two years of unemployment, women in love with their husbands do not habitually insult them before others, and a decent man, even after having just returned from viewing the corpse of his brother, doesn't throw back at his sweetheart the cup of coffee she has offered him in the endeavor to make it easier for him.

Such things create a lot of "action" on the stage, sometimes pleasant to watch for the moment. . . . But they smell more of invention than of honest observation. Falseness, even about the miseries of the lowly, always pays the same penalty: it fails to convince. (pp. 402-03)

Charles Angoff, "A Biographical Play Runs Ahead of Problem Plays," in The North American Review, *Vol. 248, No. 2, Winter 1939-40, pp. 401-06.*

WOLCOTT GIBBS

[*Gibbs was an American critic, journalist, short story writer, editor, and dramatist known for his eloquent, iconoclastic style. He was drama critic for the* New Yorker *from 1939 to 1958 and also wrote the play* Season in the Sun *(1950). In the following excerpt Gibbs demonstrates his acerbic wit by outlining the reasons why he feels* Patriots *fails as a historical drama.*]

There are, it seems to me, a good many obstacles to be hurdled by a playwright who has made up his mind to tamper with history, and we had better list them numerically:

1. A modern actor almost invariably looks jocose when made up to represent a celebrated figure out of the past. The darky butler, who is really much more like a member of the family, comes in and announces "General George Washington," but what enters is just a man of customary stature, troubled by an unusual arrangement of hair, through which he peers anxiously, like a poodle. This is, of course, nobody's fault; it is simply a condition to be faced in a trade that has to suggest giants with the best available material. I except Raymond Massey's Lincoln and Helen Hayes' Victoria from this generality, but no others that I can think of.

2. History on the stage requires a system of running reference, very unlikely in human speech. For the convenience of an audience, for instance, it is probably necessary for Thomas Jefferson to say, "Just think, it was exactly seven years ago today that I wrote the Declaration of Independence," or for Alexander Hamilton to explain (in 1800) that he would undoubtedly be killed in a duel with Aaron Burr (in 1804). Remarks like these are unquestionably helpful to customers who never survived the third grade, but they are apt to sound moderately queer when delivered in a theatre.

3. The literary talent of the playwright, curiously enough, is often inferior to the literary talent of the statesman. It is permissible, therefore, for Mr. Jefferson to produce a speech beginning "When, in the course of human events, it becomes necessary," but it is fairly unfortunate if his next lines sound as if they had been written for a B picture in Hollywood.

4. The lives of great men, superstition to the contrary, are not always terribly interesting. They are thinkers and, generally speaking, of a sedentary nature, so any dramatic action contrived for them usually results from a heightening or distortion of the facts. Thus, while it may be expedient at the box office to present Jefferson and Hamilton as the warring forces of good and evil, practically undiluted, it is also apt to be mildly distressing to the precise historian.

5. In these days, unfortunately, there is little justification for a costume piece unless some parallel can be drawn between the problems of the period and the struggle which confronts us now. That there are such parallels certainly nobody will deny. It is simply a question of whether it is advisable to bat the audience over the head with them until a state bordering on stupefaction is produced.

These in the main are my complaints against ***The Patriots,*** a play about the celebrated feud between Jefferson and Hamilton, written by Sidney Kingsley. . . . It is a worthy enterprise and, at least when Mr. Kingsley is working from his sources, clearly an eloquent one. The trouble with me was that I didn't believe for a minute that the founders of our country looked or spoke or behaved even remotely like anybody on the stage, or at least, patriotically, I hoped they didn't.

Wolcott Gibbs, "Birth of a Nation," in The New Yorker, *Vol. XVIII, No. 51, February 6, 1943, p. 31.*

GEORGE JEAN NATHAN

[*Nathan has been called the most learned and influential drama critic the United States has yet produced. During the early decades of the twentieth century, he was greatly responsible for shifting the emphasis of the American theater from light entertainment to serious drama and for introducing audiences and producers to the work of Eugene O'Neill, Henrik Ibsen, and Bernard Shaw, among others. Nathan was a contributing editor to H. L. Mencken's magazine the* American Mercury *and coeditor of the* Smart Set. *In the following excerpt Nathan asserts that, despite its faults,* Patriots *is an exceptionally intelligent and engrossing historical drama.*]

Sidney Kingsley's ***The Patriots*** represents almost everything for which I normally have no critical appetite, yet in my opinion it is, up to the time of writing, the worthiest play of this theatrical year. Its disfigurements are numerous, beginning with its very title which pokes the flag right up our noses. It relies for its final fillip upon Jefferson's eloquent inaugural address, much as Sherwood relied upon Lincoln's own ringing words to excite the Pulitzer prize committee into the conviction that Sherwood had probably also ghosted the Gettysburg Address. It unwarrantedly, by way of theatricalizing the ideological conflict between Jefferson and Alexander Hamilton, makes the latter now and again indistinguishable from the conventional melodramatic stage villain, and it at times so stacks the cards that one momentarily expects Hermann the Great to be revealed as a member of Washington's Cabinet. It goes in heavily for my pet aversion, analogies and parallels between the past and present. Its dream passage involving Jefferson and his wife is of stage valentine lace all compact, and its scene wherein Hamilton's wife learns of his infidelity is pop out of the Henry Arthur Jones bottle. And it suggests fleetingly the "there's an ugly rumor about" species of historical drama.

It is all this, and more. Yet so honest is it at bottom, so unostentatious in its deeper dramatic current, so intelligently in general handled, and so genuinely stirring in its overtones and after-image that it amounts in sum not only to the most critically acceptable full-length offering of the season but to one of the most skilful historical-biographical plays our American theatre has shown. If it has its blemishes, they are forgivable in the play's final driving effect.

Treating of the ten years in Jefferson's life just preceding his election to the Presidency, the exhibit concerns itself with his vision of the true democracy, with the plutocratic forces arrayed in all sincerity against him, and with his battle to achieve the security of the young nation and its people. With negligible rant, with some gratifying humor and with passion brewed from cold intelligence, the drama, for all its red-white-and-blue title, never descends to mere patriotic benzedrine, seldom falters on its dignified course, and always, save in a rather cinematic prologue and some of that Hamilton business, maintains its inner probity. (pp. 486-87)

Although Kingsley's play does not abandon all the customary august paralysis in the instance of its figures, it at least gestures very satisfactorily in that direction. Which is a credit to his careful research. (p. 487)

George Jean Nathan, "The Best Play of the Season," in American Mercury, *Vol. LVI, No. 232, April, 1943, pp. 486-91.*

JOSEPH WOOD KRUTCH

Sidney Kingsley's ***Detective Story*** . . . is to my mind quite the best melodrama of the year and none the worse for having a moral. Mr. Kingsley's plays have always been completely devoid of what we call "literary quality," and for that reason there is a kind of seriousness with which they cannot possibly be taken. Indeed, it is that fact rather than the undue prevalence of mere external violence which makes "melodrama" the inevitable label to apply to them. But I know no contemporary American who can take a topic—slum children in ***Dead End*** or doctors and nurses in ***Men in White***—and turn out a more stage-worthy piece, full of shrewd if not too profound observation crisply and humorously embodied in recognizable types. . . .

[In ***Detective Story***] his scene is a precinct office of the New York police; his background material is what playwrights of another age would have called "the humors" of the criminal world; and his central character is a too stern and self-righteous detective whose determination to see that the guilty are punished makes it impossible for him to keep within the letter of the law and who "beats up" an abortionist about to go free. Perhaps it is not too hard for the spectator to guess that poetic justice is going to see to it that he himself will fall a victim to his relentless determination not to understand or forgive. But the story of the uncompromising hoist with their own petard is one of the most enduringly effective of dramatic fables, and before one is too scornful of it one may well remember that Sophocles did not think it unworthy of himself. Detective McLeod in the present play has at least one important thing in common with Oedipus, for Oedipus also was a man who blustered about in his determination that the facts should come to light and who was himself destroyed when they did.

In a newspaper interview Mr. Kingsley let it be understood that he intended the ultimate implications of ***Detective Story*** to constitute a comment on, almost an allegory of, the "police state" and the danger inherent in men who are so convinced that their ends are just that they are troubled by no scruples and moved to no mercy in the pursuit of those ends. Remotely, perhaps, these implications are there, but the more obvious and immediate "problem" is the problem of criminal justice, of society's right to punish those who break its laws without sufficiently considering how they came to do what they ultimately find themselves doing. Now this is a theme on which it is very easy to be merely sentimental, and in Mr. Kingsley's defense it must be said that he avoids the usual pure black and white of the melodrama and that this is by no means a case of the wicked police persecuting the innocent victims of society. Most of his police officers are decent if rough-and-ready men; most of his criminals are really guilty, and some of them are thoroughly vicious. Over against the young veteran who stole from his employer to give a girl a good time he sets, for example, a depraved and sniveling sadist with a long record of robbery and violence. And I do not think that he ever suggests any ready answer to society's problem. It is all very well to say that to understand all is to pardon all. But could a world really survive if those of us who like ourselves to pardon did not employ others less understanding. In actual fact we have accepted Dr. Johnson's compromise, which is "knock him down first and pity him afterward." I am not sure that I know any other practicable line of conduct, and I am not sure that Mr. Kingsley thinks he does either. You can temper justice with mercy, but that still leaves the question of just how much justice and just how much tempering. (pp. 424-25)

Joseph Wood Krutch, in a review of "Detective Story," in The Nation, *Vol. 168, No. 15, April 9, 1949, pp. 424-25.*

WILLIAM BEYER

Kingsley's ***Detective Story*** makes a pertinent social comment melodramatically and deals with a police officer, one Detective McLeod, who, arrogant egotist and tyrant that he is, sees himself as perfect, but who, in the exercise of his perfection as a cop, reveals himself as totally lacking in tolerance and pity, being ruthless, even sadistic, to such an extent that his brutalities conspire to trip him up and serve as his undoing. The action, which transpires in the squad room of a Manhattan police station, provides a lusty, colorful, and brawling conflict involving the police—an ingratiatingly ribald, hard-boiled yet sentimental crew; the criminals, including first offenders as well as assorted old-timers; and the necessary confused and indignant citizenry, all of which, from McLeod on down, are highly original characters, freshly observed and lucidly presented—Kingsley at his reportorial best.

The vicious McLeod is a particularly excellent characterization and, despite his devious methods, is not without sympathy. Kingsley sees him in the round and reasonably accounts for his twisted mind, both as a man and as a cop whose personal hazards and efforts at honest law enforcement are too often turned into a mockery by the venality of our judicial system and the chicaneries of court procedure. Known criminals are allowed to go scot free, making a farce of police procedure, and it is in vengeful pursuit of such a criminal, an abortionist, that the fanatic McLeod, goes completely off the beam. The first half of the play is concerned with the total life, one might say, of the station house on a specific evening, and it bristles with authentic details, resulting in plots and counterplots out of which maze McLeod and the abortionist gradually rise to the fore. His ruthless methods have won McLeod practically no friends on the squad, and his enraged superior, Lieutenant Monoghan, after repeated warnings, brings about a showdown when McLeod's unwarranted assault on the abortionist gives him the complete authority to do so. The subsequent investigation brings Mrs. McLeod into the station house. It develops that she had had an abortion years before her marriage by the same man, a fact which McLeod had never known. The revelation is too much, and McLeod forces a separation, righteous and ruthless even in his domestic life. One of those freak accidents that are perfectly legitimate under the circumstances, a criminal jail-break, precipitates McLeod's sudden death—and leaves us shaken. Such sub-plots as need finishing are disposed of like any case on a police blotter, and we are moved to laughter, or tears as the case may be, but in every instance touched by the genuine emotions involved and the naturalness and forthrightness of the action.

The play rings true, bitingly, trenchantly so, and Mr. Kingsley has done a sound job in presenting some three dozen assorted characters that pulse with life for the brief period they are under scrutiny. As the play inevitably proceeds along melodramatic lines, some parts fit into the picture more patly than others—including the various lesser developments. When Mrs. McLeod is brought in, a suspect in the case of the abortionist, like any other, the writer is up against a truly difficult chore. McLeod's scenes with his wife are pure domestic drama, and fitting these in the middle of the play when the melodrama is going full steam is far from smooth sailing. Consequently, as pure dramatic treatment, Mrs. McLeod is poorly presented, being sacrificed to the contrived melodramatic whole. However, what the artificially fitted scenes between man and wife sacrifice in dramatic validity, the melodrama makes up for in theatrical effectiveness as a whole. (pp. 362-63)

William Beyer, "The State of the Theatre: The Season Opens," in School and Society, *Vol. 70, No. 1824, December 3, 1949, pp. 360-64.*

MARGARET MARSHALL

[*Marshall, an American editor and critic, was literary editor of the* Nation *for twenty-five years, as well as a contributing editor and drama critic. In the following excerpt Marshall observes that Kingsley's adaptation of* Darkness at Noon *lacks the complexity of Arthur Koestler's novel.*]

The power of Arthur Koestler's ***Darkness at Noon,*** both as a novel and as an explanation of one of the enigmas of our generation—those public confessions of old Bolsheviks about to die anyway—derives mainly from the dramatic conflict among three major characters, Rubashov, Ivanov, and Gletkin, each of whom comes alive as a personality at the same time that each stands as a type thrown up by the Soviet world-view and the Soviet system.

Ivanov, the head of the prison, is, like Rubashov, an old Bolshevik, but one who still believes that the end, however long deferred, justifies the means, however cruel, and that this end or aim retains its pristine purity uncorrupted by the means or by the temptations of great power. Gletkin, second in command, is the new Soviet man to whom such questions have no reality and who is impatient with Ivanov for trying to bring Rubashov round by argument and appeal instead of using his own efficient methods of "correct brutality." In the book the Soviet logic of each of these characters engages, at one point or another, the mind and even the sympathy of the reader. It is the highly intellectualized, inhuman and unhumane, logic of the fanatic, and its momentary appeal is to the fanatic element—the arrogant, self-righteous, and power-loving element—in all of us. But its convincing presentation and its power to engage us are a measure of the book's merit. The conflict among three strong men generates suspense; it also serves to lay bare the workings of the Soviet mentality as well as to probe and challenge our own basic beliefs; and it makes the final capitulation of Rubashov, or rather his return to his earlier faith, convincing. What makes Rubashov the hero of the proceedings in our Western eyes is of course the fact that this fanatic logic, though it is strong enough to carry him through a public confession, is undermined and dissipated in private by human and humanitarian "softness" and that he goes to his death in the cellar as an individual human being, not as a cipher in a historical equation.

The prime weakness of Sidney Kingsley's dramatization of ***Darkness at Noon*** . . . is that only Rubashov is allowed full stature as a personality. Ivanov is portrayed as a rather cynical but amiable old-timer going along—inclined to save his old comrade because of an early and treasured fellowship—not as a forceful and convinced revolutionary who offers a cogent and confident defense of the "logic of history" and succeeds in winning over his prisoner—before he, Ivanov, is removed and liquidated, at the instigation of Gletkin, for being too soft.

As for Gletkin, he emerges in the play as a sort of simple-minded gangster, American style, who has conceived a grudge against Rubashov. . . . [The] reasoning behind Gletkin's "correct brutality" is not sufficiently brought out; Koestler's revealing references to the social and historical forces that have helped to mold this new Soviet type—such forces, for instance, as the headlong industrialization of a backward country—are not incorporated in the play, as they might easily have been.

This seems to me one of the most damaging simplifications that had to be made—from the point of view of dramatic interest and from another point of view as well. Americans know less about the Gletkins than about the old Bolsheviks with their Western associations; they need to know more, since Gletkins are being raised up in so many quarters of the globe.

Gletkin does at least appear as a strong character—and the fiendishly logical process by which he deduces specific criminal acts as likely consequences of Rubashov's admitted casual and general remarks is convincingly handled. So is the method of "correct brutality" in which Gletkin, by the use of logic and with the aid of such tormenting goads as bright lights and examinations prolonged into days, reduces Rubashov to complete submission.

The play is episodic—the central drama of the book, the conflict among strong personalities and points of view, being largely missing—but the episodes are dramatic and telling: the episode of the dock-workers, the episode of the girl, Rubashov's lover, who has gone to her execution without a word of defense from him, and so on. (pp. 92-3)

Margaret Marshall, in a review of "Darkness at Noon," in The Nation, *New York, Vol. 172, No. 4, January 27, 1951, pp. 92-3.*

HAROLD CLURMAN

[*Highly regarded as a director, author, and longtime drama critic (1953-80) for the* Nation, *Clurman was an important contributor to the development of the modern American theater. In 1931, with Lee Strasberg and Cheryl Crawford, he founded the innovative Group Theatre, which staged the successful Broadway debut of Kingsley's first play* Men in White *in 1933. Clurman also wrote several works on the theater, including his acclaimed autobiography* All People Are Famous *(1974). In the following excerpt Clurman expresses disappointment in Kingsley's adaptation of* Darkness at Noon.]

I am confident that most people who hear about ***Darkness at Noon*** approve of its politics; I am certain that disenchanted leftists, who once looked to Moscow for miracles, will be fascinated by the play's point, which is that the rigid, materialistic functionalism of those misguided humanists, the old Bolsheviks, has led logically to the inhuman brutality of the later Soviet leaders. I am equally convinced that the average sensible theatregoer who sees the play will be left cold, because it is an elaborate mechanism which issues from no central core of real experience or intimate knowledge.

Kingsley has a gift for making theatre out of local color and documentation in such dramatic milieus as hospitals, off-center neighborhoods, detective bureaus. Being a man of the thirties, Kingsley also has a penchant for liberal social preachment. He has, however, no psychological insight, no poetic eloquence, no capacity to convey the quality of any inner state. He has pieced ***Darkness at Noon*** together from the surface of Koestler's novel, from quotes out of the writings and speeches of various Soviet spokesmen, and from the editorial repetitiousness of innumerable contemporary journalists. The result is a sort of *Reader's Digest* melodrama, intricate without suspense, psychological without characters, philosophical without mind, violent without effect. The total impression is that of cardboard operatics, reminding one both of our old anti-Nazi war films and the propaganda plays of the early Roosevelt era. (p. 23)

Harold Clurman, "From Lorca Down," in The New Republic, *Vol. 124, No. 6, February 5, 1951, pp. 22-3.*

WOLCOTT GIBBS

In ***Lunatics and Lovers,*** Sidney Kingsley, who has hitherto devoted himself to far higher, if not necessarily more difficult, things, has turned to the writing of a rackety, low-down farce. The farce form is, of course, an odd one. It has no use for sculptured and intricate wit but relies instead on a machine-gun fire of one-line jokes, rooted mainly in the basic humor of insult, malapropism, and double-entendre—or, to put it less majestically, simple dirt. The exact delineation of credible characters is also beyond its scope, the aim being only to fill the stage with a succession of extravagant caricatures, the further removed from life the better, and it does no harm—and, indeed, is probably restful for the audience—if they have appeared almost intact in a hundred such diversions before. Above all, the author is under no obligation to produce a plot, in the sense of a connected series of plausible happenings. All that he is asked to do is to confront his company of grotesques with a completely preposterous dilemma at the beginning of the play, complicate it with further lunacies in the middle, and disentangle the whole thing as rapidly and incoherently as possible at the end. Mr. Kingsley is a sufficiently experienced operator in the theatre to understand all these requirements and to follow them out to the extent of achieving the form and, to a degree, the substance of a successful farce.

The reason ***Lunatics and Lovers*** isn't quite in the first run of its kind is, I think, that its author isn't really a popular humorist at heart. His intelligence tells him what is needed, and much of the time he is able to supply it, in the form of quips of his own or else in borrowed gags so old that, like those in *Hellzapoppin,* they sound nearly new. He isn't, however, capable of the sort of sustained comic invention that gave us such tangled masterpieces as *Room Service* and *Three Men on a Horse,* and there are frequent long stretches when ***Lunatics and Lovers*** shows a good deal more effort than inspiration. It might also be said that Mr. Kingsley is a highly moral man, and at times, especially toward the end of the evening, he seems rather shocked by the depravity of his own creations, and puts in their mouths high-minded sentiments that seriously diminish their rakish charm. Altogether, I should say that while the piece . . . is very funny in spots, it is too divided in spirit and too uneven in the quality of its wit to satisfy true connoisseurs of slapstick art.

The action of the play takes place in the living room, the bedroom, and the sensationally public bath of a suite in a typical Broadway flea bag on West Forty-eighth Street. The plot—for want of a better word—has something to do with the attempts of a couple of small-time chisellers to soften up an elderly but still sporty judge to the point where he will use his influence to get them out from under an income-tax rap. Their obvious weapon is the judge's weakness for the ladies, and the time is just right for employing it, because his latest sweetmeat has left him to take up with a dentist upon whose bare back she is in the pretty habit of scrawling Anglo-Saxon monosyllables with her lipstick. By a useful coincidence, the boys' choice for her successor falls on the dentist's wife, a virtuous girl but so exasperated by her husband's behavior that she is ripe for almost anything. Since this central confusion is compounded by a secondary scuffle, involving one of the shady operators and a successful call girl (she has saved up well over seventeen thousand dollars) with a weakness for holding court in a bathtub and playing with musical toilet fixtures, you can see that Mr. Kingsley has quite a vivacious little story to tell. I won't tax you with his resolution of it, except to say that everybody winds up in the kip best suited to his spiritual needs, and that more subordinate actors and bizarre props are employed than you'd think possible in the theatre's current sad state of economy. As far as the jokes are concerned, I can only report that my emotions ranged from gratitude, when someone said to the indignant wife, "So what if she does write on your husband's back. Your children can't read, can they?," to vague melancholy, at "There's one thing about lying in the gutter—you can't fall off." The general level was probably somewhere in between. (pp. 44-6)

Wolcott Gibbs, "Standard Brands," in The New Yorker, *Vol. XXX, No. 45, December 25, 1954, pp. 44-6.*

RICHARD GILMAN

[*Gilman, an American critic and editor, displays his erudite, philosophical approach to drama criticism in* Common and Uncommon Masks: Writings on Theatre, 1961-70 *(1970) and* The Making of Modern Drama *(1974). He was a theater reviewer for* Newsweek *and* Commonweal *in the 1960s, and served as an editor on several journals. In the following excerpt Gilman declares that* Night Life, *far from being avant-garde, demonstrates a style that is sadly obsolete.*]

Scanning Broadway, the eye of the ironist is immediately rewarded, filled, satiated in quick time: there is so much generosity. So far this season we have had plays of ideas in which no one thinks, comedies from which humor has meticulously been excluded, stars who are five-pointed disks of blackness, other-directed directors, sex without love, love without sex, and sex without sex. We have also had hit flops, like *Mr. President,* which nearly everybody hates but which is sold out for all eternity, and flop hits, such as *Who's Afraid of Virginia Woolf?* which almost everybody admires but which is too "disturbing" and "negative" for the tastes of demos. And we have also had plays like ***Night Life*** around which the mists of irony swirl like complex and deadly gases.

During the intermission at ***Night Life*** a woman was heard to remark that Sidney Kingsley's drama was "simply too *avant garde*" for her. A female Rip Van Winkle, she must have awakened, at the sound of the curtain going up, from a sleep that began in 1925, or at the latest 1936, since ***Night Life*** is a stage work of such out-dated sensibility, exhausted rhetoric and antediluvian technique that to consider it advanced can have no other rational explanation. And Mr. Kingsley has surely shared the lady's sleep, his dreams filled with the early O'Neill, with Edna St. Vincent Millay and Maxwell Anderson, with the Group Theater at its ideological worst, with his own paleolithic ***Men in White*** and ***Dead End*** and with John Dos Passos' *USA*.

Mr. Kingsley's self-styled "new kind of drama" takes place in a microcosmic U.S.A., the "key club" in New York City. Now I have never been inside a key club, but I do not believe that Kingsley has been inside one either, unless he spent part of his long sleep there. For one thing, I happen to know that such establishments have girls, in bunny or other costumes, and there just aren't any tomatoes, except customers, to be seen in this one. And for another, it doesn't seem likely to me, no siree it doesn't, that a key club should be the arena where the most pressing personal, national and universal problems are thrashed out, made to yield up immense rhetorical and dramatic consequences, and ultimately resolved.

Even so, how ineptly is the implausibility put forth, how primitively does Mr. Kingsley's sad, arrested sensibility and gelid craftsmanship, which have been superseded by a dozen more pertinent kinds, arrange the evening's procedures. The single two-leveled set is filled with Representative People—a ferociously ambitious labor leader modeled on Jimmy Hoffa, a lawyer whose idealism has been shattered by the world's corruption and the H-Bomb, a lesbian movie queen, a middle-aged couple who are discovering terrible things about one another, various personages identified in the programs as "Frenchie" and "gigolo" and "Harry's girl," who pullulate and mill around and interrelate and have empathy and rapport, or show us that they lack them.

The dramatic focus—and this is one of the purportedly new dramaturgical elements—continually shifts, in Kingsley's hunger for "totality," from one character or characterological nexus to another, the utterances move from unfelt dialogue to equally unfelt and pretentious asides and spoken thoughts, the tone from bawdy to bloodthirsty to earnest to mystical to melodramatic. Throughout, a pianist knocks off pop or blues melodies, joined occasionally by a girl singer and once by the entire clientele, which does a very energetic twist—all this constitutes the other piece of theatrical trail-blazing. In the end everything is set right: the labor leader is revealed in his True Colors, the lesbian gets her Comeuppance, the lawyer has his Faith restored, the couple is reunited in Death, and Mr. Kingsley has conquered darkest, most complicated and multifarious America.

Most of the reviewers who had qualms had them about Kingsley's structure, i.e., his admittedly brilliant inventiveness was thought to result in something not quite coherent. But it was generally agreed that he has a fine ear for speech (examples: "You battled your way to the top"; "You're a worthy antagonist"; "Deep down inside, as a human being, you're . . ."), a profound awareness of psychological truth (viz.: the movie star is asked about her suicide attempt: "Why did you do it? You have everything."), and the keenest sense of contemporary anguish coupled with the wit to express it (*ecce:* "We can't get through—words don't mean anything any more." And "I don't want kids because I have a vision of a man with a pointed head pressing a button and my children frying.")

I am not ordinarily for the young on principle, but a play like ***Night Life*** next to, say, *Virginia Woolf*, cries out for a generation to get the hell out of the way. Kingsley has every right in the world except one to feel the way Ibsen did when he wrote *The Master Builder*. What disqualifies him, of course, and leaves him wholly naked to the onrushing juveniles, is the fact that he was never Ibsen. He was only Elmer Rice.

Richard Gilman, "Remembrance of Things Passe," in Commonweal, *Vol. LXXVII, No. 9, November 23, 1962, p. 232.*

ALLAN LEWIS

[Lewis, an American critic, dramatist, and scriptwriter, is the author of The Contemporary Theatre *(1962),* American Plays and Playwrights of the Contemporary Theatre *(1965), and* Ionesco *(1973). In the following excerpt from* American Plays *Lewis observes that Kingsley's later plays, aimed at commercial success, fail to fulfil the promise of his early socially conscious dramas.]*

Sidney Kingsley . . . is definitely part of Broadway's Establishment. His life is the theatre. . . . With calculated timing, he returns regularly with a new work that threatens to deal with a major issue of our time, yet never breaks the barriers of the contrived play. His most recent works, ***Lunatics and Lovers*** (1954) and ***Night Life*** (1962), are evidences of his further retreat from the serious social themes that marked his earlier success. Neither was received with critical acclaim. The irony is that what he thought popular had already become hackneyed. . . . (pp. 148-49)

In ***Lunatics and Lovers,*** Kingsley abandoned his high aim. It is a broad farce about the shady characters who frequent the back alleys of the Times Square area, a more developed story of the flotsam that paraded through the local precinct station in ***Detective Story*** and served as colorful background material; in the later play they are central characters in a medley of love, sex, adultery, and bubble baths. . . . The dialogue is brittle, the scenes often hilarious, but the play is replete with obvious trickery and corny clichés. Instead of being all-out farce, it pulls its punches and the result is romantic dribble. . . . What might have been a riotous travesty of con men conning themselves turns into a collection of gags and artificial situations in a fabricated play aimed at commercial success.

Night Life takes place in a key club, one of those recent after-hours spots where—theoretically, at least—people of importance gather. A labor racketeer and a disillusioned young lawyer are in love with a nightclub singer. The locale affords an opportunity, much as in ***Dead End*** or ***Detective Story,*** to bring in a wide range of diversified characters, including a middle-aged man and wife whose marriage is disintegrating, and a film star whose sexual appetite leans indiscriminately to both sexes. Vignettes of the main characters' past unfold as the others on stage freeze in the semidarkness, and the piano plays softly in the background as the unifying element. The development has a dramatic fascination, but the resolution is again the unexpected, poorly motivated, noble deed, as in ***Lunatics and Lovers.*** The unhappy husband is shot as he stands up to the mobster to defend the lawyer, an act of courage by the little man in defiance of rule by terror. The killer, who has always had plausible alibis for his past murders, will now be convicted for an obvious act of homicide. Everything fits in too smoothly. The labor racketeer, the center of Kingsley's attention, never becomes a full-fledged character, but is merely a straw figure on which the playwright can vent his ire. Lust, intrigue, family quarrels, are mingled in an apparently serious attempt to depict the rise of a small-time dictator.

The same is true of ***Detective Story*** and ***Darkness at Noon,*** Kingsley's other plays since World War II. In the first, Captain Macleod is too devoted to justice and honor and the law. He is a typical TV lawman, a Sir Galahad of a neighborhood precinct, which is overrun with addicts, petty criminals, and social misfits. His marriage is on the rocks because he will never bend when prescribed morality is questioned. He must break, but he does so only in death. The final scene lacks conviction and fails to prove Kingsley's point that overzealousness, whether for good or evil, can destroy the cause it serves. Kingsley's own fears are revealed. He holds aloof from commitment because to him the dedicated idealist is as destructive as the fanatic fascist. No wonder he turned to ***Darkness at Noon,*** in which Koestler had attempted to explore the psychological forces that make Rubashov put party goals above all human considerations. Kingsley is an excellent craftsman whose early plays, rising out of the social awareness of the thirties, gave hope of a developing talent. Reduced now to picturing Broadway's sideshow freaks, he offers form without content, and a reliance on pure theatricalism. His weakness is his desire to be safe. (pp. 149-51)

Allan Lewis, "The Emergent Deans: Kingsley, Inge, and Company," in his American Plays and Playwrights of the Contemporary Theatre, *Crown Publishers, Inc., 1965, pp. 143-63.*

JOHN CORRY

The years have not been kind to ***Men in White.*** Sidney Kingsley's play . . . still has its moments, but time has robbed it of its importance, and a legion of imitations has turned it into a cliché. ***Men in White*** is only a retrospective cliché, of course; the cliché was made by the imitations that followed it. The play is the progenitor of every hospital drama you have ever seen.

Men in White . . . is a melodrama, and it is as melodrama that it works best. Virtue is virtue; sin is sin, and medicine is the noblest of professions, practiced, as a saintly doctor says, by those who, if they wanted to make money, "wouldn't have chosen medicine in the first place."

The play has a great many sentiments like that, and it has language that apparently worked well enough when the Group Theater did it in 1933, but has lost its urgency now. "You're a damned, meddling young puppy," a wealthy but incompetent doctor tells the young intern who has just saved the life of his patient. "Puppy" diminishes the accusation. . . .

Lee Strasberg directed ***Men in White*** in 1933. . . . The play was applauded for its realism, but it is likely that even in 1933 the realism was not so much in the play as in the production. ***Men in White*** is full of conflict, crisis and the traumas of the sick and injured. It is only in the operating room, in fact, that it absorbs us now. . . .

[A] dozen doctors and nurses prepare themselves for an operation. They wash; they pull on sterile gloves; they are intensely quiet. This is a mime show, and it is also theater. When the plot takes over, the theater is gone. The years have taken their toll even of Mr. Kingsley's celebrated craftsmanship.

John Corry, "'Men in White' by the Quaigh Theater," in The New York Times, *July 12, 1979, p. C14.*

Kenneth (Jay) Koch

American Academy and Institute of Arts and Letters: Award of Merit for Poetry

American poet, dramatist, nonfiction writer, scriptwriter, novelist, and librettist.

© 1986 Thomas Victor

In the mid-1950s, Koch and his former Harvard classmates Frank O'Hara and John Ashbery formed what became known as the New York School of Poets. The New York poets shared the avant garde spirit of their contemporaries, the Beats. They also had much in common with Abstract Expressionist painters, including Larry Rivers, whose canvas "George Washington Crossing the Delaware" inspired Koch's comic historical pageant of the same name in 1962. Like his friends Ashbery and O'Hara, Koch applied Abstract Expressionist techniques to writing, often constructing poems as if words were units of form and sound without meaning. He was also greatly influenced by Dada and Surrealism, particularly the work of such early French Surrealists as Guillaume Apollinaire. Koch was not particularly interested in the political or psychoanalytic theories that motivated the original Surrealists; it was Surrealism's surface signatures, particularly its bizarre humor, that appealed to him, and he appropriated these for his own poetic purposes.

Despite the abstract, almost nonsensical quality of much of Koch's New York School-era poetry, represented in *Poems* (1953) and *Thank You and Other Poems* (1962), many critics consider him the most accessible New York poet. Although he has always delighted in extravagant word play, he is never deliberately obscure. Also, he imparts to his writings a keen, antic sense of humor that has been compared to that of Woody Allen and the Marx Brothers (for example, the pun on the pronunciation of his last name: "You're that famous COKE, aren't you, /That no one can drink?"). The poem "Fresh Air," from *Thank You,* may be regarded as Koch's poetic manifesto. In it he ridicules the establishment poets and academic critics of the era ("Oh, to be seventeen years old/Once again . . . and not know that poetry/Is ruled with the sceptre of the dumb, the deaf, and the creepy!"); he then hails his own muse, the breath of creative "fresh air" that will bring new life to poetry. Other poems from this period, notably *Ko; or, A Season on Earth* (1959), a mock-Byronic epic about a Japanese baseball player, reflect Koch's wild, absurdist humor and his skill at parody. Even more intensely than his later work, these poems express the sense of joy and adventure he felt in writing them.

Koch once stated that his goal as a poet is "to discover things, to communicate them, to give pleasure, to create excitement." To this end, Koch tries to maintain reader interest at its highest possible pitch throughout every poem by introducing fresh, startling images with each new phrase. An example of this technique at its most exuberant is *When the Sun Tries to Go On* (written in 1953 but not published until 1960), a disjointed litany of surrealistic images that Koch, at the suggestion of O'Hara, expanded from its original 72-line length for as long as he could sustain it. The completed poem is 2400 lines long and, some critics suggest, is to be admired as a technical feat more than enjoyed as a poem. Although reviewers praise his later collections, including *The Pleasures of Peace and Other Poems* (1969) and *The Art of Love* (1975), they express disappointment that Koch still dallies with parody and nonsense in his verse when he is clearly capable of treating more serious themes. The more recent *The Burning Mystery of Anna in 1951* (1979) and *On the Edge* (1986), while still conscientiously avoiding "seriousness," frequently reveal more heartfelt emotions, as in the poem of lost love "To Marina" in *The Burning Mystery of Anna.* These poems also utilize a simpler, more structured technique than their predecessors. Koch has written extensively for the theater, and many critics believe that his verse dramas, *Bertha* (1959) and *The Red Robins* (1979), feature some of his finest poetic writing.

Koch has made important contributions to poetry as an educator as well as through his own verse. During the late 1960s and early 1970s, he taught experimental poetry-writing classes to elementary public school children in Manhattan. His nonfiction accounts of these highly successful experiences, *Wishes, Lies, and Dreams: Teaching Children to Write Poetry* (1970) and *Rose, Where Did You Get That Red? Teaching Great Poetry to Children* (1973), became standard resources for teachers. Koch wrote about a similar program he conducted for senior citizens in *I Never Told Anybody: Teaching Poetry Writing in a Nursing Home* (1977). Koch's theory of teaching poetry appreciation is distinctly like the goal underlying his own compositions. "The true sign that one is responding to a poem correctly," he explained, "is that one begins to get pleasure from it. After one starts to get pleasure, then one quite naturally wants to understand more."

(See also *CLC*, Vols. 5, 8; *Contemporary Authors*, Vols. 1-4, rev. ed.; *Contemporary Authors New Revision Series*, Vol. 6; and *Dictionary of Literary Biography*, Vol. 5.)

FRANK O'HARA

[*O'Hara, an American poet, critic, and dramatist, was one of the most influential poets of the New York School during the 1950s and early 1960s. His poetry collections include* A City Winter and Other Poems *(1952),* Lunch Poems *(1964), and* The Collected Poems of Frank O'Hara *(1971). From 1952 until his death in 1966, O'Hara worked on the staff of New York's Museum of Modern Art; deeply influenced by the contemporary Abstract Expressionist movement in the visual arts, he collaborated with several artists to create "poem paintings." In the following excerpt, originally published in* Poetry *magazine, O'Hara defends his friend and fellow New York School poet Koch, responding to Harry Roskolenko's negative review of Koch's* Poems *in a previous issue of* Poetry. *For Roskolenko's reply to O'Hara and O'Hara's counter-rebuttal, see excerpts below.*]

> Mr. Koch, it seems, has a rare combination of words rattling about in his skull, but it is difficult to call any of his word combinations the bric-a-brac of poetry.
>
> —Harry Roskolenko, *Poetry,* July 1954

It is amusing to think of the number of gifted (even great!) poets my epigraph applies to. Though I am in total disagreement with the rest of Mr. Roskolenko's review of ***Poems*** by Kenneth Koch . . . , he has hit on something here; these very original poems have little to do with the restful and pleasant bric-a-brac he seems to prefer (he recommends the satire of another poet [Geoffrey Parsons], finally, on the grounds that "no one will be actually offended").

Mr. Koch's poems have a natural voice, they are quick, alert, instinctive and, within the limited scope of this first volume, indicate a potentially impressive variety. His technique is opposed to that Academic and often turgid development by which many young poets gain praise for their "achievement," an achievement limited usually to the mastery of one phase of Yeats (and usually the last). This is not to say that these poems do not have their precedents, but Mr. Koch intends to "make it new"—

> Once again I find the charge accounts
> And remedies not enough. You have borrowed my gas
> range,
> And the steep prunes of my kiss
> Must leave you within the graceless forest
> Garbage garage charm-account.

Mr. Roskolenko writes, "He is precious and puerile when he is not merely futile and noisy. . ."; but there is another way of reading the work. Poetry in our time may be distinguished without being frozen. I find Koch close to the light sensuality of the Cavalier poets; there is a debt, too, to those catalogues of Whitman in which the poet warmly embraces the vulgar and inanimate objects of everyday life and to the syntactical abbreviations in early Auden. Most prominent as an influence is the verbal playfulness and irony we find in recent French poets like Raymond Roussel, Benjamin Péret, Henri Michaux, Raymond Queneau (the latter's infatuation with American oddities of custom and terminology finds a native echo in this book) as well as in our own Theodore Roethke. Is

> We drank the iced tea, then
> Moved our ship slowly out to sea
> While the Infant was blasting the rose,
> O love was the engine.

or

> Ah, she was a tall, slim girl
> Not made for either office-work or repose.

precious in a pejorative sense? I think not. Not the least function of poetry is to make vivid our sense of the meaning of words. He tends to enlarge where others narrow down. Words need not be purified until the tribe has sullied them; after two generations of continual washing it is a wonder words have any color left. I do not wish to make false claims for Mr. Koch: he will undoubtedly not, from the indications of this volume, write a Gray's *Elegy*. He has the other poetic gift: vivacity and go, originality of perception and intoxication with life. Most important of all, he is not *dull*. (pp. 349-50)

Frank O'Hara, "Another Word on Kenneth Koch," in Poetry, *Vol. LXXXV, No. 6, March, 1955, pp. 349-51.*

HARRY ROSKOLENKO

[*Roskolenko was an American poet, travel writer, autobiographer, novelist, editor, and journalist. His poetry collections include* Sequence on Violence *(1938),* Notes from a Journey and Other Poems *(1946), and* A Third Summary *(1978). In the following excerpt Roskolenko provides the third installment of his debate with poet Frank O'Hara (see excerpt above) in* Poetry *magazine over Roskolenko's negative review of Koch's* Poems. *Roskolenko reasserts and expands on his original statement that Koch's poetry is precious, puerile, and lazy. The editors of* Poetry *declined to publish O'Hara's response to Roskolenko's second essay, as they felt they had "hit just the right pitch of interest." However, O'Hara's counter-rebuttal was published in 1975 in* Frank O'Hara: Standing Still and Walking in New York, *edited by Donald Allen (see excerpt below).*]

Mr. Frank O'Hara stoops to a variety of literary follies with his special pleading in the March 1955 issue of *Poetry*. The salient point of my review of Kenneth Koch's poetry [in ***Poems***] was: Mr. Koch writes lazy verse and is precious and puerile. Mr. O'Hara's argument contains irrelevant material, erroneous qualifications, and a critical method that dissolves the real value of the thing under discussion: is Mr. Koch's poetry valid or is it childish?

It is childish to me, but apparently it is not to Mr. O'Hara, which should settle the matters of taste. There are many ways of cooking a goose, but you must use fire, said a famous Buddhist chef—and I cook to my taste. For that matter, there are many ways of looking at a poem, and I've searched Mr. Koch's first book from all angles. I looked for newness, verbal excitement, inventive imagery, tension, and significant detail, but none of these elements were present. I found the book tasteless, futile, noisy and *dull*.

Mr. O'Hara then catalogues the alleged literary merits and the varieties of Mr. Koch's kind of poetry, suggesting that his work is close to "the light sensuality of the Cavalier poets." God wot! And since this is hardly modest praise, he further insists that Mr. Koch's literary influences align him with Raymond Roussel, Benjamin Péret, Henri Michaux (what astounding gall!) as well as to Whitman and Auden, but not to Mr. Gray of the *Elegy*. Poor, poor Mr. Gray! How sad to be left out of this choice group of Mr. Koch's extraordinary, though invisible influences.

But poetry is still a matter of private taste. And for those who think I am being severe, I shall quote enough of Mr. Koch's poetry to illustrate the reverse of Mr. O'Hara's curious contention. Does the following, Mr. O'Hara, contain the combined influences of Whitman, Auden, Péret, Roussel and Michaux? From **"Where Am I Kenneth?"** —

Nail Kenneth down
For I fear the crying bloomers
Of a gnome race
They come yessing among the trees
Like your Boston survivor
Nail Kenneth down

Beyond the costly mountains
Some pills are going to sleep
Frank will cover them with binding bloomers
Janice appears from multiple nowhere
The sun was a hot disk
How do you spell "dish"?

Children often work up verbal nonsense, but it's still infantilism, no matter whether you call it avant-garde or rearguard. For another example of Mr. Koch's varieties and virtues, so touchingly attested to by Mr. O'Hara, we read the following, in **"The Lanterns"**:

Dear memory, are you sure I said "bus,"
Looking out the parlor window when in the dust
The large vehicle shifted through Cincinnati?
For man how can the child be a real bust?
He has been exempted by his lack of a bust
From the symphony of birth. This is called St. Louis.

O motions! and when St. Louis receives the bus,
And she, with her bust, descends into the dust
From that physical bust, I will grow cold, Cincinnati.

And this, Mr. O'Hara, is Whitman, Auden, Péret, Roussel, and the Cavalier poets, as combined, in one fell radiation, in Mr. Kenneth Koch?

Take over, Dr. Jung and Dr. Freud! (pp. 177-78)

Harry Roskolenko, "On Kenneth Koch Again: A Rebuttal," in Poetry, *Vol. LXXXVI, No. 3, June, 1955, pp. 177-78.*

STEPHEN KOCH

The poems in Kenneth Koch's ***Thank You and Other Poems*** . . . create a world of surreal wit, a kind of word-playground, the component parts of which are always pleasant and tasty, filled with sunlight and color, with circuses, red shimmering fish, farmyards sprinkled with yellow straw and violets, with green oceans and chugging, rusty ships. (Koch's poems are drenched in the characteristic colors of Matisse, bright, unshaded, and primary.) All of his work is theatrical, and theater has led him to write some delicious little dadaistic farces collected in ***Bertha and Other Plays***.

Though he is sometimes insufferably silly, Koch is also a wit—perhaps the most polished wit writing in English, working in the discontinuous, unexpected rhythms of the Marx Brothers. The macabre is very strong in his work, but it is never even remotely depressing. On the contrary, Koch's convulsive catastrophes erupt in technicolor, but harmlessly. . . .

The most noticeable fact about Koch's work is that it is never, absolutely never, about real pain. The breezy, echoing absence of any appeal to human suffering and its dignity makes his work unique in contemporary poetry, both in and out of the New York School. (p. 5)

Stephen Koch, "The New York School of Poets: The Serious at Play," in The New York Times Book Review, *February 11, 1968, pp. 4-5.*

REED WHITTEMORE

[*An influential American poet, editor, critic, essayist, biographer, and short story writer, Whittemore is admired for the free, flowing style of his poetry. He received the Award of Merit Medal from the American Academy of Arts and Letters for his poetry in 1970 and is poet laureate of Maryland. His poetry collections include* Heroes and Heroines *(1946),* The Boy from Iowa *(1962), and* Fifty Poems Fifty *(1970). Among his other publications are* William Carlos Williams: Poet from Jersey *(1975) and* Poets and Anthologists *(1986). In the following excerpt Whittemore gives guarded praise to Koch's* The Pleasures of Peace, *expressing his wish that Koch might use his poetic gifts on less frivolous projects.*]

Some poets, some very good poets, like to stand on edges.

Wordsworth was always on the edge of bathos, and frequently fell over. Whitman was always about to lose his tonsils, and I can't say for sure that he didn't. What was Shakespeare in danger of?—Nothing maybe, unless he was in danger of being the writers he stole his plays from.

Kenneth Koch is always on the edge of nonsense or frivolity, or of a bottomless pit of images, fancies, words.

Take his well known early poem **"Fresh Air"**—it is a marvelous "fit" (as in Lewis Carroll) on the sad state of divine poesy. In it the edge he teeters on is between mock and serious, or perhaps between rational statement and yawp. The poem is a dramatic display of supermanner, with Koch trying to see how extravagantly he can gesture without dislocating his elbow.

The new book, ***The Pleasures of Peace,*** is an even more extravagant version of the same game, with gesture or manner displacing statement or content as thoroughly as Koch can manage. **"Fresh Air"** was, though tenuously, reduceable to some freshman's miserable precis—"Mr. Koch disapproves of the sterility of academic poetry and criticism"—but many of the new poems are further out. Does anybody want to interpret "O Labrador, you are the sexual Pennsylvania of our times"?

Better not try. These are anti-interpretation days. The oracle, Susan Sontag, has advised us to cultivate an erotics rather than a hermeneutics of art, and surely Koch's latest poems, like Ashbery's and many lesser gamesmen's, suggest that he agrees.

His poems may be compared musically with a long jam session (oh ancient phrase) on "Ain't She Sweet" or, more tonily, with Beethoven's "Diabelli Variations," where the original waltz is merely the departure point for the concert. Koch is a master of such music. He is marvelously various and inventive. He can play the names of the forty-eight states (he hasn't got to fifty yet) as if they were the complete works of Beethoven, and do the same with sounds, faces, islands, with the phrase "sleeping with women," with erotic proper names, in short anything he finds worthy of gaming with.

Sometimes he adds a harebrained plot, as in the poem **"Scales,"** where he follows a singer's laborious ascent of Do-Re-Mi three times, and the descent once, and then has her reach too low, hemorrhage on Fa and die.

Funny. Clever. The curse of the game. When the poems fall over the edge they are last-days-of-the-empire stuff. The reader wants to put Koch to work in a salt mine.

There are good ponderous reasons why saying something gets harder and harder in poetry, among which is the big reason that everything has been said and is being said badly and constantly. We're awash in statement. "What oft was said but ne'er so well expressed . . ." is a joke of poetic policy when practically every "what" a poet can think of has been said so oft that it has achieved the vigor of "Ain't She Sweet" before he gets to it. At least that seems to be Koch's position on truths in poetry: they are dead ducks in this age of truth over-kill, unless you treat them *as* dead, in which case the deader the better.

The title poem, my favorite, takes that deadest of ducks, peace, and improvises around it. Koch presents himself as writing a poem for peace in competition with one Giorgio *Finogle* who is also doing one. Giorgio throws himself out a window for peace, which slows up his poem. Koch keeps on, meanwhile making love for peace and parodying solemn statements of lovers.

He finishes his poem and then gives us samples—for the poem still goes on—of the reviews of it: "Great, man!" "Dead, man!" "I will expect you at six!" Meanwhile, back at the world, monkeys and boats and "all the really important mountains" are for peace, and we emerge sweaty, after 16 pages, with our freshman paraphrase: Nothing is more futile than being for peace.

Over the edge? I don't know, but I think so. I had hoped something other than the usual manner would be displayed in the poem, for the poem is in part a complaint against the manner, a complaint against the wild and futile gesticulations of pacifists. I was looking for Koch to come clean, speak straight from the shoulder about peace, about anything. He didn't, and rightly or wrongly I was disappointed. The poem is so good I would have liked it to have been serious too.

Where is the future of the mode? For the unsubtle imitators of Koch—and there seem to be a lot—the future is over the edge into dada, mockery of mockery, absolute non-statement. But for Koch the future is unclear because he obviously has the capacity, if not the inclination, to be thoroughly rationalist in his verse, and to play a number of other roles than those he chooses.

Since I like Koch but don't like the nonsense world that much of his poetry edges toward, my inclination is to pray for him to come back from the edge. I'm dubious of the results of the prayer, though. Koch might reply by writing a poem about it:

They are praying for me in
Andalusia—or is it
the bathroom?
They are praying and I hear them,
The worms,
They are perfecting me into a
service station.

Reed Whittemore, in a review of "The Pleasures of Peace," in The New Republic, *Vol. 161, No. 5, August 2, 1969, p. 23.*

DAVID LEHMAN

[*Lehman, an American poet, editor, and critic, is author of the poetry collections* Some Nerve *(1973) and* Day One *(1979). A frequent contributor of poetry and criticism to periodicals, including the* Partisan Review *and* Times Literary Supplement, *he served as an editor of* Poetry in Motion, New York Arts Journal, *and other magazines; he was also founding editor of Nobadaddy Press. Lehman cites the New York School poets Frank O'Hara, John Ashbery, and Koch as influences on his own poetry. In the following excerpt he praises Koch's long poem* When the Sun Tries to Go On *for its unpredictable, exuberant wordplay.*]

I think it was T. S. Eliot who remarked, 'It is a characteristic of great modern poetry that you can enjoy it before you understand it.' I think of this observation when reading Kenneth Koch's long poem, ***When the Sun Tries To Go On***. . . . I don't pretend to "understand" the poem; it defies conventional criticism and analysis, it is "Against Interpretation". The important thing is that the poem works. It's a completely self-enclosed world of language, where syntax and content are subordinated to the independent existence of the words themselves—where Mallarmé and Rimbaud resisted the fact of logocentrism, Koch and John Ashbery seem to accept it head on—words leading unpredictably yet ineluctably to other words, like an express train of exuberant sounds.

Sometimes it is the lining that creates a neat surprise, changing the apparent direction of the words:

Sleep
Walked carfare by the sea. A boat "pelvised"
Germany, it was so green. "Oh, then,
Can't we marry velvet?" screamed Jimmy.

More often, this disjunctive effect occurs within a line:

O cross
Head of the pennies' infant rubber sweet
Unglazed pyramidal announcing shaggy deserted melodies
Of "Kismet!"

In a kind of Flaubertian encyclopedia of the folly he loves in the world, Koch animates not only objects and places ("quiet orange Egypt") but words ("Wear out Sue, and who is she, wear 'Am I?'"). We are made to feel the exclamation-point exhilaration and celebration of the quotidian in, for example, Americana:

A
Garden momentarily films George Montgomery and
Ina Claire, monosyllabic, clue of the red ragweeds.
O now I know you! ape, red panic-car, Kismet

Of diseased, ant, hill, roadhouses, school-pigeon
Of the tippy as rainwater motorcar! Clark Gable and
  Ginger
Rogers fall beneath the wheels of this motorcar
Of cheeping staff officers.

For Koch, words are the equalizers of all things. Like a de Kooning painting, there is a pure aesthetic to the poem: the poet takes a great deal of delight in the sounds of words and his consciousness of them; he splashes them like paint on a page with enthusiastic puns, internal rhymes, titles of books, names of friends (''So/Mary Janice silvery palace Edgar Poe/ Fin giant, boat, chase, America'') and seems surprised as we are at the often witty outcome, ''like a boat/Filled with silliness''. . . . (pp. 401-02)

I know that the dissociation of language in ***When the Sun Tries To Go On*** may put off many readers. It's a poem that is perhaps most profitably read by a poet, and then read aloud. It may perhaps be a bit too long. But it's a poem that grows on you and continually astonishes you once you've entered its boundaries. (p. 403)

David Lehman, '''When the Sun Tries to Go On','' in Poetry, *Vol. CXIV, No. 6, September, 1969, pp. 401-09.*

PAUL CARROLL

[*Carroll is an American poet, editor, and critic. Among his poetry collections are* The Poem in Its Skin *(1968) and* The Luke Poems *(1971). In the following excerpt Carroll reviews Koch's collection* The Pleasures of Peace, *praising Koch's skill in capturing the excitement of poetic creativity.*]

With his ceaselessly merry spirits, irrepressible, outrageous wit, and appetite for sacrilege at the expense of such sacrosanct items as The-Poem-as-Highly-Wrought-Urn, Kenneth Koch is the Buck Mulligan of contemporary American poetry. Any workable definition of what our poetry has accomplished during the past few decades must draw on such poems as **''Thank You,'' ''Taking a Walk with You,'' ''The Artist,'' ''Lunch,'' ''You Were Wearing,''** and **''Fresh Air''**; as well as **''Sleeping with Women,'' ''Some South American Poets,'' ''Faces,''** and **''The Pleasures of Peace''.**

All poems may indeed be about poetry, as one of the commonplaces of our criticism maintains. Certainly Mr. Koch's most successful pieces are about nothing less. Each is, in fact, a variation on the one theme: the celebration of the power and the glory and the comedy of the poetic imagination. ''Excitement-prone Kenneth Koch'' was how his friend Frank O'Hara described him; and in his more frenzied, at times inspired celebrations—this applies especially to the poems in ***The Pleasures of Peace,*** his best book—he is also our Ion. Whereas the rhapsode from Ephesus celebrated the epics and hymns of Homer, Mr. Koch celebrates that splendid faculty with which men make poetry. His poems embody the poetic imagination as it rejoices in the ebullience of its health and freedom, its fecundity, its capacity for endless invention, its dear, outlandish ability to transform everyday, pragmatic reality into an Oz or a tea-party at the March Hare's house, its potency in, possibly, achieving a bit of immortality as a result of having brought forth some children of the soul.

One of Mr. Koch's most handsome features, in fact, is his apparent ability to make poetry out of anything and everything, even the most unpromising material. Nothing that exists seems unsuitable as grist for his mill. Musical scales, pennies, Snow White, Zanesville, Ohio, oblongs, the face of Calvin Coolidge, such pleasures of peace as cucumbers, the ginger from Australia, Gypsy Rose Lee, a star-shaped muffin, John L. Lewis, and ''evenings without any cucumbers''—all are strewn, higgledy-piggledy, through the pages of his book. His perpetual celebration of the imagination caught in the act of creating poetry is so invariant, in truth, that sometimes one feels that Poem X could just as well have three pages from Poem Y in the middle of it—or vice versa.

On the whole, I try to steer clear of such rarefied Alexandrian concepts as The Poem as Erased Poem; but Mr. Koch creates an environment in his books (and especially in the one under review here) in which such events as an erased poem or one composed of pieces of the reader's memory and desire can exist next to ''finished'' works of art—or in which a poem which never existed in the first place may be called into existence: e.g., three quotations from poems from ''the middle period'' (1932-1943) of ''Batorje'' occur in the middle of the long, goofy poem **''Some South American Poets.''**

''The Pleasures of Peace'' is a lengthy, consistently funny picaresque piece about writing a poem about the pleasures of peace and, by so doing, competing with another poet named Giorgio Finogle who is attempting much the same. Here's a sample of the poem's vitality: the ''A Day at the Races'' garland of blurbs from reviews and essays, laced with a nosegay from an admirer here, a brickbat from a detractor there, which occurs towards the end of **''The Pleasures of Peace'':**

''A wonder!'' ''A rout!'' ''No need for any further
  poems!'' ''A Banzai for peace!'' ''He can speak for
  us all!''
And ''Great, man!'' ''Impressive!'' ''Something new
  for you, Ken!'' ''Astounding!'' ''A real
Epic!'' ''The worst poem I have ever read!''
  ''Abominable, tasteless!'' ''Too funny!'' ''Dead,
  man!
A cop out! a real white man's poem! a folderol of
  honkie blank spitzenburger smugglerout Caucasian
  gyp
Of phony bourgeois peace poetry, a total shrig!''
  ''Terrific!'' ''I will expect you at six!''
''A lovely starry catalogue for peace!'' ''Is it
  Shakespeare or Byron who breathes
In the lines of this poem?'' ''You have given us the
  Pleasures of Peace,
Now where is the real thing?'' ''Koch has studied his
  history!'' ''Bold!'' ''Stunning!'' ''It touches us like
  leaves
Sparkling in April—but is that all there is
To his peace plea?''

In poems such as this or **''Ma Provence,''** one often senses that the poet is growing impatient to end, break away, abandon his poem, in order to get on to the next work—that is, to recapture in some new poem the intensity, the special excitement available at the origin of writing a poem, the rush of energy one can feel when the poem begins to lead into fresh, mysterious country. This might account for the fact that at times Mr. Koch's verse seems so awkward, even poorly written, adolescent despite its engaging sophistication, and often tuneless, little more than rough notes for a poem chopped into totally arbitrary lines, stanzas, and sections. But bad writing in his case turns out to be a kind of virtue. It offers the reader not the traditional, well-tailored work, but the fabric of the poem in its original state, and one can feel the needle as it begins to sew, as it were, the scissors as they begin to cut and shape. In short, Kenneth Koch offers poems which embody those precious moments: the first moments of conception and creation.

One should also be prepared to endure the curious, arid desert of feeling which exists throughout this book. Mr. Koch's chronic inability to entertain "serious" or "profound" or "relevant" experience for more than the most elusive second will also put off some readers who will probably be tempted to dismiss him as trivial or even flitty. Such criticism misses the point, as far as I'm concerned. Hundreds of good poets are writing about feelings; a handful are creating decent work about our times and this country. In his celebration of the excitement of the imagination as it begins to create, there is only one Kenneth Koch. (pp. 104-06)

Paul Carroll, "Rhapsode from Cinci," in Poetry, *Vol. CXIX, No. 2, November, 1972, pp. 104-06.*

FRANK O'HARA

[In the following excerpt O'Hara offers his final comments in his debate with critic Harry Roskolenko (see excerpts above) over Koch's Poems.*]*

Since I do not believe that "poetry is still a matter of private taste" but rather one of public responsibility, I am dissatisfied with Mr. Roskolenko's rebuttal to my remarks on Kenneth Koch's ***Poems,*** *Poetry* June 1955 [see excerpt above]. The main point against what he calls my "variety of literary follies" seems to be that Mr. Koch could not possibly be influenced by the poets I name because he is not, in his first book, superior to any or all of them, "in one fell radiation."

Who ever said he was? I do not read in the rebuttal any perception of qualities in the influences I claim which would make them antithetical to Mr. Koch's work, on the other hand. Where in his original writing about the book he misrepresented the poems, he now proceeds to misrepresent me and by the way several poets I had the temerity to mention. "What gall" indeed. As an instance, I said nothing about Whitman or Auden in general, but about the catalogues in one and the syntactical abbreviations in the other, both of which Mr. Koch does just happen to resemble in several of his poems. I qualified other influences, too, and certainly was not computing the relative statures of any poets cited. If a little anthology of what Mr. Koch's work resembles would be helpful, it can be easily drawn from these poets. I was thinking of specific poems and devices in them.

But the important issue, I think, is not that Mr. Roskolenko dislikes Mr. Koch's work, but that the principles he so dearly guards in doing it are stultifying and arbitrary. Poems are not mature, nor are they childish. I do not believe that analogies to cooking help much, either. Poetry is experience, often peculiar to the poet. The formal values to which, for convenience and expediency, we attempt to ascribe the qualities we admire in a poem are, after all, no more than conveniences. It should be understood that they are signs for the qualities, not absolute rules by which the work is judged. They have nothing to do with the poem ultimately, they are only the language in which we have fallen into the habit of discussing it, they have to do with us. My idea in writing about Mr. Koch's poems was that this language seemed to have gotten into the way of the work: Mr. Roskolenko's review was suddenly talking about childishness and maturity and responsibility. This was a disservice to poetry.

An example of what I mean is the 2nd paragraph of his rebuttal. Since when have poems been cooked of "verbal excitement," "significant detail," "tension," "inventive imagery"? You may find qualities in a poem and discuss them in these clichés, but a great poem can exist without a single one of them no matter how many "angles" you look at it from (an interesting exercise, by the way).

Again, if a poem exists, what difference does it make how old its poet is? The whole conundrum about children's art is completely passé—in the other arts Satie, Dubuffet and many others have accepted spontaneity and freedom from formalistic constraints to their benefit, basing their works in some cases on children's drawings, the work of the insane and aural or visual accidents. The public is far from lax in appreciating the special qualities this liberation has permitted, but apparently news is slow to reach Mr. Roskolenko. Infantilism has many forms.

Finally, I have read and reread the excerpts from Mr. Koch's book that Mr. Roskolenko quotes to confound me and I find my initial enthusiasm for them not a whit dimmed by the god wots that surround them. (pp. 62-3)

Frank O'Hara, "On and On about Kenneth Koch: A Counter-Rebuttal," in his Standing Still and Walking in New York, *edited by Donald Allen, Grey Fox Press, 1975, pp. 62-3.*

CONRAD HILBERRY

Kenneth Koch's ***The Art of Love*** is made up of seven verse essays (on Beauty, on the Art of Poetry, on the Art of Love, etc.), giving advice as though to an apprentice in one of those mysteries. Its long, prosy lines are easy to understand, but running all through them is a self-consciousness that is almost guaranteed to prevent shared simplicity. "The days of Allegory are over. The Days of Irony are here," Koch says in a poem called **"Some General Instructions."** In this book, irony is everywhere, residing especially in abrupt, half-comic shifts from one subject to another or from one voice to another. The tone is slippery, taking back with one hand what it gives with the other:

The problem of being good and also doing what one wishes
Is not as difficult as it seems. It is, however,
Best to get embarked early on one's dearest desires.
Be attentive to your dreams. They are usually about sex,
But they deal with other things as well in an indirect fashion
And contain information that you should have.
You should also read poetry. Do not eat too many bananas.
In the springtime, plant. In the autumn, harvest.
In the summer and winter, exercise. Do not put
Your finger inside a clam shell or
It may be snapped off by the living clam. Do not wear a shirt
More than two times without sending it to the laundry.

It is as if Koch is afraid, for a minute, that we might think he meant it. Alarmed at that possibility, he ducks away and reappears, grinning, out of the laundry.

The book parodies every advice-giving document you have ever read: *Ecclesiastes,* in the passage above; Ovid; the *Kama Sutra;* James Thurber; the table of contents of a women's magazine ("What to do during a Sex Emergency," "What are eighteen totally unsuspected enemies of love?"). Koch has a wonderfully accurate ear, and this pastiche of parody provides surprise and pleasure. But the pleasure is not as lasting as it might be, I believe, because of the tone. By mimicking one voice and then another, Koch declines to take responsibility for anything that is said—or he takes responsibility only for truisms that no one is likely to dispute ("It is true that good poetry is difficult to write") and even he puts them in such a way that we know he knows they are truisms, so he cannot be charged with naivete. He protects his own sophistication but at the expense of emotional force.

Before I sound ungrateful, let me say that the title poem, **"The Art of Love,"** maintains an exuberant energy that is somehow appropriate to the subject—which, of course, is not the art of love but the art of attracting and enjoying women. The range of tone, from affectionate to mock-sadistic, from prudent to goofy, reflects the strange variety of feelings we have about the erotic. I find in this poem more emotional drive than in the others, more tenderness even, a sense of the excitement of the encounter and the comedy and chanciness of it:

Of all compliments there
Are two kinds: those which show desire, and those
  which do not. "You look Etruscan!"
Is it a good example of the compliment without desire
(Apparently) and "You look so delicious I want to bite
  you! My God, you drive me
Crazy!" is an example of the other kind. In the one
  case the woman is left with
A high historic feeling and feeling her beauty is
  somehow eternal,
That she shares in an eternally beautiful type
Away from the sphere of our sorrow, and thus that her
  life must somehow mean something
And she be an achievement of some marvelous kind
  (which she is), and the other, more
Earthy-seeming compliment makes her feel a happy
  object of desire,
The source of fervid feelings in others, a sort of
  springtide or passage of time,
Or else a Venus, or else a sunrise, or sunset, the cause
  of sleepless evenings and gasps.

The passage begins by parodying Aristotle, let's say, or any writer in love with categories. But the parody comes in glancingly, not distracting attention from the compliments and the women. The tone, instead of dropping suddenly to call in doubt everything that has been said, maintains a poise. When the language becomes extravagant, as in "away from the sphere of our sorrow," the extravagance is delicate enough so that it does not destroy the affection. When the sentence moves from "Venus" to "gasps," we cannot mistake the comedy in this complimentary art and yet we feel the art can carry genuine admiration.

In spite of the pleasures of this poem, the book's overall impression is one of self-protection. Koch is a remarkable writer, and we know from ***Wishes, Lies, and Dreams*** and from ***Rose, Where Did You Get That Red*** that he can recognize and respect the flow of emotion and deeply conceived images in poems by grade school children and by great poets. People write what they can write, but if Koch could take the chance of appearing naked of irony, of writing something as unprotected as *Song of Myself* or "The Tyger" (both of which he uses to teach children), he might speak movingly to as many readers as he has touched through ***Wishes*** and ***Rose.*** As it is, his poems, like pop art, present great simplicity but maintain so much ironic distance that they make the ordinary reader uneasy. We can't be sure whether the artist is admiring or mocking the three-way plug or the Brillo box. This sophistication is much further from the ordinary person than straight-forward difficulty would be. A college student or lawyer can look at Brancusi more easily than Oldenburg, can read Yeats or Kinnell more confidently than Koch. He suspects that Koch and Oldenburg may be laughing at him behind their hands. (pp. 88-90)

Conrad Hilberry, "Simple Poems," in Shenandoah, *Vol. XXIX, No. 3, Spring, 1978, pp. 87-97.*

JOHN VERNON

[Vernon, an American critic and poet, is the author of The Garden and the Map: Schizophrenia in Twentieth-Century Literature and Culture *(1973),* Memory and Fiction *(1984), and the poetry collection* Ann *(1976). In the following excerpt Vernon reflects on the stages of Koch's development as a poet, beginning with the playful surrealism of his early poem "Fresh Air."]*

[Suppose] you are Kenneth Koch in 1955, thumbing through an issue of the *Hudson Review* at the New York Public Library, and you find yourself practically gagging for the lack of fresh air. The metaphor is so obvious and simple and true as to be, well, fresh—and funny as well:

Blue air, fresh air, come in, I welcome you, you are an
  art student,
Take off your cap and gown and sit down on the chair.
Together we shall paint the poets—but no, air! perhaps
  you should go to them, quickly,
Give them a little inspiration, they need it, perhaps they
  are out of breath,
Give them a little inhuman company before they freeze
  the English language to death!
(And rust their typewriters a little, be sea air! be
  noxious! kill them, if you must, but stop their poetry!
I remember I saw you dancing on the surf on the Côte
  d'Azur
And I stopped, taking my hat off, but you did not
  remember me,
Then afterwards, you came to my room bearing a
  handful of orange flowers
And we were together all through the summer night!)

This poem, **"Fresh Air,"** is still one of Koch's best and most lasting. The almost helpless and naively angry voice with its nervous, sudden outbursts, crazy rhapsodic asides, and, above all, its willingness to be silly—something Koch, I think, gradually lost as his humor became more confident, and his reputation more established—this voice was something American poetry had been without since Kenneth Fearing. The opening section of the poem, in fact, is a kind of homage to Fearing's "End of the Seer's Convention." . . . Not only is [the opening section] funny; it is also, of course, the very fresh air Koch was calling for. Whatever we think of poets like Corso and Koch today, we have to admit that American poetry hasn't been the same since. They—and others, like Ginsberg, Ferlinghetti, O'Hara, Olsen, Duncan, Spicer, and Creeley—introduced a new freedom into the very language of poetry, into the substance of that language. Poets like Lowell, Berryman,

Plath, Merwin, Bly, and many others not associated with the Beats all underwent radical transformations in their styles in the fifties and sixties, not necessarily in imitation of the Beats, but simply because the atmosphere around them was so electrically charged with change.

Koch's later work has moved more toward a kind of playful, pure surrealism, prosaic like **"Fresh Air,"** but usually eschewing both the direct statement and the wonderful silliness of that poem. Like most poets of the New York school, he often spices his poems with references to pop culture, deliberate clichés, archaisms, or both academic and romantic phrases and words, all for their campy, ironic effect. These devices were first used by Frank O'Hara—to whom Koch and Ashbery owe so much—and by now, ten years after his death, have become somewhat stale through overuse. The resulting campy surrealism sounds the same no matter who is writing it. . . . The most curious and interesting aspect of this kind of poetry is that the humor derives from attacking or undermining most of our fundamental notions about poetry and poetic language. If poetic language is concentrated, heightened, symbolic, and musical, then poetry becomes humorous by being flat, prosaic, and deliberately clumsy, the latter device learned from, of all people, Ogden Nash. In fact, Koch's rhythms—especially the deliberate effect of having too many words on a line—are strongly related to Nash's. (pp. 312-15)

John Vernon, "Fresh Air: Humor in Contemporary American Poetry," in Comic Relief: Humor in Contemporary American Literature, *edited by Sarah Blacher Cohen, University of Illinois Press, 1978, pp. 304-23.*

DENIS DONOGHUE

[Donoghue is an Irish literary critic and scholar and a professor of English and American literature. In addition to writing and editing several works of criticism, including two books about William Butler Yeats and Seven American Poets from MacLeish to Nemerov: An Introduction *(1975), Donoghue has contributed articles to* Hudson Review, Sewanee Review, *and other American and British journals. In the following excerpt Donoghue praises Koch's* The Burning Mystery of Anna in 1951, *observing that Koch's method of exploring themes in his poetry is "revery, rather than argument or summary."]*

In ***The Art of Love*** (1975) Kenneth Koch said that some poets like to save up for their poems, others like to spend incessantly what they have. Spendthrift is better than thrift, according to Koch, because the pocket is bottomless, "your feelings are changing every instant," and the available combinations of language are endless. In practice, as in the practice of ***The Art of Love,*** the big spenders write on the assumption that if you shoot a lot of lines, some of them are bound to hit the mark. If you feel inclined to out-Byron the Byron of *Don Juan,* you can write a long poem like Koch's ***The Duplications*** (1977), keeping the stanzas going with a little plot and a lot of virtuosity, rhyming Hellas with fellas, and so forth.

Virtuosity takes verve. Koch's poems are attractive not because they draw us into the charming circle of their rhetoric but because they "so serenely disdain" to edify us: they maintain power by rarely choosing to exert it. When they fail to be attractive, it is not because they take themselves too seriously but because they presume upon their grace and leave it compromised.

The Burning Mystery of Anna in 1951 is a new collection of ten fairly long poems, written in a loping, phrasal style, casual in its connectives if careful enough in its general direction. The poems have sturdy themes (anxiety; light and shadow; love; loss), but the themes are not taken as if they stood waiting to be glossed, explored, and understood. They are not even means to an end: rather, means of discovery, pursued not in the hope that they will lead to an end but that they will postpone every proffered end, endlessly. In **"The Language of Shadows"** Koch writes that

> . . . Everything's
> extinguished in desire
> In fact and action

and he wants to fend off extinction by postponing fact and action, lest desire, too, die. The method is revery rather than argument or summary. It is what Wallace Stevens meant by "the hum of thoughts evaded in the mind"; evaded, presumably, so that thinking may persist.

Not themes, then, but talk, an aesthetic of talk, as in ***The Art of Love*** and one of the new poems, **"The Problem of Anxiety,"** where desultoriness gives the poet's mind room to move and whatever time it needs to say something helpful to somebody. Nearly any theme will do. "One sidewalk leads everywhere, you don't have to be in Estapan." Koch likes to come upon things when they are just about to happen; like water about to boil, the telephone about to ring, Sarajevo an hour before the event. More interested in Sarajevo than in its cause, he likes to pick up a theme the first moment it becomes available and give it an unofficial future according to his revery.

The risk is that revery becomes whim or some other form of self-indulgence. Koch is not immune to this vanity. Like nearly every other poet of the so-called New York School, he has produced yet again the usual garrulous dribble about what it was like, back in 1951, to rap with Frank and Larry and John and Jane on West 10th Street. . . . James said we must concede to the artist his *donnée,* and so we must, but this particular *donnée* has been done to a self-regarding turn so often that I hope it has now been done to death.

The superb poems in ***The Burning Mystery of Anna in 1951*** are **"In the Morning," "The Boiling Water,"** and **"To Marina,"** each not only good but virtuous in the sense described in ***The Art of Love*** as

> excellence which does not harm
> The material but ennobles and refines it.

"To Marina" ends the book, heartbreakingly, and tells why the kissing had to stop and why the love could not stop. The aesthetic of talk hates to stop talking, but sometimes it must, and **"To Marina"** is a love poem desolate in its conclusion. . . . **"In the Morning"** and **"The Boiling Water"** are nearly as good, nearly as virtuous with the civility of good talk, but they do not bring one, as **"To Marina"** does, close to tears. (p. 49)

Denis Donoghue, "New York Poets," in The New York Review of Books, *Vol. XXVII, No. 13, August 14, 1980, pp. 49-50.*

ROBERTA BERKE

[Berke, an American poet and critic, is the author of the poetry collection Sphere of Light *(1972) and the critical study* Bounds out of Bounds: A Compass for Recent American and British Poetry *(1981). In the following excerpt from* Bounds out of Bounds, *Berke*

discusses Koch's connections with the Surrealists and the New York School poets.]

[Although the New York Poets] share an urban environment, each is so distinct that many people (including some of the New York poets) question whether they can be regarded as a group at all. Yet they are friends and collaborators, are frequently published in the same magazines and have left a collective mark on a second generation. In addition to this (and New York City) these poets share three common ideas which shaped their work.

The first of these concepts in Surrealism. As we have seen, younger poets in the fifties were confronted by the paramount influence of Eliot and the New Critics. The academic poets accepted this and wrote in forms and about subjects which could be understood within the limits set by the New Critics. Fortified by Olson's theory of Projective Verse, the Black Mountain poets attempted to write "open verse." The Beat poets rebelled not only against the New Critics, but against criticism itself, and their life-style and poetry were bohemian and neo-Romantic. The Extremist poets wrote about emotional states that had been off-limits for the genteel academic poets. The New York poets also rejected establishment literary criticism; but instead they applied certain canons of *art* criticism to their poetry. Most of these poets earned their livings as art critics, which meant that (despite occasional lip-service paid to Surrealist anti-art and anti-rational attitudes) they were accustomed to looking at works of art and to writing with strong visual imagery. Although "surreal" has acquired the wider meanings of "irrational" and "dream-like," when Apollinaire first used the term he was describing an attempt to reproduce in art the processes of the unconscious mind. André Breton, whose *Surrealist manifestos* codified the movement from 1924 onward, used "automatic writing" as the criterion to judge if a work was surrealist or not. Automatic writing is the aspect of Surrealism most relevant to the New York poets, whose poems often appear to have the same illogical juxtapositions of subject matter as dreams. These poets used surrealist techniques as what John Ashbery called "an expanded means of utterance," one of several devices for "getting into remoter areas of consciousness." This is part of the "widening of awareness" which many poets and others were seeking in the sixties and which we have set as a criterion for poetry.

The second concept which characterized the New York poets is the importance of the Present Moment. Just as dreams often seem to take place in an enormous present time, so the poems of the New York poets were concerned with what was happening in the immediate moment. History on a grand scale and myths were ignored, except for the mock-epics of Koch and Ashbery's dream landscapes, both of which are too private to be universal myths. "It's time to write one of my 'I do this, I do that' poems," said Frank O'Hara. Present actions preoccupied the New York poets, just as the action painters (whom the poets knew and wrote about) used automatic painting to reach the unconscious. The New York poets' emphasis on the present means that their poems are not intensely detailed studies in perspective but that they are wide rather than intense, like the large fields of flat color painted by some Abstract Expressionists. Certain New York poems seem to be "abstract" in the sense that they lack one definite subject or narrative sequence. Their flow of ideas and images does not stop long enough for us to see the outlines of the poets' personalities behind them; the poets themselves are abstract.

The third concept which the New York poets shared is the importance of the Ordinary: everyday events and speech. This may seem paradoxical, since these poets were attracted to Surrealist ideas, but after some early flings with French imitations, most settled into the colloquial diction and concern with common events that was typical of American poets such as Whitman and Williams. "We are in America and it is all right not to be elsewhere," affirmed Frank O'Hara.

When reading the New York poets it helps to keep in mind these three shared concepts which led to such diverse results and to read in a casual manner, with our critical guard temporarily down. Many New York poems do not disclose the secret of their charm through close repeated readings or the laborious teasing out of every in-group reference any more than do those Japanese paper flowers which seem so marvelous when they open under water but become a sodden wad of tissue if we try to dissect them. (An exception must be made for certain of John Ashbery's complex poems, which reward close reading.) But, if the New York poets are granted this relaxed acceptance, the reader must demand in return that the poems be effective on the very first reading. Many New York poems will not stand the stress of repeated readings because they were written to capture a moment or a mood rather than make grand philosophical statements. The reader must also be prepared to find that the conventional signposts that guide him or her into a poem—such as "what is this about?" and "what happens next?"—have been stolen or spray-painted with nonsense. (pp. 90-2)

Kenneth Koch is at first glance just as much a surrealist as the other New York poets. But soon it is apparent that he is cleverly piling up his images not into the serious *croquembouche* of the French Surrealists but into good old American custard-pie slapstick. Koch's irreverent wit distinguishes him from O'Hara and Ashbery, who are usually grouped with Koch as the "Big Three" of the New York poets. Rather like Woody Allen, Koch can be quite zany in a particularly New York deadpan style. In a long poem about misunderstandings, he says: "I thought Axel's Castle / was a garage; / And I had beautiful dreams about it, too—sensual, mysterious / mechanisms: horns honking, wheels turning. . . ."

The Ordinary, which other New York poets so revere, Koch tips upside down and shakes silly. Williams himself doesn't escape as Koch parodies "This Is Just to Say":

> I gave away the money that you had been saving to live
> on for the next ten years.
> The man who asked for it was shabby
> and the firm March wind on the porch was so juicy and
> cold.

Koch has written books about teaching poetry to children and to old people and teaches at Columbia University. His satires are more than mere jokes: they have a serious purpose of literary and social criticism. He is especially adroit at pushing the trendy concerns of our Present Moment to their absurd extremes, as in **"The Artist,"** his parodies of South American poets and his poem about poets' feuds, **"Fresh Air"**: Summer in the trees! 'It is time to strangle several bad poets. . . . / Here on the railroad train, one more time, is the Strangler. / He is going to get that one there, who is on his way to a poetry reading. / Agh! Biff! A body falls to the moving floor. . . . / Here is the Strangler dressed in a cowboy suit / Leaping from his horse to annihilate the students of myth!"

Koch has attempted long poems and a comic epic, ***Ko, Or a Season on Earth,*** which is not entirely successful, since its effects tend to dissipate as it lengthens. More rewarding are the shorter poems in his collections ***Thank You and Other Poems*** and ***The Pleasures of Peace.*** His earlier poems show a certain amount of influence from Kenneth Patchen (and, to a lesser extent, Marianne Moore). Although some of Koch's poems do not move beyond light verse, he has a glinting eye for the details of human folly and an exuberant imagination that make him refreshing reading. (pp. 102-03)

Roberta Berke, "'Neon in Daylight': The New York Poets," in her Bounds Out of Bounds: A Compass for Recent American and British Poetry, *Oxford University Press, 1981, pp. 90-106.*

JOHN BOENING

Every book of poems by Kenneth Koch seems to be a new beginning, a starting over, a trying-out of new voices, styles and idioms. One has to admire the energy and the audacity of a middle-age poet who seems ready and willing to try anything once in what is beginning to look like a frenetic search for a way of saying things. Like his previous collection, ***The Burning Mystery of Anna in 1951*** . . . , [***Days and Nights***] is an anthology. It contains long poems, short poems, prose poems, precious poems ("Botticelli, Giorgione, / the works"), bad poems ("O wonderful silence of animals. . . ."), "bed" poems (sixteen pages of free and not-so-free associations with the word *bed* entitled, aptly, **"In Bed"**) and a good (moving, intimate, smiling, tender, touching and inventive) poem called **"With Janice"** which is worth the price of the book.

Except for **"In Bed,"** which has 102 "stanzas" . . . , the title poem **"Days and Nights"** is the longest. It reads like the kind of ars poetica one would expect from a Woody Allen character coming out of the old Thalia after a particularly murky foreign film, with an anxiety level gunned to a fast idle and the world a willing ear. **"The Green Step,"** on the other hand, is like a movie itself, and an intriguing one at that. It is the one "prose" piece in ***Days and Nights,*** more suitably called "lyric fiction" than poetry. The "story" has eight parts, more often consequent than subsequent, all melodic and richly textured, like the interactive visual scenes (and films) styled after *Blow-Up.*

The other poems in this collection are not very attractive, and they are interesting only insofar as they demonstrate Koch's determination to work in the greatest possible variety of forms and modes. Perhaps this trial-and-errror approach to the creation of a poetic oeuvre will be justified by its occasional successes, but it seems a shame that there is so little building, so little cumulation, so little gathering-forth in Koch's work. It seems as if a great strength is being dissipated rather than husbanded, and it is poetry's loss that this is so.

John Boening, in a review of "Days and Nights," in World Literature Today, *Vol. 58, No. 1, Winter, 1984, p. 105.*

JOHN HOLLANDER

The appearance of Kenneth Koch's ***Selected Poems, 1950-1982*** is a long-overdue pleasure, and although those who admire his work as much as I do cannot help but regret certain favorites among his earlier poems that got lost in selection, this volume is of great value. It will allow unfamiliar readers to perceive, and knowing ones to reflect upon, the consistency of a joyful and energetic mode through over thirty years of, given that consistency, amazingly unrepetitive writing. Koch's continuing celebration of the playful sublime has always constituted a sort of gaudy tent, pitched among the ruins of high seriousness; a welcome sight in the intense heat, it has dispensed souvenirs and guidebooks (not to the ruins, but to itself) and orange juice, frequently blue in color, with such diligence and reliability that one has finally come to realize that the classical ruins were only random rubble, and that the tent was one of the unnamed goddess's authentic temples after all. The tent was striped with the bright, old colors of the New: Ariosto's proclaimed intention of writing of *cosa non detta in prosa mai, ne in rime*—what had not been said in prose before, nor verse—was inscribed on balloons in bunches. That the poet's true originality soared higher than those balloons of French modernist and *avant-gardiste* novelty may not have been discernible to most of the tourists over the years was, given the eternal nature of poetic reception, almost inevitable. But this lovely book should enable readers to participate more knowingly in the celebrations.

Koch's favorite kind of poem seems to be the set of variations, and the variation structure is itself varied and revised throughout his work. The first poem of his I ever read (in 1957?) was the wonderful **"The Artist,"** a sort of visionary journal and scrapbook of a sculptor whose projects evolve from steel cigarettes and a cherrywood avalanche to a scheme of almost global proportions. (p. vi)

Plans, doubts, hopes, fears, the whole paraphernalia of confidences in any artist's or writer's book of *son coeur mis à nu,* surround the records of the creation and reception of what would look today like a series of examples drawn from the fashionable art of the past two decades. But this poem was not "influenced" by Pop Art; rather, so much of the framing of both objects and hunks of environment which went on subsequent to its publication seem to have been dully literal, even if unwitting, illustrations of it. (Here the relation of true poetry to false art perhaps mirrors that of art to nature: Whistler was once accosted by a lady who remarked that she had been walking on the Embankment and that the Thames looked just like one of his *Nocturnes,* to which the artist replied that Nature seemed to be creeping up.) The elements of Koch's artist's oeuvre were mythological and paradigmatic, with the result that they became, in this Whistlerian-Wildean sense, literally prophetic. **"The Artist"** is one mode of variation on the variation theme, the "what next?"-ness that such patterns inevitably engender being tied here to the narrative of an artistic career. From the early **"Collected Poems"** to the more recent **"In Bed,"** Koch is at work on what will be next. The hilarious and beautiful **"Lunch"** from his first book is itself a Banquet of Sense, what used to be called a "travelogue" of exotic lunches. (p. vii)

The whole poem concludes with a consideration of, and a gleeful escape from, the problems raised by its own injunction, "Let us give lunch to the lunch." Both the problems and the injunction itself are more in the line of S. J. Perelman—one of the major unavowed influences on the fiction and poetry of a whole generation of American writers—than of French poetry. Koch's ongoing homage to Ariosto, in the *ottava rima* of his narrative poems ***Ko*** and ***The Duplications*** (alas, not included in this selection: who could ever forget the opening of the former of these, the only epic or romance ever *literally* to begin *in medias res* with the word "Meanwhile"?), is matched by his continual delight in the tones of poems like Whitman's

"Respondez" or "Apostrophe," and in the parable that his free verse is always preaching about itself, in what is really a very neoclassical way of moralizing, as Pope did from the form and function of his couplets, about lines of life from lines of verse. Koch's characteristic scheme of apostrophe, particularly of long and awkwardly named things and beings, is perhaps ultimately Whitmanic as well, but only in style. More deeply, it may have been a poem like (but I suppose that there isn't any other poem "like") Stevens's "Someone Puts a Pineapple Together" that helped Koch see what there was to be seen; even more than the more obvious format of the "Thirteen Ways of Looking at a Blackbird," the series of exuberant misreadings of the pineapple on the table in the shaft of light from the planet of the imagination falling upon it remains a rhythmic model for his sequences of surprising verbal moves.

As I mentioned earlier, I miss some favorite poems here (**"The Young Park," "The Scales," "The Interpretation of Dreams"**—all from ***The Pleasures of Peace***). But this volume includes almost all of the poems in ***Thank You,*** and all of them in the splendid recent volume, ***The Art of Love,*** whose title poem forms an Ovidian, didactic tetrad with three others (**"Some General Instructions," "The Art of Poetry," "On Beauty"**). Their late manner is more that of a teacher than of an eternal ephebe—one may compare the *Duck Soup*-like *mise en scène* of the poet's early **"Fresh Air"** with his more recent *ars poetica,* just as he himself invites you to look back at the early **"The Circus"** through (or is it past? over? under? around?) the later poem, which purports to try to remember the occasions on which the first was composed. In these poems, the wild turns of the earlier ones are there in smaller scale, and the parody of the didactic mode enables a literal one to work under the disguise of its own caricature. The shift in successive strophes toward the end of **"The Art of Love"** from the stand-up comic through the mellowed air of practical wisdom to the realm of the powers for which all poetry longs may be seen in

> Zombie-itis is love of the living dead. It is
> comparatively rare.
> If a woman likes it, you can probably find other things
> she likes that you will like even more.
>
> Ten things an older man must never say to a younger
> woman:
> I) I'm dying! 2) I can't hear what you're saying! 3)
> How many fingers are you holding up?
> 4) Listen to my heart. 5) Take my pulse. 6) What's
> your name?
> 7) Is it cold in here? 8) Is it hot in here? 9) Are you in
> here?
> 10) What wings are those beating at the window?
> Not that a man should stress his youth in a dishonest
> way
> But that he should not unduly emphasize his age.
>
> The inability to love is almost incurable. A long sea
> voyage
> Is recommended, in the company of an irresistible girl.
>
> To turn a woman into a duck, etc., hypnotize her and
> dress her in costume.
>
> To make love standing in water, see "Elephant
> Congress" in the *Kama Sutra* (chap. iv).
> During a shortage of girls, visit numerous places; give
> public lectures; carry this volume.

—where "a duck, etc.," is absolutely masterful. These poems, and **"Days and Nights"** and the very moving **"With Janice"** are marked by an imaginative maturity always wanting to brood on its own childhood, and never failing to startle us in old-new-old ways. (pp. ix-xi)

John Hollander, in a review of "Selected Poems, 1950-1982," in The Yale Review, *Vol. 74, No. 4, July, 1985, pp. vi-vii, ix-xi.*

PETER STITT

Kenneth Koch has fought all his life to replace solemnity and deep meaning in poetry with playfulness, parody, and a liveliness of imagination. Some of this he announced in the early poem **"Fresh Air,"** one of whose more active characters is the Strangler:

> Summer in the trees! "It is time to strangle several bad
> poets."
> The yellow hobbyhorse rocks to and fro, and from the
> chimney
> Drops the Strangler! The white and pink roses are
> slightly agitated by the struggle,
> But afterwards beside the dead "poet" they cuddle up
> comfortingly against their vase. They are safer now,
> no one will compare them to the sea.

Shortly thereafter the Strangler kills "the maker of comparisons / Between football and life."

Serious folks, creators of simile and analogy, traditionalists—these are the poet's targets. As for what Koch advocates, even there he keeps tongue in cheek:

> Is there no voice to cry out from the wind and say what
> it is like to be the wind,
> To be roughed up by the trees and to bring music from
> the scattered houses
> And the stones, and to be in such intimate relationship
> with the sea
> That you cannot understand it? Is there no one who
> feels like a pair of pants?

The passage begins in the voice of a weeping romantic, modulates into the tougher exuberance of a Whitman, and concludes in pure joking. Poems like this one leave the reader thinking that the poet has no commitment to anything other than gesture and punch line. Koch said of himself as a member of the New York School, "I think we may have been more conscious than many poets of the surface of the poem, and what was going on while we were writing and how we were using words. I don't think we saw any reason to resist humor in our poems."

Well, there is humor and there is humor. In his early poems Koch was very much an advocate of the really abominable fooling around that passed for surrealism in American poetry of the early sixties. The genuine surrealists of Spain and France were so clear about what they were doing that it is amazing so many American poets and critics failed to understand. Real surrealism always has a purpose, be it sexual, psychological, social, or sassy. Too often American imitations retain the surface play but abandon the underlying purpose, as Koch does in these lines from **"Summery Weather":** "As for pure dance / With oranges, / 'All my factories / Need refilling,' / The corpse said, falling down between them. / 'Okay okay / Here's a banana and a bandana / The light on a bright night, / With which, to finish, my personal challenge.'" Happily this phase did not last long in Koch's career. And while the poems he produced then are often unreadable, the practice of nonsensical writing probably contributed to the imaginative liveliness and good humor of his later work.

Koch's greatest commitment as a poet is to not making very much sense, to not taking things very seriously. In a late poem, **"To Marina,"** he explains of things he had written and said long ago that "To you / It seemed a position, to me / It was all a flux, especially then." Like most modernists, Koch is a bookish poet many of whose pieces are written in reaction to things others have written. These need not be poems; the ur-text can be something so debased and common as a sex manual or a Dear Abby column—as is the case in the longest poem in [***Selected Poems: 1950-1982***], **"The Art of Love."**

At first it is hard to know how to take **"The Art of Love,"** which is full of advice like this: "Nailing a woman to the wall causes too much damage / (Not to the wall but to the woman—you after all want to enjoy her / And love her again and again). You can, however, wrap tape around her arms, waist, ankles, and knees / And nail this to the wall." I must confess to having been considerably comforted by the words of Sandra M. Gilbert, who said in her 1976 review in *Poetry* [see *CLC,* Vol. 8], "It's clear, for instance, that there's an enormous gulf between the author of ***The Art of Love*** and its mad speaker, whose grotesque lecture not only parodies but seriously subverts encyclopedists of sexual self-help from Andreas Capellanus and the author of the *Kama Sutra* to Havelock Ellis and Alex Comfort."

The poem is utterly crazy and utterly wonderful. Its speaker is a naïve little man compelled to tell us everything, which he does with great enthusiasm. . . . The influence of the surrealist phase can be palpably felt, but here its techniques serve more worthy ends than in the early work. The poem is highly imaginative and admirably well-designed. The system it presents is complete and self-contained. At one point the speaker mentions a great number of questions about love that need answering; before the poem is over, they have all been answered. (pp. 640-42)

Peter Stitt, "Tradition and the Innovative Godzilla," in The Georgia Review, *Vol. XXXIX, No. 3, Fall, 1985, pp. 635-48.*

DENIS DONOGHUE

I have just read ***On the Edge*** in galleys. A book in two parts, the first is a sequence of impressions of Africa, the second a flight of autobiography: both poems are winningly free-wheeling, written so engagingly that you would easily make the mistake of thinking this kind of poetry an unarduous matter of throwing words in the air and watching them land in good order. Not so. To write like Koch, you have to have a lot of power and keep most of it in reserve. So the poetry moves daringly but unpretentiously between past and present, memories and currencies of sentiment jostling one another within the strong propriety of the cadence. Koch is a superb craftsman: that is, you don't need to take any special notice of his craft, it exerts due pressure without adverting to itself as pressure.

Denis Donoghue, in a review of "On the Edge," in Commonweal, *Vol. 112, No. 21, November 29, 1985, p. 677.*

PAUL HOOVER

[Hoover, an American poet, is the author of such poetry collections as The Monocle Thugs *(1977),* Somebody Talks a Lot *(1982), and* Nervous Songs *(1984). In the following excerpt Hoover argues that Koch is an accomplished poet who deserves the same respect as his "serious" contemporaries.]*

What is to be done with Kenneth Koch? His poetry is intelligent, amusing, and dear, and he is one of the originals of his brilliant generation, but one senses an enormous labor of hesitation on the part of reviewers and critics: is it, and can comic art ever be, really major? Is Koch's achievement at the point of its first summation only a charming quirk, unworthy of mention in the critical histories of the era? James Breslin's *From Modern to Contemporary: American Poetry, 1945-1965,* devotes chapters to Olson, Ginsberg, Lowell, Levertov, James Wright, and Frank O'Hara, as well as a page and a half to John Ashbery, but the index makes no mention of Koch. Even Ashbery's blurb on the back of ***Selected Poems*** suggests desolation: "This long-awaited collection should at last establish Kenneth Koch for what he is: one of our greatest poets." He has been overlooked and under-reviewed.

Charm is heroic, but the central tradition doesn't think so, and Koch suffers the reputation of a writer of light verse. If it hadn't been for O'Hara's underlying elegiac quality, in for instance "The Day Lady Died," he would probably have suffered the same fate. The suspicion is that, in spite of some touching later work dealing with old loves and the memory of friends, Koch simply isn't serious enough. He declines the maudlin urgencies of the central tradition in favor of the cavalier elegance of his wit. It's an elegance, however, without presumption and false height. Koch's humor, like Byron's is democratic and delights in its accessibility. Compare, for example, *Don Juan* and the ottava rima of Koch's ***The Duplications,*** 1977, a comic epic that is unfortunately not represented in ***Selected Poems.*** One wants to use the expression "inspired silliness," bearing in mind the origin of the word "seely," meaning happy or blessed. The humor of both men is heroic because it is not low, but rather creates an "aery charm" that is finally terribly sincere.

Like all "comic" poets, Koch is moralistic and didactic at heart, but he is not essentially a satirist. He stings mildly with parody, and his targets are usually works of art, not political situations or public figures. **"Variations on a Theme by William Carlos Williams"** uses Williams' famous poem about the plums as a basis for further invention, not as a way of demeaning Williams. Koch's humor is generous and tends not to congratulate itself on the superiority of its point of view. That is, the inherent sophistication of his project—and the pretension that might go with it—is deflated by the openness of his wit. He is too funny to be sanctimonious or mean, even in **"Fresh Air,"** the comic manifesto in which The Strangler kills several bad academic poets. The poem is one of the most useful statements of poetics of the period in its rejection of the pompous, maudlin, and drear, and it is written without the sternness and systemization that can accompany such works. In some ways, Koch is a Horatian and romantic at the same time. His whimsical common sense is in contrast to Robert

Bly's hyperthyroidal embracement of spiritual presences, for Koch embraces the world for its delightful actuality rather than lamenting its losses. While Bly is out of Wordsworth, filling his work with personification, forced empathy, and pathetic fallacy, a pose that is finally cartoonish and unreal, Koch stares with amusement at a bottle of sparkling soda.

When Koch is meditative, a major mode for Ashbery, he becomes Vergilian and teacherly. In fact, his finest middle work can be found in ***The Art of Love*** (not in the title poem as much as in the classic **"The Art of Poetry"** and **"Some General Instructions"**), a book which represents a triumph of "making it new" by ignoring Pound's anti-Vergilian dictum. The wit in these instructive works helps maintain tension, and they are masterpieces of sustained tone in a relaxed idiom. There is an overwhelming feeling of naturalness in these longer discourses that broadens the parameters of reference. Anything might be essayed in and seem "correct" in the context, and when enough is done the poem can simply end, as **"The Art of Poetry"** does, with the line: "Now I have said enough." Eliot had convinced the generation after him to be dramatic and imagistic, and along comes Kenneth Koch with rhetoric and generalization, as if he wanted to rewrite Horace's *Ars Poetica* for our time. While doing so, Koch makes Eliot's impersonal theory of poetry seem fussy and irrelevant. The self, too, is an object and actor in the world, equally available for reference. Even one's own poems can present themselves as topics. Thus **"The Circus"** in ***The Art of Love*** begins with a reference to **"The Circus"** in his first book, ***Thank You.***

Koch is also a romantic in his use of the catalogue. It's the gesture to the actual that counts, not the laden rhetoric attempting a seamless unity. In fact, his poetry is at its best when the structure allows for one-liners, as in **"Sleeping With Women"** and **"Alive for an Instant"** with its wonderful ending: "I have a baby in my landscape and I have a wild rat in my secrets from you." Even the love poem **"To You,"** beginning "I love you as a sheriff searches for a walnut . . ." is essentially a catalogue (cf. E. B. Browning's "How Do I Love Thee," which it may parody). In the narrative mode, the occasion is sometimes a journey, a strategy reminiscent of A. O. Barnabooth (Valery Larbaud) and Raymond Roussel, acknowledged masters for the former editor of *Locus Solus*. The attitude, too, is sometimes that of the delightfully eccentric amateur.

Like all the New York poets, Koch sees art as a part of life, so there is little self-consciousness in referring to it. The criticism of Shklovsky, Bahktin, and other formalists makes such apparent artifice almost obligatory, yet as a romantic formalist Koch never poses as the ardent technician, foregrounding his metrical or formal strategies. He is first a poet of excitable content, and he tends to use forms that allow for his charm and quiet asides. Often, like Ginsberg, he uses a long line, though he is hardly "bardic and Melvillean" in breath. One senses, in fact, the bemusement of the poet when such earnest expectations as "voice" and "breath" arise. His is an intentionally "light" poetry that offers an antidote to the relentless seriousness and historicity of, for example, Charles Olson. Koch's only dicta seem to be charm and liveliness (energia), the aesthetic pleasure that Sartre, in "Why Write?", prefers to call "aesthetic joy." His poetry has the air of "generosity" Sartre calls for: ". . . whatever the subject a sort of essential lightness must appear everywhere and remind us that the work is never a natural datum, but an *exigence* and a *gift*." It is Koch's lightness, with its freedom of access to a variety of emotions, that distinguishes him as a true artist, as opposed to the Arnoldian insistence on "high seriousness" that results in a comic—even ridiculous and burlesque—melancholia or pretension to importance. Arnold writes, in "The Study of Poetry," of the "power of liquidness and fluidity in Chaucer's verse . . . dependent upon a free, a licentious dealing with language, such as is now impossible." He goes on to characterize Chaucer as a less than classic author, in contrast with Dante: "The substance of Chaucer's poetry, his view of things and his criticism of life, has largeness, freedom, shrewdness, benignity; but it has not this high seriousness." Arnold is writing, of course, as an enemy of the French influence, an influence that arrives in Koch's work not by way of Christian de Troyes and Chaucer, but through Apollinaire, the French Symbolists, and the surrealists. Seriousness becomes a matter of forced gravity, a poetic tone that is established even before the "criticism of life" begins. Insistent seriousness inevitably leads, therefore, to manipulation and untruth.

Those who extend the Arnold tradition of severity in the guise of morality, such as John Gardner in *On Moral Fiction,* continue to mistake earnestness for true seriousness. Thus Gardner prefers the poetry of Linda Pastan, Dave Smith, Galway Kinnell, Howard Nemerov, Anthony Hecht, and William Meredith to that of Ginsberg, Ashbery, and Koch, among others working in the new poetics. There is an almost grandiose mediocrity to Gardner's choices, as if the only standard were the avoidance of "largeness, freedom, and shrewdness." A sense of play or adventure is sacrificed to the demands of (Say it!) middle-class moralism, rationalism, and Christianity. It is enough for Gardner simply not to be creepy: "Bad art is always basically creepy; that is its first and most obvious identifying sign," Poe, Baudelaire, Kafka, Goya, Beckett, Beowulf, Eliot of *The Wasteland,* and Gardner's own *Grendel* notwithstanding. Ironically, in **"Fresh Air,"** it is Kenneth Koch who gives definition to the slimy and the creepy, the bad poets "bathing the library steps with their spit" or "gargling out innocuous (to whom?) poems about maple trees and their children." Thus The Strangler leaps on Linda Pastan and "they fall to the moving floor."

Certainly the poetry of Kenneth Koch isn't the "godless terror of John Hawke's *The Beetleleg*" (Gardner), but neither is it the sentimental reminiscence of one's father singing *The Old Rugged Cross,* Gardner's personal emblem of truth in life and art. In fact, Arnold, Gardner, and mainstream critics like Helen Vendler argue for the values of a dominant social group, and Koch is marginal to that experience in the French influences, wit and urbanity, and the lack of yearning in his poetry. It is thus quite true that he doesn't speak to the central experience of American life, but neither did Eliot, Pound, Crane, Stevens, and Moore. Their work was also "creepy" and idiosyncratic, as all great writing is on first examination.

Koch, like William Carlos Williams, writes some poems that challenge the reader by being aggressively "minor" or "slight." Consider, for example, Williams' "This is Just to Say" or Koch's **"Ma Provence."** Such poems are simply amusing, and we have been led to believe that poetry, whatever else it it, must not entertain. Ironically, it's the smallness and simple pleasure afforded by such work that reveals its ambitions, not only as moral but also as potentially major art. In this context, it's interesting to note, as Ted Berrigan did in a talk at Naropa Institute, that the root of the word *amusement* is *muse*. Art is that which "stirs the muses," and it often does so most effectively in its resistance to known frames and expectations. The new is moral in its freshening of perception and defiance of the central (and therefore institutionalized) definition of art. But "largeness, freedom, and shrewdness" will appear at first to be "creepy" to those who desire only the familiar, a reaction that has politically conservative implications. The irony with Williams and Koch is that the strangeness of their art, and its "revolutionary" implications, is its delight in the ordinary. (pp. 14-16)

Paul Hoover, "Seriousness," in The American Book Review, *Vol. 8, No. 6, November-December, 1986, pp. 14-16.*

Larry (Jeff) McMurtry

Lonesome Dove

Pulitzer Prize: Fiction

American novelist, essayist, and scriptwriter.

Lonesome Dove (1985), McMurtry's epic-length novel of cowboy life, chronicles the events of a cattle drive from Texas to Montana during the 1870s. Reviewers praise the novel as a humorous yet sincere tribute to the American West. Previously, McMurtry wrote about his fascination with Texas's myth-filled past in his essay collection *In a Narrow Grave* (1968). As a novelist, however, he made his reputation with novels designed to shatter myths of the heroic West. Many of his novels, including *The Last Picture Show* (1966) and *Terms of Endearment* (1975), set in modern-day rural Texas, portray characters plagued by dissatisfaction, frustration, and loneliness. In contrast, *Lonesome Dove* endows the humble men and women it depicts with an almost legendary aura.

Lonesome Dove's protagonists are Augustus McCrae and Woodrow Call, cattlemen from Lonesome Dove, Texas, who embody the ideals of cowboy heroism. McMurtry's own interest in cowboy myth started while he was growing up on his father's livestock ranch near Archer City, Texas. His grandfather, also a cattle rancher, experienced frontier life first-hand and transmitted his romantic ideals to younger generations. *Lonesome Dove,* McMurtry explains, ''grew out of my sense of having heard my uncles talk about the extraordinary days when the range was open. In my boyhood I could talk to men who touched this experience and knew it, even if they only saw the tag end of it. I wanted to see if I could make that real, make that work fictionally.''

Critic John Horn calls *Lonesome Dove* McMurtry's ''strongest, most cogent narrative to date.'' Reviewers observe that McMurtry confines his story to the conventions of the Western genre, including such archetypal characters as the wily Indian villain Blue Duck and the good-hearted strumpet Lorena. At the same time he imbues these familiar elements with new life, using them to construct a fresh and poignant story that maintains reader interest throughout the novel's generous length. McMurtry particularly delighted critics with his portrayal of McCrae and Call, who emerge as both heroic and endearingly human. By endowing the time-honored formula of the Western with his superior literary gifts, critics suggest, McMurtry does not so much transcend the genre as fulfill its richest possibilities.

(See also *CLC,* Vols. 2, 3, 7, 11, 27; *Contemporary Authors,* Vols. 5-8, rev. ed.; *Contemporary Authors New Revision Series,* Vol. 19; *Dictionary of Literary Biography,* Vol. 2; and *Dictionary of Literary Biography Yearbook: 1980*.)

CHRISTOPHER LEHMANN-HAUPT

[It's] a highly visual, almost cinematic world that Mr. McMurtry has brought to life in ***Lonesome Dove.*** Language matters, but

its main job is to create scenes of terrific action to which the characters react with humorous homespun taciturnity. There's hardly a frame in this story that you couldn't splice from the memory of Westerns past.

Yet just because it's a well-worn genre that the author is working doesn't mean he can't be original or deeply affecting. The main action of ***Lonesome Dove*** may be as trite as a cattle drive. Lorena may be another ''whore with the proverbial heart of gold.'' Many of the novel's episodes may smack a little of the tall tale. But Mr. McMurtry has a way of diverting the progress of his cliches in odd and interesting ways.

Though men are driven powerfully by their love for women in this story, by the end not a single Jack has got his Jill. Though the savage Blue Duck does truly terrible things to some of our favorite people—including the massacre of Janey, the resourceful half-wild child who pops up to charm us in one of the novel's meandering subplots—there is never the expected showdown that a thousand shoot-'em-outs have led us to expect.

Most curiously of all, money is never a serious issue in the story. True, there is poverty, theft, gambling and people who do things for material gain. The Hat Creek Cattle Company may be richly rewarded if it succeeds in getting the herd to Montana. But the novel's main action arises out of behavior that nobody really understands, least of all the people who do the acting. There are codes to follow and destinations to reach and goals to be achieved but none of them make much sense under close examination, and there are some characters in the book who consider them outright crazy. And that of course is how the West was won. . . .

But Mr. McMurtry isn't celebrating the winning of the West. He takes his people to their point of triumph and then a few steps beyond, to their point of craziness. After thousands of miles and hundreds of pages, Captain Call ends up back in Lonesome Dove, wondering what the whole thing was all about.

But there's no point in theorizing. Mr. McMurtry certainly never does. Anyway, if ever there was a place and a time in history when there was little room for theory, then the time of the American frontier was it. As for action, ***Lonesome Dove*** has it all and then some.

Christopher Lehmann-Haupt, in a review of "Lonesome Dove," in The New York Times, *June 3, 1985, p. C20.*

WALTER CLEMONS

Though he ceased being a full-time Texan 15 years ago, Larry McMurtry is still the best Texas writer alive—an ambiguous title he declared his own uneasiness about back in the '60s when he took to wearing, to his publishers' horror, a black sweat shirt emblazoned MINOR REGIONAL NOVELIST. In recent years he's written good and bad novels set as far afield as Hollywood, Washington and Las Vegas. The poor ones, such as ***Cadillac Jack*** and ***Somebody's Darling,*** weren't commercial potboilers. They were handmade experiments that didn't happen to turn out well.

McMurtry has written astringent essays about his heritage as the descendant of ranchers and cowboys. "All through my youth I listened to stories about an earlier, a purer, a more golden and more legendary Texas that I had been born too late to see," he wrote in 1975. "In time ... I came to regard that earlier, more legendary Texas as a long, romantic, and somewhat repetitive collective invention, not unlike the Yugoslav epics." Four years ago he ruffled feathers in his home state by chastising Texas writers for dwelling on its past at a time when its urban scene cried out for a Balzac or a Dickens.

With perfect inconsistency, he's now produced a marvelous novel about a cattle drive from Texas to Montana in the 1870s. Lonesome Dove is a meager town on the Mexican border, equipped with one whore and one piano, the latter shared by the local bar and the church. Two former Texas Rangers, retired and becalmed after long years of putting down the Comanches, run a livery stable with pigs on the porch and rattlesnakes in the springhouse. The partners are white-haired Gus McCrae, easygoing, humane and loquacious, and Capt. Woodrow Call, ramrod-stiff and solitary. . . .

A companion from the past shows up: Jake Spoon, a ladies' man with a slow grin and melting brown eyes. Jake is wanted for an accidental killing in Arkansas, and his unreliablity will have tragic consequences. But he promises fortunes to be made in Montana, and his old friends are inveigled into conducting a cattle raid south of the Mexican border and driving their acquisitions north to begin a new life.

Lonesome Dove shows, early on, just about every symptom of American Epic except pretentiousness. McMurtry has laconic Texas talk and leathery, slip-hipped machismo down pat, and he's able to refresh heroic clichés with exact observations about cowboy prudery, ignorance and fear of losing face. During the opening chapters, I thought this was a man's book, not likely to interest women readers. That was a mistake. McMurtry is unfailingly acute on the life of women in this man's world. Lorena Wood, introduced as the classic sporting woman with a heart of gold, surprises us at every turn of the narrative with unexpected glints of inarticulate stubborness, shrewdness and determination. She's especially good in receiving the attention of lovestruck cowboys whose dazed crushes she recognizes for what they are—the well-meant compliments of men to whom horses are more real than she is.

It's a good sign in a novel this long, I think, that one doesn't want to read it fast and cut to the chase. The first horrible death on the drive northward—a young Irishman stirs up a nest of water moccasins during a river crossing—produces a quiet scene of deeply affecting grief. The book pauses for a glorious comic brawl in San Antonio's Buckhorn Saloon and, later, for a frightening street fight in which Woodrow Call's iron self-control breaks into madness. McMurtry's longest earlier novel, ***Moving On,*** was interesting, shapeless sprawl. This time he keeps dozens of characters in motion in far-flung locales without confusion or tedium. The whole book moves with joyous energy. . . .

McMurtry is a funny writer and a large-hearted one. "When was you the happiest, Call?" Gus McCrae inquires of his partner. "Happiest about what?" Call bleakly asks, stumped for an answer. "It don't suit you, so you managed to avoid it," McCrae says about happiness. "I don't guess I've watched you punish yourself for thirty years to be totally wrong about you. I just don't know what you done to deserve the punishment." This conundrum is never solved in the book, but McMurtry's heart is with McCrae. It's a pleasure . . . to be able to recommend a big popular novel that's amply imagined and crisply, lovingly written. I haven't enjoyed a book more this year.

Walter Clemons, "Saga of a Cattle Drive," in Newsweek, *Vol. CV, No. 22, June 3, 1985, p. 74.*

JOHN HORN

Lonesome Dove is Larry McMurtry's loftiest novel, a wondrous work, drowned in love, melancholy, and yet, ultimately, exultant.

In ***Lonesome Dove,*** as in all of his previous stories, McMurtry lays the hope and despair of ordinary people's lives side by side. He celebrates a world abundant with calamity and a human spirit wistful but prevailing.

McMurtry's backdrop is America's 19th-Century West, a post-Civil War land of cowboys, cattle, sagebrush and myth. That's hardly a surprise: Today's West has long been his homeland and the source of his genius. His novels, which include ***The Last Picture Show*** and ***Moving On,*** have been chronicles of the modern-day frontier, ruminations on how the Old West is slowly—but inexorably—being swallowed by a more mechanical, less romantic civilization. In ***Lonesome Dove***, the chronicler of today's West turns to yesterday's West to drink, as it were, directly from his source.

McMurtry's characters are as attached to the land as they ever will be to each other. The inhabitants of Lonesome Dove, the Texas city from which this story rises, have been born spang into the hands of the land, to wander it and learn the sadness of it until, eventually, it hands them back. "The earth," remarks Gus McCrae, the novel's central character, "is mostly just a boneyard. But pretty in the sunlight."

Indeed, the presence of the land for the characters in ***Lonesome Dove*** is as much a controlling factor as it was for Molly in ***Leaving Cheyenne*** or for Danny in ***All My Friends Are Going to Be Strangers.*** Here, as there, the land plays a role of its own. It dictates the action.

But although the land and the people in those earlier works remained vivid, the narratives in which they were set were vague, sometimes rambling. In ***Terms of Endearment,*** for example, setting and character were well-crafted, but the story as a whole did not linger in the memory.

Writing ***Lonesome Dove,*** though, McMurtry has produced a compelling and memorable epic without sacrificing the fine detail with which he has always worked. This is his strongest, most cogent narrative to date. And that is its triumph.

It is an eager crowd that leaves the comforts of Lonesome Dove behind. Yet, the cowboys aren't even sure why they're abandoning their Texas sticks. Perhaps Manifest Destiny has pointed them north. Perhaps not. "Me and Call have always liked to get where we started for," Gus says, "even if it don't make a damn bit of sense."

Gus is a high-plains philosopher, drifting between his cattle and his thoughts. He's happy to do most any job, however dangerous, as long as he doesn't have to leave his saddle. He's as uncomfortable with a shovel as he is with an empty bottle of liquor. He'd rather be an outlaw than a doctor or lawyer. Whatever he would be, on his horse, with his shoulder-length gray hair flowing in the wind, Gus is a figure of enchantment, a crafty and fearless warrior.

There are two women in Gus's life. Lorena, as delicate as a desert rose, is a reluctant prostitute whose dreams of San Francisco and a better life propel her north with the cattle company. Clara is Gus' old—but constant—flame. Unlike Lorena's beauty, hers is earthy. She is as fused with the land as he. When we first see her, she's milking a cow on her ranch, a remote outpost hunkered down defiantly in the wilderness.

There is a glorious individuality in both Clara and Lorena. McMurtry's women have always been his superior creations; these two are no exception. They are, if implicitly, feminists; Clara more so than Lorena. They are also leaders—willful, passionate and charismatic.

Lorena loves Gus most. Gus loves Clara most. But more than Clara, Gus loves his freedom. Men capable of happy marriage don't seem to interest McMurtry much at all. Still, the evolution of Gus' relationship with Lorena is deeply interesting and, in this historical novel, deeply contemporary. From mutual contempt, their relationship changes into a love so strong that sex, somehow, weakens it. Gus and Lorena become [the] best of friends, dependent on the other, yet often unable to express their needs and their hopes. As painful as that might be, their discovery of each other is compelling, poignant reading. Gus is determined to make Lorena his friend and lover but is willing to watch Lorena fall deeply for another man with the prescience that everything will work its way out, more or less. . . .

Throughout this masterful work, there is hope and an understated sense of gratitude. As one cowhand puts it neatly, near death and facing the amputation of his gangrenous leg, "It's a fine world, though rich in hardships at times."

At the end of the journey, no riches wait. The journey is riches enough.

John Horn, in a review of "Lonesome Dove," in Los Angeles Times Book Review, *June 9, 1985, p. 2.*

NOEL PERRIN

[*American essayist, nonfiction writer, and critic Perrin specializes in writing about country living, as in his essay collection* First Person Rural: Essays of a Sometime Farmer *(1978) and its sequels,* Second Person Rural *(1980) and* Third Person Rural *(1983). His other publications include* A Passport Secretly Green *(1961) and* Giving Up the Gun: The Japanese Reversion to the Sword, 1543-1879 *(1979). In the following excerpt Perrin praises* Lonesome Dove *for its fresh approach to the Western novel and the engaging dialogue of its characters.*]

Lonesome Dove is a very small Texas town, right on the Mexican border. In it, somewhere around the year 1880, live two former captains in the Texas Rangers: Woodrow Call and Augustus McCrae. Both are in vigorous middle age.

These days they are running a combination ranch and livery stable—or at least Call is. Gus McCrae mainly loafs around the ranchhouse with a whiskey jug, though he does participate in night raids into Mexico to steal horses and cattle. (Sometimes they are merely reclaiming stock which Pedro Flores, the fierce hacienda owner to the south, had previously crossed the river to steal in Texas. Traffic both ways is brisk.) . . .

This could be the beginning of any number of western novels. All the standard elements are present. Turn the key, and the clockwork figures will start shooting, drinking, roping cows, whoring . . .

It happens instead to be the start of one of the best westerns I have ever read. It certainly is the best of Larry McMurtry's, and he has written good ones before.

One thing that makes the book so good is the sheer sweep of the plot. Quite early on—though not before we've been on a night raid to Mexico and encountered herds moving both ways—the two Ranger captains decide to pull up stakes and go to Montana. Texas has gotten too tame for them. (p. 1)

Most of the book is taken up with innumerable adventures that occur on this long journey. McMurtry never falters. Each river crossing or Indian fight or meeting with settlers or encounter with the U.S. Cavalry (a sorry lot, in this book) is freshly realized. There is the same sense of grand drama that you get from going down the river with Huck and Jim—and the same generous helping of tragedy within a humorous book, too.

Except in this way, though, ***Lonesome Dove*** is not much like *Huckleberry Finn*. It is, quite amazingly for a western, more like the novels of that mannered Englishwoman, Ivy Compton-Burnett.

What I mean by that is that the book has a great many scenes in which nothing happens except that people talk—and they talk so well you never want them to stop. This is a rare thing in westerns. It is rare even in the novels of Larry McMurtry.

He has, of course, been a gifted writer of dialogue right along—way back since ***Horseman, Pass By*** in 1961.

But his subject matter (when it hasn't been Hollywood) has been Texas, and the convention in Texas novels and westerns in general has been that good people aren't articulate—or bad ones, either, usually. Strength and silence go together. Some little prissy weak-willed easterner may gab a lot, but westerners speak through action. True, one special variety of straight-faced joking has always been allowed, even encouraged, but that's a limited vein to mine.

McMurtry's success with ***Lonesome Dove*** comes in great part from the wonderful talkers with which the book is filled. Three of them stand out: Gus McCrae; a tough rancher named Wilbarger who claims to have gone to Yale when young; and a brilliant woman around 40 named Clara, whom Gus once hoped to make his third wife. The book is 800 pages long; I would gladly have listened to any of the three for another 800 pages. . . .

How can a book stay a western with all this talk? Easy. For every conversationalist, there are two or three silent people. Captain Call hates chatter as much as Gus loves it. Lorena almost never speaks to a customer. There is a buffalo hunter named Big Zwey who can easily go a week between sentences. The combination works.

The book is not, of course, perfect. It has at least three faults, one of which it shares with the work of Compton-Burnett. Her dialogue may be three-dimensional, but her characters are mostly one-dimensional. So are most of McMurtry's. In fact, many of them don't have even one dimension, they just have a single trait. Big Zwey's is his helpless silent unrequited love for an ex-whore named Elmira. Bolivar's is his passion for beating dinner bells with a broken crowbar. One cowboy is recognizable chiefly by his habit of vomiting whenever he gets drunk, which he does at every possible opportunity.

McMurtry has been devising one-trait characters all his life. Billy, back in ***The Last Picture Show,*** cared only about sweeping with a broom, and often swept his way right out the poolroom door in Thalia, Texas, and on to the outskirts of town. There are such people in almost every McMurtry book; they are a useful device when you're writing broad humor. But ***Lonesome Dove*** is deeper and sadder and more complex than these early books, and in its context the one-trait characters sometimes become an irritant.

A second flaw in the book is that it changes tone about a hundred pages in. I suspect that McMurtry originally intended a more superficial and more easily humorous book than the one he wound up writing.

And a third flaw is that he keeps introducing characters that he then makes no use of. . . .

It would be an ungrateful critic indeed, though, who spent much time worrying about flaws—or even who wondered too much why it is that with only one exception the women in the book are bored and disgusted by men who love them. The only sensible response to this book is to do a little dance of pleasure, and then to start hoping that McMurtry has another one as good still in him. (p. 13)

Noel Perrin, "Larry McMurtry's Western Epic," in Book World—The Washington Post, *June 9, 1985, pp. 1, 13.*

NICHOLAS LEMANN

The practice of trail-driving herds of beef cattle over long distances from ranch to railhead flourished for just a moment after the Civil War and before the widespread use of barbed wire. It was the tiniest fraction of our national experience and did not directly involve more than a few thousand people. But maybe more than anything else—more than wars, more than slavery, more than urbanization or immigration—it has animated a part of our imagination out of which flows a vital branch of popular culture. Cowboyana in the form of dime fiction and stage shows flourished even before the short era of the trail drives ended. It nourished movies and television when they were young. Even today, it seems to be everywhere: in clothing, in advertising, in political rhetoric.

Unlike other themes that have obsessed us, though, the trail drive has not made the transition from low art to high art very well. The South has *Gone With the Wind* but also Faulkner; the cowboy has *Red River* and J. Frank Dobie. It seems mysterious that so rich a subject has not produced a great novel—perhaps it has become so stylized that there is no juice left in it.

Readers who held out hope have been getting sustenance for years from the rumors that Larry McMurtry was writing a big trail-driving novel. As much as anyone, he knows the subject: he comes from a large west Texas family that he has described as "cowboys first and last," and his essays show that he has done considerable digging around in obscure first-hand accounts of trail drives. Also, if the myth-making machine has expropriated the subject, well, Mr. McMurtry knows about that too. It is hard to think of an American novelist who has been so lucky in Hollywood for so long (***Hud, The Last Picture Show, Terms of Endearment***) without becoming a part of it. By now a cowboy novel probably would have to show some underlying awareness of the movies. Mr. McMurtry seems ideally equipped for that.

At its beginning, ***Lonesome Dove*** seems to be an antiwestern, the literary equivalent of movies like *Cat Ballou* and *McCabe and Mrs. Miller*. The novel's title comes from the name of a Godforsaken one-saloon town on the dusty south Texas plain near the Rio Grande. Two former captains in the Texas Rangers have retired from the long wars against Indians and Mexicans to run the Hat Creek Cattle Company—when a customer wants horses or cattle, the former lawmen drop into Mexico at night and steal them. One of the captains, Augustus McCrae, is a lazy, hard-drinking, falsely erudite old coot; the other, W. F. Call, is strong and silent in circumstances that don't call for strength or silence. Surrounded by a motley crew of cowboys, Mexicans, old Rangers and flea-bitten animals, they have been living this funky life for nearly 15 years.

Then an old Ranger comrade of theirs rides into town, on the lam because he accidentally killed a man in Arkansas. He suggests they drive a herd of cattle to the unsettled country in Montana, where he has been on his wanderings. In no hurry to stop the picaresque fun, Mr. McMurtry lets the idea of a cattle drive gradually take hold among his characters. Call steals some horses and a herd of cattle and lines up some cowhands; grumbling and wisecracking and pulling on his jug, McCrae ambles along; the old friend brings the town prostitute as his guest.

As they get under way, the novel's scope begins to become clear. Mr. McMurtry weaves a dense web of subplots involving secondary characters and out-of-the-way places, with the idea of using the form of a long, old-fashioned realistic novel to create an accurate picture of life on the American frontier, from Mexico to Canada, during the late 1870's. He gives us conversationless cowboys whose greatest fear is that they will have to speak to a woman, beastly buffalo hunters, murderous Indians, destitute Indians, prairie pioneers, river boat men, gamblers, scouts, cavalry officers, prostitutes, backwoodsmen; open plains and cow towns; the Nueces River and the Platte and the Yellowstone. Everything about the book feels true; being anti-mythic is a great aid to accuracy about the lonely, ignorant, violent West.

Mr. McMurtry plows right into the big themes. The lack of a good reason for Call and McCrae's epic trail drive—"Here you've brought these cattle all this way, with all this inconvenience to me and everybody else, and you don't have no reason in this world to be doing it," McCrae says to Call at one point—makes the drive seem oddly profound. It becomes a way of exploring whether what gives our lives meaning is the way we live (as Call and McCrae believe, though in different ways), or what we accomplish, or nothing at all. The trail drive and the turns of plot provide many loves and deaths by which to measure the degree of meaning in the frontier's codes and imperatives. Even Call and McCrae's ages—just at the far edge of middle age—are conducive to mellow, sad tallyings-up.

The characters in ***Lonesome Dove*** seem always to be putting their horses into easy lopes that could be sustained all day, and this is the way Mr. McMurtry writes. His writing is almost always offhand and laconic, with barely any sustained passages intended to be beautiful or fervent. He always has time for another funny minor character to pirouette on stage, or for McCrae to produce a new bon mot. And he leisurely pursues familiar themes—two friends in love with the same woman (***Leaving Cheyenne***), a 17-year-old coming of age (***The Last Picture Show***), a formidable middle-aged woman surrounded by terrified men who love her (***Terms of Endearment***). During the last decade or so, the idea that eccentricity is the best way to deal with life has permeated Mr. McMurtry's work, and he makes an awfully good case for it again here. The question is whether it is possible to be eccentric and "major" in the same novel.

The scenes that best put the matter to rest are the most traditionally Western ones—the gunfights, stampedes, hangings and horse-stealings. Every one of these is thrilling and almost perfectly realized. In describing violence, Mr. McMurtry does not need to raise the stakes with labored prose—they are already high. When a young boy rides into a nest of poisonous snakes in a river and dies of the bites, or when McCrae singlehandedly fights off a band of Indians on an open plain with only a dead horse for shelter, it is unforgettable.

Such moments give ***Lonesome Dove*** its power. They demonstrate what underlies all the banter, and they transform Call and McCrae from burnt-out cases into—there is no other word—heroes. They are absolutely courageous, tough, strong, cool, loyal, fabulously good fighters. They and their men live through incredible travails, and, once they get to Montana, it is a paradise, worth everything. When McCrae explains the journey to the woman he loves by saying "I'd like to see one more place that ain't settled before I get decrepit and have to take up the rocking chair," it is moving, not silly. Whether this response is justified by the grandeur of their mission to tame the frontier, or conditioned by popular culture, it is there and cannot be denied.

All of Mr. McMurtry's antimythic groundwork—his refusal to glorify the West—works to reinforce the strength of the traditionally mythic parts of ***Lonesome Dove,*** by making it far more credible than the old familiar horse operas. These are real people, and they are still larger than life. The aspects of cowboying that we have found stirring for so long are, inevitably, the aspects that are stirring when given full-dress treatment by a first-rate novelist. Toward the end, through a complicated series of plot twists, Mr. McMurtry tries to show how pathetically inadequate the frontier ethos is when confronted with any facet of life but the frontier; but by that time the reader's emotional response is it does not matter—these men drove cattle to Montana!

The potential of the open range as material for fiction seems unavoidably tied to presenting it as fundamentally heroic and mythic, even though not to any real purpose. If there is a novel to be written about trail-driving that will be lasting and deep without being about brave men—and about an endless, harsh, lovely country where life is short but rich—it is still to be written. For now, for the Great Cowboy Novel, ***Lonesome Dove*** will do.

Nicholas Lemann, "Tall in the Saddle," in The New York Times Book Review, *June 9, 1985, p. 7.*

An Excerpt from *Lonesome Dove*

In the clear late afternoon light they could see all the way back to Lonesome Dove and the river and Mexico. Augustus regretted not tying a jug to his saddle—he would have liked to sit on the little hill and drink for an hour. Although Lonesome Dove had not been much of a town, he felt sure that a little whiskey would have made him feel sentimental about it.

Call merely sat on the hill, studying the cattle. It was clear to Augustus that he was not troubled in any way by leaving the border or the town.

"It's odd I partnered with a man like you, Call," Augustus said. "If we was to meet now instead of when we did, I doubt we'd have two words to say to one another."

"I wish it could happen, then, if it would hold you to two words," Call said. Though everything seemed peaceful, he had an odd, confused feeling at the thought of what they had undertaken. He had quickly convinced himself it was necessary, this drive. Fighting the Indians had been necessary, if Texas was to be settled. Protecting the border was necessary, else the Mexicans would have taken south Texas back.

A cattle drive, for all its difficulty, wasn't so imperative. He didn't feel the old sense of adventure, though perhaps it would come once they got beyond the settled country.

Augustus, who could almost read his mind, almost read it as they were stopped on the little knob of a hill.

"I hope this is hard enough for you, Call," he said. "I hope it makes you happy. If it don't, I give up. Driving all these skinny cattle all that way is a funny way to maintain an interest in life, if you ask me."

"Well, I didn't," Call said.

"No, but then you seldom ask," Augustus said. "You should have died in the line of duty, Woodrow. You'd know how to do that fine. The problem is you don't know how to live."

"Whereas you do?" Call asked.

"Most certainly," Augustus said. "I've lived about a hundred to your one. I'll be a little riled if I end up being the one to die in the line of duty, because this ain't my duty and it ain't yours, either. This is just fortune hunting."

"Well, we wasn't finding one in Lonesome Dove," Call said. He saw Deets returning from the northwest, ready to lead them to the bed-ground. Call was glad to see him—he was tired of Gus and his talk. He spurred the mare on off the hill. It was only when he met Deets that he realized Augustus hadn't followed. He was still sitting on old Malaria, back on the little hill, watching the sunset and the cattle herd.

R. Z. SHEPPARD

[***Lonesome Dove***'s] great length and leisurely pace convey the sense of a bygone era, while the author's attachment to misfits and backwaters never goes out of style. Neither does his premise: two aging gunfighters give it one more shot. Gus McCrae and Woodrow Call are descended from the noble buddy system of American literature. Exotically paired males, like Natty Bumppo and Chingachgook, Ishmael and Queequeg, Huck and Jim, fling themselves at the wilderness and sooner or later paddle into the mainstream. . . .

The urge to move comes as natural to McCrae and Call as the need to hang a thief. Yet they seem chained to an emotionally dead past. "The most unfree souls go west, and shout of freedom," said D. H. Lawrence. This includes Lorena, the local whore with the 14-karat ventricles, who joins the drive north because she has never lived any place cool. She also motivates much of the action when kidnaped by Blue Duck, an Indian whose specialty is killing settlers and selling their horses and children. ***Lonesome Dove*** has the highest mortality rate of any novel in recent memory. Characters are shot, stabbed, hanged, drowned, trampled, struck by snakes and lightning. "Gravediggers could make a fortune in these parts" is the sort of manly banter encountered on every other page. When the guys get dreamy, it is for Lorena or a horse.

But smile when you say cliché. McMurtry is a storyteller who works hard to satisfy his audience's yearning for the familiar. What, after all, are legends made of? The secret of his success is embellishment, the odd detail or colorful phrase that keeps the tale from slipping into a rut. During a thunderstorm, a cowboy is amazed to see little blue balls of electricity rolling on the horns of cattle. "You stayed gone a while" is poetry compared with "Long time, no see."

McMurtry also knows a thing or two about ambivalence. Though far from Freud's Vienna, McCrae and Call intuitively understand the meaning of *Civilization and Its Discontents:* "Me and you done our work too well. We killed off most of the people that made this country interesting to begin with," says McCrae. Call silently disagrees: "Nobody in their right mind would want the Indians back, or the bandits either. Whether Gus had ever been in his right mind was an open question."

Lonesome Dove is not the place to ask it. McMurtry's lip service to psychological conflict is lost to his outsize talent for descriptive narrative. Filmmakers should have no trouble finding visual thrills. The standard stream crossing is perked up by an attack of water moccasins; there is a choice between a dandy sandstorm and a typhoon of grasshoppers; Blue Duck is a menacing piece of work with his necklace of amputated fingers; a bear fights a bull to a draw; and a dead hero is packed in salt and carted more than a thousand ceremonious miles to his grave. There are also long, featureless stretches that add up to the reading equivalent of driving across Texas. But McMurtry knows exactly what he is doing in this sentimental epic. He is an uncommonly shrewd judge of book flesh.

R. Z. Sheppard, "It's a Long, Long Tale Awinding," in Time, *Vol. 125, No. 23, June 10, 1985, p. 79.*

THE NEW YORKER

[***Lonesome Dove***] basically concerns a cattle drive from southernmost Texas all the way to the highlands of Montana back in the late eighteen-seventies, around the time Montana was beginning to be made safe for settling (or, actually, as the novel reveals, it was at precisely this time that brash exploits by characters such as these were going to make that north country safe for settling, although it sure as hell wasn't yet); and it's a wonderful book. McMurtry's ongoing capacity for fashioning fully living characters—filled with contradictions and teeming with fellow-feeling—is in full bloom here; he's created dozens of them, and he's managed to keep them all vividly distinct. Reading the book, one begins to think of the novelist himself as trail driver, guiding and prodding his characters along: some tarry; others bolt and, after a long, meandering chase, have to be herded back into the main herd; others fall out and stay behind; still others just die off. Why does he, I marvel—how *can* he—keep driving them along like that, from the lazy, languid Rio Grande cusp of Chapter 1 to the awesome Montana highlands past page 800? In many ways, McMurtry strikes me as not unlike his character Captain Call, the leader of the drive, who *just does it,* and keeps on doing it as, one by one, all conceivable motivations and rationales slip away. And yet, unlike Call, McMurtry seems overflowing with empathy for every one of his creatures—a lavishment of love which makes his ability, his negative capacity, to then just let them go (after lavishing so much compassion in the fashioning of them), to just let them drift into ever more terrible demises—all the more remarkable.

I have so many questions I'd like to ask McMurtry about how he does it. But he wouldn't much cotton to my coming around and asking them. I know; I tried once. . . . I started out pouring forth praise and appreciation and heartfelt readerly thanks, and then headed into my few questions. And all the while he stared back at me, completely indifferent. The sheer extent of his indifference was terrifying. I ended up stammering some sort of gaga apology and bolting.

A few weeks ago, two of McMurtry's more recent novels were reissued in paperback—timed, I suppose, to coincide with the hardcover publication of ***Lonesome Dove.*** They included new prefaces, and these prefaces helped me to appreciate the icy reluctance to talk about his own writing with which he'd greeted me that day. "I rarely think of my own books, once I finish them," he records in the preface to ***Cadillac Jack,*** "and don't welcome the opportunity, much less the necessity, of thinking about them. The moving finger writes, and keeps moving;

thinking about them while I'm writing them is often hard enough." In the preface to ***The Desert Rose*** he plays a variation on this theme: "Once I finish a book, it vanishes from my mental picture as rapidly as the road runner in the cartoon. I don't expect to see it or think about it again for a decade or so, if ever." But those prefaces nevertheless suggest the contours of some answers to the sorts of questions I wanted to ask: questions about creators and creatures, free will and determinism—finally, I guess, about grace. At one point, he writes about the way one of his characters, Harmony, in ***The Desert Rose,*** "graced" his life during the time he was writing about her. (That's a good, an exact, word; I remember how she graced my life, too, as I read about her.) "In my own practice," he notes, "writing fiction has always seemed a semiconscious activity. I concentrate so hard on visualizing my characters that my actual surroundings blur. My characters seem to be speeding through their lives—I have to type unflaggingly in order to keep them in sight." Later, he records that he was "rather sorry," as he finished the book's composition, when Harmony "strolled out of hearing."

Characters stroll out of hearing all the time in ***Lonesome Dove,*** and strolling's not the half of it. They lurch, career, and smash out of hearing: they get snakebitten, drowned, hanged, gangrened, struck by lightning, bow-and-arrowed. The untamed West of ***Lonesome Dove*** is a tremendously dangerous wilderness. McMurtry offers a luminous epigraph to his epic, some lines from T. K. Whipple's *Study Out the Land*: "All America lies at the end of the wilderness road, and our past is not a dead past, but still lives in us. Our forefathers had civilization inside themselves, the wild outside. We live in the civilization they created, but within us the wilderness still lingers. What they dreamed, we live, and what they lived, we dream." It occurs to me that as a reader I stand in somewhat the same relationship to McMurtry as that which Whipple suggests obtains between us and our forebears. Here McMurtry has gone and done it—created this tremendous epic massif. All the while, as he was doing it, he must have been envisioning us someday reading this epic; and now we, as we read it—or, anyway, I, as I read it—try to imagine what it was like for him doing it, making it, living through the writing of it. And the thing I keep wondering about, in my clumsy, gawky fashion, is this: Did he, too, feel the sorrow, the poignant melancholy, that he engenders in us as, one by one, he disposed of those, his beloved characters; or was he able merely to glory in the craft of it, the polish, the shine? Are they—his characters—more or less real for him than they are for us? (pp. 20-2)

A review of "Lonesome Dove," in The New Yorker, *Vol. LXI, No. 27, August 26, 1985, pp. 20-2.*

WHITNEY BALLIETT

[In ***Lonesome Dove***] the Hat Creek Cattle Company . . . is owned by the novel's principal figures: Captain Augustus McCrae, a former Texas Ranger, probably in his fifties, who was born of well-to-do people in Tennessee, spent a year at a Virginia college, and has been widowed twice; and Captain Woodrow F. Call, also a former Ranger, probably in his fifties, who was born in Scotland and was raised in this country and, though never married, has one child. McCrae and Call are opposites. Call is short, industrious, humorless, taciturn, and commanding. He is puritanical to the ironic point of refusing to acknowledge his son. He has a ferocious temper and is a deadly fighter. He is impossibly stubborn. McCrae is three or four inches taller than Call, and he talks endlessly in his cannon voice, said to be audible a mile away. He leans toward philosophy, he likes to read the Prophets, and he is lackadaisical until stirred. He passes his time in Lonesome Dove (he and Call have lived there ten years) drinking whiskey, playing cards, talking, laughing, making sourdough biscuits, and visiting the town whore, the beautiful Lorena Wood. Although McCrae and Call have no great obvious affection for one another, they have gradually grown into indivisible, complementary halves, and when one of them is eventually done in, the other immediately begins to dwindle. They form a curious and affecting two-in-one fictional creation, a yin and yang that McMurtry has experimented with before. . . . (p. 153)

The book itself comes in two parts. The first includes the opening section in Lonesome Dove and a section near the end of the novel set in the house of Clara Allen, who lives outside Ogallala, Nebraska, on the North Platte. Here McMurtry . . . works at a kind of two-part character. Clara is Gus McCrae's old by-the-creek sweetheart and the wife of a slow-witted Kentucky horse trader, and July Johnson is a sheriff who is half her age. Dickensian coincidence, which McMurtry flourishes stylishly throughout the book, brings them together. Clara hires Johnson as a hand on her horse ranch, and he falls in love with her. He is weak, indecisive, and inarticulate, while she is outspoken, perverse, intelligent, selfish, high-strung, and angry. . . . She is the sort of charging, red-cheeked out-of-reach beauty that introverted men fall stupidly in love with. American fiction has few full-scale female protagonists; Clara Allen is a Jamesian exception. The second part of ***Lonesome Dove***—its very long middle section—concerns the cattle drive, and this is the work of McMurtry the commerical traveller, the seller of books-that-turn-so-easily-into-movies. The cattle drive is highly visual. There are hailstorms, sandstorms, snowstorms, cloudbursts, thunderstorms, and a locust plague. People are killed by guns, knives, hanging, lightning, snakes, Indians, and gangrene. There is a terrible kidnapping, involving Lorena Wood and a vicious Indian, Blue Duck, who unaccountably talks like an early James Cagney thug. There is a terrifying battle between a grizzly bear and a bull. Yet this calamitous crush never develops the momentum its parts demand; the book never quite gets free of the glutinous pace McMurtry sets in the opening pages.

McMurtry doesn't do much about demythicizing his subject. He skirts the worst clichés of Western writing, and throughout he is simply matter-of-fact. His prose is even and bare, his dialogue is sufficiently baggy. (The way the prototypes of McMurtry's characters spoke might be difficult to follow today—just as Mark Twain's attempt to get Jim down accurately in *Huckleberry Finn* tends to stymie most contemporary readers.) But one yearns for more *texture* in ***Lonesome Dove.*** The settled West of the eighteen-seventies was often seedy and makeshift, and although McMurtry implies this again and again, he does not give us enough descriptions. . . . (pp. 153-54)

The book needs an endpaper map. McMurtry is as vague about place as he is about time, and it would have helped us across the Great Plains. It would also have shown us the newly laid tracks of the Union Pacific, which McMurtry's light-footed cattle somehow never cross. (p. 154)

Whitney Balliett, "Captain McCrae and Captain Call," in The New Yorker, *Vol. LXI, No. 38, November 11, 1985, pp. 153-54.*

ERNESTINE P. SEWELL

[Sewell, an American critic and professor, publishes scholarly articles on literature in such periodicals as Scarecrow *and* West-

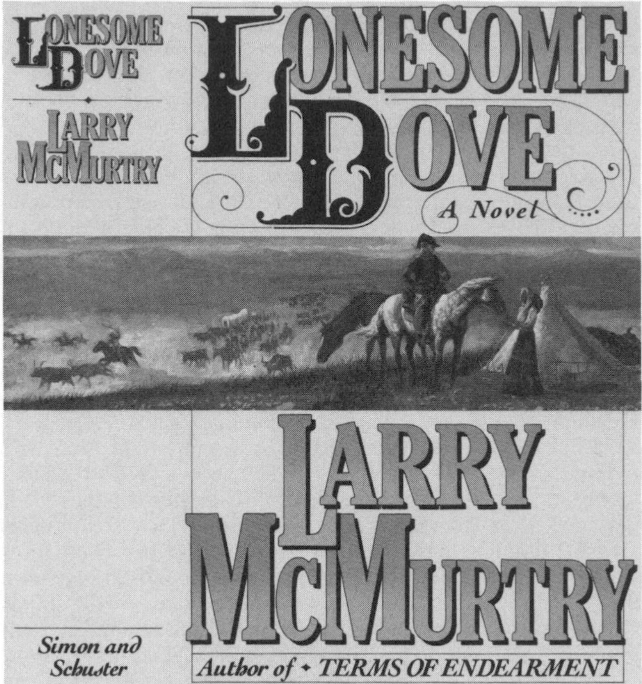

Dust jacket of Lonesome Dove, *by Larry McMurtry. Simon and Schuster, 1985. Jacket design by George Corsillo. Jacket painting by Shannon Stiruweis. Courtesy of Simon & Schuster, Inc.*

ern American Literature*; the literature of the Southwest is one of her academic specialties. She also coedited* Confronting Crisis: Teachers in America *(1980). In the following excerpt Sewell explains how Call, Gus, and Jake in* Lonesome Dove *illustrate three aspects of a single mythic figure, the Cowboy-God.*]

A panoply of big sky, the surging of mighty waters, vast expanses of grassland, a cattle drive studded by adventure and misadventure: these—with or without a camp cook for comic relief, a soiled dove for romance, a thundering herd of horses, and some Indians—will fulfill the expectations of those readers who judge western fiction by the use of conventions set to a formula. For that audience, Larry McMurtry's novel ***Lonesome Dove*** proves eminently satisfying. (p. 219)

Even a naive reader, however, is aware soon that this Western offers more than action. There is clearly a focus on the Texas Rangers, not without reason it would seem. McMurtry had accused Walter Prescott Webb of failing to be true to his commitment to write as a historian in *The Texas Rangers* (***In A Narrow Grave*** ...). Though Webb had published his tome in 1935, no one had faulted his glorification of the Rangers. The public gullibly accepted the "glaring whitewash" until McMurtry's critique in ***In A Narrow Grave*** in 1965. . . . Nor did that publication really set the record straight. Instead, McMurtry was labeled the enfant terrible of Texas letters for attacking Webb and his fellows of the literary triumvirate—J. Frank Dobie and Roy Bedichek. The fact is that only now are academicians interested in an unbiased picture of the Rangers. True, they served Texas in her hour of need, but they were violent, ruthless men who thought all non-whites to be subhuman. Should one look on Call and Gus and Jake as a composite of the Texas Ranger, he emerges as a man capable on the one hand of rustling, murder, hanging, atrocity, and injustice; and on the other of sentiment, gentleness, and heroism. In other words, the Rangers were men with feet of clay, not deities to be sanctified by a historian practising "symbolic frontiersmanship" (***Narrow Grave*** . . .).

History, however, is not McMurtry's territory: storytelling is. About his technique, he has written: "My first concern has commonly been with texture, not structure" (***Narrow Grave*** . . .). As the trail drive, which gives the novel structure, moves along, so the texturing process, which gives the novel depth, develops. McMurtry's texturing may be thought of as interlarding, enriching the whole.

The search motif is major. Each of the characters is a seeker after something. As they pursue their separate dreams, their stories are interlarded into the texture of the whole.

Call's dream is for a life of adventure and excitement where he can be again a captain of men, where he can ride the Hell Bitch, his horse, into the face of danger and prove to himself and his men that his strength lies in upholding frontier ideals of masculinity. Gus throws in with Call though he attempts to dissuade him from making the drive. They had done their duty, made Texas "safe for bankers and Sunday-school teachers." . . . Why should they subject themselves to the hazards of the trail? Texas is their place. Why not stay at Lonesome Dove and enjoy life? However, Gus is willing to go, for the trail will take him to Ogallala, where he will see Clara, whom he has dreamed about and loved from afar for fifteen years. Jake's aim in life is aimlessness. He is a gambler, a womanizer, and a bluff. Not a mean sort, just childlike, he wants only to satisfy his appetites: the challenge of a game of cards and the pleasure of a woman.

Lorena, the soiled dove, wants a cool place to escape the wretched heat of Texas and a man she can trust. San Francisco sounds cool and Jake appears willing to assume responsibility for her. . . . Newt, the sixteen-year-old waif, may be said to be searching for love. He holds fast a secret and hallowed love for Lorena and anticipates the time when he will speak to her. Also, he seeks a father.

To sum up texture thus far, a reader may begin to see parallels with Don Quijote. McMurtry writes that when he was twelve, he discovered the old knight on his adventures, imperiling the lives of others as well as himself for a ridiculous dream. Further parallels with Don Quijote would be counterproductive, though with little imagination one could construct a Procrustean apparatus, with particular reference to the Absurd: two herds of rustled horses collide head-on in the night; Call leaves in April with cattle enough for five ranches, knowing they will not reach Montana until winter; the cook gives the boys foods a survivalist would turn down; a swarm of snakes kills one of the boys; the Kiowas and Comancheros, led by the most villainous Blue Duck, commit inexpressible atrocities; a corpse is hauled from Montana to Texas. Are these instances for real? Or is McMurtry creating effect? Or is the absurdity an example of the ambivalence common to his works? Perhaps this statement from ***In A Narrow Grave*** will clarify McMurtry's use of borderland incredibilities: "nowhere else, except possibly California, can one find a richer mixture of absurdities" than in Texas. . . .

More significant to this study is McMurtry's further comment about Don Quijote: "Not long after I entered the pastures of the empty page, I realized that the place where all my stories start is the heart faced with the loss of its country, its customary and legendary range" (***Narrow Grave*** . . .). This is the dilemma of the three Rangers. Call is restless for the old life and "tried hard to keep sharp'' in the event some threat arose. . . . Gus, humorously philosophical about the sociological changes coming about in the land he had helped to tame, intends to enjoy life, keeping his whiskey jug handy and frequenting the Dry Bean, where the alluring Lorena keeps an upstairs room. Jake, uncaring, feels ''rather impermanent'' about life and makes no laments. . . .

With this insight into the characters, one may continue to penetrate the density of the novel. McMurtry has written: ''. . . our emotional experience remains largely unexplored, and therein lie the dramas, poems, and novels. An ideal place to start, it seems to me, is with the relations of the sexes'' (***Narrow Grave*** . . .).

The self-destructiveness of love negated is found in Call's story. Except for the close like-marriage feeling he has for his horse, the Hell Bitch, he rejects relationships for they may lead to emotional involvement. Yet Call is not infallible. He had made a mistake once, a mistake that ''seemed to undermine all that he was, or that people thought he was. It made all his trying, his work and discipline, seem fraudulent, and caused him to wonder if his life made sense at all.'' . . . The saloon girl Maggie, whose love for him had shone from frightened, despairing eyes, had borne his child, but Call had rejected her and her child, for he could not bring himself to admit that he had betrayed his tenets. Call is an empty shell, committed only to the image of himself as a Texas Ranger.

Jake's lack of emotional depth brings him to a tragic end. Incapable of love and the loyalty love asks, he drifts ever downward to an ignominious end.

The loss of humanity when sex is abused is dealt with by McMurtry in some minor sequences about the men into whose hands Lorena fell when she was but seventeen, men who sold her body for their own profit. And the depravity man is capable of is sickeningly revealed when Lorena is stolen from the cow-camp and turned over to Kiowa renegades and Comancheros.

But the depths of emotional experience that make ***Lonesome Dove*** literature in the most respected sense are found in the relationship Gus has with Lorena and the love he entertains for Clara. (pp. 220-22)

Clara, denying the sexual self its gratification and growing in independence as she matures, is the counterparted alter-ego of Lorena, for whom sex is a natural activity and in whom the inner force lies dormant.

Lonesome Dove is, then, a work of art that makes use of a cattle drive for structure and receives texture mainly through the search motif and the love theme, with the Absurd lending ambivalence to the credible and the incredible.

There are other symbolic interlardings. The wild Texas bull is zoomorphically the three Ranger/Cowboys themselves. Uncontrollable, he bellows and paws the ground, frightens the boys, falls behind to lollygag with the cows, or lopes ahead to lead the herd. He dashes fearlessly into battle with an enormous grizzly, and, one-eyed and one-horned, wearing the scars of that unequal battle, he brings the herd to Montana.

Gus has two pigs that go along on the drive. They symbolize the change of Texas from a land of ranching empires to a state cut up into small farms for Tennesseans and others who bring domesticity to the frontier.

Newt's initiation into manhood is confirmed by Call's gift of the Hell Bitch, for the measure of a cowboy is how well he rides and Newt had proved himself on the trail. Also, Call gives him his Henry, his buffalo gun, an act which marks the surrender of his phallic self to which he, Call, has been untrue. A last gift is his father's watch, the traditional gift of father to son.

Further, there is the symbolic subplot of July Johnson and Elmira, which serves as a foil to the Gus-Clara story. July, the Fort Smith sheriff, searches for Jake to bring him to the gallows for shooting the mayor. But he gives up that search to follow his soiled dove, Elmira, who has run away on a whiskey boat to follow her gunman-lover Dee somewhere north. Elmira, murdered by Indians, disappears from the story line and July is drawn into Clara's community, the fate awaiting Gus had Clara allowed him to remain with her.

Obviously the trail drive satisfies the aficionados of western fiction, appealing to the frontier spirit that Americans share and to the American dream that there is an Eden awaiting the stalwart. The search motif and the love relationships give the book universal appeal. But the power of the book rests in the awesomeness of the myth of the cowboy. The myth, heretofore foisted upon gullible audiences by Hollywood, can now be drawn from the fiction of one who knows the myth, Larry McMurtry, who admits to being haunted by it and recognizes that he will never be free of it (***Narrow Grave*** . . .).

In the myth the Cowboy is the God. And ''the god has abandoned Texas. Only the guards hear the music of his leaving. . . .'' (***Narrow Grave*** . . .). The God may have been Old Man Goodnight, or Teddy Blue, or McMurtry's own Uncle Johnny—any horseman whose ''mythos celebrates those masculine ideals appropriate to the frontier'' (***Narrow Grave*** . . .). McMurtry, heir to the legacy of ranchers, heard the music of the god's leaving, and he believes that, though the last cowboy has made the last drive, the Cowboy has become a mythic ''figure of romance as remote and appealing as King Arthur'' (***Narrow Grave*** . . .).

In ***Lonesome Dove*** the Cowboy-God is a Freudian composite of the three old Rangers: Call is Super-ego; Gus, Ego; and Jake, Id. Taken as one, the three embody the idea of Cowboy, the man on horseback, full of the joy of life, accepting the tragedy of life, brave, daring, hard-working, loyal, reliable, proud, stoic, often ascetic, straightforward, restless, independent, and not without a sense of humor. Each of the Rangers is consistent within the Freudian concept. When Jake the Id dies, nothing seems to go right anymore. When Gus's tempering Ego is gone, Call becomes a confused old man. He had adhered rigidly to the higher conscience and had achieved his goals. He had performed his duties, but he had failed to become ennobled by his acts, for he lacked the chastening of the Ego which would allow him to compromise his ideals and descend to Gus's level of humanity where all men make mistakes and redeem themselves someway. To view the three as one is to realize the Cowboy-God.

That the three-in-one figure is by authorial intent is strengthened by the motto Gus painted on the sign of the Hat Creek Cattle Company: *Uva uvam vivendo varia fit* . . . , which may be translated ''The cluster of grapes—many-sided, parti-colored, diverse—through living, begets one grape.'' The three, like a cluster of grapes, so various, are finally, after much ripening by the vagaries of life, one, the Cowboy-God.

The boy Newt cannot bear his father's name. He may be of Call's seed, but he is actually the product of the Cowboy-God. Perhaps he hears the music of the God's leaving—ironically, the bellowing of the Texas bull? The impact becomes even more dramatic when the reader sees that Newt and the other boys will eventually be drawn into the feminine urban world, for there are no more frontiers, only a world tamed for town-builders.

During the latter decades of the 1800s the West became less and less a man's world. The Feminine Principle, symbolized by Clara, inexorably swallowed up the cowboys, pulled them into her domain, be it her growing ranch community in Nebraska or, to move to the contemporary scene, one of the metropolitan centers spreading out over what was once rural (***Narrow Grave*** . . .). The Feminine Principle will diminish the cowboy, for his confidence will be destroyed when he leaves his man's world (***Narrow Grave*** . . .). July Johnson will become Clara's husband, bereft of his manly stature; Dish, top hand on the trail, will stay on at her ranch, "the extreme romantic, sentimental to the core" (***Narrow Grave*** . . .), idealizing Lorena and responding to Clara's will.

Lorena is the Cowboy-God's Love-Goddess. Despite all the abuse she has suffered and the horror she has faced, Lorena remains beautiful and worship-worthy. Jake had admitted: there was "a distance in her such as he had never met in a woman. Certain mountains were that way, like the Bighorns. The air around them was so clear you could ride toward them for days without seeming to get any closer. And yet, if you kept riding, you would get to the mountains. He was not so sure he would ever get to Lorie." . . . Within the household of the ranch-woman, the Love-Goddess may or may not live on: she is forever unreachable. Her spirit has gone with the Cowboy-God.

One reviewer of ***Lonesome Dove*** has said: McMurtry "writes with a new power and harnesses his awesome skills to the fullest" and "has distilled the westering experience to the essence" (Leonard Sanders, *Fort Worth News-Tribune,* Aug. 16, 1985). Let it be added that McMurtry, who has himself heard the music of the departing God, has elevated the Cowboy in the Call-Gus-Jake figure to that mythically heroic stature where he remains forever superior to other men and to his environment, his legends, however exaggerated or absurd they may seem, firmly rooted in the true western frontier experience. (pp. 223-25)

Ernestine P. Sewell, "McMurtry's Cowboy-God in 'Lonesome Dove'," in Western American Literature, *Vol. XXI, No. 3, November, 1986, pp. 219-25.*

Sam Shepard

A Lie of the Mind

New York Drama Critics Circle Award: Best Play

(Born Samuel Shepard Rogers, Jr.) American dramatist and screenwriter.

A prolific dramatist, having won eleven Obies, a Pulitzer Prize, and, most recently, a New York Drama Critics Circle Award for his play, *A Lie of the Mind* (1986), Shepard began his career in the off-off Broadway movement of the early 1960s. Influenced by the theory of "transformations," a technique practiced by the experimental theater company, the Open Theater, in which actors would rapidly shift personalities from scene to scene, Shepard's early works, noted for their powerful imagery, violence, and fascination with the American West, were innovative in their use of structure and fantasy. In the 1970s Shepard's style became more realistic, although his plays retained the mythic quality that had come to be associated with his work. Drawing from his own difficult family life, and his relationship with his alcoholic father, Shepard wrote *Curse of the Starving Class* (1976), *Buried Child* (1978), *True West* (1980), and *Fool for Love* (1983), exploring in each the emotional and often violent complexities of human relationships.

"I think there's something about American violence that to me is very touching," Shepard explains. "In full force it's very ugly, but there's also something very moving about it, because it has to do with humiliation. There's some hidden, deeply rooted thing in the Anglo male American that has to do with inferiority, that has to do with not being a man, and always, continually having to act out some idea of manhood that is invariably violent. This sense of failure runs very deep—maybe it has to do with the frontier being systematically taken away, with the guilt of having gotten this country by wiping out a native race of people, with the whole Protestant work ethic. I can't put my finger on it, but it's the source of a lot of intrigue for me."

A Lie of the Mind, seen by critics as a synthesis of Shepard's "family" plays, deals with the victims of such violence. Beaten to the point of brain damage by her husband, Jake, Beth is slowly recuperating under the watchful eye of her loveless parents and her vengeful brother. Jake, thinking that he has killed her, is holed up in his boyhood bedroom in the care of his over-protective mother. Geographically distant, but emotionally bonded by the obsessive love Beth and Jake continue to feel for each other, these families are explored and revealed. In a style which blends both the fantastic and realistic elements of Shepard's previous work, the playwright once again explores the power of enmeshed family relationships and the conflict of "the human heart divided against itself."

Most critics agree that at four hours, *A Lie of the Mind* would benefit from editing. Some find the work repetitive, treating familiar characters and themes less skillfully than in earlier plays, and to no new end. But many reviewers see *A Lie of the Mind* as a step forward, incorporating both humor and a sense of hope to create Shepard's most accessible work to date.

(See also *CLC*, Vols. 4, 6, 17, 34, 41; *Contemporary Authors*, Vols. 69-72; and *Dictionary of Literary Biography*, Vol. 7.)

FRANK RICH

[*An American drama and film critic, Rich is a frequent contributor to several publications, most notably,* The New York Times. *In the following excerpt Rich explores those qualities which have led him to judge* A Lie of the Mind *"the unmistakable expression of a major writer nearing the height of his powers."*]

Late in Act I in Sam Shepard's new three-act . . . play, ***A Lie of the Mind,*** a man named Jake . . . stands at the edge of the California bedroom he grew up in, peering into an inky night. Behind Jake, picked out by a spotlight on his bed, is a small leather box containing the ashes of his father, an alcoholic Air Force pilot who had deserted his family. Ahead of Jake, far off in the mysterious distance and illuminated only by a high green moon, is a woman whose nude back beckons with the mesmerizing lure of a distant, flickering neon sign along a desolate Western highway. The woman is Jake's wife, Beth . . . , and she is literally a highway away, back at her own childhood home in Montana.

The sight of Jake poised in the blackness between these two primordial magnetic poles—the father he can't escape and the woman he can't stop loving—is only one of many astonishing images in the altogether transporting play. . . . And it may be the one that best envelops the sweep of the whole. By the time ***A Lie of the Mind*** is over, Jake will have to achieve a symbolic reconciliation with the old man, and he will have to cross the gulf . . . that separates his bedroom from Beth's. The journey is far more difficult than it sounds. Not only did Jake help incite his father's drunken death long ago, but he has also just tried to kill Beth.

This being a Shepard play—even if in his recent, relatively realistic mode—the story of how Jake gets from where he is to where he ends up is not about one man's travels between two geographical or even psychological points. Indeed, after Act I, Jake's pivotal position in the play is usurped by his younger, milder brother. . . . Once the author reaches his final curtain—a domestic tableau of familial and romantic love lost and found, as eternal as a homecoming in a John Ford western—our vision has widened beyond both brothers, their phantom father and Beth to take in a larger landscape. Mr. Shepard has illuminated those archetypal genetic fates we all share, finally to transcend them to find that urge for salvation, that hunger for love, that allows us, like Jake, to go on.

A Lie of the Mind may be its author's most romantic play. However bleak and chilly its terrain—some of it unfolds, in more ways than one, in a blizzard—no character, alive or dead, is beyond redemption: There is always hope, as Mr. Shepard's closing metaphor has it, for a miraculous "fire in the snow." And the work's buoyancy doesn't end there. By turns aching and hilarious—and always as lyrical as its accompanying country music—***A Lie of the Mind*** is the unmistakable expression of a major writer nearing the height of his powers. Mr. Shepard has written more innovative, let alone tidier, plays, as well as those that achieve a firmer sense of closure. But these four hours pass like a dream, with scene after scene creating a reverberant effect.

Sometimes the play echoes through Mr. Shepard's recent work. Jake and Beth could be Eddie and May, the combustible fools for love; their parents and siblings are amalgams of those in the family trilogy of ***Curse of the Starving Class, Buried Child*** and ***True West.*** This play also seems to ricochet through American dramatic literature: As it shares O'Neill's vision of mirror-image fathers and sons locked in mutually destructive combat, so it contains flaky Williams mothers . . . and, once it moves surprisingly from darkness to light, a pop-art domestic absurdity reminiscent of Albee's *American Dream*. Mr. Shepard's inheritance from Mark Twain remains apparent, too: Men are forever running off to the lonely road, hoping as one Huck-sounding character explains, to escape the "feebleminded women in civilization." Only now the frontier has run out: As Jake's mother ruefully notes, the West is no longer big enough for every loner to start a new town of his own.

The play's most powerful reverberations, however, are prompted by those pure Shepard inventions that deliver the evening's inseparable poetry, action and content. It's the one, shimmering constant in this work that characters are mistaking the living for the dead, one brother for another brother, sons for fathers, sisters for wives—even, at one loony point, a man for a deer.

Such repeated confusions—some of which are acted out through the author's signature scenes of metamorphosis, in which "a whole life turns upside down in a flash"—create a cumulative dramatic sensation not quite like that produced by any other American playwright. We feel we are passing through the turbulent magnetic fields of the play's two interlocked families, almost palpably experiencing the knotted blood ties that keep tugging at the characters on stage.

These ties, as immutable as a tribal code, also seem to be the lies of the title. It is the roles the characters play in their eternal family scenarios, the mythic stories that are re-enacted ritualistically in generation after generation, that dog Mr. Shepard's people. . . .

Mr. Shepard's characters burn down their homes, run away, lose their memories, try out their new roles (Beth actually is, to delicious comic effect, an actress)—and yet fail to escape the family pull. But if, as Jake's mother says, "love is a disease," it still "makes you feel good while it lasts." Mr. Shepard seems to believe in the saving possibilities of love between men and women, if not between parents and children. Love is the play's only "plain truth." It's the characters who drive away a lover who end up in exile; they are spoken of as "lost" or "dead," even if they're alive.

A Lie of the Mind eventually bleeds its personal story into a larger cultural mythos: The final reconciliations are played out in counterpoint to both Hollywood clichés and the tradition-bound folding of a flag. As both writer and director, Mr. Shepard has filled the play, past the brim at times, with virtuosic sequences mixing the colloquial and the fantasist.

Frank Rich, "'A Lie of the Mind,' by Sam Shepard," in The New York Times, *December 6, 1985, p. C3.*

LINDA WINER

When Sam Shepard's ***A Lie of the Mind*** is good—which is a little over half its four hours . . .—it is splendid: as wildly funny, touching and harrowing as anything this unsettling Pulitzer Prize-winning movie idol has written.

But when it's bad—unfortunately, about two hours' worth—his marathon rambles between self-parody and tedium.

Shepard . . . seems unable to separate inspired madness from muddle—especially in the overtly autobiographical parts about his late father.

When everything soars, we're truly grateful to be so intimate with his unique vision, his rural-mythic rhapsodies, [and] his brutally beautiful images. . . . Other times, we yearn for a director with the distance to say, "Cut."

The surreal horror-comedy, which Shepard calls a "little legend about love," is really two stories that try to be epic—but never really come together in something bigger than their individual uneven parts.

In more than 40 plays, Shepard already has brought us weird homecomings in ***Buried Child,*** dual-personality brothers in ***True West,*** obsessive love in ***Fool for Love.*** The best of ***Lies*** uncovers more rich, primal dirt in the tension between roots and freedom. As his characters so often fear for themselves, unfortunately, now he's stuck.

Linda Winer, " 'Lie of the Mind' Seesaws from Great Madness to Grating Muddle," in USA Today, *December 6, 1985, p. 6D.*

VARIETY

A Lie Of The Mind is a mesmerizing, emotionally raw play that once again pulls the viewer into Shepard's distinctive world of distilled reality and hungry hearts. . . .

Lie is another important play by a major American dramatist with a compelling, *sui generis* style. . . .

As in ***Buried Child, Curse Of The Starving Class, True West*** and ***Fool For Love,*** obsessive family relationships are at the center of the new play. Its counterpoint story line of two families—those of a wife-beating roughneck and the woman who has suffered brain damage from his fists—makes for a more complex structure than previous Shepard works. There's also more robust comedy which director Shepard clearly has encouraged.

Shepard's male characters tend to be exposed, throbbing ganglia whose behavior springs from primitive instinct unfettered by social restraints, while his women are colonized victims whose emotional and sexual resources are essential to the men. In ***Lie,*** the brutish wife-beater and childlike battered wife are upper-case exemplars of this vision of the genders, while their respective relatives reflect the author's perception of the family as a minefield from which there's no escape. . . .

Texture, tone and subtext take precedence over narrative in Shepard's plays, which require a suspension of conventional expectations from audiences. At nearly four hours, ***Lie*** is too long and the second act drags badly, but the power of the writing and the roughhewn archetypal thrust of the characters pull the audience forward. Although there's no mistaking Shepard for any other playwright, his ability to magnify the obsessiveness of emotional desperation recalls the work of such forebears as Faulkner, Flannery O'Connor and Carson McCullers. . . .

The least sentimental of writers, Shepard has a sympathy for the excesses of self-destruction in his seemingly ignoble characters. Like Faulkner he writes about "the human heart in conflict with itself" and does so with a theatrical power that's unique.

A Lie Of The Mind demands that the audience tune in to his wavelength and most will be willing to do that.

Humm., "A Lie of the Mind," in Variety, *December 11, 1985, p. 136.*

MEL GUSSOW

In Sam Shepard's exhilarating new play, ***A Lie of the Mind,*** two families are divided against themselves and armed against each other. One family, on stage right, is Californian, fatherless and matriarchal. The other, stage left, is nomadic, Montanan and patriarchal. It would be no leap of the imagination to suggest that, as in a western movie, the Californians are homesteaders, the others are hunters. However, Shepard's new western story is not really a tale of rivalry on the range, but of interior domestic violence, the damage that one does to filial, fraternal and marital bonds—and the love that lingers in the air after the havoc has run its natural course. . . .

The play is in earnest, but it is never portentous. For all the violence, actual and imagined, it is, on one level, a sardonic comedy, with many pertinent comments to make about the need for individuals to belong to families and about the legacies that pass back and forth between parents and offspring. Without altering the idiosyncratic nature of his art, Shepard has made his work available to a greater public. His new play follows a clear naturalistic plotline, with characters who behave like normal, irrational human beings. There are no monstrous beasts beating at the door or space invaders dropping down in backyards. The playwright sees his characters in all their fallibility. This means that mother love can be overweening, that fatherhood can trigger patricide. Shepard has seldom written a more hair-raising yarn than the one he tells about how [Jake's] father died in Mexico, how the son egged his father into a drinking competition from bar to bar to the United States border, a contest that ended with the father being run over by a truck.

Both highly personal and accessible, ***A Lie of the Mind*** is a synthesis of—and an advancement over—themes and motifs that have been preoccupying the playwright since he first emerged on a public stage in the 1960's. For the record, one omission is food; that favorite Shepard image, the open refrigerator crammed with produce, does not appear in the new play. The early plays were riffs of language and absurdist ballads. These were followed by a folkloric, mystic phase, in which legendary badmen and heroes battled for supremacy. Later, arts, sports, commerce and celebrity entered his ken. Having gone through a panoply of periods, in ***Buried Child,*** written in 1978, this immensely prolific writer began exploring the question of family, as sons were forced to come to terms with their genetic origins.

Buried Child was followed by ***Curse of the Starving Class, True West*** and ***Fool for Love,*** each dealing, in various ways, with parents and children, sibling and marital rivalry. ***A Lie of the Mind*** completes a Shepard full house of family plays. The works share psychological topography. Each of the quintet, in its own way, deals with the family as a force of nature, surviving all leave-taking. These elements are unified in ***A Lie of the Mind,*** a play of penetrating originality. (p. 3)

On first look, Sam Shepard and Tennessee Williams would seem to have little in common, except for the quality of their work and their gift for creating memorable titles. But they are also connected as playwright-poets of the American heartland. I mean "heartland" in two senses, both emotional and geographic. Shepard's characters—prodigal sons and fathers, abandoned mothers and daughters—long to come back home and put things in order. Each is looking for "one, good solid ally," and the ideal is for everyone to be "in cahoots.". . . . Underlying the lies of the mind is an urgent quest for love and tranquility. (p. 7)

Mel Gussow, "Sam Shepard Revisits the American Heartland," in The New York Times, *December 15, 1985, pp. 3, 7.*

JACK KROLL

The true artist starts with his obsessions, then makes them ours as well. The very young Sam Shepard exploded his obsessions like firecrackers; in his crazy, brilliant early plays he was escaping his demons, not speaking to ours. But in his recent family plays (including the Pulitzer Prize-winning ***Buried Child***) he has simmered down, shaping his music rather than wailing it. He is, in fact, taming himself so that he may speak to us rather than dazzle or shock us. You could say that his new, big . . . , courageous ***A Lie of the Mind*** is about the taming of Shepard's violent, bedeviled spirit. But what makes it a notable event is that his complex act of self-knowledge and self-discipline becomes a revelation for us. Shepard has said that until recently he was afraid of love. This has as much to do with the artist as with the man; in opening himself up, Shepard has opened his audience to him. . . .

A Lie of the Mind is likely to gain Shepard his widest audience yet as a playwright; there's no doubt that this play will be produced all over the country. The crowds that will flock to it will have a lot to talk about. Shepard may be taming his spirit, but he will never be domesticated. ***A Lie of the Mind*** orchestrates Shepard's preoccupation with doubles: man-woman, father-son, truth-fantasy. But now the orchestration is symphonic. Shepard doubles the doubles; he deals with not one but two families, interlocked in love and hatred. . . .

These families are Shepard's most incisive explorations of the people he grew up among, the dislocated, deracinated working-class Westerners whose odyssey brought them to California. These people are battered travesties of the American pioneer energy, but something of that energy survives in their often comically desperate attempts at survival. Shepard is their William Faulkner; like Faulkner, he writes about them with a powerful blend of wild humor and tragic force. What keeps ***A Lie of the Mind*** spirited through four hours is largely its mad, gutbucket humor, which is never absent as the play moves from its various dark places to a wintry, purging light of redemption. No one beats Shepard at giving mythic resonance to events while laughing at them. It is in these redemptive resolutions that Shepard takes his greatest risk. Some of them are dubious in concept and language, such as the American flag that plays a large part at the end and in the first-kiss-in-20-years reconciliation between Baylor and Meg. . . .

Such faults are overridden by the play's humanity, animal warmth, loony hilarity and above all by its bravely romantic renunciation of the "lie of the mind," the ego-driven distortions that subvert the capacity to love.

Jack Kroll, "Savage Games People Play," in Newsweek, *Vol. CVI, No. 25, December 16, 1985, p. 85.*

WILLIAM A. HENRY, III

Many playwrights master technique, a fair number possess innate narrative gifts, but only a few achieve a genuine, persuasive voice. When plays are described as depicting reality, the statement cannot be taken literally: a set is recognizably a set, not a house or a tree, and speeches palpably differ from authentically aimless conversation. What makes a set seem real, what enables dialogue to stand for experience is the writer's capacity to create an alternative world, distinctively his own, and lure audiences into it. That talent is the true measure of voice, a blend of personality and vision.

Sam Shepard's voice has often seemed querulous or cruelly funny. Even as he was attracting an avid following as perhaps America's foremost active playwright, critics sensed in his plays a compulsive urge toward violence, a lack of compassion, a reveling in the bizarre. His comic scenes made viewers wonder whether he was laughing with or at his characters. His work has shifted from expressionist flights of fancy to a kind of grim, weird naturalism and has tended more and more to portray families as the poisoned wellspring of human evil. He has brought to life the same fumbling, feckless dreamers from the heartland that Tennessee Williams did and, like Williams, has shown a special sensitivity to the yearnings of women. But having seen the world with cold comprehension, he has lacked the perception or perhaps the will to envision a possibility of kindness, of decency, of morally redemptive hope.

Until now. Shepard, 42, last week unveiled ***A Lie of the Mind,*** the newest, longest . . . and best of his 40-odd plays. . . . ***Lie*** superficially resembles yet another Shepardian slice of life among borderline psychotics of the underclass. It opens with the confession of an uncontrollably jealous man . . . who has beaten his innocent wife . . . and left her for dead. Before it is over, characters have been shot, pummeled, enslaved and murdered. Yet the play's real action is a coming to terms with the past by the families of both the wife beater and the wife, and it ends with a flickering flame and a folded flag that symbolize the restoration of order.

More than in any other Shepard play, the combat leads to catharsis. It also results in an apparent union, all but unprecedented for him, between two wholly sympathetic characters. And because Shepard has directed the play to be uproarious, it casts new light on all his work. In retrospect, his eerie lowlifes seem more farcical, less perversely heroic.

William A. Henry, III, "Achieving a Vision of Order," in Time, *Vol. 126, No. 24, December 16, 1985, p. 83.*

VICTORIA RADIN

A Lie of the Mind is a terrible disappointment. . . . [It] seems a kaleidoscopic blur, verging at times on self-parody, of the themes of all his later works. Shepard has said that during rehearsals he allowed the actors to continue to evolve the play, and it is possible that he was rather too eager to listen to them. The work has an unfinished quality, both less poetic and less precise than his other recent works. . . .

Here we are again, after ***Buried Child*** and ***Curse of the Starving Class,*** in the badlands of the lower-middle-class Western American family—Shepard's contribution to American drama's obsession with the hearth (the "diaper play" as one critic named it). His cartoon hyperboles of dynastic disintegration, with their mixture of violence and grotesque humour, put him closer to Charles Addams than to O'Neill, Miller or Tennessee Williams. . . .

Shepard's persistent theme is how love, or ties, or "lies" go wrong, that men can't live with women—or without them. (Women have the same trouble with men, though that is less important to him.) "Love—that crock of shit", says Jake's mother. "It's another disease—only it makes you feel good while it lasts." There is little evidence in any Shepard work that love ever makes you feel good: love, or this distempered, incurable obsession, a lie of the mind, is a poison, or curse, which is helplessly handed down from one generation to another. In the past, these generations were segregated into different plays. ***A Lie of the Mind*** brings them together, but says nothing new on a subject Shepard has treated more cogently.

Victoria Radin, "Cursing Tales," in The Times Literary Supplement, *No. 4319, January 10, 1986, p. 39.*

An Excerpt from *A Lie of the Mind*

MEG: Well, what is it? I'd like to know. I mean what is the big fascination about standing out there in the cold for hours on end waiting for an innocent deer to come along so you can blast a hole through it and freeze your feet off in the process?

BAYLOR: It's deer season. You hunt deer in deer season. That's what you do.

MEG: Look at this. You've got blood all over your pants and shirt. You look like you've been in a war or something.

BAYLOR: Just rub that stuff into my feet and stop tryin' to pick a bone with me. I'm too tired to argue.

(*Pause.* MEG *keeps rubbing* BAYLOR'S *feet.* BAYLOR *keeps his eyes closed.*)

MEG: *(After pause)* Maybe you just wanna be alone. Maybe that's it. Maybe it's got nothing to do with hunting. You just don't want to be a part of us anymore.

BAYLOR: *(Eyes closed)* You've still got the greatest hands in the world.

MEG: Maybe it really is true that we're so different that we'll never be able to get certain things across to each other. Like mother used to say.

BAYLOR: Your mother.

MEG: "Two opposite animals."

BAYLOR: Your mother was a basket case.

MEG: She was a female.

(*Pause.* BAYLOR *opens his eyes, looks at* MEG, *shakes his head, then closes his eyes again.*)

BAYLOR: *(Eyes closed)* Meg, do you ever think about the things you say or do you just say 'em?

MEG: She was pure female. There wasn't any trace of male in her. Like Beth—Beth's got male in her. I can see that.

BAYLOR: I'm her father.

MEG: No. She's got male in her.

BAYLOR: *(Opens eyes, leans forward, points to himself)* I'm male! I'm her father and I'm a male! Now if you can't make sense, just don't speak. Okay? Just rub my feet and don't speak.

(BAYLOR *leans back, close his eyes again.* MEG *keeps on rubbing his feet. Pause.*)

MEG: She was like a deer. Her eyes.

BAYLOR: Oh, brother. How do you manage to get things so screwed up? No wonder yer daughter's in the shape she's in. A deer is a deer and a person is a person. They got nothing' to do with each other.

(*Pause*)

MEG: Some people are like deer. They have that look—that distant thing in their eyes. Like mother did.

BAYLOR: Your mother had that distant thing in her eyes because she'd lost her mind, Meg. She went crazy.

MEG: She was just old.

BAYLOR: Yeah, she almost took us to the grave with her. You and me'd be a lot younger today if we'd stuck her in a rest home when the whole thing started.

MEG: *(Still rubbing his feet)* I know what it is.

(*Pause.* BAYLOR *opens his eyes.*)

BAYLOR: What! What's what *what* is?

MEG: The female—the female one needs—the other.

BAYLOR: What other?

MEG: The male. The male one.

BAYLOR: Oh.

MEG: But the male one—doesn't really need the other. Not the same way.

BAYLOR: I don't get ya.

MEG: The male one goes off by himself. Leaves. He needs something else. But he doesn't know what it is. He doesn't really know what he needs. So he ends up dead. By himself.

ROBERT BRUSTEIN

[*An American drama critic and the artistic director of the American Repertory Theatre Company, Brustein is well-known and highly respected for both his devotion to excellence in all aspects of theater production and his beliefs in theater's "higher purpose." As the dean of Yale University's School of Drama from 1966 to 1979, Brustein introduced many innovative, and often controversial, dramatic techniques. His criticism, including* The Theatre of Revolt *(1964),* The Culture Watch *(1975), and* Critical Moments: Reflections on Theatre and Society, 1973-1979 *(1980), is highly regarded for the way it places drama within a social context and for its prose style. In the following excerpt Brustein finds* A Lie of the Mind *a disappointing addition to Shepard's body of work due, largely, to the recent domestication of Shepard's style.*]

A Lie of the Mind is Sam Shepard's most ambitious play to date, the closest he has come to entering the mainstream of American drama. . . . Thus Shepard seems to be following the pattern of all serious American dramatists since O'Neill—beginning with a small but passionate coterie of devoted admirers, and then achieving popular suppport and media recognition. In Shepard's case, this recognition has been enhanced, and complicated, by his celebrity as a movie actor, which has exacerbated the tension between his public and private careers. A similar tension was partly responsible for that neglect suffered by most reputable American playwrights after their greatest success (followed perhaps by a revival of interest when the playwright died or reached some venerable birthday). Clifford Odets got smothered by Hollywood; Arthur Miller ran out of usable material; Tennessee Williams lost control of his form; William Inge turned to increasingly hysterical plots; Edward Albee sacrificed his absurdist power for mythical drawing-room comedies modeled on T. S. Eliot. On the other hand, O'Neill, with whom Shepard is most frequently compared, wrote his greatest plays years after Broadway had abandoned him.

For that reason, any cautionary remarks about Shepard's future are premature, though I must admit I found ***A Lie of the Mind*** disappointing—a big canvas on which the colors run in smeared, sometimes slipshod fashion. True, Shepard's play writing has never been neat, but then it has never been very accessible either. What is strange for Shepard enthusiasts is how closely this one resembles a play by Lanford Wilson or Tennessee Williams. Ever since ***Curse of the Starving Class,*** Shepard has been moving away from extravagant characters, dream actions, and hallucinatory riffs into a more domestic style. With ***Buried Child,*** arguably his finest work, he managed to make the family play a structure for subterranean probes into the American nightmare. Now, however, those relationships between violent and sensitive brothers, loony mothers and children, fathers and alienated sons, husbands and estranged wives, have increasingly moved to the center of his plays, while whatever was fantastic and demonic has gone to the fringes. ***A Lie of the Mind*** goes delightfully haywire in the last of its three long acts, but for most of its four-hour length the action and the characters are relatively recognizable, even endearing eccentrics.

In short, Shepard is beginning to domesticate himself as a writer. . . . Composing more and more out of his actual as opposed to his dream experience, Shepard is moving inexorably toward the heart of American realism, where audiences have the opportunity to identify him as a family member like themselves—son, brother, lover, husband. This has advantages: greater clarity, concentration, and recognition. It also has disadvantages, in that Shepard is now displaying what he has in common with the spectator rather than what the spectator unwittingly shares with him. Another disadvantage is that as Shepard's life gets increasingly familiar from interviews, his work seems to get increasingly biographical—and confined. The brothers in ***A Lie of the Mind*** remind us of the ones in ***True West;*** the husband and wife recall the brother and sister in ***Fool for Love.*** The California family comes from ***Curse of the Starving Class,*** the Montana family from ***Buried Child.*** Worse, one finds oneself speculating about more personal links: whether the enmity between the dead father and his son is based on Shepard's own published filial feelings, whether the hero's jealousy over his actress wife has any bearing on his relationship with Jessica Lange, whether the character's brain-damaged dialogue has been influenced by that of his close friend Joseph Chaikin, a recent stroke victim. One is tempted, in short, to confuse fiction with reality, imaginative creation with biographical gossip.

A Lie of the Mind begins with a frenzied telephone call from Jake to his brother Frankie, saying that he has killed his actress wife, Beth. . . . Beth, however, is alive, though the assault has damaged her brain. (pp. 25-6)

Beth has moved from a California hospital to her Montana home, where her father spends his days hunting venison. When Frankie arrives to try to reconcile Beth to Jake, her father, Baylor, mistaking him for a deer, shoots him in the leg. ("In my prime, you'd have been dead meat, son.") Beth's family, particularly [her brother] Mike, is primed for vengeance. . . .

Back in California, Jake is preoccupied with the ashes of his own father, an alcoholic Air Force officer who had abandoned the family. . . . When Jake finally goes to Montana to find Beth, Mike trusses him like a horse, putting an American flag in his mouth for a bit. (Baylor is mighty upset by this desecration of the "flag of our nation.") While Baylor and his dotty wife carefully fold the flag, Jake announces his love for Beth—"I love you more than this earth. . . . Everything lied—you—you're true. I love you more than life.". . .

It may seem odd to describe such idiosyncratic characters and bizarre behavior as normal or domestic. Yet the eccentricities, while often amusing, sometimes seem willed, like the studied gothic in Beth Henley or Tennessee Williams, and at the heart of this work is a rather conventional, even somewhat banal, love story. "I love you more than this earth" is not a line one would ever expect to find in a Shepard play.

Nor would one expect to find such crude symbolism as the flag business at the end. Even his title lacks the customary, instinctual Shepard resonance. What ***A Lie of the Mind*** could use is a really exacting editor, one who might have persuaded the playwright to pare away irrelevancies and obesities from his rather bloated text, while encouraging him to examine more closely its themes and situations. (p. 26)

[This] play wears you down rather than works you up. The dialogue is a little too declarative, the plotting a little too undisciplined, the characters a little too unforgettable, to persuade you that the motor energies come out of inspiration rather than will. (p. 27)

Robert Brustein, "The Shepard Enigma," in The New Republic, *Vol. 194, No. 4, January 27, 1986, pp. 25-6, 28.*

GERALD WEALES

[Weales, an American drama critic, is a winner of the George Jean Nathan Award for drama criticism and the author of numerous books on drama as well as a theater critic for such journals as Commonweal *and* The Georgia Review. *His books include, among others,* Tennessee Williams *(1965),* The Jumping-Off Place: American Drama in the 1960's *(1969), and his most recent work,* Canned Goods as Caviar: American Film Comedy in the 1930's *(1985). In the following excerpt Weales finds the serious aspects of* A Lie of the Mind *compromised by the play's cartoonish atmosphere.]*

Sam Shepard's new play, ***A Lie of the Mind,*** runs for more than four hours, but its length does not herald structural innovation in his drama. He is still working in short scenes, as he has been since he turned up off-off-Broadway in the 1960s. In the new play, he cuts back and forth between two families and their homes on opposite ends of the stage, jumping from one painful or comic sequence to the next. The play, as one expects with Shepard, is absorbing, but a kind of attenuation has set in. It has no images as sharp and compelling as the corn shucking in ***Buried Child*** or the nude man with the lamb in ***Curse of the Starving Class;*** nor does it manage the intensity of ***True West*** or ***Fool for Love,*** even though many of the scenes are two-person encounters.

Shepard is on familiar ground in ***A Lie of the Mind,*** dealing once again with the disintegration of the American family, as in ***Curse*** and ***Child,*** and with the violence and mutability of sexual love, as in ***Fool for Love.*** . . .

The play is sprinkled with moments in which a character displays love, affection, protectiveness toward another, but the effect of the play as a whole is to suggest the impossibility of a happy relationship between a man and a woman or a healthy closeness within a family. . . .

The most startling thing about ***A Lie of the Mind*** is the broad comedy in it. . . . With ***A Lie of the Mind*** the cartoon quality of the characters becomes pervasive, so much so that the knockabout often robs the play of the kind of powerful image that Shepard so often comes up with when a potentially comic situation or character turns suddenly painful or lyric. . . . All of the characters are overstated, but none of them has quite the flamboyance of the two mothers. Shepard has been having a run on peculiar mothers—in ***Curse,*** in ***Buried Child,*** in ***True West***—but the two in ***A Lie of the Mind*** win blue ribbons for eccentricity. (p. 86)

A major new Shepard play is always an occasion, but ***A Lie of the Mind*** seems to have extended Shepard's staying power without enriching his art. In the past, he has used his taste for caricature in the interest of dramatic or visual truth. Here the serious side of the play is so compromised by the cartoon atmosphere that Shepard sometimes seems to be mocking the themes that have given substance and force to so much of his recent work. (pp. 86-7)

Gerald Weales, "Great Divide: Shepard's 'Lie of the Mind'," in Commonweal, *Vol. CXIII, No. 3, February 14, 1986, pp. 86-7, 89.*

PAUL BERMAN

In Philip Rahv's famous classification, palefaces are the American writers who cultivate sensibility, refinement, education and discipline. Henry James, for instance. Redskins are the half-baked mystics, the primitives, the gross naturalists, the writers whose strength is experience and energy. Whitman, for instance. The division between these types is deep. Critics who like James rarely like Whitman, and vice versa. . . .

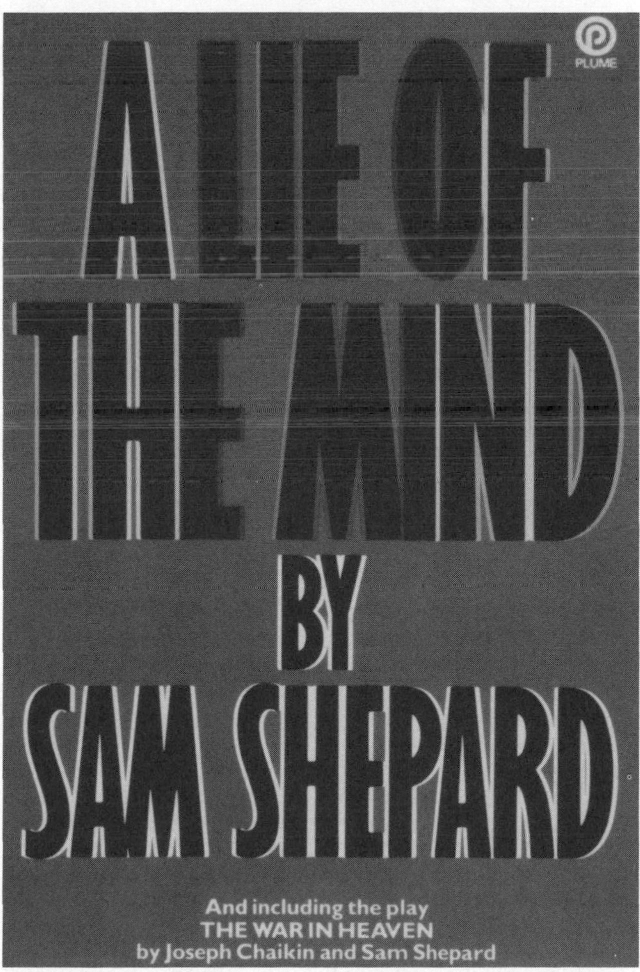

Dust jacket of A Lie of the Mind, *by Sam Shepard. New American Library, 1986. Jacket design by Hildegarde Ambusch-Karsh. Courtesy of New American Library.*

Shepard is, of course, the reddest redskin who ever lived. He gives the impression that he would rather knock your ears off with an electric guitar than do anything so prissy as to write a play. "I don't want to be a playwright," the playwright said in a program note fifteen years ago. "I want to be a rock and roll star." (p. 215)

He has constructed a bleak picture of American life as a cultural badlands dotted with a few national myths as barren of meaning as cactus is of nutrient. This picture meshes perfectly with his abrasive physicality and spontaneity to make scary scenes of astonishing bitterness. "I thought it was going to be turkey dinners and apple pie and all that kinda stuff," says the young woman in ***Buried Child.*** Goes the reply: "Well I hate to disappoint you." "I'm not disappointed! I'm fuckin' terrified!" A long evening of this makes you feel you've been sitting too close to a madman banging a drum. But it's not a sensation you'll easily forget.

He commands a voice that is well known in American theater. It is the voice that comes to us, perhaps, from Clifford Odets—the eulogistic catch in the throat, the voice of dazed regret or of a slightly embittered nostalgia. In Shepard you hear this voice at the end of plays like ***Buried Child*** and ***Fool for Love,*** only since he's not exactly a realist, the voice seems slightly disembodied, and the mood it produces is odd. You feel moved without understanding why; and the combination of being moved without exactly "getting it" is one of his striking effects.

He has developed several theatrical innovations, though the word "developed" may be too strong, since Shepard seems to have entered the theatrical avant garde with the ease of a man entering his own living room, to paraphrase Trotsky. . . . The playwright has jettisoned conventional theater space and time in favor of space and time that are determined by the emotions of his characters. He has made feelings the basis for action and done away with the ordinary restraints on behavior, so that consciousness and not behavior determines the narrative. He has drawn his characters with a kind of spontaneous line instead of striving for anything coherent. And he does all this with perfect unselfconsciousness. Taken together, his novel techniques produce a kind of crazy fluency, coherent one moment and not the next—which is how people generally are.

The fluency above all is what makes Shepard seem a man of today. By this I mean to distinguish him from what is usually called "modern." The modern style is fragmented and angular, and the audience is intended to piece together a significance. But "todayism" has the quality of an unbroken stream, and the audience is not meant to piece together anything at all. . . .

Shepard has cultivated a peculiar comic sense. He is a parodist with a pan as dead as a doornail. There are few punch lines, few opportunities to laugh out loud, few lines that seem funny when read instead of performed. Yet a sense of the ridiculous runs through a large amount of his work. . . .

Such are the achievements of Sam Shepard. There is, however, a difficulty in the redskin vocation that can't be ignored, though in the atmosphere of Shepard celebration it often is. The difficulty is what to do when a redskin's genius falls short. All writers should be geniuses at all times, of course; but sometimes they are not, and then something must be done. Palefaces fall back on their learning, intelligence and taste. But rough-and-ready redskins, what have they to fall back on? Rahv didn't take up this problem in his essay, but it is a grave one. The redskin is always in danger of plunging into the autodidact's vat of sins—into pretension, pomposity, sentimentality, tastelessness and grandiosity. From brilliant originality to painful amateurism is but a moment's leap.

The gap between the best work of a redskin writer and the worst is therefore almost always immense. For that reason the best had better be spectacular, and the worst had better not come too often. . . . In Shepard's case, no one has wanted to acknowledge just how bad the worst can be. Partly that's because of his origins in the embattled avant-garde of the 1960s, whose advocates have naturally preferred championing their hero to making critical judgments about him. But mostly it is because of his cleverness at parody. You tend to think that an author as devilishly satirical as Shepard couldn't possibly be sentimental, that Sam the rock-and-roller could never be guilty of artiness, that the American pop culture mythology could never mystify a man like that. (p. 216)

[Lapses] in the work of Sam Shepard are anything but infrequent.

His new play, ***A Lie of the Mind*** . . . is a regrettably good example. The play opens with a husband telephoning his brother to say he's beaten his wife to death. Words are sharp. The husband is so dislocated he doesn't know which state he's in, just somewhere out West. And the combination of these elements—the West and the anonymous highway, the antagonistic brothers, the brutality between men and women—evokes Shepard's strong points so powerfully you find it hard to believe that subsequent scenes are going to descend into mush.

The wife survives, though she is brain damaged. And the rest of the play becomes a melodrama of recuperation, of a wife recognizing her love in spite of being beaten nearly to death, of a husband recognizing his love in spite of being a violent brute—a play, in short, of the highest, which is to say sappiest, inspirational elements. The originality that we associate with Shepard, the break with realism, the harsh vision of cultural myths, the focus on struggle, the hostility that he portrays so crudely and powerfully, are barely evident. . . . There are the usual prose excesses about hot, dry winds coming off the desert. . . . There are the purposeless metaphors, such as the image of a fire in the snow with which the play ends. There are the animadversions on American mythology, for instance on the flag, that imply grand themes without in fact establishing any. There are the family complexities, the fierce loyalty of brother for brother, brother for sister, that become tragically tangled when husband's brother visits battered wife, who falls in love with the wrong sibling. And none of this plays any better than it sounds.

Shepard has always been a very stageable playwright. The family hostility that he has so often dramatized makes for simple but effective theater configurations. Two characters occupy opposite ends of the stage and fire away, as in ***Tooth of Crime,*** his most interesting play; or they circle each other like fighting animals, as in ***True West*** or ***Fool for Love.*** In plays like these the physical opposition of the actors, as performed on the small stages which suit Shepard's work, makes a vivid image of hatred and bonding, his favored theme. I won't say that these simple stagings render him the most enjoyable of playwrights, but they have been effective, and they have done a lot to cover up weaknesses in the scripts.

A Lie of the Mind, however, with its tale of two families, is too ambitious for such simple staging. Shepard's theme of love *redux* and health *redux* doesn't lend itself to angry circling or squaring off. Instead he divides the stage down the middle, husband's family on the left, wife's on the right, and gives us parallel scenes. Husband on stage left lies on the bed attended by family standing up, and wife on stage right lies on a bed attended by family standing up, and the play as a whole sits in front of you like a stalled train. (pp. 217-18)

[You] march out of the theater filled with a sense that Shepard has gone long-winded, misty-eyed and soft all at once.

Frank Rich has written that ***A Lie of the Mind*** "is the unmistakable expression of a major writer nearing the height of his powers" [see excerpt above]. This statement is unmistakably wrong. It would be pleasant to declare that the American theater has produced a new genius, and that Shepard is the man. But the reality is more modest. Shepard has an instinct for staging certain aspects of the 1960s revulsion for the American mainstream, and this instinct has led him to fashion several theatrical innovations, for which he should be celebrated. But he's not a major playwright and the effort to become more than what he is has led to fiascos like ***A Lie of the Mind.*** (p. 218)

Paul Berman, in a review of "A Lie of the Mind," in The Nation, *New York, Vol. 242, No. 7, February 22, 1986, pp. 215-18.*

DAVID KAUFMAN

Theatergoers who discover Shepard with his newest work, ***A Lie of the Mind,*** will never suspect that he is touching on the same tired themes that he ostensibly resolved in his last five plays. Each of Shepard's last five plays is concerned with some variation of the family; and each is about as different from the other as an episode of *Dynasty* is, say, from an episode of *As the World Turns*.

Much has been made of how Shepard has continued the O'Neill tradition of dramatizing the tragedy of America through the tragedy of the family. But despite reports to the contrary, Shepard's American family is not yours nor mine so much as it is the one that we *fear* might live across the hall or down the street or in some place we may have visited without ever getting to know any of the inhabitants. Shepard engages our attention by tapping our paranoia and feeding it back to us in quasi-surrealistic stage terms. (p. 39)

If, via Shepard, O'Neill's American family has come of age, it has not lost its innocence or its naiveté so much as it has simply gone crazy.

If, as Frank Rich suggests in his original review of the play, "***A Lie of the Mind*** is the unmistakable expression of a major writer nearing the height of his powers" [see excerpt above], then Shepard is a less viable contender for the title of Great Playwright than we might have assumed. . . . When the drama opens, Jake is phoning his brother Frankie from the road to report that this time when he beat his wife Beth, he surely killed her. (pp. 39-40)

In what will become a tedious rhythm and overbearing symmetry, this first scene dissolves into a second which finds Beth, Jake's wife/victim, in a hospital bed, while *her* brother Mike nurses her. With rare exceptions for the duration of the play, the scenes alternate from one family to the other in a contrived fashion. In fact, the mechanical structure of ***A Lie of the Mind*** is more elementary, more obvious, than *any* other play I can think of. . . . Yet Shepard's message, if he has one, remains as blurry and as deliberately cryptic as usual. The heavy symbolic gestures, the bits of stage business, look like random insertions into the first draft. At best, they justify themselves as beautiful gestures, but they fail to justify the raw material of the play or the tissue that surrounds them. . . .

Instead of plot, Shepard supplies episodes, vignettes, and long monologues as background exposition and family histories. All is dressed up with countless theatrical moments that typify his plays even as they fail to amount to a coherent statement. . . .

A Lie of the Mind is an amalgam of a number of Shepard plays that precede it. It is also filled with references to the life and works of Tennessee Williams: Beth making vague, repeated allusions to her having been lobotomized, reminding us of Williams' beloved sister Rose; Jake's father, appearing in absentia as perhaps the pivotal moving force in the play, recalling the paternal Wingfield in *The Glass Menagerie* who fell in love with "long distance" and abandoned the family. . . . But rather than borrow superficial traits and devices from Williams, Shepard should have heeded the far more substantial advice of his "Production Notes" or preface to *Menagerie:* "When a play employs unconventional techniques, it is not, or certainly shouldn't be, trying to escape its responsibility of dealing with reality, or interpreting experience, but is actually or should be attempting to find a closer approach, a more penetrating and vivid expression of things as they are." It is also instructive to note that Tom Wingfield (for our purposes, synonymous with Williams) gave us "truth in the pleasant disguise of illusion." In all of his works, Shepard presents illusion as if it were automatically some version of poetic truth.

The major problem with Shepard's dramas is that the themes are never clarified or resolved. Instead, they are kept shrouded in vagueness. Shepard's obsession with ambiguity probably originated with the 60's sensibility of open-ended possibility. When, in ***A Lie of the Mind,*** Beth's mother Meg says, "Please don't scream in the house—this house is very old," this is obviously meant to be a pregnant line—"This house" as America itself, so fragile and maligned that it can topple at any moment. But what is the point, Mr. Shepard? Is this a new or valuable insight? Or is it a comforting cliché fed to us in the guise of a puzzle, encouraging us in our smug desperation.

The legacy of American theater criticism insists that there is always a gap waiting to be filled. It is our grave misfortune that Sam Shepard, the contemporary fill-in, proves more symptomatic of the vacuum than the substance we yearn to fill it with. Despite our better judgment, Shepard has made a virtue out of a liability. By presenting the sort of heavy symbolism that no playwright has gotten away with since Ibsen, and that every self-respecting playwright—including Williams and Albee—had taken pains to avoid, Sam Shepard evidently satisfies the contemporary band of hungry critics, always anxious to locate a messiah today who can be crucified tomorrow. Shepard's gimmick is his dressing up the emperor in old clothes; but it's so long since we've seen this style of finery that the garments look new to us. Whether the clothes are new or old, the point is that our generation has more to learn from nursery rhymes of yore than from a play by Sam Shepard. (p. 40)

David Kaufman, "In Search of a Playwright," in Chronicles: A Magazine of American Culture, *Vol. 10, No. 3, March, 1986, pp. 38-40.*

SHEILA RABILLARD

In the context of the American icons Shepard imports into [his] later plays, his stress upon the phatic and conative functions of theatrical discourse becomes a revelation of an American phenomenon: this is the culture of theatricality, where all speech is for the sake of its power to command attention and words are thus a tool of violent dominance. . . . This is a phenomenon in which, we realize, we participate as we sit in the theatre submitting to demands that we listen, gazing at spectacular displays that command, "look at me." In Sam Shepard's theatre we play the role of victims subject to that violent American theatricality and at the same time play the audience with the power to feed or deny the all-pervading hunger to be seen, to be heard.

Shepard's most recent play, ***A Lie of the Mind*** (1986), provides an uncomfortable test case for this hypothesis. It is difficult to argue that, with this play, narrative interest and psychologically realistic characterization are disturbed so as to focus attention on the structures and language of performance. To be sure, there is an almost unrealistic extremity of violence in the play and, as in previous Shepard dramas, an intrusive object to disrupt the decorum of the set—a deer carcase. In the New York production of the play directed by Shepard himself, live country music played as overture and during two intermissions set a tone of cheatin', hurtin', and drinkin', and by suggesting stereotypical roles added a degree of abstraction to the drama. In comparison to previous plays, however, ***A Lie of the Mind*** allows much more of its realistic illusion to remain intact.

If there is an exploration of theatricality here it lies in this play's novel focus on women. With some warrant, actress Joyce Aaron once complained that her friend Shepard had written no good female roles. Shepard is recorded as telling an interviewer that there was "'more mystery to relationships between men.'" In ***A Lie of the Mind,*** however, particularly in the character of Beth, Shepard creates much richer women's roles than ever before. . . . Through the women's roles, he examines the difference—and the threat—of female theatricality.

Under Shepard's direction, ***A Lie of the Mind***'s women characters have a stage presence different from the men's. Much of the play's humour comes from the women's lines, because they are self-regarding in a way that the men are not; they act as their own audiences, and see themselves as they are seen. . . . [When] the women hold the stage, the spectators at this play are not the victims of a violent commandeering of attention, but sharers in the women's self-regarding gaze. The men, in contrast, played their roles with no trace of self-mockery.

There are some curious implications, not only in the sexually differentiated performance styles, but also in the plot of ***A Lie of the Mind.*** While here, as in other plays, man may strive to hold an audience, affirming himself by performing and controlling, woman perceives herself as others see her and defines herself in those terms. Even for herself an object, her performing entails an entirely different kind of dependence upon an audience. What does it mean, then, when the character Beth plays a loose woman in a local theatrical performance? The logic of the plot shows that, perceived as a tramp, she is one. This shift in identity is what her husband Jake fears, and what drives him to beat her with passionate brutality. And, brain-damaged by his jealous assault, she enters a childlike state; in this condition her affections are completely indiscriminate, and she cuddles happily with Jake's brother in lieu of him. Under

Shepard's direction, Beth dresses in the gaudiest clothes she can find in the final scene, with a tellingly ambivalent effect: she looks equally like a child playing dress-up and like a hooker. This is not, in short, an *Othello* play but almost *Othello* inside-out; the dangerousness of woman's performance is confirmed—the curious alliance between what she appears to others and what she is. ***A Lie of the Mind*** may indicate the direction Shepard's writing will take in the future; in all of the plays that precede it, however, Shepard exposes the violence of male, rather than the dangers of female, theatricality. (pp. 67-9)

Sheila Rabillard, "Sam Shepard: Theatrical Power and American Dreams," in Modern Drama, *Vol. XXX, No. 1, March, 1987, pp. 58-71.*

Dan Simmons

Song of Kali

World Fantasy Award: Best Novel

American novelist and short story writer.

Song of Kali (1985), Simmons's first novel, impressed critics as a satisfyingly gruesome and suspenseful horror tale as well as a powerful morality fable. Simmons, an elementary-level educator who specializes in teaching gifted children, began contributing stories and novellas to *Twilight Zone, Omni, Galaxy,* and other magazines in the early 1980s, with the friendly encouragement of science fiction writers Harlan Ellison and Edward Bryant. Simmons credits Ellison with helping him through a particularly difficult point in his story-writing career in 1981. "Harlan told me," Simmons reminisced, "in his usual tactful way, that if I didn't keep writing he would personally rip my nose off." Simmons completed *Song of Kali* the following year; since then he has written a second horror novel, *Carrion Comfort,* and a mainstream novel, *Phases of Gravity*.

In *Song of Kali* the Hindu goddess Kali emerges as a symbol of malignant evil. Simmons depicts Calcutta as a repellent, violent city where bloodthirsty worshippers of the goddess terrorize an American journalist and his family, ultimately kidnapping his young daughter for use in a ritual of human sacrifice. Simmons explained that the idea for the novel originated with the cultural shock he experienced while traveling through India on Fulbright scholarship in 1977: "I've lived in cities before, and wasn't afraid of them, but Calcutta was different. The cultural chaos and poverty there make it hard to be objective. Some of the people I was with just didn't see it; it was as if all they saw was the flowers. I had this strange sense of deja vu."

Reviewers emphasize that, although the scenes of death and mutilation in *Song of Kali* follow the new trend of explicitness in horror literature pioneered by writers such as Stephen King and Clive Barker, Simmons uses these shocking devices with serious intent, not merely to thrill the reader. Within its framework of unrelentingly gory events, Simmons himself asserts, the novel contains a strong message against violence, which he believes alienated many prospective publishers of *Song of Kali*. "Several editors wanted a shoot-'em-up, get-revenge ending, which I refused to do," he reported. "I was trying to show a way for [the journalist hero] to *break* the cycle of violence, without making the ending of the novel anticlimactic." Several critics commend the message inherent in Simmons's depiction of the battle between good, represented by the journalist and his family, and the evil embodied in the Kali worshippers. They also praise as particularly effective the author's evocation of the Indian city as a brutal, hellish place, a landscape not without metaphoric implications. Comments critic Bob Collins: "Simmons's vision of Calcutta is stunningly realistic, yet horrifyingly suggestive of a world rendered catatonic through brutalization, where the 'unthinkable' has become routine."

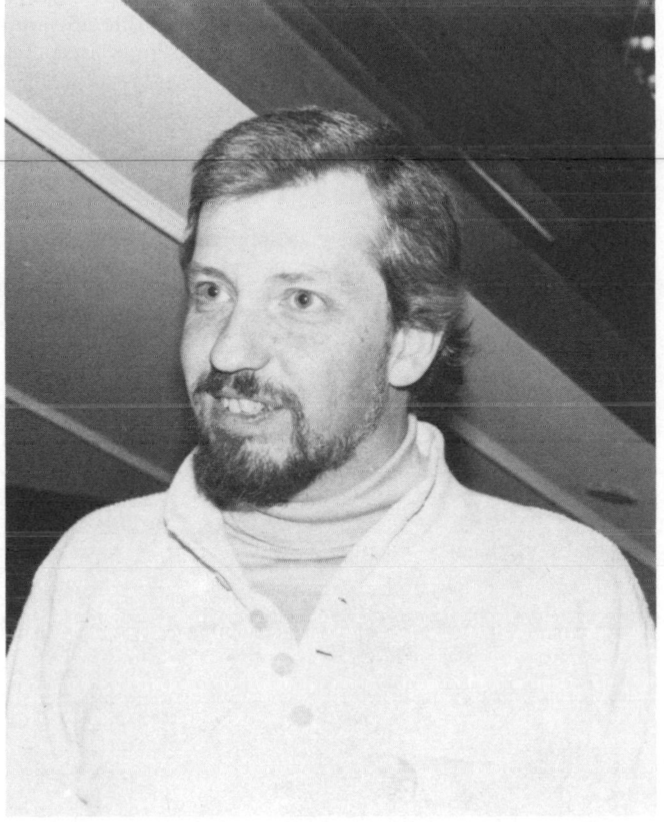

Courtesy of Robert A. Collins

EDWARD BRYANT

[Bryant, an American short story writer, critic, and novelist specializing in science fiction, won the Nebula Award for best short story in 1979 and 1980. His works include Among the Dead and Other Events Leading Up to the Apocalypse *(1973) and* Wyoming Sun *(1980). Bryant, who met Simmons at a writer's conference in 1981, encouraged Simmons's efforts at fantasy writing. In the following excerpt Bryant describes the qualities of* Song of Kali *that are most impressive.]*

I highly recommend the first Dan Simmons novel, ***Song of Kali***. . . . A couple of years ago, Dan asked me if I'd read the manuscript for ***Kali*** and make comments. Trying to be a decent friend, I agreed. The manuscript sat around for a while until one day when I decided to try reading the first chapter or two while I was eating lunch. I ended up reading the entire book that afternoon, virtually in one sitting. ***Song of Kali*** is that gripping.

This isn't, strictly speaking, a horror novel in which things jump out of closets going, "Booga, booga!" But it is a suspense novel of terror in which the monster is a city: Calcutta. Simmons presents this Indian metropolis as a teeming, festering, purely evil hellhole. Writer Robert Luczak, his wife and infant child, have gone there so Luczak can find and interview a mysterious and missing poet named M. Das. It doesn't take long before the protagonist is in 'way over his head.

Simmons' novel is about real people confronting tangible evil. One of the reasons I liked it was because this author's voice is a lead in the growing chorus that also includes Clive Barker. Dan Simmons understands terror and what that does to readers, authors, and characters. In ***Song of Kali,*** he actually uses some of the gut-level material that Stephen King, say, drew upon in *Cujo* and *Pet Sematary*. He deals with parents and children and the fragility of life. But where King finally flinches, Simmons doesn't. (pp. 19-20)

Edward Bryant, in a review of "Song of Kali," in Mile High Futures, *December, 1985, pp. 19-20.*

FAREN MILLER

Song of Kali is [a] novel where the supernatural appears, and is almost overwhelmed by the impact of reality. But what a reality! The book takes place in modern Calcutta, a monstrous city that might seem to be an American's lurid fantasy of the Third World, if Simmons didn't portray it with such conviction and authority. A city of ten to fifteen million people, immense slums, disease and misery in grotesque abundance, Calcutta is so appalling that its dark gods are not a Lovecraftian intrusion but a natural extension of its essence.

To this place comes the narrator, an American writer on assignment to seek out a noted Indian poet who seems to have reappeared, under strange circumstances, years after he was thought dead. The writer brings his Indian-born wife and their child with him, for a visit that seemed straightforward enough when viewed from New York. Their subsequent entanglement with Kali worshippers, and perhaps the bloodthirsty goddess herself, could be the subject of feverish pulp fiction, in lesser hands, but Simmons raises it well above that level with fine characterization, prose that rarely escapes control, and—above all—a keen moral sense. The evil of Kali is not an antique peril but a horror very much of our time, a shadow present within all of us, and not to be countered by further mindless violence.

Horror fanciers may shy away from a book described in such terms, so let me state clearly that ***Song of Kali*** is as harrowing and ghoulish as anyone could wish. Simmons makes the stuff of nightmare very real indeed.

Faren Miller, in a review of "Song of Kali," in Locus, *February, 1986, p. 13.*

DAN SIMMONS

"An absolutely harrowing experience. I actually felt as if I were in Calcutta—the sounds, the reek, the cloying humidity....Dan Simmons is a compelling writer."
—F. Paul Wilson, author of *The Keep*

SONG OF KALI

TOR HORROR

Cover of Song of Kali, *by Dan Simmons. Tor Books, 1985. Cover art copyright © 1985 by Jill Bauman. Reproduced by permission of Tor Books/Tom Doherty Associates.*

An Excerpt from *Song of Kali*

Some places are too evil to be allowed to exist. Some *cities* are too wicked to be suffered. Calcutta is such a place. Before Calcutta I would have laughed at such an idea. Before Calcutta I did not believe in evil—certainly not as a force separate from the actions of men. Before Calcutta I was a fool.

After the Romans had conquered the city of Carthage, they killed the men, sold the women and children into slavery, pulled down the great buildings, broke up the stones, burned the rubble, and salted the earth so that nothing would ever grow there again. That is not enough for Calcutta. Calcutta should be *expunged*.

Before Calcutta I took part in marches against nuclear weapons. Now I dream of nuclear mushroom clouds rising above a city. I see buildings melting into lakes of glass. I see paved streets flowing like rivers of lava and real rivers boiling away in great gouts of steam. I see human figures dancing like burning insects, like obscene praying mantises sputtering and bursting against a fiery red background of total destruction.

The city is Calcutta. The dreams are not unpleasant.

Some places are too evil to be allowed to exist.

SCIENCE FICTION CHRONICLE

Here [in ***Song of Kali***] we have an adventure story set in modern India with intimations of the supernatural, but nothing ever explicitly stated. The protagonist is sent by a magazine to investigate a collection of new verse by a famous Indian poet supposedly dead some ten years before. Shortly after he arrives, he is told that the poet did in fact die, but that he was brought back to life during a forbidden religious ritual. Still others tell him the man never died, merely concealed himself from the outside world. Whatever opinion you eventually retain, there is no question that the novel is a powerful experience, and frequently a repulsive one. Simmons is an author to watch.

A review of "Song of Kali," in Science Fiction Chronicle, *Vol. 7, No. 10, July, 1986, p. 40.*

BOB COLLINS

[*Collins is editor-in-chief of* Fantasy Review. *In the following excerpt Collins praises Simmons for making* Song of Kali *a powerful moral statement as well as a gripping suspense novel.*]

Song of Kali [is] a mesmerizing study of cult violence set in Calcutta.

Experiencing this novel . . . is somewhat like spending an evening in the rotting heart of a human compost heap. Simmons's vision of Calcutta is stunningly realistic, yet horrifyingly suggestive of a world rendered catatonic through brutalization, where the "unthinkable" has become routine. . . .

Into the city's cauldron of death and despair Simmons sends his protagonist (a poet/journalist freelancing for *Harper's*) along with his part Indian wife and infant daughter. He is looking for M. Das, a world-class poet, thought dead for the past decade, until some new poems apparently by Das surface in New York. He takes his family along partly to please his wife, partly to comfort himself: in fact, the narrator's touching paternal delight in his daughter's developing personality, provides a continuous foil for the city's appalling brutalism, and at last a focus for his personal confrontation with the forces of evil.

Since there *is* an element of suspense in the novel, I won't spoil it for you by rehearsing more of the plot. The book, though, is no mere entertainment/thriller. The narrator's gradual immersion in the city's feverishly irrational cult of violence, which centers around the Hindu goddess Kali, is obviously meant as symptomatic of a new "world-mood" invading our era; similarly, the narrator's final, heroic rejection of the revenge impulse provides a model for "breaking the cycle" of violence. (p. 13)

Bob Collins, "Dan Simmons: 'New Frontiers' in the Cult of Violence," in Fantasy Review, *Vol. 9, No. 9, October, 1986, pp. 13-14.*

Wole Soyinka

Nobel Prize in Literature

(Born Akinwande Oluwole Soyinka) Nigerian dramatist, poet, novelist, autobiographer, scriptwriter, and critic.

Acknowledged by many critics as Nigeria's finest contemporary dramatist and one of its most distinguished men of letters, Soyinka is also the first African to win the Nobel Prize in Literature. "There is no question at all that I think the Nobel Prize is for my drama," Soyinka remarked. "And I think the prize is a recognition of the whole African literary tradition on which my work is based, by the outside world and by the African world itself."

Although he composes some of his poetry in his tribal language, Yoruba, and is a chief proponent of a national language, Swahili, Soyinka writes mostly in English, which is still the common language of post-colonial Nigeria. His poetry, novels, and nonfiction works, along with his published playscripts, attract an international readership. Beyond any Western influences, however, Soyinka is a distinctively African writer, a chronicler of his traditional Yoruban culture as well as the turbulent history of modern Nigeria. The most significant aspect of his work, critics observe, lies in his approach to literature as a serious agent of social change and his commitment to promoting human rights in Nigeria and other nations. The humor and compassion evident in his writings, as well as his chilling portrayal of the consequences of political greed and oppression, add a universal significance to his portrayals of West African life.

Soyinka specialized in literature, with a particular emphasis on drama, at University College Ibadan and at the University of Leeds in England. He began his writing career while still a student. One of the earliest demonstrations of his gift for satire is his poem "Telephone Conversation," in which he dramatizes an African student's confrontation with a racist English landlady. An early one-act play, *The Invention* (1959), also attacks racism with satire, depicting the administrators of South Africa's apartheid system as a group of mad scientists engaged in gruesome experiments. By the mid-sixties, through productions of his plays in Ibadan and Ife as well as in London and New York, Soyinka established his reputation as an admirably skilled playwright. Reviewers discovered that he was equally adept at various styles, including comedy, as in *The Lion and the Jewel* (1959), political commentary, as in *Kongi's Harvest* (1964), and tragedy, as in *The Strong Breed* (1964).

Soyinka writes primarily for a Nigerian audience, and his writings may be best appreciated with some understanding of that region's politics and culture. A recurring figure in his work is Ogun, the Yoruban god of war, fire, and metal, known for his violent temper as well as his beneficence. Soyinka chronicles Ogun's legend in his long poem "Idanre," featured in *Idanre and Other Poems* (1967), and *Ogun Abibiman* (1977). Modern Yorubans worship Ogun as the guardian of highways, and so Soyinka uses motor vehicle accidents as metaphors for Ogun's destructive power in his experimental drama *The Road* (1965).

Courtesy of Universal Photos

In his tragedies *The Strong Breed* and *Death and the King's Horseman* (1976), he incorporates dance, music, and other elements of traditional Yoruban performance to create the effect of cathartic ritual, a technique he also uses in his adaptation of Euripides's *Bacchae*, first produced in 1967.

Although he can depict West African life in loving detail, Soyinka is an unflinchingly honest observer of his land and people. In a remark often cited by critics, he once disparaged the Negritude movement espoused by such African writers as Senegal's President Leopold Senghor, declaring that "a tiger is not forever shouting about his tigritude" and that the duiker antelope need not "prove his duikertude; you will know him by his elegant leap." He calls for African artists to abandon superficial, sentimental attitudes towards their culture that are merely remnants of patronizing European value systems. His drama *A Dance of the Forests* (1959), commissioned for the celebration of Nigeria's independence in 1960, warns his countrymen not to live in nostalgia for Africa's past glories and neglect urgent problems in the present day.

Much of Soyinka's work, then, is inseparable from his activities as a political dissident. Soyinka never hesitated to speak out against human rights violations in other nations, as well as the policies of such right wing Nigerian leaders as Colonel Yakubu Gowon. Soyinka was so troubled by the prospect of Nigeria's imminent war with Biafra in 1967 that he traveled to the enemy camp, hoping to make a personal appeal for peace. The Gowon regime reacted by jailing Soyinka without charges, mostly in solitary confinement, for nearly two years. His prison diary, *The Man Died* (1972), and his poetry collection *A Shuttle in the Crypt* (1972) chronicle this traumatic experience. Reflecting on the Nobel committee's decision, Kenyan novelist Ngugi wa Thiong'o commented: "It's good for once to see the intellectual product of Africa being recognized. But we have to remember that many writers and intellectuals in Africa are actually in jail for following in the tradition of Wole Soyinka."

Some reviewers divide Soyinka's work into pre- and post-prison phases. Although satire and social and political commentary have always been a staple of Soyinka's work, even in such lighthearted examples as his early drama *The Lion and the Jewel*, critics discern an increased anger, pessimism, and devotion to political themes in his work after 1967. Two of Soyinka's most popular dramatic pieces, his one-act comedies about the fraudulent Christian evangelist Brother Jeroboam, illustrate this view. Reviewers describe *The Trials of Brother Jero* (1960) as a good-natured farce about human frailty and temptation. *The Metamorphosis of Brother Jero* (1974), however, derives its humor from a sardonic attack on right-wing military regimes. In his plays Soyinka repeatedly denounces the succession of military-run governments that have appeared in Nigeria and other African nations. *Kongi's Harvest* (1964) is a general indictment of authoritarianism, while the satirical *Opera Wonyosi* (1977) and *A Play of Giants* (1984) feature readily identifiable caricatures of Jean-Baptiste Bokassa, Idi Amin, and other notorious statesmen.

One of the most striking aspects of Soyinka's career is the versatility evidenced by his many creative activities. He has earned respect as a producer, director, and actor as well as a dramatist, staging many of his own plays as well as those of other writers with his performance companies, the 1960 Masks and the Orisun Theatre; he also presented productions in Europe and North America. He has written radio dramas, for example, *Camwood on the Leaves* (1960), and experimented with filmmaking. In 1970 the American dramatist and actor Ossie Davis directed a film version of *Kongi's Harvest*. Soyinka played the role of Kongi, and also prepared the film's screenplay.

In its award announcement, the Nobel committee described Soyinka's style as "vivid, often harrowing, but also marked by an evocative, poetically intensified diction." Many critics praise Soyinka's writings for these qualities, particularly their graceful lyricism. Soyinka's novels, *The Interpreters* (1965) and *Season of Anomy* (1973), earned less admiration than his dramas, and many critics complain of their difficult, intricate narrative structures. Reviewers generally react more warmly to his poetry and plays than to his prose. A notable exception is *Ake: The Years of Childhood* (1980), described as an affectionate yet characteristically unsentimental reflection on his boyhood in a southwestern Nigerian village. *Myth, Literature, and the African World* (1976), a collection of essays based on lectures Soyinka delivered at Cambridge, provides insight into Soyinka's literary philosophy. It also reflects the author's extensive career in academia, as chairman of the drama departments of both Ife University and University College at Ibadan as well as a visiting lecturer at colleges in England and the United States. Critics reserve their most enthusiastic praise for Soyinka, however, as a dramatist. As Femi Osofisan declares, "The talent is awesome, unique, exemplary. . . . This singular personality bestrides the Nigerian theatre like a mortal reincarnation of Ogun, the 'axe-handed one'."

(See also *CLC*, Vols. 3, 5, 14, 36 and *Contemporary Authors*, Vols. 13-16, rev. ed.)

ADRIAN A. ROSCOE

[*Roscoe, an English critic and professor of African literature, is the author of* Mother Is Gold: A Study in West African Literature *(1971). In the following excerpt from* Mother Is Gold, *Roscoe examines the contrasts between traditional African culture and Western influences in Soyinka's poetry and drama.*]

Soyinka is a poet of twilight zones, be they between night and day or day and night, life and death, or death and life. They are areas of transition for which he has an abiding fascination; for they are those areas in which he can most fully explore certain basic facts about life and death. ***The Road*** alone is enough to suggest that no other poet or dramatist in the English language has explored so extensively, and with such rapt fascination, that shrouded middle passage between death, fleshly dissolution, and arrival in the other world.

Grey, then, is a dominant colour. Soyinka calls a whole section of ***Idanre and Other Poems*** *grey seasons;* but the colour, in fact, pervades his work as a whole. In **'I think it Rains'**, a poem whose tension springs from its subtle opposition of wet and dry, fruit and sterility, we find the stanza:

> I saw it raise
> The sudden cloud, from ashes. Settling
> They joined in a ring of grey; within
> The circling spirit. . . .

One can see, too, that the ideas implied by [the] choice of colour are borne also by words like 'wisps', 'smoke', 'febrile', and 'ashes'. In **'Season'**, we find 'wood-smoke', 'shadows from the dusk' and 'the wilted corn plume'. **'In Memory of Segun Awolowo'** ends with the lines

> Grey presences of head and hands
> Who wander still
> Adrift from understanding.

(pp. 49-50)

Soyinka, who would agree with Pound's dictum about loading the language of verse with as much meaning as it can bear, is often a difficult poet. He dictates the terms on which a reader must approach him; and, apart from an occasional explanatory note, no concessions are offered. To complicate matters further, Soyinka is a poet for whom the traditional Yoruba cosmology is a potent fact in his imaginative life, and, thus, in the art he creates. Without a working knowledge of the Yoruba background, his work cannot fully be understood; and this presents a handicap even to non-Yoruba Nigerians. The Yoruba cosmology, embodied in Ifa, the traditional religious system of his people, constantly underlies his work and has provided growth points for his artistic development. An essential point about Soyinka, then, and one which firmly marks him off from his fellow West African poets, is that *he is still working within a traditional system;* a system which allows him to explore the problems of creation and existence from a philosophical home base. He has not felt obliged to cast off traditional thinking and dress himself in the tattered remnants of alien philosophies. Not for Soyinka the myth-building problems of Yeats or Blake's desperate cry, 'I must create a system or be enslaved by another man's.' And this, perhaps, is why his scorn of negritude has always sounded so confident. Its disciples' prideful strutting was, in any case, a natural target for his satiric mind; a mind that seems always to have been convinced of man's absurdity, his innate imperfection, and the futility of his grandiose assertions. There was something further. More acutely than anyone else, Soyinka seemed to detect an element of the spurious in negritude's professed objective of reaching back for cultural roots. Christian and westernised, its disciples were, in effect, reaching back for what was no longer there. There was a celebration of convenient symbols and trophies from the past—the external *bric à brac* that could easily be appealed to—but not the *essence* of the past, its systems of thought, which had been discarded for ever. Where they hoped to assert their African-ness by praise poems for the mask or in verse sung to African instrumental accompaniment, Soyinka has worked with the essence itself. He has never renounced it; his appeal to it is spontaneous and natural. Nor is this mere lip service, for he is imaginatively engaged with a tradition that still happens to be alive. He is the only West African poet who, in this philosophical sense, can be said to do so. Hence his complete lack of nostalgia, his lack of that melancholy recollection of a dying world that marks so much West African verse. One cannot wax nostalgic about current affairs. With Soyinka there is no problem of authenticity.

This is not to say that he rejects the modern world with its new insights and its expanding scientific knowledge. His education in Nigeria and England has enabled him to absorb much that is modern; he is learned in the modern disciplines, and his style itself—recognisably modern—is evidence of absorption and adaptation. A modern grafting has been performed on a vigorous traditional plant. Or, to state it in his own way, he has achieved 'the ideal fusion—to preserve the original uniqueness and yet absorb another essence'. It means that Soyinka's work can be both strongly local and excitingly universal. (pp. 50-1)

There is an attractive human-ness about Ifa, for its gods lived among men, and usually shared man's foibles. It also offers a convincing reading of the universe, especially in its insistence on a divine balance of forces, which, as a rule, ensures harmony, but which results in chaos when the balance is disturbed. Ifa has not only survived; it has become modernised. Such is its flexibility that Sango, the god of thunder and lightning, has, with perfect ease, become also the god of electricity. Ogun, a god of prodigious power and responsibility, the deity associated with iron and metals generally, with war, exploration, artisans, and creativity, is now also the god of the roads and the god of workers. He would preside as naturally over Ibadan's Department of Metallurgy as Jeremy Bentham over the London School of Economics. There is, then, in Ifa, besides its human-ness, an open-ness and flexibility which have allowed it to survive into the modern world. It also enjoys what Sowande calls 'a Diversified Unity, and not a Unified Diversity likely to come apart at the seams'. (pp. 51-2)

'Idanre', Soyinka's account of Ogun's creation pilgrimage to the earth, is, to date, by far his most extensive and ambitious poem. Firmly based in the traditional Ifa system and containing within itself those main lines of thought that have marked Soyinka's verse throughout his career, this is a darkly powerful piece of work that in parts has a strong flavour of the mythopoeic about it. (p. 56)

Ogun is the rather satanic hero of the poem. Since he is 'the septuple one', the god who carries seven gourds with him into battle, it is not unfitting that the poem should be divided into seven sections. The first is *deluge . . .* , a scene of violent primeval activity, where, in a raging storm and Cimmerian darkness torn only by lightning flashes, earth is in the process of creation. . . . In the fury of this storm, the first of the actual season (Ogun's season) in Nigeria, and, for the poet's purpose, seen as the first storm of creation, Ogun is beginning his pilgrimage to earth. He is the god of the creative essence—the rain he brings promises new life. He is also of course the god of war who tempers his promise of life abundant with the threat of death. It is a sort of bloody conferring of life and death together. (pp. 56-7)

There is violence in the first section; but it is violence fraught with the promise of life. In the second section, *. . . and after,* the promise, in keeping with the strangely dual nature of Ogun, is not completely fulfilled; or at least, it is fulfilled and then instantly blighted. The threat of doom hangs over a scene that appeared to be growing increasingly 'blissful'. We thus find stanzas celebrating the joy of Ogun's coming balanced, inevitably, by stanzas insisting on the bloody side of his mission. The wine girl, for example, who, Soyinka tells us, is a representational fusion of Sango and Ogun, first appears in a scene of relaxed, sunny happiness. . . . But this rich serenity is shattered in an instant when, in the very next stanza, the girl appears as the dead victim of a hideous car smash. The lovely wine girl becomes 'a greying skull / On blooded highways', her lone face filled with sadness. Only moments before, Ogun, as the god of creation and of the harvest, had smiled his peace upon her; now, as the god of the road, as the god of war, he greedily slaughters her. . . . After some fine surrealistic writing, in which the poet describes some childhood fantasies, the section ends with Ogun bringing order to the world. He makes harmony out of dissonance, imposes a pattern on chaos, teaches the whole of creation to dance and sing. . . . (pp. 57-9)

Ogun's path, . . . his pilgrimage to earth, is an annual event, 'one loop of time'. The same point is made more firmly in the third section, *pilgrimage*. The journey Ogun is making is both his first pilgrimage and the annual pilgrimage he has been making ever since. This is how the Yoruba account for the seasons, and for the strange flow of human existence which is marked by waves of joy and waves of sadness, waves of plenty and waves of drought, waves of life and waves of death—all following, one after another, in an endless cyclical motion. (p. 59)

After section four, which describes Ogun and the gods settling down to an earthly existence, we reach section five, *the battle*. As its name suggests, it is given over to the bloodier side of Ogun's life on earth. As the poet explains, Ogun, having reluctantly been made king of Ira, gets drunk while leading his men into battle. Instead of destroying the enemy, he turns on his own warriors and wreaks appalling carnage among them. His men shout to try and bring him to his senses; but all to no avail. . . . He is called a murderer, a cannibal; but the cries fall on deaf ears. 'His being incarnate', says the poet, 'Bathes in carnage, anoints godhead/In Carnage.' To the cries of help, Esu, the troublesome god of fate, who also happens to be present, will not listen either. . . . Eventually, the drunken god grows sober; he realises his mistake: 'Passion slowly yielded to remorse'. . . . Aside from its mythic basis, its attempt to explain a universal pattern, this section clearly has a contemporary relevance. (pp. 59-60)

Section six, *recessional,* is an important stage in the poem's development, and one in which the more personal statement, the conclusions drawn from the night's experience, are emphasised. It recounts the return journey, the poet coming home from his night spent in the woods and rain. The night is ending; so, too, its furious cataclysmic upheavals. Dawn approaches. One central reflection seems to emerge from the night's events. While the previous sections of the poem have been insisting on the cyclic pattern of Ogun's pilgrimage, its eternal inevitability, Soyinka now seems to ask: Are we, in fact, slaves to this pattern? Is it really so inevitable? Can it, indeed, be broken? In a sense, the Yoruba system within which Soyinka is working, itself provides one answer. For, as Soyinka reminds us, the Yoruba believe that Atunda, slave to the first deity, 'Either from pique or revolutionary ideas . . . rolled a rock down on his unsuspecting master, smashing him to bits, and creating the multiple godhead.' The significance of this is that Atunda's action created diversity. Hence, Ogun, though a monstrously powerful god is, after all, only one god among many; his annual visitation, and the mixed blessings associated with it, represents but one pattern, though, of course, an important one. But Atunda brings a promise of diversity, variety of patterns; and he is praised heartily for it. The section becomes not only a celebration of diversity, but a vigorous plea for it. It is only a short step now to an *apologia* for the artist's independence, for the importance of uniqueness, of individuality. There is a plea for boldness, new directions, unfettered private growth and exploration—a plea, above all, for freedom in a myriad forms.

Incredibly, we find that Ogun, who seems to be all things to all men, can help here: is he not a bold innovating character himself? Is he not, after all, the god of adventurers and explorers? (p. 61)

The emphasis in section seven, *harvest,* returns to the promise of peace and plenty. Parts here read like a magnificent fulfilment of J. P. Clark's poem 'The Year's First Rain', which ended with an image of the earth 'Swollen already with the life to break at day'. Ogun withdraws into the forests, there is 'A dawn of bright processions', and then . . . :

> The first fruits rose from subterranean hoards
> First in our vision, corn sheaves rose over hill
> Long before the bearers, domes of eggs and flesh
> Of palm fruit, red, oil black, froth flew in sun bubbles
> Burst over throngs of golden gourds.

This is writing of a rare sensuous quality, unequalled by any other West African poet. Soyinka is describing the promise fulfilled, the promise heralded by the storm and the bloodshed. Reflecting on his country's sad contemporary history, which has parallelled Ogun's bloody pilgrimage, he laments that it is this and 'the brief sun-led promise of earth's forgiveness' that are awaited to round out, to complete, the cycle. Yet even in this final section, Ogun's dual nature as creator and killer, and the doom of repetition that he symbolises, are insisted on; for the closing stanza of this dark poem states that the golden harvest is already, in its egregious ripeness, moving towards decay, towards 'resorption in His alloy essence'. The cycle must go on.

The poem, then, with its dark backcloth and its epic resonances, provides convincing testimony not only to Soyinka's stature as a poet, but also to his ability to work within the traditional Ifa system. That there was something both timely and timeless about its inspiration is suggested in Soyinka's Preface . . . :

> ***Idanre*** lost its mystification early enough. As events gathered pace and unreason around me I recognised it as part of a pattern of awareness which began when I wrote ***A Dance of the Forests.*** In detail, in the human context of my society, ***Idanre*** has made abundant sense. (The town of Idanre itself was the first to cut its bridge, its only link with the rest of the region during the uprising of October '65.) And since then, the bloody origin of Ogun's pilgrimage has been, in true cyclic manner most bloodily reenacted.
>
> (p. 63)

Wole Soyinka is West Africa's finest dramatist. Here is a man richly endowed with literary skill, whose work, which has poured forth abundantly in a career still in its early stages, bears the marks of a refined sensibility, stringent critical standards, and, above all, great creative energy. . . . As we have seen, by temperament a satirist, he moves about the West African scene like some marvellously gifted Malcontent, fiercely thrusting at the corruption, intrigue, and vaulting ambition which he witnesses on every side. And his blows strike home, for on two occasions he has been sent to prison.

His education and training, in Africa and the United Kingdom, partly account for his position as the West African dramatist in whom the theatrical traditions of Europe and the homeland are most successfully synthesised (though perhaps symbiosis is a more appropriate word, since both traditions are strongly alive in him). London critics have said that his roots go deep into western traditions and that he is following at a distance in the footsteps of men like Jonson and Webster. While they are right in believing that Soyinka has been receptive to such influences, it must be emphasised at the same time that his work is essentially African in material and inspiration. As our discussion of his verse revealed, Soyinka is a Yoruba who acknowledges his roots and clings to them; he is not, in any sense of the word, *déraciné*. (p. 219)

The following examination of Soyinka's works is divided into three sections. The first will discuss Soyinka as a satirist and take ***Dance of the Forests*** and ***The Road*** for special treatment; the second treats of Soyinka's interest in language as an instrument of satire; and the third offers a detailed examination of the plays' synthesis of features African and western.

'Satire in the theatre', Soyinka observed in 1965, 'is a weapon not yet fully exploited among the contemporary dramatists of Nigeria, fertile though the social and political scene is for well-aimed barbs by the sharp, observant eye.'' . . . But Soyinka's interest in satire does not stem from that *annus horribilis,* 1965. One of his early poems, **'Telephone Conversation',** published in 1962, was a memorable sally into this field, drawing applause from many sides, and especially from the South African critic Ezekiel Mphahlele. Even earlier, however, came ***A Dance of the Forests,*** written for Nigeria's Independence Celebrations, and performed by The 1960 Masks, Soyinka's own company; it is the most complex satirical play which the author has so far written. Here indeed was a stroke of bold imagination that pointed up the breadth, depth and sincerity of Soyinka's vision; for in a play offered to a nation on the euphoric occasion of its Independence, the immediate victim of the satire is that nation itself; in a play ostensibly celebrating a country's birth, the talk is all of death, delusion, and betrayal. Indeed, flying in the face of all the cherished teachings of negritude, Soyinka has chosen to de-romanticise his people and their history with a boldness scarcely paralleled since the days of Synge and O'Casey. (p. 220)

We learn at once that Soyinka's vision ranges far beyond the present, even if this is his immediate concern; his theme is a large one, his frame of reference nothing less than the past, present, and ongoing stream of human existence. There is to be, then, a great gathering of the tribes at a momentous time in their history. It is a fitting occasion for the nation to show its medals and resurrect its trophies—a time to recall historic heroism of the sort that will provide inspiration for future endeavour. 'The accumulated heritage—that is what we are celebrating', declares Council Orator Adenebi. . . . Such is the spirit of the occasion; such the pride and hope of a nation at a great turning point in its history. But Soyinka possesses the satirist's passionate, almost pathological, obsession for the truth. Those heady with the excitement of the present must be bullied into setting their experience within the framework of historical fact; they must be allowed to glimpse some of the abiding truths of the human condition. Those who stand in the present and drug themselves with memories of former glories, like Orator Adenebi, whose absurd musings spiral ever further away from reality, must be faced with the grim reality behind their dreams.

The living, then, are anxious to call up from the dead a host of mighty heroes, celebrate the Gathering of the Tribes with a vision of past splendour; and in an empty clearing in the forest (with a startling piece of stagecraft), the soil breaks and there arise from the dead two pathetic human figures—a sorry link indeed 'for the season of rejoicing'. The Dead Man has behind him a wretched history of misery, thwarted hopes, and betrayal; The Dead Woman, his wife, sorrowful, and pregnant 'for a hundred generations', has an equally miserable past, and is soon to be delivered of a half-child, her baby who symbolises the future.

Soyinka allows us to see the details of their past in a Faustian recreation of the Court of Mata Kharibu, a mythical king who represents the 'glorious' history to which the living look back with nostalgia. Soyinka's purpose here is clear, for, as he observes elsewhere, the past 'clarifies the present and explains the future'. As Soyinka sees it, Africa's past is a sadly inglorious one. Thus, here in this shrine of historic magnificence, in this reign to which living Africans look back with pride, we find a whore as queen, and a king unrivalled in barbaric ferocity; a king who will brook no opposition to his every whim, who fears, like all tyrants, the independent mind, and will sell into slavery even his most devoted subjects. Dead Man is one of them, sold for a cask of rum because he dared to think for himself and suggest that he and the king's warriors should only go to war in a just cause. A figure of mutating significance, Dead Man is here representative of ordinary, thinking, reasonable mankind. (pp. 221-22)

Dead Man's history also includes involvement with the slave-trade, Africa's most traumatic historical experience. Soyinka gives his audience the brutal truth that the Kharibus of Africa's past had as much blood on their hands as the white slavers. At this point in a play notable for its Janus-like viewpoint, we begin to find Africa's inglorious past pointing a finger towards the present and the future. . . . There is a strong hint that Africa too easily accepts its chains, be they inflicted by strangers or brothers. More startling, however, is the clear implication that the chains are, and always have been, a permanent feature of the landscape. The 'new' ship in which Kharibu and all his ancestors would be proud to ride suggests modern forms of slavery that the author's fellow Africans are blindly accepting. It is as though Soyinka sees the whole of African history in the crushingly powerful image of a great slave galley sailing down the straits of time, from the dim past down to the present and on towards the horizon of the future. (pp. 223-24)

And what of the present? 'The pattern is unchanged,' says Dead Man, who was 'one of those who journeyed in the market-ships of blood', and who is now visiting the modern world of the living. It is a lesson in disillusionment, for, as he is at one point reminded, 'Your wise men, casting bones of oracle/Promised peace and profit/New knowledge, new beginnings after toil . . .' Treated abominably in the past, he and his wife are abominably treated in the present. The bearers of bitter truth about an inglorious history, they are given at the Gathering of the Tribes the cold welcome of beggars at a feast. . . . It is a measure of the subtlety of Soyinka's art that the satire here works on two levels; for this shocking treatment of guests, and, furthermore, guests from the dead (we have stressed their importance often enough), is immediately recognised as a flagrant violation of rules of conduct upon which African societies pride themselves. At a more profound level, we are meant to witness in this behavior not only a wilful blindness to the truth about the past, but also an arrogant rejection of that past as it is enshrined in these two represenative figures. . . .

The experience of Dead Man and his wife is clear enough. It is a case of *plus ça change*. Men treated each other appallingly in the past; they treat each other appallingly in the present; they will treat each other appallingly in the future. (p. 224)

Such, then, is Soyinka's message for the happy occasion of Nigeria's Independence Celebrations—a sobering reminder of some basic, and abiding, truths about mankind in general and about Africans and their history in particular. Events since 1960 have proved with a vengeance the accuracy of at least that part of his vision which dealt with the future. But in addition, ***A Dance of the Forests*** supplies proof, if proof is needed, that Soyinka saw the need for national self-criticism six years before Achebe raised the subject as a matter of urgency in the pages of *Présence Africaine*. Soyinka's satiric vision is a curious affair—partly Swift's savage indignation, partly the Conradian 'horror', and partly the Wordsworthian lament over 'what man has made of man'. It informs every part of this difficult but remarkable play.

An equally difficult and powerful piece of satire is Soyinka's ***The Road*** published in 1965. From the very title of the play (a work that stands in relation to pieces such as ***The Lion and the Jewel*** like *Hamlet* to *Twelfth Night*), one realises that here is a further exploration of a subject which has fascinated Soyinka throughout his literary career. [The] road here is a fertile central motif. At one level it is any Nigerian road beside which the main scenes of the play are acted or danced. At another level, it is the proverbial road of life, along which all men must travel, individually or collectively as nations. Closely associated with this is the idea of the road of progress, a notion lightly ridiculed in Soyinka's poem **'Death in the Dawn'.** Above all, however, it is the road between life and death which runs precisely through that hazy landscape between this world and the next that so fascinates Soyinka. Along this highway the dead must travel.

Watching over the road, lurking behind all the events of the play, is Ogun, the greedy god who feeds on the butchery that the roads daily provide. Ogun lives on death and needs feeding regularly. The lorry drivers in the play are his devotees, their festival is his festival. Significantly, during their masquerade in his honour, they carry a dog tied to a stake as a sacrificial offering. Ogun's driver followers are notorious killers of dogs that stray onto the road. . . . But Ogun shows little care for his own (one recalls the manner in which he slew his warriors when king of Ira). Hence so many of the road's 'heroes' in the play—Zorro, Akanni the lizard, Sigidi Ope, Sapele Joe, Saidu-Say, Indian Charlie, Humphrey Bogart, Cimarron Kid, Muftau, and Sergeant Burma—are dead. Hence so many of the play's central figures are probing towards death, or are actually dead and undergoing decomposition, their voices ghosting forth from this twilight zone in a most unnerving manner. . . .

[Soyinka chooses] a middle ground, a sort of no-man's land belonging neither to the world of the flesh nor the spirit. . . . (p. 228)

This dark middle area, reminiscent of many of Soyinka's poems, effortlessly grows suggestive of ideas other than those of death and dissolution. It suggests, for example, the overall position of Africa, caught, in Mabel Segun's memorable words, 'hanging in the middle way'. Soyinka portrays a hideous mingling of cultures that he finds in this middle state, though he does so with a complexity, a subtlety, and a revulsion, unparalleled in those innumerable publications that exhibit the cultural clash through stale commonplaces.

Professor himself is the best illustration of this. With his Victorian outfit of top hat and tails, all threadbare, with his academic title, earned through prowess in forgery, with his past connection with the Christian church, and his clear leanings towards Ifa, he is a sort of amphibious creature, neither right African nor right European; neither wholly spiritually oriented nor wholly materialistic. We have mentioned already the psychological problems of modern Africa: there are definite suggestions of schizophrenia or mere lunacy in Professor, and Soyinka wants us to notice them. A veritable aura of symbolism surrounds this weird scoundrel. It is no mere chance that he is dressed in Victorian garb. In part, presumably, Soyinka is making the common joke that Africa follows absurdly, at a distance, the fashions of Europe, and never actually catches up. Similar jibes are found in Achebe and Nicol. But he is also hinting that Professor represents the first real nineteenth-century encounter with the West, and furthermore, the subsequent history of that encounter. Hence, almost everything about this creature is betwixt and between. He is partly a genuine seeker after the Word, which means here knowledge of the essence of death, and partly a genuine criminal, bold, selfish, and rapacious. It is the sort of contradiction that suggests the familiar Afro-European dichotomy. . . . (p. 229)

If Professor is an unpleasant mingling of Africa and Europe, so, too, are the play's drivers and thugs. They are men with names inspired by American crime and western films, men like Say Tokyo Kid who can affect a tough Chicago gangster's drawl ('I don give a damn for that crazy guy and he know it') yet sing traditional Yoruba praise songs and worship Ogun. With his tough talk, his alleged scorn for Professor's spiritualism (belied by his belief that there are 'a hundred spirits in every guy of timber' he carries), Say Tokyo represents an ugly fusion of the traditionally African and the hard-headed materialism of an alien culture. (p. 230)

The play is also a bitter attack on Nigerian society as a whole: here is the scathing criticism of ***A Dance of the Forests*** in a wormier form. It is as though Soyinka, in his deliberate choice of the Agemo idea, is trying to say that he sees the whole of his contemporary society dissolving into the rottenness and stench of death. Apart from Murano, who is deaf, dumb, dead (and therefore, impotent), there is not a single undiseased figure in the play. The whole dark scene is pervaded by vice and greed in all its forms. The sun never seems to rise in this play. It is a picture of unrelieved gloom and decadence, where a dog-eat-dog morality rules supreme. . . . To complete this revolting picture, Soyinka ensures that a representative of all ranks of society is included: his country must be seen to be corrupt from top to bottom. The law, as represented by Particulars Joe, is corrupt in the most blatant manner; the Church stands as an empty shell behind the entire play, irrelevant and powerless. Chief-in-Town, a modern version of the traditional Oba, is a political representative who keeps a gang of thugs in hire and distributes opium. The common people, like Samson and Kotonu, prey on one another like hyenas.

The Road is Soyinka's writing on the nation's wall. He draws a society that is on the road to death and dissolution, a society for which there seems no hope. Perhaps, like Professor, who speaks of death as 'the moment of our rehabilitation', this society will have to die before it learns the truth. Rebirth is only possible after the descent from life is complete. This movement itself is foreshadowed by the mask at the end of the play which sinks slowly until 'it appears to be nothing beyond a heap of cloth and raffia.'

In ***A Dance of the Forests*** and ***The Road,*** a whole nation was under attack. In other plays, too, the satirical element has figured strongly; but there it is not a whole society but particular members of it who come in for abuse. Soyinka particularly loathes those who possess power and use it dishonestly, those whose selfishness drives them to keep the people in a state of ignorance and subservience.

In ***The Swamp Dwellers,*** Kadiye is the target, a fat village priest who remains 'smooth and well-preserved' even in times of drought by exploiting the simple piety of those whom he represents before the local god. He lies upon the land and 'choke(s) it in the folds of a serpent'. In ***The Trials of Brother Jero,*** Jeroboam himself is under attack, an eloquent fraud working as a Beach Prophet and striding the boards like some strange character from mediaeval times. He cuts a striking figure with his heavily-bearded face, his rod of office, long flowing hair, white gown and fine velvet cape—all of them aids to deceit. The West African scene is alive with weird scoundrels of this sort. In a lighter vein, ***The Lion and the Jewel*** focuses its attack on Lakunle, a westernised schoolteacher who appears ridiculous with his modicum of book learning, his complete vacuity of wisdom and his preposterous arrogance; he is a man who feels elevated enough to call his people 'a race of savages' and sees himself as the prophet of a new order. Despising ancestral ways, he is determined to drag his community into the vulgar daylight of the modern world. Soyinka would probably call ***The Lion and the Jewel*** a recreational piece. But ***Kongi's Harvest*** appeared during the years of Nigeria's gathering storm and strikes a more urgent and 'engaged' note. At the heart of his country's afflictions he sees politicians with their lust for power and their illiberal vision. He has stated elsewhere that it is not the continent's writers but its politicians who have shaped 'the present philosophy, the present direction of modern Africa', and he asked, 'is this not a contradiction in a society whose great declaration of uniqueness to the outside world is that of a superabundant humanism? Hence ***Kongi's Harvest,*** theatrically a rather dull play, is a fierce onslaught on West Africa's modern breed of politicians, and especially on Kongi himself, the President of Isma and a modern version of Mata Kharibu complete with all the image-making paraphernalia of the twentieth century. . . . After the more general satire of ***A Dance of the Forests*** these, then, are some of the individual victims chosen as targets in the plays that have followed. (pp. 231-33)

Reaping the harvest of a past dominated by the spoken word, Soyinka is deeply interested in the rhetorical arts. Hence no doubt his special penchant for the dramatic form and the appearance in each of his plays of at least one outstanding orator. We usually find, too, a carefully ordered range of linguistic styles, which not only affords Soyinka a necessary variety of voices, but constitutes a basic item in his satirical armour as well. . . .

As a satirist vitally concerned about language and style, Soyinka stands in line with distinguished predecessors. It is enough to recall the names of Skelton, Swift, Pope, and Sterne to establish how consistently the great satiric tradition of English letters has opposed itself to the abuse of language. (p. 234)

Where historically the abuse of language has been decried mainly in its literary manifestations, satire in the modern world has attacked its debasement by propagandists and political machinery. George Orwell, the twentieth century's Swift, provides a useful example. In Orwell's view, the decline of a language 'must ultimately have political and economic causes'; bad politics encourage the abuse of language, and the slovenliness of our language leads to woolly thinking. (p. 235)

Now, Orwell and Soyinka can be taken as kindred spirits. . . . We have already cited Soyinka's complaint that 'the present philosophy, the present direction of modern Africa was created by politicians' (including men who felt it necessary on two occasions to strip him of his freedom). It is not surprising, therefore, that politicians and their abuse of language should become a theme of his plays.

Kongi's Harvest offers perhaps the best example. Here traditional African politics, which placed the power of ruling in the hands of local chieftains, is being ousted by the politics of Kongi with his passion for dictatorship in the modern style. It is a familiar case of the traditional ways in conflict with the forces of change. The old order is represented by Oba Danlola and his followers, whose choice of language sharply marks them off from Kongi's party of modernists. Their style has a concreteness of metaphor and imagery which recalls the traditional Yoruba verse. . . . (p. 236)

The difference between the era which Danlola represents and Kongi's new dispensation is seen in the play as largely one of language. Having dismissed Danlola and his followers as 'a backward superstitious lot', Kongi is firmly committed to building a political machine that is recognisably modern and recognisably western. Hence, the linguistic style which Soyinka gives to the tyrant and his minions is fraught, not with the metaphor and proverbial wisdom of Old Africa, but with the 'washer words' and politico-scientific jargon of the modern world. (p. 237)

Thus, Kongi's harvest is to be 'a harvest of words', and Soyinka will shape his satire accordingly. Kongi has decided that there must be a deliberate break with the past—essentially a political break of course, but involving a cultural and linguistic break as well. . . . The effort is hard to sustain, and of course Soyinka's point is that their new style is a gross affectation; but on the whole, they succeed and we hear the familiar jargon that a man like Orwell loathed so passionately. 'Progressive forces', 'a step has already been taken in that direction', 'contemporary situation', 'reactionary', 'positive stamp', 'scientific image', 'positive scientificism', 'so-called wise ones', 'clean break'—the cliches pour forth, and one half expects to hear 'consensus', 'escalation', 'dialogue', 'credibility gap', and 'all-time highs' thrown in for good measure. (pp. 238-39)

The whole movement of the play is towards the great Festival of the New Yam, traditionally the responsibility of Danlola; Kongi plans to 'secularise' this event, ceremonially ring out the old order, and assert his supremacy as the fountainhead of all meaningful power in the country. . . . In the event, the show is a fiasco, and the play ends in the style of Danlola, though he is on his way into exile when the curtain falls. (p. 240)

Lakunle's style in ***The Lion and the Jewel*** is a clear window through which we see his worthless values. This is a much less serious play than ***Kongi's Harvest,*** but nevertheless the style given to Lakunle represents a deliberate attempt to reflect the encroachment of western values upon African mores.

Lakunle, the torch-bearer of modernity in his community, is in love with Sidi, an unlettered village nymph; but the foxy old Bale of the village, Baroka, wants her too, and the play becomes an amusing struggle between these rivals, who represent, once again, the old order and the new. Lakunle is a fervent disciple of romantic love (that recent western import into West African society) and a champion of all those freedoms for which the feminists have struggled. He sketches for his beloved the splendid life that will be hers if only she will consent to marry him without his paying the traditional bride price. . . . Sidi of course is disgusted with this 'strange unhealthy mouthing' and retreats, leaving Lakunle to complain wearily and comically. . . . This is all light satire, but it has its point. The conflict is between the champions of two worlds, and Baroka, the spokesman of tradition, wins the fight; the modern, westernised representative not only loses but is the laughing stock of the play. It is as if Soyinka, even in this gay comedy, cannot resist taking sides; as if he, in company with satirists in general, is on the side of conservatism, seeing in tradition a bedrock of sanity that will defy the swirling torrents of change and revolution. But it is not as simple as this, for Soyinka's very achievement consists in his own coming to terms, artistically, with the modern world. A clue to his real position probably lies in the fact that it is largely the trivia, that superficies of western life that Lakunle espouses—western life observed at one remove in the streets of Lagos. Thus, Soyinka is no doubt saying to his people, 'Don't throw away your heritage (which still has much to offer you) for the glossy manifestations of western life. Look at Lakunle and see how absurd it would be.' (pp. 240-42)

The Trials of Brother Jero is dominated by the personality and style of the holy fraud himself, whose oratory is cultivated to deceive, whose rhetoric serves duplicity rather than divinity. . . . As usual, the play uses two contrasting styles. Jero's is one, and the second belongs to the plain folk who are his victims. Their language is as humble as their status, and in moments of deepest sincerity it becomes mainly West African pidgin. In the . . . scene on the beach, an emotional prayer session is in progress under the direction of Chume, the assistant prophet whose wife Jero has seduced. The petitions are frankly materialistic but, coming from the poor, touchingly human for all that. They are punctuated regularly with Amens, and the whole effort builds to a tremendous climax as these humble people whip up their emotional fervour. . . . (pp. 243-44)

Thus we can understand Soyinka's fundamental interest in language. Language as a key to man's inner being; language as a mirror of social standing; language as an instrument of deceit and oppression; language as a device for sheer entertainment; language as a vehicle for man's deepest utterances; language as a source of comedy; language as an instrument of satire—Soyinka is keenly aware of all these facets and explores them energetically in his plays.

Although Soyinka's work reveals a definite blending of African and western elements, the basic material out of which the plays are fashioned is overwhelmingly indigenous. The elements of African pre-drama, for instance, are here in force, as a brief survey of the plays will reveal.

Soyinka's first play was called, significantly, ***A Dance of the Forests,*** and its opening words indicate that it is meant to partake of the nature of a dance. The resurrected ancestors were rejected by the living 'So I took them under my wing', says Aroni. 'They became my guests and the Forests consented to dance for them.' And the dance, thus, is a common feature throughout the play. The villagers dance around the totem carved for the festivities, there is the dance of the Half-Child, offspring of the Dead Woman, and a dance by the god Eshuoro and his jester, called the Dance of the Unwilling Sacrifice. Ritual is added to dance at one point when a dancer is followed by a young girl acting as an acolyte who sprinkles the dancing area as she goes. This itself is followed shortly by a solemn recitation by a dirgeman, urging everyone to stand back and 'Leave the dead/Some room to dance', and then by Agboreko's oracular consultation. At the climax of the play we find the ceremonial masking of the three 'earthly protagonists', who, ridden and possessed by the various spirits which the Interpreter calls up, 'chorus' the future in the manner of the religious masks of Egungun and Voodoo.

The Lion and the Jewel is a lively combination of dancing, singing, and drumming. A particularly memorable feature is the Dance of the Lost Traveller, a re-enactment in mime form of an important event occurring prior to the time period of the play, and about which the audience must be informed. It was the unexpected visit of a Lagos photographer whose car broke down as it passed near the village. Sidi chooses villagers to dance the different parts of 'devil horse' (car) and python; and persuades Lakunle (warmly African beneath his western veneer) to dance the part of the stranger. . . . The stranger's arrival and short stay in the village are then mimed, and, to simulate the car wheels, four dancers roll the upper halves of their bodies to the accompaniment of throbbing drums.

In the same play, Baroka wins Sidi by spreading abroad a rumour that he is impotent—a rumour that leads to the performance of a frankly sexual 'dance of virility', carried out exclusively by the ladies. It is a wild triumphant affair in which the Bale's sexual life from his days of great potency to his final 'defeat', is acted out with enormous gusto. Sadiku, his eldest wife, leads a dancing group of younger women in pursuit of a male, who rushes about, dancing in tortured movements as defeat draws near, and is finally 'scotched', to the unbounded delight of the ladies. It is a bold piece of theatre (made nicely ironic by having the dancers burst on stage at precisely the moment of Sidi's seduction) which not even Aristophanes could have bettered.

In the other plays, too, traditional elements feature strongly. ***Kongi's Harvest,*** for example, reaches a grand climax at the Yam Festival, which is a veritable orgy of feasting, dancing, chanting, and parading, all to the frenzied accompaniment of dozens of pounding pestles. As we have seen in ***The Road,*** Soyinka's note *For the Producer* with its reference to the mask idiom, is evidence enough of the tradition in which he is working. A play replete with dirge and praise singing, and which contains a festival in honour of Ogun, god of iron, it serves to indicate how deeply the roots of Soyinka's art are sunk in African traditional practice.

But the most interesting example of how Soyinka uses pre-dramatic material can be found in ***The Strong Breed,*** a dark, powerfully moving play built around the scapegoat idea, one of the most ancient conventions devised by social man for the easing of his collective conscience. In the village of the play, there is a New Year's Eve ritual in which the evil of the old year is cleansed away for the beginning of the new. The theme is introduced by a sick girl, who appears dragging an effigy or 'carrier' that is to be beaten, hanged, and burnt so that it will carry away her illness. . . . It is a clear example of pre-drama at the heart of a most moving play.

Traditional material, then, features strongly. What of those elements borrowed fromt the West? Some of these are extremely simple, yet fundamental. For instance, the plays have a text, and, therefore, a fixed form, which in itself is a basic departure from traditional practice. The improvisation of the early Yoruba troupes would be unthinkable in any of the Soyinka plays which we have discussed. Again, the texts are in English and the plays are designed for western stages rather than for the traditional open square.

There are, too, several techniques learnt from European practice that give Soyinka's art a flexibility and freedom it would otherwise lack. A day in the life of Brother Jero, introduced to the audience by the Prophet himself, and then acted out by him, represents a device more likely to have been learnt from Brecht or Pirandello than from Africa. The flashback technique, for which Soyinka has been criticised by Martin Esslin, is likewise a western borrowing. . . . A divided stage is used in the first section of ***Kongi's Harvest,*** for the play alternates between two scenes; it is a device used memorably in the Isherwood-Auden play *On the Frontier,* and, of course, it is common in films and in television plays. Soyinka might have borrowed it from any one of these sources; there is no evidence of it in the dramatic tradition inherited from his forefathers. His plots, too, reveal an ingenuity inspired more perhaps by Ben Jonson than by indigenous models. Certainly there is no plot in Yoruba Folk Opera to match the complexity of ***The Lion and the Jewel*** or ***A Dance of the Forests.***

Western influence emerges, too, in the matter of characterisation. Soyinka's figures have a degree of psychological depth and complexity which vernacular drama has never achieved. Professor, in ***The Road,*** to take but one illustration, is a distinctly African personality in a distinctly African play, but the bewildering complexity of his character, the shadows of the past that enshroud it, its aura of insanity, its weird admixture of the criminal and spiritual—all this is felt to have been made possible only by Soyinka's knowledge and imitation of western dramatists.

Soyinka has rapidly emerged as West Africa's most distinguished dramatist, and indeed he is beginning to claim attention as one of the foremost English-speaking playwrights of our time. As a satirist he is certainly in the front rank. As a poetic dramatist, he has few equals. (pp. 244-48)

Adrian A. Roscoe, "Drama" and "Progress in Verse," in his Mother Is Gold: A Study in West African Literature, *Cambridge at the University Press, 1971, pp. 13-70, 176-248.*

C. TIGHE

[In the following excerpt, which originally appeared in Journal of Commonwealth Literature, *Vol. 10, April 1976, Tighe comments on the difficulties Soyinka experienced in translating the horrors of his prison experiences into the literary works* The Man Died *and* A Shuttle in the Crypt.*]*

The main problem in Soyinka's ***The Man Died*** and ***A Shuttle in the Crypt*** is that of creating a language for describing twenty-five months of solitary confinement and all its attendant horrors and dangers.

Any attempt to come to grips with the poems must start with ***The Man Died.*** Many of the poems would make no sense at all unless one knew in detail about the civil war and the events recounted in the prison notes. Soyinka says that the poems are a 'map of the course trodden by the human mind' during his two years of solitary confinement, and that they reflect his dogged insistence that he should survive at all costs. He also points out that we are not presented with the actual struggle against a vegetable existence. Though he barely hints at it, we are presented with the fight for his sanity. Nevertheless, I am not convinced that either ***The Man Died*** or ***A Shuttle in the Crypt*** were conceived purely as works of literature, or that they are solely memoirs of what contortions the human mind can be put to by inhuman oppressors. There is a strong element of self-advertisement, almost 'monument erecting', for the powers of his survival. It may be simply the process of the prison experience engendering a survival-by-ego attitude, or it may be a post-imprisonment reshaping of the effects of the experience. ***The Man Died*** carries the marks of both these possibilities, but ***A Shuttle in the Crypt*** is a fascinating and more honest sketch for ***The Man Died.***

The poetry shows clearly that Soyinka's mental health was a fragile thing. The 'Animystic spells' were designed to induce a state of self-hypnosis by constant repetition, and while the original 'spell' had some sense, preserved and consolidated something of Soyinka, often he found it impossible to shape his thoughts clearly, so that the 'spells' served to preserve a feeling or a mood, rather than a meaning:

> My memory at last proves tenacious. That
> 'mantra' will serve. Utter words, order moods
> if thoughts will not hold.
>
> (pp. 186-87)

The exhortation 'Utter words', looks straightforward enough, but the very act of writing caused Soyinka terrible trouble. The uttering of words does in some ways channel and order thought, and in a situation where communication is completely sealed off, words and the very idea of language itself can take on some very strange aspects. For Soyinka the act of writing was an admission of loneliness and a tribute to the work of his tormentors. At the same time he was haunted by the belief that a thought did not exist until it was written down and given shape. Language was the only means he had of preserving his sanity and yet to actually use his gifts as a writer was to break his stoic-isolationist resolve: 'I need nothing. I seek nothing. I desire nothing.' It may be that 'Not to create or think is best' but this abstention will not preserve his sanity or help him make sense of his situation. To find that he was credited with a 'Confession' was a subtle damnation and a logical extension of the 'plastic surgery' already done on his public image. . . . (pp. 187-88)

Soyinka has always been obsessed with words and the image of himself using words; the figure he cuts in prison is as much a problem of Ideals as it is of the correct posture, the noble stance, and the appropriate verbal noises. I don't mean that Soyinka is not an idealist or that he has nothing to say, but that his imprisonment has not helped to correct his tendency towards verbosity. The diction of these poems ('solecisms', 'palanquins', 'interstices', 'reversion', 'suturing') is awkward and strained. The high number of equally strained puns and the generally mystic atmosphere give the impression of imitation poetry and of 'difficulty'. Soyinka's attitude to his own poetry is ambivalent, since to occupy the mind with absolutely nothing and to withdraw in upon himself was one alternative, and it is only through a twisted kind of logic that he managed to justify his own existence and the desire to write. His awkwardness in explaining this desire makes it plain that he had compromised his image of himself. . . . This awkwardness and confusion are rare in ***The Man Died*** since most of that book has been put through a kind of post-imprisonment ego-blender which disguises the real moments of doubt and fear.

A Shuttle in the Crypt is more honest in its confusions than ***The Man Died.*** The fears and doubts are not resolved in the poetry and we have to accept this state as an integral part of the prison experience. (pp. 188-89)

[Both] ***The Man Died*** and ***A Shuttle in the Crypt*** show an inability to write about himself without becoming too concerned with his own image of himself and retreating behind a thicket of explanations, none of which explains very much. Soyinka finds that the subject of his imprisonment is fascinating, but that his innermost experiences were so painfully compromised that it is impossible for him to approach them.

The fact that the poetry had a definite function makes it difficult for us to come to grips with it:

> Eyes
> That grow as stamens need
> A yeast of pollen. Shun
> Visions
> Of the unleavened, look sooner on the sun.
>
> Hold
> As they, bread as breath
> Is held and spent, discarding
> Weights of time
> In clutching and possessing—yokes of death.
>
> Light the old hearths
> With salt and oil, with tubers
> Camwood, chalk and antimony
> What they tell us, these
> Dark ancestors of doom?

These poems are literally incantations understood only by Soyinka. It is not just the struggle to find an adequate language to describe what is happening but a struggle to admit the internal effects. The language that emerges is not successful, but it is as valid as any other through its attempts at honesty and honest portrayal.

While Soyinka's attempts to write were a compromise, his attempts not to write, to cut himself off from his surroundings and withdraw into a void were both frightening and unacceptable. . . . When Soyinka reached the tenth day of his fast he wrote:

> I anoint my flesh
> Thought is hallowed in the lean
> Oil of solitude . . .
> I anoint my heart
> Within its flame I lay
> Spent ashes of your hate—
> Let evil die.

In ***The Man Died*** he writes of this experience:

> I felt a great repose in me, an enervating peace of the world and the universe within me, a peace that truly 'passeth all understanding'.

That he should have come so near to destroying himself haunted Soyinka, and that he should come so close to forgiving the 'mind butchers' brought him to a low level of despair:

> I have returned again and again to this night of the greatest weakness and lassitude, to the hours of lying still on the stark clear-headed acceptance of the thought that said: it is painless. The body weakens and the breath slows to a stop.

All Soyinka's alternatives were fraught with danger and it was a case of choosing the lesser danger and ensuring the survival of the body, if nothing else. The fact that he did survive mentally intact is a tribute to his determination.

Most of the poems in ***A Shuttle in the Crypt*** are concerned with statements of belief. The **'Four archetypes'** illustrate the plight of the visionary, the exile, and the intellectual and are a direct comment on Soyinka's own position. They reach out to ***A Dance of the Forests*** and ***The Detainee*** and they illustrate some of the ideals and some of the stranger confusions of the other prison poems. . . . (pp. 190-91)

Like many other poems in this volume, **'Hamlet'** reaches its climax with a pun (many of them are much worse than this one.) Usually the puns are a method of side-stepping the real questions that the poetry raises, a sheepish, grinning, half apology for what is being said. It is as if he finds his subject far too painful to discuss seriously and dismisses it with a pun, avoiding any attempt to articulate fully what he feels. At times the puns express an attitude of 'well this isn't a serious poem anyway so . . .', an avoidance and apology for dragging unpolished and angry feelings before an audience; two examples are the pun on 'creepers' . . . and the last effort of desperation in 'Orphans of the world / Ignite!'. . . . The final pun in **'Hamlet'** reveals an emotional undercurrent, which makes it impossible for Soyinka to write without the protection of a joke. (pp. 192-93)

A thread of question and answer runs through these poems. The end of **'Joseph'** leaves the idealist in a very weak position; **'Hamlet'** is the idealist forced into action; in **'Gulliver'** the idealist pays for his action and becomes an exile; and in **'Ulysses'** the image of the self as idealist is said to be an illusion in spite of all his trials and wanderings:

> . . . our lighted beings
> Suspended as mirages on the world's reality.

It is not surprising that after his imprisonment Soyinka felt 'rootless'. The experience was almost incommunicable, and to return home must have been something of an anti-climax. . . . In this light, ***The Man Died*** is very much a re-assertion of personality and character.

> I never feel I have arrived, though I come
> To journey's end.
>
> The quest
> Is all, endless
> The home-coming
> Respite
> Before the gathering of the outward crest.

(pp. 193-94)

Soyinka's best poetry arises when he treats his own situation obliquely. When he is writing specifically about himself the portrait is not necessarily an accurate one; the punning, the ego, the lack of concentration and the pain all obscure what Soyinka is really trying to write about. When he writes about the madmen, the fears he had for his own sanity and the difficulties he has in trying to write about his own experiences are clear. . . . It is precisely when Soyinka is not trying to give us the horrors that he is most effective. His attempts to describe the beatings end up as attempts at overworked and cheapening indignation or subside into jibes and grim, punning humour. . . . Soyinka is most successful in talking about himself when he is talking about other people. Here he is aware of the problems of finding a language and he does not debase the experience with exhortations to participate in the horror. The same sort of idea can be seen at work when Soyinka suddenly realizes that his situation and that of the hanged men is almost identical: '. . . at this wake / none keeps vigil. None.' In **'Vault Centre'** the absence of horrors and the concentration upon the pigeons above the cell make the tragedy eloquent enough without any forcing. . . . (pp. 194-96)

In **'Procession'** Soyinka openly despairs of being able to say anything about the hangings. . . . He finds himself 'Floating on lakes to cries of drowning.' He survives but:

> What may I tell you? What reveal? . . .
>
> What may I tell you of the five
> Bell-ringers on the ropes to chimes
> Of silence?
> What tell you of the rigors of the law?

(p. 196)

C. Tighe, "In Detentio Preventione in Aeternum: Soyinka's 'A Shuttle in the Crypt'," in Critical Perspectives on Wole Soyinka, *edited by James Gibbs, Three Continents Press, Inc., 1980, pp. 186-97.*

FEMI OSOFISAN

[*Osofisan, a Nigerian critic and dramatist, is the author of* A Restless Run of Locusts *(1975),* The Chattering and the Song *(1977), and* Morountodun and Other Plays *(1982). In the following excerpt Osofisan explains Soyinka's approach to drama as traditional cathartic ritual.*]

Let us acknowledge here that we are writing at a privileged moment. Fifteen years have passed since Ṣoyinka first came into the lime-light as a playwright and gradually, in the course of those years, the once baffling and near-exotic universe of his creative works—that is, the community of Yoruba cosmology in which are coeval the three historical, actual and prospective planes of entity; in which the animal and vegetable essences are correspondent; in which the acknowledged deities are both anthropomorphic and symbiotic, each fusing in his personality a series of antinomies; as well as the comprehensive union of religious and secular intuition in the traditional Yoruba—all these are now familiar after the works of scholars like Bọlaji Idowu and of culture patrons like Ulli Beier. Ṣoyinka's work right from the start took this knowledge for granted and were hence condemned for being inscrutable even by his own compatriots, heirs to three centuries of Christian and Muslim indoctrination. Indirectly then, Ṣoyinka has helped to reintegrate us into the world of our ancestors. Ogun, his personal patron god, is no longer a pagan abstraction, nor are the rest of the opulent Yoruba pantheon. Moreover, there have been critics like Gerald Moore, Oyin Ogunba, Eldred Jones, and Abiọla Irele to bring to our doorstep the once elusive jewels of Ṣoyinka's poetic quarrying, so that even a metaphysical quest like ***The Road*** can now be valued sympathetically.

We are writing at a moment that is at once privileged and painful. Within that period of fifteen years Ṣoyinka has been twice behind prison bars, has suffered personal humiliation at the hands of corrupted power, and at the moment has chosen, in defence of truth, the agonizing rigour of exile, an eternal victim, like his own Igwezu, of the absurdity of history and of his own lucidity. At that harrowing cost, he has emerged as one of the Strong Breed, those pathetically heroic characters who haunt his plays as self-appointed scapegoats of the relentless ritual of communal purification and rejuvenation. (pp. 151-53)

It is evident . . . that Ṣoyinka's influence has been quite extensive on contemporary Nigerian theatre, indeed, on the entire field of literary creativity in the country. His other activities as novelist and poet are, unfortunately, beyond the compass of this essay, but as if these were not enough achievement for one man, Ṣoyinka is also the country's first modern incarnation of the Malvarian idealist and activist, the romantic who voluntarily risks his own security and even survival in a daring, physical intervention in political violence. "The poet," he once declared, "ignores reality only at the peril of truth." Such personal forays into the political arena could not, of course, but breed strong enemies, or strong admirers, and it is clear that their impact on the country's history could be properly assessed only by political scientists. Nevertheless, Ṣoyinka's style of living, no less than his artistic achievement, has attracted a considerable number of acolytes. Of the writers and playwrights of the writer's generation, many consciously model themselves after Wọle Ṣoyinka. . . . Naturally, Ṣoyinka's influence has been more visible in the theatre. Young Funmi Joshua's first major play, for instance, entitled *Theme for Music,* the first serious play to be set in a Northern rural environment, and based on a theme of purgation and the ritual unearthing of sin, is overtly influenced by the structural and linguistic mechanics of ***Madmen and Specialists.*** That play also partly influenced the writer's own ambitious drama, *The Chattering and the Song* in which an attempt was made to probe the state of hysteria and neurosis which results from the impact of sociocultural disorder upon a group of very sensitive youths, the ultimate chaos and pathos of our intimate relationships in such circumstances. In like manner, Rasheed Gbadamọṣi's *Echoes from the Lagoon* is a direct offspring of ***The Road,*** sharing that kinship with Bọde Ṣowande's *Whispers in the Night*. And novelist Kọle Ọmọtọṣọ's recent excursion into the field of drama yielded *The Curse,* an absurdist play inspired by Ṣoyinka's plea that "the time has now come when the African writer must have the courage to determine what alone can be salvaged from the recurrent cycle of human stupidity." We could multiply these instances of direct or indirect influence by Wọle Ṣoyinka and not exhaust the list, but perhaps we should rather turn to his plays and attempt to gather in a nutshell the harvest of fifteen years of fecund creativity.

Of course, this kind of summary can only be ambitious, for Ṣoyinka is almost a theatre factory by himself. . . . All through his prodigious productivity, however, run two major connecting threads; namely, a seriousness and consistency of theme, and the gradually ripening use of theatre mechanics.

Ṣoyinka's plays are the first on the Nigerian stage to deal with themes more profound than the surface sociological disorders which make, for instance, for much of the comedy of Henshaw. This is because Ṣoyinka's plays, according to Eldred Jones, "deal with things that matter; things that are worth troubling about." And Jones goes on to expatiate: "They are concerned with the fate of man in his environment, the struggle for survival; the cost of survival; the real meaning of progress; the necessity for sacrifice if man is to make any progress; the role of death—even the necessity for death in man's life." All these elements can, in fact, be neatly summarized in one principal thematic pre-occupation—that is, the playwright's ceaseless probing of the meaning and the machinery of societal self-renovation, both on the individual and collective planes. It is this unabating concern which immediately underscores Ṣoyinka's kinship with the traditional artists, a link further strengthened by his similar recourse to a bivious channel of exploration. For traditional drama has always from its origins strained into two theatrical categories, this recurrent communal need for cleansing and restoration. On the one hand is the "popular tradition," whose ultimate purpose is to impart physical and psychological therapy, the release and satiation of long, stifled emotions, through the mechanics of satire, comedy, and masquerade; and on the other hand, is the "ritual tradition" which reaches towards the same kind of restoration but on a far more profound, more solemn level, through the mechanics of rite and cultic symbolism.

Wole Soyinka's plays are similarly divisible along that established bifilar convention. Thematically unified by the same conscious response to the burden of communal excess and anguish, the plays are structurally designed like our traditional repertory into two broad patterns of celebration. The first group would comprise those plays which seek the exorcism of collective pain or incoherence on the purely sociological level, that is, by using the dramatic resources of the popular stage whose main elements, we said, are caricature and masquerade, plus an implicit or explicit moral censure. Into this category, for instance, would fit such plays as ***Kongi's Harvest, The Jero Plays,*** and the revues collected in ***Before the Blackout.*** The second group of Ṣoyinka's plays are metaphysical in content and mood: the cathartic exploration of communal chaos now assumes a ritualistic structure, and invariably concludes on a tragic tone. Such are the plays included in Ṣoyinka's first volume of ***Collected Plays*** of 1973 and together they illustrate what, in Soyinka's own terms, is "a recognition of the occasional feeling of hopelessness which by writing about it I can exorcise."

These two categories are necessarily broad: within their compass, the urgency of Soyinka's obsessive quest extends like proboscises into a diversity of theatrical modes. It is this element in fact which most amazes in Soyinka's theatre, the endlessly varying emphases on different aspects of the cathartic process, as well as the playwright's growing mastery of theatrical techniques. Each play as it were, takes root within the flesh of its antecedent, but blossoms into an entirely novel theatrical phenomenon. The dramatic lens swings continually on the same thematic fulcrum, but gives shifting shots of the spectacle. Thus, the drama of the environment's decay may be captured by the playwright from the angle of humanity's recurrent struggle with power and sycophancy (***Kongi's Harvest***), or of the corruption of contemporary life (***The Lion and the Jewel***), or of the corrosion of faith (***The Swamp Dwellers***). Similarly, the stimulus for dramatic ritual may initiate from *hubris,* like the Professor's eschatological quest in ***The Road,*** or from compassion and an innate heroic impulse, as Eman's voluntary acceptance of the carrier role in ***The Strong Breed,*** or from collective disorientation as in ***Madmen and Specialists.*** But the neo-Shakespearean mechanics of ***The Lion and the Jewel,*** for instance, disappear in ***Kongi's Harvest,*** the latter play which is constructed upon the comprehensive celebrative structure of the "popular tradition"; and the same advance is visible, if on a different level, in the progress from ***A Dance of the Forests*** to ***Death and the King's Horseman.*** The tiger of Ṣoyinka wears its stripes but it does not refuse, like Negritude's manatee to grow away from the foetus.

A clearer knowledge of these different elements of Ṣoyinka's dramatic progress is available from a close and chronological analysis of the plays. Let us draw our first illustration from the works which we identified above as being of the lineage of the "popular tradition". Two plays here should suffice: the progress from ***The Trials of Brother Jero*** to ***Jero's Metamorphosis*** illuminates, even more than Jero's, Ṣoyinka's own artistic metamorphosis. The two plays feature the same rascal protagonist, Brother Jero, in a hilarious tussle with those who offer potential threat to his apostolate, but in the latter play, both the dramatic mood and the thematic focus alter radically. The first play is an exercise of tremendous fun, but in the second, comedy yields place to satire, a satire even more pungent because of the play's greater structural harmony and its greater insertion into the relevance of contemporary history.

Ṣoyinka offers in ***The Trials*** a plot that is appropriately simple: the whole scene, Jero forewarns, is going to be a piece of animated journal: ". . . my whole purpose in coming here is to show you one rather eventful day in my life, a day when I thought for a moment that the curse of my old Master was about to be fulfilled." This curse, we eventually find out, in a rather simplistic use of flashback, is that the Daughters of Discord—that is, women—shall be the cause of Jero's ruin and downfall. They are incarnated here specifically in the personalities of Amọpe, Chume's cantankerous wife, and of the unnamed girl who goes bathing every morning by Jero's church. It is through Amọpe that we unite with the supplementary plot, involving Jero's relationship with his flock. Of these, Chume is the conspicuous prototype, with his blind faith and devotion, his nagging domestic frustration. "Strange dissatisfied people," muses Jero, "I know they are dissatisfied because I keep them dissatisfied. Once they are full, they won't come again. Like my good apprentice, Brother Chume." . . . Chume's single obsession we find out, is to beat his troublesome wife, but Jero will not allow him until . . .

It is this moment that forms the kernel of dramatic action and irony, fed upon the time-worn mechanics of suspended recognition. For, even while prevailing upon Chume not to beat his wife, Jero suddenly discovers that the woman creditor who came to camp at his doorstep even that morning, forcing him to make a hasty undignified exit through his window, is none other than the same Amọpe, Chume's wife. From that moment, the reaction is predictable. . . . But the plan misfires, and Jero is unmasked. For the first time Chume comes to discover Jero's abode, as well as the identity of his wife's creditor. The whole truth rapidly unfolds in his mind; when next we see him, he is pursuing Jero with a cutlass. However, the day will still be Jero's. With the aid of a new convert, one aspiring Member of Parliament who has come to practise his speeches on the beach, Jero has Chume locked up in an asylum. The play ends with the Member of Parliament making complete obeisance before the figure of Jero.

Technically, the play follows a linear exposition, with a logical concatenation of events welded together by successive soliloquys by Jero. Thus, it is not really ambitious or complex structurally, a point which makes it an ideal choice for small or amateur group productions. It is this also, perhaps paradoxically, that places the play in spite of its popularity all along the West African coast, in an inferior category in the whole of Ṣoyinka's corpus. The playwright will in later plays make use of progressively fewer soliloquys, and broaden the moments of comic relief provided by scenes of mass action or frenzy (such as when Chume presides over the praying flock in Jero's absence). (pp. 155-60)

In ***Metamorphosis,*** we discover right from the opening of the play that both the social context of action as well as Jero's personal fortunes have changed since ***The Trials.*** We learn that it is "no longer his rent-troubled shack of ***The Trials*** but a modest whitewashed room, quite comfortable. . . . On the wall, a large framed picture of a uniformed figure at a battery of microphones indicates that Jero's diocese is no longer governed by his old friends the civilian politicians." The allusion to the contemporary Nigerian situation is apparent enough; it is to become even more clarified by the reference to the public execution of robbers, a phenomenon that has remained a post-war reality in this country. This is the whole basis of Jero's present confrontation. The authorities, in order to enhance the tourist trade, have decided to erect a National Public Execution Amphitheatre on the Bar Beach, a plan which necessarily entails the expulsion of all the various religious groups which have taken permanent residence on the beach. Only one group would be exempted. "Such a body," reads the Government confidential file which has illicitly come to Jero's possession, "will say prayers before and after each execution, and where appropriate will administer the last rites to the condemned. They will be provided a point of vantage where they will preach to the public on the evil of crime and the morals to be drawn from the miserable end of the felons." . . . As a matter of fact, the Salvation Army has already been chosen by the Cabinet Office for this function, but Brother Jero's aim is to secure the "spiritual monopoly" for himself, by uniting all the rival Apostolic sects under his leadership.

The choice of the Salvation Army offers Jero great inspiration—it is the very image, on a spiritual level, of the nation's new leadership, especially with its tradition of brass bands and parades, its uniforms and epaulettes, its hierarchical organization, and its neo-military protocol. Jero's principal assets are two-fold: first, the former Confidential Secretary to the Tourist Board who, on a trip with her chief to effect the eviction, is transported by Jero's preaching, turns convert on the spot, and is baptized Rebecca; and the second asset is the government file marked "Top Secret," in which all the plans for the Amphitheatre are detailed, and which is brought to Jero by Rebecca. In that file, are the incriminating details of deals made by the Board's Chief Executive Officer concerning the award of contracts for the Amphitheatre. These two assets, allied with his customary cunning, prove sufficient for Jero to blackmail the CEO into signing off the "monopoly on spirituality" to Jero's newly formed body, the Church of the Apostolic Salvation Army (CASA).

It is evident from that summary that our playwright has adopted a new stance in his response to historical events. The tiger is no longer content merely to parade his stripes, he bares his fangs and pounces, and the victim is no longer hidden behind metaphors. . . . As in ***Kongi's Harvest,*** power and its empty pomp are the objects of Şoyinka's satire in this play. The attraction of power, the reluctance to relinquish it when obtained, and its ultimate corrupting force constitute for Jero the psychological weakness of his antagonists which he can usefully exploit. It is a deep knowledge of human nature that, once again, leads him to make a striking prophecy. We have seen this before in ***The Trials,*** when the process of converting the Member of Parliament inspired Jero with an extraordinary insight into the future: "Yes, brother . . . I saw this country plunged into strife. I saw the mustering of men, gathered in the name of peace through strength." . . . And now the Civil War has taken place with all its bloodshed and anguish, a new government is installed, bringing its own rapid disillusionment, and prophecy is no longer possible now free of bitterness or grim humour: "Suppose I tell you, Shadrach," says Jero, "that it has come to the ears of the rulers that a certain new-formed religious body has prophesised long life to the regime, that this mysterious body has declared that the Lord is so pleased with their er . . . spectacular efforts to stamp out armed robbery, with the speed of the trials, the refusal of the right to appeal, the rejection of silly legal technicalities and the high rate of executions, that all these things are so pleasing to the lord that he has granted eternal life to their regime?" . . . The statement is lucid enough about the clinging power and dark incentives of the new regimes.

Jero's Metamorphosis is a daring mimic of the antics of power, but also a mimic that deliberately contains a moral indictment. The protagonist and his minions become a caricaturistic symbol of the rising regimes of our continent. And we are meant to be horrified, through the laughter, by the quality of this new leadership, the new Messiahs composed, as Shadrach says, of "thieves, robbers, rapists and cut-throats" motivated solely by self-interests and naked greed, and with an inherent callousness demonstrated in the plan to commercialize human executions. Jero's final sentence is the supreme contemptible dismissal of their posturing—as his new-formed Salvation Army marches out, he sits down, grins amiably, and says: "After all it is the fashion these days to be a desk General." (pp. 161-62)

If the two plays discussed above reflect primarily the playwright's change of mood, owing to greater political disenchantment and personal experience of physical humiliation, the two plays with which we shall close this essay bring us also the evidence of progress, in technical terms, towards the achievement of complete structural harmony. Or perhaps the appropriate word is not progress, but evolution, a conspicuous evolution towards what we confidently recognize as an African form of drama in its direct reliance on traditional mechanics. Traditional drama, to reiterate, resolves the collective traumas both through the relief of laughter and the catharsis of ritual. Şoyinka, in all the plays of his tragic cycle, similarly reaches for exorcism through theatrical mechanics which grow progressively ritualistic in conception. The departure comes from the fact that, whereas the traditional artist submits identity to art, sacrificing lyric passion to the perfection of repeated and inherited patterns, Şoyinka continuously imposes his own personality in the insistence on either highlighting specific aspects of ritual, or even creating other patterns entirely within the conventional mould. His drama thus becomes at its best a symbiosis of rhetorical and ritualistic traditions, fusing an essentially intellectual preoccupation with the structural machinery of rite.

The achievement is best realized, in our opinion, in his latest play, ***Death and The King's Horseman,*** but the initial process begins from ***The Strong Breed.*** Together the plays show a thematic concern that has remained fundamentally the same from play to play; namely, the playwright's almost obsessive inquiry into the essence and the apparatus of the society's self-rejuvenating process. Behind this quest is the belief, shared with the traditional artists, that society seasonally accumulates a burden of guilt and sin dangerous to its health and sanity, and which can be purged only through the shedding of blood. For Şoyinka this process equates to nothing less than a tragic cycle—firstly, in the notion of prerequisite destruction and violence before the advent of rain and harvest, and secondly, because this harvest, in order to be at its most fecund, must first feed on a ritual victim, taken from society's strongest stock. That scapegoat, especially in societies where the burden is hereditary, continuously fascinates Şoyinka, becoming for him the most palpable incarnation of our tragic fate—a symbolic hero whose role in the community seems to elucidate that of the artist. "Soyinka," asserts Eldred Jones, "sees society as being in continual need of salvation from itself. This act of salvation is not a mass act; it comes about through the vision and dedication of individuals who doggedly pursue their vision in spite of the opposition of the very society they seek to save. They frequently end up as the victims of the society which benefits from their vision. The salvation of the society then depends on the exercise of the individual will."

It is clearly this preoccupation that forms the central theme of both ***The Strong Breed*** and ***Death and the King's Horseman.*** In other plays this need for ritual and exorcism, and the penalty it entails in human terms impresses the playwright to such a powerful extent that it leads, sometimes, to an obsession with death itself, as seen for instance in Professor's "part intellectual, part psychic" grope towards its essence in ***The Road.*** It is, the playwright seems to forewarn, essentially a journey of *hubris,* with its inevitably disastrous aftermath. That warning is plain enough in ***Madmen and Specialists,*** where the Old Man attempts to raise a cult of the absurd as a counter to a painful moment of history in which the ascendant element is absurdity itself, and men are cowed by the repeated horror of power-elites stifling society's regenerative sources. In this limited essay, however, we shall talk only of the two plays in which Şoyinka shows a paramount concern about the sacrificial tools of the communal catharsis, and poetically explores the consequences of a possible crick in the fatal wheel.

The evolution from ***The Strong Breed*** to ***Death and the King's Horseman*** is not in the alteration of theme but rather, in a deepening of it, and the process is one of technical ripening. The heroes of both plays may as well be kinsmen—they both belong to families which, traditionally, are called upon at appropriate moments to be the medium of community's spiritual and physical restoration. There are variations, however, to the portraits of these channels of psycho-physical relief. Eman of

The Strong Breed is a young man, and is a fugitive, when we first meet him, from his village and from his burdensome inheritance. Pursued even in his refuge by "his blood," just as prophesied by his father, his drama becomes the tragedy of Oedipus: a picture of man vainly striving against the shackles of fate, and of the community paying the price of this abortive challenge through the harvest of malediction and terror. Elesin's portrait in ***Horseman*** is a slight variant: he is the father rather than the son, and his ordeal is not to carry a symbolic boat but to give up his life whenever the reigning Ọba dies.

This death, which must be voluntary, bears an analogous significance to Eman's in its ritual context. In Act 3, for instance, we are reminded of Eman's father warning his son about the inescapable demand of his blood when one of the market women angrily confronts Sergeant Amusa: "You ignorant man. It is not he who calls himself Elesin Oba, it is his blood that says it. As it called out to his father before him and will to his son after him." As the emissary of the living to their forefathers, Elesin must on the king's funeral day, reach the Alafin, halted at the gates of the territory of the ancestors, in order that the royal spirit may not be cast adrift in aimless wandering, nor the world of the living become "wrenched from its course."... But as it happens—and this particular story is drawn from an actual historical occurrence—the white District Officer intervenes at the crucial moment of Elesin's suicide, and the ultimate consequence is the death both of Elesin himself and of his heir, Olunde, the eldest son who tries to retrieve the family's honour.

Soyinka, in the preliminary notes to ***Horseman,*** warns that the play is "a choric lament not a tragedy of individual limitation." The statement is a clarification of the technical progress we mentioned above. For ***The Strong Breed*** remains on that level of "tragedy of individual limitation," borrowing the discursive structure of the Western theatrical tradition. The principal elements of this are quite familiar: there is firstly the dramatic scaffolding, built on a unilinear scenic sequence; secondly, there is the tendency towards a classical monothematic purity, in which the tragic is untainted by comedy or vulgarity; thirdly, the dramatic accent is on dialogue and verbal logistics, the banishment from stage of violence and of physical gestures other than the most stylized; and finally, there is always the implication of a physical separation between actors and audience, one active, the other passive, merely recipient. All these elements are basic to the structure and conception of ***The Strong Breed.*** The disposition of scenes, for example, is inspired essentially by the European tradition, even though a conscious attempt has been made to alter the conventional chronological sequence by the use of flashbacks. Eman's ordeal, from the moment he decides to rescue Ifada by substituting himself as carrier to the moment of his death, follows a discernible, logical progression, and the drama is still constructed in heroic terms around his central personality. The resources of dance and ritual are severely pruned, and laughter occurs sparingly only in the scene recalled from youth, involving Omae and the Tutor at the initiation camp. The influence of the early-century symbolist theatre is conspicuous in the figurative presence of the Girl and of Ifada, and in the dark significance of the former's effigy. But, of course, we are dealing on the thematic level, with a purely African phenomenon, fully comprehensible perhaps only to an African consciousness; only the technique remains basically Western, in its discursive framework, despite its poetical reworking.

In ***Horseman,*** however, the playwright turns away from the Western tradition, but the play does not merely hang upon the framework of ritual: the play is the ritual itself. Technique and theme weld fluidly to yield a theatrical experience in which both actors and audience are meant to participate, and this participation extends farther beyond the province of the emotional to the psychical, beyond mere physical exhilaration to the deeper spiritual fulfilment. The dramaturgical accent now is not on the chaos of an individual disjunction, but rather on the all-pervading personality of Iku, Death itself, celebrated like a primordial deity. It is not on the limitations of a heroic revolt, but on the seemingly immutable tribal ethos of traditional Yorubaland. It is not on tragic pathos, but rather its aftermath, the collective catharsis. "The confrontation in the play," explains Soyinka in the notes, "is largely metaphysical, contained in the human vehicle which is Elesin and the universe of Yoruba mind—the world of the living, the dead and the unborn, and the numinous passage which links all—transition."

Hence, the dramatic elements alter accordingly: dialogue, for instance, deepens beyond the level of dramatic wit and becomes a celebration of the primal word, when language reverts to its pristine existence as incantation, and "the movement of words is the very passage of music and the dance of images." Rarely before in all of Soyinka's repertory has language or spectacle approached the tragic splendour of that moment when Elesin at the end of the third act dances slowly to a gradual death, the words beating against a background of keening female voices:

Elesin: *(his voice is drowsy)*
I have freed myself of earth and now
It's getting dark. Strange voices guide
my feet.

Praise-singer. The river is never so high that the eyes
Of a fish are covered. The night is not
so dark
That the albino fails to find his way. A
child
Returning homewards craves no
leading by the hand
Gracefully does the mask regain his
grove at the end of day....
Gracefully. Gracefully does the mask
dance
Homeward at the end of day,
gracefully....

(Elesin's trance appears to be deepening, his steps heavier....)

Iyaloja: It is the death of war that kills the
valiant,
Death of water is how the swimmer
goes
It is the death of markets that kills the
trader
And death of indecision takes the idle
away
The trade of the cutlass blunts its edge
And the beautiful die the death of
beauty
It takes an Elesin to die the death of
death...
Only Elesin dies the unknowable death
of death...
Gracefully, gracefully does the
horseman regain
The stables at the end of day,
gracefully,...

This is the main structural pattern of this play, namely, a continuous upsurge, of song and antiphony, of dance and dirge, poetry and incantation in which, inevitably, actors and audience unite into a fluid chorus. The only other moment comparable to this, and perhaps as equally stirring, is the close of "Hemlock" in ***Kongi's Harvest,*** when Danlola and his retinue dance together "for the last time" at the portentous approach of doom. Here also, woven subtly within the dance and prolonging it, are similar threads of foreboding, though we shall not grasp their full import until the end of play. . . . (pp. 162-68)

But the Elesin fails in his duty, and the cause, in Soyinka's interpretation, is to be discovered not only in the sacrilege of the District Officer's intervention, but also in Elesin's concupiscence, his tenacious love of earth and flesh, as he himself later confesses: ". . . my weakness came not merely from the abomination of the white man who came violently into my fading presence, there was also a weight of longing on my earth-held limb." Thus the familiar "clash of cultures" theme, repugnant to Ṣoyinka, is carefully avoided here, and the emphasis placed upon a more profound exploration of the unpredictable temper of Death. Olunde, the first son and heir, heroically takes the place of his father to accompany the king. When his corpse is unveiled before Elesin in detention, he becomes overcome with shame and kills himself. And that is the signal for tragedy, for this death is now merely gratuitous, void of meaning. . . . The link with funeral rites such as *agemo* is therefore apparent. For we are dealing here not with an intellectual probe, a close analysis of the essence of death such as in ***The Road,*** but with a celebration, of the very process of death itself, with its pure impression on the consciousness. Of course, we are concerned essentially with the same kind of crisis; that is, the exorcism of the terror of the unknown, but where Elesin is the medium through whom the ritual is processed, Professor is an intruder into the rite, at a brief eloquent moment of suspension ("transition"), and his death is not valuable in communal terms as a symbolic restorative, only as a penalty for *hubris*. Hence, Professor's tragic end is heroic but only in the Atowoda sense, as pathfinder, discoverer, incarnation of the stray, rebellious will. We are not called upon to undertake any such journey of discovery in ***Horseman,*** only to participate, in a rite which begins, goes through a moment of defilement, but then is finally restored and terminated. At first we are enthralled by the vitality of the scene, enlivened by Elesin's infectious humour and histrionics; then we are gradually drawn into the dilemma of choices involving the Pilkingses; and finally, we are made to share in the pathos of Elesin's tragic end. Once again, as in ***The Road*** or ***The Strong Breed,*** it is death that wins, for even now Elesin is still accorded his befitting respects, and the community, appeased at last, can turn its mind towards the future. "Now," enjoins Iyaloja, "forget the dead, forget even the living. Turn your mind only to the unborn". The whiteman's intrusion into the process of burial creates a human tragedy in Elesin's double loss, but it does not and cannot halt the age-old funeral tradition.

In a play of such sombre implications, the Western classical tragedian would automatically excise all suggestions of laughter, an element judged in his own aesthetics as being diversionary, if not downright vulgar. But traditional African art willingly incorporates humour within the polythematic matrix of ritual, both for dramatic emphasis in the mingling of genres, and also for verisimilitude, in the reflection of the complexity of existence. Likewise, in ***Horseman,*** the mournful atmosphere of ritual is continually relieved by laughter, and the result is similarly an intensification of the final tragic pathos. In fact—and again in a way perhaps fully comprehensible only to an African consciousness—the ritual victim himself, Elesin, who should be expected to be overcome by sorrow at the prospects of losing his life, is paradoxically the very vehicle of much of the laughter. . . . (pp. 169-71)

Still the best moments of comedy are those which feature Sergeant Amusa, the dutiful "Native Administration" policeman under the orders of Mr Pilkings, the District Officer. His semi-literacy and—of a Christian convert—lingering superstitiousness provide easy material for fun, underlining his kinship with such delightful predecessors as Lakunle of ***The Lion and the Jewel*** and Brother Chume of *The Jero Plays*. . . . Amusa's personality thus serves, in contrast to Elesin's, to bring a useful emphasis to the progress mentioned above in Ṣoyinka's theatre. For if Amusa links up with recognizable characters in Ṣoyinka's earlier works, the personality of Elesin is unique. No other protagonist in his theatre is similarly conceived as a dual medium of laughter and pathos. Danlola possesses Elesin's exuberance, but his sense of humour is finally damaged by his anger and indignation; Kongi's megalomania is humourless; Demoke is mostly obsessed by his burden of guilt; Eman, driven by hereditary anguish, is hounded to the ultimate tragic reckoning; the Beros, father and son, have been warped beyond laughter by the impact of rampant cruelty and carnage; Professor is completely eaten in by an erratic mystical quest; Elesin alone preserves his easy, infectious mirth. If the comic and the hilarious prevail in those earlier plays, it is largely channelled through the chorus of acolytes and apprentices with which the protagonists surround themselves. And the main character is, therefore, usually portrayed in sharp contrast to this clowning, histrionic chorus as a serious, profound if adventurous thinker, the inspired and eloquent medium of a metaphysical exploration. In ***Horseman,*** however, to reiterate, we are concerned not with an exploration, but simply with a statement, of which Elesin is the personification. He does not need to probe or question; he accepts; his dilemma is not born of an inner rebellious Will, but from external sources; and the confrontation unwinds itself not in physical and vertical lines, but horizontally, in the collision of two differing and equally valid communal ethos. It is undoubtedly this which explains both the mechanics of the play, as well as Elesin's singular personality. Accepting the communal praxis, revelling in his role as companion of the Alafin, he can afford to give free rein to his ebullience.

Thus, since the significant point is not the fact of Elesin's death but the manner of it, the play remains a celebration purely in traditional ritual terms, in which *agon* is always a subsidiary component. The external element from which springs the confrontation becomes catalyst to, not the central newel of dance. . . . Thus, conflict is confined to its proper place in ritual, fused in harmoniously, as successfully as laughter and pathos are wedded, as the movement of play is conveyed not by sterile verbal fencing, but through recurrent chant and antiphony, dance and mime, and the incantatory power of the Verb. The tiger is in full splendour now: what will the future bring, I wonder? (pp. 171-74)

Femi Osofisan, "Tiger on Stage: Wole Ṣoyinka and Nigerian Theatre," in Theatre in Africa, *edited by Oyin Ogunba and Abiola and Irele, Ibadan University Press, 1978, pp. 151-175.*

EUSTACE PALMER

[In the following excerpt Palmer examines Ṣoyinka's humorous, satirical early novel The Interpreters, *as well as his darker post-prison fiction* Season of Anomy.]

At the Scandinavian African Writers' Conference held in Stockholm in 1967, Ṣoyinka delivered a lecture which has had important consequences for the development of African literature. In it he urged his fellow African writers to cease their preoccupation with the past and focus their attention instead on those forces which threaten the disintegration of African society. . . . He himself realized that before Africans could understand the present there must be a remorseless confrontation with the past and he has used the past meaningfully and effectively in his poems and plays. Ṣoyinka was merely suggesting that an unduly prolonged preoccupation with the sins of the imperialists and their allies might lead African writers to neglect the chaotic state of the continent in contemporary times and to ignore the responsibilities of Africans themselves for its present state. When Ṣoyinka delivered his lecture most African countries had already become independent, some over a decade earlier, and the first military coups had taken place in Ghana, Nigeria, Sierra Leone and other places. The Congo (Zaïre) had had its disastrous civil war and the Nigerian Civil War was just beginning. African society was indeed going through a turbulent period of readjustment in the wake of the traumatic consequences of the imperialist occupation. Although the policies of the imperialists were no doubt partly responsible for the problems of readjustment, African countries had been independent long enough for Africans themselves to take responsibility for a large proportion of the mess. Wole Ṣoyinka was pointing out that the African writer, being among the most sensitive minds in his community, has a duty to act as the conscience of his nation. In the task of discovering new values he has a very important role to play, but he can only play it effectively if he faces up to the truth and forces his countrymen to see themselves as others see them; he must alert them to the debasement of standards in their community, to the prevalence of corruption, incompetence, nepotism, brutality, injustice, poverty, social inequality, materialism, hypocrisy and snobbery. The African writer in contemporary times must be socially committed and involved, and he must be prepared to expose his society's shortcomings and suggest alternative scales of value.

The consequence of Soyinka's call is that in the later 1960s and early 1970s the focus in African writing shifted from historical, cultural and sociological analysis to penetrating social comment and social satire. Of course, Achebe had in a sense anticipated Soyinka with the publication of *A Man of the People* in 1966, but his novel was rather too political, whereas Soyinka was asking for attention to be paid to the presence of decadence in all areas of African society. His call has been heeded by several writers, but he himself had showed the way with the publication of his first novel, ***The Interpreters,*** in 1965. This novel is probably the most comprehensive exposé of the decadence of modern African society that has so far been published. It has, however, given rise to sharp controversy among critics and readers. On the one hand are those like Professor Jones who give it unqualified praise; on the other hand there are those like Derek Elders and the present writer who do not believe that the novel is the accomplished masterpiece it has been claimed to be. Soyinka has become such an established figure in the African literary canon that it is almost sacrilegious to register an opinion of his work which falls short of total praise. Let it be said at the outset that the relevance of Ṣoyinka's exposure of decadence is not in question; but in conformity with the general critical method of this study, all aspects of the novels discussed—both message and technique—must be examined for a balanced evaluation. Even where technique is concerned one is aware that Soyinka does certain things extremely well—much better than most other African novelists—but one is also uneasy about the language and structure of the novel. In raising questions about these two aspects of Soyinka's art one is, in fact, articulating the responses of hosts of intelligent readers who find them not just difficult but rather affected. One is not merely objecting to structural unorthodoxy. The practice of novelists like Sterne, Virginia Woolf, Conrad and Ngugi—to name only a few—has attuned the mind of the modern reader to novels which do not progress in linear time but which are perfectly acceptable because even in their apparent haphazardness they obey a formal logic of their own, and the reader is convinced that no other structural principle could have been devised to make the author's points effectively. Soyinka, like Ngugi in *A Grain of Wheat,* makes use of flashbacks, but where one can see a kind of logic and inevitability in their use in Ngugi's novel it is difficult to make the same case for Soyinka's. The density of the novel's verbal texture which has been so often hailed by critics can easily degenerate into a pointless wordiness. I shall try to demonstrate these points by a detailed consideration of the novel's structure.

The novel starts with all five or six interpreters at a nightclub in Lagos; a hundred and five pages and six chapters later, when Egbo is discovered in a drunken stupor in his girlfriend's flat, we realize that the story has hardly moved at all in present time. Instead, Soyinka has taken us back in a number of flashbacks whose purpose presumably is to throw some light on the characters of his interpreters. (pp. 240-42)

At the start of Chapter 7 we return to the present and to Sagoe in Dehinwa's bedroom and it is only now, as Sagoe, having woken up from his drunken stupor, makes his way to Sir Derinola's funeral, that the narrative really moves forward. From now on the story moves consistently forward with the solitary exception of the flashback to the scene of Egbo's first encounter with Simi. Soyinka does try to suggest something of a closely knit narrative with the stories of Sagoe, Lazarus and Noah, and the Uguazors and Faseyis; but in reality the narrative consists of independent episodes which are thematically and symbolically rather than causally and logically linked together. There is no doubt that the flashbacks in the first half of the book throw a considerable amount of light on Sagoe, Egbo and Sekoni; but there is little logic in their arrangement, and the linking devices, where they occur, are very tenuous. It would be a large claim to say that Soyinka uses flashbacks as adroitly as Ngugi does. The work begins to look increasingly like a clever pastiche consisting of a series of highly entertaining episodes which nevertheless add up to a picture of life.

If there are reservations about the novel's structure, there can be none about the thoroughness of the satire at society's expense. Soyinka's wide-ranging wit takes in all sections of a corrupt society—the brutal masses, the aimless intellectuals, the affected and hypocritical university dons, the vulgar and corrupt businessmen, the mediocre civil servants, the illiterate politicians and the incompetent journalists. The focus is largely on the five brilliant interpreters of this society—Sagoe the university educated journalist, Egbo the foreign service official, Sekoni the engineer and sculptor, Kola the artist and teacher of art and Bandele the university lecturer. All are talented intellectuals who have retained their African consciousness although they were largely educated in the western world. Yet their western education enables them to look at their changing society with a certain amount of detachment. They are therefore uniquely qualified to be interpreters of this society. The reader is impressed by their honesty, sincerity, moral idealism, concern for truth and justice and aversion to corruption, snobbery and hypocrisy; but anyone who assumes that Soyinka presents all the interpreters as models of behaviour will be completely misreading the novel. He is careful to expose their selfishness, egoism, cynicism and aimlessness. Indeed the conduct of the intellectuals both in and out of the university is a major preoccupation of Soyinka's in this novel. The aimlessness and superficiality of the lives of most of the interpreters is patent. With the exception of Sekoni and Bandele they all seem to be lacking in wholeness and solid core; this is seen in Egbo's inability to decide between a life of power in the creeks and the tedious routine of the foreign office, and in Sagoe's pointless chat about his drink lobes. When Sekoni dies the weaknesses are glaringly brought out as Egbo, unable to bear the grief and the funeral, flies to the refuge of his grove; Sagoe is characteristically awash in beer and vomit for a week and Kola is completely unable to work. Only the strong and resourceful Bandele retains his composure and takes upon himself the onerous task of consoling Sekoni's unfortunate father.

Egbo, who is possibly the sharpest intellect among them, is also the most selfish, egoistic and cynical. In a sense he is typical of all the interpreters in that he has to make a choice between the apparently aimless life he lives in modern Lagos and a return to traditional society. All modern young men and women who face the problem of hammering out new values for themselves in a rapidly changing and largely unsatisfactory situation have to make similar choices. (pp. 244-45)

Sagoe is much more human than Egbo. He is also the most important of the interpreters since it is largely through his activities as a journalist that we are made to see the antics of contemporary Nigerian society. We applaud his consideration and sympathy when he joins the small band of eleven mourners and takes a wreath from Sir Derinola's cortege to bestow on the poor man's. We contrast his humanity with the brutality of the Lagos crowd during the pursuit of Noah. He is even considerate in his treatment of Chief Winsala and Sir Derinola. Nevertheless, the unattractive aspects of his character are apparent. His piercing gaze strips Nigerian society bare, but his own shortcomings are simultaneously exposed. He can be irreverent, cynical and, when steeped in beer as he often is, aimless and irresponsible. He can muse over which political party a taxi driver thugs for, but on discovering that he has no money on him to pay his taxi fare is dishonest enough to bluff his way out of the jam by pretending to be a police officer and threatening to arrest the driver. His integrity and concern for truth and justice make him champion Sekoni's cause when the latter is so brutally treated by his employers, and he justifiably registers his disgust at the connivance of his own newspaper bosses with the proprietors of another paper to suppress the truth. But he lacks the courage to pursue matters to their logical conclusion and resign his job as he once weakly threatened to do. Instead he takes refuge in his pointless voidante philosophy.

The voidante philosophy serves the same purpose for Sagoe as Egbo's grove does for the latter; it provides a refuge from the frustrations of life in Nigeria. (pp. 247-48)

At his job Sagoe is thoroughly professional, but rather selfishly so, since he sees all the participants in the events he observes primarily as actors in a sensational newspaper drama, thus blinding himself at times to real human suffering. Fortunately he is reclaimed at the end for the world of humanity by Dehinwa who consents to marry him and gets him to burn his books of enlightenment. Instead of a recourse to voidancy, therefore, he finds a much more respectable and effective refuge in the solid Dehinwa.

Kola, the artist of the group, has few of Sagoe's redeeming features while sharing his cynicism and selfish professionalism. He always sees people in terms of their suitability as sitters for his painting; and as long as he gets his sitters and is able to concentrate on his work he does not care how much misery he causes. (p. 249)

Of the entire group of interpreters, Sekoni the engineer elicits the greatest sympathy. If he is also the most vulnerable it is precisely because of his basic honesty and courage and his determination not to compromise his principles and sacrifice his insights in order to accommodate the reactionary elements in his society. Apart from an occasional display of temper provoked by his frustration in a soulless society and heightened perhaps by his stutter, Sekoni seems almost entirely free of any flaws. Nor does he show any signs of the inadequacy that plagues Sagoe, Egbo and Kola. Indeed, in spite of his eventual madness, there is a wholeness in Sekoni which is quite lacking in Egbo, Sagoe, Kola and Lasunwon. He always seems to move on a plane of mysticism, conveyed not just by his stutter but also by his unusually concentrated and poetic language. (p. 250)

Sekoni appears like an almighty creator feeling the surge and the pulse of power beneath his fingers and relishing his success as he compels the primeval forces of nature to bend to his will. Perhaps there is a slight suggestion that Sekoni's dreams are too grandiose for the reality of the situation. Nevertheless, the passage celebrates the triumph of human ingenuity and power. Of course the contrast between these magnificent dreams and the mundane tasks Sekoni is assigned is most marked, and it justifiably elicits Sekoni's wrath. When his ingenious power station is condemned through a combination of jealousy, stupidity, conservatism and corruption Sekoni batters it to pieces himself and goes mad. The Sekoni story poignantly demonstrates the destruction of brilliance and originality by a narrow-minded and corrupt society. There is also the suggestion that through this destruction the vast potential of the country, which someone of Sekoni's vision would have succeeded in harnessing, remains untapped. The ruined power station is therefore symbolic on more than one level; and Sekoni himself emerges as a genius of the first order, as a man of vision and imagination and above all as a man of integrity. (p. 251)

Bandele, who is perhaps the most perfect of the interpreters, is the embodiment of Soyinka's positive values in this novel. There is hardly a flashback to Bandele's past, with the result that his presentation is not as detailed as Egbo's or Sagoe's; by the same token he seems to be the least talkative of them all. Yet there is no doubting the effectiveness of his presence throughout the novel. Apart from being Soyinka's spokesman and therefore the norm of conduct, he is the conscience of the members of his class and generation. Like Soyinka his creator he is not only aware, as the others are, of the shortcomings of his society, he can also achieve a certain measure of detachment and see with great clarity the weaknesses of his fellow interpreters. He can always be relied on to criticize the foibles of his friends sharply, whether it is Egbo's indecision in facing the choice confronting him, or Sagoe's selfish brand of journalism or Kola's indiscretions with the Faseyis. And there is no doubt that on each occasion we and the author endorse his judgement. Bandele's habitual reticence is the correlative of much more heightened powers of observation than the others. On several occasions Soyinka stresses the difference between his reactions and those of the other interpreters to the same people and situations—to Peter, the Oguazors, Lazarus and his group, Joe Golder and the Faseyis. And he emerges as easily the most courteous, the most tolerant and the most compassionate. (pp. 252-53)

The difference between Bandele and the other interpreters is most clearly revealed in the Lazarus scenes where we find him genuinely trying to unravel and understand the circumstances of the albino's 'death' while the others are being cynical. . . . [From] this moment onwards Bandele's criticism of his friends becomes more scathing as he points out their selfishness and their indifference to human suffering.

With the events of the novel moving towards their disastrous climax Bandele becomes more and more aloof from the others, an almost superhuman creature presiding in judgement over not only the other interpreters, but this corrupt society as a whole. . . . His moral superiority at the end is fully justified by his earlier flexibility. He has also earned the right to look down on the others because his conduct has been free from censure. It is this inflexibility and this inexorableness of his judgement which the images describing him towards the end are meant to suggest. (p. 253)

Although the interpreters have their shortcomings, they are distinguishable by their honesty, courage, moral idealism and concern for equity from the generality of the Nigerian public whose frivolities Soyinka so brilliantly exposes through their eyes. The satire is most scathing when directed against that pillar of the establishment, Ibadan University. As the seat of higher learning, the source of the nation's higher level of manpower and the home of academics who are presumably engaged in the pursuit of truth, the university ought to be a powerful agent of change in this society. But the attitude of its members makes it hopelessly inadequate for the task. Soyinka strips off the veneer of respectability to reveal the malevolence, pettiness, vulgarity, affectation, hypocrisy and cruelty that go on underneath. The university group is largely seen through Sagoe's eyes during the Oguazors' party. The sentence which introduces the group is a perfect epitome of what goes on: "A buzz of wit, genteel laughter and character slaughter welcomed them from the drive and they entered the house of death.' . . . It suggests the repulsiveness of what is going on underneath the genteel surface. The hallmark of the group is affectation and insincerity. (p. 255)

The satire on the university group is particularized in the attack on the ridiculous Professor Oguazor and his beloved consort, the formidable Caroline. Professor Oguazor is an enormous figure of fun who, having worked his way up the establishment ladder and achieved a professorship, feels he ought to deny the African in him and adopt a conspicuously English lifestyle; but his attempt to live the life of an Englishman has disastrous consequences, for his speech, mannerisms and home in general are a grotesque parody of the actual thing. In his pathetic striving after a western life-style which he clearly does not fully understand, he merely degenerates into ridiculousness of speech and vulgarity of taste. The plastic fruits and other artificial decorations in his home, which Sagoe so effectively ridicules, are an indication not just of a life-denying sterility or unnaturalness, as Professor Jones suggests, but of vulgarity and a complete misunderstanding of western culture. (pp. 256-57)

The behaviour of the university group is symptomatic of what goes on in the nation as a whole. This in itself is a sad comment on the university which, as the seat of higher learning, might have been expected to possess better values and standards of conduct than the mass of the people. Yet the sad fact is that in most African countries universities can lay no greater claim to virtue than the nations they are meant to serve. They manifest the same prejudices and at times demonstrate the same capacity for corruption that is to be found outside the learned walls. (p. 260)

The social comment gets added point with the description of the activities at Sagoe's newspaper offices. The contrast between the slum surroundings and the opulence of the boardroom is insisted on, as is that between the filth of the general lavatory and the comfort of the 'neuter lavatory' used by the top officials. . . . With admirable economy Soyinka exposes the managing director's corruption and lack of a proper order of priorities. The newspaper's boardroom, which is, in a sense, an expression of the managing director's personality and tastes, suggests not only extravagance and corruption but also vulgarity and lack of real taste. (p. 261)

Soyinka's satire broadens out to include the masses whom he shows to be ruthless and bloody-minded particularly in their harassment of the young thief who turns out to be Noah. The religious references in this section to the thief Barabbas who was actually freed by the Jewish masses highlights the Lagos crowd's malevolence. Soyinka's bitterness and scorn are apparent in spite of the calmness of tone. He certainly brings out not only the hypocrisy of people who fawn on leaders who are ten times more fraudulent than Noah, but their brutality and bloodlust, which is particularized in the driver who with grim concentration tries to crush the thief's legs as he goes past his bonnet. Nor does Soyinka forget the politicians, even though most of the novel is concerned with social rather than with political corruption. The mindless stupidity of Chief Koyomi is ruthlessly exposed through Sagoe's journalistic antics. In reply to the chief's demand for a concrete proposal from him, Sagoe, in a moment of tremendous cynicism, has proposed a plan for the utilization of excrement. He does not know that the chief will take it very seriously and make the proposal in a speech in Parliament which is an almost verbatim report of his proposal. (pp. 262-63)

The final scenes of the novel bring to the surface the tensions and conflicts which have broken out among the interpreters and some of their associates. Bandele has moved farther and farther apart from his friends whose aimlessness, cynicism and selfishness he has now all too clearly seen; Egbo is moving away from Simi the courtesan who is portrayed as both attractive and destructive, yet he seems unable to decide conclusively to cast his fortunes with the young undergraduate who carries his child; Kola is on the point of coming to an understanding with Monica Faseyi who is now about to be separated from her husband. Instead of a resolution of conflicts, therefore, the final scenes move towards a falling apart. The night of the gathering at Kola's exhibition is one, not of harmony, but of 'severance' in which Kola admits that every man is going his way. . . . The events of the previous few days have taken a severe toll on them all, and the novel ends in disillusionment and pessimism.

Most critics have shown awareness of the fact that Soyinka's language and style suggest that this is very much a poet's novel. The poetic quality is imparted not only by the host of allusions, cryptic images and metaphors, but also by the liberties with syntax and vocabulary one normally associates with poetry. The net effect is of tremendous density of texture, compactness and economy of language. Soyinka, by means of fusion of images, suggestive allusions and metaphors reverberating far beyond themselves, can condense into a brief paragraph what other novelists might need a whole page to say. (p. 264)

It must surely be conceded that of all anglophone writers Soyinka exhibits the most complete control over the language. One notes the judicious use of pidgin for Matthias's speech and the effective mimicking of the half-educated man's speech for satirical purposes. (p. 265)

The discussion so far should have suggested that Soyinka's ability to realize a scene is probably greater than that of most other African novelists. So many of his scenes are memorable. . . . The effective realization is partly due to his use of language which sweeps the reader vividly along, and partly to his concern for the details of movements and gestures. In the wrestling scene in the nightclub, for instance, Soyinka describes almost every aspect of the thug's and Bandele's movements. . . . The use of detail can also be effective in the portrayal of the inner thoughts of individuals giving us interesting passages of introspection, as with Egbo's guilty ruminations after his loss of innocence in Simi's bedroom. Above all, it is probably the quality of Soyinka's dialogue which contributes most to the liveliness of his scenes. Very few other African novelists equal him in this regard.

Soyinka's presentation of character is also sure. Even the minor characters are established by the few words they utter or by a striking image. . . . In a novel in which the characters are legion, it is a tribute to the novelist's powers that so many of them are substantial. The only lapses seem to be the portrayal of Noah and Lasunwon who remain shadowy figures, Lasunwon to such an extent that the reader tends to forget that he is one of the interpreters; he only seems to be distinguished by his habitual stupidity. Soyinka achieves great variety in his characters: there are the aimless but brilliant interpreters, the pillars of rectitude and sound thinking like Bandele, the arrogant, affected but vulgar academics, the social climbers like Faseyi, the embodiments of corruption like Sir Derin and Chief Winsala, the stupid politicians like Chief Koyomi, and the courageous, blunt and genuine ones like Mrs Faseyi, Monica Faseyi, Dehinwa and the female student. He has managed to encompass a tremendous amount of life in this novel.

Finally there is the quality of his humour. ***The Interpreters*** remains one of the funniest novels from the pen of an African. At times the comedy takes the form of farce as in the closing stages of the Oguazor's party. It can also be created by the author's occasionally sarcastic tone of voice. But usually it is simply comedy of character. People like Sagoe's managing director, Professor Oguazor and Ayo Faseyi are bound to be comic whenever they appear. ***The Interpreters*** will remain a book about which a good many readers will have reservations. But even these will in the last resort pay tribute to the comprehensiveness of the scope of its satire and to the powerful view of life that it presents.

The difference in tone between ***The Interpreters*** and Soyinka's second novel, ***Season of Anomy,*** is revealing. Where he has contrived some hilarious scenes in the earlier work, the mood of ***Season of Anomy*** is unmitigatedly grim. It was published some eight years after ***The Interpreters*** and a lot had happened during that period to affect Soyinka's outlook profoundly. There had been two military coups in Nigeria involving great bloodshed and violence, a bitter civil war with ugly allegations of genocide, the death of a number of promising personalities like Okigbo in the strife, a military dictatorship with political parties abolished and the normal democratic processes suspended, and Soyinka's own imprisonment and eventual voluntary exile. The situation of the African continent had deteriorated to the point of bleak hopelessness. To many, it seemed that the continent was retrogressing to a state of barbarism where the ordinary human being was deprived of all rights and his life was of no account to the authorities. . . . The immediate post-independence phase of social and political corruption and intellectual dishonesty was now giving way to a bleaker phase of dictatorship, victimization, thuggery and violence organized occasionally at the highest level, and a prevailing atmosphere of fear. If ***The Interpreters*** raised the curtain on a kind of comic opera, ***Season of Anomy*** takes us into a chamber of horrors to reveal the full extent of human degradation and inhumanity.

The novel is about the evil consequences of greed and lust for power and the apparent futility of any such attempt to introduce proper values into a society where power-drunk rulers interpret any such action as a threat to their hold on power, and see it as their duty to eliminate the instigators. At a first glance, ***Season of Anomy*** might not seem to equal ***The Interpreters*** in structural complexity and although Soyinka still retains his mastery over the episode, the best scenes in ***The Interpreters,*** like the Oguazors' party, seem livelier than the best scenes of ***Season of Anomy.*** Yet, taken as a whole, this new novel gives the impression of greater compactness and power and is altogether a more satisfying work of art than ***The Interpreters.*** For in it Soyinka skilfully interweaves a number of elements—reality and fantasy, the literal and the allegorical, the modern and the classical, African nature myths and rituals and European archetypal allusions—into a compact whole. There is also a series of interesting and functional contrasts: the natural rhythms of life associated with the community of Aiyero are set against the unnatural activities of the dictators; the regenerating, life-affirming rituals play against the Cartel's appetite for slaughter; and Ofeyi's idealism as he sets out on his quest through the devastations of this contemporary waste land is set against the corruption of the authorities and their henchmen.

Images and symbols from the world of vegetation, fertility and the natural processes are central to the meaning of ***Season of Anomy.*** This is evident in the names of Aiyero's institutions and in the titles of the various sections of the novel. Significantly, the head of the ideal and self-sufficient society of Aiyero is called 'Custodian of the Grain'. The grain suggests not merely food, but germination, revitalization, fertility, healthy luxuriance and prosperity. It represents the germ of a promising idea which will grow into a powerful movement that will (it is hoped) eventually revitalize the entire country bringing material prosperity, spiritual health and a concern for the proper values. The images therefore suggest Aiyero's potential role in the propagation of a decent life for all.

The relevance of the headings of the various sections is readily apparent. The first, which is mainly about Aiyero, the home of the grain, is called 'Seminal'. It thus suggests the sowing of the idea which is to grow and spread its roots throughout the entire country. This is the beginning of the attempt to infiltrate the country with the Aiyero ideal of moral and spiritual purity, and since the authorities are corrupt, the dissemination of the Aiyero ideal means sowing the seeds of discontent. The second section is called 'Buds', because the grain having been planted and the seeds of discontent sown, they have now sprouted and put forth buds. Consequently this section concentrates on Ofeyi's evangelizing activities. However, the use of this metaphor from the world of vegetation does not necessarily suggest complete success in the infiltration of the Aiyero ideal, for the corruption of the all-powerful authorities completely inverts what should have been the logical fruition of nature's processes. Thus 'Buds' involves not just the spreading of the Aiyero ideal of moral and spiritual purity, but also the authorities' growing uneasiness and their first counter-attack in the hounding of Ofeyi who is forced on to the defensive. The title of the third section makes the point even clearer. 'Tentacles' suggests not only the people's growing discontent, and the spreading of the Aiyero roots into other parts, but also the Cartel's plans for a vicious counter-attack. In fact, the tentacles also belong to the Cartel. Ironically 'Harvest' is not about the successful fruition of Aiyero's ideals, but a harvest of blood and murder; and 'Spores' suggests not the preparation of the grain for another sowing season but the grim putting together of the mutilated pieces. The vegetation myths are thus inverted; the landscape is not healthy and flourishing but barren and death dealing, and the harvest is a harvest of blood and corpses.

Other images and metaphors from the natural processes, the seasonal rhythm and the world of vegetation recur throughout the book, serving like motifs binding the whole. But there is always a hint that the luxuriance and fertility they suggest is an illusion. (pp. 266-69)

The pervasive images of natural healing processes in this novel are set over and against images of disease and attempts to subvert those healing processes. On the one hand we are told of the healing powers of the women of Gborolu. . . . But on the other hand whenever healing powers are attributed to the Cartel the note of irony is unmistakable: 'What they are doing now, uproot it where they can, destroy the men whom they hold responsible for the spread of the virus of thought.' . . . The images of healing associated with the dentist are usually of drastic surgical or dental processes to remove the decayed or carious portions before they infect the whole. Humanity in general is seen to be grievously sick of a cancer which is gradually spreading its tentacles to the whole and against which there is apparently no remedy. . . . (p. 270)

The Cartel is appropriately associated with images of the unnatural and the abnormal. It is the snake which must be scorched before it has time to strike or a monster-child that the rationalists have given birth to. Unlike Aiyero, which observes the natural rhythm, the Cartel is committed to unnatural and abnormal growth. In a novel which lays so much stress on germination and vegetation rituals, the Cartel, true to its reputation for inverting nature's processes, 'plants' live cows (the members bury a live cow in the dead of each night) to ensure lasting ascendancy. And their harvest is a terrible harvest of evil directed against the people. Ultimately the aim of the Cartel is the unnatural mummification of the people. . . . (p. 271)

The novel starts with the presentation of Aiyero society which is regarded by the rest of the country as an eccentric anomaly, simply because its quasi-communistic system ensures material prosperity, justice and equity and demonstrates concern for the welfare of every individual. It is most significant that while the descendants of other communities are lured by the attractions of the cities, the descendants of Aiyero, having experienced other values throughout the world, discover that what they left in Aiyero is superior to anything else and therefore always return. Aiyero society is vibrantly life affirming, the need for a commitment to truth and a better life having been the impulse behind the establishment of the community. Where the rest of human society seems to be defeated by life, the inhabitants of Aiyero affirm their vigorous commitment to life. This is suggested by the nature of Aiyero's rituals. Even the funeral rites commemorating the death of the Custodian of the Grain are enacted in terms of regeneration, rebirth and fertility. The description of this ritual is one of the most powerful in the novel, reminding us of the magnificent presentation of Sekoni's dreams in ***The Interpreters.*** (pp. 271-72)

The ideal community of Aiyero is clearly noted, then, for both its material prosperity and its spiritual and moral health. However, the fact that the head of this society is called 'Custodian of the Grain' suggests either that Aiyero wishes to conserve the grain for itself or that it is unaware that it could be disseminated to the world outside and thus become a powerful force for change. For, idealistic though this society is, it has limitations which Ofeyi is quick to observe and of which even its own leaders are becoming increasingly aware. Its much-vaunted virtue is too introspective. Its descendants are untouched not just by the world's corruption, but by the plight of mankind. In their view, to spread the message of Aiyero would be evangelism, evangelism is a form of aggression and they find no virtue in aggression. But Ofeyi points out to them that as a consequence of their refusal to evangelize a smell of mould and stagnation clings to the place. The Custodian's wish that a stranger should succeed him in his office is an indication of his own growing awareness of the need for Aiyero to move outwards. It is therefore essential to the very survival of Aiyero and its ideal of clean and decent living that it should abandon its self-regarding complacency and be prepared to evangelize. (pp. 273-74)

The cocoa plant and the Cocoa Marketing Corporation also clearly have symbolic functions in the novel. Even in a very literal sense the cocoa plant is held to be the chief source of the country's prosperity. But the reference to it as the golden pod containing nectar and ambrosia suggests its association with the life of happiness enjoyed by the classical gods. The cocoa therefore symbolizes both material prosperity and happiness, healthy God-given luxuriance and contentment; in short, the good life that every Nigerian is entitled to. The idealistic Ofeyi's cocoa promotion campaign which he launches in his capacity as public relations officer for the Cocoa Marketing Board is therefore nothing less than the attempt to give every Nigerian a chance of a decent life, and to expose the greed of the rulers who have made that life impossible. The Cocoa Marketing Board should be the agent for making the good life available to every citizen. In practice, however, it falls short of this.

It is not too difficult to see the similarity between the cocoa drive and the Aiyero ideal. Both symbolize the good life. In fact, Aiyero represents a realization of the ideal good life which the cocoa plant is supposed to give to every Nigerian citizen. It is therefore perfectly natural for Ofeyi to think of the idea of linking Aiyero with his cocoa promotion campaign. The cocoa plant, like Aiyero, is also associated with images of germination, fertility and growth. In this corrupt society, however, the people are deprived of the good life which the cocoa plant should give them as of right, because the greedy authorities have sought to appropriate it all for themselves. They sell to the people, not the genuine thing, but a severely adulterated form: cocoa-wix, cocoa-bix and cocoa-flavoured sawdust.

During his visit to Aiyero, Ofeyi characteristically discovers that Aiyero soil is cocoa-earth; he thus thinks up the clever scheme of starting a model cocoa plantation within the communal where the seedlings would be nurtured to maturity but he also envisages the parallel progress of the new idea: 'the birth of the new man from the same germ as the cocoa seed, the Aiyero ideal disseminated with the same powerful propaganda machine of the Cartel throughout the land'. In becoming equated with the Aiyero ideal the cocoa-seed thus becomes the grain, which will eventually give rise to buds, tentacles, harvest and spores. The growth of the cocoa plant—the healthy virile shoot—suggests the nursing of pure vigorous ideals in Aiyero for export to the world outside, particularly to youth. The people of Aiyero are for once prepared to make a concession to outside ideas and set aside acres of virgin land for the scheme. The growth of the cocoa plant is also paralleled, of course, with the growth of the new man in Aiyero who will eventually carry the Aiyero message of a decent life to the outside world. The story of the Aiyero communal thus becomes not just the story of the cocoa plant from seed to ripening but also of the parallel life of the child (the child destined to become the ideal man) from seed to maturity.

Ofeyi's scheme to use the Cartel's own propaganda machine to develop a new type of man who would boost his crusade for a purer society means of course that he will have surreptitiously to attack the rulers responsible for the corruption and the erosion of what should be the good life. Most of the songs he composes to boost the campaign therefore have a double edge to them, exposing the Cartel's greed. Each contains a hidden dose of anarchy, for Ofeyi is really calling for a revolution. (pp. 274-75)

The ruling Cartel is typical of the system of government of a good number of independent African states; it is a dictatorial regime consisting of civilians backed by military might, the commandant-in-chief of the armed forces being one of its arms. Its realization that its power is not based on the will of the people makes the Cartel highly suspicious of anyone who shows the slightest signs of deviating from its wishes. The number of people that the Cartel bribes and corrupts into connivance is legion. Some are ordinary individuals who have to pay with their lives later; some are members of the judiciary. Nor are the police and the medical services exempt. When bribery fails bullying tactics are used. The Cartel will stop at nothing to achieve its dastardly ends and the kind of life it offers the people is one of unmitigated misery, fear and degradation.

Although this novel is less concerned with social corruption than ***The Interpreters,*** Soyinka does give some attention to social comment. This comes out especially in the lively scene describing the unveiling of the chairman of the corporation's new fountain. Soyinka very skilfully captures the chairman's thoughts revealing his stupidity, incompetence and vulgarity; in the new dispensation this is the kind of man who becomes chairman of an important corporation. As in ***The Interpreters,*** Soyinka concentrates attention on the stuffiness and artificiality of the gathering. The conversation between the journalist Spyhole and Zaccheus certainly brings out the stiff formality, and there is a distinct suggestion that in spite of this stiff exterior there is vulgarity simmering underneath.

Through Spyhole's reveries we get an insight into the chairman's tasteless extravagance. Like the managing director of Sagoe's newspaper company in ***The Interpreters,*** the chairman shows an unseemly anxiety to acquire the material artefacts that he feels are in keeping with a certain social position. It is an elaborate marble fountain with an effigy of St George and the dragon that is about to be unveiled, a monument to bad taste and extravagance. . . . The irony surrounding the extravagant fountain itself is obvious. It is a cocoa fountain, which in this novel should suggest that it is associated with the good life and the fight against corruption. But its use here is an empty facade since the chairman is one of the most corrupt people in the land. So also is the symbolism of St George and the dragon. The scene ends, of course, in general confusion due partly to Ofeyi's clever ruses. The cocoa-pod containing Iriyise, who is about to do one of her dances, refuses to open, while clouds gather overhead. Once more the symbolism is clear; because of the menace of corruption the cocoa-seed with its promise of the good life is not allowed to emerge.

Although the members of the Cartel inevitably impress the reader as a most unattractive quartet, Soyinka does not employ much depth and subtlety in their characterization. We know very little of Chief Biga, who hardly makes an appearance in the novel, except that he is a crude muscleman—the hatchet-man of the Cartel. This is also true of the commandant-in-chief who is little better than a caricature. It is a pity that Soyinka does not devote more attention to the presentation of the men from whom so much bestial evil springs. However, he is rather more conscientious with Batoki and the Zaki Amuri. The former's brutality and cynicism are obvious, and yet in a very powerful scene, the kind of scene that only Soyinka among African novelists can create, we see that Batoki who holds an entire nation in dread cannot keep order in his own household. Perhaps Soyinka intends his domestic disorderliness to be symbolic of his personal corruption; but he really gets underneath the skin of his virago of a wife as the latter defies Batoki. We meet this woman only once, and yet Soyinka's presentation is so sure that no one can deny that she is forcefully *there.*

If Batoki is the brains of the Cartel, the Zaki Amuri, the most deadly and sinister of the lot, is the real power, and the power is very forcefully enacted. Behind his taciturnity and apparent indifference lurks the most venomous malignity. The dominant impression conveyed at his court is of moral and social corruption and tyranny. (pp. 276-78)

Ofeyi, the hero of the novel, is as courageous and idealistic as Sagoe and his friends in ***The Interpreters*** without possessing any of their unattractive qualities. He is significantly attracted to Aiyero from the very start, through an unconscious identification with the community's values. This is partly why the Custodian wishes to select him as his successor. Initially he is quite prepared to use peaceful methods to undermine the Cartel, the Aiyero idea being one such method. However, he is forced to change his views both by the failure of the Aiyero mission in the wake of the Zaki Amuri's onslaught and by his meeting and association with the dentist, whose symbolic name suggests that he advocates drastic action to remove the decayed portion of society before the whole is infected. The dentist sees violence as the only means of getting rid of a dictatorial regime and Ofeyi's development is in the direction of a gradual acceptance of the dentist's position. He is forced to accept that he and the dentist are kindred spirits: 'Violence is not what I want from here. Just the same, the sowing of any idea these days can no longer take place without accepting the need to protect the young seedling, even by violent means.' In a rapidly disintegrating situation such as that presented in the novel, even the most peaceloving are sometimes forced to abandon their principles and take refuge in violence, for violence breeds violence.

The dentist, for his part, is single-minded in his devotion to his philosophy of violence as the solution to the country's problems. It is right to talk of his 'philosophy of violence' for he is not simply a crude trained assassin. His conduct is backed by a carefully thought out and articulate rationale which is so impressive that Ofeyi often finds it unassailable: 'There is a pattern even to the most senseless killing. All that we must do is to take control of that violence and direct it with a constructive economy.' Soyinka skilfully demonstrates the dentist's cool, quiet professionalism, which comes out even in his tone of voice. He is neat and efficient in his methods and completely unsentimental. Even after the most sensational killing his voice betrays no touch of elation or of vindictiveness. He has just done a job of work well; he mentions it only in passing and goes on to other matters. Unlike some others, like Ofeyi, who waver under the influence of various dilemmas, the dentist derives strength from the unshakable conviction that his attitude and course of action are right.

Ofeyi's companion, Iriyise, undergoes a striking transformation in the novel from Lagos night-club girl to one of the society's real moral agents. The fact that she is immediately attracted to Aiyero during their first visit there is an indication of her own moral idealism. In the symbolic framework of the novel she is one of the forces dedicated to promoting the nation's moral and spiritual health. She responds to the vegetative, life-affirming rituals of Aiyero and in doing so becomes complete. . . . She is also, of course, the cocoa princess, the leading figure in Ofeyi's cocoa promotion campaign. Iriyise is associated with the images of vegetation, germination and fecundity associated with Aiyero and the cocoa plant, and after the establishment of the cocoa plantation in Aiyero she appropriately plays a prominent role in tending the young seedlings. 'Now she could even tell a blight on the young shoot apart from mere scorching by the sun. Her fingers spliced wounded saplings with the ease of a natural healer. Her presence, the women boasted, inspired the rains.' . . . An agent of healing, a source of inspiration who is in tune with the natural rhythms, she is also naturally a great vitalizing force.

One of the major consequences of the Cartel's manoeuvres in Cross-River is Iriyise's abduction and Ofeyi's subsequent quest in search of her. To link this more tightly with his theme Soyinka uses the parallel classical analogy of the abduction of Eurydice, the wife of Orpheus. It is quite clear that both Ofeyi and Iriyise are intended to be Nigerian variants of Orpheus and Eurydice.

The legend of Orpheus and Eurydice is about the high-handed rape of innocence by an immoral and irrational despot (Pluto) and also about the courage, determination and loyalty of the consort. Orpheus is an ideal figure who, because of the excellence of his artistry, has become the type of the accomplished musician. In certain variants of the legend Pluto is represented as a snake. The abducting agent is therefore associated with evil. Soyinka makes some alterations in his own adaptation of the legend to suit the demands of his theme. Thus, unlike Orpheus, Ofeyi's quest for his partner is successful, since he is able to rescue Iriyise and take her back to the realms of life, and he himself survives at the end. Otherwise Soyinka retains most of the details and attributes of the characters. Thus, the abducting agent here is the sinister Zaki Amuri—the all-powerful and corrupt despot of Cross-River—and he abducts Iriyise like Pluto in order to minister to his lust. Like Eurydice, Iriyise is a beautiful dancer and artistic performer, and Ofeyi like Orpheus is a musician, a determined and courageous idealist who refuses to be intimidated by the threats of the all-powerful seducer. The use of the Orpheus and Eurydice legend thus helps Soyinka to bring out the Cartel's villainy and Ofeyi's moral idealism.

As in most quest tales, Ofeyi's search takes him through a kind of waste land. The quest itself has a much greater significance than the mere search for Iriyise. As Ofeyi puts it: 'I am sure every man feels the need to seize for himself the enormity of what is happening, of the time in which it is happening. Perhaps deep down I realize that the search would immerse me in the meaning of the event, lead me to a new understanding of history.' . . . Ofeyi seeks then to see a pattern in the apparently chaotic jumble.

Soyinka skilfully ensures that every major event in Ofeyi's quest corresponds with some detail of the Orpheus legend. The landscape through which Ofeyi and his companion Zaccheus journey is bleak and forbidding in the extreme, possibly the harshest created in all literature. It is an arid, barren landscape of disease, death and devastation. As in the Orpheus legend, Ofeyi meets a number of people whom he asks for help in his quest. The beginning of what can be termed his descent into the 'underworld' is his meeting with Ahime on whose advice he looks for Iriyise in the mortuary. The mortuary is naturally a place of death, a real Hades; and the harrowing sight of bodies in drawers or on dissecting tables in various stages of post-mortem surgical mutilation is as scarifying as anything to be seen in Hades.

The local native Christian church, ironically named 'Tabernacle of Hope', where Ofeyi continues his search, also has suggestions of the underworld. Spooky, according to Zaccheus, it leaves on Taiila and the reader the impression of a subterranean camp. But the place which most resembles Hades is Temoko, the prison-cum-lunatic-asylum-cum-leprosy-camp, which is a veritable chamber of disease, death and horrors. The strong man, Suberu, whose major task is significantly to cow the inmates into submission and prevent them from escaping, is most probably meant to be a variant of Cerberus, the three headed dog who guards the entrance into Hades. His original personality has been eroded, and he has been brainwashed and reduced to the level of an animal trained almost automatically to do his master's bidding.

In its presentation of violence and horror this novel possibly surpasses Ouologuem's *Bound to Violence*. It is possible that in the creation of some of these scenes Soyinka has in mind the turbulent events immediately preceding the first Nigerian coup. But there are also suggestions here of the state of the country under military rule. Certainly, the civilian rulers of the three regions—the Zaki Amuri, Chief Biga and Chief Batoki—are meant in a vague way to recall the three regional premiers of the northern, eastern and western regions of Nigeria before the coup. Zaki Amuri, like the emir, is a traditional Muslim ruler, and Cross-River suggests the North. But the dictatorial methods of the three rulers and the quasi-military discipline they impose suggest the post-coup situation, not just in Nigeria, but in many African countries. Then there are such glaring similarities between the massacre of Aiyero men and aliens in Cross-River and the massacre of Ibos in northern Nigeria which led to Biafra's declaration of independence and the Nigerian Civil War. Of course, Soyinka has written a novel and not a historical document, and he has quite legitimately altered some of the historical details and distorted some of the personalities to suit the needs of his work of art. Generally, the novel is meant to be a parable of the events in Nigeria both before the coups and during the military regime. Soyinka is expressing his detestation and horror at the cruelty and injustice that characterized the conduct of government in his country during both periods.

The worst atrocities in the novel are perpetrated in Cross-River itself where the Zaki has given orders for a campaign of genocide. The reader watches spellbound as helpless multitudes are massacred while the police, army and other forces of law and order stand idly by. Soyinka lays stress on the dehumanization and brutalization resulting from such lunatic acts. Men have become reduced to the level of animals in their hunt for others or in their attempt to escape. (pp. 279-83)

Contemporary Nigeria, like ancient Egypt, seems to be under the blight of a plague, specifically, the plague of dogs—human beings who in their rapacity and lust for human blood have been transformed into jackals. The human mind itself has undergone a bestial transformation. Soyinka also vividly demonstrates the human degradation, the absolute demoralization and collapse of the human will. The gruesome episode in which a group of villagers hunt down and ritualistically slaughter a helpless victim concentrates both the degradation and the mindless, almost purposeless cruelty. . . . The hunters set about their murderous mission with the dispassionate efficiency of people doing a job that has to be done. It is almost as though they have been conditioned to murder. Again and again Soyinka pauses to consider the psychology of mass murder and genocide. What is it that makes a populace engage in the mass slaughter of those against whom they could have no personal grudge? How is one to explain 'the unholy glee upon the faces of women, even of children' as they perpetrate these atrocities? Was the blood-lust just a legacy of the climate? Was the reason to be sought in the environment like other forms of pestilence like the tsetse-fly? 'Or was there a truly metaphysic condition called evil, present in epidemic proportions that made them so open to the manipulations of coldly unscrupulous men? There had to be a cause beyond mere differences in culture, beyond material envy . . .'. . . .

A few spots of brightness enliven the almost unrelieved gloom of this bleak landscape, taking the form of the activities of a few morally upright individuals. Apart from Ofeyi himself there is the efficient and hospitable doctor, conscientiously carrying out his duties of proper healing in the midst of carnage and slaughter; there is the kindly guide Elihu, who takes Ofeyi and his companions through their tour of the Tabernacle of Hope in search of Iriyise; there is Aliyu the deformed watchman who impresses us with his tremendous courage and loyalty in the face of overwhelming odds even when his own life is at stake; and there is the courteous Lieutenant Sayi who gives Ofeyi vital help in his search. Above all there is the pure and idealistic Taiila. She originally intended to become a nun since she considered this a healing profession, a form of beauty and a refuge of peace. But realizing that a withdrawal from the complexities of the world into a life of peace would represent a stultification of her own potential as a healing agent, she postpones her decision to be a nun and comes to Nigeria where she achieves an actual realization of her healing potential in the tour of the Tabernacle of Hope with Ofeyi. Taiila and the dentist represent the two opposing forces in Ofeyi's nature—the pull towards peace and the pull towards violence which the search for Iriyise will inevitably involve. It is significant that Ofeyi meets both on the same day and they are all together at the end. Ofeyi is immediately drawn to Taiila because she represents this peaceful side of his nature, and she, for her part, thinks that they were destined to meet so that she can save him from the almost inevitable disaster that the quest involves. There are occasions when Ofeyi is tempted to give up the search and settle for a life of peace with Taiila. But she herself realizes later that to abandon the search would be to abandon all attempts at introducing some decency into an otherwise chaotic world. It is thus the dentist who wins in the end.

The novel moves towards a horrifying climax in the scenes at the prison / lunatic asylum of Temoko. In a sense, the prison is Hades from which Iriyise, like Eurydice, is eventually rescued. But it is also a microcosm of the society with which we have been presented. Here, in their most concentrated forms, are the criminal lunacy, unnatural diseases, plagues, deformities and inversions of the natural processes which afflict the world as a whole. The leper scenes suggest that blend of the grotesque, the pathetic and the comic which Soyinka can so admirably achieve.

The conclusion is one of the few question marks that one would like to place against this novel. In the general confusion of the leper fight, engineered, we are made to believe, by the dentist, Ofeyi is able to rescue Iriyise from the seemingly impregnable fortress of Temoko; they join some of the other refugees from Cross-River and trek back to Aiyero. This is a thriller-like end to a story which has hitherto left the impression that Temoko is impregnable, that it is virtually impossible to outmanoeuvre the Cartel because of their superior force, and that anyone who dares oppose them is doomed to destruction. The escape of Ofeyi and Iriyise is inherently improbable. Ofeyi is much too lucky to survive up to the end in the midst of all this vindictive carnage. However, Soyinka's motive, in altering both the conclusion of the classical legend and what should have been the logical outcome of the story, is clear. He wishes to hold out a ray of hope in an otherwise darkening atmosphere. The Aiyero idea has been checked but not defeated. In the escape, it is retreating back to source to reorganize itself and wait for a more favourable moment to strike again. The survival of the dentist, Iriyise and Ofeyi reinforces this hope. The impression left at the end is that they move upwards from the realms of death back to life. . . . (pp. 284-86)

Eustace Palmer, "Wole Soyinka: The Interpreters, Season of Anomy," in his The Growth of the African Novel, *Heinemann Educational Books Ltd., 1979, pp. 240-87.*

DONALD CAMPBELL

Besides being a fine poet and novelist, Wole Soyinka is Nigeria's foremost dramatist, probably best known to international audiences for his exciting African version of ***The Bacchae*** of Euripides. As the title suggests, [***Requiem for a Futurologist***] is much concerned with the folly of prediction, being the story of an astrologer who is hoist with his own petard. The Reverend Dr Godspeak Igbehoden is a futurologist whose successful predictions, made on television, have won him fame and fortune. These predictions have been presented with the help of an assistant, Eleazar Hosannah, and are, in fact, a series of clever hoaxes. One night, during a live transmission, Hosannah takes his master completely by surprise when he announces that Godspeak is dead. Thereafter, no one will believe that Godspeak is alive. A crowd gathers at his house to view his body and refuse to believe that he is still alive, even when he appears before them. His death has been announced on television, therefore he cannot possibly be alive. This conviction is, of course, the true target of Soyinka's social satire, which takes its inspiration from an obscure eighteenth-century controversy involving Jonathan Swift.

Although it is a well-written play, with a secure and fluent structure and characters who leap off the page, Soyinka's dramatic argument unfortunately loses some force for non-African readers by virtue of a minor deficiency that this publication might so easily have corrected. Despite the assertion that 'the action is set in a town in Nigeria but could be in most places', there are elements in the play that seem to contradict this. References to the national characteristics of Ghana and Zambia are likely to puzzle non-Africans, as will the presence of two minor characters, a Babalawo and an Egungun Masquerade. It should not have been too difficult to include a few simple notes to clarify such matters and remove an irritation which, although minor, mars one's reading of an otherwise polished piece of dramatic writing. (pp. 247-48)

Donald Campbell, in a review of "Requiem for a Futurologist," in British Book News, *April, 1986, pp. 247-48.*

Henry (Splawn) Taylor

The Flying Change

Pulitzer Prize: Poetry

American poet, critic, editor, translator, and nonfiction writer.

Critics praise *The Flying Change* (1985) as Taylor's most mature, well-crafted poetry collection to date. In *The Flying Change,* Taylor, a native of Virginia, writes about the Southern countryside and his love of horses, as he has done in previous collections such as *The Horse Show at Midnight* (1966). However, critics emphasize, the poet never treats his subjects in a pastoral manner. Taylor shows the horror and violence of country life as well as its beauty, describing rural life with humor and unflinching realism. ''Henry Taylor's work has all the ring and authority of an American Hardy,'' critic R.H.W. Dillard asserts, ''intensely aware of the darkness that moves around us and in us.''

(See also *Contemporary Authors,* Vols. 33-36, rev. ed. and *Dictionary of Literary Biography,* Vol. 5.)

Photograph by Sky Preece. Courtesy of Henry Taylor.

DANIEL L. GUILLORY

[In ***The Flying Change***] Taylor, a poet-professor, explores . . . nagging ambiguities, which persist like faces which cannot be linked to names (in **"The Way It Sometimes Is"**). Taylor lives in a rural world marked by tragedies: a blacksmith severing his finger, a horse cutting its throat on barbed wire. But beauty lives here, too, in the form of a dragonfly, ''the green-eyed snakedoctor / with wings out of old histories of aviation. . . .'' [The poet speaks] to the general reader, revealing the terror and the beauty of a world we recognize as real.

Daniel L. Guillory, in a review of ''The Flying Change,'' in Library Journal, *Vol. 110, No. 20, December, 1985, p. 114.*

JOSEPH PARISI

Only city dwellers write pastorals: only those who view the countryside from the highway think the scene idyllic. Country folk know better; what on the surface seems bucolic conceals a harsher, more brutal reality. It is the two sides, the beastly and the beautiful, that Taylor reveals in these artfully crafted lyrics [***The Flying Change***]: the lovely, rolling fields are littered with the bodies of the dead (cattle or a murdered woman), and the land gives up a harvest only after struggle, labor, sweat. This is an abiding, abundant place, but it's kept in bounds by barbed wire. If there is serenity in the woods, there is also loneliness; rewards come to those who are strong, and then usually only after heartache. Chopping wood, shoeing horses, reliving the past—the mix of nostalgic pleasure and rue makes these thoughtful and often slyly amusing poems a more subtle, realistic type of pastoral, and Taylor makes a most rewarding guide to the acreage.

Joseph Parisi, in a review of ''The Flying Change,'' in Booklist, *Vol. 82, No. 14, March 15, 1986, pp. 1, 056.*

REED WHITTEMORE

[*An influential American poet, editor, critic, essayist, biographer, and short story writer, Whittemore is admired for the free flowing style of his poetry. He received the Award of Merit Medal from the American Academy of Arts and Letters for his poetry in 1970 and is poet laureate of Maryland. His poetry collections include* Heroes and Heroines *(1946),* The Boy from Iowa *(1962), and* Fifty Poems Fifty *(1970). Among his other publications are* William Carlos Williams: Poet from Jersey *(1975) and* Poets and Anthologists *(1986). In the following excerpt Whittemore praises Taylor for his finely controlled, traditional approach to poetry.*]

In one of the elegant short poems of [***The Flying Change***], Henry Taylor begins by imagining himself, in old age, ''grappling for the memory that might seem to make long life worthwhile.'' Many poems in our time could end with such a line—it would be a dandy depressant—but Mr. Taylor (who is not yet in old age, still managing to creak to American University and teach) then simply gives up the imagining to let himself be handed a real-life vision of the worthwhile:

> . . . I blinked and
> looked down the driveway
> in time to see six deer come over the fence out of
> nowhere, their sharp feet
> barely printing the ground, and melt into the woods
> toward absolute purity of style.

Let me not try to explicate the worthwhileness of those deer, but set them up against seeing a horse, on a lazy day, suddenly ripping himself apart on a fence, ''leaving chunks of his throat skin and hair on every barb for ten feet.'' The connection is close. The deer appeared on a lazy day too. What the worthwhile does in rural Virginia is give jolts to lazy days.

What it also does is make lazers into poets. Like most of us, Mr. Taylor has a bone to pick with his own dull routines, and as a poet he is always grateful for the unexpected. He knows, though, that he is lucky to have the routines that he has. His is a life out where there *are* horses and deer, and though he is no stranger to suburbs, his mind-fix is country. What underlies the worthwhile there is the reflectiveness that goes with sitting on porches and looking at air: the condition of not doing.

Looking at air can be maddening, a great reason for wanting jolts, and in a time when idleness mostly means watching TV it seems un-American. Watching TV narrows the mind's reception-screen, reducing drift, making idleness seem to be going somewhere; but Mr. Taylor won't have that. His senses have to be ready, in the sense of open, even if being open means ''doing absolutely nothing / for minutes, hours or a whole afternoon.'' Yoga? No, just a poet going about his business, which seems comically like a nonbusiness to the businesslike. Mr. Taylor likes it that way, comedy and all.

And his comedy can be good—he is a wit—but it has no cuteness to it. His mood is somber. The worthwhile keeps being elusive and the dailiness keeps moving in, taking over. The father, yardkeeper and teacher in him has to be served, so he serves, but not with wild dedication. In the end his dedication is to distraction from serving. The ancient state of distraction is where the ''worthwhile'' is sure to show up. Every time.

So poets like Mr. Taylor have walked up and down the earth distracted for ages and ages. Theirs is an odd profession, but traditional, and Mr. Taylor is a traditionalist. His distraction is orderly, well-formulated, well-paced, being modeled after the poetic meditators of the pre-imagist days who didn't pose for a photograph by the driveway. They thought it could be an occasion for leisurely later reflecting upon the nature of all of life's moments, life itself as a moment, and so on.

Among 20th-century poets, Mr. Taylor is with Robert Frost—and more recently Howard Nemerov—in trying to carry on with this old and honorable, but now unfavored, mission of the art. He enjoys such reflections, reaching (but modestly) for what, remember, we even used to call wisdom.

The last poem in this book, **''At the Swings,''** is such a reacher. In it, Mr. Taylor takes a familiar parental moment—a trip with small children to a playground—and manages to distract himself from their brief, happy floatings there by weaving in with that experience thoughts of related, similarly evanescent love moments, moments that make him, he has to admit, weepy.

If he really had the thoughts at the playground, he was probably much too busy weaving and weeping to have pushed the children as high as they would have liked to go; but the poem doesn't have to worry about the children. It does its own pushing, out and away from children's swings.

Much contemporary verse is now so flighty, so persistently thoughtless, that in contrast the steadiness of this volume, its persistence in exploring the mental dimensions of a worthwhile moment, is particularly striking, a calmness in the unsettled poetic weather. Henry Taylor is a fine writer, and the Washington poetry community is lucky he is here.

Reed Whittemore, ''Pastoral Poet's Jolts for Lazy Days,'' in Washington Times, *March 24, 1986.*

An Excerpt from *The Flying Change*

Hawk

> Last year I learned to speak to a red-tail hawk.
> He wheeled above me as I crossed a field;
> he screamed; I pulled a blade of grass, set it
> against my lips, and started screaming back.
>
> We held that conversation for half a mile.
> Once in a while he calls me out of the house
> and I comb a border for the right blade of grass.
> I used to wish I might learn what it is
>
> we mean to one another; now, I keep
> the noise we've mastered for itself alone,
> for glimpses of his descent toward dead elms,
> and a heart that will not mind when I am gone.

R.H.W. DILLARD

[Dillard is an American poet, critic, novelist, and short story writer. His works include the poetry collections The Day I Stopped Dreaming about Barbara Steele and Other Poems *(1966) and* The Greeting: New and Selected Poems *(1981) and the novels* The Book of Changes *(1974) and* The First Man on the Sun *(1983). An instructor at Hollins College, where Taylor earned his master's degree, Dillard, like Taylor, served on the editorial staff of the* Hollins Critic. *In the following excerpt Dillard praises* The Flying Change *as Taylor's finest work to date.]*

Henry Taylor has for all of his poetic career been drawn inexorably to questions of time and mutability, of inevitable and painful change in even the most fixed and stable of circumstances. At the age of twenty-three—in the poem, **''Things Not Solved Though Tomorrow Came''** in his first book, ***The Horse Show at Midnight*** (1966)—he was already writing convincingly and feelingly of the losses and betrayals and almost desperate love in the heart of a middle-aged man. Nine years later, in his second book, ***An Afternoon of Pocket Billiards,*** he wrote as earnestly and convincingly of ''the kinds of breakings / there are, and the kinds of restraining forces.'' A yearning for freedom (and escape from time and attendant change) wars continually in his poems with an awareness of necessary failure, necessary loss, necessary change. The verse itself embodies the tension of those polarities: a poetry of plain talk and individual identity cast in traditional forms, rigorously controlled. The result of this long-term struggle, in the poems of this new collection published in Taylor's forty-fourth year [***The Flying Change***] is an even more convincingly wrought resolution, a poetic surrender to and triumph in the necessity of learning to live in a world in which "If you need a change, just stand here, / by God, and you'll get it."

The book, despite its light moments and the restraint of its well-modulated voice, is marked by a violence of language and of fact: a murdered woman ripens in a field, a horse rips his throat out on a barbed wire fence, a bull pounds into a fence and drives a poet to want "to shoot / that fucker, just to see him jump and fall," and even the old saw "There's more than one way to skin a cat" takes on graphic reality. These are the poems of a poet who, on the one hand, presses against the very edge of known things (stepping into a tub during a lightning storm, "I step in, lie back, and let it come"), and, on the other, heads home through the dark with the assurance that "you / can't see a thing, but you'll get there." Or, as he puts it in the beautiful title poem, **"The Flying Change,"** even while recognizing "that age will make my hands a sieve . . . I hold myself immobile in bright air, / sustained in time astride the flying change."

This collection marks, then, a coming of age for a poet who has foreseen this moment throughout his work. Henry Taylor's work has all the ring and authority of an American Hardy, intensely aware of the darkness that moves around us and in us, knowing that "you and I become / whatever words we may / have come so far to say." I urge you to buy and read this powerful and valuable book.

R.H.W. Dillard, in a review of "The Flying Change," in The Hollins Critic, *Vol. XXIII, No. 2, April, 1986, p. 15.*

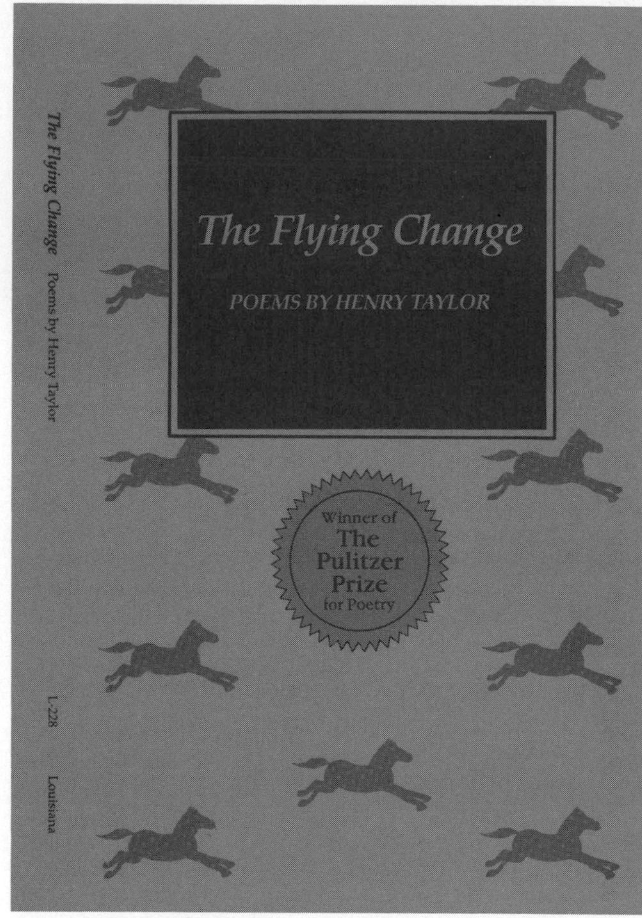

Dust jacket of The Flying Change, *by Henry Taylor. Louisiana State University Press, 1985. Courtesy of the publisher.*

PETER STITT

[*Stitt, an American critic, is the author of* The World's Hieroglyphic Beauty: Five American Poets *(1985). In the following excerpt Stitt describes Taylor's careful control of his subject matter.*]

In ***The Flying Change,*** which has . . . been given the Pulitzer Prize for poetry, Henry Taylor writes the poems of a country squire. Most of the time this country life is all too settled, predictable and complacent; the squire, after all, enjoys all the pleasures of a farmer's life with none of the risks. Indeed, the gentleman farmer may pursue pleasures for which the real farmer has neither time nor inclination, as in **"Evening at Wolf Trap":**

Once, outside the theater's weathering walls,
we sat on the grass with wine and cheese,
French bread and fruit; and as we ate, our talk
was sometimes interrupted by a small crowd

farther down the hill, throwing a frisbee.

Happily, Mr. Taylor is aware of the danger of such inherently unintense, unpoetic material to his work, and that is why he calls his book ***The Flying Change.*** In the title poem he explains that this equestrian term refers to the changing of a horse's lead in mid-jump; as poet, it is his desire to "hold myself immobile in bright air, / sustained in time astride the flying change."

Thus in the best poems here we find something altogether different from the joys of preppy picnicking. Mr. Taylor seeks for his poetry the kind of unsettling change, the sort of rent in the veil of ordinary life, that he expresses in **"Heartburn,"** where he realizes,

you can still make a wrong step
on rough ground, in the dark, and not
quite cripple yourself.

The confidence of this mature attitude serves Mr. Taylor well in such poems as **"Landscape With Tractor,"** where he discovers a body in a field, and **"As on a Darkling Plain":**

The years pile up, but there rides with you still,
across old fields to which you have come back
to invent your home and cultivate the knack
of dying slowly, to contest your will
toward getting death behind you, to find a hill
where you can stop and let the reins go slack
and parse the dark swerve of the zodiac,
a face whose eyes find ways to hold you still.

They hold you now. You turn the chestnut mare
toward the next hill darkening to the west
and stop again. The eyes will sometimes change,
but they ride with you, glimmering and vast
as the sweet country you lost once, somewhere
between the Blue Ridge and the Wasatch Range.

In addition to being a deftly written Petrarchan sonnet, this poem is attractively mysterious in subject matter. Whose face is it that allures the poet across the years? And what precisely does the lost country—surely more than just land—represent? Mr. Taylor's sense of nostalgia for his home territory is a traditional American feeling and one of the strengths of this solidly written, hauntingly conceived volume. (p. 22)

Peter Stitt, "Landscapes and Still Lives," in The New York Times Book Review, *May 4, 1986, pp. 22-3.*

DAVID SHAPIRO

[*American poet and critic Shapiro writes frequently about contemporary poetry and the visual arts. His own poetry collections include* January *(1965),* A Man Holding an Acoustic Panel *(1971), and* To an Idea *(1983). In the following excerpt Shapiro admires the craftsmanship evident in* The Flying Change.]

In a recent issue of *The New Virginia Review,* Henry Taylor has published a poem, **"Frank Amos and the Way Things Work,"** that concerns the theme of architecture as poetry, poetry as architecture. Taylor carefully builds up a dialogue with the retired builder of his house as a patient anti-hero now enduring radiation treatment. What I admire in this poem's sturdy craftsman-like tercets controls the poems in his Pulitzer Prize-winning text, ***The Flying Change***: the poem as house, as space, as dwelling.

Taylor's poems concern boundaries and the pride of boundaries: "three acres of grass bounded / by road, driveway, and vegetable garden?" in **"Landscape with Tractor,"** a corpse is found in this field, and the poet, like any trapped protagonist, wonders aloud like an average chorus: "what dope deal, betrayal, / or innocent refusal, brought her here, / and to know she will stay in that field till you die?" (In the film *Blue Velvet,* a severed ear is discovered; but Taylor would never accept such parodistic surrealism.) He does not have an agitated love of the fragment and is an anti-modernist in pursuit of states of grace: a frisbee floating like milkweed, women's hands, the charming old songs in their illegible syllables.

Taylor's poems enlarge our sympathy for those in the trades, as in his poem, **"Cutting Torch,"** since the poet evidently regards his own work as studying the "shapes flame can make." In an epoch of wandering electrons, where the television cartoon seems to have replaced the pietistic hearth, Taylor tries to revive the agrarian ideal with an emphasis on fidelity, discipline, tact, and family. A rather bitterly ironic poem on skinning cats, **"More Than One Way,"** uses Frost's darkest tone of skeptical prudence to move us toward "The genuine task." But the mordant traditionalism can also become a mannerism. At least, Taylor has to beware his own facility in scorching us with irony: "Cut off the nose button from underneath, / and it will stay with the skin; but whatever care you take, / there are two shapeless holes where the eyes used to be." Evil is formlessness, as for the poet Steele, but the tone of **"Provide, Provide"** could be less lugubriously about mutilation and more about the disasters of fideism. The positive aspect of this mordancy in Taylor is the underlying sense of a rage for justice. In **"Shapes, Vanishings,"** there is a section about a childhood confrontation with a geometry teacher that has the exact ring of the power-plays of the totalitarian classroom. Jung, by the way, recounts such a story in his autobiography, with the same scarcely suppressed sense of durable fire. A therapist might call this mere "injustice-collecting," but the poet at his best gives us a cathartic scene, then modulates to his final prudent detachments: "Therefore, / if ever she almost stops me again, / I will walk on as I have done once already, / remembering how we failed each other, / knowing better than to blame anyone." Of course, regionalism is involved in the very idea of a place where one can stroll past old teachers. Taylor is a poet of white clapboard houses that have existed "longer / than anyone now alive."

That is why Taylor can be such a satisfactory poet: **"At the Swings,"** with his two sons, the poet is thoroughly immersed in a meditation of the permanence of human prayers. This is a learned meditation, with a combination of the mysticism of Traherne and the worship of Wordsworth, and the poet polarizes the poem between a lament for his wife's mother, ill in the hospital, and praise for his sons lifting in a moment's perfection that will soon be lost. As in all of Taylor's most richly felt poems, lived place and time are the beginning of the poem's "site specificity." You cannot decontextualize this poem, which begins with the flattest factuality: "Midafternoon in Norfolk, / late July." Of course, Taylor is not an empiricist but is exactly going to swerve from those facts to the moralizing landscape and inscape where he makes his late Romantic *protest on behalf of value*—I use Whitehead's singular phrase. The playground is indeed the place where Taylor can find a holy impermanence, "that dappled moment at the swings."

The so-called "Pop" artist George Segal once remarked to me that he was involved with the presentation of ordinary flesh. Taylor is also making a kind of life-cast of ordinariness, as in his wonderful Pnin-like bathos of **"The Aging Professor Considers His Rectitude."** Taylor has a dream of purity but has learned to accept the dangers of the magnetizing everyday. Sometimes this attitude can become perilously demotic, as in this complete **"Airing Linen"**: "Wash and dry, / sort and fold: / you and I / are growing old." A bit of Frost's backward-looking pup. But the strength of Taylor, as in his beautifully asymetrical [**"The Flying Change"**]—the first part in a troubling, lucid prose that for this poet is a real audacity and deviation—is his acceptance of an antinomian aesthetic: "I schooled myself to drift away / / from skills I still possess, but must outlive." Taylor's affection for his region is faithful and unmixed and produces the sweet variety of his moderate pastorale. (pp. 348-50)

David Shapiro, in a review of "The Flying Change," in Poetry, *Vol. CXLIX, No. 6, March, 1987, pp. 348-50.*

Peter (Hillsman) Taylor

The Old Forest and Other Stories

PEN/Faulkner Award for Fiction

American short story writer, dramatist, novelist, and editor.

The Old Forest and Other Stories (1985) features selections from five decades of Taylor's writing career, from the late 1930s to the mid 1980s. Taylor's work gained a following through the years as it appeared in the *New Yorker, Kenyon Review,* and other periodicals, as well as in previous collections such as *A Long Fourth and Other Stories* (1948) and *In the Miro District and Other Stories* (1977). The publication of *The Old Forest,* however, provided a perspective on Taylor's career as a whole, and earned Taylor critical acclaim as one of the foremost contemporary authors of short fiction.

Taylor is closely identified with the Southern Renaissance or Agrarian movement that his mentors at Vanderbilt University and Kenyon College, Allen Tate and John Crowe Ransom, helped to develop in the 1920s and 1930s. Like other Agrarians, Taylor works from a more objective, humanist perspective than such Southern Gothic writers as William Faulkner and Flannery O'Connor. His writings are concerned exclusively with a particular milieu: the lives of upper-middle class Southerners from the 1930s to the early 1950s, a time when the industrialization and urbanization of the "New South" began to erode the genteel agrarian bulwark of the privileged whites. Taylor's stories evoke a sense of history with references to the South's past, while demonstrating the unsettling shifts in manners and morality experienced by his characters. "My feeling is that stories ought to be about something that's over and done with, so you can judge it properly," Taylor stated. Taylor describes the culture of this bygone era with gentle irony and a leisurely, conversational narrative style that the author acknowledges as an inheritance from his family's storytelling tradition.

Taylor also acquired from his apprenticeship with the poets Tate and Ransom, as well as his friendship with his contemporaries Randall Jarrell and Robert Lowell, an appreciation for poetry which has profoundly influenced the composition of his stories. He begins most of his stories by writing in verse. "I can't sustain it very long, but I try to finish a story in verse, then go back and put it into prose." By concentrating on word choice and rhythm, Taylor explained, he achieves a poetic compression in his fiction: "In a story you have very limited space, so every sentence has to do more. I have a theory that a story ought to do as much as a novel, and a poem ought to do as much as a story. In fact, if a poem doesn't do a great deal more with its language, then it's not as good as a story."

The Old Forest offers critics an opportunity to trace Taylor's thematic and stylistic consistencies through the decades. They particularly admire his meticulous recreation of a world that, through his descriptions, becomes uniquely his own, with its richly detailed observation of social manners and customs. Several critics observe that although the stories in *The Old Forest* are set in a particular time and place, their concern with morality and the particularities of human behavior transcend the boundaries of period fiction. "The South is his setting, but Taylor could as well be writing about any society in transition," comments reviewer J. D. McClatchy. "He has an eye for a slow crack in the social veneer, a new tone in a child's voice."

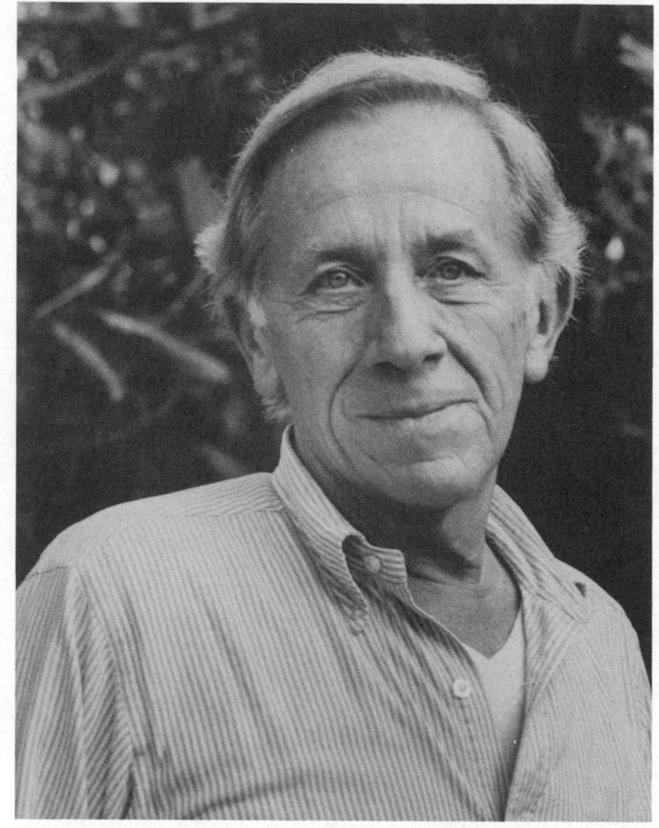

(See also *CLC,* Vols. 1, 4, 18, 37; *Contemporary Authors,* Vols. 13-16, rev. ed.; *Contemporary Authors New Revision Series,* Vol. 9; and *Dictionary of Literary Biography Yearbook: 1981.*)

PAUL GRAY

Only two of [the 14 pieces collected in ***The Old Forest and Other Stories***] have not already appeared somewhere in Peter Taylor's six previous collections of short stories. But this is, essentially, a new book. . . . [The] selection of these stories reveals a continuity and cohesion in Taylor's art that were less visible before. The settings are similar: the U.S. South during the 1930s and '40s, not the bogs or backwaters but growing cities like Memphis and Nashville. There, in the author's composite portrait, a well-ordered world is losing both energy and its faith in itself. . . .

[**"The Old Forest"**], which makes its first appearance in book form, takes place during some cold December days in Memphis, 1937. Nat Ramsey, the scion of a good family, has a minor automobile accident a week before he is to marry Caroline Braxley, a debutante of equally impeccable social standing. Unfortunately, he is not alone in that car; Lee Ann Deehart, a young working woman with whom he has enjoyed an innocent but romantic friendship, runs away from the scene and disappears. Complicated codes of honor come instantly into play. It never occurs to Nat not to tell his fiancée about Lee Ann's presence; Caroline and her parents in turn have no interest in censuring him or his presumptive faithlessness. The problem is that the wedding will remain in jeopardy until the woman can be found; having her turn up pregnant or dead after the ceremony would create insufferable scandal. By the time the search for Lee Ann ends, Nat has learned much about areas of life from which his class has conspired to shield him. And with no visible effort, Taylor has spun out a marvelously intricate and fragile web of isolated society.

Taylor's people realize that their behavior is circumscribed by customs, often the very ones they cherish most and work hardest to preserve. They also sense that they should not be too content with their restrictions; they want to understand more than their experience allows. In **"Promise of Rain,"** a father recognizes the moment when his youngest son, almost grown and increasingly remote, finds the path his life will follow: "I was 50, but I had just discovered what it means to see the world through another man's eyes. It is a discovery you are lucky to make at any age, and one that is no less marvelous whether you make it at 50 or 15. Because it is only then that the world, as you have seen it through your own eyes, will begin to tell you things about yourself." . . .

With each infrequent appearance of a Peter Taylor book (the last one came out in 1977), reviewers and fellow writers wonder again in print why the author remains a secret to the vast reading public. . . . Taylor's only novel, ***A Woman of Means*** (1950), occasioned no commercial breakthrough. Audiences should have found him, nonetheless; his work is not difficult, only miraculously engaging and evocative.

Paul Gray, "Codes of Honor," in Time, *Vol. 125, No. 5, February 4, 1985, p. 74.*

BRUCE ALLEN

Peter Taylor is one of the Southern writers who became prominent after World War II—one whose roots are in the classical short story of epiphany as practiced by Chekhov, Henry James, and James Joyce, as well as in the class- and tradition-conscious matrix of his native Tennessee. His stories are loose, ruminative chronicles of social and family conflict and of gradually earned individual self-understanding.

In a typical Taylor story, a grown or aging man looks back on his childhood (**"The Little Cousins"**) or on his adult relationships with family (**"Porte Cochere"**), and indulges critical, often disillusioning second thoughts about the codes he has lived by. The Southerner's pride in social order and personal gentility is sometimes shown up as supercilious myth (**"The Death of a Kinsman," "Two Ladies in Retirement"**), sometimes embraced even harder as a means of maintaining, not just decorum, but emotional equilibrium (**"Rain in the Heart"**). Parents manage empathy with those odd, alien creatures: their children (**"Promise of Rain"**). And cautious, timid people surreptitiously admire the scarcely imaginable lives of people more adventurous than they (**"A Friend and Protector"**).

These stories, plus seven others, make up [***The Old Forest and Other Stories***], which is basically a companion volume to Taylor's 1969 ***Collected Stories.*** (p. 25)

A few [stories] are downright weak: **"A Walled Garden,"** for instance, is a monologue unimaginatively derived from Browning, and **"Allegiance"** is a pallid imitation of Jamesian introspection at its archest and flattest.

But several others show Taylor at his very best. **"A Long Fourth"** is an ambitious, complex portrayal of a Nashville matron who's forced to notice the similarities between her own domestic problems and those of her Negro maid, and also the shallow cruelty her family regards as social superiority. This realization veers close to the shock-of-recognition quality of some of Flannery O'Connor's stories.

"The Scoutmaster" is a moving, seriocomic depiction of one family's fall away from innocent complacency into contact with some uncomfortable and unwelcome facts of life, and its consoling recollection of "golden days when a race of noble gentlemen and gracious ladies inhabited the South."

"The Gift of the Prodigal" is an elegant story about an elderly, ailing widower's loving-disapproving relationship with his wayward son, a charming, much-married troublemaker whose constant appeals for aid and understanding, far from alienating his father, ease the old man's insularity and loneliness and bring him into refreshing intimacy with a "life that is not my own."

In **"The Old Forest,"** whose action is set in 1937 and remembered almost a half century later, a young Memphis businessman's essentially innocent involvement with a girl from his city's "demimonde" threatens his imminent marriage and leads to an eye-opening confrontation with his own, and his class's, social and moral nature. Its crisis of action occurs in a wooded area that once was primeval wilderness; its shape is a simultaneous enclosure and expansion—and it's a memorable dramatization of Taylor's continuing fascination with the marginal man slowly entering and apprehending a larger, more complicated world he never made, and was never prepared for, but knows he belongs to. (pp. 25, 27)

Bruce Allen, "Short Stories of Life in the South during the '30s and '40s," in The Christian Science Monitor, March 26, 1985, pp. 25, 27.

J. D. McCLATCHY

[Peter Taylor's ***The Old Forest and Other Stories***] has been sifted from the work of forty years, a period during which he has earned a reputation as a master of the once neglected and now again fashionable short story. He would not be mistaken for the new hard-bitten breed of storyteller—Anne Beattie, say, or Raymond Carver. Taylor writes in a deliberate, even leisurely manner, with a strong, moralizing narrative voice. He has a Southerner's way of *talking* a story, not just telling it.

The South is his setting, but Taylor could as well be writing about any society in transition. He has an eye for a slow crack in the social veneer, a new tone in a child's voice.

In **"Porte Cochere,"** two grown sons have returned home for an uneasy reunion with their old father on his birthday: "He had given them a freedom unknown to children in the land of his childhood, yet from the time they could utter a word they had despised him and denied his right to any affection or gratitude. Suddenly, stepping onto the landing, he screamed down the stairs to them, 'I've a right to some gratitude!'" In other stories, and in other ways, husbands say the same thing to their wives, masters to their servants. The family—the one made by blood, the one made by custom, and the extended family of blacks and whites in the South—is Taylor's focus, and he charts its unsettled balances of power. **"The Gift of the Prodigal," "The Little Cousins,"** and [**"The Old Forest"**] are especially vivid. If we miss the depths and quirks of character that stories by John Cheever or Eudora Welty provide, still we can savor Taylor's sturdy style and the wisdom of his pained, bemused nostalgias. (pp. 73-4)

J. D. McClatchy, in a review of "The Old Forest and Other Stories," in Saturday Review, *Vol. 11, No. 3, May-June, 1985, pp. 73-4.*

JOHN RAE

I had not read Peter Taylor before. I had not even heard of him. I came to [***The Old Forest and Other Stories***] without particular expectations. I came without yardsticks, too. Even now, having read the stories, I would not know where to place him. When the American critics tell me that he is one of the best short story writers ever, I cannot be sure that I understand what all the meanings of that 'best' are.

This coming to a writer fresh and innocent of pretensions to professional criticism has an advantage. You can go in straight and say what you think without worrying overmuch whether you are in step or out of step with the opinions of others.

Peter Taylor's stories disturbed me. They left me feeling uneasy as I am sometimes left uneasy by a dream, the elements of which are unremarkable in themselves but unsettling in sequence because they do not connect. I do not mean that Taylor is some sort of literary Dali. He deals with the real world, but he seems to be exploring the curiously disconnected nature of that reality. In **'Rain in the Heart'** the army sergeant is left with the sense that no moment in his life had any relation to another. It was as though he were living a thousand lives. And the ageing aunt in **'Allegiance'** knows that the actual is 'but the sum of a thousand accidents'.

The events described in the stories are given an apparent cohesion and meaning by being set in a particular time and place. Does that not conform to our own experience? The purposeless, accidental flow of events is given a pattern by the context in which it occurs: a marriage, a career, a location and so on. Taylor's location is the Southern States, notably Tennessee during the period between the Great Depression and the Second World War.

The sense of place and time are skilfully evoked. Exactness—midwinter, Memphis, Tennessee, 1937 in [**'The Old Forest'**]—but none of that ostentatious littering of the landscape with the bric-à-brac of the period. There are writers whose work is said to be well-researched but whose descriptions read like the catalogue for a sale of memorabilia. Taylor's descriptions of Tennessee in the 1930s are not well-researched; they are accurately recalled.

A number of stories are in the first person. They avoid the label 'autobiographical'' by changing the point of view: in **'The Old Forest''** the middle-aged man recalls his own youth; in **'Promise of Rain'**, it is the father remembering his son's youth; in **'The Gift of the Prodigal'**, the father describes his current dependence on his prodigal son. The relationship between generations, especially between father and son, is a subtle and recurring theme in the stories.

One generation observing the experience of another is one of the factors that gives Taylor's stories their particular resonance. But his use of time is more complex than that. You are made aware of other, more remote periods. The old forest is primeval. White settlers were ambushed there by Chickasaw Indians. The trees were mature when Hernando de Soto passed that way. The sergeant in **'Rain in the Heart'**, unable to realise the hopes of his brief visit to his young wife, looks out of the window at the site of a bloody Confederate victory. In history, too, events occur but do not connect. Historians (one of whose volumes the sergeant is reading) make patterns where none are.

If I give the impression that Taylor's stories have a sad, pessimistic quality, that is how I found them. But the sadness is not sentiment or nostalgia; and the pessimism is brave not bitter. What is sad is that the disconnected events of life do not add up to something more. Some of Taylor's characters try to escape from this reality by living vicarious lives, like the father of the prodigal who pretends to deplore his son's escapades but longs to hear more about them. 'I am listening. I am listening gratefully to all he will tell me about himself, about any life that is not my own.'

The stories are told in a voice that inspires immediate confidence. Told not written. The style is relaxed and economical despite the complex psychological texture of some of the stories. It reminded me of the contrast between real story-telling and the self-conscious cleverness that often passes for literature nowadays. There are undoubtedly clever writers around but the difference between them and Taylor is this. Nowhere in Taylor does the style distract your attention from the narrative, like a precocious child calling 'Look at me—I'm well written'. Yet re-reading the stories, on the lookout this time, I could recognise the supreme craftmanship and the consistent accuracy in the choice of words.

The only times my confidence hesitated was over certain passages of dialogue. There are occasions where Taylor uses his young characters to say things which in form and insight appear to be beyond their range, some of Caroline Braxley's statements in **'The Old Forest'** being a case in point.

I came to Peter Taylor's stories without particular expectations. I shall never do that again because I now know that he is a writer all of whose work I want to read. He is a superb storyteller, with an outstanding talent for exploring within a particular society and period 'the terrible unrelated diversity of things'. (pp. 29-30)

John Rae, 'A Thousand Accidents,'' in The Listener, *Vol. 114, No. 2920, August 1, 1985, pp. 29-30.*

An Excerpt from *The Old Forest and Other Stories*

At noon the snow was still falling. My father stood at a front window in the living room, wearing his dark smoking jacket. He predicted that it might be the deepest snowfall we had ever had in Memphis. He said that people in other parts of the country didn't realize how much cold weather came all the way down the Mississippi Valley from Minneapolis to Memphis. I had never heard him pay so much attention to the weather and talk so much about it. I wondered if, like me, he was really thinking about the old forest out in Overton Park and wishing he were free to go out there and make sure there was no sign of Lee Ann Deehart's having come to grief in those ancient woods. I wonder now if there weren't others besides us who were thinking of the old forest all day that day. I knew that my father, too, had been on the telephone that morning—and he was on it again during a good part of the afternoon. In retrospect, I am certain that all day that day he was in touch with a whole circle of friends and colleagues who were concerned about Lee Ann's safety. It was not only the heavy snow that checked his freedom—and mine, too, of course—to go out and search those woods and put his mind at rest on the possibility at least. It was more than just this snow, which the radio reported as snarling up and halting all traffic. What prevented him was his own unwillingness to admit fully to himself and to others that this particular danger was really there; what prevented him and perhaps all the rest of us was the fear that the answer to the gnawing question of Lee Ann's whereabouts might really be out there within that immemorial grove of snow-laden oaks and yellow poplars and hickory trees. It is a grove, I believe, that men in Memphis have feared and wanted to destroy for a long time and whose destruction they are still working at even in this latter day. It has only recently been saved by a very narrow margin from a great highway that men wished to put through there—saved by groups of women determined to save this last bit of the old forest from the axes of modern men. Perhaps in old pioneer days, before the plantation and the neoclassic towns were made, the great forests seemed woman's last refuge from the brute she lived alone with in the wilderness. Perhaps all men in Memphis who had any sense of their past felt this, though they felt more keenly (or perhaps it amounts to the same feeling) that the forest was woman's greatest danger. Men remembered mad pioneer women, driven mad by their loneliness and isolation, who ran off into the forest, never to be seen again, or incautious women who allowed themselved to be captured by Indians and returned at last so mutilated that they were unrecognizable to their husbands or who at their own wish lived out their lives among their savage captors. I think that if I had said to my father (or to myself), "What is it that's so scary about the old forest?", he (or I) would have answered, "There's nothing at all scary about it. But we can't do anything today because of the snow. It's the worst snow in history!" I think that all day long my father—like me—was busily not letting himself believe that anything awful had happened to Lee Ann Deehart, or that if it had it certainly hadn't happened in those woods. Not just my father and me, though. Caroline's father, too, and all their friends—their peers. And the newspapermen and the police. If they waited long enough, it would come out all right and there would be no need to search the woods even. And it turned out, in the most literal sense, that they—we—were right. Yet what guilty feelings must not everyone have lived with—lived with in silence—all that snow-bound day.

JOHN CLUTE

Peter Taylor's new collection, ***The Old Forest,*** may be the best possible introduction to this American writer, whose tales of the northern borderlands of the Old South are among the more impressive accomplishments of 20th-century fiction.

Families from the South come north to settle in Tennessee, in cities like Memphis or Nashville, and most of Taylor's stories are about the maintenance there of something like civilisation in the jungles of entrepreneurial America. But that is too simple by far. His best tales are couched as reminiscences whose seeming tranquillity is utterly deceptive. Taylor may be deeply empathetic with the fragile mores of his transplanted ladies and gentlemen, but in his quiet way can be a satirist of the most taxing severity. Not one story fails to begin gently; not one fails by its close to have interrogated the very basis of the lives depicted. A humane, moral, important book.

John Clute, "Death in Venice," in New Statesman, *Vol. 110, No. 2839, August 16, 1985, p. 28.*

KARL MILLER

There is an occasion in *Sense and Sensibility* when the three sisters go for a walk and perceive, in the distance, the coming-on of an interesting horseman. His approach casts something of the spell cast by that long take in the film *Lawrence of Arabia* where a mirage shimmers on the horizon and sways towards the watcher in the stalls to be read in due course as a man mounted on a camel. The sisters in Jane Austen's novel perceive a single rider, whom they eventually distinguish 'to be a gentleman': but this, too, could be called a mirage. The occasion is almost over by the time we are able to gather that there have been two riders, one of them a servant. An invisibility of underlings is among the features of her fiction which might encourage one to think of it as grounded in the delineation, and in the perceptions, of a social class. No such grounding, no such principle of invisibility, can be found in Dickens.

I am assuming that it may be all right to talk of classes with reference to the work of writers who did not themselves do so. Backward-ranging comparisons, and a risk of anachronism, are likely to enter into an experience of Peter Taylor's fine stories [in ***The Old Forest and Other Stories***], for his is an art which makes much of the existence of traditions, and of a deep past. At all events, it seems clear that the stories exhibit Austen's dedication to a class, and that the class he is concerned with carries points of resemblance to the Austen gentry. His people are the gentlemen and gentlewomen of the Southern Midwest, in and around Memphis, Tennessee, and Nashville, during the Thirties and early Forties of the present century: the Second World War is approaching, though you would hardly suspect it until, here and there, it happens, and uniforms are worn. We are shown, therefore, a new Ante-Bellum South, in which the old one survives, at times preposterously, and in which the survival of a way of life is feared for. Taylor cares about the old-fashioned society girls of the region, about the 'narrow natures' among its monied males, about their 'pantywaist' prissiness. He imitates and impersonates the old-fogey father, or the shrinking young man who, even when he is called up into the Army, has yet to say goodbye to all that status and heritage, kin and kind, and class. The servants are black, and they supply the personnel for the firings which so often impend. But they are far from invisible to the author—unlike the region's poor whites, who are very rarely seen: there is no white poor, and there is little sign of government—it's as if affluence, and influence, rule. The servants are ill-treated by the whites they fascinate: but the author is not to be classed among these hard masters, with their talk of *noblesse oblige* and 'good families', of such-and-such a black being on, or off, 'the place'—in the sense of the estate.

This *noblesse* has in it a *jeunesse* which no doubt memorialises Taylor's own youth, and some of its sprightlier members have learnt to speak of slavery in a high-souled manner which has perhaps been obtained from the Agrarian school of writers. Kate claims: 'The Southern master was morally responsible, which is more than can be said for the industrial sweatshopper.' She is arguing with her vehement brother, who has been reading Spengler, and believes that Kate has been reading those Agrarian 'fellows at the University in Nashville'; he has brought to the family home, this 'hotbed of Southern reactionaries', his prig girlfriend, his 'comrade', a seeker of revolution. The household, that of an ear-nose-and-throat surgeon, is exercised by the projected firing of a negro handyman who is said to smell, and whose grim old aunt sends the wife, Kate's mother—whose husband is known to her as Sweetheart, and whose Spenglerian son is known to her as Son—into a bravura fit of indignation. Here as elsewhere, Taylor's style is reminiscential ('The worst of it was . . .'): he belongs to the fireside school of writers, but with few traces of folksiness or, in the British sense of the word, ingratiation. His black folks won't please those prigs of the present day who are on the look-out for a revolutionary correctness in the matter of colour and class, and who are prepared to investigate the short story. But his black folks are intensely and humanely imagined—and, as we are bound to feel, remembered. At the same time, we are also bound to feel that the narrators who perceive them, and whom we may sometimes distrust and disapprove of, are parts of Peter Taylor, and that his imagination is in some measure controlled by the values he is remembering.

A case could certainly be made to the effect that the stories—with their yarning attention to the familial, tribal and provincial pieties and occasions of a Southern gentry—incorporate stereotypes built to protect the way of life that is feared for. The blacks are warm, kind, and seldom the enemies of their masters, who in turn are apt, when young, to be more dependent for affection on their nurses than on their parents. But the blacks are also like animals. One tale is about Jesse, who breaks out and disgraces himself from time to time and is then rescued by his affluent white couple: the two are failures of a sort for whom his disgraces are somehow talismanic. When Jesse gets drunk and devastates his master's office, he is shown as a shambling simian, run amok. Elsewhere, in a soliloquy only nominally directed at her daughter's beau, and nakedly expressive of her panic and anxiety and of her attempts to subdue that daughter, a snobbish female garden-freak remarks: 'When I used to come back from visiting my people at Rye, she would grit her teeth at me and give her confidence to the black cook. I would find my own child become a mad little animal.' Confidence is again at issue in another story, **'The Scoutmaster'**: 'she was one of the few young girls who never—Never once! Aunt Grace could vouch for it. *She* had the girl's confidence—never stepped outside the front door to say good night to her date.' In this collection of stories, confidence is awarded to Aunt Grace, a strung-up white gentlewoman, and to black servants whose virtues are thought by successive narrators to be those of animal inferiors. Their thinking so is a story that is told in several of the stories. But we need not think that Peter Taylor thinks so, and a case could be made to the effect that he thinks very differently.

Aunt Grace's assurance in **'The Scoutmaster'** concerning her niece relates to what is perhaps the only episode in the collection where sexual behaviour is exposed and put at issue. By a family which has returned early from a rain-check ball-game, the niece is discovered to have been necking with her beau. This is deemed flagrant by the father, who expels the beau and calls him an animal, a 'common dog'. The maidenliness of some of the narrators lets us know that this is not the South of Tennessee Williams. But it neither contradicts nor is contradicted by the works of Williams, who has his own sweet bird of youth, and his Aunt Grace.

A story which might seem to promise an account of sexual conduct is the one that gives the book its underweening title. The old forest is a grove of ancient trees—a numinous, sinister spinney in the midst of Memphis. The narrator drives up to the old forest with an old flame of baser stock than the society girl he is about to marry in an effulgence of rites and ceremonies. An accident happens. 'Since the driver of the truck, which was actually a converted Oldsmobile sedan—and a rather ancient one at that—had the good sense not to put on his brakes and to turn off her motor, the crash was less severe than it might have been.' It is maidenly of the narrator to make a maiden of the Oldsmobile, and to lend her the charm of antiquity. The ceremonies that surround the impending marriage are not of recent date. The forest is old. And the Oldsmobile is an old girl. The old flame slips off into the grove and the

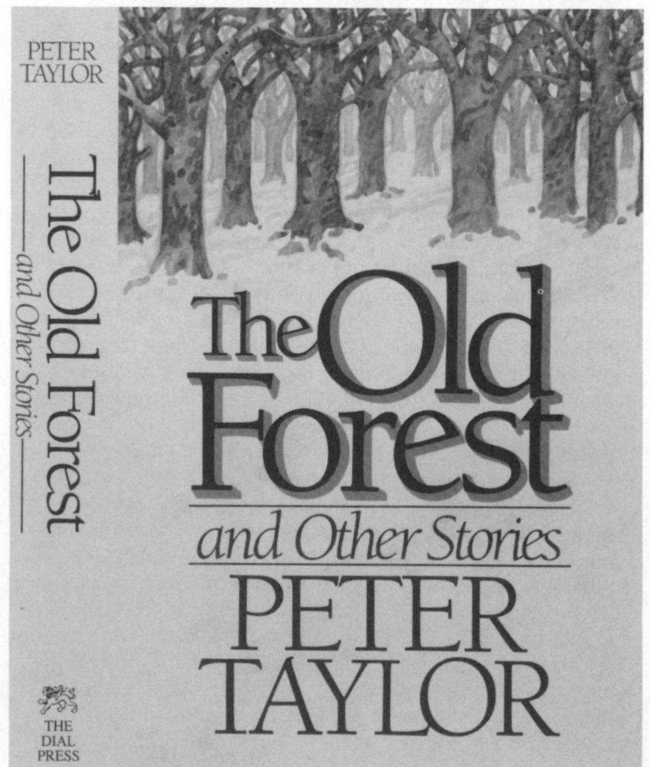

Dust jacket of The Old Forest and Other Stories, *by Peter Taylor. The Dial Press, 1985. Jacket by Terrence Fehr. Courtesy of Doubleday & Company, Inc.*

rest of the story is spent searching for her, under the threat of disgrace. The narrator's fiancée conceives an understanding of the category of girl to which Lee Ann, the refugee, belongs. They are free women—despised and envied by the society girls.

The fiancée ends the tale in a state of bitter excitement which pays tribute to the way of life, the virtues, of these other less maidenly girls, of a class just below—and then on down—the gentry. Such free spirits read Malraux and go together to Classical concerts; they band together in a proud clandestiny. By the end, the narrator has decided to take a university degree and maybe proceed to teach—a rashness in the eyes of upper Memphis: 'Though it clearly meant that we must live on a somewhat more modest scale and live among people of a sort she was not used to, and even meant leaving Memphis forever behind us, the firmness with which she supported my decision, and the look in her eyes whenever I spoke of feeling I must make the change, seemed to say to me that she would dedicate her pride of power to the power of freedom I sought.' These last words seem overworked, and do not fully convince. Nor does Lee Ann's weird sisterhood.

This is not the only story to close on an edifying note. It is fortunate on occasion, one story concludes, 'to see the world through another man's eyes': 'Because it is only then that the world, as you have seen it through your own eyes, will begin to tell you things about yourself.' Such endings make one conscious of an unending South, and of the dispensing of a sententious Southern comfort. There are stories here which resemble certain poems by Frost in their delivery of morals—those things of the past, as they're sometimes represented. It is possible to be fond of those things, given what we know of the quality of their absence and avoidance in strains of fiction contemporary with Taylor's and very different from his. But it may be that they produce blemishes in the course of the collection. The work of both Frost and Taylor, moreover, is available to a nostalgic interest in past and place, to a touristic, 'Janeite' cultivation of old words and good old days—of passages like the following:

> Once their father—the two of them would recall—had come through the strawberry patch behind the old house on the Nolansville Pike and found Uncle Jake and Father playing mumble-the-peg while Uncle Louis did all the berry picking. And when Uncle Louis saw his father stripping off his belt to give his brothers a whipping he ran to him and told him that he, the eldest brother, was to blame for not making them work and that he should receive the punishment. My grandfather had turned and walked to his house without another word.

Like Frost, Taylor may possibly have been subjected to polemical snubbing: he would seem to have been neglected by the journals of the urban American intelligentsia which date from, or recall, the era of comrades and reactionaries. Like that narrator of his, he took to teaching in the universities, where, in old age, he remains—a professor at the University of Virginia; both within the university system and beyond he has been honoured for his fiction. Nevertheless, there would appear to be many, on both sides of the Atlantic, to whom his name is unfamiliar. In writing about him, I have had to guess at the opinions of a very accomplished and fairly prolific writer, getting on now for seventy, who was effectively without a biographical identity, as far as I was concerned. For all I know—and it is evident that I should have known more—he could be a well-known Southern liberal.

Karl Miller, "Memphis Blues," in London Review of Books, *Vol. 7, No. 15, September 5, 1985, p. 15.*

JOHN FIELD

Peter Taylor's stories [in ***The Old Forest and Other Stories***] are set in Tennessee in the 1930s. He writes about families, and especially about the women in those families. He even strikes a polemical note in support of this departure from the direction of much American male writing:

> It is of course because these girls like Caroline are regarded as mere old-fashioned society girls that the present generation tends to dismiss them, whereas if it were their fathers we were writing about, the story would, shocking though it is to say, be taken more seriously by everyone . . . And why not judge their daughters and wives in much the same way? Isn't there a need to know what they were like, too?

This is a lengthy collection, and Taylor's relaxed tone slips at times from the masterful to the rambling. But the best stories, such as **"The Little Cousins,"** have an impressive assurance. In this one, a small boy is overwhelmed amidst a scene of joy by a sense of grief and loss. Far from being corny, it is at moments like this, when the easy tones of reminiscence or conventional conversation belie the unspeakable surge of feeling, that Taylor is at his most effective and touching. (pp. 34-5)

John Field, in a review of "The Old Forest," in Books and Bookmen, *No. 361, November, 1985, pp. 34-5.*

JACK MATTHEWS

In this latest collection of Peter Taylor's fiction [***The Old Forest and Other Stories***], he demonstrates how committedly he is the short-story-writer equivalent of a "novelist of manners" and how capable he is of making stories out of material and forms that give him a distinct place in contemporary letters.

The milieu of the stories is specific: it is pre-civil-rights southern upper-middle-class. Beyond this distinction, place means nothing: stories that take place in Nashville might just as well take place in Memphis and, of course, vice versa. Cliché and originality blend; we recognize the types immediately, but almost as quickly understand their individuality, their credibility as characters.

In [**"The Old Forest"**], referring to the girls in old Memphis, Taylor writes, "They considered themselves heirs to something . . . [including] old country manners and old country connections." This story, possibly the richest in the book, is about a young man who is engaged to a girl of the "MCC" (Memphis Country Club) class. One day in a snowstorm, he takes another girl with "unknown origins" for a drive; there is a collision, and the girl jumps from the car and disappears, by running off into the "old forest" remaining from the city's legendary and mysterious past. The forest is symbolic of this past, along with those darker mysteries of human motivation, and her disappearance is a momentary return to her "unknown origins."

This key situation is explicit from the beginning of the story: the story itself has to do with the working out of its premises—

its effects upon the principal characters, the finding of the lost girl, trying to understand her motive for running away, and, most subtly, watching what must be played out from the implications of character and class. It is a fascinating story with progressive revelations of seemingly inevitable consequences from the behavior of the characters who know themselves in terms of the stratified society that has named and sorted them.

A delicate snobbery pervades this story along with most of the others, but snobbery is a human condition, always most easily detected from without or after the fact. In **"A Friend and Protector,"** we see dramatized the familiar notion that in the older South blacks were somehow forced or invited to live the unlived lives of crime and violence that their white masters/employers denied themselves. Such labeling borders upon psychosociological cant, however, and cannot do justice to the humanity of the narrator's wealthy and powerful uncle nor that of the black man, Jesse, whose lunacies are just as credible and eventuate in an odd sort of dignity that seems to come from somewhere outside the narrative.

Taylor writes against most of the current fashions—black humor, radical juxtaposition, and membership in the thrill-a-line club are alien to him. His narrative voice is often earnestly verbose, and he works at narrative summary so relentlessly that whole paragraphs read like popular case histories. But then, that is the voice of gossip speaking, too, and the gossip in these stories is virtually unique in today's fiction. It is about a society that is dense, cussed honor-bitten, and stubbornly vestigial. Sometimes, the density is almost suffocating; sometimes the monotonous voice (unchanging from one story to another) is tiresome. But in reading this latest book, one is reminded that the short story (partly because it *is* short) is a most tolerant and commodious form—and isn't it good that there is room in this genre for the particular sorts of excellence to be found in ***The Old Forest and Other Stories?*** (pp. 118-19)

Jack Matthews, "Peter Taylor's Most Recent Fiction," in The Kenyon Review, *n.s. Vol. VIII, No. 1, Winter, 1986, pp. 118-19.*

Anne Tyler

The Accidental Tourist

The National Book Critics Circle Award: Fiction

American novelist, short story writer, critic, nonfiction writer, and editor.

The Accidental Tourist (1985) is Tyler's tenth novel, and her first to win a National Book Critics Circle Award; two of her previous novels, *Morgan's Passing* (1980) and *Dinner at the Homesick Restaurant* (1982), were nominated for the prize. Like most of Tyler's fiction, *The Accidental Tourist* is set in Baltimore, where the author has lived since 1967. Critics observe that Macon Leary in *The Accidental Tourist* resembles the main characters in several other Tyler novels. For instance, like the hero of *Celestial Navigation* (1974), Macon must choose between lonely security and the uncertain comforts of human love. Also, like the sibling protagonists of *Dinner at the Homesick Restaurant,* he has a close yet ambivalent relationship with his brothers and sisters. Critic Jessica Sitton recognizes in *The Accidental Tourist* "the signature element" of all Tyler's work: "Lovingly drawn, eccentric characters who come into conflict with themselves and each other as they either slip or jostle their way through life, simultaneously nurtured and stifled by their families and their past."

Some critics observe that, although Tyler's characterizations often verge on satire, her gentle wit and concentration on the realistic details of her characters' lives make their situations believable and, often, touching. Macon is a middle-aged author who craves order and stability in life. "The Accidental Tourist" is the series name of a set of guidebooks he is writing for unadventurous Americans who seek the comforts of home, such as fast food and homogenized milk, when they are forced to travel abroad. When domestic tragedy shatters Macon's timid existence, Tyler details his struggles to cope, and critics note her ability to stimulate reader sympathy for Macon, as well as laughter at his often absurd predicaments. Tyler also makes plausible the emotional struggles of Macon's Welsh corgi, Edward, who critic Mary Flanagan opines "may well prove as notable a literary canine as the Dog of Flanders." Most reviewers agree that Tyler's compassionate yet unsentimental character studies, as well as her warm sense of humor, are exquisitely demonstrated in *The Accidental Tourist*.

(See also *CLC*, Vols. 7, 11, 18, 28; *Contemporary Authors*, Vols. 9-12, rev. ed.; *Contemporary Authors New Revision Series*, Vol. 11; *Something about the Author*, Vol. 7; *Dictionary of Literary Biography*, Vol. 6; and *Dictionary of Literary Biography Yearbook: 1982*.)

© 1986 Thomas Victor

JONATHAN YARDLEY

[*Yardley is the author of* Ring: A Biography of Ring Lardner *(1977) and a frequent contributor to and book reviewer for several magazines and newspapers, including the Knight Newspapers,* New Republic, Sewanee Review, Life, *and* Partisan Review. *In the following excerpt Yardley praises* The Accidental Tourist *for its many exceptional qualities, describing it as a moving, deeply significant novel.*]

With each new novel . . . it becomes ever more clear that the fiction of Anne Tyler is something both unique and extraordinary in contemporary American literature. Unique, quite literally: there is no other writer whose work sounds like Tyler's, and Tyler sounds like no one except herself. Extraordinary, too: not merely for the quietly dazzling quality of her writing and the abidingly sympathetic nature of her characters, but also for her calm indifference to prevailing literary fashion and her deep conviction that it is the work, not the person who writes it, that matters. Of ***The Accidental Tourist*** one thing can be said with absolute certainty: it matters.

It is a beautiful, incandescent, heartbreaking, exhilarating book. A strong undercurrent of sorrow runs through it, yet it contains comic scenes—one involving a dog, a cat and a clothes dryer, another a Thanksgiving turkey, yet another a Christmas dinner—that explode with joy. It is preoccupied with questions of family, as indeed all of Tyler's more recent fiction is, but there is not an ounce of sentimentality to be found in what it says about how families stick together or fall apart. There's magic in it, and some of its characters have winning eccentricities, yet more than any of Tyler's previous books it is rooted firmly, securely, insistently in the real world.

That world is of course Baltimore, which in Tyler's fiction, as indeed in actuality, is both a place and a state of mind. By now Baltimore belongs to Tyler in the same way that Asheville belongs to Thomas Wolfe, Chicago to James T. Farrell, Memphis to Peter Taylor, Albany to William Kennedy; like these writers, she at once gives us the city as it really exists and redefines it through the realm of the imagination. When the protagonist of ***The Accidental Tourist,*** Macon Leary, drives along North Charles Street, he is on the map; when he arrives at Singleton Street, he is in uncharted territory. But there can be no question that Singleton Street, though fictitious, is real . . .

> He was beginning to feel easier here. Singleton Street still unnerved him with its poverty and its ugliness, but it no longer seemed so dangerous. He saw that the hoodlums in front of the Cheery Moments Carry-Out were pathetically young and shabby—their lips chapped, their sparse whiskers ineptly shaved, an uncertain, unformed look around their eyes. He saw that once the men had gone to work, the women emerged full of good intentions and swept their front walks, picked up the beer cans and potato chip bags, even rolled back their coat sleeves and scrubbed their stoops on the coldest days of the year. Children raced past like so many scraps of paper blowing in the wind—mittens mismatched, noses running—and some woman would brace herself on her broom to call, 'You there! I see you! Don't think I don't know you're skipping school!' For this street was always backsliding, Macon saw, always falling behind, but was caught just in time by these women with their carrying voices and their pushy jaws.

Singleton Street is not Macon's natural territory. Though by no means wealthy, he belongs to that part of Baltimore north of downtown where houses are detached, have yards, are shaded by trees; this is the world in which he grew up and in which until quite recently he lived all his life. But now, at the age of 43, he is finding that world come apart on him. A year ago something unspeakably awful happened; his 12-year-old son, Ethan, off at summer camp, was murdered in a fast-food restaurant, "one of those deaths that make no sense—the kind where the holdup man has collected his money and is free to go but decides, instead, first to shoot each and every person through the back of the skull." Now he has been left by Sarah, his wife of 20 years, who has been devastated by her son's death and believes that she must start life over because "I don't have enough time left to waste it holing up in my shell," a shell she thinks Macon played a crucial role in constructing.

So there he is, alone in the house with Helen, the cat, and Edward, the rowdy little Welsh Corgi to whom he stubbornly clings because the dog was Ethan's. Macon is a creature of firm if peculiar habit who believes that a system can be devised to meet each of life's difficulties; his stratagems for breakfast, bedclothes and the laundry are nothing if not ingenious, even if they don't exactly work. Change and disruption frighten him, which makes him perfectly suited to be the author of guidebooks "for people forced to travel on business," accidental tourists who, like Macon, hate travel and much prefer to be at home:

> He covered only the cities in these guides, for people taking business trips flew into cities and out again and didn't see the countryside at all. They didn't see the cities, for that matter. Their concern was how to pretend they had never left home. What hotels in Madrid boasted king-sized Beauty-rest mattresses? What restaurants in Tokyo offered Sweet'n'Low? Did Amsterdam have a McDonald's? Did Mexico City have a Taco Bell? Did any place in Rome serve Chef Boyardee ravioli? Other travelers hoped to discover distinctive local wines; Macon's readers searched for pasteurized and homogenized milk.

It is as Macon heads off on one of his research trips that his life begins to change. The veterinarian who has boarded Edward in the past now refuses to accept him—"Says here he bit an attendant," the girl tells Macon. "Says, 'Bit Barry in the ankle, do not readmit' "—so in desperation Macon pulls into the Meow-Bow Animal Hospital. There Edward is cheerfully admitted by "a thin young woman in a ruffled peasant blouse," with "aggressively frizzy black hair that burgeoned to her shoulders like an Arab headdress." Her name is Muriel Pritchett, and when Macon returns to reclaim Edward she tells him that she is a dog trainer on the side, with a specialty in "dogs that bite." As Edward's bad habits become steadily worse, Macon at last turns to her in desperation. It is the beginning of the end of his old world.

He'd been right on the edge. His grief over Ethan's death and the pain caused by Sarah's desertion had just about done him in, just about turned him into "some hopeless wreck of a man wandering drugged on a downtown street." Enter Muriel—Muriel with her "long, narrow nose, and sallow skin, and two freckled knobs of collarbone that promised an unluxurious body," Muriel babbling away like "a flamenco dancer with galloping consumption," Muriel with her bewildering array of odd jobs and her pathetic young son by a broken marriage and her rundown house on Singleton Street. Love at first sight it is not: "He missed his wife. He missed his son. They were the only people who seemed real to him. There was no point looking for substitutes."

But life deals things out whether you're looking for them or not. Muriel, a fighter all her days, fights her way into Macon's heart: "Then he knew that what mattered was the pattern of her life; that although he did not love her he loved the surprise of her, and also the surprise of himself when he was with her. In the foreign country that was Singleton Street he was an entirely different person. This person had never been suspected of narrowness, never been accused of chilliness; in fact, was mocked for his soft heart. And was anything but orderly." The accidental tourist has become a traveler—"Maybe, he thought, travel was not so bad. Maybe he'd got it all wrong"—whose journeys now are in the heart, whose world has grown larger than he had ever before imagined possible.

Where those journeys at last lead him is Tyler's secret, though it is no indiscretion to say that in the novel's final pages he faces wrenching, painful choices. But those choices are really less important than the change that has already taken place. Macon Leary has been given the gift of life. A man who had seemed fated to spend the rest of his days in a rut—"Here he still was'! The same as ever! *What have I gone and done?* he wondered and he swallowed thickly and looked at his own empty hands''—has been given new connections, with himself and with others.

This is the central theme of Tyler's fiction: how people affect each other, how the lives of others alter our own. As are her previous novels, ***The Accidental Tourist*** is filled with connections and disconnections, with the exaltation and heartbreak that people bring to each other; she knows that though it is true people need each other, it is equally true ''that people could, in fact, be used up—could use each other up, could be of no further help to each other and maybe even do harm to each other.'' The novel is filled as well with the knowledge that life leaves no one unscarred, that to live is to accept one's scars and make the best of them—and to accept as well the scars that other people bear.

And in ***The Accidental Tourist*** there are many others: the large and bumptious Leary family, Macon's wonderfully unpredictable boss, the people of Singleton Street, and most certainly Edward, the funniest and most loveable dog within memory. They occupy what indisputably is Tyler's best book, the work of a writer who has reached full maturity and is in unshakable command, who takes the raw material of ordinary life and shapes it into what can only be called art. The magical, slightly fey and otherworldly tone of her previous books is evident here, but more than ever before Tyler has planted her fiction in the hard soil of the world we all know; ***The Accidental Tourist*** cuts so close to the bone that it leaves one aching with pleasure and pain. Words fail me: one cannot reasonably expect fiction to be much better than this.

Jonathan Yardley, ''Anne Tyler's Family Circles,'' in Book World—The Washington Post, *August 25, 1985, p. 3.*

JOSEPH MATHEWSON

In Anne Tyler's new novel, ***The Accidental Tourist,*** the central character is a man named Macon Leary. Macon writes homespun travel books for people who don't want to travel, businessmen whose main concern is how to pretend they've never left home. ''I am happy to say,'' runs a typical entry, ''that it's possible now to buy Kentucky Fried Chicken in Stockholm.'' If Macon Leary himself were reviewing ***The Accidental Tourist,*** he might produce something like this:

''Anne Tyler is one of our most prolific and accomplished novelists. . . .

''The many readers of [***Dinner at the Homesick Restaurant***] responded to the warmth and poignancy of a story about a family who couldn't live with each other or without. Those readers will naturally expect to find Miss Tyler's hallmarks on anything else she writes: depth, compassion, a fine eye for details, language that wouldn't embarrass your grandmother, and, of course, a story set largely in Baltimore, Maryland, where Miss Tyler lives herself. Those readers will not be disappointed in her tenth novel, ***The Accidental Tourist.*** Far from it.

''But getting back to Baltimore, I would say that Miss Tyler doesn't just live there. She is at home there, and she makes us at home with a group of characters who are as real as your own family. And you know how it is with family. You grow up with them. You get a certain idea about your Uncle Fred, and that idea doesn't change much. You don't even want it to change. If Uncle Fred turns out to be a bank robber or a Republican—well, if that's the way he was going, that's the way he should go. Anything else would be too unsettling.

''And here is the one real reservation I have about ***The Accidental Tourist:*** Miss Tyler is just first-rate at creating these fully rounded people who all their lives have seen no reason to change, who have made resistance to change a sort of negative philosophy. Why, even the dog, Edward, who is a fully rounded dog, is also resistant to change. But the nature of life sometimes forces us into changing, whether we want to or not. That's one of the things Miss Tyler's story is saying. But she's done such a bang-up job of making me believe in the fixed qualities of her people that I had a few bad moments when some of the characters did begin to change, when the ice broke up around them and they started floating back to the mainstream of life, so to speak.

''For example, the central character hates the thought that he might get involved in talking to strangers on planes or trains. He always takes along a 1,198-page novel called *Miss MacIntosh, My Darling* and dips into it at random whenever trouble threatens. This strikes me as a highly practical idea; so, late in the book, on a bumpy flight, when this man actually engages in conversation with a frightened old lady and smiles to reassure her, I must confess to wishing that he still had his nose in *Miss MacIntosh.*

''This will tell you that I am a grumpy sort of a fellow and not easy to please. When I add that Miss Tyler does finally make me believe in the changes she's bringing about—cheer for them, almost—you will see how much she's accomplished. In fact, I will go as far as to say that, with the publication of ***The Accidental Tourist,*** the fall publishing season can be counted a success.

Dinner at the Homesick Restaurant is a bigger book, and, in ways, more ambitious. But I had the feeling that the grown-up characters in it didn't have much relation to the children they were when Miss Tyler first introduced them. They were like wonderfully detailed portraits pasted over the snapshots of somebody else. In ***The Accidental Tourist,*** Miss Tyler is working on a smaller canvas, but the portraits are all of a piece.

''The new book is also very funny, much more so than its predecessor; and because it's a very touching book as well, there is something about the alternation of laughter and tears that puts me in mind of the great Victorian novelists. And I will go way out on a limb here and admit that the novelist I have especially in mind is Charles Dickens. There is almost that kind of size and eccentricity to Miss Tyler's characters. Her writing has a lot of Dickens's humanity, too, as well as a certain lack of fear, which came more easily to his own century that it does, alas, to ours.

''By this I mean that Miss Tyler isn't afraid to be sentimental—what other modern writer gives us views of dead characters enjoying a happy afterlife?—and she isn't afraid to be hopeful. Not exactly optimistic. This is a sober, elegiac hopefulness, but it's still in a class by itself. These days, the few good writers who also dare to be hopeful provide themselves with the safety net of an ultimate worldly cynicism (like John Irving). Miss Tyler does her act without the net.''

Joseph Mathewson, ''Taking the Anne Tyler Tour,'' in Horizon, *Vol. 28, No. 7, September, 1985, p. 14.*

RHODA KOENIG

The accidental tourist of Anne Tyler's novel [***The Accidental Tourist,***], Macon Leary is not at home anywhere on the planet. "Energy saving was a hobby of his"—one that takes up a lot of time. Before entering a movie theater, Macon plans a "strategy"—toting up the advantages of an aisle seat versus one in the middle, figuring out how to avoid a noisy child—until his companion loses any interest in the show. Before going to sleep, he connects the percolator and electric skillet to the clock-radio so he can wake up to coffee and popcorn for breakfast in bed (leaving two eggs out all night would be courting food poisoning).

When one of his hedges against anxiety is pruned away, Macon becomes easy pickings for a woman with a strategy of her own. On his way out of Baltimore, with a plane to catch, Macon finds that the vet can't take his corgi, and in desperation turns to the Meow-Bow Animal Hospital. Behind the counter is Muriel Pritchett, a divorcée whose tongue hangs out as far as any of her boarders' (her third question to Macon is "You're not married?"). From then on, ***The Accidental Tourist*** is the story of Muriel's pursuit of Macon, her determination to rope him in and to hound him into being a free spirit.

Muriel has more to contend with than Macon's fussy habits, however. While she's sniffing around, asking him if he'd like some animal training, a chat, a hot dinner, or, heh-heh-heh, anything else, Macon is brooding about his lost wife and his dead son. Sarah Leary (for twenty years "they'd stayed two distinct people, and not always even friends") has moved out after their only child has been killed in the holdup of a fast-food restaurant. The boy appears to us in flashbacks and in Macon's dreams, but he never, so to speak, comes alive—he seems like a contrivance, a reason for Sarah to leave Macon on his own, and for us to regard him as a *sympathetic* anal-retentive instead of just a boring one. And Muriel, a skinny, frizzy-haired young sloven in spike heels and Fu Manchu nails, is the good-natured zany of I don't know how many crummy movies and theater-party plays who revives the tired middle-aged man. (I was surprised she didn't ask him to prove his love by walking barefoot in the park.) The action is unbelievably predictable—Macon gets pulled into Muriel's cheerful, slipshod life and starts enjoying it; Sarah turns up and pulls him back ("There are worse things than boring, I've decided," she says, rather unromantically); and finally Macon, prompted by a freak accident, returns to Muriel. Muriel has a small son whom she dresses in little-gentleman outfits; Macon not only takes him shopping for some real boy clothes but runs into his mother-in-law. When Macon says he is leaving her, Sarah actually tells him, "I suppose you realize what your life is going to be like. You'll be one of those mismatched couples no one invites to parties." And when Macon walks out, instead of going to tell Muriel (she's in the same building), he unaccountably gets a taxi on the next block; it doubles back, and, of course, just at that moment Muriel appears so Macon can scoop her up. I can't be the only person who feels she's reading a movie.

The minor characters are people we've seen before, too—but we've seen them before in Anne Tyler novels, and they have a quirkier and more authentic sound. "It's my opinion sex is overrated," says Macon's unmarried middle-aged brother. "For one thing, it's rather messy. And then the weather is such a problem. When it's cold you hate to take your clothes off. When it's hot you're both so sticky. And in Baltimore, it does always seem to be either too cold or too hot." Macon's boss, the spiffily dressed Julian Edge, is a dashing, even reckless fellow ("He was the kind of man who would make a purchase without consulting *Consumer Reports*"). (p. 59)

The Accidental Tourist also gleams with Anne Tyler's bright bits of observation, the imaginings of her intelligent, wary mind. "When Macon was small, he used to worry that his mother was teaching him the wrong names for things. 'They call this corduroy,' she'd said, buttoning his new coat, and he had thought, *But do they really?* Funny word, in fact, corduroy. Very suspicious." The corgi "snoozed on the couch beside him, curled like a little blond cashew nut with a squinty, blissful expression." She doesn't sentimentalize Muriel, whose conversation rambles all over the map ("She used words as a sort of background music") and who is tiresomely preoccupied with astrology and insecurity. (Tyler also, wisely, does not change Macon into a fun-loving, regular guy; he just changes in the way he regards Muriel, seeing her improvised life as evidence of her bravery and resourcefulness.)

Yet a veil of sentimentality does hang over this novel, which gently tolerates, even canonizes the banal. Tyler's characters, with their poky lives and pinched aspirations, live in a world without culture or beauty, a world of junk food, soap operas, slimy polyester clothes. The Learys, forever correcting other people's grammar, never open a book. (Macon does take a novel on his plane trips, but as "protection against strangers.") While John Cheever, say, would transmute this drabness with his crazy passionate poetry, Tyler pats it on the head, pinning a sort of Drabbies Liberation badge on everyone. As in the guidebooks Macon writes, stubborn ignorance and fear of life are made not only acceptable but cute. ***The Accidental Tourist*** is pleasant enough to read, but irritating when you stop—all that resignation and mediocrity bathed in lethargic sunshine! When I open a book, I look for a friend, but in Anne Tyler I find only relatives. (pp. 59-60)

Rhoda Koenig, "Back in Your Own Backyard," in New York *Magazine, Vol. 18, No. 34, September 2, 1985, pp. 59-60.*

LARRY McMURTRY

[*An American fiction writer and critic, McMurtry has been called the best regional writer the Southwest has yet produced. While earlier "cowboy" novels were idealized epics of courage and nobility, McMurtry's works tend to demythologize the American West, using satire and black humor to portray characters who share the basic human experiences of frustration, loneliness, and loss. His best known novels include* Horseman, Pass By *(1961),* The Last Picture Show *(1966),* Terms of Endearment *(1975), and the Pulitzer Prize-winning* Lonesome Dove *(1985). In the following excerpt McMurtry discusses the way in which Tyler reintroduces her customary themes of sibling bonding and the hapless male protagonist in* The Accidental Tourist.]

In Anne Tyler's fiction, family is destiny, and (nowadays, at least) destiny clamps down on one in Baltimore. For an archeologist of manners with Miss Tyler's skills, the city is a veritable Troy, and she has been patiently excavating since the early 1970's, when she skipped off the lawn of Southern fiction and first sank her spade in the soil which has nourished such varied talents as Poe, Mencken, Billie Holiday and John Waters, the director of the films *Pink Flamingos* and *Polyester*.

It is without question some of the fustiest soil in America; in the more settled classes, social styles developed in the 19th century withstand, with sporelike tenacity, all that the present century can throw at them. Indeed, in Baltimore *all* classes appear to be settled, if not cemented, in grooves of neighborhood and habit so deep as to render them impervious—as a bright child puts it in ***The Accidental Tourist***—to everything except nuclear flash.

From this rich dust of custom, Miss Tyler is steadily raising a body of fiction of major dimensions. One of the persistent concerns of this work is the ambiguity of family happiness and unhappiness. Since coming to Baltimore, Miss Tyler has probed this ambiguity in seven novels of increasing depth and power, working numerous changes on a consistent set of themes.

In ***The Accidental Tourist*** these themes, some of which she has been sifting for more than 20 years, cohere with high definition in the muted (or, as his wife says, ''muffled'') personality of Macon Leary. . . . (p. 1)

Like most of Miss Tyler's males, Macon Leary presents a broad target to all of the women (and even a few of the men) with whom he is involved. His mother; his sister, Rose; his wife, Sarah; and, in due course, his girlfriend, Muriel Pritchett—a dog trainer of singular appearance and ability—regularly pepper him on the subject of his shortcomings, the greatest of which is a lack of passion, playfulness, spontaneity or the desire to do one single thing that *they* like to do. This lack is the more maddening because Macon is reasonably competent; if prompted he will do more or less anything that's required of him. What exasperates the women is the necessity for constant prompting.

When attacked, Macon rarely defends himself with much vigor, which only heightens the exasperation. He likes a quiet life, based on method and system. His systems are intricate routines of his own devising, aimed at reducing the likelihood that anything unfamiliar will occur. The unfamiliar is never welcome in Macon's life, and he believes that if left to himself he can block it out or at least neutralize it.

Not long after we meet him, Macon *is* left to himself. Sarah, his wife of 20 years, leaves him. Macon and Sarah have had a tragedy: their 12-year-old son, Ethan, was murdered in a fast-food joint, his death an accidental byproduct of a holdup.

Though Macon is as grieved by this loss as Sarah, he is, as she points out, ''not a comfort.'' When she remarks that since Ethan's death she sometimes wonders if there's any point to life, Macon replies, honestly but unhelpfully, that it never seemed to him there was all that much point to begin with. As if this were not enough, he can never stop himself from correcting improper word choice, even if the incorrect usage occurs in a conversation about the death of a child. These corrections are not made unkindly, but they are invariably made; one does not blame Sarah for taking off.

With the ballast of his marriage removed, Macon immediately tips into serious eccentricity. His little systems multiply, and his remaining companions, a Welsh corgi named Edward and a cat named Helen, fail to adapt to them. Eventually the systems overwhelm Macon himself, causing him to break a leg. Not long after, he finds himself where almost all of Miss Tyler's characters end up sooner or later—back in the grandparental seat. There he is tended to by his sister. His brothers, Porter and Charles, both divorced, are also there, repeating, like Macon, a motion that seems all but inevitable in Anne Tyler's fiction—a return to the sibling unit.

This motion, or tendency, cannot be blamed on Baltimore. In the very first chapter of Miss Tyler's first novel, ***If Morning Ever Comes*** (1964), a young man named Ben Joe Hawkes leaves Columbia University and hurries home to North Carolina mainly because he can't stand not to know what his sisters are up to. From then on, in book after book, siblings are drawn inexorably back home, as if their parents or (more often) grandparents had planted tiny magnets in them which can be activated once they have seen what the extrafamilial world is like. The lovers and mates in her books, by exerting their utmost strength, can sometimes delay these regroupings for as long as 20 years, but sooner or later a need to be with people who are *really* familiar—their brothers and sisters—overwhelms them.

Macon's employer, a man named Julian, who manages to marry but not to hold Macon's sister, puts it succinctly once Rose has drifted back to her brothers; ''She'd worn herself a groove or something in that house of hers, and she couldn't help swerving back into it.'' Almost no one in Miss Tyler's books avoids that swerve; the best they can hope for is to make a second escape, as does the resourceful Caleb Peck in ***Searching For Caleb*** (1976). Brought back after an escape lasting 60 years, Caleb sneaks away again in his 90's. . . .

The Accidental Tourist is one of Anne Tyler's best books, as good as ***Morgan's Passing, Searching for Caleb, Dinner at the Homesick Restaurant.*** The various domestic worlds we enter—Macon/Sarah; Macon/the Leary siblings; Macon/Muriel—are delineated with easy skill; now they are poignant, now funny. Miss Tyler shows, with a fine clarity, the mingling of misery and contentment in the daily lives of her families, reminding us how alike—and yet distinct—happy and unhappy families can be. Muriel Pritchett is as appealing a woman as Miss Tyler has created; and upon the quiet Macon she lavishes the kind of intelligent consideration that he only intermittently gets from his own womenfolk.

Two aspects of the novel do not entirely satisfy. One is the unaccountable neglect of Edward, the corgi, in the last third of the book. Edward is one of the more fully characterized dogs in recent literature; his breakdown is at least as interesting and if anything more delicately handled than Macon's. Yet Edward is allowed to slide out of the picture. Millions of readers who have managed to saddle themselves with neurotic quadrupeds will want to know more about Edward's situation.

The other questionable element is the dead son, Ethan. Despite an effort now and then to bring him into the book in a vignette or a nightmare, Ethan remains mostly a premise, and one not advanced very confidently by the author. She is brilliant at showing how the living press upon one another, but less convincing when she attempts to add the weight of the dead. The reader is invited to feel that it is this tragedy that separates Macon and Sarah. But a little more familiarity with Macon and Sarah, as well as with the marriages in Miss Tyler's other books, leaves one wondering. Macon's methodical approach to life might have driven Sarah off anyway. He would have corrected her word choice once too often, one feels. Miss Tyler is more successful at showing through textures how domestic life is sustained than she is at showing how these textures are ruptured by a death.

At the level of metaphor, however, she has never been stronger. The concept of an accidental tourist captures in a phrase something she has been saying all along, if not about life, at least about men: they are frequently accidental tourists in their own lives. Macon Leary sums up a long line of her males. Jake Simmes in ***Earthly Possessions*** is an accidental kidnapper. The lovable Morgan Gower of ***Morgan's Passing,*** an accidental obstetrician in the first scenes, is an accidental husband or lover in the rest of the book. Her men slump around like tired tourists—friendly, likable, but not all that engaged. Their characters, like their professions, seem accidental even though they come equipped with genealogies of Balzacian thoroughness. All of them have to be propelled through life by (at the very least) a brace of sharp, purposeful women—it usually takes not only a wife and a girlfriend but an indignant mother and one or more devoted sisters to keep these sluggish fellows moving. They poke around haphazardly, ever mild and perennially puzzled, in a foreigh country called Life. If they see anything worth seeing, it is usually because a determined woman on the order of Muriel Pritchett thrusts it under their noses and demands that they pay some attention. The fates of these families hinge on long struggles between semiattentive males and semiobsessed females. In her patient investigation of such struggles, Miss Tyler has produced a very satisfying body of fiction. (pp. 1, 36)

Larry McMurtry, "Life Is a Foreign Country," in The New York Times Book Review, *September 8, 1985, pp. 1, 36.*

An Excerpt from *The Accidental Tourist*

"What do you do, Mr. Leary?"

"I write guidebooks," Macon said.

"Is that so? What kind?"

"Oh, guides for businessmen. People just like you, I guess."

"*Accidental Tourist,*" Mr. Loomis said instantly.

"Why, yes."

"Really? Am I right? Well, what do you know," Mr. Loomis said. "Look at this." He took hold of his own lapels, which sat so far in front of him that his arms seemed too short to reach them. "Gray suit," he told Macon. "Just what you recommend. Appropriate for all occasions." He pointed to the bag at his feet. "See my luggage? Carry-on. Change of underwear, clean shirt, packet of detergent powder."

"Well, good," Macon said. This had never happened to him before.

"You're my hero!" Mr. Loomis told him. "You've improved my trips a hundred percent. You're the one who told me about those springy items that turn into clotheslines."

"Oh, well, you could have run across those in any drugstore," Macon said.

"I've stopped relying on hotel laundries; I hardly need to venture into the streets anymore. I tell my wife, I say, you just ask her, I tell her often, I say, 'Going with the *Accidental Tourist* is like going in a capsule, a cocoon. Don't forget to pack my *Accidental Tourist*!' I tell her."

"Well, this is very nice to hear," Macon said.

"Times I've flown clear to Oregon and hardly knew I'd left Baltimore."

"Excellent."

There was a pause.

"Although," Macon said, "lately I've been wondering."

Mr. Loomis had to turn his entire body to look at him, like someone encased in a hooded parka.

"I mean," Macon said, "I've been out along the West Coast. Updating my U.S. edition. And of course I've covered the West Coast before, Los Angeles and all that; Lord, yes, I knew the place as a child; but this was the first I'd seen of San Francisco. My publisher wanted me to add it in. Have you been to San Francisco?"

"That's where we just now got on the plane," Mr. Loomis reminded him.

"San Francisco is certainly, um, beautiful," Macon said.

Mr. Loomis thought that over.

"Well, so is Baltimore too, of course," Macon said hastily. "Oh, no place on earth like Baltimore! But San Francisco, well, I mean it struck me as, I don't know . . ."

"I was born and raised in Baltimore, myself," Mr. Loomis said. "Wouldn't live anywhere else for the world."

"No, of course not," Macon said. 'I just meant—"

"Couldn't pay me to leave it."

"No, me either."

"You a Baltimore man?"

"Yes, certainly."

"No place like it."

"Certainly isn't," Macon said.

But a picture came to his mind of San Francisco floating on mist like the Emerald City, viewed from one of those streets so high and steep that you really could hang your head over and hear the wind blow.

RICHARD EDER

Anne Tyler, you might say, is as funny as a crutch. Who else has so clear a sense of pain and can summon up the gleefulness that does not heal it but allows us to swing across it?

I don't know if there is a better American writer going. When a writer is good enough, he or she, by definition, is impossible to compare; the vision is too individual. But I can't think of another major novelist who so plainly is still gaining on herself.

There are several characteristics, it seems to me, of a Tyler novel. One is the made-up quality of her characters. They and their lives are invented for the pleasure and instruction to be had from them. They are odd but utterly recognizable; mirrors set at an extravagant angle to catch what is going by. The author stands a certain distance away; they are not chunks torn out of a psyche or a childhood. They do not in the first instance stand for anything but themselves, yet they manage to stand for a great deal more.

Second, along with their inventedness—first you think: how beguiling; only then do you think: how true—goes a kind of respect. Tyler gives them room to exercise their qualities. Like somebody walking a dog—it is more like the dog walking the person—she will stop or wander off to accommodate them instead of dragging them along her route and at her pace. It can be a fault; and there is a characteristic loss of momentum from time to time in a Tyler novel, as if the direction had been temporarily mislaid.

Finally, she manages a three-way sensibility. Tyler knows how things are supposed to feel. She knows how they do feel, in fact, and she knows how they might feel in some barely imaginable better world. Out of this difficult triple balance, formal, real and visionary, comes the memorableness of her people.

These qualities are apparent in her new novel, ***The Accidental Tourist.*** Its protagonist, Macon Leary, is an oddity of the first water, and yet we grow so close to him that there is not the slightest warp in the lucid, touching and very funny story of an inhibited man moving out into life. . . .

As the book begins, Macon's wife leaves him. It is a splendid scene: The two of them are driving home from the beach. It is raining and Sarah, his wife, is terrified of driving in the rain. Macon won't stop, though; he has a system for this kind of driving. In a few pages, Tyler gives us a carful of unhappiness and 20 years of marriage. Sarah can no longer live with this kind, intelligent, careful man who is utterly enclosed in his systems. . . .

Macon retreats gratefully for a while, but his heart is uneasy, and Edward bites people. Macon calls a pet-training agency, and on his doorstep Muriel appears. (p. 3)

Muriel senses the life that Macon bottles up, and is determined to release it. But Tyler endows her zeal with frailty, transforming her spiny and appealing character into something quite unforgettable. When Sarah decides to return to Macon, and Macon wavers, Muriel is genuinely wounded. Like Tinker Bell's in *Peter Pan*—I suspect a distant relationship—her magic flickers and fails. It will take Macon's own power of choice, which he has never up to then used, to resolve things.

The whole last part of the book takes on a growing suspense, constructed entirely out of Tyler's ability to personify moral choice both gravely and winningly amid a carnival of comical events. Macon feels bound to Sarah. And yet, "you can use a person up," he reflects. "Who you are when you are with somebody may matter more than whether you love her."

In terms of who he has been and who he is becoming, it is brilliantly stated. Tyler has written an endlessly diverting book whose strength gathers gradually to become a genuinely thrilling one. (p. 10)

Richard Eder, in a review of "The Accidental Tourist," in Los Angeles Times Book Review, *September 15, 1985, pp. 3, 10.*

MARY FLANAGAN

Macon Leary is a quiet man, determined to remain untouched by life. The reluctant hero of Anne Tyler's tenth novel has lost his only son in a senseless and brutal murder. His wife Sarah has left, exasperated with his appalling calm and tedious routines. When ***The Accidental Tourist*** begins, he is faced with the bleak prospect of life alone in his Baltimore house. Well, not quite alone.

He cannot bring himself to part with Edward, his son's incorrigible corgi. Edward may well prove as notable a literary canine as The Dog of Flanders. There, however, the resemblance ends. His personality is resistable at best, his caprices ungovernable and his habits a menace to life and limb. Macon, in his desolation, clings to the dog, reserving for him the compassion of which his human relationships are barren. (p. 40)

In [Macon's] physical and spiritual impasse, Edward constitutes the single random influence. He is Macon's shadow self: aggressive, erratic, above all undisciplined. He is also pathetic in his mute anxiety, at once brute and lost child, with the child's constant need for reassurance. His bad behaviour is escalating rapidly. Mailmen are savaged and no cyclist is safe. And when he traps Macon's brother in the pantry for 12 hours, the dog pound and worse are imminent. Clearly, Edward must be controlled.

No one, least of all Macon who is literally and physically crippled by his affection for the animal, has been able to exert much influence. In desperation, Macon turns to Muriel Pritchett, an eccentric and garrulous dog trainer whom he first met at the Meow-Bow Hospital. Nearly 20 years Macon's junior, and a graduate, with honours, of the school of hard knocks, Muriel holds down a bewildering variety of very odd jobs, gallantly maintaining herself, her house and her wheezing son Alexander. She is a devotee of thrift shops and an avid reader of the women's mags. Not the sort of girl for Macon. But social barriers are lowered in the daily obedience sessions wherein Muriel couples alarming strength of mind with a profound understanding of the canine psyche.

The taming of Edward runs a parallel course with the liberation of Macon. Muriel accomplishes both. She possesses in abundance the qualities which Macon lacks: courage and vitality. Muriel is a fighter. But her feisty exterior conceals a quirky vulnerability which Macons finds endearing and ultimately addictive. To the astonishment and indignation of the Learys, he and Edward move into her chaotic house on Singleton Street. Here, indeed, is a foreign country, alternately threatening and intriguing—and teeming, it turns out, with unsuspected life forms. Macon begins to find solace in the slums and among the lower orders.

Life on Singleton Street with its multiracial population, chiefly unemployed, is admirably rendered, as is the contrast between its urban squalor and a prissy East-Coast establishment. Macon shuttles between the two, alternately repelled and lured by his former insulated existence. But in the end he has travelled too far. He can't get back. He can only go on, fearfully at first, and later, in the Paris denouement, with joy. Freed of the mean restrictions of common sense, he enters into something like a state of grace. "The real adventure, he thought, is the flow of time; it's as much adventure as anyone could wish."

Because of the author's fine qualities of heart and intellect, her novel transcends the genre in which one is tempted to place it: that of the middle-aged, middle-class person in quest of Identity. Anne Tyler is especially good at turning the banal into the engrossing: dog walking, furniture outlets, the ritual consumption of a baked potato. The details are myriad but not cumbersome. They are worked confidently into the novel's fabric, creating a sense of ease and familiarity. An impeccable ear for the American idiom allows character to be conveyed almost exclusively through dialogue. Her freshly-laundered prose is consistently neat and sweet, eschewing passive verbs and keeping the tone crisp but never brittle. ***The Accidental Tourist*** is very funny, but its comic strength lies in balance rather than irony. The humour is that of a writer who knows her characters to the quick and is very fond of them. Yet she can keep an appropriate distance, supplying just the right quantum of pain to prevent the text sliding into sentimentality. Rancour and self-conscious cynicism are refreshingly absent. ***The Accidental Tourist*** is the sort of book that, having finished, one begins immediately to miss. (pp. 40-1)

Mary Flanagan, "Return Flights," in Books and Bookmen, *No. 360, October, 1985, pp. 40-1.*

ADAM MARS-JONES

[*Mars-Jones, an English short story writer and critic, is the author of* Fabrications *(1981). In the following excerpt Mars-Jones observes that in* The Accidental Tourist *Tyler demonstrates a fresh, perceptive style that compensates for the more sentimental passages in the novel.*]

The Accidental Tourist is the title not only of Anne Tyler's new novel but also of a series of guide books for business travellers written by the book's hero, Macon Leary. These guides enable his readers to deny the difference of other places by reproducing the patterns of their lives at home. . . .

The Accidental Tourist series is produced in effect by a lucrative neurosis; and it is a sublime bit of novelistic business. It gives Tyler all the advantages of having an artist hero (not having, for instance, to invent a working life to counterbalance a private drama), and none of the disadvantages. Macon Leary's job is perfectly expressive of him, and involves little or no distorting feedback, since he is represented on the cover of his books not by a name but by a logo: a winged armchair. . . .

The strange thing about the book's occasional patches of cuteness or banality (and the Accidental Tourist motif is undoubtedly hammered home) is that they are always surrounded by passages that treat the same material with confident freshness.

So Macon's relationship with his dead son is well conveyed by spasms of memory, such as a remembered conversation about cinema seats (Macon wants a strategy for nobbling the best seats, Ethan just wants to see the film), or a reference to Macon always having treated Ethan as a sort of exchange student; less successfully by dreams in which Ethan is falling off a merry-go-round, calling "Catch me!", and Macon is unable to reach him. . . .

[Macon's dog, Edward] develops personality problems of his own when Macon, having broken a leg, moves back in with his brothers and sister. Edward takes the plot between his teeth when he becomes so unreliable that a dog-trainer becomes an urgent necessity; the dog-trainer, Muriel Pritchett, young and deeply disorganized, becomes the second woman in Macon Leary's life.

Edward's range of mood and gesture is brilliantly depicted throughout, from his posture when he is delivered to kennels, "standing upright now and clinging to Macon's knees, like a toddler scared of nursery school", to his hot breath and the oddly intimate dampness of his teeth, when he bites.

The opposed eccentricities of the two households, Muriel's desperately courageous mess and the Learys' compulsive regularity, make for entertaining reading. As Macon is drawn more and more to Muriel, so his young employer Julian, hitherto a preppy playboy, starts paying court to Macon's sister Rose. For once, the author's desire for a plot-twist takes precedence over truth to character: Rose has been portrayed with such dry sexlessness that when she mentions Julian's romantic interest in her the reader is cued to diagnose virgin dementia. Much more satisfying is the moment some time after their marriage when Rose moves back with her brothers, and then Julian moves in too, even mastering "Vaccination", a rebarbative family card-game that could have been devised for its spouse-repellent qualities. Julian's obsession has always been with the household as much as with Rose.

Macon's romantic destiny is less smoothly dramatized. In particular, there are two key moments, one when Sarah claims him back and another when he stays awake all night to make his final decision between the two women, which are oddly rushed or evaded. In a book which rejoices in its ability to fill in the corners with bright reticulated detail, these slight central skimpings are all the more surprising.

Any American novel which elevates the ordinary and finds it full of complex grace is likely to stand in John Cheever's lyric shadow; and this is true particularly of one moment in ***The Accidental Tourist,*** when Macon, picking up his passport from a safe deposit box, is moved by the assistant's tact in looking elsewhere while he rummages. But Anne Tyler, when she doesn't settle for a pathos that her own best form makes irrelevant, achieves a distinctive comic combination of warmth and astringency, one which is likely to make her in her turn a powerful influence.

Adam Mars-Jones, "Despairs of a Time-and-Motion Man," in The Times Literary Supplement, *No. 4305, October 4, 1985, p. 1096.*

DIANE JOHNSON

[*Johnson is an American novelist, critic, and biographer whose novels, such as* Fair Game *(1965),* The Shadow Knows *(1974), and* Lying Low *(1978), focus on the personal and social alienation of modern women. In the following excerpt Johnson discusses the qualities that define the fiction Jonathan Yardley labeled "hick chic"; she finds that* The Accidental Tourist *is exemplary of this detailed, yet distanced fiction of small town or rural America in its refusal to confront reality.*]

> Sam pulls in at the Sunoco and springs out of the car to let Mamaw out. Mamaw has barrel hips and rolls of fat around her waist. She is so fat she has to sleep in a special brassiere. She shakes out her legs and stretches her arms. She is wearing peach-colored knit pants and a flowered blouse, with white socks and blue tennis shoes.
>
> The man at the next table was also on his own. He was eating a nice pork pie, and when the waitress offered him dessert he said, "Oh, now, let me see, maybe I will try some of that," in the slow, pleased, coax-me drawl of someone whose womenfolks have all his life encouraged him to put a little meat on his bones.
>
> Amos Grundy and Sam Spangler sit over a checkerboard. Amos Grundy wears a purple shirt, vest, sleeve garters and slippers. His thin gray hair is bowl-cut. His neck is wrinkly, hands gnarled. Sam's face and ears are red. His gum boots sit by his chair. There's a dog, a hooked rug, caned chairs. The two men have been playing checkers for over thirty years and keep a running tally.

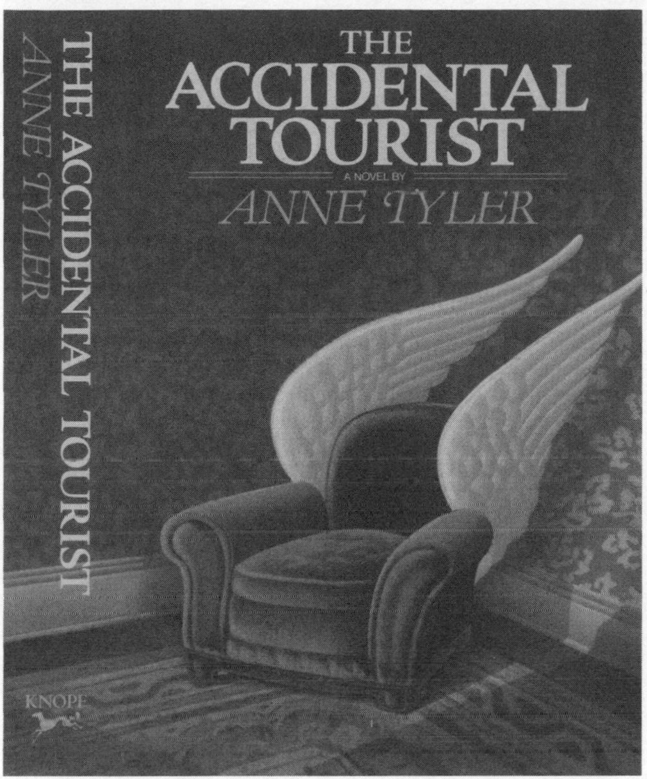

Dust jacket of The Accidental Tourist, *by Anne Tyler. Knopf, 1985. Jacket illustration and design by Fred Marcellino. Courtesy of Alfred A. Knopf, Inc.*

The first two passages are from Bobbie Ann Mason's *In Country* and Anne Tyler's ***The Accidental Tourist*** respectively, and the last is my description of a picture by Norman Rockwell, with the men's names taken from the caption. The similarity of the two excerpts from books to each other and to other recent writing, and, in subject and technique, to pictures by Rockwell (as this writer sees them), makes one notice the techniques that are common to these works of the new fiction with their fashionable settings in rural or small-town America among lower-middle-class people—what Jonathan Yardley has called "hick chic." These novels share a meticulous, literal description, the faintest hint of caricature, and a long narrative distance in which the author is very detached, a viewer rather than an interpreter. . . .

[A] summary [of ***The Accidental Tourist***] scarcely conveys the richness of descriptive detail, the apt but unaffected diction, the assurance and charm, the engaging characters, high comic tone, and wonderful ear for small-town language: "Rose laid a king on Porter's queen, and Porter said, 'Stinker' "—which is probably what Amos Grundy and Sam Spangler say too. Tyler's version of Baltimore, like Mason's small town, suggests all of small, middle, rural America.

Everyone has remarked the popularity of such settings in recent fiction, though with some difference of opinion about what such popularity means. Is it a reaction against the artistic domination of New York, as some have suggested? Or Tobacco Road-style realism, where "sweat, usually in the background of arcadia, now glistens in the foreground," in Ann Hulbert's apt phrase? In this view, the city as the locus of adventure, despair, boredom, terror, and anomie, has exhausted its traditional metaphoric possibilities, and writers have had to move to small towns, finding there, instead of the sweetness and charm we like to remember, the tedium and despair of anywhere else. . . . (p. 15)

But what does strike one as new has to do with their method, in particular, of narrative distance. Most familiar is the sort of traditional novel as practiced by James or Bellow, in which you see through the eyes of the characters. For the past several decades we've also had a sort of fiction of the self, where the character is identified with the real life of the author, who seems to go on to lead the character's life (Erica Jong, Philip Roth). Now we could say that this is fiction of the "other," in which the authors, very detached, describe mostly what can be seen, and the clarity of visual detail strangely objectifies the characters. The process that describes the surface also makes that surface relatively impenetrable: "Her skin is flawless. Her frosted curls resemble pencil trimmings." As when looking through the wrong end of a telescope, the detail seems fine and bright but the object seems far away and small. Because you cannot at a distance identify with the characters, you are cut off from them and feel their "otherness."

In the traditional novel, the hero or heroine, though foolish or luckless, and however related to the actual author, was also the reader, a more articulate, differently placed, or cleverer you, whose perceptions widen your own. Mr. Sammler or Maggie Tulliver know more than you do, however much you may worry about their fates. In these new books, the "other" knows less about himself than you know about him. You experience a poignant realization that the hero or heroine is never going to find out the things that you and the author know about his or her situation, while the character just experiences a mute feeling, usually of disappointment. (pp. 15-16)

The characters in Mason's short stories are flat . . . , and in Anne Tyler, but flat is a term that was not intended by its creator (E.M. Forster, I think) to be denigrating, simply descriptive of a method of characterization that these new works of fiction employ with success. If the characters are somehow thinner, they are also wider, like run-over cartoon cats. In Forster's example, Mrs. Micawber is a flat character because, not wanting to focus the book on her, Dickens concentrated her qualities (foolishness, loyalty) into a tag phrase ("I never will desert Mr. Micawber") and allowed the repetition of that phrase to do the work of presenting her. The more widely flattened characters in the books of Tyler and Mason are the sum of a number of observed qualities of dress, speech, action, observed the way a painter might see them, carefully, in full color, in a keen-eyed way (in the way of Norman Rockwell), exaggerating to the brink, but not over the brink, of caricature.

Anne Tyler's Muriel wears "a V-necked black dress splashed with big pink flowers, its shoulders padded and its skirt too skimpy; and preposterously high-heeled sandals." We also know that she has dark-red painted fingernails, nearly black lipstick, frizzy hair—all signifying her poor taste, lower social class, and so on. It will emerge that these sluttish costumes conceal a heart of gold. Although throughout the book Muriel's vulgarity, brashness, and lack of "good taste" are constantly detailed, the effect is not of derision but of a celebration of eccentricity, communicated by visual signals, as on a TV screen. Any quality of satire must be in the mind of the beholder, with the author maintaining an even tone of exemplary charity, neutrality, and geniality. In these and in other works by these two writers, males in particular are seen as frail, domestic, and helpless, presented with an indulgence that borders on sympathy, while the women, creations of female authors who understand the sturdiness of women, are presented as pluckier and left to fend for themselves.

"The pictures focus not on the rich or mighty, but on everyday Americans and the pleasures of home, outdoors, and family that all of us can enjoy," writes Ronald Reagan in his foreword to *Norman Rockwell's Patriotic Times*. Art critics used to warn us not to admire Rockwell's works. Back then we were told that however amusing we might find them, they were infected with easy sentimentality, and that while they might seem by exaggerating the length of an adolescent's neck or detailing an old person's wrinkles not to be flinching from the awkwardness of youth or age, they were in fact trivializing these tormenting life phases the way a funny birthday card is meant to ameliorate the fleeting of time, but in doing so conceals "reality," which, in the fashion of the times, it was seen as our duty to confront.

Whether or not one is entitled to evade or obliged to confront unpleasant details of the human condition, and whether this choice is a matter of fashion, it is true that people have long been imprinted with a view of seriousness heavily biased toward confrontation, having at the same time a strong inner impulse to have things put in a comforting way. It may be that writers now are turning from confrontation. Certainly this new mode of combining an almost photorealistic surface with a strongly ameliorative point of view meets with warm approval, and after all, amelioration has always been one province of literature, though we usually call it myth.

The Accidental Tourist is irresistible and, in its way, gripping. On one level you are terrified that Macon will stay with his dull wife. But on a deeper level you know you are in the mode or in the hands of an author who will not permit terrible disappointment, although either resolution (Sarah or Muriel) could be "real." The larger strategy is to urge a whole agenda of comforting, consoling ideas, among them that spunkiness and *joie de vivre* win over dullness; that social class doesn't count; that affection can cure allergies; that when you are traveling in France, a likable personality will get you invited to dinner by French people; that you are likely to find real bargains in the flea market; that you can return to childhood and invite others back with you; that legs mend, mean dogs can be trained, and, above all, that the dead do not suffer. When Macon is called to identify the dead body of his murdered child, the boy looks peaceful, and he does not look like himself. The pain of bereavement passes, and like Macon you will get another little boy anyway.

All of these ideas are powerfully attractive. It's just that they are not true. . . . In ***The Accidental Tourist,*** only the discarded wife Sarah, who hasn't succeeded in her attempts at liberation, seems to have strayed in from someone else's novel, a realistic novel about woman's lot, and can't quite make it in this one—she hasn't enough personality or oddness. (She has the only bit of bleak realism, when she confides to Macon after her return that she hasn't slept with anyone else during the separation.) (pp. 16-17)

When Macon wakes up in the middle of the night in Muriel's shabby house to the sound of merriment, we are shown a similar view of benign and reassuring social order:

> Who would be playing a game at this hour? And on this street—this worn, sad street where nothing went right for anyone, where the men had dead-end jobs or none at all and the women were running to fat and the children were turning out badly. But another cheer went up, and someone sang a line from a song. Macon found himself smiling. He turned toward Muriel and closed his eyes; he slept dreamlessly the rest of the night.

Our wishes are equally fulfilled by Anne Tyler's account of a holdup:

> He went grocery shopping with her unusually late one evening, and just as they were crossing a shadowed area a boy stepped forth from a doorway. "Give over all what you have in your purse," he told Muriel. Macon was caught off guard; the boy was hardly more than a child. He froze, hugging the sack of groceries. But Muriel said, "The hell I will!" and swung her purse around by its strap and clipped the boy in the jaw. He lifted a hand to his face. "You get on home this instant or you'll be sorry you were ever born," Muriel told him. He slunk away, looking back at her with a puzzled expression.

These are in a sense Reaganesque dream novels, where the poor are deserving and spunkiness will win. In the real world of the newspapers people are brutalized, and killed in holdups. But perhaps it is tiresome in the reader to insist upon reality. After all we don't require it in our president. Is Muriel's version of life more satisfying? Or in the long run does this kind of folksy escapism fail to satisfy? The great works of the past by their form console us for the harshness of human reality that they confront. But perhaps confrontation is not the national mood, and these are books of our times. (p. 17)

Diane Johnson, "Southern Comfort," in The New York Review of Books, *Vol. 32, No. 17, November 7, 1985, pp. 15-17.*

JESSICA SITTON

Readers familiar with Anne Tyler's work will recognize the signature element in her latest novel, ***The Accidental Tourist:*** lovingly drawn, eccentric characters who come into conflict with themselves and each other as they either slip or jostle their way through life, simultaneously nurtured and stifled by their families and their past. . . .

What holds this novel together is a fascination for the fateful, haphazard nature of life—the seemingly random series of events that throw incompatible people together—and for the small habits and manners that people engage in to defy the chaos. Tyler's characters often seem wrapped in cellophane: they rustle through their world, observe their surroundings, yet remain insulated, yearning to be touched even as they shrink away.

Macon Leary, the quintessential accidental tourist, is just such a character, reminiscent of the stodgy Pecks in ***Searching for Caleb:*** "You're not holding steady, you're ossified. You're encased. You're like something in a capsule. You're a dried-up kernel of a man that nothing penetrates. Oh, Macon, it's not by chance you write those silly books telling people how to take trips without a jolt."

The problem with Macon Leary is that he seems so numb, so engaged in his task of just sliding through life, that he's a difficult character to become enthralled about. I kept reading, not for Macon's sake but for Tyler's, because I still delight in her exquisite use of nuance and detail to elaborate on a scene, and the wise, off-hand observations on human frailties that her characters so often engage in. While her other works have had ordinary, plodding characters, trapped into patterns of their own making, they also possessed some inexplicable, endearingly quirky spark that Macon lacks. These elements give the reader a greater understanding of and sympathy toward an otherwise tedious character. As a result of this lack, it's difficult to understand Macon's actions, and when he finally stops sliding and takes a decisive move at the end of the novel, not only Macon but the reader as well is jolted out of the comfy armchair. What might have been a momentous decision seems just as random as all the other events leading up to it.

A writer's 10th book should come as a landmark. For Tyler, it was her ninth book, ***Dinner at the Homesick Restaurant*** (1982), that, to borrow the words of John Updike's *New Yorker* review, represented "a new level of power." ***The Accidental Tourist*** is a less complex work, and suffers in comparison for it lacks the intricate character development achieved in ***Dinner*** through illuminating shifts in narrative perspective. While it possesses many of the charming details and off-the-wall characters that Tyler can so deftly describe, ***The Accidental Tourist*** reads like a much earlier book, as though the author has slipped back to a more comfortable, less adventurous style.

Jessica Sitton, in a review of "The Accidental Tourist," in San Francisco Review of Books, Spring, 1986, p. 12.

JOHN BLADES

Nobody, it seems, doesn't like Anne Tyler—and with cause. In an age of dissonant, aggressive fiction, Tyler has established herself as a voice of sweet reason, the heiress apparent to Eudora Welty as the earth mother of American writers. With her warm but mildly disquieting vision of family life, her lovably neurotic characters, her quiet but reverberant prose, Tyler has managed to disarm all but the most calloused readers. . . .

It therefore seems rude, not to say irreverent and unpatriotic, to suggest that Tyler may not be ready for beatification, to propose that her fiction may be so marked by imperfections, her vision so distorted and/or confused, as to permanently exclude her from the company of saints, as well as from the pantheon of significant contemporary writers.

For all Tyler's seductive qualities—the great charm and coziness of her fictional universe, her compassion for misfits, and, not least, her soothing, almost tranquilizing voice—there is something annoyingly synthetic about the work itself. However wise and wonderful, her fiction is seriously diluted by the promiscuous use of artificial sweeteners, a practice that has made Tyler our foremost NutraSweet novelist. . . .

[With] the publication of ***The Accidental Tourist,*** Tyler goes to the head of her class, surpassing such highly skilled (and far less disingenous) NutraSweet novelists as John Updike, Elliott Baker, John Irving and Gail Godwin. On its most basic level, the book is a tragedy. Macon Leary, the author of a series of guidebooks for people who dislike travel, breaks up with his wife, Sarah, after—and largely as a result of—the murder of their teenage son in a Burger Bonanza.

During the course of the novel, Macon meets another woman, Muriel, who is not only younger but his opposite in almost every way: brash, embarrassingly unpredictable, full of life, fun and energy, where he is solemn, withdrawn and such a bizarre creature of routine he's barely alive. When Sarah reappears in Macon's life, suggesting reconciliation, the plot resolves itself into a familiar triangle, with Macon torn between Sarah's safe, comfortable but paralyzing domesticity and the much more uncertain but adventurous possibilities that Muriel offers.

In raw synopsis, ***The Accidental Tourist*** sounds cruelly realistic and painful, not to mention soap operatic, all of which, to one degree or another, it cannot help but be. But that does not allow for Tyler's indefatigable optimism and cheery disposition, her talent for making even the flakiest characters appealing, for extracting humor from even the most grievous human predicaments.

Nor—more to the point—does it take into account Tyler's cockeyed humanism, with which she manages to turn ***The Accidental Tourist*** into a situation tragicomedy, a burlesque imitation of life. Without some sweetening, some levity and sunlight, Macon Leary's suffering would be nearly unbearable. But in her efforts to humanize Macon, to ease both his and the reader's burden, Tyler loads him down with so many cuddly tics and personality disorders she all but destroys his humanity. . . .

And, almost compulsively, Tyler lightens her plot with elements of farce, further shredding what few remnants of believability remain. Macon's dog chases a visitor up a tree. In her desperation to hear another human voice, the pathetic Muriel, who works for the Meow-Bow Animal Hospital, calls the number that gives her the recorded time. On the final page of the book, Macon goes for a sitcom taxi ride that delivers him into the waiting arms of Muriel.

That semi-happy fadeout may send most readers away with a smile, feeling warm all over, courtesy of Tyler's latest "life-affirming" novel. But it also leaves several nagging questions: Such as how a writer can affirm life without ever seriously facing it? Or whether Anne Tyler, with her sedative resolutions to life's most grievous and perplexing problems, can be taken seriously as a writer? . . .

Tyler might well be speaking of herself—though without irony—when she says that Jeremy, the artist in ***Celestial Navigation,*** does not seem to understand that "humanity was far more complex and untidy and depressing than it ever was in his (or her) pieces."

In similar fashion, Tyler's gallery of eccentrics—from Jeremy Pauling to Morgan Gower to Macon Leary—may seem quite cute and engaging on paper, but in the flesh—not that they could be made flesh—they would probably be insufferable.

From the evidence, Tyler does seem to recognize that humanity is more complex than she is willing to acknowledge in print; what isn't so clear is whether she simply chooses to ignore the realities or to wish them out of existence by creating a saner, more sanitized world.

That world centers on Baltimore, where most of Tyler's novels have been set, and she has been deservedly praised for re-creating the city and its neighborhoods in crisp and evocative detail. For all its geographic accuracy, however, it is a place that doesn't exist outside her own imagination. For all its relation to the real world, Tyler's Baltimore—as well as those homey, endearing creatures who inhabit it—might well be located on the shores of Lake Wobegon.

John Blades, "For NutraSweet Fiction, Tyler Takes the Cake," in Chicago Tribune, *July 20, 1986, p. 37.*

Fred(erick James) Wah

Waiting for Saskatchewan

Governor General's Literary Award: Poetry

Canadian poet.

Wah reported his satisfaction at winning the Governor General's Literary Award with his tenth book, *Waiting for Saskatchewan* (1985): "I've been publishing for twenty-five years, and the award is a validation. It means what I'm doing is O.K. in the eyes of my peers." He added, "I've never considered myself a very popular writer. I've always considered myself more of an experimental writer. I like to play around and try different forms. But this book is probably more accessible because it has more narrative, and maybe because I'm getting better."

Wah, in fact, uses a different stylistic approach in each of the four sections of *Waiting for Saskatchewan*. The first section is a selection from Wah's long poem *Breathin' My Name with a Sigh* (1981) and is the closest to traditional verse. The second, "Grasp the Sparrow's Tail," is a "poetic diary" of a trip Wah made to China, his father's homeland, in 1982, while the third section, "Elite," takes the form of short prose paragraphs and reflects on Wah's childhood memories of his father. The final section, "This Dendrite Map: Father/Mother Haibun," uses the prose form of the "Elite" poems closing each piece with a more traditional Japanese haiku line; in these poems Wah is meditating on his current life. These four sections are united, then, by a common theme: Wah's search for his own racial and cultural heritage and, more specifically, an understanding of his own father and of their relationship.

Wah's paternal grandfather, the poet notes, was a Chinese immigrant railroad worker who married a woman of European ancestry. Born in Swift Current, Saskatchewan, Wah's father was sent to live with relatives in China at the age of four or five, and did not return to Canada until he was nineteen. "I remember him saying several times that he was outside both the Chinese and Anglo communities here," Wah recalled. "Neither side trusted him totally. I think the trauma of it was responsible for his singularity, his inner anger. . . . He had a deep anger, something inside him that I can feel myself."

For critics, the most striking aspects of *Waiting for Saskatchewan* are its emotional intensity and its experimental form. In several of the poems, Wah revisits China and the Saskatchewan prairie land where his father lived; here the poet connects his current observations with his feelings and memories in order to assemble a meaningful picture of his father's life. Through this symbolic search for his departed parent, Wah also tries to comprehend his own identity. Reviewers describe this process as profoundly moving, as it expresses the dynamics of the father-son relationship through imagery that is clearly focused, energetic, and immediate in its impact. Wah's attention to the rhythmic form of his poems, influenced by his experience as a jazz musician and shaped by his careful attention to the natural patterns of spoken language, also elicited praise from critics. "A consummate craftsman with one eye on the line and one ear on the breath," in reviewer Judith Fitzgerald's summary,

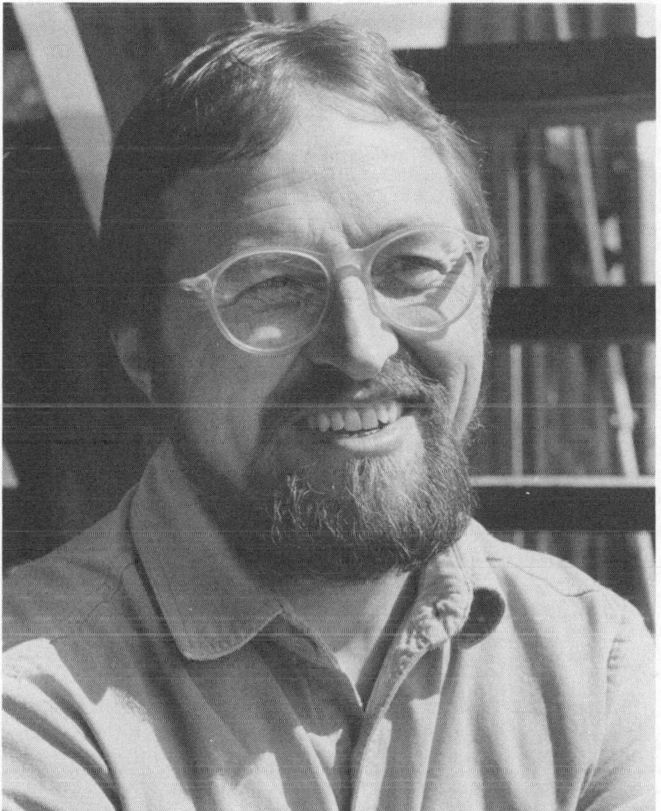
Photograph by John Goddard

"Wah constructs poems from the fabric of imagination and binds them together with threads of energy."

(See also *Contemporary Authors*, Vol. 107.)

GLADYS HINDMARCH

[Hindmarch is a Canadian short story writer and critic. Her publications include A Birth Account *(1976) and* The Peter Stories *(1976). In the following excerpt Hindmarch examines the thematic and structural beauties of* Waiting for Saskatchewan.]

Fred Wah's ***Waiting for Saskatchewan*** is a beautiful book composed in a difficult key—say E with its four sharps instead of C or G. On the surface, there are new sounds, a sense of space, a time for silence, rhythms which vary as intricately as the sounds in the title do. Say it aloud. Waiting for Saskatchewan. Waiting for Saskatchewan. The beat, the wai-wan, the ting-kat, and the sas-chew delight my ear. The title conveys senses to me of waiting (for something to happen), weight (as in measure), and of turning over, gaining speed—the Cree word *Saskatchewan* cannot be said slowly and has as its etymological source *swift current, fast-flowing river.*

Surfaces disappear as I read and listen to this work written in four parts in four forms. The book begins with father-family centred selections from Wah's jazz-influenced long poem, ***Breathin' My Name with a Sigh.*** Take a deep breath and read all that is written here with no pause from *wait* to *swift:*

> Waiting for Saskatchewan
> and the origins grandparents countries places converged
> europe asia railroads carpenters nailed grain elevators
> Swift Current

This opening passage announces themes which will recur—origins, convergences (europe and asia), the horizontal (railroad) and vertical (elevator), work in building railroads and elevators but also cafés and houses (and poems) to be nailed, constructed. His grandfather, Chinese, and grandmother, English, met/mated/converged here and Wah asks "why on earth would they land in such a place / mass of pleistocene." And that question is repeated on a personal yet universal level throughout:

> Are origins magnetic lines across an ocean
> migrations of genetic spume or holes, dark
> mysteries within which I carry further into the World

The poet manages to convey a sense of space and time (half the world, back thousands of years) and continuity (genetic spume) with a why which is suggestive of the size of a whale's blowhole, the depth of a black hole in space. His father married a woman of Swedish origin and Fred's children are blond, so now "through blonde and blue-eyed progeny father's fathers" genes are carried into the world by women with the "clan name Wah from Canton."

Many of the ***Breathin'*** poems play the vertical of mountain/elevator/horse/man against the horizontal of train tracks/magnetic lines/facial lines or arms which reach out/embrace through generations—father, mother, child. One of the simplest poems in the entire text conveys father and mother from what I take to be a young boy's point of view:

> IN THE ARMS OF THE FAMILY
> IN THE ARMS
> IN THE CENTRE OF THE ARMS
> IN THE BODY
> IN THE ARMS
> OF THE FAMILY
> IN THE ARMS OF MY FATHER
> SKY
> OF MOTHER NIGHT
> IN THE ARMS OF US ALL OUR HOLDING
> IN HIS/HER ARMS THEN
> HIS MOTHER'S MY GRAND
> FATHER'S
> ARMS

What I see are the arms holding, embracing, reaching back, holding, embracing, grandparents and grandparents' grandparents, back further to the point people began, to before then sky (air) night (space before earth). Of course sky and night also suggest the curve and darkness of the womb and of individual nights and "the centre of the arms" where the reader-boy is.

The second section of the book is a *utaniki,* a poetic diary of poetry and prose named after a difficult tai-chi movement, Grasp the Sparrow's Tail. Most of this diary was written while Wah was travelling with his wife, Pauline, in China, then revised and published in Japan. There is a particularly powerful prose piece about sightings of his father which begins:

> About a year after you died I saw you. You were alone in a car and passed me going the other way. You didn't look at me.

He sees his father alone out in the open in a park doing Grasp the Sparrow's Tail. He sees him on a bicycle in a crowd. He sees his black crew-cut, his frown, his hands on chopsticks at a roadside eatery. And then near Buddhist caves near Datong:

> you walked past me going the other way and brushed my arm. Yes, brushed. I could see it was intentional and our eyes met for an instant as you turned and glanced over the head of the baby boy you were carrying. Though you didn't say anything your face still talked to me.

These appearances are startling, direct, tender, immediate. Here is a dead father who still feels pain, who still hurts, who still has force, who still worries and wonders. Here is a totally masculine man with creosote eyes and a "body that still moves with emphasis and decision," who tenderly holds "out a green flag at the end of a train." Wah has managed to write from a depth of feeling somewhat akin to that marvellous William Carlos Williams poem where the doctor dances naked in front of his mirror at night: masculine voices not afraid to say I love my household, I feel lonely, I hurt.

In the "Elite" pronounced eee-light section, we go back to where the world began for Fred Wah—"Swift Current Saskatchewan is at the centre." There are ten parts to this sequence, each a variable-length paragraph, each with its own measure, most to be read quickly with deep breaths and then little grabs as the runs continue. Like the ***Breathin'*** section, they are straight North American—trombones and saxophones as contrasted to flutes and dulcimers, the energy and speed of hockey or country dances rather than the pauses and reflectiveness of the *utaniki* and later the *haibun-haiku.* Although the sounds are intricate, the beat is pronounced, the syntax is strictly Wah playing loud and clear. Some of the sentences are a paragraph long, like thirty-two bars; others work in smaller units of four and eight. All of them, all, contain sharp images rooted in memory and race. One of my favourites is **"Elite 9":**

> When you returned from China via Victoria on Hong Kong island and they put you in jail in Victoria on Vancouver Island because your birth certificate had been lost in the Medicine Hat City Hall fire and your parents couldn't prove you were born in Canada until they found your baptismal records in the church or in the spring of 1948 when we moved to Nelson from Trail during the floods while Mao chased Chiang Kai-shek from the mainland to offshore Taiwan and the Generalissimo's picture hung in our house and on a wall above some plants and goldfish in the Chinese National League house down on Lake Street or when you arrived in China in 1916 only four years old unable to speak Chinese and later in the roaring twenties when each time Grampa gambled away your

> boat passage so you didn't get back to Canada
> immigration cells on Juan de Fuca Strait or
> when your heart crashed so young at fifty-four
> as you fell from mom's arms to the dance floor
> did you see islands?

I like this piece because it attempts to convey a life in a single sentence and almost succeeds in doing so. I like it because of the islands—particularly the last ones on the dance floor. I like it because of its sound—note the strongest stresses all fall on verbs and nouns (frequently place names); note how the "or" where the reader grabs a quick breath is scarcely heard. The rhythm feels so natural it's like a great hockey player skating gracefully and scoring a goal—no wasted movement, all the time in the world, yet fast and powerful with the surprise at the end. I like it because I identify with the four year old on a train and boat to China waiting to go home to Saskatchewan probably before he even arrived in Canton, but then waiting and waiting for fourteen years only to arrive at last and to be put in jail. His languagelessness. A novel could be written about what is said here in one paragraph, one question. I like it because of the whole mixture of its images—the certificate burned in a fire, the goldfish beneath Mao's picture, the gambling grandfather, Juan de Fuca Strait, the Medicine Hat City Hall fire, the couple dancing in each other's arms—there is an energy to each. I like it because it is so Canadian—the subject and the voice is from here, nowhere else. The forms may come from everywhere—the Japanese, the I Ching, Barthes, Bowering, Brossard, Kearns, Kroetsch, Nichol, Marlatt, Olson, Williams, and several others whose works have been absorbed and heard clearly—but the voice is straight Wah in top performance.

The Elite is a café Wah's father ran when he returned from China—no more elite than the Regal, the New Star, the Diamond Grill. In these cafés we see father and later son making coffee ("twenty cups of ground in the cloth sack") in stainless steel urns, we see the trays of butter, and the night-shift workmen, and the sign turning on in the morning before the darkness breaks, in short the "synchromesh of everything starting to work." We also hear the sounds of a household at 4:30 a.m. when the father gets up to go to work. Everything is so familiar. We get glimpses of the son polishing the father's shoes, of a hockey arena, of small-town life. But always we return to the mixed race—"never white enough. But you weren't pure enough for the Chinese either. You never knew the full comradeship of an ethnic community." My favourite glimpse of Wah's father is when he manages a hockey team and a picture is taken with the brim of the hat "turned down, Chicago gangster style." And my favourite sentence depicting the two of them together: "When I fish now sometimes I feel like I'm you, water, glassy gaze, vertical, invisible layers, the line, disappearing." Just as in the previously quoted origin section where "magnetic lines across an ocean" interplay with the vertical and perhaps cosmic holes, here the direct surface—"Sometimes I feel like I'm you"—transforms into a dual image of the vertical man juxtaposed with the horizontal layers of water. I see a line moving from their eyes and arms into a deep layer of water (consciousness and self) and disappearing: Him, his father, his father's father, his father's father's father fishing, living, being fully alert, and, inevitably, a glassy gaze, a blurring, a death.

"This Dendrite Map: Father/Mother Haibun" are twenty-one pieces written in prose informed by a haiku sensibility and concluded with informal haiku lines. The tone of these pieces is much less boisterous than that of the "Elite" section. In

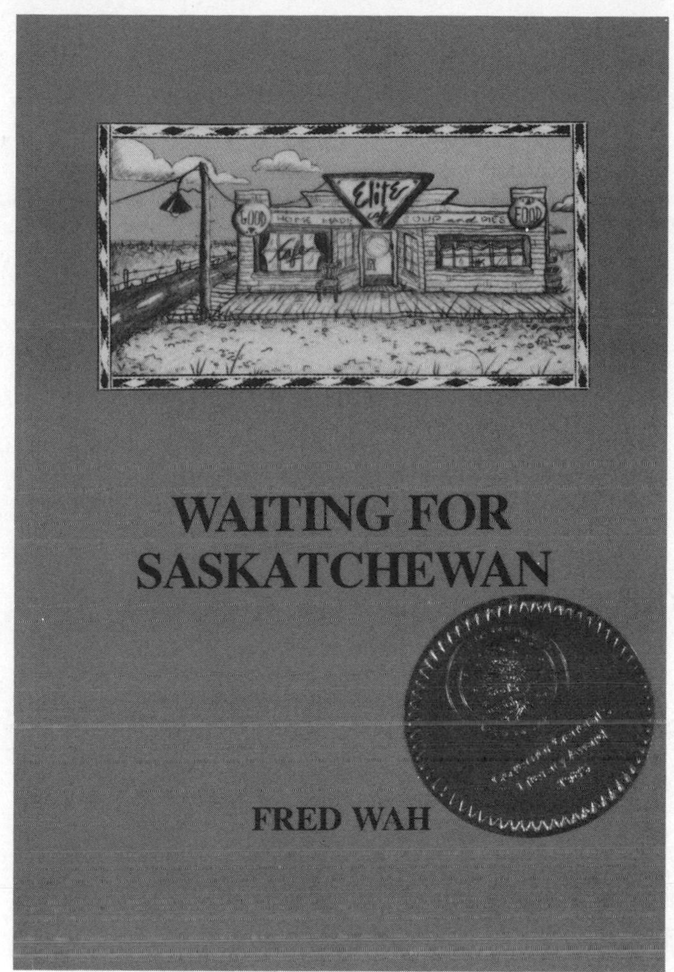

Cover of Waiting for Saskatchewan, *by Fred Wah. Turnstone Press, 1985. Copyright © 1985 Fred Wah. Cover design by Darlene Toews. Reproduced by permission of Turnstone Press, Winnipeg, Canada.*

anatomy, dendrite is "the branching part at the receiving end of a nerve cell," and, in geology, "a stone or mineral with branching, tree-like markings." Wah uses both meanings throughout the text—"this dendrite map I'm finally on now for no reason but time." He attempts to come to terms with both why he was born as he was / is and the fact that he, too, will die. . . . His anger is present, yes, but tempered. It's as if the very cells on the edge are fully alert and so full of current or life that each event contains its own death or end like the "black bear, eating, high up in the thin wild cherry trees in the gulley this morning, sun just coming up" transformed by the end of the poem to "pits in the shit."

These pieces capture moments well. Sometimes it is a picture of the "kids each year on the first day of school in front of the flowers in their new clothes," other times "your quick body as you'd flourish off a check during a busy noon-hour rush," other times "China rainbow over your youth vertical like on the prairies that rainbow stood straight up into the sky." I'm left with impressions of colours—September flowers, rainbows, Japanese plum blossoms, ravens, amaryllis, brown grass, black beans, golden flower, corn, tomatoes, "gold-toothed clicks ink mark red green on lottery blotting paper," "a rare white moose," "stain the fence red." I'm also left with a sense of spacious time because each piece has a meditative quality, a moment-thought.

Waiting for Saskatchewan is a beautifully composed book with the four forms making the shape of it unique: parts 1 and 3 echo each other as do 2 and 4, but 2 also balances 1 as 4 does 3. As I said at the outset, it is composed in a difficult key—say E. Some sounds are completely familiar but the juxtapositions are not; the rhythms have range and a power of their own; the pace of the book is original and pleasing; the images, particularly those of father-son, are deep. Throughout the book a motif-image in one section is picked up and returned to in another—family, home, café, caves, mountains, continents, oceans, lakes, geology, maps, genealogy, lines, branches, trees, no language, writing with a pen, arms, eyes, anger, hurt, delight in skin-body-dance-being present, death. It's one of the best books a Canadian has ever written. Read it aloud. Eeelight in the sound and hereness/thereness of it. (pp. 10-12)

Gladys Hindmarch, "Dendrite Map," in Brick: A Journal of Reviews, *No. 27, Spring, 1986, pp. 10-12.*

NORBERT RUEBSAAT

[***Waiting for Saskatchewan***] brings forward the (usually hidden, usually silent) dialogue between fathers and sons which is the (often unacknowledged) basis of discourse in patriarchies. This discourse, veiled as, say, "epic poetry," or "the novel," or, latterly, as "The Evening News," is a language by which certain power relations in our culture are organized and maintained.

Fred Wah addresses this subject matter in the form of a journal. The journal is an ambiguous form. It mixes "private" and "public" utterance, political statement and personal sentiment in ways that are unexpected and hard to control. Thus it challenges prevailing ways of thinking about things. We realize, for example, that the division of speech into strict forms of address might be simply another way in which patriarchies divide and rule things.

In this text, you're constantly confused about who you are as reader. You don't know if you're supposed to be listening to an intimate confession (like the one Jack Spicer is said to have made to his scarecrow) or whether you're involved in political debate. Wah further exacerbates this confusion by keeping you in doubt also about whether you're reading "poetry" or "prose": you discover as you go along that these divisions might be further tools in the repressive arsenal.

This is a terrific book. Fred Wah handles the baroque intricacies of the father/son enterprise—the confusions between power and eros, intimacy and estrangement, physicality and abstraction, etc.—with an aplomb and clarity that's fascinating. At first I thought he was "poeticizing" the matter too much, turning the subject of the book (his father) into an object by which to discuss poetry. On further reading, though, I realized the form-subject matter tension here worked perfectly: it is precisely in analysing the discourse of the father-son debate via a "poetic" strategy that Wah makes the "power" relationship come forward and become conscious. By applying the (ambiguous) idioms of poetry/prose, of "the journal" and the "poetry book" to the father-son proposition, he opens some new ground in which a kind of honest talk can occur.

The book begins with a long warm-up section, taken from Wah's previous ***Breathin' My Name with a Sigh*** book. Here the voice, mainly in traditional verse mode, searches for its subject: "my father hurt- / ing at the table / sitting hurting / at suppertime / deep inside very / far down inside / because I can't stand the ginger / in the beef and greens / he cooked for us tonight / and years later tonight / that look on his face / appears now on mine . . ." In this section, Wah finds (or we hear Wah finding) his father's "self" appearing in the son's body. Wah is now middle-aged, and he senses—knows—his father's physiognomy, his physicality both as a memory and as action.

This sense of discovering the father in the "landscape" of the self is taken one step further in ***Waiting for Saskatchewan***'s second section, a travel journal, or *utaniki* (Japanese), as Wah calls it. Here Wah follows the image of his father into the landscape and geography of his father's (and his own) past in China. He "sees" his father everywhere, across the ethnic and cultural gulf: "We travel all day to the Inner Mongolian grasslands in a small passenger van. Through the bus window I catch yet another glimpse of 'you'." Fred's never been to China before, but his father grew up there, so, mythically, Fred remembers it, of course.

This section (also previously published, in private edition, as ***Grasp the Sparrow's Tail***) contains beautiful juxtapositions of the "poetic" and "prosaic" voice. Each "diary" entry is followed by a poetic treatment or working of the material (memory and landscape) to give it music. I found the oscillation thus created (two voices in counterpoint) an interesting and oblique way of getting into this type of "search."

This jazz duo effect is carried one step further in the book's third part, "Elite". . . . Here the two voices (poetry and prose, father and son, yesterday and today, etc., etc.) are carried over into single, nominally prose pieces (Wah calls them "prose poems"). The search now moves from China—or from the body, where it began, through China, the land of myth—to Swift Current, Saskatchewan, where Fred spent his own early youth. He tries to "find" his father here (say in the Elite Café he ran) to establish a sense of place (taking this cliché by the horns here) where father and son might (physically, spiritually) coexist. Ancestral landscape this is sometimes called. He doesn't succeed too well, discovering or remembering that his father had a less developed sense of place (less longing, perhaps) than the son: "Did any shape of such places ever displace the distancing in your eyes? You looked out at it all but you never really cared if you were there or elsewhere. I think you were prepared to be anywhere."

This ability of his father's to be anywhere (and thus perhaps nowhere) sharply delineates his (here fictional, poetic or biographical) experience from Wah's own. Here Fred steps out of his father's clothes and persona. The last part of the book, *haibun*, as he calls its texts—"short prose written from a haiku sensibility and, in this case, concluded by an informal haiku line"—explores this new, emancipated sensibility. It's the strongest part of the book, by far, and really demonstrates what Wah's poesis can accomplish when it's on. Written from the "perspective" of Nelson, the Kootenays, where Wah currently lives and grew up, the language is both distant and intimate, involved with and distracted from its subject. It's both here and there: "I was back in Buffalo when you died and when I came out for your funeral at the end of September there was snow on Elephant Mountain as far down as Pulpit Rock from Ernie's house the lake quiet my mother alone suddenly, months unused, unusual, I knew you best in winter . . ." It's almost laconic, a long prose riff, and then the haiku line hits you at the end of each one like an icicle stab—"Road's nearly empty, only a few pickups with firewood.'' This, to me, is very powerful stuff; it joins the two voices, father and son, past and present, no place and here, in a powerful, respectful, yes, one can say it—an *Eastern* way.

I found myself thinking a lot about my own father while reading this book. And about the broader issues of ethnicity and region, body and place, that play into this discourse and make it so peculiarly Canadian, so peculiarly Western. . . .

The boy is aware that his father's body (and perhaps his tongue) comes from elsewhere, can never be really *here* as it is the son's privilege to be. And yet that ''other'' becomes—in middle age, say—as familiar as the ''self'' is. This on-going rupture, therefore, between the body and its landscape, between speech and the world. Passed down through generations.

This is what I experience, I guess, as the specifically ''male'' discourse (along with the specifically ethnic or Canadian or ''B.C.'' discourse) in this book. The placement of the male body, self, into landscape has always been a troublesome, often violent exercise in the history of the ''West'': love and terror, violence and intimacy, etc., mixed in baroque, unpredictable, unprepared ways. Fathers and sons, the ruptures and struggles and loves between them, have a lot to do with this on-going saga. This book begins to develop a more civilized, a circumspect approach to this plot. It's a very cautious approach, more civilized and formal and careful than I could ever manage. But the poetry or prose or diction—the language strategy works, makes sense and meaning. The issue is firmly addressed and spoken. (pp. 139-42)

Norbert Ruebsaat, in a review of ''Waiting for Saskatchewan,'' in Event, *Summer, 1986, pp. 139-42.*

JEAN HILLABOLD

In this pastiche of new poems, formerly-published poems and journal entries [***Waiting for Saskatchewan***], Saskatchewan-born Fred Wah explores his multicultural roots.

The theme of a son's search for his lost and enigmatic father blends seamlessly with the theme of a Canadian poet's search for an ethnic identity he can use. Some of Wah's vignettes of a childhood in Swift Current show an almost slapstick collision of cultures. . . . Between the scenes of a boyhood that includes church, hockey and fishing, there are hints of the unspoken fear and hardships in father Wah's life. . . . Like the distant city in another country, the essence of father Wah's life (and of the speaker's inherited patterns of thought and feeling) remains on the ''periphery,'' faintly visible.

The speaker's search for the truth of his life, and of the lives before his, resembles his description of fishing:

> Line going deep into the lake or flung out onto
> the surface glaze river current, layers of dark-
> ness, invisible fish.
>
> (**''Elite 6''** . . .)

Although descriptions of icy rivers are not unusual in the work of Saskatchewan writers, Wah's river seems to have a distinct ability to flow through several continents and several timeframes at once.

In another piece, written in dialogue, the poet (or the character he presents) discusses with a friend his motives for thinking and writing about his father. The speaker says: ''I feel lucky I'm part Chinese when I see a river.'' (**''Father/Mother Haibun 9''** . . .)

An unpunctuated piece in the first section of the book begins: ''getting at how the river in its mud banks flows downstream.'' (untitled . . .)

Images of river and land serve as metaphors for time-strata and the flow of blood and history. . . .

[The section ''Grasp the Sparrow's Tail''] is named for a position in T'ai chi, an old Chinese system of exercise that has gained popularity in North America. The purpose of t'ai chi seems to be to increase the flow of energy in the body; the various positions make a fitting motif for a poet's journey to parts of the world that are both strange and familiar to him.

The speaker's practice of t'ai chi contrasts with his father's patterns of movement, ending in a dramatic death:

> You moved your body on the go even when
> you stood head and shoulders arms too swing
> with the talk rhythm to hardworking feet (I
> loved to shine your alligator shoes, special, for
> going out only) and then you died dancing.
>
> (untitled . . .)

There is nothing original about a poet's search for ancestral and personal identity, or in descriptions of the prairie landscape and reminiscences of childhood but Fred Wah brings a keen eye to familiar territory.

Jean Hillabold, ''Wah's Rivers,'' in Briarpatch, *July-August, 1986, p. 28.*

MARC CÔTÉ

Immediacy of perception is the most striking aspect of Fred Wah's poetry. This makes, however, for a challenging read. But if one understands the dismissal of standard grammar (replaced by a rhythmical, musical one) and if one reads this poetry more slowly and thoroughly than usual, there are plenty of rewards.

Perhaps Wah's experiences with language (his father was part Chinese, and he studied linguistics) and music (he plays jazz trumpet) best inform his poetry and enable him to assemble poems shaped by their emotional and intellectual content. Despite the difficulties this causes, the clarity and complexity of Wah's perceptions are realized. The reader need never be lost.

The drive behind the book becomes clear as one reads on: ***Waiting for Saskatchewan*** is a search. The poet is searching for himself, his dead father, himself in his dead father, and his dead father in himself. Through this search, Wah creates himself. He becomes the sum of his past and present, his lineage and language. . . .

There is nothing tranquil about Wah's memories of his father. In the first two sections of the book the father is referred to in present tense. He is alive and spotted frequently by his son. These occurrences are disturbing. But they are part of ''the 'inging' of a / life like an arrow.'' They are part of making the past present.

The last two sections of the book contain prose poems that are the result of the search. These are easier to read, more accessible. There is a feeling of resolution that carries both grammatically and emotionally as the father is constantly referred to in the past tense. This half of the book is less challenging, less demanding, but more fulfilling.

In ***Waiting for Saskatchewan*** there are no lyrical passages, rich in description. The book is a successful, alive, and significant attempt to ". . . really gain sight of / word's imprint to pose itself as action on the world. . . ." It is also the achieved end of a man creating himself through his work and his world. (pp. 26-7)

Marc Côté, in a review of "Waiting for Saskatchewan," in Books in Canada, *Vol. 15, No. 6, August-September, 1986, pp. 26-7.*

An Excerpt from *Waiting for Saskatchewan*

Father/Mother Haibun #4

Your pen wrote Chinese and your name in a smooth swoop with flourish and style, I can hardly read my own tight scrawl, could you write anything else, I know you could read, nose in the air and lick your finger to turn the large newspaper page pensively in the last seat of those half-circle arborite counters in the Diamond Grill, your glass case bulging your shirt pocket with that expensive pen, always a favourite thing to handle the way you treated it like jewellry, actually it was a matched pen and pencil set, Shaeffer maybe (something to do with Calgary here), heavy, silver, black, gold nib, the precision I wanted also in things, that time I conned you into paying for a fountain pen I had my eye on in Benwell's stationery store four dollars and twenty cents Mom was mad but you understood such desires in your cheeks relaxed when you worked signing checks and doing the books in the back room of the cafe late at night or how the pen worked perfectly with your quick body as you'd flourish off a check during a busy noon-hour rush the sun and noise of the town and the cafe flashing.

High muck-a-muck's gold-toothed clicks ink mark red green on lottery blotting paper, 8-spot (click, click)

JUDITH FITZGERALD

As George Bowering writes in the Introduction to ***Loki Is Buried at Smoky Creek*** (1980), Fred Wah "offers spirit, not history". Wah's poetry and prose poems pull towards the magnet of discovery in terms of form and content. Not only does Wah embark on a voyage aimed at fixing "the story" of himself in relation to all not himself (which has nothing to do with self-centredness), he also explores the shape and sound of writing on and beyond the page.

Some of the work included in his most recent collection, ***Waiting for Saskatchewan,*** made its debut in ***Breathin' My Name with a Sigh*** (1981). Wah writes in "A Prefactory Note": "Some of the poems . . . are included in this book to give some shape to the range of forms a particular content ('father') from that long poem has generated". An example?

my father hurt-
ing at the table
sitting hurting
at suppertime
deep inside very
far down inside . . .

A consummate craftsman with one eye on the line and one ear on the breath, Wah constructs poems from the fabric of imagination and binds them together with threads of energy. (p. 39)

Judith Fitzgerald, "Hammering Out Postmodern Kinks," in Cross-Canada Writers' Quarterly, *Vol. 8, Nos. 3 & 4, 1986, pp. 39-40.*

George F. Walker

Criminals in Love

Governor General's Literary Award: Drama

Canadian dramatist and scriptwriter.

Criminals in Love (1984), Walker's eleventh play, was a major success of the 1984-1985 theatrical season in Toronto. It was also an unprecedented triumph for the Factory Theatre, a Toronto group dedicated to supporting nontraditional Canadian drama. Walker has been closely associated with the Factory Theatre, formerly known as the Factory Lab Theatre, since it staged his first play, *Prince of Naples,* in 1970. "I have a freedom and involvement with the Theatre that has continued to the present day," Walker has stated. "The Factory spirit is eclectic, unpredictable, and heroic. Something will get started there in one-twentieth the time that it would take in another space." Critics regard Walker as a leader in the Canadian alternative theater movement; his plays have also been performed in the United States, Australia, and the United Kingdom. Such early dramas as *Prince of Naples* and *Beyond Mozambique* (1974), consist of anarchic, cartoonlike assemblages of satirical media references and grim social commentary. In later plays, including *Theatre of the Film Noir* (1981) and *Better Living* (1986), Walker retains his antinaturalist style while using more formal structures.

According to reviewers, *Criminals in Love* evidences Walker's characteristic black humor as well as his refusal to offer neat resolutions for the troubled situations he depicts. The play's action occurs in a lower-class urban area similar to Toronto's East End, where Walker has spent most of his life. His hero and heroine, the teenage lovers Junior and Gail, find themselves bullied and manipulated into joining a terrorist conspiracy organized by Junior's disreputable relatives.

Critics describe *Criminals in Love* as a witty, engrossing drama, an insightful depiction of poverty and social injustice combined with a parody of second-rate crime melodramas. They describe Junior and Gail's predicament as genuinely moving, even though surrounded by such farcical elements as the bizarre philosopher-derelict William, who befriends the young couple. Some reviewers fault Walker for indulging too heavily in absurdist comedy, obscuring the poignant story of the lovers with improbable, unsatisfying plot developments as the play progresses to its climax. Critic Paul Walsh, however, expresses a more positive response to the drama's resolution. "The exhilarating honesty and imaginative flair of the play," he comments, "and above all its sincere and painfully black sense of humor, make this vision of urban waste not only bearable but revivifying."

(See also *Contemporary Authors,* Vol. 103.)

STEPHEN GODFREY

[For] the first act at least, [***Criminals in Love***] is one of the funniest plays to be seen in a long time.

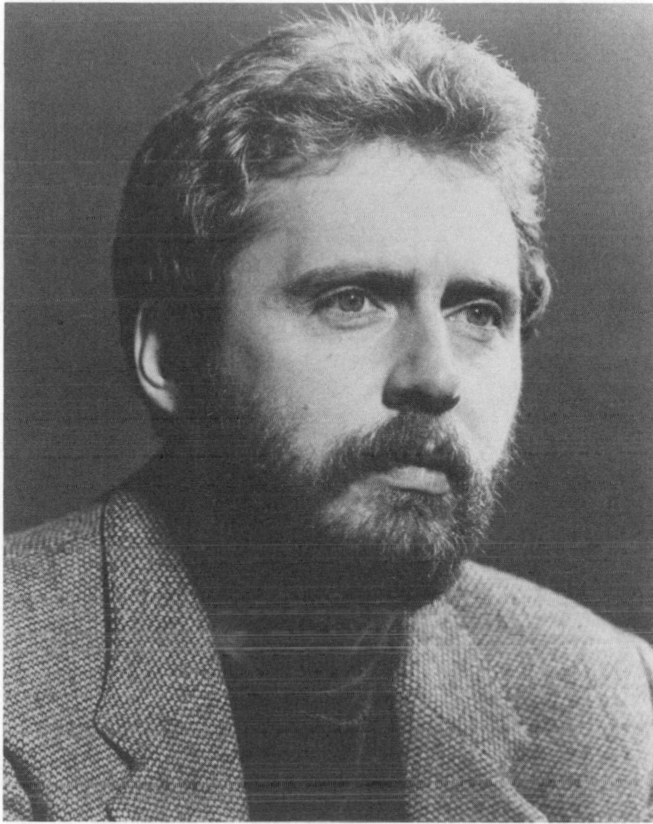

Courtesy of Great North Artists Management, Inc.

Walker works best when the story is ripe for parody, and in this vision of teenage love and crime in Toronto's east end, he skewers all expectations. These working-class people, terrified about an uncertain future, appear to have been weaned on B-movies, Philosophy 101 and a paperback copy of *I'm OK, You're OK.* The young anti-hero, Junior Dawson . . . is something of a wimp, who frets about his "destiny" and is only redeemed by his love for his no-nonsense girl friend, Gail. . . . Junior has a chance encounter with William . . . , a particularly rancid street bum given to saying un-bum things like "You have a devastating aptitude for logical debate," just before Junior must pay a visit to his father . . . , in jail as a chronic offender who "never got more than 50 yards away from the scene of the crime."

Because of his father, Junior Dawson must put up with what is basically his common-law aunt, Wineva Dawson . . . , a born leader with a flair for quelling all argument by particularly aggressive kissing. Even Gail's best friend, Sandy . . . , an entrepreneur who tries her hand as a hooker in case she has to resort to it in some financial emergency, eventually joins in Wineva's criminal plans. . . .

During the first act, [a] balance is beautifully maintained, not only because the storyline develops in a way that, under the circumstances, has a faint logic, but also because the wisecracks are tempered by sparks of genuine feeling in the relationship of the young lovers. In one brilliant scene after another, the play speeds along with the momentum of wit coming effortlessly from its overripe characters.

But by the second act, all becomes a little unhinged. Despite a hilarious scene between Senior Dawson and William the bum, the story gets bogged down in the tiresome schemes of the increasingly strange Wineva. . . . Gail notes she is being "pulled along at a breakneck clip by events," in the kind of overly self-conscious writing that ***Criminals in Love*** has previously tempered with humor.

Stephen Godfrey, "'Criminals in Love' Hilarious Despite Flaws in Second Act," in The Globe and Mail, *Toronto, November 8, 1984, p. E5.*

VARIETY

Working class dreams of elevated love and a better life get squashed in this sometimes comic, mostly confusing new play by George F. Walker [***Criminals in Love***]. . . .

The laughs are fresh in the first act but get mired in improbable development of the story and some of the main characters after intermission.

The set is working class Toronto, and Gail and Junior are the young star-crossed lovers. Junior is a shipping clerk who comes from a long line of losers, notably his dad, who is in jail for basically being a bad crook. The pair are befriended by William-the-Bum, a garbage-strewn wino whose eloquent philosophy surfaces amid his daily rantings.

Junior is lured into the family legacy of crime by his aunt, a frenetic, schizoid thief, who masterminds an elaborate theft. Along for the ride is Gail's friend Sandy, who picks up information about the underground as a general preparedness for life. . . .

Walker allows the action to become undone in the second act. William buys a three-piece suit and becomes a philosopher king, and Wineva's . . . criminal plans escalate to revolutionary heights. The sentiment that the couple will probably remain trapped in their history is blocked out by the slapstick.

Devo, in a review of "Criminals in Love," in Variety, *December 12, 1984, p. 130.*

PAUL WALSH

Criminals in Love not only addresses the desires and anxieties of the 80s but accosts them with a relentless and uncompromising explication of the decade's terrifying epithet: "No Future." . . . Walker opens his eyes and ears to the present to search out and formulate questions so new and tentative that, as the notes to the text point out, question marks are frequently and deliberately omitted. The exhilarating honesty and imaginative flare of the play, and above all its sincere and painfully black sense of humour, make this vision of urban waste not only bearable but revivifying.

Criminals in Love traces the search of the bewildered and vulnerable Junior Dawson for a way out of the dead-end predicament called his life. It is a predicament that Junior summarizes early in the play: "If you put all the things of life along a ruler . . . legacy is at one end and destiny is at the other." What terrifies him is that he's come to believe that for him both poles are the same: "Fuck all is what I came from. Fuck all is where I'm going." With a faith mixed of desire and despair, Junior looks to his strong-willed, practical girlfriend Gail for salvation from his "true destiny." Gail, who hates it when Junior says "shit like that," is desperate to find work so she will "know there's something I can do to control things. Keep things moving. Whatever happens." This is precisely what the world of the play will not allow: "whatever" inevitably happens before either of them can find the time or the means to understand it, much less control it.

As Junior tries to decide how to explain to his jailbird father that he wants to end their relationship, he meets William, an ironically philosophical bum. William, one of Walker's finest stage creatures, not only recognizes the pervasive fear of destiny "as a concept of the mind and soul" but announces that he is "the inventor of the modern connotation." Junior adopts him as an improbable confidant and tutor and, together with Gail and her entrepreneurial girlfriend Sandy Miles, they try to sort things out. Each event deepens the complications until they find themselves plummeting into the great abyss with William's words echoing behind: "Pretend you're a feather. Think about it. Try to float down. Gently."

Criminals in Love is a play Walker says he has been avoiding for some time. Blending B-movie scenarios with an environment that resembles his own east-end Toronto, it speaks with an authenticity that renders even the zaniest improbabilities and clichés acutely real. Extravagant characters and exaggerated situations are made possible by an inexorable logic that refuses to compromise with the desires of the audience for the diversion of last-minute resolutions or facile moralizing. Instead, we are led through a plot of turns and twists to the same nightmarish experience endured by the characters. As we try to make sense of a process that constantly eludes us, we want to believe that things will work out for these people because we have come to care for them. Our desires are as impotent as theirs. In the end, love conquers nothing; but, and it is here that Walker's tentative optimism shows through, love refuses to be conquered.

In 1980, Walker was considered one of Canada's "most abstruse and esoteric playwrights." Today he is also one of Canada's most popular playwrights. As his popularity increases, his plays grow more complex, demanding, and troubling. What separates ***Criminals in Love*** from the despair it explores is its humour, integrity, and its commitment to say things that need to be said. The need to articulate intimates new and possible futures, or, at least, the possibility of a future, that, once thought and spoken, can become possible for the audience. And it is Walker's absolute respect for his audience and his actors that make his plays so demanding. No easy answers or else no future. (pp. 144-145)

Paul Walsh, in a review of "Criminals in Love," in Canadian Theatre Review, *No. 45, Winter, 1985, pp. 144-45.*

JAMES HARRISON

To categorize Walker's work is impossible. His ability to make biting comments on personal and social issues—at which he is without match in English Canadian Theatre—keeps us continually guessing; it is a major reason for his success, though not necessarily a talent that works in his favour. His productions and plays have the tendency to totter between acute perceptions of man's struggle with will and fate, and a satire of those very perceptions. Too often his sharp, satirical wit is allowed to work against the substance of his material. The ornamentation outshines the wearer. The result is a juvenile self-awareness that defeats the work's potential to challenge an audience with real issues, with moments of undeflected emotion. . . .

[*Criminals in Love*] has a number of strong ideas and potentially moving emotional conflicts; the loyalty of a son to a father—in life a tie that is often impossible to break; the parody of an intellectual sixties radical clinging to sophomoric ideals of revolution; the wonderful, quizzical way that the love of the young can inspire the old; and most evident and interesting, the unresolvable confrontation of fate or destiny with will and intelligence. (p. 11)

It is a truism to say that a character must choose a course of action if he is to remain interesting to an audience, but in this case it bears repeating. What good drama does is place a character in either a situation where a choice exists and the character chooses to act upon it—Macbeth, Oedipus—or where the character is aware of the choice but chooses not to act until finally circumstances force him or her to act in order to preserve their

Cover of Criminals in Love, *by George F. Walker. Playwrights Canada, 1985. Cover photo by Tony Bock/*The Toronto Star. *Cover design by Lisa Dimson. Courtesy of Playwrights Canada.*

life or self-image—Hamlet, Hedda Gabler. Junior follows the second course, but Walker . . . delays his realization that he must act for so long by having him repeat over and over again his pledge of loyalty to his father that when the decision to make a firm stand occurs it has little impact. . . . This is Junior's story, but we are left in the end with the feeling that nothing in his perception of the situation or himself has been clarified or changed.

At the climax of the play, when his love for Gail comes into direct conflict with his loyalty to his father, Junior chooses to not desert his father. While the others decide to escape to Barbados, he chooses to stay and face up to his confrontation with destiny simply because, "it doesn't feel right" to leave. He makes the choice that hopefully most of us would have the conviction to make in the same circumstance; he rejects the societal standard of morality and holds on to something more real, more essential—his own sense of what is right.

But then, in one final condescending slash, Walker strips Junior of his last shred of individuality—his determination to stay—by having him agree to go with the others simply on the basis of Gail's plea to "do it for me." For the moment love defeats destiny. In the end destiny will have its way—Gail and Junior are prison bound; but to achieve the victory Walker has had to betray the individuality of his characters, an unpardonable sin in a play that contains such subtle issues and raises such important questions. If his intention was to present cartoon-like characters then he should have stuck to broader concerns; the cartoon form of presentation can't support the weight of the ideas and situations his script presents us with. As it is, the victory of destiny over love is hollow; the vital concerns and the potential repercussions of unanswered questions are deflated; and the audience suffers. By the end Walker has had Gail and Junior reject so many opportunities to either accept their dilemma or to search out a solution that we feel they fully deserve the black ace destiny has dealt them.

That *Criminals in Love* has been such a tremendous commercial success is . . . cause for rejoicing. (pp. 12-13)

George Walker deserves the recognition. His sharp perceptions, his knowledge of dramatic structuring, and his willingness to tackle intelligent themes indicate his voice will continue to be an exciting one in Canadian theatre. But because it is an artistic voice to be seriously listened to, a voice that will influence the direction theatre takes in this country, it is imperative that that voice matures, that it leaves behind the infantile squallings and adolescent rantings that carried it through its formative years, and that it speak with the emotional honesty that a mature dramaturgy and an intelligent audience demand and deserve. (p. 13)

James Harrison, "Reporting a Criminal Act," in Theatrum, *April, 1985, pp. 11-14.*

An Excerpt from *Criminals in Love*

GAIL:	What's wrong, Junior. What are you trying to avoid telling me.
JUNIOR:	Nothing.
GAIL:	Why aren't you looking at me. You haven't looked at me since you got here.
WILLIAM:	It's a sad story.
GAIL:	What is.

WILLIAM: I weep. Look, a tear on my cheek. I have been reached personally and sincerely by this tragedy.

GAIL: What tragedy.

WILLIAM: He'll tell you. In his time.

GAIL: Junior, is it a tragedy, is it a sad story. What the hell is it.

JUNIOR: Tragic? No. Not sad, either. Stupid. Nothing really. Just stupid. Dumb bad luck. My head hurts. (lays his head on GAIL's shoulder)

WILLIAM: A little comfort. There, there. Shush. Sleep. Dream.

GAIL: Please be quiet. (to JUNIOR) Tell me, honey.

JUNIOR: Tell her, William.

GAIL: How can he tell me. What's he got to do with it.

JUNIOR: He's good with words. Really. He'll tell it good. You'll probably enjoy the telling even if the story itself depresses you.

(Pause)

WILLIAM: I have your permission?

GAIL: Go ahead, William.

WILLIAM: First a summary. It has been a bad day for your loved one, my friend here. His father refused to end their relationship. Then beat him up. Later in the afternoon he got fired from his job.

GAIL: Oh Jesus.

WILLIAM: But that's not the worst. This is the worst. He has been coerced into an involvement in criminal activity.

GAIL: Oh no. Oh Jesus. (petting JUNIOR's head)

WILLIAM: That was the summary. Let me rinse my mouth and give you the poetic details. (picks up what's left of SANDY's Coke)

GAIL: Jesus. Shit.

JUNIOR: (to WILLIAM) Excuse me. (lays his head in GAIL's lap)

(WILLIAM wipes away a tear. Touches JUNIOR's arm affectionately; then GAIL's. GAIL looks up toward the ceiling)

WILLIAM: I speak now from the heart of experience. I use words like destiny and fate and despair. I talk of the great abyss which beckons us all. I speak of the great under-class of our society, the doomed, the forgotten, the outcasts. I describe the fine line which separates the lands of function and dis-function. I put it in terms which cover the spectrum. The political. The philosophical. The poetic. Occasionally I use the vernacular. I talk of the great fuck-up. Of getting shafted, getting screwed up the ass. Without even a kiss. I describe the human condition. I tell you Junior's story. Your story. And if I may be so bold, our story . . . Because aren't we all in this together. Aren't we all friends here. Can't you feel the bond. Isn't this the absolute truth!

(And WILLIAM continues . . . gesticulating, wiping away tears. Fadeout.)

RICHARD PLANT

George F. Walker's ***Criminals in Love*** appears on the surface to paint a realistic picture of life among the working-class urban poor. They include an old wino, a pair of teenage lovers—Gail, unemployed; Junior, a low-paid labourer—and a third teenager who is trying her talent at prostitution. Matters are bad. Junior's filial responsibility draws them all into crime when his Aunt Wineva threatens to kill Junior's imprisoned father unless they join hers and Uncle Ritchie's scheme. But the audience responding at this level sees a happy ending when, despite the certainty they are about to be captured by the police, Junior and Gail climb into bed to celebrate their love. This audience feels sure that the truth about Wineva and Uncle Ritchie will out, and that the court will be lenient with the teenagers and old wino. Sounds like a B-movie, eh?

And in fact it is. But in characteristic fashion, Walker sends up this representation of reality. The old wino, a brilliant creation, offers Walkersque epigrams with a B-movie's pseudo-philosophical pithiness. The teenage prostitute explains she is only trying the game out in case someday she is forced into it by financial emergency. Uncle Ritchie's great plan (Wineva claims he reads five words an hour) to rob the Salvation Army is laughable in its incongruity. And Wineva is shown to be able to quell all opposition by a vigorous, powerful kiss. Even when we find her growing more bizarre as the play rolls along, we don't have to take her seriously. Her strident claims of heading a revolution to overthrow the world ("When I call the army, it comes") are hilarious delusions. The result is a scintillating parody as only Walker can write one.

But another point of view is available to his audience. At this level we see the dark side of deeper comic truth. As Walker says, "It's a play about two kids in love who have a dilemma, which becomes a crime, then a revolution." But thoughtful comedy invokes an underlying seriousness. What happens to the kids—and we must note that Junior gets his face smashed in by his father and later is shot in the leg—is damaging and beyond their control. This parody presents a disturbing picture of what is humorously referred to in the play as the line between legacy and destiny: "If you put all the things of life along a ruler . . . legacy is at one end and destiny is at the other."

A laughable truism from weak-minded Junior? Yes, but it's also a statement of how the choices in these people's lives are determined by the nature of their environment—which then casts them into action that snowballs further out of their control. It's a typical structure for farce, but only in the darkest of farces does anyone get hurt. On that level, this play is dark and thoughtful.

As the play opens, Junior has his head under Gail's sweater. We laugh at her admonishment: "God, Junior, it's time to move on . . . try some other part of my body. Sex does not begin and end at my chest." When the play ends with her holding out her sweater and Junior putting his head back in, we laugh again—but with the knowledge that Junior has not "moved on." Nor has she. They can't. (p. 17)

Richard Plant, "The Plots Thicken," in Books in Canada, *Vol. 15, No. 3, April, 1986, pp. 16-18.*

JOHN H. ASTINGTON

Criminals in Love is a decided advance in George Walker's career as a dramatist. Too often Walker seems to have been rewriting the same play, but in [***Criminals in Love***] he has found new areas to explore, largely by concentrating on a situation which is not merely an occasion for parody. The play is recognizably related to Walker's previous writing, but the emphasis in ***Criminals in Love*** is placed more on failure and less on extravagant attitudinizing. The play has one bizarre extremist, a demented, charismatic, female revolutionary, and that familiar Walker type, the philosopher bum. Derelict, flotsam of some obscure European turmoil, William still strives, in his lucid intervals, for mental structures to which experience might be made to answer:

> It's a process. It takes time. We begin in the abstract. Eventually we move on. Settling finally in the area of logic. A problem exists. A solution also. It is necessary to the laws of the universe.

The rhythm of short sentences, each of which stands on its own, and may or may not be part of a more complex progress, is a typical trick of Walker's style. The empty profundities are going nowhere: they are merely gestures, no better and no worse than the grunts or profanities that William utters when plagued by his unpredictable guts. From his earliest plays Walker has been conducting a light-hearted critique of language in the style of Stoppard, but in Gail and Junior, the loving criminals of the title, we are given characters to whom life is more than a series of gambits, and at whom we laugh in a rather different way. Gail emerges as the most genuinely intelligent figure in the play, but her instincts are not enough to save her from the web of insane consequences that entraps her boyfriend: her devotion to him pulls her down too. Junior is socially and genetically deprived. Born on the wrong side of the tracks, he is the son of a repeat offender who is so incompetent that he has never escaped more than fifty yards from the scene of a crime, and who attempts to cash bad cheques at the wrong bank. Junior is scornful of such futility, but is plagued by his sense of duty, which also keeps him uncomplainingly in a boring job. The moral dilemma represented by his father is only the start of Junior's problems: his even more unsavoury uncle involves him as an accomplice in various shady projects, at the expense of his peace of mind and health of body. In the face of complexity, Junior retreats to the simple certainties of sensual bliss. As William consoles himself with the bottle, so does Junior with sex, of a kind. The play begins with the everyday picture of two adolescents making love in a schoolyard. Junior's head is out of sight under Gail's sweater, an attention which is beginning to worry her a little:

> GAIL It's not that it's not . . . you know nice. Well, sometimes it's boring. But mostly, Junior it's well . . . Were you breast fed.
>
> JUNIOR (pulls head out) I have no problem about breasts. I've never had a breast thing in my life. I just like yours . . . that's all I can say really. And I love being under your sweater. Try to understand.

William invests their love with symbolic status, as a sign of the potential happiness of mankind, but to Wineva, the millenarian radical, love is merely a step to raw power: 'The point is you don't really care if anyone gets hurt, not really. You just can't live with the responsibility. So pass it to me. Come on pass it. Because I've solved the problem.' Neither good nor evil angel wins the battle for Junior's soul, but the play ends as it begins, with Gail and Junior entwined. She smilingly invites him under her sweater, convinced that his retreat from the world, and from words, is fundamentally sane. (pp. 65-6)

John H. Astington, in a review of "Criminals in Love," in University of Toronto Quarterly, *Vol. 56, No. 1, Fall, 1986, pp. 65-6.*

L(aurali) R. Wright

The Suspect

Edgar Allan Poe Award: Best Novel

Canadian novelist and journalist.

The Suspect (1985), Wright's first mystery novel, earned Wright the distinction of being the first Canadian to win an Edgar in the best novel category. Wright, who lives in British Columbia, was a reporter, editor, and columnist for the Calgary *Herald* before retiring in 1976 to write fiction full time. Critics familiar with her first three novels, *Neighbours* (1979), *The Favorite* (1982), and *Among Friends* (1984), observe that *The Suspect* shares their wit, elegant craftsmanship, and concern for psychological and sensual detail.

About *The Suspect,* Wright confesses, "I didn't know I was writing a mystery until I inadvertently let a policeman into the story and became very fond of him." Her detective, Karl Alberg of the Royal Canadian Mounted Police, investigates a case of murder among senior citizens in a quiet British Columbia seaside community. Reviewers compliment Wright for her picturesque settings. They also praise her intriguing and likeable portrayals of Alberg, his attractive librarian friend Cassandra Mitchell, and the eighty-year-old homicide suspect George Wilcox, whom critic John North avers "may be the most personable and sympathetic murderer ever encountered on the Canadian fiction scene."

Wright brought back Karl and Cassandra in a second murder mystery, *Sleep While I Sing* (1986). In both *The Suspect* and *Sleep While I Sing* Wright avoids dramatic tension about who the murderer is and focuses instead on the mystery of why. This method, critics note, highlights Wright's ability to sustain interest by her insight into people and her skill in creating atmosphere. Commenting on the transition from mainstream novels to detective fiction, Wright observed that writing the two mysteries was easier for her than was her previous fiction. "Writing *The Suspect* was fun," she stated, "and I learned that planning—working out the plot line in advance—doesn't kill the creative spark. A character can grow within a plot plan instead of being left unfettered. That was a real joy to discover." Wright intends to publish a third Alberg-Mitchell novel.

Ross Cameron/Quill and Quire

PUBLISHERS WEEKLY

The Canadian author [L. R. Wright] invests her new story [***The Suspect***] with the qualities that distinguished ***The Favorite*** and other novels that won her critical praise. The tight, beautifully written account of people in trouble begins when George Wilcox stops by the home of Carlyle Burke and, on impulse, bashes his host fatally on the head. Both men, supposedly friends, are retired widowers living out their 80s in a small Canadian coast town. George reports finding Carlyle's body to Karl Alberg, the local Mountie whose investigation into the background of both octogenarians arouses his suspicion of the killer. Karl's attempts to trap George anger Cassandra Mitchell, George's good friend and the policeman's love interest. Their romance is another casualty of a tragedy that ends with a poignant, unguessable development. Wright adds intriguing dimensions to each chapter with revelations about an appealing murderer and his mean victim. There is also the tang of humor arising naturally out of the mixed-up incidents, in a book that succeeds as both a straight novel and a mystery. (pp. 89-90)

A review of "The Suspect," in Publishers Weekly, *Vol. 227, No. 15, April 12, 1985, pp. 89-90.*

KIRKUS REVIEWS

Canadian novelist Wright, whose ***Among Friends*** (1984) chronicled the itchy, toe-stubbing love-and-work briar patch of a Canadian sisterhood of single women, begins this village tale [***The Suspect***], set on the "Sunshine Coast" of British Columbia, with a quite startling murder—one with comic overtones. Former history teacher and widower George Wilcox, 80, has just fatally bashed in the handsome head of ex-music teacher and widower Carlyle Burke, 85. The weapon—one of a pair of foot-high shell casings—had been snatched for the unpremeditated konk from Carlyle's shelves, as Carlyle rocked away in the radiant sunshine, saying things George did *not* want to hear. In a post-mortem moment George does think about being jailed for the tiny rest of his life, but he doesn't really want "the hustle and bustle of being arrested." He'll evade the Law as best he can. It isn't until he's snug in his own cottage that George remembers Carlyle's "goddamn parrot." Would it starve until one day someone might discover Carlyle? So back goes George to Carlyle's house and phones the local branch of the RCMP to announce he's found Carlyle dead.

In charge of the village's liveliest homicide in years is Staff Sergeant Karl Alberg, 44, divorced, and the latest respondent to an ad in a Personal column inviting friendly dating, an ad composed by Cassandra Mitchell, 41, a single librarian in this very same village. While Karl sleuthes, and interviews the irascible Discoverer of the Body, Cassandra is on the way to becoming a sounding board for both Karl and George. Testimony trickles in, clues multiply, and Karl thoughtfully observes old George boating out to give two shell casings a sea burial. Meanwhile, Cassandra's affection (and Karl's growing liking) for George clash with Karl's bloodhound procedures. At the close George spills all about a guilt-ridden and bloody past.

Wright is at her best in exploiting a convivial village ambiance, briny scenery, police in-office waggery, but finally the novel lags into sentiment and contrivance, losing its bright and funny pace. Still, generally entertaining.

A review of "The Suspect," in Kirkus Reviews, *Vol. LIII, No. 8, April 15, 1985, p. 351.*

PETER L. ROBERTSON

Wright's atmospheric novel [***The Suspect***] combines the carefully detailed ambience of a sleepy town with the creation of three fully developed, sad yet lovable characters. Remarkably, we find ourselves in complete sympathy with the old man, despite his being a murderer. Thus, the novel's somber conclusion—the death of the old man—is genuinely tragic and touching.

Peter L. Robertson, in a review of "The Suspect," in Booklist, *Vol. 81, No. 17, May 1, 1985, p. 1240.*

CAMPBELL GEESLIN

The setting for this top-notch crime novel [***The Suspect***] is a small town in Canada. The mystery is not who commits the violent murder; that's vividly revealed in the first horrifying scene. The suspense comes from the reader's need to know why a nice old man would kill his neighbor, and whether the Royal Canadian Mounted Police staff sergeant will figure out what happened and why. Garden lovers will enjoy especially the important role that flowers, plants and the weather play in this story, and the town of Sechelt is wonderfully alive and convincing. . . . ***The Suspect,*** with its solid, admirable characters and careful psychological underpinnings, is every bit as good as the novels of British writers Ruth Rendell and P. D. James. In an original, moving ending, the guilt-ridden killer reaches a surprising conclusion about his life, and the reader comes away with far more than is usually offered in this kind of novel. (pp. 16-17)

Campbell Geeslin, in a review of "The Suspect," in People Weekly, *Vol. 23, No. 15, October 7, 1985, pp. 16-17.*

JOHN NORTH

George Wilcox, a frail, 80-year-old widower living out his life at sleepy Sechelt on the B.C. Sunshine Coast, may be the most personable and sympathetic murderer ever encountered on the Canadian fiction scene. To his intense surprise, the gentle pensioner, who devotes his dwindling energies to two precious projects—volunteer work at the local hospital and the care of his beloved garden—finds himself capable of murder when he kills an even older man with a brass shell casing. Shocked, and unready for the excitement of his arrest, he automatically cleans up the scene of the crime and goes home to restore his equilibrium. Later, when it occurs to him that he may get away with it, he "discovers" the body and decides to let the police catch him if they can. . . .

Wright's ability as a story-teller is outstanding: she has created realistic and likeable characters and has sustained a sense of tension and immediacy while working out a well-balanced plot. ***The Suspect*** is a must read for anyone who likes crime novels or elegantly crafted fiction.

John North, in a review of "The Suspect," in Quill and Quire, *Vol. 51, No. 11, November, 1985, p. 23.*

JANET WINDELER

[***The Suspect***] is Wright's first work of fiction in the mystery-thriller vein, but as in her previous novels the focus is on psychology rather than plot. Set in a small town on the Sunshine Coast of British Columbia, the story opens in the sun-drenched living room of 85-year-old Carlyle Burke, seconds after he has been brutally murdered by George Wilcox, another octogenarian, who appears to have been Carlyle's friend.

A cantankerous yet likable old man who spends his days working in his garden, George soon realizes that he is going to "survive this astonishing thing." and despite a profound and burdening sense of guilt, he refuses to confess to the crime. Determined to corner George into a confession is the local policeman, Staff Sergeant Alberg, a smart, sensitive, world-weary sort who is puzzled, as we are, by the motive behind the killing. Cassandra Mitchell is the town librarian: she is wise and full of heart, and finds her loyalties torn between the two men—her old friend, George, and her new romantic interest, Alberg. As Wright unravels the secrets of the suspect's past, she constructs a complex and absorbing emotional field around these people, and her skill is such that they emerge three-dimensional and entirely convincing.

The dialogue flows naturally, the plot is neatly contrived, and if Wright edges dangerously close to sentimentality on one or two occasions, the book still ought to be read for the compelling treatment of its characters and its quiet acceptance of the world.

Janet Windeler, in a review of "The Suspect," in Books in Canada, *Vol. 14, No. 9, December, 1985, p. 24.*

Obituaries

Necrology

Milton Acorn .... August 20, 1986
Harriette Arnow......................... March 22, 1986
Simone de Beauvoir..................... April 14, 1986
Jorge Luis Borges .... June 14, 1986
John Braine .... October 28, 1986
John Ciardi............................ March 30, 1986
Arthur A. Cohen .... October 31, 1986
Mircea Eliade .... March 22, 1986
Jean Genet .... April 15, 1986
W.S. Graham .... January 9, 1986
Frank Herbert .... February 11, 1986
Laura Z. Hobson .... February 28, 1986
Julius Horwitz .... May 18, 1986
Christopher Isherwood .... January 4, 1986
John MacDonald.................... December 28, 1986
Bernard Malamud .... March 18, 1986
Juan Rulfo .... January 7, 1986
Helen Hooven Santmyer.............. February 21, 1986
Noel Streatfeild .... September 11, 1986

Simone (Lucie Ernestine Marie Bertrand) de Beauvoir

January 9, 1908 - April 14, 1986

French philosopher, novelist, autobiographer, nonfiction writer, essayist, short story writer, editor, and dramatist.

(See also *CLC*, Vols. 1, 2, 4, 8, 14, 31 and *Contemporary Authors*, Vols. 9-12, rev. ed., Vol. 118 [obituary].)

PRINCIPAL WORKS

L'invitée (novel) 1943
[*She Came to Stay*, 1954]
Pyrrhus et Cinéas (philosophy) 1944
Les bouches inutiles (drama) 1945
[*Who Shall Die?* 1983]
Le sang des autres (novel) 1946
[*The Blood of Others*, 1948]
Tous les hommes sont mortels (novel) 1946
[*All Men Are Mortal*, 1955]
Pour une morale de l'ambiguité (philosophy) 1947
[*The Ethics of Ambiguity*, 1948]
L'Amérique au jour le jour (nonfiction) 1948
[*America Day by Day*, 1952]
L'existentialisme et la sagesse des nations (philosophy) 1948
**Le deuxième sexe* (nonfiction) 1949
[*The Second Sex*, 1952]
Les mandarins (novel) 1954
[*The Mandarins*, 1956]
Fait-il bruler Sade? (criticism) 1955
[*Must We Burn Sade?* 1963]
La longue marche: Essai sur la Chine (nonfiction) 1957
[*The Long March*, 1958]
Mémoires d'une jeune fille rangée (autobiography) 1958
[*Memoirs of a Dutiful Daughter*, 1959]
La force de l'âge (autobiography) 1960
[*The Prime of Life*, 1962]
La force des choses (autobiography) 1963
[*Force of Circumstance*, 1965]
Une mort très douce (reminiscences) 1964
[*A Very Easy Death*, 1966]
Les belles images (novel) 1966
L'âge de discrétion (novel) 1967
La femme rompue (novellas) 1967
[*The Woman Destroyed*, 1969]
La vieillesse (nonfiction) 1970
[*The Coming of Age*, 1972; also published as *Old Age*, 1972]
Tout compte fait (autobiography) 1972
[*All Said and Done*, 1974; also published as *All Accounting Made*, 1972]
Quand prime le spirituel (short stories) 1979
[*When Things of the Spirit Come First: Five Early Tales*, 1982]

© Jerry Bauer

La céremonie des adieux: Suivi de entretiens avec Jean-Paul Sartre (reminiscences) 1981
[*Adieux: A Farewell to Sartre*, 1984]

*This work was published in two volumes under the same title. Vol. 1 was translated and published in England as *A History of Sex* in 1961 and *Nature of the Second Sex* in 1963.

STANLEY MEISLER

Simone de Beauvoir, the renowned French writer who regarded herself more as a Marxist than a feminist when she wrote what became a primer of women's liberation, ***The Second Sex,*** more than 35 years ago, died [April 14] at a Paris hospital. She was 78.

No cause of death was given by Cochin Hospital, but De Beauvoir reportedly had been suffering from circulation problems.

De Beauvoir, who fashioned an impressive literary career as a novelist, philosopher, essayist and writer of memoirs, was a companion of Jean-Paul Sartre, the late French philosopher, playwright and novelist, for more than a half-century.

She and Sartre set the literary and political style for young French intellectuals in France after World War II. Although the two never married, always lived in separate apartments or hotel rooms and often experimented with other love affairs, they tried to see each other daily from the time they met at the Sorbonne in 1929 until Sartre died in 1980.

"His death does separate us. My death will not bring us together again. That is how things are," wrote De Beauvoir, an atheist all her adult life, in a memoir about Sartre's last days.

Although Sartre, who refused to accept the Nobel Prize in Literature in 1964, may have been better known than his companion in the world's literary and intellectual circles, De Beauvoir may have had more readers with ***The Second Sex.*** The work, hailed as a landmark examination of the position of women in a male-dominated world, sold more than 1 million copies in paperback in the United States alone.

Nor did De Beauvoir lack recognition. Her novel ***The Mandarins***—a tale of a French writer and her relationship with a male American counterpart—won the Prix Goncourt, France's most coveted literary award, in 1954.

Although ***The Second Sex*** was often regarded as an inspiration to women's liberation movements, De Beauvoir did not join the French feminist movement until 20 years after her book was published in 1949.

"I said I wasn't a feminist," she recalled later, "because I thought that the solution to women's problems must depend on the socialist evolution of society."

But she changed her mind two decades later.

"I realized that in the past 20 years, the position of women in France had not really changed and that socialism, as it has evolved—for example, in Russia—hasn't changed women's position, either," she said.

Her death brought a flurry of reaction from feminists around the world.

Typical was that of Gloria Steinem, who said in a statement:

"It's hard to believe that somehow there's a world without her. More than any other single human being, she's responsible for the current international women's movement. Her life was as pioneering as her work. Internationally and personally, she gave women the courage to strive for freedom in work and life."

French Culture Minister Francois Leotard said of De Beauvoir: "Detesting accepted ideas and conformity, she put everything into her work, into her ideas—a struggle she led with her companion Jean-Paul Sartre."

To liberate themselves, De Beauvoir urged women to have a profession and, if possible, to refuse marriage. She looked on marriage as an obscene, bourgeois institution that put women in an inferior position.

"After all," she said, "I could have married Sartre. But I believe that we were wise not to have done so."

With Sartre, De Beauvoir said, the problem of male oppression never came up. "Sartre is in no way an oppressor," she said. "If I had loved someone other than Sartre, I still would not have allowed myself to be oppressed."

For De Beauvoir, a refusal to marry meant a refusal to have children as well.

"I've escaped most of women's bondages: maternity, the life of a housewife," she once said. But the lack of children provoked criticism of her as an intellectual philosopher who did not completely understand the role of women.

In the postwar years, Sartre regarded himself as an activist in leftist causes, and De Beauvoir was usually at his side, often risking arrest, in anti-government demonstrations put down by the police.

Born in Paris on Jan. 9, 1908, Simone Lucie Ernestine Marie Bertrand de Beauvoir was the eldest daughter of a middle-class lawyer who prided himself on his atheism. Her mother, however, was a devout Roman Catholic who insisted that her two daughters receive a convent education.

"This conflict between them," De Beauvoir said, "was a good thing for me, because it meant that I couldn't fasten on to either of them and had to decide for myself."

But she soon chose her father's way and lost her Catholic faith at the age of 15. She studied philosophy at the Sorbonne and met Sartre and another friend, Andre Herbaud, there. Herbaud gave her the nickname Castor, the French word for beaver.

"You are a beaver," Herbaud said. "Beavers like company, and they have a constructive bent." That was the nickname by which Sartre knew her all the rest of his life.

In 1929, she was named a professor of philosophy at a college in Marseilles. She later taught in Rouen and Paris before turning to literature. She wrote her first novel in 1943. By the time ***The Second Sex*** was published six years later, she had written two novels, a play, and two books of essays.

De Beauvoir said she wrote ***The Second Sex*** because she wanted to write about herself and knew she could not until she discovered first what it was like to be a woman.

After her best-selling success, she continued to write novels, a study of aging, and four volumes of autobiography, including her last work—***Adieux. A Farewell to Sartre***—published in 1981.

Her works even included a highly detailed, 200,000-word description of ***The Long March*** by Mao Tse-tung.

In 1979 her life became the subject of a widely praised film documentary.

Sartre and De Beauvoir presided over a youth and intellectual movement in the 1950s and 1960s that rooted itself in the old St. Germain des Pres district on the Left Bank in Paris. Followers called it the "existentialist movement" and insisted it was patterned after the philosophy of Sartre.

Stanley Meisler, "De Beauvoir, Writer and Feminist, Dies," in Los Angeles Times, *April 15, 1986.*

THE NEW YORK TIMES

Simone de Beauvoir, the author whose work included ***The Second Sex,*** a provocative and influential polemic on the status of women, died [April 14] at Cochin Hospital in Paris. . . .

The cause of death was not immediately disclosed, but Claude Lanzmann, the director of the film *Shoah* and a longtime friend, said she had been in poor health since undergoing an operation in March.

Miss de Beauvoir, who was for many years a central figure in left-wing French intellectual circles, also wrote novels, a play and nonfiction ranging from political commentary to autobiography.

Her death came the day before the sixth anniversary of the death of her longtime companion, the French existentialist philosopher and critic Jean-Paul Sartre, on April 15, 1980.

''Simone de Beauvoir's death stresses the end of an era,'' Prime Minister Jacques Chirac said yesterday. ''Her committed literature was representative of certain movements of ideas that, at one time, had an impact on our society. Her unquestionable talent made her a writer who deserves her place in French literature. In the name of the Government, I salute her memory in respect.''

Gloria Steinem said yesterday that ''if any single human being can be credited with inspiring the current international woman's movement, it's Simone de Beauvoir.'' Betty Friedan yesterday called Miss de Beauvoir an ''authentic heroine in the history of womanhood.''

Over the years, ***The Second Sex*** remained the book for which Miss de Beauvoir was known worldwide, and which made her an important theorist of militant, radical feminism and a heroine of the women's movement. The book, published in France in 1949 and in the United States in 1953, was her own favorite. It was translated into more than a dozen languages, was honored and excoriated, and sold more than a million copies in a paperback edition in the United States alone. The 1953 Knopf hardcover edition and a paperback edition published in 1974 by Vintage are still in print.

Its basic premise—from which it took off for more than 700 pages of compelling, exasperating indictment—was best summed up in two sentences:

''One is not born, but rather becomes, a woman. No biological, psychological or economic fate determines the figure that the human female presents in society; it is civilization as a whole that produces this creature, intermediate between male and eunuch, which is described as feminine.''

Throughout her life Miss de Beauvoir was active in causes that advanced or supported her beliefs—from a 1960's international ''tribunal'' condemning the United States role in Vietnam to the signing of a manifesto with 340 other women in 1971 admitting to having had an abortion in defiance of existing French law.

Her disillusionment with Marxism in practice was recurrent—regime after regime, from the Soviet Union through Algeria to Cuba, disappointed her hopes. But she long advocated what she thought of as the concept of authentic international revolution, and the civil rights even of those with whom she disagreed.

Although she proclaimed at 19 that ''I don't want my life to obey any other will but my own,'' she in fact spent much of her life—from 1929, when she and Sartre met as students at the Sorbonne, until his death in 1980—as the closest companion of Sartre. They lived not in the same apartment but always near each other, saw each other daily, spent their annual six-week vacation in Rome together, were completely open about their liaison.

''We have,'' she said once, ''pioneered our own relationship—its freedom, intimacy and frankness.'' She added, with characteristic candor: ''We had also, rather less successfully, thought up the idea of the 'trio.''' She wrote that she turned down Sartre's offer of marriage because she knew he did not want it, but that their relationship was central to both their lives, and ''essential love,'' in Sartre's phrase. They made allowance, at least in theory, for ''contingent'' relationships of less importance.

As she conceded, this was not always a success, but the relationship with Sartre was always the one that mattered: ''I knew that no harm could ever come to me from him—unless he were to die before I did,'' she said once, and at another time commented that ''Since I was 21''—when she met Sartre—''I have never been lonely.''

Although her major theoretical contributions were to feminism, Miss de Beauvoir's writings, both novels and nonfiction, were also regarded as brilliant expositions of basic existential belief: that is, that man is responsible for his own destiny. ''Men may make of their own history a hopeless inferno, a junkyard of events, an enduring value,'' she wrote in 1947, a sentence that itself could be a definition of existentialism.

Sartre encouraged her literary ambitions and was credited by her with pushing her into the investigation of women's oppression that led to the rage and accusation of [***Le deuxième sexe***]. The book caused a storm of outrage in France and an equal furor in the United States. Philip Wylie called it ''one of the few great books of our era.'' Dr. Karl A. Menninger described it as a ''scholarly and at the same time pretentious and inflated tract on feminism.''

In 1954, Miss de Beauvoir's novel ***Les Mandarins (The Mandarins)*** won the Prix Goncourt and stirred scandalized delight with what were regarded as thinly disguised portraits of Sartre, Albert Camus and other leading French intellectuals. The author never admitted that it was a roman à clef, but did concede that the novel included an account of her affair with Nelson Algren, the American writer to whom she dedicated the book. It appeared in the United States in 1956.

Her first novel, ***L'Invitée***, published in France in 1943 and in the United States as ***She Came to Stay*** in 1954, concerned itself with a ''trio,'' with the triangular relationship among a man and a woman long attached and a second, younger woman. Miss de Beauvoir, although criticized for long-windedness, said that she felt she had been influenced by Hemingway, and that she admired the writing of Kafka, Proust and Joyce. She was a slow, meticulous, daily writer.

Her other novels included ***The Blood of Others*** (1948), ***All Men Are Mortal*** (1955), ***Les belles images*** (1967) and ***The Woman Destroyed*** (1968). She also wrote four volumes of autobiography—***Memoirs of a Dutiful Daughter*** (1958), ***Force of Circumstance*** (1963), ***The Coming of Age*** (1972) and ***All Said and Done*** (1974)—and a play, ***The Useless Mouths*** (1954).

A tour of China led to ***The Long March*** in 1958, just as a tour of the United States had produced—or provoked—***America Day by Day*** in 1953. Her attitude toward the United States did not mellow with age and she wrote in the early 70's: ''The moment a nationalist or a popular movement seems to threaten its interests, the United States crushes it.'' She went on to say that friends predicted the imminent collapse of the country, adding: ''Perhaps this collapse may set off a revolution on a worldwide scale? I do not know whether I shall live long enough to see it, but it is a comforting outlook."

With Sartre, she also engaged in acts of political protest. In 1970, for example, they were arrested for selling a banned Maoist newspaper—which they were doing to protest the ban, not in support of the paper's positions. In 1960, they were both banned from appearing on France's state-controlled radio or television because they had signed a manifesto supporting the right to refuse military service in Algeria, which was fighting for its independence from France at the time. Only a few years later, in 1967, they were put on a list of boycotted authors by a semi-official Algerian newspaper because of their support for Israel.

Throughout her life, Miss de Beauvoir continued her political activism, speaking out on issues, heading committees, making speeches, signing manifestos. The condition of women was perhaps her primary "cause," followed some years later by a similar outrage at the conditions of old age. These she wrote about in ***The Coming of Age*** in 1972, arguing that, for once, women had the advantage: "Old age is better for women than for men," she told an interviewer in 1974. "First of all, they have less far to fall, since their lives are more mediocre than those of most men. And then they still have their homes, their housework, cooking, their children, all the 'feminine' culture."

The problems of women in France early in this century figured in a collection of five early stories by Miss de Beauvoir that was published in the United States in 1982 under the title ***When Things of the Spirit Come First.***

Earlier, Miss de Beauvoir had written about death, specifically that of her mother, in the ironically titled ***A Very Easy Death*** (1966). Although she had never been close to her mother, the book was unusually free in its expression of emotion. Her mother had been a devout woman; her father a skeptic and unbeliever. Later, Simone Lucie Ernestine Marie Bertrand de Beauvoir, born in Paris on Jan. 9, 1908, was to say that this "disequilibrium, which condemned me to a perpetual soul-searching, largely explains why I became an intellectual." . . .

Miss de Beauvoir was somewhat humorless, uncompromising and passionate in her convictions. She remained convinced that, as she wrote in ***The Second Sex,*** a "totally new society" would be needed, but became increasingly convinced that meaningful change in the status of women would not necessarily evolve from change in the forms of government.

"I think that for the proletariat or a government representing it, to own the means of production is not enough to change the relationship between people," she said in the mid-70's. "That's what is really important, to change relationships between people."

At about the same time, Miss de Beauvoir acknowledged that "There hasn't been the change I'd hoped for" in women's condition. In 1976, some 25 years after ***The Second Sex*** she told an interviewer that she was uncertain about the coming of the hoped-for revolution.

"But the changes that women are struggling for," she said, "yes, that I am certain of, in the long run women will win." (p. B9)

"Simone de Beauvoir, Author and Intellectual, Dies in Paris at 78," in The New York Times, *April 15, 1986, p. B9.*

***THE TIMES,* LONDON**

Simone de Beauvoir, who died [April 14], was, in partnership with Jean-Paul Sartre, a leading philosopher-novelist of the existentialist school and later, on her own, a theorist of radical feminism.

She was born in Paris on January 9, 1908 into a prosperous and cultivated though not exceptionally distinguished family. Her father dabbled in the theatre both as actor and director, but was too conscious of his status as a gentleman to do so for profit.

He upheld the traditional French upper-class *ethos* with something of the same humourless rigidity with which his daughter afterwards attacked it.

Simone de Beauvoir's earnestness and intensity revealed itself at an early age. Even as a child she was tormented by doubts about the existence of God and the moral order of the universe, and these doubts prompted her first essays into metaphysics.

As an adolescent she resolved to study philosophy, not merely as part of an ordinary student's syllabus, but as a specialist. Her parents and teachers were discouraging. Philosophy, she was told, was a man's subject.

She studied philosophy in Paris together with Simone Weil with whom she might be thought to have much in common, but friendship did not ripen between the two women, and the reason may perhaps be seen in a remark of Simone de Beauvoir's that while Simone Weil was wholly concerned with problems of social justice, she herself was absorbed with the problem of the meaning of existence.

Simone de Beauvoir herself was to come in time to be absorbed with problems of social justice, but in her younger days metaphysics was her chief concern.

Preparing for the *agrégation,* she specialized in Leibniz and was nominally the pupil of Brunschvig, but in practice she was coached by two fellow students with whom she had *liaisons,* first René Maheu and then Sartre.

She passed the competition successfully when she was 21, the youngest *agrégée* in philosophy in France. Maheu, a future director-general of Unesco, soon proved too much a discreet establishment personality for her liking (she had to refer to him in her memoirs in his lifetime under a pseudonym, André Herbaut); by contrast, the uncompromising, unconventional Sartre thrilled her; meeting him she felt she "could share everything with him always".

Sartre, three years older than she, became in effect her *guru.* They formed a union which, though painstakingly distinguished from "bourgeois marriage", remained a settled partnership until his death in 1980.

In both her philosophical and her political thinking, she follows his lead, and like him she tried to express her ideas in a variety of literary forms—novels, stories and plays as well as straight theoretical essays.

Her best philosophical work, of an academic kind, was her earliest, ***Pour une morale de l'ambiguité*** (1947) and ***L'Existentialisme et la sagesse des nations*** (1948) in which she attempted to revise the conventional existentialist notion that life is "absurd" by defining it instead as "ambiguous".

The meaning of life, she suggested, is what each one of us can discover or create for himself. Similarly, she argued that there can be moral values insofar as men construct them for themselves.

Simone de Beauvoir's most successful novel was ***Les Mandarins*** (1954) a *roman à clef* about Sartre, Camus, herself and other luminaries of the French left-wing after the Liberation. The book won the Prix Goncourt, and was a best-seller, but precisely because it was so ''realist'', it was also her least characteristic and distinctive work.

In an essay on **''Littérature et métaphysique''** (1946) she explained that her aim was to write a ''metaphysical novel'', and the two books that came closest to realising this ambition were written at about the same time: ***Le Sang des Autres*** (1945) about a young girl who thirsts for the Absolute and then solves the problem of life by dying a noble death, and ***Tous les hommes sont mortels*** (1946) about a woman who dreads death and then discovers that life is an even heavier burden.

Death was a constant theme in Simone de Beauvoir's writing and became more prominent with the passage of time. ***Une mort trés douce*** (1964) is about the painful death of her mother; ***La Vieillesse*** (1970) is as much concerned with dying as with ageing; ***La Céremonie des Adieux*** (1981) is about Sartre's death. . . .

Simone de Beauvoir reached a wide audience with her journalism. She also wrote a number of travel books, one about the United States, which was bitterly hostile, and others about China and Cuba, which were correspondingly eulogistic.

In some respects her most substantial literary achievement was her autobiography. In the first volume, ***Mémoires d'une jeune fille rangée*** (1958), she describes the family and the world in which she grew up. In ***La Force des Choses*** (1963) she wrote about her reaction against that background, and about her life with Sartre.

She recalled that, after their *agrégation*, they were separated by their teaching duties, which kept Sartre in Le Havre while she was in Marseilles, and Sartre suggested that they should marry so as to be appointed to the same town. De Beauvoir firmly resisted such a compromise with her principles; if they intended to have children, she would have agreed, but as they did not, she stuck to her ''radical freedom''.

Sartre himself seems to have been relieved, continuing to live with his mother until her death many years later, and pursuing on the side his various sexual adventures.

In her efforts to keep pace with him, and enact the role of the fully liberated woman, she threw herself, according to her memoirs, into affairs with such unlikely people as Nelson Algren, a Chicago novelist, and Claude Lanzmann, a Marxist journalist 16 years her junior. In the end, she always returned to Sartre.

It was Sartre's financial success which enabled her, after 12 years of teaching, to quit the *lycée* as he had done; and soon she was earning her own living. Her tastes were frugal; Sartre and she always met, in her words, ''as equals''. The chief difference that de Beauvoir noted between Sartre and herself was that he ''was shaped by books'' whereas she was affected by ''immediate experience''.

Sartre himself, in his memoirs, *Les Mots*, confirmed that diagnosis. Simone de Beauvoir was also more robust than Sartre. As a young teacher in Marseilles she would hike for 20 miles a day in espadrilles; on visits to Greece, she would try to drag Sartre on long walks in the midday sun.

In the third volume of her autobiography, ***La Force de l'âge*** (1960) she wrote about the years in which she had become rich and famous. Fame she wore gracefully enough, but riches posed problems for her. She could rarely bring herself to spend money on clothes; with an effort of will she bought herself a small car and a modest flat near the cemetery of Montparnasse.

After ***L'Age de discrétion,*** which came out in 1968, she forsook the novel as a literary medium. A book entitled ***Quand prime le spirituel*** appeared in 1979, but it turned out to be an experiment in fiction from the pre-war years, the title an ironical reference to the ''spiritual'' philosophy of Jacques Maritain which the book was designed to refute from a perspective of atheist existentialism.

Simone de Beauvoir did not participate in Sartre's later enterprise of ''integrating existentialism with Marxism'', although she had to some extent to nurse him through the ordeal of composing his later mammoth works, and in the last years of his life, when he grew progressively more blind, she spent more and more time in his company, reading aloud to him, and helping to manage his money, which he was apt to lose or give away with reckless generosity.

Sartre once compared his life with her to that of George Henry Lewis with George Eliot and indeed, however unlike Lewis Sartre may have been, Simone de Beauvoir did have a lot in common with George Eliot.

She certainly took more seriously than Sartre some of the ideas they shared. A streak of Voltairean impishness in Sartre prompted him to proclaim himself a Marxist, for example, without the least willingness to submit to any authority, even that of Marx himself.

Simone de Beauvoir made more earnest efforts to be a good Marxist. Her most conspicuous endeavour was to work out a Marxist theory of women's liberation, and she undoubtedly succeeded in giving feminism a new look. This was a field in which she reached her widest public.

Her long study of the predicament of women, ***Le Deuxième Sexe***, came out as early as 1949, and although its impact was not immediate, it did much to make the demand for women's rights a key factor of the radicalism which emerged in Europe and America in the 1960s and 1970s.

Feminism was one thing she did not learn from Sartre. Indeed in an interview she once reproached Sartre for being a ''phallocrat'', and he denied the charge with only a mock indignation.

In 1972, she helped found a society called *Choisir,* to promote the cause of abortion and contraception on demand. Two years later she was elected President of the Ligue du Droit des Femmes. She refused, however, to have anything to do with the UN Women's Year in 1976, claiming that the Mexico Women's Conference was designed ''only to integrate women in a masculine society''.

She supported the alternative ''revolutionary feminist'' congress in Brussels.

As an active editorial director of the review *Les Temps Modernes,* Simone de Beauvoir made ''revolutionary feminism'' one of its favoured causes, and she devoted most of her articles, interviews and television appearances to this subject in the later years.

Although she remained on the far left all her life, she became with time more critical of the Soviet Union because of its persecution of dissenters and of the French Communist Party because it stood for "population not contraception".

Simone de Beauvoir was always a very readable writer, and a very likeable person. Her honesty, her sincerity, her almost Victorian high seriousness, commanded widespread respect, even from those who disagreed with her somewhat extreme opinions.

"Simone de Beauvoir: Exponent of Revolutionary Feminism," in The Times, *London, April 15, 1986.*

JULIET MITCHELL

[*Mitchell is an English nonfiction writer, journalist, and professor specializing in the topics of feminism and psychoanalysis. Her works include* Women: The Longest Revolution *(1966) and* Psychoanalysis and Feminism *(1974). With Ann Oakley she edited the anthology* What Is Feminism? A Reexamination *(1986). In the following excerpt Mitchell offers an interpretation of de Beauvoir's feminist, existentialist philosophy.*]

Simone de Beauvoir died on Monday April 14. She was revered and reviled as a feminist. The term must be understood in its fullest sense. With de Beauvoir's death, an exemplar of some of our most important values, of morality, has been lost. A light has gone out. Although I have disagreed with things she has said and did, I come here now both to praise and honour her as I always have.

Simone de Beauvoir was born in 1908 into a cultured *haut-bourgeois* family. By becoming its radical critic, she embodied and gave meaning to the best traditions of her milieu. Her version of the existential philosophy that she developed with her lifelong companion, Jean-Paul Sartre, was an extension into radicalism of the values of objectivity, universality and rationalism. She took these values to their logical conclusion and thereby made them critical, not conformist to the status quo. Her philosophy made each and every one of us responsible for ourselves and the world around us. She believed in truth, justice, equality: her feminism was a logical and a typically courageous extension of this endeavour.

As a child Simone de Beauvoir planned to become a writer; as an adolescent she decided to study philosophy. She did both. Her marvellous second novel, ***The Mandarins*** (1954), won a Prix Goncourt; at 21 she passed out of the Ecole normale superieure to become the youngest Agregée in philosophy from France. A list of her many and different publications and of her grassroot political actions makes her life seem diverse: in fact all fitted to a coherent project.

The Second Sex (1949) is an extraordinary achievement. It is, perhaps, the greatest demonstration of that branch of existentialism to which the adjective "Sartrean" is unjustly applied. Misleadingly translated, here and in America, it came to [be] seen as a feminist tract. It is, in fact, a staggeringly wide-ranging and moving treatise on the meaning of existence for "half the world".

De Beauvoir's initial thesis is that we are distinguished from animals by our ability to transcend nature, to create, to invent and shape our future. To deny any person or people their right to struggle is an oppression—it is here that the oppression of lower classes, castes or colonised nations and above all of women fits in. Oppression forces people back into immanence. "Woman" defined as the "natural", "animal", non-transcendent, is the ultimate incidence of this oppression.

It is within these terms that Simone de Beauvoir made her own life choice: not to marry or have children; but to invent her own life as a project, to produce not reproduce.

But something else than what man has made of man circumscribes our human ability to shape and create a future: age and death. For de Beauvoir her ardent fight for human choice came up against these facts of nature. She was preoccupied by the tension between the two. She did not, as is often asserted, deny the natural: she struggled with it, struggled to give it shape and dignity.

The volumes of her autobiography show her shaping her past in order to create her future. Her novels work with the tension between rational choice and irrational feelings, between creation and destruction. Though I believe she under-estimated them, she did not deny irrationality and negativity. They are released and recreated in her fiction in a way that, by definition, contains them. Thus the agony of jealousy, remorse, fear, depression, madness were not to be accepted and expressed in life but to be recreated within art—acknowledged but not indulged.

Her own presence reflected the integrity of her life project. The tensions were held in balance and given visible form in the combination of her poise and passion. It was a personal privilege to have met and talked with her; it was a privilege for all of us that she lived, wrote and acted in our times. (p. 51)

Juliet Mitchell, "Shaping the Past to Create the Future," in The Sunday Times, *London, April 20, 1986, p. 51.*

ELLEN WILLIS

[*Willis is an American journalist, essayist, critic, and editor. As a commentator on politics and popular culture, she has contributed articles to such periodicals as* Ms., Rolling Stone, Village Voice, *and* Commentary. Beginning to See the Light *(1981) is a collection of her essays from the 1970s. In the following excerpt Willis, who is a founder of the radical feminist group Redstockings, discusses de Beauvoir's relationship with the Women's Liberation Movement.*]

On May Day, the remnants of my old radical feminist group Redstockings held a memorial for Simone de Beauvoir. I had wanted to go, but couldn't make it, so I heard about it from a friend: Ti-Grace Atkinson talked about going to de Beauvoir's funeral, women spoke about her impact on their lives, someone read a message from Shulamith Firestone. Listening to this account, it occurred to me that in a way my relationship to de Beauvoir had always been secondhand, mediated and refracted by other feminists. When I first got involved in the women's liberation movement, I knew de Beauvoir only through ***The Mandarins,*** which I'd read, naively, as a novel (a good way to read it, I still maintain). After joining the movement I dutifully began ***The Second Sex,*** but abandoned it halfway through; it was too detached and distanced, too much the product of a French cultural and philosophical framework, to compete with the overpowering immediacy of all the discussion about *our lives* that permeated those early days of activism. (The woman who recommended it to me had discovered it at a time when America's idea of a feminist was a little old lady brandishing an umbrella.) Not till years later, when I was able to give the book the attention it deserved, did I fully appreciate de Beauvoir's impact on the politics of the feminists I was closest to—as well as those I most bitterly disagreed with.

Nearly four decades after it was first published in France, despite all the commentary the feminist movement has produced in the meantime, dated and parochial as it is in many respects, ***The Second Sex*** remains the most cogent and thorough book of feminist theory yet written. With its exhaustive portrayal of the ways in which male domination and female subordination penetrate every aspect of everyday life and shape our cultural myths and fantasies, it offers detailed evidence for the basic claims of second wave feminism—that male supremacy is a coherent system of power relations, and that "the personal is political."

If de Beauvoir's existentialist perspective is too innocent (and perhaps too arrogant) for a postmodern, poststructuralist era, it's metaphorically appropriate to her subject. Since the denial of personal autonomy defines women's oppression—and since patriarchal ideology holds that allowing women autonomy would destroy civilization if not the human species itself—a moral defense of freedom is necessarily at the heart of feminism. And for the feminists of my generation, so many of whom were "liberated"—that is, had consciously set out to earn a living, sleep with whom they pleased, and avoid traditional wife-and-motherhood—the collision between our sense of entitlement to freedom and men's stubborn assumption of dominance was not only a political (and personal) struggle but a grand moral drama. De Beauvoir's rendering of woman as the subject seeking transcendence, only to be forced into the position of Other and trapped in immanence, expressed that drama with a clarity that almost made up for her coolness.

De Beauvoir's influence pervades the early radical feminist critiques of Marxism. It was de Beauvoir who first pointed out the reductionism of Engels's attempt to trace women's oppression to the formation of classes, who insisted that sexuality and reproduction had to be primary categories for understanding women's lives; it was also de Beauvoir who argued—even more problematically from a conventional leftist point of view—that social conditions did not *cause* oppression; rather, people responded to those conditions by *choosing* to oppress. "Historical materialism," she wrote, "takes for granted facts that call for explanation: Engels assumes without discussion the bond of *interest* which ties man to property; but where does this interest, the source of social institutions, have its own source?"

Engels and other historical materialists did have an implicit answer to this question: interest had its source in the desire for survival and material comfort. But by de Beauvoir's time it was clear that this common sense approach to the question could not explain the rise of fascism, the failure of revolutionary socialism in western Europe, or the totalitarian perversion of the Russian Revolution. De Beauvoir built her philosophy on the idea that the human subject has an intrinsic impulse toward freedom, but this was if anything less useful than materialism for understanding the dynamics of domination and submission. Her solution to the problem was blaming oppression on "the imperialism of human consciousness," which, she argued, "included the original category of the Other and an original aspiration to dominate the Other." Of all her dubious appeals to a priori truths about human nature, this one seems to me the weakest. And I think it's no coincidence that subsequent feminist thinking about the roots of male supremacy has been muddled at best.

Many radical feminists who considered themselves materialists in the Marxist sense, who saw women as an oppressed class struggling in behalf of their interests (redefined as sexual and emotional in addition to economic), were also deeply influenced by ***The Second Sex.*** The political formulations that came out of this mix—the dominant tendency in Redstockings—were rich in paradox, like theologians' explanations of how God's divine plan is ineluctable but human beings have free will. Feminist materialists argued that while men's sexual class interests determined their oppression of women, and in fact all men did oppress women, any individual man *could* choose not to oppress women. Therefore, each man bore personal moral responsibility for his acts; determinism could never be an excuse for letting men off the hook. Similarly, women submitted to men so long as they had to to avoid punishment, and resisted whenever they felt it was possible: either way, they were acting in their interest. And yet there were always women who (for what mysterious reasons?) chose to take risks, to step out there ahead of everyone else. Sometimes others followed, and then you had a movement.

On the question of "where interest has its source," the feminist materialists suggested that the desire for survival, comfort (including love, sexual pleasure, emotional support), and freedom all played a role. On the surface, their understanding of male supremacy wasn't much like de Beauvoir's. In the materialist view, men's stake in their power over women was quite practical—it gained them money, leisure time, and domestic service, not to mention love, sexual pleasure, and emotional support on their own terms. But if you looked more closely at this list of goodies, it wasn't quite so simple. Could you assume, for instance, that sexual dominance was inherently more pleasurable than mutual desire? Or that it made "material" sense to choose love corrupted by the concealed rage of the oppressed over love with an equal partner? Lurking behind the materialist analysis was the de Beauvoirian assumption that oppressors were attached to power for its own sake.

For other factions of radical feminists, this assumption was quite overt. The New York Radical Feminists' manifesto, for example, argued that men exercised power over women to satisfy their egos. As they saw it, men did not value their power because it allowed them to demand women's services, but rather, demanded the services to affirm their power. Ironically, this idea was elaborated in a way that offended de Beauvoir's most basic beliefs about the artificiality of gender: cultural feminists who believed that women's problem was the ascendancy of "male values" attributed the drive for power not to the imperialism of human consciousness but to the imperialism of the phallus.

As a Redstocking, I was basically in the materialist camp, but with a difference; I thought the best tool for understanding sexuality and family life, the keys to patriarchal culture, was psychoanalysis. The radical feminist movement was, of course, resolutely anti-Freudian; here, too, classical Marxist thinking merged with de Beauvoir's. Like that other exemplary female intellectual, Hannah Arendt, whose insistence on evaluating Adolf Eichmann in rational moral terms led her to deny his patent lunacy, de Beauvoir resisted any view of human will that challenged the primacy of deliberate moral choice. Her refusal to admit the potency of unconscious fantasy and conflict not only forced her to assume a primary will to dominate; it also implicitly defined women's response to their oppression in highly moralistic terms. In the universe of ***The Second Sex,*** the female rebel was the existential heroine. And of course the paradigmatic female rebel was Simone de Beauvoir herself.

For many contemporary feminists, de Beauvoir's life has been an inspiration as well as her work; indeed, her work—not only

The Second Sex but the novels and the memoirs—is, among other things, a testament to a certain kind of life. It's easy for female rebels to idealize that life, to think of it as liberated without quotation marks. But in fact de Beauvoir was no more able than the most traditional housewife to transcend or circumvent male supremacy; her path involved its own complicated set of sacrifices, tradeoffs, and illusions. Part of the price she paid for being Simone de Beauvoir was to live more in her mind than in her body. De Beauvoir never questioned the patriarchal assumption that human freedom depends on the conquest of nature. Her relationship with Sartre was, judging by her own accounts, far more cerebral than sensual. Like most women who put a high priority on independence she had no children—and while it's a sexist fiction that all women want to be mothers, it's also a fact that so long as motherhood carries drastic social penalities, the decision to avoid it (and relinquish its erotic pleasures) is not exactly free.

Self-reflection on such matters was not de Beauvoir's strong point. Seeing herself as freer than she was, she denied the full import of her struggle—just as many of her radical feminist children, seduced by the politics of moral example, imagined they could make the revolution simply by changing their own lives. But de Beauvoir had to struggle alone; when she stepped out there, few were ready to follow. Partly because of her groundbreaking work, things are different now. In a sense, recognizing the limitations of that work and of that female rebel's life, is the best way to honor them. (p. 38)

Ellen Willis, "Rebel Girl," in The Village Voice, *Vol. XXXI, No. 21, May 27, 1986, p. 38.*

TI-GRACE ATKINSON (INTERVIEW WITH CAROL ANNE DOUGLAS)

[*American essayist, nonfiction writer, and critic, Atkinson earned fame during the 1960s and early 1970s as a feminist author, lecturer, and activist. Her publications include* The Institution of Sexual Intercourse *(1968) and the essay collection* Amazon Odyssey *(1974). Atkinson credits de Beauvoir for inspiring her involvement with political feminism, as well as her interest in philosophy; the two knew each other well as colleagues in the women's movement. In the following excerpt from an interview with Carol Anne Douglas, a member of the collective that publishes the feminist periodical* Off Our Backs, *Atkinson recounts her experience of attending de Beauvoir's funeral in Paris.*]

I first wrote Simone de Beauvoir in 1965, having read ***The Second Sex***. . . . I had never been political before, but I thought we should do something to change things. I wanted to organize with her, but she wrote back saying that she thought women would have to organize within national boundaries. Much later, she changed her mind about that.

My becoming a feminist and the kind of feminist I became was due to her. She sparked my interest in philosophy. I was so enamoured of her work that whatever she did, I was ready to copy, although I developed an interest in different kinds of philosophy.

So we corresponded from that time. I sent her things like Valerie Solanas' S.C.U.M. Manifesto, which she copied and distributed all over Europe. Over the years, I went to Paris for translations of my work, meetings and lectures, and I always saw Beauvoir. She was a support for me in a deep sense, a support and a model.

The first time I met her, in her apartment in the early '70s, I was astonished by how extremely vibrant she was, and so ravenously curious. Most of all, she was generous. She didn't seem to have a competitive bone in her body, which may have had to do with producing so many books. The combination of her contribution and her personal virtues made her really unique and a special loss.

She also introduced me to many French feminists who later became friends—Christine Delphy, Monique Wittig, Liliane Kandel, Francoise Pasquier and German feminist Alice Schwarzer. The group of women who met through Beauvoir is like a family, there are intense bonds between us.

When I was told about Beauvoir's death, I was called out of a class I was teaching on Kant and told that National Public Radio wanted to interview me about someone who had just died. It never occurred to me it was Beauvoir. When I went to the phone and heard, I felt a vacancy in my solar plexus.

I did the interview after I finished teaching the class. When I got home, there were calls from French feminists who wanted me to hear from them instead of over the media.

I wanted to be in Paris and witness that process of being put into the earth. It was financially insane to go, but impossible not to go.

French feminists told me the media there had minimized Beauvoir's role as a feminist, so they wanted a strong feminist presence at the funeral, attendees and flowers.

I learned that flowers by wire take more than three days, so they wouldn't arrive in time in Europe. So I spent a day and night calling all the feminists and groups in my address book and whoever I could think to ask if they wanted me to buy flowers for them in France, and they could pay me back later. I feel very bad that I didn't have time to systematically call everyone of every tendency. Most of the people I called had politics similar to mine because they were the people I know.

I arrived in Paris with the money to buy 29 bouquets for feminists groups (including *off our backs*) and individuals on Saturday morning, the day of the funeral. A French feminist met me and I went to shower and then went immediately to a florist. It took three hours for three French feminists and I to select and make up 29 bouquets. The French custom is to make a large banner with the name of the giver and secure it over the flowers, which made it all the more important that we had so many from feminist groups. The French feminists were thrilled. They decided to carry the American bouquets in the funeral cortege (procession) because there were nowhere near enough Americans there to carry them. I was very touched. There were also flowers from many French feminists, and from feminists in Spain, Belgium, Australia, Germany, the Netherlands and Iranian feminists in exile and African feminists. Fifty-four feminists from Madrid took a bus to be at the funeral.

When we were taking the flowers to the mortuary, women passing on the street eagerly asked us if they were for Beauvoir. They wanted to know when and where the funeral was because it had not been publicly announced.

The fact that the conservative government of Premier Jacques Chirac had recently taken office may have had something to do with the lack of publicity. The government dissolved the Ministry for the Rights of Women and fired Minister Yvette Roudy the week Beauvoir died. The ministry was replaced by a committee on the human condition.

At the morgue, which was in the hospital, the procession began. At first there was a big truck with prepared floral arrangements, then came the hearse and the family. I couldn't figure out where the coffin was, whether it was with the flowers or with the family—Beauvoir's sister. I had missed viewing the body because I didn't understand that a woman in government I knew was asking me inside for that reason. Perhaps it was just as well, because they nail the coffin shut and that would have been hard to watch.

Three to four thousand people, about ninety percent women, and the rest men in their 30s, walked behind the hearse. We walked from the hospital to Montparnasse Cemetery, a large cemetery in the center of Paris, across the street from Beauvoir's apartment. It was hard to walk there because it was the same route we had taken to visit her at her apartment. Everyone seemed to be walking alone with her thoughts.

The cemetery has 12-foot high walls with a solid steel, 12-foot high gate.

Some people who had been at the morgue had driven straight to the cemetery instead of joining the cortege, so they were already there.

The truck with the other flowers—not ours—went in, then the hearse. Then the gates clanged shut. A few women who had walked close to the hearse jumped inside. But the vast majority of us were left standing at the steel door. We were dumbfounded. I thought maybe it was a malfunction. Everyone was very quiet. We couldn't hear anything on the other side.

The gates didn't open for over an hour.

When it seemed clear that something was going on, I thought of climbing the wall. Christine Delphy offered to give me a boost. But I was in another country, so it was hard to know what I should do. I thought maybe we should chant, "Beauvoir, Beauvoir, Beauvoir."

By the time we had collected ourselves, the gates opened and the people who had attended the funeral left.

We were told that the only speaker at the funeral had been a man, Claude Lanzmann of the socialist journal *Les temps modernes,* a socialist publication on which Beauvoir and Sartre had worked. Lanzmann had been Beauvoir's lover in the '50s. He read from her work—the autobiographical book about her early life, ***Memoirs of a Dutiful Daughter.***

We walked into the cemetery, and some women who knew where to go led me to the grave site. A friend had asked me to put a white rose in the grave for her, so I was taken up to a hole in the ground. The tomb stone at the top said Jean Paul Sartre; I felt as if I was at the wrong funeral. I dropped the flower in and fled.

A woman later explained that Beauvoir had a plot next to Sartre and she was going to be cremated later that week and buried there.

Afterwards, the women felt depressed, but we didn't talk about it, perhaps because we were different nationalities.

That night, a group of French and other feminists had dinner together in a rented room in a restaurant. We talked about Beauvoir, teased each other, and laughed. It was funny with so many women who write, but it was hard for us to talk about Beauvoir's death and funeral. There was a concern not to increase each other's sadness.

I did say that I felt incomplete because I didn't see Beauvoir into the ground, and women said we'd go to the cemetery together the next day.

The next morning it was raining lightly. We went to the deserted cemetery. The evening before, women had arranged all of the flowers by the grave. I was able then to say goodbye to her.

Women from the center for documenting Simone de Beauvoir filmed the cemetery. They interviewed Christine Delphy and she started talking about Beauvoir's work. I said, "We still have her work, that's not why we're sad. It's who she was as a woman."

I had to leave on a five o'clock plane. We kept hugging each other. Christine Delphy said how grateful French feminists felt for the American flowers. "They took the edge off our pain," she said. It was enough to make you stop writing and send flowers for the rest of your life.

I wrote letters of protest over the shutting of the gates and the fact that there was only a male speaker at the funeral to many people in France. I don't know whose decision it was to shut the gates. Some said it was the government, because they didn't want people to be all over the cemetery as they were at Sartre's funeral, where there were hundreds of thousands. But there were not nearly so many people in this procession. (pp. 2-3)

Ti-Grace Atkinson, "Adieu, Adieu, Ma Mère Politique," an interview with Carol Anne Douglas, in Off Our Backs, *Vol. XVI, No. 6, June, 1986, pp. 2-3.*

PEGGY KORNEGGER

I read that Simone de Beauvoir had died as I passed a newspaper dispenser early this week. There was a small paragraph on the front page: Simone de Beauvoir dead at age seventy-eight, six years to the month, almost to the day, after her lifelong companion, Jean Paul Sartre, died on April 15, 1980.

It is hard for me to grasp that she is no longer with us; I feel an absence, a lack—as when someone suddenly stops speaking and leaves the room silent behind them. We have the memory of her words, but not the anticipation of more to come.

For me, Simone de Beauvoir was, above all else, a *chronicler.* She chronicled her own life (in four volumes: ***Memoirs of a Dutiful Daughter, The Prime of Life, Force of Circumstance, All Said and Done***), her mother's death (***A Very Easy Death***), and, most recently, her final years with Sartre and his death (***Adieux: A Farewell to Sartre***). I keep thinking: who now will chronicle the final chapter of her life? As strange as it sounds, I find it difficult to imagine her not doing it herself. Her voice has been such a vital part of my life for the past sixteen years. I have been moved by her writing—fiction, nonfiction, and autobiography—as by few other works. My own life experiences are so tied up with memories of reading her books. Remembering the books almost evokes those experiences.

The Second Sex was one of the first books I read when I began to get involved in the women's movement in 1970. I remember the excitement of reading books *by* women, *about* women; so little of my formal education had included women writers up to this point. My last semester in college women's studies classes were offered for the first time, and this is where I was introduced to Simone's work. However, as far as I knew this one book was all she had written (most of her books were out of print in the United States). It wasn't until two years later, while traveling in Europe, that I discovered her autobiography and two of her books of fiction. I can recall riding the trains of Europe with a woman friend, both of us writing in our journals and reading Simone de Beauvoir's autobiography. In ***The Prime of Life,*** Simone, too, is traveling all over Europe and writing. She became something of a heroine to us: a strong, independent woman refusing to marry, writer, intellectual, political activist. My visual images of that trip include *her* images, as well. I see her hiking across the fields of France and sitting in Paris cafes with Sartre; I see myself visiting those same cafes and feeling thrilled at being where other writers had been before me.

Back home in San Francisco, working at a full-time secretarial job, I sustained myself by reading more of her fiction (wonderful stories like those in ***The Woman Destroyed,*** and the novels that fictionalized her own life story, ***She Came to Stay*** and ***The Mandarins***). I stayed up late at night reading, writing, and staring out the window at the city lights, trying to imagine myself as a writer, like her, moving the world with my words.

In 1973 her groundbreaking book on old age, ***The Coming of Age,*** was published in the United States. Just as ***The Second Sex*** had opened my eyes to the oppression of women, this book made me see how our society devalues older people. It was amazing to me how Simone de Beauvoir always seemed to be "ahead of her time" in her political/social observations; her work preceded by many years the political movements that fought for the rights of women and older citizens.

It takes a great deal of courage to look at things that most people would rather ignore. Simone had that courage, not only in her nonfiction studies but also in her writings about her own life. I have never read any more unflinchingly honest or moving accounts of death and dying than those she gives us at the end of ***Force of Circumstance*** and throughout ***A Very Easy Death*** and ***Adieux.*** They are painful to read, but they also touch some very deep and universal truths in human experience. I identified strongly with much of what she wrote. Her thoughts on her future death and her life in retrospect are filled with a strange beauty and poignancy which moved me greatly. So much so that in 1974, while a graduate student in women's literature, I wrote her a "fan letter," telling her how much her work had meant to me. I didn't really expect a reply, but she did write back—a handwritten note, in French, warmly telling me how much it meant to her to have achieved such an identification with another woman.

It seems odd to me now, as I hold the note in my hands, that I have something that she once wrote—and that she herself is no longer alive. The finality and absence of death are so hard for the human mind to accept. In ***Force of Circumstance,*** Simone mourned the fact that with her death "all the books I've read, all the places I've seen, all the knowledge I've amassed . . . will be no more. . . . That unique sum of things, the experience that I lived, with all its order and randomness . . . all the things I've talked about, others left unspoken . . . there is no place where they will live again." And although I think I know *exactly* what she meant by that, I look at her handwritten words before me, and at all her lovingly dog-eared books on my bookshelves, and I can't help but feel that the finality she feared and hated so may not be entirely true.

The day after she died, a co-worker of mine told me that he, too, had read one of her books while riding the train in Europe and he'll never forget that particular trip because of the experience. In today's mail I received a postcard from a friend in New York who was being helped through the weeks of her father's hospitalization by reading ***Force of Circumstance.*** There are so many of us who, with our very individual and unique memories and lives, have been changed and enriched by Simone de Beauvoir's writing. The power of her voice even now, speaking across the fact of her physical death, is so strong that those who have read her books feel sadness at her passing as if we had known her intimately.

While I was leafing through her books today, re-reading passages here and there, I came across the following quote. It says best what her life's work, writing, meant to her: "Words without doubt, universal, eternal, presence of all in each, are the only transcendent power I recognize and am affected by; they vibrate in my mouth, and with them I can communicate with humanity. They wrench tears, night, death itself from the moment, from contingency, and then transfigure them. Perhaps the most profound desire I entertain today is that people should repeat in silence certain words that I have been the first to link together." If this indeed was her most "profound desire," it has been fulfilled many times over. She was an extraordinary woman. (p. 6)

Peggy Kornegger, "Remembering Simone de Beauvoir," in Sojourner, *Vol. 11, No. 10, June, 1986, p. 6.*

NICOLAS TREDELL

[English editor and critic, Tredell, author of The Novels of Colin Wilson *(1982), is a contributing editor to* PN Review. *In the following excerpt Tredell analyzes the enduring appeal of de Beauvoir's writings.]*

The French writer Simone de Beauvoir died in a Paris hospital on 14 April. She was 78. If many who never knew her will feel a sense of personal loss at her death, this is due, to a significant extent, to her remarkable autobiographies—***Memoirs of a Dutiful Daughter*** (1958), ***The Prime of Life*** (1960), ***The Force of Circumstance*** (1960) and ***All Said and Done*** (1972). These range over her struggles against her conventional upbringing, her student days at the Sorbonne, her lifelong relationship with Sartre, her experiences as a young teacher in Marseilles, the darkening political scene of the 1930s, Paris in the years of war and occupation, her own rise to fame (along with Sartre and Camus) in the heady atmosphere of Left Bank existentialism, the foundation of the journal *Les Temps Modernes,* the bitter conflicts over the Algerian war, her travels to the USA, Russia, Cuba, China and elsewhere, her friendships with Nelson Algren and Claude Lanzmann, the events of May 1968, the campaign against the Vietnam War, the growth of the feminist movement. The autobiographies can seem artless and anecdotal—this is part of their attraction—but in fact, they are carefully shaped and comprise an incomparable contribution to the cultural and political history of the twentieth century.

Assessment of de Beauvoir's fiction has been complicated by her autobiographical output and by her fame. Her novels have been too easily seen as *romans à clef*—for instance, her first novel, ***She Came to Stay*** (1943) has been taken as a transliteration of the tangled relationship between de Beauvoir, Sartre, and Olga Kosakievicz. ***She Came to Stay*** was followed by ***The Blood of Others*** (1945) and ***All Men are Mortal*** (1946). ***The Mandarins*** (1954), which won the Prix Goncourt, is a serious, substantial, consistently absorbing study of the self-questionings and shifting commitments of a group of intellectuals in a

France emerging from war. Like George Eliot and Doris Lessing, de Beauvoir is concerned to explore in this novel the relationship between 'private' and 'public' life. Her later fiction includes that telling analysis of consumer society, ***Les Belles Images*** (1966) and the unsparing ***The Woman Destroyed*** (1968).

Her pioneering, enormously influential study ***The Second Sex*** (1949) contends: 'One is not born a woman, one becomes one'. It explores the construction of femininity from a number of perspectives, for instance biological, psychoanalytic, Marxist, literary, historical, sociological. Its importance has been both theoretical and practical: it gave help and support to women struggling for autonomy at a time when, not least on the Left, such aspirations were hardly recognized, and it has continued to do so. De Beauvoir's theoretical positions were staunchly backed up by her way of life, with its rigorous refusal of marriage and motherhood.

While Sartre, in his last years, saw his intellectual influence waning and his political hopes checked, de Beauvoir, though she shared many of his political disillusionments, lived to see feminism become an important movement, to be acknowledged as one of its twentieth-century pioneers, and to commit herself fully to feminist causes. At the end of ***The Second Sex,*** she had declared that she was not a feminist and that women's liberation would come about automatically as a result of socialism; but in interviews with Alice Schwarzer (reviewed *PNR* 43), she affirmed, in 1972: 'I really am a feminist.' She allied herself with the radical *Mouvement de la Libération des Femmes,* signed the manifesto of the '343 sluts'—women who publicly declared that they had had abortions, at a time when abortion was still banned in France—and took up the MLF slogans of free abortion on demand, free contraception, and free motherhood. She continued to maintain, however, that feminism must link itself with socialist struggle. From some feminist positions, she was to be criticized as too Cartesian and rationalist, and too remote from emotions and instincts. But her approach and example are likely to endure.

De Beauvoir was much possessed by death. The rich enjoyment of life conveyed in her autobiographies is both enhanced and threatened by a strong sense of the void. ***A Very Easy Death*** (1964), a lacerating and poignant record of her mother's death from cancer, and ***Adieux: A Farewell to Sartre,*** a moving and restrained chronicle of Sartre's last years are twentieth-century *ars moriendi,* explorations of ways of dying in modern secular culture. With medieval precision, but without the consolations of faith, she bears unflinching witness to the atrocities of dying. But she was also concerned with the problems of longevity; ***Old Age*** (1970) is a humane and accessible study of a topic that, with more people living longer, will become increasingly important.

Her achievement and appeal as a writer, and the links between her writing and her feminist and socialist commitments, are well summed up in her remarks in the transcript of the Simone de Beauvoir film (1979) published in *PNR* 35: 'I just wanted to speak . . . to people as if I were whispering in their ear, and to write in a way that made people identify with my heroes and heroines or help them benefit from what I was saying . . . I really tried to excise as many things as possible from my own experience, to explain everything which could be explained about it, so that it could be of use to other people.' (pp. 7-8)

Nicolas Tredell, "Simone de Beauvoir," in PN Review, *Vol. 13, No. 1, 1986, pp. 7-8.*

Jorge Luis Borges

August 24, 1899 - June 14, 1986

(Also wrote with Adolfo Bioy Casares under pseudonyms of B. Suarez Lynch and H(onorio) Bustos Domecq) Argentinian short story writer, poet, essayist, critic, and scriptwriter.

(See also *CLC,* Vols. 1, 2, 3, 4, 6, 8, 9, 10, 13, 19; *Contemporary Authors,* Vols. 21-24, rev. ed.; and *Contemporary Authors New Revision Series,* Vol. 19.)

PRINCIPAL WORKS

Fervor de Buenos Aires (poetry) 1923
Luna de enfrente (poetry) 1925
El idioma de los Argentinos (essay) 1928
Cuaderno San Martín (poetry) 1929
Evaristo Carriego (essay) 1930
Discusión (essays and criticism) 1932
Historia universal de la infamia (short stories) 1935
[*A Universal History of Infamy,* 1972]
Historia de la eternidad (essays) 1936
Poemas, 1922-1943 (poetry) 1943
Ficciones, 1935-1944 (short stories) 1944
[*Ficciones,* 1962; also published as *Fictions,* 1965]
El aleph (short stories) 1949
[*The Aleph and Other Stories, 1933-1969* (revised edition), 1970]
Otras inquisiciónes, 1937-1952 (essays) 1952
[*Other Inquisitions, 1937-1952,* 1964]
Obras completas. 10 vols. (essays, short stories, and poetry) 1953-67
Manual de zoología fantastica [with Margarita Guerrero] (prose) 1957; also published as *El libro de los seres imaginarios* [revised edition], 1967
[*The Imaginary Zoo,* 1969; also published as *The Book of Imaginary Beings* (revised edition), 1969]
Poemas, 1923-1958 (poetry) 1958
Antología personal (poetry and prose) 1961
[*A Personal Anthology,* 1967]
El hacedor (prose and poetry) 1961
[*Dreamtigers,* 1964]
Labyrinths (short stories and essays) 1962
Obra poetica, 1923-1967 (poetry) 1967
[*Selected Poems, 1923-1967,* 1972]
Nueva antología personal (poetry and prose) 1968
Elogio de la sombra (poetry and prose) 1969
[*In Praise of Darkness,* 1974]
El informe de Brodie (short stories) 1970
[*Doctor Brodie's Report,* 1972]
**El oro de los tigres* (poetry) 1972
Borges on Writing (interviews) 1973
El libro de arena (short stories) 1975
[*The Book of Sand,* 1977]
**La rosa profunda* (poetry) 1975
Historia de la noche (poetry) 1977
Obras completas (poetry and prose) 1977
Obras completas en colaboración [with Adolfo Bioy Casares, Betina Edelberg, Margarita Guerrero, Alicia Jurado, Maria Kodama, Maria Esther Vázquez] (short stories, essays, and criticism) 1979
Prosa completa. 2 vols. (prose) 1980
Siete noches (lectures) 1980
[*Seven Nights,* 1984]
Antología poética, 1923-1977 (poetry) 1981
Atlas [with Maria Kodama] (prose) 1984
[*Atlas,* 1985]

*These works were translated and published as *The Gold of the Tigers: Selected Later Poems* in 1977.

JORGE LUIS BORGES (INTERVIEW WITH AMELIA BARILI)

[*An Argentinian, Barili is the book review editor of* La Prensa, *a Buenos Aires newspaper. In the following excerpt Barili, who interviewed Borges several times during his final years, leads the writer in a discussion of the philosophical aspects of his fiction. The interview took place in Argentina in November, 1985.*]

I met Jorge Luis Borges in 1981, when I returned to Buenos Aires from a job at the BBC in London and began working for *La Prensa*. He received me very kindly, remembering that during the 1920's, when he was not well known, *La Prensa* had been the first newspaper to publish him. Later I returned to see him frequently. Sometimes he would dictate a poem that he had been composing during a long night of insomnia. After typing it, I would put it in his desk near his collection of Icelandic sagas, a precious gift from his father.

Sometimes we would walk to a nearby restaurant, where he would eat something very simple. Or we would go to a bookstore, searching for yet another book by Kipling or Conrad in an English edition for friends to read to him. People would stop to greet him, and he would jokingly tell me they must have mistaken him for someone else. His fame as a writer seemed to burden him, and he often regretted that he had to go on living so that Borges the writer could weave his literary fantasies.

One morning shortly before he left Argentina in November, we spoke about his recent work, his beliefs, his doubts. I did not know it would be our last conversation before his death in Geneva. We started by discussing one of his latest books, ***Los Conjurados*** (***The Conspirators***), in which he calls Geneva "one of my homelands."

Where does your love for Geneva come from?

In a certain manner, I am Swiss; I spent my adolescence in Geneva. We went to Europe in 1914. We were so ignorant that we did not know that was the year of the First World War. We were trapped in Geneva. The rest of Europe was at war. From my Genevan adolescence I still have a very good friend, Dr. Simon Ishvinski. The Swiss are very reserved people. I had three friends: Simon Ishvinski, Slatkin, and Maurice Abramowicz, a poet who is now dead.

You remember him in ***Los Conjurados.***

Yes. It was a beautiful night. Maria Kodama (Borges's secretary, traveling companion and, during his final weeks, wife), Maurice Abramowicz's widow and I were at a Greek tavern in Paris, listening to Greek music, which is so full of courage. I remembered the lyrics: "While this music lasts, we will deserve Helen of Troy's love. While the music lasts, we will know that Ulysses will come back to Ithaca." And I felt that Maurice was not dead, that he was there with us, that nobody really dies, for they all project their shadow.

In ***Los Conjurados*** *you also speak about one of your nightmares. Do some repeat themselves?*

Yes. I dream of a mirror. I see myself with a mask, or I see in the mirror somebody who is me but whom I do not recognize as myself. I arrive at a place, and I have the sense of being lost and that all is horrible. The place itself is like any other. It is a room, with furniture, and its appearance is not horrible. What is atrocious is the feeling, not the images. Another frequent nightmare is of being attacked by beings who are children; there are many of them, very little but strong. I try to defend myself, but the blows I give are weak.

In ***Los Conjurados,*** *as in all your work, there is a permanent search for meaning. What is the sense of life?*

If life's meaning were explained to us, we probably wouldn't understand it. To think that a man can find it is absurd. We can live without understanding what the world is or who we are. The important things are the ethical instinct and the intellectual instinct, are they not? The intellectual instinct is the one that makes us search while knowing that we are never going to find the answer. I think Lessing said that if God were to declare that in His right hand He had the truth and in his left hand He had the investigation of the truth, Lessing would ask God to open His left hand—he would want God to give him the investigation of the truth, not the truth itself. Of course he would want that, because the investigation permits infinite hypotheses, and the truth is only one, and that does not suit the intellect, because the intellect needs curiosity. In the past, I tried to believe in a personal God, but I do not think I try anymore. I remember in that respect an admirable expression of Bernard Shaw: "God is in the making."

Even though you present yourself as a nonbeliever, there are in your works some references to mystical experiences that have always puzzled me. In the story **"The God's Script"** *you say: "From the tireless labyrinth of dreams I returned as if to my home, to the harsh prison. I blessed its dampness, I blessed its tiger, I blessed the crevice of light, I blessed my old, suffering body, I blessed the darkness and the stone. Then there occurred what I cannot forget nor communicate. There occurred the union with the divinity, with the universe." It seems that when you accept your circumstances and you bless them, then you come back to your center, and clarity dawns upon you. In the story* **"El Aleph"** *too, only when you accept your circumstances do you get to see the point where every act in the whole history of the cosmos comes together.*

This is true. It is the same idea. Since I do not think often about what I have written, I had not realized that. Nevertheless, it is better that it should be instinctive and not intellectual, don't you think? The instinctive is what counts in a story. What the writer wants to say is the least important thing; the most important is said through him or in spite of him.

Another idea that appears in many of your stories is that of the union of all creatures. In **"The God's Script"** *the pagan priest realizes that he is one of the threads of the whole fabric and that Pedro de Alvarado, who tortured him, is another one. In* **"The Theologians,"** *Aureliano and Juan de Panonia, his rival, are the same; and in* **"The End"** *Martin Fierro and El Negro have one and the same destiny.*

That is true. But I do not think about what I have already written; I think about what I am going to write—which is usually what I have already written, lightly disguised. Let's see. These days I am writing a short story about Segismund, one of the characters of *La Vida Es Sueño*. We will see how it turns out. I am going to read *La Vida Es Sueño* again, before writing the story. I thought of it some nights ago. I woke up; it was about 4 o'clock and I could not get back to sleep. I thought, let's use this sleeplessness. And suddenly I remembered that tragedy by Calderón, which I must have read 50 years ago, and I told myself, "There is a story here." It should resemble (but not too much) *La Vida Es Sueño*. To make that clear, it is going to be titled **"Monologue of Segismund."** Of course, it will be quite a different soliloquy than the one in that play. I think it is going to be a good story. I told it to Maria Kodama, and she approved of it. It has been some time since I wrote a story. But that is the source of this one.

What is the source of **"The God's Script"?** *When the priest says the fact that a prison surrounded him was not an obstacle* *to his finding the clue to the hidden language, I thought that was similar to what happened with you and your blindness.*

I lost my sight some years later. But in a certain way there is a purification in the blindness. It purifies one of visual circumstances. Circumstances are lost, and the external world, which is always trying to grab us, becomes fainter. But ***The God's Script*** is autobiographical in another sense. I united there two experiences. Looking at the jaguar in the zoo, I thought the spots on the jaguar's skin seemed to be a writing; that is not true of the leopard's spots or the tiger's stripes. The other experience was the one I had when, after an operation, I was forced to lie on my back. I could only move my head to the right or left. Then I put together the idea that occurred to me, that the jaguar's spots suggest a secret writing, and the fact that I was virtually imprisoned. It would have been more appropriate to the story for the main character not to have been a priest from a barbarian religion but a Hindu or a Jew. However, the jaguar had to be placed in Latin America. That impelled me toward the pyramid and the Aztecs. The jaguar could not appear in other scenery. Although Victor Hugo describes the Roman circus and says that among the animals there are "*jaguars enlacés,*" that is impossible in Rome. Maybe he mistook leopards for jaguars, or maybe he did not mind that sort of mistake, just as Shakespeare didn't.

Like the kabbalists, you try to find in that story the sense of God's writing. You consider that the whole cosmos could be present in one word. How do you personally conceive the beginning of the universe?

I am naturally idealistic. Almost everyone, thinking about reality, thinks of space, and their cosmogonies start with space. I think about time. I think everything happens in time. I feel we could easily do without space but not without time. I have a poem called **"Cosmogony"** in which I say it is absurd to think the universe began with astronomical space, which presupposes, for example, sight, which came much later. It is more natural to think that in the beginning there was an emotion. Well, it is the same as saying, "In the beginning was the Word." It is a variation on the same theme.

Can we find a relationship among the various conceptions about the origin of the universe among the Greeks, the Pythagoreans, the Jews?

Strangely enough, they all start with astronomical space. There is also the idea of the Spirit; that would come prior to space, of course. But in general they think of space. The Hebrews believe that the world was created from a word of God. But then that word should exist prior to the world. Saint Augustine gave the solution to that problem. Let's see, my Latin is poor, but I remember that phrase: "*non in tempore sed cum tempore Deus creavit* . . . I do not know what . . . *ordinem mundi.*" That means, "Not in time but with time God created the world." To create the world is to create time. If not, people would ask, what did God do before creating the world? But with this explanation they are told that there was a first instant without a before. This is inconceivable, of course, because if I think of an instant I think of the time before that instant. But they tell us that, and we rest content with the inconceivable. An infinite time? A time with a beginning? Both ideas are impossible. To think that time began is impossible. And to think that it doesn't have a start, which means that we are going, in Shakespeare's words, to "the dark backward and abysm of time," is also not possible.

I would like to come back to the idea of the word as origin of the world. For example, in the Hebrew tradition there is a search through cryptographic and hermeneutic methods for that exact word.

Yes, that is the kabbala.

Not long ago Haaretz, a newspaper in Israel, reported that computer experiments on the Bible had discovered in Genesis a secret clue that had remained hidden up to then and that is too complicated to have been thought of by human beings. The letters that form the word "Torah" appear all through Genesis, one by one, is strict order, at regular intervals of 49 letters, perfectly integrated into the words that compose the text.

How strange that the computer would be applied to the kabbala! I did not know that they were making those experiments. It is beautiful, all that.

Is it necessary to prove that the Scriptures are the revealed word of God in order to believe in the existence of God, or is that something that is felt regardless of proofs?

I cannot believe in the existence of God, despite all the statistics in the world.

But you said you believed some time ago.

No, not in a personal God. To search for the truth, yes; but to think that there is somebody or something we call God, no. It is better that He should not exist; if He did he would be responsible for everything. And this world is often atrocious, besides being splendid. I feel more happy now than when I was young. I am looking forward. Even I don't know what forward is left, because at 86 years of age, there will be, no doubt, more past than future.

When you say you are looking forward, do you mean looking forward to continuing to create as a writer?

Yes. What else is left for me? Well, no. Friendship remains. Somehow, love remains—and the most precious gift, doubt.

If we did not think of God as a personal God but as concepts of truth and ethics, would you accept Him?

Yes, as ethics. There is a book by (Robert Louis) Stevenson in which we find the idea that a moral law exists even if we don't believe in God. I feel that we all know when we act well or badly. I feel ethics is beyond discussion. For example, I have acted badly many times, but when I do it, I know that it is wrong. It is not because of the consequences. In the long run, consequences even up, don't you think? It is the fact itself of doing good or doing bad. Stevenson said that in the same way a ruffian knows there are things he should not do, so a tiger or an ant knows there are things they should not do. The moral law pervades everything. Again the idea is "God is in the making."

What about truth?

I don't know. It would be very strange for us to be able to understand it. In one of my short stories I speak about that. I was rereading *The Divine Comedy,* and, as you will remember, in the first canto, Dante has two or three animals, and one of them is a leopard. The editor points out that a leopard was brought to Florence in Dante's time and that Dante, like any citizen of Florence, must have seen that leopard, and so he put a leopard into the first canto of the *Inferno*. In my story, **"Inferno, I, 32,"** I imagine that in a dream the leopard is told it has been created so Dante can see it and use it in his poem. The leopard understands that in the dream, but when he awakens, naturally, how could he understand that he exists only so a man could write a poem and use him in it? And I said that if the reason he wrote *The Divine Comedy* had been revealed to Dante, he could have understood it in a dream but not when he awoke. That reason would be as complex for Dante as the other one was for the leopard.

In **"The Mirror of Enigmas,"** *you say, quoting Thomas De Quincey, that everything is a secret mirror of something else. That idea of the search for a hidden sense is in all your work.*

Yes, I think so. It is a very common human ambition—is it not?—to suppose everything has an explanation and to think we could understand it. Let's take as an example the various conceptions about the origin of the world, of which we spoke a while ago. I cannot imagine an infinite time, nor a beginning of time, so any reasoning about that is barren, since I can't conceive of it. I haven't arrived at anything. I am just a man of letters. I am not sure I have thought anything in my life. I am a weaver of dreams.

Since we have spoken about the kabbala, that is, about the studies to decipher the word of God, let's speak about the Bible. What do you think about the inspiration of the Bible?

What I find very strange is the fact that the Hebrews did not take into account the various authors or the different epochs when the books were written. It is strange to see everything in the Bible as a creation of the Spirit, which inspires those who write it, through different epochs. It is never thought, for example, that the works of Emerson, Whitman and Bernard Shaw have the same author. But the Hebrews took writers that were many miles and centuries apart and attributed their work to the same Spirit. It is a strange idea, is it not? Nowadays we think of authors, even of entire literatures, as consecutive. But they didn't. They saw everything as written by one author, and that author was the Spirit. Maybe they thought the circumstances of the writing do not matter, that the circumstances are trivial, that history is trivial. "The Bible"—the name is plural—comes from "the books" in Greek. It is a library, really, and a very heterogeneous one too. It is evident that the author of the Book of Job cannot be the author of Genesis, nor can the Song of Songs or Ecclesiastes and the Book of Kings have the same author. It is as if the individuals did not matter, nor the epochs, nor the chronological order. All is attributed to only one author, the Spirit.

One of the fundamental books of the kabbala, the "Sefer Yezirah" ("Book of Creation"), deals with the 10 Sefirot. That term means "numbers," and they are taken to be an emanation from God, the Ein-Sof. Should we think, then, that the First Being is a cipher, that He is abstract?

I feel that the First Being, the Ein-Sof, cannot be defined. It cannot even be said that He exists. Even that is too concrete. Then you cannot say that He is wise or that He knows. Because if He knows, then there are two things—the known and the One who knows. And that is too detailed for God. He should be an indefinite divinity. And then from there spring forth the "10 emanations," or Sefirot, and one of them creates this world. It is the same idea as the Gnostics had, that this world was created by a subaltern god. (H. G.) Wells had that idea also. That way you explain imperfections such as evil, diseases, physical pains, so many things. Because if an absolute God had made the world, he would have done it better, no? Instead, He has made our bodies, which are very liable to err, decompose and become diseased; the mind also decomposes, and it fails with age, and, well, there are so many other objections.

In the "Zohar" ("The Book of Splendor"), which Gershom Scholem considers the most important literary work of the kabbala, there are many speculations about life after death. Swedenborg describes in detail hells and paradises. Dante's poem is also about hell, purgatory, paradise. Where does this tendency of man come from, to try to imagine and describe something that he cannot possibly know?

In spite of oneself, one thinks. I am almost sure to be blotted out by death, but sometimes I think it is not impossible that I may continue to live in some other manner after my physical death. I feel every suicide has that doubt: Is what I am going to do worthwhile? Will I be blotted out, or will I continue to live on another world? Or as Hamlet wonders, what dreams will come when we leave this body? It could be a nightmare. And then we would be in hell. Christians believe that one continues after death to be who he has been and that he is punished or rewarded forever, according to what he has done in this brief time that was given to him. I would prefer to continue living after death if I have to but to forget the life I lived. (pp. 1, 27-9)

Jorge Luis Borges, "Borges on Life and Death," in an interview with Amelia Barili, in The New York Times Book Review, *July 13, 1986, pp. 1, 27-9.*

ALFRED J. MACADAM

[*MacAdam, an American critic and professor specializing in Latin American literature, is the author of* Modern Latin American Narratives: The Dreams of Reason *(1977). He serves as editor of* Review: Latin American Literature and Arts *and contributing editor of* Handbook of Latin American Studies. *MacAdam recalls Borges's visit in 1984 to the Center for Inter-American Relations, which publishes* Review. *In the following excerpt MacAdam offers his personal impressions of Borges.*]

The death of Jorge Luis Borges on June 14, should have surprised no one. Did we expect this fragile man in his eighties to live forever? I think we did. Why not? For most of us Borges had always been there, and we simply assumed he always would be. He was immortal.

Borges's last visit to the Center for Inter-American Relations took place in 1984, when Alastair Reid, A. John Coleman and I interviewed him about his having been awarded the T. S. Eliot Prize. It was a classic Borges performance: While always cordial and polite, he was constantly making outrageous or impertinent remarks; while always self-effacing, he was clearly proud of his artistic achievements. We were more than happy to be his straight men and to revel in the irony of his comments about his earlier writings and his relationship with T. S. Eliot. When I foolishly asked him what he thought of Eliot's poetry, he replied with a straight face that in his opinion Eliot was "much too cerebral." That Jorge Luis Borges would dare call anyone else too cerebral was the kind of *mise en abyme* we had come to expect from him, although the audience, it must be said, gasped. While his baroque, inexhaustible stories reflect our world, Borges himself was not really of this world. He was really a nineteenth-century man adrift in the late twentieth century, the last Victorian, an old-fashioned Argentine *criollo viejo*. He was the kind of person Ezra Pound had in mind when he wrote:

They will come no more,
The old men with beautiful manners.

An age has truly come to an end.

Alfred J. MacAdam, "Jorge Luis Borges: 1899-1986," in Review, *No. 36, January-June, 1986, p. 4.*

WILLIAM D. MONTALBANO

Jorge Luis Borges, a blind man of soaring and fantastic vision who became the dean of Latin American letters, died [June 14] in Switzerland. Borges, who often complained that he had lived too long, was 86.

Death came to the master Argentine storyteller in a chalet on the shores of Lake Geneva to which he had moved only a week [before]. At his side was 41-year-old Maria Kodama, whom Borges met when she was a teen-age student of literature and had employed for the past decade as a secretary and companion. They were married . . . April 26. "For love," Borges said.

Borges had left his cramped and stuffy apartment in downtown Buenos Aires at the end of 1985 aware that little time remained, his lawyer, Osvaldo Vidaurre, said Saturday. He said Kodama had called him . . . to say her husband was dead. "I feel very alone," he quoted her as saying.

"He knew he had cancer of the liver," Vidaurre said. "Before leaving for Geneva he had undergone an analysis, including a biopsy. The doctors told him it was incurable and irreversible."

Vidaurre said it was Borges' wish to die and be buried in Geneva, the city where he spent his adolescence and which "he knew like the back of his hand." Word of his fatal illness was kept secret. When a European reporter recently asked Borges how he liked Switzerland, Borges said that he was "mysteriously happy."

By nightfall [June 14], newspapers with identical banner headlines sold briskly to Argentines lining up for movie and theater seats: "Borges Is Dead." President Raul Alfonsin expressed sorrow, and his government issued a formal decree of mourning.

Spurning novels, which he dismissed as too often "full of padding," Borges focused on poems and terse, dreamlike and often ironic short stories of fantastic speculation hewn with great verbal and narrative power.

One critic called him "the founder of fabulization." Another said he was "a jeweler of words." The late Andre Maurois once observed that Borges had identified his own talent in describing metaphysicians on his imaginary planet Tlon: "They seek neither truth nor likelihood. They seek astonishment."

Borges won scores of awards and titles from universities around the world, but never the Nobel Prize, although he was bridesmaid for at least two decades. He once said that denying him the prize had become a Scandinavian tradition. Borges' work in a 60-year career fills 35 volumes. In his later years, he often denigrated his early work as "overwritten . . . baroque . . . affected and dogmatic." Those works he himself liked best included ***The Cipher,*** a book of poems, ***The Book of Sands*** and ***Dr. Brodie's Report.***

Borges was born Aug. 24, 1899, in a district of Buenos Aires called Palermo, which Borges' stories of his youth would make famous as a knife fighters' part of town.

The son of a diplomat, Borges learned English from a nanny before he learned Spanish. He spoke it with intimidating fluency and a trace of an Irish lilt. Returning to Buenos Aires from Switzerland in 1921, he edited a literary magazine and wrote poetry for a decade until turning to the short stories of a bygone, idealized Buenos Aires—work that first drew international attention.

A gradual failing of his sight blinded Borges in 1956 when he was head of Argentina's national library. In an autobiography accompanying his book ***El Aleph,*** Borges acknowledged "God's splendid irony in granting me at one time 300,000 books and darkness." Thereafter, he dictated poems and short prose pieces.

In his later years, Borges was the undiscerning host to would-be and has-been writers, journalists, teachers, critics and nearly anyone else who asked to see him. Hands wrapped around a gnarled cane, he would hunch forward on an old-fashioned sofa and gab. Once, for a visitor, he recited "The Lord's Prayer" in Old Norse. He liked the power of the language, he said.

As he grew older, visitors increasingly asked Borges about death. "When she was 99, my mother would lie in there every night," Borges said one day, gesturing toward the bedroom, "and pray to die before she was 100." Borges' mother, Leonor, to whom he was devoted, died in 1976 before her 100th birthday.

At a literary gathering here last October, a questioner asked Borges—who variously described himself as a conservative, an atheist and an anarchist—whether the idea of death was more difficult for a non-believer.

"On the contrary," Borges replied. "It is much easier. The believers are pretty crazy: They must be punished or rewarded. Who am I to deserve a punishment or a reward? Clearly, nobody. The fact of believing that death is absolute gives great tranquility, a great serenity. I believe that if they told me that I would die tonight, I would feel relieved, but one knows so little of oneself that perhaps I would be terrified. I don't know, but I feel rather impatient. I have lived too long."

William D. Montalbano, "Borges, Dean of Latin American Writers, Dies," in Los Angeles Times, *June 15, 1986.*

LEWIS H. DIUGUID

Argentine author Jorge Luis Borges, a master of parable and paradox whose appeal was international but who never gained widespread popularity, died [June 14]. . . .

The most lengthy of Borges' works fell short of 30 pithy pages, but many critics ranked him with the rollicking novelists who created, at length, the Latin American literary renaissance.

Borges' life and style often seemed as paradoxical as the tales he spun in such narrow volumes as ***Dreamtigers, Fictions*** and ***Labyrinths.*** A blind man, he was a master of description, provoking indelible images with a spare use of words, yet he carries to his grave the key to enigmas in many of his perplexing stories.

He was considered by some a consummate modernist, yet he said in an interview 10 years ago that "when I went blind in 1955, I decided not to read any more contemporary writing."

Widely acclaimed for his limpid Spanish, the only language in which he published, Borges declared that "English is by far the better language." He spoke it perfectly and taught English literature. And yet, when the conservative Borges' Chilean contemporary, communist lyric poet Pablo Neruda, said, "Very little can be done with the Spanish language," Borges bitingly replied, "That's why nothing has been done."

What Borges did in Spanish, most of it translated into the world's major languages, was 20 volumes of poems, short stories, essays and collections. The early stories, especially those rooted in the Argentine pampas, often seemed uncomplicated. Later efforts provoked lengthy literary criticism.

"People are always searching for too much in my work . . . finding profundities," Borges said. "Most people think everything I write is a parable."

Critic Anatole Broyard detected a swing back from the mazes and imaginary beasts that populated Borges' middle period on reviewing ***Dr. Brodie's Report,*** translated into English in 1970:

"He has begun to write 'realistic' or 'straightforward' stories . . . woven around a plot,' and often little else. In some cases, Borges has descended from the metaphysical to the supernatural. . . . He seems to be doubting the value of the very qualities that earned him his reputation."

While critics often compared Borges to Franz Kafka for his convolutions or Edgar Allan Poe for his sense of fantastic, the author cited as his principal precursors Robert Louis Stevenson, Rudyard Kipling, G. K. Chesterton and Thomas De Quincey.

It was not only Neruda's lyricism or politics that irritated Borges, but also the fact that he had won the Nobel Prize. Borges often was nominated and his defensiveness on not being chosen was characteristically cast in self-effacement. "When the literature of the second half of the 20th century is studied, the names will be different than we hear now," he said. "They will have found hidden writers. People who won Nobel Prizes will be forgotten." Adding a pinch of enigma, he added: "I hope I will be forgotten."

On another occasion Borges said, "I almost don't exist."

Borges was not a popular author among Argentina's readers. The exceptions were the few stories of knife-throwing gauchos brawling in bordellos. He wrote authoritatively two pieces with the same title, **"The Idiom of the Argentines,"** about the mix of Spanish, Italian and local invention that makes listening a diversion in Buenos Aires.

As a young man, after studying in Europe, he edited a couple of iconoclastic literary magazines that failed to sell. As his subject matter lost its Argentine roots, he found small but fervent readership, through translations, abroad.

"I don't like to be read in terms of an atlas," he said. The reader "should read me and forget all about me. He should read just for the story."

A related aspect of Borges' unpopularity at home was his distrust of the volatile passions that gripped Argentina in the last half of his life. In the early 1940s he was municipal librarian of Buenos Aires and bitterly opposed to the rise of Juan D. Peron, the dictatorial populist with an admiration for Mussolini.

Peron jailed Borges' mother briefly and had the librarian demoted to chicken inspector after he signed an anti-Peron manifesto. Peron went into lengthy exile after a coup in 1955. While Borges feared his return, the "shirtless ones" (peasants) and a considerable portion of the intelligentsia agitated for Peron's restoration.

As that passion became predominant, Borges, by then director of the National Library, was quoted less and less in the Buenos Aires press. Although less heard, he was often seen—guided by his cane, making his way through the down-town streets of the capital.

With the restoration, through elections, of Peron in 1973, Borges began to spend considerable time teaching in the United States and listening to Dixieland jazz.

After Peron's death, his widow was succeeded by military rule, which quickly turned brutal. Borges, with his international stature, came under pressure to speak out against the arbitrary seizure and killings of suspected left-wing guerrillas. Reluctantly at first, and later more forcefully, he did so—although again, the majority probably was against him at the time.

When the military's popularity was ebbing and the generals started the 1982 Falklands War in a bid for renewed support, Borges published in the mass-circulation daily *Clarin* a touching antiwar poem on the deaths in the South Atlantic of two young innocents sent by the opposing sides to battle. "They buried them together. Snow and corruption know them," the lines concluded.

It was as close as Borges came to political poetry on a continent that is famous for its poet-politicians.

Lewis H. Diuguid, "Noted Author Jorge L. Borges Dies in Geneva," in The Washington Post, *June 15, 1986.*

CHRISTOPHER HITCHENS

[Hitchens, an English political journalist who is Washington correspondent for the Nation, *is the author of* Inequalities in Zimbabwe *(1981) and* Cyprus *(1984). In the following excerpt Hitchens reminisces about a visit he had with Borges when the aging writer still lived in Argentina and recounts some of Borges's observations on literature and politics.]*

This is my country and it might be yet,
But something came between us and the sun.

As the old man threw off these lines, he turned his blind, smiling face to me and asked, 'Do they still read much Edmund Blunden in England?' I was unsure of what might give pleasure, but pretty certain in saying that Blunden was undergoing one of his eclipses. 'What a shame,' said Jorge Luis Borges, 'but then you still have Chesterton. I used to live in Kensington, you know. What a writer. Such a pity he became a Catholic.'

The changes of pace in a conversation with Borges seemed alarming at the time, but in retrospect showed nothing but one's own nervousness. He was always searching for a mutually agreeable topic, and seemed at times to fear that it was he, lonely, sightless and claustrated, who might be the dull partner in chat. When he found a subject that would please, he began to bubble and grin, and even to tease.

I had made my way to Maipu 994, near the Plaza San Martin, and found apartment 6B after a great deal of discouragement. Argentine government officials, usually so quick to sing of the splendours of their country, became curiously *diminuendo* when I asked if Borges was well enought to receive visitors. 'He does not welcome guests, Senõr. He does not welcome invitations either. It is better not to trouble him.' At last I simply dialled his number, imagined him working his way across the room as it rang, and was rewarded with an invitation to call upon him.

This was at the height of General Videla's pogrom against dissent, and I had already learned that a private telephone conversation in Buenos Aires was a difficult thing to have. Borges didn't care about this, partly because he heartily approved of the generals then in power. He gave me the couplet from Blunden as an instance of his feeling for Juan Peron, the vulgar mobster who had persecuted him and his family. But we didn't touch upon this until much later. He wanted to discuss English and Spanish as mediums of literature. 'I was speaking Spanish and English before there were any such languages. Do you know that in Mexico they say, "I am seeing you" when they mean, "I will see you"? I find the translation of the present into the future very ingenious. But when I think of the Bible I think of King James. And most of my reading is in English.'

He had a great respect for *Martin Fierro,* the demotic gaucho epic that is the distinctive Argentine ballad. And he had a feeling for the folklore of the country's numerous and futile wars. But he disliked the ornate pageantry that sometimes substituted for tradition in Buenos Aires, 'the showy pomp and circumstance—the hypocrisy'. His religion, he said, was presbyterian if anything, and he had some Portuguese Jewish influence in his family. It was this latter aspect that had helped stir the malice of Peron and, though he did not realise it, was the reason for the coolness of General Videla's people as well.

Back to England. 'I began to learn Old English when I went blind in 1955, and it helped me to write **"The Library of Babel".** I made a special pilgrimage to Lichfield once, because of Dr Johnson. But I hated Stratford.' 'Did you learn Old Norse?' 'No, not really, that is—no. But would you read me some Kipling?' 'With pleasure.' 'Then make it 'The Harp Song of the Dane Women'. And please read it slowly. I like to take long, long sips.'

> What is a woman that you forsake her,
> And the hearth fire and the home acre,
> To go with that old, grey widow-maker . . .

When I had finished he sat for a while and said, 'Kipling was not really appreciated in his own time because all his peers were socialists. Will you come and read me more Kipling tomorrow?' I said yes.

Next day I led him down a spiral staircase on my arm, and took him to lunch. He talked of how reverse and obverse were the same to him, so that infinity was almost banal. He said that he always felt utterly lost when he was dreaming, which was perhaps the source of the recurrent labyrinth in his writing. I asked him why he had always been so polite about Pablo Neruda, and he replied that while he much preferred Gabriel Garcia Marquez, he didn't want anyone to think that he was jealous of Neruda's Nobel Prize for literature. 'Though when you see who had has it—Shaw, Faulkner. Still, I would grab it. I feel greedy.' He said later that 'not giving me the Nobel Prize is a minor Swedish industry.'

I read him lots more Kipling and Chesterton until the time came to part. Could I come back again? Alas, I had to fly to Chile that evening. 'Ah, well if you see General Pinochet, please present him with my compliments. He was good enough once to award me a prize, and I consider him a gentleman.' I don't remember what I answered to that, but I do remember that it made a perfect match with the rest of his general conversation. He delighted in saying that the Videla government was one of 'gentlemen rather than pimps'. He explained to me the precise etymology of the Argentine slang for pimp, which was *canfinflero* or, as he also relished saying, 'cunter'. Though he was aloof from the cold war ('Why should we choose between two second-rate countries?') he loathed the idea of the mob and the many-headed. For him, English literature was a respite from all that. 'My ***Dr Brodie's Report*** is taken from Swift. And **"Death and the Compass"** is like Conan Doyle in 3-D.'

Long before war broke out between his homeland and his beloved England (words like 'folk' and 'kin' recurred in his talk), Borges had seen through the Videla régime. He had signed a public protest about the 15,000 'disappeared', which was perhaps the more powerful for having been so belated. He had spoken against the idea of a *macho* war with Chile over the stupid issue of the Beagle Channel. And his poem deploring the Falklands was as ironic and eloquent as anything written in Buenos Aires could afford to be. For a man who told me that 'I spend my days alone, in daydreams and the evolution of plots,' he was astoundingly alive to 'the outside' and peculiarly ready to take risks. I can never hear the sneer about 'ivory towers' without reflecting that Borges, who was confined to one by his blindness, managed to make honourable amendments to his cherished point of view.

As I left him, he said he would like to give me a present. I made the usual awkward disclaimers about how he shouldn't think of such a thing but he pressed on and recited a poem which he told me I would not forget. Looking me in the eye, as it were, he said:

> What man has bent o'er his son's sleep, to brood
> How that face shall watch his when cold it lies?
> Or thought, as his own mother kissed his eyes,
> Of what her kiss was when his father wooed?

This remains the only Dante Gabriel Rossetti sonnet I can unfailingly recall. (pp. 12-13)

Christopher Hitchins, "Jorge Luis Borges," in The Spectator, *Vol. 256, No. 8241, June 21, 1986, pp. 12-13.*

THE NEW YORKER

When the news reached us of the death, at eighty-six, of Jorge Luis Borges, in Geneva, on June 14th, it brought not just the pang we felt at the loss of his wise, beguiling presence but also the peculiar shiver of disquiet that his writings often generate. In our issue of June 2nd, [*The New Yorker*] published a poem of his, in which he speculates on his death. It begins:

> Which of my cities
> am I doomed to die in?
> Geneva,
> where revelation reached me
> from Virgil and Tacitus
> (certainly not from Calvin)?

In retrospect, the poem's appearance has about it that very shiver of coincidence which we have come to call Borgesian, after the Master—for we have found that reading certain of his stories and poems has the effect of casting quite ordinary happenings in a strange, vertiginous light. One of Borges' chosen Spanish words was "*asombro*," which means "astonishment," or, better, "awe." Awe was what Borges found at the heart of great literature; awe was what he felt about the myriad chance crossings in human existence—"the webbed scheme," as he called it—and awe was what, through his quirky essays, his disturbing fictions, his fantastic stories, and his meditative poems, he aroused in his readers. In a famous essay of his, **"Kafka and His Precursors,"** he demonstrates how after we have read the world through Kafka's eyes we find his influence even in writers who came before him in time. So it is with Borges: once we have read him, we sense his curious presence everywhere—in the past, in chance happenings, in the context of our own lives.

More than any other writer, Borges lived in and through literature. For him, reading was a form of time travel; his favorite writers were his friends; and, before his blindness finally descended, he had learned a whole library by heart. From a very early age, he had understood that it was his destiny to be a writer; and, indeed, no one has done more honor to that solitary office. Yet Borges never failed to point out the ironies implicit in making written sense of the world: a book, once written, mocks the writer by outlasting him, and the eternities created by the imagination are rendered ironic by the inevitability of death. Even so, for Borges it was only in writing that the living moment could be held, saved from oblivion; and literature, the sum of those written moments, was, for him, consolation enough. Just as literature had given him life, he turned his life into literature—literature of a spare and wondrous variety—and the facts of his life, such as his blindness, became metaphors in his writing. "When writers die," he once said, "they become books, which is, after all, not too bad an incarnation."

It is not every writer who adds to his work by his presence; but as Borges' writings infiltrated other languages he was much sought after, and late in his life he grew prodigal with his time, travelling to different countries, giving many lectures and interviews, appearing on international television, and answering endless questions with unfailing courtesy. . At one time, his readers felt themselves to be members of a secret society; now they are legion. Many who had read him came to hear him, and carried away, as a talisman, an image of him that added affection to awe: frail, soft-spoken in both English and Spanish, his hands clasping a walking stick in front of him, he mesmerized his listeners with his careful phrasing, his modesty, his wit, the warm and often mischievous humor of his spoken asides. We recall a conversation we had with him just over a year ago, in which he talked about his travelling; he referred to it, characteristically, as "seeing the world." "When I am at home in Buenos Aires," he told us, "one day is much like another. But when I travel—and you must realize that for me, since I am blind, travelling means merely changing armchairs—friendly ghosts materialize one by one and talk to me about literature, and about my own works, most generously. For a writer, that is great luxury. I feel blessed by it, I feel lucky." Besides his books, his gentle ghost is very much with us. (pp. 19-20)

"The Talk of the Town," in The New Yorker, *Vol. LXII, No. 20, July 7, 1986, pp. 19-20.*

HERBERT A. KENNY

[*Kenny is an American editor, poet, nonfiction, and juvenile fiction writer. Among his works are* A Catholic Quiz Book *(1947) and* Literary Dublin: A History *(1974). In the following excerpt Kenny offers a brief personal reminiscence about Borges, whom he met during the author's visit to Harvard in 1968.*]

With Jorge Luis Borges's death it is incredible to look back and realize that he did not get the Nobel Prize for Literature, which was given to Pearl Buck, John Steinbeck, and some Spanish and Italian poets who were not nearly so widely read nor one-quarter so influential. Worse still, it was given to William Golding at the very time that Borges had achieved his eminence. Was it that he offered no moral lessons, but wove his artifice for its own beauty, putting literature above the real world? For him literature was the real world. He was a conservative who was intent not on changing the world but on appreciating it, in both senses of that word.

To sit and read the *Commedia* with him and hear him expound was to make Dante's *Inferno* as real as Scarsdale. To enter into his own mirror world where time warped away into layers of dreams was to walk on air that became as palpable as the pages of the book.

One can say of Borges that he was a dear man. His soul was without bitterness. Neither his blindness, nor the loss of his mother, whom he tremendously admired, nor his unhappy marriage, nor the neglect of critics, nor the indignities he suffered under Argentine dictators wrenched outrage from his lips. I first met Borges when he came to Harvard in 1968. He had only recently married, and his wife, Elsa, spoke no English and found American university life unattractive. I introduced him to John Van Dell, a Salem, Massachusetts, jeweler who was born in Argentina, and his wife, Jean, of Portuguese background, both of whom spoke Spanish well. Borges and John immediately hit it off. On such difficulties as marriage presented to a lifelong bachelor (Borges was 68), John became his counselor.

Sunday after Sunday we all convened in the Van Dell back garden, where John cooked halves of chicken and sides of beef gaucho-style, while Borges sat and dreamed or wined and dined. I don't think he was ever happier. Together we read and argued about *Martin Fierro,* that Argentine classic, and John told of his days riding with the gauchos. "John romanticizes the gauchos!" Borges would say, who romanticized them a bit himself.

I last saw him in Dublin in 1982, when he flew over to join in celebrating the centenary of the birth of James Joyce. It was a Bloomsday celebration, and scholars from all over the world were on hand. I presented myself to Borges, and we sat together in the Great Hall of Dublin Castle, and he immediately began to talk of Salem, its authors, its history, the Van Dells, and the exuberant gaucho cookouts. His spirit was as serene as ever.

Herbert A. Kenny, "Jorge Luis Borges, RIP," in National Review, *New York, Vol. XXXVIII, No. 13, July 18, 1986, pp. 20-1.*

JOHN STURROCK

[*Sturrock, an English critic and editor of the* Times Literary Supplement, *is the author of* The French New Novel *(1969) and* Paper Tigers: The Ideal Fictions of Jorge Luis Borges *(1978). In the following excerpt Sturrock discusses the philosophy of Borges as expressed in both his life and his writings.*]

Borges died on 14 June, in Geneva—which bare fact virtually calls for an 'English papers please copy,' as they used to say, so complacently scant and grudging were the notices which we were given to read at the time. There was much Englishness about him, starting with his mother's family, which *was* English, but obvious also in the plain way that he wrote, and in the humour with which he used to deprecate his own high literary standing. Anglo-Saxon was the strange hobby of his old age, because it was northern and pleasantly formal, and in his earlier days, before his eyesight got too weak, he had read more in English literature than in any other. Critics might say, because there were labyrinths and what seemed like anxiety in his stories, that he followed on from Kafka: Borges himself said, rather, from Kipling. But none of this saved him when he died from being a foreigner, and a writer, hardly worth the column-inches of our barbarically parochial papers.

Borges was an old man, in his 87th year, a few weeks married, working—word had it—on a screenplay for a film about Venice. He had been ill for months but was well enough by June to have gone home to Buenos Aires if he had wanted to: perhaps Buenos Aires was not home enough to reclaim this comfortless man, who had learnt in his old age to travel the Western world, first-class and rather gloriously, as a late-maturing literary lion. He chose to stay on in a hotel in Geneva and to die there. The interviewers—did anyone ever give more interviews than Borges, or should it be the same interview more times?—were always asking him about death, and whether he was worried by it, and his answer was no, he wasn't, that he looked forward to it, that he was tired. This answer echoed what he once wrote about his own father, whom he admired for his invincible modesty and for being 'impatient for death' after he had had a stroke. It was the answer, too, of someone addicted to narrative, who was far from presuming that his own life had made a good story but was comforted by the nearness of a dénouement.

Geneva was not just anywhere for Borges—he had old and supportive memories of the place. There is an entry for it in the slight, peripatetic pages of his ***Atlas:*** 'Of all the cities on this planet, of all the diverse and intimate places which a man seeks out and merits in the course of his voyages, Geneva strikes me as the most propitious for happiness. Beginning in 1914, I owe it the revelation of French, of Latin, of German, of Expressionism, of Schopenhauer, of the doctrine of Buddha, of Taoism, of Conrad, of Lafcadio Hearn and of the nostalgia of Buenos Aires. Also: the revelation of love, of friendship, of humiliation and of the temptation to suicide.' Facing which compacted reminiscence there is a photograph of the mild, more or less sightless Borges sitting, both hands folded on his stick, as they so often were, before some Calvinist memorial, stony and overbearing, with a group of robed predestinarians staring out above the head of this shy and sceptical man who thought that all such large ideas, of God, grace or free will, were good only for playing about with, and not for committing yourself to, when there was every chance that they answered to nothing at all in the actual, probably soulless constitution of the universe.

Borges lived in Geneva as an adolescent, from 1914 until 1919. With hopelessly poor timing his lawyer father had decided, very impulsively, that the family should go in the summer of 1914 to be Europeanised, as the better-off Buenos Aires families then did. But the Grand Tour fell foul of the Great War; they were stuck in Geneva. So Borges went to a lycée there, adding new languages to his native Spanish and practically native English, which he had got from an English grandmother and from his English governess, Miss Tink. Miss Tink, for all the monosyllabic innocence of her name, had a bad cousin, John, who may well also have influenced the child Borges, because he was one of the street-corner 'hoodlums' who later fascinated him, partly for being so brave as well as bad, when they fought, and partly because he saw them as ideal compendia of the local mythology, the fallen descendants of something more honourable in the nation's past and at the same time an essential inclusion in its literature. Seen from Switzerland, Buenos Aires toughs like John Tink looked like just the sort of stereotype Borges wanted, defined by distance and already more than half imaginary.

Geneva encapsulated for Borges his introduction to the frontierless world of the mind. In a story which he wrote in 1972, called **'The Other',** the old Borges confers with the young, the old one sitting, as a grand visitor to Harvard, beside the Charles River in Boston, the young one beside the Rhone in Geneva, as the eager representative of his immaturity. In Geneva he grew for ever beyond the confines of Argentina, laying down other literatures and philosophies on top of whatever he had met with as a boy. The philosophy especially, idealist or oriental and quietist, alienated him from the simple empiricism in which he might otherwise have grown up. After a course of Schopenhauer, and of the seamlessly idealist Bishop Berkeley, he was an 'Argentinian strayed into metaphysics', as he later wryly put it, as if to apologise for holding such a futile interest before compatriots whom he mainly thought too backward to share it. Geneva was a great good place because it was to him like a library, a truly eclectic experience for someone who believed that being Argentinian was an opportunity to gather in cultural goods from wherever you wanted. And can we even be sure that the other 'revelations' he lists, the 'humiliation' and 'temptation to suicide', did not also come from his reading? When writing or talking about himself Borges was fearlessly misleading and saw no call to separate real events from imagined, on the grounds that he no longer knew or cared greatly which was which. He had an unusual sense of the power of repetition, of how a memory repeated over and over, as he freely repeated some of his own memories, grows increasingly unreal as it enters into the equivocal realm of literary art. To memorialise one's own life a single time, in an autobiography, is to try to keep facts merely as facts: to do it more than once and in the same terms is to ensure that the factual becomes the legendary. And if, like Borges, you have gone in more for reading and thinking than for the bolder kinds of living, there is even less cause to hold to puritanical, possibly deceptive distinctions between first and second-hand encounters with life.

In 1919, set free by the peace, the Borgeses moved on to Spain, and then in 1921 back to Buenos Aires. Apart from one more, much briefer time in Europe, in 1923, Borges was then nearly forty years at home, until at the start of the Sixties the quite sudden ubiquity of his reputation as a writer drew him out from Buenos Aires: he was invited to move as ambitiously about the world in the body as he had long done, discreetly and undemandingly, in the mind. In Spain he started to write seriously, though what he wrote was not yet in the wonderfully spare manner of later on. Spain then had its Ultraistas, or noisy and insolent modernists, and the Expressionism which Borges had picked up in Switzerland gave him his entrée there. He was mad for Walt Whitman, for parataxis (he never lost his belief in that: the shock cuts of such enlightened directors as Josef von Sternberg were a chief reason why he loved the movies, and his own finest stories make tremendous if unobtrusive capital out of them), and first and foremost for metaphors. Of these he had so many to hand that when his father, who was trying to write a novel, ran dry, Borges offered him spares of his own, which that father of exemplary modesty 'accepted out of resignation'. Borges himself produced a fine story about a werewolf, as a typical item of cultural emigration from Europe to Latin America, but no one would publish it. He wrote essays, including one whose subtitle was 'Towards an Aesthetic of Spanish Brothels' and in which the allurements of the girls were highmindedly neutralised by being assimilated to those of Quevedo's poetry; and a collection of poems entitled, according to Borges, 'either *The Red Psalms* or *The Red Rhythms* . . . in free verse and in praise of the Russian revolution, the brotherhood of man, and pacifism'. Bolsheviks, like brothels, were too furious a theme to stay for very long in Borges's delicate imagination, and theirs was certainly the first and the last revolution he ever warmed to. (p. 6)

He took either a poor view of politics, or, most of the time, no view at all, which wasn't easy or always wise, as a citzen of Argentina. Politics caught up with him only once, under Peron in the Forties. Peron was a fascist and a populist who liked to put down the smart, salon-dwelling European culture for which Borges stood. Borges had been for the Allies in the war of 1939-45, and he was against Peron, who had been for Hitler and Mussolini. Borges signed manifestos against the dictator and the dictator, famously, took his job away from him. It wasn't much of a job, something like number three in a local library, but it was a political appointment and he was promoted to oversee chicken and rabbit sales in a street-market, because chickens and rabbits were just the sort of wimpish creatures an intellectual ought to feel kinship with. Borges did not accept the appointment: he resigned and was out of work. He turned, because it was all there was for him to do, to teaching and lecturing, which he went on doing for most of the rest of his life: ***Seven Nights*** is the text of seven lectures given in Buenos Aires in 1977, but the subjects are ones he could have lectured on at almost any date after 1930—Dante, the *Thousand and One Nights,* Buddhism, the *Kabbala,* Nightmares, Blindness, Poetry. These are old lectures remembered—which is to say, refined by time, in that temporal process of distortion and oblivion which Borges saw it as his task to mimic.

The political credit which he earned by standing out against Peronism, he later dissipated. He was far too tame and olympian to be a hero to younger, angrier South American writers, nothing of a nationalist, too openly a conservative. In later life, when the test case of Cuba arose, Borges was sardonic towards Castro, to the point of preferring not to name him, and ungenerous towards the Argentinian Che Guevara, who died in what Borges clearly thought was a rotten cause, even though he might at a pinch have been found room in the writer's own mythology of Argentina, as a legendary *bravo*. During the bad days of military juntas in Argentina Borges seems to have kept silent, to have not wanted to know. Against Peron he had made a public statement, that 'dictatorships foment oppression, dictatorships foment subservience, dictatorships foment cruelty; even more abominable is the fact that they foment stupidity.' In the time of Peron maybe stupidity *was* the most abominable effect, in the later time of the *desaparecidos* it was not: things had got too murderous for Borges's fastidious argument to be even worth restating. But in some of his later stories there are signs that he saw the savageries of Argentina's history as no longer a safely catalogued stereotype, and more as topical threat. (pp. 6-7)

Borges's conservatism was frequently offered as the reason why he never got the Nobel Prize, because it was not what the very progressive Swedish Academy liked, especially in writers from Latin America, who do well to show themselves as radical and indigenous, and not, like Borges, as aloof and rootless. This is more likely to be true than another, literary reason why he did not get given the prize, which is that he was simply too literary, that he wrote about literature and not, as Nobel Prize-winners are meant to, immediately about life. The Nobel Prize is a simpleminded affair, invented for writers who are realists, but Borges was that for only a few years, when he began: a realist and a romantic, because the two go together. The first collection of poems which he published in the Twenties was called ***Fervor de Buenos Aires,*** and it displayed a zest for local colour and for aggressive imagery of which the older Borges was not proud: there is a story, his own presumably, that when he eventually became head of the National Library in Buenos Aires he used this delegated power of life and death over his own bibliography to remove, first the copies of his earlier books, now disowned, and then the entries in the catalogue that had once led people to them. Certainly, when some of the poems from ***Fervor*** and from his other early collections were brought into his ***Obras Completas*** in the late Sixties, the style had been quietened down and the unity of his oeuvre retrospectively established. In a preface Borges measured the change in himself between 1924 and 1969 with his usual incomparable neatness: 'In those days I sought out sunsets, suburbs and unhappiness; nowadays, mornings, the centre and serenity.'

What turned Borges into Borges was the knowledge he came to that realism was no closer to reality than any other form of words. Reality is simple and sensuous, language complicated and intellectual; Borges will not have it that there can be a canonical account of things, an *écriture blanche* from which all other accounts are deemed to depart in greater or lesser measure, according to how far they are 'stylised'. In a lecture on 'Poetry' in ***Seven Nights*** he disputes an 'idea attributed to the short story writer Horacio Quiroga' (a realist if ever there was one, seeming to write eyeball to eyeball with his native Uruguayan landscapes) that 'if a cold wind blows from the bank of the river, one must write simply "a cold wind blows from the bank of the river."' That sentence, decrees Borges, is 'as complex as a poem by Gongora or a sentence by Joyce'. Some such shock comparison was needed, to expel the tenacious idea that realism has ontological privileges denied to other literary modes. Realism for Borges is merely one form of idealism, one way of arranging words. Because things themselves are beyond words the writer is free to arrange words as he will, in the delusion, it may be, that he is also arranging things, but Borges is always adamant that reality will never tell *him* what to do when he is writing, even if he must be its slave when he is not.

The world is much richer in its infinite particularities than the disarmingly few generalisations we are able to rise to in our language. Between the uniqueness of our experience, and the by definition 'iterable' (as Derrida has it) signs that are all we have with which to represent it, there is a gap which only the foolish—the realists—would fancy themselves competent to span. Borges, more sensibly, delights in what to more earnest souls seems a grievous discrepancy and in the succinctness of his own writing makes a memorable virtue of language's necessary power of abstraction. He has the Platonic idea that it is by forgetting, or by leaving things out, that we become creators. Total recall is a disaster, the affliction of those too enamoured of a naive realism. One of Borges's most sardonic stories is that of Funes the Memorious, a young unfortunate unable to clear his memory of anything at all, and so for ever debarred from the least creative act. He mercifully dies, very young, of a 'congestion', lost to literature for having been unable to penetrate the secret of language.

Only in the Thirties did Borges take to writing fiction or, better, fictions, a plural called for by the brevity and manifest fictitiousness of what he wrote. In 1935, he published a set of short pieces called ***The Universal History of Infamy,*** stories of malfeasance none of which were of his own first making. Borges was not here telling stories but retelling them, playing 'the irresponsible game of a diffident man lacking the nerve to write stories but who amused himself by falsifying and twisting the stories of others'. Of others, or of no one—because the stories are from stock, they have no rightful owners. Borges does what he wants to do with them an then returns them, puts them back into circulation. These versions, in fact, are object lessons in originality. Borges's major premise is that by this time the literary world is saturated with stories, so that to suppose that one might somehow be able to add entirely new ones is presumptuous. Storytellers do not own the stories that they tell, though they may put their mark on them. Borges asks that they remain modest and not, as they usually are, possessive. The most modest of all Borges's storytellers is Pierre Menard, 'the author of *Don Quijote*', who after great labours produces two and a bit chapters of a text which already exists. Not the same text at all, urges Borges, because Menard's verbatim feat was achieved nearly three centuries after Cervantes and by a man whose native language was French: but that is not an argument that he himself believes for one moment, because Borges is anti-author, as anti-author in his whimsical way as Roland Barthes in his more hectoring one.

Borges never mistook literature for life. Literature is better for us than life because it is more interesting, and more interesting because it has been planned, whereas life is so dishearteningly plotless. Borges's finest stories—**'The Library of Babel', 'Tlon, Uqbar, Orbis Tertius', The Garden of Forking Paths', 'Death and the Compass', 'South', Pierre Menard'**—are narratives of heroic ingenuity, the exquisitely planned fantasies of a remarkable intelligence. Their subject is narrative itself, its forms, its syntax, and above all its seductiveness. Borges did not think that literature improved us, but he did think that it diverted us; his own, in its ironic, unassuming way, is for some of us the most diverting there is. (p. 7)

John Sturrock, "Goodbye to Borges," in London Review of Books, *Vol. 8, No. 14, August 7, 1986, pp. 6-7.*

HECTOR BIANCIOTTI

[Bianciotti is an Argentinian-born novelist, journalist, and editor who writes for the Parisian daily newspaper Le Monde. *He also coedited an edition of Borges's work for the French publishing house Gallimard. In the following excerpt from an article that previously appeared in* Le Monde *in a longer form, Bianciotti recalls visits he made to Borges in Geneva during the author's final illness.]*

Toward the end of 1985 Borges had to undergo a series of medical examinations in Buenos Aires. He did not feel well; day by day the ground became less firm beneath his feet. This did not stop him from going to Geneva for the holidays—he wanted to spend them in the city of his adolescence. In mid-January he was taken to a hospital where, after suffering a hemorrhage, he had to submit to painful medical tests. I visited him there. We chatted, as if we were carrying on a dialogue from the night before, in bits and pieces. He talked of an old friend of Samuel Johnson who published a book under the title *The Joys of Madness,* and of Cocteau, whom he liked, at least partly, and he recited one of his poems to me. He told me that for some time the luminous fog that covered over his vision had turned violet, a color he detested. Then he described in detail the preface he had started to write—the night before, in the hospital—for the Pléiade edition of his work.

It was clear to me that his condition was grave. I remembered that he liked to cite the example of Socrates on his last day, when he refused to talk of death and went on discussing ideas with his friends, not wanting to make pathetic statements of farewell; he sent away his wife and children and nearly dismissed a friend who cried, because he wanted to talk in peace—simply talk, continue to think.

Borges would not express even the usual irritation at being in hospital. He made jokes about the food they gave him—soups and purées whose tastes were indefinable. "It could," he said, "be made of silk, of marble, of an extract of clouds." He was animated by this conversation, and Maria Kodama and I asked him if he would get up and walk with us in the corridor. Not without some fears, he accepted. At first trembling, he finished by holding himself straight and firm. He smiled, and in a voice that was weak but that became heavy and jarring and strong when he recited Anglo-Saxon or Icelandic texts, he chanted—one might say "intoned"—the last verse of the ballad of Maldon, just as we were leaving the corridor.

> He released his beloved falcon into the forest
> and entered the battle.

Two weeks later, he was back at his hotel. He could have returned to his house in Buenos Aires. He had reasons to do so; he feared what would happen to his old editions of Anglo-Saxon sagas. He decided to stay in Geneva, the city of his youth; he wanted to be near the lake. He worked to the end on a scenario for a film on Venice. He was glad to have visitors, always happy to talk to people capable of carrying on a dialogue with his vast memory and of contributing something unexpected to it.

One day he surprised me by asking me to bring him the works of Molière, the *Poèmes barbares* of Leconte de Lisle, and Michelet's *La Mer*. And then a few days later, the entire work of Remy de Gourmont, whom, he told me a little later, he thought of as his elder brother. "It's very unfair that he should be forgotten while I'm famous." In the evening the nurse read to him from Voltaire: "The best French prose, perhaps the best poems ever written." . . .

During the last months, he had two great wishes: first, to marry Maria Kodama, his student, his accomplice in the study of Anglo-Saxon and Icelandic literature, his fervent and attentive companion, his Antigone and his scribe—and he married her. Aside from this, he wanted to live in the old quarter of Geneva he had known when he was young, and the unfindable was found for him: an apartment on a very quiet *place,* where he could hear from time to time the sounds of nearby bells. As if he had the innocent power of great poets to transform reality and somehow make it resemble their own, the narrow little street on which the building stood had no name and no number at the door. There he felt at home, arrived, finally, at the center of the labyrinth. His happiness was so intense that the inextricable pattern that his steps, as he put it, had worn down (*"fatigué"*) for nearly eighty-seven years, now disappeared and, liberated, he could make his own way to the clouds.

When he was a student in Geneva, where the writer in him was born, a friend told him he must have some visiting cards. Borges's idea of what should appear on them as his "profession" could not have been more modest: "*Jorge Luis Borges, contemporain.*" And now we have had the great luck to have been his contemporaries.

Hector Bianciotti, "The Death of Borges," in The New York Review of Books, *Vol. XXXIII, No. 13, August 14, 1986, p. 11.*

JOHN G. COPELAND

[*Copeland, an American nonfiction writer, editor, and essayist, assisted in the publication of an American collection of Borges's short stories,* Cuentos *(1958). Copeland became friends with Borges in 1955, while studying at the National University in Buenos Aires, and met him again in the 1970s. In the following excerpt Copeland relates his personal impressions of Borges, as well as his appreciation of the author's writings.*]

I first encountered Borges—the writer, not the man—in the home of Manuel Gleizer in Buenos Aires in 1955. I had come to Argentina as a graduate student, to study at the Faculty of Philosophy of the National University and to get to know Argentina and the Argentines, a presumptuous enterprise which only a young man would undertake. Buenos Aires was, and is, one of the major centers of publication in that part of the world and I soon found myself wandering about in bookstores—mostly of second-hand books—and reading voraciously. A friend suggested that I meet Gleizer, who had published some of the first works of Borges, Mallea and others; I arranged to meet him at his home. Gleizer was a small, kindly man whose Spanish bore a slight European accent and who demonstrated a profound enthusiasm for Argentine writers. He immediately asked if I had read Borges. I had to confess that I did not know him. A few hours later I left his house with a first edition of ***Ficciones,*** which I had persuaded him to sell me.

I have the bad habit of reading stories out of the order suggested by the author and that night I opened ***Ficciones*** at random and read **"El jardin de senderos que se bifurcan"** (**"The Garden of Forking Paths"**) and then **"El milagro secreto"** (**"The Secret Miracle"**). I remember that Borges' style impressed me because of its laconic, synthetic quality. I was fascinated by the world of temporal and spatial mazes I found within the stories—a world whose concepts of time and identity were mostly new to me and whose mixture of reality and fantasy I had only encountered before in Argentine literature, in a less sophisticated way, in certain stories of Quiroga and Lugones. I read all that night, until I had read the entire collection. In the following weeks I searched out Borges in many bookstores in the city and was able to acquire copies of most of the books he had written: ***El idioma de los argentinos, Historia de la eternidad*** and ***Otras inquisiciones,*** essays; ***Poemas, 1923-1953; Evaristo Carriego,*** biography; the ***Antología clásica de la literatura argentina,*** written with Pedro Henriquez Ureña; and more collections of stories; ***La muerte y la brújula, El aleph*** and ***Historia de la infamia.*** Although I read the works in the order I found them, not in the order they were written, they had a certain unity of style and content that made me anxious to meet their author.

During that period I began to talk to Argentine friends and acquaintances about Borges. Although he was firmly established in literary and intellectual circles in Buenos Aires—a number of articles had been written about his work and two book-length studies (Adolfo Priesto's *Borges y la nueva generación* and Marcial Tamayo and Adolfo Ruiz-Díaz' *Borges, enigma y clave*) had appeared—he was not so well-known to the general public in Argentina. The average Argentine reader, to judge by the displays in bookstores, seemed more inclined to read foreign authors (Ray Bradbury's stories were much in evidence at that time) than to read the works of one of their own. Although my financial condition was anything but happy, I resolved to correct that oversight and used to carry around copies of Borges to give to friends and to send to those who had extended their hospitality. (It would be interesting now to discover the history of those books, which traveled from person to person during the year I was there.)

I met the "other" Borges at a cocktail party given by Gilbert Chase, cultural attaché at the American Embassy. Ignorant of the niceties of protocol, I had gone to the Embassy without appointment to see if interviews could be arranged with certain writers who interested me. (At the time, I had conceived the idea of a collection of short stories by Argentine authors in English translation—a project I subsequently completed, but which never "found a publisher," to use a Spanish expression.) Chase granted me an immediate interview and queried me about my purpose in being in Argentina, my studies at the National University and my interest in Argentine literature. He promised to do all he could to further my plans. A few days later I found myself at his home and was introduced to most of the writers I had wanted to know, including Borges.

In the following weeks I met Borges on a number of occasions: at a cocktail party, followed by a more intimate dinner, at the apartment of Bioy Casares and his wife, Silvina Ocampo; at a meeting of the Argentine Writers Society, to which I accompanied Borges, who introduced me to his colleagues; and on several occasions when I accompanied him on walks through the center of the city during the restless summer of 1955, when political and military events were taking place which were to lead to the overthrow of Perón. I found that although much of Borges' personality is revealed or hinted at in his works—his profound erudition, his ability to recreate the books he had read, his deep attachment both to the reality and the myth of Argentina, his extraordinary ability to express himself—they had not prepared me for the agony he expressed when we discussed the situation of Argentina at that time, an agony which was derived from his intense love of country; nor did they prepare me for the delight and the curiosity which had led him to explore the most hidden parts of his city, Buenos Aires, whose history he knew so well. I discovered that a secret alley, the shadows cast by the iron grillwork on stone carvings of some colonial house he knew, or the shades of color of certain buildings at certain hours of the day could produce in Borges an innocent and youthful enthusiasm and surprise. (One of Borges' favorite words in English was "wonder"; he never lost that ephemeral quality.) Although he was functionally blind at the time, he knew those details so well that I forgot that the man on my arm could not see.

I also remember particularly a warm evening when we went to one of his favorite places, a sidewalk café (*confitería*) on the corner of Maipú and Córdoba, near his apartment. We sat down inside, at a small table in a corner. He spoke to me of the city and the pampa, of the *compadre* and the *gaucho,* of his parents and ancestors, in a voice which had a certain timeless quality and which trembled with emotion as he recalled some event of special importance to him. His words recreated happenings as if he were seeing them for the first time. Listening to him, I entered his world, in which something fantastic and incredible lies just beneath the common and the ordinary. The next day he sent me a copy of *Borges, engima y clave,* in which he had written "*en memoria de una conversada noche de Buenos Aires.*" Without realizing it, we had talked until dawn.

I left Buenos Aires at the end of 1955. Perón had been overthrown that August and Borges, who had become a symbol of the opposition, was named Director of the National Library. I was not to see him again until he appeared in Boulder in March of 1976.

Yet Borges was not to leave my life. A year or so after my return to the United States I was contacted by Paul Cooke of Monticello College, who was publishing a series of books in Spanish, dealing with the short story in various Spanish American countries. He requested that I compose a volume on Argentina. After some consideration, I suggested that we limit the collection to stories by Borges, to whom I felt I owed so much.

In the following years I also maintained contact with Borges in my university classes. Graduate seminars allowed me to "recreate" some of the stories and essays which I had read before and to explore the stories of his more recent works, ***El informe de Brodie*** and ***El libro de arena,*** collections which proved, if proof were necessary, that the years had not diminished the skill or the invention of the storyteller. As I read the stories of the more recent collections I found myself smiling as I recognized some ideas, devices and techniques as one recognizes old friends. Other things, mostly the things which Borges himself has pointed out in his preface to ***El informe de Brodie***—the "straightforward manner," anticipated some years ago in his story **"La intrusa,"** the interest in Nordic and Icelandic myth and saga, the omission of surprise from the stories, to mention only a few—were new and welcome innovations. Having re-encountered Borges the writer, I was delighted to learn that chance would also allow me to re-encounter the man.

And so we met again. Not in Buenos Aires, but in Boulder. Conversing not in Spanish on the streets of his beloved city or in a *confitería* or in the homes of his friends, but mostly in English, at the Sheraton, at the University and at the homes of my friends.

The years had been kind to Borges. His mind was clear and sharp; two operations had partly restored his vision; he walked and stood erect; he had the energy of a much younger man, as the strenuous lecture tour of American universities on which he embarked in 1976 proved. During the four days he spent in Boulder he not only gave a public lecture at the University, but also spent a morning with my graduate class, worked on a short story he was writing with Donald Yates of Michigan State University, who accompanied him on his tour, and granted numerous interviews to both professional and student journalists. He retained his sense of wonder at the world, as I noticed when he pronounced the words "Boulder, Colorado" as if they had some cabalistic, magic quality. His interest in conversation, which, he noted, is one of the gifts not denied to the blind man, was undiminished, just as he had lost none of his ability to recreate for his listeners the episodes and anecdotes on which he had drawn for his tales.

In March, 1977, Borges and I met again, now in Buenos Aires, at the home of his sister. Borges talked of a promise he had made to his father to rework a novel, *El caudillo,* which his father had published in Spain in a very limited edition many years before. And of the edition of Borges' collected poetry which he was proof-reading at the time. This led naturally to a discussion of poetry, particularly of the poetry of New England, for which Borges had a special fondness (he recited and we discussed some of his favorite lines from Robert Frost). I reflected later that time and space play only a minor role in conversations with Borges. We had not initiated a conversation in that room in Buenos Aires; we resumed one, perhaps the same one we had begun in 1955. I also noted that although Borges did not ignore the circumstantial in his conversation or in his literature, he frequently, through a secret alchemy, converted it into the universal.

Throughout his life, Borges searched, perhaps in vain, to penetrate the murky web which governs our lives. Memory was his guide and one of his most persistent memories was that of the period he had spent in Geneva, from 1914 to 1918. During those years he acquired the French language, the Latin language and the German language, and he immersed himself in Walt Whitman and the German expressionist poets. Referring to those years in his lecture in Boulder, he said:

> They revealed to me the common experiences of love, of friendship, and also of three essential languages.
>
> The first, of course, was French. And when I think of French, I think of Voltaire, I think of the eighteenth century, I think of Flaubert, I think of Verlaine, and perhaps above all of Hugo. Those are essential experiences, I suppose all men have had them, and that's as it should be.
>
> Then I was also taught Latin. And Latin is a very precious language. Since after Latin disintegrated into Spanish, Portuguese, Italian, Rumanian, and French, those languages are still wistful for Latin—they still feel homesick for Latin. And that can be said also of the English and the German languages. Those languages are always trying to be Latin. You find that very clearly in the works of Milton, or Sir Thomas Browne, for example, and, of course, in Spanish you have Quevedo and Góngora; those are all trying to write in the Latin that already had been used by the Spanish writers, by Seneca, and so on. And so I got Latin, I got the economy of Latin. In Latin there is no padding; every word stands for itself. In other languages there are articles and meaningless gadgets of language, but in Latin every word stands out.
>
> Well, I got French, I got Latin, and then when I read in English Schopenhauer's *Welt als Wille und Vorstellung,* I taught myself German in order to read the text in the original . . . Well, I discovered German, I found my way into the German expressionist poets, and one day I was browsing over a German expressionist anthology when suddenly I came across these strange words: "Als ich in Alabama meinen Morgenspaziergang machte." The word *Alabama* struck me, seemed outlandish in German, then I came to the name of the writer, and the name was a

name I had already run across reading William James's *Variety of Religious Experience*. (My father was a professor of psychology.) The name was Walt Whitman, of course. Then I said, why should I be reading Walt Whitman in German? This is all falseness.

So I ordered Walt Whitman's *Leaves of Grass* from London and got a copy—I remember a slim, green-bound volume—and as all young men are, I was swept off my feet by Whitman even as I was swept off my feet by Victor Hugo before and by other writers. And, as all young men do, I tried my best or my worst to be Walt Whitman and I wrote many poems in free verse . . . And some two years ago, I translated Whitman's "Song of Myself" into Spanish. The translation came off very well. Of course, that merely means that Whitman is such a fine poet that he can survive poor translators. He can make his way even through translators. Even through Borges being a translator. That book sold very well, and in a sense I paid back my debt to Walt Whitman.

My 1917 or 1918 debt to Walt Whitman.

So there you have the three facts: we have the French language, the Latin language, the German language, and we have also Whitman and the German expressionist poets, and the reading of German poetry. . . .

The importance of the memory of Geneva is shown in Borges's story **"El otro"** in which he described an encounter between himself in Cambridge at age seventy and that other self, Borges at nineteen in Geneva. And less than two weeks before his death, *The New Yorker* published his poem **"The Web"** in which, with eerie prescience, he wrote:

Which of my cities
am I doomed to die in?
Geneva,
where revelation reached me
from Virgil and Tacitus
(certainly not from Calvin)? . . .

What language
am I doomed to die in?

Borges died on June 14, 1986 in Geneva, city of several languages, where at nineteen he had set out on his literary quest.

And so there will be no more encounters with Borges the man, but as I read his pages, his haunting voice will live in memory—just as Borges the writer, distiller of dreams, will persist in tradition.

John G. Copeland, "Homage to Borges," in The North American Review, *Vol. 271, No. 3, September, 1986, pp. 75-8.*

JAMES GARDNER

[*Gardner, an American critic, is a frequent contributor to* The New Criterion. *In the following excerpt Gardner details the cultural and literary influences that shaped Borges's fiction.*]

The most urgent criterion we can apply to any writer is whether we will miss him once he's gone. For it is possible to admire a writer's work in a cool and critical way without ever feeling that we ourselves have been somehow diminished by his death, without ever feeling an almost selfish yearning to possess what he might have gone on to produce. The recent death of Jorge Luis Borges provokes this feeling; and there are not many other contemporary writers about whom this can be said. Even though the Fates were kind to Borges, granting him eighty-six years out of eternity, still it would have seemed a more fitting destiny had he survived to the Biblical longevity of his mother, who died not long ago at the age of ninety-nine, or had he equalled the heroine of one of his best stories, **"La señora mayor,"** who passed away at one hundred. Although death was a recurring theme in his writings, and Borges even claimed to look forward to his appointed hour, one persists in feeling that those remote and snowy outposts of the human spirit that are attained in extreme old age would have been the perfect home for the noble fragility and profound introspection that were always the mark of the author.

Jorge Luis Borges was born in Buenos Aires in the summer of 1899, into a well-to-do and educated environment that would help to mold the cosmopolitan character of his future life and literature. His father, a lawyer and professor of psychology, had in him a rich admixture of Italian, Jewish, and English blood, while his mother, who was a translator of Melville and Virginia Woolf, was of native Argentine stock. For the first fifteen years of his life, Borges lived on the outskirts of Buenos Aires. In 1914, he moved with his family to Geneva, where he stayed for four years gaining considerable proficiency in Latin, French, German, and English. After three years in Spain, where he found welcome among a group of avant-garde artists who called themselves the *ultraístas*, he returned with his family to Buenos Aires. For the next few years, Borges was active as a critic and poet in the capital. His principal prose works began to appear in the 1930s, starting with ***Historia universal de la infamia (A Universal History of Infamy)***. In 1937, he took a high position at a branch of the Buenos Aires municipal library, but he was dismissed with the arrival of Perón in 1946. He resigned from the civil service and made his living by lecturing on English literature until Perón was overthrown in 1955. Borges was then nominated to head the Buenos Aires Public Library, but by that time he had become almost completely blind, a fact which was to alter considerably his life and literature. For his remaining years, he devoted himself to writing and lecturing, as well as to travelling all over the world. He was married twice, and at the time of his death he had just moved to Geneva.

Despite his extensive travels and cosmopolitan education, which induced him to set his stories and poems in many different regions of the world, Borges throughout his life was very much attached to his native city, which figured frequently in his work, especially in his early years. He claimed that in his dreams and nightmares he found himself returning over and over again to specific points in its landscape. Though it was Borges who was destined to put his hometown on the international literary map, Buenos Aires was the center of a concentrated, fervid culture even in the period in which he was developing. As he wrote of it in one of his early poems:

Las calles de Buenos Aires
ya son la entraña de mi alma. . . .
La ciudad está en mi como un poema
que no he logrado detener en palabras.

(The streets of Buenos Aires have become the center of my soul. . . . The city is inside me like a poem I haven't quite put into words.)

These lines are quoted in an essay on Borges by the critic Victoria Ocampo, for whose literary magazine *Sur* he and many of the leading Argentine writers of his day worked. When she founded a publishing house by the same name, Borges translated Kafka, Woolf, and Faulkner for her. He also collaborated on many projects with fellow Argentine writers, like Silvina Ocampo, Victoria's sister, and with Adolfo Bioy-Cesares. These collaborations constitute one half of Borges's entire output, and range from satirical assaults on imaginary artists and politicians to primers on Buddhism and Nordic and Anglo-Saxon literature. Although the Argentine writers of Borges's youth were conscious of their standing apart from the distant wellsprings of European culture, there is a general sense among them of trying to keep up with developments abroad, consciously cultivating a cosmopolitan environment through allusions to the most recent European writers and painters, and delighting to fill their pages with quotations in French, German, and English.

To many, Borges has come to represent just such a cosmopolitan breadth of interests and erudition. He was learned in many languages and cultures; he knew many cities and men. In one interview, reprinted in a volume called *Borges at Eighty* (published . . . in 1982), he expressed regret that the language he got stuck with was Spanish. It was his contention that his temperament, in keeping with his ancestry, was more British than Iberian, and that the literature he loved best was the English he had imbibed from his earliest days rather than the Spanish literature that he really did not begin to study until he was in his twenties.

But in his many interviews, Borges never resisted the temptation to say something shocking in an offhand way, and in this case he was perhaps misstating the nature of his gifts. For though he had much in common with English mystical writers like De Quincey and Coleridge, he ultimately lacked their common sense. He was actually closer in spirit to the cabalistic temperaments of Spaniards like Raymond Llull, Calderón, and Quevedo. That is to say, there is something especially Hispanic about his achievement, and to understand this precise "Spanishness" would go far toward explaining the intricate workings of Borges's literary personality.

All national cultures are influenced by other national cultures. While weaker nations tend to produce pale imitations of those greater powers upon which they border, greater powers evolve their own organic style, usually by assimilating to themselves many foreign elements. Spain is perhaps unique in being a great power (at one time the greatest) whose artistic personality developed through the juxtaposition, rather than the confluence, of many diverse tendencies. In Spanish art and literature these tendencies exist as many autonomous parts, like tesserae in a mosaic.

Spain has always been the receiver of other cultures: from the Celts, who overran the Iberians in the fourth century, B.C., and the Romans, who two hundred years later overran the Celts; from the Germanic tribes who came in two waves in the fifth and sixth centuries; from the constant, menacing, and unassimilable presence of Islam for almost eight hundred years; from the Hapsburg presence in the sixteenth century and the Bourbon in the eighteenth. These influences, together with the early hospitality Spain showed to the Jews, have each left a different mark upon the Spanish people, as though a single block of fine marble were being worked upon by many gifted sculptors, none of whom had ever bothered to glance at what his neighbors were doing. In addition to this, Spain led the world in the colonization of the Americas, sending over far more men than the English did and interacting far more enthusiastically with the cutlure they found there. We do not find in Spain the give-and-take of other cultures, the assimilation or evolution. Rather, once a cultural influence is caught in the peninsula, it remains there in a state of permanent juxtaposition with such other cultures as it follows or precedes.

It is this kind of pluralism, then, this typically Spanish hodgepodge, that characterizes the poetry and prose of Jorge Luis Borges. More than any other writer of modern fiction, he does not merely embody his influences; he discusses them in the very process of their acting upon him. It is for this reason that in his short fictional pieces he is always happiest when he can pretend that he is writing an essay, carefully commingling imaginative authors with those real creatures—French, Irish, Icelandic, and Arabic—who have constituted the most direct influences upon his character.

Although Borges is always subtle in the extreme, and never overbearing, there is something in his writing which merits his being called a "strong poet." That is, he is able to see in everything a reflection of himself: everything, including earlier authors, is transformed into what he can use in the extension of his own character. His attitudes toward those earlier authors are evident in both his short fictional pieces and his literary essays, many of which are collected in ***Otras inquisiciones (Other Inquisitions).***

One effect of this impulse to absorb other authors into his own literary personality was that, although Borges considered himself an Anglophile (which included his liking American writers), he was often unable to accept English prose and poetry on their own terms. For him, among the most important English-language writers were Sir Thomas Brown, Robert Burton, Coleridge, De Quincey, Poe, and Whitman. The first four are there because they appealed to Borges's mystical side. His admiration for Poe had more to do with his taste for nineteenth-century France than with anything American. Whitman, on the other hand, was a totemic figure to Borges, as he has been to many South American writers, who have made him into something far more exotic than we consider him to be here at home.

Thus, Borges's idiosyncratic tastes present a skewed version of the literature of our language. There are many great authors whom he simply does not know what to do with. He has little place in his understanding for Milton, for instance, or for Dryden and the Petrarchan sonneteers like Sydney and Spenser. And he has an exaggerated affection for other, minor writers, like Wilde, Blunden, and William Morris. All this is not to say that his tastes are without subtlety; there are simply some virtues to which he cannot respond and some vices which he is too willful to reprove.

In one telltale passage, Borges draws a parallel between Whitman and Valéry which, as usual, explains more about him than it does about them. He is quick to admit that ostensibly there is nothing in their poetic practice to connect the two men. Whitman was an ebullient populist, Valéry a dandified aesthete. But Borges finds them both preeminently important insofar as everything they wrote was studiously autobiographical, that is, a meticulous, self-dramatizing construction of themselves. In the same way, Borges possesses a startling personality that appears with thrilling clarity through over a half century of literary output. Like Valéry, he is a dandy and aesthete, though he has far less faith than Valéry had in the absolute value of words or in the ludic foundation of poetry.

Like Whitman, he writes only when there is something that he wants to say. For him, poetry is therapeutic, and in his many poems he left memorable records of his emotional vicissitudes, which require us to take them more seriously than we would mere wordplay.

The exhilarating profusion of literary personalities which Borges uses to define himself probably has much to do with his distinct brand of privacy, in which he placed between himself and the external world an army of illustrious predecessors, defending himself against his immediate circumstances by taking refuge in the safety of things distant and things past. From the extreme south of the world, Argentina, he repeatedly showed an avid yearning to reach, at least in his mind, the farthest outposts of the north—the proverbial most northerly point, or *ultima thule,* that has figured for so long in the Southern imagination. He similarly went back to Anglo-Saxon times, acquiring an understanding of the earliest forms of our language. He delighted in all the strange and alien details of *Beowulf* and the *Song of the Road,* and he even went so far as to learn Old Norse. He was eternally intrigued by the mysterious ceremony and indestructible otherness of imperial China, as well as by such offbeat places as the American Wild West and postwar Prague. But again, despite the attentiveness he showed to details of local color, and despite his great skill at literary pastiche, Borges was never able to accept these cultures on their own terms; they are invariably altered through the prism of his own predilections.

Borges was not at home in the modern world. He said repeatedly that he was not a modernist and that he would have preferred to have been born in the last century. Although there is something indisputably contemporary in his prose writings, as well as in his poetry, his fealty to the formal innovations of this century has long been in doubt. He rarely discussed twentieth-century poets, and men like Eliot and Pound seem to figure not at all in his thinking.

The artistic climate in which he grew up was that of *modernismo,* which was in a sense antithetical to what is meant by "modernism" in other Western languages. In Spanish, it represented the attempt on the part of Latin American writers—pre-eminently Rubén Darío, with the publication of a book of prose and poetry entitled *Azul* (1888)—to cultivate a more cosmopolitan and less provincial artistic taste, resplendent with all the peacocks, cloth-of-gold, and brocades of Symbolist painting and decadent poetry. In the present century this fashion was most assiduously cultivated by Leopoldo Lugones, whose sultry, orchidaceous style constituted a source of ongoing horror and delight for Borges.

If Borges was for most of his life an anti-modernist, it is nevertheless true that in his early years—both in Spain, where he formed part of the *ultraístas,* and later in Argentina, where he founded, with several other young writers, a variety of short-lived avant-garde reviews—Borges was more attentive to the formal innovations of modernism than he would be in later years. The first two volumes of his poetry he never allowed to be published; his earliest published book was a collection entitled ***Fervor de Buenos Aires*** (1923), in which he shares with his generation an affection for free verse. These poems usually alternate between the traditional eleven-syllable line of Spanish verse and lines of arbitrary length. Already in 1923 we can hear the soft-spoken clarity of voice and the tenacious sense of place that would characterize his poetry for sixty years to come:

Habré de levantar la vasta vida
que aún ahora es tu espejo:
cada mañana habré de reconstruirla.
Desde que te alejaste,
cuántos lugares se han tornado vanos
y sin sentido, iguales
a luces en el día.

(I shall have to leave this larger life, which is
but a mirror of you. On every morrow I shall
have to make it anew. Ever since I left you,
how many places have become meaningless,
like lights in the daytime.)

In his next book of poems, ***Luna de enfrente*** (1925), a slightly jauntier tone sets in. It manifests itself in the overarching lines that take their inspiration from Whitman. Borges was not the first foreigner to be inspired by Whitman, of course—across the sea Apollinaire and Blaise Cendrars had also learned from him—but with Borges and other South American writers (like Pablo Neruda) there was a sense of discovering in Whitman something essentially native to their culture. We of the United States tend to see the culture of Latin America as being different from our own. But for the writers of Chile and Argentina the crucial distinction is to be drawn between the two sides of the Atlantic—Europe and the Americas—not between north and south. Thus they can claim Whitman as their own, as is evident in such lines as these from Borges's **"Mi vida entera" ("My Entire Life")**:

Aquí otra vez, los labios memorables, único y
  semejante a vosotros.
He persistido en la aproximación de la dicha y en la
  intimidad de la pena.
He atravesado el mar.

(Here yet again, those memorable lips, unique
and yet like your own. I have continued to know
the approximation of happiness and the intimacy of pain. I have crossed the sea.)

At this time Borges was also influenced by the French Symbolists, and his affection for Whitman did not keep him from including in his second book a few poems in *versos de catorce;* that is, in verses composed of roughly fourteen-syllable lines, which bear the influence of the French alexandrine.

El humo desdibuja gris las constelaciones
Remotas. Lo inmediato pierde prehistoria y nombre.
El mundo es unas cuantas tiernas imprecisiones.
El río, el primer río. El hombre, el primer hombre.

(Grey smoke reduces the remote constellation
to a grey outline. The immediate loses its name
and prehistory. The world becomes a few tender
imprecisions. The river is the first river. The
man, the first man.)

These tendencies, Whitmanesque and French Symbolist, were continued in his next book of poems, ***Cuaderno San Martin*** (1929), which was the last volume of poetry that he would publish for thirty-one years. When Borges finally emerged from this period of poetic silence, during which he produced his most memorable prose works, he was transformed, at least prosodically, into another person entirely. He now favored two extreme poetic forms: Baudelairean prose-poetry on the one hand, and the hendecasyllabic sonnet on the other. In one poem, entitled **"Un poeta del siglo XIII" ("A Poet of the Thirteenth Century")**, he even salutes the sonnet form:

¿Habrá sentido que no estaba solo
Y que el arcano, el increíble Apolo
Le había revelado un arquetipo,

Un ávido cristal que apresaría
Cuanto la noche cierra o abre el día:
Dédalo, laberinto, enigma, Edipo?

(Will he [the poet] have known that he was not alone, that the mysterious and unbelievable Apollo had revealed to him an archetype, a grasping chalice that would seize as much as night conceals or day discloses: Daedalus, the labyrinth, the enigma, and Oedipus?)

This poetry that Borges writes after 1960 is far more accessible stylistically. But he returns more often to literary and historical themes, dedicating sonnets to Poe and Emerson, as well as to such unsual poets as Jonathan Edwards, the theologian. One of the probable reasons for this turning away from visually compelling poetry in loose meters toward intellectual poems of the strictest formalism was the gradual blindness that overtook Borges in the late 1950s. It is plausible to suppose that the onset of this condition—which left him, so to speak, immured within himself—probably accentuated that deeply introspective part of his personality. For a man bereft of sight, it is usually easier to write poetry than prose, and easier to write formal poetry than the more relaxed sort, for it becomes more necessary than ever that the words be held and worked upon by the memory, and the memory is best served by a rigorous form. Borges explained his renewed interest in formalist poetry by saying that he simply found it easier to write that way.

Indeed, Borges's poetry was always more imaginative than inventive, and as he grew older he came to like the security of these tried and true forms, which he would fill with startling ideas, though at the same time he simplified his syntax to an easeful level that avoided the two extremes of artificiality and conversational flaccidity.

The prose works of Borges do not reveal the same degree of formal variety, for he seems to have discovered early on the way in which he wanted to write. Borges was always a miniaturist. None of his works extends beyond roughly six thousand words. He never attempted a novel, although it is not inconceivable that he could have done so with considerable success. The general form of his prose work is found in his so-called *ficciones,* which are really precisely wrought essays on imaginary and nonexistent subjects. The form he chose to imitate was usually that of the scholarly article. It is worth wondering why he never thought to extend this to the length of an entire book, since the style is as much the style of books as of articles. Perhaps he realized that his stories were primarily the treatment of a single imaginative impulse; perhaps he felt (no doubt rightly) that their jewel-like concision could not fill out a larger form.

The principal strategy in Borges's fiction is the inclusion, side by side, of precise references to real people, places, and texts and precise references to imaginary people, places, and texts. Because the imaginative and actual tend to revolve around the arcana of numerology and cabalistic mysticism in his stories, there is a constant sense of the subject passing in and out of focus—until one despairs of ever sorting out reality and imagination.

One of the virtues of Borges's fiction is the superb precision and polish of the Spanish. Another is a fine and at times almost imperceptibly subtle humor, which retains its completely straight face while holding up to ridicule the soberest of literary and historical essays, like, for example, the present one. It was doubtless part of Borges's literary mission that as I write these words, with the sobriety the subject calls for, I am constantly reminding myself that I sound suspiciously like that voice which he enjoys parodying.

It is as though I am writing about a character as imaginary as Pierre Menard, the eponymous hero of one of Borges's most popular and most insistently quoted stories. Probably it surprised the humble Borges that so much was always being made of this story, but there persist to this day certain circles in which it is quoted without explanation as the key point in any discussion of literature, or, indeed, of anything else. The story claims to be little more than a bibliography and analysis of the works of Pierre Menard, a twentieth-century writer and pedant who has undertaken to write, in seventeenth-century Spanish, a version of *Don Quixote* that will be in every detail identical to the original. Through concerted study, the hero of the piece manages to reproduce exactly whole sentences on end, and the author of the "essay" energetically makes much of the result, considering it to be much better than the original, since Cervantes was merely expressing himself in his own language while Menard was mastering an alien idiom and an archaic style. The piece is good fun, but any attempt to adduce it in support of the more abstruse claims of structuralism or deconstruction—for instance, that literature is merely a language game, closed off from the world it ostensibly refers to—would doubtless have produced in its author one of those charming admissions of total mystification that he made so often in his interviews.

Another Borges story that has become totemic for the wrong reasons is **"The Library at Babel,"** in which the narrator, who has spent his life in the massive and seemingly endless structure of the library, presents, in tracing the bizarre history of the institution, what is doubtless intended as a metaphor of man's quest for meaning in the universe. As might be expected in the context of contemporary literary criticism, much has been made of this story, which can be understood to reduce everything to a text or to a rigorously ordered system. What exactly Borges meant by it is hard to say. Perhaps the best answer lies in his principal inspiration, the cabala, that arcane system of scriptural interpretation whose enigmatic questions are intended to enhance our wonder at the inscrutable mystery and invisible order of the universe.

In the first of Borges's collections of fiction, ***Historia universal de la infamia*** (1935), Borges depicted various cases of evil in history. Throughout the book, he is as much at home in eighteenth-century China as he is in the antebellum South or in the New York gangland of the 1920s. He is at pains never to offer explanations for the behavior of his protagonists, since he is interested in presenting their transgressions as almost neutral acts of the physical universe. Here and in other later "fictions"—like ***Historia de la eternidad*** (1936), ***Ficciones*** (1941), ***El Aleph*** (1949), and ***El informe de Brodie*** (1970)—Borges shows himself over and over again to be essentially antimodernist. Although the form this antimodernism takes may seem in a curious way contemporary, it could be argued that Borges was merely returning to an earlier form of fiction writing, in which the author took care to persuade the reader that in his hand the reader was holding a piece of expository prose of as great an objective validity as any history of the Roman Empire. Borges's short prose pieces in ***Historia universal de la infamia,*** for instance, call to mind those popular short stories of the late nineteenth century that described historical crimes in exotic places, by writers like Louis Couperus and Villiers de L'Isle-

Adam, whom Borges is likely to have read. The expository form also afforded Borges the opportunity to parody that bookishness which, he claimed, had been developed in him at a very early age. This same bookishness, as well as a general sense of privacy, probably convinced him early on that he would never excel in a mode of fiction that attempted to depict reality by conventional dramatic means. But that Borges was better at characterization than he thought is reflected in those occasional and thoroughly persuasive passages of dialogue that are sometimes included within the context of his expository fiction.

An interesting parallel suggests itself between Borges and Italo Calvino, and in their differences as well as in their similarities you will find manifested the shifting loyalties of a generation. For, while the recently deceased Calvino remains very much a writer of the moment, Borges, one is sad to report, has probably had his day. This is not to say that he is no longer read, or no longer admired, since the spate of laudatory articles that his death occasioned handsomely confirmed the esteem in which he had been held internationally for a generation. And yet, he no longer means to the general literary public as much as he did only ten years ago.

On one level, the similarity between the two writers is uncanny and unavoidable. Though Calvino wrote novels, which Borges never did, both writers are most effective at diminutive fiction work, both like to show off in a frivolous way their fanfare of erudition, and both have a great affection for mathematical and semantic models of the universe, expressed in the labyrinths of Borges and the invisible cities of Calvino. Yet despite their similarities, a single and minute difference reveals the gap of an entire generation. For Borges saw himself as something of a cabalist, and Calvino considered himself something of a semiotician. In Borges, the repeated forays into numerology, puns, labyrinths, and puzzles presuppose a direct if occult correspondence between the adventitious ciphers on the page and the secret workings and orders of the universe as a whole. In the case of Calvino, however, an almost identical set of machinery purports to explain nothing of the universe in all its infinite secrets, but rather makes bold to reduce the entirety of the universe to the symbols on the page. It is the notion of the system itself, rather than that which underpins it, that means so much to the Italian author.

Now generations manage through a kind of natural selection to choose for their own uses not necessarily the fittest authors but rather those authors who are most apt to give them what they want, and to reveal them to themselves in as flattering a way as possible. It is in this sense that both Calvino and Borges, irrespective of the level of excellence that each attained, were pushed by an eager public into the forefront of fashion for reasons that were not directly germane to the standards of their writings. In the Sixties, when Borges first attained a large audience outside of Argentina, he could readily be assimilated into a culture that had turned its back upon the drab realities that surrounded it, that craved disorder, exoticism, and the illogic of dreams. That Borges would probably not have looked with much sympathy upon such developments had nothing to do with the role that such co-optation required him to play. But the lords of taste have repented in due course, as they always will, of their earlier orthodoxies, and the reigning taste for postmodernist neatness and order, along with suspenders and bow ties, has found in Calvino an Author more to their liking.

But Borges was a hammer and Calvino merely an anvil. Somewhere in the early Seventies, Calvino evolved into that affection for semiotics for which the way had been paved by years of French intellectual agitation. Borges, on the other hand, did not change with the times. Rather, the writing he had practiced for over two generations was finally found to fit a context, and so he was taken on by the young crowd and lionized by them. One of the things that must strike most of the readers of his early writings is that they reveal a man very much like the later Borges, whom all the world would cherish, but who would have to wait until he was in his sixties before the larger public had any use for him. His poetry, it is true, had changed its form from something akin to Whitman into a formalism as punctilious as any in modern times. But his philosophy, taking its inspiration from Surrealism and Dadaism, returns constantly to the same motifs, so that even in his earliest poetry we find the fascination that dreams, mirrors, labyrinths, and puzzles always exerted upon his imagination.

One more author with whom Borges might profitably be compared is Nabokov, whose novel *Pale Fire* attempts to do precisely what Borges specialized in throughout his life, namely to parody the pettiness and wayward self-importance of literary scholarship. Just as Nabokov presented *Pale Fire* as an authoritative edition of a long poem, together with a preliminary essay and abundant notes, so Borges is constantly pretending—as in **"Tlon, Uqbar, Orbis Tertius"** (which includes notes on three imaginary books) and **"Pierre Menard"**—that he is writing nothing more than a dispassionate bibliography and discussion of a writer or a subject. Thus, although it is difficult to say whether any of the three men, Borges, Calvino, and Nabokov, learned anything from one another, it is striking that they should all be writing "fictions" that are in many ways quite similar. But of the three men, I belive that Borges practices this sleight of hand with the foremost artistry, since he attempts and succeeds in attaining something higher than mere humor. When Calvino tries his hand at "fictions," he is almost trying to show off how well he can get along without the traditional baggage of fiction. Nabokov tells a story, it is true, but since he is principally creating parody of a rather exotic order he is not especially interested in making his characters live and breathe. In Borges, however, the characters that are spun out of the dour context of the scholarly essay are instilled with a life of their own, and they are able to move us in a way that those of Nabokov cannot, and those of Calvino seldom do. Borges was not as comic and entertaining as Nabokov, nor as willfully inventive as Calvino, but you will find in him an unlimited sympathy for human beings and the irreducible vitality of the characters thus created, even through such an economy of means, places him in a higher order of creativity. (pp. 16-24)

James Gardner, "Jorge Luis Borges, 1899-1986," in The New Criterion, *Vol. X, No. 2, October, 1986, pp. 16-24.*

OCTAVIO PAZ

[Paz, a Mexican poet, critic, nonfiction writer, editor, and translator, is revered as one of the finest modern poets writing in Spanish, and praised for his criticism and political writings as well. His works include Luna silvestre *(1933),* El laberinto de la soledad *(1950),* Corrente alterna *(1967), and* One Earth, Four or Five Worlds *(1985), as well as studies of Claude Levi-Strauss and Marcel Duchamp. Greatly influenced by Borges in his youth, Paz made friends with many of Borges's literary associates such as Silvina Ocampo and Adolfo Bioy Casares before finally meeting*

the older poet in 1971. In the following excerpt Paz offers a few personal reminiscences of Borges, then analyzes the highly individualistic aesthetics of Borges's style.]

I began to read Borges in my youth, when he was not yet an author of international renown. In those years his name was a kind of password into a circle of initates, and the reading of his works was the secret cult of a few adepts. In Mexico, around 1940, we adepts comprised a group of young men, along with an occasional less enthusiastic older partisan: José Luis Martínez, Alí Chumacero, Xavier Villarrutia, and a few more. Borges was a writer's writer; we used to follow him through the journals of that era. In successive numbers of *Sur*, I read the series of remarkable stories that later, in 1941, would make up his first collection of *ficciones:* ***El jardín de los senderos que bifurcan.***

I still have the old edition, with its stiff, blue marbled leather binding, its white letters, and, in darker ink, the arrow pointing toward a south that was more metaphysical than geographical. I have not stopped reading it and conversing silently with its author. The man disappeared behind his work (this was before publicity converted him into one of its victim-gods); at times I even fancied that Borges himself was a fictional being.

The first person who spoke to me of the real man, with amazement and affection, was Alfonso Reyes. He had great regard for Borges. But did he admire him? Their tastes were very different. They were united by one of those happy anti-coincidences that bring together people of the same profession: for Borges, the Mexican writer was the master of prose; for Reyes, the Argentine was a curious spirit, a felicitous eccentricity. Later, in Paris in 1947, my first Argentine friends—José Bianco, Silvina Ocampo, and Adolfo Bioy Casares—were also great friends of Borges. They told me so much about him that without my ever having met him I came to know him as if he were my friend, too.

Many years later, I at last met Borges in person. It was in Austin, in 1971. The meeting was proper and reserved. He didn't know what to think of me, and I had not forgiven him for that poem in which he exalts—like Whitman, but with less justification—the defenders of the Alamo. My patriotic passion did not allow me to perceive the heroism of those men; and he didn't perceive that the siege of the Alamo had been an episode in an unjust war. Borges was not always able to grasp the difference between true heroism and mere bravery. Being one of Balvanera's ruffians is not the same as being Achilles: both are figures of legend, but the first is a product of circumstance, while the second is an *example*.

Our other encounters, in Mexico and in Buenos Aires, were happier. Several times we were able to speak a bit more easily, and Borges discovered that some of his favorite poets also were mine. He celebrated these coincidences by reciting passages of this or that poet, and the conversation was transformed, for an instant, into a sort of communion. One night, in Mexico, my wife and I helped him slip away from the assault of some importunate admirers; then, in a corner, amid the noise and the laughter of the party, he recited to Marie José some verses of Toulet:

Toute allégresse a son défaut
Et se brise elle-meme.
Si vous voulez que je vous aime,
Ne riez pas trop haut.
C'est à voix basse qu'on enchante
Sous la cendre d'hiver
Ce coeur, pareil au feu couvert,
Qui se consume et chante.

(Every joy has its fault, and breaks apart of its own accord. If you want me to love you, do not laugh too loud. It is in a hushed voice that one delights, under winter's ash, this heart that, like the banked fire, smolders and sings.)

In Buenos Aires we could talk and stroll leisurely about, enjoying the weather. He and María Kodama took us to the old Lezama Park; he wanted to show us, I don't know why, the Orthodox Church, but it was closed. We contented ourselves with walking along the moist little paths, beneath the trees with their towering trunks and singing foliage. Finally we paused before the monument to the Roman she-wolf, and Borges ran his excited hands over the head of Remus. We ended up in the Café Tortoni, famous for its mirrors, its golden moldings, its generous cups of hot chocolate, and its literary ghosts. Borges spoke of the Buenos Aires of his youth, that city of "patios hollow like bowls" that appears in his earliest poems—an invented city and, nevertheless, mistress of a reality more durable than the reality of the stones: that of the word.

That evening I was surprised by his dispiritedness about the situation in his country. Although he rejoiced in Argentina's return to democracy, he felt more and more remote from what was happening there. It is hard to be a writer in our bitter countries (it may be so everywhere), above all if one has become a celebrity and is besieged by those twin enemies, treacherous envy and devout admiration, both of them myopic. Moreover, by then Borges no longer recognized the time that surrounded him. He was in another time. I understood his uneasiness. I, too, when I walk the streets of Mexico, rub my eyes with wonder: Is this what we have made of our city? Borges confided to us his decision to "go away to die somewhere else, maybe in Japan." He wasn't a Buddhist, but the idea of nothingness as it appears in the literature of that religion, attracted him. I say *idea* because nothingness cannot be anything but a sensation or an idea. If it is a sensation, it lacks any restorative and calming power. On the other hand, nothingness as an idea calms us, and at the same time gives us strength and serenity.

I saw him again last year, in New York. We found ourselves for a few days in the same hotel with him and María Kodama. We dined together. Eliot Weinberger joined us unexpectedly, and the talk was of Chinese poetry. At the end of the evening, Borges recalled Reyes and López Velarde, and, as always, he recited some lines of the latter, those beginning: *Suave patria, vendedora de chía* ("Gentle fatherland, seller of *chía*. . ."). He interrupted himself, and asked me: "What does *chía* mean?" Confounded, I responded that I could not explain it, except as a metaphor: "It is an earthy taste." He nodded his head. It was too much and too little. I consoled myself with the thought that to express the transient is no less difficult than to describe eternity. He knew that.

It is difficult to resign oneself to the death of a dear and admired man. From the moment we are born, we expect to die, yet death surpises us. In this instance the expected is always the unexpected, always the undeserved. It doesn't matter that Borges died at 86; he wasn't ripe for death. Nobody is, whatever his age. One may invert the philosophical phrase and say that all of us—old men and children, adolescents and adults—are fruits picked before their time. Borges survived Cortázar and Bianco, two other beloved Argentine writers; but the short time he survived them does not console me for his absence. Today Borges has become what he was when I was 20: some books, an oeuvre.

He cultivated three genres: the essay, the poem, and the short story. The division is arbitrary. His essays read like stories; his stories are poems; and his poems make us think, as though they were essays. The bridge connecting them is thought. It is therefore useful to begin with the essayist. Borges's was a metaphysical temperament. Hence his fascination with idealist systems and their lucid architecture: Berkeley, Leibnitz, Spinoza, Bradley, the various Buddhisms. His was also a mind of uncommon clarity, united with the fantasy of a poet attracted by the "other side" of reality, so that he could not help but laugh at the chimerical constructions of reason. Hence the homage to Hume and to Schopenhauer, to Chuang-Tzu and the Sixth Empire. Although in his youth the verbal extravagances and the syntactical labyrinths of Quevedo and Browne appealed to him, he was not like them. He makes one think more of Montaigne—for his skepticism and his universal curiosity, though not for his style. Also of another of our contemporaries, who is today a bit forgotten: George Santayana.

Unlike Montaigne, moral and psychological enigmas did not interest Borges much; nor did the diversity of the customs, habits, and beliefs of the human animal. History did not excite him; the study of complex human societies did not attract him. His political opinions were moral, even aesthetic, judgments. Although he expressed them with bravery and with honesty, he did so without truly comprehending what was going on around him. At times he affirmed, for example, his opposition to the Perón regime and his rejection of totalitarian socialism; at others he slipped up, and his visit to Chile when it was under military dictatorship, as well as his facile epigrams against democracy, caused consternation among his friends. Later he repented. One has to add that always, in his certainties and in his errors, he was consistent with himself and honest. He never lied or knowingly justified evil, as many of his enemies and detractors have done. Nothing was more foreign to Borges than the ideological casuistry of our contemporaries.

All such matters were beside the point. He kindled to other subjects: time and eternity, identity and plurality, the self and the other. He was enamored of ideas. It was a contradictory love, corroded by multiplicity: behind ideas he did not find the Idea (call it God, Nothingness, or the First Principle), but rather a new and more profound plurality, that of himself. In seeking the Idea he found the reality of a Borges who was broken up into successive manifestations. Borges was always the other Borges unfolding into another Borges, until infinity. The metaphysician and the skeptic fought within him; and though it seemed that the skeptic won, skepticism gave him no peace. Instead, it multiplied the metaphysical ghosts. The mirror was its emblem. An abominable emblem: the mirror is the refutation of the metaphysical and the condemnation of the skeptic.

His essays are memorable, mainly for their orginality, their diversity, and their style. Humor, sobriety, acuity—and suddenly, an unusual twist. Nobody else had written that way in Spanish. Reyes, his model, was more correct and fluent, less precise and also less surprising. Reyes said fewer things with more words. The great achievement of Borges was to say the most with the least. But he did not exaggerate. He did not fasten on to the sentence, like Gracián, with the needle of genius, nor did he convert the paragraph into a symmetrical garden. Borges served two opposed divinities: simplicity and strangeness. Frequently he brought them together, and the result was unforgettable—the naturalism of the uncommon, the strangeness of the familiar. This skill, perhaps inimitable, gives him a unique place in the literature of the 20th century. When still very young, in a poem dedicated to the shifting and changing Buenos Aires of his nightmares, he defined his style: "My verse is about interrogation and proof, in order to obey that which is hidden." This definition embraces his prose as well. His work is a system of linked vessels, and his essays are navigable streams that empty naturally into his poems and stories. I confess my preference for the latter. His essays do not help me to comprehend either the universe or myself; they help me rather to understand better Borges's own surprising inventions.

Although the subjects of his poems and stories are quite varied, he has a single theme. But before touching on this point, let us clear up a confusion. Many deny that Borges was really a Latin American writer. The same charge was made against the early Darío; but it is an insult no less perverse for being repeated. The writer belongs to one land and one blood, but his work cannot be reduced to nation, race, or class. Moreover, one can reverse the accusation and say that the work of Borges, for its transparent perfection and for its limpid architecture, is a living reproach to the dispersion, the violence, and the disorder of the Latin American continent. The Europeans were amazed by the universality of Borges, but none of them observed that his cosmopolitanism was not, and could not have been, anything but the point of view of a Latin American. The eccentricity of Latin America consists in its being a European eccentricity: it is a different way of being Western, a non-European way. At once inside and outside the European tradition, the Latin American can regard the West as a totality, and not with the fatally provincial vision of a Frenchman, a German, an Englishman, or an Italian. No one saw this better than a Mexican, Jorge Cuesta; and an Argentinian, Jorge Luis Borges, realized it in his writings better than anyone else. The real theme of these discussions should not be Borges's lack of Americanness, but rather the acceptance once and for all of his work as an expression of a universality implicit in Latin America since its birth.

Borges was not a nationalist. Still, who but an Argentine could have written many of his poems and stories? He also suffered from an attraction to the darkness and the violence of America. He felt it in its lowest and least heroic manifestation—the street brawl, the knife of the bullying and resentful *malevo*. A strange duality: Berkeley and Juan Iberra, Jacinto Chiclano and Duns Scotus. The law of spiritual gravity governs Borges's work: the macho Latin faces the metaphysical poet. The contradiction that informs his intellectual speculations and his fictions—the struggle between the metaphysical and the skeptical—reappears violently in the field of feelings. His admiration for the knife and the sword, for the warrior and the ruffian, was perhaps the reflection of an innate inclination. In any case, it appears again and again in his writings. It was perhaps a vital and instinctive response to his skepticism, his civilized tolerance.

In his literary life this tendency expressed itself as a love of debate and of individual affirmation. In his early days, like almost all the writers of his generation, he was a part of the literary vanguard and its irreverence. Later he changed his tastes and ideas, not his attitudes. He stopped being an extremist, but continued to cultivate his witty tone, his impertinence, his brilliant insolence. In his youth, the target had been the traditionalist spirit, and the commonplaces of the academies and the conservatives. In his mature years, respectability transformed him: he became youthful again, ideological and revolutionary. He mocked the new conformism of the iconoclasts with the same cruel humor with which he had poked fun at the old one of the traditionalists.

He did not turn his back on his times, and he was brave when faced with the circumstances of his country and of the world. But above all he was a writer, and the literary tradition seemed to him no less alive and present than current events. His curiosity ranged in time from contemporary subjects to ancient ones, and in space from the close at hand to the far off, from gaucho poetry to Scandinavian sagas. He studied and quickly mastered the other classicisms that modernity has discovered, those of the Far East and of India, of the Arabs and the Persians. But this diversity of reading and plurality of influences did not turn him into a tower of Babel: he was not confusing or prolix, but clear and concise. Imagination is the faculty that associates, that builds bridges between one object and another; it is the art of correspondences. Borges had this faculty in the highest degree, joined to another no less precious: the intelligence to stick to the essential, to weed out parasitic growths. His was not the historian's skill, or the philologist's, or the critic's; it was a writer's skill, an active skill that retains what is useful and throws out the rest. His literary loves and hatreds were profound and reasoned, like those of a theologian, and violent, like those of a lover. He was neither impartial nor fair. He could not be: his critical faculty was the other arm, the other wing, of his creative fantasy. Was he a good judge of himself? I doubt it. His tastes did not always coincide with his genius, nor his preferences with his true nature. Borges did not resemble Dante, Whitman, or Verlaine, but rather Gracán, Coleridge, Valéry, Chesterton. No, I am mistaken: Borges resembled, above all Borges.

He worked in traditional forms and, except in his youth, the changes and violent innovations of our century scarcely tempted him. His essays were truly essays; he never confused this genre, as is now the custom, with the treatise, the dissertation, or the thesis. In his poems, free verse predominated at first; later, canonical forms and meters. For an extremist poet, he was rather timid, especially if the somewhat linear poems of his first books are compared with the odes and the complex constructions of Huidobro and other European poets of that period. He did not change the music of Spanish verse or reshape its syntax: he was neither Góngora nor Darío. Nor did he discover poetic heights or depths, as did some of his contemporaries. Still, his verses are unique, unmistakable; only he could have written them. His best verses are not sculpted words; they are sudden lights or shadows, gifts of unknown powers, true illuminations.

His stories are extraordinary for the felicity of his fantasy, not for its form. When writing works of the imagination, he did not feel attracted to the adventures and verbal vertigos of a Joyce, a Céline, or a Faulkner. Always lucid, he was not swept away by the passionate wind of a Lawrence, which sometimes stirs up clouds of dust and at other times clears clouds from the sky. Equally distant from the serpentine sentences of Proust and the telegraphic style of Hemingway, his prose surprises by its balance—neither laconic nor prolix, neither languid nor clipped. This is a virtue, and a limitation. With such a prose one can write a story, not a novel. One can sketch a situation, fire off an epigram, seize the shadow of a moment, not recount a battle, recreate a passion, penetrate a soul. His originality, in prose as in verse, is not in his ideas and forms but in his style, a seductive alliance of the simplest and the most complex; in his wonderful inventions; and in his vision. It is a unique vision not so much for what he sees as for the place from which he sees the world and himself. A point of view, more than a vision.

His love of ideas was extreme. Absolutes fascinated him, although he ended up disbelieving them all. As a writer, on the other hand, he felt an instinctive distrust of extremes. A sense of measure almost never left him. He was baffled by the excesses and the enormities, the mythologies and the cosmologies of India and of the Nordic peoples, but his idea of literary perfection was of a limited and clear form, with a beginning and an end. He thought that eternities and infinities could fit on a page. He frequently spoke of Virgil, and never of Horace. The truth is that he resembled not the former, but the latter: he never wrote, nor did he try to write, a long poem, and he always kept within the limits of Horatian decorum. I do not mean that Borges adhered to the poetics of Horace, but rather that his tastes led him to prefer measured forms. In his poetry and in his prose, there is nothing cyclopean.

Faithful to such an aesthetic, he invariably heeded the counsel of Poe that a modern poem should not have more than 50 lines. But it is curious, modernity: almost all the great modern poems are long poems. The characteristic works of the 20th century—I think, for example, of Eliot and Pound—are animated by one ambition: to be the divine comdies and the paradises lost of our age. The belief that sustains all these poems is this: that poetry is a total vision of the world, or of the drama of man in time. It is history and religion. I said before that the orginality of Borges consisted in having discovered a point of view. For this reason, some of his better poems take the form of commentaries on our classics—Homer, Dante, Cervantes. Borges's point of view is his unfailing weapon: he turned all traditional points of view on their heads, and obliged us to regard the things we see and the books we read differently. Some of his fictional pieces read like stories in *A Thousand and One Nights* written by a reader of Kipling and Chuang-Tzu; some of his poems remind one of a poet from the *Palatine Anthology* who might have been a friend of Schopenhauer and Lugones. He practiced the so-called minor genres—stories, short poems, sonnets—and it is wonderful that he should have achieved with them what others have attempted with long poems and novels. Perfection has no size. Often he attained it by the insertion of the unusual into the ordinary, by the alliance of the interrogative form with a perspective that, by mining some appearances discovers others. In his stories and in his poems Borges interrogated the world, but his doubt was creative, and brought into being the appearance of other worlds, other realities.

His stories and his poems are the inventions of a poet and a metaphysician. Thus they satisfy two of mankind's central faculties: reason and fantasy. It is true that Borges does not provoke the complicity of our feelings and passions, dark or light: piety, sensuality, anger, compassion. It is also true that his works tell us little or nothing about the mysteries of race, sex, and the appetite for power. Perhaps literature has only two themes—one, man among men, his fellows and his adversaries; the other, man alone against the universe and against himself. The first is the theme of the epic poet, the dramaturge, and the novelist; the second, the theme of the lyric and metaphysical poet. In Borges's works, human society and its many and complex manifestations, which run from the love of two people to great collective deeds, do not appear. His works belong to the other half of literature, and all have a single theme: time, and our repeated and futile attempts to abolish it. Eternities are paradises that become prison sentences, chimeras that are more real than reality—or perhaps I should say, chimeras that are no less unreal than reality.

Through prodigious variations and obsessive repetitions, Borges ceaselessly explored that single theme: man lost in the labyrinth of a time made of changes that are repetitions, man preening before the mirror of unbroken eternity, man who has found immortality and has conquered death but neither time nor old age. In his essays this theme is transformed into paradoxes and antinomies; in the poems and stories, into verbal constructions that have the elegance of mathematical theorems and the wit of living beings. The discord between the metaphysician and the skeptic is insoluble, but the poet makes of it transparent edifices of interwoven words: time and its reflections dance upon the mirror of our immediate awareness. These are works of rare perfection, verbal and mental objects made according to a geometry at once rigorous and fantastic, rational and capricious, solid and crystalline. All these varations on a single theme tell us one thing: the works of man, and man himself, are nothing but configurations of evanescent time. He said it with impressive lucidity: "Time is the substance of which I am made. Time is a river which carries me off, but I am that river; it is a fire which consumes me, but I am that fire." The mission of poetry is to throw light upon what is hidden in the folds of time. It took a great poet to remind us that we are, at the same time, the archer, the arrow, and the target. (pp. 30-4)

Octavio Paz, "In Time's Labyrinth," translated by Charles Lane, in The New Republic, *Vol. 195, No. 18, November 3, 1986, pp. 30-4.*

John (Anthony) Ciardi

June 24, 1916 - March 30, 1986

American poet, essayist, juvenile poet, nonfiction writer, and translator.

(See also *CLC*, Vols. 10, 40; *Contemporary Authors*, Vols. 5-8, rev. ed., Vol. 118 [obituary]; *Contemporary Authors New Revision Series*, Vol. 5; *Contemporary Authors Autobiography Series*, Vol. 2; *Something about the Author*, Vols. 1, 46; and *Dictionary of Literary Biography*, Vol. 5.)

PRINCIPAL WORKS

Homeward to America (poetry) 1940
Other Skies (poetry) 1947
Live Another Day (poetry) 1949
Mid-Century American Poets [editor] (poetry) 1950
From Time to Time (poetry) 1951
**The Inferno* [translator] (poetry) 1954
As If: Poems New and Selected (poetry) 1955
I Marry You: A Sheaf of Love Poems (poetry) 1958
The Reason for the Pelican (juvenile poetry) 1959
Thirty-Nine Poems (poetry) 1959
How Does a Poem Mean? [editor] (textbook) 1960
I Met a Man (juvenile poetry) 1961
In the Stoneworks (poetry) 1961
**The Purgatorio* [translator] (poetry) 1961
In Fact (poetry) 1962
The Wish-Tree (juvenile fiction) 1962
Dialogue with an Audience (essays) 1963
Person to Person (poetry) 1964
An Alphabestiary: Twenty-Six Poems (poetry) 1966
This Strangest Everything (poetry) 1966
The Achievement of John Ciardi: A Comprehensive Selection of His Poems with a Critical Introduction (poetry) 1969
**The Paradiso* [translator] (poetry) 1970
Lives of X (poetry) 1971
Manner of Speaking (essays) 1972
The Little That Is All (poetry) 1974
Fast and Slow: Poems for Advanced Children and Beginning Parents (juvenile poetry) 1975
For Instance (poetry) 1979
A Browser's Dictionary and Native's Guide to the Unknown American Language (dictionary) 1980
A Second Browser's Dictionary and Native's Guide to the Unknown American Language (dictionary) 1983
Selected Poems (poetry) 1984
The Birds of Pompeii (poetry) 1985
Doodle Soup (juvenile poetry) 1985
Good Words to You: An All-New Browser's Dictionary and Native's Guide to the Unknown American Language (dictionary) 1987

*These works were published together as *The Divine Comedy* in 1977.

© Jerry Bauer

JOHN CIARDI (INTERVIEW WITH VINCE CLEMENTE)

[*Clemente, an American poet, critic, and editor, is the founding editor of* The Long Pond Review, *as well as the editor of* West Hills: A Walt Whitman Journal. *His works include* Snow Owl Above *(1977) and* Broad Bill Off Conscience Bay *(1982); he also edited the festschrift* John Ciardi: Measure of the Man *(1987). In the following excerpt from an interview with Clemente in June, 1984, Ciardi reflects on his life and career.*]

VC: Years ago you wrote, ''Nothing is really hard but to be real.'' Is this yet the impetus behind the poems you write?

JC: If you will grant the reality of fantasy, yes.

VC: Yours has been described as the quintessential ''American voice,'' that of the wiseguy with a big heart. Is there any truth to this?

JC: Everyone is out to turn a phrase. I have never thought of myself as anything as impressive as a ''quintessential American voice''—who could live in such a thought. I hope I shall always by quick to spot a con (if that makes me a wiseguy); I'd like to be quicker in compassion but I sometimes fail through stupidity or preoccupation. None of these terms is mine: I am an old man; insofar as one can say so, I think I have survived ambition; I would like to live my days in some engaged, self-engaging way that includes congenial people without damning those people I am happy to avoid.

VC: In ***Live Another Day*** (1949), in the **"Foreword to the Reader of (Some) General Culture,"** you outline your *ars poetica,* thirteen principles out of which you write your poems. These include: "that a poem should be understandable," that "Poetry should be read aloud" and be "about the lives of people," that "the subject create its own form." Would you care to revise these principles? Are they at work today, thirty-five years later, in the making of a Ciardi poem?

JC: I would never have written such a piece today. I have become less positive and much more ignorant than I was when I wrote it.

VC: During your visit, June 3, 1984, to the Walt Whitman Birthplace as its Poet-in-Residence, you revealed a darker side, warning of Russian missiles less than thirty miles off Long Island shores, while we load Europe with ours, pointed at the Russians. You insisted that "The human race is playing some kind of joke on itself."

Against such a monition, are you ready to write off the element of hope, carried in lines from **"Thoughts on Looking into a Thicket,"** from ***As If*** (1955):

> . . . I believe
> if there is an inch or the underside of an inch
> for life to grow on, a life will grow there;
>
> if there are kisses, flies will lay their eggs
> in the spent sleep of lovers; if there is time,
> it will be long enough.

Are you saying, we've run out of time?

JC: The distance I gave was not thirty miles but three hundred. Russian nuclear subs are cruising international waters off our coast, as our submarines are cruising in return off what coast Russia offers. With luck I will die of natural causes blissfully due to my own bad habits. But I do believe beyond a doubt that the bombs will go off, and that the human race has been practicing self-destruction since the first, the present difference being that our ability to destroy is now total—total and, I think, irreversible. Mankind has never been capable of any folly it did not commit.

So far we have just missed. A ten- or twenty-year difference in the technological time-table would have left Hitler with the nuclear bomb and missiles. I cannot doubt that in the end he would have been happy to take everything with him. Nor can I believe that Hitler was the last Hitler. Yes, it will happen. It will happen so certainly that I no longer have time to waste worrying about it, as I have no time to waste in worrying about my own death.

And yes, a life will grow there—everywhere—but some mutant successor species whose sages will preach that the human species was put on earth to prepare the way for their holy frogginess or fungoidicity, or whatever the new holiness becomes.

VC: "A man is what he does with his attention." Is this the pith of what life has taught you?

JC: If life is subject to aphorisms, this one is as fit as any to rule.

VC: In the fall of this year [1984], your ***Selected Poems*** will be published, the book you took "forty years to write." ***Selected*** will include, intact, only one of your volumes, ***Lives of X,*** my favorite Ciardi volume and, I'm sure, an authentic, neglected American classic. In an early letter, one dated November 15, 1978, you write: "My book ***Lives of X*** was autobiographical and went as deep as I could reach into roots. I gave it everything I had. I will even claim I brought to American poetry a kind of fictional technique that amounted to multiple expansion. No book of mine was more important to me and none was ever more thoroughly ignored." Would you care to add anything? Have you gotten over the hurt of this neglect?

JC: I included all of ***Lives of X*** in the ***Selected Poems*** because I hope it will be read this time around. I don't know why it went so unnoticed the first time out. I know I have published lesser books that attracted much more attention.

A poet's own estimate of his work is likely to be self-seeking. I am wary of what other poets have told me about their own merit, wary enough to make no great assertions about my own. I think it is a readable book. I tried to make it readable. It pleases me when I reread it, and I am not one to fall in love with every precious word I ever committed to paper. Often enough, I tend to shudder on reading an old poem. What can I say? If it had been read and disliked, that would be a judgment to learn to accept. Instead it has been simply enough ignored. I wish it hadn't been, and I would like it if someone noticed it this time out.

I don't think I feel hurt because of this neglect of the book—I have other things to do I do feel it deserves better, and ego with us all, I would like someone to read it and like it a foolish wish, perhaps, but I did not invent it: it comes as an occupational disease.

VC: The notion of just what constitutes an authentic "American voice" in American poetry—is this notion at the root of your anger, as you wrote in the November 15, 1978, letter about Lowell commending you for a poem: "I had a longish poem about Italy in the *Atlantic* some years back, and when Robert Lowell wrote to praise its Italo-American voice, I took offense. Did the S.O.B. suppose I had used an American-English inferior to his, one that I had inherited and made mine, less American-English than his?"

JC: America is an anthology of people and accents. I don't think about becoming "an authentic American voice." Was Whitman authentic to the Creole? Emily Dickinson to the cowboy? Robert Frost to a Texan wheeler-dealer? I try to find the voice in which each poem wants to speak. Let the total theorize itself.

Lowell's card was really an effort to be gracious, and why should I offend a man who says he likes one of my poems? In so doing he assumed that his ancestors had somehow made him more American than I was, and that a poem about my Italian-named ancestors was less American than his life-study blathers about Grandfather Winslow (some of his worst stuff). He didn't mean to be smug about it, he was just bred to it. The S.O.B. label belongs on his assumption rather than on him, but fatheads write good poems, too.

VC: Could there be a *Late-Century American Poets* book for you? If so, which poets would you sound out? What are some of the questions you would ask them? If such a book is not possible—then why not?

JC: I have already suggested to you, and as it would take too long here, I see no way to achieve a consensus on which living poets are doing the best work—not in this fragmented poetic scene. This is a poetic age in which no ten people admire the same thing. As I say, I have suggested to you elsewhere how to run an impartial poll. Perhaps that might lead to a *Late-Century American Poets*. But I doubt it.

VC: You always had faith in an audience for poetry, your "reader of (some) general culture," the 600,000 plus readership of the old *Saturday Review*. Does such an audience exist today?

JC: I no longer think about the reader of (some) general culture. A man is what he does with his attention. Poetry—any of the arts—is for those with a willing attention and must not be diluted for those who haven't formed an attention.

VC: Looking back over your forty years of writing poems, are you still able to insist you are a "saying" poet rather than a "singing" poet? With which John Ciardi are you most comfortable?

JC: I am always happy when a poem manages to break into song, if only for a line or two. Bless all birds. But I think I am basically a "saying" poet rather than a "singer."

VC: "I am an American man of letters . . . with Jefferson, Tom Paine, and even—God save the mark, Emerson—at the roots of my mind and feeling," you write in a letter. What have been the rewards and the responsibilities of such a life in this Republic?

JC: Isaac Asimov once said, "I don't long for the good old days when there was no servant problem. Back in those days, I'd have been a servant."

I suppose I might have found life good had I turned out to be Sheik of an oil-bearing desert. In my lineage of camel-grooms, I like the way it has gone for me in this Republic. The Republic has left me free to my choices. It says in the Constitution that we all have a guaranteed right to make fools of ourselves. I have taken every chance to reap the rewards of that guarantee. If forced to action, I mean to fight to defend that right, which includes the right to be wrong, queer, or just kooky. And how can I defend that unless I defend those kooks and queers who think (wrongly of course) that I am kooky and queer?

VC: I'm sure you don't object to being called a "survivor," and I recall the lines in the Willie Crosby poem, "Survival in Missouri"—"Having survived a theology and a war / I am beginning to understand / the rain." And as a "survivor," you attended last year's reunion of the 73rd Bomb Wing, as one of three living members of an original crew of eleven.

In a recent autobiographical essay, you included a parable of a cormorant that "turned up in the swimming pool" of your Key West home, and "a pussy cat that tried to stalk it":

> "Like the holy ghost!" my neighbor said. "A visitation!" "Shit," I told him, "that bird is a bush pilot and knew exactly what it was doing in the most practical terms." Bush pilots do crash now and then, but first they line themselves up and fly. And they don't let themselves be drawn off their flight plans by imagining that pussy cats may turn into symbolic lions. Only poet-preachers do that.

Is this, then, our final glimpse of "Lucky John," the "bush pilot," surviving scrape after scrape, outwitting the impractical "poet-preachers"?

JC: Yes, I think of myself as a survivor. I have survived the Catholic Church, the guilt-twisted and poverty-crimped years of my crazy adolescence, the Japanese airforce (with some assistance from the USAAF whose clear intent at one time was to incinerate me). I have survived the delusion that I could improve the world by frenzied political stumping for lost causes, and the dream that my vote on anything would be counted as if it counted. In the end I have even survived ambition. Dare I think that I have survived the adolescence of my own children—they are now in their thirties and I begin to hope. Through it all what I have loved has stayed in place. I would like to think I am entitled to veteran's benefits: I have no more wars to go to, but there is still time (perhaps as much as ten or fifteen years by actuarial tables) and I want to concentrate on how to live the days of those years as richly as I can, to whim, sometimes to iron whim, but out of all debt except to time and what I love.

About the cormorant—I was talking more about my neighbor than the bird. My neighbor worried about the bird in ways I thought were silly. I saw at once that it knew what it was doing and that it was more than a match for the cat. You are trying to turn it symbolic, but it wasn't. I don't know why or how it stumbled into our swimming pool. The pool happens to be hemmed in by houses and trees, and cormorants need a long runway for takeoff. The bird sized up the one open lane that would serve, waddled off to it, stood backed against the fence, sighted a line under an arching bougainvillea, then climbed steeply for thirty feet to clear the house beyond, and was gone.

Meanwhile the cat kept stalking but (wisely) backing off, and my neighbor kept chortling alarms to which the bird and I were indifferent because it knew what it was doing, and I could see that it knew it. All I find in the story is the difference between silliness (bleeding heart silliness) and knowing how. I have always admired those things in us and in nature that know how.

VC: Again and again, you insist you write only "unimportant poems." But in your heart of hearts, aren't you certain you've written some that will last, that will be around long after both of us are gone? As a poet, mustn't you believe this?

JC: Since your question is pitched to ape-ego, I referred it to my ape and he said, "Yes, of course. Your every poem will live forever." What can you expect from an ape?

As nearly as the rational man can be summoned, the question becomes, "Are you not assuming that only important (big-message) poems will survive?" My thought is that if I can keep the poem small enough, I may yet get it down to human size. I don't see much future for *important declamation*. As above, I don't know how much future there is to foresee for the human race. What does survive—I would at least like to believe—will do so because it is emotionally true to our smallness, not because it is *important* to some Holy Ghost of declared eternal principle. As an international project, I propose that we begin to bury selected chemicals in the Sahara so arranged that when the sands fuse in the last fission-fusion go-round, the buried canisters will solidify into a glassed-in message in as many languages as possible, the message being *Jenny Kissed*

Me. If there must be a last message for the species, let it be that. (pp. 11-17)

John Ciardi, "A Man is What He Does with His Attention," in an interview with Vince Clemente, in Poesis, *Vol. 7, No. 2, 1986, pp. 1-17.*

DAN JAFFE

[*Jaffe, an American poet, critic, and editor, is the editor of BkMk Press. His books include* Archibald MacLeish: Mapping the Tradition in the Thirties *(1967) and* First Tuesday in November *(1971); he also coedited* Frontier Literature: Images of the American West *(1979). In the following excerpt Jaffe, who was a friend of Ciardi's for many years, introduces two Ciardi poems, inviting the reader to admire the poet's clear yet richly complex style.*]

As Spring 1986 began, John Ciardi died, in mid-flight as the great ones often do, work in progress next to him on his desk. No doubt his poems and books will keep appearing, assuaging the grief of his friends while at the same time reminding us of the dimension of our loss.

The two poems that follow illustrate John Ciardi's power and honesty, the man of spirit and the man of flesh. Consider the range of scholarship and the complexity. Consider, too, how he keeps connected to everyday experience. Try to paraphrase the poems and you will find yourself in a torrent that defies easy explanation. That is not to say John Ciardi is admirable because difficult. Rather it is to point out how he disliked oversimplification, how he would not romanticize even himself. These poems move from pancakes to the stars, from the mythic to the momentary, from the coolly logical to the rashly human, from the elegant to the colloquial. Consider, for example, the rich ambiguity of "Reason is prattle till you come to bed." What a wonderful undermining of the mind that has become unhinged from the human connection. What a dramatic unity, in itself full of verbal irony, yet trumping so well all the lines it follows.

This is just to say that John Ciardi was a poet who would not let us forget the stuff of our magnificent confusions.

Always While Nothing Happens
The Same Again

Whenever I order pancakes I remember
why I never order pancakes. I don't care
how lovingly the waitress is the Virgin Mary
imploring me to eat everything on my plate:
They still taste like fried pulp scooped from a tank
for recycling supermarket shopping bags.

Three times a day I stand by the bar's GENTS
feeding a video cigarette machine
till it flashes CHOOSE to music, and I must decide
which of twenty-four brands of cancer-sticks
I equally really do not want: They all
taste like whiffs of a defoliant spray.

When I order another bourbon, Tim says, "Sure,
if you let me call you a cab." Still nothing happens
but a post-hypnotic imperative in which "cab"
must be the trigger word. In a later life
I say to the corpse, 'Why did you make me do it?"
But by then I am home and sleeplessly dead for sleep.

When I put Mozart on the cassette player
the Age of Reason, minueting in order
cuts courtly figures as if to perfect choices.
—Damn my accusers! Could even Laplace suppose
that Oedipus in his self-disgusting hex
found any solution in Jocasta's bed?
Always while nothing happens the same again.

When sleep unglues to the stink of inconclusion,
the virgin waitress keeps shoving under my nose
a heap of mush stabbed full of half-smoked butts
stained with blood syrup. "Finish everything!"
she weeps from the ray of her unbearable love,
accusing me of all she suffers for me.

Damn my defenders! As if she did not know
there is no word can push us past ourselves
to do what is not in us. I wanted him dead
for plotting to do me a good I have rejected.
As Oedipus sniffed sour meat. Though he pretended
not to know what sow he held in his arms.

The Logician's Nocturne

The fundamental characteristic of matter
is its existence. Nothing can exist
apart from its particular properties.
Properties, in existing, interact.
In interacting, particles—who knows how?—
form into cells particularly themselves.
Already creatures, these particular cells
colonize their properties and evolve
to a reflexive cognition. Reflexive cognition
characteristically recognizes matter
in the forms of what perceives it. So perceived,
we are the assumptions of our own reflexes.
And why strain to see through them? At such ease
as creatures shape to in their shaping nests,
I tend the environment of your undressing
to rondures from whose eloquence I learn
reason is prattle till you come to bed.

(pp. 41-2)

Dan Jaffe, "Tribute to John Ciardi," in New Letters, *Vol. 52, Nos. 2 & 3, Winter & Spring, 1986, pp. 40-2.*

ROBERT O. BOORSTIN

John Ciardi, the poet and professor who was internationally acclaimed for his translation of Dante's *Inferno,* died [March 30] at the John F. Kennedy Medical Center in Edison, N.J., after suffering a heart attack. Mr. Ciardi, who made his home in Metuchen, N.J., was 69 years old.

The author of some 40 books of poetry and criticism, including many volumes of children's verse, Mr. Ciardi taught for many years at Rutgers University and Harvard and served as poetry editor of the magazine *Saturday Review* from 1956 to 1972.

An outspoken poet and critic known for his sharp and witty images, Mr. Ciardi won praise for his verses, which spoke honestly to children, and for the 1959 poetry textbook ***How Does a Poem Mean?*** He was outspokenly critical of traditional poetry aimed at youngsters, which struck him as "written by a sponge dipped in warm milk and sprinkled with sugar."

His many collections of poems for adults, which ranged from war verses to love lyrics and occasional flights of fancy, also met with favorable reactions from critics, who praised him for his honesty.

"He is singularly unlike most American poets with their narrow lives and feuds," wrote the critic and poet Kenneth Rexroth. "He is more like a very literate, gently appetitive, Italo-American airplane pilot, fond of deep simple things like his wife and kids, his friends and students, Dante's verse and good food and wine."

But it was for his translation of the *Inferno,* first published in 1954 and still a familiar volume on college campuses, that Mr. Ciardi was perhaps best known.

"Here is our Dante," the critic Dudley Fitts wrote of Mr. Ciardi's translation. "Dante for the first time translated into virile, tense American verse; a work of enormous erudition which (like its original) never forgets to be poetry."

John Anthony Ciardi was born in Boston on June 24, 1916, the only son of Italian immigrant parents. In 1921, two years after his father was killed in an automobile accident, the family moved to Medford, Mass., where the young Ciardi peddled vegetables to the neighbors and attended public schools.

Mr. Ciardi began his higher studies at Bates College in Lewiston, Me., but transferred to Tufts University in Boston, where he studied under the poet John Holmes. He received his degree in 1938, and won a scholarship to the University of Michigan, where he obtained his master's degree the next year and won the first of many awards for his poetry.

In 1940, at the age of 24, Mr. Ciardi published his first book of poetry, ***Homeward to America.*** The book was well received, and Mr. Ciardi hoped to concentrate only on his writing, but finances forced him to take a job as an English instructor at Kansas State University.

In 1942, he enlisted in the Army Air Corps, and served as a gunner aboard a B-29 in the aerial offensive against Japan. He was decorated with the Air Medal and oak-leaf cluster.

After the war, Mr. Ciardi returned briefly to Kansas State, before being named instructor, and later assistant professor, in the Briggs Copeland chair at Harvard University, where he stayed until 1953.

While at Harvard, Mr. Ciardi began his long association with the Bread Loaf Writers Conference at Middlebury College in Vermont, where he lectured on poetry for almost 30 years, half that time as director of the program.

During his years at Bread Loaf and at the *Saturday Review,* Mr. Ciardi established a reputation as a tough, sometimes harsh, critic. His review of Anne Morrow Lindbergh's 1956 book *The Unicorn* touched off what the *Review*'s editor, Norman Cousins, described as "the biggest storm of reader protest" in the magazine's history. Mr. Ciardi defended his stand, noting that it was "the reviewer's duty to damn" when warranted.

Mr. Ciardi left Harvard to join the faculty of Rutgers University, where he taught until 1961, when he left the academic world to devote himself full-time to literary pursuits.

Among his many books were ***Other Skies,*** a 1947 collection praised for its stark images of World War II; ***From Time to Time,*** and a poetry anthology, *Mid-Century American Poets.* His children's books included ***The Reason for the Pelican*** and ***Mummy Slept Late and Daddy Fixed Breakfast.***

"What has any poet to trust more than the feel of the thing?" Mr. Ciardi once wrote. "Theory concerns him only until he picks up his pen, and it begins to concern him again as soon as he lays it down. But when the pen is in his hand he has to write by itch and twitch, though certainly his itch and twitch are intimately conditioned by all his past itching and twitching, and by all his past theorizing about them."

Mr. Ciardi, who served as a president of the National Institute of Arts and Letters, was the recipient of numerous awards and honorary degrees. In 1956, he received the Prix de Rome from the American Academy of Arts and Letters, and in 1982, the National Council of Teachers of English gave him its award for excellence in children's poetry.

During the last 10 years, Mr. Ciardi had become addicted to etymology, the study of the origin of words, and had just completed a third volume of his ***Browser's Dictionary.*** Since 1980, he had produced a weekly etymology feature for National Public Radio, entitled *Word in Your Ear.*

Robert O. Boorstin, "John Ciardi, Poet, Essayist and Translator, 69," in The New York Times, *April 2, 1986, p. B6.*

JOHN FREDERICK NIMS

[*Nims, an American poet, translator, and critic, is admired for his witty, intellectual verse, represented in* The Iron Pastoral *(1947),* Knowledge of the Evening *(1960),* A Local Habitation *(1985), and his other collections, including* Selected Poems *(1982). In the following excerpt from a lecture Nims gave at the University of Missouri at Kansas City ten days before Ciardi's death, Nims examines the many complex facets of the poet's personality, from scholar to colloquial observer of modern life.*]

It is not easy to know, when about to explore the poetry of John Ciardi, where to enter so diverse a region and how to proceed when once there. It is hardly too much to say that here—as Dryden said of Chaucer—here is God's plenty. There are similarities with Chaucer: the record of a pilgrimage, the many interests, the amused warm tolerance for human folly so long as it is neither cruel nor pretentious. Chaucer too was a man of affairs, worldly wise in a time when men were inclined to be more spiritual than now. We may think of the poet as being maladroit, like Baudelaire's albatross, once he leaves his airy realm and comes down to earth. But many have been effective when dealing with things of this world; we would have to put John Ciardi among them. If you wanted advice on the stock market, he could give it to you. If you wanted to know about real estate values or the best buy in a used car, he could tell you. If you wanted to know how to raise roses or get rid of moles in your lawn, he knew that too. If he had inherited the mom and pop grocery on the corner, likely enough he would have developed it into a worldwide chain. If he had gone into politics, he might have been our Governor Cuomo. Only a strong commitment to poetry prevented him from realizing some of the abilities hs has sacrificed for it. The multifarious interests, the many lives he has led, account for the variety of his poetry, and for the difficulty of covering it in a hasty survey.

"The many lives of poetry." In an early birthday poem he speaks of

> An album of myself . . .
> seen year by year
> Posed in the changing fashions of its skin . . .

and a quarter of a century later he confesses, "I was not able to make one life of all / the presences I haunted. . . ." At every age he has been, like Montaigne, a student of himself. He has been a soldier and then a householder, observing a quieter world from his patio. Through these observations he has become a naturalist and particularly an ornithologist, the very Audubon of poets. Always he has had a sharp eye for what is authentic and what is pretentious in the human creature; watching it, he could hardly fail to be at times a satirist. Books have been part of his life from his earliest years; he is known as a scholar, a word-watcher, an adventurous and entertaining etymologist. He has been a translator, a teacher, a lecturer, an editor, the author of a dozen or more books for children. A citizen, a political commentator. "I am an actor too," he says in ***Lives of X.*** He calls himself "a missionary bee / sucking for souls." He even says, "Were I to dramatize myself,"

> I'd say I am a theologian who keeps meeting
> the devil as a master of make-up. . . .

A missionary? a theologian? It is a little hard to see Ciardi wearing, together with his twenty or more other hats, the kind of biretta worn by the priests of his childhood. If he ever had worn one, we can be sure that he would have transformed it into a cardinal's hat, and been active in running the Mafia out of Sicily—unless indeed he had become head of it.

Through the *persona* of Leonardo da Vinci he once wrote:

> You know how or you don't. But to know how
>
> is first to be born of a people, to be
> the bearer of their seed—son, husband, father.

These are the lives—those of son, husband, father, with the sense of being born of a people—that we will glance at first in what might be thought of as our Ciardi sampler, our little anthology of the pleasures his work affords us.

The poet finds what are probably the deepest and truest sources of his work in the emotions that give us poems of three generations. All are *dynamic* relationships—I wondered briefly if *dynastic* would be too pompous a word. The author of ***A Browser's Dictionary*** would know that both words come from the same root—and that there is *dynamite* in that family. I was reassured to find that he himself had used *dynastic* in his **"Letter to Mother,"** the first poem in his first book:

> And it is good to remember that this blood, in
> another body, your body, arrived.
> There is dynastic example in a single generation
> of this blood, and the example good. . . .

In fact, more than three generations are present. There are poems that go back to a grandfather in Italy,

> Father's father,
> photographer- and Sunday-scrubbed and scarved,
> Sorrento painted behind him . . .

and to a grandmother who "in *her* tribe's dark, kept herbs and spells / and studied signs and dreams. . . ."

The first section of ***Selected Poems*** is called "Tribal Poems," as was a section of ***As If*** almost thirty years before. Several members of the tribe are as colorful as Aunt Mary, who "loved us till we screamed" and who died of eating twelve red peppers, fried in oil, after a hard day's work, thereby undergoing "red-hot transformation / from gluttony into embalmer's calm."

Dominant in the poems of family feeling is the mother. Thirty-five years after that early **"Letter to Mother,"** ***The Little That Is All*** was dedicated to her "in loving memory." But from the very beginning the love between mother and son is never without tension. **"Letter to Mother"** can say, "It was good, it was all good." But it can also say, "Mother, I can promise you nothing." Passionate and simple, from a hearty peasant background, the mother was "instinctual," says her son, "as peasantry breeds in any Apennines. . . ." He was just as passionate, but without her background—growing up as he did amid books, classes, the excitements of city life in a new land. He found he could not continue to share, for one thing, the unquestioning fervor of her Catholicism:

> Once on a shelf
> a candle lit a plaster saint
> and I knelt in a blaze of self.
> The reek of guilt would leave me faint
> where my mad mother stretched my soul. . . .

Nor could his mother share all of his interests:

> By flashlight under the covers
> . . . there
> in the cave safe from Mother,
> I read my eyes out of my head. . . .

Some of her practices would have seemed superstitious to the citizens of her adopted country, although their own ancestors had been just as superstitious not so many decades before:

> When we poured
> concrete for a new house, she leaned over
> the half-filled forms muttering,
> and dropped in a penny, a crucifix, a key,
> then pricked her finger and shook out
> a drop of blood. . . .
> She was using everything she knew anything
> about, and she knew she was using it.

"That," her son comments, "is my kind of savage," for her superstitions were based on blood and bone and the vitality of her beliefs, not just on the number 13 or black cats or ladders or the meaningless obsessions of people walking the streets—"ritualists," the poet calls them, "without conviction."

The love between mother and son was complicated because husband and father had been killed, when the child was only three, in a traffic accident—a loss that "maddened the woman, and then wasted her witless," a loss "that had been the blood / and error and evil of all my Mother's tears. . . ." More and more she saw the father in the son; more and more he saw that his "best chance was to play the husband" and (especially on those occasions when she was punishing him) to win her over with his rough affection. "Then *she*'d cry, / and I'd have to stop bawling to comfort *her*." He came to be protective not only as a husband might have been, but even as a father. As she grew weak and fey with age, he could say, "I think perhaps this woman is my child." Perhaps her son's best tribute to her is in ***Lives of X:***

> history's daughter
> tall from her root of love, my comic source,
> my radiant witch of first-made lunacies,
> and priestess of the tongues before a man. . . .

The poet can hardly have remembered his father, who was felt, however, as a powerful presence: "the deepest grave I know." In **"My Father Died Imperfect as a Man,"** we read

> My mother lied him to perfections . . .
>
> So history lied my father from his death,
> she having no history that would let him be
> imperfect and worth keeping vigils with.
> She made a saint of him. And she made me

kneel to him every night. When I was bad
he shadowed me. And always knew my lies.
I was too young to know him, but my bed
lay under him and God, and both their eyes

bored through the dark to damn me as I was. . . .

Much of what he remembered was an imaginative creation, as when he described how his father, out of his savings, had bought "ten piny lots" in the country, which he liked to visit on Sunday and make plans for:

when he sat on a stone with his wine-jug and cheese
beside him,
his collar and coat on a branch, his shirt open,
his derby back on his head like a standing turtle. A big
man he was. When he sang *Celeste Aida* the woods
filled as if a breeze were swelling through them. . . .

—Well, I have lied. Not so much lied as dreamed
it. . . .

In a time when the vogue was for children to enjoy composing, and profiting from, exposés of their parents, Ciardi, though aware of shortcomings, could regard his own with admiration, respect, and love; it is with something like exaltation that he proclaims: "I am the son of this man and this woman."

In ***Selected Poems,*** the "Tribal Poems" are followed by a group called "I Marry You" (the title of a 1958 volume), subtitled "A Sheaf of Love Poems." In the last of the group, the poet returns to his tribal memories:

My father did read some. But it was
his mountain he came from, not the mind
of man. He had ritual, not ideas. . . .

Such ancestral pieties also inform the love poems; marital love as consecrated by ritual is the theme of more than one of them. **"Epithalamion After a War"** begins, "Now by a ritual of legality / You are my flesh's darling, my mind's encounter. . . ." Of the dozen or so love poems in ***I Marry You,*** only four are reprinted in ***Selected Poems.*** Is that because love poems are harder to write, and for that reason less likely to succeed, than other tribal poems—particularly when they are poems of happy love, as these are? When Keats babbles about

More happy love, more happy, happy love
Forever warm and still to be enjoyed . . .

he is looking not at flesh and blood but at ceramic figures, their imagined emotions far above "all breathing human passion." We must all have noticed that there are fewer poems—though more verse—about blissful love than about love star-crossed or unrequited. The lover who feels fulfilled has other things to do than moon over his typewriter. As Yeats says, had he been happy in love, he "might have thrown poor words away / And been content to live." The difficulty is that poems of happy love, having few ironies to invoke, may seem not only simple-hearted but simple-minded. The poems to Ciardi's mother, also poems of love, are gripping because they are not simply poems of "more happy, happy love"; they are poems about the interplay between love and what threatens to destroy it. But the poems of ***I Marry You*** seem to offer the most untroubled and luminous vistas in all of the poetry. The beauty of the loved woman is described as the stuff of which all legend is made: "There is no other body in all myth. . . ."

But since beauty is a magnet for evil as well as for good, myth does not confine itself to the annals of happiness. When Yeats warns, "there's a light in Troy," he is not referring to the glory of Helen's hair. Something of the same feeling is in our poet's praise of his love: "The raiders' ships / All sailed to your one port. . . ." In these poems, the electric charge is not in the love, which is unclouded, but in the lover, sometimes torn between the spiritual and the sensuous:

Bravo and monk (the heads and tails of love)
I stand, a spinning coin of wish and dread. . . .

Or it is in reality itself. In the most moving poems, there is a realization of the conflict between timeless and legendary beauty and the contingency, the chanciness, of an existence made up of whatever is begotten, born, and dies. This is the thought of the love poem whose first line is its title:

The deaths about you when you stir in sleep
hasten me toward you. Out of the bitter mouth
that sours the dark, I sigh for what we are. . . .

The chill of apprehension is felt also in **"To Judith Asleep"**:

. . . my fear and miser's panic
That time shall have you last, and legendry
Undress to old bones from its moon brocade. . . .

Yet the realization that love is imperiled, that time must have a stop, teaches us to cherish what we cannot long possess. That realization sparks a defiance that is, at least for the moment, a protection against the conturbations of *timor mortis*. In **"Men Marry What They Need. I Marry You,"** this defiance is explicit:

I marry you from time and a great door
is shut and stays shut against wind, sea, stone . . .
I marry you by all dark and all dawn

And have my laugh at death.

After the marriage poems we have poems to the children. Ciardi has written about as many books for children as for us overgrowns—but I think not many poems about them. Is it because it is as hard to write children-poems as to write love poems? Are the tots too cute and adorable—at least in the verse about them? Swinburne saw them that way, as in the poem he had the nerve to call "Étude Réaliste," which begins:

A baby's feet, like sea-shells pink,
Might tempt, should heaven see meet,
An angel's lips to kiss, we think,
A baby's feet. . . .

Gerard Manley Hopkins, poet and holy man, admitted that such "rot about babies" made him see things King Herod's way.

But as the children grow older and more refractory, dramatic tensions begin and the interest picks up. The poet finds himself, in regard to them, in the position his mother was in toward him. But, perhaps because of his own early experience, he has more understanding and tolerance than her traditions permitted her to have. The father-son polarity is felt first in **"Boy"**:

He is in his room sulked shut. The small
pouts of his face clenched. His tears
as close to holy water as I recall
any font shining. A boy, and fierce
in his sacrament, father-forced this two-
faced way love has.

Racked by the need for extending sympathy and for enforcing discipline, the father concludes:

> I confess
> I don't know my own reasons or own way.
> May sons forgive the fathers they obey.

Later poems are about forgiving, but with an amused tolerance he had not quite learned when he wrote **"Boy."** What gives the poems to his son Benn, like those to his mother, their credibility is their upsetting candor. In all of the family poems we are in the presence of a spirit warm, tolerant, sympathetic, forgiving. But never blindly so; it sees, but makes allowance for, the imperfections in all of us. In **"My Father Died Imperfect as a Man"** is the sentence, "Love must intend realities." Ten years later, in ***The Little That Is All,*** it became the substance of the one-liner called **"Exit Line"**: "Love should intend realities.—Good-bye." Ten more years, and the poet returns to the insistent "must" in ***Selected Poems.*** But with the people he loved, though he saw the realities almost too vividly, it was never "Good-bye". A truer summary of his feelings is to be found just a few lines from the end of the **"Epilogue"** to ***Lives of X***: "Let what I love outlive me and all's well."

There is one life he is closer to than to any of these: his own. "Closer," he says, "than mother and son." He regards himself with not only the same unsparing honesty as he regards others, but with a frankness that is ironic, if not openly sarcastic. Looking at a photo of the soldier he was, he can say,

> The sgt. stands so fluently in leather,
> So poster-holstered and so newsreel-jawed . . .
> My civil memory is overawed.

The "fine bravura look of calm," he confesses, is a deception. The poet allows himself no heroics in his own regard. There are several poems of self-criticism, or even of self-derision. In **"Coming Home on the 5:22,"** he can mock the "prosperous well-tailored plump / middle-aged man" he has become, showing off by leaping from the train before it comes to a stop. That incident leads to further self-analysis:

> How did this fat and foolish man
> come over me? He is not I.
> Yet I am he, though I began
> as something else. When did I die?
> Well, tell the truth: not I but they.
> All those I tried in prayer or play,
>
> Like trying on a self . . .
>
> I used to say this sort of thing to God.
> He didn't like an idiot for a son.
> I wasn't pleased myself, so I changed style. . . .

A poet, in writing about himself, becomes a divided personality: observer and observed. "No mind can engender till divided into two," said Yeats, who also observed that "We make out of the quarrel with others, rhetoric, but of the quarrel with ourselves, poetry." A dramatic example of the poet quarreling with himself is Ciardi's **"Tenzone."** The title is literary, one of only two or three such in ***Selected Poems.*** It could allow us a pedantic romp into fields of genre, source, influence, parallels. **"Tenzone"** is a two-part poem: in the first part Soul accuses Body of abandoning the higher reality that it, the Soul, aspires to, and of corrupting its talent, if any, to devote itself to such earthy pleasures as big cars, bourbon, good clothes, "cash, freeloading, and the more expensive bitches." "He actually likes it here," Soul concludes in disgust. In the second part, Body, in matching stanzas, answers the "eternalist of boneyards" by saying that Soul by itself is ineffective,

> a glowworm. A spook. A half-strung zither
> with a warped sounding box. . . .

At any rate no poet, because "the poem is belly and bone." In defiance of Soul, Body admits that it does want the physicality of the here and now:

> And, *yes,* I want it all—
> grab, gaggle, and rut—as sure as death's no breather.

The poem will remind us of Yeats's "A Dialogue of Self and Soul," which, though in imagery and diction very different, is a similar debate. As Yeats has My Self say,

> I am content to live it all again
> And yet again, if it be life to pitch
> Into the frog-spawn of a blind man's ditch . . . ,

so Ciardi has Body say to Soul:

> Yes, I like it here. Make it twenty times worse
> and I'd still do it over again, even with you
> like a monkey on my back. . . .

In the most recent of his dual poems, in which the poet wakes up "inanely happy," there is a joyful reconciliation between the mind and its "animal." The poem is called **"Happiness"**; it is appropriately the first poem in his most recent book. The two poems that follow it, equally exultant, are **"The Glory"** and **"Praise."**

As a gunner in a B-29 in the South Pacific, Ciardi had another kind of life, close to death. The poems that deal with these experiences remind us more of the starkness of Wilfred Owen than of the romanticism of Rupert Brooke: grim accounts of bomber missions and their casualties, of what goes on in the mind of a downed pilot in an isolated jungle, or of one who, without provisions on his rubber raft, drifts in mid-ocean toward his lonely death. These accounts are not preserved in the ***Selected Poems.*** The only poem there that copes with the reality of modern war is **"The Graph,"** from ***Lives of X.*** In this he can confess, "I studied dying all that year," and can tell us what some of the lessons were like:

> I practiced thinking I had died last week
> and could relax with nothing more to lose.
> Still in the night sweat before every mission
> a wet rag whispered: "By this time tomorrow
> you may have burned to death. . . ."

Another time he found himself in a cave facing a concretion of corpses that had been charred to mummies by the flamethrowers. In the open mouth of one was a living rat, working there like an obscene tongue. But only in that poem is there so grim a glance at the horrors of war. Ciardi plays down the heroics, and his own part in them. His epigraph for the group of war poems in ***As If*** is a line from Melville's "The March into Virginia": "All wars are boyish, and are fought by boys. . . ."

He saw integrity and heroism in those campaigns, and gave them the honor they deserve. If the spirit of irony seems to prevail, it is because he saw so clearly the difference between the heroic and the heroics. His attitude was no less ironic toward himself, as we see in his best known war poems, **"Elegy Just in Case"** and **"On a Photo of Sgt. Ciardi a Year Later."** Long after the war he wrote a poem with the title, **"Ten Years**

Ago When I Played at Being Brave.'' His final comment on that period of his life would seem to be the title he gave the section of war poems in his ***Selected Poems***: he called it ''Bang Bang.''

A life the poet lived after the war is referred to in the title of a poem in ***From Time to Time:*** **''Image of Man as a Gardener After Two World Wars.''** It begins:

In the dead hour of the afternoon,
When the sun has overshot the sky
. . . I stand
Hosing, householding my lawn.

In poem after poem we see the poet as householder. In ***Selected Poems,*** a group subtitled ''On the Patio'' has twice as many poems as the ''Bang Bang'' section. It is there that he can say, ''Now I sit / Happy to look at what I look at. . . .'' In these poems the ironies are quieted. Much of what he looks at is in the landscaping around the patio. No mere chaise lounge gardener, he knows and lets us know the sometimes painful pleasure of working with soil, compost, burlap, wax, a grafting knife.

One of the poems in ***From Time to Time*** is called **''The Cartographer of Meadows.''** Looking at nature first from near the house, he begins to be a naturalist in the wider world, scanning with scientific exactness what is to be seen there. Everything is specific: ''I have never seen,'' one poem insists, ''a generalized blue jay.'' When he looks at bees he sees them not merely as a buzzy blur, but as ''hunchback bees in pirate pants and with peg-leg / hooks. . . .'' When he sees a deer, neck-deep in mist, he does not see just a moving head. He sees ''A brown swan with a mythic twist of antlers. . . .''

Ciardi's nature poems are rare, like Frost's, in that they are based on the realities of nature. The writers of sentimental verse like to fancy that birds are talking to *us,* really piping sweet somethings in our ear. Frost—and Ciardi—know better. (pp. 283-93)

Ciardi knows . . . that whatever there is between man and the rest of nature, it is not rational communication. He ''intends realities'' when he looks at the world, just as when he looks at the people in it. He is unsentimental in recognizing that nature is by no means always endearing. We are surrounded by oddities, mysteries, horrors. One section of ***Selected Poems*** is called ''Thickets''—looking at nature, we are always looking into a thicket of the inscrutable. **''Thoughts on Looking into a Thicket''** has to do with a spider who resorts to one of the strangest and unseemliest of camouflages—it can make itself look like bird droppings, to attract butterflies and such who regard that as their gourmet fare. Planning to eat, they light there and are eaten.

Frost is reported to have said that he had never written a nature poem. He too took what he needed from wild nature to tell us something about our human nature, often no less wild.

We might be surprised to find that in ***I Marry You,*** which is subtitled ''A Sheaf of Love Poems,'' the first poem (**''Snowy Heron''**) after the dedicatory one is about a bird. It begins: ''What lifts the heron leaning on the air / I praise without a name. . . .'' St. Francis, seeing ''the heron on his two soft kissing kites,'' might have praised God for it. ''Cry anything you please,'' says the poem, ''But praise. By any name or none / . . . And doubt all else. But praise.'' In the same ''Sheaf of Love Poems'' is **''Two Egrets,''** birds that are

like two white hands
washing one another
in the prime of light. . . .

What the two, there in their ''lit heaven,'' remind the poet of is ''a prayer / and the idea of prayer.''

These nature poems, then, are really love poems, poems of the praise which is prayer. Even in the poem about the spider dabbling in its mucky *trompe l'oeil,* the poet professes: ''I believe in the world to praise it. I believe / the act in its own occurrence.'' If the birds of the world could get together (as in Chaucer's ''The Parlement of Foules'') to pick a laureate for their nation, they might well pick John Ciardi, among his other lives a knowledgeable ornithologist. He mentions many kinds of birds, as we might expect from one who in his **''Bird Watching''** tells how he thumbs through a field guide to identify one that is a

miracle while it
is happening, and then instantly incredible forever. . . .

Gulls seem to have been an early favorite, ''ultimate bird / everywhere and everything pure wing and wind / are. . . .'' But later on there are mentions of birds more likely to be seen from the patio or in the neighborhood, birds of at least a dozen different species. These are by no means all of the birds on his life list; there are also birds imagined or read about: the dodo, the Rhino-bird. The sight of even a dead bird ''pasted to muck'' inspires his **''Small Elegy''**—seventy lines and more, not one of them mawkish, leading to deeper considerations:

Have I lost most by wanting less?
I have not happened anywhere
on more regret than I could lose,
nor on more love than I could bear;
nor on more pity than I could give
the small sad days to which we live.

In **''Back Home in Pompeii''** birds stand for the animation that was buried under ash and lava:

Back home in Pompeii
birds crunched underfoot,
stones flew away,
statues began to bow. . . .

Twenty-five years later, the lines gave a title to his 1985 volume, ***The Birds of Pompeii.***

A reference to birds can take us into yet another of his lives. About the warbler of **''In Some Doubt but Willingly,''** he writes:

What an engine this dawn
has going for it on
the limb I cannot find. . . .

Very well: the bird is an admirable little engine. But for engines in general—and in his work generalities turn to particulars—he has a limited admiration. There are exceptions. Possibly remembering his father's death in a traffic accident, he does like the safety of big cars. When he mentions a brand name, it is likely to be Cadillac. In his **''Memo: Preliminary Draft of a Prayer to God the Father,''** he can say:

Thank you for the expensive car, its weight and
 sure tread
that makes it reasonable to go reasonably fast. . . .

In spite of his war experiences, he seems comfortable with the planes that take him so many places:

There is no cloud I cannot mount
and sip good bourbon as I ride. . . .

The power mower that helps civilize the environs of the patio comes in for several mentions; it is the subject of his **"On the Orthodoxy and Creed of My Power Mower"**—a title that illustrates his tendency to ascend from particulars to a more reflective and imaginative level. In the poem, the power mower is a dangerous beast, needing to be wheedled and placated by its priest from the service department. Though fascinated by its might, the poet is not wholly at ease with this frenzied thing. Twenty-five years before, he had similar misgivings about farm machinery at harvest:

Look: there are monsters in the wheat
. . . all an enormous mouth . . .
Contraptions of intestines, a surreal sex,
A planned miscarriage, a hybrid, spit-and-gum
Lopsided, cockeyed, mad, impossible theorem

That works. Or almost works. . . .

Confronted by many products of the modern world, Ciardi is contentedly behind the times. In **"Obsolescence"** he expresses his discomfort with "an Omni-Function Digital Synchro-Mesh / Alarm wrist watch that beeps *Caro nome* / (also available with *Vissi d'arte*)." He prefers the old ways of telling time:

I know time only as a circle. Star time.
Rotation and orbit time. Dark and lit as tides. . . .

Because I am obsolete, I cannot read it.

As obsolete, he is in many ways Horace's "laudator temporis acti se puero"—a praiser of the good old days, when he was a boy. Most satirists are. Ciardi not only distrusts some of the products of the modern age; he also has a shrewd eye for its follies. When one is as sharp an observer of humanity as he is, one cannot fail to be indignant; indignation can inspire verses, said Juvenal, if all else fails—not that anything else has failed our poet. We have seen a good deal of irony at his own expense: satiric views of himself as soldier, himself as prosperous citizen. The vein of satire grows stronger in the later books. It is directed at Washington, D.C., and its leaders in such jabberwocky-like poems as the **"Ballad of the Icondic"** (Ike and Dick), at the Internal Revenue Service, at people who build air-raid shelters in their back yards (he once said he was going to build a platform out there, take up a bottle of bourbon, and settle down to watch the spectacular finale). He has poems against officialdom and bureaucracy, against red tape and blue movies, against those who administer cultural programs. As a poet who watches the language and believes in "his own profession, which is in praise / of the enlarging word," he is especially sensitive to mishandlings of the language that turn it into cant and jargon. **"Elegy Just in Case"** burlesques the officialese with which next of kin are informed:

"Missing as of inst. oblige,
Deepest sorrow and remain—"

A recent example of this kind of satire takes a line from Dante as its title, **"Donne ch'avete intelletto d'amore,"** in order to parody, by reducing to an absurdity, the trivialization of emotion by our psychosocial jargon. The title contrasts modern interfacing with the romantic but idealistic love that Dante is exalting in *La Vita Nuova;* it is the first line of the famous canzone whose opening might be translated as

Ladies, who have understanding of what love is,
 I wish to speak to you about my lady,
 Not that I can ever praise her enough. . . .

It goes on to say such things as

An angel in heaven offers a prayer, in the mind of God,
 Saying, "Lord, down on earth is to be seen
 A creature so marvellous in the effulgence
 Of her soul that the splendor is felt even up here.
 Heaven, in which nothing is lacking except that
 She be here with us, implores you, Lord,
 To convey her hither, and so prays every saint. . . .

The modern couple talk like this:

Mary and I were having an emotion.
"Thank you for having this emotion with me,"
Mary said, "I needed a reinforcement
of my identity through an interaction.
Have you accomplished a viable realization?"

"I know it was a formative experience,"
I said to Mary, "and yet, as I critique it
at my own level, I still feel under-achieved. . . ."

"Is that susceptible of remediation . . .?
 May I suggest
a release-therapy impromptu now,
and a more fully structured enactment later?"

They go on to talk about how "an optimal interpersonal encounter should emphasize mutuality" and how "approval is to be strongly indicated as tendency re-inforcement in trait development . . . relating fully to . . . raised consciousness. . . .' Our poet concludes with a prayer: "O intellect of love, may I prove worthy!"

There are other lives of Ciardi I wish I could consider: his life as fantasist or fabulist, for instance, as expressed in such poems as **"In the Hole."** Or the lives he has imagined himself into: those of Ulysses, Launcelot, Hamlet, Leonardo—many others. Or his life as guardian of the language, as shown in his talks on public broadcasting and in the volumes of ***A Browser's Dictionary.*** Or his life as translator of one of the noblest of poets. Or his life as observer of the process of writing, as revealed in such poems as **"An Apology for Not Invoking the Muse,"** in which he and Erato, Muse of lyric and love poetry, have a discussion about talent, in which he is much too modest, or as revealed in **"An Interruption,"** in which he and Aphrodite have a talk. She is not one of the nine licensed Muses, though she does like to horn in on their function; Ciardi probably likes to hobnob with a Muse who is not Establishment.

The life that has united all of these other lives, that has made them liveable and will make them live, is of course his life as poet. Though I have not dwelt specifically on this life, I hope that this little anthology of quotations has given some notion of its richness. I do not believe I know of another poet of the time who has more unsparingly translated the events and interests of his several lives into poetry, or another of whom it might more accurately be said, as a great predecessor said of his own life work,

> Camerado, this is no book,
> Who touches this touches a man.

(pp. 294-99)

John Frederick Nims, "John Ciardi: The Many Lives of Poetry," in Poetry, *Vol. CXLVIII, No. 5, August, 1986, pp. 283-99.*

JOHN STONE

[*Stone, an American poet and nonfiction writer, is a practicing physician and educator specializing in cardiology and emergency medicine as well as the author of the poetry collections* The Smell of Matches *(1972),* In All This Rain *(1980), and* Renaming the Streets *(1985). In the following excerpt Stones pays tribute to Ciardi in a trenta-sei, a stanzaic poetic form invented by Ciardi.*]

A Trenta-Sei for John Ciardi
(1916-1986)

Love should intend realities: goodbye.
—John Ciardi

In the beginning was the word, as noted
(in the end, too, if truth be known)—
Mercy next, then Love, and, gravel-throated,
a distinctive Grace enduring as the stone.
From these were made a better man than most.
We say good-bye today, old crow, gruff ghost.

In the end, too, if truth be known,
was clean white paper writing under a pen—
a gift of hand, eye, ear, and knucklebone
from Boston to Vermont and back again
to Jersey, Georgia, Key West—in every state
he came to talk and stayed to celebrate

Mercy next, then Love. And, gravel-throated,
the man became the word on which he fed
until he fed us all—and what he quoted
was from the major kingdom in his head
comprised not least of children's poems—crows,
pythons, sharks with teeth in rows.

A distinctive Grace enduring as the stone
or bronze or steel sculptors bring to life
he brought to his—and ours—though not alone,
for one enduring grace became his wife:
To her he'd bow and gratefully concede
that men have always married what they need.

From these were made a better man than most
who moved the word from mind to pen to writing
and made the books from wisdom and a host
of wars he never seemed to tire of fighting
especially those he thought he'd surely win
(as well as some he reveled in like sin).

We say good-bye today, old crow, gruff ghost.
That's never worked before—and will not now.
No good comes of good-bye. Instead, a toast
(in whatever form the authorities will allow)
to you—to us—in minor fifths and thirds.
Along the way you found we'll find the words.

(pp. 203-04)

John Stone, "A Trenta-sei for John Ciardi (1916-1986)," in The American Scholar, *Vol. 56, No. 2, Spring, 1987, pp. 203-04.*

Jean Genet

December 19, 1910 - April 15, 1986

French dramatist, novelist, poet, autobiographer, essayist, and scriptwriter.

(See also *CLC,* Vols. 1, 2, 5, 10, 14; *Contemporary Authors,* Vols. 13-16, rev. ed.; and *Contemporary Authors New Revision Series,* Vol. 18.)

PRINCIPAL WORKS

Notre dame des fleurs (novel) 1943
 [*Our Lady of the Flowers,* 1949]
Chants secrets (poetry) 1945
Miracle de la rose (novel) 1946
 [*The Miracle of the Rose,* 1965]
Les bonnes (drama) 1947
 [*The Maids,* 1954]
Pompes funèbres (novel) 1947
 [*Funeral Rites,* 1969]
Querelle de Brest (novel) 1947
 [*Querelle of Brest,* 1966]
Haute surveillance (drama) 1949
 [*Deathwatch,* 1961]
Journal du voleur (autobiography) 1949
 [*The Thief's Journal,* 1954]
Oeuvres completes. 4 vols. (novels, dramas, and poetry) 1951-53
Le balcon (drama) 1957
 [*The Balcony,* 1960]
Les nègres: Clownerie (drama) 1959
 [*The Blacks: A Clown Show,* 1961]
Les paravents (drama) 1961
 [*The Screens,* 1962]
Lettres à Roger Blin (letters) 1966
 [*Letters to Roger Blin: Reflections on the Theater,* 1969]
The Complete Poems of Jean Genet (poetry) 1981
Treasures of the Night: The Collected Poems of Jean Genet (poetry) 1981
Un captif amoreux (novel) 1986

MEL GUSSOW

Jean Genet—playwright, novelist, poet and one of the revolutionary artists of the 20th century—died [April 15] in the Paris hotel where he lived. He was 75 years old.

According to a representative of Genet's publisher, Librairie Gallimard, the author had been suffering from throat cancer and had been undergoing renewed radiation treatment.

A short, bald man with a compact, muscular body, Genet was an exceedingly private person, despite his notorious personal

© Jerry Bauer

life. The Paris hotel room in which he died had been his home for several years, but even his publisher did not know how to reach him. Reportedly the room was pristine and cell-like, and all of his possessions fit into one small suitcase. His mail was delivered to his publisher's office; even the address on his passport was Gallimard's.

A self-confessed criminal and an ex-convict, Genet was a *poète maudit* in the classic French tradition, a pioneering author of confessional novels and a dramatist of the first magnitude. Along with Samuel Beckett, he was a towering figure in the experimental theater of the mid-century. Genet's plays, ***The Maids, Deathwatch, The Balcony, The Blacks*** and ***The Screens,*** each a raging subject of controversy—as was the author throughout his lifetime—are among the most influential and consequential in the international repertory.

''Jean Genet has left us,'' said Jack Lang, former Minister of Culture in France, ''and with him, a black sun that enlightened the seamy side of things. Jean Genet was liberty itself, and those who hated and fought him were hypocrites.''

Attacked and even vilified, imprisoned as a thief, prostitute and pimp, Genet was an outlaw in life and in art. But from his life he created an art of the blackest blasphemy, a distorted mirror image of the society that bred him. As surprising as it still seems to those unfamiliar with his work, he was, at heart, a moralist, albeit one of a fiendish variety.

Reviewing ***The Screens,*** Genet's play condemning the French role in Algeria, Harold Clurman said that the author had earned the right to his "epic nihilism." Genet, he said, "is one of the few creative dramatists of our epoch. From the holocausts of the day he lights his own flaming torch. It illuminates what we are, what we have wrought, what we must renounce."

Genet was also an actor in the play of his life, putting on masks, rearranging facts to suit his purpose and clouding himself in mystique. In 1952 Jean-Paul Sartre published *Saint Genet: Actor and Martyr,* a massive volume that sanctified Genet and apparently, for a time, provoked the author into a severe case of writer's block. All his life, Genet resisted categorization and, one might say, canonization.

The first question, as yet unanswered, is whether he was born, or made, a criminal (and an artist). He was born, illegitimate, in Paris on Dec. 19, 1910, and his mother abandoned him. Until the age of 7, he was a foundling; at 21 he saw his birth certificate and discovered that his mother was Gabrielle Genet. He never learned the name of his father.

As a youth living with foster parents in the country, he was an altar boy. When he stole some money from his foster mother's purse, she called him a "little thief" and, as Genet told the story, from then on he lived out that role and whatever role that was imposed upon him. As he said, "Abandoned by my family, I found it natural to aggravate this fact by the love of males, and that love by stealing, and stealing by crime, or complicity with crime. Thus I decisively repudiated a world that had repudiated me."

His adolescent delinquency led him to a reformatory, where he was confined for a number of years. According to his account, when he was 21 he escaped from the reformatory and joined the French Foreign Legion, which he subsequently deserted. For the next 10 years he led a nomadic and often criminal life in Europe, often expelled from countries or expelling himself, as was the case in Nazi Germany. In that "nation of thieves," he said, he saw "no special act" in being a thief.

Back in France, he spent much of the Occupation in jail—and it was there that he began to write. His first work was a poem, ***Under Sentence of Death,*** memorializing a fellow prisoner who was executed for murder. The poem came to the attention of Jean Cocteau, who became the first of Genet's many artistic mentors and one of his strongest champions. Soon after, he began writing a book in pencil on brown paper. When the manuscript was confiscated, he started anew. As ***Our Lady of the Flowers,*** it was published in a limited edition in French in 1943, and in English in 1949. That novel was the genesis of his extraordinary career.

At first, that career was restricted to fiction—or fantasies based on reality, his self-inventions—but in the late 1940's he began writing plays, beginning with ***Deathwatch.*** In his first play, as in his books, Genet turned evil on its head, treating it as if it were sainthood. The most sainted figure in ***Deathwatch,*** not seen on stage, is Snowball, a king of crime.

Genet's next play, ***The Maids,*** was based on the true story of two sisters who murdered their employer. In Genet's version, the roles were to be played by actors, although in the original Paris production, in a concession to the celebrated actor-director Louis Jouvet, the roles were played by women. As in his subsequent plays, the characters assumed guises, enacting rituals of domination and violence.

The Maids, his first play to be staged in Paris (in 1947), brought him artistic credibility and even respectability, but the following year, after still another conviction for theft, he was faced with the prospect of a sentence of life imprisonment. Artists rushed to his defense with a petition—signed by Sartre, Cocteau, André Gide and Paul Claudel, among others. Genet was pardoned, which is not to say that he subsequently avoided crime. It was later reported that, for a time, he ran a bookstall by the Seine that was stocked with stolen volumes.

Deathwatch and ***The Maids*** had only brief runs Off Broadway, but his next two plays, ***The Balcony,*** and ***The Blacks*** (as translated by Bernard Frechtman), were critical and public successes in America and elsewhere. Opening at Circle in the Square in 1960, in a production directed by Jose Quintero, ***The Balcony*** ran for 672 performances. The following year ***The Blacks,*** directed by Gene Frankel, began a run of 1,408 performances and became a home for scores of talented black actors.

The Balcony, which takes place in Madame Irma's House of Illusion, reverses the civilized order. In this phantasmagorical brothel, ordinary citizens act out elaborate sexual, religious and political fantasies. Outside, a revolution is in progress, and in Genet's turnabout, the mock figures assume real-life roles. The result is a bizarre hall of mirrors, refracting a state of national and psychic emergency.

The Blacks was his "clownerie," or clown show, in which black actors put on white masks to play—and to mock—their white aggressors, as represented by a colonial society. The central ritual enacted is the murder of a white woman. As with ***The Balcony, The Blacks*** is a comedy, one of the most diabolical variety.

Genet's next play, ***The Screens,*** was his longest and most ambitious, lasting more than five hours and calling for a cast of 40. An epic accusation against his native country for its role in North Africa, it was published in 1960 but was not staged in France until 1966, in a production directed by Roger Blin (who staged the original production of *Waiting for Godot*). ***The Screens,*** reached America in 1973 in a monumental production presented by the Chelsea Theater Company.

Genet's theater could be regarded as a natural outgrowth of his confinement—and his isolation—in prison. As Richard N. Coe wrote in his book *The Vision of Jean Genet*: "Solitude, then, with all its complexities, its rewards and its terrors, is Genet's main theme." For him, Genet was "the poet of solitude."

Influenced by Verlaine, Rimbaud, Pirandello, Sartre and, perhaps most of all, Antonin Artaud (and his Theater of Cruelty), Genet, in turn, had affected playwrights of his time and later, including Eugene Ionesco, Fernando Arrabal, Amiri Baraka and Peter Weiss.

In addition to ***Our Lady of the Flowers,*** Genet wrote the books ***The Miracle of the Rose, Funeral Rites, The Thief's Journal*** and ***Querelle.*** Reviewing ***Funeral Rites,*** V.S. Pritchett said, "In the most literal sense of the phrase, Genet is a writer who has the courage of his convictions. Out of the lives of criminals, and following a tradition in French literature, he has built an erotic mystique, even a kind of metaphysic." He was, said Pritchett, "the autodidact of the jails." . . .

On two crucial political occasions he visited the United States: in 1968 to write about the Democratic National Convention for *Esquire,* and in 1970 when he activated a friendship with members of the Black Panthers.

In the last decade, so far as is known, he did no writing, but his plays continued to be produced with regularity. ***The Balcony,*** was staged this winter both by JoAnne Akalaitis at the American Repertory Theater in Cambridge and by the Comédie Française in Paris—earning the ultimate imprimatur of respectability for an artist who luxuriated in his iconoclasm.

Mel Gussow, "Jean Genet, the Playwright, Dies at 75," in The New York Times, *April 16, 1986, p. 25.*

THE TIMES, LONDON

The French novelist, playwright and poet, Jean Genet, one of the most original and provocative writers of his generation, died [April 15].

According to his own autobiographical, ***Journal du Voleur,*** he was born in the public maternity hospital in Paris on December 19, 1910, the illegitimate son of Gabrielle Genet and of an unknown father.

Abandoned by his mother at birth, he was placed, at the age of seven, as a foster child with a peasant family in Le Morvan.

There, according to his friend and biographer, Jean-Paul Sartre, he began to steal to compensate himself for being the only person in the village who did not possess property of his own. When caught, he refused to reform but instead made what Sartre considers to have been the basic "existentialist choice"—to be a thief.

This "choice" was consistent with the pattern of behaviour that led to the next important recorded event in Genet's life: entry, at the age of 15, into the *colonie agricole,* or juvenile reformatory, at Mettray.

After enduring the extremely harsh conditions which characterized French treatment of juvenile offenders of the period, Genet enlisted at the age of 19 in the French Foreign Legion. He then deserted, and proceeded to lead an itinerant life as a beggar, thief and homosexual prostitute in the capitals of Europe. . . .

He records some of his experiences at Mettray in his second novel, ***Miracle de la Rose*** (1946), and events in his later life in the ***Journal de Voleur*** (1949).

In 1942, while serving a sentence at Fresnes, Genet used the sheets of brown paper from which he was supposed to make paper bags to compose his first novel, ***Notre Dame des Fleurs.*** The manuscript of this extraordinary evocation of the world of French criminals, prostitutes and homosexuals, was eventually smuggled out of prison, and privately published in 1942, probably with the help of Jean Cocteau.

His crucial meeting with Sartre took place in May 1944, and sections of his third novel, ***Pompes Funèbres,*** which contain a remarkable study of France during the Occupation, were published in Sartre's review, *Les Temps Modernes.*

In 1947, Louis Jouvet produced Genet's play, ***Les Bonnes,*** at the Théâtre de l'Atelier. This account of how two maid servants indulge in fantasies of murdering their mistress took some time to be fully appreciated, and became recognised as a major work of the modern theatre only after the plays of Ionesco and Beckett had made audiences more familiar with the Theatre of the Absurd.

Genet's earlier play, ***Haute Surveillance,*** a presentation of how one rather inadequate criminal, wishing to obtain the status of a great evil-doer, murders one of his fellows in a condemned cell, was produced in the following year, but created such a storm of protest that no new theatrical work by Genet was produced in France until ***Les Nègres,*** in September 1959.

Genet called it a *clownerie* on the theme of race relations and it had highly successful runs in both Paris and New York.

In spite of this underwriting of the cult of revolutionary violence, which Sartre was also to develop, it was probably the success of ***Les Nègres*** which led the French authorities to lift their unofficial ban on Genet's most brilliant play, ***Le Balcon,*** which was produced in Paris in May 1960 with Marie Bell in the leading role.

This play had already had a controversial world premiere in the Arts Theatre Club in London in 1957, when Genet so disapproved of the production that he had to be restrained by force from climbing on to the stage to denounce it.

In 1966, his fame and notoriety reached their high-water mark with the production at the Odeon-Theatre de France of his play, ***Les Paravents,*** a satire of the French army and settlers in Algeria which so infuriated ex servicemen's organizations that a special force of police had to be called out to protect the theatre.

It was, nevertheless, awarded the Palmarès de la Critique for the theatrical season, and served as the final nail driven by General de Gaulle into the coffin of *L'Algérie Française.* For a former convict, the situation was not without its irony.

Although all Genet's prose works were originally published in privately circulated editions, permission was received in 1951 for his ***Oeuvres Complètes*** to be openly published by Gallimard. There was stronger resistance in England and America to the importation of his work, and his prose works had to wait until the early 1960s before being officially translated.

Genet's works often reveal a far more critical attitude to evil than he himself officially adopted, and go some way to justify Cocteau's claim that it would one day be necessary to treat him as a *moraliste.*

Whatever final judgment may be made on Genet's achievement as a writer, it is certainly true to say that not even the Marquis de Sade went further in exploring the potentialities and disappointments of evil.

"Jean Genet: Literary Exploration of Evil and Cruelty," in The Times, *London, April 16, 1986, p. 18F.*

BART BARNES

Jean Genet, 75, a critically acclaimed French dramatist, poet and novelist who drew upon his personal experiences to write of a seamy underculture populated by thieves, murderers and homosexual prostitutes, died of throat cancer [April 15] at the hotel room in Paris where he had lived for years.

Mr. Genet was regarded by critics as one of the great French writers of this century, but his story themes, in which traditional morality was almost always inverted to make heroes and saints of the likes of pimps and killers, also scandalized and offended many ordinary readers.

He was probably best known for his autobiographical ***Thief's Journal,*** a work published in 1949 that recounts details of a life of crime and petty thievery in the subcultures of Europe during the 1930s. Mr. Genet was also widely known for his novel, ***Our Lady of the Flowers,*** a celebration of crime, betrayal and homosexuality written while in prison during the 1940s, and for his plays, ***The Maids, The Balcony, The Blacks,*** and ***The Screens.***

Among his most enthusiastic admirers was the late French existential philosopher and writer Jean-Paul Sartre, who called him a "liar, thief, pervert . . ." and also a "saint and a martyr."

Sartre, author of *Saint Genet,* an extensive study of Mr. Genet's life and works, said, "With each book, this possessed man becomes a little more the master of the demon that possesses him."

Born in Paris, the illegitimate son of a French prostitute, Mr. Genet was raised in a state foundling home until he was 7, when he was placed with peasant foster parents in the Massif Central region of France. When he was 10, his foster mother accused him of stealing some change from her purse, and according to Sartre, the incident proved to be a pivotal experience that would determine the course of the rest of his life.

"I answered yes to every accusation made against me, no matter how unjust," Sartre quoted Mr. Genet as saying. "Yes, I had to become what they said I was. . . . I was coward, thief, traitor, queer: whatever they saw in me."

One act of juvenile crime led to another, and Mr. Genet spent most of his adolescence in reform school where he remained until he was 21. He joined the French Foreign Legion but deserted after only a few days and during the decade before World War II, he traveled through Europe as a beggar, thief and homosexual prostitute. "For a time I loved stealing, but prostitution appealed more to my easygoing ways," he wrote later in ***Thief's Journal.***

"Abandoned by my family, I found it natural to aggravate this fact by the love of males and that love by stealing. . . . Thus I decisively repudiated a world that had repudiated me."

Mr. Genet was in prison during most of the German occupation of Paris in World War II, and he had been in 13 jails and thrown out of five countries by the time he was 35. But it was also while in prison that he began to write, initially on the brown paper that prisoners were expected to use to make paper bags.

In addition to ***Our Lady of the Flowers,*** Mr. Genet also wrote ***Miracle of the Roses, Funeral Rites*** and ***Querelle de Brest,*** while in prison during the 1940s. All were characterized by lyrical eroticism, and in each the main characters pursued sin and corruption with dedication and enthusiasm.

Jailed a 10th time for theft in 1948, Mr. Genet faced a mandatory life sentence in prison, but he was pardoned after a delegation of leading French intellectuals including Sartre, Andre Gide and Jean Cocteau intervened on his behalf.

It was about then that he turned his energies towards poetry and drama. He wrote ***The Blacks,*** probably his best-known play in the United States, in 1959, and two years later it ran for 1,408 performances in an off-Broadway run. The play, which had an all-black cast including some wearing white masks, involves the ritual murder of a white woman, and its production in the United States coincided with the beginnings of a rising black consciousness and feelings of rage over racial oppression.

At one point one of the characters declares, "We have masked our faces in order to live the loathsome lives they have ordered. . . . We are what they would have us be." A version of ***The Blacks*** was produced at the Kennedy Center in 1973 by the D.C. Black Repertory Company, despite an unsuccessful lawsuit by Mr. Genet attempting to stop the production on the grounds that he had not been consulted and had not received his royalties.

Mr. Genet visited the United States in 1968 to cover the Democratic National Convention in Chicago for *Esquire* Magazine. His account brought a rebuke from British journalist Henry Fairlie who wrote that "There was only one thing more violent than the behavior of Mayor Daley's police at Chicago, and that was the reporting of it by Jean Genet. . . ."

He spent two months in the United States in 1970 meeting with leaders of the Black Panther Party. "What made me feel close to them immediately is the hate they bear . . . their wish to destroy a society, to beat it—a wish which was mine when I was very young," Mr. Genet said.

In 1983 Mr. Genet was awarded France's prestigious Grand Prix National des Lettres for his accumulated works, but he did not attend the ceremony. The award saluted him as a man who has "followed his destiny into the darkness."

Bart Barnes, "Jean Genet Dies: Poet, Playwright, Novelist," in The Washington Post, *April 16, 1986.*

NEW STATESMAN

'Saint Genet', Sartre called him, knowing that saintliness ascribed to an habitual criminal, sentenced to life imprisonment in 1948, would shock and tease.

Like all the best jokes, Sartre's was serious. Jean Genet . . . spent much of his life and work 'undermining' the established order in an effort to cleanse it. Constantly, in the novels and plays produced between 1942 and 1961 which established him as one of Europe's most important post-war writers, he demonstrated the anarchic brutality of Law and Order. He uncovered the blasphemies of organised religion. He demonstrated the obscenities of racism and sexism and made clear the connections between them.

Predictably it was his fate to be called anarchic, blasphemous and obscene. Parisians tore a theatre apart during ***The Blacks.*** British Customs & Excise seized his books in 1956. Anthony Blond battled to publish him legally in England.

To the end of his life Genet was pre-occupied with power. Who has it, and how? Who suffers under it, and why? His own childhood and early manhood, passed in some of Europe's harshest prisons, enabled him later to recognise unconscious complicities between oppressor and oppressed. His own homosexuality provided the starting point for his brilliantly disturbing analyses of gender. Prison life's incessant masturbatory daydreams taught him the delights and dangers of confusing reality and fantasy. Later in his work he traced those complicities and confusions: between coloniser and colonised, black and white, rich and poor, prisoner and warder, men and women.

Harold Hobson defiantly called Genet one of the last two great European writers to be formed by Christianity. Certainly he never forgot the power of the Word. Power, he recognised and taught, lies with those who successfully impose upon us their definitions of brutality, blasphemy, obscenity, anarchy, Law and Order.

For which lesson, and many others, most grateful thanks.

"Adieux: Farewell to Simone and Jean," in New Statesman, *Vol. 111, No. 2873, April 18, 1986, p. 4.*

HAROLD HOBSON

[Hobson, an English critic, editor, nonfiction writer, biographer, and novelist, writes theater reviews for The Christian Science Monitor *and the Sunday* Times *of London. His books include* Verdict at Midnight: Sixty Years of Dramatic Criticism *(1952),* French Theatre Today: An English View *(1953),* The French Theatre Since 1830 *(1978), and* Theatre in Britain *(1984). In the following excerpt Hobson, who was personally acquainted with Genet, offers a sympathetic view of the dramatist.*]

The death of Jean Genet disposes of the most persistent myth in modern literature. It is generally supposed that the revolution which has overtaken the contemporary theatre—the abandonment of decency of language, bourgeois morality, and all that ever went with an evening dress—was originated in the Fifties by Beckett, Osborne and Brecht. This is not true. The man who replaced the drawing-room with the *pissoir* is the man who has just died full of pride and honour.

For it was as early as 1947 (nearly a decade before the Great Trio) that Louis Jouvet produced ***Les Bonnes*** in Paris thereby creating a scandal. Genet was a man of middle height, and in his greatest days he looked like a well-to-do boxer whose face has suffered a good deal of battering in the ring. It had not always been so. He was the son of a prostitute and an unknown farmer. In his early life he wandered round Europe earning his living as a male whore, making his home in public lavatories. (He knew every such place in Paris that had a seat.) He was a traitor and an idolater of murderers. He was obsessed with perverted sex. "I hate London," he once said to me. "You can't smile at a pretty boy in Piccadilly without getting arrested." He had come for two months but stayed only two days. It should be noted that he was a man of exquisite courtesy, and spoke French with the same stylistic purity as he wrote it.

With such a cruel childhood, and endowed with such (then) unusual tastes, with no friends but pimps and whores, it is hardly surprising that Genet's work is subversive. In plays like ***The Blacks, Les Bonnes, Le Balcon*** he undermined society and conventional morality to such an extent much of his work was banned in Paris. His novels, ***Notre Dame des Fleurs, Miracle de la Rose*** and his poem, ***Le condamné à mort,*** are equally directed against society and equally laudatory of evil and the sordid.

Genet wrote prose better than he did poetry, and ***Le condamné à mort*** is comparatively little known. Nevertheless, it is crucial in the development of his work, for it was in watching the last 40 days in the life of one Maurice Pilorge that he became able to identify the Guillotine with the Cross. The terrible fate of this ravishingly beautiful young murderer seems, said Genet, to raise him "to a height so prodigiously glorious as the body of Christ rising into the perennial sunshine at midday." Pilorge had murdered his lover Escudero for a few francs and was executed by the hangman Desfourneaux on March 17, 1939, at the prison of St-Vrieux. "My sleepless nights," says Genet, "are haunted by the beauty of body and face of my friend Maurice Pilorge." The falling of the guillotine on the murderer's neck has the aspect of an embrace, and criminal death became in Genet's sight a bond between an assassin and Christ. This is why from 1939 on the elevation of the Host appeared to Genet to be the greatest achievement of European art.

In later years Genet became the friend of innumerable French intellectuals. But his British admirers have never understood how a man so notoriously evil could have so vast an admiration for the Christian Mass. Only Lindsay Kemp, who played the whore Divine in an adaptation of ***Flowers,*** has some inkling of comprehension. As the infinitely wearied Divine, dragging himself across the stage of a Regent Street theatre like one dazed by sleep or soporifics, to the sound of a great organ, Kemp in some sense united the sorrows of a common murderer with those of Christ.

Harold Hobson, "Poet of Flowers of Evil," in The Sunday Times, *London, April 20, 1986, p. 49a.*

RICHARD GILMAN

[Gilman, an American critic and editor, is recognized for his erudite, philosophical approach to drama criticism in Common and Uncommon Masks: Writings on Theatre, 1961-70 *(1970) and* The Making of Modern Drama *(1974), a study of the changes in dramatic art over the past century. Gilman served as theater critic for* Newsweek *and* Commonweal *in the 1960s, and as literary editor on several journals including* Commonweal *and* The New Republic. *In the following excerpt Gilman explains how Genet's experiences as a criminal and outcast shaped his creative works.*]

Jean Genet died [April 15] at the round age of 75. I have to reach for him in memory, recover the sense of him that had been so strong when his works were coming out; his last play, ***The Screens,*** appeared in 1960, and his fiction was all done by then too. For those to whom it's only cultural rumor, I need to say that he was as central a figure in the theater, and in consciousness generally, as anyone during the '50s and '60s. As late as 1970, when he appeared on the Yale campus during the Black Panthers trial in New Haven, we nudged each other excitedly when we saw him and expected apocalyptic wisdom, though none came.

An astonishingly short man (five foot two: the same height as his mentor and exegete, Sartre), stocky, with a bashed-in nose like an ex-boxer's, he was there to lend his prestige to the Panthers, who wisely didn't look this gift horse in the mouth. For he had once written: "I do not love the oppressed. I love those whom I love, who are always handsome and sometimes oppressed but who stand up and rebel."

He made himself felt as part of a climate in which notions of ritual, violence, and cruelty—in the meaning of Artaud, with whom he had some affinity—were animating the practices of fiction and theater. A transvaluator of values to an extreme beyond Nietzsche, a bearer of news from the dark side, he had written to all good citizens like us that "each object in your world has a meaning for me different from the one it has for you. I refer everything to my system, in which things have an infernal significance." . . .

There are those who saw . . . Genet's whole work as a manipulation, of fashionable negation and despair. It wasn't true, even though he indeed saw keenly into our, and his own, bad faith and not so secret guilts. "We shed our sicknesses in our books," D. H. Lawrence once wrote, which is what Genet did. In ***The Miracle of the Rose,*** he wrote that his aim in the book was "to relate the experience of freeing myself from a state of painful torpor, from a low shameful life taken up with prostitution and begging . . . under the sway of the glamour . . . of the criminal world. I freed myself by and for a prouder attitude."

It's impossible to separate the homoerotic basis of his writing—and the position of homosexuality in the world that condemned him—from his aesthetic procedures. For drama in particular he helped set free the nature of theater itself: the use of "mirrors," substitutions—of roles for roles, images for people, appearance for things. He was the poet-exposer of the nature of power, real and imaginary, in modern theatricalized society. His plays were frightening, dizzying perspectives where nothing was trustworthy and where hatred was more than a literary emotion.

Yet this exponent of the perverse who said that he admired the pimp for being "the man who has not been taken in by love" had his prouder, nobler attitude as well. Nothing from the realm of "humane" art, the universe of virtuous discourse, surpasses in beauty and humble generosity these words of Jean Genet's: "Talent is courtesy with respect to matter. It consists in giving song to what was dumb." "My victory is verbal," he once wrote, and left us its memorials.

Richard Gilman, "Jean Genet, 1910-1986," in The Village Voice, *Vol. XXXI, No. 17, April 29, 1986, p. 91.*

NATIONAL REVIEW

Novelist, playwright, prose master, and Parisian cult anti-hero, Jean Genet was a striking figure in that he cared enough about Western culture to attack it in every conceivable detail. Nothing important went un-negated. To his credit, he was not indifferent. All of the West's virtues he depicted as vices; all of its vices became for him virtues. His anti-morality possessed a kind of Cartesian consistency.

His five novels, from ***Our Lady of the Flowers*** (1943) to ***The Thief's Journal*** (1949), constitute his most important body of work. They are autobiographical, the facts often merging into mythologization, and they exhibit a remarkably resourceful rhetoric, which functions to transform values into anti-values. If property is a positive value, Genet becomes a thief. If life is a value, Genet affirms murder. Naturally, or rather unnaturally, Genet celebrates homosexuality. He supported the Algerian insurgents, the Black Panthers, the Baader-Meinhof gang, the Japanese Red Army terrorists, the rioters at the 1968 Democratic convention in Chicago (in *Esquire,* among the chic consumer ads). He supported, of course, the Palestinian terrorists. His experimental dramas dynamited the conventions of the theater.

"Jean Genet has left us," said François Mitterand's former Minister of Culture, Jack Lang. "Jean Genet was liberty itself, and those who hated and fought him were hypocrites." Genet would have richly enjoyed a sentiment so fatuous. He died at 75 in a Paris hotel room as bare as a monk's cell.

"Jean Genet, R I P," in National Review, *New York, Vol. XXXVIII, No. 10, June 6, 1986, p. 21.*

NICOLAS TREDELL

[*English editor and critic, Tredell, author of* The Novels of Colin Wilson *(1982), is a contributing editor to* PN Review. *In the following excerpt Tredell comments on Genet's political and artistic concerns.*]

Genet's life had the aura of legend: abandoned at birth by his mother, he became a ward of the state and in 1917 was fostered by a peasant family in Le Morvan. (p. 8)

In Fresnes prison in 1942, he wrote his first published poem, ***Le Condamné à Mort,*** and began to write his novel, ***Our Lady of the Flowers,*** on sheets of brown paper from which convicts were supposed to make bags. These sheets were confiscated, but he began again in notebooks and completed the work. ***Our Lady of the Flowers*** combines the argot of thieves and the slang of proscribed sexual practices with the liturgies and imageries of religion, of royalty and of classical and romantic poetry. To read it is to enter a strange, inverted world, sordid and glittering: the prison, with its 'odor of urine, formaldehyde, and paint' becomes a baroque palace of the mind; pimps and murderers turn, without idealization or redemption, into saints and madonnas; the solitary convict, masturbating on his stained straw mattress, becomes a master of rituals that do not mystify but maintain, even in extreme reverie, a peculiar rigour. As ***Our Lady*** puts it: 'Poetry is a vision of the world obtained by an effort, sometimes exhausting, of the taut, buttressed will . . . It is not an abandonment, a free and gratuitous entry by the senses; it is not to be confused with sensuality.' The themes and approaches of ***Our Lady*** were taken up and varied in ***Miracle of the Rose*** (1946), ***Funeral Rites*** (1947), ***Querelle of Brest*** (1947) and ***The Thief's Journal*** (1949).

While his literary fame grew, Genet had been sentenced to life imprisonment. Apparently he had assumed responsibility for a crime committed by a friend killed in the street fighting at the Liberation of Paris. An appeal to the government by Sartre, Cocteau and others led to a free pardon in 1948. Sartre had first met Genet at the Café de Flore in 1944, and, compelled by Genet's life and work, he produced, in 1952, the massive *Saint Genet, Actor and Martyr*. This is a brilliant, astonishing book that tries to surpass and control Genet's texts even as it acknowledges that they cannot be controlled, that they will always remain unassimilable. According to Sartre, Genet thought the study largely true, but disliked it intensely; later, Genet claimed it was really about Sartre, not himself. Genet and Sartre's paths diverged as time went on; for instance, Genet was angered by Sartre's relatively measured response to the Arab-Israeli conflict. Genet's resistance to turning crime and sexual deviance into objects of knowledge and patronising compassion, his scepticism of progressive penal reform, and his anarchic inclinations give him some affinities with a later thinker: Michel Foucault.

Genet's concern for ritual, ceremony and role-playing had strong theatrical elements. His ballet ***Adame Miroir*** was danced to Milhaud's music in 1946. 1947 saw the publication of one play—***Deathwatch***—and a staging of another—***The Maids.*** His best-known play, ***The Balcony,*** was put on in 1957. ***The Balcony*** dramatizes an image of society as a brothel, a 'house of illusions' in which clients act out various roles, such as judge, bishop, general; the analyses of the complicity of apparent opposites, and of the dependence of supposedly primary upon supposedly secondary categories, anticipate deconstruction: 'my being a judge is an emanation of your being a thief.' Genet so much disliked the first production of ***The Balcony,*** at the Arts Theatre in London, that he tried to climb on to the stage to denounce it. In contrast, he commended Roger Blin's 1959 Paris production of ***The Blacks*** as 'of the order of perfection.' ***The Blacks*** enacts and explores its themes of colonialism and race hatred through ceremony and role-playing—for example, a black plays the part of a white woman whom another black pretends to murder, the white grotesques who look on reveal themselves, at the end of the play, as black actors. ***The Blacks*** can be linked with the political analysis and the endorsement of violence in the work of Fanon. ***The Screens,*** which deals with the Algerian war, was mounted in Paris, again by Blin, in 1966, despite demonstrations, violence and bomb threats. These local difficulties apart, it is not an easy play to stage, though some scenes have great potential—for instance, the scene in which, as two colonists talk, one Arab after another enters to draw flames at the foot of painted orange trees.

In later years, Genet lived privately, sometimes emerging to give interviews for money or to lend his support to violent radical groups such as the Black Panthers and the PLO, whose 'criminal' and 'terrorist' aspects doubtless appealed to him. His ***Poèmes*** were published in 1966. His life seemed to take on an ascetic quality; he stayed in hotels and had few possessions; he preferred Morocco to France. In an interview on BBC2 late last year, when asked how he now spent his time, his reply echoed St Augustine: *'J'attends la mort.'* (pp. 8-9)

Nicolas Tredell, "Jean Genet," in PN Review, *Vol. 13, No. 1, 1986, pp. 8-9.*

Frank (Patrick) Herbert

October 8, 1920 - February 11, 1986

American novelist.

(See also *CLC,* Vols. 12, 23, 35; *Contemporary Authors,* Vols. 53-56, Vol. 118 [obituary]; *Contemporary Authors New Revision Series,* Vol. 5; *Contemporary Authors Autobiography Series,* Vol. 2; *Something about the Author,* Vols. 9, 37; and *Dictionary of Literary Biography,* Vol. 8.)

PRINCIPAL WORKS

The Dragon in the Sea (novel) 1956; also published as *Twenty-First Century Sub,* 1956; also published as *Under Pressure,* 1974
Dune (novel) 1965
Destination: Void (novel) 1966
The Eyes of Heisenberg (novel) 1966
The Green Brain (novel) 1966
The Heaven Makers (novel) 1968
Santaroga Barrier (novel) 1968
Dune Messiah (novel) 1969
Whipping Star (novel) 1970
The God Makers (novel) 1972
Soul Catcher (novel) 1972
Hellstrom's Hive (novel) 1973
Children of Dune (novel) 1976
The Dosadi Experiment (novel) 1977
The Jesus Incident [with Bill Ransom] (novel) 1979
God Emperor of Dune (novel) 1981
The White Plague (novel) 1982
The Lazarus Effect [with Bill Ransom] (novel) 1983
Heretics of Dune (novel) 1984
Chapterhouse, Dune (novel) 1985
Man of Two Worlds [with Brian Herbert] (novel) 1986

BOB COLLINS

Frank Herbert, 65, celebrated author of the Dune series, as well as two dozen other best-selling science fiction novels, died [February 11, 1986] in Madison, Wisconsin, of complications following cancer surgery.

At the time of the operation at the University of Wisconsin Hospital, Herbert was working, according to his agent Kirby McCauley, on a seventh volume in the Dune series with his author/son Brian Herbert.

Scheduled for May release . . . is Herbert's earlier collaboration with son Brian, ***Man of Two Worlds.*** It is billed as a "send-up" of the science fiction *genre* in which the existence of the earth, unknown to earthlings, depends upon the imaginative powers of an alien race, one which militaristic earth is about to destroy. The anti-hero is a half-breed (half alien and half human), the only individual in the universe who understands the situation.

Photograph by Jay Kay Klein

Dune, Herbert's all-time bestseller was made into a lavish movie in 1984, and has sold more than twelve million copies in fourteen languages world-wide; but, as Herbert was fond of reminding interviewers, the novel was rejected by twenty-two publishers before Chilton of Philadelphia agreed to bring it out in 1965. Also, professional critics gave it bad reviews, but word-of-mouth praise largely on college campuses, soon made it a best-seller, prompting reprints of Herbert's earlier novel, ***Dragon in the Sea,*** and quick sales of several new novels. The extraordinary depth and detail of Herbert's imaginary world, the desert planet of Arrakis, reminded many fans of J.R.R. Tolkien's Middle Earth, and ***Dune*** soon drew a cult of admirers. Always popular among college students, for several years Herbert made the lecture circuit, and many observers credited the author with popularizing the new discipline of ecology.

Herbert was born in Tacoma, Washington in 1920, and was educated at the University of Washington, Seattle. At the same time that he worked as reporter and editor at a series of West

Coast newspapers, Herbert served his apprenticeship as a fiction writer contributing stories to science fiction magazines, beginning with **"Looking for Something"** in *Startling Stories*, 1952. After turning to full-time writing in 1966, he settled at Mercer Island, Washington, ten years after the publication of his first novel. This novel, published by Doubleday in 1956, earned him considerable success, but another ten years passed before ***Dune*** established him as a dominant figure.

The Dune series, originally a trilogy, grew to six books with the publication of ***Chapter House: Dune*** last year. Other titles in the series are ***Dune Messiah*** (1971), ***Children of Dune*** (1976), ***God Emperor of Dune*** (1981), and ***Heretics of Dune*** (1984).

Herbert had recently signed a contract for the filming of one of his novels outside the Dune series: ***The Green Brain*** (1966), concerning mutated insects with hive-intelligence. Other novels outside the series include ***The Eyes of Heisenberg*** (also 1966), about genetic engineering, ***The Heaven-Makers*** (1968), on immortality, ***The Santaroga Barrier*** (1968), about an isolated near-Utopia, ***Destination: Void*** (1966), about machine-intelligence, ***The Whipping Star*** (1970), and ***The Dosadi Experiment*** (1977), about alien intelligence.

In recent years Herbert had varied his output with novels on lighter topics, often in collaboration, as in ***The Jesus Incident,*** with Bill Ransom in 1979, ***Without Me You're Nothing,*** with Max Barnard (1980), ***The Lazarus Effect,*** again with Ransom (1984), and the recent collaborations with his son Brian.

Perhaps because of his academic following, Herbert's works were taken seriously both within and without the science fiction community. "Herbert's omnivorous curiosity, nourished by years of developing background for good newspaper stories, found a natural outlet in science fiction," observes critic/biographer Willis McNelly. "He was never content with surface appearances, real or fictional; he taught himself to be a professional photographer, a student of comparative religion, a wine expert, a deep-sea diver, a pilot, a lay Jungian analyst. Herbert was an ecologist long before it was fashionable. ***Dune*** may indeed be one of the very best science fiction novels ever produced. It is superior in almost every way. On one level it's a rattling good story, on another a thinly-veiled allegory on the world's insatiable appetite for oil (Arrakis/Iraq, melange/oil); a parable of the concept that absolute power corrupts absolutely; or a series of answers to the questions What is a human being? and When is any being truly human?" (pp. 6, 14)

Bob Collins, "Death of a Prophet," in Fantasy Review, *Vol. 9, No. 2, February, 1986, pp. 6, 14.*

BURT A. FOLKART

Frank Herbert, who carved the futuristic planet "Dune" from his fertile imagination, peopling it with diabolical bureaucrats plagued by paranoia and driven in a search for a life-prolonging chemical, is dead. . . .

Herbert, a former journalist whose science fiction novels grew out of a news story he wrote in 1958 about efforts to control shifting sand dunes on the wild Oregon coast, had cancer. (p. 3)

Although Herbert's arid land came to be known as "Dune" to his millions of fans, the author had titled it Arrakis or Rakis and on it he placed a messianic protagonist named Paul Atreides, a mystical ruler of the nomadic Fremens. Atreides, drawn with overtones of an Arabian sheik (he would become Paul Maud'dib or prophet), had progeny who metamorphosed over several volumes into combinations of human beings and mammoth sand worms.

In a sequel, Atreides' son, Leto, aided by melange, a spice (drug) that made both immortality and intergalactic travel possible, ruled thousands of years, while the most recent book in the series—***Chapter House: Dune***—dealt with a conspiratorial sisterhood manipulating the civilizations that came after.

Although his work was originally rejected by several publishers, Herbert lived long enough to see ***Dune*** made into what critics found a mundane but technically interesting motion picture while the royalties from his work established him as a wealthy man in a literary genre populated generally by paupers.

The popularity of the politically metaphoric series even generated an encyclopedia, where the characters and plots were annotated and cross-referenced for Dune aficionados.

Bookstores commonly referred beginning sci-fi fans to the series for their first brush with things galactic, while the original ***Dune*** volume became the only work of fiction mentioned in that bible of the 1960s, *The Whole Earth Catalogue*.

Herbert credited the successes of ***Dune*** to timing, for his tales of transforming the face of a barren land touched the heart of the ecology movement. The fact that a drug helped in that transformation 9,000 years in the future endeared it to the Beatniks and the Flower Children of the current era. And although those revolutionaries moved from street corners and into corporations, they continued to buy the ***Dune*** series, which has never been out of print in either hard cover and paperback since the initial volume was published in 1965.

Herbert attended the University of Washington, where he became intrigued by psychology and education. He was a correspondent for the Hearst newspapers in Vietnam, and also was a devotee of Jungian psychology, which, simplistically put, holds that universal symbols common to all cultures transcend any language.

His first novel, ***Dragon in the Sea,*** was published in 1955 and over the years he produced 20 books ranging from the home programming of computers to a revenge novel about an American biologist whose family is killed by Irish terrorists.

But science fiction remained his forte and his favorite.

The ***Dune*** series, he said in a 1984 interview with *The Times,* was an allegorical effort to point up his basic distrust of modern political leadership.

"These charismatic leaders ought to have a sign on them: 'Warning! May Be Dangerous to Your Health.'"

But he also wanted to be remembered for the pleasure he provided his readers.

"There's no way to stop academia from taking up science fiction," he said in an interview soon after his work began attracting the attention of literary scholars.

". . . You can analyze a thing to death," he said, "(but) a science fiction writer has to remember that he's in the entertainment business and you can't shortchange the reader." (pp. 3, 39)

Burt A. Folkart, "Frank Herbert, Author of 'Dune' Series, Dies," in Los Angeles Times, *February 13, 1986, pp. 3, 39.*

DON D'AMMASSA

Frank Herbert became one of the major names in the science fiction field with only his second novel, ***Dune,*** serialized in *Analog* in 1963-1964. The novel draws heavily on Herbert's favorite concerns in the construction of his novels, the ecology and humanity's place within it, our attempts to alter our own physical and intellectual natures, the forms that intelligence itself might take, and the nature of messianic religions. Although he wrote many other novels, some of them superior to the ***Dune*** books, the original novel and its five published sequels are invariably the works one most often connects with his name.

Herbert's first published novel, ***Under Pressure,*** is a taut psychological story of submarine warfare in the near future, when oil has become even more precious a commodity than it is today. A less successful novel, ***The Green Brain,*** followed ***Dune*** and is most noteworthy for its suggestion that attempts by humans to take control of the Earth's ecology might result in other evolutionary changes to neutralize our influence.

The fact that Herbert did most of his writing in the science fiction genre does not mean that he considered science a panacea for the ills of the world. Mankind develops a viable artificial intelligence in ***Destination: Void,*** but in that novel and two comparatively recent sequels, ***The Jesus Incident*** and ***The Lazarus Effect,*** both in collaboration with Bill Ransom, the creation gets out of control and turns on its makers. The mixed blessings of genetic engineering are examined in ***The Eyes of Heisenberg.***

The Santaroga Barrier is perhaps Herbert's most tightly written story, set in [a] reclusive community whose resistance to standard marketing techniques results from their use of a drug that has caused them to evolve a kind of communal consciousness. ***The Heaven Makers*** is a variation of the humans-as-property plot and is perhaps the least noteworthy of Herbert's novels. The Bureau of Sabotage was introduced in ***Whipping Star,*** which also featured an unusual form of intelligence, a star itself. A sequel, ***The Dosadi Experiment,*** was more successful.

The first two sequels to ***Dune, Dune Messiah*** and ***Children of Dune,*** continued the basic story, examined in more detail the dangers inherent in a cult such as that which [was] founded around the charismatic Paul Atreides, as well as detailing the complex ecological structure of the planet Arrakis, but as novels they were considerably weaker. After a gap of five years, Herbert returned to that same universe for another three novels, ***God Emperor of Dune, Heretics of Dune,*** and ***Chapterhouse: Dune.*** This second trilogy was set millenia after the original stories, and now we can see the evolution of entire cultures as well as the beginning of serious evolutionary divergences in humanity itself.

The most interesting of Herbert's recent novels was ***The White Plague,*** in which a scientist avenges the murder of his family by setting loose a plague that might well wipe out the human race. Herbert suggested that there might be viable alternative societal structures in ***Hellstrom's Hive*** and looked once again at religious fanaticism in ***The God-makers.***

Although not a frequent writer at shorter length, Herbert found time to turn out a few dozen short stories, the most notable of which were **"Try to Remember"**, **"A-W-F Unlimited"**, **"The Mary Celeste Move"**, **"The Tactful Saboteur"**, and **"Committee of the Whole"**, as well as a novel about the American Indian, ***Soul Catcher,*** and assorted non-fiction. He was recipient of both the Hugo and Nebula awards for achievement in the field.

Perhaps Herbert's biggest contribution to the genre was that ***Dune***'s broad appeal introduced science fiction to readers outside the normal science fiction spectrum. His departure deprives us of one of the most significant voices in the field, as well as one of the more talented writers.

Don D'Ammassa, "Frank Herbert," in Science Fiction Chronicle, *Vol. 7, No. 7, April, 1986, p. 24.*

WILLIS E. McNELLY

[American editor, essayist, and poet, McNelly has edited several science-fiction anthologies as well as The Dune Encyclopedia *(1984), a reference work dealing with Herbert's* Dune *novels. In the following excerpt McNelly discusses both Herbert's personality and the ideas that informed his first two novels,* The Dragon in the Sea *and* Dune.]

I like to think that when Frank Herbert died last February 11, he murmured the Litany against Fear: "I must not fear. Fear is the mind-killer. Fear is the little-death that brings obliteration. I will face my fear." (p. 352)

As a life-long student of the psychology of C. G. Jung, he . . . knew that death is an inexorable part of the structure of life. He well realized that both life and death are Jungian polarities. "We begin to die from the moment of conception," he once told me, stating the old truth as if it were fresh and new. For him—indeed, for all of us—it *is* new, for each person must discover that truth for him/herself and learn that however mortality or immortality treats us, flesh will fade. Frank had learned that secret decades ago, and I like to think that he approached his end without fear, faced it with composure.

It is something of the measure of his success as a writer that virtually every major paper in the country printed an extensive obituary. Some dutifully repeated the AP dispatch sent over the wires from the Madison, Wisconsin hospital where he died, but others carried a more detailed story. Even the papers of the Eastern Establishment—the Baltimore *Sun,* the New York *Times* and the Washington *Post*—carried no mere canned wire service obits but lengthy memoirs written by journalists who knew his work well. Those writers neither condescended to him or science fiction nor praised him beyond his merits or achievements. Frank would have appreciated that little fact. A journalist himself, he had a passion for the truth, and when facts—or a life, even his life—are presented with objectivity, he would have been satisfied.

Not that he was dispassionate or completely objective himself. Far from it. Anyone who ever met Frank for more than two minutes knew how strongly he felt about so many things—good wine, wind power, ecology, scuba diving, aerial photography, computers, the environment, solar heating—the list is virtually endless. He also had the capacity of instantly charming those who listened to him. For he loved to talk. Lord, how he loved to talk—to fellow writers, to interviewers, to fans, to his friends, his family, large audiences, small groups. His voice—a voice that at first hearing seemed too highly pitched for this bearded bear of a man—was rich, resonant, full of intensity. It was at times questioning, even querulous. At other times it was almost pontifical, and indeed he sometimes seemed to voice his opinions as if they were *ex cathedra* pronunciamentos.

Yet for all of his success both as a writer and as an apologist for the causes he held dear, he never took himself too seriously. He could poke fun at himself too, knowing full well that the human tendency to follow heroes was a constant cause of trouble throughout history. "If you want to follow me as a guru," he often said, "come with me to Guyana and we'll found Herbert-town and you can have the Kool Aid concession." So much for heroes and feet of clay.

His first great commercial success was ***Dune*** although even that book did not become a best seller until several years after its initial hard and paper back editions. . . . In 1968 he told me that he had made no more than eighteen or twenty thousand dollars from the book including the money Campbell paid him for first serial rights in *Analog*. He was a working journalist even then, not devoting himself to full time science fiction writing until some years later when he could afford the luxury. The book and its sequels made him a lot of money eventually of course. More importantly, the commercial success of ***Dune*** paved the way for large advances, bigger printings, best-seller status, and heavy subsidiary sales for many other writers. Every member of the SFWA owes Frank Herbert and ***Dune*** considerable gratitude.

His first novel was published in *Astounding/Analog* under the name ***Under Pressure***. It wasn't the name he preferred. ***Dragon in the Sea*** was the title he liked best and he often spoke of it as "Good old Dragon." Yet anyone who read that mid-1950s book might well have recognized the incipient major talent at work. This early book provided no mere hint or tentative suggestion of what Herbert would later develop in ***The Dune Chronicles***. Rather, it is a fully developed, serious novel that still rates as one of his best. In it Herbert shows the same control of ideas, concepts, characters, and psychological insights combined with action-adventure that made ***Dune*** a masterpiece. What strikes the reader who approaches the book today three decades after its writing is its contemporary tone. Its problems could well be those of the late 1980s; its ecological sense is current, and its psychological insights into problems faced by men at war are as real as those of Vietnam POWs. The fullness of detail with which Herbert filled his ***Twenty-first Century Sub*** (still another title) reads like a blueprint for America's modern nuclear submarines. The novel is crammed with a careful consideration of modern problems such as the role of oil in a petroleum-starved world or the vexatious question of "security." He was proud of the book, particularly proud that submariners continually read it and wrote him telling how well he had detailed their fears and hopes.

Dragon also provides an early statement of the parable of life, death, and resurrection that so absorbed Herbert in ***Dune*** and its sequels. Citing the passage from *Isaiah* that gives the novel its name, one character says, "'In that day the Lord with his great and strong sword shall punish leviathan the piercing serpent, even leviathan that crooked serpent, and he shall slay the dragon that is in the sea.'" When the dragon in all of us is slain, Herbert seems to be saying, then there shall be peace. That concept is most assuredly another Jungian notion. In the later novel the dragon in the sea became the dragon in the sand ocean of Arrakis, Shai Hulud, Old Father Eternity, the sandworm whose seed becomes melange, the spice that gives virtual eternal life.

This may not be the place to discuss ***Dune*** and the remainder of the Chronicles. But it is surprising to realize that ***Dune*** was only Frank's second novel, although he wrote a dozen or more following it. Each of those later books has its own strengths—and sometimes weaknesses—but it is ***Dune*** by which we will all remember him. Campbell recognized its merits at first reading, but he also believed that Frank had written himself into a hole with his creation of Paul Maud'dib, the nearly omnipotent super-hero.

"Congratulations," he wrote Herbert, "you are the father of a 15-year old superman! But I betcha you aren't gonna like it . . ." In this instance, at least, Campbell was wrong, for Herbert always claimed that it had never been his intention to create a genuine superhero, a messiah who would save the world or the universe as the case may be. Instead it was his belief that heroes carry the seeds of their own destruction, that the consequences of our actions must always be considered before we undertake any action. In this belief he echoed Aristotle's notion of the tragic flaw, the *hamartia,* the overweening pride that brings about its own destruction.

One of the many messages of ***Dune*** itself was that ecology is the science of understanding consequences. Few readers in fact, perceived that implicit concept in the novel, lost as they were in the intricacies of the story itself. Certainly they did not apply it to the sequels. It was a simply enough problem, he once told me. "Where does Arrakis get its oxygen?" he asked. He then pointed out that, lacking any green plants, the planet has no chlorophyll base and hence no natural oxygen. Its atmosphere comes from the digestive processes of the sandworm, and if you limit the sandworm by reintroducing water to the planet, you'll have an oxygen catastrophe on Arrakis. He never wrote about it though, perhaps feeling that he wanted to concentrate on melange—still another by-product of the sandworm—and what its diminution would do to the known universe. He wanted to talk about the uses and abuses of power. Melange was merely his instrument for telling that story of corruption. Nonetheless he felt that the oxygen problem would have been an inevitable consequence of the ecological redemption of Arrakis. Ideas have consequencès, he often said, and he pursued those ideas in book after book.

Critics have carped at some of his later books, saying that portions of those novels often read like extended orations. For him the act of writing was not quite identical to sending a message, certainly, but he saw no reason not to embed ideas into the structure of what he wrote. It's a fine line as many of us know, and if he occasionally slipped over the edge and became too talky, the sermonic tone may be the result of his fiercely held opinions. Yet he was always aware that he had to compete in the marketplace, fight for the couple of bucks someone might shell out for one of his books before boarding a plane. It was a competition he gloried in, because when all is said and done, he was an entertainer, not a prophet or guru; entertain us he certainly did.

His sense of scenè was almost unequalled, and some very well drawn characters people his books. Jessica remains one of the very best science fiction portraits of a woman, and the various Idahos, Atreides, and even the villainous Harkonnens will long be remembered. (pp. 352-55)

In the end it seemed that Frank approached all of God's creation as if it were magically beautiful, yet he could also warn us that unless we understood the full consequences of our actions, we might be in for serious trouble. An eternal optimist, he never really believed it though. (p. 355)

Willis E. McNelly, "In Memoriam: Frank Herbert, 1920-1986," in Extrapolation, *Vol. 27, No. 4, Winter, 1986, pp. 352-55.*

Christopher (William Bradshaw) Isherwood

August 26, 1904 - January 4, 1986

English-born American novelist, autobiographer, and screenwriter.

(See also *CLC,* Vols. 1, 9, 11, 14; *Contemporary Authors,* Vols. 13-16, rev. ed., Vol. 117 [obituary]; and *Dictionary of Literary Biography,* Vol. 15.)

PRINCIPAL WORKS

All the Conspirators (novel) 1928
The Memorial: Portrait of a Family (novel) 1932
**Mr. Norris Changes Trains* (novel) 1935; also published as *The Last of Mr. Norris,* 1935
Sally Bowles (novella) 1937
Lions and Shadows: An Education in the Twenties (autobiography) 1938
**Goodbye to Berlin* (novel) 1939
Prater Violet (novel) 1945
The World in the Evening (novel) 1954
Down There on a Visit (novel) 1962
A Single Man (novel) 1964
A Meeting by the River (novel) 1967
Kathleen and Frank (autobiography) 1971
Christopher and His Kind, 1929-1939 (autobiography) 1976
***People One Ought to Know* [with Sylvain Mangeot] (verse) 1982

*These works were published as *The Berlin Stories* in 1946.

**This work was written in 1925.

BILL EDWARDS

Christopher Isherwood, 81, best known as writer of the stories on which the hit tuner *Cabaret,* which won seven Tonys as a stage musical, Grammy for best original cast album and eight Oscars for the film version, was based, died [January 4] at his Santa Monica Canyon home, after a long battle with cancer.

Attending him was his longtime friend and companion Don Bachardy, who said Isherwood was first diagnosed as having cancer of the prostate gland in 1981.

Born in Bisley, England, in 1904, he wrote many novels but the stories from the 1939 novel, ***Goodbye To Berlin,*** which he later expanded to ***The Berlin Stories*** grew into his most popular work. . . .

Educated at Cambridge University, his early novels, ***All the Conspirators*** and ***The Memorial,*** were written while still a student and were written in the style of montage, flashback and fast-paced dialog—cinematic devices that recurred in his later works.

In 1929, he went to Berlin to visit his good friend, poet W. H. Auden and remained after Auden left, giving English lessons to support himself. He left Germany in 1933 with a wealth of historical knowledge about the rise of Nazism. His first success, ***The Last Of Mr. Norris,*** published in 1935, was a comic novel about a typical figure in the bourgeois decay that preceded Hitler's rise to power.

About ***Goodbye to Berlin,*** Isherwood disclaimed autobiographical significance by saying, "I am a camera with its shutter open, quite passive, recording, not thinking." In 1964, however, Walter Allen in his *The Modern Novel* said of Isherwood, "He is a trick-photographer of enormous skill, whose art consists in posing his bizarre characters at unexpected angles, in shocking juxtaposition to the terrifying tragic background of historical events."

Besides his novels, during the 1930s Isherwood collaborated with Auden on three plays: ***Dog Beneath The Skin, The Ascent Of F6*** and ***On The Frontier.*** The latter was received coolly at its 1938 London opening as Britishers were complacent by the recent signing of the Munich pact of appeasement.

Isherwood and Auden were on their way to China when the play opened. They were going to report on the Sino-Japanese war. That trip yielded the travel book, ***Journey To A War,*** published in 1939, the year in which both Auden and Isherwood came to America (both became citizens in 1946) with Auden settling in New York and Isherwood in California.

Isherwood had worked as a script-writer for Gaumont-British during the '30s and after his arrival in Hollywood he started writing dialog for MGM. Not long in Hollywood, he adopted the Hindu philosophy of Vedanta and collaborated and/or wrote several books on that religion, including translation from Sanskrit of *The Bhagavad Gita, Crest-Jewel Of Discrimination* and *Rama-Krishna And His Disciples.*

Over the years, Isherwood worked on filmscripts for Warner Bros., 20th Century Fox and other studios. Many of his commissioned scripts never made it before the camera, including his adaptation of Carson McCullers' *Reflections In A Golden Eye.* Ironically, WB's 1967 version of that novel was scripted by Chapman Mortimer and Gladys Hill.

Isherwood's screen credits include ***The Sailor From Gibralter, The Loved One, Diane, I Am A Camera, The Great Sinner, Adventure In Baltimore, Forever And A Day,*** and ***Rage In Heaven.*** He also wrote for tv.

In 1945 he wrote ***Prater Violet,*** a novel about the making of a movie. That was followed by ***The Condor And The Cow: A South American Travel Diary.*** In 1954 he wrote his first novel with an American setting, ***The World In The Evening.***

Down There On A Visit, considered by many as Isherwood's best novel, was published in 1962 and that was followed in 1967 by ***A Meeting By The River.*** But it was not until publication of ***Christopher And His Kind,*** a memoir that explored his own homosexuality that he came out publicly.

In a 1972 interview, he said, "I have written about homosexuals in my novels and in taking up the cause of one minority, that of homosexuals against the dictatorship of heterosexuals, I have spoken out for all minorities. And we are all minorities in one way or another. For me, as a writer, it's never been a question of sex, but of otherness, of being a member of a minority, of seeing things from a slightly different angle."

In a project he labeled "The Autobiography of My Books," he found a need to understand his family and early childhood better. His study resulted in the 1972 ***Kathleen And Frank: The Autobiography Of A Family.***

In recent years, he has been guest lecturer at California colleges.

Bill Edwards, "Christopher Isherwood, 81, Dies," in Daily Variety, *January 6, 1986.*

THE NEW YORK TIMES

Christopher Isherwood, who was best known for the stories he wrote in the 1930's that served as the basis for the play and movie ***I Am a Camera*** and the musical *Cabaret,* died of cancer [January 4] at his home in Santa Monica, Calif. He was 81 years old. . . .

Much of Mr. Isherwood's work was at least quasi-autobiographical, as was ***Goodbye to Berlin,*** the collection of six short stories that, with the earlier book set in Berlin of the 1930's, ***The Last of Mr. Norris,*** are most immediately associated with his name. In a 1972 interview the English-born writer acknowledged, "With me, everything starts with autobiography," but in ***Goodbye to Berlin,*** in its most famous line, he disavowed his own involvement.

"I am a camera with its shutter open," he wrote, "quite passive, recording, not thinking." But he himself figured in the book as "Herr Issyvoo," a judging eye on the dissolution of German society in the years of pre-Hitler Berlin and on his own alienation from the England of the same years.

It was from this phrase that John van Druten took the title of his play *I Am a Camera,* which essentially was an adaptation of the story ***Sally Bowles.*** The play, with Julie Harris in the starring role, won the New York Drama Critics Award in 1952 and was later made into a movie. It returned to Broadway in 1966 as the hit musical *Cabaret,* starring Joel Grey. It scored an equal success as a movie in 1972, with Mr. Grey and Liza Minnelli winning Academy Awards for their performances.

When the two books were released under the title ***The Berlin Stories*** in 1946, Orville Prescott wrote in *The New York Times:* "In fact, his abilities are so great it would be regrettable if he never wrote the major novel of which he seems capable." Alfred Kazin, reviewing the same book, had already decided that "Isherwood is a real novelist, a real *minor* novelist."

In addition to his novels, Mr. Isherwood wrote plays, collaborated on several books about Vedanta, the religion to which he was a convert, did some translations and wrote a biographical book about his parents, ***Kathleen and Frank.***

Aside from his writing and Vedanta, Mr. Isherwood was perhaps most deeply involved with the legitimizing of homosexuality. An acknowledged homosexual, he said at a forum on homosexuality and literature in 1974 that he hoped the goal of the homosexual-rights movement would be "To victory! To be recognized as entirely natural and not to be questioned at all."

Christopher William Isherwood was born in High Lane, in rural Cheshire, on August 26, 1904, the first child of Francis and Katherine Isherwood. His father was killed in World War I, becoming to his son "Frank his Hero-Father," a perpetual obligation. His relationship with his mother was even more complex and continued to be a major struggle and preoccupation of his life until her death.

He went to St. Edmund's School, a preparatory school in Surrey, where he met W. H. Auden, later a literary collaborator and lifelong close friend. He went on to Repton, a public school, and to Corpus Christi College at Cambridge, leaving before he got a degree. Mr. Isherwood briefly studied medicine at the University of London, and published his first book while there, in 1928. It was a novel of family relationships entitled ***All the Conspirators.*** He wrote of his Cambridge years in ***Lions and Shadows: An Education in the Twenties,*** published in Britain in 1938 and the United States in 1947.

His second novel, ***The Memorial,*** was published in 1932, when he was living in Berlin, where he had gone in 1929; he left Germany in 1933. His first success, ***The Last of Mr. Norris,*** was published in 1935. By 1938, Virginia Woolf was recording in her diary, "'That young man," said W. Maugham, "holds the future of the English novel in his hands."' Mr. Isherwood was a friend of Maugham and is believed to have been the model for the figure of Larry in Maugham's novel *The Razor's Edge*.

In 1938, too, he and Auden traveled to China to report first-hand on the Chinese-Japanese War. The result was a book titled ***Journey to a War.*** With Auden, Mr. Isherwood left Britain for the United States in 1939; he became a naturalized United States citizen in 1946. The departure of the pair gave rise to some controversy about whether they had left to avoid the war; they were caricatured by Evelyn Waugh in *Put Out More Flags,* as two despicable poets, Parsnip and Pimpernel.

At about this time, Mr. Isherwood wrote to a friend, "I have discovered what I didn't realize before, or what I wasn't till now, that I am a pacifist." During the war, he worked as a conscientious objector at a Quaker refugee hostel.

Soon after, Mr. Isherwood went to the West Coast, settling in Santa Monica, where he remained for the rest of his life. In part, this move reflected his lifelong fascination with the cinema and cinematic techniques; he had done some work as a scriptwriter in Britain, and in the United States he went to Hollywood first to write dialogue for Metro-Goldwyn-Mayer. He said some years later that he had written "a fantastic large number of scripts." The best known may be his adaptation, with Terry Southern, of Evelyn Waugh's *Loved One*.

Mr. Isherwood's novel ***Prater Violet*** has a plot that revolves around the making of a movie. After a travel book about Latin America, ***The Condor and the Cow,*** he wrote his first novel with an American setting, ***The World in the Evening,*** in 1954. Mark Schorer described it as "a brilliant enigma"; other critics were less impressed. ***Down There on a Visit,*** published in 1962, comprised four episodes in the life of the narrator, Mr. Isherwood. It was a characteristic blend of autobiography and fiction. Herbert Mitgang, in [*The New York Times*] described it as a minor work but said Mr. Isherwood wrote "with coolness and purpose." Another critic, Gerald Sykes, wrote that the novel was "excellent," perhaps Mr Isherwood's best to date.

Then came ***A Single Man,*** detailing one day in the life of George, a homosexual. David Daiches, the critic, called it "a sad, sly report on the predicament of the human animal." In 1967, Mr. Isherwood wrote ***A Meeting by the River,*** an account of two brothers, one of whom intends to become a Hindu monk; the book was generally considered a failure. A play devised from it by Mr. Isherwood and Mr. Bachardy opened and closed nearly simultaneously on Broadway in 1979. Richard Eder, in [*The New York Times*] described it as "an exercise in High Twaddle."

Kathleen and Frank published in 1977, was well received. Thomas Lask, in [*The New York Times*], saw it as a "gesture of reconciliation" with Mr. Isherwood's parents. In the previous year, ***Christopher and His Kind*** which was very heavily autobiographical and candid about Mr. Isherwood's homosexuality, was published. In 1980, in an interview, Mr. Isherwood said, "All of my autobiographical books are sort of novels."

A slight, slender man with a craggy face, Mr. Isherwood interspersed his writing with occasional stints as a guest professor of English at nearby universities. He was a member of the National Institute of Arts and Letters.

Mr. Bachardy said [January 5] that Mr. Isherwood had been "feeling pretty good" until illness began to interfere with his writing. At the time, Mr. Bachardy said, he was still working on the second volume of biography to cover the period from 1939 to the present, picking up where ***Christopher and His Kind*** had left off.

He said that Mr. Isherwood had been about two thirds through and that the rest could be edited from his notes.

"Christopher Isherwood Is Dead at 81," in The New York Times, *January 6, 1986, p. B7.*

STEPHEN SPENDER

[Spender is an English man of letters who rose to prominence during the 1930s as a Marxist lyric poet and as an associate of Isherwood, W. H. Auden, C. Day Lewis, and Louis MacNeice. While his poetic reputation has declined in the postwar years, his literary stature has, nevertheless, grown. Spender believes that art contains "a real conflict of life, a real breaking up and melting down of intractable material, feelings and sensations which seem incapable of expression until they have been thus transformed." In the following excerpt Spender discusses the influence of Isherwood on his friends, particularly as he portrayed them in fiction, and recalls his own final visits with his lifelong friend.]

Old friends of Christopher Isherwood who knew him over a period of 50 years must feel, I think, that his death, in an almost literal sense, takes away something of themselves. This something may well be a persona that he created for them—one which if not more real than their own idea of themelves is at any rate more exciting.

He had the gift of making people feel that they were characters in a world of his invention. I have had this feeling several times recently when reviewers of my *Journals 1939-1983* have quoted verbatim Isherwood's description, in his early autobiographical book ***Lions and Shadows,*** of the young poet Stephen Savage. I have the feeling that Stephen Savage is more like the young Stephen Spender than I myself ever was.

In the same book, Isherwood has a character called Chalmers, who was in 'real life' the novelist Edward Upward, then his closest friend. He describes Chalmers when they were both Cambridge undergraduates, hating the university and inventing for themselves a shared fantasy world called Mortmere, in which characters were often based on dons and undergraduates and which filled the pages of stories and poems which they sent to each other almost daily. The surrealism of the Mortmere world overlapping that of the university resulted in a kind of hallucinatory realism, a world of people with characters exaggerated to the point of caricature seen against a background of objects which were symbolic and animistic while remaining in their heightened way real.

Isherwood's fiction has so much the appearance of cinematic photography that it is easy for readers lulled by application of the much-quoted phrase 'I am a Camera' to forget the Mortmere side of his writing. Although Isherwood dropped the purely fantastic side of Mortmere, something of it persisted in his fiction and conversation.

Here in ***A Single Man*** (1964) is a Mortmeresque vignette, a scene taking place in an American university faculty dining room:

> George goes through into the serving room. On the counter are steaming casseroles from which the waitresses dish you out stew, vegetables or soup. Or you can have salad or fruit—or a strange deadly-looking jelly which is semi-transparent, with veins of brilliant green. Gaz-

> ing at one of these jellies with a kind of unwilling fascination, as though it were something behind glass in a reptile house, is Grant Lefanu, the young physics professor who writes poetry.

Christopher's conversation was sprinkled with phrases like 'That strange, deadly-looking jelly—yes, I think I'll eat that,' said with much emphasis and ending with a kind of bark of a laugh, his eyes gleaming. He inhabited a world in which he cast roles for things as well as people. Everything came alive, one was conscious of demonic forces playing practical jokes.

The taking over of one's own personality by the imagined personality which Christopher imposed on one—what Gore Vidal called Christopher's 'cloning' of a friend—could be disconcerting. Edward Upward—the oldest surviving friend of all—has recently been quoted as saying about Jean Ross, the original of Sally Bowles: 'I don't think Jean ever liked the portraits of her as Sally. She thought that had just been a small part of her life.' I can well believe this, because in the Berlin stories Christopher had succeeded in creating a character so much more like Jean than she was like herself.

This happened even with Christopher himself so that, in writing about Jean in his straightforwardly autobiographical ***Christopher and his Kind,*** he confesses that he cannot remember what Jean actually said to him on some occasion, so has to invent it for her in the idiom of Sally Bowles. And, after the publication of ***Sally Bowles*** Jean in effect changed her character, becoming a serious Communist who went around selling the *Daily Worker*, and looking after her daughter by Claud Cockburn who, for a short time, was married to her.

Gerald Hamilton, the scoundrel whose adventures are the subject of ***Mr. Norris Changes Trains,*** saw very quickly the advantage of taking over the role of Mr Norris and of using the fictitious realer-than-Gerald-Hamilton character as a useful *alter ego* which enabled him for the rest of his life to play the role of lovable villain.

It was partly on account of this, but doubtless more on account of his own self-portrayal as Mr Issyvoo, Christopher, Chris, etc, that Isherwood became deeply concerned with questions of truth in his fiction—whether in some cases he had not been unfair to the originals; in others (Gerald Hamilton's for example) whether he had not provided a cover-up; but, above all, whether in his own self-portrayal, in the Berlin stories, he had not suppressed the importance of his own homosexuality.

Perhaps a more crucial question for Christopher was whether he could create a book true to his vision of life without introducing into it the Isherwood figure who acts as a kind of intermediary between the life and characters described and the reader. He failed to do this in his attempt at a Bloomsburyish novel, ***The World in the Evening*** (which had a shadowy portrait of Virginia Woolf as heroine) but he succeeded miraculously in ***A Single Man,*** a novel about an English professor in California who is afflicted with grief at the recent death of his friend and life-companion. Here Isherwood calls upon all the resources of his own experience and nevertheless succeeds in creating a character, George, who is in no way a self-portrait.

The fact of his homosexuality and his identification with other homosexuals was the one and only political cause which Christopher wholeheartedly embraced. It led to his becoming a kind of hero of the Gay community. In his personal life his aim was to achieve a lasting relationship. And all who knew Christopher will feel that his greatest personal triumph and happiness was his relationship with his friend, 30 years younger than himself, the portrait-painter and draughtsman, Don Bachardy.

I visited Christopher and Don at their house in Santa Monica several times during the past three years, the most recent being last September. Christopher was up and about, though at moments in considerable pain. He seemed to listen intermittently to the conversation going on around him rather than participate in it, though he would occasionally, eyes blazing, take up something that was being said, and make some pronouncement—one such being when I remarked that members of our literary generation had, on the whole, had happy lives. Christopher burst out: 'Gee! That's true. We've had the happiest! We've been the luckiest!' And, later on, someone having mentioned hero-worship: 'That's one thing I believe in. The fact that we've had heroes was the most important thing in our lives.'

But the impression he made in recent years was of being withdrawn, reflecting, meditating perhaps. All this time Don was doing two or three drawings of him a day. His mind, I think, had moved into a region where no one, unless perhaps Don, could follow him; his religion—Vedanta—which was more important to him than a friend from his English past could realise.

Stephen Spender, "The Secret of Issyvoo," in The Observer, *January 12, 1986, p. 46.*

JULIAN SYMONS

[An English writer, Symons has been highly praised for his contributions to the genres of biography and detective fiction. His popular biographies of Charles Dickens, Thomas Carlyle, and Edgar Allan Poe are considered excellent introductions to those writers. Symons is better known, however, for such crime novels as The Immaterial Murder Case *(1945),* The Thirty-First of February *(1950), and* The Criminal Comedy of the Contented Couple *(1985). Symons notes that his works in this genre "have all been based on the view that a crime story can have the depth and subtlety of characterisation, the moral and social point, of what is generally called a 'straight' novel." In the following excerpt Symons describes the effect of Isherwood on younger writers in the 1930s and discusses Isherwood's literary shortcomings and successes, in particular, his highly praised "I am a camera" narrative technique.]*

This article might be called "without knowing Mr Isherwood": yet in the 1930s it was impossible for any young writer not to feel that he knew Christopher Isherwood as a personality, even though we had never set eyes on him. He was known through the autobiographical ***Lions and Shadows*** as the creator with Edward Upward of Mortmere, that fantasy world of the Other Town where anything might happen if it sufficiently outraged reality, and the drinkers at the Skull and Crumpet turned every night into animals.

Then we knew him also as the figure depicted and invoked by Auden, with "squat spruce body and enormous head" whose "strict and adult pen" would "warn us from the colours and the consolations . . . make action urgent and its nature clear". And he seemed present in person, very much so, in the plays full of jokey but menacing warnings which he wrote together with Auden, ***The Dog Beneath The Skin, The Ascent of F.6*** and the more political, less successful ***On The Frontier.*** Most clearly of all we knew him through the character Herr Issyvoo, the camera eye recording the shady, sad lives of Mr Norris,

Sally Bowles, and Germans under the threat of Nazism, with an avoidance of moral comment extraordinary for the time.

In retrospect the camera eye detachment that made Isherwood a background figure in ***Mr Norris Changes Trains*** and ***The Berlin Stories*** can be seen as a brilliant Jamesian technical device, through which the narrator reveals himself while directing the spotlight on to other people. Of course the people in the spotlight are characterised too. Isherwood worked from living models, but it does not really matter that the original of Mr Norris was a whimsical homosexual rogue named Gerald Hamilton, that Sally Bowles was drawn from the erratic Bohemian Jean Ross, and that Germans described in the Berlin stories all had their actual counterparts.

The effects achieved through this blend of fiction and reality, aided by the restraint which kept Herr Issyvoo in the background and the similar restraint that made Nazism only a menace of distant thunder almost thoughout, mark ***Goodbye To Berlin*** and ***Sally Bowles*** as true works of art. The detached sympathy Isherwood gives to his characters works better than any outright lament of condemnation could do.

Isherwood's first two novels, ***All The Conspirators*** and ***The Memorial,*** were intelligent and powerful attacks on the institution of the family in particular and British society in general, marred by insistent modernities of style. With ***The Berlin Stories*** he discovered the truth (for him, though not for everybody) that style should be as unobtrusive as a well-fitting suit, so that "you hardly know whether you've got it on or not". ***The Berlin Stories*** are a triumphant justification of this style, and they were written in Isherwood's early thirties. It seemed that fictions about European society which had the span of Balzac or Zola might lie ahead.

But this never happened. What went wrong? Permanent self-imposed exile from Britain after 1939, the colours and consolations of Hollywood, the attractions of Eastern mysticism for a never-very-convinced socialist, were partly responsible. More artistically damaging, however, was the post-war possibility, which Isherwood seems to have felt almost a duty, of writing openly about homosexuality. In ***The Berlin Stories*** and ***Mr Norris*** things are suggested, hinted at, joked about, but never elaborated or assessed in moral terms. There was nothing dishonest in such reticence, it was a necessary effect of art.

The later ***Christopher and His Kind,*** by contrast, is not simply insistently homosexual. It also contains passages of dismaying emotional crudity in which Christopher past is rebuked by Christopher present for his coarseness, calculation and cruelty. The style remains easy, unobtrusive, charming, but it no longer fits the material.

In the end Christopher was not, as many thought he would be, a major writer. When he abandoned *The Lost,* the vast episodic novel of which ***The Berlin Stories*** are the surviving fragments, he gave up what proved to be his only important subject. But the stories remain, and they capture a time, a place, and the people of a disintegrating society in a moving and masterly way. They are a unique achievement.

Julian Symons, "Goodbye to Isherwood," in The Sunday Times, *London, January 12, 1986, p. 45.*

EDWARD UPWARD

[English novelist and critic, Upward received critical acclaim early in his career, his nightmare visions of reality being compared to those of Albrecht Dürer and Franz Kafka. With the publication of his first novel, Journey to the Border *(1938), he became actively involved in the Communist party and gave up writing, having decided that "trying to produce a political statement and not an artistic statement . . . just wouldn't do." He revived his writing career with the 1962 publication of* In the Thirties, *a novel portraying a poet's struggle to reconcile both his political and artistic beliefs. Today Upward is known less for his own work than for his influence on such contemporaries as Isherwood and W. H. Auden. In the following excerpt Upward remembers his long friendship with Isherwood, recalling their early collaboration on the fantastical "Mortmere" stories, and noting his own continued influence on Isherwood's works in progress.]*

Sixty-five years ago Christopher Isherwood and I became friends when we were at Repton together in the History Sixth being prepared for university scholarship exams by G. B. Smith—the idiosyncratically brilliant 'Mr Holmes' whose teaching methods are so amusingly described in the opening pages of Isherwood's ***Lions and Shadows.*** Isherwood says of me that my 'natural hatred of established authority' impressed him greatly, and that he felt it was a weakness in him not to share it. He quite enjoyed his life in a public-school community where he found that 'cunning and diplomacy could so easily defeat brute force'. He had not, however, enjoyed life during the first world war years at his prep school, where the headmaster was constantly telling him that he ought to try to behave in a manner more worthy of his hero father, a regular army officer who had been killed at Ypres.

It is possible that a rebelliousness which was to develop in him at Cambridge (and afterwards) against the beliefs and attitudes of his upper-middle-class family had been implanted in him at this prep school, but his rebellion—unlike mine—never became primarily political: it took the form of a deliberate choice to be a homosexual. (He makes clear in his autobiographical ***Christopher and His Kind*** that he did not regard homosexuality as something inborn in him, and that he enjoyed the one heterosexual experience he had.) What attracted me to him and him to me at Repton so strongly and so immediately had nothing to do with homosexuality: it was above all the recognition in each other of someone who wanted more than anything else in the world to be a writer. Mr Holmes was before long twitting us with having become a mutual admiration society, but he was only partly right. Besides being excited by each other's writings we were also extremely frank in criticising the faults we saw in them. And we educated each other from the start not only by mutual criticism but by introducing each other to books and poems we had separately become enthusiastic about.

We wrote to each other during holidays and visited each other at our homes, and once I stayed with him in Cheshire at Marple Hall where his 'wicked' uncle lived. I'm not sure whether we ever actually referred to this uncle between ourselves as 'wicked', but with his curling lip and his manner of speaking as it were sideways through his mouth he struck me as more than slightly sinister. There was a small erotic painting hung on the wall of one of the lavatories and in his library there were books by Havelock Ellis from which Christopher and I read passages to each other with relish. Some years later Christopher was to discover that this uncle was the same Kind as himself, though with an especial preference for guardsmen which Christopher never had. After the publication of Christopher's ***Mr Norris Changes Trains*** the uncle revealed all to him, and made him an allowance which helped him to live as a writer, though it sometimes arrived cruelly late. When I think now of Marple Hall, which crumbled and was demolished some years ago, I am reminded of the wonderful first paragraph of Poe's *The Fall of the House of Usher* and of the remarkably mature and almost as wonderful first paragraph of Christopher's pre-Mortmere story **'The Horror in the Tower'** about the coprophagous Kester, eleventh Lord Wranvers.

Mortmere was the imaginary village that Christopher and I created and wrote stories about for each other at Cambridge. They had titles such as **'The Little Hotel'** (a brothel for necrophiles) and **'The Leviathan of the Urinals'** and **'The Garage in Drover's Hollow'** (about an extremely sinister car-wrecker). He would write a story and put it on the table in my sitting-room late at night when I was asleep in my bedroom and I would read it with delight at breakfast, and a morning or two later he would find a story by me on his table. Only one Mortmere story has ever been published—'The Railway Accident' which I wrote at the age of 24 after I had left Cambridge. I'll say no more here about Mortmere. It has been brilliantly written about by Christopher in ***Lions and Shadows,*** which has always been my favourite among all his books, not just because I and other friends of ours come into it but because I think it is the wittiest and the richest in texture and the most consistent in tone.

At Cambridge and in the vacations he also worked hard at producing his first novel, which he read aloud to me throughout one night. It held my attention and my admiration from beginning to end, but I think we both realised that it would need much rewriting to make it publishable. Although after we had both gone down from Cambridge he was never again to read the whole of any other novel of his aloud to me, he spent many hours with me at his house or mine pacing the floor and planning out aloud the next novel he intended to write—***The Memorial***—and I would suggest solutions to the problems he came up against, and even when he completely rejected my solutions they often stimulated him to find his own. I remember being particularly excited by the time scheme he thought up—with my eager encouragement—for ***The Memorial.***

In later years when he was often abroad and we could not meet he always sent me draft typescripts of his novels for my criticisms and suggestions before he sent in the final version to his publisher. After he went to live in America he sent me no typescripts till some while after the end of the war. This was not because of the bitter letter I wrote to him in answer to his in which he told me he had become a pacifist. Auden never forgave me for it, but Christopher fully understood my indignation, and before long I understood that his pacifism was absolutely genuine. After the war when he became able to write again he sent me draft typescripts of all his later novels and he wrote me many letters in which he discussed the problems that had come up in his writing. I had few letters from him after 1981, when his cancer was first diagnosed, but I kept in touch with him by phone every year.

I am dreadfully aware of the inadequacy of this article as an expression of my feelings for him. If I hadn't had the luck to know him I should never have known how marvellous human life at its best can be.

Edward Upward, "Christopher Isherwood," in The Spectator, *Vol. 256, No. 8219, January 18, 1986, pp. 17-18.*

MICHAEL DE-LA-NOY

Since the death of Christopher Isherwood I have had time in which to learn that attempting to write an appreciation of his work is as difficult—assuming one was so stupid—as trying to imitate it. After numerous abortive stabs I decided to relax, so I opened his autobiography, ***Christopher and His Kind,*** entirely at random, at a passage recalling a birthday party in Amsterdam, washed-out by rain and attended by 'an oddly assorted all-male party'. But what a party, when Christopher Isherwood gets down to his typewriter 40 years later: Gerald Hamilton, with 'an air of nervously expecting the police to appear'; Stephen Spender, simmering with sly giggles 'yet also basically inattentive, perhaps because he was composing a poem'; Brian Howard, with his searching and testing eyes 'made restless by his need for a drink'; Howard's Bavarian boy friend, Toni, 'ill at ease in his expensive clothes'; E. M. Forster, beaming through his spectacles, 'probably enjoying himself most because Bob Buckingham was with him'. Not only are we immediately in the presence of a marvellous reporter, but translated to a world as extinct as the dodo, in which everybody knew everybody else, travel was cheap and 'live and let live' really was the motto of the day.

Christopher And His Kind appeared in 1977, when Isherwood was 73, and has been regarded by some people as an unnecessary, even an unfortunate, finale to his literary achievements, letting the cat out of the bag about his own involvement in the novels and displaying an unseemly degree of narcissism. It has also been used as the ultimate weapon with which to castigate Isherwood for his alleged inability to build on early success. But to complain that after the 'Berlin' books Isherwood somehow failed to realise his potential, that he should have gone on to write the great novel of the 20th century, is to miss the whole point about Christopher Isherwood. It is true, and it is sometimes forgotten, that he was first and foremost a novelist; even so, his excursions into travel, the theatre and biography were perfectly legitimate, and often very successful (his life of his parents is superb). But not only was he first and foremost a novelist, he lacked, most of his life, the ability to create a character with a life detached from his own, which made him into the quintessential autobiographical novelist, a salient fact not in itself a disaster but bound to circumscribe anyone. His autobiography may not have been so ingeniously constructed as his novels but in essence it was only an extension of them.

Isherwood laboured under two far more potent disadvantages than the inability, until quite late in life, to invent a truly independent character, immense ambition and very early success. He seems to have been around for ever, but in judging his work it is also a fact that the output by which his reputation has to be measured is really quite small. In 57 years he wrote only 10 novels, of which ***Prater Violet*** is no more than a diverting novella, and the first two, ***All the Conspirators*** and ***The Memorial,*** are now important only in so far as they provided, for a very young man, the experience of writing and the excitement of being published. Isherwood was just 21 when he began work on ***All the Conspirators,*** published in 1928 when he was 24, and it bears many of the hallmarks of a young man in a hurry. He had read and admired the right people—James Joyce, E. M. Forster, Virginia Woolf—and he was full of enthusiasm and self-confidence. He knew, or thought he knew, how to write a novel. But remembering, 30 years after the book had first appeared, that when Cyril Connolly waxed lyrical about ***All the Conspirators*** he had referred to its author's 'austere and conscientious assumption of a cooperative and intelligent reader', Isherwood took a sly swipe at literary criticism. 'If you want to test your own cooperation and intelligence,' he advised a new generation of readers, 'see if you can understand, for example, the first three and a half pages of the last chapter!'

That remark epitomises two crucial aspects of Isherwood, his sense of humour and his lack of self-importance (a necessary egotism in an autobiographical writer is another matter). And it was his humour that very quickly raised his work above the level of mere confessional autobiography, that stamped it with a genius for comic characterisation in the mould of Evelyn Waugh. With only his third book, ***Mr Norris Changes Trains,*** the first of two pre-war novels to be set in Berlin (Isherwood was to deny that they were *about* Berlin), he found, almost overnight, his unique tone of voice. At one fell stroke he had become a master of both construction and style. Still as a very young man (he was only 31) he had proved himself to be, what he remained for the rest of his long life, a compulsively readable writer. You have only to complete the first page of ***Mr Norris Changes Trains*** to be instantly gripped. By the end of the first short chapter, a portrait of Mr Norris has been painted with the consummate skill of a mature artist. This novel, and the next two books, ***Lions and Shadows*** (set in Cambridge and London) and ***Goodbye to Berlin,*** deservedly remain among his most popular for the simple reason that they reveal, even on the most cursory examination, a watertight control of plot and atmosphere. And all three appeared within the space of four years.

The now extinct world into which Isherwood emerged as a writer was populated, besides such eccentric characters as Gerald Hamilton (who became Mr Norris) and Brian Howard, by literate editors, and even by publishers some of whom could write. Cape having rejected Isherwood's second novel, it was one of the lively editors, John Lehmann, who recommended ***The Memorial*** to Leonard and Virginia Woolf at the Hogarth Press. And four years later, in 1936, it was Lehmann who published, in the first number of his hugely influential magazine *New Writing,* an extract from a work which eventually became ***Goodbye to Berlin.*** 'To Christopher, Berlin meant Boys' Isherwood wrote in his autobiography, throwing away with casual nonchalance what anyone else would have saved up for the opening sentence of a novel. And indeed, Isherwood does seem to have spent much pleasurable time and energy in pursuit of the ideal friend. But if only at a sub-conscious level, that chase was also a hunt for autobiographical material, and despite the fact that after ***Goodbye to Berlin,*** and excepting the slim entertainment ***Prater Violet,*** there were no more novels for 15 years, as the books of Isherwood's last years disclose he never ran out of material.

I doubt whether the lure of Hollywood script-writing supplies the total explanation for this 15-year gap. Surely Isherwood was to some extent haunted by success, needing to find not so much new material (he had plenty stored up without falling back on his American experience) as new ways in which to manipulate it. With ***The World in the Evening,*** published in 1954 and dedicated to Dodie Smith, whose best selling romantic novel *I Capture the Castle* he greatly admired, he experimented, perhaps not altogether successfully, by dispensing with 'Christopher' himself. In ***Down There on a Visit,*** which appeared eight years later (again after John Lehmann had published an extract, this time in the *London Magazine*), 'Christopher' promptly reappeared. His nerve restored, and perhaps taking seriously complaints that all those years in America had failed to produce a novel set in the New World, Isherwood, far from falling away from his youthful promise, was now on the verge, at the age of 60, of producing what was surely not just his masterpiece but one of the most remarkable novels of the 20th century.

Until 1964, Isherwood had written copiously around the subject of homosexuality, but he had never attempted to write a homosexual novel. Not only did he now take on that daunting task, but he set it within the compass of one day and focused it upon the often unsympathetically perceived persona of a middle-aged man. His 'hero' appears unwisely waddling to the telephone with his trousers round his ankles (most sensible people take the 'phone off the hook when they go to the lavatory), and ends his day, as it turns out, on his death bed, taking time off, before expiring, for a final bout of masturbation. Put thus crudely, it sounds pretty grim. In fact, ***A Single Man*** is a genuine work of art, the consummation of a life not just devoted to boys but to the very serious business of being a writer.

But without the boys, would Isherwood have written at all? Like a great many homosexuals, he was fascinated by himself, to the point where he spent a life-time exploring the universe of which he was the very conspicuous centre, indeed, to such an extent that being homosexual became as essential to Isherwood the writer as it was to Isherwood the man, and in a way not true of any novelist before him. Forster did not need to be homosexual to write *A Passage to India.* Isherwood did need to be homosexual even to accomplish ***A Meeting by the River,*** his last and quite needlessly neglected novel, a clever interplay of correspondence between two brothers. Yet the ultimate triumph is that Isherwood transcended personal limitations—those relating to his homosexual experience and to the autobiographical nature of his fiction—that might have dragged a lesser craftsman down to the level of the author of *A Boy's Own Story,* the most ludicrously overpraised gay trash of recent years. Isherwood broke quite new ground by making his restricted material accessible to everyone. To speak of Christopher Isherwood as a homosexual writer makes sense, yet at the same time it is strictly irrelevant. Trapped as he was by his own intuitive approach to his life and his work he could never have been a great novelist; what matters is that he was a writer of genius, a brilliant entertainer and one of the finest prose stylists of his generation.

Michael de-la-Noy, "Goodbye to All That," in Books and Bookmen, *No. 365, March, 1986, pp. 8-9.*

JOHN BOORMAN

[*English director, screenwriter, and author, Boorman began writing film criticism at the age of seventeen. He later worked for the Independent Television News and eventually headed the B.B.C. Documentary Film Unit. His first feature film,* Catch Us If You Can, *a comedy starring the English pop group, The Dave Clark Five, was released in England in 1966. Since that time Boorman has been involved in several films, both in England and the United States, directing them all and occasionally writing and producing them as well.* Deliverance *(1972),* Excalibur *(1980), and* The Emerald Forest *(1985) are among his most prominent works. In the following excerpt Boorman, a friend of Isherwood's, reminisces about the author's life in Hollywood and discusses the impact of cinema on his writing.*]

"I am a camera," wrote Christopher Isherwood in ***Goodbye to Berlin.*** Despite the guile and perennial popularity of those stories, that famous line has consigned him to the status of, at best, a minor master and, at worst, a marginal figure. For is he not in his novels simply describing real events and characters, and does he not, after all, appear in them as a character under his own name? Is he really a novelist at all? Like a crackle of electricity, he seems to jump the terminals, short-circuit the mysterious process by which a great writer subsumes his raw material and passes it through the murky acids and leaden depths of the unconscious before it flows out again at an even voltage onto the page.

I believe that "I am a camera" meant something quite different. Isherwood understood that it was impossible for writers to observe life in the old way once they, and their readers, had experienced the cinema. The movies were an overwhelming presence, interceding between perception and memory, a refracting glass slid between conscious and unconscious. The reader's view of experience had been fractured, altered out of mind, and nothing would ever be the same again. Isherwood addressed us as fellow moviegoers, fellow fans.

Crossing the novel with film sent his work into free-fall, and multimedia was born. ***Goodbye to Berlin*** became the stage play *I Am a Camera,* which was then filmed. The movie, in turn, went back to the stage as a musical, *Cabaret,* which, in due course, became a film again. The songs were appropriated as staple standards for light entertainment TV shows. Sally Bowles, who personifies the spirit of a time, and Berlin as a metaphor, became symbols of naughtiness and decadence like the cancan and Paris of another period. The hype got louder and the echoes diminished.

Isherwood's ironically onanistic writing presaged the cult of celebrity. The Andy Warhol invented by Andy Warhol is based on the Isherwood technique of re-creating yourself as a work of art. Stephen Spender said that the young Stephen Spender as depicted in Isherwood's novel ***The Memorial*** is much more like the young Stephen Spender than he ever was himself [see excerpt above].

Of all the couples I got to know when I first started visiting Los Angeles more than twenty years ago, Christopher Isherwood and Don Bachardy had the only "marriage" that survived. Also, atypically, they never moved house or changed the furniture. My wife and I often went for dinner to the little house perched up in the Santa Monica canyon, set back from the sea. My mind's eye would drift to the Hockney portrait of the two of them, which, again, looked so much more like them than they did themselves. We know Isherwood so intimately from his works, he has used himself up so completely for them, that I often felt there was nothing left of him in life, that the creature who remained was a fraud, even an imposter. (pp. 53-4)

This is the movie experience again.

The movies reflect the monochromatic twilight of memory and fantasy that we inhabit for much of our waking and sleeping lives. We used to perceive this as a shameful escapism, but now we accept it more readily as one of several levels of perception, indeed, realities, that make up consciousness.

Isherwood's writing uniquely acknowledges this relationship with cinema, and with these other levels of perception—as his life did. Perhaps what he saw so clearly is only becoming apparent to the rest of us as cinema goes into decline. As a writer, he was marooned, beached by the explosion of the movies, saw them as central to a world where reality was losing its grip. Now we can see movies as a transition, a magical limbo on the path to the television, which purports to loop us back to reality, but, instead, blurs all distinctions so that no one can tell the difference anymore. (pp. 54-5)

"I am a camera" was the cry of a prophet, the shutter of doom. This awareness of the power of the cinema comes to the fore in ***Prater Violet,*** perhaps Isherwood's masterpiece, certainly the best novel ever written about the process of moviemaking. It tells how the refugee Austrian Jew and distinguished director Friedrich Bergmann is hired by a British film studio to make a kind of Ruritanian operetta of surpassing banality. The studio looks for a German-speaking English writer to help Bergmann with the script, and lights on Isherwood. . . .

The impending World War II looms over Bergmann and Isherwood as they work on this frivolous concoction, and Isherwood intertwines the making of the movie with the political events that are dragging Europe to the brink of an abyss. Bergmann is a magnificent portrait—the archetypal, yet vividly individual director. . . .

Isherwood is transfixed by Bergmann's charm and power. He is the pliant willing pupil, and, perhaps because of this, he finds it impossible to write anything good. Bergmann reads his pages, grunts, then improvises the scene, bringing it all alive—to Isherwood's admiration and dismay. He realizes that Bergmann does not really need a collaborator. "but . . . stimulation and sympathy. . . . he needed an audience." (p. 55)

In contrast to Bergmann's wisdom, brilliance, and skill, Isherwood in his familiar way presents himself as silly and venal. His self-abasement is amusing, yet it also makes us uneasy, as though there is a hidden sexual element in it. But his relationship with Bergmann deepens and ripens in the white heat of making the film. He starts out as a pupil, becomes a fellow conspirator, a comrade in arms, and, finally, a friend. The two men end up with a profound understanding of each other, yet still conscious of being actors in a drama.

After the end-of-shooting party, Bergmann and Isherwood walk home in silence. In a brilliant internal monologue, Isherwood speculates about love and fear and death and identity. . . .

He comes to understand that, trapped as we are in the self, escape is possible through metaphoric projection, through making or watching movies. (p. 56)

Isherwood moved to Los Angeles, attracted by Aldous Huxley's exploration of drugs, the homosexual community, a guru who eventually led him to Hinduism, and the movies. Although he wrote screenplays from time to time, he never entered the system. It was the ambience that interested him. He was a fan, the fascinated observer, but he did not want to play the jester in one of Bergmann's studio palaces. He knew everybody, of course, and was able to worship the stars as stars, while at the same time being perceptively critical of them as private persons. I asked him once if he knew Greta Garbo. "Very well," he replied. In fact, she would often call at his home late at night, wanting him to go for moody strolls. He recalled one night when she was ringing the doorbell and he whispered to his friend, "Who'd have thought we would end up hiding under the bed to avoid going for a walk with Garbo?" (pp. 56-7)

Tawdry, silly, and despised, Hollywood still lured great men to pay court to its princes. Many of them paused with Isherwood: Tennessee Williams, William Faulkner, Bertolt Brecht, and others. One photograph of a picnic shows Isherwood eating with Charlie Chaplin, Igor Stravinsky, and Thomas Mann.

Thomas Mann's daughter proposed marriage to Isherwood, a device to acquire British nationality that would protect her in her anti-Nazi activities just before the war. Isherwood was so opposed to marriage as an institution that he could not bring himself to do it. He persuaded his friend W. H. Auden to marry her in his stead. Some time later, Mann and his entire family assembled in America and arranged for a family photograph. He politely introduced each member to the photographer. When he arrived at Auden, he said, "This is my son-in-law," and finally he indicated Isherwood. "This," he said, "is the family pimp."

Christopher Isherwood's life's work was his own life. He wrote of its every aspect, save one: the Hollywood experience, the movies. In his last years he did attempt this, but I don't know how far he got. Perhaps he felt he had said it definitively in ***Prater Violet,*** but I was always fascinated by his stories of stars like James Dean and Marilyn Monroe, whom he knew well, and regretted that he did not commit them to paper.

He and Don were passionate movie-goers. You saw them at screenings, waiting for the lights to go down, with innocent excitement in their eyes. They came to my first screening of *Deliverance*. My guests were invited afterwards to dinner at Edgar Gross's house in Beverly Hills. We had finished the meal before Joan Didion and her husband, John Gregory Dunne, staggered in, distraught and smeared with dirt and oil. They had blown a tire on the freeway coming from the screening. They discovered that neither could change a wheel. Joan's novel *Play It As It Lays* was being filmed at the time. It was about a disturbed woman who continuously drives the freeways, whose tire punctures . . . Chris was delighted with this. It was perfect. Life limping in the wake of the movie of the book; the imagined event looping back into the life of its inventor; film and reality on collision course.

On my last visit to his house, I inspected the hundreds of drawings and paintings that Bachardy had made of Isherwood. I had persuaded Don to sell me a painting of him and was invited to choose one of several. I picked out one in which a twisted smile tore the face asunder. Isherwood giggled with pleasure, as though I had confirmed his own opinion. "Oh, no," he said, "you can't have that one, that mustn't escape." I took one of the others. My daughter, Katrine, was with me, and the four of us went for dinner. Katrine, an outrageously flamboyant dresser, wore a hat adorned with a white dove. A springy wire attached it to her hat—and it seemed to hover over her.

Chris was spellbound by Katrine and her hat. He gazed at them all through dinner, his eyes sparkling, a grin fixed on his face, speechless. The hat perfectly expressed for him how wonderfully ludicrous life was. It was a movie hat that had somehow escaped into real life. These moments of synchronicity filled him with sublime happiness.

During the last year or so of Isherwood's life, Don Bachardy made one or two portraits of him each day. Bachardy's technique is quite disconcerting. He requires you to sit quite still, posing, for fifty minutes. He seats himself no more than eighteen inches from your face, which he surveys in intense detail, and then meticulously records what he sees with pencil and charcoal. You feel he has seen right through you, that it is impossible to hide.

The Isherwood portraits show him in a subtle range of moods, but never at his most characteristic: eyes blazing, grinning like an evil sprite that has been purged and excoriated by literary confession and religion, yet always threatening to burst out in an orgy of depravity.

It was as though Don was trying to restore the reality that had been squandered in those books, lost at the movies, trying to fix him, definitively, to prevent him from slipping away. If he could somehow make the perfect drawing, then Isherwood would live forever. And in his books, and in Don's drawings he will. (p. 57)

John Boorman, "Stranger in Paradise," in American Film, *Vol. XII, No. 1, October, 1986, pp. 53-7.*

SARAH CAUDWELL

[*Caudwell is the daughter of English writer and actress Jean Ross, a woman widely believed to have been the model for Isherwood's fictional creation, Sally Bowles. In the following excerpt Caudwell finds, despite the supposed verisimilitude of Isherwood's "documentary" prose style, that his rendering of Sally Bowles owes more to a sexist literary convention than to reality.*]

There is a new revival of *Cabaret* on at the moment—an event of the kind which, in my mother's lifetime, would have inspired some bright young journalist to ring up asking to interview 'the real Sally Bowles'.

Such interviews were invariably a disappointment on both sides: the journalists always wanted to talk about sex and my mother always wanted to talk about politics. . . .

[My mother] never liked ***Goodbye to Berlin,*** nor felt any sense of identity with the character of Sally Bowles, which in many respects she thought more closely modelled on one of Isherwood's male friends. (His homosexuality could not at that time be openly admitted.) She never cared enough, however, to be moved to any public rebuttal. She did from time to time settle down conscientiously to write a letter, intending to explain to Isherwood the ways in which she thought he had misunderstood her; but it seldom progressed beyond 'Dear Christopher . . .' (p. 28)

The plain, almost documentary quality of Isherwood's style has beguiled a wide audience into believing that the events and characters of ***Goodbye to Berlin*** are closer to factual reality than is commonly the case with a novel. Isherwood, himself, however, has somewhere pointed out that, to be 'lifelike', it is neither necessary nor sufficient for a work of fiction to be literally true to life: what is essential is that it should accord with the reader's expectations of life—expectations based not only on direct experience but on the conventions of existing literature. The most significant differences between Sally and her supposed model are attributable, it seems to me, to his having preferred convention to reality.

The convention does not permit an attractive young woman to have much in the way of intellectual accomplishments and Isherwood follows it loyally. . . .

Above all, the convention requires that a woman must be either virtuous (in the sexual sense) or a tart. So Sally, who is plainly not virtuous, must be a tart. At this point the relationship between reality and convention becomes strained almost to breaking-point, since what Sally actually does (as opposed to the author's opinion of why she is doing it) is the direct opposite of what one would expect in a woman determined to exploit her attractiveness for commercial advantage. Persistently and perversely, she fails to go to bed with anyone with any money. . . .

The author seems not unaware of the contradiction. 'For a would-be demi-mondaine,' he writes anxiously, 'she seemed to have surprisingly little business sense or tact.' In short, since she is not a successful tart, his solution is to represent her as an unsuccessful one.

Unsuccessful? As a tart? The reader may accept Isherwood's judgment of her talents as insufficient for success as a singer or an actress. But as a tart? She is, we are told, young, beautiful and elegant and presumably possessed of at least that minimum of social graces instilled by an expensive English boarding school: to fail, with these advantages, in a profession not generally reputed intellectually exacting argues a singular lack of application. The reader despairs of her—the girl is impossible.

And, as Isherwood draws her, so she is. What on earth, if her motives are those he imputes to her, is she doing in Berlin at all? Her upper-middle-class background would have afforded her, surely, ampler opportunities than the bars and nightclubs of Berlin to find a rich man to keep her, and that with all the safeguards of a respectable marriage. Her way of life is inexplicable save as a deliberate repudiation of that possibility, of any possibility of making her sexual relationships the subject of a commercial bargain. Or can she really imagine that she will be freer, more emancipated, if she is kept by a series of men rather than one?

My mother certainly would not have thought so. To depend for a living on providing sexual pleasure, whether or not in the context of marriage, seemed to her the ultimate denial of freedom and emancipation. . . .

She did not see the question as one of personal morality, but as a political one. What roused her to moral indignation was not the way women behave, seldom even the way men behave, but the existence of any system which offered women no other means of livelihood. She tried to explain this to the bright young journalists.

'They asked if I was a feminist. Well, of course I am, darling. But they don't think that feminism's about sex, do they? It's about economics.' (p. 29)

Sarah Caudwell, "Reply to Berlin," in New Statesman, *Vol. 112, No. 2897, October 3, 1986, pp. 28-9.*

John D(ann) MacDonald

July 24, 1916 - December 28, 1986

American novelist, short story writer, and nonfiction writer.

(See also *CLC*, Vols. 3, 27; *Contemporary Authors*, Vols. 1-4, rev. ed.; *Contemporary Authors New Revision Series*, Vols. 1, 19; and *Dictionary of Literary Biography*, Vol. 8.)

PRINCIPAL WORKS

The Brass Cupcake (novel) 1950
Wine of the Dreamers (novel) 1951; also published as *Planet of the Dreamers*, 1953
Ballroom of the Skies (novel) 1952
Cancel All Our Vows (novel) 1953
The Executioners (novel) 1958; also published as *Cape Fear*, 1962
A Flash of Green (novel) 1962
The Girl, the Gold Watch, and Everything (novel) 1962
A Key to the Suite (novel) 1962
**The Deep Blue Goodby* (novel) 1964
**Nightmare in Pink* (novel) 1964
**A Purple Place for Dying* (novel) 1964
The Quick Red Fox (novel) 1964
Bright Orange for the Shroud (novel) 1965
The House Guests (nonfiction) 1965
Darker than Amber (novel) 1966
A Deadly Shade of Gold (novel) 1966
One Fearful Yellow Eye (novel) 1966
The Girl in the Plain Brown Wrapper (novel) 1968
No Deadly Drug (nonfiction) 1968
Pale Gray for Guilt (novel) 1968
Dress Her in Indigo (novel) 1969
The Long Lavender Look (novel) 1970
A Tan and Sandy Silence (novel) 1971
The Scarlet Ruse (novel) 1973
The Turquoise Lament (novel) 1973
The Dreadful Lemon Sky (novel) 1975
Condominium (novel) 1977
The Empty Copper Sea (novel) 1978
Other Times, Other Worlds (short stories) 1978
The Green Ripper (novel) 1979
Free Fall in Crimson (novel) 1981
Cinnamon Skin (novel) 1982
The Lonely Silver Rain (novel) 1985
Barrier Island (novel) 1986
A Friendship: The Letters of Dan Rowan and John D. MacDonald (letters) 1987

*These works were published as *Three for McGee* in 1967; also published as *McGee*, 1975.

TOM DEMORETCKY

Mystery writer John D. MacDonald, the 70-year-old creator of fictional detective hero Travis McGee, died [December 28]. . . .

In a 1985 interview, MacDonald told *The Newsday Magazine* that he had a working title for the end to his enormously successful detective series: *A Black Border for McGee*. A folder with the title on it remained empty in his home on Siesta Key, an island off Sarasota, Fla. . . .

"Mind you, when McGee dies there won't be many people around to mourn him," he said in the interview, adding that the strapping knight-errant would end "unmourned, unhonored and unsung."

Such is not the case for MacDonald, who wrote 77 books, of which 30 million copies were printed in the United States alone. In 1972, the Sharon, Pa., native received the Edgar Grand Master award, the highest honor bestowed by the Mystery Writers of America. He was considered by many of his peers to be the finest mystery writer in America. Among his admirers is friend and fellow writer Kurt Vonnegut, who said, "To diggers a thousand years from now, the works of John D. MacDonald would be a treasure on the order of the tomb of Tutankhamen." . . .

In 1950, MacDonald published his first book, ***The Brass Cupcake.*** By 1964 he had published 33 books. He began the Travis McGee series at the request of his publisher, Fawcett Gold Medal Books. The first volume was ***The Deep Blue Good-by.*** McGee was originally to be called Dallas McGee, but the assassination of President Kennedy in 1963 caused the writer to rename his protagonist, a character who made his living in the salvage business, lived on a houseboat in Fort Lauderdale and engaged in philosophical conversations with his neighbor, an economist named Meyer. Frequently, McGee's "salvage" work meant helping friends by busting his way through bad guys.

While MacDonald denied that he wished to be McGee and said he resented being asked about that, McGee's musings reflected MacDonald's beliefs on such subjects as nature and the environment. One of his non-McGee novels, ***Condominium,*** reflected his views on the rapid buildup of Florida.

Tom Demoretcky, "Writer John MacDonald, 70, Dies," in Long Island Newsday, *December 29, 1986.*

PENELOPE McMILLAN

John D. MacDonald, one of the most prolific and successful of action-adventure writers, died [December 28]. . . . He was 70.

MacDonald, a longtime resident of Sarasota, Fla., died at St. Mary's Hospital in Milwaukee, Wis., of complications following heart by-pass surgery, said Claire Ferraro, associate publisher at Ballantine, Del Rey and Fawcett books in New York. He had been hospitalized since September.

Best known as the creator of Travis McGee, the eccentric antihero detective who became the '60s answer to Raymond Chandler's Philip Marlowe, MacDonald's career spanned more than 40 years, including at least 77 books and 500 short stories.

In all, his books have sold more than 70 million copies. Of these, 21 were novels about McGee, the salvage expert-amateur detective and adventurer who lived on a Florida houseboat, the "Busted Flush," won in a poker game.

Beginning in 1964, with ***The Deep Blue Goodbye,*** McGee solved crimes and, indulging his creator's dislike for many of the trends and customs in contemporary life, delivered shrewd commentaries on modern life as the mysteries unraveled.

In McGee mysteries and other novels as well, MacDonald's voice was one of a social historian, particularly of the Southern coast. In a first person McGee-MacDonald voice, the detective lamented the "locust population" of large cities advancing south, and the sad transformation of Florida's paradise of birds and marshes turned "flashy and cheap, tacky and noisy."

In ***Barrier Island,*** published [in 1986], MacDonald sketched "the laid-back life of golf, boating, long cool drinks, the peculiar callousness bred by hot climates and luxurious comfort, better than anybody since Graham Greene," author Stephen Vizinczey said in a review. He won two major awards, the Edgar Grand Master award from the Mystery Writers of America in 1972, and the American Book Award's mystery competition in 1980.

John Dann MacDonald was born in Sharon, Penn., on July 24, 1916. He attended the Wharton School of Finance and the Syracuse School of Business, then received a master's degree from the Harvard School of Business in 1939.

He earned his first paychecks from pulp magazines, selling stories while serving in the U.S. Army during World War II. He spent 30 months in the China-India-Burma theater, mostly with the Office of Strategic Services, and rose to the rank of lieutenant colonel.

In the first four months after he was discharged he wrote 800,000 words, and virtually never stopped writing. At first, he lived in Utica, N.Y., selling to the pulps as well as to Esquire and Cosmopolitan, often using a number of pseudonyms. When he had earned $6,000 from writing, he moved his wife and son to Texas.

Over the next three years, they moved some more, back to upstate New York, to Mexico and finally to Florida, where MacDonald had lived since 1949.

In 1950, his first book, ***The Brass Cupcake,*** was published. By 1964, when his first McGee mystery appeared, he had already written 43 novels.

"When McGee was created, I set about coldly to devise a character who would be likable, yet substantial enough for me to be involved with for a series," the publicly reticent MacDonald said in a rare interview, in 1973. "In the first novel, he was too somber. . . . I threw it out. In the second version, he was too much of a smart-ass—too quick and funny, too much of a winner. But by my third try, a character emerged that I enjoyed: a physically tough man who was vulnerable, yet strong."

He admitted that McGee, moralistic yet supremely knowledgeable about travel, food, drink and women, was "my Walter Mitty projection, in the sense that every banker likes to think secretly that he can pull off that big job."

In a 1984 television interview, he called his hero a "tattered knight on a spavined steed."

In later years, the non-McGee novels tackled corporate swindles and greed, as in the 1977 ***Condominium,*** about corporations grabbing land in Florida, or ***One More Sunday*** (1984) about spiritually bankrupt evangelical church leaders who raise funds through television and computers.

A lover of boats—like McGee—MacDonald also enjoyed chess, poker and was once a semi-pro bridge player. A disciplined writer, he kept regular hours, working from 8:30 a.m. to 6 p.m., producing from 900 to 9,000 words a day.

He put off writing, he said, only to travel with his wife or to go fishing. . . .

His editor, Leona Nevler, said Sunday she believed MacDonald had been working on another Travis McGee novel before his final illness. There have been rumors for years of a "final" book, called ***Symphony in Black,*** in which McGee dies.

Penelope McMillan, "Adventure Book Writer John D. MacDonald Dies," in Los Angeles Times, *December 29, 1986.*

C. GERALD FRASER

From a modest beginning in 1946 with the sale of a short story for $25, Mr. MacDonald's writing career blossomed to produce about 70 books. Of those, 21 made up the highly successful

Travis McGee series—about the adventures of a tough, cynical, philosophical knight-errant who lives on a houseboat in Florida.

Three-quarters of his books were published originally as paperbacks. His prodigious literary output also included 500 short stories.

In 1972 he won the Mystery Writers of America's Grand Master Award. In 1980 he won the American Book Award for his hard-cover mystery ***The Green Ripper.*** In 1955 he won the Ben Franklin Award for the best American short story, and in 1964 he received the Grand Prix de Littérature Policière for the French edition of ***A Key to the Suite.***

Robin W. Winks, a professor of history at Yale University, said [in 1985] in *The New York Times Book Review* that "Mr. MacDonald's books are always about boats, and hot sun, and the putative glamour of resort life, as much as they are about the persistence of evil and the near-randomness of honesty."

The Travis McGee series began in 1964 with the first appearance of McGee—a 6-foot-4, 212-pound thinking man's Robin Hood—in ***The Deep Blue Good-By,*** and four others were published within a year. Since then all the Travis McGee novels have made best-seller lists, and some have been No. 1.

Mr. MacDonald gave each Travis McGee novel a title that included a color, such as ***Bright Orange for a Shroud, Darker Than Amber, A Deadly Shade of Gold, Dress Her in Indigo, The Girl in the Plain Brown Wrapper, The Green Ripper*** and ***The Long Lavender Look.***

Movies and made-for-television films have been produced from some of his novels. ***The Executioners*** became the movie ***Cape Fear.*** And ***A Flash of Green*** . . . , was based on the novel.

Although mysteries were his métier, Mr. MacDonald published other works, including ***Condominium,*** a 1977 best-selling novel about greedy developers of substandard apartment complexes in Florida; a nonfiction work, ***No Deadly Drug,*** about the trial of Dr. Carl Coppolino, a New Jersey doctor accused of killing his wife, and ***Nothing Can Go Wrong,*** a book about a cruise that he wrote with Capt. John J. Kilpack.

Mr. MacDonald's final work [is] a non-fiction book, ***A Friendship: The Letters of Dan Rowan and John D. MacDonald,*** on the correspondence between the comic and the author. . . .

In describing his fiction, Mr. MacDonald said in a 1970 interview with *The Washington Post* that "most of my published novels are of the folk dancing category, the steps, the patterns traditionally imperative, the retributions obligatory."

"Within these limits I have struggled for freshness, for what insights I can muster, for validity of characterization and motivation, for the accuracies of method and environment which enhance any illusion of reality," he said.

During most of his career, Mr. MacDonald wrote daily, for seven to nine hours, with a break for lunch and another at the cocktail hour. He used expensive bond paper, explaining, "I think the same situation is involved as painting and sculpture," he said in *The Post*. "If you use the best materials you can afford, somehow you have more respect for what you do with it."

He said he rewrote "by throwing away a page, a chapter, half a book—or go right back to the beginning and start again."

"I enjoy the hell out of writing because it's like an Easter egg hunt," he once said. "Here's 50 pages, and you say, 'Oh, Christ, where is it?' Then on the 51st page, it'll work. Just the way you wanted it to, a little better than anything in that same area ever worked before. You say: 'Wow! This is worth the price of admission.'"

Suspense writing was "like a mental exercise" to Mr. MacDonald. "Once you accept the limits of what you're doing, you try to do the best within those limits," he said.

C. Gerald Fraser, "John D. MacDonald, Novelist, Is Dead," in The New York Times, *December 29, 1986.*

RICHARD PEARSON

John D. Macdonald, 70, an independent-minded and commonsensical storyteller whose mysteries about characters such as Travis McGee, a knight errant sleuth and boatman, made him one of the most popular mystery writers of modern times, died [December 28] . . . in a hospital in Milwaukee.

He had been hospitalized since undergoing heart surgery in September and had been in a coma since Dec. 10. . . .

Apart from his skill as a storyteller, Mr. MacDonald had a finely tuned sense of time and place. Most of his books are set in Florida, and he wrote about its beaches and seascapes and skies, with their invitations and promises, perhaps as well [as] anyone writing.

And he invited his readers to share his particular view of the world: a wearisome place inhabited by contrary people, no doubt, but a place entirely worth saving for the right-minded likes of you and me. For Mr. MacDonald, this would include everybody but the bad guys.

And for the bad guys there is Travis McGee, the self-styled "salvage consultant" who will get you back not only your property but also your dreams. The people McGee helps have no other recourse, and so his fee—half of whatever he recovers—is less important than the fact that he is upholding right and reason.

He is 6 feet, 4 inches tall, weighs about 200 pounds, and has the permanent tan of a man who lives on a houseboat in the tropics and takes care of himself. He is good with his fists, and he knows how to use guns and other weapons. He won the house boat in a card game, and he calls it "The Busted Flush." But his strongest suit is old-fashioned virtue: loyalty, honesty, tenacity.

It goes without saying that McGee and his creator are two entirely different people. But it is also true that McGee is made to embody the things that Mr. MacDonald admired most. And these qualities plainly were appealing to a vast audience of readers. He is full of comments on consumerism, changing life styles and technologies, and the virtues of work.

Not the least appealing thing about him is the fact that he takes his "retirement in installments" at a time of life when he is able to enjoy it. This allows him to inveigh against "plastic credit cards, payroll deductions, insurance programs, retirement benefits, Green Stamps, time clocks, newspapers, mortgages, sermons, miracle fabrics, deodorants, check lists, time payments, political parties, lending libraries, television, actresses, junior chambers of commerce, pageants, progress and manifest destiny." . . .

Lamenting to McGee about the world economy, Meyer could give the following impassioned lecture:

> There is a debt of perhaps 2 trillion dollars out there, owed by governments to governments, by governments to banks, and there is not one chance in hell it can ever be paid back. There is not enough productive capacity in the world, plus enough raw materials to provide maintenance of plant plus overage, even to keep up with mounting interest. . . .
>
> What is triggering it is the crisis of reduced expectations. All over the world people are coming to realize that their children and grandchildren are going to have it worse than they did, that the trend line is down. So they want to blame somebody. They want to hoot and holler in the streets and burn something down.

That does not mean, however, that there is no hope. . . .

Before Travis McGee emerged from the presses, Mr. MacDonald had published 43 other novels.

Determined to establish a series character, he refused to allow the first McGee book to be published until he had written four of them and was satisfied with his work. He first planned to write 10 McGee novels, then 12. Though 21 have emerged, McGee and his world continue to evolve.

As the number of books increased, so did the scars on the McGee back, the lines on the boyish face, and an ache in the aging heart. For victory is not without price. Time and fortune often took from him women he loved, persons who could not be replaced.

As McGee gained in years so Mr. MacDonald's reputation continued to grow. Such works as ***Condominium,*** the story of the people living in a new but unsafe building on the Florida coast, and ***One More Sunday,*** the saga of a family of television preachers, were best sellers that reached an even wider audience than those who follow his mysteries.

Collections of his early pulp short stories were lapped up by an adoring public. Even his correspondence is valued: His most recent book was ***A Friendship: The Letters of Dan Rowan and John D. MacDonald.***

But the McGee books stand as a separate body of work. The title of each includes a color code. It is said that one remains. Its title contains the word ''black'' and tells of the death of McGee. It was composed years ago and was to be published following Mr. MacDonald's death.

Richard Pearson, ''John D. MacDonald: Writer of Popular Mysteries, Dies at 70,'' in The Washington Post, *December 29, 1986.*

CHAUNCEY MABE

James Baldwin fled to Paris to find the peace to write about America. Sinclair Lewis, William Faulkner and Thomas Wolfe all wrote about their hometowns—and thereby earned the mockery and disdain of friends and relatives. Ernest Hemingway is considered the prototypical American novelist, yet only one of his books is set within the United States.

Many such examples can be cited to illustrate the uneasy relationship that often exists between a writer and the places both where he lives and where he sets his stories.

Thanks to the late John D. MacDonald, few places have a greater hold on the popular literary imagination than Fort Lauderdale, the setting for the 21-volume Travis McGee adventure series. For 20 years, readers have come from all over the world to visit Bahia Mar marina, named in the books as the place where the fictional McGee moored his houseboat, *The Busted Flush,* at Slip F-18.

Yet, had it not been for MacDonald's zeal for privacy, the dedication ceremony that will mark a slip at Bahia Mar as a literary landmark [on February 21] might well be taking place in Sarasota instead of Fort Lauderdale.

''He selected Fort Lauderdale as the setting for the Travis McGee series because he knew he could not cope with the swarms of people who would want to meet him if the series was successful,'' says Walter Shine, MacDonald's friend and bibliographer. ''It turned out he was right.'' . . .

Like untold numbers of readers, Shine first became acquainted with MacDonald when he picked up a Travis McGee novel in an airport. From the first paragraph of ***The Quick Red Fox,*** which describes a nasty February breeze coming off the ocean into the Bahia Mar yacht basin, Shine was hooked for life.

''The first time I came to Fort Lauderdale, I docked my boat and ran—*ran*—to Bahia Mar to find Slip F-18,'' Shine says with a laugh. ''It was 1969, I was no kid. I was distressed to learn there is no F-18 slip.''

Hundreds if not thousands of literary pilgrims have shared Shine's dismay, says Dick Graves, Bahia Mar marketing director. ''People come from as far away as Europe looking for Slip F-18, and there's never been one,'' he says.

[The] dedication will change all that, providing the faithful a proper shrine. Various dignitaries, headed by Fort Lauderdale Mayor Bob Cox, will be on hand as Slip F-602 is summarily redesignated as Slip F-18. A plaque will identify it as a literary landmark and Bahia Mar will permanently dock its sightseeing boat (named *The Busted Flush,* of course) in the slip. . . .

The idea for the landmark designation came from Jean Trebbi, of the Florida Center for the Book, but Shine was consulted to locate the most logical spot for the heretofore fictional Slip F-18.

That's because no one knows more about Travis McGee—or John MacDonald—than Shine and his wife, Jean. In fact, MacDonald referred questions about McGee to Shine with the remark, ''He knows more about Travis than I do.''

Shine, who now lives in North Palm Beach, has given each of MacDonald's books no less than three readings. ''They get better every time,'' he said.

The Shines carried on a 10-year correspondence with MacDonald and met with him several times. MacDonald dedicated ***The Lonely Silver Rain,*** the last Travis McGee book, to them.

Although MacDonald worked in a crime/adventure genre with some of his books, including the Travis McGee series, he was no hack. In recent years, he had enjoyed critical acclaim to match his popularity. Even when he was writing primarily to entertain he was too much a true craftsman to be less than honest.

Thus, the portrait of Fort Lauderdale that emerges in the Travis McGee series is often less than flattering. This reflects the concern that MacDonald had for environmental issues, and it pervades much of his writing, both fiction and non-fiction. He hated what he called ''the uglification of America,'' Shine says.

Yet, Trebbi says, the Travis McGee books do present Fort Lauderdale in a positive light.

''McGee longs to escape from the encroachment of the modern world as exemplified by the growth of Fort Lauderdale,'' she says. ''But the area also provides a location where he finds the best in himself and he is able to rescue some humanity for others here.''

In struggling to explain the appeal of Travis McGee, *The Busted Flush* and Bahia Mar, both Shine and Trebbi are quick to point out that McGee is not a detective, nor are the books mysteries.

''The action may parallel something like detective fiction, but Travis McGee is a salvage consultant,'' Trebbi says. ''Frequently, he finds himself salvaging a human life that has become sunken into the muck and mire. He is not really solving crimes and bringing people to justice. He is always retrieving what was lost within some individual. He's a maverick, a classic American type, and that takes him out of any genre.''

''I think there is a special flavor to McGee that captivates you the way MacDonald's other books do not,'' Shine says. ''The reader is embued with a romantic notion that desperately wants it all to be true, a longing to go to Travis McGee's place and meet him. This landmark is great, because now the reader won't have to imagine it all.''

Chauncey Mabe, ''Behind a Literary Landmark,'' in News/Sun-Sentinel, *Fort Lauderdale, February 15, 1987, p. 106.*

Bernard Malamud

April 26, 1914 - March 18, 1986

American novelist and short story writer.

(See also *CLC,* Vols. 1, 2, 3, 5, 8, 9, 11, 18, 27; *Contemporary Authors,* Vols. 5-8, rev. ed., Vol. 118 [obituary]; *Contemporary Authors Bibliographical Series,* Vol. 1; *Dictionary of Literary Biography,* Vols. 2, 28; and *Dictionary of Literary Biography Yearbook: 1980.*)

PRINCIPAL WORKS

The Natural (novel) 1952
The Assistant (novel) 1957
The Magic Barrel (short stories) 1958
A New Life (novel) 1961
Idiots First (short stories) 1963
The Fixer (novel) 1966
Pictures of Fidelman: An Exhibition (short stories) 1969
The Tenants (novel) 1971
Rembrandt's Hat (short stories) 1973
Dubin's Lives (novel) 1979
God's Grace (novel) 1982
The Stories of Bernard Malamud (short stories) 1983

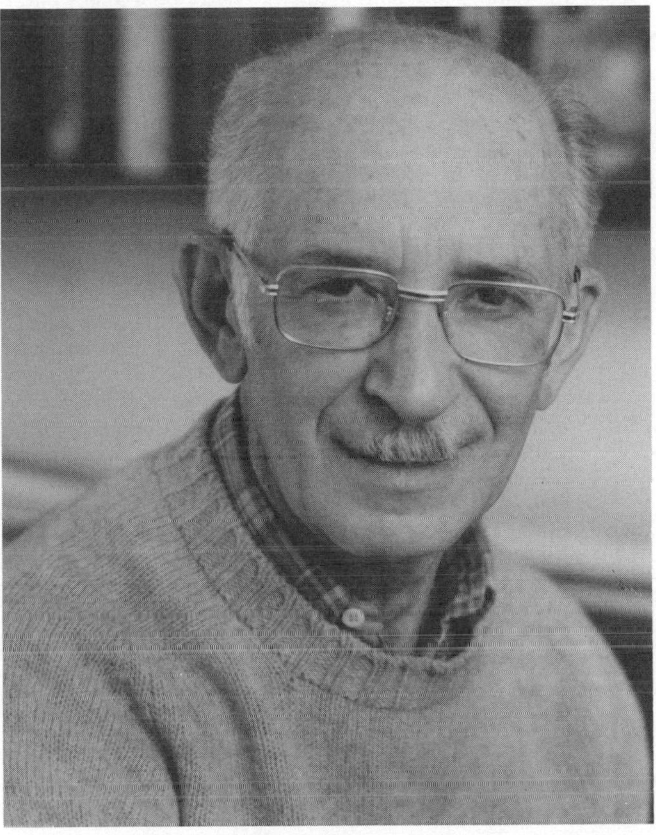

DAVID REMNICK

Bernard Malamud died in New York [March 18]. Heart surgery a few years ago left him weak at times but, bless the man, he was just about finished with another novel before his gentle voice and tough spirit gave out at the age of 71.

When a writer as fine and mysterious as Malamud dies after a long and productive life, his readers lose almost nothing, really. His life is a lasting open book. Still, if you loved a writer—and Malamud was the sort of writer you could love, not just admire—you feel almost angry at his passing.

The work is complete, sealed. Death put a lid on the magic barrel. What was in that last novel? Malamud's publishers say it's a comedy about a Jewish shopkeeper living in the old American West and you can only hope the book was almost done.

Malamud gave singular voice to all that is strange, emblematic and magical in his characters' lives. Malamud's lives, of course, were mainly Jewish lives, but for some odd critical and journalistic reasons, he was lumped together with a more comic spirit (Philip Roth) and a more cerebral one (Saul Bellow). All three produced Jewish-American literature, but they never comprised a yeshiva of fiction. Malamud's stories—and he was best in shorter work—are little miracles that cannot be jammed into any critical duffel bags. They are elusive; simple at first, then as dark and awesome as genuine spiritual experience.

He believed deeply that "art tends toward morality":

> It values life. Even when it doesn't, it tends to. My former colleague Stanley Edgar Hyman used to say that even the act of creating a form is a moral act. That leaves out something, but I understand and like what he was driving at. It's close to Frost's definition of a poem as 'a momentary stay against confusion.' Morality begins with the awareness of the sanctity of one's life, hence the lives of others—even Hitlers, to begin with—the sheer privilege of being, in this miraculous cosmos, and trying to figure out why. Art, in essence, celebrates life and gives us our measure.

Malamud's best work—the stories in ***The Magic Barrel*** and ***Rembrandt's Hat*** as well as ***The Assistant*** and the better parts of ***The Natural*** and ***The Fixer***—will always delight and stun because of the way they both portray and transcend a particular character and world: a shopkeeper and his spiritual crisis, an aging ballplayer and his secret. His prose was direct, clear and swift. At his best he had the ear of a poet. Here are the first sentences of **"Idiots First":**

"The thick ticking of the tin clock stopped. Mendel, dozing in the dark, awoke in fright. The pain returned as he listened. He drew on his cold embittered clothing, and wasted minutes sitting at the edge of the bed."

The iambic accents of that first sentence, the clarity of the image, the choice of "embittered" to describe a man's clothing: a master is at work.

As surely as his Roy Hobbs was a natural home run hitter, Malamud was a natural storyteller, and to an interviewer from *The Paris Review,* he made a little narrative of his own life. It is worth listening to:

> My father was a grocer; my mother, who helped him, died after a long illness, died young. I had a younger brother who lived a hard and lonely life and died in his fifties.
>
> My mother and father were gentle, honest, kindly people, and who they were and their affection for me to some degree made up for the cultural deprivation I felt as a child. They weren't educated but their values were stable. Though my father always managed to make a living, they were comparatively poor, especially in the Depression, and yet I never heard a word in praise of the buck. On the other hand there were no books that I remember in the house, no records, music, pictures on the wall. On Sundays I listened to somebody's piano through the window. At 9 I caught pneumonia, and when I was convalescing my father bought me the Book of Knowledge, 20 volumes where there had been none. That was, considering the circumstances, an act of great generosity.
>
> When I was in high school he bought a radio. As a kid, for entertainment I turned to the movies and dime novels. Maybe ***The Natural*** derives from Frank Merriwell as well as the adventures of the Brooklyn Dodgers in Ebbets Field.
>
> Anyway my parents stayed close to the store. Once in a while, on Jewish holidays, we went visiting, or saw a Jewish play—Sholom Aleichem, Peretz and others. My mother's brother, Charles Fidelman, and their cousin, Isadore Cashier, were in the Yiddish theater.
>
> Around the neighborhood the kids played chase the white horse, ringolevio, buck-buck, punchball and one o'cat. Occasionally we stole tomatoes from the Italian dirt farmers, gypped the el to ride to Coney Island, smoked in cellars and played blackjack. I wore sneakers every summer. My education at home derived mostly from the presence and example of good, feelingful, hard-working people. They were worriers, with other faults I wasn't much conscious of until I recognized them in myself. I learned from books, in the public schools.
>
> I took to literature early and wanted to be a writer. At 8 or 9 I was writing little stories in school and feeling the glow.

Malamud's sensibility was shaped in part by his reading the masters of short fiction—Chekhov, Hawthorne and Poe—but he was a distinctly Jewish writer even if Sholom Aleichem and the Yiddishists were not his direct masters.

> I was sharing an office [at Oregon State University, where he was teaching] with a colleague who often wished aloud that he were a Jew. I understood the sentiment. I was glad I was, although my father had his doubts about that. He had sat in mourning when I married my gentile wife, but I had thought it through and felt I knew what I was doing. After the birth of our son my father came gently to greet my wife and touch his grandchild. I thought of him as I began ***The Assistant*** and felt I would often be writing about Jews, in celebration and expiation, though perhaps that was having it both ways.
>
> I'm an American, I'm a Jew, and I write for all men. A novelist has to, or he's built himself a cage. I write about Jews, when I write about Jews, because they set my imagination going. I know something about their history, the quality of experience and belief, and of their literature, though not as much as I would like.

Think of those stories and you think of a figure in a painting by Chagall, a man with his feet on the dusty sidewalks and his head in heaven. If that makes Bernard Malamud a kind of giant, so be it.

David Remnick, "The Voice of a Natural: Bernard Malamud and His Miraculous Tales," in The Washington Post, *March 20, 1986, pp. D1, D8.*

MERVYN ROTHSTEIN

Bernard Malamud, the novelist and short story writer who won two National Book Awards and the Pulitzer Prize for his chronicles of human struggle, died [March 18] at his Manhattan apartment. He was 71 years old.

Mr. Malamud's work showed a regard for Jewish tradition and the plight of ordinary men, and was imbued with the theme of moral wisdom gained through suffering.

Mr. Malamud was considered by many critics to be one of the finest contemporary American writers. The critic Robert Alter said that stories like **"The First Seven Years," "The Magic Barrel," "The Last Mohican," "Idiots First"** and **"Angel Levine"** will be read "as long as anyone continues to care about American fiction written in the 20th century" [see *CLC,* Vol. 27].

The author once described himself as a chronicler of "simple people struggling to make their lives better in a world of bad luck." One of his last appearances was at the PEN Congress in New York in January when he read from his works.

In his work, Mr. Malamud often combined fantasy and reality to create a world that was both the same and different from the one we live in.

In **"Angel Levine,"** a black, rather seedy-looking angel appears to a retired Jewish tailor; in **"The Jewbird,"** a Yiddish-accented vagabond makes his way into an urban Jewish household in the form of a crow; in **"Idiots First,"** the Angel of Death, alias Ginzburg, pursues a desperate Jew trying to scrape together money to send his idiot son to California on the midnight train.

"Malamud has been in the fable business, so to speak," the critic Alan Lelchuk wrote [see *CLC,* Vol. 27].

Mr. Malamud's first novel, ***The Natural,*** an allegory about the rise and fall of a baseball player, was published in 1952. It is different from most of his work in that there are no Jewish characters. After the book was made into a movie starring Robert Redford in 1984, Mr. Malamud said in an interview that he was grateful for the film because it allowed him "to be recognized once more as an American writer" as opposed to a Jewish writer. But ***The Natural*** is similar to his later novels and stories in that it lies in the realm of a morality play.

"Malamud has always had a fondness for telling tales arranged for the purpose of a specific moral lesson," Mr. Lelchuk wrote.

"Neither realism nor surrealism has been his forte through the years," he continued, "but the fable, the parable, the allegory, the ancient art of basic storytelling in a modern voice; through this special mode he has earned his high place in contemporary letters."

The Assistant, his second novel, and the one many critics consider his best, was published in 1957. Set in the Depression, it tells of a Jewish grocery-store owner and his Italian assistant, and it, too, is much like a morality play.

The Fixer (1966) was inspired by the ordeal of Mendel Beiliss, a Jew tried and acquitted of ritual murder in Kiev in czarist Russia of 1913. ***The Magic Barrel,*** the author's first collection of short stories, was given the National Book Award in 1959.

On the basis of ***The Assistant*** and ***The Fixer,*** critics began to think of Mr. Malamud as a "Jewish writer" along with Saul Bellow and Philip Roth.

Mr. Malamud, however, said that he found the label of "Jewish writer" inadequate. He said that the three writers shared more differences than similarities, and that, in his case, Jewishness was more a spiritual than a cultural or a religious quality.

"I was concerned with what Jews stood for," he said, "with their getting down to the bare bones of things. I was concerned with their ethicality—how Jews felt they had to live in order to go on living."

And at another time he commented: "Jewishness is important to me, but I don't consider myself only a Jewish writer. I have interests beyond that, and I feel I'm writing for all men."

Mr. Roth agreed with Mr. Malamud. "The Jews of ***The Magic Barrel*** and the Jews of ***The Assistant*** are not the Jews of New York City or Chicago," Mr. Roth wrote. "They are Malamud's invention, a metaphor of sorts to stand for certain possibilities and promises."

Mr. Malamud's later works—***Pictures of Fidelman, The Tenants, God's Grace*** and to a lesser extent, ***Dubin's Lives***—got mixed reviews. Many critics cited a growing bleakness in his work, saying that as he left his Jewish milieu for academic and other settings his work took on a flinty emptiness without the poignance and meaning that characterized his earlier novels. His argument with God, they said, seemed to wither into a seminar.

Others, however, saw a growth in these works—his handling in ***The Tenants*** of the cultural and psychological upheaval among blacks caused by the rise of nationalism, separatism and racial pride; the powerful presence of nature in ***Dubin's Lives,*** something new for an author whose works for the most part had urban settings, and the concern with man's survival in the nuclear age in ***God's Grace.***

Bernard Malamud was born April 26, 1914, in Brooklyn, the elder of two sons of Russian Jewish immigrants, Max Malamud and the former Bertha Fidelman.

His father ran a small grocery, working 16 hours a day—he served as a model for the Jewish grocer in ***The Assistant.*** Looking back on his childhood, Mr. Malamud would recall that there were no books in his home, no cultural nourishment at all except that on Sundays he would listen to someone else's piano through the living-room window.

He attended Erasmus Hall High School in Brooklyn, and in 1936 he received his B.A. from the City College of New York. After graduation, he worked in a factory, in various stores and as a clerk in the Census Bureau in Washington, writing in his spare time.

In 1940, he got a job teaching at Erasmus Hall Evening High School, and he would continue to teach in New York City evening high schools until 1949. While he was teaching, he earned an M.A. at Columbia University in 1942.

Mr. Malamud often said that the advent of World War II and the Holocaust first made him sure that he had something to say as a writer. Until then, he said, he had not given much thought to what it meant to be Jewish, but the horror of the war—as well as the fact that he married a gentile woman, Ann de Chiara, in 1945—made him question his own identity as a Jew and compelled him to start reading about Jewish tradition and history. He knew then, he said, that he really wanted to write.

"The suffering of the Jews is a distinct thing for me," he once explained. "I for one believe that not enough has been made of the tragedy of the destruction of six million Jews. Somebody has to cry—even if it's a writer, 20 years later."

In 1949, he got a job teaching English at Oregon State University, where he stayed until 1961, becoming an associate professor. He wrote four books there—***The Natural, The Assistant, The Magic Barrel*** and his third novel, ***A New Life*** (1961), which is set in the Pacific Northwest at a college not unlike Oregon State.

In 1961, he went to teach at Bennington College in Vermont, where he taught for more than 20 years, with the exception of two years he spent as a visiting lecturer at Harvard from 1966 to 1968.

In 1963, he published ***Idiots First,*** another story collection. That was followed by ***The Fixer*** (1966), ***Pictures of Fidelman,*** stories about one central character (1969); ***The Tenants,*** a novel about the conflict between two writers, one Jewish and the other black (1971); ***Rembrandt's Hat,*** more stories (1973); ***Dubin's Lives,*** a novel about a biographer in midlife that many critics consider one of his best (1979); ***God's Grace,*** a novel (1982), and ***The Stories of Bernard Malamud*** (1983).

Mr. Malamud was a firm believer that a story should tell a story. ''With me, it's story, story, story,'' he once said. ''Writers who can't invent stories often pursue other strategies, even substituting style for narrative. I feel that story is the basic element of fiction though that ideal is not popular with disciples of the 'new novel.' They remind me of the painter who couldn't paint people, so he painted chairs.

''The story will be with us as long as man is. You know that, in part, because of its effect on children. It's through story they realize that mystery won't kill them. Through story they learn they have a future.''

He did not find writing an easy task. ''The idea is to get the pencil moving quickly,'' he said. ''Once you've got some words looking back at you you can take two or three—or throw them away and look for other. I go over and over a page. Either it bleeds and shows it's beginning to be human, or the form emits shadows of itself and I'm off. I have a terrifying will that way.''

In his writing, he prized the idea of swift transition—changing a scene in one sentence between paragraphs—and he thought he might have achieved that talent by studying intercutting in motion pictures. ''I was influenced very much by Charlie Chaplin movies,'' he said, ''by the rhythm and snap of his comedy and his wonderful, wonderful mixture of comedy and sadness.''

He acknowledged that sadness was one of his prime topics. ''People say I write so much about misery,'' he said, but added, ''you write about what you write best.''

He described the essential Malamud character as ''someone who fears his fate, is caught up in it, yet manages to outrun it; he's the subject and object of laughter and pity.''

In addition to the Pulitzer and the National Book Awards, Mr. Malamud won the Rosenthal Award of the National Institute of Arts and Letters, Vermont's 1979 Governor's Award for Excellence in the Arts and the 1981 Brandeis Creative Arts Award. He was a member of the American Academy and Institute of Arts and Letters, which in 1983 presented him its Gold Medal in Fiction. From 1979 to 1981 he was president of the PEN American Center. . . .

[His] publisher, Farrar, Straus & Giroux, announced the establishment of a Bernard Malamud literary award, to be administered by PEN.

For many years, Mr. Malamud did not become involved in social issues, arguing that for an author writing was involvement enough. But as president of PEN, he protested the repression of writers in the Soviet Union and South Africa and the curtailing of First Amendment rights.

Although he granted occasional interviews, Mr. Malamud led an intensely private life. In *The Ghost Writer,* Philip Roth created a character named E. I. Lonoff, a novelist ''deeply skeptical of the public world,'' whose ideas of work and esthetic purity obliged him to live a life of solitude. A number of critics have suggested that Lonoff was a portrait of Mr. Malamud.

Mr. Roth was a good friend of Mr. Malamud, and it is perhaps he who best summed up Mr. Malamud's work. Noting that Mr. Malamud was once supposed to have remarked that ''all men are Jews,'' Mr. Roth said:

''What it is to be human, and to be humane, is his deepest concern.''

Mervyn Rothstein, ''Bernard Malamud, Author, Dies at 71,'' in The New York Times, *March 20, 1986, p. D26.*

***THE TIMES,* LONDON**

Bernard Malamud, one of America's leading novelists and short story writers, died on March 18 at the age of 71.

As a Jewish novelist it was his perpetual misfortune to be overshadowed by his contemporary, Saul Bellow, whose greater range of experience and powers of invention enabled him to produce a succession of lavishly-conceived novels with a fluency denied to Malamud.

Nevertheless Malamud remains inimitable in his exploration of a predicament which in his work, can be seen as not merely Jewish, but as the fate of all individuals who are compelled to struggle—often through no fault of their own—through lives devoid of richness.

And it was his achievement to describe poverty of experience with a compassion which exalts the sufferings of his protagonists and—especially in the short stories—transfigures their longings to matters of eternal value.

At times the world of Malamud seems to exchange realism for emblem; to hold its inhabitants in an aura of Chagall-like innocence.

Bernard Malamud was born on April 26, 1914 in Brooklyn, of Russian immigrant parents. His father was a grocer, in whose store—necessarily itinerant from neighbourhood to neighbourhood in pursuit of business—Malamud and his brother worked as children. This world, barely suspended above the margin of poverty, was to provide the backcloth for perhaps his finest novel, ***The Assistant.***

At nights the store's back room provided the study where Bernard first tried his hand at fiction, in the dark hours after Malamud senior had given up the futile struggle with his accounts.

Malamud was educated at Erasmus Hall, New York, where his creative desires took more purposeful shape, and at New York City College. Later he went to Columbia University. From 1940 to 1949 he taught in various New York schools, and then joined the staff of Oregon State University where he stayed until 1961. Thereafter he taught at Bennington State College, Vermont.

His first novel, ***The Natural*** (1952), published when he was nearly forty, had no Jewish characters. And it is in other respects—it [tells] the life of a great baseball player in the form of a version of the Grail myth—uncharacteristic.

With ***The Assistant*** (1957) Malamud received international acclaim. The novel tells the story of a young gentile drifter who robs a Job-like, Jewish grocer in Brooklyn during the Depression. Out of an at first unwilling remorse, the thief takes on the grocer's many sorrows, goes to work for him and, after his death elects to 'become' him by having himself circumcised. As a treatment of the theme, 'all men are Jews' it was a work of rare charity and life affirmation.

A New Life (1961), a largely satirical novel about an ex-alcoholic Jew who goes to teach at a fearful 'cow college' in the Pacific North west, had richly comic passages, but was not, on the whole, accounted a success.

The Fixer (1966) was, and remains, Malamud's most ambitious novel. But it is not his best. An attempt to take Bellow on his own ground—that of the 'big' book—its subject matter, based on true history of a poor Jew wrongly accused of ritual murder in Tsarist Russia, made a successful movie, starring Alan Bates. It also collected a Pulitzer Prize and National Book Award. But despite its evident technical mastery some air of artificiality prevented all but a small minority from citing it as the masterpiece it was evidently intended to be.

Nevertheless Malamud was now established as America's second Jewish novelist (Mailer was in literary terms a spent force; Salinger had long retreated into silence; Philip Roth had proved insubstantial after a meteoric start.) But he was plainly outranked by the more versatile Bellow and this is said to have worried him even to the point of making writing more difficult.

Pictures of Fidelman (1969), a picaresque frolic in Italy, certainly represented the nadir to that point. But ***The Tenant*** (1971) and ***Dubin's Lives*** (1979) indicated a welcome return of form and confidence. In these novels, whose protagonists were both writers, Malamud intelligently examined the question of whether art confers freedom and whether the search for truth actually makes its realisation more likely.

But it is Malamud's short stories which will probably give more enduring pleasure than any of the novels he wrote after ***The Fixer,*** although all his work was of the highest integrity.

In a collection like ***Rembrandt's Hat*** (1973) he is capable, in a few, spare, pages, of distilling the sublimity in suffering of protagonists beaten down by poverty, locked in the loneliness of their own inarticulacy or utterly deceived in their opinion of the world's kindness.

It is in this that his supreme gift lies.

"Bernard Malamud: Compassionate Observer of Human Experience," in The Times, *London, March 20, 1986.*

FRED LUTZ

[Malamud] was not a highly polished literary stylist. Sometimes, in fact, he seemed to be writing with a blunt instrument. Nonetheless, he was a natural story teller, and his characters were invariably so vivid and likable, his plots so intriguing and his themes so profoundly moving, that he was often regarded as one of the major American writers of this century. He quite possibly deserved to win a Nobel Prize, but he never did.

Many readers know Malamud from two popular novels that were made into films, ***The Fixer,*** which won the Pulitzer Prize and the National Book Award for fiction in 1967, and ***The Natural*** (1952).

These two books, respectively about a handyman falsely accused of ritual murder in czarist Russia and an aging baseball player trying to salvage his hard-luck life in America, have the same theme in common with all of Malamud's novels and stories: The inevitability of human suffering and the necessity of making a new life afterward.

The Natural was Malamud's first novel, and suffering is at its very heart and soul. Roy Hobbs, the hapless lonely hero . . . , is told something by a woman that Malamud himself obviously believed: "We have two lives, Roy, the life we learn with and the life we live with after that."

Malamud was Jewish, and the lives he examined in his work were usually Jewish, which was forever earning him comparison with such other important American Jewish writers as Saul Bellow and Philip Roth. But Malamud's Jewish heroes—who always eventually became universal heroes—seldom have either the glamour or the prosperity of Bellow's and Roth's.

Instead, Malamud was more interested in those who had to struggle and suffer.

In ***Dubin's Lives*** (1977), his aging protagonist is a biographer, a thinly disguised alter-ego for the author, and Malamud's description of him might apply equally well to his creator: "He was tired of [writing] the obits but stayed with them because he liked summarizing people's lives. The editor had asked him to emphasize successful careers but he sometimes managed to slip in a failed life."

Malamud managed to slip in more than a few failed lives in his work, but the purpose of it is always the same: His fictional people can then learn through their trials how to reconcile their own disappointments, their own strong passions and obsessions, with the moral obligations they feel to start life over again.

This is also the way Malamud deals with his other primary subject, the ethical import of being Jewish.

As critic Jason Epstein once noted, "***The Assistant,*** Malamud's novel of 1957, is about little other than the question of what it means to be a Jew." And: "To be a true Jew, for Morris Bober, the book's exemplary character, is 'to do what is right, to be honest, to be good.' It is also, according to the rabbi who delivers the eulogy over the dead Bober, to suffer and endure, 'but with hope.' Hope is decisive for Malamud" [see *CLC,* Vol. 27]. (p. 1)

The sense of wonder at our being in the cosmos is sometimes an edgy one for Malamud. As a character in a short story called **"The German Refugee"** says, "There were a few large stars in the sky and they made me sad."

Another character in the story **"My Son the Murderer,"** yells, "Everything's temporary. Why should I add more to what's temporary? My gut feels temporary. The goddamn world is temporary. On top of that I don't want temporary work. I want the opposite of temporary, but where is it?"

In Malamud, something close to the opposite generally lies in people learning to care about other people more than themselves. (pp. 1, 4)

[Malamud] especially liked the short-story form for its "fast payoff."

One of his collections of short stories, ***The Magic Barrel,*** also won a National Book Award (1959). And in these stories Malamud frequently shows vividly and quickly his special talent, which is for capturing the flashpoint where painful self-knowledge becomes a sort of moral epiphany.

In **"Idiots First,"** for example, a poor and dying father, desperate to provide for his retarded son by sending him away, meets the personification of death in a train station. After some pitifully realistic begging that has gone before, this mortal meeting seems a breathtaking leap into sheer imaginative genius, with Malamud making his point in a kind of emotional explosion: If we care enough about those we love, our own well-being is only of secondary importance.

But perhaps little of the foregoing suggests enough of what was another of Malamud's great gifts, his sly and wonderfully earthy sense of humor, which he could always express in just a few deft lines.

In a short story called **"The Letter,"** for example, a man is described as ". . . angular . . . with deep-set bluish eyes and craggy features that looked as though they had been hacked out of a tree."

Or, in the novel ***God's Grace*** (1982): "Calvin Cohn was alone, forlorn. When he raised his head the silence all but cracked his neck."

Malamud could also achieve fast comic results with his witty dialogue, such as this from ***The Assistant:***

"'What do you need, Louis?'

'Cut out the wisecracks, Helen. Would it interest you that I would honestly like to marry you?' He paled at his nerve.

She was surprised, touched.

'Thank you,' she murmured.

'Thank you ain't good enough. Give me yes or no.'

'No, Louis.'

'That's what I thought.' He gazed blankly at the ocean."

Seriocomic rejections like this are nearly always survived, though. And that's because most of all, Malamud's love for his fellow human beings shines through all his work, through nearly all the characters he created, like a strong beacon for a safe moral harbor.

His Jewish heroes invariably become simply human heroes, everyday and universal, people who can understand the language of the heart.

As one of Malamud's characters reflects in the short story **"Black Is My Favorite Color":** "What I'm saying is . . . for me there's only one human color and that's the color of blood." (p. 4)

Fred Lutz, "Malamud's Art Celebrated Life," in The Blade, *April 13, 1986, pp. 1, 4.*

PHILIP ROTH

[*Roth is an American fiction writer and critic best known for the novels* Goodbye, Columbus *(1959),* Portnoy's Complaint *(1969), and his Zuckerman novels, including* Zuckerman Bound *(1985). Critics commonly refer to him as a Jewish writer, and his works are included among the best examples of contemporary American fiction. The three most prevalent subjects of his work—sexuality, Jewish-American life, and the role of the artist in modern society—have been a source of controversy throughout Roth's career: he has been praised for the skill and insight with which he treats these subjects, as well as denounced for what some critics have perceived as gratuitous obscenity and ethnic libel. As a literary artist, Roth is esteemed for his consummate use of language for the purposes of humor and satire. In the following excerpt Roth recalls some of the key moments in his friendship with Malamud, paying tribute to the dignity of the man and to the moral artistry of his work.*]

In February 1961 I traveled west from Iowa City, where I was teaching in the Writers' Workshop of the university and finishing a second book, to give a lecture called "Writing American Fiction" at a small community college in Monmouth, Ore. A close buddy from my graduate school days at the University of Chicago was teaching there and had arranged the invitation. I accepted not only because of the opportunity the trip afforded me to see, for the first time in five years, my friends Bob and Ida Baker and their small children, but because Baker promised that if I came out he'd arrange for me to meet Bernard Malamud.

Bern taught nearby at the state university in Eugene, Ore. He'd been in Eugene (pop. 50,000) since leaving New York (pop. 8,000,000) and a night school teaching job there in 1949—12 years in the Far West instructing freshmen Oregonians in the fundamentals of English composition, and writing his unorthodox baseball novel, ***The Natural,*** his masterpiece set in darkest Brooklyn, ***The Assistant,*** as well as four or five of the best American short stories I'd every read (or ever will). The other stories weren't bad either.

In the early 50's I was reading Malamud's stories, later collected in ***The Magic Barrel,*** as they appeared—the very moment they appeared—in *Partisan Review* and the old *Commentary*. He seemed to me then to be doing no less for his lonely Jews and their peculiarly immigrant, Jewish forms of failure—for those Malamudian men "who never stopped hurting"—than was Samuel Beckett, in his longer fiction, for misery-ridden Molloy and Malone. Both writers, while bound inextricably to the common life of the clan, severed their racial memories from the larger social and historical setting, and then, focusing as narrowly as they could upon the dismal, daily round of resistance borne by the most helpless of their *landsmen,* created, improbably, parables of frustration charged with the gravity of the grimmest philosophers.

Not unlike Beckett, Malamud wrote of a meager world of pain in a language all his own—in his case, an English that often appeared, even outside the idiosyncratic dialogue, to have in large part been clipped together from out of what one might have thought to be the least promising stockpile, most unmagical barrel, around: the locutions, inversions and diction of Jewish immigrant speech, a heap of broken verbal bones that looked, until he came along in those early stories to make them dance to his sad tune, to be of no use to anyone any longer other than the Borscht Belt comic and the professional nostalgia-monger. Even when he pushed this parable prose to its limits, Malamud's metaphors retained a proverbial ring. In his most consciously original moments, when he sensed in his grimly told, impassioned tales the need to sound his deepest note, he remained true to what seemed old and homely, matter-of-factly emitting the most touchingly unadorned poetry to make things even sadder than they already were—"He tried to say some sweet thing but his tongue hung in his mouth like dead fruit on a tree, and his heart was a black-painted window."

The 46-year-old man that I met at the Bakers' little house in Monmouth, Ore., in 1961 never let on that he could have written such a line, neither then nor in all the years I knew him. At first glance Bern looked to someone who'd grown up among such people like nothing so much as an insurance agent—he could have passed for a colleague of my father's, employed, as he was during the 30's and 40's, by the downtown Newark district office of the Metropolitan Life. When Malamud entered the Bakers' hallway after having attended my lecture, and stood there on the welcome mat removing his wet overshoes, I saw a conscientious, courteous, pinochle-playing workingman of the kind whose kibbitzing and conversation had been the background music of my childhood, a stubborn, seasoned, life insurance salesman who does not flee the snarling dog or alarm the children when he appears after dark at the top of the tenement stairwell—soberly reassuring in dark fedora and black overcoat, and carrying beneath his arm one of Metropolitan Life's large, black, oblong ledgers, the collection book which to me, as a boy, looked like a scaled-down portent of the coffin—to try to pry out of the poor breadwinner the half a buck that will prevent his policy from lapsing. He doesn't frighten anyone but he doesn't make the place light up with laughter either: he is, after all, the insurance man, whom you can only beat by dying.

That was the other surprise about Malamud. Very little laughter, no display at all of the playfulness that flickered on and off even in those barren, underheated, poorly furnished flats wherein were enacted the needs of his entombed, let alone of the eerie clowning that is the charm of ***The Natural.*** There were Malamud stories like **"Angel Levine"**—and later **"The Jewbird"** and **"Talking Horse"**—where the joke seemed only an inch away from the art, where the charm of the art was just the way it humourously hovered at the edge of the joke, and yet during all our meetings, over 25 years, I remember him telling me two jokes. Jewish dialect jokes, recounted very expertly indeed—but that was it: for 25 years two jokes were enough.

There was no need to overdo anything other than the responsibility to his art. Bern didn't exhibit himself and he didn't consider it necessary to exhibit his themes, certainly not casually to a stranger, if even among the friends he liked to assemble in the civilized setting of his own living room. He couldn't have exhibited himself even if he'd been foolish enough to try, and foolish enough to try he couldn't have been either—never being foolish was a small part of his larger burden. S. Levin, the Chaplinesque professor of *A New Life,* teaching his first college class with a wide-open fly, is hilariously foolish time and again, but not Bern. No more could Kafka have become a cockroach than Malamud could have metamorphosed into a Levin, comically outfoxed by an erotic mishap on the dark back roads of mountainous Oregon, and sneaking homewards, half-naked, at 3 A.M., the Sancho Panza beside him a sexually disgruntled, barroom waitress dressed in only one shoe and a bra. Seymour Levin the ex-drunkard and Gregor Samsa the bug ingeniously embody acts of colossal self-travesty, affording both authors a weirdly exhilarating sort of masochistic relief from the weight of sobriety and dignified inhibition that was plainly the cornerstone of their staid comportment. With Malamud as with many writers, exuberant showmanship, like searing self-mockery, was to be revealed only through what Heine called *Maskenfreiheit,* the freedom conferred by masks.

The sorrowing chronicler of human need clashing with human need, of need mercilessly resisted—and abated glancingly if at all—of blockaded lives racked with need for the light, the lift, of a little hope—"A child throwing a ball straight up saw a bit of pale sky"—preferred to present himself as someone whose needs were nobody's business but his own. Yet his was in fact a need so harsh that it makes one ache even now to consider the sheer size of it. It was the need to consider long and seriously every last demand of an overtaxed, overtaxing conscience torturously exacerbated by the pathos of human need unabated. That was a theme of his that he couldn't hide entirely from anyone who thought at all about where the man who could have passed himself off as your insurance agent was joined to the ferocious moralist of the claustrophobic stories about "things you can't get past." In ***The Assistant,*** the petty criminal and drifter Frank Alpine, while doing penance behind the counter of a failing grocery store that he'd once helped to rob, has a "terrifying insight" about himself: "that all the while he was acting like he wasn't, he was a man of stern morality." I wonder if early in adult life Bern didn't have an insight no less terrifying about himself, maybe more terrifying—that he was a man of stern morality who could act *only* like what he was.

Between our first meeting in Oregon in February 1961 and our last meeting this past summer at his home in Bennington, Vt., I rarely saw Bern more than a couple of times a year, and for several years, after I'd published an essay about American-Jewish writing in *The New York Review of Books* which had examined ***Pictures of Fidelman*** and ***The Fixer*** from a perspective he didn't like—and couldn't have been expected to—we didn't see each other at all. In the mid-60's, when I was frequently a guest for long periods at the Yaddo artists' colony in Saratoga Springs, N.Y., a short drive from Bennington, he and his wife, Ann, would have me over when I felt like escaping for a few hours from the Yaddo solitude; in the 70's, when we were both members of the Yaddo corporation board, we'd see each other at one of the biannual meetings; when the Malamuds began to take refuge in Manhattan from the Vermont winters, and I was still living in New York, we'd meet occasionally near their Gramercy Park apartment for dinner; and when Bern and Ann visited London, where I'd begun spending a part of my time, they'd come to have dinner with Claire Bloom and me.

Though Bern and I ended up most evenings talking together about books and writing, we hardly ever alluded to each other's fiction and never seriously discussed it, observing a discreet, unwritten rule of propriety that exists among novelists, as among rival teammates in sports, who understand just how much candor can be sustained by professional fellow-feeling that develops from something more binding than mere neighborliness but is still less ardent than blood brotherhood, however deep the respect may run. Blake says "opposition is true friendship," and though that sounds very bracing, particularly to the argumentative, and subscribing to its wisdom probably works out well for everyone in the best of all possible worlds, among the writers in this world, where resentment, touchiness, uncertainty and pride can make for a rather potent explosive, one learns to settle for something a little more amicable than outright opposition if one wants to have any true writer friends at all. Even those writers who just adore opposition usually get about as much as they can stand from their daily work.

It was in London that we first arranged to meet again after the 1974 *New York Review* essay and the exchange of letters about it that was to be the last communication between us for a couple of years. His letter had been characteristically terse and colloquial, a single sentence, sounding perhaps a little less fractious than it looked all alone on that white sheet of typing paper and inscribed above the signature in his tiny, measured hand. What I'd written about ***Fidelman*** and ***The Fixer,*** he informed me, "is your problem, not mine." I wrote right back to tell him that in time he might come to see that by my exposing fictional skeletons he was perhaps not wholly aware of himself, I'd probably done him a favor of precisely the kind William Blake advocated. I didn't have quite the gall to mention Blake but that was more or less my tack: what I'd written would help him out. Not too awful as these exchanges go, but not one likely to ennoble either of us in the history of correspondence.

The London reconciliation didn't take long for Bern and me to pull off. At 7:30 P.M. Claire's doorbell rang and there, as expected, on the dot as always, were the Malamuds. Under the porch light I gave Ann a hug and a kiss, and then, with my hand extended, plunged past her, advancing upon Bern, who with his own outstretched hand was briskly coming up the step toward me. In our eagerness each to be the first to forgive—or first perhaps to be forgiven—we wound up overshooting the handshake and kissing on the lips, rather like the poor baker Lieb and the even less fortunate Kobotsky at the conclusion of **"The Loan."** The two Jews in that Malamud tale, once immigrants together out of steerage, meet after many years of broken friendship and, at the back of Lieb's shop, listen to the story of the afflictions in each other's lives, stories so affecting that Lieb forgets all about the bread in his oven which goes up in smoke. "The loaves in the trays," the story ends, "were blackened bricks—charred corpses. Kobotsky and the baker embraced and sighed over their lost youth. They pressed mouths together and parted forever." We, on the other hand, went into the house for a perfectly cooked dinner and thereafter remained friends for good.

In July 1985, just back from England, Claire and I drove north from Connecticut to have lunch and spend the afternoon with the Malamuds in Bennington. The summer before they had made the two-and-a-half-hour trip down to us and then spent the night, but Bern wasn't equal to the journey now. The debilitating after-effects of the bypass surgery and stroke of three years earlier had begun increasingly to sap his strength, and the effort not to submit without a fight to all the disabling physical problems had begun to beat him down. I saw how weak he'd got as soon as we drove up. Bern, who always managed, regardless of the weather, to be waiting in the driveway to greet you and see you off, was out there all right in his poplin jacket, but as he nodded a rather grim welcome, he looked to be listing slightly to one side at the same time that he seemed to be holding himself, by dint of willpower alone, absolutely still, as though the least movement would bring him down. It was impossible to discern in him even a remnant of the stolid, resolute insurance agent I'd envisaged years ago. The 46-year-old transplanted Brooklynite that I'd met in the Far West, that undiscourageable round-the-clock worker with the serious, attentive face and the balding crown and the pitiless Eugene, Ore., haircut, whose serviceable, surface mildness was in no way intended to mislead anyone about the molten obstinacy at the core, was now, without question, a frail and very sick old man, whose tenacity was just about used up.

It was his heart and the stroke and all the medication that had done the damage, but to a longtime reader of the man and his fiction it couldn't help but appear as though the pursuit of that unremitting aspiration that he shared with so many of his characters—to break down the iron limits of circumstance and self in order to live a better life—had finally taken its toll. Though he'd never said much to me about his childhood, from the little I knew about his mother's death when he was still a boy, and about the father's poverty and the handicapped brother whose lamentable fate had become Bern's responsibility, I imagined that he'd had no choice but to forgo youth and accept adulthood at a very early age. And now he looked it—like a man who'd had to be a man for just too long a time. I thought of his story **"Take Pity"** and that unforgettable exchange between Davidoff and Rosen in what is perhaps the most excruciating parable that he ever wrote about life's unyieldingness even to—*especially* to—the most unyielding longings. When quizzed by Davidoff, a heavenly census-taker, about how a poor Jewish refugee died, Rosen, himself newly arrived among the dead, replies, "Broke in him something, that's how." "Broke what?" "Broke what breaks."

It was a very sad afternoon. We talked in the living room before lunch; Bern asked Claire about her daughter's opera career, they talked about singers and singing, and then he went on to speak about his own two children, but concentration was a struggle for him, and though his was a will powerless to back away from any difficult task, it was disheartening to realize how imposing a challenge just pursuing a conversation with friends had become.

As we were leaving the living room to have lunch outdoors on the back porch, Bern asked if he might read aloud to me later the opening chapters of a first draft of a novel. He'd never before read to me or asked my opinion of a work-in-progress and I was surprised by the request. I was also a little perturbed, and wondered throughout lunch what sort of book it could be, conceived and begun in the midst of all this hardship by a writer whose memory of even the multiplication tables had been clouded now for several years and whose vision, also impaired by the stroke, made shaving every morning what he'd wryly described to me as "an adventure."

After coffee Bern went to his study for the manuscript, a thin sheaf of pages perfectly typed and neatly clipped together. Ann, whose back had been bothering her, excused herself to take a rest, and when Bern settled back at the table it was to begin to read, a little formally, in his quiet insistent way, to just Claire and me.

I noticed when he sat down that all around his chair, on the porch floor, were scattered crumbs from his lunch. A tremor had made eating a little bit of an adventure too, and yet he had driven himself to write these pages, to undertake once again this ordeal. I remembered the opening of ***The Assistant,*** the picture of the aging grocer, Morris Bober, dragging the heavy milk cases in from the curb at 6 o'clock on a November morning. I also remembered the exertion that had killed him—near financial disaster and physical collapse, he nonetheless goes out at night to shovel six inches of fresh March snow from the sidewalk in front of the imprisoning store. When I got home that evening, I re-read the pages describing the grocer's last great effort to do his job. "To his surprise the wind wrapped him in an icy jacket, his apron flapping noisily. He had expected, the last of March, a milder night. . . . He flung another load of snow into the street. 'A better life,' he muttered."

It turned out that not too many words were typed on each page and that the first-draft chapters were extremely brief. I didn't dislike what I heard because there was nothing yet to like or dislike—he hadn't got started, really, however much he wanted to think otherwise. It was like having been led into a dark hole to see by torchlight the first Malamud story ever scratched upon a cave wall. What was awesome wasn't what was on the wall but, rather, contemplating the power of the art that had been generated by such simple markings.

I didn't want to lie to him but, looking at the thin sheaf of pages in the hands of that very frail man, I couldn't tell the truth, even if he was expecting it of me. I said simply, and only a little evasively, that it seemed to me a beginning like all beginnings. That was quite truthful enough for a man of 71 who had published 12 of the most original works of fiction written by an American in the past 35 years. Trying to be constructive, I suggested that perhaps the narrative opened too slowly and that he might better begin further on, with one of the later chapters. Then I asked where it was all going. "What comes next?" I said, hoping we could pass on to what it was he had in mind if not yet down on the page.

But he wouldn't let go of what he'd written—at such cost—as easily as that. Nothing was ever as easy as that, least of all the end of things. In a soft voice suffused with fury, he said, "What's next isn't the point."

In the silence that followed, before Claire eased him gently into a discussion of the kind of character he was imagining as his hero, he was perhaps as angry at failing to master the need for assurance so nakedly displayed as he was with me for having nothing good to say. He wanted to be told that what he had painfully composed while enduring all his burdens was something more than he himself must have known it to be in his heart. He was suffering so, I wished I could have said that it *was* something more, and that if I'd said it, he could have believed me.

Before I left for England in the fall I wrote him a note telling him that I was off, and inviting him and Ann to come down to Connecticut the next summer—it was our turn to entertain them. The response that reached me in London some weeks later was pure, laconic Malamudese. They'd be delighted to visit, but he reminded me, "next summer is next summer."

He died on March 18, three days before spring. (pp. 1, 40-1)

Philip Roth, "Pictures of Malamud," in The New York Times Book Review, *April 20, 1986, pp. 1, 40-1.*

RICHARD GILMAN

[American critic and nonfiction writer, Gilman has published several books, including Common and Uncommon Masks: Writings on Theatre 1961-70 *(1970) for which he won the George Jean Nathan Award for drama criticism, and* The Making of Modern Drama *(1974), a study of the changes in dramatic art over the past century. Gilman has served as drama critic or literary editor for various periodicals, including* Commonweal, Newsweek, The New Republic, *and* Partisan Review. *His "progressive criticism" earned him the American Academy and Institute of Arts Morton Dauwen Zabel Award in 1979. In the following excerpt Gilman analyzes Malamud's writings, particularly for their "humanistic values," and praises the author for his evocative short stories.]*

Malamud was known for having had "compassion," "moral wisdom," a concern for the "ordinary man." True, but was that what made him a good writer? . . .

If anything, what we might call the humanistic values of his writing gave him an air of being a little out of date—earnest, kindly, thoughtful. His gaze was on the perennial, instead of conjuring with our confusions and chaos and inventing brilliantly in order to confront and combat them. He was a storyteller in an era when most of our best writers have been suspicious of straightforward narrative. Nobody thinks of him as an innovator, unless being among the first to bring the rhythms and intonations of Jewish, or Yiddish, speech to formal prose counts as innovation.

He himself contributed to the image of a somewhat old-fashioned, or unfashionable, champion of the spirit, a humanist in a literary era in which humanism is almost anomalous. Again and again he used the word "human" in the occasional interviews and speeches he gave: "My work . . . is an idea of dedication to the human. . . . If you don't respect man, you cannot respect my work. I'm in defense of the human." And he spoke of art as "sanctifying human life and freedom."

So what's to object, as he might have put it? Those lofty, sonorous phrases, more mottoes than anything else, left me uncomfortable when they came from him and leave me so when they come from others. It isn't enough to speak of defending the human or respecting man, or rather it sounds a bit self-serving and even pompous. Did he think it was what was expected of him? To shift the burden to us, isn't it naive to say that he "touched our hearts"? Bad fiction, melodramas, kitsch touch our hearts too, bring tears more reliably, certainly in greater floods, than does good writing.

It seems to me that Malamud was usually at his weakest when he sought or fell into too direct a way to our emotions, when he was most self-consciously "humane." I think of stories like **"Black Is My Favorite Color," "The Lady of the Lake,"** and **"The Loan,"** each brought down by predictable sentiment, and even more of novels such as ***The Fixer,*** at once heavy, pseudo-lyrical, and tendentious; ***The Tenants,*** where social painfulness isn't fully transmuted into imaginative truth; and ***God's Grace,*** embarrassingly cute in a mode of fantasy—jocose, biblically flavored science fiction—to which he wasn't suited.

To what, then, was he suited? to begin with, there is that swift rooting of so many of his protagonists in an occupation or a past. His opening words located his characters: "S. Levin, formerly a drunkard"; "Davidov, the census-taker"; "Manischevitz, a tailor"; "Fidelman, a self-confessed failure as a painter"; "Kessler, formerly an egg-candler." Having so placed them, relieved of the necessity to develop them, yet having granted them a specificity that kept them from being parabolic, he moved them quickly into position to experience their fates. These are destinies of self-recognition—ironic, painful, lugubrious, or threnodic—and they are, when all is working well, revelatory of the morally or psychically unknown, or not yet known. And along the way, there are the pleasures of the text, the little fates of language: . . .

From **"The Magic Barrel":** "Life, despite their frantic yoohooings, had passed them by."

From **"The Girl of My Dreams":** ". . . he pitied her, her daughter, the world. Who not?"

From **"The Death of Me":** "His heart, like a fragile pitcher, toppled from the shelf and bump bumped down the stairs, cracking at the bottom." (p. 40)

From ***Dubin's Lives:*** "On the road a jogger trotted toward him, a man with a blue band around his head. He slowed down as Dubin halted. 'What are you running for?' the biographer asked him. 'All I can't stand to do. What about you?' 'Broken heart, I think.' 'Ah, too bad about that.' They trotted in opposing directions."

From somewhere: "exaltation went where exaltation goes."

He was neither a realist nor a fantasist. He was both. I don't mean he alternated between reality and fantasy, but that at his best the line between the two was obliterated. Observation gave way to imagining. Without strain, experience flowed into dream. In some stories characters and properties literally move up into the air, as in Chagall, with whose paintings these tales have been justly compared. "He heard an odd noise, as though of a whirring of wings, and when he strained for a wider view, could have sworn he saw a dark figure borne aloft on a pair of magnificent black wings'' (**"Angel Levine"**). ''He pictured, in her, his own redemption. Violins and lit candles revolved in the sky'' (**"The Magic Barrel"**). Even a story like **"The Jewbird"** (to my mind perhaps his finest), a piece that appears all whimsy and allegorical effort, is anchored in pebbly actuality, an actuality into which the bird flies, scattering meanings as he does feathers, an agent of our own self-knowledge.

In a culture where quantity is god it may seem demeaning to say that Bernard Malamud was a better short-story writer than novelist. Yet a case can be made that many great or good writers of fiction in English have been better makers of stories than of novels: Hawthorne, to go way back, Lawrence, Hemingway, Fitzgerald, Cheever, Flannery O'Connor. She wrote in a letter of 1958 about a short-story writer ''who is better than any one of them, including myself. Go to the library [for] a book called ***The Magic Barrel*** by Bernard Malamud.'' (He was immensely pleased, for he greatly esteemed her.)

To be sure, the novels have their pleasures, but even in the best of them his predilection for the shorter form often shows itself, straining against what novels are supposed to be. Books as good as ***The Assistant*** and ***Dubin's Lives*** are, I think, more notable in some ways for their nearly self-contained sequences than for their architectonics and narrative continuity. He may have called ***Pictures of Fidelman*** an ''Exhibition'' because he saw that it would otherwise be taken for a novel (it was by most anyway) and faulted for its lack of development. It wasn't easy for him to follow a fiction through a long, complicated course to its end. His wish for those qualities of epiphany, of revelation and decisive verbal triumph, kept breaking through.

What makes his place in literature and our memories secure isn't his themes or subjects. It isn't his nobility of purpose, his compassion or moral understanding, in short, his humanism. Or rather it's not those qualities in themselves, as detached and detachable essences. One wants to say to the sentimental admirers of his fiction (as well as to those erstwhile admirers who found him growing ''cold'' in his later work) that imaginative writing isn't the exemplification of preexisting values and virtues. It is their discovery, against all odds, in the shocks and surprises of the unfolding tale. The imagination teaches us newly. It doesn't instruct us in what we already know, and it certainly doesn't grant us our comfortable, ''humane'' wishes.

''It's not easy to be moral,'' thinks Cronin, the protagonist of **"A Choice of Profession."** It's at least as difficult to shed moral light in fiction, where the recalcitrance of words, their pressure toward the familiar—and hence the unenlightening—is constant and unyielding.

''Creativity,'' Arthur Koestler wrote, ''is the defeat of habit by originality.'' Habit was for Bernard Malamud, as for all true writers, the enemy from which you wrest the victories you can, replacing, through a series of miracles, the banalities or weariness of language with its grace. (pp. 40-41)

Richard Gilman, ''Malamud's Grace,'' in The New Republic, *Vol. 194, No. 19, May 12, 1986, pp. 40-1.*

Jaroslav Seifert

September 23, 1901 - January 10, 1986

Czechoslovakian poet.

(See also *CLC*, Vol. 34.)

PRINCIPAL WORKS

Město v slzách (poetry) 1920
Samá láska (poetry) 1923
Na vlnách T.S.F. (poetry) 1925
Slavík zpívá špatně (poetry) 1926
Hvězdy nad rajskou zahradou (essays) 1929
Poštovni holub (poetry) 1929
Jablko z klínà (poetry) 1933
Ruce Venušiny (poetry) 1936
Osm dnů (poetry) 1937
[*Eight Days*, 1985]
Zhasněte světla (poetry) 1938
Světlem oděna (poetry) 1940
Kamenný most (poetry) 1944
Přílba hlíny (poetry) 1945
Ruka a plamm (poetry) 1948
Píseň o Viktorce (poetry) 1950
Maminka (poetry) 1954
Koncert na ostrově (poetry) 1965
Odlévani zvonů (poetry) 1967
[*The Casting of Bells*, 1983]
Halleyova kometa (poetry) 1969
Morový sloup (poetry) 1977
[*The Plague Monument*, 1977; also published as *The Plague Column*, 1979]
Deštnik z Piccadilly (poetry) 1978
[*An Umbrella from Piccadilly*, 1983]
Všecky krásy světa (memoirs) 1981
Býti básníkem (poetry) 1983
The Selected Poetry of Jaroslav Seifert (poetry) 1986

© Lütfi Özkök

JERRY COHEN

Nobel prize winner Jaroslav Seifert, a Czechoslovak poet who was little known outside his homeland but considered a national treasure by his countrymen, died [January 10] at age 84 in a Prague hospital of an apparent heart attack.

Seifert, who went through as many phases as a poet as Pablo Picasso did as a painter, for years had suffered from a variety of ailments, including heart problems and diabetes. . . .

"He was a very European poet," said Michael Heim, associate professor of Russian and Czechoslovakian literature at UCLA and currently a visiting professor at Harvard. Thus, Heim said, his work cannot be likened to that of any poet writing in English.

His many different phases, Heim said, ranged from "an ebullient period" when Seifert began writing in the 1920s, to a surrealistic phase in the 1930s, to vehement patriotism during the Nazi occupation and, finally, "a mediative, philosophical stage" toward the end of his life.

But throughout, Heim said, a stream of sensuality, "even eroticism," pervaded his writing, just as the celebration of his homeland and his native Prague was omnipresent in it.

His poetry, said James Ragan, director of the USC graduate school's professional writing program, "was at all times optimistic, reflecting a championing of the human self. I think that's primarily why he was awarded the Nobel Prize, because he suggested a new liberated spirit in writing (behind the Iron Curtain) after the Stalin era."

Both Heim and Ragan said Seifert's poems—he wrote 30 volumes—are hard to come by in this country. "Two volumes are available in very limited editions, one poorly translated," Heim said.

Seifert himself once said that non-Czechs found his work difficult to appreciate because "the inner rhythm" of his poetry defied translation. Critics have said he would have gained international recognition long before the Nobel award had he written in a more widely read language.

Although he was a Communist as a youth, he became disillusioned with the party in the late 1920s. Thereafter, he was in and out of party favor during the turbulent decades that followed in Czechoslovakia. The state-run news agency, in announcing his death [January 10], described him as "a prominent Czech poet, national artist (and) winner of the 1984 Nobel Prize for Literature."

At the time of the Nobel award, Seifert, who had suffered a heart attack in 1983, was unable to travel to Stockholm to accept it. A son and daughter served as his proxies at the ceremony. . . .

Seifert was born into a working-class family, and he recounted in memoirs written in the 1970s how his mother, a staunch Catholic, gave his father, a committed Social Democrat, a communist medallion while he gave her a crucifix upon their marriage. "This shows how democratic the conditions were in our family," he wrote.

Seifert's early poetry, Heim said, was "innovative and playful and some say it is his best work." Although, so far as is known, he never was imprisoned during the Nazi occupation, his poetry in the early 1940s was fervently independent.

After the war, he became editor of a trade union daily and edited a literary daily while still producing the lyrical poems that his countrymen found so captivating. But he soon was at odds with authorities—after having briefly praised the Soviet Union in his writings—when he expressed disillusionment with the Communist takeover in a volume called ***The Song of Viktorka.***

And publication of his new works was suspended after a 1956 speech in which he criticized state cultural policies. He never became active in Prague's dissident scene, preferring instead to live and write in relative seclusion.

However, beginning in the 1960s, he gradually was rehabilitated during the stirrings of the so-called "Prague Spring," when Czechs sought to replace Soviet-line communism with a system that allowed more personal freedom.

But when Soviet troops crushed the democratic movement in 1968, he again fell into disfavor, particularly after he signed a human rights petition that called for the government to abide by the Helsinki Accords.

In his later years, dissidents and the government alike paid respect to Seifert, even though he still was not accorded the privileges and publication advantages granted fully approved writers. Some of his work was censored or published in editions so limited that they quickly sold out.

Seifert spent the last years of his life in a villa in a quiet district of Prague, surrounded by his vast collection of cactus plants—and still writing. He once said, "I'm being laughed at for being old and still writing love poems, but I shall write them until the end."

One of those poems, **"And Now, Goodby"** contained these lines:

> To all those million verses in the world I've added just
> a few.
> They probably are no wiser than a cricket's chirrup.
> I know. Forgive me. I'm coming to the end.

Jerry Cohen, "Czech Poet Jaroslav Seifert, 84, Dies," in Los Angeles Times, *January 11, 1986, p. 22.*

HERBERT MITGANG

Jaroslav Seifert, the Czechoslovak poet who won the Nobel Prize for Literature in 1984, died of a heart ailment [January 10]. . . .

Although his work was little known outside of Czechoslovakia, mainly because of the difficulties of translating what he called its "inner rhythms," Mr. Seifert was beloved by his countrymen, both as a poet and as a symbol of freedom of expression for writers under an oppressive regime. In 1968, he condemned the Soviet invasion of his country and was one of those who signed Charter 77, an appeal to the Government for greater freedom.

In a sense, Mr. Seifert wrote his own epitaph in a poem, **"And Now Goodbye"**—published some 15 years ago in a book called ***The Plague Column*** and translated by Ewald Osers—that summed up his life as a man of letters:

> To all those million verses in the world I've added just
> a few.
> They probably were no wiser than a cricket's chirrup.
> I know. Forgive me. I'm coming to the end.
>
> They were not even the first foot-marks in the lunar
> dust.
> If at times they sparkled after all it was not their light.
> I loved this language . . .
>
> But I make no excuse.
> I believe that seeking beautiful words
> Is better than killing and murdering.

Mr. Seifert was the first Czechoslovak writer to win the Nobel Prize. The Swedish Academy said his work was "endowed with freshness, sensuality and rich inventiveness, and provides a liberating image of the indomitable spirit and versatility of man."

Nearly 30 volumes of his poetry were published, but he was relatively unknown in the United States except among scholars and Americans of Czechoslovak origin. When he received the Nobel Prize, only one of his books—***The Casting of the Bells,*** translated by Tom O'Grady and Paul Jagasich, and published by The Spirit That Moves Us Press in Iowa City—was in print, in an edition of 1,000 copies.

Mr. Seifert was born in 1901 in a working-class district in Prague, where he received his education in the secondary schools. He began his career as a journalist for various Prague dailies and periodicals. In 1930, he became editor-in-chief of *Nova Scena,* a theater monthly, and throughout the 1930's and 40's he continued to write for daily newspapers, including *Prace.*

At the same time, he became active in protecting the rights and liberties of authors and journalists. He served as acting chairman of the Union of Czechoslovak Writers in 1968 and as chairman in 1969-70.

While earning his living as a journalist, he also began to write poetry. For his books of verse he received state prizes in 1936,

1955 and 1968. He was honored by the Government in 1966 and named a National Artist.

In the 1920's, he was enthusiastic about the Russian Revolution and joined the Communist Party. But he broke with it after a trip to the Soviet Union, and in 1929 joined the Social Democratic Party.

During the German occupation in World War II, his poetry embodied patriotic themes. But in the postwar period it was criticized as disloyal, bourgeois, escapist and a betrayal of his class. During the thaw of 1968, when a little more freedom was permitted, he criticized his Government's cultural policies.

Mr. Seifert got into trouble with the authorities in 1968 when he went on television to read a statement by the Writers Union chastising the Warsaw Pact countries for "grossly distorted and unsubstantiated attacks from abroad aimed at the ranks of the Czechoslovak writers." Later, the censorship office banned publication of the statement.

When he was unable to go to Stockholm to receive the Nobel Prize personally because of illness, the Czechoslovak Government refused to give an exit permit to his son-in-law and secretary, Daribor Plichta, to accept the prize in his behalf.

A bilingual edition of ***The Plague Column*** (called ***The Plague Monument***) was published in 1980 by the Czechoslovak Society of Arts and Sciences. The translation was by Lyn Coffin, with a preface by William E. Harkins, professor of Slavic languages at Columbia University. . . .

[In 1985], another of Mr. Seifert's books of verse came out in English. ***An Umbrella From Piccadilly***. translated by Ewald Osers. . . .

In a review of that book in *The Times Book Review* on June 30, 1985, Michael Henry Heim wrote that while the poems take few risks, they show "the afterglow of a dazzling output," with an "absolute fidelity to intimate lyric, a love of women (for themselves and as symbols of humanity), of Prague (for itself and as a symbol of Czechslovakia), and harmony of language."

Mr. Seifert's death was reported without comment in Moscow [January 10] by the Soviet press agency Tass. It said of him merely that he was a Nobel Prize winner and People's Artist of Czechoslovakia.

The Czechoslovak Cultural Minister, Josef Svagera, was named head of a commission to make funeral arrangements. As a People's Artist, Mr. Seifert is entitled to a state funeral. He is not looked upon officially as a writer, however, because he is no longer a member of the state-controlled Writers Union.

Herbert Mitgang, "Jaroslav Seifert, Czech Poet, Is Dead," in The New York Times, *January 11, 1986, p. C29.*

EWALD OSERS

[A Czechoslovakian translator, poet, and critic, Osers has translated many works from the original Czech and German into English, including poetry by Seifert. He has also published a collection of his own poetry, Wish You Were Here *(1977). In the following excerpt Osers affectionately recalls his friendship with Seifert.]*

A translator of poetry, if he has a more than casual interest in the work of a particular poet, is bound to develop a personal relationship—almost an *alter ego*—with his author. I have therefore to confess, unashamedly, to an acute sense of personal loss at the death on January 10th, in Prague, of Jaroslav Seifert.

On reflection this sense is not just due to the translator's identification with the poet. Seifert had the kind of personal warmth, an almost child-like openness, that made me feel, even on our first meeting six years ago, that we had known one another for years.

Of course I had been familiar with Seifert's work ever since I came across his poetry as a schoolboy in Prague, in the 'thirties, and he has always held a major place in my affections. When I compiled my first anthology of modern Czech poetry during the war, in cooperation with an English poet (*Modern Czech Poetry*,. . . 1945), I chose four poems of Seifert, including a passage from his wartime cycle ***Robed in Light***. (One of the most heartening moments came [in 1984] when, in a conversation with Seifert which I recorded for a TV company, I told him that out of his entire oeuvre this was my favourite poem. He smiled and said it was his favourite poem too. What more can a poet's translator wish for?) These four poems published in 1945—without then causing the slightest ripple—were, as far as I am aware, the first Seifert poems to appear in English.

During the 'fifties and 'sixties, with their political and cultural upheavals, with Seifert's prolonged illness and silence, and again with his reemergence as a major poetic figure, I tried to keep in touch with his work—but there were other poets, Czech and German, to whose work I devoted a lot of time. And then, in the late 'sixties and early 'seventies Seifert's 'new style'—his description—his mature old-age poetry, nostalgic and lyrical but never flabby, gripped me by the throat. It was then that *London Magazine* began to publish my translations from ***The Plague Column*** and later, from ***An Umbrella from Piccadilly***. Terra Nova Editions, now sadly defunct, brought out a beautifully produced translation of ***The Plague Column*** even before its official publication in Prague, BBC Radio 3 twice broadcast a 40-minute excerpt from the cycle, and the Young Vic staged a (not perhaps altogether successful) scenic version. A few years later *London Magazine* Editions published ***An Umbrella from Piccadilly***. Again there were two BBC Radio 3 broadcasts (plus a further re-broadcast when Seifert was awarded the Nobel Prize in 1984) and a reading in St James's church as part of the Piccadilly Festival.

Meanwhile, almost incredibly, Seifert continued to write poetry and several poems from his latest volume, ***To Be a Poet,*** were published . . . in *London Magazine*.

All this happened before the Nobel Prize. Thus, when the Prize was awarded to Seifert, his name was no longer as unknown as it would have been otherwise, and we who had been involved in translating and publishing his poetry had the delighted satisfaction of a trainer whose patience has justified all his hopes and brought him a classic winner. Sadly—though he saw and approved the manuscript—he did not live to see the publication of what will be the biggest volume of his poetry in English, ***The Selected Poetry of Jaroslav Seifert,*** over 70 poems covering the whole span of his work, from 1921 to 1984. . . .

Over the last few years, on every visit to Prague, I spent a couple of hours at Seifert's home. I have never known anyone who, though physically crippled and in and out of hospital, had his cheerfulness and serenity. I have never known a person in his eighties who had his youthful, lively, curious and inquiring mind. He would question me on conditions in England—literary, social and political—and, a regular listener to the BBC, showed himself astonishingly well informed. There was in him, at the same time, a child-like innocence and the wisdom of a man who came from a poor working-class background, who owed his achievements solely to himself, one who had known (and survived) all the writers, poets and intellectuals of his generation at home, and many from abroad, and who had kept the common touch. Crippled in his chair, his crutches leaning against his desk, suffering from a number of complaints, he was yet full of fun, ready to laugh, telling anecdotes.

He had been expecting death for a long time, he had said his goodbye to the world in a number of poems over the past fifteen years, but he hated the thought of leaving the world he loved with all his senses, of leaving Prague, his beloved native city, of never seeing beautiful women again, looking at paintings, hearing Mozart's music or reading poetry.

No one who knew him, no one who was his friend, can forget him. (pp. 130-32)

Ewald Osers, "Jaroslav Seifert, 1901-1986," in London Magazine, *n.s. Vol. 26, Nos. 1 & 2, April & May, 1986, pp. 130-32.*

WILMA A. IGGERS

[Iggers, a Czechoslovakian critic and professor of German, writes about Czech, Bohemian German, and Jewish literature. Her works include Karl Kraus: A Viennese Critic of the Twentieth Century *(1967) and* Die Juden in Böhmen und Mähren *(1986). In the following excerpt Iggers offers an overview of Seifert's career, discussing his work in relation to Czechoslovakian literature and politics.]*

Jaroslav Seifert appeared on the cultural and political scene in 1920, at the age of nineteen, with the publication of his first book of poems ***Město v slzách (The City in Tears).*** He was one of the writers, most of them poets of the same generation, who banded together in an organization called Devětsil. Despite the fact that "épater les bourgeois" was written large in their program, the impact of bourgeois culture penetrated into every nook and cranny of their existence. It was Karel Čapek's translation of Apollinaire's poem "Zone" which became of inestimable importance to that very fertile generation of young Czech poets. Devětsil was remarkably international. The group's publications contained articles by foreign writers in foreign languages, even in German, although German was almost taboo in many circles. The members' poetry, however, kept its distinctly Czech character. Jiří Wolker, Vítězslav Nezval, Jaroslav Seifert—they all wrote about the simplest things, experiences of daily life, utensils, plants, and snow, only occasionally crossing over from literal meanings to metaphorical ones.

Whereas Seifert's writings underwent subtle changes in the course of time, with the exception of his poetist period, which will be discussed shortly, his themes remained relatively constant: the beauty of Prague, beautiful young women, his friendships, and, again and again, his mother. Closely linked to his mother were his detailed memories of his parents' home in Žižkov, a poor working-class neighborhood of Prague. Although he is regularly referred to as coming from a working-class family, his father was actually an unsuccessful businessman. His early phase is generally referred to as proletarian, but little of it actually is, apart from enthusiastic exclamations about the Soviet Union and expressions of solidarity with the poor. Thus the poem **"Slavnostní den" ("A Festive Day"),** which demands that workers also be able to eat the dishes one finds in gourmet restaurants, a poem that was severely criticized, shows him more as a would-be bourgeois than as a proletarian.

As some of his Marxist critics charged, Seifert was waiting for the revolution but was not engaged in bringing it about. The focus of Devětsil was not primarily political but poetic. Insofar as it was political, as in the case of the popular, self-professed communist poet Jiří Wolker (1900-24), its Marxism was moralistic and nostalgic. Purity and gentleness, love of man, not for his heroism but for his weakness and humiliation, were the essence of its poetry. However, even Wolker's gentle moralism was attacked by Vítězslav Nezval (1900-58), one of the most prominent members of the group, who claimed that art had no purpose beyond being art. This was the first step which was to lead to poetism, the one ism which originated in Czech literature.

The poet and authority figure round whom the young leftists such as Wolker gathered in the years immediately following World War I was Stanislav K. Neumann (1875-1947), who in 1921 published an anthology of verse by various poets called *Sovětské Rusi* (For Soviet Russia), to which Seifert also contributed. Neumann proclaimed that contributions must be clear and understandable to the average reader and must identify ideologically with the socialist world and the socialist revolution. After the model of the Soviet organization Proletkult, a Czech counterpart was founded in 1921. The Czech phase of proletarian literature was brief, however. By 1922 Devětsil, under the leadership of the critic Karel Teige, turned to poetism, which was to combine a philosophy stressing the joy of life, turning life itself into poetry, and the struggle for a communist revolution. It was to encompass not only poetry but all the arts. Teige stressed the role of fantasy, fun, and the absurd as outlets of man's irrational side. The poetists now withdrew from political poetry, but not from politics.

Predictably, the carnival atmosphere did not last, and already in Seifert's collection of 1925, ***Slavík zpívá špatně (The Nightingale Sings Badly),*** death, battlefields, and gas masks, along with love and nature, are among his themes. Death also is the climax in "Akrobat," a poem published by Nezval in 1927. As was often the case with the poetists earlier, the setting is a circus, but rather than gaiety, the mood here is one of disaster. The proletarian phase of Devětsil was followed by disillusionment and, more accurately in some cases, by relief that after years of devotion to the cause, the still-young poets could consider their own enjoyment part of their program. From efforts to look at the shortcomings of the world, they turned to feelings and the subconscious, thus preparing the way for surrealism. They turned from discipline to an attitude of "enjoying the moment." Although the models of proletarian poetry had originated in Russia, the poetist ones were to be found in the West, particularly in France. The intoxication of the senses and adventures of the imagination were stressed and not German *Innerlichkeit* or the "Russian soul."

The most outstanding of the poetists was Nezval. Talented, imaginative, and sensuous, he led a bohemian, anarchic life and combined childlike playfulness with a terror of the supernatural. In comparison with Seifert, Nezval's poetry was more varied, more fantastic, and richer in surprises. Seifert in his poetist collection ***Na vlnách TSF (On the Radio Waves;*** 1925) no longer dreamed of socialism but experienced the many symbols of the exotic world: Paris, Italy, the sea. Nonetheless, did the many paraphernalia of dissembling—masks, costumes, makeup—which we find in Nezval's contemporary poems as well as in Seifert's not suggest different faces behind the smiling ones not only with Nezval but also with Seifert?

It was in 1922 that Seifert gave a lecture at a public meeting which was to have a strong impact first on Nezval and then on Devětsil as a whole. There he pointed out that for poetry to have an impact on workers, it not only has to be intelligible to them but also enjoyable as entertainment. Cowboy films, circuses, and soccer would qualify, and it was up to the artists to bridge the gap between intellectuals and proletarians. The proper function of poetry was to be an outlet for emotions, and its former function, persuasion, could be taken over by posters and caricatures. The poetry of the poetists revealed a kinship to dada. Seifert and Teige called for a break with older esthetic traditions. Modern art was to be sought not in the studios of painters but in dance bars with the sounds of the first jazz bands, in coffeehouses and music halls, and in the lights of Paris boulevards. Seifert nevertheless saw in this art a pre-image of the world of socialism. With the October Revolution in the background of their consciousness, the majority of young poets and artists in the Devětsil circle then believed that a new social transformation was beginning, and many of them, including Seifert, were members of the Communist Party. As the whole world was to become poetic, painting and the writing of poems were to be replaced by picture poems and photomontages. Together with constructivism, poetism implied the belief that, with the help of modern technology, revolutions would lead to the beauty of which they dreamed.

Despite his professed allegiance to the Devětsil movement and his flirations with Mallarmé, Rimbaud, and Verlaine, Seifert remained a very traditional and even primitive poet. František X. Šalda, the most respected critic of the time, wrote: "Seifert's poetic world in ***Samá láska*** (***All Love;*** 1923) is in no fundamental respect different from the simple world of a little Prague official: film, sports, engineering, longing for Paris, of which he has the same kind of ideas which every little suburban dressmaker could have."

It seems surprising that in spite of their turn to poetism, the members of Devětsil continued to consider themselves communists. In 1929 seven writers, including Seifert, signed a manifesto rejecting the new leadership under Klement Gottwald, who was to become President of Czechoslovakia in 1948, and were expelled from the party. Though some later reapplied for membership, Seifert became a Social Democrat and, with the exception of a brief period in 1948, seems to have remained one in spirit. His volume of poems ***Osm dnů*** (***Eight Days;*** 1937), written on the occasion of President Masaryk's death, underscores his strong identification with the beloved president and the republic. In 1929 Seifert was also dropped from Devětsil for reasons which are not entirely clear.

In the late twenties and thirties the mood of Czech poetry reflected an atmosphere of death, nightmares, and ugliness, for which no satisfactory explanation has been given; it came before the economic depression hit Czechoslovakia with full force and before the Nazis began to threaten its existence. Seifert seemed little affected by this mood. In fact, it was in 1933 that he published ***Jablko z klína (An Apple from the Lap),*** in which the main theme is love. With these simple, sometimes balladesque poems, Seifert reached new heights of popularity, while Nezval gradually became the almost totally isolated standard-bearer of surrealism. In the thirties and early forties the pendulum of Czech literature swung back to tradition. Social themes generally gained ground at the expense of personal poetry, and concern about national survival moved into the foreground. By then the energy of the Czech avant-garde was spent, and the formal dissolution of the surrealist group in 1938 was merely a gesture after the fact. The disaster which struck the Czechoslovak Republic was reflected in some of Seifert's best collections, such as ***Zhasněte světla*** (***Turn Off the Lights;*** 1938), ***Světlem oděná*** (***Dressed in Light;*** 1940), referring to Prague, ***Kammený most*** (***The Stone Bridge;*** 1944), and others, which reasserted his attachment to the national heritage. With his genuinely positive temperament, Seifert increasingly has been for many Czechs a rock of security to whom they looked in times of adversity ever since he spoke out at the writers' association meeting in 1956 on behalf of imprisoned and silenced writers. This view is also reflected in the many enthusiastic tributes to him from all over the world since he received the 1984 Nobel Prize; only the press in Czechoslovakia has limited itself to brief factual statements.

A politically very different group with which Devětsil actually had many points of contact was "Pátečníci," the "Friday group," also known as the "pragmatic group" around President Masaryk, which met on Fridays at the "Castle" or in the home of Josef and Karel Čapek (1887-1945; 1890-1938) and included both Čapeks and the leftist novelist Vladislav Vančura (1891-1942), a member of Devětsil. The Čapeks, who had spent their apprenticeships in France and Germany respectively, contributed considerably to the international dimension of Czech literature. A cosmopolitanism analogous to that of the Friday group and of Devětsil could also be found mutatis mutandis in the Catholic group of writers, including Jaroslav Durych (1886-1962) and Jan Čep (1902-74), influenced by Gabriel Marcel and Paul Claudel. With all of them, a universalist note predominated until the threat of Nazism brought about a turn to national themes. At the same time the old Czech tradition of satire continued. The political cabaret, *Červená sedma* (The Red Seven), under the direction of Eduard Bass, flourished in the early years of the Republic. Despite censorship, a practice which was difficult to reconcile with democracy, satiric magazines of various political orientations were published. Seifert was the editor of one, *Sršatec* (The Porcupine), from 1923 until 1925; in addition, artists from Seifert's circle such as Adolf Hoffmeister (1902-73) and František Bidlo drew political caricatures. Jaroslav Hašek (1883-1923) and his *Adventures of the Good Soldier Schweik* are too well known to be discussed in this brief summary.

A unique institution in Prague from the second half of the twenties until the Munich Accord was "Osvobozené divadlo," the "Liberated Theatre." Strongly influenced by American movies, dada, and the Soviet revolutionary theatre, it stressed nonconformist, militant social and political satire. One innovative feature of the "Liberated Theatre" was the combination of theatre, dance, and song, another the clever dialogues of Jiří Voskovec (1905-81) and Jan Werich (1905-80). The audiences were primarily left-wing intellectuals, and it goes without saying that Seifert and his friends saw every one of the programs. Of similar importance was the composer, dramatist, and producer. Emil František Burian (1904-59), a member of Devětsil who became the artistic director of D-34 (=*divadlo* [theatre]; "34" became "35" et cetera in successive years). Influenced by Brecht and the poetists, his repertory included—before the theatre was closed in 1938—not only Czech works such as *Schweik* but also, for example, Georg Büchner's *Leonce und Lena* and *Villon,* a play based on the French poet.

A much more intimate picture of Seifert than that gathered from his poetry is found in his only major prose work, a book of reminiscences, published in Toronto in 1981 and in Prague in a somewhat shortened version in 1983 under the title ***Všecky krásy světa* (*All the Beauties of the World*)**. The title, originally a phrase in Smetana's *Bartered Bride,* came to Seifert via Teige's introduction to the volume *Devětsil* (1922), in which he stated that all the beauties of the world should be the subject of poetry. The book for the most part consists of reminiscences written in haphazard order as they seem to have occurred to him, with extended digressions. Events are only rarely placed in time, so that the reader has to rely on a knowledge of the Czech cultural scene.

There are two main differences between Seifert's prose and his poetry. First, whereas the poetry generally hovers *above* mundane reality, the prose deals with what moved the poet—and with "what was in the air" at different times of his life. Second, although the poetry reflects his longing for beauty and goodness in the midst of evil, the reminiscences concentrate almost entirely on the positive. Memories of conviviality, of the warmth of his childhood home despite its poverty, and of love and beauty in nature far outweigh the episodes of Nazi terror and the references, only hinted at, to the situation after 1948. The negative note which does appear concerns the quick passage of time, the increasingly frequent deaths of his friends, and the expectation of his own death. Despite the infirmities of old age, among the themes on which he dwells most fondly are detailed memories of food and drink, and, repeatedly, his delight in beautiful young women.

Prague is the central focus of Seifert's work, and he sees it as one, with layers of the 1970s superimposed on those of the 1910s and 1950s. Being conservative by temperament, he resents modernizations which obstruct or merely change beautiful views. The Žižkov he loves is the old workers' section of the city with its *pavlače* (wooden corridors which run along the backs of many Prague houses on every floor), dirt, smells, and often quaint characters. Much of the housing referred to in Kafka's *Trial* is clearly located in the same Žižkov. Undoubtedly Seifert and Kafka saw the same scenes, only with different eyes. In stream-of-consciousness fashion, Seifert moves from subject to subject within chapters. The one called ("Důvěrné sdělení") "Confidential Communication," for example, begins with Seifert's being interviewed by a young woman editor. Her first naïve question—when did his love for Prague begin—leads him to reminisce about his trips to relatives in nearby Kralupy and the view of the Prague skyline along the way. Then, without transition, he moves on to a sketch of the classic poet of Prague, Jan Neruda, and Neruda's view of Prague. This leads him to an account of demonstrations he witnessed in Žižkov against increases in the price of bread as well as to scenes in church and at political meetings, which are followed by a detailed paragraph about the parklike slope Petřín on the left bank of the Moldau and the lovers in Letná Park. When he refers to the disaster which befell other European cities, he may have in mind the problematic question of Czechoslovakia's twice in recent times offering no organized resistance to aggression but thereby saving Prague, the most precious national possession. Despite the statement of his avant-garde days, the beauty he reminisces about in this quasi-summary of his life is not inspired by poetism but by the traditions of nineteenth-century literature, including its leisurely narration and its *Kleinmalerei*.

In spite of Seifert's nostalgia for the past, his reminiscences reveal no tension between past and present, only the realization that by now most of the beauty of his life lies in his memories. He grinds no axes, fights no battles, unlike the other writers remembering the same period, and only subtly identifies himself with good and against evil in whatever form. In contrast, the memoirs of Vítězslav Nezval, who obviously comes to mind, are filled with tensions between communists and pragmatists, between individuals, and even between Nezval's bohemian life in the city and the bucolic country life of his parents. Karel Honzík, who in *Ze života avantgardy* (*From the Life of the Avant-garde;* 1963) left us one of the liveliest pictures of the Czech avant-garde, contrasts its excitement and inventiveness with the dull passivity of the Western world, which watched indifferently as Czechoslovakia was sacrificed to an illusory world peace. Because of its depiction of minute details of life from pre-World War I days on, ***All the Beauties of the World*** is an invaluable source for the kind of information to which not even the fashionable "history from below" school pays much attention, whether it be the description of a delicatessen window, Seifert's father's businesses, or the cafés, bars, and back rooms where early twentieth-century literati congregated.

One could say much more about ***All the Beauties of the World*** than the present framework permits. The very genesis of the book, which originally was to be a text for a volume of photographs, is interesting. As Jan Vladislav wrote in a . . . letter, it contains not a single negative portrait, even of persons such as Marie Majerová (1882-1967), about whom Seifert had no illusions. There is a thematic parallelism among ***All the Beauties of the World,*** the 1929 essay collection ***Hvězdy nad rajskou zahradou (Stars over Paradise Garden),*** and Seifert's recent ***Býti básníkem (To Be a Poet).*** Together with his poetry, his reminiscences might be viewed as a detailed, documented ode to life.

In the speech which he prepared for the Swedish Academy upon receiving the Nobel Prize, Seifert explained his view of himself as a lyric poet and of the lyrical position within his world view. He explained the unusually strong interest in lyric poetry among the Czechs as an outgrowth of Czech history, with its periods during which direct political expression was silenced and religious expression was problematic. However, though lyrical expression flowing from the emotions and senses of the individual and identifying with external objects not only suits the Czechs generally but him as a lyric poet in particular, he is seriously concerned about its exclusiveness. Convinced that a tension among the three approaches—rational, lyrical, and pathetic—is necessary, he views the rational, i.e. the conceptual, as dominant in the present world to a dangerous extent. The component he finds lacking, especially in Czech life and culture, is that of pathos, which represents a volitional-moral perspective. The most striking expression of this deficiency to Seifert is the absence, or near absence, of tragedy. Therefore, despite his personal emphatic identification with the conciliatory, harmonious lyric spirit, he wishes for the inner vibration and movement of will which would result in taking stands "for what we consider just and against what is, but should not be."

When we trace Seifert's poetry from its beginning in 1920 to **"To Be a Poet"** (1983) . . . , we see a development, via some pirouettes, toward increasing simplicity and artlessness, almost prose. Seifert's poetry, at all stages of his work, is easy to understand. In fact, its very simplicity and lack of sophistication would alienate the type of person who reads poetry in the West and appeal all the more to the Czech readers. The questionable validity of the notion of universality as a criterion of the quality of literature becomes clear if we consider the fact that Seifert's cycle of poems titled ***Maminka*** (***Mother;*** 1954) is extremely popular in Czechoslovakia but would be unacceptable to Western readers. In the abstract, translatability of literature is considered a criterion of value; but actually, in concrete terms, we know that this is not the case. There are substantial parts of the codex of world literature which do not translate well, so that the position of many specific works of literature is different in each national scale of values.

The awarding of the Nobel Prize to Seifert came as a surprise to many. Unlike Havel, Kundera, and Vaculik, he has, with negligible exceptions, not been translated into Western languages. However, his kind of poetry and relationship to a broad readership may constitute a valuable challenge to the Western esoteric poets whose works are the objects of academic explications rather than of love. (pp. 8-12)

Wilma A. Iggers, "The World of Jaroslav Seifert," in World Literature Today, *Vol. 60, No. 1, Winter, 1986, pp. 8-12.*

Literary Biography

Stevie: A Biography of Stevie Smith

by Jack Barbera and William McBrien

(For Stevie Smith: see also *CLC,* Vols. 3, 8, 25; *Contemporary Authors,* Vols. 17-20, rev. ed., Vols. 29-32, rev. ed. [obituary]; *Contemporary Authors Permanent Series,* Vol. 2; and *Dictionary of Literary Biography,* Vol. 20. For Jack Barbera: see also *Contemporary Authors,* Vol. 110. For William McBrien: see also *Contemporary Authors,* Vol. 107.)

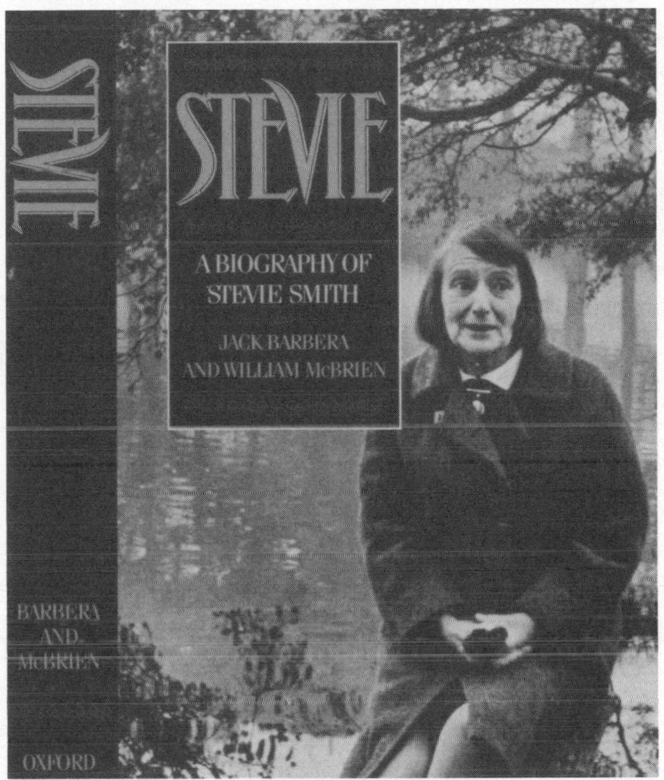

Dust jacket of Stevie: A Biography of Stevie Smith, *by Jack Barbera and William McBrien. Oxford, 1986. Jacket design by Honi Werner. Reproduced by permission of Oxford University Press, Inc. Jacket photograph by Jane Bown. Reproduced by permission of Jane Bown.*

An Excerpt from *Stevie: A Biography of Stevie Smith*

In 1939 Stevie sent some short stories to John Lehmann for publication in the magazine, *New Writing,* he was then editing, but he rejected them. She succeeded, though, in publishing two stories that year—one, a prose-poem in the *New Statesman* called "Surrounded By Children", which depicts a summer's day in Kensington Gardens and Hyde Park, and the children, some of them spoiled and unpleasant, who play there. Suddenly "a famously ugly old girl", a caricature of the author with her "wisps of grey hair carelessly dyed that is rioting out from under her queer hat", enters. She spies a luxurious perambulator and, attracted by the security it offers, tears off her clothes and climbs into it. In a gesture that is partly prophetic she stabs herself with a hatpin and draws blood. Nightmare might define the genre of this story in which Stevie seems to depict her struggle to climb back into the condition of infancy or, as once she described it in a poem, to "Storm back through the gates of Birth." In "Childhood and Interruption" Stevie depicts the attractiveness of the pram:

And underneath the pram cover lies my brother Jake
He is not old enough yet to be properly awake . . .
For a little while yet, it is as if he had not been born
Rest in infancy, brother Jake; childhood and
  interruption come swiftly on.

And in a poem written much later, "To Carry the Child", Stevie says that "To carry the child into adult life / Is to be handicapped."

This is a poem central to an understanding of Stevie and the perils she risked in her effort to preserve such qualities of childhood as the originality, freshness and directness she deemed essential for a poet. But carrying the child throughout life often entails the perpetuation of attitudes and behavior that are painful, isolating, and paralysing. Many of Stevie's friends remember times when they were surprised by her childish behaviour: Racy Buxton, for example, who was pushed aside by Stevie when walking with her on a path to the sea. "I don't want to see your back," Stevie had said, "I want to see the sea." And Lady Lawrence, who recalls "the impishness which at one party led (Stevie) gleefully to pick out all the smoked salmon in the sandwiches, leaving the bread and butter for the rest." Elisabeth Lutyens wrote: "She would *demand* company—someone to talk *at*—insist on being driven round and about and having her creature comforts catered for. Given these—and she had her own way of childishly screaming for attention—she could reward you by being very, very funny, with a devastating gift of observation and awareness of the ridiculous in our human predicament."

In "To Carry the Child" the "man in the poem is meant to have the child in him and to feel the nuisance it can be," Stevie wrote, "but then to see it is a nuisance for the child, too, and that where the two of them exist together, then each has a right to exist, and some value." She wrote the poem in her sixties, when she must have given thought again, in a calmer way, to Rosamond Lehmann's disapproval of Pompey's "little-girlness", and her view that failing to grow up keeps one at a kind of anarchistic and destructive level. Her last stanza even incorporates some of Rosamond Lehmann's diction:

But oh the poor child, the poor child, what can he do,
Trapped in a grown-up carapace,
But peer outside of his prison room
With the eye of an anarchist?

And in a stanza that seems poignantly autobiographical, Stevie wrote

The child in adult life is defenceless
And if he is grown-up, knows it,
And the grown-up looks at the childish part
And despises it.

JOHN MELLORS

[Mellors, an English critic and nonfiction writer, frequently contributes reviews to London Magazine *and the* Listener. *He has written two autobiographical works,* Shots in the Dark *(1974) and* Memoirs of an Advertising Man *(1976). In the following excerpt Mellors praises* Stevie *as a thorough and fascinating biography of Smith.]*

Stevie Smith lived for some forty years with her aunt, the 'darling Lion', in Palmers Green, North London. The aunt-niece relationship was ideal for Stevie. An aunt is of a different generation and not so close as a mother. Living with her sister, or with a husband, or a lover, would have been far more difficult. Stevie had a fear of being committed and regarded herself as more suited for friendships than for love or marriage. 'I love life,' she said, 'but only because I keep myself well on the edge.' Pompey, who is obviously Stevie herself, lightly fictionalized, in ***Novel on Yellow Paper,*** says she is 'a *toute entière* visitor'; she likes visits because they go on for so long but no longer, though they can recur. Visits to friends are perfect for someone who does not want to be committed, who prefers living 'on the edge'.

Fortunately for her biographers, Stevie was no recluse, even though she often complained of being 'lonely'. She was as sociable and talkative, in correspondence and conversation and also in her novels and poems, as she was suspicious of commitments. Consequently, Jack Barbera and William McBrien have a wealth of raw material, and although [***Stevie: A Biography of Stevie Smith***] is not the authorized biography they acknowledge that they have been given access to all sources. It will be interesting to see whether the authorized biography, when that is published, projects a different Stevie Smith from the one who emerges from the pages of ***Stevie.*** Barbera and McBrien have given an apparently full and certainly fascinating account of Stevie Smith's life and writings, and of the opinions of those writings held by critics, friends and the author herself. As American academics they are aware that English readers will expect their book to be 'in the American tradition of the beaver'. They confess to having 'beavered' but they hope it was not at the expense of 'lightness of touch'. They have, in fact, drawn the pattern of their subject's life in a clear, workmanlike way, and if they sometimes include trivial and irrelevant details (e.g. of church records showing that Stevie's aunt and great-aunt had contributed to a church building fund in 1908) they never allow the reader to feel that he cannot see the wood for the trees.

What sort of a writer was Stevie Smith? How good was she? When her first book was published in 1936, ***Novel on Yellow Paper,*** Raymond Mortimer praised it for its poetry and humour and John Hayward wrote to her to say that he had fallen under the book's 'strange and delicious spell'. That was how I felt when I read it a few years later, still in my teens. I found myself writing a (never published) 'Novel in Green Covers', in which I set out to imitate Stevie Smith's style. Was ***Novel on Yellow Paper*** a literary breakthrough? Perhaps it attracted a young reader so strongly because it represented a new way of undermining the literary establishment, the writers of mandarin prose. Hemingway had frontally assaulted the garrison with his own weapons and tactics. Stevie Smith attacked in a more roundabout way, writing as people chatted, adapting the stream of consciousness of Joyce and Woolf and Dorothy Richardson and turning it into a gossipy stream of talkativeness, a 'writing out loud' technique, so to speak.

Looking again now at ***Novel on Yellow Paper,*** more than forty years after first reading it, what do I think? It still has the great merit of making you read on. I picked it up to look quickly at the first one or two pages and found myself reading thoroughly and avidly past page 20, and page 30, and so on. Not, however, with unmixed admiration this time. For all the enjoyment, and recognition of the 'poetry and humour', this time I found myself agreeing, too, with the view of Edwin Muir, expressed in *The Listener* in 1936: he found the book 'compellingly exasperating'.

Stevie Smith's is, of course, one sees now, a hit-or-miss style, and the misses are more evident today. She herself (through Pompey, her narrator) called the book 'a foot-off-the-ground novel that came by the left hand', and she warned the 'foot-on-the-ground' reader that 'this book will be for you a desert of weariness and exasperation'. Perhaps most readers read as they walk, one foot on, one foot off, the ground, so that while they enjoy and admire they also, from time to time, are exasperated.

However, before the opinions of forty-years-on are taken as testimony that Stevie Smith's prose has not worn as well as a one-time addict might have expected, let me add that the old magic can still work, and work powerfully. There are passages in ***Novel on Yellow Paper*** which are utterly delightful and quite unlike the work of any other author. (pp. 96-7)

Perhaps life 'on the edge' is harder to endure than life in the middle. Barbera and McBrien bring out with skill and sympathy the loneliness behind Stevie Smith's humour and wit, her fears of old age, illness and death, her hankering after suicide (which she once attempted), and, above all, her compulsion to write, whether it was prose or poetry, fiction or criticism. Of her own poems she commented: 'people in rather odd circumstances are what most of my poems are about, mixed up with arguments, religious difficulties, ghosts, death, fairy stories, and a general feeling of guilt for not writing more.' If Stevie Smith kept herself 'on the edge' of life, every time she wrote she plunged into her work, wherever it might take her, looking with a clear eye on comical incongruities as well as on pain and sorrow and—something she particularly feared—'feebleness'. (pp. 97-8)

John Mellors, "Living on the Edge," in London Magazine, *n.s. Vol. 25, No. 8, November, 1985, pp. 96-8.*

JOHN CAREY

[Carey is an English critic whose works include Milton *(1969),* Thackeray: Prodigal Genius *(1977), and* John Donne: Life, Mind, and Art *(1981). In the following excerpt Carey reflects on Smith's personality and finds the biography good in reporting factual*

material about Smith though not a penetrating analysis of her life and work.]

''Venomous'', ''devious'', ''emphatically not a nice character'', are some of the tributes paid to Stevie Smith by reminiscing friends, in Jack Barbera and William McBrien's biography, ***Stevie.*** The consensus seems to be that she was fun to meet, provided you had a pressing engagement somewhere else very soon afterwards.

Stevie, of course, knew she was a problem, and kept saying so in her poems. ''I am not God's little lamb, I am God's sick tiger''. What made her sick originally was her father—another sick tiger who had decided, quite abruptly, to cure himself. He walked out on the family when Stevie was three and got a job with the White Star Line. A snapshot shows him trimly uniformed on a planked deck. Postcards would arrive at the Smith semi (''Off to Valparaiso love Daddy''), but apart from these communiqués he took no further interest in family affairs.

Stevie seems to have been wounded deeply enough to distrust life ever after. One of her poems is about a princess who ties the word ''Fear'' round her throat, runs off into a dark forest, and stays there gazing at her reflection in a stream. The forest Stevie ran into was 1 Avondale Road, Palmers Green, a large, private house where she lived for over 60 years with a large, private aunt to look after her. It must be the drabbest existence of any English poet.

Researchers who gained access to the shrine in later years reported aghast on the faded wallpaper, the neolithic stone sink, the wheezing gas fires. But Stevie loved it, because it was safe and changeless. From it she could venture forth into the dazzling, treacherous outside world, or as much of it as could be conveniently reached by the Northern Line.

Prompted by a kind of frozen anguish, she tried to stay the little girl her father had abandoned. Even when elderly she wore skimpy frocks, ending near the top of her thighs, and affected an adolescent giggle. Real children were not impressed by Stevie's juvenile disguise. They shouted ''Witch'' at her through the garden gate. But it was not something she could outgrow. ***Novel on Yellow Paper,*** with which she captivated the literary world in the 1930s, is written in slangy, mock-infantile jargon, dotted with Dorothy Parker Americanisms of the sort a schoolgirl might pick up. Her poems, too, pretend to be guileless and childlike—though sinister lines poke through the prattle like bones through grass. No other 20th-century poet has evolved so distinctive a voice, and we can deduce from this account of her life that it was compounded out of pure pain. . . .

[Stevie] was a wicked observer of people. The account of her visit to Buckingham Palace to collect her Gold Medal for Poetry in 1969 is one of the book's funniest episodes. Stevie contended that she ought to be given a meal at the Palace, as it was a long way from Palmers Green. Or at any rate sherry: she was always a couple of glasses below par, she said. When it was explained that refreshments were not available, she inquired anxiously whether the Palace had lavatory accommodation. She bought a special hat for the occasion, from a church jumble sale, and took along a new poem about death ''to cheer up Her Majesty''. She could not help noticing that the royal smile got rather fixed. Poetry, the medallist concluded, ws not absolutely Ma'am's favourite subject. ''I'm sure H.M. would rather pin it on a doggy-dear than me.''

This keenness made Stevie an uncomfortable lover. Her name was linked with several men, George Orwell among them, and before the war she had an affair of sorts with a young German, known to her set as ''Stevie's Nazi boyfriend''. Whether she ever relinquished her maidenhood remains moot. The composer Elisabeth Lutyens, a close friend, said she thought Stevie would consider it all a ridiculous gymnastic act, and would watch the male's capers unblinkingly with her intelligent black eyes. Stevie once told Miss Lutyens with glee about a young man she was in bed with inquiring ''Are you enjoying yourself dear?''

The price of such derision was loneliness. Stevie's resolve to stay on the edge of life, in case she got hurt, meant she was hurt all the time by what she took to be people's neglect of her true worth. She kept herself very narrow—paid no attention to art or music, and never bought a volume of contemporary poetry. ''Lefty good-hearts'' amused her, and she refused to centre her thoughts on anything as ''frivolous'' as politics—which meant, essentially, that she could not be bothered with other people's troubles, having enough herself. . . .

She balanced on wit and ridicule like a stilt-walker. Her anti-Christian poems (on which these biographers soft-pedal, presumably out of respect for American piety) use laughter with shattering seriousness—as when the poet meets some saintly children who proclaim ''Our Bog is dood'', and threaten to kill her when she asks what Bog and dood are. It is the history of religious intolerance, inscribed in nonsense verse.

Seeing self-important words, of the kind religions are composed of, trip over themselves, always tickled her. She became convulsed with laughter when she read in a local paper the misprint ''Is there life beyond the gravy?''

The two American admirers of Stevie who have written this account liken themselves to beavers—which seems apt. Their log-pile of fact and gossip has hollow spaces inside (the housekeeping Aunt, who meant more to Stevie than anyone, remains largely a blank). But it holds water remarkably well as an explanation of the precarious psyche Stevie's writings reflect. The official biography, when it surfaces, will have to be good to dislodge this.

John Carey, ''The Story of Stevie,'' in The Sunday Times, *London, November 10, 1985, p. 45.*

CHRISTOPHER REID

[*Reid is an English poet, journalist, and critic. Critics identify him with the group of young British poets of the late 1970s whose bizarre, witty observations of everyday life became known as the Martian school of poetry. His poetry collections include* Arcadia *(1979) and* Katherina Brac *(1985). In the following excerpt Reid states that* Stevie: A Biography of Stevie Smith *is a useful, if infelicitously written, study of Smith.*]

It is clear that studies of the life and work of Stevie Smith are at that uneasy stage where the desire to see her reputation properly established is still mixed with, and to some extent hampered by, a sense of guardianship on the part of those engaged in promoting her status. The behaviour of Smith's executor, James MacGibbon, is significant in this respect. . . . [He] explicitly withholds approval from the biography by Jack Barbera and William McBrien [***Stevie: A Biography of Stevie Smith***]. ''This is not an authorized biography'', he announces categorically on the same page as Barbera and McBrien thank him for his co-operation; and a few sentences later he tells us: ''The authorized biography is in preparation.''

Stevie: A Biography of Stevie Smith is certainly not a flawless work, and one is free for the moment to imagine that the "authorized" life will improve upon it, but MacGibbon's judgment in this case remains questionable.

Such facts as the biographers reveal about Smith's early life, and about the two great thwarted love-affairs that she endured, confirm the suspicion that ***Novel on Yellow Paper*** is essentially an autobiographical work. It is also, significantly, a work that elevates self-obsession to the level of a literary device: we are left in no doubt that Pompey's chattering commentary, and what it tells us about her wilful, capricious, freely-associating and insistently *modern* mind, are more important than whatever scraps of narrative may have been scavenged from memory in the course of the book's improvised progress. Pompey, who has the egotist's giveaway habit of referring to herself in the third person ("the cleverest living Pompey"), is an unabashed buttonholer, and at one point, in allusion to Coleridge, addresses her remarks to "Mr Wedding-Guest-Reader". Teased and taunted thus, the reader soon comes to recognize spiritual kinship with the novel's many characters for whom Pompey may sometimes declare affection, but who tend to be treated by her with a great deal of not very gentle mockery. The jeering note is frequently sounded at the expense of friends and lovers alike, and for all the come-hitherish charm of its narrative manner the final effect of the book is a bleak one.

The life of its writer evidently struck many of her acquaintances as bleak, too. One of these has confessed to the present biographers that she "couldn't imagine why she (Stevie) found life worth living"; and Smith herself once wrote: "The capacity women have for just hanging on is depressing to contemplate." Illness in childhood, the failure of her parents' marriage, unfulfilled love, a job that bored her, long periods of literary neglect and an anxious dependency on fragile friendships were all part of her lot. Where human affection was concerned, her closest and most satisfactory tie seems to have been with the aunt who for more than sixty years shared her house in Palmer's Green, and who is celebrated in ***Novel on Yellow Paper*** as "the Lion Aunt of Hull". It is a measure of the importance of this bond that when Pompey is rash enough to make sport of her aunt in fancy-dress costume, she instantly qualifies her remarks with an apology: "Darling Auntie Lion, I do so hope you will forgive what is written here. You are yourself like shining gold"—and so on. At the same time, of course, one is obliged to note that the offending words, which may really have hurt the aunt in Palmer's Green, stand obstinately unrevised.

Barbera and McBrien have clearly been diligent in their researches, but their handling of material is not always as subtle or as adroit as one might wish. Their book gets off to a wobbly start with a coy account of the jumble-sale hat worn by Smith when collecting a gold medal from Buckingham Palace. An indiscriminate use of index-cards may be responsible for the occasional bathetic lurch on later pages, as when we are informed that "1910 was a year of other noteworthy events, in addition to Stevie's prize for perfect school attendance . . . Edward VII died, and George V became king". The authors' literary pronouncements, too, can be embarrassing. It is dismaying, for example, to read that "like all writers, Stevie was captivated to the end of her days by the magic imagination engenders", such banalities having no justifiable place in a work of this or any other kind.

Generally speaking, however, the team may be judged to have produced a clear, orderly, informative and, above all, sympathetically disposed account of their subject. It may be left to the "authorized" biographer to make literary sense of the evidence, and to tackle the important questions, first, of how Smith evolved her unique poetic and narrative style, and secondly, of how this style may have related to the fierce egotistical streak that so many of her acquaintances mention; but meanwhile, *pace* the poet's no doubt well-intentioned executor, here is a book that usefully suggests lines of inquiry to the interested reader. In the absence of anything better, it cannot be so abruptly dismissed.

Christopher Reid, "The Unbuttoned Buttonholer," in The Times Literary Supplement, *No. 4313, November 29, 1985, p. 1369.*

HERMIONE LEE

[Lee, an English critic and professor of literature, has written several studies of modern authors, including The Novels of Virginia Woolf *(1977) and* Philip Roth *(1982). She also edited* Stevie Smith: A Selection *(1983), a sampler of Smith's prose and poetry. In the following excerpt Lee complains that Barbera and Mc-*

Smith in August, 1919. By permission of James MacGibbon, Executor of the Literary Estate of Stevie Smith, and McFarlin Library, The University of Tulsa.

Brien's biography evidences a dull prose style and inept scholarship, which fails to do justice to the bright, witty poet.]

> Nobody heard him, the dead man
> But still he lay moaning
> I was much further out than you thought
> And not waving but drowning.

That, as Jack Barbera and William McBrien would say, is 'a whiff of vintage Stevie,' and a good test of their biography [***Stevie: A Biography of Stevie Smith***] is to see what they do with it. We hear of some funny things Stevie Smith said in 1953. Then the poem is quoted, and the biographers comment: 'Of course, the humour of this poem is black humour . . . The dead speaker's incongruous liveliness is funny, what with his explanations, his moaning, and his cries of "no no no".' Then there is a footnote which tells us that Stevie may have been misremembering a newspaper story she kept, headlined 'Needless Dash to Bather on Rubber Float', 'about a man who was thought to be in trouble when he was only waving to a friend on shore.' And after that we go on to the depressing factors in Stevie's life at the time, like her bad knee and her tax problems.

Nothing and everything is wrong with this. It's a well-meaning attempt to say something useful about the poem and 'relate' it to the life. But it's as if Stevie Smith were writing in one language and her biographers in another. The poem's peculiar voice—at once stoical and desperate, urgent and aloof, childishly direct and edgily disenchanted—is washed up on the page amid a sea of insensitive paraphrase, banal platitudes of the 'In her heart Stevie was sad even when she laughed' school, solemn unconscious comedy and awkward negotiation between the life and the work.

Stevie Smith's apparently naïve rendering of herself in writing which is also evasive, or jokingly off-hand, or blankly 'simple,' or austerely classical, should surely set off warning lights for biographers wanting to use the poems and fiction as 'evidence.' But Barbera and McBrien wade in blithely, using (for instance) 'I like to get off with people' as possible indication of an affair with George Orwell.

Certainly she's not easy to write about. There's a temptation either to sweeten her into a cute, dotty English spinster (as in the play *Stevie*), or to idolise her as a daemonic Blakean genius, as in Michael Horovitz's soppy reference to 'the astonishing unimpeachable fact of her.' The life is not a biographer's dream. The runaway naval father, the 'house of female habitation' in Palmers Green with sick mother, sister and Aunt (and then just Aunt), the middle-class education at Palmers Green High School (where Stevie, we are told, was 'a delightful leader in mischief') and North London Collegiate, the long dull 'job-job-job' from 1923 to 1953 as secretary to Newnes and Pearson, the growing reputation in the 1930s, the commuting between suburban life, visits to friends and London literary parties, the 1950s neglect, depression and suicide attempt, and the 'come-back' in the Sixties with readings and broadcasts: none of this promises much excitement, unless you count a school theatrical appearance with Flora Robson in *Ali Baba* or a conversation with the Queen on winning the Gold Medal for Poetry.

In part, then, the biographers have to rely on reminiscence and gossip. They've certainly talked to a lot of people, and have arrived at a striking and unamiable picture of a difficult woman whose childlike unworldliness involved an almost neurotic dependence on the Aunt and impossible demands on her friends. Once she descended on a family whose house was full and whose son had measles, behaved importunately, complained of neglect, and put them into a revengeful poem. In Venice, she insisted on eating rice pudding, shopping for safety pins and sitting by the canals after dark—'Most exhausting,' said her hosts. She was a notorious cadger of late-night lifts to Palmers Green. Francis King thought her a dangerous gossip, Rosamond Lehmann said she couldn't take criticism, Olivia Manning found her tricky and malicious, and Elizabeth Lutyens called her a bullying egotist.

She put people straight into her stories and poems, and got into trouble: there's a gripping anecdote about the effects of her unkind portrayal of the writer Betty Miller and her then insufferable 10-year-old son Jonathan. Stevie and her publishers were always worried about libel, and not for nothing does ***Novel on Yellow Paper*** begin: 'Goodbye to all my friends, my beautiful and lovely friends.'

Fortunately, Stevie Smith isn't only portrayed by the mixed depositions of her 'beautiful and lovely friends.' She speaks for herself through a large number of essays, letters and interviews (some already collected in Barbera and McBrien's anthology . . . , ***Me Again.***) These are of enormous interest: we can see how the allusiveness and echoes that pack her apparently naïve poems go back to her commonplace book of the 1920s, and how her detestation of 'Lefty Goodhearts,' or middlebrow publishers ('England's Bane'), or Zionism, or (even) opponents of the death penalty add up to a die-hard, pragmatic Toryism that—like it or loathe it—goes all through her work.

The best moments are when she is simply quoted: 'As far as the public goes poetry might be one of those branch lines scheduled for closing'; 'Wouldn't it be fun to have an Answerphone that said "They have all gone into the world of light?"' But all too often this material is paraphrased or summed up by her busy, dull interpreters ('Stevie concludes with her thoughts on the relation between vulgarity and evil') whose language deadens hers.

And that is the main problem. These worthy, foot-on-the-ground commentators treat the poems with such laborious ineptitude, and write a prose of such dogged banality, that it's as if some wicked ironical fate has attracted them to this most playful, quicksilver, tough and elusive of minds. One can't be grudging about their labours, and the authorised biography (this one is tolerated but not commissioned by the executor: Stevie's feuds go on beyond the grave) will have to work hard to catch up. It's cruelly tempting, though, to re-apply Stevie Smith's cross words in her review of the New English Bible: 'Everything that was bright is dulled, what was sharp, blunted. Does their great labour, then, serve only to smudge and betray?'

Hermione Lee, "Foot off the Ground," in The Observer, *December 1, 1985, p. 18.*

PENELOPE FITZGERALD

[*Fitzgerald, an English novelist, biographer, and critic, won the Booker Prize for her third novel,* Offshore *(1979). Her other works include the novels* The Golden Child *(1977) and* At Freddie's *(1982), as well as a biography of artist Edward Burne-Jones, published in 1975. In the following excerpt Fitzgerald characterizes* Stevie: A Biography of Stevie Smith *as an accurate if uninspired chronicle of Smith's life.*]

This life [***Stevie: A Biography of Stevie Smith***] is described (twice) in a foreword as not being the authorised one, in allusion to an unfortunate dispute over the bones of a poet who might be thought, from a biographer's point of view, not to have had much of a life at all. Her family came from Hull to London and "the high-lying outer northern suburb" of Palmer's Green. The father, as her poems tell us, deserted them, and no. 1, Avondale Road became "a house of female habitation" for Stevie, her mother and her aunt for the rest of their lives.

"This can't be the right street," said my daughter, taken as a child to see the poet, but it was, and, however sought-after she became, Stevie refused to be dislodged from the House of Mercies. The Lion Aunt tended her, then in later years she tended the Lion Aunt, struggling upstairs with trays. She fell in love perhaps twice, but not very much. As a writer she made a brilliant start, was overlooked in the early 1950's, then came into her own. During the Sixties she became very well known indeed as a reader, disconcertingly dressed in white stockings and gym slip, intoning her own poetry to hymn-tunes and half-tunes, like a child singing in its cot through a long afternoon. In March 1971 she died of a brain tumour, leaving many friends and countless unknown admirers, among whom were Professor Barbera from the University of Mississippi and Professor McBrien from New York. They have spent ten patient years on tracing her uncollected work (***Me Again*** . . .), in producing the present book, and in getting the hard wrung permission to print it.

Any life of Stevie which is to be more than a collection of funny stories must be a spiritual biography. She needed, and showed, a particular kind of courage. She turned her child's size to advantage by suggesting a goblin's magical power, and, at the same time, a reproach—"you have weaned me too soon, you must nurse me again." She suffered, too, the wound of the bright school-leaver who has to go straight into an office:

> Dark was the day for Childe Rolandine the artist
> When she went to work as a secretary-typist.

"I felt this was what I deserved for not having worked better at school. I felt in disgrace, so at once became ambitious for learning." Office tedium was one of the causes of "nerviness", the inner darkness. Stevie, capable as she was of deep joy, said that one had to stay unhappy to write poetry. She had no real difficulty about that. Outside and beyond herself she observed the fates of animals, sad paragraphs in the newspaper, people talking on the bus, and above all the behaviour of her friends. Often the friends disliked being used as subject matter, but Stevie couldn't help it, and (as she explained in **"The Story of a Story"**) didn't see why, as an artist, she should have to help it.

From all this she concluded that staying alive is like being in enemy territory. Death, on the other hand, did not alarm her because it was always on call if needed. "One mustn't bore anyone with the idea," she added. All the same, in July 1953 she called unsuccessfully on Death, cutting her wrists in the Newnes Pearson office. This stands as one of the marking-points on her life, together with the day ten years later when she grew exasperated with the failing Lion Aunt, and hit her.

The Barbera and McBrien method, however, hardly allows for marking-points as they make their painstaking way through many hundreds of interviews and documents. There's a certain flatness, but also a splendid fairmindedness and accuracy; particularly on textual and publication details (they are now collaborating on a bibliography.) They have given the right value, too, to Stevie's struggles with Christian doctrine, which made her, she said, "a backslider as an unbeliever."

Smith with her aunt, Margaret Spear, whom she called "the Lion of Hull." From Stevie: A Biography of Stevie Smith, *by Jack Barbera and William McBrien. Oxford University Press, 1987. Courtesy of Jack Barbera.*

There are, perhaps, some wrong emphases. There should, I believe, have been more, by way of background, about the strange poetry movement, or mania, of the 1960's, with its mass readings (twenty-four hours on end, I remember, at the Round House). I also missed the pathos of Stevie's last two years, when she set herself, in the empty, shabby House of Mercies to cook and "do" exactly as the Lion Aunt had done before her. But I think this is a fine, painstaking biography, and it shows what Stevie herself demanded as the "judging quality"—that is, absolute attention.

Penelope Fitzgerald, "Absolute Attention," in The Times Educational Supplement, *No. 3623, December 6, 1985, p. 21.*

JOHN HORDER

[Horder is an English poet, critic, and journalist whose poetry collections include The Child Walks Around Its Own Grave *(1966) and* A Sense of Being *(1968). In the following excerpt Horder, who became friends with Smith during the last decade of her life, faults Barbera and McBrien for poor scholarship in their biography of the poet.]*

There is no rhyme or reason for this first 'unofficial' biography of Stevie Smith, the poet [***Stevie: A Biography of Stevie Smith***]. I was one of her many friends during the ten years of her life up to her death in 1971. At heart she remained the omnipotent child who expected the whole world to revolve around her. The strength and weakness of this impossible position can be found in her poem **'To Carry the Child',** the last four lines of which say it all:

> But oh the poor child, the poor child, what can
>   he do,
> Trapped in a grown-up carapace,
> But peer outside of his prison room
> With the eye of an anarchist?

In fact, Stevie's complete autobiography is to be found in her poems and fictions like ***Novel on Yellow Paper.*** So what are these two American academics up to apart from accumulating more cash for their old age? In Chapter 1 they retell the already much retold story of when Stevie received the Gold Medal for Poetry:

> Needing a hat for her trip to Buckingham Palace, Stevie went to the jumble sale sponsored by St John's Church in Palmers Green. She acquired a second-hand one, according to the then Vicar of St John's, and 'everybody thought it was killingly funny that that hat was going to go up to the Queen!' . . . On the day she went to the Palace she decided against wearing the hat she'd acquired at St John's. *But, as is true of much about Stevie's life, the detail has become the stuff of legend.* (My italics).

But what need have we of the legend when we have Stevie's magnificent poems? This last sentence is the complete give-away of Barbera and McBrien's parasitical method throughout: in amassing this vast conglomeration of trivia, they are constantly dealing in supposition rather than fact. This has nothing to do with the writing of serious literary biography.

In fact, the only authentic account of Stevie's visit to the palace is to be found in Kay Dick's heart-warming and incisive interview in *Ivy and Stevie*. . . . No matter what Hugh Whitemore lifted from precisely the same material for both the play and the film *Stevie*. Here is the same material regurgitated with acknowledgement to Hugh Whitemore! It makes me puke. I am certain it would have had the same effect on Stevie.

John Horder, in a review of "Stevie: A Biography of Stevie Smith," in New Statesman, *Vol. 110, No. 2855, December 13, 1985, p. 28.*

SUSANNAH CLAPP

[*Clapp is an English critic and editor. In the following excerpt Clapp describes* Stevie *as a thorough if not especially perceptive biography.*]

[***Stevie: A Biography of Stevie Smith***] gets off to a bad start with its title. The writer called Stevie Smith was also a celebrity called Stevie—a spiky sprite who was famous for being unfashionable. This creature thrived on being a spinster, which licensed her to be a bit cuckoo, and on speaking her hard words from a spindly frame decked out like a schoolgirl's—as if it were a feat to think behind a fringe. For Stevie Smith the writer it was comfortable, though not always convenient, to live out of the centre of London: for Stevie the celebrity it was a triumph—an acquaintance is cited here as drawling that her 'ability' to live in Palmers Green while moving in London literary circles was 'the most compelling thing about her'. First-named throughout this book, by biographers who apparently never met her, Stevie Smith and her work are draped in Palmers Greenery. Would a biographer of Hughes call him Ted?

It is not easy to write a forceful narrative about a woman who never changed her house, her job or her companion. From the age of three, when her father ran away to sea—prompted, one poem suggests, by a baleful look shot by the poet from her pram—Florence Margaret Smith lived in her Palmers Green house; from her mid-twenties, nicknamed Stevie after the jockey Steve Donoghue, she lived there alone with her aunt, producing three novels and a torrent of poems and articles, and working as a secretary at Newnes and Pearson's publishing company. Nor is it easy to write a clear-sighted account of a gifted writer who is wily, opinionated and defensively self-descriptive: 'This is a foot-off-the-ground novel,' explains the narrator of ***Novel on Yellow Paper.*** 'And if you are a foot-on-the-ground person, this book will be for you a desert of weariness and exasperation.' Jack Barbera and William McBrien approach their subject with generous and indiscriminate zeal. They have talked to a great many people, waded through an enormous amount of newsprint, and found everything interesting: the fact that Stevie Smith once came third in an egg-and-spoon race; the idea that 'commonplace neighbours' should have provided her with 'telling details of actual life'. They have made some delightful discoveries—for example, that Stevie Smith loved these lines by an unnamed satirist:

> Hush, hush, it couldn't be worse
> Christopher Robin is having his nurse.

And they make some peculiar gestures towards imaginative analysis. Stevie Smith's mother once won a prize for a short story in a local Eisteddfod: Barbera and McBrien say that her daughter's literary career could be seen as an 'emulation'. Can they be serious?

The zeal of these biographers wavers when they turn to discussing what Stevie Smith wrote. This is a book in which the celebration of talent comes to seem almost as important as the talent itself. Barbera and McBrien give considerable emphasis to the publishing history of each volume, and to the views of contemporary critics: much less to their own opinions. When ***Novel on Yellow Paper*** appears, we are told of the 'mandarin approval' of 'wits so exquisite and discriminating' as Raymond Mortimer, Noël Coward and Desmond Shawe-Taylor; on the publication of a book of poems a flurry of plaudits—'grimly entertaining', 'brilliantly funny and intimate'—is produced. Barbera and McBrien summarise and categorise her output according to theme; they treat her address to her subject-matter and her characteristic effects as if they were monosodium glutamate—we learn of ***Novel on Yellow Paper*** that 'style ennobles' a plot which could be found in a woman's magazine, and that many of her humorous remarks 'arise out of sadness but transform it by wit'.

Stevie Smith's poems are full of transformations and translations: a frog may become a prince, a typist gets sucked into the seascape of a Turner canvas in her lunch-hour. But what gives her verse its distinctive ring is her way of putting together the humdrum and the elevated in situation and vocabulary. In her poems large events happen to, or inside, people with names like patent medicines; slang runs up against over-proper English, and narrative description drops in and out of direct speech without warning: 'Dust to dust, Oh how frightful sighed the mourners as the rain began.' She casts doubt on the most booming phrase by closing it with a trick of the tongue: 'World without end ahem'. Barbera and McBrien praise the poem in which this last phrase appears for the facility with which it 'spots the comic amid immortal longings', but her verse as often moves in the opposite direction, giving dignity to the neglected or the apparently absurd.

These are also poems in which accidents happen: which play on the accidents of language and on the idea of accident. Stevie Smith's verse is full of near-misses and near-matches: shifts in metre, lines which bump or straggle, half-rhymes which can set up a sinister tinkle, as in **'The Murderer':**

She was not like other girls—rather diffident,
And that is how we had an accident.

Barbera and McBrien detect an 'incongruous liveliness' in the speaker of her most famous poem [**'Not Waving but Drowning'**], but do not note the dissonant wail which settles 'moaning' into 'drowning'. In her verse, allusion to earlier poets frequently carries the suggestion of another near-miss, expressing not a resonant continuity but a falling-off. Stevie Smith, who took a lugubrious satisfaction in 'loamishly sad' Victorian verse, turned Tennyson's lament for lost delights into a dirge about desiccation:

Cold as no love, and wild with all negation—
Oh Death in Life, the lack of animation.

There are a variety of accidents in these poems—a bold leap between rocks turns into a tumble, a giant hat whisks a fiancée away to a desert island, people drown, get lost or are fatally misunderstood—and not all these mishaps are unwelcome. There are also poems in which people experience themselves as being beside the point, or are urged to consider that there may not be a point:

You are only one of many
And of small account if any,
You think about yourself too much.
This touched the child with a quick touch.

Stevie Smith fought a sustained and admirable battle with Christianity, and the best of her poems carry the conviction that, however disagreeable, it isn't odd to feel accidental.

Her drawings—whose variable relationship to particular poems is examined with pertinacity by Barbera and McBrien—offer a mix of the idiosyncratic and the not-entirely-human which is characteristic of much of her verse. Ferocious, capering, drooping figures with currant eyes and sardonic mouths, they sprout unexpected personal effects—an umbrella, a fancy hat, a bunch of curls like cabbages. They have grace, and the comic appeal of sculptures wearing gloves. Both her drawings and her poems show people caught in a lifetime's grimace or grin: 'With my looks I am bound to look simple or fast . . .' Barbera and McBrien, perhaps prompted by a letter in which Stevie Smith explained that one volume of her work could be divided into poems which were self-portraits and those which were 'about being dead or dotty', are on the *qui vive* for confession and revelation. They tell us that a poem about suicide is 'immensely personal', and that lines dealing in dream, loss and tears 'read like autobiography'. It isn't clear why they consider some verses more autobiographical than others, though they tend to attach confessional significance to particularly glum lines: 'poignant' is a word they favour, and we are told that one poem 'seems poignantly autobiographical'. But the distinctive quality of Stevie Smith's poems depends on the elusiveness of their speakers: she elides dialogue and comment, kidnapping voices to express what an individual would never say. Lady 'Rogue' Singleton is courted with a jingling rhyme which dashes her hopes of a glamorous match:

Come, wed me, Lady Singleton,
And we will have a baby soon
And we will live in Edmonton.

Her reply has the boom of drawing-room melodrama, as well as the jumbled idiosyncrasy of thought:

I am not a cold woman, Henry,
But I do not feel for you,
What I feel for the elephants and the miasmas
And the general view.

In an essay she wrote for *Medical World* in 1956, Stevie Smith talked of the tricks fatigue played with what she saw and what she wrote, of how everything became 'just a bit off-beam'. Off-beamness can snuggle into cuteness. But it can also suggest a discrepancy between how people appear and what they are, and produces some stunning first lines: 'She is not Indian, she's ill'; 'Drugs made Pauline vague.' This may be what Barbera and McBrien mean when they talk of 'vintage Stevie'.

Stevie Smith's aunt thought her niece's writing was 'unnecessary'. Yet she helped it to happen: by her devotion, by running their house for more than forty years, by embodying attitudes about which her niece was both skittish and reverent. 'People think because I never married, I know nothing about the emotions,' Stevie Smith told a friend. 'When I am dead you must put them right. I loved my aunt.' In ***Novel on Yellow Paper*** Margaret Annie Spear is presented as staunch, sensible and surprising: a bossy housekeeper, fearful with her curling tongs; a church-going Tory, munching game pie and beer at midnight. Barbera and McBrien add some details to this picture: they stress the degree to which Miss Spear spoiled her niece—according to one friend, Stevie Smith was incapable of warming her bedtime milk by herself; they emphasise the bleakness towards the end of her life when the poet explained that her aunt had been equipped with a hearing-aid, but 'there doesn't seem much to say.' And they tell us that Miss Spear looked like Gertrude Stein. However, they provide very little of the aunt's own voice: two fragments from her correspondence are quoted, showing considerable dash, some malice, and uncritical loyalty towards her niece; other letters are mentioned as being 'long' or 'characteristically loving'. And they make little attempt to work out to what extent the 'Auntie Lion' of ***Novel on Yellow Paper*** who is described as 'a genuine bit of Old Fielding' was actually a bit of Stevie Smith: the poet may have had an interest in creating a large eccentric to whom she could play the gamine.

Stevie Smith was quick to point out the disadvantages of having a husband, with their 'boring old father-talk' and their capacity for turning their wives into wimps, 'so often delighted to tell you how splendidly bullying their husbands are . . . it is as if they would say, You may not think it but I am married to a tiger.' Yet she reaped some of the benefits of having an old-fashioned wife—a life outside the home, with solicitude and hot milk to come back to. And while she was sceptical about the '*à deux* fix', and urged flight from its miseries in her verse, she did not entirely share her aunt's position on romance: Miss Spear said that she could 'understand liking a man, but not being in love with him'. The novels contain some mooning, and some rather strenuous celebration of the opposite sex.

Barbera and McBrien identify the love-objects of her first two novels. The Karl of ***Novel on Yellow Paper*** was a Karl in real life: a German student who kissed her at the foot of the Duke of York's steps. The Freddy of this and her next novel, ***Over the Frontier,*** turns out to be an Eric: an insurance man and attender of a Palmers Green social club, who is described here by one friend as 'weak and unimpressive', and by Eric's niece as 'tall, dark-haired . . . good-looking'. Eric was once spotted with her in a derelict mansion—not 'doing anything interesting . . . just sort of crawling around'. In a passage she deleted from ***Novel on Yellow Paper*** Stevie Smith explained that Freddy wasn't her lover—but only because he didn't seize his moment.

These biographers produce several rather different views about what Stevie Smith got up to with men: a 'probably not' from her sister, a 'never took the last fence' from Elisabeth Lutyens, and one anecdote about the poet waking up in bed with a man and the memory of having 'done some terrible things'. They discuss the possibility of a particularly grim coupling between Smith and George Orwell in a London park, and link this lightly and improbably with her verses about liking to be 'tightly kissed'. They also report that she claimed to have been pursued by Orwell—with an uncertain degree of nudity—through the corridors of Bush House. Her bifurcated portrait of Orwell in ***The Holiday*** suggests interest, but not passion; her furious letter to him, claiming that he had cheated her out of a radio broadcast in 1942, suggests some intimacy, but is not evidently that of a woman scorned. Barbera and McBrien don't come to any firm conclusion of their own, although, in a passage which goes beyond even Stevie Smith's gloomy view of the rigours of wedded life, they propose that chronic fatigue made her 'ill-fitted for marriage, its physical tasks, and perhaps even for sex'.

The romantic entanglements in Stevie Smith's novels are described with the revolving self-preoccupation of adolescence. Freddy is languished over, grumbled about, patronised and treated so much as A Relationship that, although his social habits are sketched, his character is extinguished. Men are only one occasion for the many excursions and debates in her fictions, fictions which test the elasticity of 'the talking voice that runs on' by discoursing on sex education, proof-reading, the Church of England and Dionysus—and can seem to congratulate themselves on doing so. These fictions have the elliptical urgency of notes to an intimate; they can also, as David Garnett complained in a letter quoted by Barbera and McBrien, become 'an impenetrable dossier of private day-dreams'.

Some of the incidents and arguments of her novels are treated more cogently in poems. Some of them might have been better not treated at all. Stevie Smith went to Germany in 1931, and in ***Novel on Yellow Paper*** she hits out at 'all its whimpering lovey dovey get-all-together . . . its Movements, and Back to Wotan'. Yet the same novel agonises with apologetic disingenuousness over a friend who 'got married to a man that is a Jew, and the sort of Jew not like Herman or Bennie that has an artistic temperament working overtime on all cylinders, but just a plain ordinary safe businessman of a Jew with a whole hell of a great idea about money'. In ***Over the Frontier*** she is 'in despair for the racial hatred that is running in me . . . Do we not always hate the persecuted?' Barbera and McBrien assert that hers was 'the usual pre-war attitude of the English': but it wasn't the attitude of many of her friends, some of whom broke with her because of her statements.

Taken together, Stevie Smith's novels could be seen as a continuous discussion about the state of middle-class England confronted by war. The party-going narrator of ***Novel on Yellow Paper*** becomes a boundary-crossing secret agent in ***Over the Frontier,*** and a melancholy debater of the end of Empire in ***The Holiday.*** But the central preoccupations of these books are more closely intertwined with those of her poems. Pompey Casmilus, the Hermetically-named narrator of ***Novel on Yellow Paper***—patron of poets and thieves, intermediary between this world and the underworld—goes under cover, or underworld, in ***Over the Frontier.*** In ***The Holiday*** her identity changes, or splits: this unequivocally female narrator is in love with her cousin 'Caz', who is 'quite mad about death'; she loiters with him beside lakes and sarcophagi—the scenery to which Pluto snatched Persephone. Read consecutively, these novels can be seen as a flight from ordinary romance and friendship towards death; Stevie Smith considered writing a novel called 'Married to Death'. It is a flight in which there is little of the romantic swoon: as in many of her poems, death is seen as a good match.

In fact, Stevie Smith rarely ran from her friends: she liked to go visiting, and she liked to be given lifts back to Palmers Green. The liveliest passages in this biography are descriptions by friends of her behaviour. Much of Barbera and McBrien's prose has a muffled quality: page after page is filled with accounts 'based on' what someone said, or on what Stevie Smith wrote. But they sometimes allow friends to speak for themselves. What they have to say is far from fulsome. According to Francis King, she was 'a great character', but 'not, emphatically, not a nice character'. Elisabeth Lutyens talks of her 'childishly screaming for attention'. Stalwart chums resented her endless cadging of car rides—one proposed writing an essay called 'Taking Stevie Home'. Taken to Venice by one couple, she spurned their plans and instituted her own regime: shopping for safety-pins during the day, and sitting by the canals at night explaining that they were beautiful. Staying

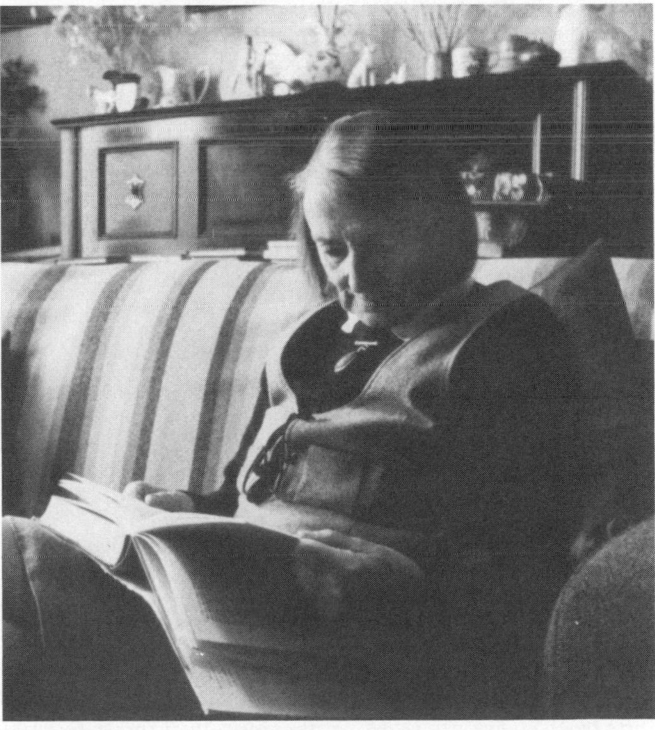

Smith at her home in Palmers Green. John Goldblatt/The Daily Telegraph Colour Library.

in Devon with another family, she flounced out of family picnics—apparently resenting the attention given to an ailing child—took to her bed, and posted grumbling letters to Palmers Green. Miss Spear, unreservedly supportive, suggested that her niece might write something about her visit, and if her hosts 'recognised themselves serve them right'; when her poem **'The Holiday'**—which speaks of 'the malice and the misunderstanding' suffered by a guest—was published in the *Observer,* it was taken to heart by more than one of Stevie Smith's hosts. Barbera and McBrien make all this worse by insisting that most of her friends agree that she 'was, basically, kind'.

This biography makes it easy to understand why Stevie Smith lost friends. She wrote harshly, in verse and prose, about their marriages and about their children—and she made her characters recognisable. In **'The Story of a Story'** she examined the trouble this caused. She gives a subtle account of the distress and annoyance experienced by one couple—in real life, Francis and Margery Hemming—when they discover a friend is writing about them. But the writer's distress has the last word: her dreamy self-absorption is mildly guyed, but her motives are held to be pure, almost lofty. The couple weep and threaten law; editors are presented as pusillanimous; the writer tells the truth, and is exiled for doing so. This is a story that it is good to believe if you want to go on writing about your friends, and it is delivered with conviction. Barbera and McBrien do not make it easy to see why Stevie Smith kept friends. Explaining that 'failing to amuse one's companions if invited to dinner or a weekend house party remains, of course, a cardinal sin in England,' they doggedly detail their subject's social manner: 'natural wit', 'never glossed over painful realities', 'quickly seized the real point of any conversation'. None of this is cheering; none of it is inaccurate; none of it captures the lively responsiveness of her letters.

'If she's really dying, send her my love,' Olivia Manning said when Stevie Smith was taken to hospital. The poet is reported to have enjoyed this. She had entertained the idea of suicide as an honourable way out since she was nine; she once tried to kill herself by slashing her wrists at Newnes and Pearson's—an attempt which Barbera and McBrien ascribe, narrowly though not unreasonably, to being fed up with her job. But she died of a brain tumour. She sat in hospital with her shaven head in a shocking-pink scarf, and without turning to the fierce and 'flower-like' Christ against whom she had battled. The poet of accidents found her vocabulary disarranged: 'I tried to say to . . . someone that I could not find the word I wanted. But instead of "word" I said "milk" first & then "snow".' (pp. 22-3)

Susannah Clapp, "Palmers Greenery," in London Review of Books, *Vol. 7, No. 22, December 19, 1985, pp. 22-3.*

PETER KEMP

Among the antique bric-à-brac—shells, sepia portraits, pictures after Landseer—bedecking 1 Avondale Road, Palmers Green, where Stevie Smith passed most of her life, was a pot of dried honesty. Spiky and brittle, it might have been a symbol of that other kind of honesty she made her own. For, as Jack Barbera and William McBrien's biography [***Stevie: A Biography of Stevie Smith***] keeps reminding you, uncomfortable candour was her forte. Her poetry romps along playfully, then suddenly pipes out disconcerting truths. Discomfiting frankness also featured in the reviews she wrote: casting a critical eye over religious books, she provoked pained outcries from vicarages and deaneries by her insistence on Christianity's cruelty. Her fiction—flitting, like her verse, over human savagery, instability and impermanence—also ruffled feelings by over-directness. Friends used as raw material felt she didn't so much write stories as tell tales. 'Charles is grieved at your having put Prue in your book,' one acquaintance reprovingly writes. Another, nettled by mention of her husband's 'fat little behind on the piano stool', felt Stevie had 'a warped way of looking at things'.

Stevie shows you—among some *longueurs* and irrelevancies—where this way of looking at things came from. What emerges from its narrative is a badly shaken childhood followed by an existence of paralysed fixity. A major jolt to Stevie's stability, it seems, came when she was three, and her father, cutting loose from the family semi in Hull, drifted off to a life at sea from which he never returned. Stevie had scarcely settled down from this when another upheaval hit her. Contracting tubercular peritonitis, she had to leave the 'house of female habitation' she was sharing in Palmers Green with her mother, sister, aunt and great-aunt for three years of recurrent residence in a convalescent home. One lasting effect of this was an inability to sleep other than in total darkness (any glimmer of light awoke memories of the convalescent wards). Another was a lifelong hankering for security.

At Avondale Road, Stevie recalled 'although Fear knocked hard / Upon the door', the occupants 'did not let him in'. Shutting out anxiety became her main preoccupation. 'I want more security,' she declared, was her watchword. One threat to stability, she sensed, was involvement with other people: 'sex,' she believed, 'is a tyrant's weapon'; her favourite classical plays were *Phaedra* and *The Bacchae,* reminders of passion's destructive turbulence; in a poem like **'Goodnight',** she gives a hauntingly horrible glimpse of marital intimacy gone wrong. It was safer, Stevie felt, to keep 'on the edge'—though, in her poetry, that image takes on a worrying, different connotation. 'Children who paddle where the ocean bed shelves steeply / Must take care they do not paddle too deeply,' she reminds herself. Her best-known poem, **'Not Waving But Drowning',** is about a fatal plunge from the shallows into the depths. What underlies its sinking feeling is Stevie's awareness of life's precariousness. Tremors go through all her writing when she contemplates 'the fearful business of being a human creature'. In a weird way—combining the prankish melancholia of Edward Lear with Tennyson's flinchings from man's animal nature—she can seem like a late-Victorian still reeling from the impact of Darwinism. In her verses, it's 'pig unto pig' as a glutton gobbles ham. Often, she sees herself as a beast, 'God's sick tiger', liable to bite. One poem warns against the practice of photographing infants on tiger-skins: animality is already within—for 'the child is the young of its species / Alike with that noble, vile, curious and fierce'.

As photographs and reminiscences here document, Stevie's defence against life's beastliness was to try to remain the schoolgirl she'd been shielded and cosseted as. Got up in juvenile jumpers and tunics, Peter Pan collars and Alice bands, she retained a girlish giggle and hoydenish ways—tumbling merrily into clumps of nettles or coming a cropper on Ivy Compton-Burnett's slippery lino. Invited to Buckingham Palace to receive a Gold Medal, she reacted like a little girl attending her first party in a strange home: would they give her things to eat? was a lavatory handy? Meeting her in her mid-fifties, a Swiss professor sternly noted her 'childlike posture' and 'demeanour' which was 'not that of a mature, responsible grown-up person'.

This, of course, was the point. Responsibility was something Stevie shunned—partly contriving to preserve a child-like persona because of the survival to the age of 96 of the 'Lion Aunt' who looked after her. The most important person in Stevie's life, she stays something of a cipher in this book. Though there's reference to her 'broad North Country accent', her voice is scarcely heard—except in a revealing letter urging Stevie, who is having an exasperating holiday, to write a tart story about her hosts ('if they recognised themselves serve them right').

'I loved my aunt,' Stevie said not long before dying. Whether she loved anyone else remains obscure. Barbera and McBrien gamely track down possible *amours*—a German chum, a North London neighbour, even George Orwell (improbably rumoured to have been involved with Stevie in a nude scamper round Bush House)—but nothing much is uncovered. Stevie never 'took the last fence' when it came to sex, a lifelong friend avers; her biographers settle for the verdict that she 'could hardly be called an adept'.

It's hard to see how she could have been, given her investment in juvenility. Acquaintances, recalling the pampering she demanded, emphasise that she was 'competitive with children', regarding them as 'rivals' for attention, chocolates and cream cakes. Behind the moppet disguise, though, was adult *angst*. At times, she shows a nightmarish sense of her situation: there's a piece by her in which a 'famously ugly old girl', envious of the security represented by a pram, climbs into one and stabs herself with a hat-pin. Suicide was always a comforting prospect for Stevie. 'In Death is sorrow shed,' one of her poems rejoices; many of them dote on decease; prominent among her objections to Christianity was its embargo on self-slaughter. As it transpired—though she once, worn down by feelings of neglect, slashed her wrists in the windowless office where she'd drudged for years—Stevie never opted out of life in this way. Instead, she tiptoed round its periphery, with her sharp dark eyes missing nothing. (pp. 27-8)

Peter Kemp, "Honest Stevie," in The Listener, *Vol. 115, No. 2943, January 16, 1986, pp. 27-8.*

MICHAEL HOROVITZ

[*Horovitz, an English poet, editor, and critic, founded the Beat-influenced poetry magazine* New Departures *in 1959. His own poetry collections include* Declaration *(1963),* Growing Up: Selected Poems, 1953-1978 *(1979), and* A Celebration of and for Frances Horovitz *(1984). In the following excerpt Horovitz defends* Stevie: A Biography of Stevie Smith *against hostile critics such as Hermione Lee (see excerpt above).*]

The English reviewing establishment seems to have closed its ranks against this first biography [***Stevie: A Biography of Stevie Smith***] of the spritely sibyl Brian Patten has dubbed 'Blake's purest daughter'. For me it's a triumph of what the authors themselves concede is 'the American tradition of the beaver, as opposed to the English tradition of the butterfly'. This is perfectly apt, since they are Americans from a younger generation than their subject, and never met her; since Stevie Smith was—and her writings remain—so particularly butterflylike; and since these writings and other primary sources are so lavishly quoted throughout.

Messrs Barbera and McBrien (B-M hereafter) had already completed a salutary course of field-work by co-editing ***Me Again*** . . . , their highly entertaining and instructive miscellany of uncollected Stevieana. Among the thousands of papers they perused on their further researches was a soldier's fan letter saying, 'You remind me of a laughing butterfly flickering over the head of James Joyce.' Stevie's flights of fancy, wordplay and imagination were faster and looser than Joyce's or Blake's—though the lightness could be deceptive, with serrated blades in its sheen or a subtle sting in the tail. She kept her muse free to be spontaneous, darting in and out of gardens and air pockets and shifting fairy woods their grandiose master-plans forbade. Joyce's verbal-butterfly pub-crawls were passing diversions from an intently (and honourably) beaverlike pursuit not unlike that with which B-M track Stevie's progress. Their scholarship, at once resourceful and ingenious though by definition plodding, for the most part illuminates without disrupting its subject's complex impulses, movements and effects.

Nevertheless, Hermione Lee for one has rebuked them for making Stevie's life and work seem boring [see excerpt above]. She does this in much the same terms as I—perhaps too waspishly—chided her ***Stevie Smith: A Selection*** (. . . 'designed especially for students') in the *Spectator* on 24 November 1984. Sixty of B-M's 580 pages are made up of notes to their exposition—a smaller fraction than the 30 pages set aside in Miss Lee's 224. My calling the latter 'inappropriately laboured', and her extrapolations 'sometimes laughably perfunctory', seems to have touched a nerve, because her *Observer* piece on B-M (1 December '85) in turn accuses them of 'banal platitudes' and 'laborious ineptitude'. Yet—by contrast to her book and to her review of theirs—B-M's commentaries are factual, judicious, pithy, always helpfully substantiated and scrupulously acknowledged. Miss Lee ridicules their 'worthy, foot-on-the-ground' approach, although the self-effacing beaver's industry is the very thing that keeps Stevie's elusively zig-zagging wings so steadily in focus. Any attempt to pin down her soul in words would be foolish indeed, but we should thank these men for giving us such a clear and unassuming itinerary of its chronological manifestations.

The text is most charmingly embellished with photographs and drawings from every phase of her development, and the biographers are particularly good on Stevie's sketches, and her relationship to other artists and writers:

> . . . Often, next to poems about rejection, loss and despair, her childlike drawings playfully wink at the reader as if to say, 'it is legitimate to express anger or sorrow, but then one must laugh', or, 'this is a volume of poetry, but one need not be "serious" about it'. Stevie's decorating her text was subversive—not that other poets hadn't done so, other 'eccentrics' such as Blake and Lear. But doodles are personal, and T. S. Eliot had made popular the notion that good poetry is impersonal. It would have been as unlikely for him to decorate his serious poems with doodles as it would have been for him to sing them. During the heyday of New Criticism, poems were supposed to be well-wrought objects. Such a metaphor minimises the relevance of things external to the text. 'If Stevie's poetry is more fashionable today than it was in the '50s, so too is the metaphor of a poem as a voice. In terms of such a metaphor an author's drawing need not be dismissed as a frill or crutch, for it can be taken as another voice or statement. Whether a poem and drawing are in harmony or counterpoint, and how

they colour each other, become matters of interest.

It's true that the simultaneous grace and incongruity of her illustrations was matched by the boldly off-key or sad-clownish tones in which she would sing some of her verses in private and, increasingly over her last 15 years, in public. And her habitually breezy conversational-mental flow is indeed about as far as one could get from Eliot's stern formalistic propriety. Though he complained of 'the intolerable wrestle with words', he could never have written lines like '. . . Person from Porlock come quickly / And bring my thoughts to an end. / I am hungry to be interrupted / For ever and ever amen.' Nor can one quite imagine Eliot writing to Pound as Stevie did to a Professor Häusermann describing 'this new idea—if that's the word for it—I've had about stringing several poems together on a theme. For instance the Person from Porlock begins with (1) The Story (for ignorant types who haven't heard of it!) (2) Research material & how assinine (sic) it can be (3) the glum personal thoughts striking up (4) wishing they weren't so glum.'

Her **'Little Boy Sick'** refracts Blake's familiar symbology. 'I am not God's little lamb / I am God's sick tiger. / And I prowl about at night / And what most I love I bite / . . . upon the jungle grass I slink / Snuff the aroma of my mental stink.' But though Blake was, as she knew, 'full of contradictions', he was far from what Stevie felt herself to be, 'an unbeliever with a religious temperament'. Her depiction of a child on a tiger skin rather less cuddly than Father William's oddly mild looking mog, provides a rather more vivid case in point of Woody Allen's irrefutable, 'Okay, the lion shall lie down with the lamb, but the lamb won't get very much sleep.'

One of her earliest poems, **'Infant,'** displays an immediately striking divergence from the unalloyed ecstasy of Blake's 'Infant Joy': 'It was a cynical babe / Lay in its mother's arms / Born two months too soon / After many alarms / Why is its mother sad / Weeping without a friend / Where is its father—say? / He tarries in Ostend. / It was a cynical babe. Reader before you condemn, pause, / It was a cynical babe. Not without cause.' Three years after her birth in 1902 Stevie's father ran away to sea, abandoning his family for good. As B-M see it, 'Deprived at an early age of her terrestrial father and mother and born into a century that witnessed the death of God, this heir of Blake walked about as a child not of Innocence but solely of Experience.' I'm not quite convinced about the 'solely'. Of 'To carry the child into adult life / Is to be handicapped', Stevie did say the 'man in the poem is meant to . . . feel the nuisance it can be, but then to see it is a nuisance for the child too, and that where the two of them exist together, then each has a right to exist, and some value'; though the poem itself admits that

> The child in adult life is defenceless
> And if he is grown-up, knows it,
> And the grown-up looks at the childish part
> And despises it.

Blake viewed our mortal incarnation as a faint shadow of the eternal life at hand. Although Stevie contrived to keep at least one foot off the ground—to enjoy at least some part of carrying the child into her own gratifyingly popular old age, it was very much a child of this century of dramatically mundane upheavals and atrocities. Her other foot had been uprooted from the cosy expectations of Edwardian gentility and re-grounded with her sister and 'the Lion Aunt' in Palmers Green, thence to try and retrace a creed and culture shattered to its foundations, twice over, by unprecedentedly godless and murderous wars. A. S. Byatt thinks she connected 'her sly interest in sadomasochism, which surfaces particularly in her anxious novel of 1938, ***Over the Frontier,*** with these swinges of universal violence and physical danger.' In her 50th year she attempted suicide by slashing her wrists, having acknowledged its possibility since early childhood.

So it is no surprise that this office-worker from the suburbs, self-consigned to prowl London's socio-literary jungle, got as close to the tragi-comic vision of Beckett, as the mystical one of Blake: portraying for instance, a woeful parent and child with the caption, 'There are some human beings who do not wish for eternal life'; or to the sardonic one of another English 'spinster poet', Philip Larkin (who admired her originality and emotional realism, and came to settle in the Hull she'd left in 1906 and never revisited). Larkin's 'deprivation is for me what daffodils were for Wordsworth' reminds me of Stevie's sense that 'being alive is like being in enemy territory'. And her reluctance to take the longest journey in 'the *à deux* fix', or to contemplate maternity, shares something with his strain of 'Get out as early as you can, / And don't have any kids yourself'. . . . It seems to me very much to her credit that she robustly maintained her independence over her five adult decades—ones in which single women encountered far stiffer opposition than they're so often likely to today.

The strangely bad press the biography and also Stevie's character as it emerges therefrom have thus far received, is surely

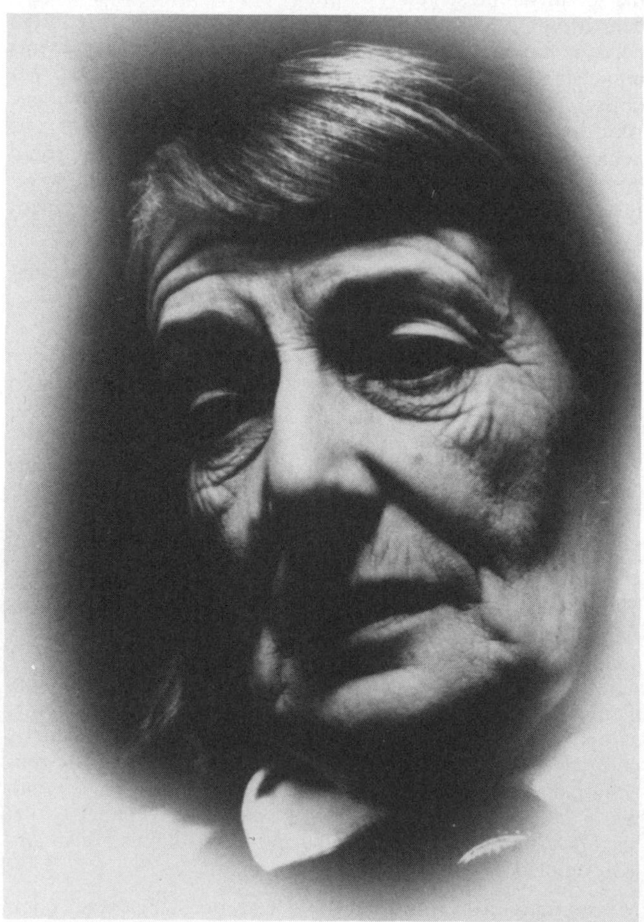

Smith in the final year of her life. National Portrait Gallery, London.

unjustified. If she'd done no more than made a better job than most of fulfilling the Blakean injunction she was oft wont to cite—'Little creature, form'd of joy & mirth, / Go, love without the help of anything on earth'—she'd deserve our unqualified respect. What Barbera & McBrien expose is the enormous range of her achievement, and the enormous odds against which it was won. Their exploration reveals 'the secret life' Forster wanted novels to probe. It shows just how much farther out than we thought Miss Smith actually was, and how often not waving but drowning. (pp. 30-1)

Michael Horovitz, "A Laughing Butterfly," in The Spectator, *Vol. 256, No. 8221, February 1, 1986, pp. 30-1.*

KAY DICK

[Dick, an English novelist, critic, editor, dramatist, and scriptwriter, publishes both under her own name and the pseudonym Jeremy Scott. Her novels as Kay Dick include By the Lake *(1949) and* The Shelf *(1984). Among her nonfiction works is* Ivy and Stevie: Ivy Compton Burnett and Stevie Smith: Conversations and Reflections *(1971), a collection of extended interviews with the two writers. Barbera and McBrien used* Ivy and Stevie *as a reference source for their biography and also interviewed Dick. In the following excerpt Dick faults the biographers for an unimaginative, trivia-obsessed approach to a subject that she proposes requires a more sensitive technique.]*

I declare an interest: with my consent much of the material used by these two biographers [in ***Stevie: A Biography of Stevie Smith***] has been taken from my book, *Ivy & Stevie* (still available, dear readers, in paperback), and from additional info I supplied. . . .

When these two American academics came first to have tea with me for Stevie chat, I was, admittedly, a trifle disconcerted to discover as I handed round the cucumber sandwiches that one of these gentlemen was busily tape-recording our tea talk. Assuming a hostess's privilege I soon put a stop to that.

In view of my involvement in this biography I was naturally eager to read it. Especially so because I could not grasp how two people could write a biography together. Who did what? Which paragraphs belong to one or t'other? I did express my incomprehension. Alas, my apprehension appears to have been justified, and is shared by Stevie's executor whose obligatory foreword is a sharpish dissociation, pointing out that an authorised biography is now being written. This is Frances Spaulding (author of *Vanessa Bell*) who, I would guess, will supply what the Americans fail to do, namely speculation of an imaginative kind, pertinent to such a vivid character as Stevie whose actual life was not in any way dramatic, in the ordinary sense that is. . . .

As to the McBrien and Barbera text, well, let us be fair, it is clearly (at enormous length) a work of industry. There's a heavy tread of feet from all those people interviewed—a case of not seeing the wood for the trees. Conscientiously Stevie's birth to death data is herein recorded—recorded is the word to describe the joint prose style. One gains the impression that the authors have followed, diligently, all details in Stevie's diary (I write metaphorically here), and listed each and every item. Imagine, as I will do, one day's entry: "Woke up from bad dream. Kissed Lion Aunt goodmorning. Ate lightly boiled egg for breakfast. Went to work for my baronets in London town (such a slog from Palmers Green). Met George Orwell for lunch—cup of tea in Hyde Park. Back to office where wrote more pages of ***Novel on Yellow Paper.*** End of workday (yawn, yawn!).

"To party at Inez Holden's, best friend (how nice to be a rich girl!). Accepted several weekend invites: must check on what creature comforts will be offered. Did, eventually, get an admirer to drive me back to Palmers Green. Kissed Lion Aunt now asleep. Thought about a poem before going to sleep. Hey Ho!"

I fantasize of course, but you get the feeling, and the overall unsatisfactory tone of this biography.

What I think (and let me not be called insular) is that both these American professors have failed to understand the Englishness of Stevie. That mixture of the Lion and the Unicorn in her, and in her work. The mixture in her of the fantastical and, to quote her (*I&S*) her "basic sensible" view of facts. What is lacking here is Stevie's sighting of life and death, joy and pain, her driven instinct to trap these mysteries in her poetry and prose. She attempted suicide, and welcomed death. I asked her "But you wouldn't like to be dead?" Her response was near enthusiastic: "I think it would be marvellous." This has not been explored with imagination.

Then there is that extraordinary relationship between Stevie and the Aunt. Stevie was the Unicorn and Aunt the Lion. Between them existed a love affair—non sexual of course—rather than an ordinary kinship. No other relationship could compete with Stevie for Aunt's enduring and uncritical love. The professors cannot quite appreciate this: they view it all as mere domestic background. No, in spite of the niceness and diligence the American professors reduce Stevie to a state of ordinariness: without appreciating that they are so doing. And ordinary was the last thing Stevie was. The high pitch of Stevie's melancholic exuberance (yes the two often go together) is missing. There is no sparkle to this Stevie, no true link with the Stevie of the poems, those 1000 gems, all so vivid, witty, teasing and shrewd about the 1000 ways in which human beings savage each other under the guise of duty and love. Altogether a sadly inadequate biography in which the subject is suffocated in trivia.

To end and let me record an extract from one of Stevie's letters to myself (reprinted in the biography): "If you attempt to be more melancholy than me I shall be more than furious: I shall be *hurt*. I felt too low for words last weekend, but worked it off for all that in a poem, and *Punch* like it, think it *funny* I suppose. It was touching, I thought—called **'Not Waving But Drowning.'**"

This is one of her most famous and quoted poems. Congratulations to *Punch*, even if they did think it "funny". Well, perhaps *Punch* were not so far out with their "funny", because its humour is the slanted kind of comic tragedy which distinguishes all of Stevie's poetry. Heart-rending in the main this poetry is, with its acceptance that so much of life is heartrendingly funny. *Punch* was right!

Kay Dick, "Stevie Wonder," in Punch, *Vol. 290, No. 7572, February 5, 1986, p. 49.*

ROY JENKINS

The adult Stevie Smith once gleefully picked all the smoked salmon out of the sandwiches at a reception, leaving the other guests nothing but bread and butter. The child—she was called Peggy then—would decide which hymn she would sing in church (usually it was "Once in Royal David's City") and proceed to sing it, regardless of what everybody else was singing. There was a freakish, anarchic, selfish streak in her that eludes definition. Her diligent and commendable biographers nearly catch it [in ***Stevie: A Biography of Stevie Smith***].

They try hard: they have interviewed an enormous number of people who knew her and were happy to tell tales about her. She made a good acquaintance, but a bad friend, and there are many prepared to relate the problems she caused them. When a poem of hers described the "malice and the misunderstanding, the loneliness and the pain" of a holiday spent with friends, several families fell over each other in the rush to claim that theirs was the ghastly time that inspired it. She knew she was difficult, but she exorcised so many of her feelings in her writing that the wounded friends and animosity must have been a price worth paying. When she started reviewing, she wrote of longing to "say what I think in a vigorous and highly offensive manner—and avoid the consequences". But, as Olivia Manning, Rosamond Lehmann, Elizabeth Lutyens and others would agree, grown-ups cannot do that.

What she could do was to write poetry. Her ***Novel on Yellow Paper*** and its prose successors have great charm—the charm, as a critic said, of "a laughing butterfly hovering over the head of James Joyce"—but it is in her poetry that her singular, wry, sad and funny spirit resides. She once said that many of her poems were about pain and isolation "but once the poem is written, the happiness of being alone comes flooding back." Yet writing was not always easy—"by contrast, peeling potatoes is so nice."

This is in many ways a fine book. . . . The problem comes with her maturity. Over-eager to account for every month of her later years, the authors spend far too long among the trees without standing back to survey the wood. It is a common fault in biography—irritating, though not in this instance ruinous. When floundering, the instinct is to fall back on quoting Stevie Smith herself, and thus regain the reader's interest. She knew the feeling. She once decided that Coleridge had got firmly stuck while he was writing "Kubla Khan" and had unfairly blamed his intrusive visitor for spoiling his poem:

> I am hungry to be interrupted
> For ever and ever amen
> O person from Porlock come quickly
> And bring my thoughts to an end.

Roy Jenkins, "Mind of Her Own," in The Economist, *Vol. 298, No. 7434, February 22, 1986, p. 84.*

MICHAEL HOROVITZ

[In the following excerpt Horovitz further expands on his objections to the harsh reception given by British critics such as Susannah Clapp, Hermione Lee (see excerpts above), and A. S. Byatt to Stevie.*]*

The first biography of Stevie Smith [***Stevie: A Biography of Stevie Smith***], by two scholars who'd paved the way for it by co-editing ***Me Again,*** their comprehensive and delightful anthology of her fugitive writings, got an extraordinarily rough ride from almost every one of its British reviewers. Susannah Clapp in the *London Review of Books* [see excerpt above] twitted the alleged 'indiscriminate zeal' with which Messrs Barbera and McBrien 'have talked to a great many people . . . and found everything interesting', including 'the idea that "commonplace neighbours" provided her with "telling details"'.' This objection is quickly overruled if one reflects that it's not such a crazy idea to start with, and then checks the Clapped-out version against the original: to discover

> . . . Stevie liked to think that Palmers Green was named 'after the holy-man kind of palmer who might have had his little cell on the green', but she knew that it was not. However unpromising, her little neighbourhood afforded Stevie the stuff of a writer's career. The lake in Grovelands Park, for instance, provided her sharp eye with telling details (young girls swinging arm in arm on its surrounding path, crying out to the boys, 'Okey-doke, phone me'), and inspired many of her fantasy poems 'about lakes and people getting bewitched, enchanted, *ensorcelé*.'

One wonders what business anyone who regards this sort of thing as uninteresting has pretending to review such a book. And the more so when Ms Clapp spends a paragraph suggesting it 'gets off to a bad start with its title . . . Would a biographer of Hughes call him Ted?' The answer is that it's an obtusely rhetorical question, for Stevie was the pseudonym she chose for herself and the nickname by which she was affectionately known, as she wished to be, to her audience and her peers alike. It's the right title by the same token as that by which several biographers of L. Armstrong and R. Zimmerman have in fact called them, respectively, Satchmo and Dylan; or, with Smiths in mind, as that by which Elaine Feinstein calls the empress of the blues Bessie throughout her reconstruction for Penguin's *Lives of Modern Women* series.

Other snobs and sourpusses clawed at the book's alleged dully plodding academicism. Hermione Lee's *Observer* dismissal [see excerpt above] characterised Barbera and McBrien as clumsy fools to 'wade in blithely, using "I like to get off with people" as possible indication of an affair with George Orwell.' If you look up what they actually do, you'll find an infinitely less presumptuous account:

> Bernard Crick, Orwell's recent biographer, repeats an anecdote both Anthony Powell and Malcolm Muggeridge report, in which Orwell told of having sex with a woman in a London park as they had nowhere else to go—circumstances he incorporated in his fictional tale *Keep the Aspidistra Flying*. As Crick sceptically indicates, 'The name of Stevie Smith has been persistently linked with this tale.' Kay Dick, who knew them both, derides such speculation and Sally Chilver calls the park story 'one of Orwell's leg-pulls'. Whether or not the poem **'Conviction'** refers to this incident is not known, but it was written in the years Stevie knew Orwell: 'I like to get off with people, / I like to lie in their arms, / I like to be held and tightly kissed, / Safe from all alarms . . .' The drawing Stevie placed next to the poem in the collection which, in 1942, she was readying for publication, depicts a man and woman making love out of doors, with an animal looking on . . .

This is typical of the way these biographers simply present the evidence they've lovingly collated, instead of essaying categorical conclusions from a superficial or partial selection. Ms

Lee's piece aired a number of prejudices whilst giving its readers virtually no specific information about ***Stevie.***

What the biography achieves, which these reviewers emphatically do not, is what the novelist John Rosenberg observed in Stevie's journalism—to wit, 'the unusual justice of setting forth the impressions that make up your value-judgements, not merely giving the sum pronouncements, so that the reader has recreated in miniature, for his own powers of criticism and understanding, the elements and essentials of the book in question. It is *creative* reviewing.' Not that Stevie's articles always set out to be kindly. Her contribution to a *Festschrift* for T. S. Eliot at seventy ('a very un-birthday present') found *Murder in the Cathedral* 'beautiful and strong in its feelings', but also 'abominable'. Eliot's 'terror-talk of cat-and-mouse damnation' appalled her, and she condemned him and various other writers of the day who found 'their chief delight in terrifying themselves and their readers with past echoes of cruelty and nonsense.' As she said, critics 'may turn the sharp edge of our own opinions against the author's argument . . . provided we do not use the book as a mere peg'. And as Barbera and McBrien say, 'One can disagree with an author's opinions and still enjoy that author's writings, as Stevie enjoyed Eliot's play, and as one who disagrees with Stevie's arguments against Christian doctrine can enjoy the poems which contain them. There is a zest, after all, that one can take and that Stevie took in argument.'

There's a world of difference, of course, between substantiated analysis or debate and the rush to unconsidered judgement of 'Don't-do-it-well, do-it-by-lunchtime' reviewerese. I was amazed to find the normally judicious A. S. Byatt bemoaning, in *The Times,* the absence from this book 'of anyone to whom Stevie Smith was a support, or did a good turn, or offered understanding.' Her relationship with the 'Lion Aunt of Hull' is explored in immaculate detail by Barbera and McBrien. No-one who reads the biography even sketchily could be in any doubt as to the niece's absolute devotion; they constituted an unshakable rock of mutual support throughout the sixty-two years they lived together in what they called the little 'House of Mercy' in London N13.

Ms Byatt's review also recycled the myth fostered by Hermione Lee of Stevie's allegedly 'die-hard Toryism', declaring that 'her political convictions were instinctively conservative.' She became a professional writer when single women had a much tougher struggle to survive than today. One could set against these suggestions that she was at all deeply committed to conservatism, with a small or large 'c', this biography's information that in the late 50s she turned to reviewing 'for the *Daily Telegraph,* a paper that paid well, Stevie thought, but was "dodgy . . . politically".' The strategies and policies of Robin Hood, Kingsley Martin's *New Statesman,* David Astor's *Observer,* and the Orwell phase of *Tribune* were manifestly closer to her heart.

Barbera and McBrien strip away the overplayed surface image of her as primarily whimsical and clownish. First impressions of her occasional moods and public masks taken at face value have fuelled some whimsical and clownish non-criticisms. Terence de Vere White noted, in the *Irish Times,* that **'Not Waving but Drowning',** her most celebrated poem, was written in the year that she tried to commit suicide—only to trail his coat grotesquely: 'on that occasion I suspect she may have been waving not drowning.' This commentator saw fit to sneer at the biographers' 'tireless amassing of detail' but clearly hasn't bothered to read the relevant sections of their study. Barbera and McBrien make the point that she did it in the Newnes publishing office she'd suffered for all of thirty years: 'I got frightfully tired. I didn't want to be there.' They cite the poem of loathing at her imprisonment—so far from cheery waving: 'Dark was the day for Childe Rolandine the artist / When she went to work as a secretary-typist / And as she worked she sang this song / Against oppression and the rule of wrong: / It is the privilege of the rich / To waste the time of the poor.' All this is in the chapter on 1950-53, **'Not Waving',** which demonstrates just how and why Stevie was probably more depressed than ever before or after in the spring of 1953. The shooting star of her early success with ***Novel on Yellow Paper*** had long ago fizzled out, and since her fiftieth birthday the previous autumn her health and finances, the dreaded job and her cherished literary career, were plummetting to rock bottom. . . . Hermione Lee had it that 'The poem's peculiar voice . . . is washed up on the page amid a sea of insensitive paraphrase, banal platitudes, solemn unconscious comedy and awkward negotiation between the life and the work.' It seems to me that the biographers carry out this intensely tricky negotiation most delicately and effectively, and that it's the eagerly censorious paraphrase and wilful distortions of de Vere White and Ms Lee which are insensitive, derisory and banal.

Barbera and McBrien's account is overall, by contrast, no more devious or awkward than Stevie's own: 'on 1 July 1953, Stevie attempted the ultimate escape by slashing her wrists. She wrote to Anna Browne explaining she just couldn't stand the strain of work any more, but expressing deep contrition for what she had done and for the terrible distress it had caused Aunt.' It's difficult to imagine anyone slashing their wrists for kicks, but Stevie of all people, and in this context, was quite patently *not* waving. A close reading of this book as of every one of hers reveals that, like so many who act the fool now and then (and indeed, like the 'poor chap' in her poem who 'always loved larking') she was fundamentally very serious indeed, sometimes desperate, often sad at heart, and almost invariably 'much further out' than the 'They' all around her thought. What solemn unconscious comedy that it's fallen to the lot of such similarly unimaginative observers today to pass such likewise unfeeling judgements on her actual life story, for posterity to retail.

The question remains, why has ***Stevie*** been so multilaterally damned? I've two tentative theories. One, because American professors are deemed inappropriate to enlighten the trail of so quintessentially English a spirit. It's true that many U.S. theses are very boring—but this isn't one of them. It might fall flat on a reader uninterested in its subject, but such a reader (like some of these reviewers) is clearly ill advised or foolish to embark on it. The obvious commitment and care, and the lively yet thoroughgoing method of Barbera and McBrien, akin to an intellectual Woodward and Bernstein, will prove extremely rewarding (entertaining as well as instructive) to the common reader *wanting* to know more about this unique, brilliant and elusive author—as long as he or she is not prone to literary xenophobia.

The other possible reason is that these biographers weren't authorised with a *carte blanche* by Stevie's literary executor. A certain amount of extraneously insidious denigration, if not an outright whispering campaign, may be operating between the lines of some of the more patronising put-downs. The official biography has now been commissioned from someone else, guaranteed Faber-able. But it's not as though this one is any sort of opportunistic sensationalising of a 'hot property', or a tissue of arbitrary interpretations or sloppy researches designed only to echo tendentious assumptions. On the contrary, its integrity and preoccupation with ascertainable facts are beyond question, and the main reiterated complaint seems to be that these men have worked so hard and so well, producing a portrait that requires the (re)viewer to take a moderately commensurate bit of time and trouble looking into its four hundred pages.

The last word had best go to Penelope Fitzgerald who knew Stevie well, and thanked the biographers, in the TES [see excerpt above], for 'a splendid fairmindedness and accuracy: this is a fine, painstaking biography, and it shows what Stevie herself demanded as the ''judging quality''—that is, absolute attention.' Would that the other reviewers had earned their keep, by paying it back in kind. (pp. 9-12)

Michael Horovitz, ''Stevie Again—Reviewers Reviewed,'' in Stand Magazine, *Vol. 28, No. 1, Winter (1986-87), pp. 9-12.*

The Passion of Ayn Rand

by Barbara Branden

(For Ayn Rand: see also *CLC,* Vols. 3, 30 and *Contemporary Authors,* Vols. 13-16, rev. ed., Vol. 105 [obituary].)

An Excerpt from *The Passion of Ayn Rand*

She had been at Paramount for almost six months when Richard Mealand learned that . . . *The Fountainhead* was no longer being submitted to publishing houses. Appalled, he offered to personally recommend it to any house of her choice. She had not thought to ask Mealand for help; she rarely asked anyone for help. It was characteristic of her that even when a friend would have been delighted to offer assistance, but did not know it was needed, her fierce independence prevented her from asking. If ever help were forthcoming unasked, she reacted with astonished pleasure; she never took it for granted—so much so that people who knew her were often startled by the extent of her gratitude when they did her the smallest of services, offering the kind of assistance one automatically offers a friend. Her gratitude was indicative of two facts: the extent of her passion for self-responsibility and how rare it had been in her life that a hand was held out to her in simple human kindness. Perhaps the second is in part the sad result of the first: an independent spirit is expected to take care of herself, to give help, not receive it; those strong enough to bear burdens are given still heavier burdens to carry. And the Atlas who was Ayn Rand never shrugged. But it appears that the cause can also be found in her alienation from people, which led to a formality and aloofness of manner that intimidated those who might have wished to offer help; her manner made them feel that she might interpret good will as a pitying insult.

Ayn told Mealand that she would like her novel to be submitted to Little, Brown, which had a reputation for good salesmanship of serious novels. Mealand introduced her to the editor, Angus Cameron. Six weeks later, Cameron called to say they were rejecting the book. When she came to pick up her manuscript, against normal publishing procedure he showed her the report written by a member of the firm's editorial board. To the end of her life, Ayn remembered the wording of that report: "This is a work of almost-genius—'genius' in the power of its expression—'almost' in the sense of its enormous bitterness. I wish there were an audience for a book of this kind. But there isn't. It won't sell." This was typical, Cameron told her, of the other reports he had received. All had praised the novel—all had predicted commercial failure.

"Of the whole history of *The Fountainhead,*" Ayn said in later years, "this was the most depressing. I told Frank when I got home that if they had told me it's a bad novel, then okay, that's their bad standards. But to have it rejected because of its *greatness*—because it's *too good*—that's really a feeling of horror."

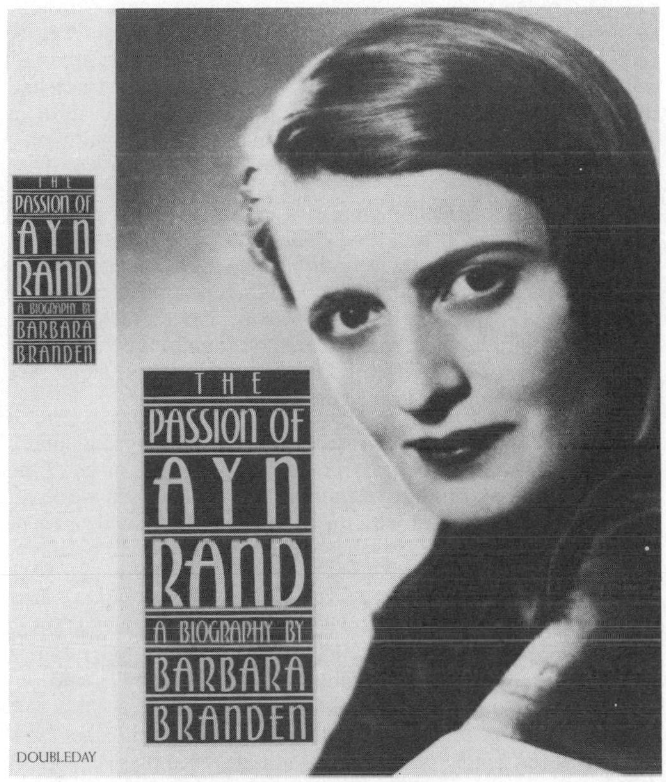

Dust jacket of The Passion of Ayn Rand: A Biography, *by Barbara Branden. Doubleday, 1986. Jacket photo by Talbot. Jacket design by Cathy Saksa. Courtesy of Doubleday & Company, Inc.*

GEORGE GILDER

[*An American writer, Gilder's early work,* Sexual Suicide *(1973) was a negative look at the feminist movement. A former speechwriter for Nelson Rockefeller, Richard Nixon, and Robert Dole, Gilder focuses in his more recent works,* Wealth and Poverty *(1981) and* The Spirit of Enterprise *(1984), on the strengths of capitalism, and, more specifically, supply-side economics. In the following excerpt Gilder praises Branden's biography for its balanced view of the rationalist philosophy expressed by Rand in her life and fiction.*]

Her coffin bore a dollar sign six feet tall; her first best seller celebrated a rape; her masterwork bears a dedication naming both her husband and a young lover 25 years her junior. Entirely dominant in her own marriage and the creator of some of literature's most forceful heroines, she fervently upheld a code of male supremacy and hero worship; a lifelong atheist and enemy of faith, she expressed a persistent belief in a "benevolent universe."

Through a life fraught with contradictions, she denied the logical possibility of contradiction and dismissed as morally depraved anyone who dared to persist in disagreement with her. She was in some ways a monster as well as a prodigy. Yet by relentlessly attacking the "unspeakable evil" and creative impotence of socialism at the time of its greatest ascendancy and by celebrating the moral and practical imperative of capitalism at its nadir—in books that commanded the fealty of millions—she was one of the great benefactors of the modern world.

Her masterpiece, ***Atlas Shrugged,*** stands as the most important novel of ideas since *War and Peace*. Yet this implacably intellectual work was first roundly hated and condemned and then obdurately ignored by America's intelligentsia. The book was saved for posterity by the word of mouth of masses of mostly non-intellectual readers who continue to buy her novels at the rate of some 300,000 copies a year and read them over and over for inspiration and guidance.

Who was Ayn Rand? The answer emerges at last in a superb biography [***The Passion of Ayn Rand***] written with much of the sweep, drama and narrative momentum of the great works of Ayn Rand herself—and with the psychological insight and sensitivity that forever eluded her. The author is Barbara Branden, for 19 years Ayn Rand's closest friend. Also the former wife of Nathaniel Branden, Rand's lover and leading apostle, she brings to the biography unique insights into the sexuality of this great writer. Working with some 50 hours of biographical tapes, she achieves a remarkable balance of intimacy and objectivity in telling the tempestuous story of a flawed but heroic woman, who bore the moral defense of capitalism on her back like Atlas for nearly two decades, and never shrugged. (pp. 1, 10)

Born in Petrograd in 1905 as Alice Rosenbaum, daughter of a Jewish pharmacist, Rand lived through all the early horror and chaos of the Bolshevik Revolution, the brutal expropriation of her father and other shopkeepers, the murder and dismemberment of the Russian royalty and their children. Then through a series of dramatic events stirringly told by Branden, Rand finally made her way to the United States, which had served for her as a promised land ever since her first encounter with the movies of Cecil B. DeMille. After several months with relatives in Chicago, she traveled to Hollywood where through an amazing series of coincidences she was adopted as a protegé by DeMille himself. But after a few years as a screenwriter, she found herself struggling through the Great Depression in an intellectual environment in which the Soviet charnel house she had managed to escape was widely seen as the last great hope for humanity. She resolved to tell the world what she knew of the reality behind the fatuous dream. The result was a series of prophetic novels, manifestos, and the creation of her own philosophy, Objectivism.

Ayn Rand's greatness stems from the fact that unlike the scores of other intellectual refugees from the East and defectors from Communism, from George Orwell to Arthur Koestler, she understood from the beginning that the source of the evil was the ideology of socialism itself. Unlike other critics of the morality of socialism, moreover, she never imagined for a moment that the system could work. She believed that socialism was evil and that the very essence of its evil was the suppression of the individual heroism and creativity that is indispensable to all human progress. Unlike other defenders of capitalism, she did not indulge the claims that it is somehow amoral and in a sense less idealistic than socialism. She knew that capitalism could not prevail unless its superior morality as well as its efficiency was recognized and acclaimed.

Despite the evidence of 30 years' stagnation in most socialist nations (which have been sustained only by subsidies and technologies from a generally flourishing capitalist world), many of Rand's insights are still not understood by pro-capitalist intellectuals today. Many still maintain that the system is amoral and then wonder why it is not embraced by idealistic youth. Many still ascribe the Great Depression not to a remorseless 10-year onslaught of tariffs, taxes, and tight money but to the "excesses" of capitalism. But partly thanks to her work, the consensus today is far more favorable to capitalism than the prevailing views of her time. Rand flung her gigantic books into the teeth of an intelligentsia still intoxicated by state power, during an era when even Dwight Eisenhower maintained tax rates of 90 percent and confessed his inability to answer Nikita Khrushchev's assertion that capitalism was immoral because it was based on greed.

From the early struggles of this penniless immigrant with faltering English and hated views, to the long trials of ***The Foutainhead,*** rejected by 12 publishers, released in niggling printings of a few thousand, demolished by most critics, and finally discovered by a tide of readers that continues in flood 30 years later—and on to the similar ordeal and triumph of ***Atlas Shrugged***—Rand's life story is one of the great sagas in the history of literature. With the help of long quotes from Rand that at times give the book the feel of autobiography, Branden triumphantly rises to the occasion of telling it.

Branden's work also dramatizes the flaws in Rand's philosophical scheme. One of the century's most important writers and thinkers, she was also one of its less sensitive human beings. Her obtuseness reached a climax in her sexual relationship with Nathaniel Branden when she brought her husband Frank O'Connor and her friend Barbara Branden together to endorse her heroism and rationality in seeking an affair with Barbara's husband.

Rand in 1947, preparing Atlas Shrugged. *Photograph by Julius Shulman.*

Rand maintained that the belief in an irrational sex drive, unrelated to philosophical principles, was similar to the Marxist belief in the primacy of matter. Just as Rand asserted that the material achievements of entrepreneurs reflect a spiritual creativity akin to the greatest of artists, she contended that her desire for Nathaniel's young body reflected an exalted morality. When 10 years later—she in her sixties, he in his thirties—he finally rejected her body, she took it as a philosophical betrayal. She rejected him, her leading apostle and protégé, and began a bitter vendetta that lasted to the end of her life.

Rand's basic incomprehension of familial and sexual realities undermined all her life and works. Her all-consuming rationalism rejected all relationships that were not rationally chosen, all love that was not earned by virtue, all actions that were not motivated by self-interest and personal happiness. This philosophy collapses instantly in the context of a family, the personal fabric of every society and economy. Families depend on the acceptance of unchosen commitments and relationships. They depend on altruism: service—unearned by proved virtue or assured reward—to children and relations. Although Rand's mother in Russia sold her last jewels to buy Ayn's tickets to America and Ayn's relations in Chicago agreed to accept her sight-unseen and supported her for a year after she arrived—and even though O'Connor married her chiefly to give her citizenship as her visa ran out—Rand persisted in her claim that she owed nothing to others. When she grew rich and famous, she virtually ignored her relatives and treated Frank with callous disregard. The recognition that the altruism of her unchosen relatives and Frank had saved her would have created a "contradiction" between her life and her philosophy—and such a contradiction she could not tolerate.

In her novels, she simply avoids the problem by excluding families altogether. Although she exalts sexual pleasure to a virtually religious pinnacle in her philosophy, her heroes and heroines are all childless: copulating abstractions that give birth to rationalizations rather than babies. By excluding the domain of procreative sexuality, she misses the altruistic and unconditional love at the very core of the human experience. Indeed, the uniquely prolonged helplessness of human offspring means that parental love is indispensable to human life and development.

Missing this dimension of family life, she also misses the essential altruism, the orientation toward the needs of others, that is crucial to production for the marketplace. As Rand eloquently and persuasively maintains, self-esteem and confidence is indispensable to entrepreneurial achievement. But so too is sensitivity and attentiveness to the needs and wants of others and alertness to the contributions of others. Only under socialism do favored industrialists pursue self-expression first and manufacture whatever they want—or whatever the rulers dictate. In fact, one of the great appeals of socialism to intellectuals is that it avoids the need to produce vulgar goods demanded by the masses. The planners decide what the people should need. The heroes of capitalism are not arrogant producers of goods immaculately conceived in their own minds; capitalists imaginatively serve the minds and needs of others.

Ignoring the altruistic aspect of family and business life, Rand also misunderstands the role of religions that uphold the unselfish moral codes essential to productive families and enterprises. Launching a false duality of her own, she asserts an inexorable divorce between reason and religion, and asserts the identity of Marxism and Christianity, collectivism and altruism (a view ironically shared by Marxist Liberation theology). As she eloquently demonstrates, however, the altruism of socialism and the welfare state is almost entirely bogus. A cheap charity that all too often spends the earnings of others in ways that degrade and demoralize the alleged beneficiaries, socialism is totally alien to Christian charity, which is freely chosen by the donors and made effective by love and moral teaching.

In addition, Rand fails to comprehend that her rationalism comes perilously close to a hermetic system of causes and effects—a total and mechanistic logic pervading the universe—that contradicts her assertions of free will. A world of Randian heroes would not only fail to reproduce itself; it would also find itself bound in chains of mechanistic rationality. Modern physics and mathematics both deny the sufficiency of such rationalism. Rand is objectively wrong when she asserts as an axiom that every effect must have a cause and that the perplexities of quantum theory are "mere mathematical problems." Mathematics is near the foundation of her logical system and she is inconsistent in so cavalierly dismissing its limitations. Religious commitments, including her own faith in reason and in a "benevolent universe," are crucial to a belief in meaningful free will as opposed to an irrational existentialism.

Such objections to Rand's philosophy might seem to disparage her achievement. But in fact, like every great thinker, she transcends her contradictions. In a world where most novelists lack any coherent philosophy at all, her work looms as a major triumph. Barbara Branden's own triumph is to show in full human detail the sources both of this achievement and its notable but ultimately venial flaws. (p. 10)

George Gilder, "Ayn Rand: Sex, Money, and Philosophy," in Bookworld, *Chicago Tribune, June 29, 1986, pp. 1, 10.*

TERRY TEACHOUT

[*Teachout is an editor for both* Harper's *and the conservative newsletter* Modern Times. *In the following excerpt he discusses Rand's fall from, and eventual return to, right-wing respectability. Although he finds Branden a poor stylist, Teachout does consider her work important for the numerous personal details that help to explain the peculiarities in Rand's life, work, and philosophy.*]

Rand and Nathaniel Branden around 1956. From The Passion of Ayn Rand, *by Barbara Branden. Doubleday, 1986. Courtesy of Barbara Branden.*

The history of any ideology is in large part a catalogue of purges, a sour and acrid rule to which the American Right has been no exception. One of the earliest right-wing purges carried out in this country took place in 1957 when the novelist-philosopher Ayn Rand was for all intents and purposes read out of the conservative movement. The agent of her demise was *National Review,* which elected to publish a scathing review of ***Atlas Shrugged,*** her new novel, written by none other than Whittaker Chambers.

The juxtaposition of Ayn Rand and Whittaker Chambers was (and is) an intriguing one. Ayn Rand, a Russian émigrée turned screenwriter and novelist, had written in ***The Fountainhead*** an impeccably conservative novel of ideas which sold several hundred thousand copies and was subsequently made into a popular movie starring Gary Cooper and Patricia Neal. Chambers, a reformed Communist spy turned senior editor of *National Review,* was widely accepted at the time as a conservative totem, largely because of *Witness,* his best-selling memoir. Chambers's decision to attack Ayn Rand in the pages of *National Review* was thus a fateful one, and his review of ***Atlas Shrugged,*** "Big Sister Is Watching You," was couched in terms that left no room for doubt as to the seriousness of her failures of orthodoxy:

> The news about this book seems to me to be that any ordinarily sensible head could possibly take it seriously, and that, apparently, a good many do. . . . Out of a lifetime of reading, I can recall no other book in which a tone of overriding arrogance was so implacably sustained. Its shrillness is without reprieve. Its dogmatism is without appeal. . . . From almost any page of ***Atlas Shrugged*** a voice can be heard, from painful necessity, commanding: "To a gas chamber—go!"

Ayn Rand's followers promptly inundated *National Review* with irate correspondence. Ayn Rand herself never again spoke to its editor, William F. Buckley, Jr. (Within a few years, in fact, she was calling *National Review* "the worst and most dangerous magazine in America.") But the anathema pronounced by Chambers stuck, and Ayn Rand was subsequently dismissed as a fringe figure by the majority of the American conservative establishment.

This dismissal, however, had no measurable effect on her popularity as an author. Her four novels alone continue to sell at the rate of over 300,000 copies a year. And the half-life of the Chambers anathema proved to be shorter than anyone expected. "It is normally a matter of two decades," John Chamberlain wrote in 1961 with Ayn Rand in mind, "before the young take over the seats of power in the name of what they have learned to believe twenty years ago." George Gilder, right on schedule, named Ayn Rand in the preface of his *Wealth and Poverty* as one of the people who "shaped my early economic ideas." Alan Greenspan has never made any secret of his youthful association with Ayn Rand. Most of today's younger conservatives readily admit to having read her books closely. Barbara Branden, in the final chapter of her new biography, ***The Passion of Ayn Rand,*** devotes fifteen pages to a list of public figures who take (or took) her seriously. Nearly three decades after the publication of ***Atlas Shrugged,*** it is respectable to have been influenced by Ayn Rand.

Was it a mistake to have rehabilitated Ayn Rand so thoroughly? The publication of this full-scale biography provides an excellent opportunity to reconsider her claims to recognition as a serious novelist and conservative philosopher. Mrs. Branden was closely linked to Ayn Rand, both personally and professionally, for nineteen years. She conducted over forty hours of taped interviews with Ayn Rand in preparation for a biographical sketch published in the 1962 symposium, *Who Is Ayn Rand?* Although Mrs. Branden's judgments are inevitably colored by the specifics of her troubled relationship with her subject, who had a lengthy affair with the author's first husband, the psychologist Nathaniel Branden, it is hard not to feel on reading this book that she has been at some pains to give us the facts as honestly as emotion permits.

To be sure, Barbara Branden is an excruciatingly bad stylist, trapped in the throes of what Wolcott Gibbs used to call "ladies'-club rhythm," and her swooning rhapsodies blot every page:

> One saw his warmth—the frustrated warmth of a lonely man—especially in his dealings with the animals he loved; he treated the least stray animal with the exquisite gentleness of a parent; a part of Frank always remained the boy who had stolen sick chickens from his neighbors in order to heal them. Bitterness? Contempt? Passion? These were not attributes that had relevance to Frank.

But Mrs. Branden's hopeless style is offset by her intimate knowledge of the details of Ayn Rand's personal life, and these details are undoubtedly central to the question of whether or not Ayn Rand's philosophy was as "wildly grotesque and excessive" as Whittaker Chambers claimed.

"My personal life," she wrote in 1957, "is a postscript to my novels; it consists of the sentence: *'And I mean it.'* I have always lived by the philosophy I present in my books—and it has worked for me, as it works for my characters." But did it? (pp. 69-70)

[Alice] began writing short stories at the age of nine, deciding at sixteen to earn her living as a novelist and philosopher. ("If all philosophers," she later said, "were required to present their ideas in novels, to dramatize the exact meaning and consequences of their philosophies in human life, there would be far fewer philosophers—and far better ones.") Even as a schoolgirl, she knew precisely what she despised most about the Soviet system:

> My concept of good and evil, already in the process of being formed, saw its vindication everywhere. . . . I realized they were saying that the illiterate and poor had to be the rulers of the earth *because* they were illiterate and poor. . . . It was the demand for the sacrifice of the best among men, and for the enshrinement of the commonplace, that I saw as the unspeakable evil of Communism.

Alice's opportunity to leave the USSR came in 1925 when an aunt who had moved to Chicago prior to the revolution got in touch with the Rosenbaum family. Alice resolved to learn English, move to the United States, and become a Hollywood screenwriter. ("I began to go to movies every night," she would recall. "My real enthusiasm for America, apart from its political principles, was formed then. I saw the essence of what Americans could be and ought to be.") She emigrated to America in 1926, changing her name to Ayn Rand and moving to Hollywood within a year.

A chance meeting with Cecil B. DeMille on her first day in Hollywood led to a series of jobs ranging from junior writer at DeMille's studio to head of the RKO wardrobe department, with serious writing relegated to evenings and weekends. Her play, ***Night of January 16,*** a courtroom drama which makes use of a jury composed of audience members, was produced on Broadway in 1935; ***We the Living,*** an autobiographical novel, appeared in 1936 to poor sales and negative reviews. The failures of these early efforts had no visible effect on Ayn Rand, who remained serenely confident of her own importance as an artist and thinker.

In 1943 Bobbs-Merrill published ***The Fountainhead,*** a 754-page novel about a fiercely individualistic architect "who does not exist for others" named Howard Roark. Diana Trilling's curt review of ***The Fountainhead*** in the *Nation* was typical of critical reaction to the novel:

> Ayn Rand's Howard Roark is . . . a giant among men, ten feet tall and with flaming hair, Genius on a scale that makes the good old Broadway version of art-in-a-beret look like Fra Angelico. And surrounding Howard Roark there is a whole galaxy of lesser monsters—Gail Wynand who is Power, and Peter Keating who is Success, and Dominique who is Woman. . . . Surely ***The Fountainhead*** is the curiosity of the year, and anyone who is taken in by it deserves a stern lecture on paper rationing.

The irony in Mrs. Trilling's last sentence was greater than she could possibly have known. Until 1944, frightened by bad reviews and stymied by the wartime paper shortage, Bobbs-Merrill was unable to publish editions of ***The Fountainhead*** larger than 5,000. But by 1948 over 400,000 copies of the novel had been sold, largely by word of mouth, and Ayn Rand subsequently sold the movie rights to Warner Brothers for $50,000. King Vidor directed the film version of ***The Fountainhead,*** for which Ayn Rand supplied an original screen adaptation that was shot virtually intact. She later claimed, in a form letter sent to inquiring readers, that the success of ***The Fountainhead***

> has demonstrated its own thesis. It was rejected by twelve publishers who declared that it had no commercial possibilities, it would not sell, it was "too intellectual," it was "too unconventional," it went against every alleged popular trend. Yet the success of ***The Fountainhead*** was made by the public, . . . single, individual readers who discovered it of their own choice, who read it on their own initiative and recommended it on their own judgment.

The story repeated itself when Ayn Rand first began showing ***Atlas Shrugged*** to publishers in 1956. Most were put off by the novel's thousand-page length and explicitly right-wing political stance. ("Would you cut the Bible?" she asked Bennett Cerf when he suggested shortening a chapter.) When Random House brought the book out the following year, the prestige reviewers were universally hostile. Granville Hicks, writing in the New York *Times,* dismissed ***Atlas Shrugged*** as "not in any literary sense a serious novel," while Gore Vidal announced that "Ayn Rand's philosophy is nearly perfect in its immorality." But the public ignored the critics again, so totally that ***Atlas Shrugged,*** nearly three decades after its initial publication, continues to sell a minimum of fifty thousand copies in paperback every year.

While working on ***Atlas Shrugged,*** Ayn Rand told an inquiring reporter that "it will combine metaphysics, morality, economics, politics, and sex—and it will show the tie between metaphysics and economics." She pitched the book to Bennett Cerf and Donald Klopfer of Random House as "an extreme, uncompromising, moral defense of capitalism (which presents) a new philosophy." The nature of this philosophy is succinctly explained in the novel's afterword:

> My philosophy, in essence, is the concept of man as a heroic being, with his own happiness as the moral purpose of his life, with productive achievement as his noblest activity, and reason as his only absolute.

Ayn Rand's followers have tended to accept these assertions without cracking a smile. But the way in which she chose to dramatize her "new philosophy" is revealing: her *magnum opus,* it turns out, is cast in the unlikely form of a thousand-page detective story.

As strange as it seems that a *conte philosophique* should be written in the style of Sir Arthur Conan Doyle, a casual examination of ***Atlas Shrugged*** reveals even more extraordinary oddities. All the heroes are violently colored caricatures with jutjawed names like Ellis Wyatt and Ken Danagger, all the villains spineless cretins with slimy names like Wesley Mouch and Floyd Ferris. (Nora Ephron once advanced the intriguing thesis that an Ayn Rand hero could be spotted solely by calculating the vowel-consonant ratio in his name.)

As a satire on the follies and dangers of collectivism, ***Atlas Shrugged*** has genuine merit. But as a work of imaginative literature it is unsatisfactory in the extreme. The plot is preposterous, the treatment deadly serious in its romantic utopianism. The mixture, a familiar one, has been dominating the world's best-seller lists for decades. ***Atlas Shrugged*** carries this particular strain of popular literature to its furthest limits: it is a book which permits the reader to wallow shamelessly in extravagant romance while simultaneously feeling like a real intellectual. The results, which suggest a bizarre fusion of *Gone With the Wind* and F. A. Hayek's *The Road to Serfdom,* are irresistibly appealing to the adolescent mind, and it is hardly surprising that ***Atlas Shrugged*** has proved to be such a durable

Rand and her husband Frank in 1959. Joan Kennedy Taylor.

seller. But one inevitably wonders how anyone beyond the age of sixteen or so ever found it to be, as its author so resolutely claimed, an artistically serious exposition of serious ideas.

Ayn Rand's stylistic peculiarities begin to make a kind of sense when seen in the context supplied by Barbara Branden's biography. None of Rand's acquaintances dared to challenge her on intellectual or aesthetic grounds: friends who dared to differ with her *obiter dicta* promptly ceased to be friends. But the sheer narrowness of her pronouncements was startling. Kipling's "If" was her favorite poem, Rachmaninoff her favorite composer, Victor Hugo and Mickey Spillane her favorite novelists. Ayn Rand's "lack of information," Mrs. Branden recounts,

> seemed to some of her friends appallingly evident. . . . Over the years we were to hear Ayn excoriate the "grim, unfocused malevolence" of Rembrandt—to a painter; Beethoven's "tragic sense of doom"—to a musician. . . . She would dismiss much of the history of literature as antiromantic and unstylized, and the history of philosophy, with the sole significant exceptions of Aristotle and aspects of Thomas Aquinas, as mystical, dishonest, and irrational.

This intellectual narrowness, accompanied by a starchily old-fashioned atheism of the very worst kind, inevitably led her to espouse a militantly positivistic philosophy of life. "In my novels," she wrote, "and in actual life, the alleged victories of evil are made possible only by the flaws or the errors of those who are essentially good. Evil, left to its own devices, is impotent and self-defeating." And she was as firm in her optimism as she was convinced of her personal genius. "Her proudest boast about the philosophical system she would later devise," Mrs. Branden observes, "was that if one accepted any part of it, consistency required that one accept the total of it."

Such comprehensive philosophies rarely bring peace of mind to those who develop them, and after the publication of ***Atlas Shrugged*** Ayn Rand began to despair of the ultimate conversion of the world to her way of thinking. "I had no more inspiration for fiction," she told a friend at the time:

> Fiction, to me, is ***Atlas Shrugged.*** My mission was done. . . . I no longer know where are the intelligences to which I've *always* addressed myself. I feel paralyzed by disgust and contempt. . . . And if I feel contempt for the whole culture—if it feels like I'm living in the last days of the Roman empire—then what sense does it make to continue writing?

Her response to this dilemma took the form of a systematic attempt to disseminate the philosophy outlined in ***The Fountainhead*** and ***Atlas Shrugged.*** She began lecturing around the country, drawing large crowds and evoking surprisingly enthusiastic responses. Together with Barbara and Nathaniel Branden, she founded the Nathaniel Branden Institute, a New York-based organization which conducted classes and supplied taped lectures in "Objectivism," the Randian philosophy, as well as publishing a monthly magazine called *The Objectivist*.

By 1967 the Nathaniel Branden Institute had grown sufficiently to move to a suite of offices in the Empire State Building. "It seemed time," Mrs. Branden writes, "to offer the students what they appeared to want: a social life that was integrated to their philosophical interests." What they got instead was a quasi-cult which revolved around the adoration of Ayn Rand and her fictional heroes. The psychological effects of this worship on its practitioners, as one of Ayn Rand's acquaintances recalls, were dire:

> Because they had learned the philosophy predominantly from fiction, the students of Objectivism thought they had to be like Ayn Rand heroes: they were not to be confused, not to be unhappy, and not to lack confidence. And because they could not meet these self-expectations, they bore the added burden of moral failure.

The Rand cult disintegrated in 1968 when Nathaniel Branden, who had been her lover since 1955, confessed that he was in love with a younger woman. Ayn Rand immediately broke with both Brandens and disbanded the Institute. Her later years were largely devoted to a series of futile attempts to bring ***Atlas Shrugged*** to the screen, first as a movie and later as a nine-hour television miniseries. "If all those concerned do their best," she said in reference to the first of these attempts, "the cultural consequences will be incalculable." She died of lung cancer in 1982.

"I have always lived by the philosophy I present in my books—and it has worked for me, as it works for my characters." Judging by the lavish evidence of emotional instability provided by Barbara Branden in ***The Passion of Ayn Rand,*** to take this claim at face value would require one to reject the philosophy so painstakingly set forth in ***The Fountainhead*** and ***Atlas Shrugged.*** But there are better grounds than this for rejecting the philosophy of Ayn Rand, a system of thought which is as intellectually jejune as it is internally consistent.

Conservatism has always viewed itself as an essentially tragic philosophy of compromise between competing impulses and even competing goods. The Randian world, by contrast, is elegantly self-correcting, an earthly paradise where truth is obvious, man perfectible, compromise the only deadly sin. To take such an idealistic vision seriously is necessarily to part company with conservatism as it has been construed from Burke onward. It is no accident that Ayn Rand consistently rejected the "conservative" label, preferring to call herself a "radical for capitalism." Indeed, she knew a diverse assortment of genuine conservatives ranging from Albert Jay Nock to Henry Hazlitt, and she despised the lot of them:

> I didn't conclude then that conservatives were actually hopeless traitors. Just that a lot of them were weak and cowardly. I still thought that it was an issue of ignorance. It took years for me to gradually discover that it was an amoral, *anti*-moral attitude . . . they didn't believe capitalism could be saved.

One should note, however, that Ayn Rand's utopian vision is in certain respects strikingly congruent with the political attitudes now espoused by some younger conservatives, many of them born after the baby boom. In the world of ***Atlas Shrugged*** capitalism is an absolute good, morality a distillate of hedonism, philosophy a utilitarian means to a short-term end. These premises mesh neatly with the amalgam of low taxes, isolationism, and moral libertarianism that is the "conservatism" of a new generation of congressional aides, think-tank habitués, and political activists, and Ayn Rand's current respectability may be in some measure a product of the enthusiasm of these people, who read her in high school and have continued to take her seriously ever since. ("If there is a novelist with unusual appeal among the Reagan organization," the New York *Times* correctly observed in 1981, "it is Ayn Rand, proponent of enlightened self-interest.")

This group by no means makes up the entire younger generation of conservatives, and it has yet to be seen whether its members will exercise any lasting influence on the conservative movement as a whole. But because of them we can safely assume that Ayn Rand, Mrs. Branden's sensational revelations notwithstanding, will be with us for some time to come. The thought is not a comforting one. (pp. 71-2)

Terry Teachout, "The Goddess That Failed," in Commentary, *Vol. 82, No. 1, July, 1986, pp. 68-72.*

PETER L. BERGER

[*Austrian-born American sociologist and nonfiction writer, Berger is the author of several sociological works, including* The Heretical Imperative: Contemporary Possibilities of Religious Affirmation *(1979) and* Speaking to the Third World *(1985). In the following excerpt Berger notes Branden's personal involvement with Rand, praising the fairness of Branden's biography. Berger further comments on the weaknesses of Rand's philosophy and the command of her personality.*]

Ayn Rand (1905-1982) occupies a curious position on the American intellectual scene. A lifelong outsider, without academic credentials and generally scorned by established scholars, she exerted a powerful influence through her writings and for a while was the center of a movement that elicited passionate commitment from sizable numbers of people. . . .

Rand has been influential among intellectuals on the political right, especially in its libertarian sector (thus the economist Alan Greenspan, one of her early associates, has continued to express his indebtedness to her). Amid the recent resurgence of libertarian thought in the United States, Rand serves as an ideological reference point. . . .

Barbara Branden's biography [***The Passion of Ayn Rand***] emphasizes the personal, which is rather ironic in view of Rand's disdain of emotionalism and her insistence that people must be understood by their "principles." Ms. Branden's association with Rand was long and in the end exceedingly painful. She co-founded the Nathaniel Branden Institute with her husband, Nathaniel Branden, and according to the book stood aside while he carried on an affair with Rand, also married, before he and Ms. Branden were divorced. This book is as much an exercise in self-examination as in biography, and the reader is given an inordinate amount of detail about what Ms. Branden calls "the events of 1968," when the coterie around the Branden Institute fell apart. It is understandable that these events are of great interest to Ms. Branden, and there is a certain moving quality to her evident effort to be fair to a woman about whom she has very mixed feelings. The reader who has no such association with Rand or her movement would have liked more attention to the ideas at issue.

It is these ideas, rather than Rand's undoubtedly fascinating personality, that probably hold the clue to her popularity. She set out to provide a philosophical and moral defense of American capitalism, and her success can only be explained by the paucity as well as the intellectual poverty of most comparable attempts. The critics of Rand's work were often motivated by ideological animosity; they were also, on the whole, quite right in their negative judgments. Rand's novels are ponderous, filled with characters that are, indeed, embodiments of principles rather than living human beings. Her philosophy is a vulgarized cross between Adam Smith and Friedrich Nietzsche, a flat Enlightenment rationalism aspiring to an ethic of heroism. Her epistemology of "objectivity" is roughly as sophisticated as Lenin's dialectical materialism, her morality is based on selfishness and her political program could not be realized in any modern society.

Yet Rand did understand some central realities—precisely realities that a good number of contemporary American intellectuals fail to see. Foremost among these is the reality that capitalism alone provides the institutional foundation for individual rights, which is why all forms of modern collectivism, of whatever ideological coloration, detest capitalism. Unfortunately, while capitalism does indeed require a moral defense, Ayn Rand's principles hardly provide one. Her ideas, especially as they continue to be espoused by various libertarians, still create agitation on the right. It is noteworthy that the most caustic review of ***Atlas Shrugged*** appeared in *National Review;* its author, none other than Whittaker Chambers, maintained that Rand's ideas led straight to the gas chambers. The allegation was unfair (Rand always insisted that one must never use force except in self-defense—one of her principles, actually), but it shows the degree of rage provoked by Rand in conventional conservative circles, especially those animated by religious convictions.

Rand was passionately patriotic about her adopted country. There are many things about America, though, that she never understood, and the pervasiveness of religion in this country was certainly one of them. She imagined America as she imagined capitalism, and her success is evidence of the fact that her own fantasies coincided with those of others—and probably that her own simplicities met the need of others for one simple, all-embracing explanation of everything. This makes for a movement, but it doesn't make for good philosophy or viable politics. Capitalism is part and parcel of an inevitably messy empirical reality that can never be captured in a system of axioms. A defense of capitalism that can claim to be both moral and rational will have to take cognizance of its empirical reality—something Rand was temperamentally unable to do.

It is difficult to accord an important place to Ayn Rand either as a novelist or as a thinker. And yet there is something appealing, even a touch of grandeur, about the figure who emerges from Ms. Branden's somewhat tortured account: the young woman who arrives in America clutching her Remington Rand typewriter (she took her name from it); who not only renames herself but proceeds to remake herself in the shape of her passionately held ideals; the hero-worshiper who invented improbably heroic figures in her novels and who convinced very ordinary people that they too could be heroes; the mature and successful figure who always refused compromise, no matter what the cost, and who faced bitter personal disappointment and pain with an unbending courage. One can understand why this individual, whatever her intellectual and personal foibles, could command loyalty and inspire commitment.

Peter L. Berger, "Adam Smith Meets Nietzsche," in The New York Times Book Review, *July 6, 1986, p. 13.*

Rand with friends Barbara and Nathaniel Branden and her husband Frank in 1963. From The Passion of Ayn Rand, *by Barbara Branden. Doubleday, 1986. Courtesy of Barbara Branden.*

TIM W. FERGUSON

She cried and she suffered. She fed a cat better than she fed herself. She wore a "good luck" watch. She married a passive and often pitiful man. She liked it when he called her a pet name, "Fluff." She wasn't mechanical and couldn't drive. She was often fearful of the world around her.

This was Ayn Rand, as depicted in Barbara Branden's biography [***The Passion of Ayn Rand***]. The longtime confidante finds that the novelist-philosopher who exalted reason and success and condemned the irrational and sacrificial was herself prone to many human failings. The verdict doesn't deny the possibility of triumphant man—indeed, Ms. Branden shows that in many respects Rand *was* the kind of person she wrote about—but it does suggest that in this life even romantic heroes must reckon with frailty.

The Passion of Ayn Rand . . . is the story of a literary prairie fire that has burned for 40 years, despite the best efforts of the American intelligentsia to douse it. . . .

A central and contentious element of the book is Ms. Branden's analysis that Rand, lacking the physical features she equated with femininity, was frustrated in realizing her sexual aspirations. The author follows the psychological footprints back to Rand's days in Russia, where an engineering student walked off with her unrequited love. In Ms. Branden's view, Rand could not fill the void even as she enjoyed an enduring and, in its own way, loving marriage to Frank O'Connor for half a century. A one-time actor, O'Connor was mostly a househusband at the mercy of Rand's domineering personality. She would say that he was working in a Brooklyn cigar store because he was too good for this corrupt world; his reward for letting her live out her values, even in the arms of another man, was alcoholism.

In general, when Rand assigned her wishes the status of moral imperatives, those around her suffered for it. The parade of one-time allies distanced for their disagreement included economist Ludwig von Mises and two significant but less heralded women theorists, Isabel Paterson and Rose Wilder Lane. Rand usually renounced her politically conservative friends when they stuck to some faulty premise, like belief in God. The atheist author then might consign the poor "mystic" to a virtual memory hole.

The totalitarian overtone in a woman who was a courageous foe of tyranny emerges as one of the many paradoxes of Rand's life. . . .

Yet through this, Barbara Branden retained so much respect for Rand's undeniable strength and genius that she sought and gained rapprochement with the author shortly before her death in 1982.

Ms. Branden's account includes some choice details, such as Rand's discovery of Urey, Colo., as a real-life setting for "Galt's Gulch," the mountain hideaway to which the producers of the world escape in ***Atlas Shrugged.*** The writing occasionally drifts into Randian idiom, as when people "name" emotions they experience. With a subject who disdained humor, subtlety and spontaneity, the book cannot help but be similarly disadvantaged.

At the end of it all, there is the question of Rand's impact. Still another paradox is that her fame and exposure were greatest when U.S. culture and politics were moving rapidly to the left. During the counter-evolution of the past two decades, Rand's influence has been hardly visible, although her books still sell. . . .

Rand believed that ordinary Americans hungered for stories with philosophical meaning, and they proved her right and the critics wrong. Now at last, the thinking set may be ready to take her seriously. . . . Barbara Branden has shown how Rand's abstraction of unremitting egoism, played out, failed its creator. We've begun to explore what parts of her brilliance can be reclaimed from the wreckage.

Tim W. Ferguson, "The Praxeological Prophet," in The Wall Street Journal, *July 17, 1986, p. 22.*

BILL BAILEY

Surprisingly [***The Passion of Ayn Rand***] is the first full-scale biography of the philosopher-novelist Ayn Rand. Other books have been written about her world view, literary style, and influence. Her best novels, ***The Fountainhead*** (1943) and ***Atlas Shrugged*** (1957), are still read today and heatedly discussed. But a complete life story to explain the forging of her iconoclastic nature has not been available before. Of course, anyone interested in Rand will seize this book as if fallen from heaven because of the writer's mystique. Her familiar characters Howard Roark and John Galt are so staunchly individualistic that embodiment of them in real life seems impossible. Yet Rand practiced what she preached and was a stubborn perfectionist when faced with a stifling world. At one with her art, she believed that only in fiction can the reader be led into an ideal world not possible with fact. Always the courageous writer, especially given the way she vilified many of society's sacred cows, Rand's life exemplifies adherence to lofty principles. Now the stringent ideology espoused in her books can be better understood in tandem with this biography. (pp. 216-17)

[***The Passion of Ayn Rand***] is a loving reminiscence intellectually stimulating, full of conversation, and evocative of greatness. Over a lifetime an active mind questions itself endlessly; Rand's mental meanderings carry the reader along. Branden, herself an enthusiastic philosopher, is certainly equal to the job of theoretical exegesis. Not to forget her personal life, Rand's marriage to the actor-painter Frank O'Connor is vividly told.

Since she created supermen in her fiction, Frank had much to live up to and did. Equally absorbing is the aftermath of public opinion upon the release of her books. It seemed that every constituency of American life felt somehow threatened by this Russian emigrée who advocated strength not in numbers, but in the separate person.

Altogether this biography is persuasive reading; it depicts a creative intelligence unafraid and goes far toward explicating Rand's clearly stated but difficult to emulate ideology. Other biographies will be written by those not so intimately joined to Rand, but this one will have to form a cornerstone. (p. 217)

Bill Bailey, in a review of "The Passion of Ayn Rand," in Best Sellers, *Vol. 46, No. 6, September, 1986, pp. 216-17.*

Robert Frost Himself

by Stanley Burnshaw

(For Robert Frost: see also *CLC,* Vols. 1,3,4,9,10,13,15,26,34; *Contemporary Authors,* Vols. 89-92; *Something about the Author,* Vol. 14; and *Dictionary of Literary Biography,* Vol. 54. For Stanley Burnshaw: see also *CLC,* Vols. 3, 13; *Contemporary Authors,* Vols. 9-12, rev. ed.; and *Dictionary of Literary Biography,* Vol. 48.)

An Excerpt from *Robert Frost Himself*

In Thompson's eyes Frost had broken his promise to include him on important visits abroad, yet this was no mortal sting compared to some other hurts he had suffered. Frost frequently ''invented''; he gave him conflicting accounts of events; he reinterpreted meanings. ''Don't let me fail to explain,'' he would say, but didn't explain; and then to soften the blow, he would add: ''We're both trying to understand me.'' As early as 1948, when Thompson felt they were reaching their highest accord, Frost advised, ''Don't pay attention to what I say.'' ''Don't let me throw any dust in your eyes''—precisely what he'd been doing. ''Mythologizing,'' critics hostile to Frost had been calling it; Thompson branded it ''lies.'' In fact it was neither, for what do you tell a person you cannot trust and from whom you feel you must gain protection? You befuddle him, give him conflicting accounts, force him to rage with confusion, make him unable to sort the true from the false. You know that your fate is endangered, that you cannot reach out from the grave.

Not till the final years did Thompson come to fear that Frost had often ''held back'' and had given him ''differing versions'' because *he* had failed to live up to expectations. Hadn't the poet conveyed as much in the guise of a question—''Don't you think you should drop the biography?''—reinforcing his hope with a reason—''You know too much about me''—which he knew Thompson would recognize as the opposite of the truth. Surely Kay must have ''pressured Frost into saying that,'' Thompson decided. The episode passed; bafflement reigned; the biographer's anger vented itself in hate and resentment—and in playing antipodal roles. In public: Frost's affable friend, the devoted praiser of poems, the man most avid to herald in print the eighty-fifth birthday. In private: the knowing revealer of Frost-the-monster (to Donoghue); of the nation's deceiver on the day of Inauguration; of countless slurs, gratuitous charges, hostile interpretations, and so on throughout the ''Notes.'' He admits having given the poet ''plenty of chance(s) to build up resentments against me.'' And yet as late as March 1962, Thompson could speak of their recent visit ''as one of our best.'' But from that date on their relations worsened. They met only twice, and briefly: in July and October. Thompson telephoned (December 8th) three days after Frost had entered the Peter Bent Brigham hospital. ''Was he mad at him?'' Frost asked. ''Was anything wrong?'' Three loud shouts of ''no-no-no'' came the answer, closing their last conversation. Five weeks later Thompson set down in ''a note from the heart'': ''Here I am, pretending that I'm anxious to see Frost when the truth of the matter is that I really don't care whether I ever see him again, alive or dead.''

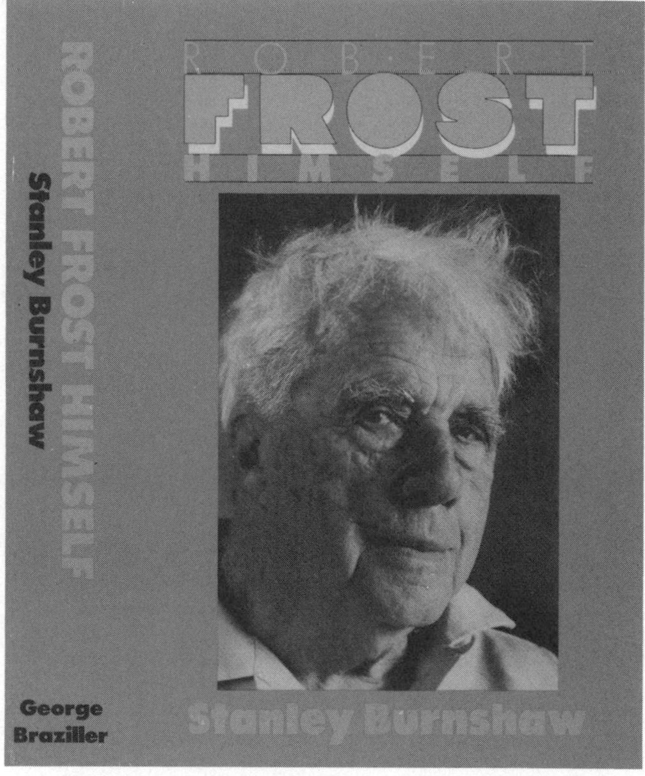

Dust jacket of Robert Frost Himself, *by Stanley Burnshaw. George Braziller, 1986. Jacket design by Levavi & Levavi. Jacket photo by Alfred Eisenstaedt,* Life, *Magazine © Time, Inc.*

ROBERT RICHMAN

[*Richman is poetry editor of* The New Criterion. *In the following excerpt Richman compares* Robert Frost Himself *favorably with Lawrance Thompson's official three-volume biography of the poet, complimenting Burnshaw for correcting Thompson's overly neg-*

ative portrayal of Frost and for offering a perceptive analysis of Frost's poetry.]

In ***Robert Frost Himself***—part memoir, part biography, part polemic—Stanley Burnshaw fulfills a request made of him by the eminent poet twenty-seven years ago. In June of 1959 the eighty-five-year-old Frost had asked his old friend, then an editor at Frost's publisher Holt, to "save" him, as the poet put it, from "Larry"—i.e., Lawrance Thompson, Frost's official biographer. (p. 85)

Thompson's three massive volumes, which appeared in 1966, 1970, and 1976 (the last written by Thompson's research assistant, R. H. Winnick, after the biographer's death in 1973), were a harsh indictment of the poet. "Nowhere," notes Burnshaw, "in the annals of literature has so marked a change of the public heart been recorded." The critics, with few exceptions, were taken in by Thompson's performance. When the second volume of what one writer would later call Thompson's "work of riddance" was published, Helen Vendler, in a review in the *New York Times Book Review,* called Frost a "monster of egotism" who left "behind him a wake of destroyed human lives." Following Thompson's lead, she accused Frost of "criminal blandness" in his dealings with his son Carol, who had killed himself with a shotgun at the age of thirty-eight in 1940. *The Years of Triumph,* as the second volume was ironically titled, was awarded a Pulitzer Prize in 1971. When the third volume came out—which the biographer had hoped to call *The Years of Glory* but which was changed to *The Final Years* after his death—one reviewer, David Bromwich, insisted that "a more hateful human being cannot have lived," while Howard Moss declared that Frost was a "mean-spirited megalomaniac" who represented "one of the worst examples of a common strain in American literary life."

It is difficult to convey the enormity of Thompson's two-thousand-page assault. But for a quick fix on the scope of Thompson's ambition the reader need only consult the famous index to the second volume. Under "Frost, Robert Lee," Thompson had listed sixty-three topical subheadings. Among these are "Anti-Intellectual," "Baffler-Teaser-Deceiver," "Brute," "Campaigner," "Charlatan," "Cowardice," "Enemies," "Escapist," "Hate," "Insanity," "Jealousy," "Murderer," "Pretender," "Punishment," "Rage," "Retaliations, Poetic," "Revenge," "Self-Centeredness," "Spoiled Child," and "Vindictive." Scarcely a single human virtue can be found. What's more, Thompson's list of negative characteristics and qualities could have easily been expanded. For example, there could have been a subheading "Cheater," for Frost's having been guilty of, as Thompson puts it, "gouging a worshiper" on a real-estate deal, or "Manipulator," for his having "cultivated" an impressive array of critics, college presidents, and book-club editors, or "Self-Absorption," for, in Thompson's words, the poet's "thoughts of suicide (which) became another lifelong game of self-indulgent pity," or, of course, "Cruelty," for his being, according to Thompson, totally responsible for the unhappiness of his family.

The man Frost called upon for help in his moment of desperation might have seemed, on the surface, deeply unsuited to the task. When Burnshaw first met Frost on a visit to the Gulley Farm in 1929 (arranged through a mutual friend, the poet Wade Van Dore), the younger man was already politically left-wing. Yet Frost, at the time the supposed epitome of Yankee individuality, found much to like in Burnshaw, and vice versa. During their first encounter Frost was "friendliness flowing steady." The truth was, Frost relished diversity. No doubt he also admired Burnshaw's taste for what the latter calls "private" poetry during such socially aware times. (One of Burnshaw's private poems had been taken by Marianne Moore for *The Dial* around this time.) Much of the second chapter, entitled "Roads Taken and Not Taken," details Burnshaw's various attempts to defend his poetic taste while working as an editor at the Communist Party weekly *The New Masses*. According to his account of those years, he bravely challenged Joseph North—an editor of *The New Masses*—about the quality of the proletarian fiction and poetry he was printing. On one occasion he foisted a copy of Frost's poem **"Provide, Provide"** on North. "We talk of 'the system,'" Burnshaw said. "There it stands in twenty-one bitter lines, and very much more." We are given a sense of what Burnshaw (and Frost) were up against from Granville Hicks's review of Frost's ***Collected Poems*** in *The New Republic* of December 3, 1930. Hicks had written that there was "one thing" Frost

> cannot do: he cannot contribute directly to the unification, in imaginative terms, of our culture. He cannot give us the sense of belonging in the industrial, scientific, Freudian world in which we find ourselves.

Burnshaw's retort to Hicks's alarmingly narrow view, fifty-six years later, is worth quoting at length:

> For purposes of narrative verse (Frost) can find not merely pathos but also, because there are certain standards implicit in that world, something close to tragedy. He can find subjects for comedy there, dramatic conflicts, objects of natural beauty. He can treat abnormality and yet keep it in its place, or he can find a theme for as illuminating a commentary on failure as Robinson ever wrote. In the contemplation of nature he can, as scores of lyrics show, find

Frost at his home in Franconia, New Hampshire, 1915. The Jones Library, Inc., Amherst, MA.

> the beginnings of paths that lead straight to the problems that have perennially perplexed the mind of man. He can, in short, find opportunity and stimulus to exercise to the full the poetic imagination.

It is precisely this kind of sensitivity to Frost's poetry, in the end, that makes ***Robert Frost Himself*** such an illuminating book. To be sure, Burnshaw has amassed a considerable amount of evidence to refute Thompson's "official" life. He demonstrates, for example, that Thompson seriously undervalued the importance of Frost's friendship with Wade Van Dore; that Thompson's personal dislike of Frost was greater than we imagined; that the poet's politics were not of the cartoonish reactionary sort; that Frost was capable of great devotion as a friend, husband, and parent; and so on. But it is Burnshaw's capacity to appreciate and understand the poetry that makes his book so persuasive. It is the kind of understanding that is nowhere to be found in Thompson's book, nor—as Burnshaw reveals—in the over one thousand pages of notes for the biography on file in a University of Virginia archive. It "is helpful, if shocking," says Burnshaw, "to realize (that) Frost's poems as poems are virtually ignored" in these notes. All of which would seem to confirm Richard Poirier's remark that Thompson "did not know how to read (the poems)."

How necessary is it to "know how to read" a poem in order to write or comprehend a poet's life? In Frost's case, as with any major writer, it is quite important. For if we read the poems literally, and conceive Frost to be primarily a poet of maxims and country wisdom, it is likely that we will see the man in equally simplistic terms—that is, as someone who is the sum of certain (selected) outward actions. If, on the other hand, we perceive the poetry as essentially ambiguous, as something that makes consistent use of strategies which question or supersede the poem's literal content (as recent critics have seen it), we will in all likelihood view the man as not simply the sum of his actions but as the sum of his actions *and* his art. Now clearly Thompson sees the poetry the first way. Literal-minded to a fault, he grants Frost no subtlety or complexity of thought. And Burnshaw sees it—along with Richard Poirier and William Pritchard, both of whom have published helpful books on Frost—in the second way. The Frost Burnshaw had in mind when he wrote this book is the author of highly complex poems and of the statements, "'Life has lost none of its mystery and its romance. The more we know of it, the less we know," and, "There will always be something left to know, something left to excite the imagination." It's heartening to find Burnshaw following Frost's lead in this, punctuating his narrative with comments such as "Yet what did I *really* know (about Frost's motivations)?" "Did a 'final' idea (in Frost's poetry) exist?" and "No poet alive could be more elusive."

Appropriately, Burnshaw devotes a considerable amount of space in ***Robert Frost Himself*** to Lionel Trilling's speech at the dinner in honor of Frost's eighty-fifth birthday. As Burnshaw suggests, Trilling's talk was the turning point in our understanding of Frost's poetry. "I have to say that *my* Frost," said Trilling,

> is not the Frost I seem to perceive existing in the minds of so many of his admirers. . . . He is not the Frost who controverts the bitter modern astonishment at the nature of human life: the opposite is so. He is not the Frost who reassures us by his affirmations of old virtues, simplicities, pieties, and ways of feeling: anything but. (At the same time) I believe that he is quite as American as everyone thinks he is, but not in the way that everyone thinks he is. . . .
>
> I think of Robert Frost as a terrifying poet.

Trilling's words caused an uproar. According to Burnshaw, "Donald Adams kept shaking his head in fury" after the speech. The next day Adams advised Trilling in *The New York Times* to "come out of the Freudian wood . . . and face the facts of life." Frost himself was visibly upset—or so it seemed. Burnshaw's most interesting revelation regarding the event, however, was Thompson's rushing away from the room at the Waldorf-Astoria immediately following the speech. (He would later write in his biography that the "'terrifying' debate was a local storm not destined to survive.") Burnshaw asked Frost afterwards, "How could (Thompson) let himself stay away after what happened?" Perhaps what Thompson was running away from was the realization that he had erred greatly in his estimation and perception of Frost's poetry, and that his life's work was deeply and irrevocably scarred as a result of it.

Stanley Burnshaw has carried out his pledge to his friend well, but not at the expense of objectivity. ***Robert Frost Himself*** places in perspective a poetic career that was not "a triumph over his enemies," as Thompson characterized it, but, as Lionel Trilling said, one that generated "the terrible actualities of life in a new way" for us. (pp. 85-8)

Robert Richman, "The 'Monster' Myth," in The New Criterion, *Vol. V, No. 3, November, 1986, pp. 85-8.*

TRIG THORESON

This book [***Robert Frost Himself***] could just as well be titled *Robert Frost and Me,* so dependent is it on the personal recollections and perceptions of the author. Readers hoping to find a short, authoritative biography of the poet will therefore be disappointed, but they will be richly rewarded in other ways. Though Burnshaw only saw Frost regularly during the poet's last years, he enjoyed an off-and-on relationship with him beginning in the 1920s; thus, Burnshaw's knowledge of his subject is clearly based on a friendly and enduring, if sometimes long-distance, intimacy. The result is a sympathetic study of a man of steadfast kindness and wit, yet one who was perfectly capable of small public insensitivities and large private errors. Of greatest interest is Burnshaw's lengthy and careful dissection of Frost's troubled relationship with his official biographer, Lawrance Thompson, whose controversial portrait of Frost as a monster of selfishness and egotism Burnshaw eagerly discredits. A fascinating work designed to correct the biographical record of a major twentieth-century poet.

Trig Thoreson, in a review of "Robert Frost Himself," in Booklist, *Vol. 83, No. 5, November 1, 1986, p. 380.*

PAUL MARIANI

[*American critic, poet, and biographer Mariani is associate editor of the* William Carlos Williams Review *and has written two books about the poet, including the acclaimed biography* William Carlos Williams: A New World Naked *(1981). Among his other works are his own poetry collections, including* Timing Devices *(1977) and* Prime Mover *(1985). In the following excerpt Mariani describes* Robert Frost Himself *as an uneven book, but still a fairer account of Frost than Lawrance Thompson's previous biography of the poet.*]

Elinor and Robert Frost in 1915, with their children (clockwise from top): Leslie, Irma, Carol, and Marjorie. George H. Browne/Robert Frost Collection, Plymouth State College.

In this new memoir and apologia for Robert Frost [***Robert Frost Himself***], Stanley Burnshaw recalls Frost's role in the inauguration ceremonies of John F. Kennedy. Frost, then in his 87th year, had prepared a prologue to **"The Gift Outright,"** the poem he meant to say that afternoon. But something went wrong: there was the bitter wind and cold, the afternoon glare interfering with the page before him, the poet's apparent nervousness before he recited from memory the poem he was giving now to the new president, and then the fumbling as he addressed Kennedy as John Finley—Finley being one of Frost's Harvard professors of 70 years before.

Burnshaw, then the poet's editor at Holt, also remembers how Frost's biographer, Lawrance Thompson, explained to him a few days later in his office in New York how the canny old poet had staged the whole affair to steal the limelight from the president. But Finley? To steal the show by muttering the name of John Finley? Burnshaw has also remembered what Frost had said to him in confidence shortly before: that he was counting on Burnshaw to save him from the man he himself had chosen 20 years earlier to be his biographer.

Frost has been dead now for 23 years. And the myth of Frost as monster—a myth generated in large part by Thompson himself—has been around nearly as long, ever since the second in Thompson's three-volume study was published in 1970 to wide acclaim and some dismay and shock. In his own lifetime, Frost had become an American institution, and Thompson's disclosures of Frost's reputedly vicious behavior and dark motives towards family and friends, once claimed for him, even if without adequate proof, were too good as revisionist gossip to be dismissed. One had needed an antidote to the complacent, two-dimensional image of the good grey poet. So there had been Lionel Trilling's assessment of Frost—given at the poet's 85th birthday celebration—as a poet who terrified. After some hesitation, Frost himself was willing to accept Trilling's portrait, though he wondered if someone would also remember the other poet who consoled. Frost—a man of large and complex gestures—could let the Trilling image stand, since he knew himself to contain all the contrarieties fear—that prime mover—might display as protective covering.

Because Thompson worked with Frost from the late 1930s until his subject's death, in which time he had access to so many of Frost's papers and intimates, many have assumed that the portrait he rendered in his biography was essentially correct, even if unflattering. And while most of the prominent critics who reviewed the second volume of Thompson's biography—the volume which disclosed the new, dark Frost—accepted the monstrous figure presented there, there were still a large number of people—critics, teachers, friends—who knew that Thompson had darkened the portrait beyond recognition. Stanley Burnshaw is only the latest of Frost's defenders, but he shows us in his memoir how he followed the poet's career from the 1920s on—though he saw him only intermittently for many years—and how he became Frost's editor at Holt in the late 1950s.

"Save me from Larry," Frost asked Burnshaw in his last years, and this Burnshaw has largely succeeded in doing in ***Robert Frost Himself.*** If the book is erratic, at times self-preoccupied and slow-moving, nevertheless Burnshaw marshals overwhelming evidence against even a semblance of objectivity in Thompson's portrait. He reveals the growing distrust between Thompson and Frost as well as between Thompson and Kay Morrison, Frost's secretary and the woman who—after Elinor Frost died in 1938—watched over and cared for Frost for the last 25 years of his life. Quoting from the 1,500 pages of notebook material which Thompson compiled and which is now at the University of Virginia (made available to scholars in 1980), Burnshaw reveals the biographer's growing antipathy and even hatred of his subject. Frost himself said on more than one occasion that one could get on as much by hatred as by love. And to bear that out, Burnshaw shows us that Thompson not only often got his facts wrong but insisted on seeing Frost's actions again and again in the worst possible light.

How difficult it is to readjust one's thinking once the worst has been suggested of someone. It is the old "Exactly when *did* you stop beating your wife" syndrome all over again. But against Thompson's "official" view Burnshaw patiently marshals the evidence of other eyewitnesses who saw Frost in a kinder if no less complex light. Among the other studies and collections Burnshaw cites are the following: ***The Letters of Robert Frost to Louis Untermeyer,*** Thompson's own ***Selected Letters*** (where Frost can speak for himself), the ***Family Letters of Robert and Elinor Frost,*** Reginald Cook's *Robert Frost: A Living Voice* (1974), then biographical studies by Sidney Cox (1957), Elizabeth Shepley Sergeant (1960), Kathleen Morrison (1974), Wade Van Doren's memoir (not yet available, but which Burnshaw has apparently seen), and William Pritchard's welcome reassessment, *Frost: A Literary Life Reconsidered.*

Having dismantled Thompson, Burnshaw then offers us in his final chapter some ways of recovering the "knowable" Frost. Who was Frost? Like Dr. Johnson, Frost was a brilliant talker, a presence whose voice (the words are Randall Jarrell's, one

Frost and his dog. Photograph by Alfred Eisenstaedt, Life *Magazine © Time Inc.*

of the poet's best critics and defenders) "was half a natural physiological process and half a work of art." When he spoke, it was as if he "dreamed aloud and the dream were a poem." For Frost poetry was as good as it was dramatic; at its best it revealed the complex, thinking, feeling human being who had uttered the words. What mattered finally for this disciple of William James was a "passionate preference" for something, a belief in something so strong one could make it happen. Though jealous for the public reputation he had worked so hard to make for himself, knowing just how fragile fame could be, he could also be generous. The evidence is still coming in that, while he could sometimes play mischief with the great (as he did with T. S. Eliot and Archibald MacLeish), he did support younger poets with his time and money. And over a lifetime's watching, he did manage to place more than a few poems where it has so far proved awfully hard to get rid of them.

What we are witnessing is, I think, the end of the generation which tried to diminish Frost's accomplishments as a poet. We know that such things happen as a counter-response to an uncritical adulation in the poet's lifetime. But Frost has survived, and his poems begin to look better than ever when placed against his contemporaries'. He seems even more modern than most of the modernists. The evidence supporting the major status of the poet is impressive and continues to pour in. Thompson's biography, overloaded with an unworkable scholarly apparatus, its index verging on the comic and the pathological, a book indifferently written and coarse in its understanding of Frost's poems, will continue to diminish as it must.

This is perhaps unfortunate for Thompson, but it was the biographer's gamble against the poet and Frost, for all his joking, knew he was playing for "mortal stakes." Burnshaw has largely succeeded in setting the record straight for his friend, Robert Frost. In time we may even get the full critical biography Frost deserves. God knows we need it. In the meantime we still have Frost's own legacy: his extraordinary poems. It is beginning to look as if they may be too tough to kill, even by the biographer. (pp. 3, 14)

Paul Mariani, "Robert Frost: The Fire and the Ice," in Book World—The Washington Post, *November 2, 1986, pp. 3, 14.*

R. W. FLINT

The greatness of poets is a topic much in abeyance these days. Audiences, teachers and most critics concentrate on what Gerard Manley Hopkins liked to call quiddity or inscape, at the expense of "the roll, the rise, the carol, the creation" that he thought is the essence of poetry—its ability to exalt, transfigure and regenerate. It's no wonder that few people realize how open the question of Robert Frost's nature and magnitude as a poet still remains. One remembers the concluding sentence of his note of thanks to Lionel Trilling for a dramatically disturbing speech at Frost's 85th birthday dinner: "No sweeter music can come to my ears than the clash of arms over my dead body when I am down."

It was a whimsical hope. Yet a good ear could have picked up a muffled clashing in recent years, though hardly enough to raise the dead. At the heart of the matter, lurking like some sinister revenant from Frost's early imaginings of backwoods terror, a very Geryon in its malign tripartite bulk, lies Lawrance Thompson's "official" biography—almost 2,000 pages of anecdote, copious quotations, amateur psychology and a swelling vein of trumped-up indignation occasionally relieved by compunction and good sense, set out in a clotted, humorless, academic prose. Stanley Burnshaw, a poet who spent a happy weekend with Frost as early as 1929, kept a sharp eye on Frost's work and became his editor at Holt, Rinehart & Winston, now presents in his excellent ***Robert Frost Himself*** both a memoir of considerable interest and an explanation of why Thompson's biography became so perverse and why it was published nevertheless.

The Frost-Thompson partnership began in friendly mutual enthusiasm in the 1940's, a fact made plain by the superiority of the first volume of the biography over its two tortured successors. Frost's accounts to Thompson of his early years obviously pleased both of them. But there was something in both men that didn't trust the public honors that arrived in force after 1915, when the second volume begins. But Frost at least understood their values for himself and could, so to speak, turn them under as recommended for every crop in his long didactic poem, **"Built Soil."** Institutions were generous to him because he responded with an eagerness unparalleled since the last years of Mark Twain. He needed the praise, of course, but his need for opportunities to roll his ideas around in public, testing them against the sound of his verse, was greater still. No such luck for Thompson, however, tied to his Princeton professorship and hamstrung by the kind of Yankee prudery that Frost understood all too well but, to his grief and surprise, was helpless to restrain.

Thompson had been recruited as the poet's traveling companion to England in 1957 and to Israel and Greece in 1961, but was conspicuously not invited on the subsequent trip to Russia. At a dinner in England, as Thompson tells it, he was seated next to an editor, and heard the poet on the editor's other side reply "in a sullen voice" to a compliment about Thompson: "He's a charming man, but charm is not enough, is it?" By then the question of who was the Johnson and who the Boswell had been lost in a struggle of egos long set on different trajectories, the poet expecting steady sympathy from well inside his work, the biographer driven by an impossible ideal of tact and respectability in public figures. If Thompson had treated the man with anything like the casual diffidence he lavished on the poetry, there would have been no struggle and very likely no biography. "The poet's faith in his young devotee," Mr. Burnshaw writes, "turned into doubt, distrust, suspicion, fear, and a cry for 'protection.'" This cry became a direct appeal to Burnshaw. "I'm counting on you," Frost said with more than usual gravity. "You will be here. I won't. . . . I want the truth. I need protection from lies, all sorts of lies."

Yet Holt, Rinehart & Winston can't be seriously faulted for publishing books that contained so much pertinent material or blamed for later persuading Edward Connery Lathem to edit them down to a single revised volume of 534 pages. It remained for Mr. Burnshaw to sweeten the consciences of everyone concerned by relating the story of Frost's last five years with a scrupulous fullness whenever his own dealings could throw light. He takes all the right positions and shows himself to have been a sensitive, generous, tactful and solicitous friend, an admirable choice for the job. Like Louis Untermeyer in the best prepolitical days of his earlier friendship with Frost, Mr. Burnshaw knew what he was getting into and gracefully rode out the storms.

But a few large issues escape him. We want to ask if academic critical biography in its new-found pride of place and with its frequent obtuseness toward the arts it ostensibly serves, can ever be trusted with figures as self-created, as aboriginal, as Frost. One must pinch oneself to remember that Randall Jarrell was a professor when he wrote the two splendid essays in *Poetry and the Age* that turned the understanding of Frost around and stimulated Trilling's fruitfully aggressive speech (an event entirely engineered by Mr. Burnshaw). Two other first-class professorial studies, Richard Poirier's *Robert Frost: The Work of Knowing* and William H. Pritchard's *Frost: A Literary Life Reconsidered,* have recently taken Jarrell's initiative several steps further in the right direction.

Frost with Dwight D. Eisenhower and John F. Kennedy at the presidential inauguration, 1961. Photograph by George Silk, Life *Magazine © 1961 Time Inc.*

Frost's most debilitating flaw, a quenchless thirst for praise and patronage, helped him become the creative teacher he often was—the primal poet in residence. Like Frost's career, the college English departments were steadily expanding and searching out new grounds for authority—in philosophy, psychology, politics, anything that came to hand. Their own weaknesses oddly complemented and camouflaged his. Mr. Pritchard has thoroughly understood all this because he unaffectedly loves the poetry and analyzes it with great skill. Mr. Poirier is more consistently analytical and less biographical. He displays an acute awareness of the vital role of the erotic in Frost, a quality that made him perhaps the best poet of marriage and domestic love in English since John Milton.

Once, after enduring a series of high-flown speeches at an anniversary dinner of the Academy of American poets, Frost rose and said: "My idea of poetry isn't of climbing on top of the earth, nor of its standing on top of the earth, but of its reclining on top of the earth and giving way to its moods. Like a spoiled actress, you know, the day after she has been on the stage." He was entertaining that way, but not really a humorist. His upbringing by a Calvinist mother turned Swedenborgian; the tone he took from his raffish, capable, courageous and dead serious Victorian father; his sleepless devotion to good work when the fit was on him—all put him in a class with other archaic masters of actuality like Eakins, Dreiser, Hemingway, Faulkner and Frank Lloyd Wright. No amount of provisional banter about his, or poetry's, essential playfulness could turn his head for long. At least Thompson understood that much when he put Frost's maxim that "humor is the most engaging cowardice" under "Cowardice" in his foolish index; for humor he had no entry at all. "But I am very wild at heart sometimes," Frost once wrote to Untermeyer. "Not at all confused. Just wild—wild." The task of reining in that wildness so that it could generate his subtly luxuriant plainness, his playfulness beyond play, his individuality beyond eloquence or conventional beauty—this was what his curious public life had helped him to achieve.

R. W. Flint, "'Not Confused, Just Wild'," in The New York Times Book Review, *November 30, 1986, p. 24.*

EDWARD J. INGEBRETSEN, S.J.

[In the following excerpt Ingebretsen commends Burnshaw for correcting Frost's negative image; otherwise, however, he deplores the numerous errors and omissions in the biography.]

Burnshaw's major contribution to Frost studies is his third chapter [in ***Robert Frost Himself***], "The Fabrication of the 'Monster' Myth," in which he examines how a poet so extensively "known"—through memoirs, reminiscences, reflections, and "portrait biographies"—nonetheless could have developed so "monstrous" a posthumous reputation. (pp. 288-89)

His treatment of the politics and mechanics of the Authorized Biography, and the failure of later Frost critics to investigate these more thoroughly, makes convincing and sober reading. But if to the making of books about Robert Frost there seems no end, it seems his poetry remains an afterthought. In the main, Burnshaw's references to Frost's poetry are merely asides.

Only one poem (**"Build Soil"**) receives extended treatment—five pages—while perhaps four or five others (notably **"The Gift Outright," "Two Tramps in Mud Time," "For Once, Then, Something"**) engage his attention for more than a page. Though Burnshaw roundly criticizes Thompson, his "Chronology" suffers by comparison to Thompson's facts. He omits all references to Frost's wide professional life, noting little more than when Frost published a collection of verse and which received Pulitzer Prizes. He includes specifically "personal" information—such as noting Robert and Elinor's 1892 "secret marriage ceremony" and Frost's hemorrhoidectomy in 1940—the latter of which even Thompson passed over discreetly. He focuses on the "social" Frost—who, in 1961, "Reads poem at Kennedy Inauguration. Visits Israel, Greece (March)."

Burnshaw's final chapter, "Toward the Knowable Frost" is also worthwhile, though still one sees him busy retrieving Frost from the categories of Thompson's notorious "Index." He admires Elinor Frost a great deal and attempts to accord her a proper place at the poet's side. But Burnshaw's first two chapters are less helpful. These "memoirs" seem as much about Burnshaw's early social activism as about Frost. But more to the point, Burnshaw's eccentric methods of quoting and citing blur the line between quotation and paraphrase. For example, on page four—the second page of the text—he slightly misquotes material from Thompson's biography; on the same page he places quotation marks around words that make them seem to be quotations, though they cannot be found in the place he cites. He quotes from Untermeyer's and Thompson's volumes of ***Letters,*** though, again, not always with accuracy. At one point he quotes Louis Untermeyer on his relationship with Frost. His reference notes to the extended quote on this page (p. 72) indicate *two* sources, though an unclear textual use of ellipses—a common error in this book—and the quotation marks make it impossible to tell where one quotation ends and another begins. He attributes line after line of dialogue and comment to Frost—though he points out that during the "over two decades" between his first meeting with Frost and his beginnings with Holt he had little personal contact with him. One extended "quote" is, in fact, a loose paraphrase of a letter he cites from Thompson's ***Selected Letters.***

Pre-publication material from the publisher notes that the volume has a bibliography; it does not. Finally, Burnshaw's notes are too often careless or erratic or both, utilizing a system of double asterisks and footnotes, and an elaborate cross-referencing system that obfuscates as much as it clarifies. Sometimes he dates personal letters he has received; sometimes he does not. . . . Sometimes he uses a "standard form" for notes, citing pages and closing with periods, though often he does not. . . .

In the introduction to his ***Selected Letters*** Lawrance Thompson invites his readers to "roll (their) own" biography. Since the poet's death, many have. All in all, one thinks, perhaps Frost's concern about biography was in order: "Trust the poems." What value is Robert Frost "Himself" in captivity if we have neglected or forgotten his poetry? (pp. 289-90)

Edward J. Ingebretsen, S. J., in a review of "Robert Frost Himself," in American Literature, *Vol. 59, No. 2, May, 1987, pp. 288-90.*

VN: The Life and Art of Vladimir Nabokov

by Andrew Field

(For Vladimir Nabokov: see also *CLC,* Vols. 1,2,3,6,8,11,15,23; *Contemporary Authors,* Vols. 5-8, rev. ed., Vols. 69-72 [obituary]; *Contemporary Authors New Revision Series,* Vol. 20; *Dictionary of Literary Biography,* Vol. 2; *Dictionary of Literary Biography Yearbook: 1980;* and *Dictionary of Literary Biography Documentary Series,* Vol. 3. For Andrew Field: see *Contemporary Authors,* Vols. 97-100.)

An Excerpt from *VN: The Life and Art of Vladimir Nabokov*

The following, then, are the factors that contributed to *Lolita*. A parodic but very important analogue to incest in the Nabokov family tree. A large family that was inclined to favor itself romantically—besides using his mother's nickname for Lolita, Nabokov used the nickname of a cousin with whom he was madly in love as a little boy, Dolly, for her nickname, and Nicolai Nabokov proposed to Nabokov's sister Elena (she refused him). Nabokov's own passionate attachment to his memory of "Colette." The "five or six" pedophiles whom he said he had known personally during his life. (The dubious sixth was a staff member at *The New Yorker* with whom he had never discussed the matter but about whom he had strong suspicions.) His reading and rereading of Havelock Ellis at various points throughout his career. The address to the jury by the young Nabokov in the trial of Nikolai Evreinov's play. And finally, his hate/take relationship with Dostoevsky and the lure of Dostoevsky's most daring undeveloped theme coupled with the use of open eroticism by his contemporaries Ivan Bunin and D. H. Lawrence in the thirties. Considering all of these vectors, *Lolita* was not a chance but virtually a fatidic development in Nabokov's career.

The story of the artist-chimpanzee [who was taught to draw and drew the bars of his cage] is very useful when we consider the novel that Nabokov actually wrote in 1953-54. His impulse by that time was to create a portrait of a man imprisoned in passion, but not in (we remember *Laughter in the Dark*) "blind passion." In his interview with Alain Robbe-Grillet, Nabokov said that for him *Lolita* was really "a certain problem" that he wished to solve in an elegant and economical fashion. The problem that Nabokov sought to resolve was threefold in nature. First, the protagonist as victim of his own or someone else's passion *(King, Queen, Knave* and *Laughter in the Dark)* had to be joined with the theme of the protagonist-artist *(Despair* and *The Eye)* who both controls and conveys the story. This synthesis, which presented a challenge far more difficult than it might first appear, required in turn that, while the narration would reside with

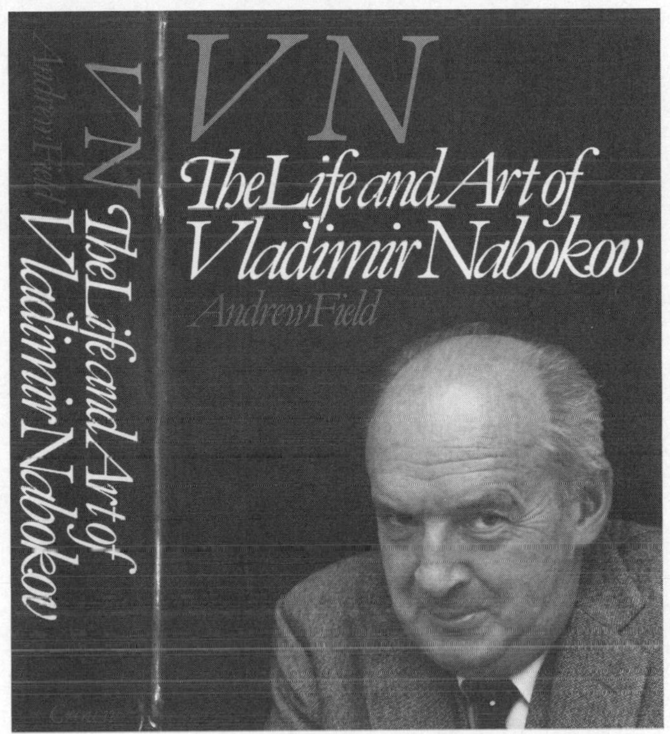

Dust jacket of VN: The Life and Art of Vladimir Nabokov, *by Andrew Field. Crown Publishers, 1986. Jacket design by Walter Harper. Jacket photograph © Philippe Halsman.*

the hero, the course of the story itself had to proceed according to inexorable rules. In such a synthesis, the hero's game must be both won and lost at the same time. And finally, there was the challenge and delight of allegorically resolving a theme, love, in terms of its extreme and seemingly mutually exclusive opposite, lechery. To put it in another way and more simply, *Lolita* is Nabokov's most mature novel and the meeting ground and perfect blending of all his habitual themes.

JIM ELLEDGE

From the beginning of his lengthy and illustrious career, Nabokov has been shrouded in mystery, due largely to his own eagerness, even obsession, to camouflage his life. His will (Nabokov died in 1977) even stipulates that his private papers are to remain unpublished until a half-century after his wife's and son's deaths. Nevertheless, in Andrew Field's fourth book on Nabokov [***VN: The Life and Art of Vladimir Nabokov***], much of Russia's most complex and beguiling émigré novelist's heretofore undisclosed and puzzling life is illuminated both accessibly and authoritatively. This study draws from many previously unavailable sources—Field's extensive interviews with Nabokov, his family, and his friends; the novelist's personal correspondence with, among others, his mother and father; his literary correspondence, including Edmund Wilson's letters; and a number of unpublished notebooks. While focusing on the man, Field never ignores the work when it serves to illuminate the hidden recesses of Nabokov's life. Field's is a captivating study in which his respect for his subject is as apparent as it is engaging.

Jim Elledge, in a review of "VN: The Life and Art of Vladimir Nabokov," in Booklist, *Vol. 82, No. 22, August, 1986, p. 1652.*

DAVID GATES

The long pursuit of Vladimir Nabokov by scholar Andrew Field would have made a good Nabokov novel—had not Nabokov already predicted such a struggle for interpretive power in his 1962 ***Pale Fire,*** a novel masquerading as a study of a poet by a mad academic. Field, as a biographer must, has been intent on reducing him to a figure in a book. Nabokov, however, who saw the figures in *his* books as "galley slaves" doing his authorial bidding, was intent on eluding such a fate. He wanted to make Field "his" biographer, someone who would construct an artful myth about his life. Field's ***Nabokov: His Life in Part,*** an incomplete biography that appeared in 1977, the year Nabokov died, so outraged his subject's sense of himself that he called out his lawyers. And Nabokov included in his last novel, ***Look at the Harlequins!,*** a swipe at "a matter-of-fact, father of muck, mucking biographist." In this new "full-length" portrait [***VN: The Life and Art of Vladimir Nabokov***], Field makes the passage his epigraph.

VN reprints verbatim much of Field's earlier biography, as well as portions of a still earlier critical study. We get fuller but essentially similar accounts of Nabokov's aristocratic family in prerevolutionary Russia, his impoverished exile in Berlin, where he became a major Russian writer, his immigration to the United States in 1940, the critical and popular triumph of ***Lolita*** in 1958 and his final years of genteel seclusions at a hotel in Montreux. It is above all the story of a survivor. When Nabokov's Russian works were banned in the U.S.S.R. and his émigré readership dispersed, he resolutely began writing in English. In this adopted language he wrote the books that guaranteed him literary immortality—and that restored him to something like his boyhood standard of living.

Few readers will be as "stunned" as Field by the news of his subject's extramarital affairs or scandalized by the two TV interviews in which Nabokov suavely poured whisky from a teapot. (He always toyed with illusion, even in his cups.) Still, there are surprises. Nabokov the Red-baiter sought out Soviet intellectuals; Nabokov the lepidopterist (he studied butterfly genitalia) wasn't the solid scientist he made himself out to be. (One entomologist calls his papers "idiosyncratic as hell.") And Nabokov the archfoe of Freud seems to have had a mother nicknamed Lolita.

The greatest surprise here is Field's new disenchantment with his subject. "He is, I reckon, a good man," Field wrote of Nabokov in 1977; this passage is not in the new book. Field now argues that it was Nabokov's "narcissism" that helped him cheerfully survive his lean years, and to create his fictive worlds. But, says Field, he "wore his fame badly" and became, at the end, a "garden-variety egotist."

The narcissism that fed Nabokov's art, Field argues, came to infect it, and he condemns the "pseudo-Olympian" late novels for their self-indulgence. But the same charge could be made against everything Nabokov wrote: it is hard to judge him by any esthetic but his own. Was he the last of the great Russian writers? A modernist in the line of Proust and Joyce? He didn't care. "I'm not interested," he once said, "in groups, movements, schools of writing and so forth. I am only interested in the individual artist." This insistence on the sovereignty of solitary genius may be narcissistic, but it is also his great legacy. His well-known devices—the pun, the double, the false-bottomed narrative, the visible author who is both enchanter and charlatan—can be mimicked. But the essential Nabokov is inimitable. He had the imagination to hear a flushing toilet as a "brief waterfall" and to see grass blades spewing from a lawn mower as "optical twittering." No writer has quite the same way of fusing icy intellect and hot sensuality; no writer yearns quite so articulately for quite the same lost paradise.

Field knows this in principle, but he still seems uncomfortable about both the man and his work. It's true that Nabokov's Jovian thunderings against, say, Dostoevski now sound silly, but Field is oddly unwilling to take seriously his critical views. He backs into reaffirming his long-held opinion that Nabokov is "as interesting as any . . . writer in this century" by saying that there is "no reason to alter it." And his peroration ("The world will not soon forget either him or his stories") is less than ringing. The result of this half-suppressed uncertainty is that ***VN,*** despite its readability and its wealth of detail, lacks both an authoritative assessment of Nabokov's importance and a sense that he was knowable in human terms. "Judge Nabokov as you will," Field concludes, throwing up his hands, "there is evidence on all sides." This refusal to have the last word in their long dialogue is Field's way of being fair to Nabokov—fairer, perhaps, than he really wants to be. But the reader can only feel cheated. (pp. 78-9)

Nabokov as a student in St. Petersburg, 1916.

David Gates, "The Perils of Narcissism," in Newsweek, *Vol. CVIII, No. 12, September 22, 1986, pp. 78-9.*

ROBERTA SMOODIN

[Smoodin is an American novelist and critic. Her novels include Ursus Major *(1980) and* Inventing Ivanov *(1985). In the following excerpt Smoodin commends Field's biography for its intriguing revelations about Nabokov's work and personal life.]*

Given the fact that Vladimir Nabokov, the most private and mendacious of great writers, designated in his will that his personal papers and letters could not be made public until 75 years after the deaths of his wife and son, ***VN: The Life and Art of Vladimir Nabokov*** by Andrew Field is certainly the most exhaustive and revealing biography of the writer we will see until well into the next century. It is a fine piece of detective work and analysis, a hybrid work that would please Nabokov, if any biography could.

Field delves into Nabokov's work with a seriousness and sensitivity that is impressive, making longshot connections between the writer's life and art that create the sense of a successfully completed jigsaw puzzle. Yet, at the same time, Field treats the writer's life as if it were a movie star's life and gives the reader juicy, gooey details about Nabokov's womanizing and literary politicking that are worthy of any good Hollywood star bio. All of this makes the book absolute heaven for the true Nabokov addict. For anyone who isn't already convinced that Nabokov's laundry lists are worthy of literary analysis, this book might prove to be as soporific as a bottle of Valium.

Field starts with the assumption that Nabokov is one of the 20th Century's great writers. The author of ***Lolita, Pale Fire, Ada,*** and earlier works such as ***Despair, Laughter in the Dark*** and ***King, Queen, Knave,*** Nabokov must be ranked with Joyce and Proust in terms of his literary achievements. More than this, though, his life was so much more varied and fascinating than theirs, and his linguistic achievements all the more stunning because of the polyglot nature of his work. In *Finnegans Wake,* Joyce, showing off his knowledge of scores of languages, performed an intricate and ultimately perplexing literary dance that did little to illumine any truths about human nature but much to demonstrate the brilliance of Joyce. Nabokov certainly was one to show off, to demonstrate with every sentence that he was more brilliant than his reader could ever hope to be. But language was not quite so pyrotechnic for him. Instead, it was the sea he swam in, and his transition from the brightest and best young Russian emigre writer to a great English-language writer is a feat that must fascinate anyone with an interest in the act of writing and the way language shapes the writer.

My bias here is clearly showing. I am one of those who would read every laundry list . . . Nabokov cached away in drawers at the Montreux Palace Hotel, where he lived his last years. I am, therefore, also one of those for whom Field wrote this book, and I found the Nabokov minutiae in it wondrous.

Nabokov, who was born in 1899 and died in 1976, was forced to flee Russia with his family when he was a teen-ager, after living a life of extreme privilege, decadence and acknowledgement of his gifts. His gypsying around Europe afterward, in England, Germany, Czechoslovakia and France, frequently in impoverished conditions, was colored by a deep sense of irredeemable loss, which became one of the great themes of his work. But he was also much feted as Sirin, his nom de plume, author of poetry, essays, stories and novels that best captured Russian emigre life.

Field describes this phase of Nabokov's life with loving detail, and communicates brilliantly the way Nabokov always lived secure in the knowledge of his own brilliance. Few other writers have enjoyed that kind of security, though they may have had more security in the more banal aspects of existence. This makes Nabokov's life both curious and interesting, and Field uses this as an important clue to the writer's vastly enigmatic personality.

The book is excellent, as well, in its analyses of two of Nabokov's greatest works, ***Lolita*** and ***Pale Fire.*** Field has done his homework, and his use of existing Nabokov scholarship and his own remarkable ability to connect reality with literature makes these chapters treats, as close as one can get to feeling privy to Nabokov's creative process. He cuts through Nabokov's frequent lies about his own work and uses the author's misdirection quite cleverly, looking for the correct path under the bogus one, and frequently seems to find it. Field's devotion, hard work and intelligence cannot be questioned.

My only quibble with Field concerns his estimation of ***Ada.*** Field dismisses ***Ada*** as the work of an overripe old writer, a writer past his prime, and calls it self-indulgent. Because of this, ***Ada*** gets little attention. As a Nabokov fan who loves ***Ada*** for its poignancy and richness, I felt cheated of Field's incisive scholarship on the subject of my favorite of Nabokov's works. But, if one's only complaint about a biography is that one wished for more, this complaint is really a compliment in disguise.

Field gives the reader many delicious Nabokov bits. Upon arriving in Ithaca after a long train ride, "Nabokov raised his hands and clapped smartly for a porter. They were perhaps hundreds of miles from the nearest porter. It was clear that Nabokov, though politically an American patriot, had in terms of his life reverted wholly to being a European." In anecdotes like this, Field captures perfectly the inner conflicts out of which Nabokov's great body of work grew. (pp. 1, 15)

Roberta Smoodin, in a review of "VN: The Life and Art of Vladimir Nabokov," in Los Angeles Times Book Review, *September 28, 1986, pp. 1, 15.*

R. Z. SHEPPARD

This is Andrew Field's third crack at the literary and biographical puzzle that was Vladimir Nabokov. The first, ***Nabokov: His Life in Art*** (1967), demonstrated the scholar's grasp of the great man's novels, stories and poems. It was a valuable guide through an intimidating maze of themes and plots; its thoroughness made it a high form of flattery. Field's credo, that a writer's "truest and most palpable biography" is his work, rang with disarming idealism. Nabokov must have been impressed and relieved; his disdain for the genre he defined as "psychoplagiarism" was well known. The acolyte was invited to the author's home in Montreux, Switzerland, where he took the inside track in Nabokovian studies and conducted the interviews that led to book No. 2, ***Nabokov: His Life in Part*** (1977).

It would appear there was more to a writer than his art. Field dutifully charted the course of Nabokov's life: his birth into a distinguished St. Petersburg family; his idyllic, multilingual youth; the Bolshevik Revolution, which stripped the clan of rank and property and launched it into exile. There were Nabokov's university years at Cambridge; his ascension as "Sirin," the pseudonymous literary star of the Russian émigré communities of Berlin and Paris; the coming of World War II; and the flight to America with Wife Vera and Son Dmitri. Colorful details from this period include Nabokov's career as a teacher at Wellesley and Cornell, his cross-country butterfly hunts, his friendship and falling-out with Edmund Wilson and the sensational success of ***Lolita,*** which freed Nabokov from the academy and allowed him to live in an old-style luxury hotel on the shores of Lake Geneva.

In retelling this story, Field frequently borrows verbatim from his earlier book. But there are some intriguing additions. His research since Nabokov's death in 1977 has enriched the European period between the wars and provided some naughty parts. The novelist's great-grandmother Nina von Korf continued a love affair with Dmitri Nabokov, the novelist's grandfather, after he became her son-in-law. This, according to Field, accounts for the theme of incest in books like ***Ada*** and ***Lolita,*** a reversal of family history in which "the man marries the daughter in order to be able to continue more easily to be her mother's lover." As a gossip, Field has it both ways. Nabokov's grandmother Maria and Alexander II "must have been fleeting lovers." In one breath, this relationship could mean that the novelist's father was the Czar's bastard son. In the next gasp, the possibility is dismissed on the ground that Alexander had another mistress at the time. There is solid evidence that Nabokov was a randy young adult and had at least one serious extramarital entanglement. There is also the assertion that he was a spiritualist who believed in communication between the living and the dead.

If so, Field can expect some late-night calls. For ***VN*** is not only a revision of ***His Life in Part*** but a revisionist view of the man and much of his art. The literary icon Field once cryptically defined as a "Russian-American writer of our time and of his own reality" is now called a "great Russian-American Narcissus." Late novels such as ***Ada*** and ***Look at the Harlequins!*** are seen as works of a "garden-variety egotist." Both books have their share of self-indulgence and preening; neither approaches the level of masterpieces like ***Lolita*** and ***Pale Fire,*** the last word on the mad pursuit of biographical reality. But viewed against the body of Nabokov's fiction, the narcissist label seems inadequate, a bit trendy and more than a little disingenuous. Field made his name studying the work and the man. Better than most outsiders, he knows the sources of Nabokov's genius, his gifts for showmanship and parody, his eccentricities and vanities. To discover at this late date that his hero was not Mother Teresa seems peculiar. (pp. FB10, FB12)

R. Z. Sheppard, "Revisions," in Time, *Vol. 128, No. 16, October 20, 1986, pp. FB10, FB12.*

JOEL CONARROE

[*American critic and professor, Conarroe is the author of* William Carlos Williams's Paterson: Language and Landscape *(1970) and* John Berryman: An Introduction to Poetry *(1977). In the following excerpt Conarroe observes that* VN *offers some interesting details about Nabokov's life, but that inaccurate and shallow observations mar the biography.*]

Whenever he replied to an inquiring stranger that, yes, he was Vladimir Nabokov, the novelist in turn would ask, "And what do you do?" as though "Nabokov" were a vocation. The well-rehearsed role he played so well—urbane, polymath émigré, playful yet aloof—is nicely documented in Andrew Field's unauthorized life, ***VN,*** his third book about the writer. Mr. Field's efforts to get past the public persona, however, have been less successful. There is a telling moment in one of the earlier books when he observes Nabokov enter a room while putting on a tie, and hears him speak to his wife: "'Darling, can I really not write about him?' . . . Then he suddenly saw me,—'Oh, I'm terribly sorry, Andrew. I didn't realize you *were* still here.' The word stress was strangely out of place." This was apparently one of the few times Mr. Field saw the author with his guard (and necktie) down; had he witnessed such spontaneity more often, his analysis of the private man would almost certainly be more penetrating.

Nabokov's public career, as Mr. Field shows, falls into four nearly symmetrical parts—an artist's seasonal cycle. Springtime was spent in St. Petersburg, where, as the novelist later said, he was "a perfectly normal trilingual child." The pampered princeling of a well-to-do family, young Volodya learned to regard himself as the center of the universe. At 16 he became a multimillionaire when his father's brother left him an estate. Almost immediately, however, the Bolshevik Revolution sent the family into relative poverty abroad, and the writer spent the summer of his life in that unmapped country called exile, deeply aware of all he had lost. During this 20-year period, in Germany, England and France, he wrote under the pseudonym Sirin a body of work in Russian that may be compared in this century, Mr. Field correctly claims, only with that of Chekhov and Ivan Bunin.

The productive autumn years, in America, lasted from 1939 until 1959, during which time he taught at Stanford, Wellesley and finally Cornell, where for a decade he played the part of intellectual dandy in the provinces and earned a reputation as a brilliant and charmingly eccentric professor. With the success of ***Lolita*** in 1958 he was able to give up teaching and move with his wife to Switzerland, spending his final 18 years in the stately Palace Hotel in Montreux. A permanent transient, Nabokov never owned a home, apparently unwilling to risk another trauma like the loss of his family's estates. It seems that he settled in contentedly wherever he happened to be, and his years in such quiet places as Ithaca, N.Y., and Montreux suggest a comment Haydn once made about his own periods of relative seclusion: "I was cut off from the world—there was no one to confuse or torture me, and I was forced to become original."

In documenting this pilgrimage through six countries (and numerous fictional landscapes), Mr. Field provides a great deal of interesting information. We learn, for example, that Nabokov was an insomniac with a lifetime history of headaches, that he had an aversion to music, that much of ***Lolita*** was written in a Buick, that he thought *Doctor Zhivago* third-rate sentimental fiction and that, when he gave up his heavy smoking, this sensuous athlete who had troubled the sleep of Wellesley undergraduates came to resemble, in his own description, "a blend of the portly poet Apukhtin and General MacArthur." Entertaining as such facts are, whether about Buicks or butterflies, they do not show what went on behind the man's carefully constructed facade; we never see the emergence of what Leon Edel, with reference to Henry James, calls the figure in the carpet. It may be, of course, that the figure cannot be revealed, since Nabokov's will stipulates that his private papers not be published until 50 years after the death of his wife and son. But even though Mr. Field recognizes that the man is "a conjecture within a conundrum," he feels adequately equipped "to describe that secret life."

As it happens, Nabokov, in whose work the subject of biography looms large, was suspicious of "mucking biographitists," who commit "psychoplagiarism" by using what an author has created to give an impression of the inner life. If the biographitist of his own peripatetic history errs, however, it is on the side not of looting the artist's canon but of substituting details for imaginative speculation and analysis.

VN, to be sure, does have a controlling thesis—Nabokov as Narcissus—but the theory is never persuasively argued, and in fact it disappears for long stretches at a time. There are those who regarded the ironic Russian as a cold-blooded creature with little capacity for deep feeling, but Mr. Field is interested neither in relating this point of view to his own consideration of self-love and creativity nor in discussing the implications for fiction of a writer's possibly distorted sense of self. When he does offer interpretive commentary, moreover—mostly quarried from his earlier studies—his critical vocabulary proves unequal to the challenge of so complex and articulate an artist. Some of his generalizations, in fact, sound remarkably naïve, as in the reference to "'pessimistic' ***Despair*** and 'optimistic' ***The Gift***" (Mr. Field is fond of quotation marks), or in the stupefying observations that Humbert Humbert desires "the destruction of all mature women" and that his "perversity is very close to homosexuality." And while carefully composed passages can be found, some wayward prose cries out for a blue pencil: "Nabokov's technique is to attempt to, quite literally, by ridicule exclude the possibility of a Freudian reading." (That sentence, with its infinitive not merely split but sundered, sounds like a translation from some mythical Nabokovian language.)

At other times the problem lies not in manner but in matter: "The following dates for public readings have been gleaned from public newspaper announcements and accounts: a reading on March 25, 1924, at the Flugerverband (Schoneberger Ufer 40); on April 18, 1924 (Fasanenstrasse, 78, am Kurfursten damm); a reading at an unspecified place. . . ." The list goes on at length, its data scarcely transmuted into digestible prose.

Nabokov once referred to Mr. Field as "absent-minded," and it does seem that his right hand is not always aware of what the left is up to. For example, following the atypically bold statement that there is not "a single actual 'sexual' scene in all of Nabokov, except for . . . one in ***Lilith,***" the critic discusses several erotic passages, including a scene "in which Van feasts on Ada's nipples," which, if not "sexual," is certainly sexual. And although his research is admirable and his knowledge of the man and the work impressive, there are lapses of fact that give one pause, such as the assertion that ***Lolita***—banned in public libraries in Cincinnati, Newark and elsewhere—"wasn't banned (except in New Zealand)."

Nabokov in Berlin, 1934. By permission of Zinaida Schakowskai.

In his earliest book, ***Nabokov: His Life in Art,*** published nearly 20 years ago, Mr. Field provided a laudatory gloss on the major novels written up to then. Ten years later he brought out ***Nabokov: His Life in Part*** (which the novelist playfully suggested be called *His Life and His Parts*), an entertaining study based on a series of interviews with the author and his wife. For ***VN,*** Mr. Field draws heavily on these works (he now sees them as preparatory exercises), revising some passages and quoting others at length. We learn, in the final chapter, that "there was a four-year legal struggle over my 1977 book about him. Nabokov was furious about what he saw as a breach of faith. The author was upset because, he contended, he had been given assurances about the general outlines of the life of Nabokov that proved to be untrue."

There is nothing like a legal dispute to arouse hostile feelings, and Mr. Field's portrayal of the Montreux years does seem to be fueled by anger. The intolerant and dictatorial novelist we encounter, no longer Narcissus, is now simply a "garden-variety egotist," a furtive tippler who wears his fame badly, openly boosting himself for the Nobel Prize (which, shamefully, he was denied) while gossiping maliciously about other writers. We read that ***Ada*** is "sprawling and self-indulgent," its characters "not people but dolphins," and we get, gratuitously, a description of a *conte à clef* by Zinaida Schakowskoi about an aging artist held prisoner by a tyrannical wife who isolates him from all natural feeling. Little wonder that with so depressing a sense of the final years Mr. Field can rise only to a half-hearted peroration: "A full-length portrait of Vladimir Nabokov then, Russian-American writer of our time and of his own reality. The world will not quickly forget either him or his stories." For the conjurer who gave us ***The Gift, Pnin, Pale Fire*** and other works of genius, this, surely, is prose too feeble, praise too faint. (pp. 7, 9)

Joel Conarroe, "What Masterpiece Was Written in a Buick?", The New York Times Book Review, *November 2, 1986, pp. 7, 9.*

JEFFREY MEYERS

[*Meyers is an American critic, literary biographer, and professor of English. Among his many books are biographies of Wyndham Lewis, Katherine Mansfield, D. H. Lawrence, and, most recently, Ernest Hemingway. Meyers has also published bibliographies of George Orwell and T. E. Lawrence, and several critical studies of contemporary authors, most notably,* Wyndham Lewis: A Revaluation *(1980). In the following excerpt Meyers praises Field's critical evaluations of Nabokov's writings and outlines the major events in the novelist's life.*]

In the 1950s my friends at Cornell raved about an idiosyncratic teacher, with a strange Russian name, who lectured on the European novel. One of his students once approached the podium at the end of a lecture and begged: "Do it again!" During World War II the aristocratic White Russian once attracted an audience of nine hundred when a Minnesota newspaper fancifully described him as a "celebrated Soviet writer and a personal friend of Josef Stalin."

Nabokov was born (like Borges, Hart Crane, and Hemingway) in 1899. His father was a leader of the right-wing Kadet Party, a member of the first Duma, minister of justice in the last provisional government, and editor of the main émigré newspaper in Berlin. Nabokov's wealthy parents adored him and each other, and he grew up in a trilingual paradise of tutors and governesses, trips to Biarritz, and butterfly hunting near their old-fashioned country house. He was driven in a Rolls-Royce to the most advanced and expensive school in Russia, and inherited millions from a pedophile uncle who ardently fondled him in public. His first poems appeared when he was 17. The family fled to Yalta after the Bolshevik Revolution, and went into exile in 1919. The loss of Russia was the worst tragedy of his life, but he maintained a defiant optimism in his works. . . .

Field's chronicle of Nabokov's ancestors [in ***VN: The Life and Art of Vladimir Nabokov***] is confusing; but he illuminates the relation of the fascinating life and works, provides sound readings of the novels, and convincingly argues that ***Ada*** is Nabokov's most overrated book. Field discusses the themes of illusion, narcissism, doubles, incest, and homosexuality, as well as the characteristic games, puns, and parodies. Nabokov wrote a perceptive book on Gogol and shared his master's "solemn deviousness, his spectral vision in art, and the peculiar intensity of his comedy."

From 1919 to 1940 Nabokov lived in England, Germany, and France; maintained a precarious existence as a teacher of English and tennis; and began his career as a Russian writer. He entered Trinity College, Cambridge, in 1919, to study French and Russian, attended lectures, took verbatim notes, and passed the exams in 1922 without ever entering the library.

After graduation he joined the émigré colony of 200,000 souls in Berlin and survived a period of wild inflation by demanding payment in hard currency. In 1922 his father was assassinated at a public meeting, by a Russian monarchist who was attempting to shoot another émigré political figure. The following year, Nabokov's engagement was suddenly terminated when he asked his fiancée for a "strange kind of kiss." He married his Jewish wife, Vera, in 1925 and remained in Nazi Germany until 1937, when they finally moved to Paris. "We were always sluggish," he explained. "Gracefully sluggish in the case of my wife, terribly sluggish in my case. We get accustomed to a place, and we just stay." He publicly expressed his devotion to his wife, but had a number of serious love affairs.

In 1940 Nabokov agreed to replace a Russian lecturer at Stanford and began his academic career in America. He was—with Wells, Koestler, and Huxley—one of the few novelists with scientific training, and continued his entomological research on field trips to the West and at museums in New York and Boston.

Nabokov taught from 1941 to 1948 at Wellesley—which provided the first comfort and security of his adult life—and from 1948 to 1959 at Cornell, where he never attended a faculty meeting. In America, he began writing in English. Edmund Wilson, who admired Nabokov's Russian novels and became his closest friend, helped establish his reputation by introducing his work to editors and publishers, and by recommending him for a Guggenheim grant. Nabokov did not—perhaps could not—help Wilson; and they later quarreled bitterly about Nabokov's masterly translation of Pushkin's poem *Eugene Onegin*.

Nabokov achieved fame and wealth when ***Lolita,*** rejected by five American publishers, was brought out by the Olympia Press in Paris and eventually became a sensational best-seller. The English publisher lost his seat in Parliament; Adolf Eichmann (in an Israeli prison) found the book offensive; and the half-million dollars in royalties allowed Nabokov to move in 1959 to a suite in the Montreux Palace Hotel. He drank heavily at the end of his life and died in Switzerland (like Joyce and Mann, Erich Remarque and Irwin Shaw) in 1977. Though Nabokov professed intense dislike of Dostoyevsky, Freud, and Lawrence, he was strongly influenced by their work. A brilliant follower of Joyce and a highly original stylist, the Russian master left three American masterpieces: ***Lolita, Pnin,*** and ***Pale Fire.***

Jeffrey Meyers, "Spectral Vision," in National Review, *New York, Vol. XXXVIII, No. 21, November 7, 1986, p. 52.*

SIMON KARLINSKY

[Karlinsky is a Manchurian-born American critic and professor of Slavic languages and literature. His publications include Marina Cvetaeva: Her Life and Art *(1965),* The Bitter Air of Exile: Russian Literature in the West, 1922-1972 *(1977), and* Russian Drama from Its Beginnings to the Age of Pushkin *(1985); he also edited* The Nabokov-Wilson Letters *(1979). Karlinsky visited Nabokov in 1973 and learned of the novelist's growing disillusionment with Field as a biographer. In the following excerpt Karlinsky cites several factual errors in* VN *and argues that poor scholarship, an insufficient knowledge of Russian culture, and an unsympathetic attitude towards his subject make Field an unfit biographer for Nabokov.]*

Nabokov's son calls [***VN: The Life and Art of Vladimir Nabokov***] an "odd concoction of rancor, adulation, innuendo and outright factual error." Is such an assessment fair? Andrew Field's first book on the subject, ***Nabokov: His Life in Art,*** subtitled "A Critical Narrative," came out in 1967, when Field was something of a Nabokov protégé. At that time, much of Nabokov's earlier work—novels, stories, poetry—was not yet translated into English. Field informed the readers of the English-speaking countries (many of whom still thought that ***Lolita*** was Nabokov's first novel) of Nabokov's output in the 1920s, '30s and '40s and asserted its importance for appreciating the writer's art. Despite a deliberately difficult scrambled structure, Field's 1967 book performed the useful task of acquainting Nabokov's admirers with the whole of his work and biography. It was written with the full cooperation of Vladimir and Vera Nabokov, who gave Field access to their archive and recollections and who helped him correct, I was told, over a hundred major errors of fact and translation when his book was already in the page-proof stage.

Between the publication of Field's first book on Nabokov and his second one, ***Nabokov: His Life in Part,*** 1977, the relationship between the writer and the biographer soured. During a visit to Montreux in 1973, I found Nabokov sad and angry about what he saw as Field's breach of confidence. To give Field a deeper perspective during his work on the first biography, Nabokov told him of some personal and family matters that were meant to be off the record and not for publication. To Nabokov's chagrin, Field intended to include this information in his new book. He also went about interviewing people in the Russian exile community whom Nabokov considered his personal enemies. As we learn from a passage at the end of ***VN,*** it took a "four-year legal struggle" to resolve what confidential information could or could not be revealed in the 1977 book.

VN is meant to be an updated synthesis of the first two books. Its distinct advantage over them is that instead of the convoluted sequence in which they were couched (in apparent imitation of some of Nabokov's narrative structures), the story of Nabokov's life and writings is told here in a coherent and chronological order. It also contains (another first) a reasonably complete index. The aim of the 1967 and 1977 books was to assert the greatness of Nabokov's literary art. In ***VN,*** Field still admires some of Nabokov's writings, but this is undermined by his seething animosity toward not only the writer himself, but also his family and ancestors. Field has clearly gone out of his way to interview a number of Nabokov's surviving Russian contemporaries who for one reason or another resented Nabokov's international success and his often aloof stance. As one of his prime sources for ***VN,*** Field cites Princess Zinaida Schakowskoi's scurrilous 1979 memoir *In Search of Nabokov,* published in Paris in Russian. Field calls it "excellent" and "essential." In fact, its treatment of Nabokov and its *ad feminam* attack on his wife Vera often border on character assassination.

I have always found Andrew Field something of a puzzle. After decades of writing on Russian literature and culture, at times brilliantly, he can still come up with statements about them that are so naive or so misinformed as to leave one gasping in disbelief. On p. 2 of the introduction to ***VN,*** Field asserts a similarity between Vladimir Nabokov and Czar Nicholas II ("a weak and foolish man") because they both "came from cosmopolitan St. Petersburg, which played with politics and culture and took a Fabergé-service picnic to the edge of a volcano." But of course the snobbish, superstition-bound court of Nicholas and Alexandra was neither cosmopolitan, nor aware of the innovative cultural flowering that marked their reign, while Nabokov's resolutely anti-monarchist family was close to the center of that flowering. The memoirs of Nabokov's father, published in English by Virgil D. Medlin and Steven L. Parsons in 1976, show the absurdity of such a juxtaposition.

At the beginning of his annotations to ***VN,*** Field recommends to the reader Renato Poggioli's *The Poets of Russia,* 1960, as one of "the best guides to early 20th-century Russian literature and culture." Uninformed and error-ridden in the first place, Poggioli's book has been rendered totally obsolete by the vast amount of critical and scholarly material published during the last two decades both in the Soviet Union and in the West on early 20th-century Russian poets. Nor does Field bother to mention some of the most important studies of Nabokov's novels that have appeared in English since the publication of his 1967 biography. After the pioneering essays by Edythe C. Haber on ***Glory*** (1977) and Alex de Jonge on ***Mary*** and ***The Gift*** (1980); after Ellen Pifer's *Nabokov and the Novel* (1980), which is an indispensable study of Nabokov's ethics and his perception of reality; and after Brian Boyd's magnificent, book-length analysis of ***Ada*** (1985), Field's discussion of the novels in ***VN,*** mostly repeated from his first two books, can't help appearing pallid and pedestrian.

But ***VN*** also contains some new conjectures, and for some of them the only appropriate adjective is "preposterous." One of these is Field's guess that in Nabokov's letters to his mother he addressed her as "Lolita." Field then qualifies as "brazen compulsion, the ultimate gesture of contempt for everything Freudian" Nabokov's later "giving his mother's nickname to the heroine of his greatest novel." But of course polite Russian usage would preclude a respectful son, such as Nabokov was, from addressing his mother by a nickname, even if such a nickname as "Lolita" existed in Russian, which it doesn't. As Dmitri Nabokov explains in the afterword to ***The Enchanter,*** Field misconstrued the actual salutation, which was *Radost'* ("My Joy").

Even more bizarre is Field's explication of the name Zina Mertz in ***The Gift.*** This is Nabokov's most attractively depicted female character (Field oddly leaves her out when discussing the pleasant and unpleasant women in Nabokov). Also, as Field is aware, Zina is the closest Nabokov came to producing a literary portrait of Vera Nabokov, née Slonim. "Zina," Field insists, "isn't a Christian Orthodox name." How could he have failed to notice that Russian life and literature are full of women named Zinaida, whose friends and family usually call them Zina? Mertz, Field admits, "is a perfectly plausible russified German Jewish name." But no, he prefers to derive it from an art movement among the German Dadaists in the '20s (the painter Kurt Schwitters, *pace* Field, coined the word Merz from the German word for "commerce"). From this, through some leap in logic, it follows that the name Zina is an "easy anagram for Nazi." First, this anagram would never work in Russian, the language in which ***The Gift*** was written (the name would have to be "Tsina"); and second, why would Nabokov want to name the irresistibly appealing young half-Jewish woman, who was in part a portrait of the wife he loved, with an anagram for Nazi?

In such passages of ***VN,*** both scholarship and common sense take a nosedive. Whatever value other portions of Field's book might offer, one thing is clear. A writer of Vladimir Nabokov's stature deserves a biographer who is more at home in Russian culture and has more respect and sympathy for the man and his achievement than Field now does.

Simon Karlinsky, "Nabokov's Life and Lolita's Birth," in Book World—The Washington Post, *December 14, 1986, p. 5.*

ROSS WETZSTEON

[In the following excerpt Wetzsteon rebukes Field for demonstrating poor scholarship and narrow mindedness towards his subject in VN.]

The unreliable narrator has been a common stratagem of novelists from Joseph Conrad to Vladimir Nabokov, but it's hardly what one expects in a biographer. Ironically, Nabokov has been cursed with his own Kinbote, a sleazy, subacademic hack named Andrew Field, whose commentary on Nabokov's "life and art" possesses all of the petty pedantry but none of the runic resonance of Charles Kinbote's commentary on John Shade's ***Pale Fire.*** A reader unaware of Field's hidden agenda might be bewildered by ***VN***'s meandering mixture of adulation and spite, discretion and innuendo, obsessiveness and laziness, but for those who know even a bit of background about the problematic relationship between the biographer and his subject, this disconcerting tone becomes a case of life not so much imitating as debasing art.

In May 1968, a year after the publication of his critical study ***Nabokov: His Life in Art,*** Field approached Nabokov about the possibility of a biography, and eventually they entered into a kind of Manchester-Kennedy arrangement, research coopera-

Nabokov at Harvard's Museum of Comparative Zoology, 1947. Photograph by Joffé.

tion in exchange for manuscript approval. Such deals are dubious, in any case, but it soon became apparent that this one was disastrous. Give Field his due—the increasingly aloof and self-enamored Nabokov was equally responsible for the mistake, clearly felt that his "cooperation" extended only as far as providing Field with dates, opinions, and papal interpretations of his work, sternly resisted anyone prying into his privacy, and regarded biography as little more than "psychoplagiarism."

Nabokov didn't want a biographer, he wanted a toady of the type Hemingway found in A. E. Hotchner. But instead of dropping the project, Field continued to ingratiate himself with Nabokov, and when the manuscript of ***Nabokov: His Life in Part*** was finished, Nabokov's predictable reaction was rage—not just at unwelcome revelations, but at misquotations, distortions, and outright inaccuracies of fact and interpretation (a distinction, of course, Nabokov was unlikely to have made). There was talk of litigation, changes and deletions were negotiated, dozens of factual errors were corrected, and the book was finally published in 1977, to the bitterness of Nabokov and his family.

A straightforward account of his disputatious relationship with Nabokov would have been both honorable and scholarly (if that's not an oxymoron), but for whatever reason Field chose to conceal the depth of their disagreement from his readers. Indeed, straightforwardness is not one of Field's most salient characteristics, a fact confirmed by the artful, not to say crafty way he misleads his readers into thinking ***VN*** is "the first full biography" when it recycles huge chunks of material, often word for word, paragraph for paragraph, from his previous two books.

In ***His Life in Part,*** Field adopts a strategy of coyness—using as his epigraph, for instance, "Hah! What Dr. Johnson would have thought about that book," or writing "three years later, when we were both wiser by far about what stresses a biography can bring to bear (in two directions)," or stating "The book you hold does not come with the recommendation of Vladimir Nabokov"—that had a devious double message: those who knew the extent of the bitterness between the author and his subject couldn't quite accuse him of hiding it, but those who didn't would only think he was modestly, even affectionately, acknowledging their inevitable disagreements.

Field is slightly more forthright in the current book: "There was a four-year legal struggle over my 1977 book about him. Nabokov was furious about what he saw as a breach of faith. The author (Field is somewhat grandiosely referring to himself) was upset because, he contended, he had been given assurances about the general outlines of the life of Nabokov that proved to be untrue. Yet though Nabokov's stance was menacing (when he was not being very genial), he never actually went to court over anything." What's most noticeable about this passage, quoted in isolation, is the use of the adversarial courtroom tactic—the innocently sly implication that Nabokov didn't sue only because he had no case. But what's most noticeable in the context of ***VN*** as a whole is the moral vulgarity that can depict a conflict between Nabokov's prickly dignity and Field's gossip-mongering as an unfortunate case of mutual misunderstanding.

In essence, then, ***VN*** is a reissue of ***Nabokov: His Life in Part*** with the juicy parts back in. And oh what revelations we're led to expect! "Astounding new discoveries made in the decade since Nabokov's death," according to the jacket. Nabokov's "secret life," according to the introduction—"It is time for all the important sealed doors to be opened." Kinbote, we will do well to recall, made similar promises.

"One of the great secrets of the Nabokov family" is trotted out in the first chapter, a liaison between Vladimir's great-grandmother and grandfather—though it's hard to understand why Field calls this a "secret," since the composer Nicolai Nabokov, the novelist's cousin, has already written about it at some length in his memoirs, published over a decade ago. Almost immediately following this nonshocker, Field intimates that Nabokov actually might have been the grandson of Czar Alexander II—but after the tease he examines the flimsy evidence and concludes, with wholly inappropriate italic emphasis, since it was he himself who raised this white herring, that "Nabokov's father was *not* the bastard son of Alexander II." And so it goes, sealed doors opening to unstifled yawns, until Field finally "reveals"—new Shakespeare manuscript discovered!—that Nabokov had extramarital affairs, drank furtively, and died suspiciously.

As for the alleged affairs, Field has apparently forgotten the high-minded stance he took in his earlier volume: "It is none of my business, nor of yours either." But even if he now concedes he was wrong in 1977, he can still be accused of hypocrisy, for in the present volume he simultaneously trumpets his few meager speculations about Nabokov's sexual adventures and squeamishly disapproves of Nabokov's reinsertion of sexually explicit passages in his Russian novels when they were translated into English—in the hopes of increasing sales, he implies with a disdainful sniff. If Nabokov were not so hostile to Freud, it'd be tempting to call this a classic case of projection.

As for that "furtive" drinking, Field reaches this conclusion on the basis of two factoids: "When he came down to greet morning visitors, he might stop for a ten o'clock whiskey at the bar,'' and the more assertive declaration that ''he poured scotch from a teapot during the course of at least two television interviews.'' And what about that ''mysterious'' death? Field quotes Nabokov's son Dmitri as attributing it to a hospital infection contracted while being treated for flu—but then goes on to characterize this account as only a ''version.'' Was Dmitri lying? Was he covering up? What's going on? ''It seems quite possible,'' Field speculates, ''. . . that Nabokov suffered from some form of cancer in his last years.'' His evidence? He has closely examined Lord Snowdon's photographs!

But there's one further ''secret door'' as yet unopened. ''What sort of brazen compulsion,'' Field asks, ''the ultimate gesture of contempt for everything Freudian, brought Nabokov to use a version of his mother's nickname for the heroine of his greatest novel? That nickname was Lolya.'' He's only warming up—this is the revelation that's going to make his career! ''Photocopies of the letters by Nabokov to his mother that were given to me have one word cut out: the salutation. It is a word about seven letters long and with the tail or hat of Nabokov's Russian *t* often showing clearly below or above the cut-out space.'' One can hear Field pausing for suspense. ''Lolita, surely, it seems to me.''

Now one has to use only elemental psychology to argue that it's more likely Nabokov deleted the endearment out of reticent regard for his adored mother, elemental pedantry to point out that when the Cyrillic *t* is handwritten in the lower case it's closer to an Arabic *m*, and elemental *arithmetic*—follow this closely, Andrew—to count the letters of L-O-L-I-T-A and discover that it has only six.

What's left after these ''astounding new discoveries''? Field's writing is alternately term-paperish (''Perhaps given the situation of Russia and the foolishness of the czar, the Russian Revolution really was inevitable''), sloppy (''an émigré train waiter finds himself on the same train with his wife whom he believes to be still in the Soviet Union, only he doesn't realize it''), and subliterate (''The first irreparable rift in their friendship''). The analysis of Nabokov's fiction is perfunctory (virtually nothing on his last three novels, as if—one can only hope—Field is finally getting bored with the subject), the conjectures about his psyche often self-contradictory (at one point Field argues that Nabokov's idyllic childhood makes Freudian interpretation irrelevant, at another he cites it as the source of what he feels is Nabokov's virtually clinical Narcissus complex), the organizing theme of Nabokov as Narcissus hyperbolic in any case (and never extended beyond a marginal metaphor), and the literary scholarship disgraceful (Field writes as if virtually nothing about Nabokov's fiction had been published in the 20 years since his first volume).

But it's Field's tone that's most disturbing—vindictive, supercilious, undercutting his surface admiration with sudden lapses into nastiness—and all the while portraying himself as a forgiving victim of a former friend. Obviously, he's not only entitled but obligated to an ambivalent view of his subject—whose life can undergo a biographer's scrutiny and emerge unscathed? But this book reads like an act of revenge in the guise of devoted scholarship—and who is a more suitable object of revenge than the person we feel has rejected our admiration?

Nabokov is both an ideal and an impossible subject for a biography—after all, the essence of his work is the transformation of memory into imagination—but the worst possible subject for a biographer like Field, who transforms imagination into memory. Ignore this wretched book, return to Nabokov's own fiction instead: ''I know more than I can express in words, and the little I can express would not have been expressed had I not known more.''

Ross Wetzsteon, ''Stale Fire: Nabokov's Nemesis Strikes Again,'' in The Village Voice, *Vol. XXXI, No. 52, December 30, 1986, p. 55.*

FERNANDA EBERSTADT

[*Eberstadt is an American critic and author of the novel* Low Tide *(1985). In the following excerpt Eberstadt praises* VN *for its vivid and objective portrait of Nabokov.*]

The life of the Russian emigré novelist Vladimir Nabokov (1899-1977) is one complicated by artifice, concealment, invention, and subterfuge. Nabokov is one of the more theatrical and self-flaunting of serious modern writers. If Saint Paul once wrote that he did not live, but died daily, one might say of the novelist Nabokov that he did not live, but re-invented himself daily. In his later years a celebrated lecturer and literary lion, Nabokov painstakingly arranged every public statement and appearance, rewriting his interviews with journalists and sometimes denying afterward (with threat of legal action) that he had made the statements recorded on tape or film. He revised three times over into a more pleasing picture his memoirs of his first forty years: its two sequels, describing his American experiences, Nabokov himself suppressed. His fiction is walled with false mirrors and paved with teasing trails designed deliberately to confound the prospective biographer—indeed, a number of his novels are prefaced with introductions rather coyly fending off the ''sleuths'' or ''the little Freudian'' who might seek personal revelations in the author's art. Moreover, in a more unequivocal effort at privacy, Nabokov in his will stipulated that his personal papers—including those same volumes of memoirs and a novel which his son Dmitri claims to be one of the author's best—might not be published until fifty years after the deaths of his wife and son (b. 1932), a provision that echoes the century-long ban on his own private archives imposed by Nabokov's raging bête noir, Sigmund Freud.

Consequently, the present-day biographer of so complex, gamesome, and devious an artist finds himself awkwardly hindered in his investigations. As the Nabokov scholar Andrew Field declares in his recently published ***VN: The Life and Art of Vladimir Nabokov***—the first complete biography of the novelist—''There are grounds to suppose that Nabokov never intended that the details of his life be known. It is the purpose of this book to describe that secret life.'' The first part of this proposition is something of an understatement; the second is a promise that Field is not able to make good on—I suspect because Nabokov, although an avid womanizer and enthusiastic literary feuder, probably did not have much relevant life outside his work. (p. 4)

[*VN*] is a rather casual although always engaging assemblage of literary criticism and biographical information.

A large amount of ***VN*** is devoted to the examination of individual stories, novels, and poems. Field's approach to Nabokov's work is pleasingly straightforward and free of critical cant. Although much of his criticism of necessity involves detective work—the unraveling of the trilingual puns and anagrams that encrust Nabokov's fiction, and the uncovering of the literary sources whose influences Nabokov himself laboriously denied—Field nonetheless avoids becoming overly in-

Nabokov and his wife Vera with their son, Dmitri, in 1960. AP/Wide World Photos.

ternal in his textual analysis, maintaining instead a salutary distance from his subject. To his great credit, Field treats Nabokov's work as would an intelligent reader, frank in his likes and dislikes, and not as a professional Nabokovian, gloating proprietarily over every verbal jest.

For biographical material, Field draws upon Nabokov's own memoirs, on extensive interviews with the author and his wife (who has repudiated the book), and on the taped recollections of Nabokov's relatives, students, friends, and colleagues, each of whose anecdotes light up piquant though quite different aspects of the artist. Field wisely chooses to quote directly from his interviews: a currently fashionable biographical method which here gives the reader an opportunity to judge for himself the credibility of these sometimes unreliable reporters and to enjoy at firsthand the highly idiosyncratic emigré cadences which mark the speech of Nabokov and his friends.

Although Field's biography is sketchy, offering (as its author himself admits) "occasional scaffolding where one would prefer a finished room," the book is acute in both its critical judgments and its understanding of Nabokov's complicated relations with the world. By the end of ***VN,*** one has the rare sense of having gained a vivid familiarity with the novelist, in all his monstrous vanity, his desperation to shock, his petty vindictiveness and vulgarity, his manic energy, playfulness, charm, and his wholehearted devotion to literature.

Biographies of great writers often tend to shake one's reverence for their subjects: great writers are often mean men, and it's difficult for their biographers to unveil that creative process by which such men in their works transcend themselves. It is *VN*'s virtue that although Andrew Field is very harsh about Nabokov as a man and a writer, his book leaves one with a portrait of an artist Olympian in both failings and accomplishments. (pp. 4-5)

Fernanda Eberstadt, "Vladimir Nabokov: Ardor and Art," in The New Criterion, *Vol. 5, No. 7, March, 1987, pp. 4-18.*

DMITRI NABOKOV

[*Nabokov, the German-born American son of Vladimir Nabokov, has translated many of his father's works. In the following excerpt he accuses Field of writing a slanderous, error-filled biography of his father.*]

> Reality would be only adulterated if I now started to narrate what you know, what I know, what nobody else knows, what shall never, never be ferreted out by a matter-of-fact, father of muck, mucking biographitist.

So says a character in Vladimir Nabokov's ***Look at the Harlequins.*** Nabokov had written 'biograffitist.' Andrew Field [in ***VN: The Life and Art of Vladimir Nabokov***], misquoting him, fumbles his epigraph and kills the pun—a fitting omen.

Wait—one must write dispassionately even when faced with slander of one's father. One must again slog through Field's grammar, style, scholarship, and innuendo to check if improvements have occurred during the book's Atlantic crossing (it appeared in the USA last year). One finds they have not. Just as the biograffitist's previous book insulted Nabokov at the time of his death, so the British edition of this one offends his memory on the anniversary of his birth.

After Field's factually competent ***VN: His Life in Part*** (1966) and a mediocre bibliography, Nabokov made the mistake of approving a projected biography. He tried, initially, to be indulgent. During the summer of 1973 Field unexpectedly became obsessed that Nabokov was somehow trying to 'manipulate' his biographer and began pumping any hostile 'source' he could find. A note in the present book assures *all* informants that their contributions have been used—no matter what rusty axes they might have had to grind.

When he saw the manuscript, Nabokov rebelled against the disinformation and innuendo that filled it. Field responded: 'I am a younger man, and I would have you consider how easy in fact it would have been for me to wait a number of years and publish a book with a title like, well, "He Called His Mum Lolita".' On 8 August 1973 Nabokov replied (in part):

> Your ignoble letter . . . arrived only now. . . . I would attribute to the workings of a deranged mind some of its wild rubbish . . . but derangement is one thing, and blackmail another, and blackmail is the word for your threats to publish my informal utterances on two afternoons of tape-recording, the garbled recollections of strangers, and the various rumors that fell into your unfastidious lap, if I continue to insist on your deleting from your book the errors of fact, the blunders of fancy, and the vulgar malice which still mar your 'revised' edition. . . .

The matter did not go to court only because our lawyers prevailed on the publisher to delete some of the worst mistakes, even if the 'style and tone' of Field's manuscript remained, as Nabokov said, 'beyond redemption.' The book was eventually published in 1977.

In the early 1980, we learned that the 'Mum' book was indeed being written, and laced with new venom now that VN was safely dead and unable to sue. The page proofs I was able to procure contained countless blunders, falsehoods and insinuations, and we supplied the American publishers, Crown, with a generous sampling of factual errors. Crown's condescending reaction was to incorporate a couple of our countless corrections (e.g. the misdating of the Russian serfs' liberation, and a detail about my motor racing) and proceed with publication.

Practically all the blunders survive in this English version, from 'biographitist' in the epigraph to a misspelling of the name 'Tatarinova' near the end of the index. Strangely, a major mistake Field has publicly admitted remains as well. (Then again, its deletion would have left a major hole in his psycho-speculation.) I refer to his contention that Nabokov, in his letters, addressed his mother as 'Lolita.' Field thought he perceived the trace of the 'tail or hat' of a cyrillic *t* where Nabokov, with a gentleman's reserve, had chosen to delete the affectionate salutation in the letters shown to Field. He decided the missing word was 'about seven letters long.' 'Lolita, surely,' he concluded (though Lolita has six, not seven, letters), and, whith characteristic recklessness, proceeded to build on what he now considered an established fact. The term of endearment was *radost* [an equivalent of 'dearest']: we have the original letters to prove it.

To list all Field's factual accidents would require a small volume, so I shall limit myself to a handful of howlers. The image of my great-grandfather dashing by (*sic*) horseback to St Petersburg from a country house in the middle of a Russian winter upon Alexander II's assassination is extraordinary: first of all, he was already in the city; besides, by 1881, more practical transport was available. Equally comical is the thought of my grandfather formally introducing his dinner guests to the servants. Field's doubts about a planned duel that caused Nabokov to agonise over his father's fate are based on misinformation about a different duel and different people. The unwise contention that Nabokov's verse ceased mentioning God after his father's assassination will be exploded when the translated poems appear in 1988. My mother's alleged participation in a hit-squad to execute Trotsky is a gem.

The sea of alcohol in which the ageing Nabokov supposedly dissolved has no more solid support than a joke of his on television, shared with the audience: a teapot of water laced with some Scotch (neither my mother nor I ever saw him even slightly tipsy). The presumed 'decline' that ensued (since fictional biography must have a denouement) presumably refers to such trifles as ***Ada, Transparent Things,*** and ***Look at the Harlequins.*** The publication of letters Field has never seen will soon settle other more personal matters.

Professor Field, who in a recent lecture accused Nabokov of 'extremly limited historical sensibility,' not only botches the details and chronology of Nabokov's work and life but is guilty as well of some incredible historical howlers. On the very first page of his introduction he enthrones Alexander II in 1868: 'seven years too late to free the serfs,' as Brian Boyd has put it, 'and an unlucky thirteen years behind the true date.' Field goes on to give the date of the Russian Revolution as 1916. . . .

Field sees his relationship with Nabokov as a battle of two titans. One tends more toward the image of a malevolent dwarf sliding through his own muck with a bulldog grip on his love/hate-object's coat tails. All one can do (to quote again from ***Look at the Harlequins***) is 'refute, then demolish by ridicule the would-be biographer's doctored anecdotes and vulgar inventions.'

Dmitri Nabokov, "Did He Really Call His Mum Lolita?" in The Observer, *April 26, 1987, p. 25.*

Robert Graves: The Assault Heroic, 1895-1926

by Richard Perceval Graves

(For Robert Graves: see also *CLC,* Vols. 1, 2, 6, 11, 39; *Contemporary Authors,* Vols. 5-8, rev. ed., Vol. 117 [obituary]; *Contemporary Authors New Revision Series,* Vol. 5; *Something about the Author,* Vol. 45; *Dictionary of Literary Biography,* Vol. 20; and *Dictionary of Literary Biography Yearbook: 1985*. For Richard Perceval Graves: see also *Contemporary Authors,* Vols. 65-68 and *Contemporary Authors New Revision Series,* Vol. 9.)

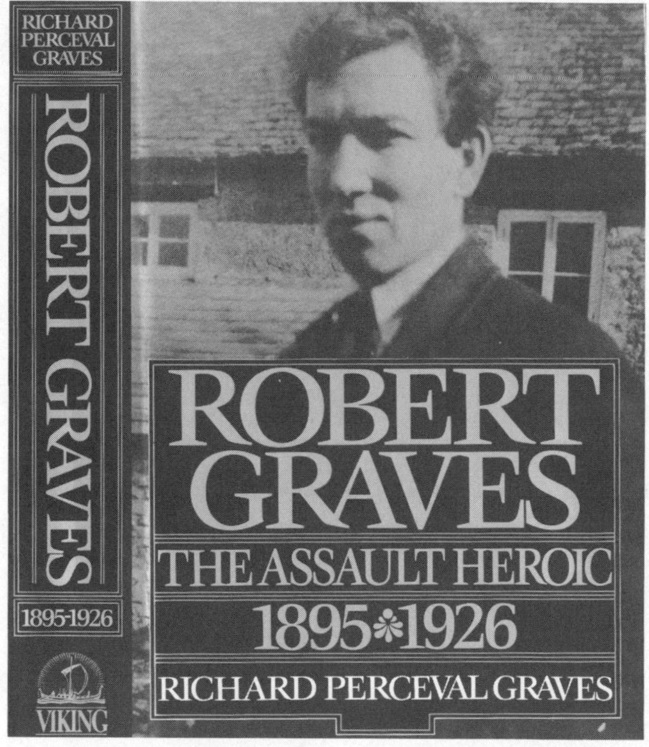

Dust jacket of Robert Graves: The Assault Heroic, 1895-1926, *by Richard Perceval Graves. Viking Penguin, 1987. Jacket design by Bob Silverman. Jacket photograph by John Graves. Reproduced by permission of George Weidenfeld & Nicolson Limited.*

An Excerpt from *Robert Graves: The Assault Heroic, 1895-1926*

[Robert] had been brought up within a literary family in which it was taken for granted that artistic achievements were of great importance. He had also found from an early age that writing poetry helped him to cope with both external pressures and internal conflicts. Bullied assiduously during his first terms at Charterhouse, where the high standards of behaviour which he had assimilated at home made it difficult for him to be accepted by his peers, he had written how:

> Green terror ripples through our bones,
> Our inmost heart-strings thrill
> And yearn for careless day.

As he became less overwrought during the middle years of his Carthusian career, his writing lost the forcefulness of these lines; but he enjoyed words and the technical challenge of experimenting with new metres and rhyming patterns, and poetry became not only an escape, but a positive pleasure. From an early age Graves had been happy to take direction from someone whom he idealized; and his pleasure in writing poetry was heightened by the close friendship which developed between himself and 'Peter' Johnstone. . . .

The stresses of Graves's wartime experiences at first strengthened his reliance both upon Johnstone and upon other male friends such as Sassoon and David Thomas; but these stresses also introduced into his work the horrifying realism of lines such as those on the 'Dead Boche', who 'scowled and stunk/With clothes and face a sodden green.' At the same time his poetry was improved by the thoroughgoing criticism which he received from his poetic mentor Edward Marsh. Towards the end of the war, recuperating from shell-shock at a convalescent home in the Isle of Wight, Robert came to see that in his poetry he had been conducting an 'Assault Heroic' in which he had ''alchemized' unhappy experiences into poetic gold. . . .

The attraction for Marjorie, followed shortly afterwards by revulsion from Johnstone and the belief that he himself had been treading down a dangerous 'pseudo-homosexual' road, was followed by marriage to Nancy. For a while Robert and Nancy appeared to have much in common and attempted to live in an enchanted world in which innocence and artistic ambition could flourish side by side; but reality kept breaking in.

The stresses of married life, together with a recurrence of shell-shock, sent Robert delving first into psychology, which immeasurably deepened both his human understanding and the interest of his best poetry; and then (under Mallik's influence) into philosophy, which threatened at one stage to make his writing utterly obscure. The additional stresses produced by years of failure to support himself by his writing, had begun to poison his relationship with Nancy, to make her ill with worry, and to induce a kind of personality crisis in Robert himself.

Whether Robert would remain an interesting minor poet, or whether he would achieve something more, must have seemed an open question in January 1926. He needed above all some strong and self-reliant person upon whose judgment he could rely, and in whose affection he could feel secure. Such a person was to hand in Laura Riding. It was she who showed him the way out of his emotional and intellectual impasse; so that within three and a half years of their voyage to Egypt, Robert was nearing the end of *Goodbye To All That,* his heroic and partially successful attempt to rid himself of all the conflicts and unhappinesses of his 'historical' past.

KINGSLEY AMIS

[*Amis made his reputation as a rebel against the postwar English intellectual establishment with his sardonic first novel,* Lucky Jim *(1954). Since then he has won acclaim as one of England's foremost contemporary novelists with such works as* Ending Up *(1974) and* The Old Devils *(1986), which won the Booker-McConnell Prize. Although best known for his satirical fiction, he has written poetry, science fiction, criticism, and numerous essays for contemporary journals. In the following excerpt Amis characterizes* Robert Graves: The Assault Heroic *as a tedious biography without insight.*]

The author of this book [***Robert Graves: The Assault Heroic, 1895-1926***] is a son of John Tiarks Ranke Graves, younger brother of Robert (I use the plain Christian name for brevity). The blurb describes him as 'a full-time biographer' whose previous subjects include T. E. Lawrence, Housman and the Powys brothers. He was helped in his present task by privileged access to unpublished memoirs by respectively Robert's mother Amelie, brother John and half-brother Perceval, together with various family diaries and letters. This is the first volume of what is intended as the definitive, very long biography.

Robert was the third child of middle-aged parents, his father, Alfred Perceval, Irish Protestant, his mother German with some Norwegian blood. He grew up in a well-off, respectable, indeed dry household, strong in morality but rich in affection too, populous in the sense that it was constantly full of relatives: there were five children of a previous marriage of Alfred's and innumerable aunts and uncles. Their comings and goings make difficult reading.

Alfred was an Inspector of Schools, also like other senior Graveses a literary man, a poet whose song 'Father O'Flynn' must be better known than any one of his son's poems. (He sold it outright in a batch, £80 the lot, being no better at money than the rest of the family.) Perhaps Robert was inspired by his father's creative example; this biographer more than most tries to clarify complicated and never really explicable events, like becoming a poet, by ascertained and easily grasped facts. Perhaps, then, and perhaps not. In rather the same way, Robert began as a poet very early, in other words he made verse-type scribbles from time to time, like many little boys who develop into writers and very many more who don't.

With the schooldays we are on firmer ground. Robert went to a lot of schools, six in all by the time he was 14, and hated every one of them. Charterhouse, where he ended up, took a turn for the better when he began to do well at cricket and boxing and later poetry, but in his last month there he wrote to his brother John that it was 'one of the vilest places on God's Earth.' In this respect Robert showed himself to be significantly like other writers and artists in general.

The reason for the prevalent unpopularity of school with creative persons is perhaps straightforward, even syllogistic. All schools, at least in the day when they were still schools, provided the entrant with inexhaustible reservoirs of opposition and competition. These are the two things most hated and most bitterly resisted by egotists. All artists are egotists. There. Not all egotists are artists, of course, and it does seem that other types, like those who eventually become industrialists or trade unionists, say, or critics, have no discernibly worse a time at school than anyone else, so perhaps we should insert some intensifier like 'screaming' before egotists in my conclusion just above.

Hereabouts somebody often pleads that the egotism is needed to get the art into being and is therefore worthwhile, though the relevant wives and husbands are not always consulted on the point. But this is a large subject. Before leaving it I might remark that artist-egotists can be cowards and dissemblers too, which is why some of them miss the conventional bad time at school.

Robert was manifestly not one of them. He left school in July 1914 and by May the following year was serving with the Royal Welch Fusiliers in France. He shirked none of the dangerous and harrowing tasks that fell to an infantry subaltern, in due course a captain, at that appalling time. He was lucky not to have died of a wound from shell-fragments and his nerves were severely affected for years afterwards. After demobilisation in 1919 he went to Oxford, got married, lived on Boar's Hill and entered the literary life. The story ends with Robert's departure for an academic post in Egypt in the company of his wife Nancy and of the American poetess Laura Riding Gottschalk, who had crossed the Atlantic on purpose to become his helpmeet and collaborator.

As told here it is not a very interesting story. All those family sources seem to have yielded precious little of much consequence. On and around Boar's Hill, for instance, Robert got to know or ran into all manner of literary figures—Bridges, Gilbert Murray, Edmund Blunden, Robert Nichols, Masefield, Yeats, T. E. Lawrence, Walter Raleigh, Siegfried Sassoon, who had been a brother-officer in France, even Vachel Lindsay—but on this showing they never did or said anything worth remembering. Here, as elsewhere, a mass of undifferentiated detail is piled up after the manner of a bad examinee, with the reader left to spot the connections and applications, if any. Even this is preferable to the author's attempts to impart relevance to his facts.

When he exerts himself to focus on his subject's actual writing it is to comment that his early religious conflicts 'fuelled his creativity,' or that the 'cornerstone' of Robert's and Nancy's relationship was 'a shared commitment to the arts,' though worse than this was surely to be feared after an introduction that begins: 'A true poem is like a spring of water in a desert land.' Golly, and here I am walking past springs of water in desert lands every day for years without ever tumbling to it that what they're like is true poems.

Something that might have alleviated matters is any show of penetration, liveliness or wit, any flicker of enjoyment in the writing or personal response to the material, were it no more than malice or boredom. But no: it is very much as if the full-time biographer of the family felt or was told that here was something he was uniquely equipped to do and had better get on with willy-nilly. The book does possess one great novelty, however: it presents Laura Riding in a favourable light.

Kingsley Amis, "Digging Up Graves," in The Observer, *September 21, 1986, p. 31.*

MARTIN SEYMOUR-SMITH

[Seymour-Smith is an English poet, critic, and biographer. His works include the poetry collections All Devils Fading *(1954) and* Reminiscences of Norma *(1971) as well as his recent criticism,* The New Guide to Modern World Literature *(1985). From 1951 to 1954 Seymour-Smith served as tutor to Robert Graves's son on Mallorca; his* Robert Graves *(1956) is the first biography of the poet. In the following excerpt Seymour-Smith compares factual data from his biography with data in* Robert Graves: The Assault Heroic *and praises Richard Perceval Graves's work as a valuable account of the poet's life from the viewpoint of a close family member.]*

This [***Robert Graves: The Assault Heroic, 1895-1926***] is the first volume of a projected three-volume 'definitive' biography of Robert Graves by his nephew, Richard Perceval Graves. It takes over where the author's father, Robert's younger brother John Graves, left off. John, who died in 1980, had been described by Robert as a 'typically good pupil of a typically good school' (to which he returned as teacher); he had for long contemplated the composition of a book called *My Brother Robert*. The outstanding virtue of his son's first volume—which almost exhausts the private information he holds, mainly derived from the diary of the poet's father Alfred Perceval Graves—is that it is a worthy completion of the task John Graves set himself. He would not have gone beyond 1931 and the death of Alfred Perceval. As Richard Perceval Graves remarks, John was 'a devout Christian, a loving father, and a most honourable, unselfish man'. The difficulties begin here. This author . . . closely resembles his father. But Robert Graves did not at all closely resemble his 'typically good' brother; nor does he resemble his 'typically good' son—who, although he has 'known' and 'loved' his uncle 'since childhood', did not know him very well at all, and was never the recipient of his confidences. Nor, for that matter, was Robert capable of speaking in the moralistic terms employed by Richard Perceval. But his family for the most part (there are exceptions) was—and is. This gives ***The Assault Heroic*** an unexpected dimension.

Graves with his family, September, 1908. Back row (left to right): Charles, Rosaleen, and Robert. Front row: Clarissa, Alfred, John, and Amy. By permission of Richard Perceval Graves.

The publication of this book puts me in a difficult position. As the author of the first biography of Robert Graves I am, naturally, proprietory. I should therefore not appear graceless when new biographies and critical studies appear. But what if I sincerely believe that they are awful and misleading? It is fortunate, then, that this book does have a genuine value.

Those who are interested in Robert Graves will thank me only if I am candid. The late John Graves, to the idea of whose book upon him Robert Graves responded with a certain sense of depression, was put out when he heard from me that I had been commissioned to write a biography of Robert. He struggled with his own understandable proprietory feelings. Eventually he was generous to me: he sent me many extracts from his father's diary that he thought would be useful, gave me his opinions about the influence of Laura Riding on Robert, and talked to me at length and frankly on the telephone. He behaved as a conscientious man should behave. What I got from him was mostly confirmatory of what I had got from Robert Graves himself (at a time when neither of us contemplated my writing a book about him): but John was also very useful in confirming my view of the impression made by the Riding-Graves relationship on outsiders. I put it on record that ***Antigua, Penny, Puce*** is in part a satire on John. I should now add that it is good-natured satire: Robert sincerely hated his brother the journalist Charles because he saw in him a caricature of his own worst faults ('Am I greedy like that?' he would ask in horror): for John he had genuine affection.

Richard Perceval Graves has been as generous to me as his father was. People had often addressed to him such remarks as, 'I suppose it is inevitable that some day you should write about your uncle Robert,' and the appearance of my book temporarily 'blunted' his 'determination', as he puts it. Happily this discouragement persisted only until he had read 'the first few chapters'. Now he has been able to concede that 'a man is entitled to his opinions,' and has 'drawn up' his 'evidence in the decent obscurity of the reference notes'. I am grateful to him for his forbearance, and recognise his difficulties—my, so to say, getting in before him, and also in the matter of what his father so intelligently told me. I was scared that so loyal a chronicler would have found me out in many an inaccuracy—but relieved to discover that he had not. Going on what Graves himself had said, I had put him at Charterhouse for seven instead of five years. I also, as he did, got the date of his confirmation wrong. Apart from that, and from a few very trifling family matters such as why did Alfred Perceval sign the pledge upon his second marriage, the differences between this author and myself are confined to matters of opinion.

Like the family of which he is so able a representative, Richard Perceval is always anxious to correct his uncle's recollections—recollections which I found, somewhat to my surprise, to be no better but no worse, either, than anyone else's. Thus he attempts to play down Robert's role in saving Siegfried Sassoon from a court-martial. He challenges my account. I sympathise with him: one of Robert's many faults was his inability to minimise his part in anything which might appear creditable in the eyes of an enlightened posterity. Perhaps he was not unique in that. In this particular matter, however, Richard Perceval is biting on granite: without Graves, Sassoon would have been court-martialled. The details are far too complicated to go into: suffice it to say that where this biographer speculates, and where he can be checked, he is mistaken. He thinks a letter written by Graves to an influential person must have been sent well after 19 July 1917. I ought in my book to have given the date of this letter, which is in the Russell Archives in Canada. It is 19 July 1917. Richard Perceval has become confused through his failure to understand the circumstances under which ***Goodbye to All That*** was written. He is frantically anxious to challenge its detail, as many of Graves's contemporaries were. He thinks that the press-cutting in which Sassoon announced his pacifism was Graves's first news of it: understandably, because in ***Goodbye*** he does so describe it, adding an elegant touch of its fluttering from an envelope to the ground. A little elementary homework, though, soon demonstrates that Graves first knew of Sassoon's pacifism a month earlier than the date of the cutting: when he received a typescript of the statement. But when he came to work on his autobiography—in a desperate hurry, needing cash and lots of it, not caring a damn what anyone except Laura thought of him, Laura in hospital with a smashed spine—he had only the cutting to hand, and so embellished his receipt of it in journalistic high style. Of such trivial carelessness come masterpieces—and many flops—and also come over-earnest misinterpretations. If Richard Perceval will now read Ronald Clark's excellent biography of Bertrand Russell (who behaved ill in this affair), then he will begin to see how it is impossible to deprive his uncle Robert of the major credit for the rescue of Sassoon—who, after all, went on to further active service, and who always recognised, if at times reluctantly, his debt to Graves in that respect. Indeed, Richard Perceval's background knowledge of both history and literature seems at times to be oddly scant, even amateurish.

The date of Robert Graves's confirmation! What can that possibly matter? But in an age of inaccuracy, in which university teachers can commit hideous solecisms in Sunday newspapers, one can only applaud his exactitude. The cumulative effect of such errors can only be disastrous. So, while I cannot give Richard Perceval any credit for his intuitions—in contrast to his uncle, he scarcely in any case indulges them. I can acknowledge that I feel chastened by his small corrections. This brings me more closely to the real virtue of his book—or of this first instalment of it, since upon the fate of the second two I must rudely speculate.

The virtue of this account of Graves's life from its beginnings until his first meeting with Laura Riding in January 1926 is its meticulous Victorian charm. The author has relied on the diaries of his grandfather, Alfred Perceval, to a large degree. A. P. was a minor Irish poet (and schools inspector) who resembled his son Robert rather more closely than the latter—until the very last days of his conscious life—recognised. At school Robert read Samuel Butler. Richard Perceval notes this, but he does not and cannot quite realise its consequences—nor, indeed, those of Robert's meeting with Laura Riding in 1926. Here he is, eighty years or so after all these things happened—rebellious son breaking with family tradition, and feeling bad about his lies and prevarications—giving us the family account of what is wrong with genius Robert. For John, I remember, it was as though it had happened yesterday; his indignation about Robert's refusal to 'take a regular job' was as fresh as it had been in the 1920s. Richard Perceval has inherited all that, and in his pages we do not say goodbye to it at all. He does not know what he is doing. But expressing his sense of this inheritance is what he is doing, and, in doing it, he has given us his best book to date.

What we have here is the first-hand account of a wayward genius from the viewpoint of one who 'loves' him—'loves' in that somewhat distant, uncarnal, strictly family sense—but cannot possibly even begin to understand him. It is priceless and invaluable. I can only wish that I had had it to refer to when I was giving my own account. Richard Perceval's integrity is absolute, his application exemplary, his own assault at this late date far more heroic than that of his uncle, from whose early rejected poem he quotes that phrase for his title. So although I have to say that this book does seem to me to be awful and misleading as an account of the processes of mind of Robert Graves between his birth and 1926, I can also say that it is a perfect family record: something that I should have thought, until I read it, impossible of achievement at this over-sophisticated instant in history. Readers who want to know what Graves grew out of and away from will find it laid out here in an astonishingly pure form.

Richard Perceval acknowledges the help of Laura Riding (now styled Ms Laura Riding Jackson). He will, he promises us, show how Ms Jackson rescued Graves from his shell shock and made him 'whole' again. This seriously worries me for the success of his enterprise in its entirety. There is no doubt at all that Laura Riding did help Graves to become 'whole' again, even if one must point out that those who change, change by virtue of their own efforts, whatever the influences upon them. But, as I was at pains to point out in my own book—much to her annoyance—she was exactly what he desired, and had desired for many years. She exists in his work from at least 1920, and perhaps even before that. Such 'miracles', as Graves liked to describe her advent, are not unusual: people, not as original as they like to think (that applies, too, to Ms Jackson), do change partners, only to discover that they have attracted the same sort of person . . . Laura was for Robert the perfection of his first wife, Nancy Nicolson: she told him what to do, but she had a vastly superior intellect and much more confidence in herself. She seemed prophetic, and she did not resist the role of prophet.

Laura was also scrupulous in the matter of Robert's family relationships. He only, as he was frequently at pains to point out, went to bed with Laura 'because Nancy told me to'. Laura saw to it as well that he appeared to be scrupulous towards his grieving parents. But simultaneously, antinomian as she was, she told him that their views 'about life'—and those of T. E. Lawrence and all his other friends, too—were ridiculous, rubbish, wrong, misguided. She knew what was wrong with everyone. She knew everything except what she would concede she did not know (some trifling detail about the universe). She still does. She wrote astonishing poems, although many find their absoluteness of knowledge and their chaste diction a bar to response. She translated such commonplace matters as her wanting another man—Phibbs—for herself, and not being able to have him because he chose to go off with Nancy instead, into cosmic terms: he was 'the devil' and her suicide attempt was an experiment with living. Graves accepted all of this and wanted to say 'goodbye to all that': to the gross little details of history like dining out or being famous or ambitious ('who's in, who's out?'). But he could not quite manage it. He remained 'ordinary', human, robust, in a manner which she—for all her sporadic radiance—could not quite achieve. Of his experience of making love to this extraordinary woman he reluctantly recorded, with the ghastly pun on his own name, 'the grave's narrowness though not its peace'. He was himself extraordinary, offputting and eccentric. Yet eventually his poems appealed to us more than hers did. Yes, she did understand the workings of the universe, and the burden of this knowledge she did bear: 'nor is it written that you may not grieve.'

She did because he thought she did. Yet this woman could never have existed as a serious entity—this woman who could engage, with her incompetent lover G. Phibbs, on a work to define the whole scope of human knowledge—had Graves not fiercely guarded her from ridicule. That is precisely the scope of his influence upon her: that, and the money and the power to appeal to the public which she did not have.

There is indeed a hideous narrowness in her. It is located somewhere within her inability to recognise that others, however misguided they may be, possess a sense of their own identity: that this causes them to resist her instructions as to how spiritually to proceed. However unpopular Graves may be for some of his nastinesses and meannesses, he is much valued for the warmth of his heart in his poetry. As his friends know, he possessed that quality in life, too—and that of candour. So **'Certain Mercies'** is the title of one of the poems he wrote while he was in bondage to her. She 'allowed' that poem, and knew what it was about. Poor Robert! And when she got rid of him, after subjecting him to ten years of chastity on the grounds that 'bodies have had their day,' and with the sudden bright announcement made at breakfast-time to the effect that Robert's rival, Schuyler Jackson, and she had revived bodies ('Schuyler and I do!'), when that happened to him, he felt much, muttered much, behaved not very well or badly—and went gratefully to a new and natural love, to be denounced and damned for it, of course, by Laura and her more satisfactory consort. He got over it within two years, although the experience scarred him. She has never got over it: the experience is even now an open wound. She has obsessively accused him of exploitation of her, use of her ideas (as if those ideas were actually owned by her—the Lord is a jealous Lord), and even of theft of notebooks left behind in 1936 in their joint Mallorcan home. The notebooks were in fact destroyed unread by Graves within a few weeks of his return in 1946. This was the man who was able to tell me, when I was going up to Oxford, 'Now you can start a Laura Riding revival,' and who would read her poems aloud, to those who would listen, with admiration as astonished as it had been twenty years before.

Graves poses again with his family on November 22, 1917. Standing, left to right, are Rosaleen, Charles, Alfred, and John. Seated are Robert, Amy, and Clarissa. By permission of Richard Perceval Graves.

But how shall Richard Perceval proceed in his account of Graves's life from 1926? He has acknowledged the assistance of Laura Riding, and has even corrected—so he believes—my version of Graves's first meeting with her. As so often, he fails to understand that much of my information comes from Graves himself—although in this instance it is supported by written evidence from William Nicolson, who was present at that meeting, and to whom Graves, seeing his guest, whispered: 'For God's sake what am I going to do?' Ms Jackson now insists that Nicolson was 'courteous' to her. Of course. That does not alter what his opinion of her was, and nor in turn is that a discredit to her. As I have written, Graves himself soon changed his mind. The matter quite often came up in conversation between us, under the rubric of 'first impressions' and their reliability or otherwise.

Richard Perceval has 'known' and 'loved' his uncle since childhood. Whatever that means, he means it. Now that he has almost run out of family material, on what information is he to proceed? He had none from his subject, and he can hardly be seen to rely upon anything I say. Will he therefore rely upon Ms Jackson? If he does that, he must soon cease to love his uncle, for Ms Jackson, although capable for a while of compromising with his apparently dutiful approach, cannot encourage it. Graves was not cold in the ground when she wrote a letter to the *Times Literary Supplement* of such ferocity and jealous hatred that it almost burned up the page. It could scarcely have appeared in Graves's lifetime. (Perhaps the editor wanted to make a point about someone.)

What does Richard Perceval think about that letter? Are the recollections of its writer to be relied upon? Will he ask me for whatever evidence I hold? Whatever be the quality of his understanding of his uncle, Richard Perceval is very clearly an honest and meticulous man. Will he quarrel when he finds himself in disagreement with Ms Jackson? (Some have.) Or will his account be, *faute de mieux,* in effect Ms Jackson's retrospective 'corrections' (as she likes to style them) of 'literary history'? Certainly she will be the first to offer to supply him with intimate details of Graves's life after she said goodbye to him for ever in 1939. Could he accept that, or is his idea of knowledge less mystical? How will he account for the tragedy of her obsession, define the original relationship?

After 1926, Graves drifted away from his family. John paid a short visit to Mallorca in the early 1930s—a visit of which he gave me useful details, all of them scrupulous but few not shrewdly critical of Laura Riding. Graves used to see his mother from time to time until her death in the 1950s. But in the main his family saw nothing of him and knew less. He used to say, 'Blood is thicker than water and much nastier,' a remark which I fear his nephew might fail fully to appreciate. His diary runs out in 1939. The papers held by various university libraries in America do not contain enough sources for a biography—or, insofar as they do, they reflect my own researches, which were mostly conducted as a check on Graves's own recollections, passed to me, for the most part, not as a future biographer but as a friend. Most of Graves's closest friends are dead or uninterviewable. Yet there is room for another account of Graves, from an angle quite different from mine. I think it will have to employ my account, however much it may criticise or even deplore it. I would indeed be glad to assist Richard Perceval. Meanwhile, whatever he may do in its successors, he has in this volume given us a rare glimpse of the errant black sheep who makes good. It is the more enchanting in that its author regards it as something altogether more objective. (pp. 19-20)

Martin Seymour-Smith, "Hello to All That," in London Review of Books, *Vol. 8, No. 17, October 9, 1986, pp. 19-20.*

PAUL O'PREY

These early, highly dramatic years of Robert Graves's life [presented in ***Robert Graves: The Assault Heroic, 1895-1926***] make quite a story, as he himself commented ironically at the end of ***Goodbye To All That,*** the brilliant, angry autobiography he wrote in 1929 when he was still only 34 years old:

> I seem to have done most of the usual storybook things. I had, by the age of 23, been born, initiated into a formal religion, travelled, learned to lie, loved unhappily, been married, gone to war, taken life, procreated my kind, rejected formal religion, won fame and been killed. (By 1926 I had also) won a prize at the Olympic Games, become a member of the senior common-room at one Oxford college before becoming a member of the junior common-room at another, (and) had a statue of myself erected in my lifetime in a London park.

Graves during World War I. By permission of Richard Perceval Graves.

Richard Perceval Graves's position as Robert Graves's nephew has allowed him access to a considerable amount of important material which was unavailable to Martin Seymour-Smith, who published the first biography of Robert Graves in 1982; as a consequence Mr. Graves reveals a number of factual inaccuracies in the earlier biography, though he thankfully and skilfully confines these academic wranglings to the 'decent obscurity' of the footnotes. He has not, however, been sufficiently ruthless in his selection of this material: we get rather bogged down in the minutiae of events which means that in almost 400 pages we travel only 31 years, while the seemingly endless list of relatives we meet can only be of limited interest to those outside the clan.

This concentration on the family seriously unbalances the book. We hear too much about relatively trivial goings on within the family, culled from the pages of a diary kept by Robert Graves's irrepressible father, the poet Alfred Perceval Graves, who a year after ***Goodbye To All That*** was published, to the acclaim of the critics and the horror of the family, replied with his own version of events in *To Return To All That;* Richard Perceval Graves shares his grandfather's concern for the reputation of the family and is not only at pains to highlight the influence the family had over Robert, but to defend it from the unpleasant things he frequently said or wrote about them all. By comparison, Robert's friendships with, for example, Siegfried Sassoon, T. E. Lawrence and Basanta Mallik, which were more important for him after he reached a certain age than were his relationships with his parents, and which are surely more important for us, receive a relatively superficial treatment.

That said, however, Richard Perceval Graves has brought out very well the conflict between inbred priggishness and natural rebelliousness that went into the forming of Robert Graves's character; he is also good at describing the early evolution of his obsession with poetry, tracing it back to a childhood love of folk song inherited from his father.

The final chapters, in which the family moves backstage slightly, are by far the most lively and interesting and this bodes well for the next volume of what I believe is intended as a trilogy; the second volume will deal mainly with the strange literary and emotional relationship between Robert Graves and Laura Riding, whose bitterly hostile reaction to the version of events as previously put forward, in good faith, by Tom Matthews and Martin Seymour-Smith, is well-known to those who have managed to decipher her numerous letters to the press on the subject. Judging from the last chapter of the present volume, however, it would appear that Mr. Graves has so far managed to remain on better terms with her and it will be interesting to see if he can thereby establish an accurate and objective account of what until now has been obscured behind a tangle of rumours, contradictions, misunderstandings and sour grapes.

Paul O'Prey, "Family Rites," in Books and Bookmen, *No. 373, November, 1986, p. 25.*

JOHN GROSS

In recent years Robert Graves has enjoyed renewed popularity as a novelist (thanks largely, no doubt, to the television adaptation of ***I, Claudius***), but his poetry, if its absence from the bookshops is any guide, has fallen out of fashion. No matter— his time will come again. The best of his poems are magnificent, and almost all of them are alive and kicking.

This doesn't necessarily make him an ideal subject for a biography. He once wrote an admirable poem called **"My Name and I,"** about the contrast between the identity imposed by society, the legal label fixed on at birth, and the inner self, "illegal and unknown." There is a gulf between them, and there is a gulf between the ascertainable facts of an artist's career and the private world in which his art takes shape.

We still want to read the lives of artists, even so, and Richard Perceval Graves, the poet's nephew, is not the first biographer of Graves to take the field—a life by Martin Seymour-Smith appeared five years ago. But apart from disagreeing with many of Mr. Seymour-Smith's conclusions, Mr. Graves has undertaken a much fuller study [***Richard Graves: The Assault Heroic, 1895-1926***], one that enjoys the advantages of intimate family knowledge and access to previously unexplored family papers.

The family connection seems unusually appropriate. Robert Graves grew up in a family with an acute sense of its forebears—as his nephew says, "People long dead were talked about as familiarly as though they had only just left the room"—and although he eventually broke free from his immediate background, he retained a great deal of family pride and the unmistakable stamp of his origins.

One grandfather was a Protestant Bishop of Limerick, who had been born as far back as 1812 (and who had been friendly with Wordsworth). The other, Heinrich von Ranke, was a professor of medicine in Munich and a nephew of the historian Leopold von Ranke, whose wife had been a Graves—the links between the two families were intricate. Robert's father was well known in his day for his poems and ballads on Irish themes; his mother was a forceful, high-minded woman, at once loving and demanding, in whom it is hard not to see the source of her son's eventual conviction that matriarchy was the natural order of things, and that there had once been a matriarchal golden age.

Graves's early upbringing nurtured his imagination and implanted a love of reading and writing; it also left him unprepared for the brutal and sordid aspects of life at his public school, which oppressed him so much that at one stage, taking his cue from an episode in the Bible, he was driven to keep the other boys at bay by shamming madness. Gradually he acquired sturdier resources to fall back on, among them his prowess at boxing, the encouragement of an enlightened teacher (George Mallory, a famous mountaineer who later disappeared during an ascent of Everest) and, by the time he was 16, the certainty that poetry was his vocation.

In his last year at school he had been one of a small minority who argued against the introduction of military service, but once World War I had broken out he thought that the only honorable thing to do was to enlist. In 1916 he was so severely wounded in the battle of the Somme that he was left quietly in a corner to die—the last thing he heard before losing consciousness was a stretcher-bearer saying "Old Gravy's got it, all right." His parents were notified that he had been killed, but a day or two later he managed to get a note to them; it reached them on his 21st birthday.

Anyone who tries to describe Graves's experience in World War I is to some extent bound to be in hopeless competition with his own account in ***Goodbye to All That,*** one of the outstanding memoirs of modern times; but Richard Graves succeeds in filling gaps and offering some fresh perspectives. He is especially alert to the immense psychological cost of Graves's wartime ordeals, and to the enduring conflict between his "anti-war principles" and his conception of "his duty as a gentleman."

In the last year of the war Graves married Nancy Nicholson, who was working on a farm at the time as a "land girl." Her father was a distinguished painter, William Nicholson, and at 18 she was already a fierce feminist, chiefly because she felt her mother, who was also a painter, had sacrificed her career to husband and children. When she was introduced to Graves's parents she showed up wearing her land girl's trousers—a firm declaration of feminist intent.

After Graves had been demobilized, the couple settled outside Oxford, initially in a cottage belonging to John Masefield. For a time Nancy ran a tiny general store; Graves studied at the university, published a tract in which he argued that poetry was "a modified descendant of primitive Magic," and produced a succession of poems that mostly proved his point.

One early admirer was John Crowe Ransom, then teaching at Vanderbilt University in Tennessee. It was in the journal Ransom helped to edit, the *Fugitive,* that Robert and Nancy first encountered the poetry of Laura Riding Gottschalk. They were impressed; Graves began corresponding with her, and when he was appointed professor of English at Cairo she was invited to join them. She accepted, and Richard Graves's first volume closes in 1926 with the three of them—and Robert and Nancy's four small children—setting sail for Egypt together.

The next volume is something to look forward to. Mr. Graves tells his story straightforwardly and unaffectedly; there is no doubt a cleverer book on Graves waiting to be written, but it is hard to imagine one that enters into his spirit with keener sympathy or more intuitive understanding.

John Gross, in a review of "Robert Graves: The Assault Heroic, 1895-1926," in The New York Times, *March 6, 1987, p. C29.*

MARTIN GREEN

[Green is an English critic whose works have been praised for their expertise in blending nonliterary perspectives—including anthropology, science, religion, and politics—into studies focusing on literature, and literary figures. His books include Science and the Shabby Curate of Poetry *(1965),* Yeats's Blessings on von Hugel: Essays in Literature and Religion *(1967),* Tolstoy and Gandhi: Men of Peace *(1983), and* The Origins of Nonviolence *(1986). In the following excerpt Green faults the biographer for leaving many aspects of Graves's family life unexplored.]*

[***Robert Graves: The Assault Heroic, 1895-1926***] describes the first 31 years of the life of Robert Graves, known most widely as the author of ***I, Claudius*** and ***The White Goddess,*** known best (i.e., most thoroughly) as a long-lived and productive modern poet. But the interest of his youth is not his early poems or the early beginnings of his philosophy but the family and class situation into which he was born—a situation which made his development as a modernist writer very striking. . . .

Graves' father, Alfred, was an "Irish" poet (author of *Songs of Killarney*) whose "Father O'Flynn" was a popular comic song. Nearly everyone in the family wrote—and read each other; after Graves, his brother Charles and then his brother John edited the literary magazine of the public school they all attended—where they published his poems. Thus Graves began to write in a situation very favorable for getting published, but quite unfavorable for himself getting the modernist message

Graves with his first wife, Nancy, and their children Catherine, David, and Jenny. By permission of Richard Perceval Graves.

of his time—the call for writers to radically alienate themselves from ruling-class society. . . .

If we compare his life-history with D. H. Lawrence's or T. S. Eliot's (both of an older generation), we see how Graves' development was retarded by his family situation. Ideas (like muscular Christianity) which young intellectuals generally shrugged off by 1910 still had power over Graves, because his family was such a potent environment for a poet. After the war, at Oxford, he went to live with John Masefield and was protected by Walter Raleigh, two of the literary old guard; he made friends with John Buchan and Lawrence of Arabia, the heroes and trumpeters of the empire. D. H. Lawrence and Eliot moved in very different circles.

And yet, even in this period, Graves was fighting against his heritage. His politics were in some sense socialist, his poetics were in some sense modernist and, most important, he was developing a revolutionary faith in matriarchy—as an historical phenomenon but one with contemporary implications. There were other aptitudes in Graves, which gradually made him as anti-establishment as Lawrence and Eliot. Though imperious and egotistic, he allowed his wife to direct their lives; though ambitious and manipulative, he alienated his protectors—''uncouth'' was Siegfried Sassoon's word for him.

Of course there were non-modernist writers who were uncouth, like Kipling; and Stalky and Kim were types not unlike Graves—who can best be aligned with Evelyn Waugh as two of Kipling's literary ''sons.'' Alfred Graves was, like Arthur Waugh, a minor man of letters and everybody's friend. Their sons became more than that, by rebelling against their fathers' blandness. But their rebellion—in a very English way—stopped short of full modernism.

This book is written by Graves' nephew and is in fact a family biography in more than one sense. It is dedicated to R. P. Graves' siblings and offspring; it discreetly reminds us that he knew the people involved personally; above all, it gives so much detail about the poet's brothers and sisters and uncles and aunts that it is a group biography of the Graveses and von Rankes. The writing therefore answers to the main interest of the subject. We see family ties restraining and pulling at these lives. Graves' mother, wanting to go to India as a missionary in her thirties, is persuaded to marry instead; religious values must cede to family ones. Alfred Graves, as soon as his son joins up, runs from magazine editor to editor with the latter's war poems and when that fails persuades *The Spectator* to publish extracts from Robert's letters from the front. (This is how literature, the family and the army went together and private blurred into public for people like the Graves.)

Unfortunately R. P. Graves misses the sharpest interest of his topic. His view of the family is familial. He sees them as colorful (eccentric), but the color is historically trivial. He does not tell us what we most want to know. For instance, how interesting, in the light of Graves' later matriarchalism, to know what his mother's Bavarian connections meant to him. He often visited Munich in the decade before 1914, when everyone was discussing matriarchal ideas. How interesting to know what *real* Irishmen thought of Alfred Graves as an Irish poet and how he felt about the difference between them and him. His innocent exploitation of Irishness in verse is a classic example of literary imperialism. And how interesting to know what contact Robert had with his aunt Rosamund, Lady Massie-Blomfield.

Lady Massie-Blomfield, sister to Alfred Graves and married into the navy, was famous in a minor way for her theories of child-rearing. She wanted parents to teach their children, while in the nursery, military drill—''About turn! . . . Forward march!''—and to greet their parents as superior officers. This was part of the semi-military moral rearmament movement of the decade before 1914, when a section of England's ruling class was preparing for war with Germany. R. P. Graves tells us nothing about Lady Massie-Blomfield, which presumably means that she had no significant encounters with Robert Graves. But even without such an encounter, as proof of how close Graves's family came to that kind of fascism, what could be more historically suggestive than this blood tie?

This book is quite satisfying, if you don't bring a historical sensibility to its topic. Graves has myriad facts to recount, and he writes easily. (Too easily: I frowned to be told that Osborne Palace was one of Queen Victoria's ''favorite haunts''—where she hung out, no doubt.) But on behalf of biography (which is an important genre), I protest that one must bring historical sensibility to such a topic. Otherwise we end up as we do here, with something close to family gossip—with a book such as Alfred Graves might have written, not Robert.

Martin Green, ''Hello to All That,'' in Book World—The Washington Post, *March 15, 1987, p. 7.*

Nancy Mitford: A Biography

by Selina Hastings

(For Nancy Mitford: see also *Contemporary Authors,* Vols. 9-12, rev. ed.)

An Excerpt from *Nancy Mitford: A Biography*

Creative imagination was never one of Nancy's strong points. The best of her fiction is closely autobiographical; the nearer she kept to her own experience, the better the result. With historical biography the problem of plot was removed; but could an intensely personal writer such as Nancy achieve sufficient detachment to write history? to write about people long dead, who had no connection whatsoever with Alconleigh, the Radletts or Fabrice de Sauveterre? The short answer is, no, she could not: she did not try. Nancy approached her biography of Madame de Pompadour exactly as though it were one of her novels, with herself as the Pompadour and Colonel as Louis XV. 'I do love it because of the shrieks. They were all exactly like ONE, that's the truth! . . . Like me, the Marquise preferred objects sculpture & architecture to paintings, (& pretty things to ugly ones & rich people to poor people—she liked pink better than brown & ladies on swings better than women baking bread) C'est comme ça it takes all sorts to make a world.' The parallels with herself and the Colonel were impossible to miss. 'Pomp literally worshipped the King, he was god to her, & never from the age of 9 thought of anybody else. Very cold, physically, which makes it perhaps understandable, her great faithfulness, no physical temptations.' Theirs was a 'delightful relationship of sex mixed up with laughter . . . After a few years of physical passion on his side it gradually turned into that ideal friendship which can only exist between a man and a woman when there has been a long physical intimacy. There was always love. As in every satisfactory union it was the man who kept the upper hand.' Versailles itself Nancy saw as a Utopia, a perpetual romping house-party offering 'a life without worries and without remorse, of a perfectly serene laziness of the spirit, of perpetual youth, of happy days out of doors and happy evenings chatting and gambling in the great wonderful palace, its windows opening wide on the fountains, the forest and the Western sky'. Nancy's Versailles was a fairyland with dear good Louis XV at its head and pretty kind Madame de Pompadour by his side commissioning wonderful works of art and caring about the poor. The blackness of Versailles, the real and terrible power of the King, the ruthless greed of his mistress, Nancy chose to ignore. She read extensively in contemporary memoirs—Voltaire, Saint-Simon, de Luynes—and in the historians of the nineteenth century—Michelet, de Tocqueville and Carlyle—but certain subjects she simply chose not to treat: the brutal religious

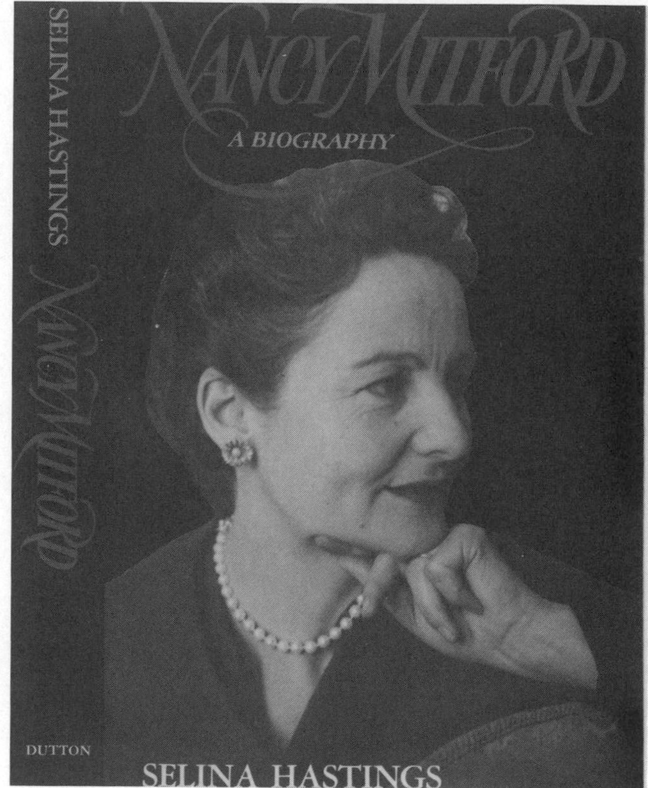

Dust jacket of Nancy Mitford: A Biography, *by Selina Hastings. Dutton, 1986. Jacket design by Nancy Etheredge. Title handlettered by David Gatti. Jacket photo by Cecil Beaton courtesy of Sotheby's London.*

persecutions of Louis's reign were skated over because 'Catholicism is a closed book to me'; and so was the touchy subject of Free-masonry: 'Nobody whose father was one could take free masons seriously. Waffling off to Oxford with his apron, I can see it now.' The result may not have been history, but it was gay and pretty, full of jokes and personalities, and it brought France and the French court alive for many people who previously had barely heard of Louis XV and Versailles.

Pompadour took Nancy a year to write, part of which she spent in a pension in the town of Versailles itself. As soon as it was finished the manuscript was sent to Raymond Mortimer who, with his wide knowledge of French history and literature, could be relied upon to spot the worst of the howlers. Although (as Evelyn had always been) shocked by her slovenly punctuation and taken aback by the extreme informality of Nancy's style (the Duc de Richelieu was 'perfectly odious', the Dauphine found many French customs 'too common for words'), Raymond was nonetheless captivated by the liveliness of the narrative: 'Your narrative style is so peculiar, so breathless, so remote from what has ever been used for biography,' he wrote to her. 'I feel as if an enchantingly clever woman was pouring out the story to me on the telephone.'

HUGO VICKERS

[*Vickers, an English biographer, nonfiction writer, editor, and critic, wrote the biographies* Gladys, Duchess of Marlborough *(1979) and* Cecil Beaton: The Authorized Biography *(1985). He also edited* Cocktails and Laughter *(1983), the reminiscences of former Duchess of Windsor Loelia Lindsay. In the following excerpt Vickers gives an overview of the biography and commends Hastings for her well-balanced, sensitive portrayal of Mitford.*]

[***Nancy Mitford: A Biography***] is the second biography of Nancy Mitford to emerge from Hamish Hamilton. The first by Sir Harold Acton (1975) is now reissued. . . . Sir Harold, an old friend, reconstructed Nancy's life from her letters, occasionally giving considered judgments on her novels and biographies and quoting Taoist dicta where appropriate. His tone is friendly and sympathetic. He warns us that Nancy will never appeal to those of us without a sense of humour and he provides convincing evidence of the veracity of Logan Pearsall Smith's theory that 'Hearts that are delicate and kind and tongues that are neither—these make the finest company in the world'. Sir Harold's book is by no means comprehensive: 'In the meantime' he writes 'I set forth on my wanderings and eventually settled in Peking, so there is a considerable blank in my vision of Nancy, a gap of nearly nine years.'

In his introduction Sir Harold declared: 'there is ample material for future biographers' and duly passed the torch to Selina Hastings, who spent at least four years researching and writing this book. Like Sir Harold she dwelt in the Diana Mosley/Duchess of Devonshire camp but she achieved the cooperation of Pamela Jackson (who reminisced) and Jessica (who loaned letters). She also received considerable help from the hero of this book, the late Gaston Palewski (who appears in Sir Harold's book, disguised loosely as 'the Colonel').

Selina Hastings confines the cast of characters in this book to the key ones—the parents, the sisters, the boyfriends and the very close friends. Possibly she could have told us more about her interrelations with friends. She charts the change in Nancy from spoilt, enraged child to the calm, thoughtful letter-writer of later years. There were early disagreements with the sisters. As the author says:

> The result was that from an early age Nancy learned to develop that highly polished veneer with which she confronted the rest of the world. Her defence—and her weapon—was the tease. Everything, however sad, painful or dispiriting, had instantly to be turned by Nancy into a joke.

Lady Selina recreates the world of effeminate men friends that delighted Nancy and enraged 'Farve'. The first major disappointment was Hamish St. Clair-Erskine, whose whims she indulged and whose debts she paid. He appealed to Nancy's maternal instincts and she believed that one day they would marry. However, the author tells us that Nancy's brother, Tom had had a schoolboy affair with Hamish and knew him for what he was: 'a vain, shallow, silly little tart'. Eventually Hamish escaped Nancy's matrimonial plans by the spiteful ruse of engaging himself (fruitlessly) to Philip Dunn's sister, Kit. Within a month Nancy was engaged to Peter Rodd. He emerges from this book as an unattractive delinquent, who proposed as a joke, philandered and drank throughout the marriage and ended his days a penniless scrounger with a piratical appearance.

Selina Hastings is especially interesting on the dramas that surrounded the publication of Nancy's novels, particularly ***Wigs on the Green*** which caused a rift with her sister Diana due to references to 'the Leader'. It also ended any relationship with Unity. In a telling letter to her, Nancy wrote: 'Oh dear I wish I had never been born into such a family of fanatics. . . . Oh how I wish I was stone-hearted like you.'

We learn that the famous 'Colonel' was not the first Frenchman in Nancy's life. She became pregnant by a Huguenot Captain called Roy André Desplats-Pilter, which resulted in a complete hysterectomy. He was followed by the Colonel with 'a face like an amiable toad.'

The central theme of this book is the love of Nancy for her 'Fabrice de Sauveterre'. Evidently he was a delightful character, but it seems to me that he caused Nancy considerable unhappiness. Like Hamish he did not love her; unlike Hamish he was a relentless *coureur* after women. At the British embassy in Paris he would select his prey and 'pressing close to her on one of the huge sofas in the Salon Jaune, bouncing up and down on the cushions while urgently hissing in her ear: "*J'ai envie de toi! J'ai envie de toi!*"' His half-invitation-half-threat: '*J'ai horreur de coucher seul*' kept Nancy in a permanent state of unease, as did the news that he had an illegitimate child, that he was to be Ambassador (or 'Embrassadeur' as they joked) in Rome, and the final humiliation as he married a divorced woman. Selina Hastings paints the story of this love with the same poignant sensitivity as Nancy's fictionalised account, ***The Pursuit of Love.***

Sir Harold Acton quoted Nancy writing that it was 'very good to have one or two blaming reviews among the praise, nothing better for sales'. At the risk of disappointing Selina Hastings I have no hesitation in recommending this book to those who enjoyed Nancy's own works. At all times it is confidently handled, balancing the fact with the fiction, setting the real-life scenes behind each novel and identifying their various inspirations. Nancy had a difficult life, unfulfilled in many ways. She bore it with fortitude, adding no stronger plea to a request or complaint than the words: 'I MIND'. In her book Selina Hastings succeeds in making us mind too.

Hugo Vickers, "The French Lady Writer," in Books and Bookmen, *No. 360, October, 1985, p. 14.*

HILARY SPURLING

[*Spurling, an English critic, biographer, and editor, is a former theater critic and literary editor for the* Spectator. *She is the author of* Handbook to Anthony Powell's 'Music of Time' *(1977) and a two-volume biography of English novelist Ivy Compton-Burnett, published in the United States as* Ivy: The Life of Ivy Compton-Burnett *(1984). In the following excerpt Spurling complains that Hastings overemphasizes the bleaker aspects of Mitford's life, neglecting the author's triumphs.*]

'Head of Bone / Heart of Stone / Sister-Hater / Mother-Baiter.' . . . Nancy Mitford's unfinished poem might serve as the text for this unexpectedly cautionary biography [***Nancy Mitford: A Biography***]. Selina Hastings locates the crisis of Nancy's life before she was three, with the birth of her sister Pamela. Nancy, turned over at birth to a beloved nanny who showed signs of defecting to the newcomer, protested so vehemently that her mother, unnerved by the ear-splitting howls of despair and rejection emanating from the nursery, retaliated with brutal logic by sacking the nanny.

The treatment was drastic but effective. Nancy never again made a fuss about anything that mattered, not even when she was dying in pain so excruciating she had to stuff a cushion in her mouth to stop herself screaming aloud. If England and America reverberated with her shrieks—she earned £22,000 in royalties in 1968, perhaps the equivalent of five times as much today—they were, as Selina Hastings points out, the shrieks of mirth that became a Mitford trade-mark: '"How we shrieked!" "Did you shriek?"—an ugly word with its underlying implication of distress.'

Lonely, unhappy, malicious, insecure, Nancy sharpened her claws on her sisters and longed for an independence which she finally achieved at 22, escaping after weeks of tantrums, tension and tears to a boarding house in South Kensington, only to return home ignominiously almost at once on the grounds that life was insupportable with no one to put away her underclothes. To the end of her life she remained appalled at the prospect of cooking herself so much as a plate of porridge for dinner on the maid's night off. Her ideal was the one she described in ***The Blessing:*** servants to change the mimosa three times a day in her bedroom.

Clothes, money, maids, mimosa and an equally unfailing supply of fresh, frivolous, shortlived jokes compensated in some sense for the frightful bleakness of an inner landscape she did not care to contemplate. Two lovers and the husband she married in between were handpicked to ensure, each in his very different way, that she should feel constantly rejected in private and often in public as well.

Nancy's hilarity reached its height in wartime with one sister—Diana Mosley—imprisoned in Holloway jail as a fascist (Nancy had called personally at the Home Office to insist on Diana's arrest), and another—Unity Mitford—washed up, demented and incontinent, after shooting herself on the day Hitler declared war. 'The last straw is Harrods don't stamp one's notepaper any more,' wrote Nancy. Invited to lecture on fire-watching as part of the war effort, she was promptly asked to stop because her affected voice and falsity of manner were more than her audience could stand.

Parts of this book read like the story of a real-life Winnie in Beckett's *Happy Days,* buried up to her neck with her world in ruins and a brave, tight, twitchy smile permanently pinned to her face. Nancy voiced neither complaints nor regrets. In later life she came increasingly to blame her troubles—barrenness, bad teeth, lack of concentration, low spirits—on indifference and neglect in childhood by her mother, whose pattern of stoical self-repression became steadily more marked in Nancy herself. Even her beloved Frenchman, Gaston Palewski, 'the Colonel' who was the love of her life, apparently addressed her as *'vous'* to the day she died.

Gaunt, emaciated, heavily drugged, unable to move or eat, she died slowly of Hodgkin's disease, a complaint that seems to have tightened its grip in the very month the Colonel finally married another: 'almost as though the pain were an expression of 30 years of suppressed jealousy, misery and rage over the disappointment of her love for the Colonel,' writes Selina Hastings in a biography that would surely have caused its subject considerable and justified annoyance. 'Oh *goodness* I thought it would make you *laugh,*' Nancy wrote sharply when her mother protested about some particularly harsh account of the Mitford upbringing: 'all clearly a caricature, what's called Meant to be Funny.'

It is perhaps a trifle rough on a joker like Nancy, who took such inordinate pains all her life to be funny, to be landed in the end with a biographer who virtually discounts her public image, the impact she made on her contemporaries, the triumphs she wrested from the wreck of a profoundly unfunny private life. Silly and tiresome as she seemed in Harold Acton's infinitely discreet memoir, Nancy seems altogether too pathetic in this one. For a fuller and more balanced account, the reader will still have to go to the short biography embedded in the Mitford family saga by Jonathan Guinness, who writes with a nephew's wariness, genuine affection and gingerly respect about this sharpest and most alarming of all his formidable Mitford aunts.

Hilary Spurling, "Screams from the Nursery," in The Observer, *October 13, 1985, p. 26.*

JAMES LEES-MILNE

[Lees-Milne is an English nonfiction writer, biographer, diarist, autobiographer, novelist, and critic. Working with England's National Trust, Lees-Milne, who is an architectural historian, preserved many historic country houses in Britain. He wrote several books on the subject, including National Trust Guide: Buildings *(1948). His other works include autobiographical writings, such as* Another Self *(1970) and* Midway on the Waves *(1985), which contain reminiscences about his friendship with Mitford. In the following excerpt Lees-Milne comments on Mitford's life and her literary talent; he also observes that, despite the handicap of never having met her subject, Hastings presents an accurate and moving portrait of Mitford.]*

[***Nancy Mitford: A Biography***] is no hagiography. On beginning it one senses that Lady Selina Hastings is bewildered by her subject, can't make up her mind how much she likes her, how much she appreciates her, how much she understands her. She can hardly be blamed. She did not know Nancy Mitford. She belongs to a much younger generation, born in fact the very year that Adolf Hitler was taking his curtain in the bunker. She comes hard on the heels of a generation which took Nancy Mitford at the value she set upon herself, a generation which too long apotheosised her. Nevertheless, Selina Hastings has done an excellent job. She has been impartial, objective and on the whole extremely fair to her subject, if not always to some others of the *dramatis personae*. She has, rather surprisingly, accepted Nancy's very unkind evaluation of her mother, the benign and sweet Lady Redesdale, as a wicked goose, which she certainly was not, and she has, I must protest, been a little too severe with Hamish Erskine. 'Vain, shallow, silly little tart', she calls him. Well—when I retrace the cloistered quads of Oxford with that beguiling, debonair, 'Brideshead' member of the *jeunesse dorée,* do I see him in that light, whatever he became later? No, I do not. It is like comparing the Bonnie Prince Charlie of the '45 with the disillusioned, sodden old bore puking in the opera box at Florence in the 1780s. It doesn't seem quite fair. Or is it?

The author has devoted much space to Nancy's childhood, upbringing and 'deb' days, and pretty silly the last seem now, even to my generation. How they strike the contemporary young, so earnest, so careworn by the insoluble problems—nuclear waste, Ethiopian famines, drug-pushing, and miscegenation—mystifies me. For the contemporary young have anyway little time for jokes and shrieks; and besides, what one generation considers funny the next invariably finds rather foolish. Even Shakespeare, who gets away with most things, hasn't always been able to keep his clowns amusing. And really the idiocy of the Bright Young Things of the Twenties, that lamentable decade, with their games of Follow-My-Leader over the counters at Selfridge's, must have been pretty hard to take by outsiders at the time.

> On Monday we went to the cinema in Oxford which was great fun only we made so much noise we were nearly turned out & then we went to tea at the Trout where we again made hay. Then we went home & shortly after left for Oxford this time to go to the ball in the town hall. It was a marvellous ball. We went and sat out in the Court of Justice & found a book with the names of people who were going to be summoned so we wrote remarks such as 'marvellous man' under their names until a policeman came & sent us away with a flea in our ear & removed ye booke. We all spilt a lot of ink & poured ink into the judge's glass of water. It was fun.

Nancy was 21 when she wrote the above account of 'fun' to her far from frivolous brother still at Eton. But 'fun' which never left her was soon transmuted by tragedy. It suffered a sea change. When her humour ceased to be silly it became bitter. And no wonder. Nancy who was essentially a virginal character, not interested in sex for its own sake, fell but four times in love, and each time disastrously. It was as though some demon impelled her to select the unattainable on whom to lavish her adoration. The first was the 'silly little tart', five years her junior, to whom it never occurred to reciprocate her romantic passion for him. When at last it got through to him that Nancy was suffering on his account, Hamish persuaded her sister Diana to tell her that nothing was doing, and pushed off.

Four of the Mitford children, Pam, Tom, Diana, and Nancy, at their home, Asthall Manor. By permission of the Literary Estate of Nancy Mitford, % A.D. Peters & Co. Ltd., London.

Within a month Nancy was engaged to Peter Rodd, a handsome, well-educated, unscrupulous, impecunious rogue. They married. He was unfaithful to her from the start. Their marriage was on the rocks before Nancy met No. 3, a Free French captain, by whom she became pregnant. This necessitated a hysterectomy operation and no possibility of children which she wanted. The captain was supplanted by a French colonel, likewise in the Resistance Movement, and a close associate of General de Gaulle. To this distinguished officer who rose to great heights in the service of his country Nancy lost her heart irrevocably. For 32 years she absolutely worshipped Gaston Palewski who made no secret of sleeping with every woman he met and before Nancy's death married a French duchess with whom he lived happily ever after. Nancy's letters to the colonel, extracts of which are printed here for the first time, reveal the suffering she underwent while keeping the stiffest of upper lips before her friends and the world in general. Written during the long periods when she was separated from him and intended as they were to entertain him who must not be bored by declarations of love, they make most painful reading. Because of the colonel she went to live in France, admired everything French and (rather tiresomely) despised everything English.

These years of unfulfilled love and secret misery coincided with the blossoming of her literary talent and immense success. In fact, misery being the well-known mother of invention, the existence of the colonel in the twilight background of her life was the begetting of the autobiographical novels, ***The Pursuit of Love*** and ***Love in a Cold Climate***. They were followed by the historical biographies, ***Madame de Pompadour, Voltaire in Love, The Sun King*** and ***Frederick the Great,*** which sold millions of copies and brought their author fortune and fame. Selina Hastings points out perceptively that Nancy approached these biographies as though they were her novels, transposing herself into the roles of the heroines and the colonel into those of the heroes.

Her letters are by far and away the best things she wrote. They are without compare for wit, gossip, analysis of books (she was a voracious reader) and a barbed malice which makes them vastly provoking and lively. They are explosives which can only be defused by time. This means that so long as any of her loved ones are still living, publication of her correspondence *in extenso* is quite out of the question. Nancy never hesitated to lambast those she was most fond of. 'The Hills are hell,' she is quoted by Selina as saying of Heywood and Anne Hill, in whose famous shop she worked during the war and who were, and remained, among her dearest friends.

For Nancy's second name was Teaze. 'Being beastly' was her favourite sport. It began with the birth in 1907 of sister Pamela of whom she became furiously jealous. So she was beastly to Pam. She was beastly to Muv. She was beastly to the Harveys, whose only fault was to succeed the Duff Coopers at the Embassy in Paris. She was rather beastly, when she dared, to her brothers-in-law, Derek Jackson and Sir Oswald Mosley. She was beastly once—indeed, very—to her favourite sister Diana in going to the Home Office during the war and exhorting the Under-Secretary of State to pack her off to prison. And yet Nancy was always forgiven. Why was this? Because her company was the best in the world. Because she made one laugh with her. Because her teasing and mockery illuminated every dark corner of one's own dreary life. Because she electrified the very air one breathed.

Yet it would be a great mistake to suppose that Nancy Mitford was all frivolity. Far from it. She took her biographies extremely seriously, researching in libraries and archives like a mole. As for Selina Hastings's account of Nancy's long and terrible illness, the tortures she endured from doctors, the raising and the dashing of hopes, the courage shown, and still the jokes, it is so poignant that it cannot be read without tears. (pp. 25-6)

James Lees-Milne, "The Pangs of Disprized Love," in The Spectator, *Vol. 255, No. 8,206, October 19, 1985, pp. 25-6.*

ANNE CHISHOLM

[*Chisholm, an American journalist, biographer, and critic, is the author of* Philosophers of the Earth: Conversations with Ecologists *(1972) and* Nancy Cunard: A Biography *(1979). In the following excerpt Chisholm praises Hastings's fresh approach to Mitford's much-chronicled life, particularly her revelations about Mitford's unhappy personal relationships.*]

During the past twelve months, the Mitford industry must surely have reached its peak. Five books about or by members of the celebrated clan have appeared, including the massive compilation *The House of Mitford* by Jonathan and Catherine Guinness. Thus even to addicts of the genre Selina Hastings's [***Nancy Mitford: A Biography***] will have something *déjà lu* about it. She has tried to skirt around this danger by making her book comparatively short, and by concentrating on her subject's personal and emotional life. The approach has led her to take a different, almost subversive attitude to the Mitford family, whose behaviour, writings and legend have hitherto, in true upper-class English fashion, concealed rather than revealed emotion.

Nancy (she was almost christened Ruby) Mitford was the eldest of the seven children, six of whom were daughters, of Lord and Lady Redesdale. According to Hastings, as a small child Nancy was utterly indulged and she never recovered from the arrival of her sister Pam, whose life she set about making a misery. The childhood we now seem to know all too well (Nancy was the first Mitford to write about it—in ***The Pursuit of Love***) emerges from this account as rather more jolly and normal than its legend; Lord and Lady Redesdale seem less bizarre than they have formerly seemed. Hastings provides the first explanation (that I have heard) of "Farve"'s famous term of abuse, "sewer": nothing to do with drains, he derived it from *sua*, the Tamil for pig. Nancy grew into a witty, spirited girl who preferred elegant and amusing young aesthetes to soldiers or bankers. . . .

[She] married Peter Rodd, who became well known for his irresponsibility, capacity to bore and numerous infidelities. She started to write novels which at first achieved only a modest success. Although, in the 1930s, as Hastings relates, both Rodds were briefly caught up in the family enthusiasm for Fascism and Oswald Mosley (even buying black shirts), they soon switched to a vaguely pink pro-Leftism and Nancy caused much family trouble by satirizing Sir Oswald and his movement in ***Wigs on the Green*** (1935)—although in deference to her sisters Diana, Mosley's wife, and Unity, Hitler's admirer, she did tone it down.

Portrait of Mitford by William Acton. By permission from the Literary Estate of Nancy Mitford, % A.D. Peters & Co. Ltd., London.

In the late 1930s Nancy went with Rodd to southern France to help the refugees from Franco's Spain. During the war, she worked in Heywood Hill's London bookshop and fell dramatically and permanently in love with a Free French colonel, Gaston Palewski. Hastings is here at her most perceptive. Although her sense of the romantic sometimes affects her prose, she takes a cool look at Palewski and evokes sympathy for Nancy, who was to be firmly placed on the margin of his existence while he was the centre of hers. "Oh, the horror of love", she later wrote in a letter. After the war Nancy moved to Paris, where she wrote her amusing autobiographical novels and later her eccentric but popular versions of French history. She corresponded copiously with her English friends and with her sisters; Hastings is curiously frugal with quotations from the correspondence with Eveyln Waugh, which contains many jokes and clues to both writers' temperaments as well as to their work. It is comforting to learn that Nancy corrected her own early writings according to U and non-U terms after the publication of her essay in ***Noblesse Oblige***. . . .

Nancy Mitford emerges from this biography as "politically immature" and emotionally undernourished. Hastings herself is tentative on political matters and most assured when writing about character and feeling. She is thoughtful about the Mitford idiom, and shows how the jokes and special words worked as a protective device. "Shriek", the Mitfordese for laughter is, as Hastings remarks, "an ugly word with its underlying implications of distress". Even more unpleasant is "scrapage", Nancy Mitford's term for pregnancy or baby (she had had two miscarriages and a hysterectomy). Hastings's verdict on Nancy's attitude to her two Fascist sisters is almost too simple: "she loved her sisters but she loathed their politics". She does not deal with how Nancy felt about her brother Tom's pro-German views, and her analysis of the causes and consequences of the extraordinary episode in 1940 when she secretly informed the authorities that her sister Diana was dangerous and ought to be imprisoned is oddly perfunctory. But the book is very readable, and the portrait of Nancy Mitford that emerges from it is much more human, if sadder and less dazzling, than any we have been given before.

Anne Chisholm, "Lonely Laughter," in The Times Literary Supplement, *No. 4,308, October 25, 1985, p. 1210.*

STEPHEN SPENDER

[Spender is an English poet, critic, essayist, nonfiction and short story writer, autobiographer, diarist, and dramatist. He rose to prominence during the 1930s as a Marxist lyric poet and as an associate of W. H. Auden, Christopher Isherwood, C. Day Lewis, and Louis MacNeice. Among his poetry collections are Vienna *(1934),* The Generous Days *(1971), and* Recent Poems *(1978); his nonfiction works include* The Destructive Element: A Study of Modern Writers and Beliefs *(1935) and* China Diary *(1982). In the following excerpt Spender observes that Hastings does not probe the psychological motivations behind Mitford's troubled relationships and presents instead the superficial details. Spender then describes three aspects of Mitford: the frivolous person, the satiric autobiographical novelist, and the flippant familial letter writer.]*

Here we are on the map of the England of Evelyn Waugh, country of upper-class eccentrics and the London of Bright Young Things and feckless adventurers: Basil Seal and Ambrose Silk—fictitious characters; Brian Howard and Peter Rodd—their real life models. Nancy Mitford's best novel, ***The Pursuit of Love*** is a province of this and of the imagination with its heroine's father, Matthew Alconleigh, 'an eccentric backwoods peer known for his defiant philistinism and the terrible force of his temper', his seven children holding their conversations about sex in the Hons' cupboard, and Kroesig—alias Waugh's Basil Seal—based on Peter Rodd, Nancy's husband, whom she later divorced.

Matthew Alconleigh is clearly a portrait of Lord Redesdale, Nancy's father, and she was in real life the first of seven children. [In ***Nancy Mitford: A Biography,***] Selina Hastings tells us that she never quite got over the birth of the second of these, her sister Pamela, to whom, when they were growing up, she behaved with studied cruelty. Nancy adored her eccentric father, but had little communication with her mother, who seemed to her cold and withdrawn.

A remark that echoes throughout this book is that made by Nancy's sister Diana in 1973, when Nancy was dying of a terribly painful variety of Hodgkin's Disease in her house at Versailles: 'The awful thing is, she doesn't come first with anybody.' Perhaps the point is too well taken—for how many of us can be certain that we are first with anybody? All the same it is surely true that Nancy was isolated—isolated in her family, of which, nevertheless, she was so much a part that this might be said to isolate her from nearly everyone not one of her sisters. Isolated, too, in the three great loves of her life, each of them seemingly designed by nature to isolate any lover who formed an attachment to him. . . . Instead of examining Nancy Mitford's psychology in choosing such non-starters, Selina Hastings is content merely to describe the characteristics in each man which made him so impossible. She gives us a great deal of surface—made of facts, for which we are thankful—but she does not get below it.

One might suggest that there were three Nancy Mitfords: 1) the rather frivolous person who in manners, speech and behaviour was a character in the Waugh-Mitford fiction, and very much a member of her family's generation; 2) the autobiographical novelist who was the satiric narrator of the life of 1; 3) the writer of letters in which she maintained a flippant tone so as at once to distance herself from, and remain on affectionate terms with her sisters. (p. 27)

One advantage of flippancy is that it is very accommodating. It can disguise disapprobation under a thick layer of frivolous epistolary usage. Nancy, with two of her sisters in love with Führers, had much to accommodate. When Unity Mitford, who had fallen for Hitler, joined the Nazi party, and wearing a special badge given her by the Führer with his autograph engraved at the back publicly declared the fact, and pronounced her hatred of the Jews, Nancy wrote her a letter which begins:

> Darling Stony-heart. We were all very interested to see that you were the Queen of the May this year at Hesselberg.
>
> Call me early, Goering dear.
>
> For I'm to be Queen of the May. Good gracious that interview you sent us, fantasia, fantasia.

There is, it seems to me, something poignant as well as brilliant about this. Using her peculiar kind of idiom Nancy is able to intermix revulsion with affection in equal proportions. Her attitude to Diana—the sister who was closest to her—excelling her in beauty and equalling her in brilliance—is more complicated. In 1933, Diana had fallen in love with Oswald Mosley, whom she was to marry three years later. Nancy I played along with Diana and 'Sir Ogre' (as she called him behind his back), and she and Peter Rodd (to whom she was then married) even joined the Blackshirts, though the statement in which she expressed her support of Mosley, in the magazine *Vanguard,* is one of conformism completely lacking in her usual vitality. By 1934 she had turned against the Fascists. But even during her phase of sympathy for the Leader, in her letters to Diana Mosley her real feelings come out:

> Darling Bodley (nickname for Diana) TPOL's (The Poor Old Leader's) meeting was fascinating but awful for him as the hall was full of Oxfordshire Conservatives who sat in hostile and phlegmatic silence. . . . I think he is a *wonderful* speaker. . . . There were several fascinating fights, as he brought a few Neanderthal men along with him and they fell tooth and (literally) nail on anyone who shifted his chair or coughed. One man complained afterwards that the fascist's nails had pierced his head *to the skull*.

This is wonderfully funny, and affectionate. It also shows a streak of cruelty, but flippancy can accommodate this.

Nancy 2, the autobiographical novelist, wished to distance herself from Nancy 1 employing the flippant style of Nancy 3, the familial letter writer, to do so. Behind all this, there is, surely a hint of hysteria. Panic becomes uppermost at the outbreak of war when, soon after Oswald Mosley had been sent to Brixton prison, Nancy went to the Home Office, to inform Gladwyn Jebb, then Principal Private Secretary of the Under-Secretary of State, that 'in her opinion Diana was as dangerous as her husband, that her frequent visits to Germany were sinister and suspicious, and that no time should be lost in putting her under arrest'. 'Not very sisterly behaviour,' Nancy admitted jauntily, 'but in such times I think it one's duty.'

Diana was indeed arrested and sent to Holloway prison, where she remained for two years on her own before the Mosley couple were reunited in married quarters. Nancy was intrigued, rather than harrowed, by her sister's predicament, wondering how it felt to be in prison. Diana apparently knew nothing of the part that Nancy had played in her fate until after Nancy's death. The sisters renewed their telephoning-each-other-every-day relationship after the war when they lived in Paris.

In the postwar period, Nancy Mitford became a best-seller, with several novels, and with historical studies of ***Voltaire in Love, The Sun King*** and ***Madame de Pompadour*** to her name. Her love-affair with the ever-busy, ever-self-important Palewski remained in a state of bemused suspension, until, one day, Palewski married the lady who was his long-standing chief liaison. For four years, at the end of the Sixties, Nancy Mitford endured with magnificent courage bouts of unimaginable pain, of the kind which, if one hears of it happening to even one person, makes life seem meaningless horror. She adored France, and one must not judge her life unhappy, just because others would have been miserable in similar circumstances. She achieved much, loved places as well as people, and was a wit who inhabited an inner world of her own sparkling imagination. (pp. 27-8)

Stephen Spender, "Nancy Mitford's Province," in The Listener, *Vol. 114, No. 2,936, November 21, 1985, pp. 27-8.*

GABRIELE ANNAN

[In the following excerpt Annan, an English critic and translator, detects an element of pity as well as reproachfulness in Hastings's attitude towards Mitford.]

In one of Evelyn Waugh's short stories there is a debutante whose comment on almost everything that happens is: "Goodness how sad." The exclamation would make an excellent title for Selina Hastings's book [***Nancy Mitford: A Biography***]: "Goodness How Sad: A Life of Nancy Mitford." At any rate, that is how her biographer seems to see her. From the birth of her sister Pam, she explains, when Nancy was three and Nanny transferred her affections to the new baby, Nancy "came first with nobody." And right at the end, when she is dying horribly slowly of leukemia, Selina Hastings quotes the third sister (Lady Mosley): "The awful thing is, she doesn't come *first* with anybody."

With the heartless *cri de coeur* "goodness how sad," Waugh mimicked the debutante voice. It was the voice in which Nancy Mitford began to write her clear, direct, free-running prose. She sobered it up as time went on, but sensibly never quite stifled it. Even in the painstakingly researched biographies she wrote in middle age it still rings engagingly in the impetuous expression of her *partis pris:* "Louvois . . . that horrible man" or "the Abbé (Bernis), his dear little face puckered with worry." When first heard, the voice was as original, fresh, and amusing as the gold digger voice of *Gentlemen Prefer Blondes,* and in her most successful novels Nancy Mitford cleverly used a first-person narrator. "The charm of your writing," Evelyn Waugh teased her in 1955, when her fame was at its height, "depends on your refusal to recognise a distinction between girlish chatter and literary language." Four years later he was *re*-reading ***Voltaire in Love*** (1957) and praising it unreservedly: "You write so deceptively frivolously that one races on chuckling from page to page without noticing the solid structure."

The two were great friends, and after Nancy followed her lover to Paris in 1946 and settled there, she and Waugh became busy correspondents. Waugh tutored her in Catholic doctrine and theology, which she needed to work up for her biographies of Madame de Pompadour and Louis XIV; she helped him with his French; and he never stopped picking holes in her English spelling, punctuation, and diction—especially her diction, because, while she was always keen to try a new word, modern coinages turned him green. . . .

Pleasure was Nancy Mitford's lodestar, the only effective antidote to sadness. The six Mitford girls' childhood is exceptionally well documented and has also given much pleasure: apart from the large autobiographical element in Nancy's novels and the memoir of her by Harold Acton (particularly enjoyable because he quotes so much from her high-spirited letters), there is Jessica Mitford's account of her youth, *Hons and Rebels;* Diana Mosley's autobiography: David Pryce-Jones's life of Unity Mitford; Jonathan and Catherine Guinness's *The House of Mitford;* and numbers of other memoirs figuring Mitfords. The merry Hons huddled in the airing cupboard are as

A portrait of Mitford's lover, Gaston Palewski, by Nora Auric. By permission of the Literary Estate of Nancy Mitford, % A.D. Peters & Co. Ltd., London.

familiar as the solemn children scribbling in the parlor of Haworth Parsonage, which was not much bigger. But were the Hons really so merry? "What's the time, darling?" Linda asks Jassy in ***The Pursuit of Love.***

> "Guess."
> "A quarter to six?"
> "Better than that."
> "Six!"
> "Not quite so good."

The boredom and frustration were asphyxiating. When Nancy published **"Blor"** (reprinted in ***The Water Beetle***), a portrait of the good nanny who eventually supplanted a succession of "cruel" or indifferent ones, her mother, Lady Redesdale, was upset because Blor emerged as the only loving character in her daughter's childhood. "Oh *goodness,*" Nancy apologized, "I thought it would make you *laugh*. . . . Of course the trouble is that I see my childhood (& in fact most of life) as a hilarious joke." This does not sound very reassuring: "shrieking" (Mitford for shrieking with laughter) can be a cover-up, and Selena Hastings spots it.

As soon as she was old enough, therefore, Nancy turned to what her father, Lord Redesdale, and his look-alike Uncle Matthew in ***The Pursuit of Love*** called "sewers." (Wilamowitz-Hastings explains that the word derives from the Tamil *sua* = pig.) Any literate, cultivated, urban male was a "sewer," and aesthetes were the most extreme form. "The oddly chosen battleground of Nancy's generation," wrote Jessica Mitford, "was that of Athletes versus Aesthetes—sometimes called the Hearties and the Arties." Jessica was the fourth sister, much younger than Nancy. Her generation's battleground was communists versus bourgeois and fascists. But for Nancy, the aesthetes represented liberty and pleasure. The way they carried on was as different as possible from the Mitford way, so brutally lacking in physical comfort, intellectual stimulation, and aesthetic enjoyment. For five years Nancy was in love with perhaps the most unsuitable sewer of them all, a devastatingly charming, effete, narcissistic, and tipsy homosexual called Hamish Erskine. She was still in love with him when, in 1931 (she was nearly twenty-seven and her first novel ***Highland Fling*** had just come out), she finally broke off their engagement. The decision made her unhappy enough to think of gas ovens, but she chose parties instead: "If one can't be happy one must be amused don't you agree," she wrote to Mark Ogilvie-Grant, another sewer.

Nearly twenty years later, in ***The Blessing,*** breakfast in bed has taken the place of parties. It comes up "pretty to look at, piping hot, and carefully presented" (Waugh can't have cared much for that sentence, if he noticed it) for sad Grace who is still in love with the husband she has left because of his unfaithfulness, as Nancy left Erskine for being generally impossible. "Not for the first time" Grace thinks "it would be difficult for someone who led such an intensely comfortable life as she did to be quite submerged in unhappiness. There were too many daily pleasures, of which breakfast in bed was not the least." Like Nancy, Grace is a stoic hedonist. Pleasure consoles.

In ***Madame de Pompadour*** "Pleasure" is a chapter heading. "Versailles in the eighteenth century," the chapter begins, "presented the unedifying but cheerful spectacle of several thousand people living for pleasure and very much enjoying themselves." This was what Nancy would have liked to believe, perhaps, but her own account of life at the court of Louis XV does not bear it out. It was full of miseries: tortures of boredom, envy, jealousy, disgrace, and injustice were exacerbated by the lack of privacy and the necessity of putting on a brave face. However, putting on a brave face was Nancy's own forte.

Madame de Pompadour was the first of the biographies. "The pure pleasure of writing without the misery of inventing," she sighed. It's true that invention was not her strong point. Her plots are weak and her characters pale, when they are not caricatures or else portraits—simple or composite—of family and acquaintances.

When ***Madame de Pompadour*** appeared in 1954, the historian A.J.P. Taylor had fun with it in the *Manchester Guardian:* "(***The Pursuit of Love***) characters have appeared again, this time in fancy dress. They now claim to be leading figures in French history, revolving around Louis XV and his famous mistress, Madame de Pompadour." Nancy was only slightly annoyed; in fact, she'd already said more or less the same thing: "I do love it (doing the biography) because of the shrieks. They were all exactly like ONE." In ***The Sun King*** she discovered that Madame Montespan's family, the Mortemarts, were Mitfords under the skin:

> She, her two sisters and their brother were always together; they were extremely brilliant. They had a way of talking . . . which people found irresistible. Their lazy, languishing, wailing voices would build up an episode, piling unexpected exaggerations upon comic images until the listeners were helpless with laughter. Among themselves they used a private language. They were malicious, but good natured.

Still, the Mitford takeover of the French court in the seventeenth and eighteenth centuries makes it come alive in a way no other writer has managed—except, of course, Madame de Sévigné and Saint-Simon, who were in the thick of it but are not much read by the middlebrow English public. As for the rest—politics and battles—well, you can see that Nancy Mitford did her homework in the Bibliothèque Nationale. She fell in love first with a Frenchman and then with France, rather as she had fallen in love with sewers: Frenchness was the antithesis of her family's ultra-English milieu, habits, and values. She set up a dichotomy and banged away at it in everything she wrote from 1945 on: the French climate is warm, the English climate cold, and the same goes for French and English houses respectively; the French countryside is more beautiful than the English, but mercifully the French prefer the town anyway, while the English prefer the boredom of country life; the English are thick, the French quick and witty; French women smell delicious and dress well, English women dress appallingly and do not smell at all. (Nancy was obsessed with clothes. When the French ambassadress visited the highbrow bookshop where she worked during the war she couldn't "sleep on account of her clothes, wondering how mine could be made over but of course they couldn't.") The litany continues: French food is delectable, English food beneath contempt; the French are interested in art, the English not; they set out to please, the English don't bother. And so on.

The Frenchman who changed Nancy's life was Gaston Palewski. Selina Hastings sums him up perfectly. He "was possessed of all the qualities that, to an English eye, epitomise the sophisticated Frenchman: he was charming, he was amusing, he was a great lover of the arts and an incorrigible womaniser.'' He became Fabrice in ***The Pursuit of Love*** and Charles-Edouard in ***The Blessing*** and ***Don't Tell Alfred,*** not to speak of his infiltrating Nancy's portraits of Louis XIV and Louis XV and other charmers of the past. She first met him in 1942 when he had been recalled from commanding the Free French forces in East Africa to become General de Gaulle's *directeur de cabinet* in London. (pp. 3-4)

By this time Nancy was living apart from Peter Rodd, whom she had married ten years earlier. As husband material, Peter Rodd was as unpromising as Hamish Erskine, though for different reasons. Instead of being gay he was a womanizer, just as fond of the bottle, and more narcissistic still. He was handsome, clever, pompous, a bore and a ne'er-do-well. ''Nearly everything he did turned out badly.'' He was exactly the same age as Nancy, but in a photograph unkindly reproduced here she looks like a cross mother restraining her grown-up son. Still for a short while she was happy: ''Well, the happiness,'' she wrote to Mark Ogilvie-Grant. ''Oh goodness gracious I am happy. You *must* get married darling, everybody should this minute if they want a receipt for absolute bliss.''

In Palewski's case the trouble was not so much his character as the fact that, through the long years of their relationship (nearly thirty), he was never in love with Nancy, though much entertained by her company. She loved him to distraction. They did not live together. He would take her out or dine at her house, spend the night, and be back in his own bed in time to be called by his valet. The woman who came first with him was the Duchesse de Sagan. In 1969 he married her. For Nancy, already showing symptoms of her final illness, ''it was almost literally a death-blow, the bitterness of it exacerbated by the fact that Gaston's wife was a divorced woman: for years Nancy had accepted the face-saving excuse that he could never marry her because he dare not risk his political career (he had been ambassador to Italy and minister for atomic energy) by marrying a divorcée. Now retired from politics, he could marry where he chose, and his choice was not Nancy. She admitted her misery to no one . . . (her) manner studiedly casual.''

Nancy's English heroines all have to learn painfully what her French ones know by instinct: to catch a man, you must devote all your energy and attention to pleasing and amusing him; you must enter into the subjects he cares about, make him comfortable, flatter him. When you have caught him you must redouble your efforts; when he begins to be unfaithful you must behave like the Duchesse de Choiseul, wife of Louis XV's foreign minister, who ''took the situation philosophically and made friends with her husband's mistresses.'' And you must never, never sulk or make a fuss.

Nancy's love was never quite requited. The other great sadness in her life was that after several miscarriages she had to have a hysterectomy. She would have loved a child. Her feeling for children comes out in her fond attitude to the wicked child-hero of ***The Blessing,*** and in the captivating way she writes about historical children: the little Duc du Maine, for instance, Louis XIV's oldest child by Madame de Montespan, or Louis XV's child-bride. . . . Perhaps her sister's lack of children was one of the things in Diana Mosley's mind when she wrote, after Nancy's death, ''her life seems almost too sad to contemplate, despite great successes with her books.''

Success not only with her books. In the *tout Paris* of the Forties, Fifties, and Sixties, Nancy was a star, and the chief adornment of the British embassy. She did not always behave well there. When the dowdy Harveys succeeded the fasionable Coopers as incumbents in late 1947, Nancy enthusiastically joined Lady Diana Cooper's game of ''Being Beastly to the Harveys'': ''We all proudly say we shan't write our names in their book.'' But, says Selina Hastings, ''true to form, Nancy had only to dine with the new Ambassador and his wife a couple of times for her to turn from hunting with the hounds to running with the hare.''

It is not the only time she sounds a little reproachful. She gives the impression that while she feels sorry for Nancy in an almost sisterly way, and very much admires her funniness, panache, and guts, she finds it more difficult to be fond of her than perhaps she thought she would when her project began. Re-reading the Mitford *oeuvre* can produce the same effect. In spite of the gaiety, jokes, charm, and apparent frivolity, there is something insistently didactic about it: frivolity, in fact, is being solemnly preached—and courage in adversity too. *Toujours gai* is the motto—the French version, really, of the British stiff upper lip, only adorned with a soupçon of silky down instead of the bristling Redesdale moustache.

There is a lot to be said for stiff upper lips, but solemnity about frivolity is hard to take, and so are its concomitants: the worship of chic, and the snobbish contempt for dowdy, unfashionable appearance, manners, and views. The mini apotheosis in ***Don't Tell Alfred*** of mousy Fanny (named after the heroine of *Mansfield Park*?) neither quite convinces nor quite makes amends. As for the lecturettes on taste in general and French architecture, decoration, *ébénisterie,* and gardening in particular, they have a place in the biographies; but in the later novels they clutter up the action like glossy magazines lying pointlessly around.

There is something prophetic about Fanny's summing up of her dashing mother, the Bolter, in ***The Pursuit of Love:***

> She was curiously dated in her manner, and seemed still to be living in the 1920's. It was as though, at the age of thirty-five, having refused to grow any older, she had pickled herself, both mentally and physically, ignoring the fact that the world was changing and that she was withering fast.... Her conversation, her point of view, the very slang she used, all belonged to the 'twenties, that period now deader than the dodo.

The difference between Fanny's present, the Forties, and ours, is that we have *le goût rétro,* and it helps to keep Nancy Mitford's books enjoyable. For they belong to their period as much as Dior's New Look, which caused her such excitement. The most dated thing about her is her recipe for success in the pursuit of love. The notion that there should be such a thing at all must be anathema to feminists of both genders.

Like her friend Waugh, Nancy Mitford was a brilliant mimic. Her comic entertainment has tremendous charm. It is a charade acted with the drawing-room curtains as back cloth. It's fun and even flattering to be asked to share the private jokes, but after a bit the mind wanders and longs for something more solid and varied. Waugh provides it. His jokes are even funnier, but his performance is given with proper scenery, suggesting a world beyond the orangerie, and on a solid stage constructed of Christian metaphysics. So his novels are comedies or tragicomedies, while hers are just fun and games. (p. 4)

Gabriele Annan, "Goodness, How Sad," in The New York Review of Books, *Vol. XXXIII, No. 13, August 14, 1986, pp. 3-4.*

WILLIAM McBRIEN

[*McBrien, an American editor, critic, and biographer, edits the scholarly periodical* Twentieth Century Literature. *With Jack Barbera, he wrote* Stevie *(1986), a biography of the contemporary English poet Stevie Smith. In the following excerpt McBrien cites several flaws in Hastings's scholarship and style, but observes that* Nancy Mitford *is an entertaining, if imperfect, biography.*]

Nancy Mitford's lover Gaston Palewski said "La famille Mitford fait ma joie," but Americans may take a different view. Her biographer calls the United States "the one nation on the face of the earth Nancy loathed above all others." John Wilkes Booth was her favorite figure in history. Surprisingly, her books have sold well here, including the snobby but droll ***Noblesse Oblige*** (recently reprinted), with its careful discrimination between "U" (upper-class lingo) and "non-U." But success in the United States did not please Nancy (although the royalties did): "Either praise or blame from govs (Americans) leaves ONE cold." Definitely not a democrat, she thought Utopia was "cottagers, happy in their cottages while I am being happy in the Big House." Nor will feminists relish her sentiment that "in every satisfactory union it was the man who kept the upper hand."

Mitford in London, 1959. By permission from the Literary Estate of Nancy Mitford, % A.D. Peters & Co. Ltd., London.

Her parents aren't easy to like either—U, eccentric, provincial in the extreme and shockingly prejudiced. Having done his duty in World War I, Lord Redesdale (Farve) retired to the purposeless life of a vanishing gentry. Hunting occupied him, but not always the conventional kind. First he hunted rats with a mongoose in a London office building, then chased his children across the countryside with a bloodhound and a mongrel terrier. Muv was "remote," a woman who rarely hugged or kissed her children and was capable of "whiplash sarcasm." As early as age 9, Nancy, the eldest child, wished her parents dead so that she could run the house and be freer to torment the siblings who displaced her. Nancy became an adept at cruelty although eventually she shifted from meanness to mirth. She discovered that "by quickly converting unhappiness or hurt into comedy, you anaesthetise the pain."

[In ***Nancy Mitford: A Biography,***] Selina Hastings, a London journalist, says that "marriage and children and a home of her own were what (Nancy) longed for," but this seems a simplistic assessment. Some part of Nancy deftly dodged all of these in her romantic pursuit of a homosexual who seemed to care only for himself. . . .

Then, on the rebound when a homosexual she desperately loved threw her over, Nancy suddenly married Peter Rodd (a k a Prod). There was little love between them, and although the Rodds stayed married until 1957, mostly they lived apart. . . .

In 1934 Peter and Nancy, who inaccurately thought of herself in those years as a socialist, wore black shirts and wrote Fascist propaganda. Years later she told her friend Evelyn Waugh: "Prod looked very pretty in a black shirt. But we were younger & high spirited then & didn't know about Buchenwald." Fascism was a family weakness. . . .

In 1938 Lord and Lady Redesdale went to the Nuremberg rally and were introduced to the Führer. Farve (how easily one falls into it) thought "that feller Hitler" was splendid and Muv was won over "by the sheer *niceness* of the man," especially after she ate tea (as the U say) with Hitler in his Munich apartment.

All in all a remarkable *histoire,* some of which Nancy Mitford deliciously recounted, thinly veiled, in novels that continue to give us pleasure, ***The Pursuit of Love, Love in a Cold Climate, The Blessing*** and ***Don't Tell Alfred*** being the best of them. Miss Hastings writes admiringly of Nancy's novels but, in quoting so amply and adroitly from the hilarious and sometimes affecting letters Nancy ceaselessly wrote, the author unwittingly persuades us that letters were finally her subject's most stunning literary achievement.

"Fiction that dare not speak its name" is how one friend of mine defines biography. Selina Hastings' chronicle of Nancy Mitford's life raises suspicions because it quotes, for instance, the words her subject spoke from her pram at the age of 3. Perhaps the author, who speaks of her subject's "courageous disregard for historical fact," has it right, but how can we tell? Elsewhere Miss Hastings reports what "de Gaulle once confided to . . . Georges Pompidou." But she provides not a shred of documentation to persuade us that we have indeed de Gaulle's dicta. There is the occasional footnote. And from time to time we're given unnecessary and incorrect information: that Yugoslavia and Czechoslovakia, for example, are "new countries . . . formed from the old Balkan Kingdoms after the end of the war."

A lot has been left out: we're given only glimpses of the brilliant and intimate friendships that Evelyn Waugh, James Lees-Milne, Harold Acton, and others have described in their own writings about Nancy Mitford. "Keep it jolly" is mostly the author's maxim: the self-deception and heartbreak go largely unexplored.

Miss Hastings is good on the period, though, especially bringing to life the décor, the clothes, the manners and the slang. Her narration is racy and the style, though not impeccable, suits its subject. Severer scrutiny might have rid the book of some clichés: "No one loved a good time more than Nancy" or "She was kept on a very short rein" (I don't *think* the author meant this literally). There are mindless generalities: French officers are described as "so flattering and funny at the dinner-table, so desperately brave at the front." Miss Hastings, seeming no less a Francophile than her subject, finds that Frenchmen like Palewski take "a pleasure in the company of women incomprehensible to the average Englishman."

The book does offer an entertaining look at a nearly extinct species. Focused on Nancy Mitford, it reveals little that touches us about the very odd and sometimes lonely life of a minor wit, but the setting is an anthropological delight. Yet courage, particularly hers, is perhaps scanted in this account. In ***Nancy Mitford,*** her friend Harold Acton writes more grippingly of the impressive gallantry with which Nancy battled Hodgkin's disease for four years. Finally she was heard to say to her French doctor, "Je veux me dépêcher" ("I want to hurry"). Then hurry away she did. Once she had written Waugh that the Last Judgment sounded like "finding one's coat after a party I hope the arrangements are efficient." Her concern, she said, stemmed from "the great importance of getting into the right set at once on arrival in Heaven."

William McBrien, "O Brave U World," in The New York Times Book Review, *August 17, 1986, p. 8.*

MERLE RUBIN

"The Mitford Girls," who provided the title and subject of a recent musical, have found a niche as minor mythological figures—figurines, perhaps—each one different, distinctively modeled, neatly labeled, curiously fascinating, but never more than peripheral. . . .

Nancy, in many ways the brightest, has always seemed the most interesting to me. Although her four early novels—***Highland Fling*** (1931), ***Christmas Pudding*** (1932), ***Wigs on the Green*** (1935), and ***Pigeon Pie*** (1940)—are very slight indeed (as she herself was first to admit), her four postwar novels, ***The Pursuit of Love*** (1945), ***Love in a Cold Climate*** (1949), ***The Blessing*** (1951), and ***Don't Tell Alfred*** (1960), are truly delightful.

Her biographies of Madame de Pompadour, Voltaire, Frederick the Great, and the Sun King are idiosyncratic, to say the least, but often entertaining. And her contributions to mapping the distinctions between "U and non-U" (upper class and non-upper class) speech have provided snobs and reverse-snobs of all backgrounds with hours of fun and argument.

This first full-scale biography of Nancy [***Nancy Mitford: A Biography***] . . . is Selina Hastings's first book. She has written Nancy's life rather as Nancy herself might have written it. It's not that she assumes Nancy's viewpoint or takes her side throughout, but she manages to look at her as Nancy might have looked at one of the characters: with affection, insight, wit, admiration, pity, and a touch of disapprobation.

Like Nancy, Ms. Hastings prefers the quick, keen judgment to sustained analysis. Discussing Nancy's attitude toward Unity's Nazism, she tells us that Nancy "tried to emphasize the ridiculous aspects of Unity's behavior, while . . . maintaining a façade of good-natured, sisterly affection. She loved her sisters, but she loathed their politics. . . ." Ms. Hastings's assessments strike me as shrewd and accurate, but, like Nancy, she is not inclined to probe complications—literary or psychological.

Yet, Hastings conveys with innate understanding the insecurity and pain beneath Nancy's polished veneer. Like an indulgent novelist, she all but rushes in to warn her heroine of impending trouble: first, of the folly of her infatuations with unsuitable men, later, of the dangers of the great love of her life, the womanizing leader of the French resistance Col. Gaston Palewski.

Of Nancy's precipitate marriage to Peter Rodd, she notes: "Nancy rather liked pompous men, and she had that undiscriminating respect for intellect often felt by those themselves lacking a formal education."

She describes Nancy's growing love of France and things French with a teasing sympathy, yet also shows us Nancy's courage in the face of adversity, from the disruptions of life in war-torn London to the disappointments and sorrows of her personal life.

This is a graceful portrait, very much in the spirit of its subject.

Merle Rubin, "First Full-Scale Biography of Nancy Mitford—and Her Sisters," in The Christian Science Monitor, *September 10, 1986, p. 24.*

Writing Against: A Biography of Sartre

by Ronald Hayman

(For Jean-Paul Sartre: see also *CLC,* Vols. 1, 4, 7, 9, 13, 18, 24 and *Contemporary Authors,* Vols. 9-12, rev. ed., Vols. 97-100 [obituary]. For Ronald Hayman: see also *Contemporary Authors,* Vols. 25-28, rev. ed. and *Contemporary Authors New Revision Series,* Vol. 18.)

An Excerpt from *Writing Against: A Biography of Sartre*

His capacity for change was heightened by his awareness that we must never expect to recognize ourselves in our completed work, that books and actions deviate like children from parental intentions. Sartre had an extraordinary capacity for change. Disliking the idea of the static self and refusing to be tethered philosophically, politically, or personally to any commitment, he believed he could transform his life like a snake sloughing off dead skin. Even physically he changed more than most people do, the slight, narrow-shouldered boy growing into the wide, squat man who was dubbed by his American friends "Mr. Five-by-Five." When he was twenty-four, his ambition, he told Simone de Beauvoir, was to become both Stendhal and Spinoza; later, applying philosophy to politics and *Realpolitik* to philosophy, he tried to negotiate a peace treaty between Marx and Freud. When this diplomacy failed, he fell back on a gigantic biography of Flaubert founded on a combination of Marxist and Freudian insights. By then the young Sartre who never voted had turned into the radical knight-errant who rode on international airlines. The mature Sartre never tired of demonstrating, agitating, signing manifestos, making politcal speeches, attending rallies, though, to seasoned politicians, he still seemed politically immature, incurably naïve. Despite his formidable intellect, he never quite arrived at what he called "the age of reason," at adult stability, though the young writer who made up his mind that success would never induce him to spend less time enjoying cafés, movies, or girls had grown into the compulsive worker who always wore moccasins to avoid wasting time on tying shoelaces. But the young man who declared that all anti-Communists were swine had turned into an old man who declared that the Communist party was the worst enemy of freedom, and the champion of individual freedom had denied freedom to the individual.

But while he took an almost perverse pleasure in asserting his own freedom through protean self-transformation, he could neither learn from his mistakes nor keep hold of his most valuable insights. He had so much faith in his ability to form new theories that he forgot the old ones: rather than build higher on an old foundation he would start all over again with a new one.

DAVID CAUTE

[*Caute is an English novelist, dramatist, essayist, and critic. His works include* At Fever Pitch *(1959),* Communism and the French Intellectuals, 1914-1960 *(1964),* Collisions: Essays and Reviews *(1974), and* The K-Factor *(1983). In the following excerpt Caute commends Hayman for his skill in assimilating the many contradictory aspects of Sartre's life into a cohesive biography.*]

Writing a full-scale biography worthy of Sartre is a prodigious undertaking: the sheer volume, variety and complexity of his literary output would deter even if the man's life had not been so replete with incident. Yet Ronald Hayman, fresh from his triumphs with Nietzsche, Kafka and Brecht, has pulled it off [in ***Writing Against: A Biography of Sartre***] with an admirable blend of industry, empathy and critical detachment capable of conveying Sartre's pivotal importance in the intellectual life of Europe from the publication of ***La Nausée*** in 1938 until the appearance of his vast, sprawling study of Flaubert in the 1970s.

Inevitably Hayman's debt to Sartre's lifelong companion, Simone de Beauvoir, is enormous—not merely the massively intimate chronicles she detonated throughout Sartre's life, but also the love letters she published after his death. These caused a scandal and a rift between *Castor* (the Beaver) herself and Sartre's literary executor, Arlette Elkaim, who inherited all of Sartre's copyrights even the private letters he had written before Arlette was born. Sartre had discovered this beautiful 19-year-old Algerian Jewess in 1956, made her his mistress and then, in a peculiarly Sartrean feat of incestuous gymnastics, his adopted daughter. While sibling incest had always fascinated Sartre, (***Les Mouches, Altona*** and ***Les Mots***), nothing he had written suggested that he might achieve a different version across a generation gap of 32 years. Turning his young mistress into his daughter was, perhaps, a way of becoming her brother.

Mr Hayman makes free use of the love letters and we would demand our money back if he didn't. What is shocking about these letters is not their contents but the bizarre freedom of information act by which de Beauvoir sublimated her personal pain and jealousy into the substitute gratification of confessor of the harem. Sartre told her every detail by letter, it was part of the contract.

In Sartre's fiction there is a great deal of sexuality but very little sex; intelligent schoolboys dithering between ***The Age of Reason*** and Moravia's *Woman of Rome* should choose the latter. It is interesting to discover that for Sartre, in Mr Hayman's words, an erection was an unsatisfactory experience because it 'felt too much like something that happened to him'. Of

Sartre in 1951. The Granger Collection, New York.

course! The organic motion so often falsely celebrated as the male act of will and dominance is almost casually dismissed by Sartre as a Pavlovian conditioned reflex, a passive thing involving no act of choice. The penis, in short, sadly reveals itself to be an *en soi* rather than a *pour soi;* Sartre concluded that its activities were 'fairly second-rate' but he continued to pursue them with extraordinary ease even into the years of rapid physical degeneration when he appeared to John Huston as 'a little barrel of a man and as ugly as a human being can be. His face was bloated and pitted, his teeth were yellowed and he was wall-eyed.' Sartre's life emerges as the clearest demonstration of the aphrodisiac power of genius and fame.

Sartre appears to have been both charming to his mistresses and horribly frank. He told one girl, 'You've arrived in my life like a dog on a putting green.' After a night with her he reported to de Beauvoir that 'her thighs are shaped like a drop of water, wider at the bottom than at the top . . .' After the war he began an affair with a woman, Dolores Vanetti, whom he first met in New York and who pointed out Stravinsky and Garbo to him in the Russian Tea Room. Here at last was a real threat to his relationship with de Beauvoir. Shaken, she asked him point-blank which of them meant more to him. Sartre replied, 'She's enormously important to me, but you're the one I'm with.' As de Beauvoir recalled the conversation, *'J'eus le souffle coupé.'* But this stoical woman had the breath to last the whole course, supervising the rota of women friends during Sartre's long and ghastly physical decline, and finally lying down next to his dead body in hospital until a nurse rebuked her.

For this reader the problem in ***Writing Against*** (not a good title) resides in the genre of literary biography which attempts to embrace the total life and work in a continuous, chronological progression. At the appropriate moment Mr Hayman steps back from the love affairs and calamitous quarrels with Camus or Merleau-Ponty to summarise and evaluate the published work. Naturally this approach has the merit of putting the work 'in context' and Hayman does an excellent job on making the connections; he shows precisely how the mistress related to ***Les Mains Sales*** and how Sartre's experience of the Cold War inspired the ***Critique de la Raison Dialectique.*** But to read in one paragraph that, 'de Beauvoir had lost 16 pounds in weight and was covered in spots,' and then almost immediately to give serious consideration to the phenomenology of ***L'Etre et le Néant*** requires an elastic temperament—although it is the temperament that Simone de Beauvoir's intellectual autobiographies also demand. Reading Mr Hayman's accounts of Koestler's several punch-ups with Camus, one is again reclining in easy voyeurism, only to be invited to change gear abruptly and ponder Sartre's definition of an authentically committed literature as enunciated in ***Qu'est-ce que c'est que la Littérature?***

As Hayman points out, Sartre's genius lies in the total work and the total man. One could add that the powerful fascination he has exercised on several generations is closely related to his ability (shared with his contemporaries Malraux and Camus) to move freely across the frontiers separating philosophy, fiction, drama and journalism; his unique capacity to relate people to ideas, the general to the particular. But that capacity withered somewhat after 1950, when the fastidious detachment from politics, the fertile attraction-repulsion conveyed by Mathieu in ***Les Chemins de la Liberté,*** finally yielded to an overwhelming preoccupation with the great, grinding wheels of historical determinism, the stifling weight of the 'practico-inert' bearing down on the individual's capacity for genuine choice and freedom of action. Unlike the hacks of socialist realism, Sartre could never contrive fictional protagonists whose destiny was to serve as puppets in a pre-orchestrated oratorio to History.

But what of violence? From 1950 onward Sartre's utterances on the necessity of revolutionary violence were regarded as scandalous by the liberal-bourgeois culture whose round table floats in mid-Atlantic. Whereas his six-year collaboration with Communism excited a deep anger (reactivated by his euphoric trip to Castro's Cuba), his subsequent declarations of solidarity with Frantz Fanon, the student rebels of 1968, and persecuted Parisian Maoists tended to evoke an exasperated scorn. Hayman conducts us through this minefield with remarkable skill, penetrating Sartre's own reasoning without necessarily surrendering to it.

Sartre contradicted himself throughout his life and, in a final, traumatic interview, virtually disowned everything he had written. It is one of the many virtues of Hayman's book that he quietly demonstrates how this very inconsistency expands rather than diminishes Sartre's stature as the most stimulating witness to the middle years of the 20th century. (pp. 34-5)

David Caute, "The Most Stimulating Witness," in The Spectator, *Vol. 257, No. 8259, October 25, 1986, pp. 34-5.*

EAMONN McARDLE

Ronald Hayman's [***Writing Against: A Biography of Sartre***] is informative, thoroughly researched and well written. Together with the recently published life of Sartre by Annie Cohen-Solal (the author of a memorable biography of Sartre's friend and *alter ego* Paul Nizan) . . . Hayman's study will doubtless provide a starting point for any future evaluation of Sartre's work.

The main phases of Sartre's career are well known. In recalling them, however, Hayman manages to present new exhibits and call upon fresh witnesses for the prosecution and the defence in order to bring his subject to life.

In the beginning was the word, or words. Sartre titled the only two sections of his autobiographical essay evoking his formative early years 'Reading' and 'Writing'. He emerged from a cosseted childhood and adolescence—indecently prolonged by the rites of passage peculiar to the once prestigious Ecole Normale Supérieure in the rue d'Ulm in Paris—possessed by a sacerdotal conception of his writerly vocation. After military service he settled down to an uneventful career as a provincial lycée teacher and devoted himself to writing.

Sartre negotiated the troubled pre-war decade by avoiding the political entanglements of his contemporaries. He immersed himself in *belles lettres* and in the study of Husserl and Heidegger. But whereas his college friend Nizan had found in Heidegger, by way of reaction, additional reasons for his commitment to Marxism, Sartre found chiefly the instruments he needed to fashion a corrosive and apolitical psychology. The fruits of this period of his life formed the basis of Sartre's later reputation.

In the novel ***Nausea*** (1938), the short story collection ***Intimacy*** (1939), the essay in 'phenomenological ontology', to quote the subtitle of ***Being and Nothingness*** (1943) and the stage play ***In Camera*** (1944), Sartre rehearsed a medley of themes that have since become commonplace: the death of God; the experience of contingency; despair; freedom; authenticity; bad faith. Popularised by a number of throwaway lines ('Man is a useless passion', 'Hell is other people'), his ideas appeared to offer to a public in the immediate post-war years an intelligible if sombre account of the human condition, 'by nature an unhappy consciousness with no chance of escaping its unhappy fate'.

A great deal of ink has flowed on these themes since then. It is of more than anecdotal interest therefore to discover here how much of what Sartre wrote on this subject was merely a *literary pose,* as he admitted in an interview with Benny Lévy published towards the end of his life and reproduced in part by Hayman: 'I talked about despair, but it's nonsense. I talked about it because it was being talked about; it was fashionable . . . I've never experienced despair, nor seen it as a quality that could be mine . . .'

So much for authenticity.

Politics caught up with Sartre in the shape of World War Two. From 1943 onwards he began to contribute to the Resistance journal *Combat* and this involvement plunged him into the maelstrom as a political commentator and controversialist after the end of the war. Unhappily for Sartre he entered the political fray just as the Cold War began to freeze the limits of political discussion for all but desperadoes. As a result the debates he joined with other figures of the left intelligentsia around the review *Les Temps Modernes* in the Forties and Fifties rarely attained the existential intensity, the vigour or the clarity of the exemplary debates of the Twenties between the Surrealists, *Clartéists* and the French Communist Party when the PCF still afforded a forum for critical discussion. The devaluation of intellectual currency in the interval that separates these two historical moments seems palpable. In Sartre's personal case the loss was threefold.

In political terms the reigning dogmatism and polarities entailed for Sartre an unconditional, if occasionally critical, alignment with the Soviet Union and the PCF between the end of the war and 1968. He performed the usual self-lobotomy of the Stalinist intellectual even while remaining outside the Party. On his return from the Soviet Union in 1954 he announced that he had found 'total freedom of criticism in the USSR . . . I met a new breed of man'. As late as the Sixties he could fend off criticism of the Soviet Union with an exercise in double think that has since become notorious: 'We mustn't demoralise (the workers of) Billancourt.' The notable exception to this counter-conformism was his public role in mobilising opposition to the Algerian and Vietnamese wars.

In the theoretical domain Sartre concluded in the Fifties on the need to develop Marxism, and he undertook to furnish it with a 'subjective' complement in order to 'reconquer man inside Marxism'. The resulting ***Critique of Dialectical Reason*** (1960) played little part, however, in the return to Marx, the recovery of utopian socialism or the rereading of Marxism and the history of the workers' movement that characterised the emergence of a New Left in France and elsewhere. Despite Hayman's claim, moreover, it is doubtful if 'existential Marxism' played any part whatever in the events of May '68, though Sartre's ***Critique*** has provided more than one academic commentator with an entirely speculative framework through which to reinterpret them. The point to note is that the ahistorical categories of the ***Critique*** could as well be applied to any 'revolution' at any time in the past. Hayman also verges upon the realm of fantasy in having Sartre father the Situationist International.

In the field of *belles lettres* Sartre was also badly scarred by his time. In ***What is Literature*** (1947) he proposed a combative

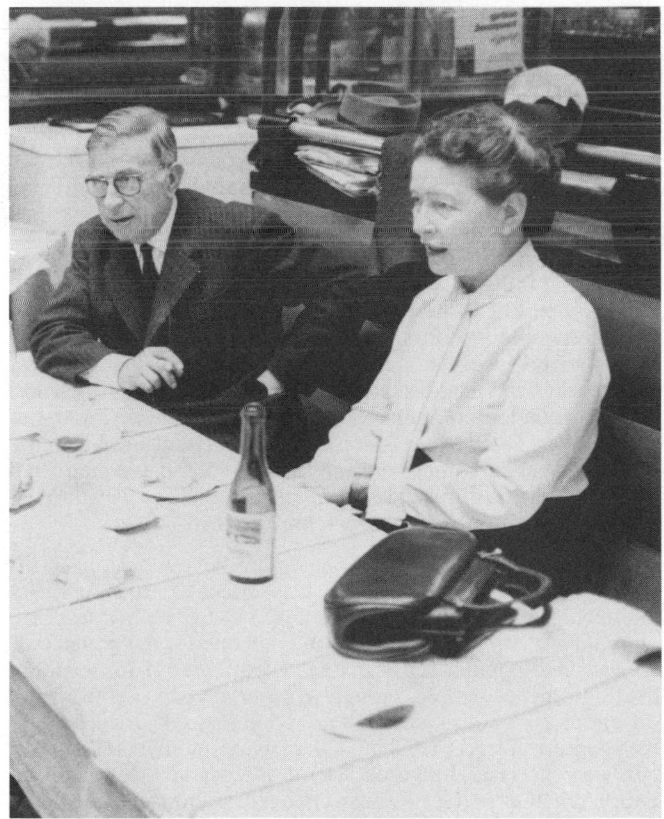

Sartre in 1964 with his longtime companion Simone de Beauvoir. UPI/Bettmann Newsphotos.

role for the 'committed' writer. On the one hand he attacked aestheticism, poetry in general and the Surrealists in particular. (Hayman offers a few interesting items on the personal sources of Sartre's hostility to poetry.) On the other he attacked the merely utilitarian considerations of socialist realism. Attempting a difficult balancing act in an effort to find a third way Sartre nevertheless fell victim in ***What is Literature*** to the very intellectual dogmatism he correctly excoriated in the positions of the Communists. His subsequent abandonment of imaginative writing illustrates better than any commentary the corner he had boxed himself into through the contradictory demands he placed on the writer.

Sartre describes in his autobiographical piece ***Words*** the curious effect that the invention of photography had had on his grandfather Charles Schweitzer who, in later life, would self-consciously 'strike an attitude' in front of others as if 'at the behest of some invisible photographer'. Hayman insists on a similar self-consciousness on Sartre's part, that he was always living autobiographically, as though with one eye on his biographers to come. Against the odds, this biographer presents a reasoned and persuasive though less than compelling case for the integrity of Sartre's 'divagations'. History may deal less kindly with one of the century's greatest self-confessed poseurs.

Eamonn McArdle, "Bad Faith," in New Statesman, *Vol. 112, No. 2903, November 14, 1986, pp. 27-8.*

JOHN STURROCK

[*Sturrock, an English critic, is the author of* The French New Novel: Claude Simon, Michel Butor, Alain Robbe-Grillet *(1969). In the following excerpt Sturrock maintains that Hayman recounts the intimate facts of Sartre's life but does not assess carefully enough Sartre's literary and philosophical work.*]

In 1970, the year he qualified as an OAP, Jean-Paul Sartre was still declaring his solidarity with certain 'acts of political violence' in the clamantly Maoist paper he was then backing, *La Cause du peuple*. But in its next issue the paper corrected this truculent senior citizen's endorsement, to read not violent 'acts' but violent 'articles.'

This was a prudent retraction, even though Sartre himself, all through a political life that got wilder and angrier the older he became, would seldom differentiate between acts and articles, so completely was he a man of words. Of too many words, for speeches and manifestos spilled from him in crushing plenty, as he responded compulsively to world events, at least after World War Two, at the same time as he went on producing philosophical and other books at times so dense and protracted they are scarcely finishable—who ever got all the way through his three cruelly obese volumes on Flaubert?

In his hopeful moods Sartre appeared to believe that this writing, vociferating and lecturing was effective, that furiously intellectual though he could not help but be, he had leverage on reality and was some sort of megaphone for the proletariat. As the great populariser of existentialism after 1945, no doubt he did influence people, though whether anyone ever lived any differently as a consequence of adopting that self-dramatisingly bleak philosophy is unclear. There were moments also, certainly in his last, drawn-out years of wretched health, when Sartre felt that in fact he had changed nothing in the world, that he had been sounding off, and that his many articles were simply that, never true, courageous and life-saving acts such as he had dreamt of accomplishing as a boy.

These reasonable and pathetic self-doubts have no place in Ronald Hayman's long, long biography of Sartre [***Writing Against: A Biography of Sartre***]. Hayman is one of those unable to doubt that Sartre brought good things about in the world. In the sentimental conclusion to his book his transfusionist view is that 'particles of Sartre are in the blood that flows through our brains,' an unhappy phrase typical I fear of the piety that undermines this biography, whose author, once afloat on an ocean of small facts, offers only the thinnest analysis of what is big and of importance in Sartre, which is his writing and thinking, literary, philosophical and political. Hayman's Sartre is seen only in close-up, as represented by what he or his associates have earlier recorded about him, and the book is full of variously appealing trivialities, such as his failure to digest raw fish on a visit to Tokyo—the sea's revenge, we can assume, for his strange and repeated fantasy in earlier days that lobsters were following him down the street.

On this intimate side, Hayman's book is diligent and interesting. Little (five foot two, no more) Sartre's rough but successful way with women plays quite a part, and for all his tremendous intelligence, humour and simplicity of life, one puzzles more and more why Simone de Beauvoir put up with him, unless he was in fact rather more charming than Hayman lets us see. But we need to be helped to *understand* Sartre as well (if not the complicated man then his multitudinous ideas) rather than merely to follow him groupie-like through a vagrant, positive but not so dramatic life. Hayman shirks the hard part, aside from some stilted recaps of what there is in the philosophical or other books, fed piecemeal into the narrative. Sartre never comes together into a whole and his reputation as thinker or writer is assumed, not justified.

Worse than this, in a way, because it is so misleading, is the absence of any perspective on events of the biographer's own, which means that not only Sartre but the political context in which he for so long agitated is presented as Sartre saw it, so that his often extreme, callous and gullible views seem worthier and more rational than they in fact were. Someone as fertile and aggressive in thought as he was asks to be stood up to. He is not stood up to here.

John Sturrock, "Angry Old Man," in The Observer, *November 19, 1986, p. 28.*

FREDERIC RAPHAEL

[*Raphael, an American-born English novelist, short story writer, scriptwriter, and critic, is respected for his screenplays, including* Darling *(1965) and* Two for the Road *(1966), as well as for his fiction. In such works as* Obbligato *(1956),* The Glittering Prizes *(1977), and* Heaven and Earth *(1985), he observes the lives of the British upper-middle class. In the following excerpt Raphael praises* Writing Against *as a well-balanced account of Sartre's life and offers his own criticisms of Sartre's political and professional behavior.*]

When France fell, Sartre spent some time in a German prisoner-of-war camp. He was exposed for the first time to the sight and sound and smell of the working class. He found that other people might be hell, but they were also mysterious and irretrievably "other". He dreamed all his life of some *rapprochement* between the intellectual and the toiler, even though he confessed that he never really liked the male half of the human race. He retained a long appetite, and appeal, for the other half. When he involved himself in post-war politics, it

Sartre in 1964. © Lütfi Özkök.

Sartre at a press conference in Paris, 1974. UPI/Bettmann Newsphotos.

was as the soon-disillusioned founder of a non-communist leftist party.

After it disintegrated under its own weightlessness, he practised protracted coitus interruptus with the Communist party, until the Hungarian Revolution led to divorce before marriage.

Sartre continued, obstinately, even crassly, to argue that Marxism was inescapable doctrine (rather than a sort of sub-language). He never saw that Marx, like the 1930s philosopher Alain, was always "writing against": he too made sense only as a critic, as an adversary. Ronald Hayman has thus chosen an appropriate, if awkward, title [***Writing Against: A Biography of Sartre***] for his excellent, well-balanced and readable account of Sartre's life and times. Annie Cohen-Solal's . . . biography takes some beating, but Hayman trumps Cohen-Solal in the clarity of his philosophical exegesis. He keeps us amused with gossip, but nearly always honours his high purpose. He is respectful but unintimidated and comes to his own sensible conclusions (for instance, he rightly sees the merits of Sartre's Freud screenplay, which others have depreciated). He rarely loses his grip on the French background, though he is wrong to query whether someone in the crowd could have shouted "You are arresting a Nobel Prize", when Sartre was almost nicked for selling *La Cause du Peuple,* a Maoist paper which he had agreed to "edit" in his old age. Although he had refused the Nobel (in 1963), it was quite natural for his fellow-citizens to refer to him, as they do to all laureates, as "un Prix Nobel".

How important was Sartre? He marked his era all right. How many afternoons did Left Bank *habitués* (and *habituées*) spend debating existentialism—*was* it a humanism?—while wearing black corduroys and drinking black coffee and hoping to catch sight of Sartre and the Beaver *dans ses oeuvres?* His philosophy in ***L'Etre et le Néant*** was famously denounced by A J Ayer as being founded on a misuse of the verb "to be" (Sartre retorted, with unusual brevity, "Ayer est un con") and he was wrong, often wilfully and wickedly, on the virtues of communism. His ideas were capriciously personal and expressed in a mystifying jargon; for all his Tolstoyan desire to liberate the working class, few of them ever understood him. He became a rabid anti-American, but his trilogy, ***Les Chemins de la Liberté*** (he never wrote the intended fourth volume) was a tribute to John Dos Passos and to Ernest Hemingway. (Mathieu, wounded and firing on the advancing Germans, is Robert Jordan *deux.*) His plays remain his best claim to fame. He was quite an actor himself and put memorable rhetoric in the mouths of men like Pierre Brasseur and those of a sequence of actress-mistresses with whom he tested, sometimes to near destruction, his special relationship with Simone de Beauvoir, the "little judge" to whose critical editing he submitted all his work.

His ignorance of fact was notorious and it is to be doubted if he ever read many of the books he denounced so fiercely, including Aron's. He loathed the bourgeois idea of art and spent huge amounts of the time indicting Flaubert (***The Idiot of the Family***), Mallarme and Baudelaire. His appreciation of Jean Genet, ***Saint and Martyr,*** was not appreciated by its subject. He had a way of writing about himself when supposedly dealing with others. He was sometimes literally his own worst enemy, though he had competition. His irresponsible rhetoric did much to license the rebellious youth whose great moment came in May, 1968, when they all but overthrew the Fifth Republic. After that date, he slowly collapsed into nodding extremism, bearing out Camus's prescient observation that he and his *Les Temps Modernes* "family" had a penchant for servility.

Frederic Raphael, "Kings of the Intellect," in The Sunday Times, *London, November 30, 1986, p. 52.*

RHIANNON GOLDTHORPE

[*Goldthorpe, an English critic, is the author of* Sartre: Literature and Theory *(1984). In the following excerpt Goldthorpe differs with Hayman on several of his interpretations of Sartre's approach to philosophy and literature.*]

Freud, according to Ronald Hayman [in ***Writing Against: A Biography of Sartre***], pushed biography decisively away from fact towards speculation; Sartre's own biographical writing veered, independently of Freud, towards fiction. While Hayman's account of Sartre's life is full of richly detailed fact and anecdote, he is by no means immune to psychoanalytic or imaginative pattern-making: all Sartre's work is "written against" the stepfather who supplanted Jean-Paul at the heart of his mother's life. Is this a reductively Freudian explanation, or a discovery of the "original choice" which, for the early existentialist Sartre, could and should be constantly called into question? Or is it the starting-point for that "totalizing" process of understanding which, according to the later Sartre, should be the goal of any biographical enterprise, and which should move dialectically between the individual, his family and class situation, and his broader historical context?

Hayman seems to encourage this last view, but shorn of its Marxist implications: Sartre, he later suggests, also wrote, either simultaneously or successively, against his patriarchal and bourgeois grandfather (who abundantly provided the superego from which Sartre believed he had been freed by the early death of his father), against the bourgeoisie, against himself (the bourgeois intellectual), against the idea of the self, against the breakdown of democracy and liberty, against anti-Stalinism, against Stalin, and, at any given moment, against everything that he had previously written.

It is true that Sartre insisted, as a moral imperative, on the need to review one's responses constantly in a rapidly changing situation. This was neither a rationalization of inconsistency nor, as Hayman would have it, a form of self-betrayal. Indeed, the difficulty with the "writing against" thesis is that it tends to underestimate the continuity in Sartre's thought and to overemphasize the contradictions between, rather than the ambiguities within, his successive intellectual positions. For instance, Hayman exaggerates Sartre's negative attitude towards the imagination. He was fascinated by it, and it dominated his work from the early phenomenological treatise ***L'Imaginaire*** to the Flaubert biography, to say nothing of his own creative writing. His attitude towards the imaginary was deeply ambivalent, rather than consistently negative: it might be a mode of escapism and self-deceptive wish-fulfilment, but it also exemplified the freedom of consciousness and its powers of transcendence. In its negation of the real it might withdraw into nihilism, it might seek to transform reality into art or to change reality itself. It was as essential to socio-political action, whether direct or indirect, as it was to creative writing and, by extension, it was essential to the link between the two. It is also implicated in Sartre's ambitious attempts to establish the total significance of an individual life and to grasp its involvement in the movement of history, while recognizing that such "totalities" could never be complete. In this perspective the Flaubert study is not, *pace* Hayman, a compensating retreat into individualism after the failure to sustain the socio-political arguments of the ***Critique de la raison dialectique.*** It is complementary, in its relative concreteness, to the abstractions of the ***Critique.*** The compensation was Sartre's direct immersion in the would-be revolution of 1968 ("L'Imagination au pouvoir!") and in the anarchism of extreme left-wing politics which followed upon (or accounted for) its collapse.

Hayman's biography is more ambitious than Annie Cohen-Solal's recent, even longer, French one . . . in that he attempts to summarize the implications of Sartre's novels, plays, major essays and complex philosophical works in a few lapidary paragraphs. The results are uneven: Sartre's "Being" (unqualified by "in-itself"or "for-itself") is not Heidegger's "Dasein", which would be better rendered by the notion of "la réalité humaine". Sartre would not have taken as a compliment the contention that his early existential biographies of Baudelaire and Genet "are nothing if not Freudian in their approach". The claim that he never lost faith in his ability "to make the signifier transparent and the signified perfectly visible" does less than justice to the growing complexity of his views on language.

But apart from evaluating his creative and philosophical writing and his forays into aesthetics, literary criticism, anti-psychiatry and social theory, any life of Sartre must read like a global roll-call of post-war political and moral crises. His hectic involvement in events as public conscience, journalist, activist and unofficial ambassador concerns Hayman far more than the minutiae of Marxist controversy, and he is particularly sensitive to Sartre's lifelong preoccupation with the ethics of violence. Like many Sartrean dilemmas, it remained unresolved both in theory and in practice.

For Hayman, this refusal to resolve and conclude, or even to complete an *oeuvre* consisting largely of massive fragments, bears witness to achievement rather than failure. Indeed, he suggests that Sartre's importance depends more on his failures than on any of his successes, and, with a biographer's *parti pris,* he considers Sartre's greatest achievement to be the trajectory of his life. His sheer persistence was heroic and, if he failed, it was because he was addicted to the impossible. It is true that Sartre, who was not given to self-aggrandisement or affectation, maintained that committed writing should, like bananas, be consumed on the spot, and he wrote off his own commitment to writing as a form of neurosis. He would have thought it right that his intellectual progeny should, as so many did, turn upon their father. But he also maintained that writing was his life. Sartre's work is his best biography.

Rhiannon Goldthorpe, "A Hero of the Unresolved," in The Times Literary Supplement, *No. 4367, December 12, 1986, p. 1404.*

S. J. Perelman: A Life

by Dorothy Herrmann

(For S. J. Perelman: see also *CLC,* Vols. 3, 5, 9, 15, 23; *Contemporary Authors,* Vols. 73-76, 89-92 [obituary]; *Contemporary Authors New Revision Series,* Vol. 18; and *Dictionary of Literary Biography,* Vols. 11, 44. For Dorothy Hermann: see also *Contemporary Authors,* Vol. 107.)

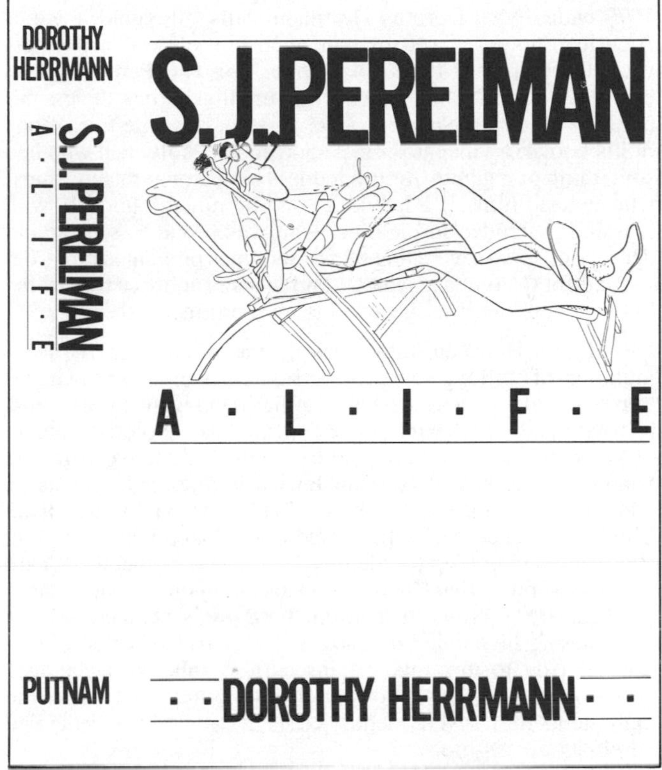

Dust jacket of S. J. Perelman: A Life, *by Dorothy Herrmann. Putnam, 1986. Jacket design © 1986 by One Plus One Studio. Jacket illustration © 1949 by Al Hirschfeld. Reprinted by permission of The Putnam Publishing Group.*

An Excerpt from *S. J. Perelman: A Life*

In February of 1931, as soon as the Marxes had returned from their engagement at the Palace Theatre in London, they summoned Perelman and Johnstone to read the script [of *Monkey Business*] to them in their suite at the Roosevelt Hotel. The writers, who were the first to arrive, flipped coins to determine which one of them would read the script. Perelman won. He later claimed that his only acting experience had been a minor role in a high-school pageant based on the life of Pocahontas. At any rate, he was not an adept public speaker, and that night his nervousness was intensified by the perhaps deliberate tardiness of Groucho and his brothers.

After a forty-five-minute wait, the audience started drifting in . . . first, the Marxes' father, then Herman Mankiewicz with his brother Joseph, then a Paramount scriptwriter, three of the Marxes and their wives, their lawyers, dentists, accountants—and several dogs, including Zeppo's Afghans, who had devoured the upholstery of his car that afternoon, and Chico's wirehaired terrier, which immediately started fighting with the Afghans. Finally Groucho and his wife arrived.

There were at least twenty-seven people and five dogs in the room. As soon as they had all more or less settled themselves, Sid began reading the script, including all the technical terms. It took about an hour and a half. During the reading Harpo, the dogs and several people went to sleep.

"But Perelman went on reading," said Arthur Sheekman, Groucho's gag man. "Valiantly, I thought. I would have shot myself on page 25."

After Sid had finished reading, there was a deathly silence. Finally Chico asked Groucho, "Well, what do you think?" Groucho took the cigar out of his mouth and said, "It stinks," whereupon all the guests, including the dogs, got up and left the room.

Fully convinced that he and Johnstone would be fired the next day, Sid was surprised to learn that the Marxes thought the script might work if it was thoroughly overhauled. He and Johnstone spent the next five months rewriting it. They were joined by other Marx Brothers writers: Arthur Sheekman, Nat Perrin, J. Carver Pusey and Solly Violinski. The brothers also threw in suggestions, as did Herman Mankiewicz and Norman McLeod, the director.

One of Groucho's criticisms of Sid was that his humor was too literary and convoluted for a mass audience. It was during the making of *Monkey Business* that their lifelong battle began about whether screen comedy can ever afford to be intelligent or intellectual.

Groucho particularly objected to a love scene between himself and Thelma Todd, in which Sid had written that Groucho was to jump up and say, "Come, Kapellmeister, let the violas throb, my regiment leaves at dawn." Then he was supposed to parody a famous scene from the popular film *The Merry Widow* with Mae Murray. Groucho told Sid, "The trouble is that the barber in Peru won't get it," meaning Peru, Indiana. Perelman tried to convince him that the scene would reveal Groucho's genius for parody. But he could not convince Groucho, and the *Merry Widow* scene was deleted. Sid's "Come, Kapellmeister" line remained in the picture, however, and he confessed that whenever he saw *Monkey Business,* he felt a sense of triumph when he heard Groucho say it.

JONATHAN YARDLEY

Sidney Joseph Perelman was one of the great comic writers of the century, in this or any other language, and his death in 1979 ended what Dorothy Herrmann calls "the golden age of American humor," yet the comedian himself was neither especially funny nor especially agreeable. The Perelman who emerges in Herrmann's admiring, intelligent but lifeless biography [***S. J. Perelman: A Life***] is, to borrow the title of one of his books, a vinegar puss: a sour, melancholy man who had something of a genius for unkindness in personal relationships, who fancied himself a ladykiller and humiliated his wife with real and pretended infidelities, who was prone to self-pitying depressions "so severe that they sometimes prevented him from writing for as long as a year," and whose snobbery toward the lower orders did not disguise his own origins in them.

His life, as Herrmann describes it, was devoted to the accumulation of "a long series of personas—man about town, intrepid world traveler, dashing Lothario, elegant dandy—that he tried to don in a search for self-identity, an adolescent dream of grandeur inevitably doomed to failure." A native of Rhode Island and the son of Russian-Jewish immigrants, he was an odd—and uncomfortable—mix of cultures: on the one hand "his Jewish ancestry, with its tradition of skepticism, learning and restless searching for identity," and on the other the "Yankee philosophy" that "believed in speaking one's mind, standing against the crowd and in pinching one's pennies, seldom squandering his money on cabs, gifts for friends or other luxuries." Add to this mix the insecurities inherent at being a poor boy in a rich boys' college (Brown), and you have all the ingredients for a severe identity crisis; it haunted and bedeviled Perelman all his life.

It was also, obviously, the mix out of which his humor grew. Himself a bundle of contrasts and contradictions, Perelman had a penetrating eye for them in other individuals and in society as a whole. He became best known for his play with words—the mind-bending puns, the non sequiturs, the incongruities—but his humor was more complex than that. More than a mere punster, he was a master of malice and ridicule; he was able to get away with directing it at others because he had the wisdom to direct it at himself as well. Even as Perelman himself played the boulevardier for all it was worth, in his impeccably tweedy clothes and neatly trimmed moustache, in his comic pieces he turned that boulevardier into a figure of fun, thus making himself seem less superior to the common lot of us than he actually thought himself to be.

Considering that his humor had so sharp an edge to it, the widespread affection with which he was regarded by his many readers is something of a mystery, one that Herrmann does not attempt to explore. But this is consistent with her biographical method, a genuine oddity of which is that although it analyzes Perelman the man at considerable length, it analyzes Perelman the humorist and writer scarcely at all. Surprisingly little of his work is directly quoted—did his estate place her under restrictions that she does not mention in her acknowledgements?—and even less of it is subjected to searching criticism. Considering that the only reason Perelman commands biograhical attention is that he was a humorist and writer, this is a strange omission indeed.

On the purely biographical material, by contrast, Herrmann is diligent and often interesting, though she is inattentive to chronology and never manages to work up much narrative steam. Her discussion of Perelman's early years is thorough, especially his intimate friendship with an eccentric character named Nathan Weinstein, who changed his name to Nathanael West, wrote *Miss Lonelyhearts* and *The Day of the Locust,* and eventually became Perelman's brother-in-law. West was a major if somewhat elusive influence in Perelman's life long after his death in 1940 in a motor accident, and his sister Laura's emotional dependence on him contributed to the many difficulties and discomforts of her marriage to Perelman.

But on the evidence that Herrmann presents, it can only be concluded that the principal difficulty in that marriage was Perelman himself. He was inattentive, indifferent and unfaithful to Laura, and his treatment of his two children bordered on the cruel: "Like so many temperamental men of genius, he found children tiresome nuisances, which was perhaps the reason he preferred animals and birds. . . . Boisterous children and sulky adolescents were difficult to control, and he took revenge on their behavior in his humor—exaggerating their faults to grotesque proportions." But he was madly in love with his mynah, Tong Cha, of whom one acquaintance said: "Tong Cha was a lot like Perelman. He made horrible noises and pecked at you constantly until he drew blood."

Perelman's life, like the lives of most writers, was a constant struggle to pay the bills, one not really alleviated until he collaborated on a successful play, ***One Touch of Venus,*** and, later, won an Academy Award for his contributions to the screenplay for ***Around the World in 80 Days.*** He spent a lot of time in Hollywood, which he hated, working on films of little or no distinction; he "divided his time between commercial writing and pieces of a literary nature, a pattern that would remain more or less set for the rest of his life." The best of the "literary" work, if that is the word for it, was done for *The New Yorker* in the '40s and '50s, when he was able to temper his bitterness with irreverence and self-mockery; the later work too often is that of "an angry, cantankerous man, condemning almost everyone and everything."

Perelman once wrote:

> If I were to apply for a library card in Paris, I would subscribe myself as *feuilletoniste,* that is to say, a writer of little leaves. I may be in error, but the word seems to me to carry a hint of endearment rather than patronage. . . . In whatever case I should like to affirm my loyalty to it as a medium. The handful of chumps who still practice it are as lonely as the survivors of Fort Zinderneuf; a few more assaults by television and picture journalism and we might as well post their bodies on the ramparts, pray for togetherness, and kneel for the final annihilation. Until then, so long and don't take any wooden rhetoric.

Perelman was a miniaturist and a caricaturist, and he knew that it was no mean thing to be either; to be both, and to raise both to the level of art, was a rare and enduring accomplishment.

Jonathan Yardley, "Perelman beyond Price: The Life of a Comic Master," in Book World—The Washington Post, *July 27, 1986, p. 3.*

GENE LANGLEY

The Roaring '20s. The Jazz Age. The decade syncopated to the talents of brilliant cartoonists, caricaturists, and writers gilding everything with zany irreverence, peppy put-ons, and practical jokes on everybody.

"Put an egg in your shoe and beat it" was a college wisecrack made in 1924 by that preeminent creature of the '20s, S. J. Perelman. But the decade grew older, and Perelman grew up.

Ambitious to be a cartoonist, he first drew for his college magazine, *The Brown Jug,* at Brown University, then later for *Judge* magazine. His work was decorative, artistic, up-to-date, but soon not quite as funny as the captions.

His first cartoon for *Judge* was entitled "The Flighty Pair." It has a rather surreal quality, with two men being tossed in the air through clouds: "Don't breathe a word, Casper—but I think Lord Percy is horribly fastidious."

"You said it, Dalmatia. He even insists on being measured for his coat of arms."

As his captions grew longer and better, the drawings disappeared, and he joined the company of writers such as Robert Benchley, James Thurber, and Dorothy Parker.

Dorothy Herrmann gives us an even-handed, on-the-mark study of the often-sad, often-angry, but well-tailored man behind the jester. [***S. J. Perelman: A Life***] lays out the topography and sociology of Perelman's life, his marital and family problems, his infidelities and wandering ways, his difficulties with friendships.

Elegant Nathanael West, later famous for his novels *Miss Lonelyhearts* and *The Day of the Locust,* became one of Perelman's best friends at Brown, giving him an example of how to dress well. Later he became his brother-in-law when Perelman married West's sister Laura. The death of Mr. West in a car crash was a crucial tragedy in the Perelmans' lives.

Perelman wrote for all the popular arts: print (books and magazines, including *The New Yorker*); Broadway (he launched Mary Martin on her career with his hit ***One Touch of Venus***); Hollywood (he won an Oscar for his screenplay for ***Around the World in Eighty Days***). Later he wrote scripts for TV.

His first successful book, ***Dawn Ginsbergh's Revenge,*** had been endorsed by none other than Groucho Marx, who quipped: "From the moment I picked up your book until I laid it down, I was convulsed with laughter. Someday I intend reading it."

Thus encouraged, Perelman worked on two of the Marx brothers' films, ***Monkey Business*** and ***Horse Feathers.*** The manic Marxes and the literary Perelman were an explosive combination from the beginning, and it was an experience he would complain about for the rest of his life.

But he complained about most everything. Publishers, critics, whoever might dare try to edit his copy. He had a long list. He could not stand—among many, many things—the A. A. Milne stories. In a tale about a sea serpent that wanted to devour the creator of Winnie the Pooh, he versified: "He wants to eat that A. A. Milne, / Whose writings are so quaint, / I'm glad of that because they fill me / With a tendency to faint."

Many projects and scripts foundered along the way. One outstanding failure was an effort to get rich on Broadway with a show he wrote with Ogden Nash and caricaturist Al Hirschfeld. Maybe this prompted the line "A hush fell over the audience, and had to be removed by the ushers."

Perelman's intricate use of words belongs to the printed page. But he eventually felt that the age of written satire, parody, and whimsy had passed him by.

Human folly, as he saw it through his steel-rimmed spectacles, was magnified to the point of absurdity, and his own humanity redeemed it with laughter.

Here he is, using some of that language in a piece taking off on inflation:

> As recently as 1918, it was possible for a housewife in Providence, where I grew up, to march into a store with a five-cent piece, purchase a firkin of cocoa butter, a good second-hand copy of Bowditch, a hundredweight of quahogs, a shagreen spectacle case and sufficient nainsook for a corset cover, and emerge with enough left over to buy a balcony admission to *The Masquerader* with Guy Bates Post, and a box of maxixe cherries.

Humor writing is no joke, and if his humor darkened at the end, nevertheless he was still sketching some brilliant captions for the world around him. In fact, he wrote that "Before they made Perelman, they broke the mold."

Gene Langley, "'Before They Made Perelman, They Broke the Mold'," in The Christian Science Monitor, *August 20, 1986, p. 20.*

JOHN LAHR

[Lahr, an American critic, novelist, biographer, essayist, editor, and scriptwriter, writes about theater and the entertainment industry in Up Against the Fourth Wall *(1970) and* Automatic Vaudeville: Essays on Star Turns *(1984). His other notable publications include* Prick Up Your Ears: The Biography of Joe Orton *(1978) and his acclaimed biography of his father, the actor-co-*

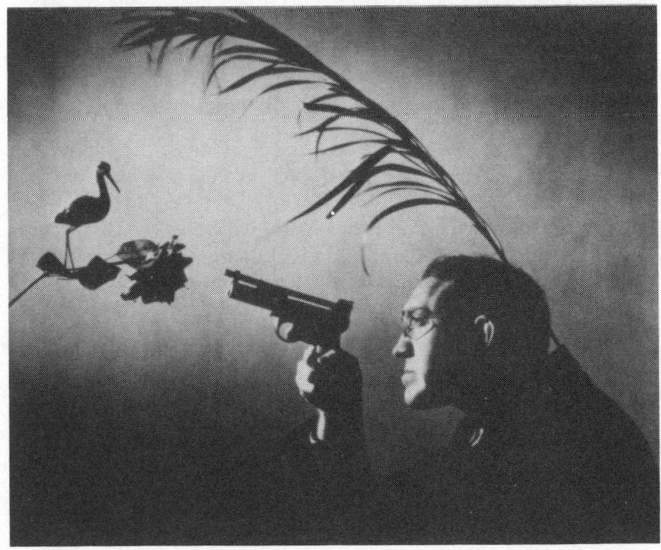

Portrait of Perelman, 1935. Photograph by Ralph Steiner.

median Bert Lahr, Notes on a Cowardly Lion *(1969). Bert Lahr starred in* The Beauty Part, *a play by Perelman and Ogden Nash, in 1962. In the following excerpt Lahr characterizes* S. J. Perelman: A Life *as a mediocre biography that fails to convey either Perelman's humor or his brilliant prose style. Lahr offers his own interpretation of the comedian's life.*]

''Button-cute, rapier-keen, wafer-thin and pauper-poor is S. J. Perelman,'' wrote the humorist, caricaturing both himself and *Time* magazine style. ''He raises turkeys which he occasionally displays on Broadway.'' This comic disingenuousness is charming enough to forgive Perelman anything, and it was intended to. Perelman's speciality was intellectual burlesque; and his literary high jinks allowed him, like the great performing stage clowns he so admired, to admit his infantile emotions in public and make a good buck in the bargain. In life, as Dorothy Herrmann's frumpy biography, ***S. J. Perelman: A Life,*** amply documents, the writer was also narcissist-nice and erudite-empty.

Perelman (who died in 1979 at the age of 75) contended that the great 20th-century American comedians were Jewish and that the immigrant experience was the clue to their prodigious heritage of laughter. ''They were wrestling with English as a foreign langauge,'' he told the critic Kenneth Tynan. ''They'd take an Anglo-Saxon cliché like 'I disbursed a goodly sum' and make it funny by pronouncing it the wrong way.'' Perelman, of course, was also talking indirectly about his own comic attack. His fustian style, which mixed the sludge and swank of English speech into an elegant parody of elegance, showed off his own assimilation into mainstream culture.

Born in 1904, Sidney Joseph Perelman was a first-generation American, the only son of Joseph and Sophie Perelman, who moved from one failed business to another until they found themselves raising chickens on a farm in Providence, R.I. Perelman's laughter got even for a long history of regrets: his stalled parents, his looks, his failure to graduate from Brown University. ''I'm highly irritable,'' he wrote, ''and my senses bruise easily and when they are bruised, I write. It's a strange way for an adult to make a living, isn't it?'' In Perelman's case, ''adult'' was an honorary title. The swagger of his lapidary prose broadcast his self-absorption and his obsession with mastery. In print, he laughed at his wife's alcoholism, his detachment from his children, whom he called ''the dwarfs,'' and his own compulsive infidelity (he was cheating on Laura Perelman two days after he married her in 1929). ''I am,'' he joked, ''what the Puritans call a womanizer. It's a sort of lay preacher.''

Always guarded, Perelman lived at a distance from himself, and his laughter kept the havoc of his real life also in long shot. ''He ran away from trouble,'' says his former editor Robert Gottlieb. ''He ran away from real emotional or psychic engagement.'' Perelman, like all comedians, was the main object of his affections, and his own greatest invention. In print—whether in his reminiscences of silent-film-going in ''Cloudland Revisited,'' his hilarious travel adventures or his *New Yorker* ''casuals''—he never strayed far from the contours of himself. A resolute miniaturist, he preferred to call his form of literary entertainment *feuilletons* and himself ''a writer of little leaves.'' The genre, in Jimmy Durante's words, was a form of ''non-friction.''

''As a comic writer, you develop a comic 'persona' for yourself,'' Perelman said. ''And that is what turns into yourself. I don't know who the real 'you' is.'' Perelman of the comic turn is a mixture of shlepper and sophisticate, a combination, as Paul Theroux put it in his introduction to Perelman's posthumous ***Last Laugh,*** ''of Sad Sack and Pierre Loti.'' Even at college, where he edited the satire magazine and harbored ambitions to become a professional cartoonist, Perelman cut a raffish, spiky figure. He worked himself up into the class ''wag,'' proclaimed in the yearbook as ''our leading sophisticate, (who) fought the good fight against Babbittry, Sham, Hypocrisy, and Mediocrity. All are supposed to quiver before the vicious slashes of his pen and pencil.''

By 1924, Perelman had migrated to New York City to try and live by his witticisms. His reputation for humor grew faster than his bank balance; but in 1929, at the age of 25, his first book, ***Dawn Ginsbergh's Revenge,*** catapulted him into the aristocracy of success. He subsequently thought this work ''dated'' and refused to allow its republication. But his surrealist cartoons were increasingly matched by a prose style whose puns, wisecracks, non sequiturs and baroque flourishes aspired to comparable surreal astonishments.

At first, Perelman imitated Stephen Leacock, George Ade and Ring Lardner. ''I was such a shameless Lardner thief I should have been arrested,'' he said. But by the mid-1930's, Perelman was an innovator of his own combative brand of literary slapstick. At his best, in an early story, **''Scenario,''** a collage of on- and off-screen clichés that roll on for three pages without a paragraph, Perelman could make a stunning improvisational riff out of dead rhetoric: ''It's a hisTORical drama, Mr. Biberman, it'll blow them outa the back of the houses, it's the greatest thing in the industry, it's dynamite! Pardon me, officer, is that General Washington? Bless yer little heart, mum, and who may yez be, savin' yer prisince? Honest Brigid the applewoman of Trinity, is it?''

Perelman spent a lifetime taking potshots at the gonifs and greedheads of Hollywood, while at the same time hungering for a big hit. His flirtation with the movies began in the early 30's when he collaborated in the writing of the Marx Brothers' ***Monkey Business*** and ***Horse Feathers;*** it continued through the decade when he and his wife signed on as a $1,000-a-week screenwriting team for B movies; and it concluded in the 50's, with Perelman winning an Oscar for ***Around the World in 80 Days.*** Perelman later characterized this migration of literary talent to Hollywood with typical asperity. ''Wave a paycheck at us and we could turn in our own wheelbase, strip ourselves inside out like a glove: the most agile, biddable, unblushing set of mercenaries since the Hessians,'' he wrote in ***Westward Ha!*** Perelman was even more outspoken about the Marx Brothers, who gave him a leg up into literary legend: ''Anybody who ever worked on any picture for the Marx Brothers said he would rather be chained to a galley oar and lashed at ten-minute intervals.''

Groucho, who himself was hell on a short fuse and whom Perelman always referred to as Cuddles, had his own version of events. To him, Perelman had been merely a hired (and haughty) hand. Perelman, he told the press as late as 1972, ''could write a funny line, but never a script. When he was writing for us, he was working with four other men. He thought he was the greatest writer in the world and didn't want to be identified with comedians . . . thought we were too low. After we became successful, he came out and said he wrote a great part of the Marx Brothers. This just wasn't true. We had good writers, but he wasn't one of them.''

Plot, characterization, range and depth of emotion were not part of Perelman's comic bag of tricks. He was a writer, as F.

Scott Fitzgerald said, of "exquisite tact," who preferred caricature and wordplay. "My humor is of the free association kind," he said, "and in order to enjoy it you have to have done a good bit of reading. It's a heavy strain for people who haven't read much." This always posed problems when trying to transfer Perelman's antic spirit from the page to the stage. "He writes great dialogue," the impresario Mike Todd once said of Perelman, "but it's strictly *New Yorker*." The low comics for whom Perelman wrote humanized his words and made them their own. For this, Perelman never quite forgave them.

Although he had his Broadway hit when he teamed with Ogden Nash and Kurt Weill in ***One Touch of Venus,*** Perelman's greatest theatrical achievement was ***The Beauty Part*** with Bert Lahr, which closed because of the New York newspaper strike of 1962-63 and remains one of Broadway's most memorable casualties. On opening night a man laughed so hard at Lahr's interpolation of Perelman's redbaiting hysteric, Nelson Smedley, that he had to stuff a handkerchief in his mouth to shut up. Lahr thought the material the best he'd ever had; but later, regrettably, he refused to take the play to England. Perelman turned on him in print.

"I'm frozen in my period," Perelman said toward the end of his career, a verdict as true of his psyche as his style of humor. Anger was a way of feeling alive, and Perelman cultivated his fine fury. "I don't believe in kindly humor. I don't think it exists," he said. In his travel reportage he sought out places "filled with things I can be hostile about."

The writer needed imbroglio and provoked it everywhere. He rowed with shopkeepers near his Pennsylvania farm who banished him from their stores and refused him service for his bad temper. He rowed endlessly with publishers (especially Random House's Bennett Cerf, on whom Perelman took revenge as "Barnaby Chirp" and "Emmett Stag"; the latter surname translates as *cerf* in French). He rowed a lifetime with his wife, Laura, whom he had decided to divorce in the year she died. "I'm a bleeder," he said of the writing on which he worked six days a week, keeping office hours and producing 125 words a day. But he also made others bleed. "Those part-time chimpanzees masquerading as children" bore the brunt of his indifference and his inability to love. At 15, Perelman's son robbed a woman at knifepoint; several years later, he was arrested again and charged with assault, robbery and attempted rape. Perelman refused to talk about it; but the man whom Paul Theroux has characterized as a "cheery soul" was actually intermittently blocked by yearlong depressions and on lithium.

Perelman's problems with dramatic structure seem to have been inherited by his biographer, whose previous literary venture was titled ***With Malice Toward All. S. J. Perelman: A Life*** misses almost every opportunity for narrative tension. The story of this master of parody often reads like a parody of biography. "Perhaps he felt that (Nathanael) West, who disliked sentimentality, might find any reference to grief distasteful," Ms. Herrmann writes of Perelman's pathological denial of feeling, in this case over the death of his brother-in-law, West. "Or perhaps like many supersensitive men of genius, he avoided harsh reality, preferring to live instead in a dreamland of romance, an adolescent fantasy world where death and horror do not exist."

Perelman's preoccupation with the cliché, baroque language and the elegant variation appears to have had no salutary effect on Mrs. Herrmann's unsmiling prose, which is chockablock with non sequiturs and dead words: "He began to lose a comic writer's most precious gift—his sense of humor." Ms. Herrmann paraphrases large chunks of Perelman's uncompleted memoir, ***The Hindsight Saga;*** quotes interminably from Josephine Herbst's lackluster novel about the complicated relationship among Laura, Nathanael West and Perelman; and gleans no point of view from the secondary sources she strings together. . . .

Perelman is indisputably in the vanguard of modern American comic writers, but he was never as interested in the nature of American life as in his pukka response to it. His laughter rarely takes on big issues, only the small fry. This may limit his resonance, but not his achievement. "I am content to stitch away at my embroidery hoop," he said. "I think the form I work can have its own distinction." In this, at least, Perelman was right. (pp. 3, 28)

John Lahr, "'I Don't Believe in Kindly Humor'," in The New York Times Book Review, *September 7, 1986, pp. 3, 28.*

L. S. KLEPP

It's to S. J. Perelman's everlasting credit that he didn't cut the comedy. He never succumbed to any temptation or blandishment to quit clowning around and get down to serious work, so the austere, brooding 900-page meditation on the ins and outs of angst that he might have composed remained unwritten, even though his own life supplied enough to keep an entire platoon of Middle European metaphysicians happily depressed for years.

Dorothy Herrmann gives us all the particulars [in ***S. J. Perelman: A Life***]: a lonely childhood in Providence, where his father failed at chicken-farming; a combative marriage with Laura, sister of his friend Nathanael West; his infidelities and hers; the juvenile delinquencies of their son; West's early death in a car crash. But I suspect that Perelman, an interpid worrier, would have achieved a considerable measure of gloom even without these troubles. "What I really am, you see, is a crank," he told Jane Howard in 1962. "I'm highly irritable, and my senses bruise easily and when they are bruised, I write. It's a strange way for an adult to make a living, isn't it?"

He bruised easily, but he didn't write easily. Perelman was the Flaubert of humorists, laboriously polishing his prose in the spartan office he kept in a rundown Sixth Avenue walk-up, where the view was blocked and so, often enough, was Perelman. It was a rare day when he finished a page of copy. He had to take pains, because what distinguishes his humor is the degree to which it depends on style alone for its comic effects. He created no memorable comic characters, no Walter Mitty or Bertie Wooster, and invented only perfunctory plots. His *New Yorker* pieces were almost entirely a matter of parody, dismembered clichés, and highly wrought nonsense. The art that went into them was appreciated by friends and admirers like T. S. Eliot and Somerset Maugham and by British critics, though not so much by American reviewers, who kept after him to attempt something important, preferably a darkly comic novel in the manner of West. But Perelman, who had already collaborated on a strained, facetious Roaring '20s novel called ***Parlor, Bedlam and Bath,*** was not about to get mixed up with long fiction again. It's just as well. Parody is the soul of his work, and brevity is the soul of parody.

Divided souls take refuge in irony, and Perelman was a small army of self-contradictions. Herrmann makes this clear by quoting a dozen of his friends, who agree on very little except that he was complicated. He seems to have been shy and debonair, a brilliant conversationalist who often had nothing to say, a fundamentally cold and remote man who was basically kind and a romantic at heart. He was also an Anglophile, impeccably dressed in London-tailored tweeds, who, when he moved to London in 1970 following his wife's death, discovered that he didn't care for the English; a scriptwriter on two great Marx Brothers movies (***Monkey Business*** and ***Horse Feathers***) who couldn't stand the Marx Brothers; a fastidious aesthete whose one consuming ambition was to write a Broadway hit; a hater of Hollywood ("a dreary industrial town controlled by hoodlums of enormous wealth") who had a tender nostalgia for the place. But these ambivalences, which probably were responsible for his frequent depressions, inspired the convoluted brilliance of his best work.

Herrmann's biography is well organized, judicious, Freud-free, and blandly written, with occasional lapses of grammar and usage. (At one point Perelman's father is seen "pouring over" socialist tracts in his spare time.) She is sometimes so intent on ferreting out the discord and depression that plagued her subject that she slights his work. But she is mostly clear, interesting, and sensible, and she quotes some good things, including this autobiographical fragment:

> Perelman's life reads like a picaresque novel. It began on a bleak shelf of rock in mid-Atlantic near Tristan da Cunha. Transplanted to Rhode Island by a passing Portuguese, he became a man of proverbial strength around the Providence wharves; he could drive a spike through an oak plank with his fist. As there was constant need for this type of skilled labor, he soon acquired enough tuition to enter Brown University. . . . Retired today to peaceful Erwinna, Pa., Perelman raises turkeys which he occasionally displays on Broadway, stirs little from his alembics and retorts. Those who know hint that the light burning late in his laboratory may result in a breathtaking electric bill. Queried, he shrugs with the fatalism of your true Oriental. "*Mektoub,*" he observes curtly. "It is written."

L. S. Klepp, "Laughing on the Outside," in The Village Voice, *Vol. XXXI, No. 37, September 23, 1986, p. 50.*

STEFAN KANFER

"Button-cute, rapier-keen, wafer-thin and pauper-poor is S. J. Perelman . . . that he possesses the power to become invisible to finance companies . . . that he owns one of the rare mouths in which butter has never melted are legends treasured by every schoolboy."

This was about as much personal information as Humorist Sidney Joseph Perelman ever intended to disclose. But his natural reticence went with him when he died at the age of 75 in 1979. Dorothy Herrmann, author of a previous book about American wits, ***With Malice Toward All,*** begins [***S. J. Perelman: A Life***] by calling her subject "brilliant" and ends by labeling his work "sublime." Between these terminals she presents a cloth-bound gossip column featuring a morose and promiscuous figure who never came to terms with his beginnings.

Perelman in his later years. © Nancy Crampton.

Perelman's parents were Russian-Jewish immigrants who raised poultry on a small Rhode Island farm. In one of many psychobiographical pole vaults, Herrmann says, "As soon as he could afford it, he began buying only the most expensive custom-made English clothes. They were so beautifully tailored they gave the impression their wearer had never suffered poverty, hardship and the terrible smell of thousands of chickens dying." That Perelman's similarly attired literary colleagues were not all fleeing from the aroma of guano is irrelevant; once the feather complex has been formulated, all facts must bend to fit it.

Like many youths of his generation, Perelman absorbed himself in pulp literature and vaudeville. When he became a cartoonist and writer at Brown University, the melodramatic phrase coupled with the antic gesture were indispensable parts of his technique. Another campus satirist derived from the same origins: Nathan Weinstein, soon to be better known as Nathanael West, the author of *Miss Lonelyhearts*. The two men were close friends, then relatives when Perelman married West's sister Laura. It was not, Herrmann reports, a conventional union. Early on, the Perelmans went to Hollywood, where a fellow scenarist, Dashiell Hammett, once noted, "Last night I ran into Sid . . . and wound up by doing a little pimping for him." Soon afterward, Hammett and Laura had a brief fling. It was, Herrmann speculates, "perhaps her way of punishing Sid for his numerous infidelities."

In fact, the great sorrow of the Perelmans' lives did not have a sexual cause. In December 1940, West and his new wife

Eileen (the title character of *My Sister Eileen*) were killed in an automobile accident. Laura slowly descended into alcoholism. Perelman mourned privately and rarely discussed his brother-in-law. He went on to write film scripts and plays that failed too often, and he turned out the pieces, mostly for *The New Yorker,* for which he is remembered: the collisions of Britishisms and Yiddishisms, the classic parodies of James Joyce and Raymond Chandler, the explosive lampoons of popular culture.

There were more than a few moments of contentment. Despite their difficulties, the Perelmans remained married for 40 years, until Laura's death in 1970. During that period, S. J. contributed to two of the wildest Marx Brothers films, ***Horse Feathers*** and ***Monkey Business,*** and he became lionized in Britain and the U.S. as the reigning master of the comic essay.

But Herrmann's thesis is a stubborn one, and her subject must play Pagliacci to the end. Editors and women friends are brought on to recall a "contained," "testy, easily depressed man," "cranky to be considered this 'national treasure' and not sell." Herrmann adds that after the failure of his last play, ***The Beauty Part,*** in 1963, "(Perelman) began to lose the comic writer's most precious gift—a sense of humor." This will come as a great surprise to readers who enjoyed Perelmania in five later collections of essays as well as a number of saline interviews and commentaries. It is true that personally Perelman was never Mr. Sunshine and that he always craved more recognition and rewards than he received. So did Mark Twain, W. C. Fields, Ring Lardner and many other American humorists.

For future scholars, Herrmann provides a number of valuable interviews. But her prying litany of misery displays few insights about her subject and little analysis of his unique combination of spontaneity and polish. The famous collection ***The Most of S. J. Perelman*** offers a series of works that are far more revealing—and one title that is unfortunately prescient. **"De Gustibus,"** it says, **"Ain't What Dey Used to Be."**

Stefan Kanfer, "Feather Complex," in Time, *Vol. 128, No. 15, October 13, 1986, p. 100.*

The Life of Langston Hughes, Volume I, 1902-1941: I, Too, Sing America

by Arnold Rampersad

(For Langston Hughes: see also *CLC,* Vols. 1, 5, 10, 15, 35; *Contemporary Authors,* Vols. 1-4, rev. ed., Vols. 25-28, rev. ed. [obituary]; *Contemporary Authors New Revision Series,* Vol. 1; *Something about the Author,* Vols. 4, 33; and *Dictionary of Literary Biography,* Vols. 4, 7, 48.)

An Excerpt from *The Life of Langston Hughes, Volume I, 1902-1941: I Too, Sing America*

On the afternoon of his first day out he took his dinner, then returned to his seat to stare out of the train window and brood on what he had left behind and the life that awaited him now in Mexico. Cheerlessly he thought of his angry mother and his forbidding father. In particular, he brooded on his father's hatred of blacks; nothing else in James Hughes so alienated his son. In a year when W. E. B. Du Bois was predicting the coming of race war, when Marcus Garvey was preparing a grand meeting in New York with the cry "Back to Africa," when the Ku Klux Klan was in resurgence and blacks were being lynched with impunity, his own father sneered at "niggers." Blacks seemed to Langston, even at the distance from which he sometimes viewed them, the most wonderful people in the world. This was the main legacy of his grandmother through her heroic tales, and of the Reeds, and of the black men and women in church who had loved him as a child.

The sun was setting as the train reached St. Louis and began the long passage from Illinois across the Mississippi and into Missouri, where Hughes had been born. The beauty of the hour and the setting—the great muddy river glinting in the sun, the banked and tinted summer clouds, the rush of the train toward the dark, all touched an adolescent sensibility tender after the gloomy day. The sense of beauty and death, of hope and despair, fused in his imagination. A phrase came to him, then a sentence. Drawing an envelope from his pocket, he began to scribble. In a few minutes Langston had finished a poem:

> I've known rivers:
> I've known rivers ancient as the world and older than the flow of human blood in human veins.
>
> My soul has grown deep like the rivers.
> I bathed in the Euphrates when dawns were young.
> I built my hut near the Congo and it lulled me to sleep.
> I looked upon the Nile and raised the pyramids above it.

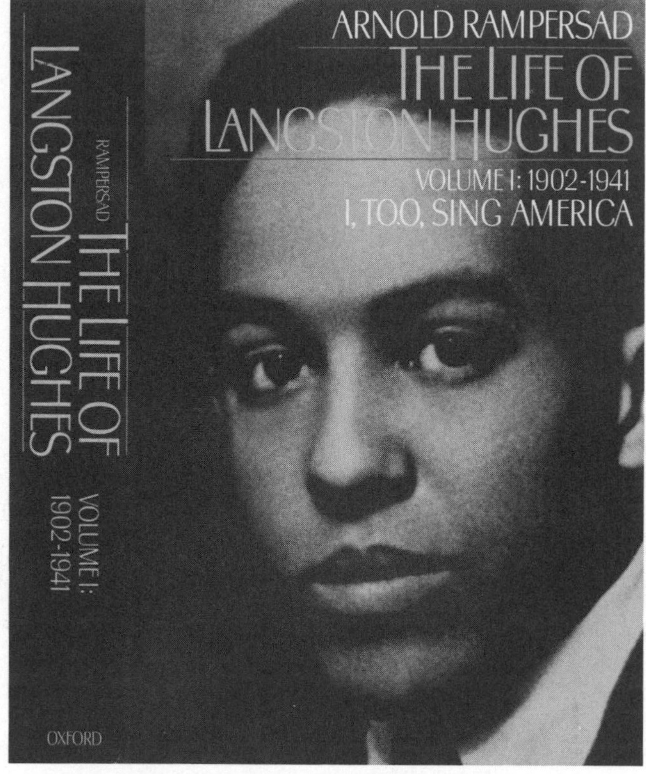

Dust jacket of The Life of Langston Hughes, *by Arnold Rampersad. Oxford, 1986. Jacket design by Honi Werner. Jacket photo by Nickolas Muray. Courtesy of Oxford University Press, Inc.*

> I heard the singing of the Mississippi when Abe Lincoln went down to New Orleans, and I've seen its muddy bosom turn all golden in the sunset.
>
> I've known rivers;
> Ancient, dusky rivers.
>
> My soul has grown deep like the rivers.

With its allusions to deep dusky rivers, the setting sun, sleep, and the soul, "The Negro Speaks of Rivers" is suffused with the image of death and, simultaneously, the idea of deathlessness. As in Whitman's philosophy, only the knowledge of death can bring the primal spark of poetry and life. Here Langston Hughes became "the outsetting bard," in Whitman's phrase, the poet who sings of life because at last he has known death. Balanced between the knowledge of love and of death, the poetic will gathers force. From the depths of grief the poet sweeps back to life by clinging to his greatest faith, which is in his people and his sense of kinship with them. His frail, intimidated self, as well as the image of his father, are liquidated. A man-child is born, soft-spoken, almost casual, yet noble and proud, and black as Africa. The muddy river is his race, the primal source out of which he is born anew; on that "muddy bosom" of the race as black mother, or grandmother, he rests secure forever. The angle of the sun on the muddy water is like the angle of a poet's vision, which turns mud into gold. The diction of the poem is simple and unaffected either by dialect or rhetorical excess; its eloquence is like that of the best of the black spirituals.

KIRKUS REVIEWS

[***The Life of Langston Hughes, Volume I, 1902-1941: I, Too, Sing America*** is a] sympathetic, yet clear-eyed portrait of one of America's most controversial writers that also manages to be a sweeping depiction of the black experience in this country and abroad during the first four decades of the 20th century.

Hughes is an ideal subject about which to construct this type of biography-cum-social history; he was at or near the epicenter of much of the cultural, social and political turbulence that marked those years. Rampersad (English/Rutgers) records both Hughes' life and the era's shocks and aftershocks with admirable clarity and a fine sense of their larger implications. During the first 40 years of his life (the period covered here), Hughes came in contact with most of the major figures in both black and white artistic and civil-rights circles—W.E.B. DuBois, Countee Cullen, Alfred Knopf, Carl Van Vechten, Josephine Baker, Paul Robeson, Ernest Hemingway, Arthur Koestler, Richard Wright, among others. Rampersad delineates each of them in vignettes that capture their personalities in a few evocative details. There is his description of an exchange between Hughes and Josephine Baker, for example, in which "La Bakaire" falls into a pseudo-Chevalier accent when telling Hughes "how I . . . have learn zee loop-zee-loop." "An English never learned in the slums of St. Louis," is Rampersad's straight-faced comment. The locales are equally colorful, ranging from the Congo to Harlem during the "Renaissance"; from the Paris of "Bricktop" to Moscow in the mid-30's; from Loyalist Spain to Hemingway's Cuba; from the South of the Scottsboro Boys to the Carmel of Robinson Jeffers and Vachel Lindsay.

Rampersad does not shy away from the ambiguities and ironies in Hughes' life—his possible homosexuality, his refusal to acknowledge the injustices in Soviet society even when confronting them face to face during a trip to Russia, his willingness to accept financial assistance from "capitalist" patrons while espousing the socialist cause. Rampersad resolutely refuses to "beautify" his subject. And, as might be expected, the author is just as evenhanded in his evaluations of Hughes' writings. Strengths and weaknesses are both pointed out; successes and failures are analyzed with equal care.

Neither exposé nor hagiography, this is a near-perfect example of the biographer's art, balanced and thought-provoking. One eagerly awaits the appearance of Volume II.

A review of "The Life of Langston Hughes, Vol. I, 1902-1941: I, Too, Sing America," in Kirkus Reviews, *Vol. LIV, No. 13, July 1, 1986, p. 1005.*

Hughes in 1923. Photograph by Nickolas Muray.

JOHN GROSS

Langston Hughes was only 21 when he wrote the poem that first made him famous, **"The Weary Blues."** More than two years passed before he was ready to show it to the world; then, in 1925, he submitted it as one of his entries for a competition for black writers, a widely-noted affair (the judges included Eugene O'Neill and Alexander Woolcott) culminating in a banquet at the Fifth Avenue Restaurant, where it was announced that **"The Weary Blues"** had won first prize in the poetry section. After the announcement, the poem was recited—magnificently, according to Arnold Rampersad in his new biography of Hughes [***The Life of Langston Hughes, Volume I, 1902-1941: I, Too, Sing America***]—by the writer James Weldon Johnson:

> Down on Lenox Avenue the other night
> By the pale dull pallor of an old gas light

It must have been a very powerful moment.

Hughes had, in fact, already published widely in magazines. His first important poem, **"The Negro Speaks of Rivers,"** had been accepted by W.E.B. Du Bois for *Crisis,* the N.A.A.C.P. magazine, while he was still a few days short of his 19th birthday. (Some 10 years later, as his fame began to spread to Latin America, it was to be translated into Spanish by Jorge Luis Borges.)

Still, if any one event can be said to have started him on his career as a professional writer, it was the Fifth Avenue banquet. Among the guests there, no one had been more enthusiastic about **"The Weary Blues"** than Carl Van Vechten, the white author and critic who was already becoming known as a champion of "the Harlem renaissance." Mr. Van Vechten recommended Hughes to Alfred A. Knopf, and within three weeks of his winning the prize a collection of his poems had been signed up for publication.

With this first volume, and still more with his second collection, ***Fine Clothes for the Jew,*** it became clear that black America had found a distinctive poetic voice. (And if excessively respectable black reviewers denounced him for writing about "trashy" or "repulsive" subjects, it only seemed to underline his authenticity.) But what was much less clear, unless you were prepared to take his sunny public image at face value, was what Hughes himself was actually like.

He came out of a rich and complicated background. His maternal grandmother, who was part-Indian, had originally been married to an Abolitionist who lost his life in the raid on Harpers Ferry. His great-uncle, the first black American to hold municipal office by popular vote, had ended his career as a Congressman. On both sides of his family he had socially prominent white forebears—on his mother's side he was connected to a Virginian family who numbered among their ancestors the 17th-century English poet Francis Quarles.

His childhood, on the other hand, was hardly calculated to give him much sense of family pride. All but abandoned by a father who despised other blacks (and whom Langston came to hate in turn), and neglected by a mother who dreamed of a career on the stage, he was mostly cared for by his grandmother. It was an upbringing that left lasting wounds.

One obvious result was a tendency to keep his guard up. In later life, for all his sociability, friends often found something passive and enigmatic about him; they wondered where his deepest feelings lay. It is one of the many merits of Arnold Rampersad's excellent biography that he conveys this quality and explains it where he can (largely in terms of Hughes's childhood), without claiming to have all the answers.

Nor, as he shows, does a sensitive portrait of Hughes have to be a solemn one. He writes with appropriate liveliness about a career that was marked by a succession of footloose adventures, warm friendships, sharp quarrels and dramatic gestures. We are given graphic accounts (amplifying and sometimes correcting Hughes's own published versions) of the writer's early voyages as a sailor to Africa and Europe, of the wide assortment of jobs he ran through, of the degree of calculation he could show—a sensible one, under the circumstances—in managing his literary career.

His dealings with his wealthy and elderly white patron, Charlotte Mason (who liked to be called "Godmother") make a particularly gripping episode. It was a relationship that, quite apart from its financial advantages, brought out in him strong elements of both emotional dependency and the fear of being smothered; it also involved him, eventually, in ugly disputes with Mrs. Mason's other major black protégée and his former friend, the novelist Zora Neale Hurston.

His final break with "Godmother" coincided with and perhaps helped to hasten his move to the political far left, at the beginning of the 1930's. Mr. Rampersad's book contains enough reminders of the racism that had confronted Hughes since childhood to make it easy enough to understand why he should have taken up a radical position; but—given his intelligence and independence in other matters—they are not enough to explain away his woeful subservience for a decade or so to the official Communist line (signing statements in *The Daily Worker* supporting "the recent Moscow trials of the Trotskyite-Bukharinite traitors," and so on and so forth).

The most interesting chapter of the 1930's section deals with his visit to the Soviet Union in 1932-33—in particular, with the period he spent in central Asia, some of it in the company of another foreign visitor, Arthur Koestler. The two men got on well, but in comparison with Koestler's misgivings about what he had seen, Hughes's attitude comes across as irresponsible and giggly.

By the beginning of the 1940's, however, he was edging away from the Communists, and by 1941 he was being denounced by them as a turncoat. At which point Mr. Rampersad breaks off, leaving you eager to see what he makes of the rest of the story, and confident that his second volume is going to be as good as his first.

John Gross, in a review of "The Life of Langston Hughes, Volume I, 1902-1941: I, Too, Sing America," in The New York Times, *September 30, 1986, p. C16.*

GWENDOLYN BROOKS

[American poet Brooks is renowned for her moving, perceptive descriptions of urban black life. She received the American Academy of Arts and Letters Award for her poetry in 1946, and in 1950 became the first black author to win the Pulitzer Prize with her collection Annie Allen. *She was also honored as poet laureate of Illinois in 1969. Brooks began her personal acquaintance with Hughes when she was sixteen. In the following excerpt Brooks commends* The Life of Langston Hughes *for its absorbing depiction of the poet's life and milieu and offers her own impressions of Hughes.]*

What was Langston Hughes? An overwhelmer. Long ago I felt it was proper to say he had "a long reach / strong speech / remedial fears / muscular tears." I gave him titles: "Helmsman, hatchet, headlight." And I suggested: "See / one restless in the exotic time! and ever, / till the air is cured of its fever."

Well, the time is still exotic. The air is not cured of its fever. Hughes is not here to be restless, but his product is here, still restless and capable of quite an agitation, a continuing agitation. Schoolchildren, elders, laborers, maids, doctors, nurses, filing clerks, miners, computer dabblers, salespeople at Macy's and Marshall Field's have heard of Langston Hughes and his compulsions—and many can quote from his poetry. An increasing number of scholars and textbook builders find him interesting to study.

Who he was is a smallish part of what he was. He was born in Joplin, Mo., on Feb 1, 1902—James Langston Hughes, a little tan black who had a quizzical love for his mother, a pure hatred for his father and a cool, selective response to the maternal grandmother who was chief among his upbringers. In [***The Life of Langston Hughes, Volume I, 1902-1941: I, Too, Sing America***], Arnold Rampersad describes the poet's childhood as virtually loveless. As for his mother, Carrie, we are told that he "loved her hopelessly." His grandmother, Mary Sampson Patterson Leary Langston, was "of Indian, French, and some African *(sic)* ancestry," and was "born free" in

North Carolina. Although he lived with her on and off until he was 13 years old, he did not cry when she died in 1915.

His father he remembered only too sharply: "I hated my father." And the father, Hughes said, "hated Negroes. I think he hated himself, too, for being a Negro. He disliked all of his family because they were Negroes." James Hughes was tightfisted, uncharitable, cold. He and his wife, Carrie, were separated early. There was an attempt at reconciliation when Langston was 5 years old, but it ended, in the midst of an earthquake in Mexico. Langston's mother—who had joined her husband in Mexico City, where he was working as secretary to the general manager of the Pullman Company—fled Mexico and marriage, and bestowed her little son on her mother in Lawrence, Kan. For many years she was to deposit him with her mother while she worked at jobs in other towns or even in other states, and many times Langston felt rejected.

Sometimes, when his mother was angry with him, she would say, "You're just like Jim Hughes. You're as evil as Jim Hughes." There were good times, however. His mother introduced him to music halls, the public library, operas and the joys of reading.

In school in Topeka (his mother had to fight the school board to secure admittance to the all-white Harrison Street School), the seemingly "gentle and kind" teacher would say loudly for all the class to hear, as she removed licorice sticks from the grasp of a white pupil, "You don't want to eat these; they'll make you black like Langston. You don't want to be black, do you?" Because he was a superior student, she had to give him excellent grades, but she taunted him steadily, and did nothing when his classmates slapped, stoned or snowballed him. In spite of the one-sided warfare, Langston loved school.

His mother married Homer Clark and moved to Lincoln, Ill., and after the grandmother's death she asked Langston to join her there. He was headed for a discovery that was to enchant the rest of his life. As a schoolboy in the eighth grade, he discovered that he could put words together to make what seemed, to him, magic. The next year the Clarks moved to Cleveland and Langston entered Central High School, where he became a regular writer of poetry and stories in the school's monthly magazine. Early models recommended to him by Ethel Weimer, his much-respected English teacher, were Walt Whitman, Carl Sandburg, Edgar Lee Masters, Edwin Arlington Robinson, Amy Lowell, Vachel Lindsay.

Hughes visiting Central Asia in 1932, with Kolya Shagurin, Shaarieh Kikilov, and Arthur Koestler. From The Life of Langston Hughes, *Vol. I, by Arnold Rampersad. Oxford University Press, 1986. By permission of Harold Ober Associates Incorporated and Yale Collection of American Literature, Beinecke Rare Book and Manuscript Library, Yale University.*

His first book, ***The Weary Blues,*** appeared in 1926. By then he had become one of the best-known black writers in the country. He had already been to Africa and lived in Mexico and France, and in the years before World War II, as he traveled all over this country and abroad—there was a trip around the world in 1932 that included a long journey through the Soviet Union—he became a world figure.

The Harlem Renaissance, joyfully tackled in this book, is one of the most popular subjects encountered on campuses across the country now. If a school wants to recognize blacks and blackness at all, it confronts the Harlem Renaissance. Langston Hughes was its best-loved star. Countee Cullen, Claude McKay, Zora Neale Hurston, Alain Locke, Jessie Fauset—all provocatively introduced here—and others achieved italics, but who comes instantly and powerfully to mind when "the Harlem Renaissance" is mentioned? Langston Hughes. And this despite the fact that he could mischievously fly in the face of Renaissance taboos.

This first volume of ***The Life of Langston Hughes*** sparkles when it is involved with Hughes's devotion to his craft, with his eagerness to polish this, to hone that. "Although he wrote steadily, Hughes worried about the quality of his work: almost never in his life would he be sure about his own estimate of a poem," Mr. Rampersad says. Elsewhere he writes, "Hughes had clearly shown already that he saw his own art as inferior to that of either black musicians or religionists—inferior to the sweet trumpeters and moaners in cabarets, inferior to the old black woman in the Amen corner, who cries to Jesus 'Glory! Hallelujah!'" However, Mr. Rampersad avows that "his sense of inferiority definitely empowered rather than debilitated Hughes."

I cannot agree with Mr. Rampersad when he says that Hughes, in response to personal encounters with racism, "subdued his rage and kept his balance. . . . (He) was simply not very vulnerable to insult." I met Langston Hughes when I was 16 years old, and saw enough of him in subsequent years to observe that, when subjected to offense and icy treatment because of his race, he was capable of jagged anger—and vengeance, instant or retroactive. And I have letters from him that reveal he could respond with real rage when he felt he was treated cruelly by other people.

He judged himself the adequate appreciator of his own people, and he judged blacks "the most wonderful people in the world." He wanted to celebrate them in his poetry, fiction, essays and plays. He wanted to record their strengths, their resiliency, courage, humor.

> I, too, sing America.
>
> I am the darker brother.
> They send me to eat in the kitchen
> When company comes,
> But I laugh,
> And eat well,
> And grow strong.
>
> Tomorrow,
> I'll be at the table
> When company comes.

Nobody'll dare
Say to me,
"Eat in the kitchen,"
Then.

Besides,
They'll see how beautiful I am
And be ashamed—

I, too, am America.

But long before he died in 1967, Langston Hughes had decided that "they" intended never to "see how beautiful" he was. He, "the darker brother," early consigned to "the kitchen" and left there, was not to be considered lovely or cherishable on any foreseeable sunny morning. And "they" were not going to "be ashamed" either. Just at the birth of America's most recent racial hot time Langston Hughes found himself increasingly sardonic, less and less concerned that "the darker brother" be seen as beautiful by "the fairer brother."

Indeed, early on he was claiming, "America never was America to me." . . . (pp. 7, 9)

Hughes in Moscow, 1933, holding the Russian translation of his novel Not without Laughter. *From* The Life of Langston Hughes, *Vol. I, by Arnold Rampersad. Oxford University Press, 1986. By permission of Harold Ober Associates Incorporated and Yale Collection of American Literature, Beinecke Rare Book and Manuscript Library, Yale University.*

Mr. Rampersad's first volume has the appeal of any easy-reading novel. The reader is quickly and steadily empathetic, experiencing—with appropriate itch, anger, fear, misery, joy, affectionate irritation, anticipation, exhilaration, triumph, horror, sorrow or pain—childhood sensitivities, youth's traumas and semi-delights and self-discovery; travels in Mexico, Africa, the Soviet Union, Spain, China, Japan; textures and levels of relationships; illness, wrong career choices, triumphs and defeats; pleasing or disillusioning encounters with very important people; a stint in Hollywood; political adventures and misadventures.

Through the years, there has been much debate about the degree of Langston Hughes's "literary quality." It is a pleasure to see in this book a quotation cleanly edifying. One of the children of Arna Bontemps, Hughes's close friend and sometime collaborator, said, "According to my father more than once, almost from the start of their relationship he had recognized in Langston an original, authentically American artist, a grand creative figure like Mark Twain or Walt Whitman, in spite of his flaws as a writer, and thus essentially beyond criticism. No new rival, no matter how accomplished, could diminish Langston's standing in the national literature." Arna Bontemps "admired other black writers, but he never lost that lofty view of Langston." Mr. Rampersad adds, "He saw Hughes, with all his shortcomings, as a man of literature, as nevertheless a figure of epic proportion."

This volume closes on a disturbingly negative note—recounting the time in early 1941, after the pact between Hitler and Stalin, when Hughes, disillusioned with the Soviet leader he had admired and praised since 1932, said he regretted some of the things he had written and found himself attacked from the left and the right at once. It leaves those of us who knew Langston Hughes eager for Volume Two, hoping that it will disclose for us the subtle largeness, the remarkable symbol-radiance that enriched our lives, that made us better people. I reached the last page feeling that this detailed and hardworking volume had not allowed me to review that largeness (except, of course, in the stubbornness of my stimulated memory). Long ago, in tribute, I said of this overwhelmer: "Mightily did he use the street. He found its multiple heart, its tastes, smells, alarms, formulas, flowers, garbage and convulsions. He brought them all to his table-top. He crushed them to a writing-paste. He himself became the pen."

Arnold Rampersad understands that fact. Out of that street, however, the symbol-radiance of Langston Hughes rose high. We will have it in sight, I believe, when we have reached the last page of the next volume of this work by the capable, serious Mr. Rampersad. (p. 9)

Gwendolyn Brooks, "The Darker Brother," in The New York Times Book Review, *October 12, 1986, pp. 7, 9.*

DAVID NICHOLSON

[In the following excerpt Nicholson praises Rampersad's illuminating portrait of Hughes and discusses the political and artistic ideas expressed in Hughes's poetry.]

In rooting his art so specifically in black art forms such as jazz and the blues, Langston Hughes strove to reflect an American reality ignored or distorted by other American writers. His art was grounded in his life, a life that embodied the classic American theme of a search for identity. Like another American hero, he was always in revolt against the bourgeoisie, always ready to light out for the territory of his own imagination.

This first volume of [***The Life of Langston Hughes, Volume I, 1902-1941: I, Too, Sing America***]—well written and thoroughly researched by Arnold Rampersad, a professor of English at Rutgers—ends in early 1941 with Hughes "broke and ruint" and prone in a California hospital bed, suffering from an illness he described variously as arthritis or sciatica because he was unwilling to admit he had contracted a venereal disease. He had other problems as well. His poem **"Goodbye Christ"**—written nine years before—had been reprinted as part of a leaflet and used in a fundamentalist protest. In the resulting furor. Hughes was branded a communist and denounced by religious leaders. He had been evicted from his Harlem apartment. And, galling for a man who had earlier vowed to live solely from his writing, the first volume of his autobiography, ***The Big Sea,*** for which he had had grand hopes, had sold fewer than 2,500 copies. Even more galling, Richard Wright's *Native Son*—released at the same time as ***The Big Sea*** and a book Hughes thoroughly disliked—had sold more than 200,000 copies in three weeks, a total exceeding all of Hughes' sales in nearly 20 years of writing.

It was not an auspicious time for the writer once dubbed the "Poet Laureate of the Negro Race"—a title Hughes may or may not have bestowed on himself but which, given his propensity for keeping his eye on the main chance, he was not shy about exploiting. Only 19 when he first published in national magazines—the children's *Brownies' Book* and the *Crisis* (W.E.B. Du Bois founded the former and edited the latter)—he published his first book of poems. ***The Weary Blues,*** just three years later in 1924. He had traveled to several African countries, to England, France, Russia, Japan, China, Cuba and Haiti. He had read and lectured throughout the world and across the United States. He had traveled with Arthur Koestler in Russia; roomed with Henri Cartier-Bresson in Mexico; reported on the Spanish Civil War with Ernest Hemingway; and with Theodore Dreiser represented the League of American Writers at the 1938 Congress for Peace Action in Paris.

In 1941, then, at the dramatic moment Rampersad chooses to end his first volume, the man who once called his writing "a tightrope of words," adding, "and God help you if you fall the wrong way," appears to have suffered his final fall from grace. But while Hughes may have been down, he was not out. He would recover from his illness and, before his death in 1967, publish six additional volumes of poetry, seven of fiction, a second volume of autobiography, plays, essays and histories.

He was a man of extraordinary tenacity and resilience, and Rampersad, like the best biographers, uses the facts of Hughes' life to illuminate the public poet and the private man. Everything is here, including—in response to claims in an earlier biography—a denial that Hughes was homosexual. Though handled frankly and tastefully, this continued discussion of Hughes' sexuality seems unnecessarily intrusive. Of more consequence are the details of Hughes' wanderings, his publications, his fervent (though not always well-reasoned) socialist leanings, and his involvement with and support of the members of the Harlem Renaissance with whom he is most often linked (though his career easily outspans any of that group), as well as younger writers such as Wright, Ralph Ellison, Margaret Walker and Alice Walker. Throughout this comprehensive and enthralling account of Hughes' life and his development as a writer, Rampersad offers a precise assessment of his work and its importance. In fact, this may be the best biography of a black writer we have had.

In forging his individual style, Hughes broke with the genteel tradition of Afro-American letters. His contemporary Countee Cullen used elevated forms such as the sonnet for his similarly elevated subject matter; Hughes early wrote in free verse, perhaps helped, Rampersad speculates, by the examples of Walt Whitman and Carl Sandburg. He soon came to use black common speech and to write of ordinary people—his ***Fine Clothes to the Jew,*** which Rampersad calls Hughes' "most brilliant book of poems, and one of the more astonishing books of verse ever published in the United States," was soundly criticized, not because of its title, but because many found his portraits of gamblers, musicians and prostitutes offensive. Though Hughes occasionally wrote in dialect that aped the work of Paul Laurence Dunbar, his mature style was simple and elegant, framed with the rhythm, tone and color of the blues. And, unlike Dunbar, he never felt that in using the vernacular he had betrayed his talents.

In this regard—creating art that in content and form fall "deliberately within the range of authentic blues emotion and blues culture"—Hughes proves an important international influence. Nicolás Guillén, the national poet of Cuba, began on Hughes' advice to use the rhythms of the drum-based, call-and-response *son* in his work; Léopold Sédar Senghor and Léon Damas would cite him as essential to their development of the French African and Caribbean literary movement-cum-philosophy known as *Negritude*.

Hughes' writing was of course important to him. He clung to it with remarkable tenacity—though he slipped more than once on his tightrope, he always recovered—for it gave him his sense of himself and provided his links with other blacks. To put it simply, writing was all Hughes had.

His background included courageous and distinguished men: His grandmother's first husband died of wounds received in John Brown's momentous raid on Harper's Ferry and as a child, Hughes slept under his bullet-riddled shawl. His great-uncle was John Mercer Langston, "the first black American to hold office . . . by popular vote," lawyer, U.S. minister to Haiti, acting president of Howard University, and congressman from Virginia. But while Hughes grew up hearing of the deeds of those who had come before him, his immediate family life was the kind which produces broken, unfulfilled men.

His mother longed to act on the stage; lacking talent, she resorted to theatricality in her own life. His parents' marriage did not last, and he spent much of his childhood with his grandmother in Lawrence, Kansas. His mother married again, this time to an itinerant "chef cook," and when Hughes was reunited with her after his grandmother's death, the family moved from town to town. He spent much of his high school years in Cleveland, living alone when his mother fled in search of his stepfather.

Hughes seems to have seen his natural father fewer than a half-dozen times, and they were always in conflict. He would write of him, "My father hated Negroes. I think he hated himself, too, for being a Negro." It was a view of the world and himself that Hughes could not countenance. The richness of his grandmother's legacy compensated for the paucity of parental love in his life—in her house he learned black history, racial pride and, just as important, black folkways. It is not insignificant, then, that Hughes wrote **"The Negro Speaks of Rivers,"** the race- *and* self-affirming poem that would first bring him to wide notice, while on a train en route to Mexico and a year with the father he already knew he hated. . . . (pp. 1-2)

If Hughes was "anxious for love and a settled identity," he found it in his relationship with his black audience. He wanted, he wrote in his journals, "To create a Negro culture in America—a real, solid, sane racial something growing out of the folk life, not copied from another, even though surrounding race." In his elevation of black folk forms, he succeeded as well or better than his contemporaries or any of those who have come after him. (p. 2)

David Nicholson, "Langston Hughes: Lives of the Poet," in Book World—The Washington Post, *January 4, 1987, pp. 1-2.*

CHRISTOPHER HITCHENS

[*Hitchens, an English political journalist who is Washington correspondent for the* Nation, *is the author of* Inequalities in Zimbabwe *(1981) and* Cyprus *(1984). In the following excerpt Hitchens commends Rampersad's portrayal of Hughes's inner struggles and conflicts.*]

Langston Hughes was born to struggle. Not only was he born black in the era of Jim Crow, but he was born to a family that was extremely conscious of its responsibilities to 'The Race.'

His grandmother's first husband had fallen with John Brown at Harper's Ferry, and the infant Langston was made to sleep under his bullet-riddled shawl. His great-uncle, John Mercer Langston, was that rarity, an elected black Congressman (and the American minister to Haiti). The fact that Langston Hughes's immediate family was poor, divided and self-hating by contrast with these paragons was a fact that could only increase his self-consciousness—both as a poet and as a political animal.

Arnold Rampersad's finely written and carefully researched book [***The Life of Langston Hughes, Vol. I: I, Too, Sing America***] does not say so explicitly, but makes it clear that Hughes had no talent for politics. He was in effect compelled to take stands. As a conspicuously bright student he spent much time in white schools and classes, and had little choice but to bear himself bravely when subjected to vulgar abuse and discrimination. We learn from Rampersad that he was introduced to the Marxist classics by Jewish fellow-students who were his allies against bigotry. As a political *poet,* Hughes made a distinct impression with **'Goodbye Christ' and 'Good Morning Revolution,'** as well as with plays on the Scottsboro case and other outrages of racialism. But as a political *animal* he merely served as a black ornament to the legion of Thirties fellow-travellers.

Hughes in Carmel, California, about 1935. John D. Short, Jr.

The nadir was probably his signature on a pro-Stalin round robin in the *Daily Worker* at the time of the purges. The most pathetic was certainly his attempt to form a workers' theatre company with Whittaker Chambers. So, despite some good moments in Spain and a stirring and moving speech (quoted at length here) at the famous anti-fascist writers' meeting in Paris, he was not an original. He kept seeking the private and personal life that circumstances had denied him, and it is in mapping this search that Rampersad makes his claim as a skilled biographer.

Above all, Hughes was black. His best essay, **'The Negro Artist and the Racial Mountain,'** which appeared in *The Nation* in 1926, was an appeal for writers and performers to be themselves. Hughes became the clearest and most appealing voice of the Harlem Renaissance by arguing for the integrity of jazz, the blues of Bessie Smith and the boom of Paul Robeson. As Rampersad writes: 'On each of the few occasions in his life when his internal pressures proved too great to bear, the cause would be private rather than racial.'

This may appear at first sight to be a distinction without a difference, since most of Hughes's dilemmas arose directly out of such 'pressures' as his father wishing to be white. Still, it's a distinction that's usually made too little rather than too much. Hughes had a wretched time sexually, for example, and there is no evidence that colour played much of a part in his unhappiness. Rampersad leaves open the question of his homosexuality, and by including an erotic paean to a girl named Susanna Jones (written when Hughes was still at school) makes the mystery more absorbing.

Like a number of black American writers, Hughes could not decide whether he was an alienated African whose culture and history had been stripped from his people, or an American who was denied a full share in the national patrimony. . . .

Hughes took a square look at life all right, and knew what he was talking about. But he doesn't seem to have been able to resolve this conflict in his impulses. This volume closes with him 'broke and ruint' in a hospital in California, unwilling to admit that he had been stricken by anything so crude and unromantic as venereal disease.

Rampersad's book is a portrait of an age as well as a life study. There are well-drawn passages about Du Bois, about Mary McLeod Bethune, about the intellectual *macedoine* of *New Masses* and the Popular Front. But through it all comes the impression of a man who, driven to combat, would rather have been listening to Billie Holiday.

Christopher Hitchens, "Whitman's Darker Brother," in The Observer, *January 18, 1987, p. 22.*

ROBERT J. BUTLER

For many years a full and clear understanding of Langston Hughes' poetry has been obscured by a number of stereotypes which have clouded our view of his personal life. Labelling him as a failed radical, many critics have dismissed his poetry as lacking in sufficient nerve and energy. Others have regarded Hughes as a naive primitivist, arguing that his work is marred by a romantic softness and lack of intellectual substance. Still other critics have accused the poet of having sold out to several white patrons and have found his work lacking in the necessary militancy and "relevance."

Thanks to Arnold Rampersad's excellent biography [***The Life of Langston Hughes, Vol. I, 1902-1941: I, Too, Sing America***], these stereotypes have finally been put to rest. As a result, doors to Hughes's writing have been opened which have heretofore been closed or only slightly ajar. The Langston Hughes who emerges from this study is an extremely complex, enigmatic figure whose life eludes any easy formulations. On the surface "charming," "innocent," and even pliant, Hughes was in fact a painfully divided man whose art sprang from the psychic tensions of his fascinating life. Unlike other scholars who have located these tensions in the pressures exerted on Hughes by a racist world, Rampersad convincingly argues that the key divisions in Hughes's mind are traceable to an anguished family life: "Hughes' (sic) greatest psychological wound had been inflicted not by racism but by parental neglect." Caught between a father who hated blacks and a mother who never understood him, Hughes developed an art which was "anchored" in equally strong desires to celebrate the black life that his father despised and to search for the sort of love which his mother was never able to supply.

The book is filled with many other fresh insights. Hughes's crucially important friendships with Arna Bontemps and Carl Van Vechten are probed in meticulous detail. His problematical relationships with other Harlem Renaissance figures such as Alain Locke, Zora Neale Hurston, and Countee Cullen are examined honestly without the biases which have blurred earlier accounts of these relationships. And his unfortunate dealings with various white sponsors are viewed in an interesting way as part of the identity crisis brought on by Hughes's troubled family life.

Refusing to glamorize Hughes as a black "titan" who somehow transcended the commercialism of the world in which he lived, Rampersad admits that some of Hughes's work is deeply flawed because he occasionally "surrendered to the market place." But Rampersad also stresses that Hughes at his best was a major poet who radically altered the course of Afro-American literature.

There is little doubt that this superb book is the definitive critical biography of Hughes and that all successive work on Hughes will owe a heavy debt to Rampersad.

Robert J. Butler, in a review of "The Life of Langston Hughes, Volume I, 1902-1941," in Best Sellers, *Vol. 46, No. 11, February, 1987, p. 437.*

The Young Hemingway

by Michael Shane Reynolds

(For Ernest Hemingway: see also *CLC,* Vols. 1, 3, 6, 8, 10, 13, 19, 30, 34, 39, 41; *Contemporary Authors,* Vols. 77-80; *Dictionary of Literary Biography,* Vols. 4, 9; *Dictionary of Literary Biography Yearbook:* 1981; and *Dictionary of Literary Biography Documentary Series,* Vol. 1.)

An Excerpt from *The Young Hemingway*

From the Italian war he brought back a pistol and a bottle of kummel shaped like a bear: authentic trophies. In his damaged leg he still carried bits of metal, equally authentic. If the war had not been so glorious as advertised, its true experience was still instructional: the whores in the government brothels who teased him for blushing; the taste of grappa; the faces of men bleeding to death; the sound of in-coming artillery; the blue eyes of a nurse; the smell of his own blood; the way dead bodies bloated in the sun. In less than a year he had become a charter member of modern times.

On this day, homeward bound, he was both more and less sure of himself than when he had left. His short war—barely three weeks at the front line—was undigested. The seven months in Italy, most of them in the Milan hospital, exposed him to a life for which he had been unprepared. He had seen and done things impossible in Oak Park. Duty drivers had not needed a father's permission to risk their lives on shell-pocked roads. Thrown in among older men, he was accepted as an equal with the privileges of an officer. In the cafes and clubs of Milan, he drank the wines, the cognacs and beers that Oak Park railed against. It had been good. And an older woman, eight years older, loved him, promised to marry him. She, too, thought him older than nineteen. He let her think so, inventing himself as he went along. They kissed as he had not kissed a girl before, lived a little recklessly, betting on the San Siro races, trying new foods in the Galleria. The world, he now knew, was larger than he had imagined; more various than he had dreamed. The moment his foot touched the Jersey pier, he was caught between two lives—the invented one he had been living and the old one waiting for him in Oak Park. Vaguely he must have known that this was the end of something.

Never again would he be the novice, never again play the innocent. During his three months on the Kansas City *Star* and during his tour in Italy, he learned that only experienced men were respected. A man must seem capable, knowledgeable and self-reliant even if, at his core, he was not. As precisely as he had studied the Chuckwill's Widow and the lake trout, he studied men's voices and their attitudes. Whomever he studied, he could imitate. He could be whomever he imagined himself to be.

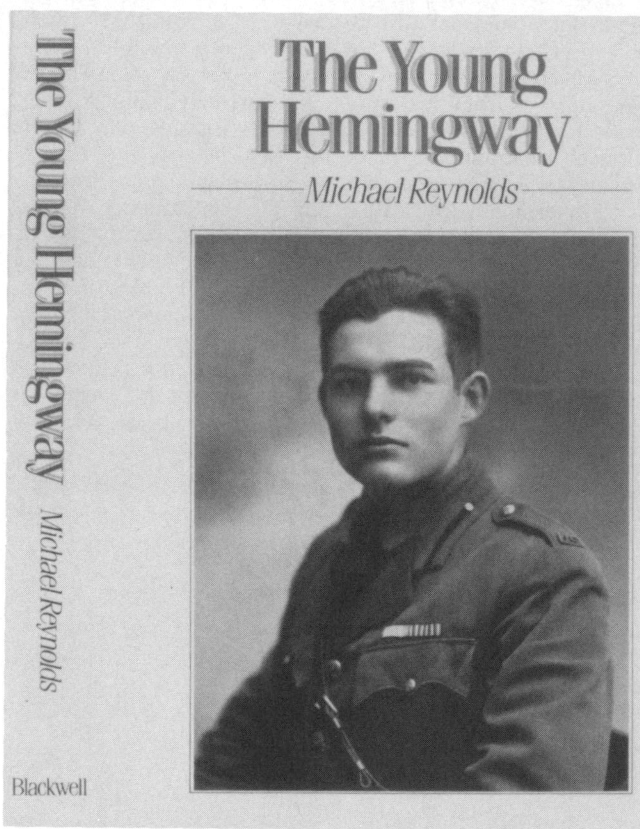

Dust jacket of The Young Hemingway, *by Michael Reynolds. Basil Blackwell, 1986. Jacket by Miller, Craig and Cocking Design Partnership.*

JOHN M. McINERNEY

In the years since his suicide in 1961, Ernest Hemingway, a Nobel Prize winner and arguably the most celebrated American author since Mark Twain, has proved to be an easy target. His distinctive style, with its repetitions and short clauses, is easy to parody, as Dwight MacDonald and others have demonstrated with devastating effect; the famous "Hemingway code" soon seemed more like existential bull, and his very public persona, with its macho posturing, began to echo hollowly.

Now, however, we see the need for another reappraisal. Some analysts are finding new depths and surprises behind the bearded, blustering façade. For example, Professor Michael Reynolds's

Hemingway and his father Doctor Hemingway, Grace, Ursula, Sunny, and Marcelline, in a Hemingway family portrait from around 1910.

new literary biography, ***The Young Hemingway***, maintains convincingly that one deliberately camouflaged source of the "Papa" Hemingway we all came to know was Oak Park, Illinois.

Reynolds's study, which focuses on three critical years from early 1919 to the end of 1922, draws upon some newly mined primary sources, like the unpublished letters of Hadley Richardson Hemingway (his first wife), as well as standard material. Using resources as various as back issues of the Oak Leaves newspaper and the minutes of Board of Education meetings, Reynolds also evokes the cultural environment to which Ernest Hemingway, a teenaged, wounded survivor of World War I service in Italy, returned in January of 1919.

That environment was a middle-class enclave on the outskirts of Chicago with a split personality. On the one hand, Oak Parkers were deeply conservative, determined to preserve fundamental values and a genteel lifestyle. On the other hand, they saw life as a contest, and they wanted Oak Park to be first in everything, from football, to the latest inventions, to the number of war heroes. Their enduring hero was Theodore Roosevelt, and they heartily endorsed his muscular Christian morality and commitment to strenuous activity.

Reynolds shows that Hemingway carried that outlook with him as he moved uncertainly through these maturing years, at the end of which he sailed off to Paris and his literary destiny. Reynolds's narrative technique, which employs many flashback and flash forward passages, occasionally becomes a bit confusing and repetitious, but he manages to make Hemingway's various transitions, from scared adventure-seeker to self-invented war hero, from rebellious son in a troubled household to alienated adult, from clumsy romantic imitating Kipling to apprentice writer learning from Sherwood Anderson, and from inexperienced student of Havelock Ellis to young husband, both clear and significant.

Ernest Hemingway never wrote about Oak Park, and after 1922 he didn't really try to go home again, but in many respects he never left. (pp. 458-59)

> *John M. McInerney, in a review of "The Young Hemingway," in* Best Sellers, *Vol. 45, No. 12, March, 1986, pp. 458-59.*

JOHN CHAMBERLAIN, JR.

In the recent spate of Hemingway books and biographies, Michael Reynolds's study of Hemingway from his early youth to the time just before his expatriate years is a welcome addition. Rendered in realistic but affectionate strokes, ***The Young Hemingway*** gently shaves the hair from Hemingway's chest. We see him as an impressionable youngster growing up in upper-crust Oak Park, Ill., inspired by the he-man ethics of Teddy Roosevelt. He is deeply influenced by town values and parental conflicts, and creates an image of a limping, shell-shocked war veteran rather than the one of the chocolate-delivering ambulance driver he was. On the dedication page Mr. Reynolds quotes from T. S. Eliot, "the end precedes the beginning." While Eliot may be a bit mystical for the gutsy Hemingway, the passage refers to the way Hemingway consciously created his image—he filled the shell from the inside out. The armor squeaks: we catch him lying about his age even to his lovers, limping excessively down gangplanks on his return from war, borrowing and embellishing war stories, becoming an overnight boxing expert, exaggerating his illnesses and, in short, making himself part of what he wrote—fiction. The book is not derisive but provides insight into a struggling human being. Mr. Reynolds, a professor of English at North Carolina State University, also shows Hemingway the writer, his early imitations and subsequent rejections of popular literature, his determination to succeed, Sherwood Anderson's benign influence on the way he lived and his ultimate decision to go to Paris. The book is both informative and entertaining. (pp. 24-5)

> *John Chamberlain, Jr., in a review of "The Young Hemingway," in* The New York Times Book Review, *March 9, 1986, pp. 24-5.*

JACKSON R. BRYER

[*American critic and editor, Bryer is the author of several books, including* The Critical Reputation of F. Scott Fitzgerald: A Bibliographical Study *(1967), and* Conversations with Lillian Hellman *(1986). In the following excerpt Bryer finds that despite his narrow focus and occasionally irritating novelistic tone, Reynolds presents a convincing picture of the young Hemingway.*]

Reynolds has usefully mined Oak Park newspaper files to show how its most famous son superficially repressed (he never explicitly set any of his fiction in Oak Park) but subliminally reflected the town's paradoxical response to the rapidly encroaching modern age: "the New so necessary for Progress, which all admired, was equally a threat to the Status Quo, which all admired." . . . This is reflected in Hemingway's fiction, Reynolds observes, where the "style and subject matter are Modern; his structure and plot line are traditional" . . . ; it

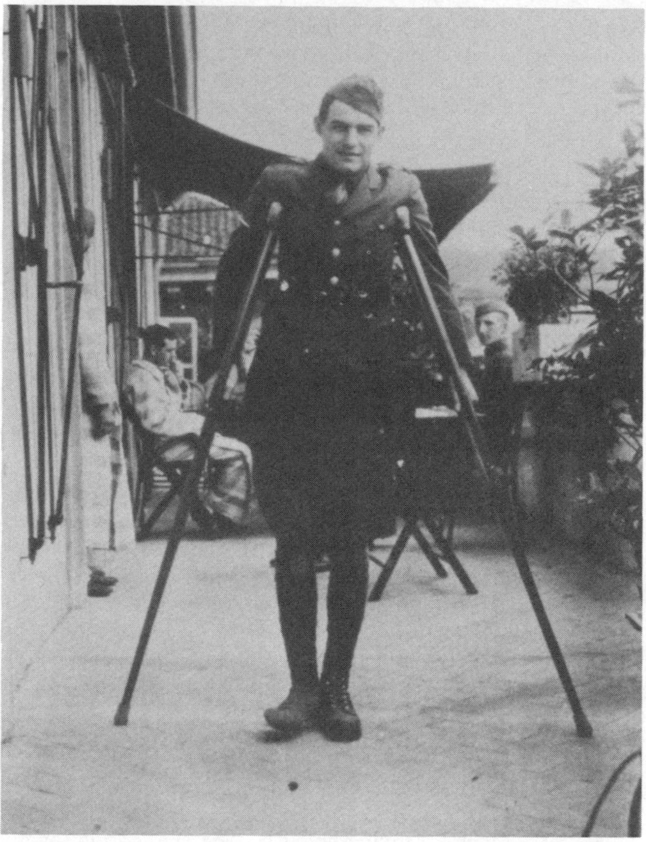

Hemingway in 1918, recuperating at a hospital in Milan, Italy. Prints and Photographs Division, Library of Congress.

is also present, as he notes, in his conservative and rather puritanical views on sex and marriage.

Reynolds has found worthwhile new family correspondence which reveals that Grace Hall Hemingway was a spiritualist . . . and documents the strong possibility that Clarence Edmonds Hemingway suffered from recurrent bouts of mental depression which began as early as 1903, when Ernest was four. . . . This correspondence also discloses the important presence in the Hemingway home of Ruth Arnold, a live-in voice student and companion of Grace's, who was eventually banished from the household by Dr. Hemingway under mysterious circumstances, and who, despite the fact that she lived with the family for eleven years, is not mentioned in any of the book-length reminiscences of Ernest's siblings. . . . Reynolds' account points up the continuous tensions within the family without assigning blame, suggesting that Ernest's later much publicized accusations against his mother may well represent sublimations of his very complicated feelings towards both his parents, especially his inability to face the truth about his father's mental illness and eventual suicide. (pp. 270-71)

Reynolds is especially persuasive in indicating how Hemingway altered the facts of his youth in retelling them later in life, whether it was in his fiction or in auto-biographical statements. Noting that "his most interesting creation was his self," Reynolds shows how Hemingway falsified the story of his wounding, invented stories about his family, and continually deceived Hadley about details of his background and activities during their courtship. His point, which is a good one, is that "whatever Truth he had to tell us was in the fiction.". . . (p. 272)

[Reynolds'] focus is narrow and impressionistic; . . . he omits a good deal which he doesn't feel is relevant to his purpose. And he tends to adopt a highly novelistic tone which can be irritating at times:

> By summer's end the Sturgeon river trout were wary, the days hot and the nights laden with mosquitoes. The trout season was about to close, but it did not matter. If a man loved a river deeply enough, nothing else mattered. The Sturgeon, the Black, the Fox, each bend and pool, the curl of water moving across the sunken log, the glitter of water all silver in the afternoon, the murmur at evening with the feeding trout raising circled ripples on the blue-black slick of it: all as he remembered and would remember always. . . .

But, while one may fault Reynolds for passages like this, his picture of the early Hemingway rings very true. (pp. 273-74)

Jackson R. Bryer, "Hemingway: A Thrice-Told Tale," in Novel: A Forum on Fiction, *Vol. 19, No. 3, Spring, 1986, pp. 270-74.*

ALLEN JOSEPHS

Michael Reynolds's ***The Young Hemingway,*** a short literary biography . . . , charts new biographical territory. Reynolds, who in ***Hemingway's First War*** demonstrated indisputably that most of ***A Farewell to Arms*** was not autobiographical, shows us what second-generation biographical critics can achieve. By writing well-conceived essays around specific important moments in the young writer's life, he avoids having to make unsound suppositions about what we cannot know. He criticizes Hemingway not to condemn him for his faults, but to show how as a writer he was able to transcend them.

Reynolds has assiduously researched Hemingway's family background and the collective attitudes of early twentieth-century Oak Park, Illinois, the hometown he would abandon but whose influence he could never escape. His conclusions illuminate as no previous work the forces and ideas, the aspirations and convictions, that coalesced in the young Hemingway. By purposely avoiding a chronological format, he is able to use the past to adumbrate the future, to describe a life that would at times overcome its failures through fiction. Whether tracing the influence of Teddy Roosevelt or Einstein on Hemingway, or discussing the often disturbing family history of the Hemingways, Reynolds pieces together a believable portrait of the young man and helps us understand why we are so fascinated by Hemingway's personal and artistic career. (p. 21)

Allen Josephs, "In Papa's Garden," in Boston Review, *Vol. XI, No. 3, June, 1986, pp. 20-1.*

JULIAN SYMONS

[An English writer, Symons has been highly praised for his contributions to the genres of biography and detective fiction. His popular biographies of Charles Dickens, Thomas Carlyle, and Edgar Allan Poe are considered excellent introductions to those writers. Symons is better known, however, for such crime novels as The Immaterial Murder Case *(1945),* The Thirty-First of February *(1950), and* The Criminal Comedy of the Contented Couple

(1985). In the following excerpt Symons finds Reynolds's book to be an excellent, though partial, account of Hemingway's early development. Symons further contends that while Hemingway created a unique writing style, his narrow interests provided few subjects.]

A sickly and neurotic family, the children of Dr Clarence Hemingway and Grace Hall, something wrong with almost all of them. Of the five children, Ernest and two of his sisters, Marcelline and Ursula, suffered from blinding headaches and insomnia. Ernest, his much younger brother Leicester and Marcelline all had weak, light-sensitive eyes. Ernest had high blood pressure, Marcelline low. Both suffered from diabetes, and so did Leicester. Bouts of severe depression affected them all, as they did their father. At least three killed themselves. Ernest put the muzzle of his shotgun to his head and pulled the trigger in 1961, five years later Ursula took an overdose of drugs after three cancer operations, Leicester after five operations shot himself in 1982. Marcelline's death in 1963 was said to be from natural causes, but Leicester suspected she had killed herself. Their father had set the example. In 1928 Dr Hemingway, distressed by money problems, diabetes, and all sorts of neuroses, had shot himself. (pp. 85-6)

Reynolds's book [***The Young Hemingway***] is excellent, a detailed realization of family background and Oak Park life. It is particularly good about Hemingway's slow development from the intelligent awkward cub journalist on a Kansas paper who joined the Missouri Home Guard, volunteered for War service like a good Oak Parker (although as a Red Cross driver, not a fighting soldier), and came back still a literary innnocent, his chief influences Ring Lardner, O. Henry and short stories in the *Saturday Evening Post*. It should be added that Reynolds's book gives only a partial picture, deliberately ignoring Hemingway's war service and his affair with the nurse Agnes von (or perhaps not von) Kurowsky. (p. 86)

Hadley Richardson on the day of her wedding, September 3, 1921. From The Young Hemingway, *by Michael Reynolds. Basil Blackwell, 1986.*

Hemingway is the classic modern case of a writer who created a style but lacked suitable subjects. It was Europe, one may say, that taught him to write, even though his tutors were American, but what was he to write about? He had no interest in other people except so far as they affected himself, no political beliefs, little cultural background. His subject was himself and the physical actions, often involving violence, that excited him. ***The Sun Also Rises*** survives as the first full flowering of the developed Hemingway style, the romantic version of his wartime experience in ***A Farewell to Arms*** plus the restraint of the style make this a moving novel, in many of the short stories style and subjects are perfectly married. (Generally the style works best in short stretches.) The rest is second-rate or secondhand as the style becomes affected or goes soggy with sentiment, the whole offering much rhetorical sound but little substance.

Perhaps the real subjects were back in Oak Park and in the family, but those were areas he forbade himself to touch or look at. In 1924 five copies of ***In Our Time*** were ordered by the Hemingway family from the Parisian publisher, then returned without explanation. Two years later his mother wrote to him scornfully about ***The Sun Also Rises,*** saying that every page filled her with a sick loathing, and that it was a doubtful honour to have produced one of the filthiest books of the year. In the years of fame and money, Reynolds tells us, Hemingway created for himself Oak Park households with large lawns, swimming pools, servants, but such places never entered his fiction, and he never returned to Oak Park, after his father's funeral. (p. 88)

Julian Symons, "Regarding the Master," in London Magazine, *n.s. Vol. 26, No. 3, June, 1986, pp. 85-8.*

WILFRID SHEED

[Sheed is an English-born American critic, fiction writer, and biographer whose works are marked by his erudition and wit. He is the son of Frank Sheed and Maisie Ward, founders of the Catholic publishing house of Sheed and Ward. The author of such works as Transatlantic Blues *(1978) and* Frank and Maisie: A Memoir with Parents *(1985), Sheed has served as a columnist for the* New York Times *since 1971. In the following excerpt he discusses Hemingway's earliest literary influences.]*

In such cases [as Hemingway's], one sometimes feels that, with so many influences latent in his work, there is hardly room for the author himself. But every writer starts off as a compendium, or revised anthology, and it is particularly useful to know that Hemingway was no exception. To hear him tell it himself, Hemingway only entered his famous ring with very dead Europeans. He never even deigned to put on the gloves with Dickens or (the bout I would like most to have seen) with George Eliot. So it is interesting to hear what he actually did read in his formative years.

According to Michael Reynolds, an old Hemingway hand who is content to cut off small slices (his last book was called ***Hemingway's First War***), Ernest first actually got into the ring

Hemingway and his wife Hadley in the autumn of 1921 with Doctor Hemingway, Leicester, Sunny, Grace, Carol, and Marcelline. From The Young Hemingway, *by Michael Reynolds. Basil Blackwell, 1986.*

with the *Saturday Evening Post,* which as late as 1919 was still his model for fiction. And his first opponent was not Flaubert at all, but one E. W. Howe, who wrote a serial called "Anthology of Another Town." Howe's sketches of small-town life would soon be superseded by Ernest's discovery of Sherwood Anderson's *Winesburg, Ohio*. But Reynolds makes the point that this kind of writing had been in the American air for some time, from Hamlin Garland through Edgar Lee Masters, and that this was the air that young Hemingway breathed first and deepest.

There is, of course, no doubt whatever that he later read the European masters, and learned a bit of this and a bit of that from them. But trying to stuff them all into his own literary pedigree seems just a characteristic display of *le snobisme*. Can anyone reading ***Up in Michigan*** really think he is watching a contest with Turgenev? It is probably commoner than not for great writers to be influenced by nobodies, the first food they eat. Pulp writers (as they are aptly called) churn out a kind of featureless, interchangeable *materia prima* which is often more malleable to the hands of genius than the works of other geniuses are likely to be. Studying under a master, you can only imitate him, feebly or well, and eventually pray for your release; but with Captain Marryat you can do whatever you like. (p. 12)

Wilfrid Sheed, "A Farewell to Hemingstein," in The New York Review of Books, *Vol. XXXIII, No. 10, June 12, 1986, pp. 5-6, 8, 10, 12.*

JAMES CAMPBELL

[*Scottish journalist, novelist, and nonfiction writer, Campbell has served as political correspondent for both the* Scottish Daily Record *and the* Glasgow Daily Record. *He is the author of several books, including* Bomber Raid *(1978) and* Essays in Anglo-Saxon History, 400-1200 *(1986). In the following excerpt Campbell finds the "flashback/flashforward" structure of Reynolds's biography disorienting, but praises his work for its "rare" portrayal of the young man who would become the writer. Campbell also discusses the reasons behind the development and eventual decline of Hemingway's writing.*]

It is rare, as well as at times being difficult, to see clearly the young man who was raised in the posh Chicago suburb of Oak Park, became a reporter as a prelude to being a writer, offered his services to the Red Cross in wartime, and always fell in love with older women. . . . Michael Reynolds's ***The Young Hemingway*** [is] therefore welcome. . . .

Reynolds uses what his publishers call a "flashback/flashforward technique", which often seems like no more than a disorientating tendency to leap about in time. . . .

Somewhere in the midst of all his activity Hemingway lost his talent. The roots of that loss are possibly sunk in the same ground from which the talent flourished: the First World War, a traumatic event from which he returned with 227 leg wounds and a limp which gradually became a swagger. Hemingway's work thereafter throve on action and woundings (and also, as

Scott Fitzgerald said, on women: "***A Farewell to Arms*** is a big book. If there's another big book I think we'll find Ernest has another wife"). The action seemed, to Hemingway, to give men's lives substance; the injuries to lend them tragedy. He would have written about death even if he had not come close to it in the war, but no doubt less profoundly and less precisely; his experience on the battlefield empowered him to see death as a living presence, and this presence inhabits all his best work. . . .

Reynolds reports that, back in Oak Park, he kept on wearing a uniform (to which he was not entitled anyway) long after everyone else had given theirs up. In effect, he kept wearing it for the rest of his life. Hemingway understood combat: he excelled in describing not so much the thrill and horror of battle (though on occassions that too) but the hopelessness of the individual caught up in it. The best writing he did is contained in the often oblique war novels and stories of the 1920s: ***In Our Time, The Sun Also Rises, Men Without Women*** and ***A Farewell to Arms***—ordered by chronology and also pretty much by merit. It is frequently remarked, in reference to his later works, that Hemingway wrote like one of his own imitators—but no imitator wrote as badly as he was capable of doing in the 1930s and 40s.

In the 1920s, in order to mix the material the First World War had given him into his boyhood experience of the lakes and woods, Hemingway developed a prose which was directly responsible to sensation, which registered minor alterations in mood, and was alert to the nuances of weather, taste and smell. It is a style that is responsive to the new cinematic age—in that it was prepared to leave out what the screen could show better—and it is, above all, a style which permits its narrative user to avoid confronting his inner emptiness. (p. 837)

As he later began to write more about the chance of glory which war offered to the outer man, leaving behind its catastrophic effects on the inner, the style became over-ripe. He never properly recaptured it until ***A Moveable Feast,*** a book written with the aid of diaries kept in Paris in the 1920s. (p. 838)

James Campbell, "Arms and the Young Man," in The Times Literary Supplement, *No. 4,348, August 1, 1986, pp. 837-38.*

Evelyn Waugh: The Early Years, 1903-39

by Martin Stannard

(For Evelyn Waugh: see also *CLC*, Vols. 1, 3, 8, 13, 19, 27; *Contemporary Authors*, Vols. 25-28, rev. ed. [obituary], Vols. 85-88; and *Dictionary of Literary Biography*, Vol. 15.)

JOHN GROSS

[*Gross, an English critic and editor, was editor in chief of Gollancz from 1956 to 1958 and has been an editorial consultant to* The Observer *since 1965. His publications include* The Rise and Fall of the Man of Letters: A Study of the Idiosyncratic and the Humane in Modern Literature *(1969) and* James Joyce *(1970). In the following excerpt Gross describes* Evelyn Waugh: The Early Years *as a flawed biography that nonetheless offers worthwhile information about Waugh not covered in Christopher Sykes's 1975 study*.]

Martin Stannard's biography of Evelyn Waugh [***Evelyn Waugh: The Early Years, 1903-39***] is the first since Christopher Sykes's 11 years ago, and Mr. Sykes's account plainly left room for a more extensive portrait sooner or later: for all its virtues it was a pioneer effort, and necessarily incomplete.

Meanwhile, however, we have been presented with the ***Diaries*** and ***Letters*** and a succession of memoirs by Waugh's friends. The prospect of a long trudge across the same territory no longer seems quite as enthralling as it once did; and since Mr. Stannard, in his first volume, spends over 500 pages taking Waugh to the age of 36, it seems reasonable to begin by asking how much of what he has to tell us is really new.

He can claim one undoubted scoop (if you can still use the term in an Evelyn Waugh context without sounding absurd). The first Mrs. Waugh—the other Evelyn, now Mrs. Nightingale—has spoken to him about the break-up of her marriage to Waugh, and given an account of it that differs significantly from Christopher Sykes's version. According to Mr. Sykes, the final fortnight in which the couple tried to patch things up was a happy interlude which ended with Waugh leaving for the country, and then finding himself betrayed. According to Mrs. Nightingale, it was very far from happy, and ended with Waugh himself deciding that they should get divorced. About what basically went wrong with the marriage she maintains a decent reserve, but she did tell Mr. Stannard that 'Evelyn was not an affectionate person. I was.'

A number of Mr. Stannard's other informants offer interesting new perspectives. The late Lady Betjeman recalls being alarmed by Waugh's advances both before and after her marriage. Lady Mosley reveals that on one occasion in Dublin he met Yeats (though nothing memorable seems to have passed between them). Sir Alexander Glen sets right Waugh's brief account of an arduous expedition he and Waugh made to Spitzbergen in 1934.

Mr. Stannard has also tracked down some obscure sources, and drawn on a certain amount of previously unpublished material. He quotes an incisive passage from a letter, for example (not included in Mark Amory's edition of the letters), in which Waugh is drawn into defending his trade as a novelist by the moralistic attacks of the then editor of the *Tablet*. He has also been able to correct ***A Little Learning,*** Waugh's one volume of autobiography, at various points—showing, for instance, that the Victorian ancestor whom Waugh portrayed as an eminently respectable physician was in fact a successful quack.

Still, neither his interviews nor his delvings in the archives have produced any bombshells. For the most part he relies on readily available sources, and for large stretches he is reduced to offering little more than a competent paraphrase of Waugh himself—drawing on the diaries and letters in particular, and even more heavily, whenever Waugh ventures among remote peoples, on the travel books.

Since this generally involves adopting Waugh's point of view, he often gives the effect of speaking from a great height. 'Tennyson Jesse was a mere detective-story writer.' Says who—Waugh or Stannard? And when he adds a comment to his direct quotations from Waugh, it tends to labour the point. 'Don't tell Hazel I am back,' writes Waugh to a friend. 'It appears that he still wished to keep Hazel Lavery at a distance,' observes Mr. Stannard.

Even when he disagrees with Waugh, he finds it hard to fight clear of him. Faced with an idiotic generalisation, he will plead that at least it represents a genuine attempt on Waugh's part to form his own judgment. He admits that Waugh's admiring comparison between high-living settlers in Kenya and artists—because both groups were out of tune with their age—is one that 'somewhat strains credulity as a general principle.' Yes indeed. 'But,' he adds, 'it was something sincerely felt by Waugh.'

While Mr. Stannard is concerned to stress that Waugh was a serious artist, he doesn't go in for much analysis of the novels. Perhaps this is just as well, given his one major effort in this direction—a strained attempt to relate the themes of ***Decline and Fall*** to the influence of Bergson and Spengler. But he makes some good incidental points—on the element of self-portraiture in Waugh's account of Rossetti, for example—and puts a little-known futuristic story, **'Out of Depth,'** to particularly effective use in discussing the writer's frame of mind in the period immediately following his conversion to Catholicism.

Rather too much space, on the other hand, is devoted to recording Waugh's literary and political opinions: they were not the most interesting thing about him. But within its limits the picture Mr. Stannard paints of Waugh himself carries conviction, and he manages to convey at least something of the daemon which drove him on. 'The school was quite ordinary,' he writes of the original of Llanabba Castle. 'It was Waugh who was strange.'

The book would have benefited from some sharper editing. It contains quite a few minor errors; and Waugh himself would surely have had mixed feelings about seeing his style celebrated by a writer who thinks that 'vacillate' means the same thing as 'oscillate,' and who spells it 'vascillate' into the bargain.

John Gross, "On the Waugh-Path," in The Observer, *October 19, 1986, p. 26.*

ANTHONY QUINTON

[*Quinton, an English philosopher and critic, is president of Trinity College, Oxford. His works include* The Nature of Things *(1973) and* Thoughts and Thinkers *(1982). In the following excerpt Quinton contrasts Stannard's method in* Evelyn Waugh: The Early Years *with that of Christopher Sykes in his 1975 biography of the novelist.*]

Evelyn Waugh is not the first writer of his epoch to receive the honour of a two-volume biography. Even in death and from the viewpoint of ceremonial retrospection he has been once again pipped at the post by an Etonian: George Orwell, treated in two volumes by Abrahams and Stansky. But Orwell has been dead for 16 years longer and this book [***Evelyn Waugh: The Early Years, 1903-39***] has a Victorian amplitude that no book about Orwell has. It calls to mind Mrs. Moorman on Wordsworth in its unrelenting fullness of detail.

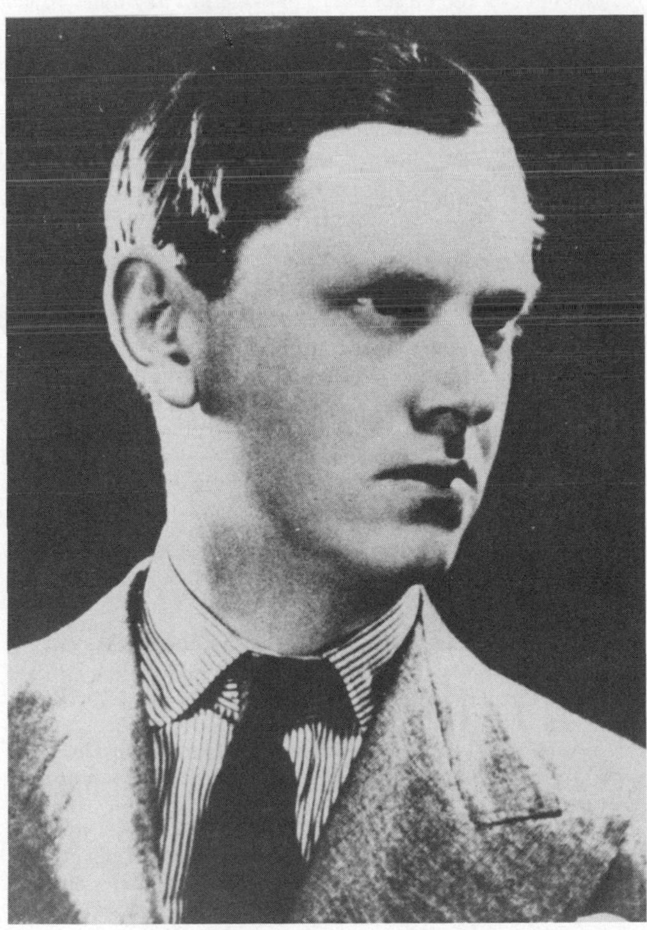

Waugh in his younger years. The Bettmann Archive, Inc.

At the outset Stannard gives proper courteous acknowledgement to Christopher Sykes, whose very thorough job on Waugh came out in 1975. He justifies giving twice as much space to their common subject's first 36 years by the consideration that much new evidence has come to light, or, which is much the same thing from the general reader's point of view, has become publishable, with the passage of time. Stannard is to Sykes much that Skidelsky has been to Harrod in the case of Keynes.

Thus it emerges that Waugh had some homosexual romances at Oxford, with the historian Richard Pares and, a more familiar friend, Alastair Graham (whose fearsome mother was the model for Lady Circumference). Stannard does not think he went all the way with Pares, judging their relationship to have been "idyllically Platonic". After the painful collapse of his brief marriage to Evelyn Gardner, affairs are recorded with Audrey, the daughter of the essayist E. V. Lucas, and with Hazel, the second, much younger wife of the fashionable painter, Sir John Lavery. We are provided with some base, but entertaining, glimpses of Waugh seeking to extricate himself from the tiresome retentiveness of the second of these ladies.

Sykes had access to all Waugh's papers, although his second wife asked him, understandably, not to quote from the love letters Waugh wrote to her. Stannard's method has been to work minutely through Waugh's own records of his life and then to seek to answer questions raised by that inquiry through interviews with surviving associates. A particular advantage he has enjoyed has been the opportunity to talk to Mrs. Nightingale, Waugh's first wife, which was not available to Sykes. Hitherto Waugh's natural resentment has tended to dominate accounts of the marital catastrophe. He was a difficult man with the typical aggressiveness of the very short: his young wife had been very ill and had gone through a lot from her fairly frightful mother to marry him; he had left her a great deal alone in order to get on with ***Vile Bodies.***

Another witness on whom Stannard has relied heavily has perhaps had a more distorting effect. The enduring vigour of Sir Harold Acton has tended to make Stannard represent Waugh as a moon circling round Acton as Jupiter. He who lives longest, it seems, gets to tell most of the story.

Sykes's book was mainly a straightforward chronicle of events and reactions. Stannard goes more thoroughly into the books. This is not simply in pursuit of biographically usable intimation. His main concern in these passages is with Waugh's ideas or outlook on the world generally. He finds it to be underlyingly consistent, despite the conversion to Catholicism and the effects of success and fame. He sees Waugh, persuasively, as persistently loyal to an ideal of order or structure, expressed at one level in his high moral valuation of craftsmanship (something he acquired in his early apprenticeship as a book illustrator) and at another in his sense of civilisation as an endangered inheritance from Rome, sustained by the Roman church against the destructive tides of humanist antinomianism.

More adventurously, he claims that the young Waugh was a student of Bergson and Spengler, two foreign worthies of whom there is no hint or inkling in Sykes. Of Captain Grimes, Stannard says that Waugh developed him "into an unmistakably Bergsonian protagonist". That is possibly rather a large structure to rear on a diary entry from Waugh's time at Lancing which records his reading Bergson.

The raw material on which the book is based is very intermittent. At some periods of his life Waugh recorded a great deal; at others practically nothing. In his early adult life he travelled a lot and, since he did so with the intention of writing it up for the reading public, he set down in full everything that happened. Stannard's text too faithfully corresponds to this distribution of recording energies. We follow Waugh step by step through various ghastly tropical places; Abyssinia, British Guiana; and an Arctic one: Spitzbergen. There are missed boats and trains, insect bites, digestive disturbances, corrupt and offensive customs officials and riverboat captains, to the point at which the after all very distinct personality of the traveller is almost obliterated.

Amid these *longueurs* there is much that is informative and much that is sensible, particularly the treatment of Waugh's relations with his kindly, fussy, deeply embarrassing father. In pursuit of his own asinine fancies Arthur Waugh failed to arrive at any reasonable relationship with his more gifted, but firmly noncricketing son, who hated being dumped at Lancing and not being properly prepared for a grander school. Stannard is level-headed about Waugh's fascination with aristocratic splendour, however moth-eaten, pointing out that it was kept in some sort of place by Waugh's artistic conscience, and did not lead him into sycophancy.

Martin Stannard has plainly been working for a long time on Waugh and, despite his preoccupation with his subject's general ideas, sees that he must be valued as a writer for the formal qualities of his work, as he himself constantly insisted. But little of Waugh's brilliance as a writer of English prose has rubbed off on his chronicler, despite respectful gestures from time to time. Can one really use the phrase "impish humour" without Arthur Marshall-style inverted commas? Of Waugh in the early 1930s he writes "he was persistently in the company of gilded youth and very much the smart man about town". There is some idiosyncratic French: *Cote d'Azure* and *soubriquet* (something that might be bestowed through a *soupirail* on a *soubrette,* no doubt).

Anthony Quinton, "Portrait of the Artist as a Short Man," in The Sunday Times, *London, November 2, 1986, p. 54.*

P. N. FURBANK

[*Furbank, an English biographer and critic, has received acclaim for his literary biographies, particularly his two-volume study of novelist E. M. Forster published in 1977 and 1978. His other works include* Samuel Butler, 1835-1902 *(1948) and* Unholy Pleasure: The Idea of Social Class *(1985). In the following excerpt Furbank characterizes* Evelyn Waugh: The Early Years *as an adequate biography of the novelist.*]

Standing back from the first volume of Martin Stannard's new biography of Evelyn Waugh [***Evelyn Waugh: The Early Years, 1903-39***] one registers the impression that, for good or evil, it is a discussion rather than a narrative. The story-line is present, indeed, but so often interrupted by argumentation over issues of fact, by summaries of Waugh's writings and by critical analyses, that we might be reading a life of some classic author (Wordsworth or Cicero) with the outlines of whose life we are expected to be familiar. This is not necessarily a criticism of Stannard, for it may be inherent in the whole genre of the "critical biography"—always in some respects an awkward one; and he has certainly amassed a great deal of new information, much of it unavailable to Waugh's earlier biographer Christopher Sykes, and can fairly claim in certain directions to be "setting the record straight". He gives us, for the first time, the views of Waugh's first wife on the breakdown of their marriage—also an account of Waugh's love-life during the ensuing years, when he suffered an unrequited passion for Teresa Jungman and was pursued, to his discomfort, by Sir John Lavery's wife. We also get, in some detail, the very good story of Waugh as Arctic explorer in Spitzbergen: his intense contempt for pemmican and skis and his ineradicable conviction of re-enacting the last days of Captain Scott.

As so often with biographies, one is brought up rather short by what is said about "heredity". It would not be fair to tease Stannard, or no more than very mildly, for holding that people inherit things like "a talent for water-colour painting"—for this is a belief dear to so many biographers. Still, it is a very odd and benighted belief, and one certainly unknown to genetic science. It is reassuring to find that Evelyn Waugh himself found it comical. "Ignorant of fashions in biological theory we still look to heredity—as our forebears looked to the stars—as the source of character", he wrote in ***A Little Learning.*** "When one of the young misbehaves, we muse: 'How like her poor uncle'; when one shows talent, we ask: 'Now where does he get that from?' and daily give intuitive assent to a proposition which confounds our reason."

Where perhaps one has more right to challenge Stannard, since he is in the business of re-interpreting Waugh, is for perpetuating certain cherished but false myths. There is for instance the gloss put on the most famous passage in ***Vile Bodies*** which makes it Waugh's *Waste Land* and an announcement of apocalyptic despair:

> "Oh, Nina, *what a lot of parties.*"
>
> (. . . Masked parties, Savage parties, Victorian parties, Greek parties, Wild West parties, Russian parties, Circus parties, parties where one had to dress as somebody else, almost naked parties in St. John's Wood, parties in flats and studios and houses and ships and hotels and night clubs, in windmills and swimming baths, tea parties at school where one ate muffins and meringues and tinned crab, parties at Oxford where one drank brown sherry and smoked Turkish cigarettes, dull dances in London and comic dances in Scotland and disgusting dances in Paris—all that succession and repetition of massed humanity. . . . Those vile bodies. . . .)

Stannard endorses the "apocalyptic" interpretation, remarking that the passage is a late interpolation, possibly influenced by the breakdown of Waugh's first marriage; and he implicitly associates it with his religious conversion.

Now it does not need very close attention to the passage to see that this will hardly do; "tea parties at school where one ate muffins and meringues and tinned crab": these affectionate words are not the ones in which a prophet announces apocalypse or turns his back upon Sodom and Gomorrah. Nor, presumably, if Waugh really had conceived a religious horror of his earlier way of life or was thenceforth to write in "outrage at a culturally degraded society", would he have gone on frequenting frivolous society or writing frivolous novels—as he did, for ***Scoop*** is no less frivolous than ***Vile Bodies*** and ***Put Out More Flags*** not much less so; his "religious" novel ***Helena*** is remorselessly bright and frivolous; and frivolous, in a sense, is even ***The Ordeal of Gilbert Pinfold.***

It is a mistake to come down too heavily on frivolity. For a frivolousness permitting of hints of compunction and glimpses of the tragic is, in Waugh's hands, a considerable artistic achievement; and it could only be sustained by a man still, and always, half in love with frivolity. . . .

A word about humour is in place here. There is much to be said against Waugh as a man; his arrogance, snobbery and unkindness sometimes grow quite horrific. But his humour, so far as one can see, remained oddly innocent. (It was, we gather, the saving grace of his family life.) As Stannard rightly suggests, one cannot rule out the possiblity that his prolonged persecution of his sometime Oxford tutor Cruttwell helped eventually to drive the poor man insane. His motives, at all events, were pretty nasty; but the form of the joke—to spend so much time *barking* under Cruttwell's windows—does just something to soften the offence.

Of course neither André Gide nor Thomas Mann would have gone barking under windows; and this puts one in mind of an illuminating remark by Martin Green in *Children of the Sun:* "throughout the period, including the years of political seriousness and left-wing commitment, English popular taste, even at the level of the popular press, was in alliance with the dandy aesthetes, in one important phase of sensibility, the sense of humour. The snob-aesthete Evelyn Waugh was closer to the mass audience of England than would seem to a foreigner credible." Martin Green's label "dandy aesthete" for Waugh strikes me as extremely helpful; but we need to add the rider "renegade aesthete". One remembers Yeats's complaint to Aubrey Beardsley that modern artists were abandoning beauty for humour, and Waugh is a latter-day case in point. As a draughtsman he dabbled in "amusing" pastiches of Nolde and Wyndham Lewis, and as a novelist he glimpsed something new that could be done by an extreme paring-away of all fictional elements apart from dialogue; but, unlike his master Ronald Firbank, he soon gave up any ambition towards radical "modernist" innovation and focused his great gifts on pleasing and entertaining the larger British public—one which found his outrageousness just of the kind that they could understand and relish. This was no prostitution of his talents, merely a drawing of limits and narrowing of horizons. He was the sort of man (Max Beerbohm was another) who takes very exact stock of his own abilities; and the mixture in him of unbridled worldly ambition with level-headed modesty as an artist is caught, if unkindly, in his own description of Constantius in ***Helena:***

> Constantius in his own eyes fell short of perfection. His talents comprised all that was needed—no more; a representative collection, not unique, but adequate; he would make do. His need was simple; not today, not tomorrow, but soon, sometime before he grew too old to make proper use of it, Constantius wanted the World.

Stannard's overall picture of Waugh's life is that "In early manhood he was swept along, at times in a hallucinatory daze, despair following on disappointment. Later he exercised a degree of control by inventing protective masks, the 'eccentric don' and 'testy colonel' of ***Pinfold.*** Increasingly he felt persecuted, an alien sensitive spirit in a crumbling civilisation. . . . He always believed himself safe behind the 'massive defences . . . the borderline of sanity', but at one point the don and the colonel became himself and, temporarily, he went mad." This is a coherent and by no means a ridiculous account, but various corrections suggest themselves. Was he ever "swept along"? He strikes one as a confirmed decision-taker: even his youthful drinking, according to his friend Dudley Carew, was "a serious, not to say deadly business" (the cry being "sustain the mood!") and had no resemblance to the helpless boozing of a Dylan Thomas. Then, the "testy colonel" was a mask already adopted by him as a schoolboy at Lancing and employed to rebuke the confessional tendencies of his friend Dudley Carew. Carew has a nice reminiscence of him at that time: "It was then Evelyn's custom . . . to glare as we passed and say: 'Soul on the hearth-rug, Carey?' and I would answer: 'Oh, Evelyn, that face!'" As for the "alien sensitive spirit in a crumbling civilisation", it is a shade too languid for a Waugh impersonation. But what most of all is lacking in Stannard's account is the intensity of Waugh's self-hatred and sense of sin—for whatever his judgment on the society surrounding him, his judgment on himself was plainly of the blackest. ***The Ordeal of Gilbert Pinfold*** is sometimes misunderstood, as it was by J. B. Priestley when he interpreted Pinfold's voices as showing him up as a "fake" (they represented "the fundamental self telling the ego not to be a mountebank"). This can hardly be the point, for the accusations that the voices bring—that Pinfold is really the Jew profiteer "Peinfeld", a shoe-fetishist, a "common little communist pansy"—are patently ludicrous, and even the victim Pinfold reflects, wonderingly, that if they had really wanted to crucify him they could have done better than that. What the voices are, rather (not too unlike the voices in Bunyan's *Grace Abounding*), is the incarnation of Pinfold's own temptations. They are Pinfold/Waugh asking himself, "Can I be the appalling sort of person who itches to call people communist pansies, would like to have people at his mercy and bully or torture them, and enjoys salacious sentimental fantasies about his own daughter's sex-life?" ("Treat her *husbandly* . . ."). This is a *malaise* (adversary "voices") which many of us suffer occasionally in a milder form, but only Waugh has managed to get it down clearly on paper, and it continues to amaze one that he could handle it with success as comedy.

Stannard's book, it must be said, suffers a little from his hit-or-miss aim with words. He writes "equable" when he means "equitable", "despoiled" when he means "spoiled", "befriended" when he means "became friendly with". Further, he continually uses the word "mystical" as a synonym both for "religious" and for "superstitious"—a very misleading habit in a book about Waugh, whose religion, according to his own account as well as Father Martin D'Arcy's, could hardly have been less mystical.

Though there is a lot that is rewarding in Stannard's book, as there was in Christopher Sykes's, this extraordinary, unnerving man Waugh has still to find his ideal biographer—in which he resembles W. H. Auden, whose life, which has the same powerful hold over our imagination, shows an odd antithetical symmetry with, and even affinity to, Waugh's. The ever-observant Martin Green points out that "as late as *Letters from Iceland* (1937) he (Auden) . . . said that he would like to write like Firbank, Beatrix Potter, Carroll and Lear, just the authors Waugh might have cited".

P. N. Furbank, "A Man in His Humour," in The Times Literary Supplement, *No. 4362, November 7, 1986, p. 1237.*

ALLAN MASSIE

[*Massie is an English novelist and critic whose novels include* Change and Decay in All Around I See *(1978) and* One Night in

Winter *(1984). Among his other works are the critical studies* Muriel Spark *(1979) and* Colette *(1986). In the following excerpt Massie observes that although Stannard fails to give a completely satisfying account of Waugh's early life and career, he provides some noteworthy information that justifies the biography.*]

Nothing can be more annoying for an author than the reviewer's trick of declaring a book to be unnecessary. If the accusation ever has any point, it should be directed at the publisher rather than the author, who has presumably chosen his subject because it interested him. It is obviously tempting to suggest that we don't need a new biography of Evelyn Waugh yet, since we have had Christopher Sykes's (1975), the ***Diaries*** (1976), and the ***Letters*** (1980); but the temptation should be resisted. Nobody after all has to read a biography unless he wants to (except a reviewer), and it is not really for a reviewer to judge whether the publishers have read the market rightly.

Mr Stannard's enterprise can anyway be easily justified. The Sykes biography was ill-balanced, very good in its way, but at its best that was the way of the memoir rather than the biography; moreover, as he wrote himself, 'the great quantity of documentary material . . . suggests to me that other biographical studies could and perhaps should be written.' Hence Mr Stannard observes, 'this itself emphasises the need for a fuller portrait'. While paying due tribute to Mr Sykes, he corrects several minor errors of dating, and sets out to offer a fuller account of Waugh's sexual relationships before his remarriage in 1937, and a different version of his marriage to Evelyn Gardner. It is true that the first of these is not very illuminating, containing little that the discriminating reader might not have gathered from Mr Sykes. Nevertheless there is more of it. Indeed since Mr Stannard takes almost as long to cover the first 36 years of Waugh's life as Mr Sykes required for its whole 63, fuller is certainly the right word.

The promised revelations about the first marriage are few. It is suggested that Waugh's sexual inexperience contributed to its failure. That surely is something we have all guessed. When two people who love each other separate after only a few months of marriage it doesn't take any great perception to realise that something has probably gone wrong in bed. Mr Stannard is certainly fairer to Evelyn Gardner, to whom he has talked, and is right to point out how she retained the friendship of Anthony Powell and many others; nevertheless it is Mr Sykes who reminds us that her marriage to John Heygate didn't last either, whatever conclusions one may choose to draw from that. Incidentally, if Mr Stannard is fairer to Evelyn Gardner, he is correspondingly unfair to Heygate, who seems to have behaved as well as it is possible to behave if you have fallen in love with a friend's wife and she with you. Waugh forgave him later, and indeed used to inquire of him in kindly fashion from Anthony Powell. He was certainly a more substantial figure than Mr Stannard allows, and his only resemblance to John Beaver in ***A Handful of Dust*** was one of circumstance, not character.

Nor is Mr Stannard illuminating on another question of Waugh's early life. He can do no more than paraphrase the account of the attempted suicide which Waugh himself offered in ***A Little Learning***: 'we shall never know how serious was his intention to kill himself; he did not know himself.' There is no mention of it in the diaries, and indeed the dates and entries in the published version cast some doubt on its probability. Its appearance on the last two pages of ***A Little Learning*** is so exactly artistically correct that one suspects the novelist's touch. At any rate it is characteristic that this doleful moment (if it existed) should have been transformed within three years into the high comedy of the false suicide of Captain Grimes. But was it the memory of that invention which prompted the autobiographer's account? Did life copy art, or art life?

Waugh in 1963. Photograph by Mark Gerson.

Mr Stannard seeks to explain Waugh; perhaps more than he should. Interpretative biography is hazardous. Lytton Strachey's practice exposed the limitation of the *leitmotif* system. He sees Waugh's aggressiveness as defensive: 'Waugh's terror of the loss of individual identity was instinct in him and permeated his art from the beginning . . .' His snobbery was self-protective; he was ever on guard against mockery and insult. No doubt this is true up to a point.

Yet he does no more than skirt a discussion of the really interesting tension in Waugh. In as much as he was a divided man, he was torn between an intellectual, and indeed emotional, adherence to order and an inborn zest for disorder. The Church, and later family life, satisfied the first, social life the second. Both are inherent in his art. He prized structure, and the unfashionable dignity and lucidity of his prose reflected this side of his nature. But he was also happy in the jungle; he revels in the anarchic characters he summons into being: Grimes, Basil Seal, Atwater, Ritchie-Hook, even Trimmer and the whole surging cast of ***Vile Bodies*** are written of lovingly. He recognised, and loved, this same desire for the beauty of order and the same relish in the banana-skins of experience and language in Wodehouse and Saki. It is what makes all three great comic writers, for comedy loves discrepancies, and yet depends on the perception of an ideal order from which man falls away and against which he rebels. Mr Stannard doesn't seem to grasp this. When Waugh described himself as being 'very happy' with the Abdication crisis—'if it had not been for Simpson this would have been a very bitter week'—he asks 'what particular pleasure he derived?' and adds, with a solemnity that would do credit to Arthur Box-Bender: 'it was not the romantic enthusiasm of the schoolgirl population or the impassioned horror of the nationalists. Perhaps it was simply that, as a Catholic, Waugh thrilled to see the head of the Church of England committing adultery' (as if he had not been doing that for years!). Well, if Mr Stannard will believe that, he will believe anything, but he does seem to have missed the joke.

Wilfrid Sheed, in a review of the ***Diaries***, wrote that 'Waugh loved order and beauty, he was cursed with perfect taste, and modern life was a jangling torment to him.' This is true, but again only up to a point. Despite his acedia, which was real enough, it is impossible to read his letters to the Lygons, to Laura Waugh, Nancy Mitford or Ann Fleming, without being aware of the zest for modern life and the comic spectacle it afforded him; which zest lived alongside any distaste which he may have felt. The great pre-war novels especially confirm this.

You can't explain Waugh with neat phrases. He is altogether too complicated, resourceful and intelligent. You can only reveal him in action, and then of course you can't compete with his self-revelation. Any biographer is on a sticky wicket (to use a phrase which Evelyn would have rejected, though it would have come naturally to Arthur or Alec Waugh). Whenever he switches from quotation to explication, from Waugh's words to his own, he starts to sound platitudinous. It is at times rather like the voice of Mr Samgrass.

Nevertheless, with these reservations, Mr Stannard has done a good job of work. There is some interesting stuff on Waugh's finances, though, perhaps because he is a don, he seems to find it surprising that a professional writer should live on advances and overdrafts. (The publisher chooses to spell this 'overdraught', though, according to Chambers, this means 'a current of air passing above or from above!) He is good on the aberration of Waugh's panegyric on the Italian Empire in Abyssinia, and good too on Waugh's theories of fiction. He quotes admirably, as befits the editor of *Evelyn Waugh: The Critical Heritage*, and, in doing so, reminds us what an acute and judicious critic Waugh could be.

There is much of interest in this book, and few admirers of Waugh will want to be without it, though few will, I fancy, be completely satisfied. All the same we should reserve judgement. Mr Stannard is only half-way through his task. It will be fair to estimate his achievement when he has published the second and more difficult volume. That will be tricky indeed; Waugh's military service poses deep problems. His marriage too will be a challenge to the biographer. In his treatment of that, Mr Stannard seems to me to have begun very well. (pp. 35-7)

Allan Massie, "Up to the Half-Way Point Mr. Stannard," in The Spectator, *Vol. 257, No. 8263, November 22, 1986, pp. 35-7.*

Lillian Hellman: The Image, the Woman

by William Wright

(For Lillian Hellman: see also *CLC,* Vols. 2,4,8,14,18,34; *Contemporary Authors,* Vols. 13-16, rev. ed., Vol. 112 [obituary]; *Dictionary of Literary Biography,* Vol. 7; and *Dictionary of Literary Biography Yearbook: 1984.* For William Wright: see also *Contemporary Authors,* Vols. 53-56 and *Contemporary Authors New Revision Series,* Vol. 7.)

An Excerpt from *Lillian Hellman: The Image, the Woman*

By her own admission, Hellman spent her first opening night drinking heavily, and the day after, nursing a hangover. A few days later, after a number of pleasant congratulatory talks with Hammett in California, she suddenly remembered her opening-night call to him when a woman claiming to be his secretary had answered the phone. Belatedly realizing that it had been 3 A.M. in California at the time and that Hammett had no secretary, Hellman raced to the airport in a fury, boarded a plane for Los Angeles, went to Hammett's rented house in Pacific Palisades, smashed the basement soda fountain and took the next plane back to New York.

Considering 1934 flight schedules from coast to coast and the time required for the trip, her story is hard enough to believe. Adding mystery is the fact that Hammett *did* have a secretary at the time, a young woman named Mildred Lewis, who had been hired by his studio as an inducement to him to work. Because of Hammett's erratic life (and because he probably *was* sleeping with her), Lewis often stayed overnight. But it was not like Hammett to keep secrets from Hellman, even if he had had a reason. If he had wanted to hide the secretary, he would not have allowed her to answer the phone—certainly not at three o'clock in the morning. As for Hellman's arrival at the house, Hammett had two black housemen, a homosexual couple, Jones and Winfield, who might have at least called Hammett when the demolition began.

Whatever the truth of the story, which was written twelve years after Hammett's death and almost forty years after it allegedly happened, it was more of a spasm of jealous anger at all the outrages and betrayals Hellman had been subjected to during their relationship, a wish-fulfillment fantasy made up of bits and pieces of jealous outbursts that had actually occurred. If she was guilty of melodrama in her plays, it would become a Hellman mechanism in her memoirs to distill a diffuse and unsatisfactory reality into a deft literary concentrate.

Dust jacket of Lillian Hellman: The Image, the Woman, *by William Wright. Simon and Schuster, 1986. Jacket design by Fred Marcellino. Jacket photograph by Vandamm Studio. Courtesy of Simon & Schuster, Inc.*

JOHN BLADES

In literature, as in politics and show business, America has a masochistic impulse to cultivate monsters, with Norman Mailer and Truman Capote at the head of the pack. Of them all, though, few have received as much care and feeding as Lillian Hellman, at least to judge by the evidence submitted in William Wright's biography of the playwright, ***Lillian Hellman: The Image, the Woman***. . . . This was never more true than during the last 15 years of Hellman's life, while she was publishing distinctive memoirs.

The most notorious of these books was ***Scoundrel Time,*** her selective reprise of the '50s witch hunts, whose chief villain was, of course, Sen. Joseph McCarthy. In defending her memoir (and the two that preceded it, ***An Unfinished Woman*** and ***Pentimento***) against charges of distortion and falsification of history, Hellman adopted the tactics of her arch adversary. She intimidated friends as well as enemies with her venomous tongue, fierce temper, black rages; she resorted to threats and petty blackmail, anything to help perpetuate her self-image as one of the century's (if not the milennium's) ranking literary and political heroines.

Hellman's personal ''McCarthyism'' is perhaps the ugliest, most hypocritical face of the playwright/memoirist that emerges from Wright's biography. The book also documents numerous examples of her faulty memory, her creative myopia and/or her ''Walter Mitty fantasies,'' high among them her romanticized portrait of her 30-year affair with Dashiell Hammett. In Hellman's remembrances, the couple might be the Katharine Hepburn-Spencer Tracy of America's literati. In truth, Wright maintains, it was often a mutually self-destructive relationship, with epic fights, long estrangements, chronic infidelities and drunken binges on both sides.

All this may tend to indicate that Wright wields a blunt instrument in his portrayal of Hellman, but his book, while largely an indictment, doesn't seem unbalanced or unsympathetic. Unlike Regina in ***The Little Foxes,*** and assorted other characters in her plays, Hellman is not a figure of consummate greed, rapacity and evil. Wright swears that he conducted ''an impartial search behind the legend,'' then goes on to take stock of her contradictions: ''fierce loves and fiercer hatreds, grand gestures and petty acts of vindictiveness, dogged adherence to principle and underhanded maneuvers, rockhard strength and frightened vulnerability.''

Nor does Wright neglect to give Hellman credit for her talents as a dramatist (''If her rank as an artist is arguable, her prestige and eminence are facts'') or as a conscientious political activist, however confused, volatile and inflammatory her radical politics could be. But, he argues, ''For all her prodigious impact on the world . . . her greatest contribution was the character she created in her memoirs.''

Unavoidably perhaps, Wright devotes a lot of space to sorting the fiction from the fact in these memoirs, with special attention to her celebrated wartime trips to Russia and Spain and to the infamously self-serving Julia chapter from ***Pentimento,*** which was almost certainly a melodramatic fabrication. As much as anything, these were what led Mary McCarthy to call Hellman a compulsive liar.

Wright's biography surely won't be the last word on Hellman. It is almost certain to provoke an immediate response both from her acolytes and her enemies. For now, though, ***Lillian Hellman: The Image, the Woman*** is the most comprehensive dossier on its perplexing subject, if not always the most gracefully written or the most unbiased. However impartial he was at the start, Wright would have to agree that what he's ended up with is a portrait of a literary monster, though not necessarily a self-made one.

John Blades, ''Playwright Hellman Cast in the Role of Scoundrel,'' in Chicago Tribune, *November 9, 1986, p. 3.*

CHRISTOPHER LEHMANN-HAUPT

In the epilogue to his new biography, ***Lillian Hellman: The Image, the Woman,*** William Wright (***Pavarotti: My Own Story*** and ***The Von Bülow Affair***) recounts how, once having contracted for his book, he wrote to his famous subject in the slim hope that she might cooperate. Within days, Mr. Wright's editor got an angry telephone call from Ms. Hellman, newspapers received an announcement appointing William Abrahams as her official biographer, and two dozen or so of Ms. Hellman's friends got notes asking them not to talk to Mr. Wright.

Hellman, newly hired as a scriptwriter for Samuel Goldwyn, arriving in Los Angeles. AP/Wide World Photos.

Sensing an element of panic in his subject's response, he writes, he asked himself why she was going to such lengths as to risk ''damage to her image as a civil libertarian if her effort at censorship became known.''

''Why did she care so much? Such a biography, or five such books, would in no way preclude an authorized version.'' As a celebrity, she had been vulnerable to insensitive attack for 50 years ''and had, on balance, little to complain about.'' What was there to be so concerned about?

Plenty, as it turns out—at least to judge from the final results of Mr. Wright's work. True, ***Lillian Hellman*** is in form a conventional chronological biography. It traces the writer's growth from her Jewish-merchant origins in the American South, through the successive stages of her career as a Hollywood screenwriter, a Broadway playwright, and a memoirist. It reports the known facts of her most significant relationships—to her husband, Arthur Kober; to her longtime companion, Dashiell Hammett, and to the multitudes of lovers, friends and enemies who rushed on and off stage throughout her embattled life.

It's also true that Mr. Wright strives for impartiality in describing the many storms of controversy that Ms. Hellman's career somehow managed to stir up. He defends the best of her plays (***The Children's Hour*** and ***The Little Foxes***) on the ground that, even if they are excessively melodramatic, as some critics have accused them of being, they continue to come alive on stage long after the works of more esteemed dramatists have grown moribund.

He tries to give her the benefit of the doubt at every turn, going as far as to put a good light on her motives when he seems to catch her telling a falsehood or committing an act of bad faith. He even brings some wit to his narrative: of her appearance as a presenter at the 1977 Academy Awards ceremonies, he writes, "Onto the huge stage stepped a tiny old lady" whose name meant for the members of the audience "a number of plays they had grown up with, a number of films they had studied and a number of books they were embarrassed not to have read."

Still, the big picture that Mr. Wright brings into focus is one that would explain why Ms. Hellman seems to have blanched at the prospect of seeing her life fall into a stranger's hands, and why she made such a pathetic attempt to keep it among friends.

For his portrait of Lillian Hellman is contradictory. Whether he is considering the chronology of her career, or interviewing her many friends and associates who *were* willing to talk to him, or reviewing the public record of her various memoirs (***An Unfinished Woman, Pentimento*** and ***Scoundrel Time***) and weighing the attacks and counterattacks involving their veracity, he is always driven to one inescapable conclusion. The divergence between the image projected and the woman herself was a considerable one, to say the very least.

How does he account for the many seeming discrepancies between reality and his subject's version of events? Again, he is scrupulous to consider all possibilities. He provokes a reader to consider, at one extreme, a political explanation—namely, that Ms. Hellman may have been almost throughout her life a member of the Communist Party. At another extreme, he suggests that "she may have worked out a compromise with her psyche: to realize wish-fulfillment fantasies and salve truths by revising her history in her memoirs and perhaps thereby forestalling a collapse into psychosis."

Once again trying to put her in the best light, he writes: "For all of her prodigious impact on the world—plays, books, loves, friends, politics, social criticism—there seems little doubt that her greatest contribution was the character that she created in the memoirs. So much attention has been given to the truth or falsity of the portrait that the creative feat has been overlooked." The question of whether or not "such a character actually existed," he goes on, doesn't "diminish Hellman's creative achievement."

In his final summing up, he chooses to celebrate her anger. "Hellman's anger revealed a hatred for the world, a hatred for the cruel mistakes of an unjust order, both natural and political, inflicted on her and others. So much of the thrust of her life was fueled by a desire to correct those mistakes—whether by irate dramas, political engagement or, on a more personal level, her doctorings of reality." And he concludes diplomatically: "At the same time, few people have ever loved the world as intensely, rejoiced so in its possibilities and grasped so eagerly for its rewards."

A reader tries to find solace in those concluding grace notes. But with the major themes and overtones of ***Lillian Hellman*** still echoing dissonantly, one is bound to find these last words ringing out of tune and weak.

Christopher Lehmann-Haupt, in a review of "Lillian Hellman: The Image, the Woman," in The New York Times, *November 17, 1986, p. C17.*

DAVID RICHARDS

Any biographer tackling author and playwright Lillian Hellman is confronted with a double challenge—on the one hand, digging up the truth of that complex and controversial life; on the other, undoing the self-aggrandizing fictions that Hellman elaborated in her best-selling memoirs—***An Unfinished Woman, Pentimento*** and ***Scoundrel Time.***

Granted, some of the undoing had already begun before Hellman's death in June 1984 at age 79. The most public attack on the integrity of her character was launched by fellow author Mary McCarthy, who charged four years earlier on *The Dick Cavett Show* that "every word she writes is a lie, including 'and' and 'the.'" (Hellman promptly slapped McCarthy with a $2,225,000 defamation suit, although she was to die before it came to judgment.)

There were plenty of others, eager to question Hellman's veracity on a wide range of events—her heroic trips to Spain during the Spanish Civil War and to Russia during the final days of World War II; the mission she supposedly undertook in the heart of Nazi Berlin to deliver a cache of money to her anti-fascist friend "Julia"; even what had long been considered the keystone of Hellman's independent temperament, her appearance before the House Un-American Activities Committee and her ringing declaration that "I cannot and will not cut my conscience to fit this year's fashions."

In [***Lillian Hellman: The Image, The Woman***] biographer William Wright attempts to get beyond "the Walter Mitty fantasies" and find "the truth behind the legend." He is the first to admit, however, that for every question answered, two more pop up. Contradictions abound. If in her memoirs Hellman inflated some episodes of her life, presumably for posterity's sake, Wright found that she also omitted true stories that legitimately confirmed her stature. She could be grand and elegant in keeping with her New Orleans birthright and a genteel upbringing that suggested the more decorous side of ***The Little Foxes,*** her most famous play. But she also carried on like a longshoreman, drank and smoked excessively and ran up a string of lovers, sometimes under the very nose of detective writer Dashiell Hammett, whom she claimed to be her one true love.

In a terse note, written shortly before she died, Hellman refused to cooperate with Wright—designating her editor at Little, Brown, William Abrahams, as her official biographer, instead. Whatever secrets lie in her private papers, remain private for the time being. Consequently, Wright ends up with lots of speculations of his own and his text is dotted with such prudent verbal caveats as "may well have been," "it might be assumed" and "it is possible that."

What accounted for the relationship between Hellman and Hammett? ("Did anyone ever see them together?" Gore Vidal

Hellman during rehearsals of her play The Little Foxes *in 1939, with actress Tallulah Bankhead and director Herman Shumlin. The Billy Rose Theatre Collection, The New York Public Library at Lincoln Center, Astor, Lenox and Tilden Foundations.*

once asked wickedly.) Wright has his ideas—among them, the theory that Hammett, subject to writer's block most of his life, simply found it easier to coach Hellman from the sidelines and play the literary game vicariously through her. But he concedes that Hammett's "unshakeable fascination with and dependence on Hellman defies several laws of natural selection and simply stands, like so much that was central to Hammett, as an unlikely, unencumbered fact."

Was Hellman a member of the Communist Party—something she long denied, although to little avail as far as her detractors were concerned? Wright doesn't know. But he argues, "her political positions—and that would include her silences almost more than her stated positions—take on a much needed logic if it is assumed that Hellman was a Party member . . . it seems highly likely she was (a secret member)."

To the fundamental question—Why did Hellman feel the need to fabricate?—Wright advances several possibilities. She was a playwright—the most successful female playwright of her time—and it is only natural that she might bring to the story of her life the same sense of well-made drama she brought to such works as ***Toys in the Attic*** and ***The Children's Hour.*** There are, too, Wright suggests, the failings of memory to consider. It was only after her career as a playwright had ceased that Hellman turned to prose and began writing about events that had transpired 30 years earlier.

Then he unleashes a corker: "At least some of Hellman's fabrications may have stemmed from a murkier area. . . . Perhaps she altered the truth . . . to meet a psychological demand for a less painful reality. There is a significant difference between a person engaged in dishonest public relations and one who is fundamentally delusional. In Hellman's case, she may have worked out a compromise with her psyche: to realize wish-fulfillment fantasies and salve painful truths by revising her history in her memoirs and perhaps thereby forestalling a collapse into psychosis."

That's getting hard to swallow. If some of Wright's theories are provocative, you can't help feeling throughout this book that you are being lured out onto the thin ice of hypothesis. If Wright persuasively dismantles the public Lillian Hellman, he never really manages to evoke the creature underneath, or even a convincing approximation. For that we're going to have to wait for future biographies, of which several are reportedly already in the works.

That's not to deny that ***Lillian Hellman,*** is absorbing, but its fascination lies mainly in the passing tidbits and anecdotes the author turns up in his delvings. When, for example, Hellman posed for the famous Blackglama ad, she misunderstood the slogan, "What becomes a legend most?", that accompanied the full-paged photograph of her, swathed in mink. The slogan was asking "What garment looks best on a legend?," but Wright tells us that Hellman interpreted it to mean, "What human raw material is most likely to develop into a legend?"

Somchow that says as much about the lady's strong drives and fierce pride as anything else in this sometimes intriguing, often conjectural volume. (pp. 1, 11)

David Richards, in a review of "Lillian Hellman: The Image; The Woman," in Book World—The Washington Post, *November 23, 1986, pp. 1, 11.*

FRANK RICH

[*American critic Rich has served as a film, drama, and television critic for* Time *and* The New York Times; *he has also contributed articles and reviews to* Ms., Esquire, *and other periodicals. In the following excerpt Rich praises Wright's biography for its objective, truthful presentation of Hellman.*]

Lillian Hellman brought out the knee-jerk in almost everyone. To her admirers, she was a paragon of integrity during a "scoundrel time"—a tough-minded writer who refused to cut either her civil libertarian's conscience or her premodernist literary style for the sake of fashion or survival. To her detractors, she was a holier-than-thou opportunist—a hypocritical Stalinist whose dishonest, self-aggrandizing memoirs adroitly snookered the public into retroactively anointing her the St. Joan of the Joseph McCarthy era. By her death in 1984, Hellman's supporters included a goodly number of the show business and intellectual elite, but her enemies list was as long as, and more eclectic than, that of an archnemesis, Richard Nixon. She had not only been attacked by the expected conservatives and neoconservatives but had also provoked varying degrees of fire, for varying reasons, from a heterogeneous array of liberals, including Elizabeth Hardwick, Irving Howe, Alfred Kazin, Murray Kempton, Diana Trilling and, of course, Mary McCarthy. It was Miss McCarthy who sparked Hellman's final act of Dickensian litigation by telling the television interviewer Dick Cavett in 1980 that "every word" Hellman wrote was "a lie, including 'and' and 'the'."

Although Hellman's $2 million libel suit died when she did, the decades-old debates reopened by the Cavett-McCarthy exchange did not. The veracity of Hellman's best-selling memoirs, the full profile of her ideology, the theatrical status of her frequently derided but constantly revived plays remained ambiguous. Perhaps these matters can never be resolved completely, but [in ***Lillian Hellman: The Image, The Woman***] William Wright, Hellman's first biographer, has separated most of the lies, big and little, from the truth. A journalist whose previous subjects include Luciano Pavarotti and Claus von Bülow, Mr. Wright seems an unlikely candidate to sort out the Hellman story. As it happens, he possesses an essential attribute that more passionate writers who either loved or reviled his subject do not: he really is an objective observer.

This worldly biography, unlike anything else written by or about Hellman, has no hidden agenda. Mr. Wright isn't interested in refighting the political wars of the past half century from the perspective of one camp or another. His main concern is facts, which he has diligently collected, documented and analyzed. The findings of his fair-minded, engagingly unfolded research often uphold the Mary McCarthy point of view.

Mr. Wright leaves no doubt, if there was any, that the pseudonymous Julia of the autobiographical ***Pentimento,*** along with other Hellman characters in ***Watch on the Rhine*** and ***An Unfinished Woman,*** is Muriel Gardiner—a woman Hellman neither knew firsthand nor assisted, as she claimed, in heroic anti-Nazi activities. ''She (Gardiner) may have been the model for somebody else's Julia, but she was certainly not the model for mine,'' Hellman said to *The New York Times* in denying the similarities between the chapter **''Julia'' in *Pentimento*** and Gardiner's own memoir, *Code Name Mary,* published in 1983. But Gardiner, who died in 1985, told Mr. Wright that Hellman had phoned her during the controversy and proposed a meeting. While the two elderly women never did get together, the biographer reasonably speculates that ''the harsh reality of (Hellman's) lawsuit against Mary McCarthy, and Gardiner's potential effect on it, may have forced Hellman to acknowledge the . . . imagined origins (of **''Julia''**) and to take steps to control the damage.'' By then Miss McCarthy had already filed an interrogatory response in court listing many improbabilities in **''Julia,''** not the least of which is that ''a celebrated Jewish antifascist'' would have been chosen for an undercover mission in Nazi Berlin.

Mr. Wright also supports the assertion of Ernest Hemingway's third wife, the journalist Martha Gellhorn, that Hellman (in her first memoir, ***An Unfinished Woman***) fictionalized her adventures with Hemingway in and out of the Spain of 1937. Under the biographer's meticulous examination, many of the ''ands'' and ''thes'' of his subject's memoirs collapse too. A serious drinker at various times but not an alcoholic, Hellman exaggerated her liquor problem in public—''from the same impulse that made her drink heavily: (Dashiell) Hammett-worship—and an almost pathetic, somewhat tomboyish eagerness to be admitted to his one-man club.'' While there's no doubt that Hellman ''suffered badly'' as a consequence of the Hollywood blacklist, Mr. Wright debunks some details of her travails, including the circumstances of the sale of her Westchester farm and her repeated declaration that she was reduced to working as a department store salesclerk.

About the only issue that stymies Mr. Wright's investigative zeal is his attempt to verify or disprove Hellman's lifelong assertion that she never joined the Communist Party. As a practical or ideological matter, the issue is ''moot in that (Hellman) adhered to the Party line more than some communists did . . . in the postwar years when many American communists openly broke with the Party. . . .'' (Hellman's subsequent acknowledgments of Soviet repression were grudging, or, in William Barrett's amusing characterization, ''wistful.'') But if Hellman lied in denying a party membership—as there's reason to speculate she might have, long after she had paid a high price for her unpopular views—why did she bother? Mr. Wright carefully considers the possible motives, from the innocuous to the principled to the malevolent, but the question is left begging on circumstantial evidence.

That issue notwithstanding, Hellman's detractors will find plenty to savor in this book. Still, it would be wrong of them to view ***Lillian Hellman*** as the stake that has finally been rammed through their old adversary's heart. In this biography, as in life, Hellman is a commanding figure in spite of—and sometimes because of—her own worst instincts. By revealing more complexities, however unflattering, than Hellman herself ever exhibited for scrutiny, ***Lillian Hellman*** may increase its protagonist's hold on center stage in the public imagination rather than force her at last to relinquish it.

Charting the discrepancies between ''the character that she created in the memoirs,'' which he calls Hellman's ''greatest contribution,'' and the real Lillian Hellman, Mr. Wright uncovers a paradigmatic American life, and he explores its many dimensions sympathetically. In the biographer's view, the fraudulence of some parts of the memoirs ''doesn't diminish Hellman's creative achievement'' as a writer, or at least as a writer of fiction. ''Hellman would hardly be the first American literary figure to indulge in touching up an unsatisfactory reality,'' he writes. ''It has gone on happily since Hawthorne inserted the 'w' in his name. . . .'' Even recounted without embellishment, Hellman's actual adventures were exciting, taking her from German-Jewish New Orleans to Broadway in its golden age, the expatriate swirl of Gerald and Sara Murphy's Côte d'Azur, Hollywood's Garden of Allah, civil-war-torn Spain, Stalin's Soviet Union and Tito's postwar Yugoslavia. With or without Julia, the cast of principal characters included, among many others, Hammett, Horace Liveright, Herman Shumlin, Ralph Ingersoll, Dorothy Parker, Sam Goldwyn and Tallulah Bankhead. That Hellman, for public consumption, successfully wrapped herself in ''Walter Mitty fantasies'' as frequently as she did in silk and mink only adds more mysterious wrinkles to the legend.

Mr. Wright has his psychological theories about Hellman—the discovery of her beloved father's infidelities may have prompted her distrust of all authority—but the woman who emerges from this book is far too independent a character to fit any neat definition, let alone any idolatrous enshrinement or venomous caricature. Hellman undoubtedly deserves full credit for having the courage of her convictions, whether fighting fiercely for the Screen Writers Guild or standing up to the House Un-American Activities Committee or even, in one of the book's funnier latter-day incidents, hitting the powerful

Hellman with Dashiell Hammett in New York, 1941. Photograph by George Karger, Life *Magazine © 1973 Time Inc.*

Hollywood agent Sue Mengers with her purse when Ms. Mengers appeared to be comparing the plight of the embezzling producer David Begelman to the persecution of blacklisted screenwriters. Balancing the toughness were a raucous, private sense of humor and a romantic, sensual nature that left even her many discarded lovers permanently smitten.

''Lillian came on with every man she met,'' said Arthur Miller, apparently one of the few men to resist the invitation. Randall Smith, a longshoremen's union organizer who carried on with Hellman while maintaining a separate acquaintanceship with her longtime lover Hammett, traces her sexual appeal less to her physical attributes (which he catalogues in oddly painstaking detail) than to ''her honesty and integrity.'' Yet Hellman also practiced what Mr. Wright calls ''a form of intellectual totalitarianism,'' attacking the motives of anyone who disagreed with her, and, for all her close relationships and humanitarianism, she was, in her friend Albert Hackett's description, ''basically contemptuous of most people.'' (She bullied secretaries no less than political antagonists.)

Hellman also had a stingy streak. Although she selflessly nursed Hammett through decades of alcoholism, whoring, illness and literary impotence, she was less than magnanimous toward his relatives in the disposal of his estate. When Eric Bentley's documentary Off Broadway play *Are You Now or Have You Ever Been* paid her tribute with a recitation of her defiant letter to HUAC, she demanded royalties. Nor would she significantly lower her Western-scale financial demands when a worshipful Chinese director made herculean bureaucratic and translation efforts so that he might stage ***The Little Foxes*** in Peking. ''Things like that never moved Lillian in the slightest,'' said her agent, Don Congdon. ''I reminded her that Arthur Miller had recently gone to China with *Salesman* and had had a good experience. Lillian said she didn't care for Arthur Miller any more and didn't much care what kind of experience he'd had.''

But, as Mr. Wright says, ''it is perhaps Hellman's refusal to go the way of a good second-rate playwright that irks her critics more than anything else.'' Hellman was primarily a writer of exceptionally well-made melodramas. Whereas Tennessee Williams ''would plumb the depths of his quirky characters and find truths that applied to everyone, Hellman plumbed the depths of her quirky characters and found quirks.'' Nonetheless, her better dramas, with their ''slamming encounters with surface reality,'' endure as those of her similar contemporaries have not. ''Who in recent decades has argued about the work of Sherwood or Odets?'' the author asks rhetorically. He is particularly perceptive in his high appraisal of the character of Regina, who, in ***The Little Foxes,*** seizes the audience's imagination and sometimes its admiration even though she proves to be money-grubbing and unscrupulous as well as smart and glamorous.

In Hellman's own mesmerizing grip on the public, one finds a similar appeal. Mr. Wright's biography replaces the saintly, often fictive Lillian Hellman of her memoirs with a flawed, real-life Lillian Hellman closer in spirit to Regina, and all the more intriguing for that. But while Regina's domain was only the turn-of-the-century South, Hellman exerted her unstoppable will across a half century of American cultural and political history. Exactly why she did so cannot be explained by the party lines of her fans or foes and, in the end, eludes even Mr. Wright's admirable research. ''Every attempt at sorting out the fundamental beliefs from the tangle of her views, stances and actions leads to no ideological bedrock—only an overriding emotion: anger,'' the biographer concludes, before ending his portrait of the most tantalizingly unfinished woman on the word ''enigma.'' Lillian Hellman, no little fox, continues to outrun anyone who might attempt to cage her. (pp. 1, 38-9)

Frank Rich, ''Slamming through Life,'' in The New York Times Book Review, *November 23, 1986, pp. 1, 38-9.*

LAURA SHAPIRO

As her own biographer, Lillian Hellman was a master of the craft of omission, a trait she shared with such great stylists as Isak Dinesen and M.F.K. Fisher. All three revive the past on their own terms, combining lucid detail with elusive prose and leaving much deliberately out of focus. Realized in a flow of beautifully turned sentences, this attitude toward the art of memoir produces wonderful books—and in Hellman's case, infuriates as many people as it enthralls.

William Wright's biography of Hellman [***Lillian Hellman: The Image, The Woman***] is the first book-length investigation of her veracity, a subject that has absorbed old lefties and conservatives for years. . . . Piecing together research, rumors, anecdotes and analysis, Wright has come up with a mass of evidence on all sides of every question. By the end we know what a great many people, including the author, think about Lillian Hellman, but we're no closer to Hellman herself than we were when she wrote her last paragraph.

On the subject of the [House Committee on Un-American Activities] appearances, Wright points out that Hellman's famous offer—she was willing to testify about herself but not about other people—was not a new moral stand; it had been tried by previous witnesses and disallowed by the committee. Like the others, she ended up pleading the Fifth Amendment. He finds nothing in contemporary newspaper accounts to back her remark that a reporter briefly disrupted the hearing by exclaiming, ''Thank God somebody finally had the guts to do it.'' Pawing endlessly at the question of whether Hellman was a member of the Communist Party, he concludes that she probably was, at least for a while. . . .

Despite his fair-mindedness as he handles the conflicting stories of these and other major questions, Wright's analysis is so tedious and hamfisted that it undermines his credibility. He puts an astonishing amount of faith in Hellman's FBI file, as if he'd never heard of the errors and misconceptions rampant in the bureau's communist watch. He even dabbles in two-penny psychology: arguing purely from anecdote, he decides Hellman was ''fundamentally delusional.'' On minor issues, his zeal for uncovering the truth becomes a mania. Why did she refer to her maternal relatives as the Newhouses when the ''dominant members'' of the family were named Marx? Why did she make so much of her childhood in New Orleans when she spent half her time in New York? Why didn't she sell her Manhattan town house instead of her Westchester farm when she needed money, since she once told someone she hated cities? Most unpleasantly, Wright frequently refers to Hellman as ''ugly'' and concludes that she may have won her many lovers though sheer sexual aggression.

Wright admits in the end that Hellman's most important and enduring creation was the character she calls "I." Whether or not such a person existed, he says, is "all but irrelevant" in view of the artistic achievement at hand. Yet the Lillian Hellman he creates in this biography is too feebly realized to be convincing either as artist or scoundrel. Biographers, no less than fiction writers or memoirists, have to build a character for us if we are to believe in their work. Wright's lack of faith permeates every page of this biography and reduces its subject to straw. Hellman deserves better—she deserves a truth at least as powerful as the one she created herself.

Laura Shapiro, "Would the Real Lillian Stand Up," in Newsweek, *Vol. CVIII, No. 21, November 24, 1986, p. 92.*

PATRICIA GOLDSTONE

[*Goldstone is an American dramatist and critic. Her plays include* The Circus Animals's Desertion, Anne in the Camps, *and* Wars of Attrition. *In the following excerpt Goldstone commends Wright's biography of Hellman but questions his assertion that Hellman's tendency to distort the truth may have been a symptom of psychosis.*]

In this meticulously researched, evenhanded and intuitive biography [***Lillian Hellman: The Image, The Woman***] of America's arguably greatest female playwright, author William Wright . . . has written three books in one. ***Lillian Hellman*** is a book about theater, a book about women and success and a book about the political forces shaping the American intellectual left since the 1930s. With a deft and witty style, Wright has woven these narrative threads together into a tapestry that depicts the beginnings of the Age of Disinformation.

Hellman in her later years. © 1986 Thomas Victor.

The most pruriently fascinating aspect of the book is of course Hellman the Woman, who appears, at least in some aspects, as monstrous as her most memorable dramatic creation, Regina in ***The Little Foxes.*** Wright delineates the Hellman who swindled the daughters of her lifelong love, Dashiell Hammett, out of their shares of their father's estate; who once threatened a reporter with evidence of his homosexuality if he published an unfavorable piece, as well as the better-known Joan of Arc of the McCarthy barricades. He presents a woman ahead of her time, a woman who was "sexually aggressive when no women were. . . . She cleaned up!" Although he presents convincing evidence that Hammett crafted the plots for her most successful plays, Wright describes their 30-year love affair as Hellman's anchor despite their many flagrant infidelities to one another. He is particularly incisive in defining their mutual attraction: Hammett's "rigorous honesty served as a brake on her shoddier impulses . . . she was like a junk-food addict who had the bad luck to fall in love with a nutritionist," while Hellman's raw ambition seemed to fire the perhaps more talented Hammett with an energy he lacked.

It is to Wright's credit that he never raises the question of whether Hellman might have used her free-floating libido to advance her career. He focuses instead on the far more disturbing question of whether the author of the battle cry of the intellectual left during the McCarthy era, "I cannot cut my conscience to suit this year's fashion," did indeed tailor her politics out of a complicated desire to achieve mythic status in her own lifetime. His chain of evidence includes Hellman's flexibility in eliminating the lesbian subplot of ***The Children's Hour*** in order to make the Broadway play into a Hollywood movie in the moral climate of the 1930s; her shocking lack of real political sophistication and, most compelling, the scandalous hypothesis that Hellman "commandeered" the life-story of freedom-fighter Mary Gardiner Buttinger as the basis for **"Julia."**. . .

It is in this last instance that the weakness of the book, if there is a weakness, emerges. In discussing the controversy that erupted in 1983 when publication of Buttinger's memoirs gave substance to Mary McCarthy's celebrated accusation that Hellman fantasized the whole relationship in order to enhance her own image, Wright raises the possibility that Hellman might have been psychotic. To posit that Hellman was mentally ill is to dismiss her as a writer by absolving her of moral responsibility, and is ultimately far more damaging than to dismiss her as a lightweight melodramatist, an oft-leveled critical charge Wright illuminates with considerable insight into the craft of the theater elsewhere in the book.

It is ironic that Wright finds it more comforting to speculate that Hellman was a secret member of the Communist Party who dissembled in order to protect her power as a propagandist. But, even here, he concludes, "In fighting 'unannounced battles,' Hellman was creating a warring and divisive atmosphere that distracted from the larger problems both she and her adversaries were completely concerned with: poverty, racial injustice, and the arms race."

If Hellman was not a Communist, and not psychotic, but simply a hungry, forceful, talented woman thoroughly in touch with the reality around her, the picture Wright has created is even more disturbing, for it means that our society, in its two-pronged quest for celebrity and for simple victories, has itself become psychotic. Although Wright makes some educated guesses about the effects of Hellman's childhood as a Jew in turn-of-the-century New Orleans, and even on a possible inferiority complex about her looks, he wisely refrains from reducing her by psychology: He leaves her a resonant enigma, a tarnished madonna for a troubled age.

Patricia Goldstone, in a review of "Lillian Hellman: The Image, the Woman," in Los Angeles Times Book Review, *January 4, 1987, p. 3.*

Appendix

The following is a listing of all sources used in Volume 44 of *Contemporary Literary Criticism*. Included in this list are all copyright and reprint rights and acknowledgments for those essays for which permission was obtained. Every effort has been made to trace copyright, but if omissions have been made, please let us know.

THE EXCERPTS IN CLC, VOLUME 44, WERE REPRINTED FROM THE FOLLOWING PERIODICALS:

The American Book Review, v. 8, November-December, 1986; v. 9, March-April, 1987. © 1986, 1987 by *The American Book Review*. Both reprinted by permission of the publisher.

American Film, v. XII, October, 1986 for "Stranger in Paradise" by John Boorman. © 1986, The American Film Institute, J. F. Kennedy Center, Washington, DC 20566. Reprinted with permission from *American Film* magazine and the author.

American Literature, v. 59, May 1987. Copyright © 1987 Duke University Press, Durham, NC. Reprinted by permission of the publisher.

American Mercury, v. LVI, April, 1943.

The American Poetry Review, v. 15, November-December, 1986 for "The Watcher" by Edward Hirsch. Copyright © 1986 by World Poetry, Inc. Reprinted by permission of the author.

The American Scholar, v. 56, Spring, 1987 for "A Trenta-Sei for John Ciardi (1916-1986)" by John Stone. Copyright © 1987 by the author. Reprinted by permission of the author.

Belles Lettres, v. 1, July-August, 1986; v. 2, November-December, 1986. All reprinted by permission of the publisher.

Best Sellers, v. 45, April, 1985; v. 45, March, 1986; v. 46, May, 1986; v. 46, September, 1986; v. 46, February, 1987. Copyright © 1985, 1986, 1987 Helen Dwight Reid Educational Foundation. All reprinted by permission of the publisher.

The Blade, April 13, 1986. Reprinted by permission of the publisher.

Book World—The Washington Post, June 9, 1985; August 25, 1985; November 17, 1985; February 2, 1986; February 16, 1986; March 23, 1986; May 4, 1986; July 27, 1986; November 2, 1986; November 23, 1986; December 14, 1986; January 4, 1987; March 15, 1987. © 1985, 1986, 1987, *The Washington Post*. All reprinted by permission of the publisher.

Booklist, v. 81, December 1, 1984; v. 81, March 15, 1985; v. 81, May 1, 1985; v. 82, December 1, 1985; v. 82, February 15, 1986; v. 82, March 1, 1986; v. 82, March 15, 1986; v. 82, August, 1986; v. 83, November 1, 1986. Copyright © 1984, 1985, 1986 by the American Library Association. All reprinted by permission of the publisher.

Books and Bookmen, n. 360, October, 1985; n. 361, November, 1985; n. 365, March 1986; n. 371, September, 1986; n. 373, November, 1986. © copyright *Books and Bookmen* 1985, 1986, 1987. All reprinted with permission of the publisher.

Books in Canada, v. 14, December, 1985 for a review of "The Suspect" by Janet Windeler; v. 15, April, 1986 for "The Plots Thicken" by Richard Plant; v. 15, August-September, 1986 for a review of "Waiting for Saskatchewan" by Marc Côté. All reprinted by permission of the respective authors.

Bookworld, Chicago Tribune, June 29, 1986 for "Ayn Rand: Sex, Money, and Philosophy" by George Gilder. Copyright © 1986 by George Gilder. Reprinted by permission of Georges Borchardt, Inc. and the author.

Boston Review, v. XI, June, 1986 for "In Papa's Garden" by Allen Josephs; v. XI, August, 1986 for "The Emperor's New Fiction" by Rosellen Brown. Copyright © 1986 by the Boston Critic, Inc. Both reprinted by permission of the respective authors.

Briarpatch, July-August, 1986. Reprinted by permission of the publisher.

Brick: A Journal of Reviews, n. 27, Spring, 1986. Reprinted by permission of the publisher.

British Book News, April, 1986. © *British Book News,* 1986. Both courtesy of *British Book News.*

The Bulletin of Science Fiction Writers of America, Spring, 1986 for "In Memoriam: Frank Herbert, 1920-1986" by Willis E. McNelly. Copyright © 1986 by the author. Reprinted by permission of the publisher and the author.

Canadian Literature, n. 112, Spring, 1987 for "Margaret Atwood's 'The Handmaid's Tale' and the Dystopian Tradition" by Amin Malak. Reprinted by permission of the author.

Canadian Theatre Review, n. 45, Winter, 1985. Copyright © 1985, CTR Publications. Reprinted by permission.

Chicago Tribune, April 27, 1986 for "'Good Mother': A 1st Novel in a Class by Itself" by Catherine Petroski; April 27, 1986 for "Joys of Family Life on Display in 'Monkeys'" by Sherie Posesorski; June 8, 1986 for a review of "The Book of Absent People" by Kate Millet; July 13, 1986 for "Linda Collins Finds Complexity in the Ordinary" by Amy Hempel; July 13, 1986 for "Worthwhile 'Kangaroo' a Real Zoo" by David Holahan; January 11, 1987 for "Boundless Love" by Sven Birkerts. © copyrighted 1986, 1987, Chicago Tribune Company. All rights reserved. All reprinted by permission of the respective authors./ July 20, 1986; October 5, 1986; November 9, 1986. © copyrighted 1986, Chicago Tribune Company. All rights reserved. All used with permission.

The Christian Science Monitor, March 26, 1985 for "Short Stories of Life in the South during the '30s and '40s" by Bruce Allen; August 20, 1986 for "'Before They Made Perelman, They Broke the Mold'" by Gene Langley; September 10, 1986 for "First Full-Scale Biography of Nancy Mitford—and Her Sisters" by Merle Rubin. © 1985, 1986 by the respective authors. All rights reserved. All reprinted by permission of the respective authors./ April 30, 1986; May 21, 1986; July 18, 1986. © 1986 The Christian Science Publishing Society. All rights reserved. All reprinted by permission from *The Christian Science Monitor.*

Chronicles: A Magazine of American Culture, v. 10, March, 1986. Copyright © 1986 by The Rockford Institute. All rights reserved. Reprinted by permission of the publisher.

Commentary, v. 81, March, 1986 for "E. L. Doctorow's 'Jewish' Radicalism" by Carol Iannone; v. 82, July, 1986 for "The Goddess That Failed" by Terry Teachout. Copyright © 1986 by American Jewish Committee. All rights reserved. Both reprinted by permission of the publisher and the respective authors.

Commonweal, v. LXXVII, November 23, 1962. Copyright © 1962 Commonweal Publishing Co., Inc. Reprinted by permission of Commonweal Foundation./ v. CXII, November 29, 1985; v. CXIII, February 14, 1986. Copyright © 1985, 1986 Commonweal Foundation. Both reprinted by permission of Commonweal Foundation.

Cross-Canada Writer's Quarterly, v. 8, 1986 for "Hammering Our Postmodern Kinks" by Judith Fitzgerald. Copyright 1986 by the author. Reprinted by permission of the author.

Crypt of Cthulhu, v. 5, June 15, 1986 for a review of "Songs of a Dead Dreamer" by Robert M. Price. Copyright © 1986. Reprinted by permission of the author.

Daily News, New York, May 19, 1986. © 1986, New York News Inc. Reprinted by permission of the publisher.

Daily Variety, January 6, 1986. Reprinted by permission of the publisher.

The Economist, v. 298, February 22, 1986; v. 300, August 2, 1986. © The Economist Newspaper Limited, 1986. Both reprinted by permission of the publisher.

Event, Summer, 1986. Reprinted by permission of the publisher.

Fantasy Review, v. 9, February, 1986 for "Death of a Prophet" by Bob Collins; v. 9, June, 1986 for "Delights of the Cosmic Macabre" by Michael A. Morrison; v. 9, October, 1986 for "Dan Simmons: 'New Frontiers' in the Cult of Violence" by Bob Collins. Copyright © 1986 by the respective authors. All reprinted by permission of the respective authors.

Forum for Modern Language Studies, v. XVIII, July, 1982 for "Confronting 'Fictions,' Past and Present: Max Frisch's 'Montauk' as Autobiography" by Barbara Saunders. Copyright © by *Forum for Modern Language Studies* and the author. Reprinted by permission of the publisher.

The Georgia Review, v. XXXIX, Winter, 1985; v. XXXIX, Fall, 1985. Copyright, 1985, by the University of Georgia. Both reprinted by permission of the publisher.

The Globe and Mail, Toronto, November 8, 1984. Reprinted by permission of the publisher.

Haunted Library Newsletter, November, 1986. Reprinted by permission of the publisher.

The Hollins Critic, v. XXIII, April, 1986. Copyright 1986 by Hollins College. Reprinted by permission of the publisher.

Horizon, v. 28, September, 1985 for "Taking the Anne Tyler Tour" by Joseph Mathewson. © 1985 by Horizon Publishers, Inc. Reprinted by permission of the publisher and the author.

The Horror Show, v. 5, Spring, 1987. Copyright 1986. Reprinted by permission of the publisher.

The Hudson Review, v. XXXIX, Summer, 1986. Copyright © 1986 by The Hudson Review, Inc. Reprinted by permission of the publisher.

Journal of Commonwealth Literature, v. X, April, 1976 for "In Detentio Preventione in Aeternum: Soyinka's 'A Shuttle in the Crypt'" by C. Tighe. Copyright by the author. By permission of Hans Zell Publishers, an imprint of K. G. Saur Limited.

The Kenyon Review, n.s. v. VIII, Winter, 1986 for "Peter Taylor's Most Recent Fiction" by Jack Matthews. Copyright 1986 by Kenyon College. All rights reserved. Reprinted by permission of the author.

Kirkus Reviews, v. LII, November 1, 1984; v. LIII, April 15, 1985; v. LIII, November 1, 1985; v. LIV, January 1, 1986; v. LIV, March 1, 1986; v. LIV, April 15, 1986; v. LIV, July 1, 1986; v. LIV, November 1, 1986. Copyright © 1984, 1985, 1986 The Kirkus Service, Inc. All rights reserved. All reprinted by permission of the publisher.

Library Journal, v. 110, February 15, 1985 for a review of "Ender's Game" by Jackie Cassada; v. 110, March 1, 1985 for a review of "When the Bough Breaks" by Barbara Conaty; v. 110, September 15, 1985 for a review of "The Triumph of Achilles" by Rhoda Yerburgh; v. 110, December, 1985 for a review of "The Flying Change" by Daniel L. Guillory; v. 111, January, 1986 for a review of "Summer" by Elise Chase; v. 111, March 1, 1986 for a review of "Going to See the Leaves" by Sherrie Tuck; v. 111, July, 1986 for a review of "One Way or Another" by Marcia Tager. Copyright © 1985, 1986 by Reed Publishing, USA, Division of Reed Holdings, Inc. All reprinted from *Library Journal,* published by R. R. Bowker Co., Division of Reed Publishing, USA, by permission of the publisher and the respective authors.

The Listener, v. 114, August 1, 1985 for "A Thousand Accidents" by John Rae; v. 114, November 21, 1985 for "Nancy Mitford's Province" by Stephen Spender. © British Broadcasting Corp. 1985. Both reprinted by permission of A. D. Peters & Co. Ltd./ v. 115, January 16, 1986 for "Honest Stevie" by Peter Kemp; v. 116, October 16, 1986 for "Suspects" by Brian Morton. © British Broadcasting Corp. 1986. Both reprinted by permission of the respective authors.

Locus, February, 1986. Copyright © 1986 by Locus Publications. Reprinted by permission of the author.

London Magazine, n.s. v. 25, November, 1985; n.s. v. 25, February, 1986; n.s. v. 25, March, 1986; n.s. v. 26, April & May, 1986; n.s. v. 26, June, 1986; n.s. v. 26, October, 1986. © *London Magazine* 1985, 1986. All reprinted by permission of the publisher.

London Review of Books, v. 7, September 5, 1985 for "Memphis Blues" by Karl Miller; v. 7, December 19, 1985 for "Palmers Greenery" by Susannah Clapp; v. 8, August 7, 1986 for "Goodbye to Borges" by John Sturrock; v. 8, September 18, 1986 for "Pushing On" by John Bayley; v. 8, October 9, 1986 for "Hello to All That" by Martin Seymour-Smith; v. 8, December 4, 1986 for "Pushing On" by Robert Flint; v. 9, April 2, 1987 for "Philistines" by Barbara Everett; v. 9, April 23, 1987 for "Charmed Lives" by Patrick Parrinder. All appear here by permission of the *London Review of Books* and the respective authors.

Long Island Newsday, December 29, 1986. Reprinted by permission of the publisher.

Los Angeles Times, January 11, 1986; February 13, 1986; April 15, 1986; June 15, 1986; December 29, 1986. Copyright, 1986, Los Angeles Times. All reprinted by permission of the publisher.

Los Angeles Times Book Review, February 3, 1985; June 9, 1985; September 8, 1985; September 15, 1985; November 24, 1985; February 9, 1986; February 23, 1986; June 29, 1986; July 6, 1986; July 27, 1986; September 7, 1986; September 14, 1986; September 28, 1986; January 4, 1987. Copyright, 1985, 1986, 1987, *Los Angeles Times.* All reprinted by permission of the publisher.

Mademoiselle, v. 92, March, 1986 for "Briefing for a Descent into Hell" by Joyce Maynard. Copyright © 1986 by the author. Reprinted by permission of the author.

Manchester Guardian Weekly, February 23, 1986. Copyright © 1986 by Guardian Publications Ltd. Reprinted by permission of Los Angeles Times—Washington Post News Service.

Mile High Futures, December, 1985. © Mile High Comics, Inc. Reprinted by permission of the publisher.

Modern Drama, v. XXX, March, 1987. Copyright *Modern Drama.* University of Toronto. Reprinted by permission of the publisher.

Mother Jones, v. XI, April-May, 1986. Copyright © 1986 by the Foundation for National Progress. Reprinted by permission of the publisher.

Ms., v. XIV, April, 1986 for "Three First Novels Confront the Ultimate Loss" by Diane Cole; v. XV, October, 1986 for a review of "God's Snake" by Joan K. Peters. © 1986 Ms. Magazine Corp. Both reprinted by permission of the respective authors.

The Nation, New York, October 11, 1933; November 13, 1935; April 9, 1949./ v. 242, January 18, 1986; v. 242, February 22, 1986; v. 242, May 10, 1986; v. 242, May 24, 1986. Copyright 1986 *The Nation* magazine, The Nation Company, Inc. All reprinted by permission of the publisher./ v. 172, January 27, 1951. Copyright 1951, renewed 1979, *The Nation* magazine, The Nation Company, Inc. Reprinted by permission of the publisher.

National Review, New York, v. XXXVIII, March 14, 1986; v. XXXVIII, June 6, 1986; v. XXXVIII, July 18, 1986; v. XXXVIII, November 7, 1986. © by National Review, Inc., 150 East 35th Street, New York, NY 10016; 1986. All reprinted with permission of the publisher.

The New Criterion, v. X, October, 1986 for "Jorge Luis Borges, 1899-1986" by James Gardner; v. V, November, 1986 for "The 'Monster' Myth" by Robert Richman. Copyright © 1986 by The Foundation for Cultural Review. Both reprinted by permission of the respective authors.

New Directions for Women, v. 15, May-June, 1986; v. 15, July-August, 1986. © copyright 1986 New Directions for Women, Inc., 108 West Palisade Ave., Englewood NJ 07631. Both reprinted by permission of the publisher.

The New Leader, v. LXVIII, December 16-30, 1985. © 1985 by The American Labor Conference on International Affairs, Inc. Reprinted by permission of the publisher.

New Letters, v. 52, Winter & Spring, 1986 for "Tribute to John Ciardi" by Dan Jaffe. © copyright 1986 The Curators of the University of Missouri. Reprinted by permission of the publisher and the author.

New Letters Review of Books, v. 1, Spring, 1987 for "Knowing Ourselves So Fiercely" by Rush Rankin; v. 1, Spring, 1987 for "Home Deliveries: Cautionary Sex & Violence" by Deborah Navas. © copyright 1987 The Curators of the University of Missouri. All reprinted by permission of the publisher and the respective authors.

The New Republic, v. 124, February 5, 1951./ v. 194, January 27, 1986 for "The Shepard Enigma" by Robert Brustein. © 1986 The New Republic, Inc. Reprinted by permission of the author./ v. 161, August 2, 1969; v. 194, March 17, 1986; v. 194, May 12, 1986; v. 195, August 4, 1986; v. 195, November 3, 1986; v. 196, February 23, 1987; v. 196, March 30, 1987. © 1969, 1986, 1987 The New Republic, Inc. All reprinted by permission of *The New Republic.*

New Statesman, v. 110, August 16, 1985; v. 110, December 13, 1985; v. 111, February 28, 1986; v. 111, April 18, 1986; v. 112, July 11, 1986; v. 112, October 3, 1986; v. 112, November 14, 1986. © 1985, 1986 The Statesmen & Nation Publishing Co. Ltd. All reprinted by permission of the publisher.

New York Magazine, v. 18, June 24, 1985; v. 18, September 2, 1985; v. 19, June 2, 1986; v. 19, September 22, 1986. Copyright © 1985, 1986 by News America Publishing, Inc. All reprinted with the permission of *New York* Magazine.

New York Post, June 7, 1985; May 19, 1986. © 1985, 1986, News America Publishing, Incorporated. Both reprinted from the *New York Post* by permission.

The New York Review of Books, v. XXXIII, June 12, 1986 for "A Farewell to Hemingstein" by Wilfrid Sheed. Copyright © 1986 Nyrev, Inc. Reprinted by permission of the author./ v. XXVII, August 14, 1980; v. XXXII, November 7, 1985; v. XXXII, December 19, 1985; v. XXXIII, August 14, 1986; v. XXXIII, October 23, 1986; v. XXXIII, November 20, 1986. Copyright © 1980, 1985, 1986 Nyrev, Inc. All reprinted by permission from *The New York Review of Books.*

The New York Times, September 27, 1933; October 24, 1936; November 21, 1939. Copyright 1933, 1936, 1939 by The New York Times Company. All reprinted by permission of the publisher./ July 12, 1979; March 12, 1985; June 3, 1985; June 7, 1985; October 31, 1985; December 6, 1985; December 15, 1985; January 6, 1986; January 11, 1986; January 27, 1986; February 3, 1986; February 27, 1986; March 20, 1986; April 2, 1986; April 15, 1986; April 16, 1986; April 23, 1986; May 19, 1986; September 4, 1986; September 8, 1986; September 15, 1986; September 16, 1986; September 30, 1986; November 17, 1986; December 24, 1986; December 29, 1986; February 25, 1987. Copyright © 1979, 1985, 1986, 1987 by The New York Times Company. All reprinted by permission of the publisher.

The New York Times Book Review, February 11, 1986; June 9, 1985; June 16, 1985; September 8, 1985; December 22, 1985; January 26, 1986; February 9, 1986; March 2, 1986; March 9, 1986; March 23, 1986; April 20, 1986; April 27, 1986; May 4, 1986; July 6, 1986; July 13, 1986; July 20, 1986; August 17, 1986; September 7, 1986; September 14, 1986; September 21, 1986; October 5, 1986; October

12, 1986; November 2, 1986; November 23, 1986; November 30, 1986; January 11, 1987. Copyright © 1968, 1985, 1986, 1987 by The New York Times Company. All reprinted by permission of the publisher.

The New Yorker, v. LXI, June 17, 1985 for a review of "I'm Not Rappaport" by Edith Oliver; v. LXI, November 11, 1985 for "Captain McCrae and Captain Call" by Whitney Balliett; v. LXI, December 9, 1985 for "Mel-O-Rols, Knickers, and Gee Bee Racers" by Whitney Balliett; v. LXII, April 28, 1986 for a review of "Kangaroo" by John Updike; v. LXII, June 2, 1986 for a review of "Cuba and His Teddy Bear" by Edith Oliver; v. LXII, December 15, 1986 for "Old World Wickedness" by John Updike. © 1985, 1986 by the respective authors. All reprinted by permission of the publisher./ v. LXI, August 26, 1985; v. LXII, July 7, 1986. © 1985, 1986 by The New Yorker Magazine, Inc. Both reprinted by permission of the publisher./ v. XVIII, February 6, 1943; v. XXX, December 25, 1954. Copyright 1943, renewed 1970; copyright 1954, renewed 1982 by The New Yorker Magazine, Inc. Both reprinted by permission of the publisher.

News/Sun-Sentinel, Fort Lauderdale, February 15, 1987. Reprinted by permission of the publisher.

Newsday, May 19, 1986. © Newsday, Inc. 1986. Reprinted by permission of the publisher.

Newsweek, v. CV, June 3, 1985; v. CVI, November 4, 1985; v. CVI, December 16, 1985; v. CVII, February 17, 1986; v. CVII, March 3, 1986; v. CVII, June 2, 1986; v. CVIII, September 22, 1986; v. CVIII, October 6, 1986; v. CVIII, November 24, 1986. Copyright 1985, 1986, by Newsweek, Inc. All rights reserved. All reprinted by permission of the publisher.

The North American Review, v. 248, Winter, 1939-40./ v. 271, September, 1986. Copyright © 1986 by the University of Northern Iowa. Reprinted by permission from *The North American Review.*

Novel: A Forum on Fiction, v. 19, Spring, 1986. Copyright © Novel Corp., 1986. Reprinted by permission of the publisher.

The Observer, October 13, 1985; December 1, 1985; January 12, 1986; August 24, 1986; September 14, 1986; September 21, 1986; October 19, 1986; November 19, 1986; January 18, 1987; April 26, 1987. All reprinted by permission of The Observer Limited.

Off Our Backs, v. XVI, June 1986 for an interview with Ti-Grace Atkinson, "Adieu, Adieu, Ma Mère Politique," by Carol Anne Douglas. Copyright © Off Our Backs Inc. 1986. Reprinted by permission of Ti-Grace Atkinson and Carol Anne Douglas.

People Weekly, v. 23, October 7, 1985; v. 25, June 2, 1986; v. 26, July 21, 1986; v. 26, September 1, 1986. © 1985, 1986, Time Inc. All reprinted by permission of the publisher.

PN Review, v. 13, 1986 for "Simone de Beauvoir" by Nicolas Tredell; v. 13, 1986 for "Jean Genet" by Nicolas Tredell. © *PN Review* 1986. Both reprinted by permission of the author.

Poesis, v. 7, 1986 for "A Man Is What He Does with His Attention: A Conversation with John Ciardi" by Vince Clemente. © Poesis. Reprinted by permission of the author.

Poetry, v. CXIV, September, 1969 for "'When the Sun Tries to Go On'" by David Lehman; v. CXIX, November, 1972 for "Rhapsode from Cinci" by Paul Carroll; v. CXLVIII, April, 1986 for a review of "The Triumph of Achilles" by Robert B. Shaw; v. CXLVIII, August, 1986 for "John Ciardi: The Many Lives of Poetry" by John Frederick Nims; v. CXLIX, March, 1987 for a review of "The Flying Change" by David Shapiro. © 1969, 1972, 1986, 1987 by The Modern Poetry Association. All reprinted by permission of the Editor of *Poetry* and the respective authors./ v. LXXXV, March, 1955 for "Another Word on Kenneth Koch" by Frank O'Hara. © 1955 by The Modern Poetry Association. Renewed 1983 by Maureen O'Hara-Granville-Smith. Reprinted by permission of the Editor of *Poetry* and the Literary Estate of Frank O'Hara./ v. LXXXVI, June, 1955 for "On Kenneth Koch Again: A Rebuttal" by Harry Roskolenko. © 1955, renewed 1983, by The Modern Poetry Association. Reprinted by permission of the Editor of *Poetry* and the Literary Estate of Harry Roskolenko.

The Progressive, v. 50, March, 1986. Copyright © 1986 by The Progressive, Inc. Reprinted by permission from *The Progressive,* Madison, WI 53703.

Publishers Weekly, v. 227, January 25, 1985; v. 227, April 12, 1985. Copyright © 1985 by Xerox Corporation. Both reprinted from *Publishers Weekly,* published by R. R. Bowker Company, a Xerox company, by permission./ v. 228, September 13, 1985; v. 228, December 20, 1985; v. 229, January 3, 1986; v. 229, January 24, 1986; v. 229, March 7, 1986; v. 229, April 25, 1986; v. 230, July 18, 1986; v. 230, November 7, 1986. Copyright 1985, 1986 by Reed Publishing USA. All reprinted from *Publishers Weekly,* published by R. R. Bowker Company, a Reed Publishing company, by permission.

Punch, v. 290, February 5, 1986. © 1986 by Punch Publications Ltd. All rights reserved. May not be reprinted without permission.

Quill and Quire, v. 51, November, 1985 for a review of "The Suspect" by John North. Reprinted by permission of *Quill and Quire* and the author.

Review, n. 36, January-June, 1986. Copyright © 1986 by the Center for Inter-American Relations, Inc. Reprinted by permission of the publisher.

San Francisco Review of Books, Spring, 1986; Fall, 1986. Copyright © by the *San Francisco Review of Books* 1986. Both reprinted by permission of the publisher.

Saturday Night, v. 101, January, 1986 for "Lady Oracle" by Victoria Glendinning. Copyright © 1986 by *Saturday Night.* Reprinted by permission of the author.

Saturday Review, v. 11, May-June, 1985; v. 12, May-June, 1986. © 1985, 1986 *Saturday Review* magazine. All reprinted by permission of the publisher.

School and Society, v. 70, December 3, 1949.

Science Fiction Chronicle, v. 7, April, 1986; v. 7, July, 1986. Copyright © 1986 by *Science Fiction Chronicle.* All rights reserved. Both reprinted by permission of the publisher.

Science Fiction Review, v. 15, August, 1986 for a review of "Songs of a Dead Dreamer" by Neal Wilgus. Copyright © 1986 by the author. Reprinted by permission of the author.

Shenandoah, v. XXIX, Spring, 1978 for "Simple Poems" by Conrad Hilberry. Copyright 1978 by Washington and Lee University. Reprinted from *Shenandoah* with the permission of the Editor and the author.

The Small Press Review, v. 19, March, 1987. © 1987 by Dustbooks. Reprinted by permission of the publisher.

Sojourner, v. 11, June, 1986; v. 12, December, 1986. Copyright © 1986 by Sojourner Inc. Both reprinted by permission of the publisher.

The Spectator, v. 257, September 13, 1986 for "Another Little Drink Wouldn't Do Us Any Good" by Anita Brookner. © 1986 by *The Spectator.* Reprinted by permission of the author./ v. 255, October 19, 1985; v. 256, January 18, 1986; v. 256, February 1, 1986; v. 256, June 21, 1986; v. 257, October 25, 1986; v. 257, November 22, 1986. © 1985, 1986 by *The Spectator.* All reprinted by permission of *The Spectator.*

Stand Magazine, v. 28, Winter (1986-87) for "Stevie Again—Reviewers Reviewed" by Michael Horovitz. Copyright © by the author. Reprinted by permission of the publisher.

The Sunday Times, London, November 10, 1985; January 12, 1986; April 20, 1986; November 2, 1986; November 30, 1986. © Times Newspapers Limited 1985, 1986. All reproduced from *The Sunday Times,* London by permission.

Sunday Today, July 13, 1986. ©by *Today.* Reproduced by permission of *Today.*

Theatre Arts, v. XLVII, August-September, 1963 for "Max Frisch: The Saga of Bahnhofstrasse" by Alan Pryce-Jones. Reprinted by permission of the author.

Theatre Arts Monthly, v. XIX, December, 1935.

Theatrum, April, 1985. Reprinted by permission of the publisher.

Time, v. 125, February 4, 1985; v. 125, June 10, 1985; v. 126, December 16, 1985; v. 126, December 18, 1985; v. 127, February 17, 1986; v. 127, June 2, 1986; v. 127, June 9, 1986; v. 128, October 13, 1986; v. 128, October 20, 1986. Copyright 1985, 1986 Time Inc. All rights reserved. All reprinted by permission from *Time.*

The Times, London, March 20, 1986; April 15, 1986; April 16, 1986. © Times Newspapers Limited 1986. All reprinted by permission of the publisher.

The Times Educational Supplement, n. 3623, December 6, 1985. © Times Newspapers Ltd. (London). Reproduced from *The Times Educational Supplement* by permission.

The Times Literary Supplement, n. 4305, October 4, 1985; n. 4308, October 25, 1985; n. 4313, November 29, 1985; n. 4319, January 10, 1986; n. 4324, February 14, 1986; n. 4332, April 11, 1986; n. 4348, August 1, 1986; n. 4350, August 15, 1986; n. 4353, September 5, 1986; n. 4362, November 7, 1986; n. 4367, December 12, 1986. © Times Newspapers Ltd. (London) 1985, 1986. All Reproduced from *The Times Literary Supplement* by permission.

Today, July 7, 1986. Reprinted by permission of the publisher.

University of Toronto Quarterly, v. 56, Fall, 1986. © University of Toronto Press 1986. Reprinted by permission of University of Toronto Press.

Tribune, v. 50, November 21, 1986. Reprinted by permission of *Tribune,* London.

USA Today, December 6, 1985; February 28, 1986; April 4, 1986. Copyright, 1985, 1986 *USA Today*. All excerpted with permission of the publisher.

Variety, December 12, 1984; January 23, 1985; December 11, 1985. Copyright 1984, 1985, by Variety, Inc. All reprinted by permission of the publisher.

VLS, n. 49, October, 1986. Copyright © 1986 News Group Publications, Inc. Reprinted by permission of the publisher.

The Village Voice, v. XXX, June 25, 1985 for ''Herb without Spice'' by Julius Novick; v. XXX, November 26, 1985 for ''Back to the Future'' by J. Hoberman; v. XXXI, April 29, 1986 for ''Jean Genet, 1910-1986'' by Richard Gilman; v. XXXI, May 20, 1986 for ''Hello Kitty'' by Jacqueline Austin; v. XXXI, May 27, 1986 for ''Rebel Girl'' by Ellen Willis; v. XXXI, May 27, 1986 for ''Cuba Si, Teddy No'' by Michael Feingold; v. XXXI, September 23, 1986 for ''Laughing on the Outside'' by L. S. Klepp; v. XXXI, December 30, 1986 for ''Stale Fire: Nabokov's Nemesis Strikes Again'' by Ross Wetzsteon; v. XXXII, February 3, 1987 for ''Motherhood is Powerful'' by Laurie Stone. Copyright © News Group Publications, Inc., 1985, 1986, 1987. All reprinted by permission of *The Village Voice* and the respective authors.

The Virginia Quarterly Review, v. 63 (Winter, 1987). Copyright, 1987, by *The Virginia Quarterly Review*, The University of Virginia. Reprinted by permission of the publisher.

Vogue, v. 176, October, 1986. Copyright © 1986 by The Condé Nast Publications Inc. Courtesy *Vogue*.

The Wall Street Journal, February 7, 1986 for ''Yesterday's World of Tomorrow'' by Hilton Kramer. Copyright © 1986 by Hilton Kramer. Reprinted by permission of Georges Borchardt, Inc. and the author./ September 10, 1986 for ''Heft and Heavy Breathing'' by Joanne Kaufman. © Dow Jones & Company, Inc. 1986. All rights reserved. Reprinted by permission of the author./ July 17, 1986. © Dow Jones & Company, Inc. 1986. All rights reserved. Reprinted by permission of *The Wall Street Journal*.

The Washington Post, March 20, 1986; April 16, 1986; June 15, 1986; December 29, 1986. © 1986, Washington Post Co. All reprinted by permission of the publisher.

Washington Times, March 24, 1986. Reprinted by permission of the publisher.

Western American Literature, v. XXI, November, 1986. Copyright, 1986, by the Western Literature Association. Reprinted by permission of the publisher.

World Literature Today, v. 58, Winter, 1984; v. 60, Winter, 1986; v. 60, Autumn, 1986. Copyright 1984, 1986 by the University of Oklahoma Press. All reprinted by permission of the publisher.

The Women's Review of Books, v. III, July, 1986 for ''Choice of Evils'' by Gayle Greene; v. III, September, 1986 for ''Dance of Life'' by E. M. Broner. Copyright © 1986. All rights reserved. Both reprinted by permission of the respective authors.

The Yale Review, v. 74, July, 1985. Copyright 1985, by Yale University. Reprinted by permission of the editors

THE EXCERPTS IN CLC, VOLUME 44, WERE REPRINTED FROM THE FOLLOWING BOOKS:

Berke, Roberta. From *Bounds Out of Bounds: A Compass for Recent American and British Poetry*. Oxford University Press, 1981. Copyright © 1981 by Roberta Berke. Reprinted by permission of Oxford University Press, Inc. In Canada by Sterling Lord Literistic, Inc.

Butler, Michael. From *The Novels of Max Frisch*. Wolff, 1976. © 1976 Oswald Wolff (Publishers) Ltd., London. Reprinted by permission of Berg Publishers Ltd.

Campbell, Ramsey. From an introduction to *Songs of a Dead Dreamer*. By Thomas Ligotti. Silver Scarab Press, 1986. Introduction copyright © 1985 by Ramsey Campbell. Reprinted by permission of Ramsey Campbell.

Jurgensen, Manfred. From "The Drama of Frisch," in *Perspectives on Max Frisch*. Edited by Gerhard F. Probst and Jay F. Bodine. University Press of Kentucky, 1982. Copyright © 1982 by The University Press of Kentucky. Reprinted by permission of the publisher.

Kieser, Rolf. From "Wedding Bells for Don Juan: Frisch's Domestication of a Myth," in *Perspectives on Max Frisch*. Edited by Gerhard F. Probst and Jay F. Bodine. University Press of Kentucky, 1982. Copyright © 1982 by The University Press of Kentucky. Reprinted by permission of the publisher.

Lewis, Allan. From *American Plays and Playwrights of the Contemporary Theatre*. Crown, 1965. Copyright © 1965 by Allan Lewis. Used by permission of Crown Publishers, Inc.

Natan, Alex. From an introduction to *German Men of Letters: Twelve Literary Essays, Vol. III*. Edited by Alex Natan. Wolff, 1964. © 1964 Oswald Wolff (Publishers) Limited, London. Reprinted by permission of Berg Publishers Ltd.

O'Hara, Frank. From *Standing Still and Walking in New York*. Edited by Donald Allen. Grey Fox Press, 1975. Copyright © 1975 by Maureen Granville-Smith, Administratrix of the Estate of Frank O'Hara. Reprinted by permission of the publisher.

Osofisian, Femi. From "Tiger on Stage: Wole Soyinka and Nigerian Theatre," in *Theatre in Africa*. Edited by Oyin Ogunba and Abiola Irele. Ibadan University Press, 1978. © Ibadan University Press, 1978. All rights reserved. Reprinted by permission of the publisher.

Palmer, Eustace. From *The Growth of the African Novel*. Heinemann Educational Books Ltd., 1979. © Eustace Palmer 1979. Reprinted by permission of the publisher.

Roscoe, Adrian A. From *Mother Is Gold: A Study in West African Literature*. Cambridge at the University Press, 1971. © Cambridge University Press 1971. Reprinted by permission of the publisher.

Salmonson, Jessica Amanda. From *Heroic Visions II*. Edited by Jessica Amanda Salmonson. ACE Fantasy Books, 1986. Copyright © 1986 by Jessica Amanda Salmonson. All rights reserved. Reprinted by permission of the publisher.

Steinmetz, Horst. From "Frisch as a Diarist," translated by Jay F. Bodine, in *Perspectives on Max Frisch*. Edited by Gerhard F. Probst and Jay F. Bodine. University Press of Kentucky, 1982. Copyright © 1982 by The University Press of Kentucky. Reprinted by permission of the publisher.

Vernon, John. From "Fresh Air: Humor in Contemporary American Poetry," in *Comic Relief: Humor in Contemporary American Literature*. Edited by Sarah Blacher Cohen. University of Illinois Press, 1978. © 1978 by the Board of Trustees of the University of Illinois. Reprinted by permission of the publisher and the author.

THE EXCERPTS FROM THE AUTHOR'S WORKS IN CLC, VOLUME 44, WERE REPRINTED FROM THE FOLLOWING BOOKS:

Aleshkovsky, Yuz. From *Kangaroo*. Translated by Tamara Glenny. Farrar, Straus and Giroux, 1986. Translation copyright © 1986 by Farrar, Straus and Giroux, Inc.

Amis, Kingsley. From *The Old Devils: A Novel*. Summit Books, 1987. Copyright © 1987 by Kingsley Amis. All rights reserved.

Atwood, Margaret. From *The Handmaid's Tale*. Houghton Mifflin Company, 1986. Copyright © 1986 by O. W. Toad, Ltd. All rights reserved.

Barbera, Jack and William McBrien. From *Stevie: A Biography of Stevie Smith*. William Heinemann Limited, 1985. Copyright © 1985 by Jack Barbera and William McBrien. All rights reserved.

Branden, Barbara. From *The Passion of Ayn Rand*. Doubleday & Company, Inc., 1986. Copyright © 1986 by Barbara Branden. All rights reserved.

Burnshaw, Stanley. From *Robert Frost Himself*. George Braziller, Inc., Publishers, 1986. Copyright © 1986 by Stanley Burnshaw. All rights reserved.

Cameron, Peter. From *One Way or Another: Stories*. Harper & Row, Publishers, 1986. Copyright © 1986 by Peter Cameron. All rights reserved.

Card, Orson Scott. From *Ender's Game*. Tom Doherty Associates, 1985. Copyright © 1977, 1985 by Orson Scott Card. All rights reserved.

Collins, Linda. From *Going to See the Leaves*. Viking Penguin Inc., 1986. Copyright © Linda Collins, 1986. All rights reserved.

Currie, Ellen. From *Available Light: A Novel*. Summit Books, 1986. Copyright © 1986 by Ellen Currie. All rights reserved.

Doctorow, E. L. From *World's Fair*. Random House, 1985. Copyright © 1985 by E. L. Doctorow. All rights reserved.

Field, Andrew. From *VN: The Life and Art of Vladimir Nabokov*. Crown Publishers, 1986. Copyright © 1986 by Andrew Field. All rights reserved.

Gardner, Herb. From an extract in an unpublished script of his *I'm Not Rappaport*, 1985.

Ghosh, Amitav. From *The Circle of Reason*. Viking Penguin Inc., 1986. Copyright © Amitav Ghosh, 1986. All rights reserved.

Gluck, Louise. From *The Triumph of Achilles*. The Ecco Press, 1985. Copyright © 1985 by Louise Glück. All rights reserved.

Graves, Richard Perceval. From *Robert Graves: The Assault Heroic, 1895-1926*. Viking Penguin Inc., 1986. Copyright © Richard Perceval Graves, 1986.

Grunwald, Lisa. From *Summer*. Alfred A. Knopf, 1985. Copyright © 1985 by Lisa Grunwald. All rights reserved.

Hastings, Selina. From *Nancy Mitford: A Biography*. E. P. Dutton, 1985. Copyright © 1985 by Selina Hastings. All rights reserved.

Hayman, Ronald. From *Sartre: A Life*. Simon and Schuster, 1987. Copyright © 1987 by Ronald Hayman. All rights reserved.

Herrmann, Dorothy. From *S. J. Perelman: A Life*. G. P. Putnam's Sons, 1986. Copyright © 1986 by Dorothy Herrmann. All rights reserved.

Kellerman, Jonathan. From *When the Bough Breaks*. Atheneum, 1985. Copyright © 1985 by Jonathan Kellerman. All rights reserved.

Ligotti, Thomas. From *Songs of a Dead Dreamer*. Silver Scarab Press, 1986. Copyright © 1985 by Thomas Ligotti.

Maso, Carole. From *Ghost Dance*. North Point Press, 1986. Copyright © 1986 by Carole Maso.

McMurtry, Larry. From *Lonesome Dove*. Simon & Schuster, 1985. Copyright © 1985 by Larry McMurtry. All rights reserved.

Merkin, Daphne. From *Enchantment*. Harcourt Brace Jovanovich, Publishers, 1986. Copyright © 1986, 1984 by Daphne Merkin.

Miller, Sue. From *The Good Mother*. Harper & Row, Publishers, 1986. Copyright © 1986 by Sue Miller. All rights reserved.

Minot, Susan. From *Monkeys*. E. P. Dutton/Seymour Lawrence, 1986. Copyright © 1986 by Susan Minot. All rights reserved.

Modarressi, Taghi. From *The Book of Absent People*. Doubleday & Company, Inc., 1986. Copyright © 1986 by Taghi Modarressi.

Povod, Reinaldo. From *Cuba and His Teddy Bear*, 1986. Copyright © 1986 by Reinaldo Povod. All rights reserved.

Rampersad, Arnold. From *The Life of Langston Hughes: I, Too, Sing America, 1902-1941, Vol. I*. Oxford University Press, 1986. Copyright © by Oxford University Press, Inc.

Reynolds, Michael. From *The Young Hemingway*. Basil Blackwell, 1986. © Michael S. Reynolds 1986. All rights reserved.

Rush, Norman. From *Whites: Stories*. Alfred A. Knopf, 1986. Copyright © 1984, 1985, 1986 by Norman Rush. All rights reserved.

Shepard, Sam. From *A Lie of the Mind*. New American Library, 1987. Copyright © 1986 by Sam Shepard. All rights reserved.

Simmons, Dan. From *Song of Kali*. Tom Doherty Associates, 1986. Copyright © 1985 by Dan Simmons. All rights reserved.

Simpson, Mona. From *Anywhere but Here*. Alfred A. Knopf, 1987. Copyright © 1986 by Mona Simpson. All rights reserved.

Spanidou, Irini. From *God's Snake*. W. W. Norton & Company, 1986. Copyright © 1986 by Irini Spanidou. All rights reserved.

Süskind, Patrick. From *Perfume: The Story of a Murderer*. Alfred A. Knopf, 1986. Copyright © 1986 by Alfred A. Knopf, Inc. All rights reserved.

Taylor, Henry. From *The Flying Change: Poems*. Louisiana State University Press, 1985. Copyright © 1985 by Henry Taylor. All rights reserved. Reprinted by permission of Louisiana State University Press.

Taylor, Peter. From *The Old Forest and Other Stories*. The Dial Press, 1985. Copyright © 1941, 1945, 1947, 1949, 1951, 1958, 1959, 1979, 1981, 1985 by Peter Taylor. All rights reserved.

Tyler, Anne. From *The Accidental Tourist*. Alfred A. Knopf, 1985. Copyright © 1985 by Anne Tyler Modarressi, et al. All rights reserved.

Wah, Fred. From *Waiting for Saskatchewan*. Turnstone Press, 1985. Copyright © 1985 Fred Wah.

Walker, George F. From *Criminals in Love*. Playwrights Canada, 1985. Copyright © 1984 George F. Walker. All rights reserved.

Wiley, Richard. From *Soldiers in Hiding: A Novel*. The Atlantic Monthly Press, 1986. Copyright © by Richard Wiley. All rights reserved.

Wright, William. From *Lillian Hellman: The Image, the Woman*. Simon & Schuster, 1986. Copyright © 1986 by William C. Wright. All rights reserved.

Literary Criticism Series
Cumulative Author Index

This index lists all author entries in the Gale Literary Criticism Series and includes cross-references to other Gale sources. For the convenience of the reader, references to the *Yearbook* in the *Contemporary Literary Criticism* series include the page number (in parentheses) after the volume number. References in the index are identified as follows:

AITN: *Authors in the News,* Volumes 1-2
CAAS: *Contemporary Authors Autobiography Series,* Volumes 1-5
CA: *Contemporary Authors* (original series), Volumes 1-120
CABS: *Contemporary Authors Bibliographical Series,* Volumes 1-2
CANR: *Contemporary Authors New Revision Series,* Volumes 1-20
CAP: *Contemporary Authors Permanent Series,* Volumes 1-2
CA-R: *Contemporary Authors* (revised editions), Volumes 1-44
CDALB: *Concise Dictionary of American Literary Biography*
CLC: *Contemporary Literary Criticism,* Volumes 1-44
CLR: *Children's Literature Review,* Volumes 1-13
DLB: *Dictionary of Literary Biography,* Volumes 1-57
DLB-DS: *Dictionary of Literary Biography Documentary Series,* Volumes 1-4
DLB-Y: *Dictionary of Literary Biography Yearbook,* Volumes 1980-1986
LC: *Literature Criticism from 1400 to 1800,* Volumes 1-6
NCLC: *Nineteenth-Century Literature Criticism,* Volumes 1-15
SAAS: *Something about the Author Autobiography Series,* Volumes 1-3
SATA: *Something about the Author,* Volumes 1-48
TCLC: *Twentieth-Century Literary Criticism,* Volumes 1-24
YABC: *Yesterday's Authors of Books for Children,* Volumes 1-2

Author Index

Author Index

Author Index

Epstein, Daniel Mark 1948- .... **CLC 7**
See also CANR 2
See also CA 49-52

Epstein, Jacob 1956- .... **CLC 19**
See also CA 114

Epstein, Joseph 1937- .... **CLC 39** (463)
See also CA 112, 119

Epstein, Leslie 1938- .... **CLC 27**
See also CA 73-76

Erdman, Paul E(mil) 1932- .... **CLC 25**
See also CANR 13
See also CA 61-64
See also AITN 1

Erdrich, Louise 1954- .... **CLC 39** (128)
See also CA 114

Erenburg, Ilya (Grigoryevich) 1891-1967
See Ehrenburg, Ilya (Grigoryevich)

Eseki, Bruno 1919-
See Mphahlele, Ezekiel

Esenin, Sergei (Aleksandrovich)
1895-1925 .... **TCLC 4**
See also CA 104

Eshleman, Clayton 1935- .... **CLC 7**
See also CA 33-36R
See also DLB 5

Espriu, Salvador 1913-1985 .... **CLC 9**
See also obituary CA 115

Evans, Marian 1819-1880
See Eliot, George

Evans, Mary Ann 1819-1880
See Eliot, George

Evarts, Esther 1900-1972
See Benson, Sally

Everson, Ronald G(ilmour)
1903- .... **CLC 27**
See also CA 17-20R

Everson, William (Oliver)
1912- .... **CLC 1, 5, 14**
See also CANR 20
See also CA 9-12R
See also DLB 5, 16

Evtushenko, Evgenii (Aleksandrovich) 1933-
See Yevtushenko, Yevgeny

Ewart, Gavin (Buchanan)
1916- .... **CLC 13**
See also CANR 17
See also CA 89-92
See also DLB 40

Ewers, Hanns Heinz
1871-1943 .... **TCLC 12**
See also CA 109

Ewing, Frederick R. 1918-
See Sturgeon, Theodore (Hamilton)

Exley, Frederick (Earl)
1929- .... **CLC 6, 11**
See also CA 81-84
See also DLB-Y 81
See also AITN 2

Ezekiel, Tish O'Dowd
1943- .... **CLC 34** (46)

Fagen, Donald 1948-
See Becker, Walter and Fagen, Donald

Fagen, Donald 1948- and
Becker, Walter 1950-
See Becker, Walter and Fagen, Donald

Fair, Ronald L. 1932- .... **CLC 18**
See also CA 69-72
See also DLB 33

Fairbairns, Zoë (Ann) 1948- .... **CLC 32**
See also CA 103

Fairfield, Cicily Isabel 1892-1983
See West, Rebecca

Fallaci, Oriana 1930- .... **CLC 11**
See also CANR 15
See also CA 77-80

Faludy, George 1913- .... **CLC 42**
See also CA 21-24R

Fargue, Léon-Paul 1876-1947 .... **TCLC 11**
See also CA 109

Farigoule, Louis 1885-1972
See Romains, Jules

Fariña, Richard 1937?-1966 .... **CLC 9**
See also CA 81-84
See also obituary CA 25-28R

Farley, Walter 1920- .... **CLC 17**
See also CANR 8
See also CA 17-20R
See also SATA 2, 43
See also DLB 22

Farmer, Philip José 1918- ...... **CLC 1, 19**
See also CANR 4
See also CA 1-4R
See also DLB 8

Farrell, J(ames) G(ordon)
1935-1979 .... **CLC 6**
See also CA 73-76
See also obituary CA 89-92
See also DLB 14

Farrell, James T(homas)
1904-1979 .... **CLC 1, 4, 8, 11**
See also CANR 9
See also CA 5-8R
See also obituary CA 89-92
See also DLB 4, 9
See also DLB-DS 2

Farrell, M. J. 1904-
See Keane, Molly

Fassbinder, Rainer Werner
1946-1982 .... **CLC 20**
See also CA 93-96
See also obituary CA 106

Fast, Howard (Melvin) 1914- .... **CLC 23**
See also CANR 1
See also CA 1-4R
See also SATA 7
See also DLB 9

Faulkner, William (Cuthbert)
1897-1962 .... **CLC 1, 3, 6, 8, 9, 11, 14, 18, 28**
See also CA 81-84
See also DLB 9, 11, 44
See also DLB-Y 86
See also DLB-DS 2
See also AITN 1

Fauset, Jessie Redmon
1884?-1961 .... **CLC 19**
See also CA 109

Faust, Irvin 1924- .... **CLC 8**
See also CA 33-36R
See also DLB 2, 28
See also DLB-Y 80

Federman, Raymond 1928- .... **CLC 6**
See also CANR 10
See also CA 17-20R
See also DLB-Y 80

Federspiel, J(ürg) F. 1931- .... **CLC 42**

Feiffer, Jules 1929- .... **CLC 2, 8**
See also CA 17-20R
See also SATA 8
See also DLB 7, 44

Feinstein, Elaine 1930- .... **CLC 36**
See also CA 69-72
See also CAAS 1
See also DLB 14, 40

Feldman, Irving (Mordecai)
1928- .... **CLC 7**
See also CANR 1
See also CA 1-4R

Fellini, Federico 1920- .... **CLC 16**
See also CA 65-68

Felsen, Gregor 1916-
See Felsen, Henry Gregor

Felsen, Henry Gregor 1916- .... **CLC 17**
See also CANR 1
See also CA 1-4R
See also SAAS 2
See also SATA 1

Fenton, James (Martin) 1949- ...... **CLC 32**
See also CA 102
See also DLB 40

Ferber, Edna 1887-1968 .... **CLC 18**
See also CA 5-8R
See also obituary CA 25-28R
See also SATA 7
See also DLB 9, 28
See also AITN 1

Ferlinghetti, Lawrence (Monsanto)
1919?- .... **CLC 2, 6, 10, 27**
See also CANR 3
See also CA 5-8R
See also DLB 5, 16
See also CDALB 1941-1968

Ferrier, Susan (Edmonstone)
1782-1854 .... **NCLC 8**

Feuchtwanger, Lion
1884-1958 .... **TCLC 3**
See also CA 104

Feydeau, Georges 1862-1921 ..... **TCLC 22**
See also CA 113

Fiedler, Leslie A(aron)
1917- .... **CLC 4, 13, 24**
See also CANR 7
See also CA 9-12R
See also DLB 28

Field, Andrew 1938- .... **CLC 44** (463)

Field, Eugene 1850-1895 .... **NCLC 3**
See also SATA 16
See also DLB 21, 23, 42

Fielding, Henry 1707-1754 .... **LC 1**
See also DLB 39

Fielding, Sarah 1710-1768 .... **LC 1**
See also DLB 39

Fierstein, Harvey 1954- .... **CLC 33**

Figes, Eva 1932- .... **CLC 31**
See also CANR 4
See also CA 53-56
See also DLB 14

Author Index

Hiraoka, Kimitake 1925-1970
See Mishima, Yukio
See also CA 97-100
See also obituary CA 29-32R

Hirsch, Edward 1950-............. **CLC 31**
See also CANR 20
See also CA 104

Hitchcock, (Sir) Alfred (Joseph)
1899-1980.................... **CLC 16**
See also obituary CA 97-100
See also SATA 27
See also obituary SATA 24

Hoagland, Edward 1932-.......... **CLC 28**
See also CANR 2
See also CA 1-4R
See also DLB 6

Hoban, Russell C(onwell)
1925-...................... **CLC 7, 25**
See also CLR 3
See also CA 5-8R
See also SATA 1, 40
See also DLB 52

Hobson, Laura Z(ametkin)
1900-1986................. **CLC 7, 25**
See also CA 17-20R
See also obituary CA 118
See also DLB 28

Hochhuth, Rolf 1931-....... **CLC 4, 11, 18**
See also CA 5-8R

Hochman, Sandra 1936-......... **CLC 3, 8**
See also CA 5-8R
See also DLB 5

Hochwälder, Fritz 1911-........... **CLC 36**
See also CA 29-32R
See also obituary CA 120

Hocking, Mary (Eunice) 1921 ..... **CLC 13**
See also CANR 18
See also CA 101

Hodgins, Jack 1938- .... **CLC 23**
See also CA 93-96

Hodgson, William Hope
1877-1918.................. **TCLC 13**
See also CA 111

Hoffman, Daniel (Gerard)
1923-.................. **CLC 6, 13, 23**
See also CANR 4
See also CA 1-4R
See also DLB 5

Hoffman, Stanley 1944- .... **CLC 5**
See also CA 77-80

Hoffman, William M(oses)
1939-......................... **CLC 40**
See also CANR 11
See also CA 57-60

Hoffmann, Ernst Theodor Amadeus
1776-1822................... **NCLC 2**
See also SATA 27

Hofmannsthal, Hugo (Laurenz August Hofmann Edler) von
1874-1929................. **TCLC 11**
See also CA 106

Hogg, James 1770-1835 .... **NCLC 4**

Holberg, Ludvig 1684-1754 .... **LC 6**

Holden, Ursula 1921- .... **CLC 18**
See also CA 101

Holdstock, Robert (P.)
1948- .... **CLC 39** (151)

Holland, Isabelle 1920-............ **CLC 21**
See also CANR 10
See also CA 21-24R
See also SATA 8

Holland, Marcus 1900-1985
See Caldwell, (Janet Miriam) Taylor (Holland)

Hollander, John 1929- ..... **CLC 2, 5, 8, 14**
See also CANR 1
See also CA 1-4R
See also SATA 13
See also DLB 5

Holleran, Andrew 1943?-.......... **CLC 38**

Hollis, Jim 1916-
See Summers, Hollis (Spurgeon, Jr.)

Holmes, Oliver Wendell
1809-1894................. **NCLC 14**
See also SATA 34
See also DLB 1

Holt, Victoria 1906-
See Hibbert, Eleanor (Burford)

Holub, Miroslav 1923- .... **CLC 4**
See also CANR 10
See also CA 21-24R

Honig, Edwin 1919-............... **CLC 33**
See also CANR 4
See also CA 5-8R
See also DLB 5

Hood, Hugh (John Blagdon)
1928-.................... **CLC 15, 28**
See also CANR 1
See also CA 49-52
See also DLB 53

Hooker, (Peter) Jeremy 1924-...... **CLC 43**
See also CA 77-80
See also DLB 40

Hope, A(lec) D(erwent) 1907- .... **CLC 3**
See also CA 21-24R

Hopkins, John (Richard) 1931-...... **CLC 4**
See also CA 85-88

Horgan, Paul 1903-................ **CLC 9**
See also CANR 9
See also CA 13-16R
See also SATA 13
See also DLB-Y 85

Horwitz, Julius 1920- .... **CLC 14**
See also CANR 12
See also CA 9-12R

Hospital, Janette Turner 1942-..... **CLC 42**
See also CA 108

Hostos (y Bonilla), Eugenio María de
1893-1903.................. **TCLC 24**

Hougan, Carolyn 19??-....... **CLC 34** (60)

Household, Geoffrey (Edward West)
1900-......................... **CLC 11**
See also CA 77-80
See also SATA 14

Housman, A(lfred) E(dward)
1859-1936................ **TCLC 1, 10**
See also CA 104
See also DLB 19

Housman, Laurence
1865-1959.................. **TCLC 7**
See also CA 106
See also SATA 25
See also DLB 10

Howard, Elizabeth Jane
1923-..................... **CLC 7, 29**
See also CANR 8
See also CA 5-8R

Howard, Maureen 1930-........ **CLC 5, 14**
See also CA 53-56
See also DLB-Y 83

Howard, Richard 1929- .... **CLC 7, 10**
See also CA 85-88
See also DLB 5
See also AITN 1

Howard, Robert E(rvin)
1906-1936.................. **TCLC 8**
See also CA 105

Howe, Julia Ward 1819-1910 .... **TCLC 21**
See also CA 117
See also DLB 1

Howells, William Dean
1837-1920................ **TCLC 7, 17**
See also CA 104
See also DLB 12

Howes, Barbara 1914- .... **CLC 15**
See also CAAS 3
See also CA 9-12R
See also SATA 5

Hrabal, Bohumil 1914-............ **CLC 13**
See also CA 106

Hubbard, L(afayette) Ron(ald)
1911-1986.................... **CLC 43**
See also CA 77-80
See also obituary CA 118

Huch, Ricarda (Octavia)
1864-1947.................. **TCLC 13**
See also CA 111

Hueffer, Ford Madox 1873-1939
See Ford, Ford Madox

Hughart, Barry 1934-....... **CLC 39** (155)

Hughes, Edward James 1930-
See Hughes, Ted

Hughes, (James) Langston
1902-1967........**CLC 1, 5, 10, 15, 35, 44** (506)
See also CANR 1
See also CA 1-4R
See also obituary CA 25-28R
See also SATA 4, 33
See also DLB 4, 7, 48

Hughes, Richard (Arthur Warren)
1900-1976................. **CLC 1, 11**
See also CANR 4
See also CA 5-8R
See also obituary CA 65-68
See also SATA 8
See also obituary SATA 25
See also DLB 15

Hughes, Ted 1930-..... **CLC 2, 4, 9, 14, 37**
See also CLR 3
See also CANR 1
See also CA 1-4R
See also SATA 27
See also DLB 40

Hugo, Richard F(ranklin)
1923-1982.............. **CLC 6, 18, 32**
See also CANR 3
See also CA 49-52
See also obituary CA 108
See also DLB 5

Author Index

Author Index

Author Index

Sartre, Jean-Paul 1905-1980...... **CLC 1, 4, 7, 9, 13, 18, 24, 44** (493)
See also CA 9-12R
See also obituary CA 97-100

Sassoon, Siegfried (Lorraine) 1886-1967....................**CLC 36**
See also CA 104
See also Obituary CA 25-28R
See also DLB 20

Saura, Carlos 1932-...............**CLC 20**
See also CA 114

Sauser-Hall, Frédéric-Louis 1887-1961
See Cendrars, Blaise
See also CA 102
See also obituary CA 93-96

Savage, Thomas 1915- ....**CLC 40**

Sayers, Dorothy L(eigh) 1893-1957................ **TCLC 2, 15**
See also CA 104, 119
See also DLB 10, 36

Sayles, John (Thomas) 1950-.................. **CLC 7, 10, 14**
See also CA 57-60
See also DLB 44

Scammell, Michael 19??- .... **CLC 34** (480)

Schaeffer, Susan Fromberg 1941-.................. **CLC 6, 11, 22**
See also CANR 18
See also CA 49-52
See also SATA 22
See also DLB 28

Schell, Jonathan 1943- ....**CLC 35**
See also CANR 12
See also CA 73-76

Scherer, Jean-Marie Maurice 1920-
See Rohmer, Eric
See also CA 110

Schevill, James (Erwin) 1920-.......**CLC 7**
See also CA 5-8R

Schisgal, Murray (Joseph) 1926-.........................**CLC 6**
See also CA 21-24R

Schlee, Ann 1934- ....**CLC 35**
See also CA 101
See also SATA 36

Schlegel, August Wilhelm von 1767-1845................. **NCLC 15**

Schlegel, Johann Elias (von) 1719?-1749..................... **LC 5**

Schmitz, Ettore 1861-1928
See Svevo, Italo
See also CA 104

Schnackenberg, Gjertrud 1953-........................**CLC 40**
See also CA 116

Schneider, Leonard Alfred 1925-1966
See Bruce, Lenny
See also CA 89-92

Schnitzler, Arthur 1862-1931 ..... **TCLC 4**
See also CA 104

Schorer, Mark 1908-1977 ....**CLC 9**
See also CANR 7
See also CA 5-8R
See also obituary CA 73-76

Schrader, Paul (Joseph) 1946-......**CLC 26**
See also CA 37-40R
See also DLB 44

Schreiner (Cronwright), Olive (Emilie Albertina) 1855-1920 .... **TCLC 9**
See also CA 105
See also DLB 18

Schulberg, Budd (Wilson) 1914- .....**CLC 7**
See also CANR 19
See also CA 25-28R
See also DLB 6, 26, 28
See also DLB-Y 81

Schulz, Bruno 1892-1942......... **TCLC 5**
See also CA 115

Schulz, Charles M(onroe) 1922-........................**CLC 12**
See also CANR 6
See also CA 9-12R
See also SATA 10

Schuyler, James (Marcus) 1923-..................... **CLC 5, 23**
See also CA 101
See also DLB 5

Schwartz, Delmore 1913-1966.............. **CLC 2, 4, 10**
See also CAP 2
See also CA 17-18
See also obituary CA 25-28R
See also DLB 28, 48

Schwartz, Lynne Sharon 1939-.....**CLC 31**
See also CA 103

Schwarz-Bart, André 1928-...... **CLC 2, 4**
See also CA 89-92

Schwarz-Bart, Simone 1938- ....**CLC 7**
See also CA 97-100

Schwob, (Mayer Andre) Marcel 1867-1905................. **TCLC 20**
See also CA 117

Sciascia, Leonardo 1921- ..... **CLC 8, 9, 41**
See also CA 85-88

Scoppettone, Sandra 1936-.........**CLC 26**
See also CA 5-8R
See also SATA 9

Scorsese, Martin 1942- ....**CLC 20**
See also CA 110, 114

Scotland, Jay 1932-
See Jakes, John (William)

Scott, Duncan Campbell 1862-1947.................. **TCLC 6**
See also CA 104

Scott, Evelyn 1893-1963...........**CLC 43**
See also CA 104
See also obituary CA 112
See also DLB 9, 48

Scott, F(rancis) R(eginald) 1899-1985...................**CLC 22**
See also CA 101
See also obituary CA 114

Scott, Paul (Mark) 1920-1978 ....**CLC 9**
See also CA 81-84
See also obituary CA 77-80
See also DLB 14

Scott, Sir Walter 1771-1832...... **NCLC 15**
See also YABC 2

Scudéry, Madeleine de 1607-1701..... **LC 2**

Seare, Nicholas 1925-
See Trevanian
See also Whitaker, Rodney

Sebestyen, Igen 1924-
See Sebestyen, Ouida

Sebestyen, Ouida 1924-............**CLC 30**
See also CA 107
See also SATA 39

Seelye, John 1931-.................**CLC 7**
See also CA 97-100

Seferiades, Giorgos Stylianou 1900-1971
See Seferis, George
See also CANR 5
See also CA 5-8R
See also obituary CA 33-36R

Seferis, George 1900-1971 ...... **CLC 5, 11**
See also Seferiades, Giorgos Stylianou

Segal, Erich (Wolf) 1937-....... **CLC 3, 10**
See also CANR 20
See also CA 25-28R
See also DLB-Y 86

Seger, Bob 1945- ....**CLC 35**

Seger, Robert Clark 1945-
See Seger, Bob

Seghers, Anna 1900-...............**CLC 7**
See Radvanyi, Netty

Seidel, Frederick (Lewis) 1936-.....**CLC 18**
See also CANR 8
See also CA 13-16R
See also DLB-Y 84

Seifert, Jaroslav 1901-1986......**CLC 34** (255), **44** (421)

Selby, Hubert, Jr. 1928-..................**CLC 1, 2, 4, 8**
See also CA 13-16R
See also DLB 2

Sender, Ramón (José) 1902-1982.....................**CLC 8**
See also CANR 8
See also CA 5-8R
See also obituary CA 105

Serling, (Edward) Rod(man) 1924-1975....................**CLC 30**
See also CA 65-68
See also obituary CA 57-60
See also DLB 26
See also AITN 1

Serpières 1907-
See Guillevic, (Eugène)

Service, Robert W(illiam) 1874-1958.................. **TCLC 15**
See also CA 115
See also SATA 20

Seth, Vikram 1952-...............**CLC 43**

Seton, Cynthia Propper 1926-1982....................**CLC 27**
See also CANR-7
See also CA 5-8R
See also obituary CA 108

Settle, Mary Lee 1918-............**CLC 19**
See also CAAS 1
See also CA 89-92
See also DLB 6

Author Index

Tindall, Gillian 1938- . . . . **CLC 7**
See also CANR 11
See also CA 21-24R

Tocqueville, Alexis de
1805-1859 . . . . **NCLC 7**

Tolkien, J(ohn) R(onald) R(euel)
1892-1973 . . . . **CLC 1, 2, 3, 8, 12, 38**
See also CAP 2
See also CA 17-18
See also obituary CA 45-48
See also SATA 2, 32
See also obituary SATA 24
See also DLB 15
See also AITN 1

Toller, Ernst 1893-1939 . . . . **TCLC 10**
See also CA 107

Tolson, Melvin B(eaunorus)
1900?-1966 . . . . **CLC 36**
See also obituary CA 89-92
See also DLB 48

Tolstoy, (Count) Alexey Nikolayevich
1883-1945 . . . . **TCLC 18**
See also CA 107

Tolstoy, (Count) Leo (Lev Nikolaevich)
1828-1910 . . . . **TCLC 4, 11, 17**
See also CA 104
See also SATA 26

Tomlin, Lily 1939- . . . . **CLC 17**

Tomlin, Mary Jean 1939-
See Tomlin, Lily

Tomlinson, (Alfred) Charles
1927- . . . . **CLC 2, 4, 6, 13**
See also CA 5-8R
See also DLB 40

Toole, John Kennedy
1937-1969 . . . . **CLC 19**
See also CA 104
See also DLB-Y 81

Toomer, Jean
1894-1967 . . . . **CLC 1, 4, 13, 22**
See also CA 85-88
See also DLB 45

Torrey, E. Fuller 19??- . . . . . . **CLC 34** (503)

Tournier, Michel 1924- . . . . . . **CLC 6, 23, 36**
See also CANR 3
See also CA 49-52
See also SATA 23

Townshend, Peter (Dennis Blandford)
1945- . . . . **CLC 17, 42**
See also CA 107

Trakl, Georg 1887-1914 . . . . **TCLC 5**
See also CA 104

Traven, B. 1890-1969 . . . . **CLC 8, 11**
See also CAP 2
See also CA 19-20
See also obituary CA 25-28R
See also DLB 9

Tremain, Rose 1943- . . . . **CLC 42**
See also CA 97-100
See also DLB 14

Tremblay, Michel 1942- . . . . **CLC 29**

Trevanian 1925- . . . . **CLC 29**
See also Whitaker, Rodney
See also CA 108

Trevor, William
1928- . . . . **CLC 7, 9, 14, 25**
See also Cox, William Trevor
See also DLB 14

Trilling, Lionel
1905-1975 . . . . **CLC 9, 11, 24**
See also CANR 10
See also CA 9-12R
See also obituary CA 61-64
See also DLB 28

Trogdon, William 1939-
See Heat Moon, William Least
See also CA 115

Trollope, Anthony 1815-1882 . . . . . **NCLC 6**
See also SATA 22
See also DLB 21, 57

Trotsky, Leon (Davidovich)
1879-1940 . . . . **TCLC 22**
See also CA 118

Troyat, Henri 1911- . . . . **CLC 23**
See also CANR 2
See also CA 45-48

Trudeau, G(arretson) B(eekman) 1948-
See Trudeau, Garry
See also CA 81-84
See also SATA 35

Trudeau, Garry 1948- . . . . **CLC 12**
See also Trudeau, G(arretson) B(eekman)
See also AITN 2

Truffaut, François 1932-1984 . . . . . . **CLC 20**
See also CA 81-84
See also obituary CA 113

Trumbo, Dalton 1905-1976 . . . . **CLC 19**
See also CANR 10
See also CA 21-24R
See also obituary CA 69-72
See also DLB 26

Tryon, Thomas 1926- . . . . **CLC 3, 11**
See also CA 29-32R
See also AITN 1

Ts'ao Hsuëh-ch'in 1715?-1763 . . . . **LC 1**

Tsushima Shūji 1909-1948
See Dazai Osamu
See also CA 107

Tsvetaeva (Efron), Marina (Ivanovna)
1892-1941 . . . . **TCLC 7**
See also CA 104

Tunis, John R(oberts)
1889-1975 . . . . **CLC 12**
See also CA 61-64
See also SATA 30, 37
See also DLB 22

Tuohy, Frank 1925- . . . . **CLC 37**
See also DLB 14

Tuohy, John Francis 1925-
See Tuohy, Frank
See also CANR 3
See also CA 5-8R

Turco, Lewis (Putnam) 1934- . . . . . . **CLC 11**
See also CA 13-16R
See also DLB-Y 84

Tutuola, Amos 1920- . . . . **CLC 5, 14, 29**
See also CA 9-12R

Twain, Mark
1835-1910 . . . . **TCLC 6, 12, 19**
See also Clemens, Samuel Langhorne
See also DLB 11

Tyler, Anne
1941- . . . . . **CLC 7, 11, 18, 28, 44** (311)
See also CANR 11
See also CA 9-12R
See also SATA 7
See also DLB 6
See also DLB-Y 82

Tyler, Royall 1757-1826 . . . . **NCLC 3**
See also DLB 37

Tynan (Hinkson), Katharine
1861-1931 . . . . **TCLC 3**
See also CA 104

Unamuno (y Jugo), Miguel de
1864-1936 . . . . **TCLC 2, 9**
See also CA 104

Underwood, Miles 1909-1981
See Glassco, John

Undset, Sigrid 1882-1949 . . . . **TCLC 3**
See also CA 104

Ungaretti, Giuseppe
1888-1970 . . . . **CLC 7, 11, 15**
See also CAP 2
See also CA 19-20
See also obituary CA 25-28R

Unger, Douglas 1952- . . . . **CLC 34** (114)

Unger, Eva 1932-
See Figes, Eva

Updike, John (Hoyer)
1932- . . . . . . **CLC 1, 2, 3, 5, 7, 9, 13, 15, 23, 34** (283), **43**
See also CANR 4
See also CA 1-4R
See also CABS 2
See also DLB 2, 5
See also DLB-Y 80, 82
See also DLB-DS 3

Uris, Leon (Marcus) 1924- . . . . . . **CLC 7, 32**
See also CANR 1
See also CA 1-4R
See also AITN 1, 2

Ustinov, Peter (Alexander)
1921- . . . . **CLC 1**
See also CA 13-16R
See also DLB 13
See also AITN 1

Vaculík, Ludvík 1926- . . . . **CLC 7**
See also CA 53-56

Valenzuela, Luisa 1938- . . . . **CLC 31**
See also CA 101

Valera (y Acalá-Galiano), Juan
1824-1905 . . . . **TCLC 10**
See also CA 106

Valéry, Paul (Ambroise Toussaint Jules)
1871-1945 . . . . **TCLC 4, 15**
See also CA 104

Valle-Inclán (y Montenegro), Ramón (María) del 1866-1936 . . . . **TCLC 5**
See also CA 106

Vallejo, César (Abraham)
1892-1938 . . . . **TCLC 3**
See also CA 105

Van Ash, Cay 1918- . . . . **CLC 34** (118)

Vance, Jack 1916?- . . . . **CLC 35**
See also DLB 8

Walker, Margaret (Abigail) 1915- .... **CLC 1, 6**
See also CA 73-76

Walker, Ted 1934- .... **CLC 13**
See also Walker, Edward Joseph
See also DLB 40

Wallace, Irving 1916- .... **CLC 7, 13**
See also CAAS 1
See also CANR 1
See also CA 1-4R
See also AITN 1

Wallant, Edward Lewis 1926-1962 .... **CLC 5, 10**
See also CA 1-4R
See also DLB 2, 28

Walpole, Horace 1717-1797 .... **LC 2**
See also DLB 39

Walpole, (Sir) Hugh (Seymour) 1884-1941 .... **TCLC 5**
See also CA 104
See also DLB 34

Walser, Martin 1927- .... **CLC 27**
See also CANR 8
See also CA 57-60

Walser, Robert 1878-1956 .... **TCLC 18**
See also CA 118

Walsh, Gillian Paton 1939-
See Walsh, Jill Paton
See also CA 37-40R
See also SATA 4

Walsh, Jill Paton 1939- .... **CLC 35**
See also CLR 2

Wambaugh, Joseph (Aloysius, Jr.) 1937- .... **CLC 3, 18**
See also CA 33-36R
See also DLB 6
See also DLB-Y 83
See also AITN 1

Ward, Douglas Turner 1930- .... **CLC 19**
See also CA 81-84
See also DLB 7, 38

Warhol, Andy 1928- .... **CLC 20**
See also CA 89-92

Warner, Francis (Robert le Plastrier) 1937- .... **CLC 14**
See also CANR 11
See also CA 53-56

Warner, Sylvia Townsend 1893-1978 .... **CLC 7, 19**
See also CANR 16
See also CA 61-64
See also obituary CA 77-80
See also DLB 34

Warren, Mercy Otis 1728-1814 .... **NCLC 13**
See also DLB 31

Warren, Robert Penn 1905- .... **CLC 1, 4, 6, 8, 10, 13, 18, 39** (254)
See also CANR 10
See also CA 13-16R
See also SATA 46
See also DLB 2, 48
See also DLB-Y 80
See also AITN 1

Washington, Booker T(aliaferro) 1856-1915 .... **TCLC 10, CLC 34**
See also CA 114
See also SATA 28

Wassermann, Jakob 1873-1934 .... **TCLC 6**
See also CA 104

Wasserstein, Wendy 1950- .... **CLC 32**

Waters, Roger 1944-
See Pink Floyd

Wa Thiong'o, Ngugi 1938- .... **CLC 3, 7, 13, 36**
See also Ngugi, James (Thiong'o)
See also Ngugi wa Thiong'o

Watkins, Vernon (Phillips) 1906-1967 .... **CLC 43**
See also CAP 1
See also obituary CA 25-28R
See also CA 9-10
See also DLB 20

Waugh, Auberon (Alexander) 1939- .... **CLC 7**
See also CANR 6
See also CA 45-48
See also DLB 14

Waugh, Evelyn (Arthur St. John) 1903-1966 .... **CLC 1, 3, 8, 13, 19, 27, 44** (520)
See also CA 85-88
See also obituary CA 25-28R
See also DLB 15

Waugh, Harriet 1944- .... **CLC 6**
See also CA 85-88

Webb, Beatrice (Potter) 1858-1943
See Webb, Beatrice (Potter) and Webb, Sidney (James)
See also CA 117

Webb, Beatrice (Potter) 1858-1943 and **Webb, Sidney (James)** 1859-1947 .... **TCLC 22**

Webb, Charles (Richard) 1939- .... **CLC 7**
See also CA 25-28R

Webb, James H(enry), Jr. 1946- .... **CLC 22**
See also CA 81-84

Webb, Mary (Gladys Meredith) 1881-1927 .... **TCLC 24**
See also DLB 34

Webb, Phyllis 1927- .... **CLC 18**
See also CA 104
See also DLB 53

Webb, Sidney (James) 1859-1947
See Webb, Beatrice (Potter) and Webb, Sidney (James)
See also CA 117

Webb, Sidney (James) 1859-1947 and **Webb, Beatrice (Potter)** 1858-1943
See Webb, Beatrice (Potter) and Webb, Sidney (James)

Webber, Andrew Lloyd 1948-
See Rice, Tim and Webber, Andrew Lloyd

Weber, Lenora Mattingly 1895-1971 .... **CLC 12**
See also CAP 1
See also CA 19-20
See also obituary CA 29-32R
See also SATA 2
See also obituary SATA 26

Wedekind, (Benjamin) Frank(lin) 1864-1918 .... **TCLC 7**
See also CA 104

Weidman, Jerome 1913- .... **CLC 7**
See also CANR 1
See also CA 1-4R
See also DLB 28
See also AITN 2

Weil, Simone 1909-1943 .... **TCLC 23**
See also CA 117

Weinstein, Nathan Wallenstein 1903?-1940
See West, Nathanael
See also CA 104

Weir, Peter 1944- .... **CLC 20**
See also CA 113

Weiss, Peter (Ulrich) 1916-1982 .... **CLC 3, 15**
See also CANR 3
See also CA 45-48
See also obituary CA 106

Weiss, Theodore (Russell) 1916- .... **CLC 3, 8, 14**
See also CAAS 2
See also CA 9-12R
See also DLB 5

Welch, James 1940- .... **CLC 6, 14**
See also CA 85-88

Welch, (Maurice) Denton 1915-1948 .... **TCLC 22**

Weldon, Fay 1933- .... **CLC 6, 9, 11, 19, 36**
See also CANR 16
See also CA 21-24R
See also DLB 14

Wellek, René 1903- .... **CLC 28**
See also CANR 8
See also CA 5-8R

Weller, Michael 1942- .... **CLC 10**
See also CA 85-88

Weller, Paul 1958 .... **CLC 26**

Welles, (George) Orson 1915-1985 .... **CLC 20**
See also CA 93-96

Wells, H(erbert) G(eorge) 1866-1946 .... **TCLC 6, 12, 19**
See also CA 110
See also SATA 20
See also DLB 34

Wells, Rosemary 19??- .... **CLC 12**
See also CA 85-88
See also SAAS 1
See also SATA 18

Welty, Eudora (Alice) 1909- .... **CLC 1, 2, 5, 14, 22, 33**
See also CA 9-12R
See also DLB 2
See also CDALB 1941-1968

Werfel, Franz (V.) 1890-1945 .... **TCLC 8**
See also CA 104

Wergeland, Henrik Arnold 1808-1845 .... **NCLC 5**

Wersba, Barbara 1932- .... **CLC 30**
See also CLR 3
See also CA 29-32R
See also SAAS 2
See also SATA 1

Author Index

Author Index